T0389489

Middle Western Karaim

# The Languages of Asia Series



VOLUME 22

The titles published in this series are listed at *brill.com/la*

# Middle Western Karaim

*A Critical Edition and Linguistic Analysis of the Pre-19th-century Karaim Interpretations of Hebrew* piyyutim

*By*

Michał Németh

BRILL

LEIDEN | BOSTON

Library of Congress Cataloging-in-Publication Data

Names: Németh, Michał, 1980- author.
Title: Middle Western Karaim : a critical edition and linguistic analysis of the pre-19th-century Karaim interpretations of Hebrew piyyutim / Michał Németh.
Description: Leiden ; Boston : Brill, 2020. | Series: Languages of Asia, 2452-2961 ; vol. 22 | Includes bibliographical references and index.
Identifiers: LCCN 2020003868 (print) | LCCN 2020003869 (ebook) | ISBN 9789004414228 (hardback) | ISBN 9789004419377 (ebook)
Subjects: LCSH: Karaim language–History. | Karaim language–Texts. | Jewish religious poetry, Hebrew–Translations into Karaim.
Classification: LCC PL69 .N46 2020 (print) | LCC PL69 (ebook) | DDC 494/.38–dc23
LC record available at https://lccn.loc.gov/2020003868
LC ebook record available at https://lccn.loc.gov/2020003869

Typeface for the Latin, Greek, and Cyrillic scripts: “Brill”. See and download: brill.com/brill-typeface.

ISSN 2452-2961
ISBN 978-90-04-41422-8 (hardback)
ISBN 978-90-04-41937-7 (e-book)



This book is printed on acid-free paper and produced in a sustainable manner.

# Contents

## *The* peshatim*: Text and Translation*

# Preface

## Rationale

The genesis of this book goes back to 2011 when I was invited by two scholars, Mariola Abkowicz and Anna Sulimowicz-Keruth, to collaborate with them in cataloguing Karaim manuscripts and printed sources kept in Polish private holdings. As a result of our efforts, in the years 2012–2016 more than 460 items were catalogued and described in detail. Most importantly, their age and the place of origin were determined, their copyists identified (where possible), and each manuscript received a table of contents in which the incipits and genres of the Karaim works were specified and the authors and/or translators of these works identified as precisely as possible. Last but not least, we carried out a palaeographical examination of the manuscripts and determined the dialectal affiliation of each Karaim passage they contained, and briefly noted, when applicable, the main linguistic peculiarities of a particular work.[1] This paved the way for the linguistic research the results of which are presented in this volume.

Many of the manuscripts discovered in the above-mentioned private holdings turned out to be exceptionally valuable.[2] Thus, the linguistic material presented in the present volume stems primarily from these collections and was later supplemented with sources kept in the Wroblewski Library of the Lithuanian Academy of Sciences.

For the purposes of this volume, i.e. with the aim of describing the main features of Middle Western Karaim phonology and morphology, I have chosen the Karaim translations of Hebrew religious songs known as *piyyutim* (singular: *piyyut*) to be investigated. This is not only because these texts are linguistically valuable, but also because there has been no literary study that would bring the translation tradition of this genre closer to the reader.

*Piyyutim* are liturgical poems that were sung after, or prior to, standard prayers. Usually, these were elaborations on themes known from the Tanakh

---

1 The preparation of the catalogue was financed by the Polish National Science Centre in the framework of the research project 2011/03/D/HS2/00618 lead by the present writer. For a summary of our work, see Németh (2016c), where the methodology used to determine both the age of the manuscripts and the identity of the copyists is explained in detail.

2 A number of invaluable Bible translations have already been presented in Németh (2014c, 2015c, 2016a); a critical edition of ADub.III.73 is nearly ready and will soon appear in a separate book (Németh [2021]).

(see, for instance, the *piyyutim* composed for each Torah portion) or from other standard prayers. Both the Hebrew *piyyutim* and their Karaim translations (only a few Karaim *piyyutim* were written originally in Karaim) were full of poetic embellishments, which makes them linguistically, and above all syntactically, a fairly complex subject of analysis.[3]

Based on the sources kept in the private archives of the Abkowicz, Dubiński, and Sulimowicz families, altogether a total of 51 Karaim translations, more precisely *peshatim* (singular: *peshat*), of this genre were identified. Later, as a result of archival research conducted in the Wroblewski Library of the Lithuanian Academy of Sciences (Vilnius), this list has been augmented with a further 60 titles. From this vast material we selected for analysis those texts that were consistent with the objectives of the present work. Given that the focus of this volume is the history of Middle Western Karaim, we have critically edited here all the *peshatim* that originate from before the end of the 18th century and were available to us in at least one copy produced no later than the first half of the 19th century.[4] Based on these criteria, a total of 149 copies of 30 different *peshatim* were included in this monograph.[5]

This critical edition includes an elaborate introduction in which the reader is made familiar with the state-of-the-art in Karaim philological studies and, albeit briefly, *paytanic* literature. In a separate chapter, an attempt is made to summarize our knowledge of all the copyists and translators that contributed to the creation of the edited texts. Chapter 2, in turn, contains an elaborate description of Late Middle and Early Modern Western Karaim phonology and some remarks on the differences between the Late Middle and Modern Western Karaim morphological systems.

3 For further reading, see, above all, Deutsch (1905: 65–68), Petuchowski (2004: 11–19), Fleischer (2007: 365–372), Hollender (2008: 2–10), or Münz-Manor (2011). At the time the present work is being finalized, we are still waiting for Wasserman's (forthcoming) study to be published.

4 The recent history of Modern Western Karaim (i.e., from the second half of the 19th century on) has already received a decent description (see our discussion below).

5 Many Karaim manuscripts contain *piyyutim* written in Hebrew only, see, for instance, Evr II A 1185. This might be also the case with the only potentially valuable manuscript the present author knows of but has had no opportunity to see: it is a collection of prayers allegedly copied in 1690 in Lutsk and mentioned by Medvedeva (1988: 92) and stored under catalogue number A 1445 in the Russian Academy of Sciences in Saint Petersburg (formerly the Leningrad Branch of the Institute of Oriental Studies of the Russian Academy of Sciences). As is explained in chapter 1.1, however, this manuscript most likely also only consists of Hebrew texts.

## Acknowledgements

The manuscripts presented here would perhaps not have been discovered without the financial help of the Polish National Science Centre. The research conducted in the framework of the research project entitled *A catalogue of Karaim manuscripts and printed sources* (project no. 2011/03/D/HS2/00618) allowed me and my research team to find a large number of invaluable sources.

This work would not have seen the light of day had it not been for the support I received from the Alexander von Humboldt Foundation. My stay as a postdoctoral research fellow at the Seminar für Orientkunde (which was later incorporated into the Institut für Slavistik, Turkologie und zirkumbaltische Studien as the Abteilung Turkologie) at the Johannes Gutenberg University of Mainz was the most fruitful research experience I have had the privilege to be part of. Later, the Alexander von Humboldt Return Fellowship allowed me to supplement my linguistic description with further valuable observations. My thanks go to all those colleagues with whom I had the possibility to discuss the main idea of this book during my fellowship. In this respect, I owe special thanks to Professors László Károly (Uppsala), Julian Rentzsch (Mainz), and Hendrik Boeschoten (Mainz).

I am also indebted to Marek Piela (Kraków), Riikka Tuori (Helsinki), Gabriel Wasserman (Jerusalem) for their assistance in Hebraistic matters, as well as to Gabriel Wasserman, again, and Jason Lowther (Kraków) for proofreading my dissertation. It goes without saying that any errors remaining are my own responsibility.

It is also my most pleasant duty to express my sincere gratitude to Anna Sulimowicz-Keruth, Th.D. (Warsaw), Adam Dubiński (Warsaw), and Mariola Abkowicz (Wrocław) who selflessly provided me with unlimited access to the manuscripts in their possession. My hearty thanks are due, in particular, to Anna Sulimowicz-Keruth who also assisted me in establishing the identity of a number of Karaim authors, copyists, or translators.

Finally, and most especially, I owe a debt of gratitude to my wife and sons, without whose boundless understanding and perseverance this book simply would not exist at all.

# Tables, Figures and Facsimiles

## Tables



## Figures

## Facsimiles

# Abbreviations and Editorial Symbols

## Abbreviated Grammatical Terms

| | | | |
|---|---|---|---|
| abl. | ablative | liqu. | liquids |
| acc. | accusative | nas. | nasals |
| affr. | affricates | neg. | negative |
| allat. | allativus | pers. pron. | personal pronoun |
| dat. | dative | pl. | plural |
| def. art. | definite article | pl. t. | plurale tantum |
| dem. pron. | demonstrative pronoun | plos. | plosives |
| deriv. | derivative | pluperf. I. | pluperfect I |
| expr. partic. | expressive particle | pluperf. II. | pluperfect II |
| fric. | fricative | poss. | possessive form |
| fut. | future tense | postp. | postposition |
| gen. | genitive | priv. | privative |
| imperat. | imperative | sg. | singular |
| instr. | instrumental | suff. | suffix |
| interr. pron. | interrogative pronoun | superlat. | superlative |

## Abbreviated Names of Languages

| | |
|---|---|
| Ar. | Arabic |
| BHeb. | Biblical Hebrew |
| EKar. | Eastern Karaim |
| Heb. | Hebrew |
| Kar. | Karaim. |
| Lat. | Latin |
| Lith. | Lithuanian |
| MHeb. | Medieval Hebrew |
| MKar. | Middle Karaim |
| MNWKar. | Middle North-Western Karaim |
| Mod.NWKar. | Modern North-Western Karaim. |
| Mod.SWKar. | Modern South-Western Karaim. |
| MPol. | Middle Polish |
| MSWKar. | Middle South-Western Karaim |
| MWKar. | Middle Western Karaim |

| | |
|---|---|
| NWKar. | North-Western Karaim |
| PBHeb. | Post Biblical Hebrew |
| Pers. | Persian |
| PSlav. | Proto-Slavonic |
| Pol. | Polish |
| Russ. | Russian |
| Slav. | Slavonic (in general) |
| SWKar. | South-Western Karaim |
| TKc. | Turkic |
| Ukr. | Ukrainian |
| WKar. | Western Karaim |

## Other Abbreviations

| | | | |
|---|---|---|---|
| a. | after | init. | initial position |
| arch. | archaic | lit. | literally |
| b. | before | n.a. | not applicable |
| ca. | circa | med. | medial position |
| colloq. | colloquial | ms. | manuscript |
| dial. | dialectal | mss. | manuscripts |
| f. | folio | non-voc. | non-vocalized text |
| ff. | folios | r° | recto |
| fig. | figuratively | v° | verso |
| fin. | final position | voc. | vocalized text |

## Editorial Symbols

### *Used in the Transcription*

| | |
|---|---|
| ... | irrelevant fragment |
| [...] | missing or illegible fragment |
| [abc] | reconstructed fragment |
| {abc} | text added interlineally or in margins |
| {{abc}} | text crossed out or redundant |
| ⌊abc def⌉1 | fragment commented on in one footnote |
| ⌊אבג דהו⌉1 | Hebrew fragment commented on in one footnote |

### *Used in the Translation*

| | |
|---|---|
| [...] | missing or illegible fragment |
| [...?] | incomprehensible fragment |
| [?] | uncertain translation (used in the apparatus only) |
| [abc] | reconstructed fragment |
| [i.e., abc] | explanation for clarity (used in the apparatus only) |
| [see, abc] | explanation for clarity (used in the apparatus only) |
| {abc} | text added interlineally or on margins |
| {{abc}} | text crossed out or redundant in the original |
| (abc) | amplification for clarity or motivated by the structure of English |
| (~ abc) | alternative translation (used in the apparatus only) |
| ⌞abc def⌝[1] | fragment commented on in one footnote |

### *Used in Commentaries*

| | |
|---|---|
| [abc] | phonetic notation |
| /abc/ | phonological notation |
| ⟨abc⟩ | orthographic notation |
| < *abc* | borrowing; internal development |
| *abc* > | borrowing; internal development |
| ≤ *abc* | continuation without lingusitic change |
| *abc* ≥ | continuation without lingusitic change |
| ← *abc* | derivation |
| *abc* → | derivation |
| *abc* →← *cba* | blend, contamination |
| *abc* ~ *cba* | alternation |
| *ö* : *e* | relation, opposition |
| **abc* | reconstructed or not attested form |
| ***abc* | nonexistent, hypothetical, or erroneous form |
| ? | uncertain data |
| + | (in tables) a feature abundantly documented |
| (+) | (in tables) a feature present only in a few examples |

CHAPTER 1

# Introduction

## 1.1 The Oldest Western Karaim Religious Texts

The importance of Karaim linguistic material in understanding the history of Middle Western-Kipchak has been pointed out by a number of authors. The archaic nature of the native Turkic stratum of this material and its role in Turkic comparative linguistics has already been touched upon, for instance, by Kowalski (1929: xxv, lix, lxi–lxv), Pritsak (1959a: 318–320), A. Zajączkowski (1961: 37–40), W. Zajączkowski (1966: 429), Dubiński (1993 [1994]: 116), and Jankowski (2003: 131–132; 2015b: 272).[1] Still, this Karaim material cannot be effectively exploited in historical-comparative studies along with the Middle Kipchak written sources from the 13th–16th centuries (see Berta 1996: 3–7). One of the rules of the comparative method in diachronic linguistics is that the linguistic materials being compared, whether they be written in cognate or potentially cognate languages, should date, if possible, from the same time-period. However, the oldest meticulously investigated and comprehensively described Western and Eastern Karaim texts originate from the 19th and 18th centuries, respectively.[2]

Recently, however, a number of archaic Karaim handwritten sources have been discovered, some of which have been scholarly edited. Their critical editions will pave the way for much more reliable comparative-historical analyses comparing Karaim and the languages that stand closest to it, i.e. primarily the language of *Codex Comanicus* (for a description of the latter source, see, e.g., von Gabain 1959, Drüll 1980: 13–16, or Drimba 2000), Armeno-Kipchak with a written history dating back to the 16th century (for a comprehensive catalogue of sources, see Garkavec 2002; for an excellent overview of Armeno-Kipchak studies, see Tryjarski 2017), and Krymchak with its oldest source dating

1 In this respect, quite eye-catching is A. Zajączkowski's (1939a) article in which he quotes a passage from the 14th-century *Codex Comanicus* in a journal published for readers of Karaim and states that 'inanam ki har bir Karaj bunu anlar heč bir avurluchsuz' ['I believe that every single Karaim will understand this without any difficulties.'] (Zajączkowski 1939a: 3).

2 For descriptions of 19th-century North- and South-Western Karaim see, primarily, Grzegorzewski (1903), Kowalski (1929), Németh (2011b) and Olach (2013); the most comprehensive depictions of 18th-century Eastern Karaim are the works of J. Sulimowicz (1972, 1973) and Jankowski (1997).

 | DOI:10.1163/9789004419377_002

from 1785, see Polinsky (1991: 134)[3] and Jankowski (2015a: 461). Surprisingly, the source from 1785 was not taken into account in Ianbay's (2016) Krymchak dictionary.

The oldest known North-Western Karaim texts are a *qinah* authored in 1649 by Zarach ben Natan (? 1578–1657/8; see Tuori 2013: 62) copied in 1671 (B 263: 26 v°, 28 r°),[4] two religious poems by Icchak ben Abraham Troki (1533/4–1594) copied in 1686 (Evr I 699: 15 v°–16 r°),[5] an edition of which was prepared by Jankowski (2014),[6] and three works copied in JSul.I.01a, namely: the *peshat* of the *piyyut* אַשְׁמָתֵנוּ גָּדְלָה *ʾašmåṯēnū gåḏlå* with the incipit *Jazyqlarymyz ulġajdylar bijikḱa astry* (see Németh 2018a, and № 2 below), a *qinah* starting with the words *Men miskin qaldyġy*, both composed by Josef ha-Mashbir (died 1700), and the *zemer* with the incipit *Bügün Sinaj tavġa* by Aharon ben Jehuda of Troki. The latter three works were copied by ha-Mashbir himself between 1685 and 1700 in ms. JSul.I.01a, see folios 118 v°–119 v° (*peshat* № 2), 121 r°–123 r°, and 115 v°–116 r°. As far as I know, besides the first three verses of Genesis presented in 1691 by Gustaf Peringer (1651–1710) and published (with many misprints) by Tentzel (1691: 572–575), these are the only Wesern Karaim texts dating from the 17th century. Consequently, the first text mentioned, i.e. the *qinah* by Zarach ben Natan, should be regarded, for the time being at least, as the oldest written records of Western Karaim.[7] The number of sources grows after 1700, see, e.g., ADub.III.73, ADub.III.78, JER NLI 4101-8, JSul.III.05, TKow.01.

---

3 Another important Krymchak source is ms. № 1159 of the Gintsburg Collection of the Russian National Library copied most likely in 1799. It contains the Twelve Minor Prophets and some fragments of Ketuvim.

4 Mentioned in Muchowski (2013b: 86–87, 97–98), and Németh (2015b: 170, 172). Its critical edition is under preparation by the present author.

5 Copied by a person called Mordechai ben Icchak. See my remark in 2.1.2.

6 Kizilov (2007: 72) presented one of them based on an eighteenth-century copy.

7 In the scholarly literature we can find a number of assertions that the Karaim written heritage is much older—without, however, any definite philological data being provided. For instance, Šapšal (1918: 6) states that:

> 'Около XI. в. была ими переведена на родной чалтайскій діалектъ*) вся Ветхозаветная Библія. Переводъ этотъ хотя и подвергался въ послѣдующіе вѣка измѣненіямъ, но и въ дошедшихъ до насъ спискахъ вполнѣ сохранилъ свой архаическій обликъ и имѣетъ по своему лексическому составу и грамматическимъ формамъ весьма близкое сходство съ единственнымъ уцѣлѣвшимъ памятникомъ половецкаго языка—Codex Comanicus.'
>
> ---
>
> *) Такъ называютъ караимы свое нарѣчіе турецкаго языка. Нѣкоторые сближаютъ слово чалтай съ "чагатай".

A similar opinon was expressed by Musaev (1964: 8), who claimed that the Hebrew Bible was translated into Karaim in the 11th–14th centuries. On the other hand, Pritsak (1959: 323), W. Zajączkowski (1980: 161), and, after them, Csató (2011: 169) contended that the oldest South-Western Karaim Bible translations dated from the 16th century. For the time being, however,

The earliest written record of an Eastern Karaim religious text is a translation of the Former Prophets, the Books of Ruth, Esther, and Proverbs (the latter is preserved in fragments) copied between 1648 and 1687 (JSul.III.02) and presented in Németh (2016a).[8] Another early source is the prayer book *Siddur* (1734), the Eastern Karaim linguistic material of which (a collection of *selichot*) was edited by J. Sulimowicz (1972, 1973), as well as fragments of an 18th-century translation of the Bible edited by Jankowski (1997; ms. Gaster Hebrew MS 170, first mentioned by Steinschneider 1817: 38).

The source containing the oldest South-Western Karaim text is perhaps ms. A 144$_5$ (copied in Lutsk in 1690, as claimed by Medvedeva 1988: 92) stored in the Institute of Oriental Manuscripts of the Russian Academy of Sciences. However, in light of the fact that it is not listed among the many other sources kept in the Institute of Oriental Manuscripts that were used by the compilers of the largest Karaim dictionary, i.e. KarRPS, it is very probable that it does not include any Karaim portions of texts at all and was written in Hebrew only (see the list of sources in KarRPS 28–29 under the category *Молитвы и обрядовые песни* (*многие с переводом*)).

The oldest known South-Western Karaim text is perhaps JSul.I.38.11, a collection of religious songs copied between 1738 and 1744. Another important source is JSul.I.53.13, a remnant of a prayer book copied in the mid-18th century Halych (ca. 1762), a sample of which is presented in *peshat* № 6 below. Other sources in this group are JSul.III.65, an 18th-century Halych Karaim translation of the Book of Esther, and JSul.III.63 copied ca. 1778 by Jeshua ben Mordechai Mordkowicz (died 1797)—see the three *peshatim* from this source published in the present book (№ 2, 4 and 26). Of a similar age are, most likely, some fragments of JSul.I.01 (here referenced as JSul.I.01b) (see № 3, 6, 26, in our edition), and JSul.I.37-09, just to mention a few. The number of handwritten sources from Halych grows rapidly after the turn of the 19th century.

---

these facts remain unconfirmed, as none of these authors have referenced definite philological data. We must, of course, also remember that Pritsak and Zajączkowski might have known something we do not know. For instance, W. Zajączkowski (1980: 161) also stated (again, without referring to specific manuscripts), that the oldest North-Western Karaim Biblical texts originate from the 18th century, which became a proven fact following the discovery of ms. ADub.III.73 in 2014 (see Németh 2014c: 110–113; 2015c: 50–51) and TKow.01 in 2019. Finally, it ought to be mentioned here that Medvedeva (1988: 92, 98) lists a Karaite (not *Karaim*) prayer book from 1617 (ms. A 13) kept in the Institute of Oriental Manuscripts of the Russian Academy of Sciences, Saint Petersburg, but it is still to be determined whether this source contains any text written in Karaim (it is reported to be compiled in Hebrew).

8 Recently, Eljaševič (2016) has presented an Eastern Karaim text sample from a *pinkas* from Kaffa dated back to 1653–1663, but this is not a religious text, see Jankowski (2018: 41).

It ought to be mentioned that the manuscript containing Josef ha-Mashbir's authograph noted above, i.e. JSul.I.01a, also originates from Halych, but it is written in North-Western Karaim.

Demonstrably the oldest Lutsk Karaim texts date back to the early 19th century. To this group belongs JSul.I.02, partially copied by Mordechai ben Josef of Lutsk in 1807. It is a collection of religious songs composed in the 18th and 19th centuries. Its near contemporary is ms. JSul.I.38.21 as well as JSul.I.04 containing a translation of the Book of Job copied in 1814 by Jaakov ben Icchak Gugel. Equally old is JSul.I.50.06, a manuscript copied ca. 1815 and containing a translation of the Book of Esther and a modest collection of *piyyutim*. Further sources from the early 19th century exist that were potentially written in Lutsk, but establishing their exact place of creation requires additional investigation.[9] The oldest Lutsk Karaim text edited in the present work is a *peshat* of *piyyut* № 6 copied in JSul.I.37.02—a manuscript dating most likely from the mid-19th century.

Finally, two additional remarks are necessary. For decades, the short refrain of the hymn אוֹדֶה וְגַם אֶתְפַּלְּלָה *ʾōḏe wḡam ʾeṯpallå* as published in *Siddur* (1528/1529: vol. 2: 212) was considered the oldest record in Karaim. The hymn itself is a translation into Modern Greek, but its refrain is written in a Turkic language. As far as I know, this information was first published by Poznański (1913–1914: 224; see Poznański 1912–1919 in our bibliography). He, in turn, was informed by Nathan Porges (1848–1924), a rabbi in Leipzig, that the refrain of this hymn is "tatarisch"—a term used at that time by scholars to denote any kind of Turkic language, cf. the title of Poznański's referenced article (i.e. *Karäisch-tatarische Literatur*). Later, this information was repeated by several scholars, among them A. Zajączkowski (1926: 8; 1964: 794), Dubiński (1959 [1994]: 64), and Harviainen & Hopeavuori & Nieminen (1998: 36). Shapira (2003: 691–692) was the first to notice that the hymn in question was not written in Karaim even though he himself had not analysed the respective fragment linguistically and neither had he provided proper argumentation in support of his assertion. Later Jankowski (2008: 163–164; 2012: 53–54) and Aqtay (2009: 19–20) studied the text in detail and argued convincingly that this passage was definitely not written in Karaim, but rather in Crimean Turkish.

The second source that ought to be briefly discussed here is Evr I Bibl 143 listed in Harkavy & Strack (1875: 167–168) and referred to in that text as a "tatarische Uebersetzung" of a large part of the Torah (from Exodus 21:11 up

9 This group of sources includes manuscripts JSul.I.19, JSul.I.37.05, JSul.I.37.06, JSul.I.38.04, and JSul.I.38.21.

till Numbers 28:15). It remained almost completely overlooked until 2017[10] when Aleksandra Soboleva from the Vinogradov Russian Language Institute (Moscow) carried out a palaeographic examination of this source. The examination of the watermarks showed that the Italian paper it was written on dates back to the 15th century (Grishchenko 2018: 172).[11] The datating of the text and that it contains Kipchak elements seems to be supported by the brief preliminary linguistic investigation of its content, cf. e.g. אַנְגַר *aŋar* 'to him' (2 r°), קִיזְגַא *qyzġa* 'to the girl' (2 r°), טַש בִלַא *taš bilä* 'with a stone' (2 r°), טוּרְגַי *turġaj* 'may he stand' (2 r°). It is written in the Yevano-Karaitic type of Hebrew script (Mashait style) very similar to a 14th-century sample presented in Birnbaum (1954–1957, plate 391) and close to a 16th-century sample shown in Birnbaum et alii (2007: 720, 726: figure 35). The fact that it contains a translation of the Torah into a Kipchak Turkic vernacular and that it is written in a Hebrew script type characteristic of the Crimean region might, at first glance, suggest that its language is Early Middle Karaim. Nevertheless, it still requires proper analysis in order to determine, beyond a reasonable doubt, its linguistic affiliation. In Jankowski's view (2018: 39–40) it is rather written in Chagatay and we also incline towards this opinion. Recently, Shapira (2019: 289–293) argued that this translation "was made within a Rabbanite community, not in a Karaite one".

## 1.2 Scholarly Edited Western Karaim Religious Texts

The language of 19th- and 20th-century Western Karaim liturgical texts is relatively well documented. Its modern scholarly investigation began with Grzegorzewski's article (1903) which offered a detailed description of Halych Karaim based on both religious and secular text samples.[12] Some years later

10 It was briefly presented by Shapira (2006: 270), without a word of linguistic commentary. It has recently been described by Shapira as a "Kiptchak-Turkic text" (Shapira 2018: 309).

11 The following three 15th-century watermarks have been identified: 1. Sartorial scissors, small, with single-circuit handles, cf. Briquet (1907 II: no. 3746, from 1463–1473), cf. also Piccard (no. 122352, from 1466); 2. Sartorial scissors, medial, with double-circuit handles and bandelet: a type of Briquet (1907 II: no. 3689, from 1463–1467); 3. Letter L, double-circuit, italic; cf. Briquet (1907 III: no. 8282, from 1472–1485; we can treat therefore 1472 as a *terminus post quem* for the creation of this manuscript), cf. also Piccard (no. 28603, from 1473; and no. 28604, from 1471) (Grishchenko 2017, personal communication).

12 The Book of Job in Radloff's edition (? Saint Petersburg, ? 1888 or ? 1890) is unavailable. It was mentioned only by Kowalski (1929: lxxvii, 283–285) and A. Zajączkowski (1931: 31). Jankowski (2009: 507) goes so far as to claim that it might be a "ghost publication". Allegedly, it is a North-Western Karaim translation with Eastern Karaim elements (this

Munkácsi (1909) published a work on three religious poems: both the Hebrew originals and their Halych Karaim translations composed by Abraham ben Levi (Leonowicz), hazzan in Halych in 1802–1851. This was followed by another article by Grzegorzewski (1916–1918), which presented and discussed in detail the Halych Karaim interpretations of Psalms 142 and 143 (translator: Josef ha-Mashbir; Grzegorzewski provides no specific date on the manuscript he used) as well as a few other examples of folk literature. Nearly a decade later Kowalski's (1929) published *Karaimische Texte*, which still remains one of the most important works in this field. In this voluminous edition, Kowalski rightly distinguished between North-Western Karaim religious (pp. 1–54) and secular texts (pp. 55–147) and presented the linguistic material in the form of a phonetic transcription fully compliant with today's linguistic standards. Kowalski's disciple, A. Zajączkowski, continued this tradition and prepared a comparative critical edition of the Book of Psalms (A. Zajączkowski 1931–1932 [1934], 1934b) based on four manuscripts dating from the 19th and 20th centuries.[13]

The Second World War brought an end to these scholarly efforts.[14] If we take into consideration the fact that the above works were published within three decades, it is perhaps somewhat surprising that it took almost another three decades after the war before the next scholary edition of Karaim religious texts appeared, namely the above-mentioned work of J. Sulimowicz (1972, 1973) on

might result from negligent editorial work). The latter piece of information, however, is far from being certain.

13 Interestingly, A. Zajączkowski himself also prepared a copy of the Book of Psalms in a scholarly transcription, based on a manuscript that belonged to Feliks Mickiewicz, a Karaim from Troki (ms. ADub.III.69 copied between 18 Oct 1928 and 29 Jun 1929), but he did not include this source in the edition mentioned.

14 Tadeusz Kowalski was arrested during *Sonderaktion Krakau* and was imprisoned in the Sachsenhausen concentration camp until his liberation in February 1940. He died in 1948, in the age of 59, due to worsened health condition (see Zaborski 2000: 12). The private library of his protégé, Ananiasz Zajączkowski, was destroyed during an air raid on Warsaw in August 1944 (Zajączkowska-Łopatto 2013: 13). The lost collection also included Karaim manunscripts and the drafts of his own books and papers prepared for printing (see Zajączkowski 1953: 5, 1954: 7). For many years after the war his primary task was to restore the traditional Oriental Studies curriculum in Poland (Zajączkowska-Łopatto 2014: 134–139). In September 1939, A. Zajączkowski's disciple Józef Sulimowicz was preparing to defend his MA thesis (on the language of the Karaim translation of the Tanakh printed in Eupatoria in 1841) at the University of Warsaw. However, after being conscripted into the army on 23 Jun 1941, and refused permission several times by his superiors to continue his studies after the war, he only managed to obtain his MA degree in 1968 while holding the rank of a colonel (A. Sulimowicz 2013b: 5–9).

the *Siddur* (1734). The first editions of Western Karaim religious texts published after the war are Firkovičius's two books (though lacking a critical apparatus or any commentary) containing a text of the Book of Psalms (1994; without facsimile) and another of the Book of Proverbs (2000; with a facsimile). In the second decade of the 21st century, there has been a revival in text editing practice in the field. Csató (2011) presented the text of a North-Western Karaim translation of the first 16 verses of Psalm 91 along with a syntactic analysis.[15] In the same year, Jankowski (2011) published a critical edition of two prayers for Yom Kippur translated into Halych Karaim and copied in Hebrew script in 1940. Two years later Olach (2013) presented numerous samples from a 19th-century Halych Karaim translation of the Torah and the Haftarot.[16] She then went on to write three articles: a comparative edition of a short evening prayer[17] (Olach 2014) and two articles (Olach 2016a, 2016b) containing a description of a total of three 19th-century copies of Shelomo ben Aharon's morning prayer with the incipit *Ojanġyn ǯan ojan syjly*. In 2019, Cegiołka (2019) published a sample of JSul.III.01, and Jankowski prepared a critical edition of the North-Western Karaim text of the *Haggadah* based on ms. F305-49 and Malecki (1900).

Only a few Western Karaim religious texts originating from earlier than the 19th century have been critically edited so far. Firstly, we should list Jankowski's above-mentioned very important edition of two religious poems based on manuscripts from the 17th and 18th centuries (Jankowski 2014). Secondly, there are Németh's three articles, which provide a critical analysis of samples from a

15 The authoress does not mention the age of the manuscript in her work. Based on the facsimile presented on pages 183–184, we can say that the manuscript is certainly not older than the 19th century. In my opinion, it stems from the second half of the 19th century the earliest. It should also be pointed out here that transliterating the vowel point *patach* with both *ä* and *a* as Csató did in her article (see Csató 2011: 172) was an erroneous solution. Firstly, in a transliteration one grapheme must be rendered with one symbol. Secondly, this notation suggests that the *patach* was used to indicate an unrounded open front vowel, which is not the case in 19th-century North-Western Karaim.

16 The latter contains passages from the books of Joshua, Judges, 1–2 Kings, Isaiah, Jeremiah, Ezekiel, Hosea, Joel, Obadiah, Micah, Habakkuk, and Zechariah. Olach did not assign a date to the manuscript. The facsimile (only the first page of the text, see Olach 2013: 433), clearly shows that the copyist of this manuscript was Jeshua Josef Mordkowicz (see 2.2.5). The manuscript analysed by Olach has exactly the same structure as ADub.III.82.

17 North- and South-Western Karaim versions of one and the same prayer are compared. The North-Western version was taken from Firkovičius (1993: 16); the South-Western Karaim text was found in a manuscript. Again, the age of the manuscript is not established by the author: the facsimile (Olach 2014: 323) suggests that it is not older than the second half of the 19th century.

North-Western Karaim translation of the Torah (Németh 2014c) and the Book of Ruth (Németh 2015c) (based on ms. ADub.III.73 from 1720 and ca. 1720, for more information on this manuscript, see bibliography), and the critical edition of Gustaf Peringer's Karaim material from 1691 (Németh 2020). Furthermore, a short sample of the song *Men zavallyJisra'el* (*peshat* № 26) was presented and analysed by Németh (2014a) on the basis of ms. JSul.III.63 and a few other sources and, finally, the idiolect of Josef ha-Mashbir was analysed by Németh (2018a) on the basis of *peshat* № 2 found in ms. JSul.I.01a.

As far as printed primary sources are concerned, mention should be made of a number of publications containing Western Karaim religious texts from the 19th–20th centuries. The first such work is the Book of Genesis prepared for print by Zachariasz Mickiewicz and Elijahu Rojecki in 1888 in Vilnius. This was soon followed by Malecki's collections of penitentiary prayers and hymns for Yom Kippur (1890) and Passover (1900), both in North-Western Karaim. In 1895, another religious work came out in Vilnius, edited by Simcha Dubiński, which comprises 15 penitentiary prayers and dirges sung on the Shabbats of the months Tammuz and Av, which was printed in Hebrew along with its North-Western Karaim translation. The last collection of religious sources published before the Great War was a set of liturgical songs edited by Bizikowicz & Firkowicz (1909): on pages 78–79 we find one religious song translated into North-Western Karaim. All the above works were published in Hebrew script.

In the interwar period members of Karaim communities residing in Poland edited and published a large number of religious works in journals and brochures. In contrast to what appeared before the Great War, these works were mostly written in Latin script and primarily in the south-western dialect. And so, in 1927, Szulimowicz & Zarachowicz prepared for print a hectographic edition of the South-Western translation of the Book of Jeremiah based on a manuscript copied in Hebrew script by Jeshua Josef Mordkowicz. This booklet was one of the last works to be published in Karaim and written in Hebrew script. Twenty-eight copies (see Kowalski 1929: lxxviii) of it were prepared in Halych in 1927.[18] Soon after, Mardkowicz (1930) edited a collection of 23 *zemirot* excerpted from older manuscripts. One year later, a prayer (*tachanun*) appeared in Abrahamowicz's (1931) text while Szymon (Szemaja) Firkowicz (pen name *Szafir*) published a North-Western Karaim translation of Psalm 23. In 1935, the latter author prepared a collection of prayers entitled *Kołtchałar*. Finally, quite a few dirges (*qinot*) composed in memory of deceased persons

18 One copy of it survived in the archive of the Dubiński family, see ADub.III.87. Its edition will most likely form part of the project *KaraimBible* financed by the European Research Council, which will be headed by the present author in the years 2019–2024.

were published in this period, see the works of Abkowicz (1926), A. Leonowicz (1930–1931), J. Leonowicz, (1936a, 1936b), S. Leonowicz (1936), and Łobanos (1927, 1930–1931).

Mardkowicz (1932a, 1932b, 1936), the editor of the journal *Karaj Awazy*,[19] also published some religious songs; see those authored by Moses Darʿī (not living earlier than the mid-12th century, see Nemoy 1952: 133; Gintsburg 2003: 9) and Josef ben Jeshua of Derażne (died 1678, see Walfish 2011: 647). In the article it is not stated who translated Darʿī's works from Hebrew into Karaim (cf. Mardkowicz 1932b: 19). On the other hand, Josef ben Jeshua's works were most probably authored in Karaim.

After the Second World War a number of new texts appeared featuring Western Karaim religious writings. Worthy of mention here are the works of Mykolas Firkovičius, the hazzan of the Karaim community in Trakai. He prepared for print a collection of prayers (Firkovičius 1993) and two prayer books (Firkovičius 1998, 1999). In 2019, Kobeckaitė published the Book of Job.[20]

## 1.3 Existing Western Karaim Interpretations of Hebrew *piyyutim*

The present volume is based on textual material comprising 30 *peshatim* in Western Karaim (for more details, see 1.4). These are Karaim interpretations of Hebrew works. To the best of my knowledge, the works edited here make up more than a third of the total number of *peshatim* discovered in Western Karaim translation to date. During archival research conducted as a preparatory work for this book, the present author learned about the existence of 119 works that were consistently termed *peshatim* of *piyyutim* by their copyists.[21] These works are listed below according to the names of the authors of the

19 He was one of the most prominent Karaim social activists in the interwar period; for more information on him, see A. Sulimowicz (2013a).

20 It also ought to be mentioned here that no Western Karaim non-religious texts dating from earlier than the 19th century have been edited for scholarly purposes, either. The oldest source presented in Németh (2011b) dates back to the 1840s. The documents edited in W. Zajączkowski (1965), Németh (2010, 2013b, 2013c), and A. Sulimowicz (2014, 2015, 2016) date from the 19th century, too.

21 Icchak ben Icchak of Lutsk's *peshat* of שָׁבַת מְשׁוֹשִׁי *šåḇaṯ mśōśī* with the incipit *Eksildi ḥyǯlyq da janġajlyq* is termed a *piyyut* in mss. JSul.III.03 (104 r°) and JSul.I.11 (99 r°). This work, however, did not enter the present volume given that in all other available sources it is described as a *tachanun*, see ADub.III.61 (117 r°), JSul.I.01 (134 r°), JSul.I.45 (129 r°), JSul.III.63 (37 v°), JSul.III.69 (228 r°), and JSul.III.79 (280 v°).

Karaim interpretations arranged in chronological order and grouped according to whether the identity of the translators has been established (A), not been established (B), or whether even the name of the translator remains unknown (C).[22]

## A. Authors of established identity

**Josef ha-Mashbir ben Shemuel** (ca. 1650–1700)

1. *Jasly hem taryqqan ʒanly*
   Hebrew incipit: אֲנוּנָה אֲנִי וַעֲגוּמָה *ʾănūnå ʾănī waʿăgūmå*
   Dedication: Shabbats of the month Tammuz
   Location: JSul.III.03 (98 rº–99 rº)
2. *Jazyqlarymyz ulġajdylar bijikḱa astry* or *Jazyqlarymyz ulġajdylar astry bijikke*
   Hebrew incipit: אַשְׁמָתֵנוּ גָּדְלָה *ʾašmåṯēnū gåḏlå*
   Dedication: Shabbats of the month Tammuz
   Location: JSul.I.01 (118 vº–119 vº)
3. *Qoltqabyla e H joqtan bar etivčü*
   Hebrew incipit: אָנָּא יָוָי כִּי אֲנִי עַבְדֶּךָ *ʾånnå YWY kī ʾănī ʿaḇdeḵå*
   Dedication: Shabbat Teshuvah
   Location: JSul.I.01 (128 rº–130 rº)

**Mordechai ben Icchak Łokszyński** (died before 1709)

4. *E küčlü Tenrim kipligim galutumda* or *E küclü Tenri kipligim galutumda*
   Hebrew incipit: אֱיָלוּתִי בְּגָלוּתִי *ʾĕyålūṯī bgålūṯī*
   Dedication: The third Shabbat of the month Tammuz
   Location: JSul.III.73 (103 rº–103 vº)

**Mordechai ben Nisan** (died ca. 1709)

5. *Jasly da zabun bolġan*
   Hebrew incipit: אֲנוּנָה אֲנִי וַעֲגוּמָה *ʾănūnå ʾănī waʿăgūmå*
   Dedication: Shabbats of the month Tammuz
   Location: JSul.III.03 (99 rº–100 rº)

---

22 The Hebrew incipits of the originals are presented following the Hebrew orthography applied by Karaim copyists. As a location, I provide the accession number of the oldest manuscript the respective work is to be found in. Finally, in case of *peshatim* the composer of which remains unidentified, as a location I provide all the manuscripts I managed to find the respective text in.

**Moshe ben Icchak Cic-Ora** (died 1717/1718)

6. *Men synyq ummasy Jisra'elnin*
   Hebrew incipit: אֲנִי יְשֵׁנָה וְלִבִּי עֵר *ʾănī yšēnå wlibbī ʿēr*
   Dedication: Pesach (while reading the Hallel ha-Gadol)
   Location: ADub.III.78 (284 r°–285 r°)

**Simcha ben Chananel** (died 1723)

7. *Adonajdy biji Jisra'elnin*
   Hebrew incipit: אֲדוֹנָי מֶלֶךְ יִשְׂרָאֵל *ʾăd̠ōnåy melek̠ yiśråʾēl*
   Dedication: Yom Teruah
   Location: Sul.I.54.03 (1 v°–2 r°)
8. *Biji dunjanyn bijik da jalġyz Tenri*
   Hebrew incipit: מֶלֶךְ רָם וְיָחִיד *melek̠ råm wyåḥīd̠*
   Dedication: Shabbat Shirah
   Location: JSul.III.03 (85 r°–86 r°)
9. *E H Tenrim sen basladyn körgizme mana* or
   *E Adonaj Tenri sen basladyn kergizme mana*
   Hebrew incipit: אֲדוֹנָי אֱלֹהִים אַתָּה הַחִלּוֹתָ *ʾăd̠onåy ʾĕlohīm ʾattå haḥillōt̠å*
   Dedication: Parashat Va'etchanan
   Location: JSul.III.03 (107 v°–108 r°)
10. *E Tenrisi dunjanyn ol jaratuvcu*
   Hebrew incipit: אֱלֹהֵי עוֹלָם הָעוֹשֶׂה כֹּל *ʾĕlohē ʿōlåm håʿōśe kol*
   Dedication: Parashat Ki Tavo
   Location: JSul.III.03 (108 r°–108 v°)
11. *E ummasy Jisra'elnin inanuvcular bir Tenrige*
   Hebrew incipit: אַנְשֵׁי אֱמוּנָה בְּתוֹרַת אֵל *ʾanšē ʾĕmūnå bt̠ōrat̠ ʾēl*
   Dedication: Parashat Bechukotai
   Location: JSul.III.03 (106 r°–106 v°)
12. *Eger ajtsam šira oḥujum*
   Hebrew incipit: אִם אָמְרִי אָשִׁירָה לְאֵלִי וְאַנְוֵהוּ *ʾim ʾåmrī ʾåšīrå lʾēlī wʾanwēhū*
   Dedication: Sukkot (on Shemini Atzeret)
   Location: JSul.I.54.03 (3 r°–4 r°)
13. *Joḥtur senin kibik kičli da qorqunčlu Tenri*
   Hebrew incipit: מִי כָּמוֹךָ אַדִּיר וְנוֹרָא *mī kåmōk̠å ʾad̠īr wnōrå*
   Dedication: Parashat Haazinu
   Location: JSul.VII.22.02.13 (1 r°–1 v°)
14. *Joḥtur Tenrisi kibik Jisra'elnin*
   Hebrew incipit: אֵין כָּאֵל יְשׁוּרוּן יָחִיד וְנֶאֱמָן *ʾēn kåʾel yšūrūn yåḥīd̠ wneʾĕmån*

Dedication: Yom Teruah
Location: JSul.I.54.03 (1 rº–1 vº)

15. *Kelip sortun Jisraʾel*
Hebrew incipit: אַחֲרֵי בֹּא יְשׁוּרוּן *ʾaḥărē ḇo yšūrūn*
Karaim text by: Simcha ben Chananel
Dedication: Parashat Shlach
Location: JSul.III.03 (106 vº–107 vº)

16. *Kicli Tenri syrynda aziz malaẖlarnyn*
Hebrew incipit: אֵל נַעֲרָץ בְּסוֹד מַלְאֲכֵי שְׁבִיבוֹ *ʾēl naʿărås̱ bsōḏ malʾăḵē šḇīḇō*
Dedication: Parashat Eikev
Location: ADub.III.61 (137 vº–138 vº)

17. *Maẖtavludu ol Tenri Adonaj* or
*Maẖtavludu ol Tenri H* or
*Maẖtavludur ol Tenri H*
Hebrew incipit: בָּרוּךְ הָאֵל הָ׳ *bårūḵ håʾēl H*
Dedication: Sukkot (on Shemini Atzeret)
Location: JSul.I.54.03 (4 rº–4 vº)

18. *Necik joẖtu tensi qajjam Tenrige*
Hebrew incipit: אֵין עֲרוֹךְ לְאֵל יָהּ *ʾēn ʿărōḵ lʾēl yåh*
Dedication: Parashat Vayikra
Location: JSul.I.45 (140 rº–141 rº)

19. *Qajjam avalġy Tenri*
Hebrew incipit: יוֹשֵׁב קֶדֶם *yōšēḇ qeḏem*
Dedication: Sukkot (on Shemini Atzeret)
Location: JSul.I.54.03 (4 vº–5 rº)

20. *Qajjam Tenri juluvčumuz biznin*
Hebrew incipit: אָמֵן גּוֹאֲלֵנוּ *ʾåmēn gōʾălēnū*
Dedication: The first day of Sukkot
Location: JSul.I.54.03 (2 rº–2 vº)

21. *Sensen aziz Tenri da qajjam*
Hebrew incipit: אַתָּה קָדוֹשׁ יוֹשֵׁב תְּהִלּוֹת בְּנֵי אֵיתָן *ʾattå qåḏōš yōšēḇ thillōṯ bnē ʾēṯån*
Dedication: Parashat Reʾeh
Location: ADub.III.61 (138 vº–139 rº)

22. *Siviniz qulluġun H-nyn*
Hebrew incipit: אֶהֱבוּ אֶת הָ׳ דּוֹר יְשָׁרִים *ʾehĕḇū ʾeṯ H dōr yšårīm*
Dedication: Parashat Shoftim
Location: ADub.III.61 (139 rº–139 vº)

23. *Sizge caġyramen igit sözlerin e syjly erenler*
Hebrew incipit: אֲלֵיכֶם אֶקְרָא אִישִׁים *ʾălēḵem ʾeqrå ʾīšīm*

Dedication: Parashat Kedoshim
Location: JSul.III.03 (105 vº–106 rº)

24. *Ummasy Jisra'elnin zallenedi alnynda Tenrinin* or *Ummasy Jisra'elnin zellenedi alnynda Tenrinin*
Hebrew incipit: אֲנוּנָה אֲנִי וַעֲגוּמָה *ʾănūnå ʾănī waʿăgūmå*
Dedication: Shabbats of the month Tammuz
Location: JSul.III.03 (101 vº–102 rº)

**Josef ben Shemuel ben Josef ha-Mashbir** (died 1738)

25. *Maḥtavludu joġarġy Tenri jaratuvcu köklerni* or *Maḥtavludur joġarġy Tenri jaratuvcu köklerni*
Hebrew incipit: יִשְׁתַּבָּח אֵל עֶלְיוֹן *yištabbaḥ ʾēl ʿelyōn*
Dedication: Parashat Vayelech
Location: JSul.III.03 (109 rº–109 vº)

**Shemuel ben Josef ha-Mashbir** (died 1744)

26. *Men zavally Jisra'el*
Hebrew incipit: אֲנוּנָה אֲנִי וַעֲגוּמָה *ʾănūnå ʾănī waʿăgūmå*
Dedication: Shabbats of the months Tammuz and Av
Location: JSul.I.01 (126 rº–126 vº)

27. *Sizge caġyramen igit sezlerim e syjly Jisra'eller* or *Sizge caġyramen igit sezlerim e syjly erenler*
Hebrew incipit: אֲלֵיכֶם אֶקְרָא אִישִׁים *ʾălēḵem ʾeqrå ʾīšīm*
Dedication: Parashat Kedoshim
Location: ADub.III.61 (134 vº–135 rº)

**Mordechai ben Shemuel** (died 1765)

28. *E qajjam Tenrisi Jaʿaqovnun*
Hebrew incipit: אֱלֹהֵי יִשְׂרָאֵל נְשַׁבְּחָךְ וּנְפָאֲרָךְ *ʾĕlohē yiśråʾēl nšabbḥåḵ ūnpåʾăråḵ*
Dedication: The first day of Pesach
Location: JSul.III.03 (110 rº–110 vº)

29. *Necik joḥtu tensi küclü Tenrige* or *Necik joḥtur tensi küclü Tenrige*
Hebrew incipit: אֵין עֲרוֹךְ לְאֵל יָהּ *ʾēn ʿărōḵ lʾēl yåh*
Dedication: Parashat Vayikra
Location: JSul.III.03 (105 rº–105 vº)

30. *Sensen Tenri astry kötirilgen*
Hebrew incipit: אַתָּה אֵל מִתְנַשֵּׂא *ʾattå ʾēl miṯnaśśē*
Dedication: Parashat Nitzavim
Location: JSul.III.03 (108 vº–109 rº)

**Abraham ben Mordechai**[23] (died ca. 1805)

31. *Aziz küčlü Tenri sen*[24]
    Hebrew incipit: אַתָּה אֵל לְכָל רֹאשׁ מִתְנַשֵּׂא *ʾattå ʾēl lkål roš mitnaśśē*
    Dedication: Parashat Bereshit
    Location: F305-08 (96 rº–96 vº)
32. *Aziz küčlü bij ol qajjam*
    Hebrew incipit: אֵל מֶלֶךְ הַיּוֹשְׁבִי בַשָּׁמַיִם *ʾēl melek hayyōšbī baššåmayim*
    Dedication: Parashat Noach
    Location: F305-08 (97 rº–97 vº)
33. *Aziz bijim bar ol jaratylmyšlarnyn*
    Hebrew incipit: אֲדוֹן כָּל הַבְּרִיאוֹת *ʾădōn kål habbrīʾōt*
    Dedication: Parashat Lech-Lecha
    Location: F305-08 (97 vº–98 rº)
34. *Abraham avinu tüǵal etip sortun*
    Hebrew incipit: אֵיתָן אַחַר כְּלוֹתוֹ *ʾētån ʾaḥar klōtō*
    Dedication: Parashat Vayeira
    Location: F305-08 (98 vº–99 vº)
35. *Aziz Tenri birdir edi da bardyr da bolurda*
    Hebrew incipit: אֵל אֶחָד אֶהְיֶה אֲשֶׁר אֶהְיֶה *ʾēl ʾeḥåd ʾehye ʾăšer ʾehye*
    Dedication: Parashat Chayei Sarah
    Location: F305-08 (99 vº–100 rº)
36. *Aziz Tenri sensin qyluvču baġatyrlar*
    Hebrew incipit: אַתָּה קָדוֹשׁ פּוֹעֵל גְּבוּרוֹת *ʾattå qådōš pōʿēl gbūrōt*
    Dedication: Parashat Toledot
    Location: F305-08 (100 r–101 rº)
37. *Ej maḥtavlu Tenri da maḥtalġan*
    Hebrew incipit: אֵל בָּרוּךְ וּמְבוֹרָךְ *ʾēl bårūk ūmbōråk*
    Dedication: Parashat Vayetze
    Location: F305-08 (101 rº–101 vº)

---

23 Abraham ben Mordechai of Poniewież, a scholarly leader of the Lithuanian Karaims of Poniewież and Nowe Miasto, author of numerous *piyyutim* and *zemirot* (died ca. 1805; Tuori 2013: 82–83; see, primarily, Mann 1931: 745–766). In Mann (1931), we find two more individuals bearing this name: Abraham ben Mordechai (died after 1658; Mann 1931: 805), and Abraham ben Mordechai of Troki (died after 1634; Mann 1931: 1105), but as far as we know they engaged in neither scholarly or poetic activity. In this light, the author of the present volume decided to list Abraham ben Mordechai here instead of classifying him as an author of unestablished identity.

24 Given that Abraham ben Mordechai only interpreted *piyyutim* dedicated to specific weekly Torah sections, his works are presented here not in alphabetical order, but instead are arranged according to the order of the *parashot*.

38. *Atamyz Ja'aqov tüǵal kiši*
Hebrew incipit: אִישׁ תָּם בְּלֶכְתּוֹ בְּמַהֲלָכָיו *ʾīš tåm blekṯō bmahălåḵåw*
Dedication: Parashat Vayishlach
Location: F305-08 (103 rº–103 vº)

39. *Inamly kiši Ja'aqov olturdu*
Hebrew incipit: אִישׁ חָלָק יָשַׁב *ʾīš ḥålåq yåšaḇ*
Dedication: Parashat Vayeshev
Location: F305-08 (103 vº–104 vº)

40. *Ornundan balqytadyr anlatma*
Hebrew incipit: מִמְּקוֹמוֹ הוֹפִיעַ *mimmqōmō hōp̄iaʿ*
Dedication: Parashat Miketz
Location: F305-08 (104 vº–105 rº)

41. *A kimǵa uqšatasiz Tenrini*
Hebrew incipit: אֵל מִי תְּדַמְּיוּן *ʾēl mi tḏammyūn*
Dedication: Parashat Vayigash
Location: F305-08 (105 rº–105 vº)

42. *Aziz Tenri sen turǵuzduj čekĺarin*
Hebrew incipit: אַתָּה הִצַּבְתָּ גְּבֻלוֹת *ʾattå hiṣṣaḇtå ḡḇulōṯ*
Dedication: Parashat Vayechi
Location: F305-08 (105 vº–107 vº)

43. *Juluvčumuz biznin juluvčusu Jisraʾelnin*
Hebrew incipit: גּוֹאֲלֵנוּ גּוֹאֵל יִשְׂרָאֵל *gōʾălēnū gōʾēl yiśråʾēl*
Dedication: Parashat Shemot
Location: F305-08 (107 vº–108 rº)

44. *Aharaǵy ol šarajatnyn Moše*
Hebrew incipit: אֲבִי הַתְּעוּדָה *ʾăḇi hattʿūḏå*
Dedication: Parashat Vaʾera
Location: F305-08 (108 rº–109 rº)

45. *Inamlysy üv́umńun Moše*
Hebrew incipit: אַתָּה נֶאֱמַן בֵּיתִי *ʾattå neʾĕman bēṯī*
Dedication: Parashat Bo
Location: F305-08 (109 rº–109 vº)

46. *Kimdir H kibik ullu da baǵatyr*
Hebrew incipit: מִי כַהָ אֲשֶׁר *mī ka-H ʾăšer*
Dedication: Parashat Beshalach
Location: F305-08 (110 rº–110 vº)

47. *Ej Tenrim ešitüvün baǵatyrlyǵyjnyn*
Hebrew incipit: אֵלִי שִׁמְעֲךָ שָׁמְעוּ רְחוֹקִים *ʾēlī šimʿăḵå šåmʿū rḥōqīm*
Dedication: Parashat Yitro
Location: F305-08 (110 vº–111 rº)

48. *Aziz Tenrisin tüzüdüj urluġuna*
Hebrew incipit: אַתָּה כּוֹנַנְתָּ לְזֶרַע *ʾattå kōnantå lzeraʿ*
Dedication: Parashat Mishpatim
Location: F305-08 (111 vº–112 rº)

49. *Ajyrylyp sortun gufluqtan*
Hebrew incipit: אַחֲרֵי בֹא עָנָו *ʾaḥărē ḇo ʿånåw*
Dedication: Parashat Terumah
Location: F305-08 (112 rº–113 rº)

50. *Anlatuvču tüzlükĺarni joġarġy Tenri*
Hebrew incipit: אֵל עֶלְיוֹן דּוֹבֵר *ʾēl ʿelyōn dōḇēr*
Dedication: Parashat Tetzaveh
Location: F305-08 (113 rº–113 vº)

51. *Ol vaḥtta ind́adi Tenri*
Hebrew incipit: אָז בְּהַר הַמּוֹר *ʾåz bhar hammōr*
Dedication: Parashat Ki Tisa
Location: F305-08 (113 vº–114 vº)

52. *Inamlysy Tenrinin Moše ribbimiz*
Hebrew incipit: אוֹמֵן בַּחֲזוֹת כְּבוֹד אֵל *ʾōmēn baḥăzōṯ kḇōḏ ʾēl*
Dedication: Parashat Vayakhel
Location: F305-08 (114 vº–115 rº)

53. *Inamly Tenri kertidir ki*
Hebrew incipit: אֱמֶת הַשָּׁמַיִם כִּסְאֶךָ *ʾĕmeṯ haššåmayim kisʾeḵå*
Dedication: Parashat Pekudei
Location: F305-08 (115 rº–115 vº)

54. *Uqšaš barmodur küčlü Tenriġa*
Hebrew incipit: אֵין עֲרוֹךְ לְאֵל יָהּ *ʾēn ʿărōḵ lʾēl yåh*
Dedication: Parashat Vayikra
Location: F305-08 (116 rº–116 vº)

55. *Maḥtav berijiz Adonajġa*
Hebrew incipit: בָּרְכוּ אֶת הָ׳ *bårḵū ʾeṯ H*
Dedication: Parashat Tzav
Location: F305-08 (116 vº–117 rº)

56. *Sen aziz da qorqunčlu Tenri*
Hebrew incipit: אַתָּה קָדוֹשׁ וְנוֹרָא *ʾattå qåḏoš wnōrå*
Dedication: Parashat Shemini
Location: F305-08 (117 rº–117 vº)

57. *Inamly Tenri joḥtan barġa*
Hebrew incipit: אֱמֶת אֵל מֵאַיִן לְיֵשׁ *ʾĕmeṯ ʾēl mēʾayin lyēš*
Dedication: Parashat Tazria
Location: F305-08 (117 vº–118 rº)

58. *Ajtmaqlary H-nyn tüǵal ajtmaqlar*
Hebrew incipit: אִמְרוֹת יְהֹוָה אֲמָרוֹת תְּמִימוֹת *ʾimrōṯ YHWH ʾămårōṯ tmīmōṯ*
Dedication: Parashat Metzora
Location: F305-08 (118 rº–118 vº)

59. *Aziz Tenrimizǵa joḥtur tenši*
Hebrew incipit: אֵין כֵּאלֹהֵינוּ נוֹרָא עֲלִילוֹת *ʾēn kēlohēnū nōrå ălīlōṯ*
Dedication: Parashat Acharei Mot
Location: F305-08 (118 vº–119 vº)

60. *Ej syjly eŕanĺar sizǵa čaġyramyn ügüt sözĺar*
Hebrew incipit: אֲלֵיכֶם אֶקְרָא אִישִׁים *ʾălēḵem ʾeqrå ʾīšīm*
Dedication: Parashat Kedoshim
Location: F305-08 (119 vº–120 rº)

61. *Astry kertidir ki joḥtur*
Hebrew incipit: אָכֵן אֵין כֶּאֱלֹהֵינוּ *ʾåḵēn ʾēn keʾĕlohēnū*
Dedication: Parashat Emor
Location: F305-08 (120 rº–120 vº)

62. *Ej juluvčusu Jisraʾelnin*
Hebrew incipit: אֵין כָּמוֹךָ גּוֹאֵל יִשְׂרָאֵל *ʾēn kåmōḵå gōʾēl yiśråʾēl*
Dedication: Parashat Behar
Location: F305-08 (120 vº–121 rº)

63. *Inamly el üvŕatüvü byla H-nyn*
Hebrew incipit: אַנְשֵׁי אֱמוּנָה בְּתוֹרַת אֵל *ʾanšē ʾĕmūnå bṯōraṯ ʾēl*
Dedication: Parashat Bechukotai
Location: F305-08 (121 rº–123 rº)

64. *Maḥtavludur aziz Tenri ki joḥtur tüǵanḿak maḥtavyna azizliginin*
Hebrew incipit: בָּרוּךְ אֵל אֲשֶׁר אֵין *bårūḵ ʾēl ʾăšer ʾēn*
Dedication: Parashat Bamidbar
Location: F305-08 (123 rº–123 vº)

65. *Adonaj berdi ajtmaq*
Hebrew incipit: יְיָ נָתַן אוֹמֶר *YWY nåṯan ʾōmer*
Dedication: Parashat Naso
Location: F305-08 (123 vº–124 rº)

66. *Ajtty biji ol bijĺarnin*
Hebrew incipit: אָמַר אֲדוֹנָי הָאֲדוֹנִים *ʾåmar ʾăḏōnåy håʾăḏōnīm*
Dedication: Parashat Behaalotecha
Location: F305-08 (124 rº–124 vº)

67. *Ajtty Tenri kelip sortun*
Hebrew incipit: אַחֲרֵי בֹא יְשׁוּרוּן *ʾaḥărē ḇo yšūrūn*
Dedication: Parashat Shlach
Location: F305-08 (125 rº–125 vº)

68. *Adonajnyn aziz šeminin sağynčyn*
Hebrew incipit: אֶהֱבוּ אֶת ה׳ *ʾehĕḇū ʾeṯ H*
Dedication: Parashat Korach
Location: F305-08 (125 vº–126 rº)

69. *Ösťuŕulǵan edi Tora qatynda*
Hebrew incipit: אָמוֹן הָיְתָה תוֹרָה *ʾåmōn håyṯå tōrå*
Dedication: Parashat Chukat
Location: F305-08 (126 rº–127 rº)

70. *Kimdir H kibik anyn syjyndyralmadyrlar bar ḥanlyqlar*
Hebrew incipit: מִי כַּה׳ אֲשֶׁר לֹא יָכִילוּ *mī ka-H ʾăšer lo yåḵilū*
Dedication: Parashat Balak
Location: F305-08 (127 rº–127 vº)

71. *Ulluluğu qotarylsyn aziz joğarġy Tenrinin*
Hebrew incipit: יִתְגַּדַּל אֵל עֶלְיוֹן *yiṯgaddal ʾēl ʿelyōn*
Dedication: Parashat Pinchas
Location: F305-08 (127 vº–128 rº)

72. *Aziz tamaša išĺarij bilivčüĺarǵa*
Hebrew incipit: אֱלֹהַי מַה נוֹרָא *ʾĕlohay ma nōrå*
Dedication: Parashat Matot
Location: F305-08 (128 rº–129 rº)

73. *Ullu belgiĺari Tenrimiznin*
Hebrew incipit: אוֹתוֹת אֱלֹהֵינוּ *ʾōṯōṯ ʾĕlohēnū*
Dedication: Parashat Masei
Location: F305-08 (129 rº–129 vº)

74. *Inamly Moše qajjam inamlyq edi avzunda*
Hebrew incipit: אוֹמֶן אֱמוּנָה אוֹמֶן *ʾōmen ʾĕmūnå ʾōmen*
Dedication: Parashat Devarim
Location: F305-08 (129 vº–130 rº)

75. *Adonaj Tenri sen bašladyj körgüzḿa maja qabaqlaryn*
Hebrew incipit: יְיָ אֱלֹהִים אַתָּה הַחִלּוֹתָ *YWY ʾĕlohīm ʾattå haḥillōṯå*
Dedication: Parashat Va'etchanan
Location: F305-08 (130 rº–131 rº)

76. *Aziz Tenri küčlüdür syrynda jalynly malaḫlarnyn*
Hebrew incipit: אֵל נַעֲרָץ בְּסוֹד מַלְאֲכֵי שְׁבִיבוֹ *ʾēl naʿărāṣ bsōḏ malʾăḵē šḇīḇō*
Dedication: Parashat Eikev
Location: F305-08 (131 rº–131 vº)

77. *Aziz tenri da qajjamsyn*
Hebrew incipit: אַתָּה קָדוֹשׁ יוֹשֵׁב תְּהִלּוֹת בְּנֵי אֵיתָן *ʾattå qåḏōš yōšēḇ thillōṯ bnē ʾēṯån*

Dedication: Parashat Re'eh
Location: F305-08 (131 vº–132 rº)

78. *Ej doru tüzĺarnin*
Hebrew incipit: אֶהֱבוּ אֶת הָ׳ דּוֹר יְשָׁרִים *ʾehĕḇū ʾeṯ H dōr yšårīm*
Dedication: Parashat Shoftim
Location: F305-08 (132 rº–133 rº)

79. *Kim H kibik asajyšly*
Hebrew incipit: מִי כַּהָ׳ אִבֵּי עֶדְנֵי *mī ka-H ʾibē ʿeḏnē*
Dedication: Parashat Ki Teitzei
Location: F305-08 (133 r–133 vº)

80. *Aziz Tenrisi bütün dunjanyn*
Hebrew incipit: אֱלֹהֵי עוֹלָם הָעוֹשֶׂה כֹּל *ʾĕlohē ʿōlåm håʿōśe kol*
Dedication: Parashat Ki Tavo
Location: F305-08 (133 vº–134 vº)

81. *A sen küčlü Tenri da qajjam olturuvču*
Hebrew incipit: אַתָּה אֵל מִתְנַשֵּׂא *ʾattå ʾēl miṯnaśśē*
Dedication: Parashat Nitzavim
Location: F305-08 (134 vº–135 rº)

82. *Kim senin kibik aziz küčlü da qorqunčlu*
Hebrew incipit: מִי כָּמוֹךָ אַדִּיר וְנוֹרָא *mī kåmōḵå ʾaḏīr wnōrå*
Dedication: Parashat Haazinu
Location: F305-08 (136 rº–136 vº)

83. *Inamly navisi Tenrinin Moše*
Hebrew incipit: אִישׁ אֱלֹהִים בֵּרַךְ לְשִׁבְטֵי *ʾīš ʾĕlohīm bēraḵ lšiḇṭē*
Dedication: Parashat Vezot Haberachah
Location: F305-08 (136 vº–137 vº)

**Abraham ben Levi Leonowicz** (1776–1851)

84. *Joġarġy Tenri bijik ketirilgen jasyryn*
Hebrew incipit: אֵל עֶלְיוֹן נִתְעַלָּה עַל כֵּס חֶבְיוֹן *ʾēl ʿelyōn niṯʿallå ʿal kēs ḥeḇyōn*
Dedication: Parashat Vayetze
Location: ADub.III.61 (128 vº–130 rº)

85. *Moše ribbimiz atasy ol navilernin*
Hebrew incipit: אֲבִי הַתְּעוּדָה *ʾăḇi hattʿūḏå*
Dedication: Parashat Va'era
Location: ADub.III.61 (130 rº–131 rº)

**Josef ben Abraham Leonowicz** (1795–1866)

86. *Adonaj biji Jisra'elnin*
    Hebrew incipit: אֲדוֹנָי נִגְלָה בְּסִינַי *ʾăd̲ōnåy niḡlå bsīnay*
    Dedication: Shavuot
    Location: JSul.III.67 (162 vº–164 rº)
87. *E kicli Tenrim ḥabarynny ki cyhardym*
    Hebrew incipit: אֵלִי שִׁמְעֲךָ שָׁמְעוּ רְחוֹקִים *ʾēlī šimʿăḵå šåmʿū rḥōqīm*
    Dedication: Parashat Yitro
    Location: JSul.I.37.03 (9 rº–10 rº)
88. *Joḥtur H Tenrimiz kibik biznin qorqunclu*
    Hebrew incipit: אֵין כֵּאלֹהֵינוּ נוֹרָא עֲלִילוֹת *ʾēn kēlohēnū nōrå ălīlōṯ*
    Dedication: Parashat Acharei Mot
    Location: JSul.I.37.03 (15 vº–16 vº)
89. *Kicli Tenri kerti da qajjam*
    Hebrew incipit: אֱמֶת אֵל מֵאַיִן לְיֵשׁ *ʾěmeṯ ʾēl mēʾayin lyēš*
    Dedication: Parashat Tazria
    Location: JSul.I.37.03
90. *Kim barmodu H kibik kicli Tenri*
    Hebrew incipit: מִי כַּה אֱלֹהֵינוּ הַמַּגְבִּיהִי לָשֶׁבֶת *mī kå-H ʾělohenū hammaḡbīhī låšeḇeṯ*
    Dedication: Parashat Beshalach
    Location: JSul.I.37.03 (8 rº–9 rº)
91. *Sen e H aziz Tenri da qorqunclu*
    Hebrew incipit: אַתָּה קָדוֹשׁ וְנוֹרָא *ʾattå qåd̲oš wnōrå*
    Dedication: Parashat Shemini
    Location: JSul.I.37.03 (13 vº–14 rº)
92. *Sensen kicli da qajjam Tenri*
    Hebrew incipit: אַתָּה אֵל לְכָל רֹאשׁ מִתְנַשֵּׂא *ʾattå ʾēl lḵål roš miṯnaśśē*
    Dedication: Parashat Bereshit
    Location: ADub.III.61 (128 rº–128 vº)

**Zarach ben Shealtiel** (born 1799 or 1802, died probably before 1869)

93. *Ullu Tenri küčlüdir syrynda aziz malaḫlarnyn*
    Hebrew incipit: אֵל נַעֲרָץ בְּסוֹד מַלְאֲכֵי שְׁבִיבוֹ *ʾēl naʿăråṣ bsōd̲ malʾăḵē šḇīḇō*
    Dedication: Parashat Eikev
    Location: F305-11 (125 rº–129 rº)

**Jeshua Josef Mordkowicz** (1802–1884)

94. *Adonaj Tenrisi Jisraʾelnin*
 Hebrew incipit: אֲדוֹנָי אַתָּה מֵרִבְבוֹת קֹדֶשׁ בְּסִינַי *ʾaḏōnåy ʾattå mēriḇḇōṯ qoḏeš bsīnay*
 Dedication: Shavuot
 Location: JSul.III.67 (157 rº–158 rº)

95. *E qajjam Tenrisi ic dunjalarnyn*
 Hebrew incipit: אֱמֶת הַשָּׁמַיִם כִּסְאֶךָ *ʾĕmeṯ haššåmayim kisʾeḵå*
 Dedication: Parashat Pekudei
 Location: ADub.III.61 (133 rº–133 vº)

96. *Kelip sortun Moše*
 Hebrew incipit: אַחֲרֵי בֹא עָנָו *ʾaḥărē ḇo ʿånåw*
 Dedication: Parashat Terumah
 Location: ADub.III.61 (132 rº–133 rº)

97. *Kicli Tenri toḥtavcu*
 Hebrew incipit: יָהּ שׁוֹכֵן *yåh šōḵēn*
 Dedication: Parashat Toledot
 Location: JSul.I.37.17

98. *Sen e Moše qulum*
 Hebrew incipit: אַתָּה נֶאֱמַן בֵּיתִי *ʾattå neʾĕman bēṯī*
 Dedication: Parashat Bo
 Location: ADub.III.61 (131 rº–132 rº)

**Abraham ben Shemuel** (died after 1815)[25]

99. *E Adonaj Tenri šikir beremen sana*
 Hebrew incipit: יוֹדוּ לַהֿ חַסְדּוֹ *yōḏū la-H ḥasdō*
 Dedication: Purim
 Location: JSul.I.50.06 (29 rº–33 rº)

100. *Joḥtur aziz Adonaj kibik kicli* or
 *Joḥtur aziz Adonaj kibik küčlüŕagi* or
 *Joḥtur aziz H kibik küčlüŕagi*
 Hebrew incipit: אֵין קָדוֹשׁ כיוָ֞י אַדִּיר הָאַדִּירִים *ʾēn qåḏōš k-YWY ʾaḏīr håʾaḏīrīm*
 Dedication: Purim
 Location: JSul.I.50.06 (33 rº–34 vº),
 F305-08 (144 rº–145 rº), F305-09 (4 rº–5 rº)

25 Both Abraham and his father Shemuel are referred to as living persons in manuscript JSul.I.50.06 (29 rº).

**Simcha ben Jeshua Jaakov Leonowicz** (1841–1900)[26]

101. *Qajjam avalġy bij kicli Tenri*
   Hebrew incipit: מָרוֹם מֵרִאשׁוֹן *mårōm mērišōn*
   Dedication: The seventh day of Passover (Shviʿi Atzeret)
   Location: JSul.III.64 (23 rº–25 rº)
102. *Qajjam aziz maḥtavlu Tenrisi Jisraʾelnin*
   Hebrew incipit: אַתָּה קָדוֹשׁ יוֹשֵׁב תְּהִלּוֹת יִשְׂרָאֵל *ʾattå qåḏōš yōšēḇ thillōṯ yiśråʾēl*
   Dedication: The Passover Shabbat
   Location: JSul.III.64 (22 rº–23 rº)

**Icchak Boaz Firkowicz** (1865–1915)

103. *Qajjam Tenri avaldan küčlüdir bijimiz biznin*
   Hebrew incipit: מָרוֹם מֵרִאשׁוֹן *mårōm mērišōn*
   Dedication: The seventh day of Passover (Shviʿi Atzeret)
   Location: RAbk.IV.04 (1 rº–2 rº)

**Eliezer Josef ben Josef Łobanos** (1878–1947)

104. *Bijikligijni qotaramyn senin Tenrim*
   Hebrew incipit: unknown (authored by Pinchas ben Aharon Malecki, born 1854, died 1928)
   Dedication: unknown
   Location: JSul.I.49.48 (1 rº–1 vº)

## B. Authors of unestablished identity

**Abraham ben Jehuda**

105. *Ej maḥtavlu Tenri da maḥtalġan*
   Hebrew incipit: אֵל בָּרוּךְ וּמְבוֹרָךְ *ʾēl bårūḵ ūmḇōråḵ*
   Dedication: Parashat Vayetze
   Location: F305-08 (101 vº–103 rº)

**Aharon ben Simcha ben Josef**[27]

106. *Men e Tenrim jaratuvču dunjany*
   Hebrew incipit: אַתָּה אֱלֹהַי יוֹצֵר עוֹלָם *ʾattå ʾělohay yōṣēr ʿōlåm*

---

26 Hazzan in Halych in 1894–1900.

27 Possibly Aharon ben Simcha (died after 1668; Mann 1931: 869), or Aharon ben Simcha of Poswol (died after 1675; Mann 1931: 1117–1120), or Aharon ben Simcha, the father of Shelomo (lived in the 17th/18th centuries; Mann 1931: 1447; Tuori 2013: 72). The *peshat* in

Dedication: unknown
Location: F305-11 (77 rº–81 vº)

**Josef ben Mordechai**

107. *Aziz joġarġy Tenri maḥtavy qotarylsyn*
Hebrew incipit: —
Dedication: Parashat Vayelech
Location: F305-08 (135 rº–135 vº)

## C. Unknown authors

108. *Adonajdyr biji Jisra'elnin*
Hebrew incipit: אֲדוֹנָי מֶלֶךְ יִשְׂרָאֵל *ʾăḏōnåy meleḵ yiśråʾēl*
Dedication: Yom Teruah
Location: RAbk.IV.15 (174 rº–174 vº)
109. *Biji dunjanyn avaldan tamašalyqlar qyldy* or *Biji dunjanyn avaldan tamašalyḥlar qyldy*
Hebrew incipit: מֶלֶךְ עוֹלָם מִקֶּדֶם נִפְלָאוֹת עָשָׂה *meleḵ ʿōlåm miqqeḏem nip̄låʾōṯ ʿåśå*
Dedication: Purim
Location: F305-08 (145 rº–146 vº), F305-09 (5 rº–7 rº)
110. *Eger ajtsam šira ohujum Tenrińa da orun hadirlajym šeḫinasyna anyn*
Hebrew incipit: אִם אָמְרִי אָשִׁירָה לְאֵלִי וְאַנְוֵהוּ *ʾim ʾåmrī ʾåširå lʾēlī wʾanwēhū*
Dedication: Sukkot (on Shemini Atzeret)
Location: F305-08 (140 rº–141 rº)
111. *Jasly men da taryqqan*
Hebrew incipit: אֲנוּנָה אֲנִי וַעֲגוּמָה *ʾănūnå ʾănī waʿăḡūmå*
Dedication: Yom Kippur
Location: F305-41 (76 rº–77 rº), F305-08 (205 rº–206 rº)
112. *Jasly men men da taryḥqan*
Hebrew incipit: אֲנוּנָה אֲנִי וַעֲגוּמָה *ʾănūnå ʾănī waʿăḡūmå*
Dedication: Yom Kippur
Location: F305-11 (65 rº–66 vº)

---

question was written in 1709, see F305-11 (77 rº). Only one copy of this *peshat* is available—from 1878. The fact that the date of the latter manuscript is more recent is the reason why it was not included in our edition (see the text selection criteria in 1.4).

113. *Jazyqlarymyz köp boldular*
Hebrew incipit: אַשְׁמָתֵנוּ גָּדְלָה *ʾašmåṯēnū gåḏlå*
Dedication: Shabbats of the month Tammuz
Location: F305-08 (207 vº)

114. *Maḥtavludur ol Tenri H bijikŕaktir bar jaratylmyšlardan*
Hebrew incipit: בָּרוּךְ הָאֵל ה׳ *bårūḵ håʾēl H*
Dedication: Sukkot (on Shemini Atzeret)
Location: F305-08 (141 vº)

115. *Qajjam avalġy aziz Tenri čyġarġanynda bizni jerinden Gošennin*
Hebrew incipit: יוֹשֵׁב קֶדֶם *yōšēḇ qeḏem*
Dedication: Sukkot (on Shemini Atzeret)
Location: F305-08 (142 rº–142 vº)

116. *Sen e Tenrim jaratuvču dunjany baġatyrlyġyja köŕa*
Hebrew incipit: אֲנוּנָה אֲנִי וַעֲגוּמָה *ʾănūnå ʾănī waʿăgūmå*
Dedication: Shabbats of the month Tammuz
Location: F305-08 (288 rº–291 rº)

117. *Šükür eťamin saja uluslar arasyna ej H*
Hebrew incipit: אוֹדְךָ בְעַמִּים ה׳ *ʾōḏḵå ḇʿåmmīm H*
Dedication: Purim
Location: F305-08 (143 rº–144 rº), F305-67 (32 vº–34 vº)

118. *YHWH Tenrim sen bijik ettij išĺarijni*
Hebrew incipit: אֱלֹהַי אַתָּה רוֹמְמוֹת *ʾĕlohay ʾattå rōmmōṯ*
Dedication: Pesach (while reading the Hallel ha-Gadol)
Location: F305-08 (181 rº–182 rº)

119. (A *peshat* fragmentarily preserved; the incipit is missing)
Hebrew incipit: אַתָּה קָדוֹשׁ פּוֹעֵל גְּבוּרוֹת *ʾattå qåḏōš pōʿēl gḇūrōṯ* (?)
Dedication: Parashat Toledot
Location: JSul.I.37.03 (1 rº–1 vº)

The Eastern European Karaites have a long tradition of composing *piyyutim* in Hebrew. According to Tuori (2013: 60–82), a number of Karaim scholars from the 16th–17th centuries are known to be authors of such songs, such as, for instance, Yehuda ben Zerubbavel (16th–17th centuries), Yoshiyahu ben Yehuda (17th century), Abraham ben Aharon of Troki (died 1696) and his contemporary Abraham ben Aharon of Poniewież. As transpires from the archival materials I had access to, the tradition of translating Hebrew *piyyutim* into Karaim is not much more recent and can be traced back to the end of the 17th century, cf. *piyyut* № 2 authored by Josef ha-Mashbir in the late 17th century, the autograph of which has been preserved in ms. JSul.I.01 (118 vº–119 vº).

A number of additional remarks are necessary here. Firstly, Kizilov (2007) presented two works (he terms them *piyyutim*) of Icchak ben Abraham of Troki (1533/4–1594) and described them as "the earliest samples of the Karaim language" (see Kizilov 2007: 65). The case is that, on the one hand, the texts he worked on originate from sources not older than the 19th century and as such cannot be treated as among "the earliest samples of the Karaim language". These are much more recent copies. Kizilov referred to this circumstance as a "methodological problem". However, such "problems" (in fact: errors) reocurr, time and again, in his works.[28] On the other hand, the two works he presents, namely *Ne byla utrulajym* and *Jigit ojan ne juqlejsyn* are, in fact, not *piyyutim*, but *zemirot*, which transpires clearly from the archival materials.[29] Importantly, *piyyutim* (liturgical poems) and *zemirot* (paraliturgical poems) are consistently distinguished in the Karaim written heritage.[30] Later, Kizilov (2009: 162) claimed that he "managed to find quite a number of *piyyutim* by *Mashbir* in Karaim" (Kizilov 2009: 162). Yet again, however, the incipits he mentions, i.e. *Aruv aqyl ivretken*, *Adonaj Tenri kerti*, and *Aziz ǯan ojanġyn*, refer to works that are not *piyyutim*.[31] The same is true of the works of Josef ben Jeshua of

28 Cf., e.g., the statement: "to my knowledge, the earliest written usage of the term *kenesa* for the designation of a Karaite house of prayer is to be found in a poem by the Volhynian poet Joseph ben Yeshua (ca. 1648)" (Kizilov 2009: 116), but then he quotes Mardkowicz's (1932a: 20) article published in the 20th century. Obviously, it may well be that this word was already used in the 17th-century autograph (it is there, indeed, in a 19th-century copy in ms. ADub.III.102.09: 6 vº: כְּנֵסָהלַרְנִי *kenesalarny*). Nevertheless, we cannot treat a 20th-century copy as a reliable source for 17th-century linguistic data. It is an anachronism. *Nota bene*, Mardkowicz's practice of altering the original texts in his non-critical editions published in the journal Karaj Awazy was explained in Németh (2009), where the original manuscripts were compared with their editions published by Mardkowicz. Finally, some other serious turcological and linguistic shortcomings of M. Kizilov's interpretations of Karaim texts were pointed out by Jankowski (2015c: 190–192).

29 For *Ne byla utrulajym*, see JSul.I.02 (149 rº–149 vº), JSul.I.17 (76 rº–76 vº), JSul.I.19 (181 rº–181 vº), and JSul.I.38.06 (1 vº), where it is described as a *zemer* for Shabbat recited during Minchah. In the latter manuscript the author of the Hebrew original is clearly mentioned as יצחק נ֗ע הטרוקי בעֿס הזוק אמונה בכמ֗ר אברהם הזקן זצ֗ל 'Icchak of Troki, may his soul rest in Eden, the author of the book *Ḥizzuq Emuna*, the son of the honourable Rav Abraham, the aged, may the memory of the righteous be a blessing' (JSul.I.38.06: 1 rº), which supports Jankowski's (2015c: 190) argumentation in his polemics with M. Kizilov. For *Jigit ojan ne juqlejsyn* described as *zemer*, visit ADub.III.102.08 (18 rº–19 vº), and JSul.VI.12.01 (4 rº–5 rº; the author of this *zemer* is referred to as הרר מרדכי 'the Rav, Rabbi Mordecai').

30 For information on Karaite *zemirot*, see Tuori (2013: 87–112); the history and essence of *piyyutim* is well explained by Deutsch (1905: 65–68), Petuchowski (2004: 11–19), Fleischer (2007: 365–372), or Hollender (2008: 1–5). The specific way Kizilov interprets the genres of Karaim religious works was mentioned also by Jankowski (2015c: 189).

31 See: *Aruv aqyl ivretken* termed *baqqasha* in JSul.I.18 (139 vº–141 rº) (*nota bene*, Zarach ben Natan of Troki's *zemer* beginning with the words *Caġyramen rast Tenrim* was sung to the

Derażne: Kizilov (2009: 163) writes that he was "writing *piyyutim* in the Karaim language", but in the publication he refers to, namely in Nosonovsky (2007: 300), we clearly see that it is not *piyyutim* whose authorship is attributed to this sage, but rather elegies. In Kizilov (2009: 161) we read that he has discovered more "Karaim *piyyutim* by Isaac ben Abraham", but he provided no further definite data. Finally, the "*piyyut*" of Josef ben Jeshua of Derażne analysed in von Rohden (2004) also turned out to be a *zemer* (see the heading of the Hebrew work provided in von Rohden 2004: 162), and not a *piyyut*.

## 1.4 Scope of the Study: The Karaim *peshatim*

As has already been mentioned, the aim of this study was to reconstruct the way in which Western Karaim evolved between the second half of the 17th century and the first half of the 19th. The reason behind this choice was to show reliable linguistic material from the period in which the majority of the most significant changes in the Western Karaim phonological system took place.[32]

Thus, two major criteria were taken into account when establishing the scope of this study. The first was the chronology: the *peshatim* included in the present book can safely be assumed to have been written before the end of the 18th century (i.e. their authors had died before 1800). An additional prerequisite was that at least one copy of a given work should date from the first half of the 19th century. At the same time, in this edition all the discovered copies were taken into consideration by comparing them with the oldest complete versions of each text. As far as the latter versions are concerned, one of them survived in a 17th-century manuscript (№ 2), three of them are to be found in manuscripts from the 18th-century (№ 3, 6, 26), nineteen copies were created around around 1800 (№ 1, 7–12, 14–15, 17, 19–20, 23–25, 28–30), two copies originate from the first half of the 19th century (№ 13, 18) and six copies date from the mid-19th century (№ 4, 16, 21–22, 27).

The second main criterion was the genre. I wanted to find a suitably large group of texts that were consistent contentwise and the age of which would

---

melody of *Aruv aqyl ivretken*, see ADub.III.102.08: 19 v°), *Adonaj Tenri kerti qajjam* referred to both as *baqqasha* and *tachanun*, see ADub.III.102.08 (8 v°–12 r°), JSul.I.18 (141 r°–142 r°), and *Aziz ǯan ojanġyn* described as a *zemer* for Shabbats in JSul.I.02 (45 r°–48 r°), JSul.I.17 (41 v°–43 v°), JSul.I.19 (100 v°–109 r°), and JSul.III.74 (19 r°–21 r°). It is important to note that in JSul.I.19 the latter work is introduced by a lenghty heading (100 v°–103 r°) which shows the great importance this work had in Karaim religious life.

32 Only the elimination of the velar *ŋ* from the Western Karaim phonological system must have taken place earlier.

TABLE 1 The age of the texts edited in the present volume

| Age of the texts | Number of texts |
|---|---|
| 2nd half of the 17th century | 1 |
| ca. 1750 | 2 |
| 2nd half of the 18th century | 7 |
| ca. 1800 | 23 |
| 1st half of the 19th century | 37 |
| ca. 1850 | 60 |
| 2nd half of the 19th century | 16 |
| ca. 1900 | 2 |
| 1st half of the 20th century | 1 |
| **Total number of texts:** | **149** |

meet the first main criterion and had not been exhaustively researched in the past. Texts referred to as *piyyutim* have not received much attention in the scholarly literature.[33]

These critera allowed me to assemble representative linguistic material that could be presented in a single book of reasonable length, i.e. the *peshatim* 1–30 listed in 1.3 above. In the final analysis, the linguistic material presented in the critical edition (Chapter 4) consists of 149 texts excerpted from thirty-two manuscripts (see Table 2) found during an analysis of more than 500 archival items. As transpires from section 1.2, only one of these texts had been published before: the oldest version of peshat № 2 was presented in Németh (2018a).

TABLE 2 Manuscripts the *peshatim* edited were found in (arranged in chronological order)

| Accession № | Place of origin | Date of copy | Copyist |
|---|---|---|---|
| JSul.I.01a | Halych | between 1685 and 1700 | Josef ha-Mashbir |
| JER NLI 4101-8 | Lutsk | 1729 | Unknown |
| ADub.III.78 | Kukizów | ca. 1750 | Unknown |

33 Unlike, for instance, *zemirot*, see Mardkowicz (1930) or Tuori (2013). In fact, the language of the *zemirot* translated into or written in Western Karaim that I found (over seventy in number) in the manuscripts I worked on, exhibit exactly the same linguistic features as the *piyyutim* edited in this book.

TABLE 2 Manuscripts the *peshatim* edited were found in (*cont.*)

| Accession № | Place of origin | Date of copy | Copyist |
|---|---|---|---|
| JSul.I.53.13 | Halych | mid-18th c. (ca. 1762) | Unknown |
| JSul.I.01b | Halych | 2nd half of the 18th c. | Mordechai ben Shemuel |
| JSul.III.63 | Halych | ca. 1778 (before 1797) | Jeshua ben Mordechai Mordkowicz |
| JSul.I.38.09 | Halych (?) | turn of the 19th c. | Unknown |
| JSul.I.54.03 | Halych (?) | turn of the 19th c. | Unknown |
| JSul.III.66 | Halych | turn of the 19th c. | Unknown |
| JSul.III.03 | Halych | shortly after 1805 | Unknown |
| JSul.I.54.12 | Halych | early 19th c. | Unknown |
| JSul.I.45 | Halych | 1st half of the 19th c. (after ca. 1825) | Jeshua Josef Mordkowicz |
| JSul.I.46 | Halych | 1st half of the 19th c. (after ca. 1825) | Jeshua Josef Mordkowicz |
| JSul.VII.22.02.13 | Unknown | 1st half of the 19th c. | Unknown |
| JSul.III.67 | Halych | after ca. 1840 (before 1851) | Josef b. Icchak Szulimowicz (?) |
| JSul.III.64a | Halych | between 1840 and 1851 | Unknown |
| JSul.III.72 | Halych | before 1851 | Jeshua Josef Mordkowicz |
| ADub.III.61 | Halych | 1850/1851 | Jeshua Josef Mordkowicz |
| JSul.III.73 | Halych | mid-19th c. | Jeshua Josef Mordkowicz |
| JSul.I.37.02 | Lutsk | mid-19th c. | Unknown |
| JSul.I.54.09 | Halych | mid-19th c. | Jeshua Josef Mordkowicz |
| JSul.III.69 | Halych | ca. 1851 (before 1866) | Jeshua Josef Mordkowicz |
| JSul.III.79 | Halych | ca. 1851 (before 1866) | Jeshua Josef Mordkowicz |
| JSul.I.37.03 | Halych (?) | between 1851 and 1866 | Unknown |
| JSul.III.77 | Halych | between 1856 and 1866 | Jeshua Josef Mordkowicz |
| JSul.I.01c | Halych | 2nd half of the 19th c. | Jeshua Josef Mordkowicz |
| JSul.III.07 | Halych | 2nd half of the 19th c. | Jeshua Josef Mordkowicz |
| JSul.III.76 | Halych | 2nd half of the 19th c. | Jeshua Josef Mordkowicz |
| F305-08 | Poniewież (?) | 2nd half of the 19th c. | Unknown |
| JSul.I.11 | Lutsk | 1878 | Zecharia ben Chanania Rojecki |
| JSul.I.16 | Halych | 19th/20th c. | Unknown |
| JSul.I.54.15 | Unknown (Lutsk?) | turn of the 20th c. | Unknown |
| JSul.III.64b | Halych | 1st half of the 20th c. | Abraham ben Icchak Josef Leonowicz |

## 1.5 Scope of the Study: The Hebrew Originals

The present work provides *paytanic* poetry experts with material for further investigations. Some discrepancies between the Hebrew *piyyutim* and their Karaim interpretations show that this might be a promising subject of scholarly analysis.[34] One interesting example is, for instance, the passage in line 16:19–20,[35] where Heb. יִמְשׁוֹל עַמִּים בְּקַשְׁתּוֹ וּבְחַרְבּוֹ 'He [i.e. Moses] will rule over nations with his sword and bow' (JSul.III.79: 157 r°) was translated, as we can see in all the available copies, as *Erklenir uluslar istine tivil kici byla jajynyn da qylycynyn* [...] 'He [i.e. Moses] will rule over nations **not** with the power of his bow and sword [...]'. Another interesting detail is the use of the expression 'peace offerings of a buffalo' to render Heb. שֶׁלֶם מְרִיאוֹ 'a peace offering of a fatling' (JSul.III.79: 146 v°), which is attested in two different *peshatim*.[36] In the latter case, the Karaim translation is intriguing in light of the fact that all animal sacrifices in the Torah are of domestic animals. As a consequence, either we are dealing here with the Karaim word used in the meaning of 'bull', hitherto unattested, or this is simply an unusual rendering of the Hebrew original.

Given that the content of the *piyyutim* was greatly influenced by the Tanakh, the translation techniques applied in the *peshatim* are also based on the techniques we see in Karaim translations of the Hebrew Bible. A good example is the tendency to avoid anthropomorphisms when referring to God (described by A. Zajączkowski 1929), which is characteristic of both Biblical translations and, as we can now see, translations of the *piyyutim*. Unfortunately, so far only limited research has been done on the translation techniques applied in Karaim texts and their exegetic implications. The only publications in which this issue has been touched upon, besides Zajączkowski's article mentioned above, are Henderson (1826: 331–339), A. Zajączkowski (1931–1932: 191–292; 1947), Dubiński (1965a, 1965b), Altbauer (1979–1980), and Olach (2017: 235–238).

However, preparing an exhaustive analysis that contrasts the content of the Hebrew originals with their Karaim interpretations would go far beyond the final focus of this study as well as beyond the competences of its author. The

34 At this point I should express my thanks to Dr. Gabriel Wasserman (Hebrew University) for drawing my attention to certain matters connected with the relationship between the Hebrew originals and their Karaim interpretations (based on my English translations).

35 The first number indicates the number of a particular *peshat*, while the numbers after the colon refer to the number of the line of a particular work.

36 See *bujvolundan šelamim debeḥasynyn* 'than a sacrifice of a buffalo (offered) for peace offerings' (18:33–34) and *semiz bujvollary šelamimlernin* 'peace offerings of fat buffalos' (29:32); cf. Kar. *bujvol* < Russ. *буйвол* 'bufallo' (KarRPS 137).

same would be true of any attempt to identify all the Biblical or Talmudic references or allusions present in the texts. A detailed investigation of the relationship between the Hebrew and Karaim versions requires, besides Turkological training, in-depth Hebraistic skills, extensive exegetic knowledge of the Tanakh and a familiarity with the linguistic and stylistic peculiarities of *paytanic* poetry. Such a task would also require a profound grasp of the theological differences between mainstream Judaism and Karaism. The passage from Fleischer (2007: 372–373) quoted below provides a fuller picture of the language and style of this genre:

> The language of piyyut is mixed. From pre-paytanic poetry it inherited not only a link to the Bible, but one to post-biblical Hebrew as well. However, like all ancient poetry and perhaps more so, paytanut sought to turn an elegant phrase and adopt an unusual expression. Poetry's new position in the liturgy once again bestowed upon it an increasingly elitist and intellectual character. The initial search for unusual means of expression was cautious. The text was embellished here and there with lexical innovations, but remained clear and understandable. With the transition to the rhymed stage the emphasis shifts and a potent, highly organized but hermetic beauty becomes a goal. The classic paytan avoids as far as possible common words. He looks for *hapax legomena* and puzzling, brilliant or surprizing formulations. He recasts usual roots in unusual morphological forms, and imparts words with new grammatical status: nouns, adjectives, prepositions and conjunctions are transformed into verbs and vice versa. [...] The poet's language naturally became obscure in this process. Yet at this stage, as only so often in the history of poetry, obscurity was not considered flaw, rather the opposite. Piyyut at its best was the domain of learned men who delighted in its powerful phrasing and enigmatic language. [...]
>
> One of the typical paytanic stylistic means to be mentioned in this context is the frequent use of [...] emblematic designations for recurring notions, such as God, Israel, the Tora, biblical heroes, events, etc. Together they form a rich and complex network of alternative expressions [...]. Another important attribute of paytanic style is the [...] frequent embedding of biblical phrases in the paytanic text. [...] The biblical verse with its original connotations also enriched its new context with secondary meanings. [...]

We must remember, though, that the Karaim linguistic content should by no means be analysed in complete isolation from its Hebrew pattern. It is impossible to ignore the various messages conveyed by the Hebrew *piyyutim*: their content was often consulted during the editorial process in order to minimize the risk of misinterpretation. A good example is line 2:19, where the Hebrew word בָּטְלוּ 'are no more; have become extinct' was rendered as Kar. *batyl* (or *batil*) *bol-* '1. to be false; 2. to be prohibited, to not be allowed'. The Karaim word is far from being an exact equivalent of the Hebrew expression. Yet, it seems very likely that the auditive similarity between those two words led to the Karaim author's choice of this verb, even at the price of altering the meaning of the original text.

It is also worth mentioning that in the case of polysemous words used in an ambiguous context, it was often the Hebrew original that facilitated the choice of the appropriate meaning to be used in our English translation. Good examples are Kar. *qyjas* 'number, quantity; measure; value, price' attested in 11:34 in the meaning of 'value' and SWKar. *sizgir-* 'to strain (to filter)' recorded in line 9:27 in the figurative meaning of 'to refine'—cf. Heb. עֶרֶךְ 'value, valuation' and בְּמַצְרֵף 'in a melting pot, in a crucible' (a derivative of צרף 'to refine, to smelt') used in the originals (see JSul.III.69: 288 r° and JSul.III.79: 157 r°, respectively).[37]

Equally important is the fact that many Karaim fragments would have remained vague, erroneously interpreted or inappropriately translated if there had been no attempt to consult the emblemantic content of the Hebrew originals. For instance, if the English translation was based on the literal sense of the Karaim text, only, the fragment *Da rešut cerivinde cyqmasynlar bes sanalġanlar* [...] in *peshat* № 21 (line 23) would be translated as *And to a permitted war (even) five counted (people) must not go* [...]. The case is, however, that the fragment *cyqmasynlar bes sanalġanlar* refers to *five categories* of people, and not to *five people* in the figurative meaning of *any people*. Four of those categories are listed in Deuteronomy 20:5–8, whereas the fifth appears in Deuteronomy 24:5 (Gabriel Wasserman, personal communication). Thus, this fragment should be translated as *And to a permitted war five numbered (categories of people) must not go* [...].

37 We had the opportunity to consult the Hebrew originals as copied in mss. ADub.III.61 (94 r°–94 v°, 134 v°–135 v°), JSul.I.37.02 (6 r°–6 v°), JSul.I.16 (286 v°–288 r°), JSul.I.45 (100 v°–101 r°, 147 r°–147 v°), JSul.III.03 (84 v°–85 r°, 110 v°), JSul.III.67 (55 v°, 205 r°, 207 r°, 223 r°–223 v°, 248 v°–249 r°), JSul.III.69 (157 r°–157 v°, 283 v°, 286 r°–286 v°, 288 r°, 290 v°–291 r°, 294 r°–294 v°, 295 v°, 296 v°, 297 v°–298 r°, 299 r°–299 v°, 300 v°, 302 r°–302 v°), JSul.III.73 (67 v°), JSul.III.76 (51 r°–51 v°, 53 r°, 115 v°), JSul.III.77 (191 r°–191 v°), JSul.III.79 (146 v°–147 r°, 149 r°–149 v°, 152 v°–153 r°, 156 v°–158 r°, 159 r°–161 v°, 197 v°–198 r°, 265 r°–265 v°), as well as printed in *Siddur* (1528) and *Siddur* (1737).

TABLE 3 The number of verses of the Tanakh edited by scholars to date

| Karaim dialect | Verses edited | Verses edited in % |
|---|---|---|
| Eastern Karaim | 12,236 | 52.5 |
| South-Western Karaim | 687 | 2.95 |
| North-Western Karaim | 5,046 | 21.68 |

In 15:27, in turn, there is a mistranslation as a result of confusing אוֹרְךָ 'I will instruct you' with its homonym, i.e., with אוֹרֶךָ 'your light'.

An interesting task for the future would be to compare passages that contain direct references to the Tanakh with existing translations of the Hebrew Bible into Karaim. According to my own observations, the Biblical passages tend to have been paraphrased. For instance, the translation of Psalm 85:9 we see in line 18:43–44 is completely different from the one we know from later manuscripts, cf. ADub.III.69 (101 r°–102 r°) copied in Troki or B 282 (28 r°) copied in the Crimea.

There are over 140 Karaim Biblical manuscripts and printed editions in existence, and these are kept in various holdings, the most important being Polish, Lithuanian, and Ukrainian private archives, the Wroblewski Library of the Lithuanian Academy of Sciences (Vilnius), the Institute of Oriental Manuscripts of the Russian Academy of Sciences (Saint Petersburg), and the Russian State Library (Moscow). Further manuscripts are stored in other libraries, such as, e.g., the John Rylands Library (Manchester), the Cambridge University Library, and the Edinburgh University Library. Notwithstanding this fact, only a fraction of the Western Karaim Biblical manuscripts are in academic circulation. There are as far as I know, only 17 relevant publications containing scholarly edited Karaim Biblical texts, namely: Grzegorzewski (1916–1918), Danon (1921), Kowalski (1929), A. Zajączkowski (1931–1932; 1934b), J. Sulimowicz (1972; only Daniel 9:9–11), Firkovičius (1994), Jankowski (1997), Firkovičius (2000), Csató (2011), Olach (2013), Shapira (2013), Németh (2014d), Shapira (2014), Németh (2015c), Németh (2016a), Olach (2017), and Jankowski & Aqtay & Cegiołka & Çulha & Németh (2019). Compared to the total number of verses of the Karaim Hebrew Bible (which is 23,273), the above scholarly works encompass only a modest portion of the Western Karaim Tanakh (see Table 3). Hence, a comparison of the text of the *peshatim* with existing Bible translations requires extensive and intensive preparatory work consisting in the preparation of a comprehensive edition of the Western Karaim Hebrew Bible. A critical edition of ADub.III.73 is under preparation (see Németh 2021).

CHAPTER 2

# Authors and the Copyists of the *peshatim* Edited

## 2.1 Authors of the *peshatim*

The *peshatim* edited in this volume are the work of eight individuals. The authorship is in each case clearly indicated in the headings introducing the translations. Compiled below is a short biography of these individuals.

### 2.1.1 *Josef ha-Mashbir ben Shemuel*

Born probably ca. 1650,[1] died on the Shabbat of parashat Bo 5460 A.M. (see JSul.II.02: 52 r°),[2] i.e. on 3 Shevat 5460 A.M. which is 13 January 1700 according to the Gregorian calendar. In Mann's seminal work (1931: 1437) we find only 1699/1700 given as the date of his death. The son of Shemuel ha-Rodi, Josef ha-Mashbir was a Karaim scholar, poet, and hazzan in Halych from 1685 until his death. He was a native speaker of North-Western Karaim. Grzegorzewski (1916–1918: 279), Abrahamowicz (2001: 13), Akhiezer & Markon (2007: 425), Kizilov (2009: 48), and Šabarovśkyj (2013: 150) claim that he came to Halych from Derażne. Gąsiorowski (2008: 375), and Tuori (2013: 77), in turn, argue that he was born in Lithuania. Finally, Muchowski & Tomal & Sulimowicz & Witkowski & Yariv (2017: 32) occupy the middle ground, hypothesising that he moved to Halych from Derażne, but his family may have ultimately originated from Lithuania. Josef ha-Mashbir was responsible for a cultural revival in the community in Halych following a period of neglect.[3]

---

1 We know this based on Fahn's (1929: 40; *non vidi*) work, in which he published ha-Mashbir's gravestone.

2 I want to thank Anna Sulimowicz-Keruth (Warsaw) for providing me with the exact date of ha-Mashbir's demise.

3 Cf. Zarach ben Natan of Troki's elegy with the incipit *Ačy qyna avur syjyt jylajym* composed to commemorate the death of David ben Jeshua the Jerusalemite (died 1647 (5408 A.M.), see Mann 1931: 125; JSul.I.53.12: 1 r°) who visited Halych and Lutsk at that time. In that work we read: *Da keldi ol qahalyna Haličnin da kördü ol elin kečnin da hečnin* 'And he arrived in the community of Halych and saw the backwardness and vanity of the people' (JSul.I.53.12: 2 r°; the English translation of this translation in Kizilov 2009: 47 is not entirely correct). This elegy was then reprinted after being transposed into South-Western Karaim in 1933, see Mardkowicz (1933a: 11–12).

 | DOI:10.1163/9789004419377_003

TABLE 4 Authors of the *peshatim* and their native dialect

| № | Author | Native dialect | *Peshatim* № |
|---|---|---|---|
| 1. | Josef ha-Mashbir | North-Western | 1–3 |
| 2. | Mordechai ben Icchak Łokszyński | North-Western | 4 |
| 3. | Mordechai ben Nisan | North-Western | 5 |
| 4. | Moshe ben Icchak Cic-Ora | South-Western (?) | 6 |
| 5. | Simcha ben Chananel | North-Western | 7–24 |
| 6. | Josef ben Shemuel ben Josef ha-Mashbir | South-Western | 25 |
| 7. | Shemuel ben Josef ha-Mashbir | South-Western (?) | 26–27 |
| 8. | Mordechai ben Shemuel | South-Western | 28–30 |

His North-Western Karaim autograph[4] supports the view that he was born into a North-Western Karaim community or, at least, that his family had its roots in Lithuania.

Actually, it seems very likely that Josef ha-Mashbir was brought up in Troki if we juxtapose the following of facts from his biography.

Firstly, it is important to be aware of the fact that according to Fürst (1869: 85–86), Josef ha-Mashbir's teacher was Nisan the aged (*ha-zaqen*) of Lithuania, and that Josef ha-Mashbir taught his teacher's son Mordechai ben Nisan (see 2.1.3). Moreover, based on the headings introducing the copies of *peshat* № 5 in mss. JSul.III.69, JSul.III.79, and JSul.I.01c, we can say with some certainty that Nisan the aged was in fact *of Troki*. As a consequence, if we consider the fact that Nisan the aged moved from Troki to Kukizów not earlier than 1688, i.e., not earlier than the year when the Karaim community of Kukizów was established (see, e.g., Gąsiorowski 2008: 191–192)[5] and not earlier than Josef ha-Mashbir's arrival in Halych in 1685, it appears highly probable that Josef ha-Mashbir was taught by Nisan in Troki and not elsewhere.

The question remains whether he made his way to Halych directly from Lithuania or whether, according to Karaim historiographic tradition, he came from Derażne. What makes the latter interpretation problematic is the fact that the Karaim community in Derażne was destroyed long before 1685, namely in

4 Ms. JSul.I.01a: 118 v°, see 2.2.1 below.

5 The Karaim population in Kukizów included representatives of both the north-western and south-western branches. The settlers arrived in Kukizów in two waves: from Troki in 1688 and from Halych in 1692 (see Gąsiorowski 2008: 191–192).

1648–1649 during the Khmelnytsky Uprising.[6] Even though some historical evidence suggests that the community survived these revolts, the present author does not find them sufficiently convincing.[7]

The edited materials show that Josef ha-Mashbir, despite the many epithets assigned to his name, is never referred to with the appendage as '*of Derażne*', unlike, for instance, his contemporary Chananel of Derażne, the father of Simcha ben Chananel (2.1.5). His birthplace is not mentioned, either, by Simcha Icchak Łucki (born at the end of the 17th century, died 1776) in *Ner Tzaddikim* written around 1757 (see Mann 1931: 1436–1437). However, according to A. Sulimowicz-Keruth (personal communication), the ha-Rodi family must have had strong ties with the community in Derażne given that a *zichronot* written ca. 1892 by Zarach Leonowicz (1829–1894),[8] informs us that Josef ha-Mashbir's brother Jeshua and their parents (Shemuel ha-Rodi and Shelomit), were buried in Derażne (see JSul.I.01: 198 r°).

Nevertheless, the most important information from the perspective of the present work is the fact that he was a native speaker of North-Western Karaim.

Besides the five poems composed in Hebrew mentioned by Tuori (2013: 75), and the three *peshatim* edited in this volume (№ 1–3), Josef ha-Mashbir wrote at least four more religious songs in Karaim, namely: *Jah*[9] *Tenri kerti qajjam*, *Maḥtav sarnavun bašlajym*, *Maḥtavlu bij aziz Tenrim*,[10] and *Aziz ǯan ojanġyn kipĺa belijni*.[11] The latter *zemer* was even translated into Hebrew by Mordechai

6 According to Nosonovskij & Šabarovśkyj (2004: 45) the massacre might have taken place in 1650.

7 This has already been suggested by Mordechai Sułtański's in his Zecher Tzaddikim, a historiographic work from 1837/1838 (see Poznański 1920: 114) as well as by Sergjusz Rudkowski (1932: 4–5), a Karaim man of letters living in years 1873–1944. It is perhaps worth mentioning here that the data in question comes from the Russian census of 1677–1679 cited by Bałaban (1927: 50) and A. Zajączkowski (1934a: 182) in which, allegedly, a group of 6 persons of Jewish and Karaim origin are mentioned. Based on this piece of evidence, Šabarovśkyj (2013: 153–154) claims that a small Karaim community must have lived there well into the second half of the 18th century, a fact which is later contested by Muchowski & Tomal & Sulimowicz & Witkowski & Yariv (2017: 13–14). For more information, see Németh (2018a).

8 In fact, Zarach ben Shemuel ben Levi ben Jeshua ben Shemuel ben Jeshua ben Shemuel ha-Rodi. He was hazzan in Halych in 1884–1894.

9 Heb. יָהּ (one of the names of God).

10 See, in South-Western Karaim copies, F305-220 (1 r°–2 v°), JSul.I.18 (141 r°–142 r°; 136 r°–136 v°; 136 v°–138 r°, respectively).

11 See, e.g., JSul.I.17 (41 v°–43 v°).

ben Nisan (2.1.3).[12] Finally, he also composed a *qinah* with the incipit *Men miskin qaldyġy*.[13]

For further reading, see Kizilov (2009: 48–50), Šabarovśkyj (2013: 150–153), Tuori (2013: 75–78), and Németh (2018a).

### 2.1.2 *Mordechai ben Icchak Łokszyński*

Born probably in the mid-17th century in the small Karaim community of Święte Jezioro in Lithuania (see Tuori 2013: 82). He died before 1709. He was a native speaker of North-Western Karaim. The year of his death was determined by the fact that Mordechai ben Nisan (2.1.3, died ca. 1709) wrote a *qinah* to commemorate his passing, see Mann (1931: 1259–1260).[14] Mordechai ben Icchak has translated at least two *zemirot* of Zarach ben Natan of Troki into North-Western Karaim, the incipits of which are *Avaz kötüŕamin Tenriġa sarnajmen* and *Maḥtav beŕamen qajjam Tenriġa*.[15] At a certain point of his life he moved to Troki, since in the sources he is referred to as *Mordechai of Troki called Łoksynśki* [...] *ben Icchak*.[16] In ms. JSul.I.19 (59 vº), in turn, he is mentioned as the author of the Hebrew *zemer* שְׁאִי זִמְרָה נַפְשִׁי *śʾī zimrå napšī* later translated by Jeshua ben Mordechai (2.2.3) into Karaim with the incipit *Čeber zemer ajtma*. Interestingly, the above manuscript (59 vº) gives him a slightly more elaborate patronymic, namely: *Mordechai ben Icchak, the grandson of Mordechai Łokszyński*. This supports Tuori's (2013: 82) assertion that the author of שְׁאִי זִמְרָה נַפְשִׁי *śʾī zimrå napšī* and the translator of אֶשָּׂא בְּכוֹס יֶשַׁע *ʾeśśå bḵōs yešaʿ* is, in fact, one and the same person. Moreover, I find it quite probable that the Mordechai ben Icchak mentioned by Jankowski (2014: 39), i.e. the copyist of the oldest known North-Western Karaim text in Evr I 699 from 1686 (see folio 10 rº), was, in fact, "this" Mordechai ben Icchak Łokszyński.

---

12 See, e.g., JSul.I.17 (44 rº–46 rº), Hebrew incipit: אוֹרִי נְשָׁמָה הַקְּדוֹשָׁה בְּאוֹרֵךְ *ʾōrī nšåmå haqqḏōšå bʾōrēḵ*.

13 See, e.g., JSul.I.01 (121 rº–123 rº), F305-67 (64 rº–67 rº).

14 Mordechai ben Icchak's contemporary was Josef ben Icchak (see Mann 1931: 737), the author of several religious and theological works who cooperated with Mordechai ben Nisan; for instance, he wrote an approbation of the latter's *Maʾamar Mordechai* (see 2.1.3 below). Given the lack of conclusive genealogical data, we can only surmise whether Mordechai ben Icchak and Josef ben Icchak were brothers. The last mention of Josef ben Icchak is from 1710 (see Mann 1931: 739).

15 Hebrew incipits: Heb. אֶשָּׂא בְּכוֹס יֶשַׁע *ʾeśśå bḵōs yešaʿ* and Heb. אֶקְרָא אֶל עֶלְיוֹן *ʾåqrå ʾel ʿelyōn*, see RAbk.IV.15 (89 rº–90 rº; 112 vº–113 vº), respectively.

16 Cf. מרדכי הטרקי המכונה לוקסינשקי נבּת בכּמע יצחק הזקן (JSul.I.17: 79 vº).

### 2.1.3 *Mordechai ben Nisan*

A native of Troki: his father was referred to as *Nisan the aged* (ha-zaken) *of Troki* or *of Lithuania* (see the Hebrew headings that introduce the copies of *peshat* № 5). The year of his birth is unknown, yet he is believed to have been born around 1650 (see Tuori 2013: 73). He was a speaker of North-Western Karaim. In 1688 he left Lithuania and settled down in Kukizów (along with his father Nisan) to take up duties of the first hazzan of that community. He continued to perform this function until he left for the Crimea in ca. 1709. On the way, he and his son Nisan were murdered, probably at the hands of brigands (see Mann 1931: 739, fn. 1067b).[17] He authored several theological, grammatical, and religious works, among others the treatises *Dod Mordechai*[18] in 1699, and *Ma'amar Mordechai* in 1709. We know of two *zemirot* authored by him in Hebrew and translated, also by him, into Karaim: *Astry qorqunčlu bij*, and *Šükür maḥtav Tenrige.*[19]

For more information on Mordechai, his works and his relationships with his contemporaries, see Fürst (1869: 87–95), Mann (1931: 588–589, 738–739, 1257–1262), W. Zajączkowski (1976: 764), Harviainen & Hopeavuori & Nieminen (1998: 43), Gąsiorowski (2008: 23–24, 376), Tuori (2013: 73–75), and Wasserman (2016).[20]

### 2.1.4 *Moshe ben Icchak Cic-Ora*

Based on Mann (1931: 1266, fn. 617) we know that he died in 1717/1718 (i.e. in 5478 A.M.) and that in a *zemer* written in his honour Josef ben Shemuel (2.1.6) referred to him as *ha-zaqen*, i.e. *the aged*, which means that he must have died at an advanced age. In the edited sources he is called *Rabbi*, whereas his father, Icchak, is given the appendages *Rabbi* and *ha-Maskil*. Mann also attributes authorship of two *piyyutim* to him. He was most probably a native speaker of South-Western Karaim (see 2.2.9). He is referred to as a living person in a letter from Shelomo ben Aharon of Vilna issued in 1715, see Mann (1931: 1266).

---

17 Cf. the abbreviation ה״ד, i.e. Heb. הַשֵּׁם יִקֹּם דָּמוֹ 'may the Lord avenge his blood' often used alongside his and his son's name.

18 Published under the title *Sefer Dod Mordechai* (סֵפֶר דֹּד מָרְדְּכַי) in 1830 in Vienna in the printing house of Anton Edler von Schmid.

19 The Hebrew incipit of the first one is אֵל נַעֲרָץ נוֹרָא *ʿēl naʿărås̩ nōrå* (JSul.I.17: 36 rº–38 rº). The second was authored in 5461 A.M., i.e. in 1700/1701 and its Hebrew incipit is נוֹדֶה לה עַל חַסְדּוֹ *nōḏe l-H ʿal ḥasdō* (see, RAbl.IV.15: 151 vº–154 rº).

20 We also found a *zemer* authored in Hebrew by Josef ben Nisan of Lithuania and translated by Mordechai into Karaim (the South-Western Karaim incipit reads *Maḥtavlar berejim aziz Tenrige*; the Hebrew incipit: אוֹדֶה לְאֵל נוֹרָא *ʾōḏe lʾēl nōrå*, see JSul.III.74: 77 rº–79 rº). Seen in this light, it seems likely that Josef ben Nisan and Mordechai ben Nisan were brothers (see 2.1.2).

His father, Icchak, is most probably the *Jzaak syn Abrahama* mentioned in the document edited by Muchowski & Tomal & Sulimowicz & Witkowski & Yariv (2017: 47: *Jzaak, starszy, syn* […] *Abrahama z Halicza, z rodziny Cic Ora* 'Icchak the aged, the son of Abraham of Halicz, from the *Cic Ora* family') as a person buried in Kukizów. In JSul.I.53.15 (7 r°), his surname is spelled ציוּצֿיורא *Cücöre* (or *Cücöra*), which is most probably a South-Western Karaim hypercorrect form of *Cic Ora* with the *Ora* > *Öre* change triggered by the phonotactic requirements of the vowel harmony. This form may have served as the base for the Slavicized variant of this surname, namely *Czuczorowicz* (see Muchowski & Tomal & Sulimowicz & Witkowski & Yariv 2017: 78). The name of the family most likely derives from Heb. צִיץ אוֹרָה *ṣīṣ ōrå* 'glistening light'.

### 2.1.5 *Simcha ben Chananel*

The date of his birth is uncertain, but he was most likely born in Trakai, given that he was among those migrants from Trakai who established the Karaim community of Kukizów in 1688, see the document edited in Mann (1931: 886). In the latter document he refers to himself in Hebrew as הצעיר והזעיר 'young and small', which suggests that he was born sometime after 1670. He is known to have died 20 Adar II 5483 A.M., i.e. 27 March 1723 A.D. and was buried in Kukizów (see JSul.II.02: 52 r°; the place of his burial is mentioned also in JSul.III.05: 164 r°; see also Muchowski & Tomal & Sulimowicz & Witkowski & Yariv 2017: 33, 45). His father, Chananel, was the hazzan of the community in Derażne (see JSul.I.45: 101 r°). Simcha became the hazzan in Kukizów, succeeding in that post Mordechai ben Nisan (2.1.3), and thus from ca. 1709 probably until his death. He was a native speaker of North-Western Karaim and the author of a number of *piyyutim* composed in Hebrew (see Mann 1931: 1270, fn. 645) as well as a large number of Karaim interpretations of *piyyutim*, see *peshatim* № 7–24. He was a prominent copyist; in 1710 he copied Shelomo ben Aharon's *Appirion* (its Viennese copy is referenced by Poznański 1916: 98), whereas between 25 March and 31 May 1720 he created a translation of the Torah (ADub.III.73: 1 r°–343 r°).[21] Shortly afterwards, he attached a copy of four other books of Ketuvim, namely the Book of Ruth, the Book of Jeremiah, Ecclesiastes, and the Book of Esther, to the same manuscript (ADub.III.73: 344 r°–388 v°). We can only suppose that he was also the translator of the four books of Ketuvim mentioned above. This is probable in light of the fact that he was the translator of another book of Ketuvim, namely the Book of Lamentations,[22] and also because he was given the epi-

21 A critical edition of this manuscript is being prepared by Németh (2021).

22 See JSul.I.11 (4 r°–52 r°); the fact that Simcha ben Chananiel was the translator comes from the introductory passage in Hebrew on folio 28 r°. The manuscript itself originates from

thets *the translator, the divine translator, the divine translator and ha-Torani.*[23] He was also the copyist of TKow.01, a partially-vocalised manuscript containing the translation of the Torah (he finished copying this source on the first day of the parashat Vayeshev in the month Kislev 5483 A.M., i.e. on 7 December 1722 A.D.). For more information about him, his idiolect and ms. ADub.III.73, see Németh (2014c: 110–113; 2015c: 50–51; 2021).

### 2.1.6 *Josef ben Shemuel ben Josef ha-Mashbir*

Born most probably in Halych and died, according to Mann's (1931: 1438) edition of Karaite texts, in 5497 A.M., i.e. 1736/1737 A.D.[24] The son of Shemuel ben Josef ha-Mashbir (2.1.7). He died young, even before his father: in the sources he is therefore often mentioned as a 'young and wise scholar'. He was a native speaker of South-Western Karaim.

### 2.1.7 *Shemuel ben Josef ha-Mashbir*

Born 1680, died 1745/1746 according to Mann's (1931: 1438) edition of Simcha Icchak Łucki's *Ner Tzaddikim*. He was the second son of Josef ha-Mashbir (2.1.1) and the hazzan in Halych from 1738 until 1744 (after his brother Moshe, who most probably performed this function in the years 1700–1738).[25] In all likelihood he was a native speaker of South-Western Karaim or of both Western Karaim dialects. He had two sons: Moshe, who died possibly ca. 1778 (and had a son called Josef, see RAbk.IV.15: 49 r°),[26] and Josef (2.1.6). Interestingly, his

---

1878 and contains different types of texts copied by three persons. The Book of Lamentations was copied by Zecharia ben Chanania Rojecki (2.2.6).

23 See JSul.I.45 (142 v°), JSul.III.69 (295 v°, 298 r°), and JSul.III.79 (179 v°). Importantly, these honorifics were not bestowed on the other authors of *peshatim* presented in this volume; hence, the title given to Simcha ben Chananel is exceptional.

24 Mann takes this information from Simcha Icchak Łucki's *Ner Tzaddikim* (authored ca. 1757), i.e. from the work of a contemporary of Josef ben Shemuel. To learn more about Simcha Icchak Łucki, see, e.g., W. Zajączkowski (1973b).

25 See Zarachowicz (1935: 23), Gąsiorowski (2008: 456), Muchowski & Tomal & Sulimowicz & Witkowski & Yariv (2017: 33). However, for a critique of these dates, see Shapira (2002: 15), and Kizilov (2009: 377, fn. 3).

26 There is no consensus among historians regarding the time period when Moshe ben Shemuel lived and served as hazzan. Based on Mann (1931: 756, 1351) and Reuven Fahn's tombstone documentations (*non vidi*) from before the Great War, Kizilov (2009: 105, 377) claims that Moshe performed the functions of hazzan until 1778, and refutes Zarachowicz's opinion (1935: 23), later repeated by Gąsiorowski (2008: 456), that he continued to serve this function until 1792. According to the materials edited by Mann (1931: 756), a letter sent by Abraham ben Mordechai of Poniewież to Mordechai ben Nisan of Kukizów in 1783 refers to another letter, unanswered, sent earlier in ca. 1778 to Icchak ben Icchak, the hazzan of Lutsk (died ca. 1778) along with two additional letters addressed to Jeshua ben Mordechai (2.2.3) and Mordechai ben Nisan of Kukizów (the hazzan in Kukizów, died 1803). From

daughter Menucha married Mordechai ben Shemuel (2.1.8). He composed at least one *zemer* in Hebrew, which was later translated by his grandson Shemuel ben Moshe (hazzan in Halych in 1796–1801) into Karaim.[27]

### 2.1.8 *Mordechai ben Shemuel*

Born most probably around the turn of the 18th century, he served as hazzan in Kukizów in the first half of the 18th century (see Gąsiorowski 2008: 457, Kizilov 2009: 378, and Muchowski & Tomal & Sulimowicz & Witkowski & Yariv 2017: 43), possibly after Simcha ben Chananel's (2.1.5) death in 1723. He then filled the office of hazzan in Halych from 1744 until 1764 (see Zarachowicz 1935) or 1765 (see Kizilov 2009: 377). Kizilov quotes Bałaban (1909: 4), who discovered that Mordechai was listed in the census of 1765. In fact, he died on the first day of the Parashat Ki Tavo 5525 A.M., i.e. on 1 September 1765 A.D. (see the dirge composed in his memory and copied by his grandson Jeshua Josef Mordkowicz in JSul.I.01 (162 rº–163 rº)). Interestingly, he was referred to as *the divine philosopher*, *the seer*, or *the possessor of understanding* in the edited sources, see, e.g., ms. JSul.III.03 (105 rº, 110 rº). Mordechai was the father of four children, among them of Jeshua Mordkowicz (see 2.2.3) and a member of the esteemed ha-Rodi family: his father, Shemuel, was the son of Josef ha-Mashbir's brother, Jeshua. He was a native speaker of South-Western Karaim. See also 2.2.2 below.

## 2.2 Copyists of the *peshatim*

As is shown in Table 1, the material was excerpted from 149 texts preserved in thirty-two manuscripts. Of this group, 113 texts (i.e. 76% of the total) were copied by persons whose identity has been clarified, i.e. Josef ha-Mashbir ben Shemuel, Mordechai ben Shemuel, Jeshua ben Mordechai Mordkowicz, Jeshua Josef Mordkowicz, Josef ben Icchak Szulimowicz, Zecharia ben Chanania Rojecki, and Abraham ben Icchak Josef Leonowicz. The remaining 36 copies (24% of the total) are the work of fourteen different persons of unknown identity. These are the copyists of manuscripts ADub.III.78, F305-08, JER NLI

---

this correspondence we know that Jeshua ben Mordechai was addressed as 'the hazzan and the presiding judge of the Holy Community of Halych' (Mann 1931: 1350–1351), which could mean that Moshe ben Shemuel had passed away by the time the letter was written (i.e. ca. 1778) and Jeshua ben Mordechai took over his duties. However, we must treat this information with some caution: It is conceivable that two *hazzanim* were present at the same time, as was the custom in the interwar period, i.e. some communities had a junior and a senior (*ullu*) hazzan.

27 Its Hebrew incipit is כְּרוּבִים כָּל בְּנֵי עֶלְיוֹן *krūḇīm kål bnē ʿelyōn*. The Karaim incipit is *Keruvimler bar malaḫlar* (see JSul.I.02: 113 vº–114 vº).

TABLE 5 The number of copies created by each copyist (in chronological order) and their native dialect

| No | Copyist | Number of copies | Native dialect |
|---|---|---|---|
| 1. | Josef ha-Mashbir | 1 | North-Western |
| 2. | Unknown 1 (copyist of JER NLI 4101-8) | 1 | North-Western |
| 3. | Unknown 2 (copyist of ADub.III.78) | 1 | North-Western |
| 4. | Unknown 3 (copyist of JSul.I.53.13) | 1 | South-Western |
| 5. | Mordechai ben Shemuel | 3 | South-Western |
| 6. | Jeshua ben Mordechai Mordkowicz | 3 | South-Western |
| 7. | Unknown 4 (copyist of JSul.I.38.09) | 2 | South-Western |
| 8. | Unknown 5 (copyist of JSul.I.54.03) | 6 | South-Western |
| 9. | Unknown 6 (copyist of JSul.III.66) | 1 | South-Western |
| 10. | Unknown 7 (copyist of JSul.III.03) | 14 | South-Western |
| 11. | Unknown 8 (copyist of JSul.I.54.12) | 2 | South-Western |
| 12. | Unknown 9 (copyist of JSul.VII.22.02.13) | 1 | South-Western |
| 13. | Josef ben Icchak Szulimowicz (?) | 5 | South-Western |
| 14. | Unknown 10 (copyist of JSul.III.64a) | 1 | South-Western |
| 15. | Jeshua Josef Mordkowicz | 98 | South-Western |
| 16. | Unknown 11 (copyist of JSul.I.37.02) | 1 | South-Western |
| 17. | Unknown 12 (copyist of JSul.I.37.03) | 2 | South-Western |
| 18. | Zecharia ben Chanania Rojecki | 2 | North-Western |
| 19. | Unknown 13 (copyist of F305-08) | 1 | North-Western |
| 20. | Unknown 14 (copyist of JSul.I.16) | 1 | South-Western |
| 21. | Unknown 15 (copyist of JSul.I.54.15) | 1 | South-Western |
| 22. | Abraham ben Icchak Josef Leonowicz | 1 | South-Western |

4101-8, JSul.I.16, JSul.I.37.02, JSul.I.37.03, JSul.I.38.09, JSul.I.54.03, JSul.I.53.13, JSul.I.54.12, JSul.I.54.15, JSul.III.03, JSul.III.64a, JSul.III.66, and JSul.VII.22.02.13.

It is striking that the 98 copies produced by Jeshua Josef Mordkowicz make up two thirds of the total number of 149 texts. However, the linguistic description provided in this book cannot by any means be considered an analysis of this person's idiolect, only. The analysed linguistic material comes not only from him, but from 22 different hands while each text as well as each linguistic feature is treated individually, i.e. the linguistic facts are contrasted with the age of their source, the biography of the copyist, the place where the text was copied, etc. In fact, only six of the oldest copies of each *peshat* (mentioned at the end of section 1.4) were copied by Jeshua Josef Mordkowicz (see *peshatim*

TABLE 6 The copyists of the oldest variants of each Karaim *peshat*

| *Peshat* № | Copyist of the oldest version | The accession № of the oldest manuscript |
|---|---|---|
| 1 | Unknown 7 | JSul.III.03 |
| 2 | Josef ha-Mashbir | JSul.I.01a |
| 3 | Mordechai ben Shemuel | JSul.I.01b |
| 4 | Jeshua ben Mordechai Mordkowicz | JSul.III.63 |
| 5 | Unknown 7 | JSul.III.03 |
| 6 | Unknown 2 | JSul.I.54.03 |
| 7 | Unknown 5 | JSul.III.03 |
| 8 | Unknown 7 | JSul.III.03 |
| 9 | Unknown 7 | JSul.III.03 |
| 10 | Unknown 7 | JSul.III.03 |
| 11 | Unknown 7 | JSul.I.54.03 |
| 12 | Unknown 5 | JSul.VII.22.02.13 |
| 13 | Unknown 9 | JSul.I.54.03 |
| 14 | Unknown 5 | JSul.III.03 |
| 15 | Unknown 7 | ADub.III.61 |
| 16 | Jeshua Josef Mordkowicz | JSul.I.54.03 |
| 17 | Unknown 5 | JSul.I.45 |
| 18 | Jeshua Josef Mordkowicz | JSul.I.54.03 |
| 19 | Unknown 5 | JSul.I.54.03 |
| 20 | Unknown 5 | ADub.III.61 |
| 21 | Jeshua Josef Mordkowicz | ADub.III.61 |
| 22 | Jeshua Josef Mordkowicz | JSul.III.03 |
| 23 | Unknown 7 | JSul.III.03 |
| 24 | Unknown 7 | JSul.III.03 |
| 25 | Unknown 7 | JSul.I.01b |
| 26 | Mordechai ben Shemuel | ADub.III.61 |
| 27 | Jeshua Josef Mordkowicz | ADub.III.78 |
| 28 | Unknown 7 | JSul.III.03 |
| 29 | Unknown 7 | JSul.III.03 |
| 30 | Unknown 7 | JSul.III.03 |

№ 4, 16, 18, 21, 22, 27; see Table 6), and there are altogether 34 works that were copied long before he was born or could have learned to write (see Table 2).

Further biographical data on the copyists are presented below. The dialectal affiliation of the unknown copyists' idiolects and, in some cases, their possible identity is also addressed in this chapter.

### 2.2.1 *Josef ha-Mashbir ben Shemuel*

See 2.1.1. He copied a large portion of ms. JSul.I.01—mostly texts in Hebrew; the only works he copied in Karaim are the *zemer* with the incipit *Bügün Sinaj tavġa* (115 v°–116 r°), the *peshat* of the *piyyut* № 2 with the incipit *Jazyqlarymyz ulġajdylar bijikḱa astry* (118 v°–119 v°), and a *qinah* beginning with the words *Men miskin qaldyġy* (121 r°–123 r°)—the latter also being authored by him. The language of these works is uniform, and clearly North-Western in type with a number of archaic elements. Remarkably, in the text of *piyyut* № 2 we find instances of the **ŋ* > *n* change, too, in place of the expected **ŋ* > *j* shift, cf. *sana* (2:41, 43, 52) and *mašijaḥyndan* (2:46). It is highly likely that the author's idiolect was influenced in this respect by the language of the Halych Karaims amongst whom he lived from 1685 on.

It ought to be added that, in the introduction to the *peshat Jazyqlarymyz ulġajdylar bijikḱa astry* on folio 118 v° in ms. JSul.I.01a Josef ha-Mashbir writes the following: "I have translated this *piyyut* in metre into the foreign language, and I present it to the eye of the reader" (see № 2:6–7). Based on this passage we can be sure that this part of ms. JSul.I.01 was copied by Josef ha-Mashbir. For the time being, this is the only known autograph of ha-Mashbir written in Karaim.

### 2.2.2 *Mordechai ben Shemuel*

See 2.1.8. He was most probably the copyist of JSul.I.01b; his name is not recorded *expressis verbis* in the manuscript. We base our assessment on the following philological and genealogical facts:

In the heading introducing *peshat* № 3, its author, Josef ha-Mashbir (the author of the *peshat*), is referred to as 'my master, my uncle, my father-in-law' (3:1), cf. Fig. 1 below. In turn, from the *zichronot* in JSul.III.05 (254 v°: lines 6–10, 261 v°: lines 1–10)—copied by the son of Mordechai ben Shemuel, namely Moshe ben Mordechai—we learn that Mordechai ben Shemuel, who was the grandson of Josef ha-Mashbir's brother, took Shemuel ben Josef ha-Mashbir's daughter, Menucha, for his wife.[28] Mordechai ben Shemuel is thus the only per-

28 I am indebted, again, to Anna Sulimowicz-Keruth (Warsaw) for kindly providing me with this genealogical information.

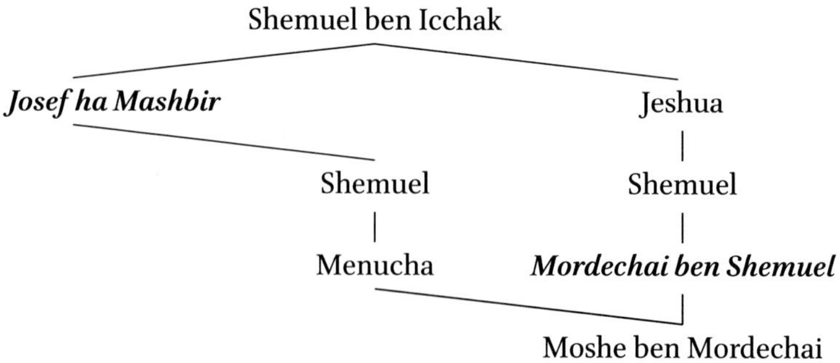


FIGURE 1 The relationship between Josef ha-Mashbir and Mordechai ben Shemuel
*Note*: The full genealogy is not presented here; only those persons who are of relevance to section 2.2.2 are indicated.

son who was, firstly, a clergyman (i.e. was trained in calligraphy), and, secondy, could have referred to Josef ha-Mashbir both as his 'father-in-law',[29] and as 'my uncle'.[30] And even if we agree that Heb. אד̃ might have also stood for 'my master' and not only for 'my master, my uncle', the use of the expression 'father-in-law' by Moshe ben Mordechai and the age of the manuscript narrows down the number of potential copyists practically to one.

As far as the Karaim portions of the text of ms. JSul.I.01 are concerned, he copied folios 59 r°, 108 r°–108 v°, and 124 r°–130 v° (in addition, he copied many other passages in Hebrew). All these passages are recorded in South-Western Karaim, i.e. in his native dialect, including the *peshat Bijine dunjanyn šira ajtajim*[31] written by Mordechai ben Nisan (2.1.3)—a native speaker of North Western Karaim (59 r°). The situation is slightly different with the *qinah* that begins with the words *Ojanġyn jüregim qyna oḥumaqqa* attributed to Shelomo ben Aharon of Poswol (born 1670, died 1745): in this dirge, originally written in North-Western Karaim, the copyist retained the NWKar. *j* (< *ŋ), see e.g. סִיְיט אֵטִיְיז *syjyt etijiz* 'grieve (imperat.2.pl)' (125 r°), איוּביוּיְינִיוּ *üvüjnü* 'your house

29 Heb. חוֹתֵן 'father-in-law' was used in the sources in a broader sense of '1. father-in-law; 2. any ancestor of one's father-in-law'.

30 Cf. the abbreviation אד̃ 1. אֲדֹנִי 'my master'; 2. אֲדוֹנֵנוּ 'our master'; 3. אֲדֹנִי דוֹדִי 'my master, my uncle'. It was very frequently used in the meaning of 'my uncle' though in *zichronot*, cf. אד' וחותני in Muchowski & Tomal & Sulimowicz & Witkowski & Yariv (2017: 30, 271). In Karaim sources, Heb. דוֹד 'uncle' was used, similarly to חוֹתֵן, to denote 'uncle' or 'any ancestor of one's uncle'.

31 The Hebrew original was composed by Abraham ben Aharon of Troki in the 17th century (see JSul.III.79: 201 r°) with the Hebrew incipit: אֲשׁוֹרֵר לַאֲדוֹן עוֹלָם בְּמוֹרָא *ʾăšōrēr laʾăḏōn ʿōlåm bmōrå*.

(acc.)' (125 v°). However, in this case the main text was copied in South-Western Karaim, whereas the copyist left the NWKar. *j*-forms unaltered when reproducing it.[32]

### 2.2.3 *Jeshua ben Mordechai Mordkowicz*

Born in the 18th century and died on the first day of the Parashat Vayakhel-Pekudei 5557 A.M. (which is 27 Adar 5557 A.M., i.e. 25 March 1797 A.D.), see JSul.I.01 (164 r°). He served as hazzan in Kukizów in the second half of the 18th century, possibly before 1771 (see Kizilov 2009: 378) and later also as hazzan of Halych succeeding Moshe ben Shemuel ben Josef ha-Mashbir in his office—most likely from ca. 1778 (but not later than 1778) until his death.[33] He had two sons: Icchak and Shemuel. His father was the grandson of Josef ha-Mashbir's brother Jeshua ben Shemuel ha-Rodi. He was a native speaker of South-Western Karaim. We know of his two translations of Hebrew *zemirot*: אִם אֶשְׁכָּחֵךְ יְרוּשָׁלַיִם *ʾim ʾeškåḥēḵ yrūšålayim* (the Hebrew original was possibly written by Icchak ben Abraham Troki, see JSul.I.17: 58 v°–59 v°, and JSul.I.19: 74 r°–76 r°; Karaim incipit: *E Jerušlem tigel šahar unutmammen senni*) and שְׁאִי זִמְרָה נַפְשִׁי *śʾī zimrå napšī* by Mordechai ben Icchak Łokszyński (2.1.2) its Karaim incipit being *Čeber zemer ajtma*.

He was the copyist of JSul.III.63, 39 folios in length, containing the works of Josef ha-Mashbir (2.1.1), Mordechai ben Icchak (2.1.2), Mordechai ben Nisan (2.1.3), Shemuel ben Josef ha-Mashbir (2.1.7), Shelomo ben Aharon of Poswol, and Icchak ben Icchak of Lutsk—i.e. texts originally written in both North-Western and South-Western Karaim. At the same time, the language of the manuscript is uniform: it is South-Western Karaim, the copyist's vernacular, with the original *ü*, *ö* and *š* consistently preserved (for a description, see Németh 2014a). A few North-Western Karaim features occur, but only in texts authored by the speakers of that particular dialect, see e.g. *jaḥšylyġyj* 'your goodness' (21 r°) and *tamašalyġyj* 'your wonders' (21 r°) in the work *Bijine dunjanyn šira ajtajim* by Mordechai ben Nisan of Troki (see also 2.3).

32 Since in this part of JSul.I.01 the vowel points have been added to the text by another hand using a different ink and quill pen based on the South-Western Karaim sound system (see 124 r°–130 v°), the vocalization is clearly non-North-Western Karaim even in the case of those words containing the NWKar. *j* (< *ŋ), see e.g. סוֹזְלֵירִיי *sözlerij* (125 v°). Words of the latter type are therefore artificial hybrids rather than really existing variants.

33 Zarachowicz (1935: 33) and, after him, also Gąsiorowski (2008: 457) claim that he served as hazzan in Halych in the years 1792–1796. See our commentary in 2.1.7.

### 2.2.4 *Josef ben Icchak Szulimowicz*

Born before 1830, died 1883. He was most probably the copyist of ms. JSul.III.67. In the bottom margin of folio 1 r° we find the following almost completely faded annotation written in pencil (in Polish) by Józef Sulimowicz (1913–1973): *r. Josef b. Izaak Szulimowicz brat mojego dziadka* 'Ribbi Josef ben Icchak, the brother of my grandfather'. The only likely explanation of this annotation is that Józef Sulimowicz decided to record the name of the copyist.[34]

As far as the Karaim content of this manuscript is concerned, Josef ben Icchak copied the works of both North-Western and South-Western Karaim authors, namely Mordechai ben Nisan (2.1.3), Moshe ben Icchak Cic-Ora (2.1.4), Simcha ben Chananel (2.1.5), Shelomo ben Aharon of Poswol, Mordechai ben Shemuel (2.1.8), Abraham ben Levi, Jeshua Josef Mordkowicz (2.2.5), and Josef ben Abraham Leonowicz. The language of the Karaim passages is consistently South-Western Karaim, i.e. they are written in Josef ben Icchak's vernacular.

### 2.2.5 *Jeshua Josef Mordkowicz*

He was born 1802 in Halych, died 1 Av 5644 A.M. (i.e. 23 July 1884, see JSul.I.01: 152 r°, 182 r°) in Halych. His mother, Esther, was the sister of the Karaim scholar and poet Abraham ben Josef Shelomo Łucki (1792–1855).[35] His father, Moshe, originated from Kukizów and was the son of Mordechai ben Shemuel (2.1.8), which means that Jeshua Josef was also a member of the esteemed ha-Rodi family. He was a disciple of Abraham Leonowicz, who later became his father-in-law: Jeshua married his daughter, Deborah (1813–1872) around 1825. A few years before that, in ca. 1821, he became the hazzan in Kukizów and remained in this position until the destruction of that community (due to fire) around 1831. He was hazzan in Halych in the years 1866–1884, and a prominent teacher and copyist of dozens of manuscripts, including copies of the whole Tanakh, see e.g. ADub.III.82–84.[36] He had great calligraphic skills and often inserted his

---

34 It ought to be mentioned that Josef ben Icchak Szulimowicz was, in fact, the brother of Józef Sulimowicz's great grandfather, and not of his grandfather.

35 For more on Abraham ben Josef Shelomo, see W. Zajączkowski (1973a).

36 Kizilov (2009: 111) writes that most of the manuscripts copied by Jeshua Josef disappeared during World War II and that he could only locate one prayer book and several letters written by him. It is certainly true that during both the Great War (see Mardkowicz 1933b: 4–5) and World War II many of the manuscripts copied by Jeshua Josef Mordkowicz were destroyed, but, apparently (and luckily for us), many more handwritten sources of his survived than Kizilov had believed. The author of the present work examined 12 manuscripts Jeshua Josef Mordkowicz had copied to extract the *peshatim* recorded there. He also copied the manuscript partially edited in Olach (2013), ms. JSul.III.01, and many other works, like for instance F305-220.

name, as the copyist, in the Hebrew headings introducing the works he had copied. A native speaker of South-Western Karaim. For an exhaustive biography of Jeshua Josef Mordkowicz, see Kizilov (2009: 110–112) as well as Zarachowicz's (1925) article based on information obtained from Shemuel Mordkowicz (1848–1930) who was not only Jeshua Josef's nephew, but also his disciple (Shemuel was the son of Mordechai Shalom ben Moshe Mordkowicz, see 2.2.17).

Of the sources edited in this work, he copied mss. ADub.III.61, JSul.I.01c, JSul.I.45, JSul.I.46, JSul.I.54.09, JSul.III.07, JSul.III.69, JSul.III.72, JSul.III.73, JSul.III.76, JSul.III.77, and JSul.III.79. In those, he copied the works of Aharon ben Jehuda of Troki, Josef ha-Mashbir (2.1.1), Mordechai ben Icchak Łokszyński (2.1.2), Mordechai ben Nisan (2.1.3), Moshe ben Icchak Cic-Ora (2.1.4), Simcha ben Chananel (2.1.5), Josef ben Shemuel ben Josef ha-Mashbir (2.1.6), Shemuel ben Josef ha-Mashbir (2.1.7), Shelomo ben Aharon of Poswol, Mordechai ben Shemuel (2.1.8), Icchak ben Icchak of Lutsk, and Josef ben Abraham Leonowicz, as well as works of which he himself is the author. He consistently used South-Western Karaim, i.e. his native tongue, in his work.[37] The rare exceptions where he left NWKar. *j* (< **ŋ*) in the texts he copied exclusively concern works originally written in North-Western Karaim, see e.g. אַלְנִייָא *alnyja* 'before you (dat. [allat.])', אוּלוּסוּייָא *ulusuja* 'to your people', סַוַוגָטְלַרִייָא *savaġatlaryja* 'to your mercies', and טָאוִייָא *tavyja* 'to your mountain' (JSul.I.46: 87 r°) copied in an *aqidah* of Mordechai ben Nisan with the incipit *Qabaqlaryn raḥmetlernin e H acqyn ulusuja*.

### 2.2.6 *Zecharia ben Chanania Rojecki*

Born ca. 1849 in Nowe Miasto (Lith. *Naujamiestis*), he was the son of Chanania and Anna. The censuses of 1850 and 1869 provide somewhat contradictory information regarding the year of his birth: in 1850 he is mentioned as a 1-year old child, whereas in the census of 1869 he is listed as a 21-year-old individual.[38] In 1869 he was still living in his home town along with his parents, brothers, and sisters. According to the editor of *Karaj Awazy*, he served as hazzan in Lutsk in the years 1879–1902 ([Mardkowicz] 1932c: 16; Kizilov 2015b: 71 repeats these dates), which suggests that he arrived in Lutsk around 1878, that is around the year when ms. JSul.I.11 was copied (we know that it was copied in Lutsk). In AGKŁ we learn that on 9 December 1892 he married Esther bat Abraham

---

37 Many archaic linguistic features were retained in the manuscripts he prepared in the first half of the 19th century (mainly the preservation of the original *ö*, *ü*, *š* [and probably of *č*, *ž*, and *ǯ*]). This is the case in JSul.I.45, JSul.I.46, and JSul.III.72. Archaic features are absent from the sources he copied in the second half of the 19th century.

38 This information was provided by Anna Sulimowicz-Keruth (personal communication).

Firkowicz (the wedding ceremony took place in Malowanka, Lithuania) and that he was aged 41 on his wedding day, which, in turn, implies that he was born around 1851. Importantly, in his marriage certificate he is referred to as the elder hazzan of the Karaim community in Lutsk. In 1902 he issued his last birth, death, and marriage certificates, which suggests that he might have died in 1902.

Manuscript JSul.I.11 contains South-Western Karaim texts: prayers for Pesach (4 r°–24 v°), as well as a complete translation of the Book of Lamentations (28 r°–52 r°) prepared by Simcha ben Chananel (2.1.5). On the other hand, the second part of the manuscript contains numerous *piyyutim* and *qinot* written in North-Western Karaim, i.e. in the copyist's native dialect. The latter group includes the works of Abraham ben Aharon,[39] Abraham ben Icchak Nowicki,[40] Josef ha-Mashbir (2.1.1), Mordechai ben Nisan (2.1.3), Simcha ben Chananel (2.1.5), Shelomo ben Aharon of Poswol, and Icchak ben Icchak of Lutsk, i.e. mostly native speakers of North-Western Karaim.[41] Some of his texts exhibit extensive intermingling between South- and North-Western Karaim standards, resulting in such hybrid forms as e.g. איציון *ič́un* (2:10) (i.e., Mod.SWKar. *icin* →← Mod.NWKar. *üč́uń*), for more examples see the editions of *peshatim* № 2 and 24.

### 2.2.7 *Abraham ben Icchak Josef Leonowicz*

Born 1857, died 1938. He was the son of Icchak Josef ben Jeshua Jaakov Leonowicz (born ca. 1829, died after 1885), i.e. a descendant of the ha-Rodi family. He lived in Halych. He was a native speaker of South-Western Karaim. On 6 November 1923 he wrote a letter in Karaim (an invitation to a wedding); based on the latter source we know that his idiolect lacked archaisms and reflected typical Halych Karaim colloquial features (see Németh 2011b: 167–170).

39 According to JSul.I.11 (123 v°), Abraham ben Aharon was the first hazzan to serve in this role in Nowe Miasto. Given that the Karaim community was established there in the 17th century (see Gąsiorowski 2009: 202, 206–207), he must have been born in the 17th century. It remains an open question whether this person should be identified as the Abraham ben Aharon hazzan in Nowe Miasto mentioned by Mann (1931: 645–647, 1080).

40 In JSul.I.11 (119 r°) he is referred to as *Abraham the aged* [...], *the hazzan of the holy community of Nowe Miasto* [...] *the son of Icchak the aged called Nowickij*. This is most likely the person mentioned by Gąsiorowski (2009: 471) and Mann (1931: 919) as the leader of the Karaim community of Nowe Miasto in the mid-18th century.

41 It is difficult to say what actually was the native dialect of Icchak ben Icchak of Lutsk (died ca. 1778). From Mann (1931: 748–749) we only learn that he was a disciple of Moshe ben Simcha (17th/18th centuries; the father of Simcha Icchak Łucki) and that he had spent several years of his life in Kukizów before "he returned to Luck and subsequently became the local Ḥazzān". However, philological data in ms. ADub.III.78 suggest that he was a native speaker of South-Western Karaim, see 2.2.9.

He copied folios 18 rº–25 rº of ms. JSul.III.64 (this part is indicated here as JSul.III.64b) containing, besides a prayer in Hebrew, the Karaim works of Mordechai ben Shemuel (2.1.8), Josef ben Abraham Leonowicz, and Simcha ben Jeshua Jaakov Leonowicz—i.e. authors who were native speakers of South-Western Karaim. The language of the text he copied consistently adheres to the Modern South-Western model, i.e. he used his native language in his work.

### 2.2.8 *Copyist of JER NLI 4101-8 (Unknown 1)*

The manuscript in question is predominantly in Hebrew. The partially vocalised Karaim translations of six works are written in post-harmony-shift North-Western Karaim. These are copied on folios 228 rº–230 rº (see *peshat* № 2), 243 vº–246 vº (*Men miskin qaldyġy* composed by Josef ha-Mashbir ben Shemuel, see 2.1.1), 247 rº–249 rº (*Esińa alajym* by Mordechai ben Nisan, see 2.1.3), 260 vº–262 vº (*Küčlü Tenrim da išančym* by Mordechai ben Icchak, most probably the person described in 2.1.2), 347 rº–348 rº (*Ačy qyna avur firjat* by Aharon ben Jehuda of Troki), and 396 vº (*Joḥtur senin kibik malaḫlary arasynda* by an unkown author).

### 2.2.9 *Copyist of ADub.III.78 (Unknown 2)*

This person copied the 625 folios comprising ADub.III.78, which were written predominantly in Hebrew. The Karaim additions cover ca. 11 folios of this manuscript and consist of works written by Josef ha-Mashbir ben Shemuel (2.1.1), Mordechai ben Nisan (2.1.3), Moshe ben Icchak Cic-Ora (2.1.4), Simcha ben Chananel (2.1.5), Shelomo ben Aharon, and Icchak ben Icchak of Lutsk. The copyist was most probably a native speaker of North-Western Karaim. One interesting thing to note about this manuscript is that the works composed originally by North-Western Karaim native speakers[42] were copied in Middle North-Western Karaim and were vocalized by the copyist. On the other hand, the *peshatim* of Moshe ben Icchak Cic-Ora and Icchak ben Icchak of Lutsk[43] were left unvocalized by the copyist, the North-Western Karaim vocalization was added later to it by another hand (using a different quill pen and different ink), and a number of South-Western forms with *n* (< **ŋ*) were left in the

42 I.e., Josef ha-Mashbir's *Qoltqabyla e H joqtan bar etivčü* (523 rº–527 vº; see № 3), Mordechai ben Nisan's *Bijińa dunjanyn šira ajtajim* (243 vº–244 rº), Simcha ben Chananel's *Joḥtur senin kibik kičli da qorqunčlu Tenri* (575 rº–575 vº; see № 13), and Shelomo ben Aharon's *Küčlü bijim kipligim* (601 rº–601 vº).

43 These are Moshe ben Icchak Cic-Ora's *Men synyq ummasy Jisra'elnin* (284 rº–285 rº; see № 6) and Icchak ben Icchak of Lutsk's *peshat* of a *zemer* with the Karaim incipit *Janġyrtajik köp maχtavlar* composed probably in 1735 (312 rº–314 vº).

text, see e.g. ייַארַטילְדִין *jaratyldyn* (6:13), ייָזִיקְלַארִינִיזְגַא *jazyqlarynyzġa* (6:69–70), טיוּזיוּניוּז *tüzünüz* (6:70), טֶנְרִינִיזְנִי *Tenrinizni* (313 r°), קִילְנִיז *qylynyz* (313 r°)—along with North-Western forms with *j* (< *ŋ) that are present in these texts, too, such as בַארִייז *baryjyz* (313 r°), כיוּציוּיְינוּ *küčüjnü* (314 r°), סיוֹזיוּיְינוּ *sözüjnü* (314 v°), טוּרוּיוּז *turujuz* (313 r°), and אוּלוּסוּיְינוּ *ulusujnu* (314 r°). In fact, since in Moshe ben Icchak Cic-Ora's *peshat* entitled *Men synyq ummasy Jisraʾelnin* (№ 6) there is no NWKar. *j* (< *ŋ), this particular text should be classified as "MSWKar. with MNWKar. vocalization" which lends credence to the assumption that Moshe ben Icchak Cic-Ora was a native speaker of South-Western Karaim. Finally, the South-Western Karaim features in Icchak ben Icchak of Lutsk's *peshat* suggest that his native tongue was also South-Western Karaim.

### 2.2.10 *Copyist of JSul.I.53.13* (*Unknown 3*)

JSul.I.53.13 is a 10 folio-long manuscript written in Hebrew and Karaim. In this source we find two works in Karaim: a short initial fragment of Josef ha-Mashbir ben Shemuel's (2.1.1) dirge *Men miskin qaldyġy* (JSul.I.53.13: 1 r°–1 v°) and Moshe ben Icchak Cic-Ora's (2.1.4) *peshat* beginning with the words *Men synyq ummasy Jisraʾelnin* (JSul.I.53.13: 7 r°–7 v°, see № 6). In other words, it contains one work originally written by a North-Western Karaim native speaker and one text by a South-Western Karaim individual. The surviving fragment of the first work, originally written in Middle North-Western Karaim, is too short to be analysed (moreover, it is not vocalized), whereas *peshat* № 6, composed in Middle South Western Karaim, was copied in the latter dialect.

### 2.2.11 *Copyist of JSul.I.38.09* (*Unknown 4*)

This person copied manuscript JSul.I.38.09, which contains two Karaim texts of Simcha ben Chananel (2.1.5), i.e. a North-Western Karaim native speaker: *Qajjam Tenri juluvčumuz biznin* (JSul.I.38.09: 4 r°–5 r°, see № 20) and *Eger ajtsam šira oḥujum* (JSul.I.38.09: 5 r°–6 v°, see № 12). The latter work is partially vocalized (on folios 5 r°–5 v°) following South-Western standards (all the other Karaim parts of this source are not vocalized). Given the lack of vocalization and the absence of any forms that would contain the reflex of MKar. *ŋ in *peshat* № 20, it is impossbile to establish the dialectal affiliation of this text without its philological context. It is only by means of an analysis of *peshat* № 12 (penned, let us emphasize once more, by a North-Western Karaim speaker) in which we see a clear predominance of forms with SWKar. *n* (< *ŋ) that we can say that the copyist himself was a native speaker of South-Western Karaim; see the forms סֵנִין קַייָמְלִיגִין *senin qajjamlyġyn* (12:12–13), יירטילמישלרננין *jaratylmyšlarynnyn* (12:19), כיונשיוליוגיונניו *künšülügünnü* (12:19), סנין בירליגין *senin birliġin* (12:20), and בגטירליקלריננין *baġatyrlyqlarynnyn* (12:22). The existence of the only NWKar. *j* (< **ŋ*) in the form בירגייא *birgeje* (or: *birgeja*) (12:16) is most probably a result of leaving a North-Western Karaim feature unaltered by the copyist who could have used a North-Western Karaim original as a source in his work.

### 2.2.12 *Copyist of JSul.I.54.03 (Unknown 5)*

The text prepared by this copyist, manuscript JSul.I.54.03, contains six *peshatim* of Simcha ben Chananel (2.1.5), whose native tongue was North-Western Karaim. These texts are written in Middle South-Western Karaim with the same linguistic characteristics featured throughout the manuscript. There are only three forms exhibiting the NWKar. reflex of MKar. **ŋ* in the whole manuscript. These are טיוזיויוז *tüzüjüz*, which appears twice (7:20; 19:12), and בִּירְגֵיֵיא *birgeje* (12:16). All the other relevant forms exhibit *n* as the continuant of MKar. **ŋ*, e.g. סַרְנַנִיז *sarnanyz* (7:14), אַוְזוּנוּזְנוּן *avzunuznun* (7:19), יָרַטִילְמִישְׁלָרִינְדָן *jaratylmyšlaryndan* (12:45), בוּיְרוּכְלָרִינְנִין *bujruqlarynnyn* (12:45–46), סָנָא *sana* (12:46, 54), קִיבְלָלַרִינְנִין *qyblalarynnyn* (12:55), אַיְטִינִיז *ajtynyz* (14:19), בֵּירִינִיז *beriniz* (14:19), גִילֵיאיִינִיזְנִי *gilejinizni* (19:12), etc. Hence, the copyist used his own South-Western Karaim idiolect in his scribal work.

### 2.2.13 *Copyist of JSul.III.66 (Unknown 6)*

The manuscript copied by this scribe consists of 188 folios, predominantly prayers written in Hebrew. As far as the Karaim portions of the text are concerned, these are six works (*vidduyim*, *tachanunim*, *piyyutim*, and *aqidot*) written by four different individuals: Aharon ben Jehuda of Troki, Josef ha-Mashbir (2.1.1), Mordechai ben Icchak Łokszyński (2.1.2), and Mordechai ben Nisan (2.1.3), i.e. native speakers of North-Western Karaim. At the same time, the manuscript is written in South-Western Karaim, which should therefore be treated as the copyist's native tongue. The few NWKar. forms with *j* (< **ŋ*) that appear only in Mordechai ben Nisan's *aqidah* with the incipit *Qabaqlaryn raḥmetlernin e H acqyn ulusuja* (JSul.III.66: 105 v°–107 r°) should be interpreted as North-Western Karaim glosses reflecting the orthography of the originals left unchanged by the copyist, see אולושוייָא *ulusuja* (105 v°), קָלִייִז *qalyjyz* (106 r°), כֵּלִייִז *kelijiz* (106 v°), and נָאבִילֵרִיִי *navilerij* (107 r°) juxtaposed alongside the other forms with *n* (< **ŋ*): אָקִילְלָרִינִיז *aqyllarynyz* (106 r°), סָנָא *sana* (106 v°), אולוסוּנְנוּ *ulusunnu* (107 r°), אָזִיזְלִיגִינְנִי *azizliginni* (107 r°), and בַּרְלִיגִינְנִי *barlyġynny* (107 r°). No other works in this manuscript contain NWKar. *j*-forms.[44]

44 These works are Josef ha-Mashbir's *Qoltqabyla e H joqtan bar etivčü* (№ 3), Mordechai ben Icchak Łokszyński's *vidduy* with the incipit *Bolġaj qabulluq alnyndan senin* (153 v°–154 r°), the latter author's *tachanunim* entitled *Qajjam Tenri ulusuna ačqyn raḥmet ešiklerin*

### 2.2.14 *Copyist of JSul.III.03 (Unknown 7)*

This scribe copied manuscript JSul.III.33, which consists of 120 folios containing a total of 22 texts in Karaim—the *peshatim* of Josef ha-Mashbir (2.1.1), Mordechai ben Nisan (2.1.3), Simcha ben Chananel (2.1.5), Josef ben Shemuel ben Josef ha-Mashbir (2.1.6), Shemuel ben Josef ha-Mashbir (2.1.7), Mordechai ben Shemuel (2.1.8), Shelomo ben Aharon of Poswol, and Icchak ben Icchak of Lutsk.[45] This means that both North- and South-Western Karaim authors from the 17th and 18th centuries are represented in this source. Nevertheless, the language of the manuscript is uniformly South-Western Karaim (with some archaic elements and many hypercorrect forms; see Németh 2014a: 252–262 for a description), i.e. this copyist, too, altered the originals according to his own South-Western Karaim idiolect.

### 2.2.15 *Copyist of JSul.I.54.12 (Unknown 8)*

This person copied a short manuscript containing two *peshatim* by Simcha ben Chananel (2.1.5) originally written in North-Western Karaim, namely № 7 and 14. The language he used is consistently South-Western Karaim with both Middle and Modern Karaim features. Yet, in *peshat* № 7, the copyist left three forms (out of four relevant forms) with the NWKar. *j* (< **ŋ*) unchanged, see *sarnajyz* (7:14), *kötürüjüz* (7:18), and *tüzüjüz* (7:20). Ergo, the copyist employed his own South-Western Karaim idiolect in his work.

### 2.2.16 *Copyist of JSul.VII.22.02.13 (Unknown 9)*

This unknown scribe copied a manuscript that contains only one work: an unvocalized version of *peshat* № 13 by Simcha ben Chananel (2.1.5). The language of the text is South-Western Karaim.

### 2.2.17 *Copyist of JSul.III.64a (Unknown 10)*

This person copied the *peshatim* of Aharon ben Jehuda of Troki, Daniel ben David the Jerusalemite, Mordechai ben Icchak Łokszyński (2.1.2), Moshe ben

---

(154 r°–154 v°) and *On qudratyn kip quvatyn* (155 r°–156 v°), as well as Aharon ben Jehuda of Troki's *tachanun* beginning with the words *Symarlaǵaj aziz Tenri* (154 v°–155 r°).

45 More precisely, *peshatim* № 1, 2, 5, 8–11, 15, 18, 23–26, 28, 30 presented below, as well as Shelomo ben Aharon's *Bijine dunjanyn šira ajtajim* (86 v°), Icchak ben Icchak of Lutsk's *tachanun* beginning with the words *Eksildi ḥyǯlyq da janǵajlyq* (104 r°–104 v°) along with his interpretation of וַיָּקֶם אֶת דְּבָרוֹ *wayyåqem ʾeṯ dḇårō* (read on the Shabbats of the month Tammuz) with the incipit *Mode bolady ummasy Jisraʾelnin* (102 v°–103 v°), and three *qinot* authored by Shelomo ben Aharon of Poswol (*Ojanǵyn jüregim qyna uḥumaqqa*, 113 r°–114 r°), Josef ha-Mashbir (*Men miskin qaldyǵy* 116 r°–118 r°), and Mordechai ben Nisan (*Esime alajym*, 118 r°–119 r°).

Icchak Cic-Ora's (2.1.4), Mordechai ben Shemuel (2.1.8), Josef ben Abraham Leonowicz, and Jeshua Josef Mordkowicz (2.2.5) on folios 1 rº–17 vº, 26 rº–31 vº of JSul.III.64. In this source, all these works, authored by the native speakers of both South- and North-Western Karaim, were consistently reproduced in South-Western Karaim.

Folio 14 rº gives a hint as to the copyist's identity: in the heading introducing the *peshat* of the Hebrew *piyyut* אֲדֹנָי אַתָּה בְּרִבְבוֹת קֹדֶשׁ בְּסִינַי *ʾaḏōnåy ʾattå bribbōṯ qoḏeš bsīnay* with the incipit *Adonaj Tenrisi Jisraʾelnin* (№ 94) we can read that it was authored by "my brother [...] Jeshua Josef [...] ben Moshe [...]",[46] which means that this part of the manuscript could have been copied by one of Jeshua Josef Mordkowicz's half-brothers: either Mordechai Shalom (died 1875) or Simcha (1828–1906)—both of them being South-Western Karaim native speakers.[47] Given that this part of the manuscript was created between 1840 and 1851,[48] it is somewhat more likely that it was Mordechai Shalom who copied the text (Simcha was aged somewhere between 12 and 23 during this time period).

### 2.2.18 *Copyist of JSul.I.37.02* (*Unknown 11*)

This manuscript contains only one text in Karaim, and that is Moshe ben Icchak Cic-Ora's (2.1.4) *Men synyq ummasy Jisraʾelnin* (№ 6). The manuscript was copied in Lutsk. It is written in South-Western Karaim with a number of archaic features preserved.

---

46 The relevant part of the heading reads as follows: וזה הפשט הראשון לפיוט אדני אתה ברבבות קדש בסיני תרגמו החכם האלהי והפלוסוף התורני כקֿש ההֿו אדוני אחי כמוֿהרר ישועה יוסף החזן והמלמד נֿי באֿד כמוֿהרר משה המלמד הזקן הישיש זצלהֿה 'And this is the first *peshat* of the *piyyut* (beginning with the words) *ʾaḏōnåy ʾattå bribbōṯ qoḏeš bsīnay*, the translation of the Torah-based hakham, the divine philosopher, his holy and glorious name, the great and honourable sage, my master, my brother, his honour, the Rav, Rabbi Jeshua Josef the hazzan and teacher, may his light shine, the son of my master, his honour, the Rav, Rabbi Moshe the aged teacher, hazzan, may the memory of the righteous be for the life of the World to Come' (JSul.III.64: 14 rº).

47 Jeshua Josef's father, Moshe ben Mordechai Mordkowicz married twice: first to Esther (see 2.2.5) and later to Malka (1786–1854). Esther was the mother of Jeshua Josef, Malka gave birth to Mordechai Shalom and Simcha.

48 These dates are based on the fact that Moshe ben Mordechai Mordkowicz (born ca. 1759, died 1840) is mentioned as a deceased person in the heading quoted above, whereas Abraham ben Levi Leonowicz, died 1851, is referred to as a living person in the heading introducing *peshat* with the incipit *Adonaj bijiJisraʾelnin* on folio 15 rº (his name is accompanied by the abbreviation נֿי).

### 2.2.19 *Copyist of JSul.I.37.03 (Unknown 12)*

This person copied the 16-folio ms. JSul.I.37.03, which comprises 14 works written by South-Western Karaim authors: Shemuel ben Josef ha-Mashbir (2.1.7; see № 27), Mordechai ben Shemuel (2.1.8; № 29), Abraham ben Levi Leonowicz, Josef ben Abraham Leonowicz, and Jeshua Josef Mordkowicz (2.2.5). The language of the manuscripts is clearly Modern South-Western Karaim. In the heading introducing the *peshat* with the incipit *Joġarġy Tenri bijik ketirilgen jasyryn* (1 v°; see № 84 in 1.3 above) the copyist calls Abraham ben Levi Leonowicz his uncle,[49] but we cannot narrow down the number of the potential copyists to any single individual owing to the fact that Abraham Leonowicz had many nephews.

### 2.2.20 *Copyist of F305-08 (Unknown 13)*

This copyist created a 322-folio manuscript containing Karaim religious texts. The linguistic features in the source are clearly Modern North-Western Karaim.

### 2.2.21 *Copyist of JSul.I.16 (Unknown 14)*

The work of this copyist is a 456-folio item containing both Hebrew and Karaim religious texts. In the latter group we find the works of Josef ha-Mashbir ben Shemuel (2.1.1), Mordechai ben Icchak Łokszyński (2.1.2), Mordechai ben Nisan (2.1.3), and Shelomo ben Aharon of Poswol. The linguistic features we find in the source clearly indicate its Modern South-Western Karaim form.

### 2.2.22 *Copyist of JSul.I.54.15 (Unknown 15)*

This person copied a short text comprising one *peshat* (№ 7) of Simcha ben Chananel (2.1.5). It was written in Modern South-Western Karaim at the turn of the 20th century. In some instances, the original *š* is retained, but there are only three words that are relevant in this case (two of them being loanwords), namely אַשְׁכָּרִילְמָגִי *aškarylmaġy* (8:7), אוֹשׁוֹל *ošol* (8:11), and מוּשׁכְנוּן *mušqnun* (7:12). It seems that in this source the use of the letter *shin* in these words is merely for orthographic purposes; see our commentary in 3.3.4.2.

## 2.3 When Two Idiolects Meet: Authors of the *peshatim* vs. the Copyists

As we see, the persons involved in the creation of these texts, i.e. the authors of the Karaim versions and those who copied them, originated from different

---

49 Cf. תרגמו אדוני דודי 'the translation of my uncle'.

Karaim communities and were native speakers of different varieties of Western Karaim. The eight authors of the *peshatim* include four native speakers of North-Western Karaim, two of South-Western Karaim, and two persons who were most probably South-Western Karaim native speakers or who might have had a native command of both dialects, see Table 4. On the other hand, as far as the native dialect of the copyists is concerned, most of them were speakers of South-Western Karaim, except for Josef ha-Mashbir, Zecharia ben Chanania Rojecki, and the unknown copyists of JER NLI 4101-8 (Unknown 1), ADub.III.78 (Unknown 2), and F305-8 (Unknown 13) see Table 5.

The analysis above enables us to answer the question of whether the texts edited in this volume reflect the language (idiolect/dialect) of the copyists or that of the authors. In other words, how slavishly did those who created the copies follow the originals? This is why in our description outlined above we took into account the entire Karaim linguistic material of the manuscripts and not only that of the edited *peshatim*.

The philological and linguistic analysis of the above-mentioned sources presented in paragraphs 2.2.1–20 clearly shows that the language of the vast majority of the sources is homogenous regardless of the kind of works they are comprised of, where the authors of these works originated from, during which time period the copied works were created, or when and where the texts were copied.[50] In summing up our observations, we can see that 20 of the 22 copyists used their own idiolect in their work. Given that the linguistic material in JSul.I.53.13 is not representative enough to shed light on the relationship between the autograph and the copy (see 2.2.10), the only clear exception is Zecharia ben Chanania Rojecki, i.e. a native speaker of North-Western Karaim who attempted, not entirely successfully, to copy some parts of ms. JSul.I.11 as if they were written in South-Western Karaim—probably as part of some kind of preparation before taking over the duties of the hazzan in Lutsk, i.e. in a South-Western Karaim milieu to which he felt an outsider (see 2.2.9). There is one reservation to our claim, namely that the copyists happened "to forget to replace" the NWKar. *j* (< **ŋ*) with SWKar. *n* (< **ŋ*) in texts originally written in NWKar. which is the only dialectal difference clearly distinguished in the unvocalized writing.[51] The presence of a few forms of this type in the analysed South-Western Karaim texts is merely of a philological nature (see our further discussion in the following chapter).

---

50 The only exceptions in this respect seem to be JSul.III.67 and JSul.III.72, which is something that will be discussed later in this book (3.3.4.2).

51 Additionally, in JSul.III.67 we find NWKar. טִירְלִיקְכָּא *tirlikḱa* 'to life' (14:13) unchanged (in a *peshat* of Simcha ben Chananel). This is the only example where a north-western dialectal feature is reflected in the vocalization of a south-western text.

CHAPTER 3

# Linguistic Description

## 3.1 Introductory Remarks

The following subchapters will outline the still insufficiently described features of Middle Western Karaim phonology and morphology. This description is based primarily on the materials critically edited in chapter 4, but occasionally it is supplemented with relevant linguistic facts discovered in other handwritten sources (either presented elsewhere or currently being prepared for print by the present author). Such an approach, however, will be limited to situations in which the respective additions will have an impact on any of the final conclusions of this book.

There are several reasons why providing a uniform linguistic description of the edited material (and creating a standardized transcription of it) was a complex task. Firstly, the edition juxtaposes the linguistic material of two Karaim dialects with markedly different sound systems. Secondly, the edited manuscripts were created in different time periods: the oldest text originates from the end of the 17th century whereas the most recent dates from the first half of the 20th century (1938 at the latest) which gives us a time range of ca. 250 years (see Table 2). Given that the phonology of North-Western Karaim was affected by consequential changes in the 17th–18th centuries and also that the South-Western Karaim sound system changed considerably in the second half of the 18th and the beginning of the 19th century,[1] several compromises were necessary in order to reconcile the phonological, phonetic, and phonotactic peculiarities of the Middle North-Western, Middle South-Western, Modern North-Western, and Modern South-Western varieties of Karaim.

Moreover, the corollary of the above is that in the concise linguistic description presented below synchronic approach had to be augmented with a diachronic perspective. While all three dialects of Modern Western Karaim are relatively well known, Middle Western Karaim is underreaserched, to say the least. Therefore, in the following subchapters only those features of Middle Western Karaim will be discussed which appear to be archaic in character and

1 See, above all, Németh (2014a, 2014b, 2015b, 2016a, 2018b) and Stachowski (2015).

 | DOI:10.1163/9789004419377_004

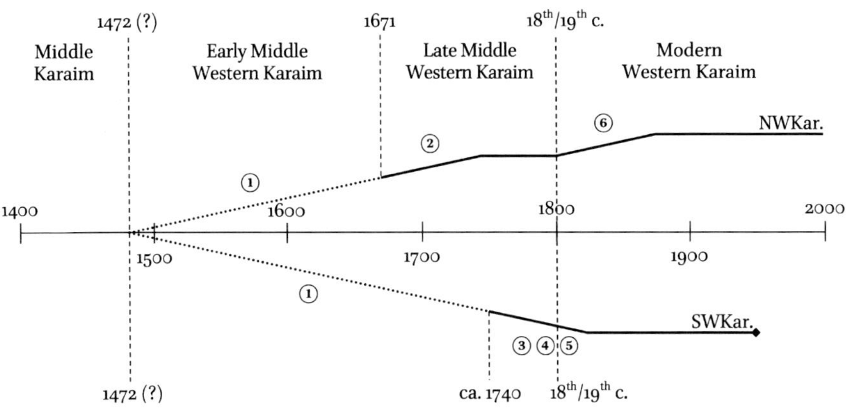


① = Elimination of *ŋ. ② = Harmony shift. ③ = Dealveolarization of č, š, ž, ǯ. ④ = Delabialization of ö, ü.
⑤ = /C/ + /i/ > [Ći]. ⑥ = Spirantization of the syllable-closing q.

FIGURE 2 The main Middle Western Karaim sound changes

are either important for understanding the nature of the transitional period between Middle and Modern Western Karaim or provide us with answers to still unanswered questions.

The names given to different periods in the history of Karaim are presented in the periodization shown in Figure 2.[2] The discussion of the absolute and relative chronology of the phonological, phonetic, and morphonological features that provided the basis for this periodization are presented in Németh (2015b: 179–182; 2016b: 272–275; 2018b) is refined in this chapter; the phenomena shown in this figure receive a detailed explanation.

The Karaim linguistic material was recorded in what are known as the Karaitic types of semi-cursive Hebrew script. Even though there are some differences between the shapes of the letters used in the 149 texts edited here (see Table 1), we can say from the outset that all of them belong, generally speaking, to the Northern-Karaitic type described by Birnbaum (1954–1957: 316). This script was used to create the main textual corpus of the manuscripts. In turn, the Hebrew headings were predominantly written in Karaite Hebrew cursive.[3]

2 The time periods with no written records are marked with dotted lines: the absolute chronology of the sound change nr. ① is unknown (*terminus ante quem*: 1671). In ⑤: C = *consonant*, Ć = *patal(ized) consonant*.

3 It should be noted that Eastern Karaim belongs, in this respect, to a different scribal tradition: the philological data strongly suggests that Crimean communities inherited a Byzantine-type script which later evolved into what became known as Crimean Yevano-Karaitic cursive (cf.

Unfortunately, no exhaustive research has been conducted so far on the origin and typology of Karaim semi-cursive scripts. I myself have discussed the palaeographic features of the semi-cursive variant used by the Karaims in Lutsk (Németh 2011b: 131–135) and have also presented a thorough orthographic description of it (Németh 2011b: 101–130). Another contribution to the subject is Olach's article (2016c) in which the authoress concentrates on the orthographical rules applied by the Karaims and states, after Birnbaum (1954–1957: 316), that the Karaim manuscripts are examples of the Northern-Karaitic type with Ashkenazic influences. Previously, the Karaitic types of Hebrew scripts have only been briefly mentioned in several works, see e.g. Jacobs (1901: 211, plate IV, no. 86), Birnbaum (1954–1957, plates 391–394) or Birnbaum's description in the second edition of Encyclopaedia Judaica (see Birnbaum & Diringer & Federbush & Maimon & Naveh & Shunary 2007: 706, 718). At the same time, however, these script types were ignored in such essential publications as, e.g., Yardeni's monograph (1997; see, for example, the schematic description of the dissemination of Hebrew scripts on page 91) or Engel's article (2013) on Hebrew script in the newly published *Encyclopedia of Hebrew language and linguistics*, which is a monumental work. Neither is the script of the Karaims mentioned in a comprehensive volume edited by Janhunen & Rybatzki (1999) on the scripts used by the Turkic peoples in the past.

The orthographic rules, or rather tendencies, described in detail in Németh (2011b: 101–130; 2013c: 260–263) also apply to the material presented here,[4] although it should be noted that the orthography of the texts edited in this volume is much more consistent and archaic. The explanation for this lies in the fact that the documents edited in Németh (2011b) were predominantly written by individuals who were not professional scribes, whereas the present edition contains the fruits of the careful and meticulous efforts of well-educated people trained in the art of copying and calligraphy.

Unusual orthographic solutions are thus rather rare. Among others, they include a few instances where labial vowels are written in an unexpected way in front of *v*, such as e.g. in מֻיווְרֵיְי *müvrej* written with a *qubutz* in JSul.I.01b (6:24),[5] a handful of examples of *t* rendered with the letter *taw* instead of

---

Lidzbarsky 1901: 452, plate IV: Manuscript writing; Birnbaum & Diringer & Federbush & Maimon & Naveh & Shunary et al. 2017: 706, 718).

4 Another description worth mentioning here is the article of Olach (2016c). Musaev (1964: 34–36) and Poppe (1965: 42) provide merely a very concise, incomplete, and faulty description of some of the spelling-to-sound correspondencies.

5 Cf. the rule that noting three *waws* and three *yodhs* in a row should be avoided described in Németh (2011b: 119–122).

the routinely used *teth*, see, for instance תֶנְרִינִין *Tenrinin* (23:11) in JSul.I.45,[6] or טֶילְמֶירְתֶימֶן *telmertemen* (5:24) in JSul.III.79, the singular use of ז״ (*zayin* with a *gershayim*) for noting *ž* in the place name דראז״נה *Deražne* (see the Hebrew heading of № 24 in JSul.I.11), the single use of the letter combination *zayin* + *tzade* for *č* in יַרַטוּבְזצוּסוּ *jaratuvčusu* (20:21) in ms. JSul.I.54.03,[7] and the very rare use of *kaph* in the segment -*qq*- to note the second (suffix-initial) -*q*-, see e.g. אָגָאלִיקְכָא *aġalyqqa* (9:17), צִיקְמַקְכָא *cyqmaqqa* (9:22), אַצְלִיקְכָא *aclyqqa* (11:12) in JSul.III.03 or אַגַלִיקְכָא *aġalyqqa* (9:17), צִיקְמַקְכָא *cyqmaqqa* (9:22), אַצְלִיקְכָא *aclyqqa* (11:12) in manuscript JSul.I.45. Furthermore, in several instances we find the undoubled letter *qoph* and *teth* used for rendering geminated consonants, e.g. אֵשִׁיטִירְגֵיי *ešit*[*t*]*irgej* (14:31), טַרְטִירְגַיְ *tart*[*t*]*yrġaj* (14:29), or קוֹרְקָנִימִיז *qorq*[*q*]*anymyz* (19:19) (manuscripts JSul.I.54.03 and JSul.I.54.12).

## 3.2 The Vocalic System

Based on the philological evidence eight vowel phonemes can be distinguished in the Late Middle Western Karaim vowel system: /a/, /e/, /y/, /i/, /o/, /ö/, /u/, and /ü/.

### 3.2.1 *The Closed* ė

We have clues but no firm philological evidence that would allow us to assume that a phonological opposition between an open /e/ and a closed /ė/ existed in Middle Western Karaim. There are a handful of forms in which, so it seems, *e* and *i* are confused and which, in turn, might suggest that a difference between [e] and [ė] may have indeed existed at the phonetic level—as was very likely the case in the language of *Codex Comanicus* or in Armeno-Kipchak (see, for instance, von Gabain 1959: 50, and Pritsak 1959b: 82). However, the question still remains to what extent can we rely on this group of words.

The Middle Western Karaim forms that might be relevant here are כֵלְגִין *kelgin* (26:16) < *kelgen*, and סֵינְדִין *sendin* (26:25) < *senden* in JSul.III.63, as well as בֵירְמִיגִי *bermigi* (12:32) < *bermegi*, and בִיזְגִיא *bizgi* (20:19) < *bizge* in JSul.I.54.03. However, if we juxtapose these four words with the abundance of forms in which the *e* sound is written correctly, we would then appear justified in saying that the occurrence of *i* is very likely a result of scribal errors.[8]

---

6 As opposed to טֶנְרִינִין *Tenrinin*, which is written five times with the letter *teth* in the same *piyyut* in the same manuscript, see 23:7, 23:6, 23:12, 23:22, 23:26.

7 This notation became more common in the second half of the 19th century for ǯ, and ʒ.

8 By way of comparison, cf., for instance, the original *e* of the morphemes listed above writ-

TABLE 7 Late Middle Western Karaim vowels

| | **Functionally front** | | **Functionally back** | |
|---|---|---|---|---|
| **High** | i | ü | y | u |
| **Low** | e | ö | a | o |
| | Unrounded | Rounded | Unrounded | Rounded |

It should be mentioned that vowel points in JSul.I.01b (created in second half of the 18th century) have been added to the text by another hand using a different ink and quill pen. For this reason, any attempts to examine the vowel system based on this originally Middle Western Karaim manuscript involve some risk of error and therefore the forms גּיוּנֵיחְלִירִימְנִין *güneḥlirimnin* (26:54–55) < *güneḥlerimnin*, and כֵּילְטִירְגִּינְצִי *keltirginči* (3:14) < *keltirginče* cannot be used as proof in this respect.

Nor do we learn anything new from the linguistic data attested in the Modern South-Western Karaim sources that would bring us beyond the state-of-the-art in this regard. As both Dubiński (1978: 36) and Németh (2011a: 72–74) argued, a closed-mid Mod.SWKar. *ė* existed only as a positional variant of /e/ standing in front of palatalized (or palatal) consonats and in the segment *ḱė* as a result of the *ky* > *ḱė* change.[9] Such an explanation might therefore be valid for the forms כּיוֹטִירְגִּינִי *kötirgini* (10:21) < *kötirgeni* [-ǵe-], כֵּיצִינְשִׁינִיז *kecinsiniz* (11:3) < *kecinseniz* [-ńi-], כֵּיטְשִׁינִיז *ketsiniz* (11:5) < *ketseniz* [-ńi-], מֵירֵיסְלִיגִּין *meresligin* (15:3) < *mereslegin* [-ǵi-], and כִּיז *kyz* < *kez* [*ḱe*-] attested in mss. ADub.III.61, JSul.III.03, and JSul.III.79.[10] The only form in which we see a *chiriq* written to represent an **e*, and one that is not followed by a palatal(ized) consonant, is טֵיגֵימִין *tegemin* (1:59) in JSul.III.03.

---

ten correctly in ***kesilgen*** (2:34), ***öküngenlej*** (2:44), ***kötürgenimizni*** (2:46), ***bilgenimbyla*** (26:23), ***azizligimizden*** (2:16–17), ***senden*** (26:22, 26:36), ***bizden*** (2:24) in JSul.III.63, as well as in ***bermegibyla*** (19:8), ***bizge*** (7:6, 7:7, 7:31, 14:20, 14:21, 14:28, 14:31, 17:5, 17:8, 17:12, 19:5, 19:8, 19:10, 19:14, 19:19, 20:10, 20:11, 20:17, 20:18, and 20:20) in JSul.I.54.03.

9 Both of these phenomena can be explained by adstratal influence of Ukrainian dialects; the respective Ukrainian phonotactic processes are described in detail e.g. in Zilynśkyj (1979: 48–49, 55), and Žylko (1958: 113–117).

10 Two similar forms can be found in JSul.I.11, namely אֵיזִימֵיזְדִּי *ezimezdi* < *ezimizde* (2:33) and טִיגִּילְלֵיר *tigiller* (2:55) < *tigeller*, but the data excerpted from this source should be, in this case, treated cautiously or even rejected. The passages in question were written in South-Western Karaim by a native speaker of North-Western Karaim and, in fact, contain a wide variety of errors, including scribal errors and artificial hybrid forms.

One interesting case to note here is the replacement of the word *kip* 'strong' with *köp* ~ *kep* 'many' in 14:20. However, this confusion is rather a result of a mistranslation, given that in the Hebrew original the word רוֹב '1. multitude; 2. greater part' is used in the respective part—cf. also BHeb. רֹב 'multitude' which could have been used, metonymically, in the sense of 'greatness' (König 1910: 428).

Also of little informative value in this respect are those four forms in which the *i* is replaced, in writing, with *e*: MSWKar. יוּרֵיגֵינִין *jüregenin* (12:11) < *jüreginin*, and בִּילֵידֵילֵיר *biledeler* (12:26) < *bilediler* in JSul.I.54.03, and Mod.SWKar. אֵירֵינְלֵירִימִיזְנִין *erenlerimiznin* < *erinlerimiznin* (17:22), and צִיגַרִיבֵיז *cyġarybez* (6:25) < *cyġaryrbiz* in JSul.III.72. All these forms are very likely either a result of assimilative changes or are simply clerical errors. The relevant linguistic material is therefore much too scarce to draw any reliable conclusions on this matter.

Even though there are no similar North-Western examples in the edited texts, there are some in ms. ADub.III.73, in a work copied in 1720 by Simcha ben Chananel, see, e.g., *beznin* > בִּיזְנִין *biznin* '(fine) linen (*gen.*)' (Exodus 39:3; 153 v°), *bezden* > בִּיזְדֵין *bizden* '(fine) linen (*abl.*)' (Exodus 39:27; 155 r°), or *egirmi* > אִיגִירְמִי *igirmi* 'twenty' (Leviticus 27:3; 205 v°). Nevertheless, with so little material to draw on we cannot once again say anything certain about the existence and phonological status of *ė* in Late Middle North-Western Karaim on the basis of the *e* ~ *i* alternation. The use of *patach* in etimologically front-vocalic words gives us, however, some additional clues in this respect, see chapter 3.2.2.

### 3.2.2 *The Harmony Shift in North-Western Karaim*

The term *harmony shift* is understood to mean here the transposition of the front vs. back vowel harmony into a consonant-harmony, whereas the time period in which this happened is termed a *transitional period*. As is described in detail in Németh (2014b, 2015b: 170–172) and Stachowski (2015), the essence of the harmony shift was that the standard Kipchak vowel harmony evolved into a different long-distance assimilatory process within which it is the consonants that agree in word forms (with regard to their degree of palatality), not the vowels. In other words, a palatal(ized) vs. non-palatal(ized) consonant harmony evolved.[11] In the initial phase of this process, Middle Western

11 In my view the Karaim linguistic material written in Hebrew script does not support the notion of the "syllabic-harmony" forwarded in Csató (1995, 1999), primarily because the continuant of the non-first syllabic *e* is consistently written with the same two vowel points as those used for noting the sound *a* (< **a*), i.e. interchangeably with both *patach* (◌ַ) and *qamatz* (◌ָ), see the examples below. Hence, no distinction was made between *a* and *'a* even though the abundance of different vowel points used in the Tiberian vocaliza-

Karaim must have developed a system of phonological oppositions between palatal(ized) and non-palatalized consonants which could easily have happened under the influence of neighbouring Slavonic languages and Lithuanian. This triggered another crucial change, namely that the phonological opposition between vowels became of minor importance, which in turn resulted in the backing of *ö*, *ü*, and *e* into *o*, *u*, and *a* (except for the word-initial *ö-*, *ü-* and the first-syllabic *e*, which remained intact). As a consequence, the vowel system was affected by the harmony shift such that *ö*, *ü*, and *e* evolved into *'o*, *'u*, and *'a* (*'o*, *'u*, and *'a* denote vowels that emerged from *ö*, *ü*, and *e* in a position following palatal(ized) consonants as a result of vowel-backing). It is important to note that the data from manuscript ADub.III.73 clearly shows that the *e* > *'a* process began to operate in word-final syllables and gradually extended towards the beginning of the words (see Németh 2014b: 361–366). Given that the difference between *ö*, *ü* and *'o*, *'u* cannot evidently be expressed in Hebrew script (see 3.2.3.1 below), it is only the illuminating distinction between *e* and *'a* that could have been used to establish the time frame of this process.

Based on the philological data collected from ADub.III.73, ADub.III.78, and B 263, in Németh (2015b: 172) it was concluded that:

> we can […] assume that the harmony shift stared to operate, in certain areas or idiolects, in the last decades of the 17th c. the latest (cf. manuscript B 263 from Trakai), whereas in other areas or idiolects it could have operated even until the 1750s (cf. manuscript [ADub.]III.73 […] and [ADub.]III.78).

The philological data excerpted from JSul.I.01a, i.e. from the autograph of Josef ha-Mashbir, support the above assertion. In his three texts copied between 1685 and 1700 (enumerated in 2.2.1) the *e* > *'a* change is clearly attested as we see the non-first syllabic *e* written with both *patach* (◌ַ) and *qamatz* (◌ָ), see e.g. אִימַינְצְלִילַיר *iḿančlilar* (2:11), גוּנַיחְלַיר *güńaḥlar* (2:13), וֵירַינְדִילַיר *veŕandilar* (2:15), מֵירַיסְלַדִילַיר *meŕasladilar* (2:27), טוֹרָילַירִין *töŕalarin* (2:38), and טוּזוּלגָין *tüzülǵan* (121 v°). Moreover, in manuscript ADub.III.73 copied by Simcha ben Chananel (2.1.5) we find a large number of forms written with both *e* and *'a*, see e.g. בִּירְגֵיֵיא *birgeje* (ADub.III.73: 116 v°, 117 v°, 118 v°) vs. בִּירְגֶייָא *birgeja* (ADub.III.73: 116 v°), or אֵיטְמֵיא *etme* (ADub.III.73: 116 r°) vs. *etḿa* אֵיטְמָיא (ADub.III.73: 116 r°). The

tion system would allow for that. For a discussion on the consonant vs. syllabic-harmony issue see, mainly, Hamp (1976), Csató (1995, 1999), Nevin & Vaux (2004), and Stachowski (2009).

latter pertains also to manuscript TKow.01, also by Simcha ben Chananel, see e.g. טיוּביוּנְדָן *tübünd́an* (TKow.01: 1 vº) or איוּסְטיוּנֵיא *üstüne* (TKow.01: 5 rº) vs. איוּסְטיוּנַיא üstüńa (TKow.01: 1 rº).

The very short text in B 263 (26 vº) from 1671 exhibits the same post-harmonic phonological features, see, for instance, אִיזְלָר אֵדִי *izĺar edi*, סוֹזוּנָה *sözüńa*, אוֹכסוּזדַן *öksüzd́an*, or כוּנְגַיא *küńǵa*. The same can be seen in manuscript Evr I 699 copied in 1686, in which we find a poem by Icchak ben Abraham Troki (1533/4–1594) in folios 15 vº–16 rº. In our view, such forms as יֵיסָא *jeśa* (< **jese*) or יֵיטְסַא *jetśa* (< **jetse*) clearly show that the text belongs to the post-harmony-shift era. We therefore disagree in this respect with Jankowski (2014) who transcribes *jesä* and *jetsä*. It is true that in Eastern Karaim texts *patach* was used for both *a* and, in non-first syllables, *e* (*ä*, in the front-vowel environment; see Jankowski 1994). But in North-Western Karaim the situation is fundamentally different given that (let us emphasize this again) **both** *patach* (ַ) **and** *qamatz* (ָ) were used to note the sound in question (see e.g. the data adduced above from mss. B 263, Evr I 699, JSul.I.01a, JER NLI 4101-8, or ADub.III.73). Therefore, in our view, it is not advisable to apply Eastern Karaim patterns to North-Western Karaim, even if we agree that *patach* may possibly have been used in North-Western Karaim, too, for *e* (*ä*). The appearance of *qamatz* in this role is, however, evidence of the ongoing *e* > *'a* shift.

If we combine what has been said above with the fact that in ADub.III.73 both *tzere* (ֵ) and *segol* (ֶ) were used to render both the non-first syllabic and the first-syllabic **e*-type vowel, we can forward the following tentative hypothesis for North-Western Karaim:

1. Originally, in the non-first syllables of front-vocalic words *patach* was used for *e* (*ä*)—as opposed to *ė* rendered with *tzere* and *segol* in the word-initial syllables. This practice was preserved in Eastern Karaim texts, but there are no North-Western Karaim texts that would document it.
2. The non-first-syllabic *e* began to alternate with *'a* during the operation of the harmony shift. This resulted in the use of vowel point *qamatz*, too, in this position (see mss. B 263, Evr I 699, JSul.I.01a).
3. During the operation of the harmony shift the difference between the value of the first-syllabic and the non-first syllabic *e*-type vowels became less distinctive, which, in turn, led to the use of *tzere* and *segol* for non-first syllabic *e*, too (see mss. ADub.III.73, TKow.01).

This hypothesis assumes the existence of two *e*-type vowels in Middle North-Western Karaim, and this also explains why the first-syllabic *e* was left intact during the harmony shift. For the time being, however, this phenomenon requires further investigation. Primarily, a much larger 17th-century Western Karaim corpus is needed. It must also be borne in mind that Middle South-

Western Karaim lacks any trace of two *e*-type vowels (*nota bene*, the vast majority of the texts edited below are written in South-Western Karaim). Taking into account all these inconclusive philological phenomena, we decided to only use *e* in our transcription and to not distinguish between *e*, *ä*, and *ė*.

For further details, see the next chapter (mainly 3.2.3.1).

### 3.2.3 *Front Labials*

In general, the evolution of the Karaim front labials can be presented as follows:

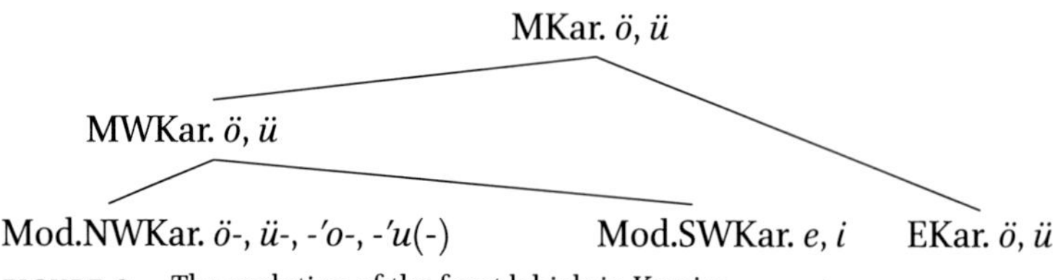


FIGURE 3 The evolution of the front labials in Karaim

The main issue addressed below is the chronology and the way the MWKar. *ö*, *ü* evolved in Late Middle Western Karaim and the first decades of Modern Western Karaim. A number of relevant special cases are also presented.

#### 3.2.3.1 MNWKar. *ö*, *ü* and Their Continuants

It is something of a challenge to say anything certain with regard to the evolution of MWKar. *ö*, *ü* in North-Western Karaim. As was mentioned above, during the same period when the so-called harmony shift was operating, an *ö* > *'o*, *ü* > *'u* change also took place. However, establishing the timeframe of this process is extremely difficult due to the fact that in most of the relevant texts written in Hebrew script a distinction could not be made either between *ö*, *ü*, and *'o*, *'u* or between *ö*, *ü* and *o*, *u* (see also Németh 2014a: 254).

To give one example, in ADub.III.68, in a source written in 1881–1882, i.e. long after the harmony shift had taken place, we see a combination of *yodh* and *waw* with a *shuruq* (יוּ) used for both *ü*- and -*'u*(-) as well as a combination of the letters *yodh* and *waw* with a *holam* (יוֹ) used for *ö*- and -*'o*- (with an additional *aleph* in the word-initial position), see e.g. Mod.NWKar. איוּציוּן *üčün* [üč́uń] (2 v°), איוֹזַינְנִין *öźannin* [öźańńiń] (2 v°), and כיוֹציוּביוּנְדַיא *köčüvünd́a* [ḱoč́uv́uńd́a] (2 v°). The same picture can be observed in ADub.III.73, which is 170 years older than ADub.III.68, see MNWKar. איוּציוּן *üčün* (19 v°), כיוֹפְּטיוּר *köptür* (19 v°), איוֹטְמֵיכ *ötmek* (19 v°), although it is important to note that the exact phonetic value of MNWKar. *ö* and *ü* in the non-initial position is uncertain in this case.

In the non-palatal-consonant environment, the vowels *o* and *u* are clearly distinguished from the sounds mentioned above, given that *o*, and *u* were writ-

TABLE 8 The notation of *ö*, *ü* in Josef ha-Mashbir's autographs in JSul.I.01a (see 2.2.1)

| | In initial position | In medial position | In final position |
|---|---|---|---|
| /ü/—without *yodh* | 18 | 52 | 6 |
| /ö/—without *yodh* | 11 | 15 | 0 |
| /ü/—with *yodh* | 1 | 27 | 3 |
| /ö/—with *yodh* | 2 | 2 | 0 |

ten consistently with the letter *waw* (with the respective vowel point), i.e.: וֹ, ו stood for *o*, whereas וּ, ו represented *u* (see also Table 21). On the other hand, *yodh* was used to indicate either the palatality of the preceding consonant or the frontness of *ö*, and *ü* in the word-initial position.

However, JSul.I.01a then provides us with very interesting data. Besides the above-mentioned spelling tendency, in ha-Mashbir's autograph we can find many examples of the original *ö* and *ü* noted with the letter *waw* only, i.e. with וֹ and וּ, respectively (of course, with an additional *aleph* if written word-initially), see the examples below.[12] Statistically, these examples can be presented as shown in Table 8.

Although the material is too scarce to say anything decisive, it is extremely interesting to observe that the spelling variants with a *yodh* appear predominantly in a medial position, whereas a spelling without the additional letter *yodh* is most characteristic of an initial position in which *ö*, and *ü* were preserved well until modern times. In other words, this suggests that the letters וֹ and וּ stood for [ö, ü] while יוֹ and יוּ (with a letter *yodh*) were used, indeed, to note [*'o*] and [*'u*], respectively. Even more importantly, in the dirge copied in ms. B 263 in 1671—i.e. in the oldest known Western Karaim text—as well as in ms. Evr I 699 from 1686 the letter *yodh* is not used in this role at all.

The above-mentioned use of יוֹ and יוּ by Josef ha-Mashbir tallies with our own observation that during the harmony shift vowel-backing began to operate in word-final syllables and gradually extended towards the beginning of the words and eventually did not reach the word-initial *ö*, *ü*, and the first-syllabic *e*. In fact, if we assume that in JSul.I.01a יוֹ and יוּ stood for *'o* and *'u* whereas וֹ and

12 To a lesser extent the same can be observed in ADub.III.78 (see № 27). However, the linguistic material taken from this source must be treated cautiously as it had originally been written in Middle South-Western Karaim and only then was a clearly Middle North-Western Karaim vocalization added to it by another hand.

ו indicated *ö*, *o* and *ü*, *u*, there would be only three examples that would contradict the tendency referred to above. Strictly speaking, there are only three words in which, on the one hand, a syllable containing the letter-combination יו (for /ü/) stands closer to the beginning of the word than a syllable in which /ü/ is recorded with the letter ו and, on the other, the letter-combination איו (/ü-/) appears word-initially: טיוּטַיטוּבְצוּ *tüťatüvčü* (2:18), אוּסְטיוּמוּזְגַיא *üstümüzǵa* (2:26), and איוּץ *üč* (2:31). All other attestations of the original *ö* or *ü* (137 in total) confirm this tendency.

Hence, there is some evidence indicating that the *ö* > *'o*, *ü* > *'u* change was an ongoing process in ha-Mashbir's time, which, after all, in light of the well attested *e* > *'a* change (see 3.2.2) would not be surprising. In other words, we can say that the *ö*, *ü* > *'o*, *'u* and the *e* > *'a* changes took place, roughly speaking, in the same time period[13] as two important components of the harmony shift.

Finally, the pivotal question of whether the different notation, i.e. the presence and absence of the letter *yodh*, is unintentional or introduced on purpose, has no unequivocal answer. We can easily find variant spellings such as אוּצוּן *üčün* (2:10) ~ אוּציוּן *üčün* (2:13), כוֹרוּפּ *körüp* (2:50) ~ כיוֹריוּפּ *körüp* (2:23, 40), or אוּץ *üč* (JSul.I.01: 115 vº, 122 vº) ~ איוּץ *üč* (2:31), טוּסלוּ *tüslü* (2:50) ~ טוּסליוּ *tüslü* (2:43), or בוּגוּן *bügün* (2:17) ~ ביוּגיוּן *bügün* (JSul.I.01: 115 vº, 122 rº).[14] Nonetheless, a twofold explanation of this orthographic phenomenon appears possible:

a. it either reflects an actual variation in pronunciation, i.e., to take one example, in ha-Mashbir's idiolect /üčün/ stood for [üčün] ~ [üčuń], or
b. it was merely a variation in spelling, i.e. in ha-Mashbir's idiolect both אוּצוּן and אוּציוּן represented /üčün/, i.e. [üčün] or [üčuń].[15]

It ought to be added here that the transcription used in this book puts to one side the above uncertainties regarding the actual realization of *ö*, *ü*. When we

13 With the reservation that in the case of Josef ha-Mashbir's idiolect the alternation of *ö* ~ *'o*, *ü* ~ *'u* was still observable, at least at an orthographic level, in those texts in which the *e* > *'a* change was already reflected in writing with no exceptions.

14 In ADub.III.73 we can also find a few examples of the letter *yodh* being skipped in the spelling of front labials, although there are no statistics available yet. See טוּביוּלְדיוּ *tüvüldü* (332 rº) ~ טיוּביוּלְדיוּ *tüvüldü* (332 rº), טוּשְׁליוּכְניוּ *tüšlüknü* (341 vº).

15 The latter is, to certain extent, supported by Middle South-Western Karaim sources, in which, alongside the dominant notation with an additional *yodh*, the labial *ö*, *ü* might also have been noted without *yodh*, see, e.g., סוּרְטֶרְסֶן *sürtersen* (3:11) or טוֹשֵׁיגִינְדֵיא *töšeginde* (3:9) (JSul.I.01b). This is even more of an important parallel as in MSWKar. there was no *'o*, *'u* and therefore, in the front-vowel environment the letters וֹ and וּ as well as יוֹ and יוּ cannot be deciphered in any other way than *ö*, and *ü*, respectively.

transcribe, say, אוּסְטיוּמוּזְגַא as *üstümüzğa* (2:26), this does not mean that the word was, in the opinon of the present writer, pronounced [*üstümüzğa*]: as far as the North Western Karaim material is concerned, the letters *ö*, *ü* in the transcription indicate, broadly speaking, "an attestation of an [ö], [ü] or of their continuants".

### 3.2.3.2 MSWKar. *ö*, *ü* and Their Continuants

In Németh (2014a: 264), it was concluded that:

> [...] since we know that the analysed texts copied by Jeshua-Josef Mordkowicz only exhibit *e* and *i* [...], and since we know that he was born in 1802, it seems valid to say that the *ö* > *e*, *ü* > *i* [process] operated in the final decades of the 18th century and ended presumably around 1800, in some idiolects or areas possibly somewhat later than the *š* > *s* process.[35] Importantly, however, both processes could have started much before 1772.
>
> 35 Shortly after submitting this article for printing I saw a Torah translation stored in the archive of Anna Sulimowicz copied by Jeshua-Josef Mordkowicz (catalogue number JSul.III.01) in which front labials are partially preserved (cf. e.g. *sözün*, *kördi*, *ivretivlerin*) whereas *š* not (e.g. *jaḥsy*, *is*). This agrees with the relative chronology presented here.

This was repeated in Németh (2015b: 174). Both papers, however, were based on a preliminary reading of only 14 handwritten prayer books and one Bible translation from Halych. Hence, even though the newly discovered Middle South-Western Karaim linguistic material of JSul.I.53.13 and JSul.I.01b corroborates the assertion that the MSWKar. front labials still tended to be present in manuscripts with religious texts copied at the end of the 18th century (see Table 10), the conclusion quoted above can be modified slightly.

Firstly, in the last few years the present writer has been fortunate to discover many more works copied by Jeshua Josef Mordkowicz which feature *ö* ~ *e* and *ü* ~ *i* alternations (see, for instance mss. JSul.I.45, JSul.I.46, JSul.III.72, and JSul.III.73).[16] We should therefore say that the *ö* > *e* and *ü* > *i* changes more likely ended in the opening decades of the 19th century and not around 1800, see Table 9. It is important to note that this still accords with the testimony of the

16 Of the sources referenced in this work, he copied mss. ADub.III.61, JSul.I.01c, JSul.I.45, JSul.I.46, JSul.I.54.09, JSul.III.07, JSul.III.69, JSul.III.72, JSul.III.73, JSul.III.76, JSul.III.77, and JSul.III.79. Let us also emphasize here that *ö*, *ü*, *e*, and *i* are clearly distinguished in the Hebrew script, see Table 21 or Németh (2014a: 253–254).

texts edited in Németh (2011b), based on which we can say that the private letters and circulars written in South-Western Karaim between ca. 1840 and 1923 by persons born between 1797 and 1857 clearly reveal no trace of the MWKar. *ö*, and *ü* (see Németh 2011b: 18–20, 22). According to our knowledge today, the most recent source in which we can still find examples of *ö*, *ü* (alternating with the dominant *e*, *i*) is probably JSul.III.73, written in mid-19th century Halych (the special case of JSul.I.37.02 will be touched upon below).[17]

TABLE 9 Hypercorrect forms with *ö*, *ü* in place of (**e*, **i* >) *e*, *i*

| Accession № | Date of copy | Hypercorrect forms | Roots vs. forms |
|---|---|---|---|
| JSul.I.53.13 | mid-18th c. (ca. 1762) | *jörimden* (6:25–26) | 1 vs. 1 |
| JSul.I.01b | 2nd half of the 18th c. | – | – |
| JSul.III.63 | ca. 1778 (before 1797) | – | – |
| JSul.I.38.09 | turn of the 19th c. | *körgünlerinde* (12:25)<br>*küčü* (12:5)<br>*künšülügünnü* (12:29)<br>*üšlerine* (12:21) | 4 vs. 4 |
| JSul.I.54.03 | turn of the 19th c. | – | – |
| JSul.III.66 | turn of the 19th c. | *ešittürejim* (3:79)<br>*körtiden* (3:23)<br>*küpligim* (3:40)<br>*ödi* (3:121)<br>*ögeninde* (3:109–110)<br>*öske* (3:14)<br>*üčümde* (3:65)<br>*üčüne* (3:125) | 6 vs. 8 |
| JSul.III.03 | shortly after 1805 | *cöriv* (8:41)<br>*köcindirme* (11:20)<br>*körekleriniz* (11:18)<br>*köreklidi* (11:37)<br>*körtiden* (26:22; 30:20)<br>*körtidü* (30:27)<br>*körtiligi* (24:53; 26:58)<br>*körtilik* (9:28; 15:15)<br>*körtilikke* (1:76)<br>*körtilikni* (23:17)<br>*körtü* (28:29)<br>*köteriniz* (23:9, 20)<br>*küp* (9:3; 11:29; 24:14; 30:23) | 8 vs. 39 |

17 The case of JSul.I.37.02 will be touched upon below.

TABLE 9 Hypercorrect forms with *ö*, *ü* in place of (**e*, **i* >) *e*, *i* (*cont.*)

| Accession № | Date of copy | Hypercorrect forms | Roots vs. forms |
|---|---|---|---|
| | | *küplegin* (1:41; 5:17, 23; 9:17; 24:30; 26:33)<br>*küplermen* (15:33)<br>*küplesin* (1:30; 24:22)<br>*küpligim* (1:48, 5:11, 26:14)<br>*küpligin* (5:27)<br>*küplikleri* (25:29)<br>*küplügimiz* (28:31)<br>*örkekler*[*in*]*in* (8:57)<br>*süzge* (11:8, 19)<br>*süznün* (11:7) | |
| JSul.I.54.12 | early 19th c. | – | – |
| JSul.I.45 | 1st half of the 19th c. | *kölme* (23:21)<br>*körtiden* (2:27; 26:22; 30:20)<br>*körtidi* (30:27)<br>*körtiligi* (26:58)<br>*körtilik* (15:15; 29:36)<br>*körtilikke* (1:76)<br>*körtini* (23:17)<br>*köstü* (8:48)<br>*küplegin* (1:41; 5:17; 26:33)<br>*küpligim* (5:11; 26:14)<br>*ücüne* (2:43) | 5 vs. 17 |
| JSul.I.46 | 1st half of the 19th c. | *biznü* (7:29)<br>*körtiden* (3:23, 62)<br>*körtilik* (3:44)<br>*körtilikni* (3:45)<br>*küplegin* (3:73, 75; 5:23)<br>*küpligim* (3:40, 64)<br>*küpligin* (5:27)<br>*küplikleri* (25:29) | 3 vs. 12 |
| JSul.VII.22.02.13 | 1st half of the 19th c. | – | – |
| JSul.III.67 | after ca. 1834 (before 1851) | – | – |
| JSul.III.64a | between 1840 and 1851 | – | – |
| JSul.III.72 | before 1851 | – | – |
| ADub.III.61 | 1850/1851 | – | – |
| JSul.III.73 | mid-19th c. | *küpligim* (4:4)<br>*küpligimiz* (28:31) | 1 vs. 2 |
| JSul.I.37.02 | mid-19th c. | *üšlerim* (30:25) | 1 vs. 1 |

TABLE 9 Hypercorrect forms with *ö*, *ü* in place of (**e*, **i* >) *e*, *i* (*cont.*)

| Accession № | Date of copy | Hypercorrect forms | Roots vs. forms |
|---|---|---|---|
| JSul.I.54.09 | mid-19th c. | – | – |
| JSul.III.69 | ca. 1851 (before 1866) | – | – |
| JSul.I.37.03 | between 1851 and 1866 | – | – |
| JSul.III.79 | ca. 1851 (before 1866) | – | – |
| JSul.III.77 | between 1856 and 1866 | – | – |
| JSul.I.01c | 2nd half of the 19th c. | – | – |
| JSul.III.07 | 2nd half of the 19th c. | – | – |
| JSul.III.76 | 2nd half of the 19th c. | – | – |
| JSul.I.16 | 19th/20th c. | – | – |
| JSul.I.54.15 | turn of the 20th c. | – | – |
| JSul.III.64b | 1st half of the 20th c. | – | – |

Furthermore, there are a large number of hypercorrect forms in which the vowels *e*, *i* < MKar. **e*, **i* were confused with *e*, *i* < MKar. **ö*, **ü* (Table 9). These errors show that some of the copyists were, at some point, unable to reconstruct correctly the original phonetic shape of a number of roots, including such commonly known words as *e-* 'to be' (> hypercorrect *ö-*), *iš* 'work, deed' (> hypercorrect *üš*), *jer* 'place' (> hypercorrect *jöri*), *kel-* 'to come' (> hypercorrect *köl-*), *kiči* 'small' (> hypercorrect *küčü*), *siz* 'you (pl.)' (> hypercorrect *süz*), and others.[18] There are approximately 84 such forms (the unreliable data from JSul.I.11 is not taken into account for the reason mentioned above in 2.2.6), and they are attested in eight manuscripts copied by Jeshua Josef Mordkowicz and the unidentified copyists labelled as Unknown 3, Unknown 4, Unknown 6, Unknown 7, and Unknown 11. In the case of Jeshua Josef Mordkowicz, however, such forms appear only in manuscripts JSul.I.45, JSul.I.46, and JSul.III.73. It is noteworthy that hypercorrect forms are absent from all those manuscripts in which there are no forms with the original *ö*, *ü* (cf. Table 9 and Table 10).

The presence of one hypercorrect form in JSul.I.53.13, i.e. יוֹרִימְדֵין *jörimden* (< *jerimden*) (6:25–26) suggests that the delabialization of *ö*, *ü* could have started

18 See Table 9. The *ö* > *ü* change in *üzü üzüne* (18:7) < *özü özüne* (in ms. JSul.I.54.03) should rather be treated as a result of an assimilative change (or a scribal error).

TABLE 10 The continuants of MSWKar. *ö, ü* in the texts edited

| Accession № | Date of copy | *ö, ü* | *ö ~ e, ü ~ i* | *e, i* |
|---|---|---|---|---|
| JSul.I.53.13 | mid-18th c. (ca. 1762) | + | (+) | |
| JSul.I.01b | 2nd half of the 18th c. | + | | |
| JSul.III.63 | ca. 1778 (before 1797) | + | | |
| JSul.I.38.09 | turn of the 19th c. | + | (+) | |
| JSul.I.54.03 | turn of the 19th c. | + | (+) | |
| JSul.III.66 | turn of the 19th c. | + | (+) | |
| JSul.III.03 | shortly after 1805 | | + | |
| JSul.I.54.12 | early 19th c. | + | (+) | |
| JSul.I.45 | 1st half of the 19th c. | | + | |
| JSul.I.46 | 1st half of the 19th c. | | + | |
| JSul.VII.22.02.13 | 1st half of the 19th c. | | | + |
| JSul.III.67 | after ca. 1840 (before 1851) | | | + |
| JSul.III.64a | between 1840 and 1851 | | | + |
| JSul.III.72 | before 1851 | + | (+) | |
| ADub.III.61 | 1850/1851 | | | + |
| JSul.III.73 | mid-19th c. | | + | |
| JSul.I.37.02 | mid-19th c. | | + | |
| JSul.I.54.09 | mid-19th c. | | | + |
| JSul.III.69 | ca. 1851 (before 1866) | | | + |
| JSul.I.37.03 | between 1851 and 1866 | | | + |
| JSul.III.79 | ca. 1851 (before 1866) | | | + |
| JSul.III.77 | between 1856 and 1866 | | | + |
| JSul.I.01c | 2nd half of the 19th c. | | | + |
| JSul.III.07 | 2nd half of the 19th c. | | | + |
| JSul.III.76 | 2nd half of the 19th c. | | | + |
| JSul.I.16 | 19th/20th c. | | | + |
| JSul.I.54.15 | turn of the 20th c. | | | + |
| JSul.III.64b | 1st half of the 20th c. | | | + |

as early as the mid-18th century. This accords with the fact that the vast majority of these hypercorrect forms are attested in manuscripts copied at the turn of the 19th century. We must therefore hypothesise that the process must have begun early enough to interfere with the idiolects of those who were still active copyists around 1800. Importantly, in JSul.I.38-11 copied between 1738 and 1744 we found a number of forms with SWKar. *e, i* (< **ö, *ü*), e.g.: סֵיזִינֵיא *sezine* 'to his word' (< *sözüne*; 1 r°), כֵּיזִינְנִי *kezinni* 'your eye (acc.)' (< *közünnü*; 1 r°). Bearing in mind what has been presented above and in 3.2.3.1, we have grounds for believing that the process began to operate, roughly speaking, not later than the first half of the 18th century, and then over time it gained strength, eventually eliminating the front labials from the sound system in the first decades of the 19th century.[19]

This chronology is also clearly visible in the manuscripts copied by Jeshua Josef Mordkowicz (1802–1884): while in his oldest texts, i.e. in JSul.I.45, JSul.I.46, JSul.III.72, JSul.III.73, we can see extensive alternation of *ö* ~ *e* and *ü* ~ *i* or the front labials being predominantly preserved (like, e.g., in JSul.III.01), the manuscripts copied in the second half of the 19th century contain almost no forms with *ö*, and *ü* (i.e. mss. ADub.III.61, JSul.I.54.09, JSul.III.69, JSul.III.79, JSul.III.77, JSul.I.01c, JSul.III.07, and JSul.III.76), see Table 10.

This edition provides further evidence that confirms our observation expressed in Németh (2014a: 254; 2015b: 174), namely that the delabialization process of *ö*, *ü* spread from word-ending syllables back towards the beginning of a word,[20] cf., for instance, *köründi* (15:9), *körimlerinden* (5:14), *özünnin* (28:30), or the alternating variants of *özünün* ~ *özünin* ~ *özinin* ~ *ezinin* (7:5), *kötürme* ~ *kötirme* ~ *ketirme* (3:24), *süründüm* ~ *süründim* ~ *sirindim* (6:25). There are only a very few exceptions to this rule, see e.g. *biznü* (7:29), and *küninnü* (3:8).

#### 3.2.3.3 The Continuants of MKar. -(*i*)*ġčü*

One quite interesting case to note is that of the MWKar. *-ivčü* suffix which forms the basis of *nomina agentis* (today often described as one of the Karaim present participles). Etymologically it goes back to the Middle Kipchak **-iġčü* derivative suffix (see Berta 1996: 592, 595). While the Modern South-Western Karaim texts analysed in the present edition display well-known variants, i.e. *-uvcu* ~ *-ivci* (see e.g. Zajączkowski 1931: 28–29), in the oldest South-Western Karaim texts three variants are used: *-uvču* ~ *-ivčü* ~ *-üvčü*, see e.g. כֵּלִיוְוצוּ *kelivčü* (JSul.III.63: 2:14), אֵטִיוְוצִיוּ *etivčü* (JSul.I.01b: 3:3, 3:67), כיוֹריוּוְיוּ *körüvčü* (JSul.I.01b: 3:4), כיוֹטיוּרוּוְצִיוּ *kötürüvčü* (JSul.I.01b: 3:68), כֵּמִישיוּוְצִיוּ *kemišüvčü*

19 Interestingly, as far as the oldest Lutsk Karaim sources are concerned (see 1.1), MWKar. *ö* and *ü* were not retained in JSul.I.02 from 1807 and in JSul.I.50.06 (ca. 1815), see e.g. אִילִיש *iliš* (< **ülüš*; JSul.I.02: 8 v°) or כֵּירֵיא *kere* (< **köre*; JSul.I.02: 9 v°), which contrasts with JSul.I.04 copied in Lutsk in 1814 by Jaakov ben Icchak Gugel where the archaic front labials are intact, see, e.g. איוּץ *üč* (1 r°), כיוּנְלֵירִי *künleri* (2 r°), איוּסְטיוּנֵיא *üstüne* (20 r°), כיוֹזליר *közler* (80 r°), סיוֹזְלֵיְדִי *sözlejdi* (100 r°) or סיוֹזְלֵירִי *sözleri* (100 r°).

20 It is important to emphasize that exactly the same applies to the way the *e* > *'a* change operated in Middle North-Western Karaim, see 3.2.2.

(JSul.I.01b: 3:77), כיוֹנְדֵירִיוְוצִיוּ *könderivčü* (JSul.I.54.03: 12:26). What is conspicuous in this case, however, is the lack of **\-*yvču* forms in the edited materials. What we have here is an asymmetric MWKar. pattern whereby in the back-harmonic environment the first syllable of the suffix always contains a labial vowel, whereas in the front-vowel environment an illabial *i*- may also occur. This phenomenon is perhaps linked to the chronology of the *ü* > *i* change.

Namely, the original, Middle Karaim form of the suffix was *-(*y*)*vču* ~ -(*i*)*včü*. Then, as is generally known, *b*, *p*, *m*, and *v* (the latter was most probably bilabial, too, see 3.3.4.1) tended to labialize adjacent vowels, which means that both *yv* > *uv* and *iv* > *üv* processes could have easily taken place suffix-initially.[21] Now, if we assume that the labialization of the initial sound of this suffix began at a time when the position of the front labials in the South-Western Karaim phonological system was already weakened (and thus the sounds *ö*, *ü*, instead of being used even more frequently, were already considerably limited), it becomes explicable why the *-*yvču* > -*uvču* operated without, it seems, exception, whereas the -*ivčü* > -*üvčü* change did not: the latter happened to be "blocked" by phonological limitations, which resulted in an alternation of the -*ivčü* ~ -*üvčü* forms. Later, the *ü* was eliminated from the sound system together with the alveolar *č* (> *c*, see below), which during the first half of the 19th century gave us the Mod.SWKar. -*uvcu* ~ -*ivci*.[22]

This is corroborated by the oldest North-Western Karaim sources. In manuscript ADub.III.73 the suffix in question bears the form -(*u*)*vču* ~ -(*ü*)*včü*—without exceptions.[23] In addition, in JSul.I.01a we also find the variant -*ivčü*, אֵטִיבְצוּ *etivčü* (JSul.I.01a: 122 r°), and כֵלִיבְצוּ *kelivčü* (JSul.I.01a: 122 v°) being good examples. However, nor was the NWKar. *-*yvču* form attested.

21 As an example of the labializing tendency, see e.g. **syzlavly* > *syzlavlu* (3:73). This is, by the way, an argument in support of the thesis that it is the forms *-(*y*)*vču* ~ -(*i*)*včü* that are older: an *uv* > *yv* change would hardly be explainable. For more on the labialization tendency mentioned here see, for instance, Pritsak (1959a: 327).

22 Seen in this light, forms like *könderivčü* (11:26) should perhaps not be regarded as exceptions to the rule that the *ü* > *i* process began in the final syllables and gradually extended towards the beginning of a word, because the first-syllabic *i*- in such forms should rather be interpreted as a continuant of MWKar. *i*- and not as resulting from the later *ü* > *i* delabialization.

23 See, for example, כיוֹטיוּבְצִיוּ *kötüvčü* (6 v°), ביוּרֵליוּבְצִיוּ *bürelüvčü* (7 r°), טיוּנְכֵיליוּבְצִיוּ *tünkelüvčü* (7 r°), איוֹלְטיוּריוּבְצִיוּ *öltürüvčü* (7 r°). I have meticuously read and analysed folios 3 r°–347 v° (the initial two folios are missing; for the last five folios, i.e. the Book of Ruth, see Németh 2015c).

As a final remark it should be added that in the SWKar. *-ivčü* (*-ivcü*) suffix, the labial *-ü* survived until surprisingly late, perhaps due to the labializing attribute of *-v-* (as was already suggested in Németh 2014a: 254); cf. *maḥtavlu* (17:3) < *maḥtavly*, *syzlavlu* (3:73) < *syzlavly*, in which the sound *-v-* triggered an *y* > *u* change despite not being adjacent to *y*, such as *maḥtavu* (16:23) < *maḥtavy*.

#### 3.2.3.4 Remarks on the Convergent Development of MWKar. *ö*, *ü* in South- and North-Western Karaim

The harmony shift and the evolution of the front labials had a profound impact on Middle Western Karaim vocalism: they shaped both of its dialects and eventually led to its transformation into two separate vocalic systems. In the north-western dialect new phonotactic constraints emerged, whereas in South-Western Karaim a phonemic merger took place between *ö* : *e* and *ü* : *i*, as a result of which these phoneme pairs fell together into *e* and *i*, respectively. Based on the philological evidence collected and analysed in recent years it became possible to establish a preliminary time frame for some of these changes (Németh 2014a, 2014b, 2015b). Now, the texts edited in the present volume make further refinement of our conclusions possible (see Table 11).

The influence exerted by Slavonic languages and Lithuanian, which have no *ö* or *ü* in their phonemic inventories, is the only reasonble explanation for why in the Late Middle Western Karaim period the phonological status of the front labials had weakened in both dialects, independently of each other. The Slavicization (assimilation) of Karaim is a historical fact: this process affected not only the Karaim lexicon, but also manifested itself in numerous structural influences (see Németh 2011b: 62–76). As a consequence, any analysis of the development of the front labials in Karaim should also take into account Slavonic phonology and phonotactics.

However, this shared Slavonic influence produced different results in the two dialects. In North-Western Karaim it resulted in a marked increase in the number of palatal consonants, which in turn paved the way for consonant harmony by, on the one hand, creating a phonological opposition between palatalized and non-palatalized consonants, and, on the other, weakening the phonological opposition between front and back vowels (see Németh 2014b: 364–366). In South-Western Karaim, in turn, *ö*, *ü* changed into *e*, *i* and it is precisely the increased frequency of use of these two sounds that resulted in a greater number of palatal consonants due to, once again, Slavonic phonotactic influences. As a consequence, both dialects have a high number of palatal consonants (compared to other Turkic languages) and no *ö*, *ü* (except NWKar. *ö-*, *ü-*), albeit as the outcome of completely different processes.

TABLE 11 The evolution of Middle Western Karaim front labials

| | NWKar. | SWKar. |
|---|---|---|
| ca. until 1650 | *ö, ü* | |
| 1675<br>1700<br>1725 | *ö-, ü-, -ö-, -ü(-) ~ -'o-, -'u(-)* | *ö, ü* |
| 1750<br>1775<br>1800<br>1825 | *ö-, ü-, -'o-, -'u(-)* | *ö ~ e, ü ~ i* |
| 1850 | | *e, i* |

TABLE 12 Modern North-Western Karaim vowels

| | **Functionally front** | | **Functionally back** | |
|---|---|---|---|---|
| **High** | i | ü- | -y(-) | u |
| **Low** | e | ö- | a | o |
| | Unrounded | Rounded | Unrounded | Rounded |

TABLE 13 Modern South-Western Karaim vowels

| | **Functionally front** | | **Functionally back** | |
|---|---|---|---|---|
| **High** | i | | y | u |
| **Low** | e | | a | o |
| | Unrounded | | Unrounded | Rounded |

It is also rather striking that, as is shown by the philological data, both the NWKar. *ö* > *'o*, *ü* > *'o*, *e* > *'a* changes, and the SWKar. *ö* > *e*, *ü* > *i* shifts operated according to similar mechanisms, i.e. they both started to occur in word-final syllables. More precisely: they were first triggered in suffixes and enclitics and then extended back towards the word-initial syllables. In my view, the reason for this convergence should be sought in the fact that in the case of the suffixes these changes were not burdened with the loss of lexical meaning. For this reason, the stem-vowels “resisted” for longer, as can be seen in the fact that the North-Western Karaim first-syllabic *e* and word-initial *ö*-, *ü*- remained intact.

#### 3.2.4 *The Modern Western Karaim Vocalic System*

Based on the above we can say that the vocalic systems of present-day North-Western Karaim emerged, most likely, in the mid-18th century, whereas the South-Western Karaim vocalism known from 20th-century written and oral material took shape a hundred years later, in the mid-19th century.

## 3.3 The Consonant System

### 3.3.1 *General Overview*

The following paragraphs provide a description of the Early Middle Western Karaim and Late Modern Western Karaim consonant systems that encompasses the period up until the end of the first half of the 19th century. To better understand the pre-19th-century philological evidence presented in this volume, the linguistic data have been interpreted in the broader context of the much better known Modern Western Karaim sources dating from the second half of the 19th century (see Grzegorzewski 1903, 1916–1918; Kowalski 1929; A. Zajączkowski 1931; Pritsak 1959a; Musaev 1964, 1977; Dubiński 1978; Németh 2011a, 2011b, 2013b–c, 2014a, 2014b, 2014c, 2015b, 2016b; Csató 2012; Csató & Johanson 2016). In the tables below the following notation are used:

C[?] consonant of uncertain phonological status and/or phonetic value
(C) disappearing consonant
*C* newly emerging consonant [italic letters]
**C* newly emerging consonant with no separate graphemic representation[24]
/C[?]/ less possible position in the phonological system

Commentary
1. *w* and *v* are not distinguished in the transcription (see 3.6). There is no certainty as to the exact distribution of these sounds and their phonemic status in Middle Karaim. For more details see 3.3.4.1 below.
2. *ł* and *l* are not distinguished in the transcription (see 3.6). These sounds were very likely positional allophones. For more details, see commentary nr. 5 and 3.3.7 below.

24 Our point of reference is the sound-to-spelling correspondence known from Hebrew.

TABLE 14 Early Middle South-Western Karaim consonants

| | Bilabial | | Labiodental | | Dental | | Alveolar | | Palatal/ pre-velar | | Velar/ uvular | | Laryngeal | |
|---|---|---|---|---|---|---|---|---|---|---|---|---|---|---|
| **Plos.** | p | b | | | t | d | | | ḱ | ǵ | k, q | g, /ġ$^{?}$/ | | |
| **Affr.** | | | | | c$^{?}$ | | č | ǯ | | | | | | |
| **Fric.** | | | f | v$^{?}$ | s | z | š | ž$^{?}$ | | | ḥ, ḫ | ġ | /ḫ$^{?}$/ | h |
| **Nas.** | | m | | | | n | | | | | | | | |
| **Liqu.** | | | | | | ł | | l | | | | | | |
| **Trill** | | | | | | | | r | | | | | | |
| **Glide** | | w | | | | | | | | j | | | | |

TABLE 15 Early Middle North-Western Karaim consonants

| | Bilabial | | Labiodental | | Dental | | Alveolar | | Palatal/ pre-velar | | Velar/ uvular | | Laryngeal | |
|---|---|---|---|---|---|---|---|---|---|---|---|---|---|---|
| | – | + | – | + | – | + | – | + | – | + | – | + | – | + |
| **Plos.** | p ṕ | b b́ | | | t t́ | d d́ | | | ḱ | ǵ | k, q | g, /ġ$^{?}$/ | | |
| **Affr.** | | | | | c$^{?}$ | | č č́ | ǯ ǯ́ | ć | ʒ́ | | | | |
| **Fric.** | | | f | v$^{?}$ v́$^{?}$ | s | z | š š́ | ž$^{?}$ ž́$^{?}$ | ś | ź | ḥ, ḫ | ġ | /ḫ$^{?}$/ | h h́ |
| **Nas.** | | m ḿ | | | | n | | | | ń | | | | |
| **Liqu.** | | | | | | ł | | l | | ĺ | | | | |
| **Trill** | | | | | | | | r ŕ | | | | | | |
| **Glide** | | w ẃ | | | | | | | | j | | | | |

3. *q* and *k* are distinguished in the transcription. These two sounds were differentiated in writing by the use of the letters ק and כ, respectively. Retaining this distinction in the transcription enables us to better understand coarticulative phenomena and the phonetics of loanwords (with the exclusion of Hebrew loanwords in which the original orthography is applied regardless of the phonetic realization in Karaim).
4. The articulation of the (pre-)velar stops might have been retracted when they occurred with tautosyllabic back vowels as a natural process so as to become at least partly uvular in that position.
5. Based on what we know from Turkic phonotactics (see e.g. Räsänen 1949: 148 ff.), we can assume that *g*, *k*, *l* must have been palatalized in front of *e*, *i*, *ö*, and *ü*—as an inherited feature. Later, as a result of the harmony shift, the number and frequency of use of the palatal or palatalized counterparts of the Late Middle North-Western Karaim non-palatal consonants increased considerably (see, primarily, Németh 2014b, 2015b). Most probably, the following set of NWKar. palatalized consonants came into existence in this period: *ṕ*, *b́*, *t́*, *d́*, *ć*, *ʒ́*, *č́*, *ǯ́*, *ẃ*, *v́*, *š́*, *ž́*, *h́*, *ḿ*, *ń*, *ĺ*, and *ŕ*.
6. *ḥ* and *ḫ* are distinguished in the transcription, but there is no certainty as to the phonemic status of *ḫ* in Middle Karaim. For more details see 3.3.4.3 below.
7. There were three main processes that further shaped the consonant system in the first half of the 19th century: **a)** the SWKar. *č*, *ǯ*, *š*, *ž* > *c*, *ʒ*, *s*, *z* dealveolarization process as described in detail in Németh (2014a); **b)** the palatalization of SWKar. c, *ʒ*, *s*, *z*, *n* > *ć*, *ʒ́*, *ś*, *ź*, *ń* (described in detail using sources from the second half of the 19th century in Németh 2011a: 74–80); **c)** the NWKar. *q* > *ḥ* change (see 3.3.2.1).

Problematic issues (only) are described in detail below.

### 3.3.2 *Plosives*

#### 3.3.2.1 *q* and Its Development

In the native lexicon *q* appeared in the back-vowel environment only (whilst *k* was used in the front-vowel environment), and it must have been either a velar or a uvular sound. In North-Western Karaim, *q* eventually underwent spirantization in the syllable-closing and suffix-initial positions,[25] which is not attested in the edited materials. The oldest attestation of the *q* > *ḥ* spirantization was found by the present author in ms. RAbk.IV.15, see, for example,

25 In a limited number of words (such as e.g. in NWKar. *jaḥšy*, SWKar. *jaḥsy*), the *q* > *ḥ* spirantization is a Middle Karaim or an inherited Kipchak feature (see von Gabain 1959: 54).

TABLE 16 Late Modern South-Western Karaim consonants

| | Bilabial | | Labiodental | | Dental | | Alveolar | | Palatal/ pre-velar | | Velar/ uvular | | Laryngeal | |
|---|---|---|---|---|---|---|---|---|---|---|---|---|---|---|
| | – | + | – | + | – | + | – | + | – | + | – | + | – | + |
| **Plos.** | p | b | | | t | d | | | ḱ | ǵ | k, q | | | |
| **Affr.** | | | | | *c | *ʒ | (č) | (ǯ) | *ć | *ʒ́ | | | | |
| **Fric.** | | | f | v | s | z | (š) | (ž$^{?}$) | ś | *ź | ḥ, ḫ | ġ | | h |
| **Nas.** | | m | | | | n | | | | *ń | | | | |
| **Liqu.** | | | | | | ł | | l | | | | | | |
| **Trill** | | | | | | | | r | | | | | | |
| **Glide** | | *w* | | | | | | | | j | | | | |

TABLE 17 Late Modern North-Western Karaim consonants

| | Bilabial | | Labiodental | | Dental | | Alveolar | | Palatal/ pre-velar | | Velar/ uvular | | Laryngeal | |
|---|---|---|---|---|---|---|---|---|---|---|---|---|---|---|
| | – | + | – | + | – | + | – | + | – | + | – | + | – | + |
| **Plos.** | p ṕ | b b́ | | | t t́ | d d́ | | | ḱ | ǵ | k, (q) | | | |
| **Affr.** | | | | | c$^{?}$ | | č č́ | ǯ ǯ́ | ć | ʒ́ | | | | |
| **Fric.** | | | f | v v́ | s | z | š š́ | ž ž́ | ś | ź | ḥ, ḫ | ġ | | h h́ |
| **Nas.** | | m ḿ | | | | n | | | | ń | | | | |
| **Liqu.** | | | | | | ł | | l | | ĺ | | | | |
| **Trill** | | | | | | | | r ŕ | | | | | | |
| **Glide** | | w ẃ | | | | | | | | j | | | | |

NWKar. ייָזִיקֿלִי *jazyḥly* (< *jazyqly*) (RAbk.IV.15: 49 r°), חַנְלִיקֿלַרְדָא *ḥanlyḥlarda* (< *ḥanlyqlarda*) (RAbk.IV.15: 49 r°), or טַרְלִיקֿטָן *tarlyḥtan* (< *tarlyqtan*) (RAbk.IV.15: 50 r°) (the fricativeness is rendered with the unusual combination of the letter *qoph* with a *raphe*).[26] Nevertheless, it is only in the sources from the second half of the 19th century that the fricative pronunciation of *q* is clearly and abundantly reflected in writing (see e.g. the linguistic material of JSul.I.11 in № 24). To sum up, there were two graphemes available to distinguish between a palatal/pre-velar *k* and a velar/uvular *q*—i.e. the letter *kaph* (כ) and *koph* (ק), respectively—and another two signs to denote the fricative nature of /q/ (namely, the letters *cheth* (ח) and *koph* with a *raphe* (קֿ)).[27]

### 3.3.3 *Affricates*

#### 3.3.3.1 The Question of *c*

The phonological status of MWKar. *c* is uncertain. As is generally known, the *c* sound is alien to the native Turkic phoneme inventory, but it eventually entered the Modern Western Karaim phonological system due to the South-Western Karaim dealveolarization process described in more detail in paragraph 3.3.5 below. Another phenomenon that introduced this sound into the phonemic inventory was the large number of Hebrew and Slavonic loanwords. Initially, it was often replaced by *č* in Karaim, but later it remained unchanged.[28] It is conceivable that, as a result of the latter process, /c/ could have entered the phonological system much earlier than the second half of the 19th century. However, there is no philological proof in support of this assumption, since no clear distinction was made between *č* and *c* in Karaim Hebrew script.

26 Ms. RAbk.IV.15 consists of handwritten passages of varying age. The one in question originates from the period between ca. 1778/1792 and 1797. The age of this part of the manuscript can be established based on the fact that in folio 49 r° the father of Josef ben Moshe ben Shemuel ben Josef ha-Mashbir (see 2.1.7) is mentioned as being deceased. Given that Josef's father, Moshe, bore the title *hazzan*, we can easily identify him and say that he passed away in ca. 1778 or 1792. In turn, another heading in folio 45 v° informs informs us that Jeshua ben Mordechai Mordkowicz (died 1797, see 2.2.3), was still alive when the text was written.

27 This concurs with our conclusion in Németh (2015b: 174), namely that this process, which is not attested in JSul.III.05, must have begun to operate after the 1780s at the earliest and ended prior to the 1880s.

28 Cf. e.g. Kar. *cadyk* 'just', *cafon* 'north', *cynamon* 'cinnamon', *cenzor* 'censor', *maceva* 'tombstone' (see KarRPS). There are, however, instances where Heb. *c* is replaced with Kar. *č*, as e.g. in *čabor* 'aspergillum', *čoref* 'jeweler'.

#### 3.3.3.2 The Question of the Alveolar Affricates

For a description of affricatives in South-Western Karaim, see 3.3.5.

### 3.3.4 *Fricatives*

#### 3.3.4.1 The Question of *v*, and *w*

The phonetic value of *v* remains speculative. We have reasons to assume that in Middle Western Karaim there might in fact have been two voiced labial fricatives: a bilabial *w* and a labiodental *v* along with their palatalized variants in NWKar., i.e. *v́* and *ẃ*—even though they were not unambiguously distinguished in writing.

Musaev (1964: 69) asserts that the bilabial *w* was a characteristic feature exclusively of the native lexicon, *en bloc*, as a continuant of the Turkic **γ*,[29] whereas the labiodental *v* was, in his opinion, present in loanwords, only. On the other hand, however, the language of the Codex Comanicus indicates that a somewhat different distribution of these sounds would also have been conceivable and, in certain positions, a labiodental *v* might have appeared in words of native origin (see von Gabain 1959: 52–53). Other authors and field researchers, including Karaim-born Turcologists (Jan Grzegorzewski, Tadeusz Kowalski, Ananiasz Zajączkowski, Omeljan Pritsak, and Aleksander Dubiński; see Németh 2011a: 94–98 for an exhaustive overview of those linguistic descriptions), posited or documented the existence of the glide *w* and the labiodental *v* for Modern Western Karaim as spoken from the late 19th century on and did not touch upon the distribution of these sounds.

In our view, the bilabial pronunciation of (**γ*) > *w* (being either a glide or a fricative) appears to be corroborated by the fact that *w* labialized adjacent vowels in the same way as the group of the three other bilabial consonants did, i.e. *b*, *p*, and *m* (see Zajączkowski 1932: 154, and our remark in 3.2.3.3).

For the time being, however, the phonemic status of the originally labiodental *v*-s of Hebrew, Yiddish, Persian, and Slavonic loanwords in Karaim must remain speculative. We know that from the end of the first half of the 19th century way until the initial decades of the 20th century both *w* and *v* were present in Western Karaim (see Németh 2011a: 96–98), but based solely on the philological evidence we cannot go any further in the reconstruction of their existence and distribution in Middle Western Karaim given that the sounds in question were written with the same set of graphemes, i.e. ב, בֿ, וו, ו. What we can assume here is only that the sound transcribed with *v* was very likely a glide in at least the majority of native lexemes. As a consequence, even though *w* and *v* are

29 The only exception is, as Musaev says, the *v*- in Kar. *vat*- 'to strike' < **uvat-*.

mentioned in tables 16–19 above, no distinction is made between these three sounds in the transcription, and they are rendered with *v*, which stands, we may say, generally for a labial approximant.

#### 3.3.4.2 The Question of *š*, *s*, and *ś*

As is generally known, the Hebrew letters *shin* (ש) and *samekh* (ס) were used in the Karaim semi-cursive script to distinguish between *š* and *s*, respectively.[30] Based on the usage of these two letters we can try to establish the chronology of the *š* > *s* change that took place in South-Western Karaim.

In Németh (2014a: 264) it was argued that:

> it seems […] justified to say that the *š* > *s* process operated in the 18th century, presumably most intensively in its final decades. This would explain why the process involved […] the idiolect of the copyist of JSul.III.03. The latter manuscript showed that the *š* > *s* change had ended before he copied it, for he only used the original **š* in loanwords and made one mistake in reconstructing it. The same manuscript, however, reflects a far-reaching alternation of *ö* ~ *e*, and *ü* ~ *i*, as well as *s* ~ *ś* in front of a syllable with *i*, and testifies that the *ö* > *e*, *ü* > *i*, *s* + *i* > *ś* + *i* processes were ongoing during the copyist's lifetime. This also means that these processes ended later than the *š* > *s* shift. […] Importanly, however, both processes could have started much before 1772.

In fact, the manuscripts which provided the basis for describing the *š* > *s* dealveolarization process in Németh (2014a: 257–264) are still representative in this matter. Nevertheless, we can supplement the above with further observations and conclusions based on a reading of additional South-Western Karaim manuscripts, including those that were copied in the 18th century or around

30 The dots above the letter *shin* used in Hebrew orthography to indicate the difference between *shin* (שׁ) and *sin* (שׂ) were not used by Karaim scribes at all. However, due to this dual use of the letter *shin* in unvocalized texts there are some examples of using the letter *shin* for [s] in Karaim texts, too, see: in JSul.I.16: קוּבַטְשִׁיז *quvatsyz* (4:18), in JSul.I.38.09: אשטרלגן *astralġan* (20:20), in JSul.I.45: כֵּימִישֵׁישֶׁין *kemisesen* (5:11), שֵׁיזִי *sezi* (9:9), in JSul.I.54.03: פּוּשְׁטָא *pusta* (19:3), in JSul.III.03: יִירִישֵׁנִיז *jiriseniz* (11:8), כֵּימִישֵׁשֶׁין *kemisesen* (5:11), טֵירְשֵׁיֵישִׁיז *tersejesiz* (15:16), in JSul.III.66: אֵישְׁלֵיטֵידִילֵיר *esletediler* (3:10), in JSul.III.67: טִיבְשִׁירִילְמֶישְׁסֶן *tivsirilmessen* (or *tivširilmessen*) (12:15). The use of the letter *shin* for /s/ in front of *i* or in front of palatal(ized) consonants is a complex matter and will be discussed separately below (see 3.3.4.3). The letter *samekh*, however, was never used for rendering *š*.

the turn of the 19th century, i.e. including texts written earlier than the oldest sources that were taken into consideration in Németh (2014a).[31]

To start with, it ougth to be stressed that the question of deciphering the letter *shin* as *š* must be treated cautiously. The orthography must have been conservative to certain extent (as is known from any kind of religious text). We must be aware of the fact that at least in some cases the copyists could have retained the orthography of the originals even if such a solution reflected an earlier stage in phonetic development that was not characteristic of their own idiolects. Moreover, the orthography is, in fact, doubly deceptive given that a large group of South-Western Karaim texts are copies of *peshatim* originally written in North-Western Karaim, i.e. they were composed in a dialect in which the *š* > *s* change had never taken place. As a result, the letter *shin* (theoretically suggesting a SWKar. *š*), might have been a slavishly copied letter *shin* either from an archaic South-Western Karaim text or from a North-Western Karaim text of any age.[32]

One noteworthy example in this context is that of ms. JSul.III.67. As we can see from Table 19, of the five *peshatim* copied in that particular manuscript, only *peshat* № 28 was originally written in South-Western Karaim. Moreover, it is only the copy of this *peshat* in which *s* (< **š*) forms predominate. All other *peshatim* included in this source were originally composed in North-Western Karaim and, at the same time, exhibit either a dominant *š* or an *š* ~ *s* alternation. A very similar phenomenon is to be observed in ms. JSul.III.72 (see Table 19).

This, of course, does not make these sources unreliable. It is simply that their analysis requires careful handling. Indeed, we have a great deal of fairly reliable data at our disposal. Most importantly, a number of *peshatim* originally composed in South-Western Karaim were relatively soon afterwards copied in the same dialect, a good illustration of this phenomenon being *peshatim* № 25, 26, 28, 29, and 30 in JSul.III.03, *peshat* № 6, composed most probably in South-Western Karaim and copied in mss. JSul.I.53.13, JSul.I.01b, and the *peshat*

31 In this respect, the most important texts are JSul.I.53.13, JSul.I.01b, JSul.I.38.09, JSul.I.54.03, and JSul.III.66. We should add here that the language of JSul.III.01, the complete translation of the Torah and the Haftarah copied by Jeshua Josef Mordkowicz (2.2.5) also corroborates the relative chronology established in Németh (2014a), namely that the *š* > *s* shift gained momentum earlier than the delabialization of *ö* and *ü*. In that manuscript *š* is retained almost exclusively in loanwords, whereas *ö* and *ü* are predominantly retained.

32 It is important to note that how many and what kind of intermediate copies existed between the North-Western Karaim originals and their South-Western Karaim copies edited in the present volumes has yet to be determined. An attempt to establish a preliminary relationship between the respective copies of the *peshatim* is presented in the introduction to each edition of the texts in chapter 4.

№ 26 in JSul.III.63 (preliminarily analysed in Németh 2014a). In these texts, the chance of distorting the linguistic picture with orthographic phenomena is marginal and only the "archaic spelling" remains as an important factor that needs to be taken into account. However, and most importantly, as we have shown in chapter 2.2 and 2.3, the manuscripts are for the most part linguistically fairly consistent and therefore reliably depictable.

Let us continue with a number of supplementary remarks regarding the absolute chronology of the *š* > *s* change. As quoted above, our view was that even though the oldest manuscripts in which the *š* > *s* change is abundantly documented originate from the turn of the 19th century (in Németh 2015b we quoted mss. JSul.III.03, JSul.III.63, JSul.III.69, and JSul.III.79; below see also mss. JSul.I.54.03, JSul.III.66, and JSul.I.54.12), the genesis of this process might, in fact, go back to much earlier times. Our argumentation was based on the fact that the same process took place in both the Lutsk and Halych varieties of Karaim despite the fact that these two communities were isolated from each other from the First Partition of Poland (1772) on, as was already mentioned in 3.2.3.2 in a slightly different context (for more details, see Németh 2014a: 263).

This observation appears to be substantiated by the fact that the word *kenes* 'advice' (< **keneš*) is attested in JSul.I.38.11 (1 vº), and that כֵּינֵיס *ašyra* 'through' is spelled twice with the letter *samekh*, i.e. as אָסִירָא *asyra* (6:9, 56), in ms. JSul.I.53.13—a manuscript created around 1762. These are the oldest examples of the *š* > *s* change.

Three comments are in order here. Firstly, there is only one text written in the Karaim language in JSul.I.53.13; all other parts of the manuscript are in Hebrew. Secondly, the *peshat* in question (№ 6) was most probably composed in South-Western Karaim. Thirdly, the fact that the word *asyra* is attested in that source twice precludes the possibility that the copyist had made a scribal error. Nevertheless, further data would be required to confirm with greater certainty that the *š* > *s* change started to operate (decades?) before 1772. For instance, we do not have those old materials from Lutsk at our disposal (see 1.1).[33]

There are considerably fewer examples of the hypercorrect use of *š* than cases where *ö* and *ü* are confused with *e* and *i* (see Table 9). In fact, there are only four words in which such a phenomenon might be expected. However, even

---

33 As mentioned in 1.1, the oldest mss. from Lutsk are JSul.I.02 (a fragment copied in 1807) and JSul.I.04 (copied in 1814). In these surces, the original *š* is mostly retained, see, for instance, יַירְלִיגָשְׁלָבְצוּ *jarlyġašlavču* (JSul.I.02: 8 vº), יַיחְשִׁי *jaḥšy* (JSul.I.02: 62 rº), בֵּיש *beš* (JSul.I.04: 1 vº), or אִיש *iš* (JSul.I.04: 3 vº), but there are some reliable examples of the *š* > *s* development, too, see e.g. *toḥtavcusu* טוֹחְטָבְצוּסוּ (JSul.I.02: 7 vº) or אֵיסֵיקְלֵיר *esekler* (JSul.I.04: 1 vº).

TABLE 18 Possibly hypercorrect forms with *š* in place of *s* (< **s*)

| Accession № | Date of copy | Hypercorrect forms | Roots vs. forms |
|---|---|---|---|
| JSul.III.63 | ca. 1778 (before 1797) | *ašajyšlyqlaryndan* (4:27) | 1 vs. 1 |
| JSul.I.38.09 | turn of the 19th c. | *künšülügünnü* (12:29) | 1 vs. 1 |
| JSul.III.03 | shortly after 1805 | *jašanġajsen* (26:37) | 1 vs. 1 |
| JSul.III.72 | before 1851 | *ulušqa* (7:12) | 1 vs. 1 |

these are uncertain in light of the double use of the letter *shin* in the unvocalized writing we mentioned towards the beginning of this subchapter and the fact that the three examples displayed in Table 18 can simply be explained in an orthographic dimension.

As far as the *terminus ante quem* of the *š* > *s* process is concerned, it should be pointed out that the private letters and circulars edited in Németh (2011b) sent between 1841 and 1923 by persons born between 1797 and 1857 (Németh 2011b: 19–20) bear absolutely no traces of the original *š* and we can treat these documents as a reliable source of knowledge on colloquial Karaim.

The texts edited here corroborate our other observation in Németh (2014a: 257–259), namely that the letter *shin*, and hence most probably also the alveolar *š*, remained unchanged the longest in loanwords. This is also true with reference to the language of JSul.III.01. The words that exhbit this phenomenon are as follows: *aškara bol-*, *dušman*, *fašman*, *mašiah*, *hammeše*, *haqadoš*, *hašgaha*, *hešbon*, *ḥyššym*, *Jehošuʿa*, *miqdaš*, *mušq*, *qamuš*, *qodeš*, *rašaʿa*, *šabat*, *šahar*, *šeḫina*, *šelamim*, *šem*, *šert*, *ševet*, *šira*, *širinik*, *šofar*, *šükür*, *tamaša*, *tešuva*, and *tišri*. Given that the above ennumeration also includes Persian loanwords, this phenomenon was in all likelihood not only orthographic in nature, i.e. it was not only a question of leaving the Hebrew spelling unchanged.

For some evidence that *š* evolved into *s* via an intermediate stage of *ś*, see 3.4.3.

The table below shows whether in the particular texts copied in the respective manuscript we can find: **1)** the original *š* retained (*š* ≥ *š*), **2)** a regular *š* ~ *s* alternation (*š* ~ *s*); **3)** *s* used predominantly in lieu of *š*, except for loanwords, in which *š* is mostly retained ((*š*) ~ *s*); **4)** *s* used only in place of the original *š*, with the exception of Hebrew words in which *shin* tends to be an orthographic feature; **5)** the letter *shin* is used for [ś] (see 3.4.3 below).

TABLE 19 The continuants of MKar. *ś̌* and the use of the letter *shin* for [ś] in edited South-Western Karaim texts (by manuscript and copy)

| *Peshat* № | Author's native dialect | Copyist's native dialect | *ś̌* | *ś̌ ~ s* | (*ś̌*) ~ *s* | *s* | ש = [ś] |
|---|---|---|---|---|---|---|---|
| **JSul.I.53.13** (mid-18th c.; ca. 1762) | | | | | | | |
| 6 | SWKar. (?) | SWKar. | + | (+) | | | |
| **JSul.I.01b** (2nd half of the 18th c.) | | | | | | | |
| 3 | NWKar. | | + | | | | |
| 6 | NWKar. | SWKar. | + | | | | |
| 26 | SWKar. (?) | | + | | | | |
| **JSul.III.63** (ca. 1778 (before 1797)) | | | | | | | |
| 2 | NWKar. | | + | | | | |
| 4 | NWKar. | SWKar. | + | | | | |
| 26 | SWKar. (?) | | + | | | | |
| **JSul.I.38.09** (turn of the 19th c.) | | | | | | | |
| 12 | NWKar. | SWKar. | + | | | | |
| 20 | NWKar. | | + | | | | |
| **JSul.I.54.03** (turn of the 19th c.) | | | | | | | |
| 7 | NWKar. | | + | | | | |
| 12 | NWKar. | | + | (+) | | | |
| 14 | NWKar. | SWKar. | + | (+) | | | |
| 17 | NWKar. | | + | | | | |
| 19 | NWKar. | | + | | | | |
| 20 | NWKar. | | + | | | | |
| **JSul.III.66** (turn of the 19th c.) | | | | | | | |
| 3 | NWKar. | SWKar. | + | (+) | | | |

TABLE 19 The continuants of MKar. *š* and the use of the letter *shin* for [ś] (*cont.*)

| *Peshat* № | Author's native dialect | Copyist's native dialect | *š* | *š* ~ *s* | (*š*) ~ *s* | *s* | ש = [ś] |
|---|---|---|---|---|---|---|---|
| **JSul.III.03** (shortly after 1805) | | | | | | | |
| 1 | NWKar. | | | | + | | + |
| 5 | NWKar. | | | | + | | + |
| 8 | NWKar. | | | + | | | + |
| 9 | NWKar. | | | | + | | + |
| 10 | NWKar. | | | | + | | + |
| 11 | NWKar. | | | | + | | + |
| 15 | NWKar. | SWKar. | | | + | | + |
| 23 | NWKar. | | | | + | | + |
| 24 | NWKar. | | | | + | | + |
| 25 | SWKar. | | | + | | | + |
| 26 | SWKar. (?) | | | + | | | + |
| 28 | SWKar. | | | | + | | + |
| 29 | SWKar. | | | | + | | + |
| 30 | SWKar. | | | | + | | + |
| **JSul.I.54.12** (early 19th c.) | | | | | | | |
| 7 | NWKar. | SWKar. | + | (+) | | | |
| 14 | NWKar. | | + | (+) | | | |
| **JSul.I.45** (1st half of the 19th c., after ca. 1825) | | | | | | | |
| 1 | NWKar. | | | | + | | + |
| 2 | NWKar. | | | | + | | + |
| 5 | NWKar. | | | | | + | + |
| 8 | NWKar. | | | | + | | + |
| 9 | NWKar. | | | | + | | + |
| 10 | NWKar. | SWKar. | | | + | | + |
| 11 | NWKar. | | | | + | | + |
| 15 | NWKar. | | | | | + | + |
| 18 | NWKar. | | | | + | | + |
| 23 | NWKar. | | | | + | | + |
| 24 | NWKar. | | | | | + | + |

TABLE 19 The continuants of MKar. *š* and the use of the letter *shin* for [ś] (*cont.*)

| ***Peshat* №** | **Author's native dialect** | **Copyist's native dialect** | *š* | *š* ~ *s* | (*š*) ~ *s* | *s* | ש = [ś] |
|---|---|---|---|---|---|---|---|
| 25 | SWKar. | | | | + | | |
| 26 | SWKar. (?) | | | | + | | + |
| 29 | SWKar. | | | | + | | + |
| 30 | SWKar. | | | | + | | + |
| **JSul.I.46** (1st half of the 19th c., after ca. 1825) | | | | | | | |
| 3 | NWKar. | | | | + | | + |
| 7 | NWKar. | SWKar. | | | | + | |
| 14 | NWKar. | | | | + | | + |
| 25 | SWKar. | | | | + | | |
| **JSul.VII.22.02.13** (1st half of the 19th c.) | | | | | | | |
| 13 | NWKar. | SWKar. | + | (+) | | | + |
| **JSul.III.67** (after ca. 1840 (before 1851)) | | | | | | | |
| 7 | NWKar. | | + | | | | |
| 12 | NWKar. | | | + | | | |
| 14 | NWKar. | SWKar. | + | | | | (+) |
| 20 | NWKar. | | | + | | | |
| 28 | SWKar. | | | | + | | + |
| **JSul.III.64a** (between 1840 and 1851) | | | | | | | |
| 6 | SWKar. (?) | SWKar. | | | | + | + |
| **JSul.III.72** (before 1851) | | | | | | | |
| 7₁ | NWKar. | | + | | | | |
| 7₂ | NWKar. | | + | (+) | | | |
| 12 | NWKar. | SWKar. | | + | | | (+) |
| 14 | NWKar. | | + | (+) | | | |
| 17 | NWKar. | | | + | | | |

TABLE 19 The continuants of MKar. *š* and the use of the letter *shin* for [ś] (*cont.*)

| *Peshat* № | Author's native dialect | Copyist's native dialect | *š* | *š* ~ *s* | (*š*) ~ *s* | *s* | ש = [ś] |
|---|---|---|---|---|---|---|---|
| 19 | NWKar. | SWKar. | + | | | | |
| 20 | NWKar. | | | + | | | |
| 27 | SWKar. (?) | | | | | + | + |
| 28 | SWKar. | | | + | | | |
| **ADub.III.61** (1850/1851) | | | | | | | |
| 1 | NWKar. | | | | + | | + |
| 2 | NWKar. | | | | | + | + |
| 5 | NWKar. | | | | | + | + |
| 8 | NWKar. | | | | + | + | + |
| 9 | NWKar. | | | | + | | + |
| 10 | NWKar. | | | | + | | + |
| 11 | NWKar. | | | | + | | + |
| 13 | NWKar. | | | | | + | + |
| 15 | NWKar. | | | | + | | + |
| 16 | NWKar. | SWKar. | | | + | | + |
| 21 | NWKar. | | | | | + | + |
| 22 | NWKar. | | | | | + | + |
| 23 | NWKar. | | | | + | | + |
| 24 | NWKar. | | | | | + | + |
| 25 | SWKar. | | | | | + | + |
| 26 | SWKar. (?) | | | | | + | + |
| 27 | SWKar. (?) | | | | | + | + |
| 29 | SWKar. | | | | + | | + |
| 30 | SWKar. | | | | (+) | + | + |
| **JSul.III.73** (mid-19th c.) | | | | | | | |
| 4 | NWKar. | SWKar. | | | + | | + |
| 28 | SWKar. | | | | + | | + |

TABLE 19 The continuants of MKar. *š* and the use of the letter *shin* for [ś] (*cont.*)

| *Peshat* № | Author's native dialect | Copyist's native dialect | *š* | *š* ~ *s* | (*š*) ~ *s* | *s* | ש = [ś] |
|---|---|---|---|---|---|---|---|
| **JSul.I.37.02** (mid-19th c.) | | | | | | | |
| 6 | SWKar. (?) | SWKar. | | + | | | + |
| **JSul.I.37.02** (mid-19th c.) | | | | | | | |
| 6 | SWKar. (?) | SWKar. | | + | | | + |
| **JSul.III.69** (ca. 1851 (before 1866)) | | | | | | | |
| 1 | NWKar. | | | | + | | + |
| 2 | NWKar. | | | | | + | + |
| 5 | NWKar. | | | | | + | + |
| 8 | NWKar. | | | | + | | + |
| 9 | NWKar. | | | | (+) | + | + |
| 10 | NWKar. | | | | + | | + |
| 11 | NWKar. | | | | + | | + |
| 15 | NWKar. | | | | + | | + |
| 16 | NWKar. | SWKar. | | | + | | + |
| 21 | NWKar. | | | | | + | + |
| 22 | NWKar. | | | | | + | + |
| 24 | NWKar. | | | | | + | + |
| 25 | SWKar. | | | | | + | + |
| 26 | SWKar. (?) | | | | | + | + |
| 27 | SWKar. (?) | | | | | + | + |
| 29 | SWKar. | | | | + | | + |
| 30 | SWKar. | | | | + | | + |
| **JSul.I.37.03** (between 1851 and 1866) | | | | | | | |
| 27 | SWKar. (?) | SWKar. | | | | + | + |
| 29 | SWKar. | | | | | + | + |

TABLE 19 The continuants of MKar. *š* and the use of the letter *shin* for [ś] (*cont.*)

| *Peshat* № | Author's native dialect | Copyist's native dialect | *š* | *š* ~ *s* | (*š*) ~ *s* | *s* | ש = [ś] |
|---|---|---|---|---|---|---|---|
| **JSul.III.79** (ca. 1851 (before 1866)) | | | | | | | |
| 1 | NWKar. | | | | + | | + |
| 2 | NWKar. | | | | | + | + |
| 5 | NWKar. | | | | | + | + |
| 8 | NWKar. | | | | + | | + |
| 9 | NWKar. | | | | (+) | + | + |
| 10 | NWKar. | | | | + | | + |
| 11 | NWKar. | | | | + | | + |
| 13 | NWKar. | | | | | + | + |
| 15 | NWKar. | SWKar. | | | + | | + |
| 16 | NWKar. | | | | | + | + |
| 21 | NWKar. | | | | | + | + |
| 22 | NWKar. | | | | + | | + |
| 24 | NWKar. | | | | | + | + |
| 25 | SWKar. | | | | | + | + |
| 26 | SWKar. (?) | | | | | + | + |
| 27 | SWKar. (?) | | | | | + | + |
| 29 | SWKar. | | | | + | | + |
| 30 | SWKar. | | | | | + | + |
| **JSul.III.77** (between 1856 and 1866) | | | | | | | |
| 3 | NWKar. | SWKar. | | | + | | + |
| **JSul.I.01c** (2nd half of the 19th c.) | | | | | | | |
| 1 | NWKar. | | | | (+) | + | + |
| 5 | NWKar. | SWKar. | | | | + | + |
| 24 | NWKar. | | | | | + | + |

TABLE 19 The continuants of MKar. *š* and the use of the letter *shin* for [*ś*] (*cont.*)

| *Peshat* № | Author's native dialect | Copyist's native dialect | *š* | *š* ~ *s* | (*š*) ~ *s* | *s* | ש = [*ś*] |
|---|---|---|---|---|---|---|---|
| **JSul.III.07** (2nd half of the 19th c.) | | | | | | | |
| 3 | NWKar. | SWKar. | | | (+) | + | + |
| 25 | SWKar. | | | | | + | + |
| **JSul.III.76** (2nd half of the 19th c.) | | | | | | | |
| 7 | NWKar. | SWKar. | | | | + | + |
| 12 | NWKar. | | | | (+) | + | + |
| 14 | NWKar. | | | | (+) | + | + |
| 17 | NWKar. | | | | | + | + |
| 19 | NWKar. | | | | | + | + |
| 20 | NWKar. | | | | | + | + |
| **JSul.I.16** (19th/20th c.) | | | | | | | |
| 4 | NWKar. | SWKar. | | | (+) | + | + |
| **JSul.I.54.15** (turn of the 20th c.) | | | | | | | |
| 8 | NWKar. | SWKar. | +(?) | | | | (+)(?) |
| **JSul.gb** (1st half of the 20th c.) | | | | | | | |
| 28 | SWKar. | SWKar. | | | (+) | + | + |

3.3.4.3 The Question of *h*, *ḥ*, and *ḫ*

In both North and South-Western Karaim texts, the fricative *h* (ה), *ḥ* (ח), and *ḫ* (כ) were consistently distinguished in writing. While the phonological status of *h* and *ḥ* is clear, it remains speculative what the actual phonetic value and the phonological status of *ḫ* were given that it only appeared in Hebrew loanwords. It may very well be that it merely served an orthographic purpose and that it was adapted phonetically for Karaim. One interpretation that suggests itself is that it was pronounced [k] given that it was written with the letter *kaph*.

But such a hypothesis does not tally with the Modern Western Karaim data: we find instances of erroneous spelling of Hebrew words containing *kaph* without *dagesh qal* in which it is replaced by the letter *cheth*, see e.g. זוֹחֵה *zoḥe* 'worthy of; well-deserved' (JSul.VII.22.22.03: 1 v°; see Németh 2011b: 327, 376) vs. זוֹכֵה *zoḫe* (2:52) < Heb. זוֹכֶה 'winner'. Moreover, according to Harviainen (2013: 454), the realization of ח (standing for an unvoiced velar fricative) equaled that of כ in the Karaite Hebrew spoken by Lithuanian Karaims in the late 20th century. Seen in this light, it is very probable that there was no difference between *ḫ* and *ḥ* in Middle Western Karaim pronunciation, either.

Nevertheless, we will maintain the distinction between *ḫ* and *ḥ* in the transcription so as to facilitate further research on this matter. The interpretation we presented above cannot be treated as the only possible one in light of the different pronunciation of ח and כ among the Karaims of Istanbul: in the latter case *cheth* was realized as a glottal stop [ʾ] whereas *kaph* (*kaph rapha*) was pronounced as a post-velar fricative [ḥ] (see Harviainen 2013: 455). Finally, we must also bear in mind the presence of a devoiced counterpart of the laryngeal *h* in the Ukrainian dialects (see Zylińskyj 1979: 125–126), which may have also had an influence on the realization of כ among South-Western Karaims.

The laryngeal pronuciation of *h* is reconstructed on the basis of the linguistic features of those Slavonic loanwords used in Western Karaim that reflect the Ukrainian-type laryngeal (glottal) articulation of PSlav. **g* (Zilynśkyj 1979: 124 ff.), see e.g. MNWKar. מִיהְלָא *myhla* 'mist' attested in a manuscript copied in Kukizów in 1720 (ADub.III.73: 4 r°; Genesis 2:7) or Mod.SWKar. דוֹטוֹהוֹ *dotoho* 'in addition' < Ukr. *до того* id., העליציי *halycyj* 'of Halych (used as a byname)' < Ukr. *галичий* id., הוֹלֹאוָוא *holova* 'head' < Ukr. *голова* id. (Németh 2011b: 277, 282, 283).

For the first traces of the *q* > *ḥ* change, see 3.3.2.1; for the first traces of the *ġ* > *h* change, see 3.3.4.4.

### 3.3.4.4 *ġ* and Its Development

The phonetic value of *ġ* remains, to certain extent, speculative. There is no doubt that the letter *gimel* was used for the velar plosive *g* and the palatal/prevelar *ǵ*. But most likely it was also used to denote a fricative velar sound in back-vowel environment. Although the sign *rafe* was already used in 18th-century Western Karaim texts to denote, beyond any shadow of doubt, fricativeness (see ADub.III.73), the material edited in this volume shows that it became widely used only around the turn of the 19th century[34] and it was introduced

34 See the *rafe* used in JSul.I.01b (but only in *Men synyq ummasy*!), JSul.I.38.09, JSul.I.54.03. In the oldest mss., i.e. in JSul.I.01a, JSul.I.53.13, JSul.III.63, it is not used at all.

simultaneously above *beth*, *gimel*, and *pe* to denote the fricative nature of the sounds rendered with the respective letters. Most likely, it was merely an orthographical innovation then. Consequently, given, on the one hand, the undoubtedly non-plosive nature of those sounds rendered with the letters *beth* (ב) and *pe* (פ) (i.e. of *v* (*w*) and *f*) that were eventually written with the letters *beth* with a *rafe* (בֿ) and *pe* with a *rafe* (פֿ), and, on the other hand, given the fricative nature of the Hebrew consonant written with the letter *gimel* without *dagesh*, we can assume that the *gimel* in back-vowel environment stood most probably for a fricative velar/uvular consonant. For this reason, in our transcription, *ġ* stands for a velar/uvular fricative sound and we leave the question open whether in certain positions or in certain period of time it might have been pronounced as a velar/uvular plosive.[35] This is also in compliance with other Middle Kipchak data.

### 3.3.5 *The* š, č, ǯ, ž > s, c, ʒ, z *Dealveolarization*

A detailed analysis of the *š* > *s* change in 3.3.4.2 was all the more important as our knowledge of the chronology of the SWKar. *š*, *č*, *ǯ*, *ž* > *s*, *c*, *ʒ*, *z* process is based on documentation of this particular change.[36] This is because all other sound pairs, i.e., *č* vs. *c*, *ǯ* vs. *ʒ* and *ž* vs. *z*, were not, or only very rarely, distinguished in writing.[37] In the critical edition, therefore, whether an alveolar *č*, *ǯ*, *ž* or rather a dental *c*, *ʒ*, *z* should be reconstructed in the respective text depended on the presence or lack of *š*. For further information, see 3.6. For some evidence in favour of interpreting the South-Western Karaim dealveolarization as a two-stage pocess, namely *š*, *č*, *ǯ*, *ž* > *ś*, *ć*, *ʒ́*, *ź* > *s*, *c*, *ʒ*, *z*, see 3.4.3.

---

35 At the turn of the 20th century the velar/uvular *ġ* was in the process of being eliminated from the sound system and would eventually evolve into *g* ~ *h* (and *ǵ* ~ *ḣ* in front-vowel environment), for more details on which, see Németh (2011a: 88–94). Importantly, the materials edited in this volume include two attested examples of the latter process, cf. the word *cyġar-* 'to take out' recorded in the forms צִיהַרִינִיז *cyharynyz* (26:10) and צִיגַרִיר *cyġaryr* (26:26) in ms. JSul.III.69 copied ca. 1851 (before 1866), and the word *qoġa* 'rush; reed' attested as קוֹהָאנִין *qohanyn* (8:49) in ms. ADub.III.61 copied in 1850/1851. These two forms are the oldest known examples documenting the *ġ* > *h* change. See also *ahalyq* in F305-08 (6:38).

36 The mazurizing features characteristic of Polish dialects were similar, but operated in a different period of time (most probably from the second half of the 12th century until the 14th century) and in different territories (see, e.g. Klemensiewicz 1974: 35–36, 44). In Yiddish, in turn, the confusion of *š*, *ž*, *č* and *s*, *z*, *c* is characteristic only of its north-western variety (see Weinreich 1963: 348–349, 353–354, and 347 (figure 5)).

37 For a discussion of the possible reasons for such a practice let me redirect the reader to Németh (2014a: 257–258).

### 3.3.6 *Nasals*

There is no trace of MKar. **ŋ* in the texts. Given the lack of relevant manuscript monuments we can only establish a *terminus ante quem* for its elimination based on the Western Karaim sound system. In the north-western dialect this must have happened before 1671 (see ms. B 263), whereas in the south-western dialect it occurred prior to ca. 1740 (see mss. JSul.I.38.11, ADub.III.78).

The [*ni*] > [*ńi*] shift known from Modern South-Western Karaim (see, e.g. Németh 2011a: 74 ff.) could have taken place simultaneously with the [*si*] > [śi] change described in 3.4.3. The pontentially palatal nature of /n/ in this position is, however, hidden behind the script.

### 3.3.7 *Liquids*

As we mentioned in 3.3.1, the sound *l* must have been palatalized in the front-vowel environment according to Turkic phonotactics. There were, however, no orthographic means of distinguishing between *ł* and *l* in the Hebrew script. Nevertheless, there are some forms of the word *tefila* 'prayer' that might tell us something about the *l*-sounds. Namely, such forms as תְפִלַהלֵיר *tefilaler* (7:2) in JSul.I.54.03, תְפִלַהמְדֵיא *tefilamde* (3:105) in ms. JSul.I.01b, and תְפִלָהמֵיא *tefilame* (6:63) in ms. JSul.I.53.13 suggest that the liquid consonant of this Hebrew loanword was pronounced differently than in the *-la-* segment of the native lexicon. In these forms, perhaps, the possibly alveolar *l*, perceived as a functionally palatal consonant, influenced the vowel in the suffix and led to the disruption of the vowel harmony.[38]

The question remains whether the *l* in, for instance, *tefilame* had the same phonetic value as the alvolar *l* when positioned in front of *i* and palatal(ized) consonants, see Németh (2011a: 85–87).

## 3.4 Assimilative Sound Changes

### 3.4.1 *The NWKar.* aj > ej *Change*

The syllable-closing glide *j* triggered an *a* > *e* shift in the north-western dialect of Karaim. We find numerous examples of this change in *peshat* № 6 in ADub.III.78, see, e.g., יוּקְלֵאיְידוֹגַאן *juqlejdoġan* (6:6–7), בוֹלְגֵיי *bolġej* (6:19), בָרְגאֵיְיסִיז *barġejsiz* (6:35), קוֹנְדַרְגֵייסִיז *qondarġejsiz* (6:36). The fact is, however, that this particular text had been vocalized after the main text had been writ-

---

38 This phenomenon is known in other Turkic languages, too, cf. Tksh. *gol* 'goal (in sports)', the plural form of which is *goller*.

ten, possibly by another person, according to North-Western Karaim standards. Hence, we cannot treat this data as reliable in this respect.[39] We did not encounter examples of the *aj* > *ej* change in any other North-Westen Karaim text edited here (in particular, in *peshat* № 2 as copied in JSul.I.01a by Josef ha-Mashbir).

There are a few examples of a similar change in South-Western Karaim copies of north-western originals, see, *cejalyġy* (3:35) in JSul.I.46 (spelled צֵייָאלִיגִי), JSul.III.07 (spelled צֵיֲיאלִיגִי), and JSul.III.77 (spelled צֵייָאלִיגִי). There is a chance that the copyists left this North-Western Karaim feature unchanged and it is not the way these words were pronounced in South-Western Karaim. However, we need much more data if we are to say anything decisive in this respect (note that *j* is not in a syllable-closing position in *cejalyġy*).

### 3.4.2 *The SWKar.* ti ~ ki, di ~ gi *Alternation*

There are a few examples of *t* and *k* as well as *d* and *g* being confused in front of *i*, i.e. a process well known from South-Western Karaim sources dating from the second half of the 19th century onwards.[40] Most of these examples are to be found in sources written after 1850, see *kivil* (< *tivil*) (27:28), *kivincigine* (< *tivincigine*) (8:12) in ADub.III.61, *kitrevik* (< *titrevik*) (3:37) in mss. JSul.III.07 and JSul.III.77, and *kislerin* (< *tislerin*) (28:19) recorded in JSul.III.64b. However, we also find two examples of this phenomenon attested in JSul.I.45 and JSul.I.46 that were most probably copied in the first half of the 19th century,[41] namely: טִייִזְלֵיר *tijizler* (< *kijizler*) (2:21) and כִיטְרֵיבִּיק *kitrevik* (< *titrevik*) (3:37), respectively. The age of these manuscripts cannot be established accurately; what we do know, however, is that the copyist was born in 1802, and thus these two manuscripts could not have been written earlier than, say, the 1820s. To date, this is the oldest known record of this linguistic feature.

---

39 It ought perhaps to be mentioned that this is the reason why in Németh (2015b: 174) it is noted that this sound change is not documented in ADub.III.78. For the same reason we cannot treat as reliable the attestation of the NWKar. *-men* > *-min* ~ *-myn* change in this manuscript. As was noted in Németh (2015b: 176), this change was still an ongoing process in the second half of the 19th century: ADub.III.68 clearly reflects a *-men*, *-ḿeń* ~ *-min*, *-myn* alternation.

40 This phenomenon was a result of Ukrainian adstratal influence (for a detailed description, see Németh 2011a: 80–85).

41 It is important to note that these sources were copied by Jeshua Josef Mordkowicz (2.2.5), who lived in Halych for decades and that the *ti*, *di* > *ki*, *gi* change was more characteristic of the Halych variety of South-Western Karaim (Németh 2011a: 84–85).

### 3.4.3 *The SWKar.* si, sĆ > śi, śĆ *Change*

One issue already raised in Németh (2014a) is the very frequent use of the letter *shin* to note *s* (also *s* < *s*) in front of *i* and palatal(ized) consonants. Since in all other positions, *s* (either < **š* or < *s*) was rendered with the letter *samekh*, and since we know from other Modern South-Western Karaim texts from the second half of the 19th century that *i* and the palatal consonants palatalized *s* and a number of other consonants, namely *c*, *z*, *ʒ*, *n*, *t*, *d*, and *l* (see Németh 2011a: 74–87), it is safe to say that in the material edited here the letter *shin* was used to render [ś] in these positions, see, for instance, כֵּילֵישִׁי *kelesi* [ḱeleśi] (8:26) (JSul.III.03), יֵשִׁישִׁי *jesisi* [jeśiśi] (8:41) (JSul.III.03), כֵּישְׁטִי *kesti* [ḱeśt́i] (8:48) (JSul.III.03), טֵירְשְׁכֵּיא *terske* [terśḱe] (8:55) (JSul.III.03), טֵירְשְׁלִיגִינֵיא *tersiligne* [terśĺiǵine] (8:56) (JSul.III.03) to take examples from one manuscript only. The observations and conclusions formulated in Németh (2014a: 258–261) still remain valid in light of the materials edited here: even the oldest documented case of this phenomenon remains the same (in ms. JSul.III.03). The *si* > *śi* process must therefore have operated in the last few decades of the 18th century at the latest and ended, at least in certain areas, presumably around the beginning of the 19th century (see Table 19).

One additional remark should be added here. The orthographic practice of using the letter *shin* to render [ś] in the position in question could only have been introduced *after* the *š* > *s* (or *š* > *ś*, see below) change took place. This is because after the *š* > *s* dealveolarization occured, the letter *shin* lost its role of denoting *š* and might have been utlized for another purpose—to render [ś]. This is the reason why these two phenomena, i.e. the elimination of *š* (at least from the native lexicon) and the notation of [ś], co-occur (see Table 20 below).

Finally, there are two words in the edited materials, namely *taset-* 'destroy' and *sesken-* 'to tremble; to shake with fear', in which it is usually the letter *shin* which is used to denote *s* (< *s*) and which does not stand in front of *i* or a palatal(ized) consonant.

The verbal base *tas et-* is attested 14 times with a *shin* and only four times with a *samekh*. The forms with the latter *shin* are *tasetkin* טָשֵׁיטְכִּין (4:15) in JSul.III.63, *tas etkin* טַשְׁאֵטְקִין (4:8) and טַשׁ אֵטְכִּין (4:34) in JSul.I.16, *tas etkin* טָשׁ אֵטְכִּין (4:8, 4:34) in JSul.III.73, טַשְׁאֵיטְכִּין *tas etkin* (1:40) in JSul.I.45, טַשׁ אֶיטְכִּין *tas etkin* (1:40) in ADub.III.61 and JSul.III.79, טַשׁ אֵיטְכִּין *tas etkin* (1:40) in JSul.III.69, טַשאֵיטְכִּין *tas etkin* (1:40) in JSul.I.01c, *tas etme* טַשׁ אֶיטְמֶיא (16:20) in ADub.III.61 and JSul.III.79, *tas etmek* טָשׁ אֵיטְמֵיק (30:14) in JSul.III.03, and טַשׁ אֶיטְמֶיק *tas etmek* (30:14) in mss. ADub.III.61, and JSul.III.69. On the other hand, the forms with the letter *samekh* are טַס אֵיטְכִּין *tas etkin* (1:40) in ms. JSul.III.03, טַס אֶיטְמֶיא *tas etme* (16:20) in JSul.III.69, and טַס אֵיטְמֶיק *tas etmek* in JSul.I.45 and JSul.III.79. The other verb is recorded in single word form, namely *seskenesiz* (15:18), writ-

TABLE 20 The continuants of MKar. *š* and the use of the letter *shin* for [*ś*] in the edited South-Western Karaim texts (by manuscripts)

| Accession № | Date of copy | *š* ≥ *š* | *š* ~ *s* | (*š*) ~ *s* | *š* > *s* | ש = [*ś*] |
|---|---|---|---|---|---|---|
| JSul.I.53.13 | mid-18th c. (ca. 1762) | + | (+) | | | |
| JSul.I.01b | 2nd half of the 18th c. | + | | | | |
| JSul.III.63 | ca. 1778 (before 1797) | + | | | | |
| JSul.I.38.09 | turn of the 19th c. | + | | | | |
| JSul.I.54.03 | turn of the 19th c. | + | (+) | | | |
| JSul.III.66 | turn of the 19th c. | + | (+) | | | |
| JSul.III.03 | shortly after 1805 | | + | + | | + |
| JSul.I.54.12 | early 19th c. | + | (+) | | | |
| JSul.I.45 | 1st half of the 19th c. | | | + | (+) | + |
| JSul.I.46 | 1st half of the 19th c. | | | + | (+) | + |
| JSul.VII.22.02.13 | 1st half of the 19th c. | + | (+) | | | + |
| JSul.III.67 | after ca. 1840 (before 1851) | + | + | + | | + |
| JSul.III.64a | between 1840 and 1851 | | | | + | + |
| JSul.III.72 | before 1851 | + | + | | (+) | (+) |
| ADub.III.61 | 1850/1851 | | | + | + | + |
| JSul.III.73 | mid-19th c. | | | + | | + |
| JSul.I.37.02 | mid-19th c. | | + | | | + |
| JSul.I.54.09 | mid-19th c. | | | + | | + |
| JSul.III.69 | ca. 1851 (before 1866) | | | + | + | + |
| JSul.I.37.03 | between 1851 and 1866 | | | | + | + |
| JSul.III.79 | ca. 1851 (before 1866) | | | + | + | + |
| JSul.III.77 | between 1856 and 1866 | | | + | | + |
| JSul.I.01c | 2nd half of the 19th c. | | | (+) | + | + |
| JSul.III.07 | 2nd half of the 19th c. | | | (+) | + | + |
| JSul.III.76 | 2nd half of the 19th c. | | | (+) | + | + |
| JSul.I.16 | 19th/20th c. | | | (+) | + | + |
| JSul.I.54.15 | turn of the 20th c. | +(?) | | | | (+)(?) |
| JSul.III.64b | 1st half of the 20th c. | | | (+) | + | + |

ten with *samekh* once as סֶישְׁכֵינֵישְׁיז in JSul.I.45, but then in four manuscripts with the letter *shin*, see שֵׁישְׁכֵינֵישְׁיז in JSul.III.03, שֶׁישְׁכֶינֶישְׁיז in ADub.III.61, שֶׁישְׁכֵינֶישְׁיז in JSul.III.69, and שֶׁישְׁכֵינֵישְׁיז in JSul.III.79.

In our view, the use of the letter *shin* in these two words is not merely an orthographic feature (cf. 3.3.4.2), but the actual phonetic value of the soud rendered with the letter *shin* in these words was [ś]. Our interpretation is based on Dubiński (1978: 135), who states that these two words were pronounced *taśet-* and *śeśken-*, and on MNém.I.01 (2 r°), where A. Mardkowicz writes: "Mówi się u nas „tasiettim" (nie „tasettim")." 'We say *taśéttim* (not *tasettim*)'. This supports the idea that the dealveolarization (3.3.5) was a two-stage process: *š, č, ǯ, ž* > *ś, ć, ʒ́, ź* > *s, c, ʒ, z*.

## 3.5 Irregular Sound Changes

The following irregular sound changes have been identified:
1. Occasionally, word final *-z* is a subject of devoicing (probably as a result of the influence of Polish phonotactics), see *tenešelmes* (< *tenešelmez*) (3:19).
2. Occasionally, we find examples of so-called *Mittelsilbenschwund*, see *utru* < *uturu* (30:5; 24:34).

## 3.6 Transcription of Karaim

In the present work a phoneme-based and etymologically motivated transcription has been used to transcribe the Karaim content of the sources—including the Hebrew *Fremdwörter* embedded in the Karaim text. To avoid using four different notation systems concurrently, a single uniform transcription is employed for the Middle North-Western, Middle South-Western, Modern North-Western, and Modern South-Western varieties of Karaim.[42]

The main sound-to-spelling correspondences described in Table 21 below concern only the Karaim linguistic material presented in the present volume. The description of the orthographic and linguistic peculiarities of the Hebrew passages and insertions require Hebraistic expert knowledge. Hebrew names are excluded for the same reasons noted above.

In the present work, a predominantly phonemic transcription is employed—with certain exceptions: see our remarks concerning *k, q; w, v, u̯; ḫ; ł,* and *l* in 3.3 above. The variant spellings are listed, if applicable, from the most frequent to the least frequent. Obvious spelling mistakes and bizarre notations are neglected.

42 In fact, the transcription can also be used to document Eastern Karaim philological data. The phonetic transcription introduced in, i.a., Németh (2011b, and 2011c) to present Modern Western Karaim was not applicable here because of the uncertainty surrounding the Middle Karaim reconstructions.

TABLE 21 Transcription of Karaim (excluding Hebrew elements)[43]

| Transcription | Possible value | SWKar. | NWKar. |
|---|---|---|---|
| *a* | a | initial position: | א (*non-voc.*), אַ, אָ |
| | | medial position: | – (*non-voc.*), א (*non-voc.*), ◌ַ, ◌ָ, ◌ַא, ◌ָא |
| | | final position: | א (*non-voc.*), ◌ַא, ◌ָא, ◌ַה, ◌ָה |
| *b* | b | initial position: | ב |
| | | medial position: | ב |
| | | final position: | ב |
| *c* | c, ć | initial position: | צ̌ |
| | | medial position: | צ̌ |
| | | final position: | ץ̌ |
| *č* | č | initial position: | צ̌ |
| | | medial position: | צ̌ |
| | | final position: | ץ̌ |
| *d* | d, d́ | initial position: | ד |
| | | medial position: | ד |
| | | final position: | ד |
| *ʒ* | ʒ, ʒ́ | initial position: | צ̌, צ̌ז |
| | | medial position: | צ̌, צ̌ז |
| | | final position: | *no attestation* |
| *ǯ* | ǯ | initial position: | צ̌, צ̌ז |
| | | medial position: | צ̌, צ̌ז |
| | | final position: | *no attestation* |
| *e* | e, ė | initial position: | אי (*non-voc.*), יה (*non-voc.*), אֵי, אֶי |
| | | medial position: | י (*non-voc.*), ◌ֵי, ◌ֶי, ◌ֵ, ◌ֶ |
| | | final position: | יא (*non-voc.*), ◌ֵי, ◌ֵיא, ◌ֶי, ◌ֶיא |
| *f* | f | initial position: | פ, פֿ |
| | | medial position: | פ, פֿ |
| | | final position: | *no attestation* |

43 In this table, those North-Western Karaim palatal or palatalized consonants that emerged due to the harmony shift (see 3.3.1) are not listed separately, since these were noted in the same way their non-palatalized equivalents were written—with the sole difference being that palatality was usually (but not necessarily) marked with an additional *yodh* if the respective consonant was standing in front of *o*, *u*, and *a*.

TABLE 21 Transcription of Karaim (excluding Hebrew elements) (*cont.*)

| Transcription | Possible value | SWKar. | NWKar. |
|---|---|---|---|
| *g* | g | initial position: | ג |
| | | medial position: | ג |
| | | final position: | *no attestation* |
| *ġ* | ġ | initial position: | *no attestation* |
| | | medial position: | גֿ, ג |
| | | final position: | *no attestation* |
| *h* | h | initial position: | ה |
| | | medial position: | ה |
| | | final position: | ה |
| *ḥ* | ḥ | initial position: | ח |
| | | medial position: | ח |
| | | final position: | ח |
| *ḫ* | ḫ | initial position: | *no attestation* |
| | | medial position: | כֿ (in Hebrew loanwords, only) |
| | | final position: | *no attestation* |
| *i* | i | initial position: | אי (*non-voc.*), אִי |
| | | medial position: | י (*non-voc.*), ◌ִי |
| | | final position: | י (*non-voc.*), ◌ִי |
| *j* | j | initial position: | יי, י |
| | | medial position: | יי, י |
| | | final position: | יי, י |
| *k* | k | initial position: | כ |
| | | medial position: | כ, ק |
| | | final position: | כ, ק (the *sofit* form ך is not used) |
| *l* | ł, l | initial position: | ל |
| | | medial position: | ל |
| | | final position: | ל |
| *m* | m | initial position: | מ |
| | | medial position: | מ |
| | | final position: | ם |
| *n* | n, ń | initial position: | נ |
| | | medial position: | נ |
| | | final position: | ן |

TABLE 21 Transcription of Karaim (excluding Hebrew elements) (*cont.*)

| Transcription | Possible value | SWKar. | NWKar. |
|---|---|---|---|
| *o* | o | | initial position: או (*non-voc.*), אוֹ<br>medial position: ו (*non-voc.*), וֹ<br>final position: וֹ (*no attestation in the non-voc. texts*) |
| *ö* | ö, 'o | | initial position: איו (*non-voc.*), או (*non-voc.*), איוֹ, אוֹ<br>medial position: יוֹ, ו (*non-voc.*), וֹ<br>final position: *no attestation* |
| *p* | p | | initial position: פּ<br>medial position: פּ<br>final position: פּ (the *sofit* form ף not used) |
| *q* | q | | initial position: ק<br>medial position: ק, כ<br>final position: ק |
| *r* | r | | initial position: ר<br>medial position: ר<br>final position: ר |
| *s* | s, ś | | initial position: ס, ש<br>medial position: ס, ש<br>final position: ס |
| *š* | š, s | | initial position: ש<br>medial position: ש<br>final position: ש |
| *t* | t, ť | | initial position: ט, ת<br>medial position: ט, ת<br>final position: ט |
| *u* | u | | initial position: או (*non-voc.*), אוּ<br>medial position: ו (*non-voc.*), וּ, ◌ֻ<br>final position: ו (*non-voc.*), וּ |
| *ü* | ü, 'u | | initial position: איו (*non-voc.*), או (*non-voc.*), איוּ, אוּ<br>medial position: יוּ, יו (*non-voc.*), ו, וּ<br>final position: יוּ, וּ |
| *v* | w, v, u̯ | | initial position: ב, בֿ, וו<br>medial position: ב, בֿ, וו, ו<br>final position: ב, בֿ, וו |

TABLE 21 Transcription of Karaim (excluding Hebrew elements) (*cont.*)

| Transcription | Possible value | SWKar. | NWKar. |
|---|---|---|---|
| *y* | y | initial position: אי (*non-voc.*), אִי<br>medial position: י (*non-voc.*), ◌ִי<br>final position: י (*non-voc.*), ◌ִי | |
| *z* | z, ź | initial position: ז<br>medial position: ז<br>final position: ז | |
| *ž* | ž | initial position: *no attestation*<br>medial position: ז<br>final position: *no attestation* | |

The phenomena described in 3.3.4.2 and 3.3.5 above not only make transcription of the letter *shin* quite a demanding task, but also that of the letters *zayin* (used for *z*, *ž*), and *tzade* (used for *c*, *č*, *ʒ*, *ǯ*). After considering all the advantages and disadvantages, the following transcribing strategy was applied to the texts written in South-Western Karaim:

1. In those manuscripts, in which the original **š* is retained, the original *č*, *ǯ* and *ž* (the latter used in loanwords, see *veža* in 14:20) are also kept unchanged.
2. In those manuscripts, in which there are only a few exceptional examples of the *š* > *s* change, the original *č*, *ǯ*, *ž* are kept unchanged.
3. In those manuscripts, in which there is a clear alternation of *š* ~ *s*, besides those readings with the original *č*, *ǯ*, *ž*, the alternative readings with *c*, *ʒ*, *z* are indicated in the apparatus.
4. In those manuscripts, in which the original *š* remained unchanged in loanwords only, while in every other instance the *š* > *s* change is attested, the original *č*, *ǯ*, *ž* are transcribed as dentals, i.e. as *c*, *ʒ*, *z*, unless they form part of a loanword.
5. In those manuscripts, in which the there are only a few examples of *š* being retained (or in which there is no trace of it at all), the original *č*, *ǯ*, *ž* are transcribed as dentals, i.e. as *c*, *ʒ*, *z*.
6. In those texts in which the actual phonetic value of the sound written with letter *shin* could have been [ś], the letter *shin* is transcribed *s* (given that the transcription is predominantly phonemic); nor in these texts do we indicate the possible palatalization of *c*, *ʒ*, *z*, *n*, *l* in this position either.

TABLE 22 Romanization of Hebrew

| **Letter** | א | ב | בּ | ג | גּ | ד | דּ | ה | ו | ז | ח | ט | י | כ | ך | כּ | ל |
|---|---|---|---|---|---|---|---|---|---|---|---|---|---|---|---|---|---|
| **Transcription** | ʾ | ḇ | b | ḡ | g | ḏ | d | h | w | z | ḥ | ṭ | y | ḵ | | k | l |
| **Letter** | מ | ם | נ | ן | ס | ע | פ | ף | פּ | צ | ץ | ק | ר | שׁ | שׂ | ת | תּ |
| **Transcription** | m | | n | | s | ʿ | p̄ | | p | ṣ | | q | r | š | ś | ṯ | t |
| **Vowel point** | ◌ִ | ◌ִי | ◌ֶ | ◌ֱ | ◌ֵ | ◌ַ | ◌ֲ | ◌ָ | ◌ֳ | ◌ֹ | וֹ | ◌ֻ | וּ | ◌ְ | | | |
| **Transcription** | i | ī | e | ĕ | ē | a | ă | å | ŏ | o | ō | u | ū | – | | | |

7. The letters *shin*, *sin*, *tzade*, and *zayin* in Hebrew words are transcribed according to their value in Hebrew, regardless of any Karaim linguistic features; the only exceptions are those words that underwent a phonetic adaptation process according to the authors of KarRPS.

## 3.7 Transcription of Hebrew

The Hebrew content is treated in two different ways in this volume, namely the titles (incipits) of the Hebrew *piyyutim* are quoted in a commonly used Hebraistic transcription, whereas the Hebrew linguistic material to be found in the *peshatim* is transcribed according to the rules described by Harviainen (2013), Machcińska (2015), and Muchowski (2017).[44] Even though Harviainen's analysis is valid primarily according to late-19th- and 20th-century standards, I decided to follow the article consistently in all the *peshatim*, including those written long before the 19th century. This is primarily because there is no study available on the Karaite Hebrew used by South-Western Karaims in the 17th and 18th century. See Table 22.

## 3.8 Morphonology and Morphology

The edited texts exhibit only a few differences compared to Modern Western Karaim morphonology and the morphology known from the existing grammars; see, primarily, the works of A. Zajączkowski (1931), Pritsak (1959a),

44 See also Harviainen (1991, 1992, and 1997), and Khan (2020) for further reading.

Musaev (1964, 1977), and Németh (2011b, 2011c). The following facts and phenomena should be mentioned in this light:

1. The abilitive *-al* ~ *-el* and inabilitive *-al-ma* ~ *-el-me* mood markers are productive, see *ajtalma* (12:5) 'to be able to speak out', *bolalmajmen* 'I am not able' (4:26), *jetelmedi* 'he was not able to reach' (12:40), *kötürelmedim* (4:14) 'I was not able to lift', *kötirelmejmen* (4:14) 'I am not able to lift', *syndyralyr* (12:29) 'will be able to break', *tyjalyr* 'he will stop (it)' (17:14).[45]
2. One pluperfect *-p edi* form is used in the texts, namely *beribedin* (26:13). A detailed description of this tense is given in Németh (2015a), and Németh [forthcoming].
3. There is one hitherto unattested example of the use of the particle *-oq*, namely in the word *oloq* 'exactly that' (< *ol* 'that'), see: *oloq saʿatny titinlenir qaḥyry da acuvu H-nyn* 'in that very hour the wrath and anger of God will fume' (30:15). It is also present in the word *alajoq* 'in the same way; as well as' (< *alaj* 'this way, so, thus') frequently used in the edited *piyyutim* and lemmatized in KarRPS. It was described as a "particle which specifies the exact time of an action" in the unpublished fragments of Ananiasz Zajączkowski's PhD thesis, see Németh (2013a: 139). The words *oloq* and *alajoq*, however, show that it should be rather interpreted as an intensifying or specifying particle. For its cognates in the Turkic languages, see, e.g., Räsänen (1957: 248), von Gabain (1959: 63), and Džanmavov (1967: 187–188); for further details see also Németh (2015c: 92).
4. The abbreviated form of the postp. *byla* 'with', the instrumental suffix *-ba* is on one occassion attested in the form *qyjasyba* (3:122) in JSul.I.01b copied in the second half of the 18th century. And even though this word was amended to *qyjasybyla* (most probably by the copyist himself), it can hardly be treated as a scribal error in light of the *byla* > *-ba* > *-ba* ~ *-be* process that undoubtedly later took place.
5. The elimination of the future case marker *-r-* in Mod.SWKar. non-abbreviated verb forms has already been described by Grzegorzwski (1916–1918: 258), Berta (1998: 311), and Németh (2011b: 47). This phenomenon is also very common in these texts, see, for instance, *caġyrymen* (11:30) < *caġyryrmen* or *qajtarymen* (15:33) < *qajtaryrmen*. In addition, we ought to mention that the *-z-* future tense marker of the negative *-ma-z-* suffix is, in one case, also syncopated, see *qalmabiz* (< *qalmazbiz*) (6:73) in mss.

---

45 From the second half of 20th century on, the sole use of the abilitive mood marker can be found in the word *bolal-* 'to be able', see A. Zajączkowski (1932: 126–127), Musaev (1964: 264, it is described here, for some reason, as an aspectual category), and Németh (2011b: 51).

JSul.III.64a, JSul.III.72, and JSul.I.37.02. Given that the elimination of the *-r-* and *-z-* shift only occurs when they perform the role of tense markers, the phenomenon itself is rather morphological or morphonological, than phonetic in nature.

CHAPTER 4

# Introduction to the *peshatim*

This chapter contains a comparative critical analysis of the *peshatim*. In each case it is the oldest vocalized and complete copy which constitutes the basis for this comparison. The critical apparatus takes into account variant readings, including all phonological, morphological, and lexical discrepancies, as well as brief etymological remarks. Erroneous forms are commented on briefly. In the footnotes, the commentaries are arranged by manuscript (in chronological order). If a comment concerns a fragment longer than one single word, the respective passage is enclosed in half square brackets, i.e. ⸤…⸣.

In the transcription, each line is matched with two numbers: the overall line number of the entire *peshat* is followed by the number of the line of the respective page. For example, the first line of *peshat* № 9 starts on the seventh line of folio 107 vº of ms. JSul.III.03:

[1] [7] פשט לפיוט פרשת ואתחנן שהוא ה׳ אלהים אתה החילות להחכם הנ̃ל יעמ̃ש

The English translation is philological and follows the structure of the Karaim text as strictly as possible. However, it must be made clear that, bearing in mind the consistent syntactic differences, the line numbers in the translation are merely guidelines for the reader. To ensure greater clarity, some complementary passages are introduced into the translation even if their exact counterparts are not present in the Karaim *peshat*. These additions are typeset in brackets.

Given the textual complexity and vagueness of many of the analysed passages, the solutions described below were chosen to facilitate the reading. For clarity's sake, personal pronouns referring to God are always transcribed with a capital letter (see, for instance, the translation in line 12:35). Proper nouns, such as personal names, names and epithets of God, names of feasts and holidays, etc., are transcribed with capital letters. The abbreviation הָ׳ standing for Heb. *ha-šēm* הַשֵּׁם 'ha-Shem (epithet of God)' is consistently transcribed as *H*. Unlike in the originals, the hyphenation used for splitting words at the end of a line is consistently indicated in the transcription even if the manuscript lacks it or it is indicated at the beginning of the second line. Based on the meaning of the Karaim text, the Hebrew original as well as the logical rhythm of the text, distinctions between a full stop, comma, colon, semicolon, and ellipsis have been introduced into the transcription even though copyists rarely used them and

 | DOI:10.1163/9789004419377_005

rarely distinguished between them. Naturally, the translation follows English standard punctuation. The translation of Biblical passages is based primarily on King James Bible 2000 and Friedman (2003).

The reason why the word *enajat* 'eye (of God)' is so often spelled erroneously, namely as *enaj at*, is exhaustively explained in A. Zajączkowski (1929: 15). The reasoning is not repeated in the apparatus.

Postpositions are transcribed as one word with the forms they follow only if there is a *shewa* below the letter preceding the postposition or if the handwriting leaves no doubts in this respect. Keeping this notation unchanged in the transcription is especially important in case of *byla*, which eventually evolved into SWKar. *-ba* ~ *-be* and NWKar. *-ba* ~ *-b́a* alternating with the original postpositional form. In other words: the orthography might be of help in establishing the chronology of the process of transformation of the postposition *byla* into the instr. suffix *-ba*$^2$.

The Hebrew abbreviations have been deciphered and explained in a separate index toward the end of this volume. If the first word of the respective line of the Hebrew original is indicated in the Karaim text it is often marked with a cantillation sign. For simplicity's sake, in the transcription it is predominantly marked with the cantillation sign *segol* (◌֒), but only in cases where a sign was used for this purpose in the edited manuscript.

Each text is preceded by introductory remarks. In these paragraphs, where necessary, the relationship between the respective copies is shown in schematic form. It should be emphasised, however, that these diagrams are only intended to visualize the textual similarities between the copies. In other words, on no account should the diagrams be treated as the *stemmata codicum* of the entire manuscripts. One fact that absolutely must be borne in mind is that the texts in particular manuscripts—often copied by several individuals over a long period of time—could have been taken from a number of different sources.

The facsimiles are presented towards the end of this volume.

# *The* peshatim*: Text and Translation*

∵

# PART 1

## *The* peshatim *of Josef ha-Mashbir ben Shemuel*

∵

**Text number:** № 1
**Karaim incipit:** *Jasly hem taryqqan ӡanly*
**Hebrew incipit:** אֲנוּנָה אֲנִי וַעֲגוּמָה *ʾănūnå ʾănī waʿăgūmå*
**Dedication:** Shabbats of the month Tammuz
**Language:** Early Mod.SWKar., Mod.SWKar.
**Number of copies:** 6

| Accession no. | Place of origin of copy | Date of copy | Copyist | Folios |
|---|---|---|---|---|
| JSul.III.03 | Halych | shortly after 1805 | Unknown 7 | 98 rº–99 rº |
| JSul.I.45 | Halych | 1st half of the 19th c. | Jeshua Josef Mordkowicz | 121 rº–122 vº |
| ADub.III.61 | Halych | 1850/1851 | Jeshua Josef Mordkowicz | 110 rº–111 rº |
| JSul.III.69 | Halych | ca. 1851 (before 1866) | Jeshua Josef Mordkowicz | 216 vº–218 vº |
| JSul.III.79 | Halych | ca. 1851 (before 1866) | Jeshua Josef Mordkowicz | 265 vº–268 rº |
| JSul.I.01c | Halych | 2nd half of the 19th c. | Jeshua Josef Mordkowicz | 130 rº–132 rº |

## 1 Introductory Remarks

This *peshat* is one of four pre-18th-century Karaim *peshatim* of the *piyyut* אֲנוּנָה אֲנִי וַעֲגוּמָה *ʾănūnå ʾănī waʿăgūmå*. The other three are № 5, 24, and 26. All the copies are vocalized.

The copies can be arranged into two groups with shared, unique features. On the one hand, the texts copied in mss. JSul.III.03 and JSul.III.69 stand very close to one other and originate, most likely, from the same root or from different, yet closely related copies. On the other hand, the *peshatim* in mss. JSul.I.45, ADub.III.61, JSul.III.79, and JSul.I.01c constitute a separate group with a number of similarities that are characteristic only of them. This observation is also interesting because all the manuscripts with the exception of JSul.III.03 were copied by the same person (JSul.III.69 and JSul.III.79 were even copied roughly in the same time period). The above is exemplified by the following discrepancies: *alnyndan özinnin* (~ *ezinnin*) vs. *alnyndan* (line 17), *synyqtyrasen* vs. *synyqtyrdyn* (24), *aruv enajatly Tenri* vs. *aruv enajatly* (25), *arynma* vs. *arytma* (30), *talaslarymny* vs. *talasymny* (37), *Tenrim* vs. *Tenri* (39), *vale küplegin* (~ *kiplegin*) *meni* vs. *vale meni küplegin* (~ *kiplegin*) (41), *avur gineḥlerimni* vs. *menim avur gineḥlerimni* (44), *turuvcularnyn istime jamanġa* vs. *turuvcularnyn istime* (47), *kelgenden* vs. *kelgenni* (50), *istime* vs. *istime senin kleginden* (50), *qabul körgin* (~ *kergin*) vs. *qabul etkin* (54), *sivgin e H qutqarma meni* vs. *sivgin meni e H qutqarma* (55), *ertemde da kecemde* vs. *kecemde da ertemde* (67), *bitiklerde* vs. *bitiginde* (68), *ulluraq* vs. *ullu* (71), *tirli* vs. *tislü* (~ *tisli*) (72), *bar* vs. *bu* (74), *osol bar* vs. *ol* (76), *jaḥsy ullu jarlyġasynny* vs. *jaḥsy ḥabarlarny tutunulġanny* (~ *tutunulġanlarny*) *bizge da körgizgin bizge ullu jarlyġasynny* (76). As a consequence, the relationship between the copies (but not necessarily between the manuscripts!) can be presented as follows (cf. also *peshat* № 5):

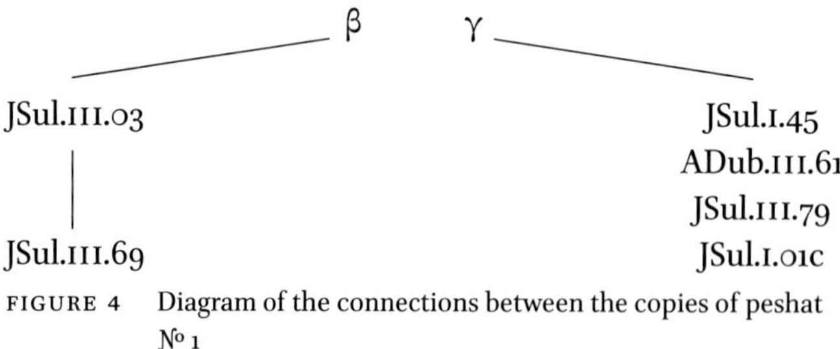


FIGURE 4 Diagram of the connections between the copies of peshat № 1

Furthermore, a number of less significant, probably *ad hoc* changes had been introduced by the copyists to improve the Karaim text.

## 2 Transcription[1] and Translation

98 rº [1] [1] ⸤והא לך פשטים יקרים לפיוט אנונה אני ועגומה: זה הפשט הראשון לפיוט
[2] [2] הזה עשאו אמ̃ו נזד משגבנו הוא אז̃ המאור הגדול כמוה̃רר יוסף המשביר בר
[3] [3] לע̃נ נב̃ת: בא̃ז כמוה̃רר שמואל הזקן ונ̃פ נשיא בית אב למשפחת הרודים
[4] [4] בעם ה׳ יעמ̃ש: אנונה אני ועגומה:⸣[2]
[5] [5] Jasly hem taryqqan ʒanly tisli qajġydan boldum men ol iḥcuvun[3]
[6] [6] bolġan Tenrige da elge burundan ḥor da acy ʒanly
[7] [7] indeldim. Ḥorlandym haligine da juvuz boldum ki jazyqlarym
[8] [8] ücün[4] qaty galutqa taslandym. Birisi kibik ol nekeslernin

---

1 Based on JSul.III.03.

2 JSul.I.45: בשם שוכן מעונה: אכתוב פשטים לפיוט אנונה: אשר תרגמו אותו כפי חכמתם אנשי תבונה: להביט לאזני עמי הארץ הבלתי מבינים לשוננו הקדושה וההגונה: וזה התרגום הראשון יקר כבת אישון תרגמו אז̃ הה̃ו כמוה̃רר יוסף המשביר נ̃ע בא̃ז כמוה̃רר שמואל הזקן ז̃ל. | ADub.III.61: בעזרת אל שומע תפלה ותחנה: אכתוב פשטים לפיוט אנונה: וזה הראשון חברו אז̃ מוה̃רר יוסף המשביר בר לע̃נ תנצ̃בהה: בא̃ז כמוה̃רר שמואל הזקן יעמ̃ש: אנונה אני ועגומה. | JSul.III.69: ואם תרצה תאמר גם פשטו שתרגמו אדו׳ זקני החכם הקדוש מוה̃רר יוסף המשביר בר לע̃נ זצו̃קל: בא̃ז הגביר המרומם ונשיא משפחת הרודים כ̃ש כמה̃ר שמואל הזקן נב̃ת וז̃יא. | JSul.III.79: ואם תרצה תאמר פשטו שתרגמו אדוני זקני החכם האלהי השלם והכולל כגק̃שת כמוה̃רר יוסף המשביר בר לעם נבר זצו̃קל בא̃ז כמוה̃רר שמואל הזקן נשיא בית אב למשחת הרו̃דים תנצ̃בהה: אנונה אני. | JSul.I.01c: זה הפשט אנונה אני ועגומה תרגמו אז̃ החכם הר̃ר יוסף המשביר זצו̃קל: בא̃ז כמוה̃רר שמואל הזקן אב משפחת הרו̃דים תנצ̃בהה: אנו̃נה אנ̃י.

3 The meaning and the exact reading of this word remains obscure. There is no equivalent either in the Hebrew original or in the other three interpretations of this *piyyut*. It is also absent from the Karaim dictionaries. Besides this attestation, the word also appears in two works of Zarach ben Natan: in one of his *zemirot* reprinted in Mardkowicz (1930: 13; the word is attested as "ichcuwun") in exactly the same context and in his dirge authored in 1649 and copied posthumously in B 263 (26 vº) as אִיחְצוּבֿוּן *iḥčuvun* in a contex that does not clarify the meaning. We found this word in the above mentioned *zemer* in the following manuscripts: RAbk.IV.15 (35 rº: אִיקְצוּבוּן *iqcubun*), JSul.I.02 (60 rº: *iḥcubun* אִיחְצוּבוּן), JSul.I.17 (47 vº: *iḥcubun* אִיחְצוּבוּן), and JSul.III.74 (24 rº: *iḥcubun* אִיחְצוּבוּן). See our remarks in the glossary.

4 ADub.III.61: *icin.* | JSul.III.69: *icin.* | JSul.III.79: *icin.* | JSul.I.01c: *icin.*

5 Or: *my.*

6 I.e., *Josef ha-Mashbir*; cf. Genesis 42:3.

7 Or: *my.*

8 I.e., *the ha-Rodi family.*

9 JSul.I.45: *In the name of God! I will write down the* peshatim *of the* piyyut (*with the incipit*) *ʾănūnå, the translation which is in accordance with the wisdom of the men of reason, to have understanding for the ears of my ignoramuses that are without understanding to our holy and respectable language. And this is the first interpretation, as beloved as the apple of the eye, which our aged master translated, the great and honourable sage, his honour, the Rav, Rabbi Josef ha-Mashbir, may his soul rest in Eden, the son of our aged master his honour, the Rav, Rabbi Shemuel, the aged, may his memory be a blessing.* | ADub.III.61: *With the help of God, He hearkens the prayer and the supplication. I will write down the* peshatim *of the* piyyut (*with the incipit*)

[1] [1] ⌊And may the beloved interpretations of the *piyyut* (with the incipit) *ʾănūnå ʾănī waʿăǧūmå* follow here. This is the first *peshat* of this *piyyut*, 98 rº

[2] [2] delivered by our master, our teacher, our crown-like stronghold, our[5] aged master, the luminary and the great, his honour, the Rav, Rabbi ⌊Josef who provides pure grain⌋[6]

[3] [3] for the elevation of the soul, may his soul lodge in Eden, the son of our[7] aged master, his honour, the Rav, Rabbi Shemuel, the aged and honourable, the patriarch of the house of the family, ⌊who rule the

[4] [4] Lord's people⌋,[8] may he rest in peace. (Incipit:) *ʾănūnå ʾănī waʿă-ǧūmå*⌋[9]

[5] [5] (1). I have become mournful and worried from ⌊all the⌋[10] troubles, I, who had earlier been [...?][11]

[6] [6] for God and the people, I was called dishonourable and sad.

[7] [7] Now, I have become condemned and unworthy, for, because of my sins,

[8] [8] I had been cast into a hard exile. I was considered as one of those contemptible (persons) among the people,

---

ʾănūnå. *And this is the first one delivered by our aged master, our teacher, the Rabbi Josef who provides pure grain* [i.e., Josef ha-Mashbir; cf. Genesis 42:3] *for the elevation of the soul, 'may his soul be bound in the bond of life'* [cf., 1 Samuel 25:29], *the son of our aged master his honour, the Rav, Rabbi Shemuel, the aged, may he rest in peace.* (*Incipit:*) ʾănūnå ʾănī waʿăǧūmå. | JSul.III.69: *And, if you prefer, say its* peshat [i.e., of the Hebrew original], *which my aged master translated, the holy hakham, our teacher, the Rabbi Josef ha-Mashbir who provides pure grain* [i.e., Josef ha-Mashbir; cf. Genesis 42:3] *for the elevation of the soul, may the memory of the righteous and holy be a blessing, the son of our aged master, the elevated master and the patriarch of the ha-Rodi family, his glorious name, his honour, Rabbi Shemuel, the aged, may his soul lodge in Eden and may his merit protect us, Amen!* | JSul.III.79: *And, if you prefer, say its* peshat [i.e., of the Hebrew original], *which my aged master, the divine and complete hakham, the High Priest, the holy and glorious name of whom is his honour, the Rav, Rabbi Josef ha-Mashbir pure with the pure* [see, 2 Samuel 22:27] *may the memory of the righteous and holy be a blessing, the son of his honour, the Rav, Rabbi Shemuel, the aged the patriarch of the house of the ha-Rodi family, 'may his soul be bound in the bond of life'* [cf., 1 Samuel 25:29]. (*Incipit:*) ʾănūnå ʾănī. | JSul.I.01c: *This is the* peshat *of the* piyyut (*with the incipit*) ʾănūnå ʾănī waʿăǧūmå, *which our aged master translated, the complete hakham, the Rav, Rabbi Josef ha-Mashbir, may the memory of the righteous and holy be a blessing, the son of our aged master, his honour, the Rav, Rabbi Shemuel, the aged the patriarch of the ha-Rodi family, 'may his soul be bound in the bond of life'* [cf., 1 Samuel 25:29]. (*Incipit:*) ʾănūnå ʾănī.

10 Lit. 'various'.

11 See, our commentary attached to *iḥcuvun* in line 5 of the transcription (fn. 3).

[9] [9] sağyslandym dunjada ne ornuna ki burundan siver men edim.
[10] [10] Qojdu meni rast terecim qajğyly ullu satyrlyğym ornuna
[11] [11] har[12] kün[13] syzlavlu boldum da syndym. [14]⸢דוֹה וזבֹה⸣.
[12] [12] Vaj mana ki ucrandym jazyqlaryma da jyğys hem zavly qatyn kibik
[13] [13] ajrycly boldum bar azizlikten ki sen e[15] Tenrim ḥorladyn meni.
[14] [14] Taberdin meni tinkelme jerlerinde qulluq etivcilernin
[15] [15] abaqlarğa jirime[16] tersligi byla jüregimnin[17] ez erklettin
[16] [16] meni. Da tar vaḥtymda raḥmetlemekten siresen meni alnyndan
[17] [17] özinnin[18] anyn ücün[19] ki byrclandym murdarlyqta ol gojlar
[18] [18] kibik ki alar arasyna tozdurdun jyjynlarymny. Ahah H qyjasa
[19] [19] unuttun ki sensen jaratuvcum da kenderivcim[20] ki bulaj tamaša
[20] [20] kemišmek[21] kemistin[22] meni. [23]⸢זנחתני פרצתני⸣.
[21] [21] Sen e[24] H rast jarğucu ahah[25] kemistin bosatma jazyqlarymny da
[22] [22] ullu buzuqluq qyldyn mana ki sirdin meni syjyncly aziz ivinden.
[23] [23] Da bu murdar galut jerimde tync bermejsen[26] mana da jaman
[24] [24] tisler byla qorqutasen meni da synyqtyrasen[27] meni acuvlu[28] ḥyssy-
[25] [25] myndan. Ahah aruv enajatly Tenri[29] kle[30] ki eger gergede
[26] [26] qazylsam ezime necikte qacma alnyndan, anlajmen ki dağyn

12 JSul.I.45: *da har.* | ADub.III.61: *da har.* | JSul.III.79: *da har.* | JSul.I.01c: *da har.*
13 ADub.III.61: *kin.* | JSul.III.69: *kin.* | JSul.III.79: *kin.* | JSul.I.01c: *kin.*
14 JSul.I.45: דוֹה. | ADub.III.61: דוה וזבה נקראתי. | JSul.III.69: דוֹה. | JSul.I.01c: דוֹה.
15 JSul.I.45: deest. | ADub.III.61: deest. | JSul.III.79: deest. | JSul.I.01c: deest.
16 ADub.III.61: *da jirime.* | JSul.III.79: *da jirime.* | JSul.I.01c: *da jirime.*
17 ADub.III.61: *jiregimnin.* | JSul.III.69: *jiregimnin.* | JSul.III.79: *jiregimnin.* | JSul.I.01c: *jiregimnin.*
18 JSul.I.45: deest. | ADub.III.61: deest. | JSul.III.69: *ezinnin.* | JSul.III.79: deest. | JSul.I.01c: deest.
19 ADub.III.61: *icin.* | JSul.III.69: *icin.* | JSul.III.79: *icin.* | JSul.I.01c: *icin.*
20 JSul.I.45: *könderivcim.*
21 ADub.III.61: *kemismek.* | JSul.III.69: *kemismek.* | JSul.III.79: *kemismek.* | JSul.I.01c: *kemismek.*
22 JSul.I.45: *kemišesen.* | ADub.III.61: *kemisesen.* | JSul.III.79: *kemisesen.* | JSul.I.01c: *kemisesen.*
23 JSul.I.45: זנחתני. | ADub.III.61: זנחתני. | JSul.III.69: זנחתני. | JSul.III.79: זנחתני. | JSul.I.01c: זנחתני.
24 JSul.I.45: deest.
25 JSul.I.45: deest. | ADub.III.61: deest. | JSul.III.79: deest. | JSul.I.01c: deest.
26 JSul.I.45: *bermedin.* | ADub.III.61: *bermedin.* | JSul.III.79: *bermedin.*
27 JSul.I.45: *synyqtyrdyn.* | ADub.III.61: *synyqtyrdyn.* | JSul.III.79: *synyqtyrdyn.* | JSul.I.01c: *synyqtyrdyn.*
28 JSul.I.01c: *qaḥyrly.*
29 JSul.I.45: deest. | ADub.III.61: deest. | JSul.III.79: deest. | JSul.I.01c: deest.
30 The meaning of this word is unclear; cf., however, *kle ki* *'even though' in line 3:20.
31 JSul.I.45: *and I.* | ADub.III.61: *and I.* | JSul.III.79: *and I.* | JSul.I.01c: *and I.*
32 JSul.I.45: deest. | ADub.III.61: deest. | JSul.III.79: deest. | JSul.I.01c: deest.

[9] [9] I, who earlier had been beloved instead.
[10] [10] My righteous judge has made me concerned in place of my great jollity,
[11] [11] I[31] have become a sufferer (suffering) every day and I have been broken. (2).
[12] [12] Woe betide me, for I met with my sins and, like an unclean woman or a woman with a discharge,
[13] [13] I have become separated from all holiness because You, O[32] God of mine, have condemned me.
[14] [14] You have pushed me to wander in the lands of those who serve
[15] [15] idols, to[33] walk with the obstinacy of my heart, You Yourself have had authority
[16] [16] over me. And in times of my tribulation You drive me away from before Yourself[34] (refusing) to take pity on me,
[17] [17] for I have disgraced myself in the uncleanness like the Gentile
[18] [18] among whom You have scattered my congregations. O Lord, have You indeed
[19] [19] forgotten that You are my creator and leader that You
[20] [20] ⌊have abandoned⌋[35] me so oddly? (3).
[21] [21] You, O[36] Lord the righteous judge, O You have resigned absolving my sins and
[22] [22] ⌊destructed me greatly⌋[37] for You have driven me from the place of Your sheltering holy home.
[23] [23] And in this unclean land of my exile, ⌊You do not give me peace⌋[38] and
[24] [24] with evil dreams You frighten me and depress[39] me with Your irate[40] wrath.
[25] [25] O ⌊pure-eyed God⌋[41], even if I would be buried in a grave
[26] [26] to escape somehow from before You, I do understand that even

33 ADub.III.61: *and to.* | JSul.III.79: *and to.* | JSul.I.01c: *and to.*
34 JSul.I.45: *You.* | ADub.III.61: *You.* | JSul.III.79: *You.* | JSul.I.01c: *You.*
35 JSul.I.45: *abandon.* | ADub.III.61: *abandon.* | JSul.III.79: *abandon.* | JSul.I.01c: *abandon.*
36 JSul.I.45: deest.
37 Lit. 'you did great destruction to me'.
38 JSul.I.45: *you have not given me peace.* | ADub.III.61: *you have not given me peace.* | JSul.III.79: *you have not given me peace.*
39 JSul.I.45: *have depressed.* | ADub.III.61: *have depressed.* | JSul.III.79: *have depressed.* | JSul.III.79: *have depressed.*
40 JSul.I.01c: expressed with a synonym.
41 JSul.I.45: *pure-eyed.* | ADub.III.61: *pure-eyed.* | JSul.III.79: *pure-eyed.* | JSul.I.01c: *pure-eyed.*

[27] [27] andada kicejtirsen istime acuvunnu[42] da tutar ⌊meni on
[28] [28] ḥyššymyn[43]⌉[44] jazyqlarym ücün[45] ec alma ʒanymdan.
[29] [29] [46]⌈ימינך תסעדני⌋. Patšahym[47] jaratuvcum on qudratyn
98 vº [30] [1] küplesin[48] meni arynma[49] jazyġymdan sahat sirtersen avur
[31] [2] ginehḥlerimni. Kör[50] da ḥajifsin istime ki astry juvuz
[32] [3] da ḥor boldum galutta da kedergi ajlandyrasen bar jaḥsy
[33] [4] saġyslarymny, jeter bolġajdy mana bu acuvun[51] muna daġy caja[52]
[34] [5] ʒanly da[53] aqlafly qysady ʒanymny ki ḥor dinine ezinin
[35] [6] tenestiredi rast da abajly[54] aziz dinimni. Da sen e[55] H jaratuvcu[56]
[36] [7] aziz ʒanymny ki icimde ajyrmaq ücün[57] meni murdar goj-
[37] [8] lardan qacanġadejin bu talasmassen talaslarymny[58].[59]מֿתי.
[38] [9] E bijik bijim qacan cyġaryrsen[60] rastlyqqa jarġularymny.
[39] [10] Qoltqa byla e qorqunclu Tenrim[61] esitkin bu qoltqamny
[40] [11] acylyġyndan ʒanymnyn da ⌊tas etkin⌉[62] bar goj qyjnavcularymny.
[41] [12] ⌊Vale küplegin[63] meni⌉[64] da jarlyġaslanajym ki daġy[65] qahalym
ücün[66]

---

42 JSul.I.01c: *qaḥyrynny.*

43 JSul.I.45: *ḥyssymyn.* | ADub.III.61: *ḥyssymyn.* | JSul.III.79: *ḥyssymyn.* | JSul.I.01c: *ḥyssymyn.* || See also next footnote.

44 JSul.III.69: *on ḥyssymyn meni.*

45 ADub.III.61: *icin.* | JSul.III.69: *icin.* | JSul.III.79: *icin.* | JSul.I.01c: *icin.*

46 JSul.I.45: ימֿינך. | JSul.III.69: ימינך. | JSul.III.79: ימֿינך. | JSul.I.01c: ימֿינך.

47 JSul.III.69: *patsahym.* | JSul.III.79: *patsahym.* | JSul.I.01c: *patsahym.*

48 JSul.III.03: a hypercorrect form of *kiplesin.* | JSul.I.45: *kiplesin.* | ADub.III.61: *kiplesin.* | JSul.III.69: *kiplesin.* | JSul.III.79: *kiplesin.* | JSul.I.01c: *kiplesin.*

49 JSul.I.45: *arytma.* | ADub.III.61: *arytma.* | JSul.III.79: *arytma.* | JSul.I.01c: *arytma.*

50 ADub.III.61: *ker.* | JSul.III.69: *ker.* | JSul.III.79: *ker.* | JSul.I.01c: *ker.*

51 JSul.III.79: *qaḥyryn.* | JSul.I.01c: *qaḥyryn.*

52 JSul.I.45: *ceja.* | ADub.III.61: *ceja.* | JSul.III.69: *ceja.* | JSul.III.79: *ceja.* | JSul.I.01c: *ceja.* || Cf. *ceja* in line 58.

53 JSul.I.45: deest.

54 JSul.I.45: *inamly.* | ADub.III.61: *inamly.* | JSul.I.01c: *inamly.*

55 JSul.I.45: deest.

56 JSul.I.45: *jaratuvcum*; a scribal error.

57 ADub.III.61: *icin.* | JSul.III.69: *icin.* | JSul.III.79: *icin.* | JSul.I.01c: *icin.*

58 JSul.I.45: *talasymny.* | ADub.III.61: *talasymny.* | JSul.III.79: *talasymny.* | JSul.I.01c: *talasymny.*

59 ADub.III.61: מֿתי תוצֿיא. | JSul.III.69: מֿתי תוצֿיא אדֿון.

60 JSul.I.45: *cyġarysen.* | JSul.III.69: *cyġarysen.*

61 JSul.I.45: *Tenri.* | ADub.III.61: *Tenri.* | JSul.III.79: *Tenri.*

62 JSul.III.03: טַס אֵיטְכִין. | JSul.I.45: טַשְׁאֵיטְכִין. | ADub.III.61: טַשׁ אֶיטְכִין. | JSul.III.69: טַשׁ אֵיטְכִין. | JSul.III.79: טַשׁ אֶיטְכִין. | JSul.I.01c: טַשאֵיטְכִין.

63 JSul.III.03: a hypercorrect form of *kiplegin.* | JSul.III.69: *kiplegin.* || See also next footnote.

[27] [27] there You would intensify Your anger[67] and Your right hand would catch[68] me
[28] [28] because of my sins in order to take revenge on my soul.
[29] [29] (4). My sovereign, creator of mine, may Your right hand
[30] [1] strengthen me ⌊to get purified⌋[69] of my sin; can it be (that) You will blot out my heavy 98 vº
[31] [2] sins? Take a look (at me) and have mercy on me, for I have become very unworthy
[32] [3] and condemned in the exile and You do avoid my good
[33] [4] thoughts, Your anger[70] seems to be enough for me, lo, even the shameless-[71]
[34] [5] -hearted and[72] uncircumcised crush my heart, for they equalise their own malicious religion
[35] [6] with my just and honourable[73] religion. And You, O[74] Lord the creator[75]
[36] [7] of my holy heart inside me, how long will You not arbitrate my contention
[37] [8] in order to save me from the unclean Gentile? (5).
[38] [9] O great Lord of mine ⌊when will You turn[76] to righteousness my verdicts⌋[77]?
[39] [10] I beg You, O, awesome God ⌊of mine⌋[78], listen to my prayer
[40] [11] (that comes) from the bitterness of my heart and destroy all my gentile tormentors.
[41] [12] But strengthen me and let me be rescued for

---

64 JSul.I.45: *vale meni küplegin*; *küplegin* is a hypercorrect form of *kiplegin*. | ADub.III.61: *vale meni kiplegin*. | JSul.III.79: *vale meni kiplegin*. | JSul.I.01c: *vale meni kiplegin*.

65 JSul.I.01c: *dağyn*.

66 ADub.III.61: *icin*. | JSul.III.69: *icin*. | JSul.III.79: *icin*. | JSul.I.01c: *icin*.

67 JSul.I.01c: expressed with a synonym.

68 Or: *hold*.

69 JSul.I.45, ADub.III.61, JSul.III.79, JSul.I.01c: expressed with a synonym.

70 JSul.III.79, JSul.I.01c: expressed with a synonym.

71 Or: *cruel-*.

72 JSul.I.45: deest.

73 JSul.I.45: *trustworthy*. | ADub.III.61: *trustworthy*. | JSul.I.01c: *trustworthy*.

74 JSul.I.45: deest.

75 JSul.I.45: *creator of mine*; a scribal error.

76 Lit. 'take out', 'draw out'.

77 I.e., *when will You find me innocent*.

78 JSul.I.45: desunt. | ADub.III.61: desunt. | JSul.III.79: desunt.

[42] [13] necik özüm[79] ücün[80] tizijmen sana jalbarmaqlarymny.
[43] [14] Sana telmertemen osol közlerimni[81] qylma bar kleklerimni
[44] [15] da sirtme özün[82] ücün[83] avur[84] gineḥlerimni. [85]עֵינַי.
[45] [16] Sana jalġyzġa telmerediler közlerim[86] e joqtan bar etivcim
[46] [17] könderivcim[87] da bar tarlyġymdan juluvcum, ki ⌊qutqarġajsen [meni]⌉[88]
[47] [18] bar[89] jaman[90] kleklerinden turuvcularnyn istime jamanġa[91] ki sen[92] e[93]
[48] [19] H Tenrim jalġyzov[94] sen[95] küpligim[96] da umsuncum. Qoltqa byla
[49] [20] aziz jaratuvcum körgin[97] qyjynymny da cydaġanymny barda kelgen-
[50] [21] den[98] istime[99] ki rast etemen terenni senin rast jarġucum.
[51] [22] Anyn ücün[100] ⌊qulaq salġyn⌉[101] avazyna tefilemnin e H ki tefile sözleri[n][102]
[52] [23] ⌊ertede da kecede⌉[103] sarnajdy sana tilim da avzum.
[53] [24] [104]⌈קוֹלִי שְׁעֵה⌋. Har caġyrġanymda sana ⌊e H⌉[105] avazymny

---

79 ADub.III.61: *ezim.* | JSul.III.69: *ezim.* | JSul.III.79: *ezim.* | JSul.I.01c: *ezim.*

80 ADub.III.61: *icin.* | JSul.III.69: *icin.* | JSul.III.79: *icin.* | JSul.I.01c: *icin.*

81 ADub.III.61: *kezlerimni.* | JSul.III.69: *kezlerimni.* | JSul.III.79: *kezlerimni.* | JSul.I.01c: *kezlerimni.*

82 JSul.I.45: *ezin.* | ADub.III.61: *ezin.* | JSul.III.69: *ezin.* | JSul.III.79: *ezin.* | JSul.I.01c: *ezin.*

83 ADub.III.61: *icin.* | JSul.III.69: *icin.* | JSul.III.79: *icin.* | JSul.I.01c: *icin.*

84 JSul.I.45: *menim avur.* | ADub.III.61: *menim avur.* | JSul.III.79: *menim avur.* | JSul.I.01c: *menim avur.*

85 ADub.III.61: עֵינַי מְצַפּוֹת.

86 ADub.III.61: *kezlerim.* | JSul.III.69: *kezlerim.* | JSul.III.79: *kezlerim.* | JSul.I.01c: *kezlerim.*

87 JSul.I.45: *kenderivcim.* | ADub.III.61: *kenderivcim.* | JSul.III.69: *kenderivcim.* | JSul.III.79: *kenderivcim.* | JSul.I.01c: *kenderivcim.*

88 JSul.III.03: *qutqarġajsen.* | JSul.I.45: *qutqarġajsen meni.* | ADub.III.61: *qutqarġajsen meni.* | JSul.III.79: *qutqarġajsen meni.* | JSul.I.01c: *qutqarġajsen meni.*

89 ADub.III.61: deest.

90 JSul.I.45: *jamandan da.*

91 JSul.I.45: deest. | ADub.III.61: deest. | JSul.III.79: deest. | JSul.I.01c: deest.

92 JSul.I.01c: *sensen.*

93 JSul.I.45: deest. | ADub.III.61: deest. | JSul.I.01c: deest.

94 JSul.I.01c: *jalġyz.*

95 JSul.I.45: *sensen.* | JSul.III.69: *sensen.* | JSul.I.01c: deest.

96 JSul.III.03: a hypercorrect form of *kipligim.* | ADub.III.61: *kipligim.* | JSul.III.69: *kipligim.* | JSul.III.79: *kipligim.* | JSul.I.01c: *kipligim.*

97 ADub.III.61: *kergin.* | JSul.III.69: *kergin.* | JSul.III.79: *kergin.* | JSul.I.01c: *kergin.*

98 JSul.I.45: *kelgenni.* | ADub.III.61: *kelgenni.* | JSul.III.79: *kelgenni.* | JSul.I.01c: *kelgenni.*

99 JSul.I.45: *istime senin kleginden.* | ADub.III.61: *istime senin kleginden.* | JSul.III.79: *istime senin kleginden.* | JSul.I.01c: *istime senin kleginden.*

100 ADub.III.61: *icin.* | JSul.III.69: *icin.* | JSul.III.79: *icin.* | JSul.I.01c: *icin.*

[42] [13] even the prayers (addressed) to You I compose are (both) for my community and for myself.
[43] [14] I direct my eyes at You with hope, (that You would) do all my wishes
[44] [15] and blot out Yourself[106] my heavy sins. (6).
[45] [16] My eyes look with hope only at You, O my creator from nothing,
[46] [17] my leader and my saviour from all my misery, ⌊may You save
[47] [18] [me]⌉[107] ⌊from all[108] the evil⌉[109] wishes of those who stand above me ⌊for the purpose of evil⌉[110], because You, O[111]
[48] [19] Lord God of mine, only You[112], are my strength and hope. ⌊I beg You⌉[113],
[49] [20] holy creator of mine, see my suffering and that I have borne everything that has come
[50] [21] upon me[114] for I justify Your judgement, my righteous judge.
[51] [22] Listen[115], therefore, to the voice of my prayer, O Lord, for
[52] [23] my tongue and my mouth sing to You words of prayers in the mornings and at night.
[53] [24] (7). In my each call to you, ⌊O Lord⌉[116], accept my voice

---

101 JSul.I.45: *qajyrġyn esitivinni.* | ADub.III.61: *qajyrġyn esitivinni.* | JSul.III.69: *qajyrġyn esitivinni.* | JSul.III.79: *qajyrġyn esitivinni.* | JSul.I.01c: *qajyrġyn esitivinni.*

102 JSul.III.03: *sözleri*; a scribal error. | JSul.I.45: *sözlerin.* | ADub.III.61: *sezlerin.* | JSul.III.69: *sezlerin.* | JSul.III.79: *sezlerin.* | JSul.I.01c: *sezlerin.*

103 ADub.III.61: *erteden da keceden.*

104 JSul.III.69: קוֹלִי. | JSul.I.01c: קוֹלִי.

105 JSul.I.45: desunt. | ADub.III.61: desunt. | JSul.III.69: desunt. | JSul.III.79: desunt. | JSul.I.01c: desunt.

106 Lit. 'for Yourself'.

107 JSul.I.45: *may You save me.* | ADub.III.61: *may You save me.* | JSul.III.79: *may You save me.* | JSul.I.01c: *may You save me.*

108 ADub.III.61: deest.

109 JSul.I.45: *from all evil and the.*

110 JSul.I.45: desunt. | ADub.III.61: desunt. | JSul.III.79: desunt. | JSul.I.01c: desunt.

111 JSul.I.45: deest. | ADub.III.61: deest. | JSul.I.01c: deest.

112 JSul.I.01c: deest.

113 Lit. 'with prayer'.

114 JSul.I.45: *me at Your request.* | ADub.III.61: *me at Your request.* | JSul.III.79: *me at Your request.* | JSul.I.01c: *me at Your request.*

115 JSul.I.45: *turn Your ear.* | ADub.III.61: *turn Your ear.* | JSul.III.69: *turn Your ear.* | JSul.III.79: *turn Your ear.* | JSul.I.01c: *turn Your ear.*

116 JSul.I.45: desunt. | ADub.III.61: desunt. | JSul.III.69: desunt. | JSul.III.79: desunt. | JSul.I.01c: desunt.

[54] [25] qabul körgin[117] da ⌊köz jummağyn⌉[118] jalbarmağymdan asyrma menden bar

[55] [26] tarlyqlarymny. Sivgin ⌊e H qutqarma meni⌉[119] bar qysyqlyqlarymdan

[56] [27] da ʒaḥtlağyn bolusqun mana ki jaryqqa cyğarğajmen bar jaḥsy

[57] [28] sağyslarymny. Baqqyn muft cydağanymny acytmaqlaryna

99 r° [58] [1] ceja gojlarnyn da sirtkin közlerimden[120] jaslarymny, ki ḥalim

[59] [2] joğundan qaruv berme alarğa jalğyz tegem[e]n[121] jasyn közlerimnin[122]

[60] [3] alnynda senin e[123] H da sana jalğyzğa tizijmen tefile sözlerimni[124].

[61] [4] [125]⌈תפלתי שמעה⌋. Tefilemni esitkin da qaruv bergin

[62] [5] mana ajtadoğac qorqmağyn zavally ki tync etermen ullu qajğy-

[63] [6] laryndan ʒanynny. Qoltqa byla ja Tenri jaman islerime köre[126]

[64] [7] tere etmegin meni da qysqartmağyn tirlik künlerimni[127]. Da

[65] [8] bu firjatym da jylamağym[128] kelsin alnyna da savağatyn byla jasartqyn

[66] [9] siveklerimni ullu qajğylar ücüne[129] jancylğanlarny. Ki budur

[67] [10] ullu qoltqalarym e H ⌊ertemde da kecemde⌉[130] ki sirinlik

[68] [11] byla jazğajsen sağync bitiklerde[131] meni ḥor miskinni.

[69] [12] [132]⌈חנני צורי⌋. Ḥajifsingin meni jaratuvcum da tolturğun

[70] [13] mana dağy[133] barda jaḥsy qoltqalarymny ki tanyğajmen aziz jollarynny.

---

117 JSul.III.03: *körgin.* | JSul.I.45: *etkin.* | ADub.III.61: *etkin.* | JSul.III.69: *kergin.* | JSul.III.79: *etkin.* | JSul.I.01c: *etkin.* || Cf. also line [3:100].

118 JSul.I.45: *jummağyn enajatynny.* | ADub.III.61: *jummağyn enajatynny.* | JSul.III.69: *jummağyn enajatynny.* | JSul.III.79: *jummağyn enajatynny.* | JSul.I.01c: *jummağyn enajatynny.*

119 JSul.I.45: *meni e H qutqarma.* | ADub.III.61: *meni e H qutqarma meni*; the repetition of the word *meni* is a result of a scribal error. | JSul.III.79: *meni e H qutqarma.* | JSul.I.01c: *meni e H qutqarma.*

120 ADub.III.61: *kezlerimden.* | JSul.III.69: *kezlerimden.* | JSul.III.79: *kezlerimden.* | JSul.I.01c: *kezlerimden.*

121 JSul.III.03: *tegemin*; probably a scribal error. | JSul.I.45: *tegemen.* | ADub.III.61: *tegemen.* | JSul.III.69: *tegemen.* | JSul.III.79: *tegemen.* | JSul.I.01c: *tegemen.*

122 ADub.III.61: *kezlerimnin.* | JSul.III.69: *kezlerimnin.* | JSul.III.79: *kezlerimnin.* | JSul.I.01c: *kezlerimnin.*

123 JSul.I.45: deest.

124 ADub.III.61: *sezlerimni.* | JSul.III.69: *sezlerimni.* | JSul.III.79: *sezlerimni.* | JSul.I.01c: *sezlerimni.*

125 JSul.I.45: תפּלתי. | JSul.III.69: תפּלתי. | JSul.I.01c: תפּלתי.

126 ADub.III.61: *kere.* | JSul.III.69: *kere.* | JSul.III.79: *kere.* | JSul.I.01c: *kere.*

127 ADub.III.61: *kinlerimni.* | JSul.III.69: *kinlerimni.* | JSul.III.79: *kinlerimni.* | JSul.I.01c: *kinlerimni.*

[54] [25] and do not close Your eyes to my entreaty, in order to make my miseries pass.
[55] [26] May you want[134], O Lord, to save me, from all the oppression,
[56] [27] and hurry to help me so that I may reveal all my good
[57] [28] thoughts. Take care that I did not bear in vain the harassment
[58] [1] of the shameless[135] Gentile, and wipe my tears from my eyes, since 99 rº
[59] [2] given the lack of capability[136] to respond them I shed the tears of my eyes
[60] [3] before You, O[137] Lord, and I compose words of prayers only to You.
[61] [4] (8). Listen to my prayer and reply
[62] [5] to me, saying, 'Do not fear, (you) helpless, for I will soothe the worries
[63] [6] of your heart'. But, I beg You, do not judge me according to my evil deeds
[64] [7] and do not shorten the days of my life. And
[65] [8] may my cry and my weep[138] come before You and, with Your mercy,
[66] [9] let my bones, broken in great troubles, be full of life. For these are
[67] [10] my great wishes, O Lord, ⌊in my mornings and night⌋[139], that You may
[68] [11] record me, the condemned miserable (man), in ⌊the books⌋[140] of remembrance with approval.
[69] [12] (9). Have mercy on me, (O) creator of mine, and also satisfy
[70] [13] all my good wishes so that I may learn Your holy ways.

---

128 JSul.I.45: *jalbarmaġym.* | ADub.III.61: *jalbarmaġym.* | JSul.III.69: *jalamaġym*; a scribal error, probably intead of *jylamaġym.* | JSul.III.79: *jalbarmaġym.* | JSul.I.01c: *jalbarmaġym.*

129 ADub.III.61: *icine.* | JSul.III.69: *icine.* | JSul.III.79: *icine.* | JSul.I.01c: *icine.*

130 JSul.I.45: *kecemde da ertemde.* | ADub.III.61: *kecemde da ertemde.* | JSul.III.79: *kecemde da ertemde.* | JSul.I.01c: *kecemde da ertemde.*

131 JSul.I.45: *bitiginde.* | ADub.III.61: *bitiginde.* | JSul.I.01c: *bitiginde.*

132 JSul.I.45: חַנֵּנוּ. | JSul.I.01c: חַנֵּנוּ.

133 JSul.I.45: *daġyn.*

134 Lit. 'love; like'.

135 Or: *cruel.*

136 Or: *power.*

137 JSul.I.45: deest.

138 JSul.I.45: *entreaty.* | ADub.III.61: *entreaty.* | JSul.III.79: *entreaty.* | JSul.I.01c: *entreaty.*

139 JSul.I.45: *in my night and mornings.* | ADub.III.61: *in my night and mornings.* | JSul.III.79: *in my night and mornings.* | JSul.I.01c: *in my night and mornings.*

140 JSul.I.45: *Your book.* | ADub.III.61: *Your book.* | JSul.I.01c: *Your book.*

[71] [14] Ancaq ne ulluraq[141] qoltqam budur ki ḥabar bergejsen mana acy

[72] [15] ʒanlyġa ajtadoġac bosattym sana e miskin bar tirli[142] jazyq-

[73] [16] larynny, alajoq[143] köpligine[144] köre[145] jarlyġasynnyn qabul etkin

[74] [17] tefilesin barda jalbaruvcularnyn[146] da jystyrġyn[147] bar[148] murdar jerlerden

[75] [18] bizni sajlanmuš[149] qullarynny. Qoltqa byla e Tenri savaġatyn

[76] [19] byla körtilikke[150] cyġarġyn ⌊osol bar⌉[151] jaḥsy ⌊[ḥabarlarny tutunulġanlarny bizge da kergizgin bizge] ullu jarlyġasynny⌉[152].

⌊הַטֵה ה׳ אָזְנְךָ עֲנֵנִי כִּי עָנִי וְאֶבְיוֹן אָנִי:⌉[153] [20] [77]

141 JSul.I.45: *ullu.* | ADub.III.61: *ullu.* | JSul.III.79: *ullu.*

142 JSul.I.45: *tislü.* | ADub.III.61: *tisli.* | JSul.III.79: *tisli.* | JSul.I.01c: *tisli.*

143 JSul.I.45: *alaj.* | ADub.III.61: *alaj.* | JSul.III.69: *alaj.* | JSul.III.79: *alaj.* | JSul.I.01c: *alaj.*

144 ADub.III.61: *kepligine.* | JSul.III.69: *kepligine.* | JSul.III.79: *kepligine.* | JSul.I.01c: *kepligine.*

145 ADub.III.61: *kere.* | JSul.III.69: *kere.* | JSul.III.79: *kere.* | JSul.I.01c: *kere.*

146 JSul.I.01c: *jalbaruvcularynnyn.*

147 ADub.III.61: *ystyrġyn.* | JSul.III.69: *ystyrġyn.* | JSul.III.79: *ystyrġyn.* | JSul.I.01c: *ystyrġyn.*

148 JSul.I.45: *bu.* | ADub.III.61: *bu.* | JSul.III.79: *bu.* | JSul.I.01c: *bu.*

149 JSul.I.45: *sajlanmus.* | ADub.III.61: *sajlanmus.* | JSul.III.69: *sajlanmus.* | JSul.III.79: *sajlanmus.* | JSul.I.01c: *sajlanmus.*

150 JSul.III.03: a hypercorrect form of *kertilikke.* | JSul.I.45: *körtilikke*; a hypercorrect form of *kertilikke.* | ADub.III.61: *kertilikke.* | JSul.III.69: *kertilikke.* | JSul.III.79: *kertilikke.* | JSul.I.01c: *kertilikke.*

151 JSul.I.45: *ol.* | ADub.III.61: *ol.* | JSul.III.79: *ol.* | JSul.I.01c: *ol.*

152 JSul.III.03: *ullu jarlyġasynny*; probably a scribal error, cf. the use of *ḥabar cyġar-* 'to announce news, to trumpet news' and *jaḥsy ḥabar* 'good news'. | JSul.I.45: *ḥabarlarny tutunulġanny bizge da körgizgin bizge ullu jarlyġasynny.* | ADub.III.61: *ḥabarlarny tutunulġanny bizge da kergizgin bizge ullu jarlyġasynny.* | JSul.III.79: *ḥabarlarny tutunulġanny bizge da kergizgin bizge ullu jarlyġasynny.* | JSul.I.01c: *ḥabarlarny tutunulġanlarny bizge da kergizgin bizge ullu jarlyġasynny.*

153 Psalm 86:1; אָזְנֶךָ *pro* אָזְנְךָ. | JSul.I.45: הטה ה׳: . (Psalm 86:1). | ADub.III.61: ותאמר אחריו מזמור הַטֵה ה׳ אָזְנֶךָ עֲנֵנִי וגו׳. (Psalm 86:1). | JSul.III.69: הַטֵה ה׳ אָזְנֶךָ עֲנֵנִי וגו׳. (Psalm 86:1). | JSul.III.79: הַטֵה ה׳ אָזְנֶךָ עֲנֵנִי וגו׳. (Psalm 86:1). | JSul.I.01c: ותאמר הטה ה׳ אזנך ענני וגו׳. (Psalm 86:1).

[71] [14] But, my great wish is that You may announce to me, the sorrowful,
[72] [15] saying, 'I absolved, O miserable one, all your sins',
[73] [16] as well as You may, according to the abundance of Your grace, accept
[74] [17] the prayer of those who pray to You, and gather, from all[154] unclean lands,
[75] [18] us, Your chosen servants. I beg You, O God, with Your mercy
[76] [19] announce as a truth ⌊all those⌋[155] good ⌊[news that were promised us and show us]⌋[156] Your great mercy.
[77] [20] ⌊'Bow down your ear, O Lord, hear me: for I am poor and needy.'⌋[157]

154 JSul.I.45: *these.* | ADub.III.61: *these.* | JSul.III.79: *these.* | JSul.I.01C: *these.*

155 JSul.I.45: *the.* | ADub.III.61: *the.* | JSul.III.79: *the.* | JSul.I.01C: *the.*

156 Reconstructed on the basis of JSul.I.01C. Absent from JSul.III.03 due to scribal error.

157 Psalm 86:1. | JSul.I.45: *'Bow down, O Lord.'* (Psalm 86:1). | ADub.III.61: *And afterwards you will say 'Bow down your ear, O Lord, hear me ...' and so on.* (Psalm 86:1). | JSul.III.69: *'Bow down your ear, O Lord, hear me ...' and so on.* (Psalm 86:1). | JSul.III.79: *'Bow down your ear, O Lord, hear me ...' and so on.* (Psalm 86:1). | JSul.I.01C: *And you will say 'Bow down your ear, O Lord, hear me ...' and so on.* (Psalm 86:1).

**Text number:** № 2
**Karaim incipit:**
1. *Jazyqlarymyz ulġajdylar bijikḱa astry*
2. *Jazyqlarymyz ulġajdylar bijikke astry*
3. *Jazyqlarymyz ulġajdylar astry bijikke*

**Hebrew incipit:** אַשְׁמָתֵנוּ גָּדְלָה *ʾašmåṯēnū gåḏlå*
**Dedication:** Shabbats of the month Tammuz
**Language:** MNWKar., MSWKar., Early Mod.SWKar., Mod.SWKar.[158]
**Number of copies:** 7

| Accession no. | Place of origin of copy | Date of copy | Copyist | Folios |
|---|---|---|---|---|
| JSul.I.01a | Halych | between 1685 and 1700 | Josef ha-Mashbir | 118 vº–119 vº |
| JER NLI 4101-8 | Lutsk | 1729 | Unknown 1 | 228 rº–230 rº |
| JSul.III.63 | Halych | ca. 1778 (before 1797) | Jeshua Mordkowicz | 38 rº–39 rº |
| JSul.I.45 | Halych | 1st half of the 19th c. | Jeshua Josef Mordkowicz | 139 rº–140 rº |
| ADub.III.61 | Halych | 1850/1851 | Jeshua Josef Mordkowicz | 118 rº–118 vº |
| JSul.III.69 | Halych | ca. 1851 (before 1866) | Jeshua Josef Mordkowicz | 230 rº–230 vº |
| JSul.III.79 | Halych | ca. 1851 (before 1866) | Jeshua Josef Mordkowicz | 286 rº–287 rº |
| JSul.I.11 | Lutsk | 1878 | Zecharia ben Chanania Rojecki | 102 vº–104 rº |

## 1 Introductory Remarks

The *peshat* edited here was composed by Josef ha-Mashbir ben Shemuel, a fact which is noted in all the respective headings except for the one copied in JSul.I.01a. The latter is an autograph made by the translator himself. All seven copies are vocalized.

There are no major differences between the copies. The minor discrepancies indicate that it is the texts copied in mss. JER NLI 4101-8, JSul.III.63, and JSul.III.69 that stand the closest to the autograph in JSul.I.01a, see *jüzümüznü* ~ *izimizni* vs. *izlerimizni* (27), *munajġanlar* vs. *qyjynalġanlar* (42). The copy in JSul.I.11 has more in common with mss. JSul.I.45, ADub.III.61, and JSul.III.79, see e.g. *qajġylar* vs. *qyjynlar* (42), *munajġanlar* (42). The latter three share several passages exclusively specific to them, see e.g. *qyjynalġanlar* (42), *byla* vs. *sartyn* (31). Based on the above, we arrive at the following diagram of the connections between the copies:

158 With a number of North-Western Karaim and hybrid forms in JSul.I.11.

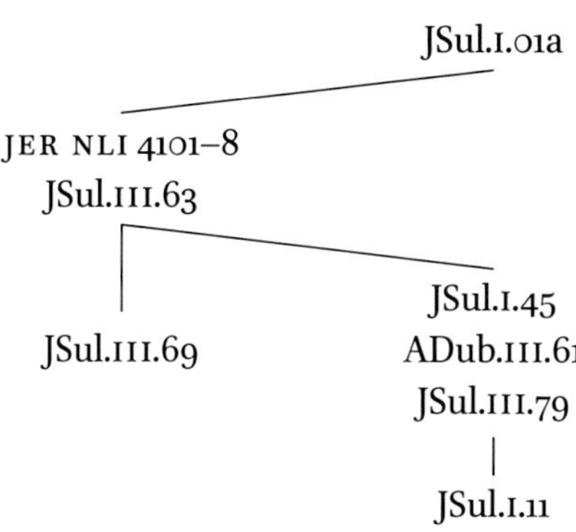


FIGURE 5 Diagram of the connections between the copies of peshat № 2

## 2 Transcription[159] and Translation

118 vº

[1] [3] ⌞... שכתוב כמו

[2] [4] ומסודר בתפלת השבת: ואם ירצה אזי שוב ומתרגם את הפיוט

[3] [5] להשמעות אזני הקק בלשון לעז להבין האנשים והנשים הבלתי יודעי׳

[4] [6] טעם מלות הפיוט עצמו וזה כדי להלאיטם יותר להתאבלות חורבן

[5] [7] ירושלם תובב להיותם זוכים כל ישראל כאחד לייעוד שמחו את ירושלם

[6] [8] וגילו בה ולאופן זה אני הצעיר תרגמתי את הפיוט במשקל בלשון לעז

[7] [9] ומציבו לעין הקורא למען ירוץ קורא בו: ויחזק הכותב ויאמץ הקורא⌝[160]

[8] [10] [161]אב״. Jazyqlarymyz ulġajdylar ⌊bijikḱa astry⌋[162]

[9] [11] da bojnumuzġa qalyn örül-

[10] [12] düĺar[163]. Vaj bizǵa[164] ki bu jazyġymyz üčün[165] bolduq Tenri-

---

159 Based on JSul.I.01a.

160 JSul.III.63: ובזה אכתוב עוד פשט של אשמתינו גדלה שתרגמו אז מו ההוה כמוהרר יוסף המשביר בר נע באז כמעד שמואל הזקן נע יעמש. | JSul.I.45: ואם תרצה תאמר גם פשטו שתרגמו אז ההו כמוהרר יוסף המשביר בר לענ נבת באז כמוהרר שמואל הזקן יעמש. | ADub.III.61: וזהו פשטו לאז מוהרר יוסף המשביר זצוקל באז כמעד שמואל הזקן אב משפחת הרודים יעמש. | JSul.III.69: ואם תרצה תאמ גם פשטו שתרגמו אז הרר יוסף המשביר בר לענ זצוקל באז מוהרר שמואל הזקן יעמש. | JSul.III.79: וזהו פשטו שתרמגו אז מוהרר יוסף המשביר בר לענ זצוקל בן שמואל הזקן יעמש. | JSul.I.11: ואם תרצה תאמר גם פשטו שתרגמו אז׳ ההו׳ כהר׳ יוסף המשביר בר באז״ כמוהרר שמואל הזקן נבת.

161 = Heb. אָשְׁמָתֵינוּ and בַּעֲוֹנוֹתֵינוּ. || Each part of the *peshat* contains a translation of two subsequent parts of the Hebrew original merged into one. In mss. JSul.I.01a and JSul.III.63, the beginning of each part is indicated with an abbreviation that stands for the first words of the two respective Hebrew portions of text. As we can see, in the Hebrew original the words that introduce each verse are arranged in alphabetical order. The latter stylistic approach is lost in the Karaim translation. || JSul.III.63: deest. | JSul.I.45: deest. | ADub.III.61: deest. | JSul.III.69: deest. | JSul.III.79: deest. | JSul.I.11: deest.

162 JSul.III.63: *astry bijikke.* | JSul.I.45: *bijikke astry.* | ADub.III.61: *bijikke astry.* | JSul.III.69: *bijikke astry.* | JSul.III.79: *bijikke astry.* | JSul.I.11: *bijikke astry.*

163 JSul.III.63: *örüldüler.* | JSul.I.45: *irildiler.* | ADub.III.61: *irildiler.* | JSul.III.69: *irildiler.* | JSul.III.79: *irildiler.* | JSul.I.11: *irildiler.*

164 JSul.III.63: *bizge.* | JSul.I.45: *bizge.* | ADub.III.61: *bizge.* | JSul.III.69: *bizge.* | JSul.III.79: *bizge.*

165 JSul.I.45: *üčün.* | ADub.III.61: *icin.* | JSul.III.69: *icin.* | JSul.III.79: *icin.* | JSul.I.11: אִיצִיוּן *icün* (a hybrid form).

166 I.e., *the one leading the prayers out of this manuscript.*

167 I.e., *Karaim*; see also line 6.

168 See, Isaiah 66:10.

169 See, Habakkuk 2:2. The phrase is used in early modern Hebrew writing, to mean: "So that the reader will read it easily and fluently."

170 JSul.III.63: *And hereby I will write down, additionally, the* peshat (*of the* piyyut *with the incipit*) ʾašmåṯēnū gåḏlå, *which our aged master translated, our teacher, the great and honourable sage, his honour, the Rav, Rabbi Josef who provides pure grain* [i.e., Josef ha-Mashbir;

[1] [3] ⌊... As is it written 118 v°

[2] [4] and arranged among prayers for Shabbat. And, if one[166] wishes, then (one should) go back and translate this *piyyut*,

[3] [5] to make it heard to the ears of the holy community, in ⌊the foreign language[1167] in order to make it understood to the men and women who do not know

[4] [6] the meaning of the words of the *piyyut* itself and to gently teach them to mourn for the destruction

[5] [7] of Jerusalem, may it be rebuilt and re-established speedily in our days, so that the whole (congregation of) Israel may have the merit (to experience) the (divine promise):

[6] [8] ⌊'Rejoice with Jerusalem, and be glad with it.'[1168] And for this purpose, I have translated this *piyyut* in metre into the foreign language, and I present it

[7] [9] to the eye of the reader, ⌊so he may run who reads it[1169]. And may the writer be strong, and the reader be mighty.[1170]

[8] [10] (1). Our sins have increased greatly

[9] [11] and have been thickly plaited around our neck.

[10] [12] Woe betide us, for because of our sin(s) we have become

---

cf. Genesis 42:3], *may his soul rest in Eden, the son of our aged master Shemuel, whose honourable repose is Eden, may his soul rest in Eden, may he rest in peace.* | JSul.I.45: *And, if you prefer, say its* peshat [i.e., of the Hebrew original], *which our aged master translated, the great and honourable sage, his honour, the Rav, Rabbi Josef who provides pure grain* [i.e., Josef ha-Mashbir; cf. Genesis 42:3] *for the elevation of the soul, may his soul lodge in Eden, the son of our aged master, his honour, the Rav, Rabbi Shemuel, the aged, may he rest in peace.* | ADub.III.61: *And this is the* peshat *of our aged master, our teacher, Rabbi Josef ha-Mashbir, may the memory of the righteous and holy be a blessing, the son of our aged master, Shemuel, the aged, whose honourable repose is Eden, the patriarch of the house of the ha-Rodi family, may he rest in peace.* | JSul.III.69: *And, if you prefer, say its* peshat [i.e., of the Hebrew original], *which our aged master translated, the Rav, Rabbi Josef who provides pure grain* [i.e., Josef ha-Mashbir; cf. Genesis 42:3] *for the elevation of the soul, may his soul lodge in Eden, the son of our aged master, our teacher, his honour, Rabbi Shemuel, the aged, may he rest in peace.* | JSul.III.79: *And this is its* peshat [i.e., of the Hebrew original], *which our aged master translated, our teacher, the Rav, Rabbi Josef who provides pure grain* [i.e., Josef ha-Mashbir; cf. Genesis 42:3] *for the elevation of the soul, may the memory of the righteous and holy be a blessing, the son of our aged master, his honour, the Rav, Rabbi Shemuel, the aged, may he rest in peace.* | JSul.I.11: *And, if you prefer, say its peshat* [i.e., of the Hebrew original], *which our aged master translated, the great and honourable sage, his honour, Rabbi Josef who provides pure grain* [i.e., Josef ha-Mashbir; cf. Genesis 42:3], *the son of our aged master, his honour, the Rav, Rabbi Shemuel, the aged, may his soul lodge in Eden.*

[11] [13] mizǵa[171] ujatlylar[172] da iḿančliĺar[173]. [174]ג״ד.
[12] [14] Jazyġyüčün[175] atalarymyznyn kesildi kohenĺar[176] naviĺar[177] da[178]
biznin
[13] [15] güńaḥĺar[179] üčün[180] eksildiĺar[181] bar zeḫutlular[182]. Jollary
[14] [16] Cijjonnun jaslydylar[183] kelivčü[184] joġundan mo'edǵa[185] da[186] qabaq-
[15] [17] lary anyn veŕandiĺar[187]. [188]ה״ו. Bolduq čerčakḱa[189]
[16] [18] bar uluslarġa[190] kültkü[191] da čajnavlar[192]. Ki ullu aziz-
[17] [19] ligimizdán[193] joḥtu ⌊bügün bizǵa⌋[194] ni[195] miqdaš ani[196] mizbeaḥ
[18] [20] ani[197] kohen tüťatüvčü[198] otjamlar. [199]ז״ח.
[19] [21] Debeḥalar da tirkiĺar[200] batyl[201] boldular da joḥtu galutumuzda[202]

---

171 JER NLI 4101-8: *Tenri alnyna.* | JSul.III.63: *Tenrimizge.* | JSul.I.45: *Tenrimizge.* | ADub.III.61: *Tenrimizge.* | JSul.III.69: *Tenrimizge.* | JSul.III.79: *Tenrimizge.* | JSul.I.11: *Tenrimizge.*

172 JSul.I.11: *ujatlyler*; a scribal error.

173 JER NLI 4101-8: *imenčliĺar.* | JSul.III.63: *imenčliler.* | JSul.I.45: *imencliler.* | ADub.III.61: *imencliler.* | JSul.III.69: *imencliler.* | JSul.III.79: *imencliler.* | JSul.I.11: *imencliler.*

174 = Heb. גְּוָעוּ and דַּרְכֵי. || JSul.I.45: deest. | ADub.III.61: deest. | JSul.III.69: deest. | JSul.III.79: deest. | JSul.I.11: deest.

175 JSul.I.45: *jazyġy ücün.* | ADub.III.61: *jazyġy icin.* | JSul.III.69: *jazyġy icin.* | JSul.III.79: *jazyġy icin.* | JSul.I.11: יִיזִיגִי אִיצִיוּן *jazyġy icün* (*ičün* is a hybrid form).

176 JSul.III.63: *kohenler.* | JSul.I.45: *kohenler.* | ADub.III.61: *kohenler.* | JSul.III.69: *kohenler.* | JSul.III.79: *kohenler.*

177 JSul.III.63: *naviler.* | JSul.I.45: *naviler.* | ADub.III.61: *naviler.* | JSul.III.69: *naviler.* | JSul.III.79: *naviler.* | JSul.I.11: *naviler.*

178 JER NLI 4101-8: *a.*

179 JSul.III.63: *güneḥler.* | JSul.I.45: *gineḥler.* | ADub.III.61: *gineḥler.* | JSul.III.69: *gineḥler.* | JSul.III.79: *gineḥler.* | JSul.I.11: *gineḥler.*

180 JSul.I.45: *ücün.* | ADub.III.61: *icin.* | JSul.III.69: *icin.* | JSul.III.79: *icin.* | JSul.I.11: איוציון *ücün* (a hybrid form).

181 JSul.III.63: *eksildiler.* | JSul.I.45: *eksildiler.* | ADub.III.61: *eksildiler.* | JSul.III.69: *eksildiler.* | JSul.III.79: *eksildiler.*

182 JSul.I.11: *zeḫutlar*; most probably a scribal error.

183 JSul.I.11: *jaslydyrlar.*

184 JER NLI 4101-8: *kelüvčü.* | JSul.I.45: *kelivcü.* | ADub.III.61: *kelivci.* | JSul.III.69: *kelivci.* | JSul.III .79: *kelivci.* | JSul.I.11: *kelivcü.*

185 JSul.III.63: *mo'edge.* | JSul.I.45: *mo'edge.* | ADub.III.61: *mo'edge.* | JSul.III.69: *mo'edge.* | JSul.III.79: *mo'edge.*

186 JER NLI 4101-8: *bar.* | JSul.III.63: *bar.* | JSul.I.45: *da bar.* | ADub.III.61: *da bar.* | JSul.III.79: *da bar.*

187 JER NLI 4101-8: *verendiĺar*; the text is not vocalized from this word on. | JSul.III.63: *verendiler.* | JSul.I.45: *verendiler.* | ADub.III.61: *verendiler.* | JSul.III.69: *verendiler.* | JSul.III.79: *verendiler.* | JSul.I.11: *veŕandirĺar.*

188 = Heb. הָיִינוּ and וְאֵין. || JSul.I.45: deest. | ADub.III.61: deest. | JSul.III.69: deest. | JSul.III.79: deest. | JSul.I.11: deest.

189 JER NLI 4101-8: *čörčekke*; a hypercorrect form of MSWKar. *čerčekke.* | JSul.III.63:

[11] [13] ashamed and embarrassed (in the presence of our) Lord. (2).
[12] [14] Because of the sin(s) of our fathers, ⌊(we have been) deprived of the priests, the prophets⌋[203],
[13] [15] and because of our transgressions ⌊the (people) with merits⌋[204] have vanished. The ways
[14] [16] of Zion have been mournful because of the lack of those who would join[205] holidays, and[206] its[207] gates
[15] [17] have been destroyed. (3). We have become laughing stock
[16] [18] of[208] all nations, (the object of their) ridicule and mockery. Because from the great holiness
[17] [19] of ours there is not (even) a shrine, or an altar
[18] [20] left today or a priest who would burn incense. (4).
[19] [21] The sacrifice and offering have become prohibited[209] in our exile, there is no

---

*čerčekke.* | JSul.I.45: *cercekke.* | ADub.III.61: *cercekke.* | JSul.III.69: *cercekke.* | JSul.III.79: *cercekke.* | JSul.I.11: צֵירְצֵיקְקֵיא *cercekḱa* (a hybrid form).

190 JSul.I.11: *uluslarda.*

191 JSul.I.45: *kiltki.* | ADub.III.61: *kiltki.* | JSul.III.79: *kiltki.* | JSul.I.11: *kiltki.*

192 JSul.I.45: *cajnavlar.* | ADub.III.61: *cajnavlar.* | JSul.III.69: *cajnavlar.* | JSul.III.79: *cajnavlar.*

193 JSul.III.63: *azizligimizden.* | JSul.I.45: *azizligimizden.* | ADub.III.61: *azizligimizden.* | JSul.III .69: *azizligimizden.* | JSul.III.79: *azizligimizden.* | JSul.I.11: *azizligimizden.*

194 JER NLI 4101-8: *bügün.* | JSul.III.63: *bügün bizge.* | JSul.I.45: *bigin bizge.* | ADub.III.61: *bizge bigin.* | JSul.III.69: *bizge bigin.* | JSul.III.79: *bigin bizge.* | JSul.I.11: בִיזְגֵיא בִיגיוּן *bizge bigün* (*bigün* is a hybrid form).

195 JSul.I.11: *ne*; an obscure form.

196 JSul.I.11: *ane*; an obscure form, cf. *ani* in line 54.

197 JSul.I.11: *ane*; an obscure form, cf. *ani* in line 54.

198 JSul.III.63: *tütetivči.* | JSul.I.45: *titetivcü.* | ADub.III.61: *titetivci.* | JSul.III.69: *titetivci.* | JSul.III .79: *titetivci.* | JSul.I.11: טִטֵטִיבְציו *titetivcü* (a hybrid form).

199 = Heb. זֶבַח and חָגְרוּ. || JSul.I.45: deest. | ADub.III.61: deest. | JSul.III.69: deest. | JSul.III.79: deest. | JSul.I.11: deest.

200 JSul.III.63: *tirkiler.* | JSul.I.45: *tirkiler.* | ADub.III.61: *tirkiler.* | JSul.III.69: *tirkiler.* | JSul.III.79: *tirkiler.* | JSul.I.11: *tirkiler.*

201 Or: *batil.* See our comment in the translation (fn. 209).

202 JER NLI 4101-8: *galutta.*

203 Lit. 'the priests, the prophets were cut off'.

204 JSul.I.11: *the merits*; perhaps a scribal error.

205 Lit. 'come to'.

206 JSul.III.63: deest.

207 JSul.III.63: *all its.* | JSul.I.45: *all its.* | ADub.III.61: *all its.* | JSul.III.79: *all its.*

208 JSul.I.11: *among.*

209 The Hebrew original has בָטָלוּ 'are no more; have become extinct' here. The similarity of this Hebrew word to Kar. *batyl* (~ *batil*) *bol-* 'to be prohibited, to not be allowed' might have influenced the translator in choosing this word to be used in the *peshat.*

[20] [22] čyġarmaq[210] ʿolalar da šelamimĺar[211]. Anyn üčün[212] bavlandylar[213]
[21] [23] kijizĺar[214] byla da syjyt eťadiĺar[215] kohenĺar[216] kijüvčü[217] qodeš
[22] [24] upraqlar[218]
119 r° [23] [1] upraqlar. [219]ט״י. Körüp[220] murdar umalar
[24] [2] Jišmaʿel da Edom eksikligin bar azizliknin bizd́an[221]
[25] [3] öz[222] murdarlyqlaryn[223] bizǵa[224] laqabladylar[225]. Da ḥökümlük[226]
[26] [4] süŕadiĺar[227] üstümüzǵa[228] ki jazyqlarymyz üčün[229] miqdašyn
[27] [5] Tenrinin meŕasĺadiĺar[230]. [231]כ״ל. Kertid́an[232] bar
[28] [6] bu iḿančlik[233] japty jüzümüznü[234] ki[235] kemištik[236] qylma
[29] [7] čeb́ar[237] micvalaryn ki Torada jazylġandylar[238]. Bolalmajbiz[239]

---

210 JSul.I.45: *cyġarmaq.* | ADub.III.61: *cyġarmaq.* | JSul.III.69: *cyġarmaq.* | JSul.III.79: *cyġarmaq.*

211 JSul.III.63: *šelamimler.* | JSul.I.45: *šelamimler.* | ADub.III.61: *šelamimler.* | JSul.III.69: *šelamimler.* | JSul.III.79: *šelamimler.*

212 JSul.I.45: *icin.* | ADub.III.61: *icin.* | JSul.III.69: *icin.* | JSul.III.79: *icin.* | JSul.I.11: *ücün* (*a hybrid form*).

213 JSul.III.69: *bajlandylar.* | JSul.III.79: *bajlandylar.* | JSul.I.11: *bavlandyler*; an erroneous hypercorrect from.

214 JSul.III.63: *kijizler.* | JSul.I.45: *tijizler.* | ADub.III.61: *kijizler.* | JSul.III.69: *kijizler.* | JSul.III.79: *kijizler.* | JSul.I.11: *tijizler.*

215 JER NLI 4101-8: *ettiĺar*; not vocalized. | JSul.III.63: *etediler.* | JSul.I.45: *etediler.* | ADub.III.61: *ettiler.* | JSul.III.69: *ettiler.* | JSul.III.79: *ettiler.* | JSul.I.11: *ettiler.*

216 JSul.III.63: *kohenler.* | JSul.I.45: *kohenler.* | JSul.III.69: *kohenler.* | JSul.III.79: *kohenler.*

217 JSul.I.01a: uncertain reading: spelled כִּיוּבְצִיוּ. | JSul.III.63: *kijüvčü*; uncertain reading: spelled כִּיוּבְצִיוּ. | JSul.I.45: *kijivcü.* | ADub.III.61: *kijivci.* | JSul.III.69: *kijivci.* | JSul.III.79: *kijivci.* | JSul.I.11: כִּיִיבְצִיוּ *kijivcü* (a hybrid form).

218 Catchword.

219 = Heb. טָמֵא and יָרְשׁוּ. || JSul.I.45: deest. | ADub.III.61: deest. | JSul.III.69: deest. | JSul.III.79: deest. | JSul.I.11: deest.

220 JSul.I.45: *körip.* | ADub.III.61: *kerip.* | JSul.III.69: *kerip.* | JSul.III.79: *kerip.* | JSul.I.11: *kerip.*

221 JSul.III.63: *bizden.* | JSul.I.45: *bizden.* | ADub.III.61: *bizden.* | JSul.III.69: *bizden.* | JSul.III.79: *bizden.* | JSul.I.11: *bizden.*

222 JSul.I.45: *ez.* | ADub.III.61: *ez.* | JSul.III.69: *ez.* | JSul.III.79: *ez.* | JSul.I.11: *ez.*

223 JSul.I.11: *murdarlyḥlaryn.*

224 JSul.III.63: *bizge.* | JSul.I.45: *bizge.* | ADub.III.61: *bizge.* | JSul.III.69: *bizge.* | JSul.III.79: *bizge.* | JSul.I.11: *bizge.*

225 JSul.I.11: *laqabladyler*; an erroneous form.

226 JSul.III.63: *ḥökümlük.* | JSul.I.45: *ḥokimlik*, spelled חוֹכִּימְלִיק. | ADub.III.61: *ḥokimlik*, spelled חוֹכִּימְלִיק. | JSul.III.69: *ḥokimlik*, spelled חוֹכִּימְלִיק. | JSul.III.79: *ḥokimlik*, spelled חוֹכִּימְלִיק. | JSul.I.11: *ḥokimlik*, spelled חוֹכִּימְלִיק.

227 JSul.III.63: *sürediler.* | JSul.I.45: *sirdiler.* | ADub.III.61: *sirdiler.* | JSul.III.69: *sirdiler.* | JSul.III.79: *sirdiler.* | JSul.I.11: *sirdiler.*

[20] [22] offering of burnt offerings and peace offerings. For this reason,
[21] [23] the priests who had been wearing holy garments strapped up themselves with felt and grieve[240].
[22] [24] [241]
[23] [1] (5). When the unclean nations 119 r°
[24] [2] of Ishmael and Esau saw the lack of all kind of holiness among us,
[25] [3] they have ascribed[242] their own uncleanness to us. And
[26] [4] they ⌊treat[243] us ruthlessly⌋[244], for because of our sins they
[27] [5] inherited the shrine of God. (6). Indeed, all
[28] [6] this shame has covered our face[245], because[246] we have stopped doing
[29] [7] His noble commandments that are written in the Law. We cannot

---

228 JSul.III.63: *üstümüzge.* | JSul.I.45: *istimizge.* | ADub.III.61: *istimizge.* | JSul.III.69: *istimizge.* | JSul.III.79: *istimizge.* | JSul.I.11: אִיסְטִימִיזְגַיא *istimizǵa* (a hybrid form).

229 JSul.I.45: *ücün.* | ADub.III.61: *icin.* | JSul.III.69: *icin.* | JSul.III.79: *icin.* | JSul.I.11: *icin.*

230 JSul.III.63: *meresllediler.* | JSul.I.45: *meresllediler.* | ADub.III.61: *meresllediler.* | JSul.III.69: *meresllediler.* | JSul.III.79: *meresllediler.* | JSul.I.11: מֵירֵיסְלַידִילֵיר *meresĺadiler* (a hybrid form).

231 = Heb. כִּסְּתָה and לֹא. || JSul.I.45: deest. | ADub.III.61: deest. | JSul.III.69: deest. | JSul.III.79: deest. | JSul.I.11: deest.

232 JSul.III.63: *kertiden.* | JSul.I.45: *körtiden*; a hypercorrect form of *kertiden.* | ADub.III.61: *kertiden.* | JSul.III.69: *kertiden.* | JSul.III.79: *kertiden.* | JSul.I.11: *kertiden.*

233 JSul.III.63: *imenčlik.* | JSul.I.45: *imenclik.* | ADub.III.61: *imenclik.* | JSul.III.69: *imenclik.* | JSul.III.79: *imenclik.* | JSul.I.11: *imenclik.*

234 JER NLI 4101-8: *jüzĺarimizni*; not vocalized. | JSul.I.45: *izlerimizni.* | ADub.III.61: *izlerimizni.* | JSul.III.69: *izimizni.* | JSul.III.79: *izlerimizni.* | JSul.I.11: *izlerimizni.*

235 JSul.III.69: *anyn icin ki.*

236 JSul.III.63: *kemeštik*; a scribal error, cf. line 37. | JSul.I.45: *kemistik.* | ADub.III.61: *kemistik.* | JSul.III.69: *kemistik.* | JSul.III.79: *kemistik.* | JSul.I.11: *kemistik.*

237 JSul.III.63: *čeber.* | JSul.I.45: *ceber.* | ADub.III.61: *ceber.* | JSul.III.69: *ceber.* | JSul.III.79: *ceber.*

238 JSul.I.11: *jazylǵandyrlar.*

239 JSul.I.11: *bolalmejbiz.*

240 ADub.III.61: *grieved.* | JSul.III.69: *grieved.* | JSul.III.79: *grieved.* | JSul.I.11: *grieved.*

241 Catchword in the Karaim text: 'garments'.

242 Lit. 'termed, named'.

243 JSul.I.45: *treated.* | ADub.III.61: *treated.* | JSul.III.69: *treated.* | JSul.III.79: *treated.* | JSul.I.11: *treated.*

244 Lit. 'pull ruthlessness upon us'. | JSul.I.45: lit. 'pulled ruthlessness upon us'. | ADub.III.61: lit. 'pulled ruthlessness upon us'. | JSul.III.69: lit. 'pulled ruthlessness upon us'. | JSul.III.79: lit. 'pulled ruthlessness upon us'. | JSul.I.11: lit. 'pulled ruthlessness upon us'.

245 JSul.I.45: *faces.* | ADub.III.61: *faces.* | JSul.III.79: *faces.* | JSul.I.11: *faces.*

246 JSul.III.69: a synonymous expression used.

[30] [8] barma ⌊Jerušalajimǵa[247] körünḿa⌋[248] qyblalaryna[249] H-nyn jylda
[31] [9] üč[250] qurlalar. [251]מנ״. Vaj bizǵa[252] ki teliligimiz
[32] [10] byla[253] ḥor ettik resimĺarin[254] ⌊Tenrinin da šarajatlaryn⌋[255]
[33] [11] da[256] özümüzd́a[257] bolduq ḥorlanġanlar. Ačyrġandyrdyq[258]
[34] [12] any saqlamajyn šertin[259] ol kesilǵan[260] birǵamizǵa[261] eki
[35] [13] keŕatĺar[262]. [263]סע״. Ullu ökt́amligimiz-
[36] [14] d́an[264] jerimizd́a[265] terśajdik[266] ters tana kibik anyn
[37] [15] üčün[267] har vaḥt tol[tur]abiz[268] ačuvlar[269]. Kemištik[270] Tora-
[38] [16] syn da tanyqlyqlaryn da töŕaĺarin[271] anar[272] köŕa[273] özümüz-
[39] [17] d́a[274] bolduq bar jamanġa učranġanlar[275]. [276]פצ״.

---

247 JSul.I.11: deest.

248 JSul.III.63: *Jerušalajimge körünme.* | JSul.I.45: *Jerušalajimge kerinme.* | ADub.III.61: *kerinme Jerušalajimde.* | JSul.III.69: *Jerušalajimge kerinme.* | JSul.III.79: *kerinme Jerušalajimde.* | JSul.I.11: *kerinme.*

249 JER NLI 4101-8: *qyblalary alnyna.* | JSul.III.63: *qyblalary alnyna.* | JSul.I.45: *qyblalary alnyna.* | ADub.III.61: *qyblalary alnyna.* | JSul.III.69: *qyblalary alnyna.* | JSul.III.79: *qyblalary alnyna.* | JSul.I.11: *qyblalary alnyna.*

250 JSul.I.45: *ic.* | ADub.III.61: *ic.* | JSul.III.69: *ic.* | JSul.III.79: *ic.*

251 = Heb. מְאַסְנוּ and נְאַצְנוּ. || JSul.I.45: deest. | ADub.III.61: deest. | JSul.III.69: deest. | JSul.III.79: deest. | JSul.I.11: deest.

252 JSul.III.63: *bizge.* | JSul.I.45: *bizge.* | ADub.III.61: *bizge.* | JSul.III.69: *bizge.* | JSul.III.79: *bizge.* | JSul.I.11: *bizge.*

253 JSul.III.63: *sartyn.* | JSul.I.45: *sartyn.* | ADub.III.61: *sartyn.* | JSul.III.79: *sartyn.* | JSul.I.11: *sartyn.*

254 JSul.III.63: *resimlerin.* | JSul.I.45: *resimlerin.* | ADub.III.61: *resimlerin.* | JSul.III.69: *resimlerin.* | JSul.III.79: *resimlerin.*

255 JSul.I.45: *Tenrinin da sarajatlaryn.* | ADub.III.61: *Tenrinin da sarajatlaryn.* | JSul.III.69: *da sarajatlaryn Tenrinin.* | JSul.III.79: *Tenrinin da sarajatlaryn.* | JSul.I.11: *Tenrinin da sarajatlaryn.*

256 JSul.III.63: *da anyn üčün.*

257 JSul.III.63: *özüm{ü}zde.* | JSul.I.45: *ezimizde.* | ADub.III.61: *ezimizde.* | JSul.III.69: *ezimizde.* | JSul.III.79: *ezimizde.* | JSul.I.11: *ezimezdi*; a scribal error.

258 JSul.I.45: *ačyrġandyrdyq.* | ADub.III.61: *ačyrġandyrdyq.* | JSul.III.69: *ačyrġandyrdyq.* | JSul.III.79: *ačyrġandyrdyq.* | JSul.I.11: *acyrġandyrdyq.*

259 JSul.I.45: *sertin.* | ADub.III.61: *sertin.* | JSul.III.69: *sertin.* | JSul.III.79: *sertin.* | JSul.I.11: *sertin.*

260 JSul.III.63: *kesilgen.* | JSul.I.45: *kesilgen.* | ADub.III.61: *kesilgen.* | JSul.III.69: *kesilgen.* | JSul.III.79: *kesilgen.*

261 JSul.III.63: *birgemizge.* | JSul.I.45: *birgemizge.* | ADub.III.61: *birgemizge.* | JSul.III.69: *birgemizge.* | JSul.III.79: *birgemizge.* | JSul.I.11: *birgemizge.*

262 JSul.III.63: *keretler.* | JSul.I.45: *keretler.* | ADub.III.61: *keretler.* | JSul.III.69: *keretler.* | JSul.III.79: *keretler.* | JSul.I.11: *keretler.*

263 = Heb. סָרַרְנוּ and עָזַבְנוּ. || JSul.I.45: deest. | ADub.III.61: deest. | JSul.III.69: deest. | JSul.III.79: deest. | JSul.I.11: deest.

264 JSul.III.63: *öktemligimizden.* | JSul.I.45: *ektemligimizden.* | ADub.III.61: *ektemligimizden.*

[30] [8] go ⌊to Jerusalem⌉[277] to appear ⌊to the⌉[278] countenance of the Lord
[31] [9] three times a year. (7). Woe betide us, given that by[279] our folly
[32] [10] we have rejected ⌊the statutes of God and His laws⌉[280]
[33] [11] and[281] we, too, have become condemned. We made Him angry
[34] [12] by not obeying His covenant, the (one) made with us two
[35] [13] times. (8). With great pride
[36] [14] we have persisted ⌊in our land⌉[282] like a disobedient calf, (and) for
[37] [15] this reason we arouse (His) anger all the time. We have abandoned
[38] [16] His Law and His witnesses and His laws and, according to that,
[39] [17] we have also joined those who have met with evil. (9).

---

| JSul.III.69: *ektemligimizden.* | JSul.III.79: *ektemligimizden.* | JSul.I.11: איוֹקְטֵימְלִיגִימִיזְדֵין *öktemligimizd́an* (a hybrid form).

265 JSul.III.63: *jerimizde.* | JSul.I.45: *jerimizde.* | ADub.III.61: *jerimizde.* | JSul.III.69: deest. | JSul.III.79: *jerimizde.* | JSul.I.11: *jerimizde jerimizde*; superfluous repetition.

266 JSul.III.63: *tersejdik.* | JSul.I.45: {*tersejdik*}. | ADub.III.61: *tersejdik.* | JSul.III.69: *tersejdik.* | JSul.III.79: *tersejdik.* | JSul.I.11: *tersejdik.*

267 JSul.I.45: *ücün.* | ADub.III.61: *icin.* | JSul.III.69: *icin.* | JSul.III.79: *icin.* | JSul.I.11: *ücün* (a hybrid form).

268 JER NLI 4101-8: *tolabiz.* | JSul.I.01a: *tolabiz.* | JSul.III.63: *tolabiz.* | JSul.I.45: *tolabiz.* | ADub.III .61: *tolabiz.* | JSul.III.69: *tolabiz.* | JSul.III.79: *tolabiz.* | JSul.I.11: *tolabiz.* || The absence of the causative form is probably due to scribal error.

269 JSul.I.45: *acuvlar.* | ADub.III.61: *acuvlar.* | JSul.III.69: *acuvlar.* | JSul.III.79: *acuvlar.*

270 JSul.I.45: *kemistik.* | ADub.III.61: *kemistik.* | JSul.III.69: *kemistik.* | JSul.III.79: *kemistik.* | JSul.I.11: *kemistik.*

271 JSul.III.63: *törelerin.* | JSul.I.45: *terelerin.* | ADub.III.61: *terelerin.* | JSul.III.69: *terelerin.* | JSul.III.79: *terelerin.* | JSul.I.11: טֵירֵילַירִין *terelárin* (a hybrid form).

272 JSul.III.69: *bunar.*

273 JSul.III.63: *köre.* | JSul.I.45: *köre.* | ADub.III.61: *kere.* | JSul.III.69: *kere.* | JSul.III.79: *kere.* | JSul.I.11: *kere.*

274 JSul.III.63: *özümüzde.* | JSul.I.45: *ezimizde.* | ADub.III.61: *ezimizde.* | JSul.III.69: *ezimizde.* | JSul.III.79: *ezimizde.* | JSul.I.11: *ezimizde.*

275 JSul.I.45: *ucranġanlar.* | ADub.III.61: *ucranġanlar.* | JSul.III.69: *ucranġanlar.* | JSul.III.79: *ucranġanlar.* | JSul.I.11: *ucranġanlar.*

276 = Heb. פְּשָׁעֵינוּ and צָעַקְנוּ. || JSul.I.45: deest. | ADub.III.61: deest. | JSul.III.69: deest. | JSul.III.79: deest. | JSul.I.11: deest.

277 JSul.I.11: desunt.

278 JSul.III.63: *before.* | JSul.I.45: *before.* | ADub.III.61: *before.* | JSul.III.69: *before.* | JSul.III.79: *before.* | JSul.I.11: *before.*

279 JSul.III.63: *due to.* | JSul.I.45: *due to.* | ADub.III.61: *due to.* | JSul.III.79: *due to.* | JSul.I.11: *due to.*

280 JSul.III.69: *the statutes and laws of God.*

281 JSul.III.63: *and therefore.*

282 JSul.III.69: desunt.

[40] [18] Haligińa[283] körüp[284] ki güńaḥĺarimiz[285] üstümüzd́adi[286] da
[41] [19] har vaḥt ulġajady[287] tarlyġymyz nečik[288] tengizd́a[289] tolġun{lar,}
[42] [20] anyn üčün[290] firjat eťabiz[291] sana[292] H[293] biz jarlylar muḥtač-
[43] [21] lar[294] tüslü[295] qajġylarbyla[296] munajġanlar[297]. [298]קר״.
[44] [22] Öküńabiz[299] sana[300] tarlyġymyzdan[301] galutta öküngánĺaj[302]
[45] [23] ačy[303] ǯanly[304] tullar da öksüzĺar[305]. Qoltqabyla körgün[306]
119 v° [46] [1] qyjyn čydaġanymyzny[307] da jarlylyq kötürǵanimizni[308] da ešittir-
[47] [2] gin bizǵa[309] mašijaḥyndan[310] ḥabarlar[311]. [312]שת״.

---

283 JSul.III.63: *haligine.* | JSul.I.45: *haligine.* | ADub.III.61: *haligine.* | JSul.III.69: *haligine.* | JSul.III.79: *haligine.* | JSul.I.11: *halegene*; a scribal error.

284 JSul.I.45: *körip.* | ADub.III.61: *kerip.* | JSul.III.69: *kerip.* | JSul.III.79: *kerip.* | JSul.I.11: *kerip.*

285 JSul.III.63: *güneḥlerimiz.* | JSul.I.45: *gineḥlerimiz.* | ADub.III.61: *gineḥlerimiz.* | JSul.III.69: *gineḥlerimiz.* | JSul.III.79: *gineḥlerimiz.* | JSul.I.11: *geneḥlerimiz*; a scribal error.

286 JSul.III.63: *üstümüzgedi.* | JSul.I.45: *istimizgedi.* | ADub.III.61: *istimizgedi.* | JSul.III.69: *istimizgedi.* | JSul.III.79: *istimizgedi.* | JSul.I.11: *istimizgede*; a scribal error.

287 JSul.III.69: *ulġajdy.* | JSul.I.11: *ulġajdy.*

288 JSul.I.45: *necik.* | ADub.III.61: *necik.* | JSul.III.69: *necik.* | JSul.III.79: *necik.* | JSul.I.11: *necik.*

289 JSul.III.63: *tengizde.* | JSul.I.45: *tengizde.* | ADub.III.61: *tengizde.* | JSul.III.69: *tengizde.* | JSul.III.79: *tengizde.* | JSul.I.11: *tengizde.*

290 JSul.I.45: *ücün.* | ADub.III.61: *icin.* | JSul.III.69: *icin.* | JSul.III.79: *icin.* | JSul.I.11: איוציון *ücün* (a hybrid form).

291 JSul.III.63: *etebiz.* | JSul.I.45: *etebiz.* | ADub.III.61: *etebiz.* | JSul.III.69: *etebiz.* | JSul.III.79: *etebiz.*

292 In JSul.I.01a: SWKar. influence, see also lines 44, and 53.

293 JER NLI 4101-8: *e H.* | JSul.I.45: *e H.* | ADub.III.61: *e H.* | JSul.III.69: *e H.* | JSul.III.79: *e H.* | JSul.I.11: *e H.*

294 JSul.I.45: *muḥtaclar.* | ADub.III.61: *muḥtaclar.* | JSul.III.69: *muḥtaclar.* | JSul.III.79: *muḥtaclar.* | JSul.I.11: *muḥtaclar.*

295 JSul.I.45: *tisli.* | ADub.III.61: *tisli.* | JSul.III.69: *tisli.* | JSul.III.79: *tisli.* | JSul.I.11: *tisli.*

296 JSul.III.63: *qyjynlar ičine.* | JSul.I.45: *qyjynlar ücüne*; *ücüne* is a hypercorrect form of *icine.* | ADub.III.61: *qyjynlar icine.* | JSul.III.69: *qajġylar icine.* | JSul.III.79: *qyjynlar icine.* | JSul.I.11: *qyjynlar icine.*

297 JSul.I.45: *qyjnalġanlar.* | ADub.III.61: *qyjnalġanlar.* | JSul.III.79: *qyjnalġanlar.* | JSul.I.11: *qyjnalġanlar.*

298 = Heb. קְרָאנוּךָ and רְאֵה. || JSul.I.45: deest. | ADub.III.61: deest. | JSul.III.69: deest. | JSul.III.79: deest. | JSul.I.11: deest.

299 JSul.III.63: *ökünebiz.* | JSul.I.45: *ekinebiz.* | ADub.III.61: *ekinebiz.* | JSul.III.69: *ekinebiz.* | JSul.III.79: *ekinebiz.* | JSul.I.11: *ekinebiz.*

300 In JSul.I.01a: SWKar. influence, see also lines 42, and 53.

301 JSul.III.63: *tarlyġymyzden*; an erroneous form.

302 JSul.III.63: *öküngenlej.* | JSul.I.45: *ekingenlej.* | ADub.III.61: *ekingenlej.* | JSul.III.69: *ekingenlej.* | JSul.III.79: *ekingenlej.* | JSul.I.11: *ekingenlej.*

[40] [18] Now, seeing that our sins are upon us and
[41] [19] that our misery ⌊keeps increasing⌋[313] all the time like the waves in the sea,
[42] [20] we cry to You, Lord[314], we, the worried miserable,
[43] [21] wracked[315] ⌊by troubles⌋[316] ⌊of all kind⌋[317]. (10).
[44] [22] We yearn for You, (to get out) from our misery in the exile, as
[45] [23] the sad widows and orphans yearn. We beg You, see
[46] [1] the suffering borne and the misery suffered by us and make us hear 119 v°
[47] [2] news[318] from Your[319] Messiah. (11)

---

303 JSul.I.45: *acy.* | ADub.III.61: *acy.* | JSul.III.69: *acy.* | JSul.III.79: *acy.* | JSul.I.11: *acy.*

304 JSul.I.45: *ʒanly.* | ADub.III.61: *ʒanly.* | JSul.III.69: *ʒanly.* | JSul.III.79: *ʒanly.* | JSul.I.11: *ʒanly.*

305 JSul.III.63: *öksüzler.* | JSul.I.45: *eksizler.* | ADub.III.61: *eksizler.* | JSul.III.69: *eksizler.* | JSul.III .79: *eksizler.* | JSul.I.11: *eksizler.*

306 JSul.I.45: *körgin.* | ADub.III.61: *kergin.* | JSul.III.69: *kergin.* | JSul.III.79: *kergin.* | JSul.I.11: כיוֹרְגִין *körgin* (a hybrid form).

307 JSul.I.45: *cydaġanymyzny.* | ADub.III.61: *cydaġanymyzny.* | JSul.III.69: *cydaġanymyzny.* | JSul.III.79: *cydaġanymyzny.* | JSul.I.11: *cydaġanymyzny.*

308 JSul.III.63: *kötürgenimizni.* | JSul.I.45: *ketirgenimizni.* | ADub.III.61: *k[e]t[i]rgenimizni*; erroneously spelled: כִּטִירְגֵינִימִיזְנִי. | JSul.III.69: *ketirgenimizni.* | JSul.III.79: *ketirgenimizni.* | JSul.I.11: *ketirgenimizni.*

309 JSul.III.63: *bizge.* | JSul.I.45: *bizge.* | ADub.III.61: *bizge.* | JSul.III.69: *bizge.* | JSul.III.79: *bizge.* | JSul.I.11: *bizge.*

310 JSul.III.63: *mašijaḥymyzdan.* | JSul.I.45: *mašijaḥymyzdan.* | ADub.III.61: *mašijaḥymyzdan.* | JSul.III.69: *mašijaḥymyzdan.* | JSul.III.79: *mašijaḥymyzdan.* | JSul.I.11: *mašijaḥymyzdan.*

311 JER NLI 4101-8: *jubančly ḥabalar.* | JSul.III.63: *jubančly ḥabarlar.* | JSul.I.45: *jubancly ḥabarlar.* | ADub.III.61: *jubancly ḥabarlar.* | JSul.III.69: *jubancly ḥabarlar.* | JSul.III.79: *jubancly ḥabarlar.* | JSul.I.11: *jubancly ḥabarlar.*

312 = Heb. שׁוּבָה and תָּמִיד. || JSul.I.45: deest. | ADub.III.61: deest. | JSul.III.69: deest. | JSul.III.79: deest. | JSul.I.11: deest.

313 JSul.III.69: *increased.* | JSul.I.11: *increased.*

314 JSul.I.45: *O Lord.* | ADub.III.61: *O Lord.* | JSul.III.69: *O Lord.* | JSul.III.79: *O Lord.* | JSul.I.11: *O Lord.*

315 JSul.I.45: *tormented.* | ADub.III.61: *tormented.* | JSul.III.79: *tormented.* | JSul.I.11: *tormented.*

316 JSul.III.63: *by suffering*; lit. 'within suffering'. | JSul.I.45: *by suffering*; lit. 'within suffering'. | ADub.III.61: *by suffering*; lit. 'within suffering'. | JSul.III.69: *by troubles*; lit. 'within troubles'. | JSul.III.79: *by suffering*; lit. 'within suffering'. | JSul.I.11: *by suffering*; lit. 'within suffering'.

317 Lit. 'various'.

318 JSul.III.63: *joyful news.* | JSul.I.45: *joyful news.* | ADub.III.61: *joyful news.* | JSul.III.69: *joyful news.* | JSul.III.79: *joyful news.* | JSul.I.11: *joyful news.*

319 JSul.III.63: *our.* | JSul.I.45: *our.* | ADub.III.61: *our.* | JSul.III.69: *our.* | JSul.III.79: *our.* | JSul.I.11: *our.*

Qajtarġyn H[320] ošol[321] qajtuvumuznu burundaġylaj[322] bijlikḱa[323] da sürtkün[324] özün[325] üčün[326] bar qylġanymyzny tüslü[327] jazyqlar. Ḥajifsingin[328] üstümüzǵa[329] körüp[330] ki har jyl biz qyna oḥujbiz[331] ⌞da jaslajbiz da čuvlajbiz⌝[332] ki Cijjon da Jerušalajim veŕandiĺar[333], da ki zoḫe tüvülbiz[334] juvutma sana[335] qarban har kün[336] ani janġajda ani[337] moedd́a[338] ani[339] šabatta eki qozular jyllyq balalary tüġaĺĺar[340]. [341]⌜וּבְיוֹם הַשַּׁבָּת שְׁנֵי כְבָשִׂים⌟.

320 JSul.I.45: *e H.* | ADub.III.61: *e H.* | JSul.III.69: *e H.* | JSul.III.79: *e H.* | JSul.I.11: *e H.*

321 JER NLI 4101-8: deest. | JSul.I.45: *osol.* | ADub.III.61: *osol.* | JSul.III.69: *osol.* | JSul.III.79: *osol.* | JSul.I.11: *osol.*

322 JSul.I.11: *burundaġylej.*

323 JSul.III.63: *bijlikke.* | JSul.I.45: *bijlikke.* | ADub.III.61: *bijlikke.* | JSul.III.69: *bijlikke.* | JSul.III.79: *bijlikke.* | JSul.I.11: *bijlikke.*

324 JSul.I.45: *sirtkin.* | ADub.III.61: *sirtkin.* | JSul.III.69: *sirtkin.* | JSul.III.79: *sirtkin.* | JSul.I.11: *sirtkin.*

325 JSul.I.45: *ezin.* | ADub.III.61: *ezin.* | JSul.III.69: *ezin.* | JSul.III.79: *ezin.* | JSul.I.11: *ezin.*

326 JSul.III.63: deest; a scribal error. | JSul.I.45: *ücün.* | ADub.III.61: *icin.* | JSul.III.69: *icin.* | JSul.III.79: *icin.* | JSul.I.11: איוציון *ücün* (a hybrid form).

327 JSul.I.45: *tisli.* | ADub.III.61: *tisli.* | JSul.III.69: *tisli.* | JSul.III.79: *tisli.* | JSul.I.11: *tisli.*

328 JSul.I.11: *ḥajifsunġun.*

329 JSul.III.63: *üstümüzge.* | JSul.I.45: *istimizge.* | ADub.III.61: *istimizge.* | JSul.III.69: *istimizge.* | JSul.III.79: *istimizge.* | JSul.I.11: *istimizge.*

330 JSul.I.45: *kerip.* | ADub.III.61: *kerip.* | JSul.III.69: *kerip.* | JSul.III.79: *kerip.* | JSul.I.11: *kerip.*

331 JSul.I.45: *uḥujbiz.* | ADub.III.61: *uḥujbiz.* | JSul.III.69: *uḥujbiz.* | JSul.III.79: *uḥujbiz.*

332 In fact, JSul.I.01a: *da jaslajbiz {da jylajbiz} da čuvlajbiz*; with an addition written by another hand (different ink and quill pen) on the left margin; cf. ADub.III.61, JSul.III.69, JSul.III.79, and JSul.I.11. | JSul.III.63: *da jaslajbiz da čuvlajbiz.* | JSul.I.45: *da jaslajbiz da cuvlajbiz.* | ADub.III.61: *da jaslajbiz da cuvlajbiz da jylajbiz.* | JSul.III.69: *da jylajbiz da jaslajbiz da cuvlajbiz.* | JSul.III.79: *da jaslajbiz da cuvlajbiz da jylajbiz.* | JSul.I.11: *da jaslejbiz da jylejbiz da cuvlejbiz.*

333 JSul.III.63: *verendiler.* | JSul.I.45: *verendiler.* | ADub.III.61: *verendiler.* | JSul.III.69: *verendiler.* | JSul.III.79: *verendiler.* | JSul.I.11: וֶֽירֶינְדִילֶיר *veŕandiler* (a hybrid form).

334 JSul.I.45: *tivilbiz.* | ADub.III.61: *tivilbiz.* | JSul.III.69: *tivilbiz.* | JSul.III.79: *tivilbiz.* | JSul.I.11: *tivilbiz.*

335 JER NLI 4101-8: deest. | JSul.I.01a: SWKar. influence, see also lines 42, and 44.

336 ADub.III.61: *kin.* | JSul.III.69: *kin.* | JSul.III.79: *kin.*

337 JSul.I.11: *ane*; an obscure form.

338 JSul.III.63: *mo'edde.* | JSul.I.45: *mo'edde.* | ADub.III.61: *mo'edde.* | JSul.III.69: *mo'edde.* | JSul.III.79: *mo'edde.* | JSul.I.11: *mo'edde.*

[48] [3] Lord[342], give us back (the opportunity) to restore

[49] [4] our kingdom as it was before and remove, for[343] this very reason ⌞all our

[50] [5] sinful deeds⌟[344]. Have mercy on us by seeing that

[51] [6] every year we sing *qinot*[345], ⌞and shed tears, and yell⌟[346]

[52] [7] because of the destruction of Zion and Jerusalem, and because we do not have the honour

[53] [8] to bring You offerings every day, or (every) month

[54] [9] or even on holidays, or even on Shabbat, (an offering of) two lambs of the first year

[55] [10] without blemish. ⌞'And on the Sabbath day two lambs …'.⌟[347]

---

339 JSul.I.11: *ane*; an obscure form.

340 JSul.III.63: *tügeller.* | JSul.I.45: *tigeller.* | ADub.III.61: *tigeller.* | JSul.III.69: *tigeller.* | JSul.III.79: *tigeller.* | JSul.I.11: *tigiller*; a scribal error.

341 Numbers 28:9. | JSul.III.63: וביום השבת שני כבצים: וכולו. (Numbers 28:9). | JSul.I.45: וביום השבת שני כבצים בני שנה וגו'. (Numbers 28:9). | ADub.III.61: וּבְיוֹם הַשַּׁבָּת שְׁנֵי כְבָצִים וגו' תם. (Numbers 28:9). | JSul.III.69: וּבְיוֹם הַשַּׁבָּת שְׁנֵי כְבָצִים בְּנֵי שָׁנָה תְּמִימִים. (Numbers 28:9). | JSul.III.79: וּבְיוֹם הַשַּׁבָּת שְׁנֵי כְבָצִים בְּנֵי שָׁנָה תְּמִימִים וגו'. (Numbers 28:9). | JSul.I.11: ותאֹמר וביום השבת שני כבצים בני שנה תמימים. (Numbers 28:9).

342 JSul.I.45: *O Lord.* | ADub.III.61: *O Lord.* | JSul.III.69: *O Lord.* | JSul.III.79: *O Lord.* | JSul.I.11: *O Lord.*

343 JSul.III.63: deest; a scribal error.

344 Lit. 'all that of ours that made all kind of sins'.

345 I.e., *dirges*.

346 JSul.I.01a: *da jylajbiz* 'and cry' added after *da jaslajbiz* by another hand on the right margin. | JSul.III.63: *and shed tears, and yell.* | JSul.I.45: *and shed tears, and yell.* | ADub.III.61: *and shed tears, and yell, and cry.* | JSul.III.69: *and cry, and shed tears, and yell.* | JSul.III.79: *and shed tears, and yell, and cry.* | JSul.I.11: *and shed tears, and cry, and yell.*

347 Numbers 28:9. | JSul.III.63: *'And on the sabbath day two lambs …' An that is all.* (Numbers 28:9). | JSul.I.45: *'And on the sabbath day two lambs of the first year …', and so on.* (Numbers 28:9). | ADub.III.61: *'And on the sabbath day two lambs …', and so on. The end.* (Numbers 28:9). | JSul.III.69: *'And on the sabbath day two lambs of the first year without spot.'* (Numbers 28:9). | JSul.III.79: *'And on the sabbath day two lambs of the first year without spot …', and so on.* (Numbers 28:9). | JSul.I.11: *And you will say 'And on the sabbath day two lambs of the first year without spot …'.* (Numbers 28:9).

**Text number:** № 3
**Karaim incipit:** *Qoltqabyla e Hjoqtan bar etivčü*
**Hebrew incipit:** אָנָּא יָיָ כִּי אֲנִי עַבְדֶּךָ *ʾånnå YWY kī ʾănī ʿabdekå*
**Dedication:** Shabbat Teshuvah
**Language:** MSWKar., Early Mod.SWKar., Mod.SWKar.
**Number of copies:** 5

| Accession no. | Place of origin of copy | Date of copy | Copyist | Folios |
|---|---|---|---|---|
| JSul.I.01b | Halych | 2nd half of the 18th c. | Mordechai ben Shemuel | 128 rº–130 rº |
| JSul.III.66 | Halych | turn of the 19th c. | Unknown 6 | 134 rº–137 vº |
| JSul.I.46 | Halych | 1st half of the 19th c. | Jeshua Josef Mordkowicz | 95 rº–99 rº |
| JSul.III.07 | Halych | 2nd half of the 19th c. | Jeshua Josef Mordkowicz | 110 vº–113 vº |
| JSul.III.77 | Halych | between 1856 and 1866 | Jeshua Josef Mordkowicz | 191 vº–194 rº |

## 1 Introductory Remarks

The content of this *piyyut* is based on Psalm 51. All the five copies are vocalized. The vowel points in JSul.I.01b were added to the text perhaps by another hand (the *niqqud* are partially of slightly lighter colour).

There are numerous differences between the copies, but these are mostly amendments of minor importance. Based on these, we can say that the *peshat* in ms. JSul.III.66 contains a number of unique elements when compared, on the one hand, with the *peshat* in JSul.I.01b and, on the other, with the version copied in JSul.I.46, JSul.III.07, and JSul.III.77, see *jalġyz raḥmetlevčü* vs. *raḥmetlevčü* (*Tenri*) (5), *bošatlyq* vs. *širinlik* (6), *ḥajifsinmeklerinnin* vs. *raḥmetlerinnin* (11), *qyblalarynnyn* vs. *ulusunnun* (14), *saġynġyn meni* vs. *saġynġyn* (14), *arytma* vs. *juvma* (17), *inčkeliklerine* vs. *inčkelikleri* (18), *tüslü* vs. *türlü* (19), *qojmady* vs. *qojmadyn* (27), *kleklerim* vs. *kleklerimbyla* ~ *kleklerinbyla* (43), *aqyllattyn* vs. *aqyllatqyn* (45), *aruv* vs. *jaḥšy* (47), *azizligi üčün* vs. *azizligine köre* (63), as well as the absence of the words *arytma* (17) and *hanuz* (109). The texts in the latter three sources are almost identical, with a few minor exceptions. Finally, both the *peshat* in JSul.III.66, and the *peshatim* in mss. JSul.I.46, JSul.III.07, and JSul.III.77 stand as a single group, closer to what we see in JSul.I.01b, as is shown in the diagram below:

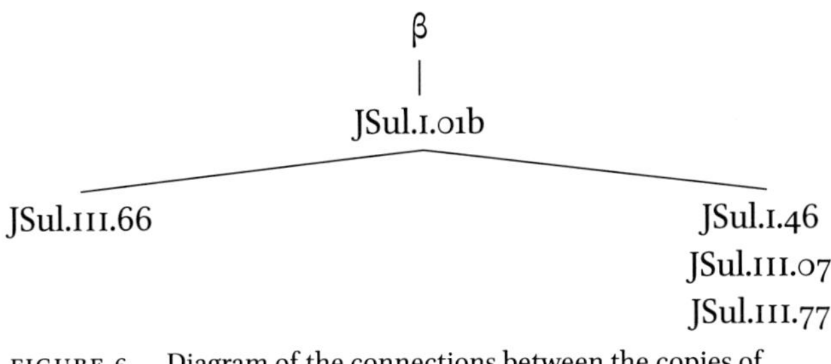


FIGURE 6 Diagram of the connections between the copies of peshat № 3

Furthermore, it is striking that the vast majority of the differences between the texts copied in JSul.I.01b and JSul.III.66 concern the initial part of the *peshat*—more precisely lines 1–66 (i.e. up to the end of part 12). In this respect, the differences between JSul.I.01b and mss. JSul.I.46, JSul.III.07, JSul.III.77 are evenly distributed throughout the text.

## 2 Transcription[348] and Translation

128 rº [1] [12] ⌊ועוד כדי לחכמיך דבר בדומהו אכתוב פשטו של אנא ה׳ כאע[349] הנק׳ בשבת תשובה שחליצו[350] ותרגמו אד וחותני מוה האלהי

[2] [13] כמוהרר יוסף באז כמהר שמואל הזקן ונב׳ יעמש ׳⌉[351]

[3] [14] Qoltqabyla e H joqtan bar etivčü[352] bar jaratylmyšlarny[353] ham[354]

[4] [15] körüvčü[355] išlerin[356] alarnyn, bilgenimde men qulun

---

348 Based on JSul.I.01b.

349 An abbreviation standing for the first three words of the Hebrew incipit, i.e., כִּי אֲנִי עַבְדֶּךָ.

350 Uncertain reading; possibly שחליצו *pro* שחילצו.

351 JSul.III.66: וכל התפלה עד לסדר הפיוט הנכבד של הרב הקדוש נע הנל אנא ה׳ כי אני עבדך ׳ ואחכ אומרים גם פשטו והוא יפה ומהודר נאה ומתוק ונאדר ׳ אשר תרגמו והמליצו והוציאו לאורה בזוך סלת חכמתו הצלולה ׳ כקש אדוננו מורנו החכם האלהי כמוהרר יוסף המשביר בר לענ יעמש בכמוהרר שמואל הזקן ונפ זצוקל. | JSul.I.46: ותתפלל כל תפלתך בשבת רחמים כסדר המסודר בתפלתה במחזור וכשתגיע לקריאת פיוט אָנָא הָ כִּי אֲנִי עַבְדֶּךָ כשתקראהו תקרא גם פשטו זה היקר מכל מחקר עשאו אז החכם האלהי והתורני המפולפל המובהק והמרומם באושר מעלת חכמתו בין קהלות בני מקרא הוא אמו כמוהרר יוסף המשביר בר לענ נבת באז כמוהרר שמואל הזקן נשיא בית אב למשפחתנו הרודים בעם ה׳ יעמש: אמר שתאתר הבית הראשון בגירסא תחל. | JSul.III.07: וכל היחוד הכתוב בשלמות בתפלת שבת רחמים וכשתגיע לפיוט אָנָא הָ כִּי אֲנִי עַבְדֶּךָ וכשתקרא של בית ממנו תאמ מיד אחד כל בית את פשטו: והפשט של פיוט זה: הוא חבורו של אז החכם האלהי כקשת כמוהרר יוסף המשביר בר לענ נבת באז כמוהרר שמאול הזקן יעמש: תרגמו להבינו לאזני עמי הארץ הבלתי מבינים לשון הקדש כדי שיתעוררו לתשובה ולמעט השית יחשוב למת לזכות ולצדקה ויקויים עמת פסוק והמשכילים יזהירו וגו׳. (The meaning of the abbreviation עמת is uncertain). | JSul.III.77: ואם תרצה להאריך בתפלה תאמר גם פשט הפיוט הנל תרגמו בלשון קדש במליצה ברורה ומפוארה איש אלהים המרביץ והמורה תורה: מובהק בכל סוד ורז סתרה: אז מוהרר יוסף המשביר זצוקל: באז הגביר המרומם ואב משפחת הרודים כמאד שמואל הזקן הנעלה יעמש: אנא ה׳ כי אני עברך.

352 JSul.I.46: *etivcü.* | JSul.III.07: *etivci.* | JSul.III.77: *etivci.*

353 JSul.I.46: *jaratylmyslarny.* | JSul.III.07: *jaratylmyslarny.* | JSul.III.77: *jaratylmyslarny.*

354 JSul.III.66: *hem.* | JSul.I.46: *hem.*

355 JSul.I.46: *körivcü.* | JSul.III.07: *kerivci.* | JSul.III.77: *kerivci.*

356 JSul.III.66: *islerin.* | JSul.III.07: *islerin.* | JSul.III.77: *islerin.*

357 I.e., *to present another* peshat *of the same* piyyut; see *piyyut* № 26 preceding № 3 in JSul.I.01.

358 Or: *master*; cf. Heb. אד.

359 Heb. חוֹתֵן 'father-in-law' was used by Karaims in a broader sense of '1. father-in-law; 2. any ancestor of one's father-in-law', cf. Heb. חתן 'to become related by marriage', whence the word derives.

360 Expressed with הא׳להי, an honorific used in Hebrew for philosophers and kabbalists.

361 JSul.III.66: *And the whole prayer, until the order* [i.e., service] *of the respected* piyyut *of the holy Rabbi, may his soul rest in Eden, beginning with the words* ʾånnå H kī ʾănī ʿab̲dek̲å. *Afterwards, they say also its peshat, (which) is a beautiful and elegant, pleasant and sweet and glorious (translation), which the glorious holy name, our master, translated, explained and published with purity of the fine flour of his clear wisdom, our teacher, the divine hakham, his honour, the Rav, Rabbi Josef who provides pure grain* [i.e., Josef ha-Mashbir; cf. Genesis 42:3] *for the elevation of the soul, may he rest in peace, the son of his honour, the Rav, Rabbi*

[1] [12] ⌊Furthermore, in order ⌊to teach you something similar[1357], I will write the *peshat* of (the *piyyut* with the incipit) *ʾånnå H kī ʾănī ʿabdekå* read on Shabbat Teshuva, which my master, uncle[358], and father-in-law[359] extracted and translated, our honourable teacher Rabbi, the divine[360], 128 r°

[2] [13] his honour, the Rav, Rabbi Josef the son of our aged master, his honour, Rabbi Shemuel, the aged, his soul is in Eden, may he rest in peace.[1361]

[3] [14] (1). I beg You, O Lord creator of all creatures from nothing and

[4] [15] the one who sees their deeds: since I know, I, Your servant,

---

*Shemuel, the aged, may the memory of the righteous and holy be a blessing.* | JSul.I.46: *And you shall pray your whole prayer on the Shabbat of Mercy, in accordance with the order* [i.e., prayer service] *that is ordered* [i.e., presented] *in its prayer in the* machzor [i.e., in the prayer book used on the holy days]*; and when you reach the reading of the* piyyut (*with the incipit*) ʾånnå H kī ʾănī ʿabdekå—*when you read it, you should also read this peshat of it, which is dear beyond all investigation. Our aged master made it, the divine and Torah-scholar hakham, the very sharp(-minded), who is lofty in the happiness of his wisdom among the communities of the sons of the Scripture* [i.e., of Karaims], *our master, our teacher, his honour, the Rav, Rabbi Josef who provides pure grain* [i.e., Josef ha-Mashbir, cf. Genesis 42:3] *for the elevation of the soul, may his soul lodge in Eden, the son of our aged master, his honour, the Rav, Rabbi Shemuel, the aged, the patriarch of the house of our family, who rule the Lord's people* [i.e., the ha-Rodi family], *may he rest in peace. He said: you should say the first verse in (accordance with) this version. Begin!* | JSul.III.07: *And (you should say) the entire* Yihud [i.e., the declaration of divine unity] *that is written in full in prayers for the Shabbat of Mercy; and when you get to the* piyyut (*with the incipit*) ʾånnå H kī ʾănī ʿabdekå, *and you read every verse of it, you should read, immediately after each stanzas, its (respective)* peshat. *And the* peshat *of this* piyyut *is a composition of our aged master, the complete hakham, his holy and glorious name, his honour, the Rav, Rabbi Josef who provides pure grain* [i.e., Josef ha-Mashbir, cf. Genesis 42:3] *for the elevation of the soul, may his soul lodge in Eden, the son of our aged master, his honour, the Rav, Rabbi Shemuel, the aged, may he rest in peace; he translated it to make it understandable to the ears of the ignoramuses, who do not understand the holy language* [i.e., Hebrew], *so that they will be roused to (perform) repentance and good deeds. May God, blessed be He, consider this for the loftiness of His Torah as virtue and righteousness* [...?], *and may there be fulfilled for the loftiness of His Torah the verse 'And they that are wise shall shine ...'* [Daniel 12:3] *and so on.* | JSul.III.77: *And, if you prefer to prolong the prayer, you may also say the* peshat *of the* piyyut *above, which the man of God translated with eloquent language, clear and glorious, from the holy language of, the disseminator and teacher of the Torah, very (scholarly) in all secrets and enigmas of its mystery, our aged master, our teacher, the Rav, Rabbi Josef ha-Mashbir, may the memory of the righteous and holy be a blessing, the son of our aged master, the elevated master and the patriarch of the ha-Rodi family, his honour, Rabbi Shemuel, the aged, the exalted, may he rest in peace. (Incipit:)* ʾånnå H kī ʾănī ʿabdekå.

[5] [16] ki sensen raḥmetlevčü[362] bar [jazyqlylarny][363] ǯomartlyġyndan[364] aziz tenriliginnin, anyn üčün[365]

[6] [17] juvudum mende jazyqly qolma širinlik[366] alnyndan qyblalarynnyn. Ḥajifsingin[367]

[7] [18] menide e Tenrim[368] köplügüne[369] köre[370] šavaġatynnyn[371].

[8] [19] [372]⌜בזכרי יום איום⌟. Jarġu kününnü[373] ol ullu da ol qorqunčlu[374] saġynġanymda töše-

[9] [20] ginde[375] jatyšlarymnyn[376], ürpejedi[377] čačy[378] gufumnun köplügünden[379] jerenči[380] iš-

[10] [21] lerimnin[381], ančaq[382] raḥmetlerin esletedirler[383] meni jalbarma sana anlavču[384] saġyšlaryn[385]

[11] [22] fikirlerimnin. Šahat[386] artmaġyna köre[387] raḥmetlerinnin[388] sürtersen[389] temgil[l]erin[390] jaman

[12] [23] išlerimnin[391]. [392]⌜גדול האצה⌟. E ullu kenešli[393] da[394] tamaša[395] išli[396]

[13] [24] kölegesinde[397] raḥmetlerinnin jarġu kününde[398] tačandyrġyn[399] meni. Da jarlyġašlanma[400]

---

362 JSul.III.66: *jalġyz raḥmetlevčü.* | JSul.I.46: *raḥmetlevcü.* | JSul.III.07: *raḥmetlevci Tenri.* | JSul.III.77: *raḥmetlevci Tenri.*

363 JSul.I.01b: *jazyqlarnyn*; the word-final *nun* was added later to change the accusative case suffix into the genetive case suffix; this is, however, an error: the verb *raḥmetle-* governs the accusative case. | JSul.III.66: *jazyqlylarny.* | JSul.I.46: *jazyqlylarny.* | JSul.III.07: *jazyqlylarny.* | JSul.III.77: *jazyqlylarny.*

364 JSul.I.46: *ʒomartlyġyndan.* | JSul.III.07: *ʒomartlyġyndan.* | JSul.III.77: *ʒomartlyġyndan.*

365 JSul.I.46: *ücün.* | JSul.III.07: *icin.* | JSul.III.77: *icin.*

366 JSul.III.66: *bošatlyq.* | JSul.I.46: or: *sirinlik.* | JSul.III.07: *sirinlik.* | JSul.III.77: *sirinlik.*

367 JSul.III.77: *ḥajifsin.*

368 JSul.I.46: *Tenri.*

369 JSul.III.66: *köpligine.* | JSul.I.46: *köpligine.* | JSul.III.07: *kepligine.* | JSul.III.77: *kepligine.*

370 JSul.III.07: *kere.* | JSul.III.77: *kere.*

371 JSul.III.66: *šavaġatlarynnyn.* | JSul.I.46: *savaġatynnyn.* | JSul.III.07: *savaġatynnyn.* | JSul.III.77: *savaġatynnyn.*

372 JSul.III.66: בזכרי יום. | JSul.I.46: בזכֹּרי. | JSul.III.07: בזכרי. | JSul.III.77: בזכֹּרי.

373 JSul.I.46: *küninnü.* | JSul.III.07: *kininni.* | JSul.III.77: *kininni.*

374 JSul.I.46: *qorqunclu.* | JSul.III.07: *qorqunclu.* | JSul.III.77: *qorqunclu.*

375 JSul.I.46: *teseginde.* | JSul.III.07: *teseginde.* | JSul.III.77: *teseginde.*

376 JSul.I.46: *jatyslarymnyn.* | JSul.III.07: *jatyslarymnyn.* | JSul.III.77: *jatyslarymnyn.*

377 JSul.III.66: *örpejedi.* | JSul.I.46: *erpejedi.* | JSul.III.07: *erpejedi.* | JSul.III.77: *erpejedi.*

378 JSul.I.46: *cacy.* | JSul.III.07: *cacy.* | JSul.III.77: *cacy.*

379 JSul.III.66: *köpliginden.* | JSul.I.46: *köpliginden.* | JSul.III.07: *kepliginden.* | JSul.III.77: *kepliginden.*

380 JSul.I.46: *jerenci.* | JSul.III.07: *jerenci.* | JSul.III.77: *jerenci.*

381 JSul.I.46: *islerimnin.* | JSul.III.07: *islerimnin.* | JSul.III.77: *islerimnin.*

[5] [16] that You are ⌊the one who has pity on all the sinners⌋[401] because of the generosity of Your divinity, for this reason
[6] [17] I have come closer, a sinner, too, to ask for approval[402] before Your countenance. Have mercy
[7] [18] on me, too, O God of mine, according to the abundance of Your mercy.
[8] [19] (2). Remembering the great and frightful day of Your verdict,
[9] [20] ⌊in the bed of my rest⌋[403] the hair of my body rises because of the abundance of my repulsive
[10] [21] deeds, but Your mercies remind me to pray ⌊to You⌋[404] who knows the thoughts[405]
[11] [22] of my reason. Can it be that according to the increase of Your mercy You will remove the stains of my evil
[12] [23] deeds? (3). O (God) of great intentions and wondrous works,
[13] [24] in the day of verdict hide me in the shadow of Your mercies. And

---

382 JSul.I.46: *ancaq.* | JSul.III.07: *ancaq.* | JSul.III.77: *ancaq.*
383 JSul.III.66: *esletediler.*
384 JSul.III.66: *e anlavču.* | JSul.I.46: *e anlavcu.* | JSul.III.07: *e anlavcu.* | JSul.III.77: *e anlavcu.*
385 JSul.I.46: *saġysyn.* | JSul.III.07: *saġysyn.* | JSul.III.77: *saġysyn.*
386 JSul.I.46: *sahat.* | JSul.III.07: *sahat.* | JSul.III.77: *sahat.*
387 JSul.III.07: *kere.* | JSul.III.77: *kere.*
388 JSul.III.66: *ḥajifsinmeklerinnin.*
389 JSul.I.46: *sirtersen.* | JSul.III.07: *sirtersen.* | JSul.III.77: *sirtersen.*
390 JSul.I.01b: *temgilerin*; a scribal error, cf. line 60. | JSul.III.66: *temgillerin.* | JSul.I.46: *temgillerin.* | JSul.III.07: *temgillerin.* | JSul.III.77: *temgillerin.*
391 JSul.I.46: *islerimnin.* | JSul.III.07: *islerimnin.* | JSul.III.77: *islerimnin.*
392 JSul.I.46: גדוֹל. | JSul.III.07: גדוֹל.
393 JSul.I.46: *kenesli.* | JSul.III.07: *kenesli.* | JSul.III.77: *kenesli.*
394 JSul.III.66: *hem.* | JSul.I.46: *hem.* | JSul.III.07: *hem.* | JSul.III.77: *hem.*
395 JSul.III.07: *tamasa.* | JSul.III.77: *tamasa.*
396 JSul.I.46: *isli.* | JSul.III.07: *isli.* | JSul.III.77: *isli.*
397 JSul.I.46: *kelegesinde.* | JSul.III.07: *kelegesinde.* | JSul.III.77: *kelegesinde.*
398 JSul.III.07: *kininde.* | JSul.III.77: *kininde.*
399 JSul.I.46: *tacandyrġyn.* | JSul.III.07: *tacandyrġyn.* | JSul.III.77: *tacandyrġyn.*
400 JSul.I.46: *jarlyġaslanma.* | JSul.III.07: *jarlyġaslanma.* | JSul.III.77: *jarlyġaslanma.*
401 JSul.I.01b: lit. 'He of all the sinners, who has mercy'; the use of the suffix *-nyn* (gen.) is, however, a scribal error in place of *-ny* (acc.); see fn. 363 in the transcription. | JSul.III.66: *the only one who has pity on all the sinners.* | JSul.III.07: *the God who has pity on all the sinners.* | JSul.III.77: *the God who has pity on all the sinners.*
402 JSul.III.66: *forgiveness.*
403 Lit. 'in the bed of my lairs'.
404 JSul.III.66: *O, to You.* | JSul.I.46: *O, to You.* | JSul.III.07: *O, to You.* | JSul.III.77: *O, to You.*
405 JSul.I.46: *thought.* | JSul.III.07: *thought.* | JSul.III.77: *thought.*

[14] [25] jarlyġašybyla[406] ulusunnun[407] saġynġyn[408] da eske[409] [keltirgin][410] meni. Da hanuz tiri

[15] [26] egenimde bu juvuz[411] dunjada resimlerinni üvretkin[412] mana[413] ki[414] jaryqlanma

[16] [27] jaryġybyla qyblalarynnyn zoẖe etkejsen meni. Anyn üčün[415] artyrġyn rastly-

[17] [28] ġynny juvma[416] meni jazyġymdan da arytma[417] güneḥimden[418] qyjasa sapun byla da kiršen[419]

[18] [29] byla juvundurġun meni. [420]⌜[421]דקדוקי מצ׳⌟. Inčkelikleri[ne][422] micvalarynnyn

128 vº [19] [1] tenešelmes[423] alarġa bir türlü[424] bahaly nerse, vale men jazyqly vaj men{im} ǯanyma[425] ki

[20] [2] ḥorladym da qajjam etmedim alarny ⌞kle ki⌟[426] jalyn[427] alarnyn bildimde ese, tek

[21] [3] hečlikni[428] quvma jeldejdi da qunušturady[429] meni ⌞jaman jecerim⌟[430] ḥotej ki kün[431] da keče[432]

[22] [4] jolda ⌞q[y]jnaldym[da]⌟[433] ese. Anyn üčün[434] güneḥlerimde[435] men bilinemen da harbir jazyġym

---

406 JSul.I.46: *jarlyġasy byla.* | JSul.III.07: *jarlyġasy byla.* | JSul.III.77: *jarlyġasy byla.*

407 JSul.III.66: *qyblalarynnyn.*

408 JSul.III.66: *saġynġyn meni.*

409 JSul.III.66: *öske*; a hypercorrect form of *eske.*

410 JSul.I.01b: *keltirginči*; a scribal error. | JSul.III.66: *keltirgin če* (unusual spelling). | JSul.I.46: *keltirginče.* | JSul.III.07: *keltirgince.* | JSul.III.77: *keltirgince.* || The *-ginče* converbial form, i.e., *eske keltirginče* 'until [You] recall', does not fit in with the context; the unclear forms in JSul.I.01b and JSul.III.66 also support this assumption. The imperative construction *eske keltirgin* appears to have originally been used here.

411 JSul.III.66: deest. | JSul.I.46: deest. | JSul.III.07: deest. | JSul.III.77: deest.

412 JSul.I.46: *ivretkin.*

413 JSul.III.66: *meni*; a scribal error.

414 JSul.III.66: deest.

415 JSul.I.46: *ücün.* | JSul.III.07: *icin.* | JSul.III.77: *icin.*

416 JSul.III.66: *arytma.*

417 JSul.III.66: deest.

418 JSul.I.46: *gineḥimden.* | JSul.III.07: *gineḥimden.* | JSul.III.77: *gineḥimden.*

419 JSul.III.66: *kirsen.* | JSul.I.46: *kirsen.* | JSul.III.07: *kirsen.* | JSul.III.77: *kirsen.*

420 JSul.III.66: דקדוקי מצותיך. | JSul.I.46: דקדּוקי. | JSul.III.07: דקדּוקי. | JSul.III.77: דקדוקי.

421 And abbreviation of Heb. מצותיך.

422 JSul.I.01b: *inčkelikleri.* | JSul.III.66: *inčkeliklerine.* | JSul.I.46: *inckelikleri.* | JSul.III.07: *incke-likleri.* | JSul.III.77: *inckelikleri.* || The context requires the dative case.

423 JSul.I.46: *teneselmes.* | JSul.III.07: *teneselmes.* | JSul.III.77: *teneselmes.*

[14] [25] remember me to be rescued ⌊with the salvation of Your people⌉[436] ⌊and recall me⌉[437]. And while I am still alive
[15] [26] in this low[438] world, teach me Your statutes, so that You would
[16] [27] honour me (by) being enlightened with the light of Your countenance. For this reason, increase Your (sense) of justness
[17] [28] in order to purify[439] me from my wrongs and ⌊to cleanse (me) from⌉[440] my sins as if You would wash me with a ⌊soap or lye⌉[441].
[18] [29] (4). (There) is no precious thing that could compare to the subtlety of Your commandments,
[19] [1] but woe betide my soul because I, the sinful, 128 v°
[20] [2] have condemned and not strengthened them; ⌊even if⌉[442] I would know ⌊what comes with them as a reward⌉[443],
[21] [3] my evil inclination would guide me and would rouse me to chase vanity—[even] if I
[22] [4] would suffer day and night on my way. For this reason, I acknowledge my transgressions and every single sin of mine

424 JSul.III.66: *tüslü.* | JSul.I.46: *tirli.* | JSul.III.07: *tirli.* | JSul.III.77: *tirli.*
425 JSul.I.46: *ʒanyma.* | JSul.III.07: *ʒanyma.* | JSul.III.77: *ʒanyma.*
426 JSul.I.46: *ḥotej.* | JSul.III.07: *ḥotej.* | JSul.III.77: *ḥotej.* || Cf. line 1:25.
427 JSul.I.46: *jallaryn.* | JSul.III.07: *jallaryn.* | JSul.III.77: *jallaryn.*
428 JSul.I.46: *heclikni.* | JSul.III.07: *heclikni.* | JSul.III.77: *heclikni.*
429 JSul.I.46: *qunusturady.* | JSul.III.07: *qunusturady.* | JSul.III.77: *qunusturady.*
430 A calque of Heb. יֵצֶר הָרָע 'evil inclination', see Genesis 6:5, 8:21.
431 JSul.III.07: *kin.* | JSul.III.77: *kin.*
432 JSul.I.46: *kece.* | JSul.III.07: *kece.* | JSul.III.77: *kece.*
433 JSul.I.01b: *qjnaldym*; a scribal error. | JSul.III.66: *qyjnaldym da.* | JSul.I.46: *qyjnaldym da.* | JSul.III.07: *qyjnaldym da.* | JSul.III.77: *qyjnaldym da.*
434 JSul.I.46: *ücün.* | JSul.III.07: *icin.* | JSul.III.77: *icin.*
435 JSul.I.46: *gineḥlerimde.* | JSul.III.07: *gineḥlerimde.* | JSul.III.77: *gineḥlerimde.*
436 JSul.III.66: *by the mercy of Your countenance.*
437 In all copies: *and until* [You] *recall me*, which is most probably a result of a scribal error repeated by the copyists; see the respective commentary in the transcription.
438 JSul.III.66: deest. | JSul.I.46: deest. | JSul.III.07: deest. | JSul.III.77: deest.
439 JSul.III.66: *cleanse.*
440 JSul.III.66: desunt.
441 Cf. Jeremiah 2:22.
442 In JSul.I.01b and JSul.III.66 expressed with *kle ki*, the meaning of which is not entirely clear. We reconstruct its sense based on *ḥotej* 'even though' used in place of *kle ki* in the other mss. Cf. line 1:25.
443 JSul.I.01b: lit. 'their reward'. | JSul.III.66: lit. 'their reward'. | JSul.I.46: lit. 'their rewards' | JSul.III.07: lit. 'their rewards'. | JSul.III.77: lit. 'their rewards'.

[23] [5] alnymdady[444] hammeše[445]. [446]⌈השכלתני שכל⌉. Kertiden[447] sen aqyllattyn meni

[24] [6] malaẖlyq usbyla vale men kötürme[448] bojunsasyn aziz Torannyn özümnü[449].

[25] [7] čynyqtyrmadym[450]. Yšandym[451] fajdaly bolma hečlik[452] malybyla bu juvuz dunjanyn ki

[26] [8] senin bernenden tojma yšanmadym[453]. Haligine qajry qajrylajym da kimge

[27] [9] qačajym[454] ki sana yšančymny[455] qojmadym[456]. Vaj menim bu tirligime ki sana bir

[28] [10] jalġyz Tenrige jazyqly boldum da bar jamanny enajatlarynda[457] qyldym.

[29] [11] [458]⌈והן לי לפוקה⌉. Da muna bar išlerim[459] tuzaqqady mana ki saqlamadym jürüme[460] kečindir-

[30] [12] meklerinbyla[461] ol berilgenler Sinaj tavynda. Anlyqbyla H[462] Tenrim rast bolusen[463]

[31] [13] sözleme[464] birgeme töre[465] sözleri[466] jarġu kününnün[467] ḥešbonunda. Ančaq[468] Toran

[32] [14] da micvalaryn da uvutmaqlaryn jazyqlylarny juvatadylar meni ki jazyqlary bošatylyr[469]

[33] [15] anlanġanlarynda jaman išlerinde[470]. Anyn üčün[471] ki rastčyqqajsen[472] sözlegenin[473]

---

444 JSul.III.66: *qaršymady.* | JSul.I.46: *qarsymady.* | JSul.III.07: *qarsymady.* | JSul.III.77: *qarsymady.*

445 JSul.III.77: *hammese.*

446 JSul.I.46: השכלת֯ני. | JSul.III.07: השכ֯לתני. | JSul.III.77: השכלת֯ני.

447 JSul.III.66: *körtiden*; a hypercorrect form of *kertiden.* | JSul.I.46: *körtiden*; a hypercorrect form of *kertiden.*

448 JSul.I.46: *kötirme.* | JSul.III.07: *ketirme.* | JSul.III.77: *ketirme.*

449 JSul.I.46: *ezimni.* | JSul.III.07: *ezimni.* | JSul.III.77: *ezimni.*

450 JSul.I.46: *cynyqtyrmadym.* | JSul.III.07: *cynyqtyrmadym.* | JSul.III.77: *cynyqtyrmadym.*

451 JSul.I.46: *ysandym.* | JSul.III.07: *ysandym.* | JSul.III.77: *ysandym.*

452 JSul.I.46: *heclik.* | JSul.III.07: *heclik.* | JSul.III.77: *heclik.*

453 JSul.I.46: *ysanmadym.* | JSul.III.07: *ysanmadym.* | JSul.III.77: *ysanmadym.*

454 JSul.I.46: *qacajym.* | JSul.III.07: *qacajym.* | JSul.III.77: *qacajym.*

455 JSul.I.46: *ysancymny.* | JSul.III.07: *ysancymny.* | JSul.III.77: *ysancymny.*

456 JSul.III.66: *qojmady*; a scribal error.

457 JSul.III.66: *enajatlaryn alnyna.* | JSul.I.46: *enaj atlaryn alnyna.* | JSul.III.07: *enaj atlaryn alnyna.* | JSul.III.77: *enajatlaryn alnyna.*

458 JSul.I.46: וה֯ן לי֯. | JSul.III.07: וה֯ן. | JSul.III.77: והן לי.

[23] [5] is ever before me. (5). Indeed, You have admonished me

[24] [6] with the wisdom of angels, but I did not accustom myself to lifting the yoke of Your holy Law.

[25] [7] I hoped to benefit from the goods of vanity of this low world, for

[26] [8] I did not hope[474] to be satisfied with Your bounty. Now, I turn back and: Whom should

[27] [9] I run to, given that I did not ⌊hope in⌋[475] You? Woe betide my life, since

[28] [10] I have become sinful ⌊in Your sight⌋[476], only God, and all the evil I have done (has been done) in Your sight.

[29] [11] (6). And, lo, all my deeds have become a snare for me because I did not care to walk with the guidance

[30] [12] given on Mount Sinai: with all this (in mind), my[477] Lord God, You will be justified

[31] [13] to say Your judgements in the accounts of Your day of verdict: it is only Your Law,

[32] [14] Your commandments, and Your (words of) consolation to sinners that comfort me, (namely) that the sins of (sinners)

[33] [15] will be absolved when they learn[478] their evil deeds. Given that You will be justified when You say

459 JSul.I.46: *islerim.* | JSul.III.07: *islerim.* | JSul.III.77: *islerim.*

460 JSul.III.07: *jirime.* | JSul.III.77: *jirime.*

461 JSul.I.46: *kecindirmeklerin byla.* | JSul.III.07: *kecindirmeklerin byla.* | JSul.III.77: *kecindirmeklerin byla.*

462 JSul.III.66: *e H.* | JSul.I.46: *e H.* | JSul.III.07: *e H.* | JSul.III.77: *e H.*

463 JSul.III.66: *bolursen.* | JSul.I.46: *bolursen.* | JSul.III.07: *bolursen.* | JSul.III.77: *bolursen.*

464 JSul.III.07: *sezleme.* | JSul.III.77: *sezleme.*

465 JSul.III.07: *tere.* | JSul.III.77: *tere.*

466 JSul.III.66: *sözlerin.* | JSul.I.46: *sözlerin.* | JSul.III.07: *sezlerin.* | JSul.III.77: *sezlerin.*

467 JSul.III.07: *kininnin.* | JSul.III.77: *kininnin.*

468 JSul.I.46: *ancaq.* | JSul.III.07: *ancaq.* | JSul.III.77: *ancaq.*

469 JSul.I.46: *bosatylyr.* | JSul.III.07: *bosatylyr.* | JSul.III.77: *bosatylyr.*

470 JSul.I.46: *islerinde.* | JSul.III.07: *islerinde.* | JSul.III.77: *islerinde.*

471 JSul.I.46: *ücün.* | JSul.III.07: *icin.* | JSul.III.77: *icin.*

472 JSul.I.46: *rast cyqqajsen.* | JSul.III.07: *rast cyqqajsen.* | JSul.III.77: *rast cyqqajsen.*

473 JSul.III.07: *sezlegenin.* | JSul.III.77: *sezlegenin.*

474 Or: *believe.*

475 Or: *trust.*

476 Lit. 'for You'.

477 JSul.III.66: *O my.* | JSul.I.46: *O my.* | JSul.III.07: *O my.* | JSul.III.77: *O my.*

478 Lit. 'meet'.

[34] [16] byla ügüt[479] sözleri[n][480] alarġa tiri egenlerinde aruv bolġajsen firjatlaryndan

[35] [17] töreleškeninde[481]. [482]⌈זדות וגאות⌋. Čajalyġy[483] jüregimnin[484] jeldedi[485] meni bar

[36] [18] öktemliklerge[486] da bu boldu ajibim[487] senin alnynda. Anyn üčün[488] tutady

[37] [19] gufumnu titrevik[489] esime alġanymda jazyqlarymny künümde[490] da kečemde[491],

[38] [20] ki jaratyldym qyjasa jaman etmek üčün[492] olturušumda[493] da turġanymda[494],

[39] [21] ha mana ki jazyġybyla atam{nyn} tolġatyldym da anam güneḥibyla[495] issitti[496]

[40] [22] meni ḥamilalyġynda. [497]⌈חשקי צורי⌋. Haligine jaratuvčum[498] kipligim[499] {bar} tarlyqtan

[41] [23] juluvčum bar klegimdi menim ki raḥmetinbyla juvutqajsen jarlyġašymny[500], da ki bu

[42] [24] bolur körkü[501] maḥtavun{n}un eger tynlasan jylamaqly qoltqamny. Ahah tergevčü[502]

[43] [25] fikirlerin aruv jüreknin[503] qoltqabyla jaḥšy[504] kleklerimbyla[505] tojdurġun synyq

[44] [26] ǯanymny[506], ki muna egirek[507] bernelerden süves[e]n[508] bolsa kertilik[509] adamnyn büv-

479 JSul.I.46: *igit.* | JSul.III.07: *igit.* | JSul.III.77: *igit.*

480 JSul.I.01b: *sözleri.* | JSul.III.66: *sözleri.* | JSul.I.46: *sözlerin.* | JSul.III.07: *sezlerin.* | JSul.III.77: *sezlerin.*

481 JSul.III.66: *töreleskeninde.* | JSul.I.46: *tereleskeninde.* | JSul.III.07: *tereleskeninde.* | JSul.III.77: *tereleskeninde.*

482 JSul.I.46: זדור.

483 JSul.I.46: *cejalyġy.* | JSul.III.07: *cejalyġy.* | JSul.III.77: *cejalyġy.*

484 JSul.III.07: *jiregimnin.* | JSul.III.77: *jiregimnin.*

485 JSul.III.66: *jeldejdi.* | JSul.I.46: *jeldejdi.* | JSul.III.07: *jeldejdi.* | JSul.III.77: *jeldejdi.*

486 JSul.I.46: *ektemliklerge.* | JSul.III.07: *ektemliklerge.* | JSul.III.77: *ektemliklerge.*

487 Or: *ajybym.*

488 JSul.I.46: *ücün.* | JSul.III.07: *icin.* | JSul.III.77: *icin.*

489 JSul.I.46: *kitrevik.* | JSul.III.07: *kitrevik.* | JSul.III.77: *kitrevik.*

490 JSul.III.07: *kinimde.* | JSul.III.77: *kinimde.*

491 JSul.I.46: *kecemde.* | JSul.III.07: *kecemde.* | JSul.III.77: *kecemde.*

492 JSul.I.46: *ücün.* | JSul.III.07: *icin.* | JSul.III.77: *icin.*

493 JSul.III.66: *olturusumda.* | JSul.I.46: *olturusumda.* | JSul.III.07: *olturusumda.* | JSul.III.77: *olturusumda.*

494 JSul.I.46: *turusumda.* | JSul.III.07: *turusumda.* | JSul.III.77: *turusumda.*

495 JSul.I.46: *gineḥi byla.* | JSul.III.07: *gineḥi byla.* | JSul.III.77: *gineḥi byla.*

[34] [16] them Your words of advice when they are (still) alive, You shall be blameless[510] (despite) of their cries

[35] [17] when You judge. (7). The haughtiness of my heart roused[511] me

[36] [18] to all proud (deeds), and this has become my shame before You. For this reason

[37] [19] shiver takes hold on my body day and night when I take into consideration my sins

[38] [20] that I did[512] while sitting or standing[513] as if I did them to do evil,

[39] [21] woe is me, for I was brought forth by my father's iniquity and my mother warmed

[40] [22] me with her transgressions during pregnancy. (8). Now, O creator of mine, my strength, my saviour from all the misery,

[41] [23] all I wish is that, in Your mercy, You would bring closer my salvation, and that this

[42] [24] ⌊would grace Your praise⌉[514]—in case You listen to my teary prayer. O, (You, the) investigator

[43] [25] of the thoughts of the clean hearts, I beg You with my good wishes, satisfy my contrite

[44] [26] heart for, lo, You prefer truth in the inward parts of a man more than gifts,

---

496 Or: *yssytty*.

497 JSul.I.46: חשְׂקי. | JSul.III.07: חשְׂקי. | JSul.III.77: חשְׂקי.

498 JSul.I.46: *jaratuvcum*. | JSul.III.07: *jaratuvcum*. | JSul.III.77: *jaratuvcum*.

499 JSul.III.66: *küpligim*; a hypercorrect form of *kipligim*. | JSul.I.46: *küpligim*; a hypercorrect form of *kipligim*.

500 JSul.I.46: *jarlyġasymny*. | JSul.III.07: *jarlyġasymny*. | JSul.III.77: *jarlyġasymny*.

501 JSul.III.07: *kerki*. | JSul.III.77: *kerki*.

502 JSul.I.46: *tergevci*. | JSul.III.07: *tergevci*. | JSul.III.77: *tergevci*.

503 JSul.III.07: *jireknin*. | JSul.III.77: *jireknin*.

504 JSul.I.46: *jaḥsy*. | JSul.III.07: *jaḥsy*. | JSul.III.77: *jaḥsy*.

505 JSul.III.66: *kleklerim*. | JSul.I.46: *kleklerin byla*. | JSul.III.07: *kleklerin byla*. | JSul.III.77: *kleklerin byla*.

506 JSul.I.46: *ʒanymny*. | JSul.III.07: *ʒanymny*. | JSul.III.77: *ʒanymny*.

507 JSul.III.66: *edirek*.

508 JSul.I.01b: *-sen* not vocalized. | JSul.III.66: *sivesen*. | JSul.I.46: *sivesen*. | JSul.III.07: *sivesen*. | JSul.III.77: *sivesen*.

509 JSul.I.46: *körtilik*; a hypercorrect form of *kertilik*.

510 Lit. 'clean' (i.e., 'justified'), cf. Psalm 51:4.

511 JSul.III.66: *rouses*. | JSul.I.46: *rouses*. | JSul.III.07: *rouses*. | JSul.III.77: *rouses*.

512 Lit. 'created'.

513 JSul.I.46, JSul.III.07, JSul.III.77: expressed with a synonym.

514 Lit. 'will be the beauty (~ adornment) of Your praise'.

[45] [27] reklerinde[515] da anyn üčün[516] jabuq uslu orunda kertilikni[517] aqyllatqyn[518] meni.

[46] [28] [519]⌜טהור עין⌟. E aruv enajatly[520] anlavču[521] aruv saǧyšlarny[522] ham[523] menimde

129 r° [47] [1] jaḥšy[524] saǧyšymny[525] anlaǧyn, da jazyqlarym eger qyzardylar ese qyrmyzy jipek kibik

[48] [2] muna šavaǧatyndan[526] qarny kibik aǧartqyn, ki anda anlarmen k[ö]plügün[527]

[49] [3] šavaǧatynnyn[528] üstümde[529] anyn üčün[530] qoltqalarymny tolturma ǯaḥtlaǧyn[531],

[50] [4] bürkündürgün[532] meni čaborbyla[533] da arynajym jazyǧymdan da qarnyn aruvluǧu[534] kibik

[51] [5] meni aǧartqyn. [535]⌜יצורי בידיך⌟. Muna fikirlerimni jaryqqa čyǧarma[536]

[52] [6] senin erkindedi ki sen büvreklerimni[537] saǧyšlarǧa[538] jarattyn. Da ol tirlikni

[53] [7] da ol ölümnü[539] bergeninde Torany[540] menim beḥirama berdin, alajoq közler[541]

[54] [8] körme[542] nedi[543] jaḥšy[544] da nedi[545] jaman da tynlamaq üčün[546] qulaqlarda mana ačtyn[547].

---

515 JSul.I.46: *bivreklerinde.* | JSul.III.07: *bivreklerinde.* | JSul.III.77: *bivreklerinde.*

516 JSul.I.46: *ücün.* | JSul.III.07: *icin.* | JSul.III.77: *icin.*

517 JSul.I.46: *körtilikni*; a hypercorrect form of *kertilikni.*

518 JSul.III.66: *aqyllattyn.* | JSul.I.46: *aqyllatqyn*; the copyist first wrote *aqyllattyn* (the first curve of the letter *teth* has been overwritten with a *qoph*).

519 JSul.III.07: טהֹור. | JSul.III.77: טהור.

520 JSul.III.66: *enaj atly.* | JSul.I.46: *enaj atly.* | JSul.III.07: *enaj atly.* | JSul.III.77: *enaj atly.*

521 JSul.I.46: *anlavcu.* | JSul.III.07: *anlavcu.* | JSul.III.77: *anlavcu.*

522 JSul.I.46: *saǧyslarny.* | JSul.III.07: *saǧyslarny.* | JSul.III.77: *saǧyslarny.*

523 JSul.III.66: *hem.*

524 JSul.III.66: *aruv.* | JSul.I.46: *jaḥsy.* | JSul.III.07: *jaḥsy.* | JSul.III.77: *jaḥsy.*

525 JSul.III.66: *saǧysymny.* | JSul.I.46: *saǧysymny.* | JSul.III.07: *saǧysymny.* | JSul.III.77: *saǧysymny.*

526 JSul.I.46: *savaǧatyndan.* | JSul.III.07: *savaǧatyndan.* | JSul.III.77: *savaǧatyndan.*

527 JSul.I.01b: *küplügün*; probably a scribal error instead of *köplügün.* | JSul.III.66: *küpligün*; probably a scribal error instead of *köpligün.* | JSul.I.46: *köpligin.* | JSul.III.07: *kepligin.* | JSul.III.77: *kepligin.* || In the original, it is PBHeb. רוֹב 'multitude' that is used in this case. Given that BHeb. רֹב 'multitude' might have been used, metonymically, in the sense of 'greatness' (see König 1910: 428), it might well be that *küplügün* and *küpligün* in JSul.I.01b and JSul.III.66, respectively, are hypercorrect forms of *kipligin* 'power, strength', and not scribal errors.

528 JSul.I.46: *savaǧatynnyn.*

[45] [27] and therefore You shall teach me the truth in a hidden place of wisdom.
[46] [28] (9). O, pure-eyed (God), the one who knows my clean thoughts, too,
[47] [1] understand my clean thoughts, and if my sins would redden like scarlet silk, 129 rº
[48] [2] (then), lo, make them white like snow, so that I would understand the abundance[548]
[49] [3] of Your mercy over me: hasten me to fill my prayers,
[50] [4] sprinkle me with a sprinkler so that I shall be purged of my sin and make me white like the whiteness of the snow.
[51] [5] (10). Behold, it is in Your power to reveal my thoughts,
[52] [6] since You have created my inward parts for contemplation. And
[53] [7] when You gave me life and death, You gave me (also) the Law[549] as a choice, as well as eyes
[54] [8] to see what is good and what is evil, and You opened also my ears to hear.

---

529 JSul.I.46: *istime.* | JSul.III.07: *istime.* | JSul.III.77: *istime.*

530 JSul.I.46: *ücün.* | JSul.III.07: *icin.* | JSul.III.77: *icin.*

531 JSul.I.46: *ʒaḥtlaǵyn.* | JSul.III.07: *ʒaḥtlaǵyn.* | JSul.III.77: *ʒaḥtlaǵyn.*

532 JSul.III.66: *bürkündirgün.* | JSul.I.46: *birkindirgin.* | JSul.III.07: *birkindirgin.* | JSul.III.77: *birkindirgin.*

533 JSul.I.01b: or: *cabor byla.* | JSul.III.66: or: *cabor byla.* | JSul.I.46: *cabor byla.* | JSul.III.07: *cabor byla.* | JSul.III.77: *cabor byla.*

534 JSul.III.77: *aruvluġun*; a scribal error.

535 JSul.I.46: יצוֹרי. | JSul.III.07: יצוֹרי. | JSul.III.77: יצורי.

536 JSul.I.46: *cyġarma.* | JSul.III.07: *cyġarma.* | JSul.III.77: *cyġarma.*

537 JSul.I.46: *bivreklerimni.* | JSul.III.07: *bivreklerimni.* | JSul.III.77: *bivreklerimni.*

538 JSul.III.66: *saǵyslarġa.* | JSul.I.46: *saǵyslarġa.* | JSul.III.07: *saǵyslarġa.* | JSul.III.77: *saǵyslarġa.*

539 JSul.I.46: *elimni.* | JSul.III.07: *elimni.* | JSul.III.77: *elimni.*

540 JSul.I.46: *aziz torany.* | JSul.III.07: *aziz torany.* | JSul.III.77: *aziz torany.*

541 JSul.III.07: *kezler.* | JSul.III.77: *kezler.*

542 JSul.III.07: *kerme.* | JSul.III.77: *kerme.*

543 JSul.I.46: *nedir.* | JSul.III.07: *nedir.* | JSul.III.77: *nedir.*

544 JSul.I.46: *jaḥsy.* | JSul.III.07: *jaḥsy.* | JSul.III.77: *jaḥsy.*

545 JSul.I.46: *nedir.* | JSul.III.07: *nedir.* | JSul.III.77: *nedir.*

546 JSul.I.46: *ücün.* | JSul.III.07: *icin.* | JSul.III.77: *icin.*

547 JSul.I.46: *actyn.* | JSul.III.07: *actyn.* | JSul.III.77: *actyn.*

548 JSul.I.01b: or: *strength,* if *küplügün* is not a scribal error instead of *köplügün,* but a hypercorrect form of *kipligin.* | JSul.III.66: or: *strength,* if *küpligün* is not a scribal error instead of *köpligün,* but a hypercorrect form of *kipligin.* | JSul.I.46: *abundance.* | JSul.III.07: *abundance.* | JSul.III.77: *abundance.*

549 JSul.I.46: *holy Law.* | JSul.III.07: *holy Law.* | JSul.III.77: *holy Law.*

[55] [9] Anlyq byla ešittirgin[550] mana bijenč[551] da quvanč[552] bijensinler süveklerim[553] ki jančtyn[554].

[56] [10] [555]⌜כלו עיני⌟. Telmerediler közlerim[556] uvunčlu[557] sözlerine[558] šavaġatynby-

[57] [11] la[559] meni köndergin[560], ḥorlamaġyn meni jaratylmyšyn[561] bujruqlarynnyn da öz[562] azizli-

[58] [12] gin üčün[563] ⌞fašmanly[564] jazyġymny sürtkün[565], alajoq öz[566] aruvluġun üčün[567]⌟[568] čajalyq-

[59] [13] ta[569] jazyġymny bitiginden tabertkin[570]. Öz[571] tenriligin üčün[572] [jašyrġyn][573]

[60] [14] qyblalarynny jazyqlarymdan da barda temgillerimni aryttyrġyn.

[61] [15] [574]⌜לך אני הושיעני⌟. Kör[575] ki sana jalġyzga telmermen ki qutqarġajsen meni barda qysyq-

[62] [16] lyġymdan e qyjaslavču[576] fikirlerimni ki jüregimde[577]. Ki kertiden[578] ömürgedejin-

[63] [17] mo[579] ačuvlanyrsen[580] mende. Anyn üčün[581] ⌞azizligine köre[582]⌟[583] bir šeminnin tüzü-

[64] [18] gün[584] atlamlarymny yzyna e jaratuvčum[585] kipligim[586] tar vaḥtymda. Aruv jürek[587]

---

550 JSul.I.46: *esittirgin.* | JSul.III.07: *esittirgin.* | JSul.III.77: *esittirgin.*
551 JSul.I.46: *bijenc.* | JSul.III.07: *bijenc.* | JSul.III.77: *bijenc.*
552 JSul.I.46: *kuvanc.* | JSul.III.07: *kuvanc.* | JSul.III.77: *kuvanc.*
553 JSul.III.66: *siveklerim.* | JSul.I.46: *siveklerim.* | JSul.III.07: *siveklerim.* | JSul.III.77: *siveklerim.*
554 JSul.I.46: *janctyn.* | JSul.III.07: *janctyn.* | JSul.III.77: *janctyn.*
555 JSul.III.07: כּלו. | JSul.III.77: כּלו.
556 JSul.III.07: *kezlerim.* | JSul.III.77: *kezlerim.*
557 JSul.I.46: *uvunclu.* | JSul.III.07: *uvunclu.* | JSul.III.77: *uvunclu.*
558 JSul.III.07: *sezlerine.* | JSul.III.77: *sezlerine.*
559 JSul.I.46: *savaġatyn byla.* | JSul.III.07: *savaġatyn byla.* | JSul.III.77: *savaġatyn byla.*
560 JSul.III.07: *kendergin.* | JSul.III.77: *kendergin.*
561 JSul.I.46: *jaratylmysyn.* | JSul.III.07: *jaratylmysyn.* | JSul.III.77: *jaratylmysyn.*
562 JSul.I.46: *ez.* | JSul.III.07: *ez.* | JSul.III.77: *ez.*
563 JSul.I.46: *ücün.* | JSul.III.07: *icin.* | JSul.III.77: *icin.*
564 JSul.III.07: *fasmanly.* | JSul.III.77: *fasmanly.*
565 JSul.I.46: *sirtkin.* | JSul.III.07: *sirtkin.* | JSul.III.77: *sirtkin.*
566 JSul.I.46: *ez.* | JSul.III.07: *ez.* | JSul.III.77: *ez.*
567 JSul.I.46: *ücün.* | JSul.III.07: *icin.* | JSul.III.77: *icin.*
568 JSul.III.66: desunt; a scribal error.
569 JSul.I.46: *cejalyqta.* | JSul.III.07: *cejalyqta.* | JSul.III.77: *cejalyqta.*
570 JSul.III.66: *taber{t}gin*; a scribal error; *taber-* was changed to *tabert-*, but the suffix-initial

[55] [9] With all this (in mind), make me to hear joy and gladness, may the bones which You have crushed rejoice.

[56] [10] (11). My eyes look long for Your comforting words, guide me with Your mercy,

[57] [11] do not condemn me; ⌊in the light of[1588] Your orders of creation and Your own holiness

[58] [12] blot out my wicked sins (and), in the same way, in the light of Your own purity,

[59] [13] ⌊make my haughty sins be thrown out from Your book[1589]. In the light of Your divinity, hide

[60] [14] Your countenance from my sins and cleanse all my stains.

[61] [15] (12). See, that I long for You only, that You may save me from all

[62] [16] my miseries: You who measure all the thoughts that are in my heart. Or will You indeed

[63] [17] forever be angry with me? For this reason, according to the holiness of Your only name,

[64] [18] align my steps (to get them back) to Your path, O my creator, my strength in times of my distress. A clean heart

---

*g-* remained unchanged (the word should read *tabertkin*). | JSul.I.46: *tabergin.* | JSul.III.07: *tabergin.* | JSul.III.77: *tabergin.*

571 JSul.I.46: *ez.* | JSul.III.07: *ez.* | JSul.III.77: *ez.*

572 JSul.I.46: *ücün.* | JSul.III.07: *icin.* | JSul.III.77: *icin.*

573 JSul.I.01b: the word has been smudged out. | JSul.III.66: *jašyrġyn.* | JSul.I.46: *jasyrġyn.* | JSul.III.07: *jasyrġyn.* | JSul.III.77: *jasyrġyn.*

574 JSul.I.46: לֹּך אנִֹי. | JSul.III.07: לֹּך. | JSul.III.77: לך אני.

575 JSul.III.07: *ker.* | JSul.III.77: *ker.*

576 JSul.I.46: *qyjaslavcu.* | JSul.III.07: *qyjaslavcu.* | JSul.III.77: *qyjaslavcu.*

577 JSul.III.07: *jiregimde.* | JSul.III.77: *jiregimde.*

578 JSul.I.46: *körtiden*; a hypercorrect form of *kertiden.*

579 JSul.I.46: *emirgedejinmo.* | JSul.III.07: *emirgedejinmo.* | JSul.III.77: *emirgedejinmo.*

580 JSul.I.46: *acuvlanyrsen.* | JSul.III.07: *acuvlanyrsen.* | JSul.III.77: *acuvlanysen.*

581 JSul.I.46: *ücün.* | JSul.III.07: *icin.* | JSul.III.77: *icin.*

582 JSul.III.07: *kere.* | JSul.III.77: *kere.*

583 JSul.III.66: *azizligi üčün.*

584 JSul.III.07: *tizigin.* | JSul.III.77: *tizigin.*

585 JSul.I.46: *jaratuvcum.* | JSul.III.07: *jaratuvcum.* | JSul.III.77: *jaratuvcum.*

586 JSul.I.46: *küpligim*; a hypercorrect form of *kipligim.*

587 JSul.III.07: *jirek.* | JSul.III.77: *jirek.*

588 Uncertain translation.

589 JSul.I.46: *throw out my haughty sins from Your book.* | JSul.III.07: *throw out my haughty sins from Your book.* | JSul.III.77: *throw out my haughty sins from Your book.*

[65] [19] jaratqyn mana e[590] Tenrim da qolajly sağyšlar[591] janğyrtqyn ičimde[592].

[66] [20] [593]⌈מתי רחום⌋. E raḥmetlevčü[594] Tenri qačan[595] qajrylyrsen[596] mana da ullu qajğylarymdan

[67] [21] juvutyrsen meni, e kiplevčü[597] bükrejgenlerni[598] juvuz etivčü[599] öktemlerni[600] da

[68] [22] kötürüvčü[601] juvuzlarny ne vaḥtny raḥmetlersen meni. Jubandyrmaqlaryn[602] ašajyš-

[69] [23] latsynlar[603] ǯanymny[604] da bašlyğyna[605] ḥanlyqlarnyn avaldağylaj qojğun bašymny[606].

[70] [24] Tašlamağyn[607] meni qyblalaryn alnyndan da vaḥtsyz almağyn menden ǯanymny[608] aziz alheminni.

[71] [25] [609]⌈נר מצוה⌋. Balquvlu janadoğan čyraq[610] kibik {jaryq}[611] Torağa da micvağa čynyq-

[72] [26] tyrğyn[612] meni, qoltqabyla e balquvum menim qaranğylyğymdada[613] ijgin onğalmaq

[73] [27] syzlavly[614] jarama da sözüne[615] köre[616] kiplegin[617] meni, qojğun meni avaldağylaj janğyrt[618]

[74] [28] künlerimni[619] da alğyšlağyn[620] bar išimni[621], qajtarğyn mana bijenčli[622] jarlyğašynny[623]

---

590 JSul.I.46: deest.

591 JSul.I.46: *sağyslar.* | JSul.III.07: *sağyslar.* | JSul.III.77: *sağyslar.*

592 JSul.III.66: *üčümde*; a hypercorrect form of *ičimde.* | JSul.I.46: *icimde.* | JSul.III.07: *icimde.* | JSul.III.77: *icimde.*

593 JSul.III.07: מתֹּי. | JSul.III.77: מתֹּי.

594 JSul.I.46: *raḥmetlevcü.* | JSul.III.07: *raḥmetlevci.* | JSul.III.77: *raḥmetlevci.*

595 JSul.I.46: *qacan.* | JSul.III.07: *qacan.* | JSul.III.77: *qacan.*

596 JSul.I.46: *qajrylysen.* | JSul.III.07: *qajrylysen.* | JSul.III.77: *qajrylysen.*

597 JSul.I.46: *küplevcü.* | JSul.III.07: *kiplevci.* | JSul.III.77: *kiplevci.*

598 JSul.I.46: *bikregenlerni.* | JSul.III.07: *bikregenlerni.* | JSul.III.77: *bikregenlerni.*

599 JSul.I.46: *etivcü.* | JSul.III.07: *etivci.* | JSul.III.77: *etivci.*

600 JSul.I.46: *ektemlerni.* | JSul.III.07: *ektemlerni.* | JSul.III.77: *ektemlerni.*

601 JSul.I.46: *kötirivcü.* | JSul.III.07: *ketirivci.* | JSul.III.77: *ketirivci.*

602 JSul.I.46: *jubatmaqlaryn.* | JSul.III.07: *jubatmaqlaryn.* | JSul.III.77: *jubatmaqlaryn.*

603 JSul.I.46: *asajyslatsynlar.* | JSul.III.07: *asajyslatsynlar.* | JSul.III.77: *asajyslatsynlar.*

604 JSul.I.46: *ʒanymny.* | JSul.III.07: *ʒanymny.* | JSul.III.77: *ʒanymny.*

605 JSul.I.46: *baslyğyna.* | JSul.III.07: *baslyğyna.* | JSul.III.77: *baslyğyna.*

606 JSul.I.46: *basymny.* | JSul.III.07: *basymny.* | JSul.III.77: *basymny.*

607 JSul.I.46: *taslamağyn.* | JSul.III.07: *taslamağyn.* | JSul.III.77: *taslamağyn.*

608 JSul.I.46: *ʒanymny.* | JSul.III.07: *ʒanymny.* | JSul.III.77: *ʒanymny.*

[65] [19] do create in me, O God, and renew the pleasant thoughts within me.

[66] [20] (13). O, merciful God, when will You turn towards me and (when) will You take me away from my great troubles (to be)

[67] [21] closer (to You), O, You who strengthen those who are bent and lower the (pride of those who are) haughty and

[68] [22] lift up those who are low; when will You have mercy on me? May Your comfort[624]

[69] [23] (to be brought to me) make my soul relish and place me[625] ahead of all the kingdoms, as it was before.

[70] [24] Cast me not away from before Your countenance and take not my soul, Your holy spirit, too soon away from me.

[71] [25] (14). Accustom[626] me to the bright[627] Law and commandment(s) as to a shiningly burning torch,

[72] [26] I beg You, O my light even[628] in my darkness, send healing

[73] [27] to my suffering wound and, according to Your word, strengthen me, regard me in a way You did before, renew

[74] [28] my days and bless all my deeds, restore unto me the joy of Your salvation

609 JSul.III.07: נֿר. | JSul.III.77: נר.

610 JSul.I.46: *cyraq*. | JSul.III.07: *cyraq*. | JSul.III.77: *cyraq*.

611 JSul.I.46: deest. | JSul.III.07: deest. | JSul.III.77: deest.

612 JSul.I.46: *qunusturġun*. | JSul.III.07: *qunusturġun*. | JSul.III.77: *qunusturġun*.

613 JSul.III.66: *qaranġylyġymda*. | JSul.I.46: *qaranġylyġymda*. | JSul.III.07: *qaranġylyġymda*. | JSul.III.77: *qaranġylyġymda*.

614 JSul.I.46: *syzlavlu*. | JSul.III.07: *syzlavlu*. | JSul.III.77: *syzlavlu*.

615 JSul.I.46: *sözine*. | JSul.III.07: *sezine*. | JSul.III.77: *sezine*.

616 JSul.III.07: *kere*. | JSul.III.77: *kere*.

617 JSul.I.46: *küplegin*; a hypercorrect form of *kiplegin*.

618 JSul.I.46: *janġyrtqyn*. | JSul.III.07: *janġyrtqyn*. | JSul.III.77: *janġyrtqyn*.

619 JSul.III.07: *kinlerimni*. | JSul.III.77: *kinlerimni*.

620 JSul.I.46: *alġyslaġyn*. | JSul.III.07: *alġyslaġyn*. | JSul.III.77: *alġyslaġyn*.

621 JSul.I.46: *isimni*. | JSul.III.07: *isimni*. | JSul.III.77: *isimni*.

622 JSul.I.46: *bijencli*. | JSul.III.07: *bijencli*. | JSul.III.77: *bijencli*.

623 JSul.I.46: *jarlyġasynny*. | JSul.III.07: *jarlyġasynny*. | JSul.III.77: *jarlyġasynny*.

624 JSul.I.46, JSul.III.07, JSul.III.77: expressed with a synonym.

625 Lit. 'my head'.

626 JSul.I.46: *rouse*. | JSul.III.07: *rouse*. | JSul.III.77: *rouse*.

627 JSul.I.46: deest. | JSul.III.07: deest. | JSul.III.77: deest.

628 JSul.III.66: deest. | JSul.I.46: deest. | JSul.III.07: deest. | JSul.III.77: deest.

[75] [29] da ǯomartlyq[629] alheminbyla[630] kiplegin[631] bašymny[632]. [633]⌈סוד דברך⌋. Ne tatyj-

[76] [30] dylar tanlajyma syr sözlerin[634] e Tenrim ki qajtqanda raša‘a jaman jollaryndan

129 v° [77] [1] jazyqlary bošatylyrlar[635]. Da ki har mode boluvču[636] jazyqlaryn jylamaqbyla da kemišüvčü[637]

[78] [2] jazyqly bolma raḥmetlenirler. Anlyq byla bolušqun[638] mana qutulma güneḥ-

[79] [3] lerimden[639] da ešittirejim[640] raša‘alarġa özümkibik[641] ki sana umsunġajlar.

[80] [4] Körgüz[642] mana bu šavaġatyjny[643] da üvretejim[644] güneḥlil[e]rge[645] jaḥšy[646] qylyqlarynny[647]

[81] [5] da bar jazyqlylar tügel[648] tešuvabyla sana qajtyrlar. [649]⌈ערוב עבדך⌋.

[82] [6] Qunušturġun[650] meni jaḥšy[651] išlerge[652] ki jarġu kününde[653] saġynmaġajsen mana raša‘a-

[83] [7] lyġymny, da bügünde[654] sürtkün[655] közlerimden jašlarymny[656] da bijendirgin küčlü[657]

[84] [8] qajġylarymdan da körgüz[658] mana e Tenrim jarlyġašynny[659]. Šavaġatyna[660] köre jaḥšy[661]

[85] [9] išlerge[662] tiri tutqun meni da ölčemegin[663] mana jamanlyġymny. Qoltqabyla

---

629 JSul.I.46: *ʒomartlyq.* | JSul.III.07: *ʒomartlyq.* | JSul.III.77: *ʒomartlyq.*

630 JSul.I.46: *alhem byla.* | JSul.III.07: *alhem byla.* | JSul.III.77: *alhem byla.*

631 JSul.I.46: *küplegin*; a hypercorrect form of *kiplegin.*

632 JSul.I.46: *basymny.* | JSul.III.07: *basymny.* | JSul.III.77: *basymny.*

633 JSul.I.46: סוֹד דבריך. | JSul.III.07: סוֹד. | JSul.III.77: סוֹד.

634 JSul.III.07: *sezlerin.* | JSul.III.77: *sezlerin.*

635 JSul.I.46: *bosatylyrlar.* | JSul.III.07: *bosatylyrlar.* | JSul.III.77: *bosatylyrlar.*

636 JSul.I.46: *boluvcu.* | JSul.III.07: *boluvcu.* | JSul.III.77: *boluvcu.*

637 JSul.I.46: *kemisivcü.* | JSul.III.07: *kemisivci.* | JSul.III.77: *kemisivci.*

638 JSul.I.46: *bolusqun.* | JSul.III.07: *bolusqun.* | JSul.III.77: *bolusqun.*

639 JSul.I.46: *gineḥlerimden.* | JSul.III.07: *gineḥlerimden.* | JSul.III.77: *gineḥlerimden.*

640 JSul.III.66: *ešittürejim*; a hypercorrect form of *ešittirejim.* | JSul.I.46: *esittirejim.* | JSul.III.07: *esittirejim.* | JSul.III.77: *esittirejim.*

641 JSul.I.46: *ezim kibik.* | JSul.III.07: *ezim kibik.* | JSul.III.77: *ezim kibik.*

642 JSul.I.46: *körgiz.* | JSul.III.07: *kergiz.* | JSul.III.77: *kergiz.*

643 JSul.III.66: *šavaġatynny.* | JSul.I.46: *savaġatynny.* | JSul.III.07: *savaġatynny.* | JSul.III.77: *savaġatynny.*

644 JSul.I.46: *ivretejim.* | JSul.III.07: *ivretejim.* | JSul.III.77: *ivretejim.*

645 JSul.I.01b: *güneḥlilrge*; a scribal error. | JSul.III.66: *güneḥlilerge.* | JSul.I.46: *gineḥlilerge.* | JSul.III.07: *gineḥlilerge.* | JSul.III.77: *gineḥlilerge.*

646 JSul.I.46: *jaḥsy.* | JSul.III.07: *jaḥsy.* | JSul.III.77: *jaḥsy.*

[75] [29] and strengthen me[664] with the generosity of Your[665] spirit. (15). How tasty

[76] [30] for my palate are Your words of secret, O, God of mine, (saying) that the sins of the wicked when they return from the the ways of evil

[77] [1] will be absolved and that all those who confess their sins with a cry and those who stop 129 vº

[78] [2] sinning will be taken pity on. With all this (in mind), help me to get free of my transgressions

[79] [3] and may I make the sinners like me hear that they should rest their hope in You.

[80] [4] Show me Your mercy and may I teach the transgressors Your good customs[666]

[81] [5] and all the sinners shall be converted to You with proper[667] repentance. (16).

[82] [6] Rouse me to good deeds so that in the day of verdict You would not remember my wickedness

[83] [7] and still today wipe out my tears from my eyes and please me

[84] [8] after (the times of) my great troubles and show me, O God, Your grace. According to Your mercy

[85] [9] keep me alive in order to do good deeds and do not measure my evilness. I beg You

---

647 JSul.I.46: *midalarynny.* | JSul.III.07: *midalarynny.* | JSul.III.77: *midalarynny.*
648 JSul.I.46: deest. | JSul.III.07: deest. | JSul.III.77: deest.
649 JSul.I.46: ער֒וב. | JSul.III.07: ער֒וב. | JSul.III.77: ער֒וב.
650 JSul.I.46: *qunusturġun.* | JSul.III.07: *qunusturġun.* | JSul.III.77: *qunusturġun.*
651 JSul.I.46: *jaḥsy.* | JSul.III.07: *jaḥsy.* | JSul.III.77: *jaḥsy.*
652 JSul.I.46: *islerge.* | JSul.III.07: *islerge.* | JSul.III.77: *islerge.*
653 JSul.III.07: *kininde.* | JSul.III.77: *kininde.*
654 JSul.I.46: *biginde.* | JSul.III.07: *biginde.* | JSul.III.77: *biginde.*
655 JSul.I.46: *sirtkin.* | JSul.III.07: *sirtkin.* | JSul.III.77: *sirtkin.*
656 JSul.I.46: *jaslarymny.* | JSul.III.07: *jaslarymny.* | JSul.III.77: *jaslarymny.*
657 JSul.I.46: *küclü.* | JSul.III.07: *kicli.* | JSul.III.77: *kicli.*
658 JSul.I.46: *körgizgün.* | JSul.III.07: *kergizgin.* | JSul.III.77: *kergizgin.*
659 JSul.I.46: *jarlyġasynny.* | JSul.III.07: *jarlyġasynny.* | JSul.III.77: *jarlyġasynny.*
660 JSul.I.46: *savaġatyna.* | JSul.III.07: *savaġatyna.* | JSul.III.77: *savaġatyna.*
661 JSul.I.46: *jaḥsy.* | JSul.III.07: *jaḥsy.* | JSul.III.77: *jaḥsy.*
662 JSul.I.46: *islerge.* | JSul.III.07: *islerge.* | JSul.III.77: *islerge.*
663 JSul.I.46: *elcemegin.* | JSul.III.07: *elcemegin.* | JSul.III.77: *elcemegin.*
664 Lit. 'my head'.
665 JSul.I.46: deest. | JSul.III.07: deest. | JSul.III.77: deest.
666 JSul.I.46: *measures.* | JSul.III.07: *measures.* | JSul.III.77: *measures.*
667 JSul.I.46: deest. | JSul.III.07: deest. | JSul.III.77: deest.

[86] [10] jarlyġašly[668] Tenrim qanly išlerden[669] qutqarġyn meni. [670]⌈פדני מכל רע⌋. Juluġun

[87] [11] meni bar jamandan da jaḥšy[671] ḥabarly etkin meni ajtadoġač[672] ešittim[673] firjatynny,

[88] [12] qorqmaġyn zavally bošatylyr[674] jazyġyn ki qabul ettim jylamaqly qoltqanny. E bijim

[89] [13] Tenrim qylġyn mana bu jaḥšylyqny[675] da qotaryrm̀en[676] bar kelivčülerge[677] baġatyrlyġynny,

[90] [14] sarnar tilim rastlyġynny. [678]⌈צורי למדתני⌋. Kör[679] jaratuvčum[680] ki nečik[681]

[91] [15] üvrettin[682] mana qorquvunnu ⌊jašlyq künümden⌉[683] alaj halide anlatamen ullu-

[92] [16] luġunnu, da eger adamlyġyma köre[684] jazyqly bolamen[685] sana muna[686] har kün[687]

[93] [17] tilim qotarady maḥtavunnu. Ahah aziz atam kör[688] ki bijenčli[689] jürekbyla[690]

[94] [18] tözemen[691] alġyšynny[692] da bošatlyġynny[693], bilemen ki sen H[694] ačasen[695] erinlerimni da

[95] [19] avzum anlatady maḥtavunnu. [696]⌈קדוש ונורא⌋. E aziz da qorqunčlu[697] Tenrim

[96] [20] tuzaġyndan güneḥlerimnin[698] azatlyqqa meni čyġarġyn[699], alajoq meni ačy[700] ǯanly[701]

---

668 JSul.I.46: *jarlyġasly.* | JSul.III.07: *jarlyġasly.* | JSul.III.77: *jarlyġasly.*

669 JSul.I.46: *islerden.* | JSul.III.07: *islerden.* | JSul.III.77: *islerden.*

670 JSul.I.46: פְּדֵנִי. | JSul.III.07: פְּדֵנִי. | JSul.III.77: פְּדֵנִי.

671 JSul.I.46: *jaḥsy.* | JSul.III.07: *jaḥsy.* | JSul.III.77: *jaḥsy.*

672 JSul.I.46: *ajtadoġac.* | JSul.III.07: *ajtadoġac.* | JSul.III.77: *ajtadoġac.*

673 JSul.I.46: *esittim.* | JSul.III.07: *esittim.* | JSul.III.77: *esittim.*

674 JSul.I.46: *bosatylyr.* | JSul.III.07: *bosatylyr.* | JSul.III.77: *bosatylyr.*

675 JSul.I.46: *jaḥsylyqny.* | JSul.III.07: *jaḥsylyqny.* | JSul.III.77: *jaḥsylyqny.*

676 JSul.I.46: *qotarymen.* | JSul.III.07: *qotarymen.* | JSul.III.77: *qotarymen.*

677 JSul.III.66: *kelivčilerge.* | JSul.I.46: *kelivcilerge.* | JSul.III.07: *kelivcilerge.* | JSul.III.77: *kelivcilerge.*

678 JSul.I.46: צוֹרִי. | JSul.III.07: צוֹרִי. | JSul.III.77: צורי.

679 JSul.III.07: *ker.* | JSul.III.77: *ker.*

680 JSul.I.46: *jaratuvcum.* | JSul.III.07: *jaratuvcum.* | JSul.III.77: *jaratuvcum.*

681 JSul.I.46: *necik.* | JSul.III.07: *necik.* | JSul.III.77: *necik.*

682 JSul.I.46: *ivrettin.* | JSul.III.07: *ivrettin.* | JSul.III.77: *ivrettin.*

683 JSul.I.46: *jaslyqlarymdan.* | JSul.III.07: *jaslyqlarymdan.* | JSul.III.77: *jaslyqlarymdan.*

684 JSul.III.07: *kere.* | JSul.III.77: *kere.*

685 JSul.III.66: *bolamen ese.* | JSul.I.46: *boldum ese.* | JSul.III.07: *boldum ese.* | JSul.III.77: *boldum ese.*

[86] [10] my merciful God, save me from ⌊the guilt of bloodshed⌋[702]. (17). Redeem
[87] [11] me from all the evil, make me ⌊receive good news⌋[703] by saying 'I heard your cry,
[88] [12] fear not, miserable, your sin will be absolved for I have accepted your teary prayer'. O, my Lord
[89] [13] God, do this good thing to me and I shall preach Your powerfulness for those to come,
[90] [14] my tongue shall sing aloud of Your righteousness. (18). See, my creator, that as
[91] [15] You have taught me to fear You from ⌊the day of⌋[704] my youth on, so do I now call
[92] [16] Your greatness, and if I am sinful to You according to my human nature, lo,
[93] [17] my tongue preaches Your praise. O, my holy father, see that
[94] [18] I wait for Your blessing and forgiveness with a joyful heart, I know that it is You, Lord[705], who open my lips and
[95] [19] my mouth calls Your praise. (19). O my holy and awesome God,
[96] [20] ⌊free me⌋[706] from the snare of my transgressions as well as ⌊save me⌋[707], Your sad servant,

---

686 JSul.I.46: deest. | JSul.III.07: deest. | JSul.III.77: deest.
687 JSul.III.07: *kin.* | JSul.III.77: *kin.*
688 JSul.III.07: *ker.* | JSul.III.77: *ker.*
689 JSul.I.46: *bijencli.* | JSul.III.77: *bijencli.*
690 JSul.III.07: *jirek byla.* | JSul.III.77: *jirek byla.*
691 JSul.I.46: *tezemen.* | JSul.III.07: *tezemen.* | JSul.III.77: *tezemen.*
692 JSul.I.46: *alġysynny.* | JSul.III.07: *alġysynny.* | JSul.III.77: *alġysynny.*
693 JSul.I.46: *bosatlyġynny.* | JSul.III.07: *bosatlyġynny.* | JSul.III.77: *bosatlyġynny.*
694 JSul.I.46: *e H.* | JSul.III.07: *e H.* | JSul.III.77: *e H.*
695 JSul.I.46: *acasen.* | JSul.III.07: *acasen.* | JSul.III.77: *acasen.*
696 JSul.I.46: קדוש. | JSul.III.07: קדוש. | JSul.III.77: קדוש.
697 JSul.I.46: *qorqunclu.* | JSul.III.07: *qorqunclu.* | JSul.III.77: *qorqunclu.*
698 JSul.I.46: *ginehlerimnin.* | JSul.III.07: *ginehlerimnin.* | JSul.III.77: *ginehlerimnin.*
699 JSul.I.46: *cyġarġyn.* | JSul.III.07: *cyġarġyn.* | JSul.III.77: *cyġarġyn.*
700 JSul.I.46: *acy.* | JSul.III.07: *acy.* | JSul.III.77: *acy.*
701 JSul.I.46: *ʒanly.* | JSul.III.07: *ʒanly.* | JSul.III.77: *ʒanly.*
702 Lit. 'from bloody deeds'.
703 Lit. 'be of good news'.
704 JSul.I.46: deest. | JSul.III.07: deest. | JSul.III.77: deest.
705 JSul.I.46: *O Lord.* | JSul.III.07: *O Lord.* | JSul.III.77: *O Lord.*
706 Lit. 'bring me out to freedom'.
707 JSul.I.46: *save me with Your mercy.* | JSul.III.07: *save me with Your mercy.* | JSul.III.77: *save me with Your mercy.*

[97] [21] qulunnu[708] avur jazyqlarymdan qutqarġyn, ki muna özün[709] bildirdin ki bolur

[98] [22] bošatlyq[710] jazyqlaryna qajtuvčularnyn[711] tešuvabyla sana anyn üčün[712] körgün[713]

[99] [23] qajtqanymny sana[714] da ḥajifsüngün[715], ki klemejsen debeḥany da bergejedim da ʿolany-

[100] [24] d[a][716] süvmejsen[717] anyn üčün[718] bu aruv qoltqamny qabul etkin[719].

[101] [25] [720]⌜ראה עניי⌟. Küčlü[721] miskinligimni da qyjynymny da synyq ǯanymny[722] alnynda

[102] [26] bügün[723] bilgin, da jaryqqa čyġarma[724] töremni[725] da jarġumnu šavaġatyndan[726] tezče[727]

[103] [27] ojanġyn, da nečik[728] jaḥšyraq[729] ʿoladan da debeḥadan süvesen[730] synyq ǯanny[731] alaj aryt-

[104] [28] tym ǯanymny[732] ančaq[733] süvgün[734], da anyn üčün[735] bu synyq tefilamny[736] širin[737] körgün[738].

[105] [29] [739]⌜שיחי בזעקי⌟. Alajoq bu tefilamde[740] qolamen ki ölgenimden[741] sortun

130 rº [106] [1] jaryqlyġyn qyblalarynnyn körgejmen[742], da tösü[743] kibik ol tenufanyn da inčigi[744]

---

708 JSul.I.46: *qulunnu savaġatyn byla.* | JSul.III.07: *qulunnu savaġatyn byla.* | JSul.III.77: *qulunnu savaġatyn byla.*

709 JSul.I.46: *ezin.* | JSul.III.07: *ezin.* | JSul.III.77: *ezin.*

710 JSul.I.46: *bosatlyq.* | JSul.III.07: *bosatlyq.* | JSul.III.77: *bosatlyq.*

711 JSul.I.46: *qajtavcularnyn.* | JSul.III.07: *qajtavcularnyn.* | JSul.III.77: *qajtavcularnyn.*

712 JSul.I.46: *ücün.* | JSul.III.07: *icin.* | JSul.III.77: *icin.*

713 JSul.I.46: *körgin.* | JSul.III.07: *kergin.* | JSul.III.77: *kergin.*

714 JSul.I.46: deest. | JSul.III.07: deest. | JSul.III.77: deest.

715 JSul.III.66: *ḥajifsingün.* | JSul.I.46: *ḥajifsingin.* | JSul.III.07: *ḥajifsingin.* | JSul.III.77: *ḥajifsingin.*

716 JSul.I.01b: *ʿolanydy*; a scribal error. | JSul.III.66: *ʿolanyda.* | JSul.I.46: *ʿolanyda.* | JSul.III.07: *ʿolanyda.* | JSul.III.77: *ʿolanyda.*

717 JSul.III.66: *sivmejsen.* | JSul.I.46: *sivmejsen.* | JSul.III.07: *sivmejsen.* | JSul.III.77: *sivmejsen.*

718 JSul.I.46: *ücün.* | JSul.III.07: *icin.* | JSul.III.77: *icin.*

719 JSul.I.46: *körgin.* | JSul.III.07: *kergin.* | JSul.III.77: *kergin.*

720 JSul.I.46: ראֹה. | JSul.III.07: ראֹה. | JSul.III.77: ראֹה.

721 JSul.I.46: *küclü.* | JSul.III.07: *kicli.* | JSul.III.77: *kicli.*

722 JSul.I.46: *ʒanymny.* | JSul.III.07: *ʒanymny.* | JSul.III.77: *ʒanymny.*

723 JSul.III.07: *bigin.* | JSul.III.77: *bigin.*

724 JSul.I.46: *cyġarma.* | JSul.III.07: *cyġarma.* | JSul.III.77: *cyġarma.*

725 JSul.III.66: *teremni.* | JSul.I.46: *teremni.* | JSul.III.07: *teremni.* | JSul.III.77: *teremni.*

726 JSul.I.46: *savaġatyndan.* | JSul.III.07: *savaġatyndan.* | JSul.III.77: *savaġatyndan.*

[97] [21] from my grave[745] sins for, lo, You Yourself have announced that there will be

[98] [22] forgiveness for the sins of those who return to You with repentance. Therefore see

[99] [23] my return to You and have mercy, for You desire not sacrifice—else would I give it—and

[100] [24] You delight not in burnt offering: (so) therefore accept my clean prayer.

[101] [25] (20). Today, You shall know my misery and suffering and (the presence of) my repentant soul before You,

[102] [26] and, through Your grace, wake up to reveal swiftly my law and my verdict,

[103] [27] but as You like a contrite heart more than burnt offering and sacrifice, so have I cleansed

[104] [28] my soul just (so that) You (will) love it, and therefore ⌊may my prayer seem amiable to You⌋[746].

[105] [29] (21). Also, in this prayer of mine I ask You that I may see the light of Your countenance after my death and

[106] [1] that I may be accepted along with my words, like the udder of the wave offering and the thigh 130 rº

727 JSul.I.46: *tezce.* | JSul.III.07: *tezce.* | JSul.III.77: *tezce.*

728 JSul.I.46: *necik.* | JSul.III.07: *necik.* | JSul.III.77: *necik.*

729 JSul.I.46: *jaḥsyraq.* | JSul.III.07: *jaḥsyraq.* | JSul.III.77: *jaḥsyraq.*

730 JSul.I.46: *sivesen.* | JSul.III.07: *sivesen.* | JSul.III.77: *sivesen.*

731 JSul.I.46: *ʒanny.* | JSul.III.07: *ʒanny.* | JSul.III.77: *ʒanny.*

732 JSul.I.46: *ʒanymny.* | JSul.III.07: *ʒanymny.* | JSul.III.77: *ʒanymny.*

733 JSul.I.46: *ancaq.* | JSul.III.07: *ancaq.* | JSul.III.77: *ancaq.*

734 JSul.I.46: *sivgin.* | JSul.III.07: *sivgin.* | JSul.III.77: *sivgin.*

735 JSul.I.46: *ücün.* | JSul.III.07: *icin.* | JSul.III.77: *icin.*

736 JSul.I.01b: or: *tefilamni*; see line 105. | JSul.III.66: *tefilemni.* | JSul.III.07: *tefilemni.* | JSul.III.77: *tefilemni.*

737 JSul.I.46: or: *sirin.* | JSul.III.07: *sirin.* | JSul.III.77: *sirin.*

738 JSul.I.46: *körgin.* | JSul.III.07: *kergin.* | JSul.III.77: *kergin.*

739 JSul.III.07: שיׄחי. | JSul.III.77: שיׄחי.

740 JSul.III.66: *tefilemde.* | JSul.I.46: *tefilemde.* | JSul.III.07: *tefilemde.* | JSul.III.77: *tefilemde.*

741 JSul.I.46: *elgenimden.* | JSul.III.07: *elgenimden.* | JSul.III.77: *elgenimden.*

742 JSul.III.07: *kergejmen.* | JSul.III.77: *kergejmen.*

743 JSul.III.66: *tešü.* | JSul.I.46: *tesi.* | JSul.III.07: *tesi.* | JSul.III.77: *tesi.*

744 JSul.III.66: *imčigi.* | JSul.I.46: *imcigi.* | JSul.III.07: *imcigi.* | JSul.III.77: *imcigi.*

745 Lit. 'heavy'.

746 Lit. 'see my prayer (as something) amiable'.

[107] [2] kibik ol terumanyn sözlerimbyla[747] qabul bolġajmen, ki čaġyrġanymda[748] sana

[108] [3] jarġu kününde[749] qutqarma meni očaġyndan[750] geḥinnomnun tezče[751] mana qaruv

[109] [4] bergejsen, ajtadoġač[752] bumodu[753] ol synyq ǯanly[754] alnymda hanuz[755] tiri ege-

[110] [5] ninde[756] bunčaġadejin[757] ⌞meni e Tenrim⌟[758] ḥorlamaġajsen. [760]⌜תדיק צרי״[759]⌟.

[111] [6] Hem[761] qoltqam[762] menim barda ulusun üčün[763] qabul bolsun sana ki dušmanlaryn[764]

[112] [7] jančqajsen[765] joqluqqa nečik[766] qurġaq orunda qubrany, da ki jalbarmaġyn

[113] [8] onča[767] ulusunnun ešitkejsen[768] da sürtkejsen[769] közlerinden[770] alarnyn jylaġan

[114] [9] jašlarny[771], da aziz šaharymyzny[772] Jerušalajimni qondarġyn da anda toḥtatqyn

[115] [10] endi e bijim qorqunčlu[773] šeḫinanny, alajoq šavaġatyndan[774] öz[775] kleginbyla

[116] [11] tüzetkin[776] Cijjonnu toḥtav šaharynny[777]. [778]⌜אומה ענייה⌟. Miskin umasyn

[117] [12] Jisra'elnin[779] bar otračlarda[780] ol tozulġanny[781], qutqarġyn any bu ačy[782] galuttan ol

---

747 JSul.III.07: *sezlerim byla.* | JSul.III.77: *sezlerim byla.*

748 JSul.I.46: *caġyrġanymda.* | JSul.III.07: *caġyrġanymda.* | JSul.III.77: *caġyrġanymda.*

749 JSul.III.07: *kininde.* | JSul.III.77: *kininde.*

750 JSul.I.46: *ocaġyndan.* | JSul.III.07: *ocaġyndan.* | JSul.III.77: *ocaġyndan.*

751 JSul.I.46: *tezce.* | JSul.III.07: *tezce.* | JSul.III.77: *tezce.*

752 JSul.I.46: *ajtadoġac.* | JSul.III.07: *ajtadoġac.* | JSul.III.77: *ajtadoġac.*

753 JSul.III.66: *bumudu.* | JSul.III.07: *bumodur.* | JSul.III.77: *bumodur.*

754 JSul.I.46: *ʒanly.* | JSul.III.07: *ʒanly.* | JSul.III.77: *ʒanly.*

755 JSul.III.66: deest.

756 JSul.III.66: *ögeninde*; a hypercorrect form of *egeninde.*

757 JSul.I.46: *buncaġadejin.* | JSul.III.07: *buncaġadejin.* | JSul.III.77: *buncaġadejin.*

758 JSul.I.46: *e Tenrim meni.* | JSul.III.07: *e Tenrim meni.* | JSul.III.77: *e Tenrim meni.*

759 An abbreviation of Heb. צָרִים.

760 JSul.I.46: תדׄיק. | JSul.III.07: תדׄיק. | JSul.III.77: תדיק.

761 JSul.III.07: *ham.* | JSul.III.77: *ham.*

762 JSul.I.46: *qoltqamda.*

763 JSul.I.46: *ücün.* | JSul.III.07: *icin.* | JSul.III.77: *icin.*

764 JSul.I.46: *dusmanlarymny.* | JSul.III.07: *dusmanlarymny.* | JSul.III.77: *dusmanlarymny.*

765 JSul.I.46: *jancqajsen.* | JSul.III.07: *jancqajsen.* | JSul.III.77: *jancqajsen.*

[107] [2] of the *terumah*, and that You may reply me swiftly when I will call to You
[108] [3] in order to save me from the fire of hell,
[109] [4] saying, 'Is this that broken hearted before me being still[783] alive?',
[110] [5] ⌊O God of mine⌋[784], may You not condemn me that much. (22).
[111] [6] And may[785] my prayer for the whole nation be accepted: that You may
[112] [7] annihilate its[786] enemies like the hay[787] in a dry place and that
[113] [8] You may hear the prayer of Your chosen people and that You may wipe out from their eyes
[114] [9] the tears (they) cried: and build our holy city, Jerusalem, and place there
[115] [10] now Your awesome divine Presence, O my lord, in the same way You would
[116] [11] ⌊do good⌋[788], through Your grace and (in accordance) with Your own wish, to Zion, Your place of living. (23). Save the miserable people
[117] [12] of Israel, dispersed on all the isles, from the bitter[789],

766 JSul.I.46: *necik.* | JSul.III.07: *necik.* | JSul.III.77: *necik.*
767 JSul.I.46: *onca.* | JSul.III.07: *onca.* | JSul.III.77: *onca.*
768 JSul.I.46: *esitkejsen.* | JSul.III.07: *esitkejsen.* | JSul.III.77: *esitkejsen.*
769 JSul.I.46: *sirtkin.* | JSul.III.07: *sirtkin.* | JSul.III.77: *sirtkin.*
770 JSul.III.07: *kezlerinden.* | JSul.III.77: *kezlerinden.*
771 JSul.I.46: *jaslarny.* | JSul.III.07: *jaslarny.* | JSul.III.77: *jaslarny.*
772 JSul.I.46: *saharymyzny.* | JSul.III.07: *saharymyzny.* | JSul.III.77: *saharymyzny.*
773 JSul.I.46: *qorqunclu.* | JSul.III.07: *qorqunclu.* | JSul.III.77: *qorqunclu.*
774 JSul.I.46: *savahatyndan.* | JSul.III.07: *savahatyndan.* | JSul.III.77: *savahatyndan.*
775 JSul.I.46: *ez.* | JSul.III.07: *ez.* | JSul.III.77: *ez.*
776 JSul.I.46: *tizetkin.* | JSul.III.07: *tiz etkin.* | JSul.III.77: *tiz etkin.*
777 JSul.I.46: *saharynny.* | JSul.III.07: *saharynny.* | JSul.III.77: *saharynny.*
778 JSul.III.07: אוֹמה. | JSul.III.77: אומה. || Cf. אוֹם עֲנִיָּה in *Siddur* (1528/1529: 202 v°).
779 JSul.III.66: *Jisra'elni*; a scribal error.
780 JSul.I.46: *otraclarda.* | JSul.III.07: *otraclarda.* | JSul.III.77: *otraclarda.*
781 JSul.I.46: *tozulġanlarny.* | JSul.III.07: *tozulġanlarny.* | JSul.III.77: *tozulġanlarny.*
782 JSul.I.46: deest. | JSul.III.07: deest. | JSul.III.77: deest.
783 JSul.III.66: deest.
784 JSul.I.46, JSul.III.07, JSul.III.77: different word order.
785 JSul.I.46: *may even.*
786 JSul.I.46: *my.* | JSul.III.07: *my.* | JSul.III.77: *my.*
787 Or: *straw ~ blackthorn ~ woodbine*; see EKar. *qubra ~ quvra* in KarRPS (372; 373).
788 Lit. 'repair'; cf. Psalm 51:18.
789 JSul.I.46: deest. | JSul.III.07: deest. | JSul.III.77: deest.

[118] [13] qaty da unutmaġyn firjatlarybyla miskin[790] muḥtačlarny[791], ⌊alajoq raḥmetlerin-

[119] [14] byla qondar[792] ol aziz jerinde[793] qalalarybyla Jerušalajimni⌋[794], da šavaġatynbyla[795]

[120] [15] köndergin[796] ary ačy[797] ǯanly[798] ulusunnu ullu tarlyqlardan jubanġanlarny.

[121] [16] [799]⌈רעה עמך⌋. Alajoq qondarġyn veren bolġan miqdašynny ki edi[800]

[122] [17] qondarylġan qyjasyba[801] kise kavodnun da ol ḥajot qodešnin[802] ki ediler navilerge

[123] [18] körüngenler[803], da anda jumuš[804] etsinler[805] alnynda senin naviler kohenler

[124] [19] nasiler da bar törečiler[806]. Da ol aziz tavda küttürgün[807] ulusunnu

[125] [20] Jisra'elni ki tynčalġajlar[808] ullu tarlyqlar ičine[809] tünkelgenler[810], ki anda

[126] [21] klersen rastlyqbyla juvutqan debeḥalarny da tügel[811] qarbanlarny anda čyġaryrlar[812]

[127] [22] mizbeaḥyn üstüne[813] tanalar. [814]⌈הושיעה את עמך וכול'⌋.

---

790 JSul.I.46: *ac.* | JSul.III.07: *ac.* | JSul.III.77: *ac.*

791 JSul.I.46: *muḥtaclarny.* | JSul.III.07: *muḥtaclarny.* | JSul.III.77: *muḥtaclarny.*

792 JSul.I.46: *qondarġyn.* | JSul.III.07: *qondarġyn.* | JSul.III.77: *qondarġyn.*

793 JSul.I.46: *jerde.* | JSul.III.07: *jerde.* | JSul.III.77: *jerde.*

794 JSul.I.46: the copyist or some other person has included the note explaining that this fragment should follow the subsequent part of the clause, i.e. that it shoud be read after the fragment beginning with *da savaġatynbyla* in line 119 and ending in *jubanġanlarny* in line 120.

795 JSul.I.46: *savaġatynbyla.* | JSul.III.07: *savaġatyn byla.* | JSul.III.77: *savaġatyn byla.*

796 JSul.III.07: *kendergin.* | JSul.III.07: *kendergin.* | JSul.III.77: *kendergin.*

797 JSul.I.46: *acy.* | JSul.III.07: *acy.* | JSul.III.77: *ycy*; a scribal error.

798 JSul.I.46: *ʒanly.* | JSul.III.07: *ʒanly.* | JSul.III.77: *ʒanly.*

799 JSul.I.46: רעֹה. | JSul.III.07: רעֹה. | JSul.III.77: רעה.

800 JSul.III.66: *ödi*; a hypercorrect form of *edi.*

801 JSul.I.01b: amended to: *qyjasybyla.* | JSul.III.66: *qyjasy byla.* | JSul.I.46: *qyjasy byla.* | JSul.III .07: *qyjasy byla.* | JSul.III.77: *qyjasy byla.*

802 JSul.I.46: *haqodešnin*; i.e. used with the Hebrew definite article; cf. JSul.III.07 and JSul.III .77. | JSul.III.07: *haqodešnin.* | JSul.III.77: *haqodešnin.*

803 JSul.III.66: *köringenler.* | JSul.III.07: *keringenler.* | JSul.III.77: *keringenler.*

804 JSul.I.46: *jumus.* | JSul.III.07: *jumus.* | JSul.III.77: *jumus.*

805 JSul.I.46: *eterler.* | JSul.III.07: *eterler.* | JSul.III.77: *eterler.*

806 JSul.I.46: *tereciler.* | JSul.III.07: *tereciler.* | JSul.III.77: *tereciler.*

807 JSul.III.66: *küttirgin.* | JSul.I.46: *kittirgin.* | JSul.III.07: *kittirgin.* | JSul.III.77: *kittirgin.*

[118] [13] hard exile and do not forget the miserable[815] worried (people) and their cries, and, through Your mercy,
[119] [14] build also the holy place of Jerusalem along with its walls, and, through Your grace,
[120] [15] guide there Your sad people (being) gladdened after (the times of) great misery.
[121] [16] (24). Likewise, rebuild the destroyed shrine of Yours which was
[122] [17] built according to the measure of the throne of Your reputation and (according to the measure) of the living sanctity that
[123] [18] appeared to the prophets, and ⌊may the prophets, priests and all the judges serve[1816] there before You.
[124] [19] And graze Your people, Israel, on the holy mountain
[125] [20] so that they may repose, they who wandered in great miseries, and there
[126] [21] You shall wish for the sacrifices and true offerings brought to You with righteousness: there shall they offer
[127] [22] bullocks upon Your altar. ⌊'Save your people,' and so forth.[1817]

---

808 JSul.I.46: *tync alġajlar.* | JSul.III.07: *tync alġajlar.* | JSul.III.77: *tync alġajlar.*

809 JSul.III.66: *üčüne*; a hypercorrect form of *ičine.* | JSul.I.46: *icine.* | JSul.III.07: *icine.* | JSul.III .77: *icine.*

810 JSul.I.46: *tinkelgenler.* | JSul.III.07: *tinkelgenler.* | JSul.III.77: *tinkelgenler.*

811 JSul.III.07: *tigel.* | JSul.III.77: *tigel.*

812 JSul.I.46: *cyġaryrlar.* | JSul.III.07: *cyġaryrlar.* | JSul.III.77: *cyġaryrlar.*

813 JSul.I.46: *istine.* | JSul.III.07: *istine.* | JSul.III.77: *istine.*

814 Psalm 28:9. | JSul.III.66: ותאמר הוֹשִׁיעָה אֶת עַמֶּךָ וּבָרֵךְ אֶת נַחֲלָתֶךָ וּרְעֵם וְנַשְּׂאֵם עַד הָעוֹלָם. (Psalm 28:9). | JSul.I.46: הוֹשִׁיעָה אֶת עַמֶּךָ וגו׳. (Psalm 28:9). | JSul.III.07: אָז יַעֲלוּ עַל מִזְבַּחֲךָ פָרִים: הוֹשִׁיעָה אֶת עַמֶּךָ וגו׳. (Psalm 51:19) | JSul.III.77: הוֹשִׁיעָה אֶת עַמֶּךָ וּבָרֵךְ אֶת נַחֲלָתֶךָ וּרְעֵם וְנַשְּׂאֵם עַד הָעוֹלָם: בָּרוּךְ ה׳ לְעוֹלָם אָמֵן וְאָמֵן. (Psalm 51:19, Psalm 28:9, Psalm 89:52).

815 JSul.I.46: *ravenous.* | JSul.III.07: *ravenous.* | JSul.III.77: *ravenous.*

816 JSul.I.46: *the prophets, priests and all the judges will serve.* | JSul.III.07: *the prophets, priests and all the judges will serve.* | JSul.III.77: *the prophets, priests and all the judges will serve.*

817 Psalm 28:9. | JSul.III.66: *And you will say 'Save your people, and bless your inheritance: feed them also, and lift them up forever'.* (Psalm 28:9). | JSul.I.46: *'Save your people …' and so on.* (Psalm 28:9). | JSul.III.07: *'Then shall they offer bullocks upon your altar. Save your people …' and so on.* (Psalm 51:19; Psalm 28:9). | JSul.III.77: *'Then shall they offer bullocks upon your altar. Save your people, and bless your inheritance: feed them also, and lift them up forever. Blessed be the Lord forevermore. Amen, and Amen.'* (Psalm 51:19, Psalm 28:9, Psalm 89:52).

# PART 2

## *A* peshat *of Mordechai ben Icchak Łokszyński*

∵

**Text number:** № 4
**Karaim incipit:** *E küčlü Tenrim kipligim galutumda*
*E küclü Tenrim küpligim galutumda*
*E küclü Tenri kipligim galutumda*
**Hebrew incipit:** אֱיָלוּתִי בְּגָלוּתִי *ʾĕyålūṯī*[1] *bḡålūṯī*
**Dedication:** The third Shabbat of the month Tammuz
**Language:** Early Mod.SWKar., Mod.SWKar.
**Number of copies:** 3

| Accession no. | Place of origin of copy | Date of copy | Copyist | Folios |
|---|---|---|---|---|
| JSul.III.63 | Halych | ca. 1778 (before 1797) | Jeshua Mordkowicz | 39 rº–39 vº |
| JSul.III.73 | Halych | mid-19th c. | Jeshua Josef Mordkowicz | 103 rº–103 vº |
| JSul.I.16 | Halych | turn of the 20th c. | Unknown 14 | 288 rº–290 rº |

## 1 Introductory Remarks

All copies are vocalized. In JSul.III.63, the poem is termed *qinah*, but in the two other manuscripts it is described as *piyyut*. JSul.III.63 contains a form exhibiting the NWKar. **ŋ* > *j* change, namely *saja* (4), which suggests that it was copied on the basis of a North-Western Karaim original. The versions in JSul.III.73 and JSul.I.16 differ in just three instances, see *Tenrim* vs. *Tenri* (4): *Tenri* vs. *Tenrim* (5), *saharlaryn* vs. *saharlary* (7), and *aziz kohenlerimnin* vs. *kohenlerimnin* (26). In contrast to the latter two copies, the one in JSul.III.63 exhibits a number of unique differences, see *kötürümen* vs. *men kötiremen* ~ *men ketiremen* (4), *qaḥyrlarbyla* vs. *qaḥyr byla* (6), *tilsizlendim* vs. *tilsiz boldum* (14), *kötürelmedim* vs. *kötirelmejmen* (14), *qojdular* vs. *alar qojdular* (16), *azašqanlaryn tozulġan* vs. *tozulġanlaryn* (26), the use of *ki* (12), *bu* (13), etc. The following tentative diagram of the connections between the copies can be drawn:

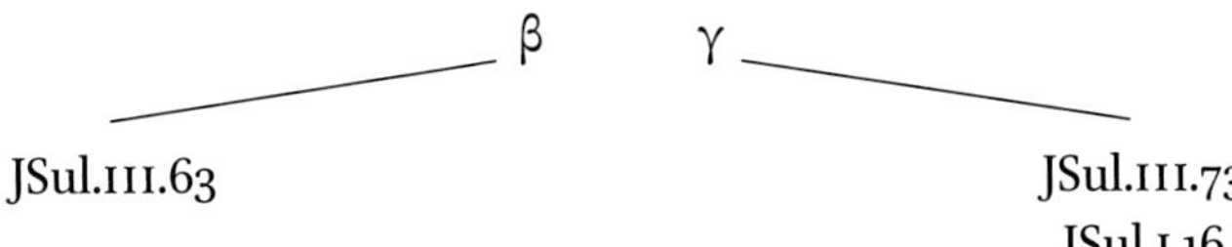


FIGURE 7 Diagram of the connections between the copies of peshat № 4

1 Spelled אֱיָלוּתִי in *Siddur* (1737: 26 vº).

## 2 Transcription[2] and Translation

39 rº

[1] [3] ⌊ובזה אכתוב עוד פשט אחת מתורגם על קינת איילוֹֿתי בגֿלותי שהוא נקראת בעת הצהרים

[2] [4] במנחת שבת שלישות משבתות תמוז שתרגמו אזֿ מוהֿרר מרדכי נֿע בכמֿער יצחק נֿע

[3] [5] וזו היא הפשט תאֿמ כנגין הגירסא ׳ אוולוֹֿתי בגֿלותי⌉[3]

[4] [6] E küčlü[4] Tenrim[5] kipligim[6] galutumda saja[7] jalġyzġa kötürümen[8]

[5] [7] közlerimni[9]. E Tenri[10] tölevčü[11] öčler[12] raša‘alarġa bajlanġyn

[6] [8] qaḥyrlarbyla[13] qaratetme barda[14] qonšularymny[15]. Sedomnun šaharlaryn[16] kibik

[7] [9] aḥtarġyn jerlerin Edomnun, ki alar ediler veren etivčüler[17] sarajlarymny.

[8] [10] Quvġun ačuvbyla[18] da ⌊tas etkin⌉[19] alarny e H tübünden[20] ol köklernin[21].

[9] [11] ⌊והפזמון אחר כל בית: *Quvġun ačuvbyla*.⌉[22] ⌊זכוֹר חרֿפת⌉[23]

---

2 Based on JSul.III.63. In JSul.III.73 and JSul.I.16, the punctuation mark *sof pasuq* is used to indicate both sentence or clause endings and the verse boundaries of the Hebrew original. In the latter role, *sof pasuq* is not taken into consideration in the transcription. The sentence endings are reconstructed based on all three copies.

3 JSul.III.73: וזה הפשט לפיוט איילותי בגלותי הנאמר במנחה שלישית משבתות תמוז תרגמו אמֿו ההֿו כמוהֿרר מרדכי נבֿת באמֿו כמוהֿרר יצחק המכונה לוקסינשקיי יעמש: איֿלותי בגֿלותי. The spelling of the surname (לוקסינשקיי) suggests the reading *Loksynśkyj*. | JSul.I.16: הא לך פשטו חברו כמוהֿרר מרדכי נבֿת בכמֿעד יצחק המכונה לוקשינשקיי זצלֿהה. The spelling of the surname (לוקשינשקיי) suggests the reading *Lokšynśkyj*.

4 JSul.III.75: *küclü*. | JSul.I.16: *kicli*.

5 JSul.I.16: *Tenri*.

6 JSul.III.73: *küpligim*; a hypercorrect form of *kipligim*. | JSul.I.16: *kipligim*.

7 JSul.III.73: *sana*. | JSul.I.16: *sana*.

8 JSul.III.73: *men kötiremen*. | JSul.I.16: *men ketiremen*.

9 JSul.III.73: *osol közlerimni*. | JSul.I.16: *kezlerimni*.

10 JSul.I.16: *Tenrim*.

11 JSul.III.73: *televci*. | JSul.I.16: *televci*.

12 JSul.III.73: *ecler*. | JSul.I.16: *ecler*.

13 JSul.III.73: *qaḥyr byla*. | JSul.I.16: *qaḥyr byla*.

14 JSul.III.73: *osol barda*. | JSul.I.16: *osol barda*.

15 JSul.III.73: *qonsularymny*. | JSul.I.16: *qonsularymny*.

16 JSul.III.73: *saharlaryn*. | JSul.I.16: *saharlary*; a scribal error.

17 JSul.III.73: *etivciler*. | JSul.I.16: *etivciler*.

18 JSul.III.73: *acuv byla*. | JSul.I.16: *acuv byla*.

19 JSul.III.73: טָש אֵטְכִין. | JSul.I.16: טַשְׁאֵטְקִין.

[1] [3] ⌊An hereby I will write a *peshat* of the *qinah* (with the incipit) *ˀĕyålūṯī bḡålūṯī* which is recited in the early afternoon 39 r°

[2] [4] on the third of the Shabbats of Tammuz, at the *minchah*[24], which our aged master, our teacher, his honour, the Rav, Rabbi Mordechai translated, may his soul rest in Eden, the son of the Rav Icchak, whose honourable repose is Eden, may his soul rest in Eden.

[3] [5] And this *peshat* you will say as a sung version (Incipit:) *ˀĕyålūṯī bḡålūṯī*⌉[25]

[4] [6] (1). O, my[26] powerful God, my strength in my exile, to You alone ⌊I will⌉[27] lift

[5] [7] my eyes. O God[28] who pays revenge[29] to the wicked, commit Yourself

[6] [8] to punish with wrath all the neighbours of mine. Destroy the lands of Edom as

[7] [9] (You did with) the cities of Sodom, for they were them who devastated my palaces.

[8] [10] Persecute with anger and eradicate them, O Lord, from below the skies.

[9] [11] ⌊And the refrain after every verse: 'Persecute with anger …'⌉[30] (2).

20 JSul.III.73: *tibinden.* | JSul.I.16: *tibinden.*

21 JSul.I.16: *keklernin.*

22 JSul.III.73: *Quvġun* :והפזמון (Heb. והפזמון 'and the refrain is:'). | JSul.I.16: *quvġun acuv byla.*

23 JSul.I.16: desunt.

24 I.e., *afternoon prayer service.*

25 JSul.III.73: *And this is the* peshat *of the* piyyut (*with the incipit*) ˀĕyålūṯī bḡålūṯī *the one recited at the* minchah [i.e., at the afternoon prayer service] *on the third of the Shabbats of Tammuz, which our master, our teacher, his honour, the Rav, Rabbi Mordechai translated, may his soul lodge in Eden, the son of our master, our teacher, his honour, the Rav, Rabbi Icchak called Łokszyński, may he rest in peace.* (*Incipit:*) ˀĕyålūṯī bḡålūṯī. | JSul.I.16: *Here is its* peshat [i.e., of the Hebrew original], *deliveredy by his honour, the Rav, Rabbi Mordechai, may his soul lodge in Eden, the son of Icchak, whose honourable repose is Eden, called Loksinskij, may the memory of the righteous be for life of the World to Come.*

26 JSul.I.16: deest.

27 JSul.III.73. *I do.* | JSul.I.16: *I do.*

28 JSul.I.16: *my God.*

29 Or: *punishment.*

30 JSul.III.73: *and the refrain is: 'Persecute …'.* | JSul.I.16: *persecute with anger ….*

[10] [12] Saġynġyn ḥaraplamaġyn da rusva[jla]maġyn[31] ʿAmonlularnyn da Moʾavlylarnyn, turġan

[11] [13] künlerinde[32] heḫalynda joġarġy Tenrin[in][33] körgenlerinde[34] ol keruvimlerni.

[12] [14] Muna ajttynyz ki[35] qulluq etmejbiz, ančaq[36] jaratuvčuġa[37] köklerni[38]. E

[13] [15] ḥor ulus muna biz haligine körebiz[39] bu[40] tenrilerinizni turadoġanlarny,

[14] [16] qaryštym[41] da tilsizlendim[42] da ullu ḥorluġumdan kötürelmedim[43] közlerimni[44].

[15] [17] ⸤Quvġun ačuvbyla da ⸤tas etkin⸣[45] alarny e H tübünden ol köklernin.⸣[46] [47]⸢כלֹהֿ הדֿר⸥

[16] [18] Tavusqun hörmetin[48] ulanlarynyn Tatarnyn, ki qojdular[49] verenlikke čeber[50]

[17] [19] [o]runlaryn[51] jerimnin qačqan[52] künümde[53] tarlyġybyla ǯanymnyn[54] uvučundan[55]

[18] [20] avančynyn[56] da jaman iščinin[57]. Da küčsüz[58] quvatsyz büreldim[59] Jizreʿelden

[19] [21] jerine Jišmaʿelnin, da qojdular uv ašyma[60] da zahürmen[61], da ičirdiler[62] mana

[20] [22] sirke vaḫtynda ullu suvsaplyġymnyn, da čajpadylar[63] da öltürdüler[64]

---

31 JSul.III.63: *rusvalajmaġyn*; a scribal error. | JSul.III.73: *rusvajlamaġyn*. JSul.I.16: *rusvajlamaġyn*.

32 JSul.I.16: *kinlerinde*.

33 JSul.III.63: *Tenrin*; a scribal error. | JSul.III.73: *Tenrinin*. JSul.I.16: *Tenrinin*.

34 JSul.I.16: *kergenlerinde*.

35 JSul.III.73: deest. | JSul.I.16: deest.

36 JSul.III.73: *ancaq*. | JSul.I.16: *ancaq*.

37 JSul.III.73: *jaratuvcuġa*. | JSul.I.16: *jaratuvcuġa*.

38 JSul.I.16: *keklerni*.

39 JSul.III.73: *kerebiz*. | JSul.I.16: *kerebiz*.

40 JSul.III.73: deest. | JSul.I.16: deest.

41 JSul.III.73: *qarystym*. | JSul.I.16: *qarystym*.

42 JSul.III.73: *tilsiz boldum*. | JSul.I.16: *tilsiz boldum*.

43 JSul.III.73: *kötirelmejmen*. | JSul.I.16: *ketirelmejmen*.

44 JSul.I.16: *kezlerimni*.

45 JSul.III.63: טָשֵׁיטְכִּין.

46 JSul.III.73: *quvġun*. | JSul.I.16: *quvġun*.

47 JSul.I.16: desunt.

48 JSul.III.73: *hermetin*. | JSul.I.16: *hermetin*.

49 JSul.III.73: *alar qojdular*. | JSul.I.16: *alar qojdular*.

[10] [12] Remember the insults and the disgrace of the Ammonites and the Moabites in the days they stood

[11] [13] at the altar of the God above, and saw the cherubim.

[12] [14] Lo, you said: 'We will not serve (the cherubim), but only the creator of the heavens'. O,

[13] [15] you dishonourable people, behold, we now see your gods (still) existing,

[14] [16] I have become ashamed and speechless[65] and because of my great shame I was[66] not able to lift my eyes.

[15] [17] ⌊Persecute with anger and eradicate them, O Lord, from below the skies.⌋[67] (3).

[16] [18] Withdraw[68] Your esteem for the sons of Tatars for they have devastated the nice

[17] [19] places of my land in the day of my escape—⌊with misery in my heart⌋[69]—from the hands of

[18] [20] my malefactors and evil-doers. And I wandered powerlessly and helplessly from Jezreel

[19] [21] to the land of Ishmael, and they put poison and wormwood into my food, and gave vinegar to drink

[20] [22] in the times of my great thirst, and they punished and ⌊killed

---

50 JSul.III.73: *ceber.* | JSul.I.16: *ceber.*

51 JSul.III.63: *urunlaryn*; probably a scribal error (or an assimilation). | JSul.III.73: *orunlaryn.* | JSul.I.16: *orunlaryn.*

52 JSul.III.73: *qacqan.* | JSul.I.16: *qacqan.*

53 JSul.III.73: *kinimde.* | JSul.I.16: *ancaq.*

54 JSul.III.73: *ʒanymnyn.* | JSul.I.16: *ʒanymnyn.*

55 JSul.III.73: *uvucundan.* | JSul.I.16: *uvucundan.*

56 JSul.III.73: *avancynyn.* | JSul.I.16: *avancynyn.*

57 JSul.III.73: *iscinin.* | JSul.I.16: *iscinin.*

58 JSul.III.73: *kicsiz.* | JSul.I.16: *kicsiz.*

59 JSul.III.73: *bireldim.* | JSul.I.16: *bireldim.*

60 JSul.III.73: *asyma.* | JSul.I.16: *asyma.*

61 JSul.III.73: *zahirmen.* | JSul.I.16: *zahirmen.*

62 JSul.III.73: *icirdiler.* | JSul.I.16: *icirdiler.*

63 JSul.III.73: *cajpadylar.* | JSul.I.16: *cajpadylar.*

64 JSul.III.73: *eltirdiler.* | JSul.I.16: *eltirdiler.*

65 JSul.III.73, JSul.I.16: expressed with a synonym.

66 JSul.III.73: *am.* | JSul.I.16: *am.*

67 JSul.III.73: *persecute ...* | JSul.I.16: *persecute.*

68 Lit. 'bring to an end' or 'destroy'.

69 Lit. 'with the misery of my heart'.

[21] [23] seksen min jyjynyn aziz[70] kohenlerimnin. ⌊Quvġun.⌉[71] [72]⌈המּמוני פצעוני⌋

[22] [24] Uvalttylar meni jarčyqladylar[73] meni čerüvü[74] Kesarnyn[75] da Aspasjanosnun[76],

[23] [25] tepter ettiler meni veren ettiler meni jyjynlary Titosnun[77] da [Ad]irjanosnun[78],

[24] [26] taberdiler meni öz[79] jerimden quvdular öz[80] jerlerine, da taspoldu menden

[25] [27] umsunču[81] ḥajifsinmeknin. Quvdular meni azaštyrdylar[82] meni, neginče[83] ki[84]

[26] [28] bolalma{j}men yštyrma[85] ⌊azašẖanlaryn tozulġan⌉[86] elimnin. Juttular meni da čajpadylar[87]

39 v° [27] [1] meni, da tol{tur}dular qarynlaryn ašajyšlyqlaryndan[88] jerimnin. Quvġun[89] ... [90]⌈שׁבִֿי עֲנִיָּה⌋

[28] [2] E miskin ummasy Jisra'elnin olturġun qarajdoġač[91], ki bardy umsunč[92] tynč[93]

[29] [3] etme aqibatynny, da uvuturmen seni da raḥemtlermen seni ešitkenimde[94]

[30] [4] ošol[95] firjatynny, tügenir[96] gineḥin[97] e ǯymaty[98] Cijjonnun, arttyrmasty artyq

[31] [5] dušman[99] olǯalama[100] jerinden seni. Alaj ajtady šeẖina muna men turarmen öč[101]

---

70 JSul.I.16: deest.

71 JSul.III.73: *quvġun acuv byla.* | JSul.I.16: *quvġun acuv.*

72 JSul.I.16: desunt.

73 JSul.III.73: *jarcyqladylar.* | JSul.I.16: *jarcyqladylar.*

74 JSul.III.73: *cerivi.* | JSul.I.16: *cerivi.*

75 Heb. קיסר, i.e., Caesar (full name: Gaius Julius Caesar).

76 Heb. אספסיאנוס, i.e., Vespasian (full name: Titus Flavius Vespasianus).

77 Heb. טיטוס, i.e., Titus (full name: Titus Flavius Sabinus Vespasianus).

78 JSul.III.63: *Andirjanosnun*; a scribal error. | Heb. אדריאנוס, i.e., Hadrian (full name: Publius Aelius Hadrianus).

79 JSul.III.73: *ez.* | JSul.I.16: *ez.*

80 JSul.III.73: *ez.* | JSul.I.16: *ez.*

81 JSul.III.73: *umsuncu.* | JSul.I.16: *umsuncu.*

82 JSul.III.73: *azastyrdylar.* | JSul.I.16: *azastyrdylar.*

83 JSul.III.73: *negince.* | JSul.I.16: *negince.*

84 JSul.III.73: deest. | JSul.I.16: deest.

85 JSul.III.73: *ystyrma.* | JSul.I.16: *ystyrma.*

86 JSul.III.73: *tozulġanlaryn.* | JSul.I.16: *tozulġanlaryn.*

87 JSul.III.73: *cajpadylar.* | JSul.I.16: *cajpadylar.*

[21] [23] a multitude of eighty thousand holy[102] priests of mine⌋[103]. Persecute[104]... (4).

[22] [24] The armies of Caesar and Vespasian have dispersed and split me,

[23] [25] the crowds of Titus and Hadrian have trampled and destroyed me,

[24] [26] they have cast me out from my own lands and have driven me to their own lands

[25] [27] and my hope for mercy has been lost. They have persecuted me and mislead me to the point that

[26] [28] I am unable to gather those of my people who are dispersed. They have swallowed me and destroyed

[27] [1] me and they ⌊have become satiated⌋[105] with the pleasures of my land. Persecute[106]... (5). 39 v°

[28] [2] 'O, miserable community of Israel, sit and observe that there is still hope

[29] [3] to soothe your confidence; and I will console you and I will have mercy on you when I will hear

[30] [4] your cry; your sin comes to its end, O, community of Zion, your enemy will not keep

[31] [5] taking you captive from your land any more.' So did say the divine Presence of God, 'Behold, I stand up to take revenge:

---

88 JSul.III.63: a hypercorrect form of *asajyšlyqlaryndan.* | JSul.III.73: *asajyslyqlaryndan.* | JSul.I.16: *asajyslyqlaryndan.*

89 JSul.I.16: *quvġun acuv byla.*

90 JSul.I.16: desunt.

91 JSul.III.73: *qarajdoġac.* | JSul.I.16: *qarajdoġac.*

92 JSul.III.73: *umsunc.* | JSul.I.16: *umsunc.*

93 JSul.III.73: *tync.* | JSul.I.16: *tync.*

94 JSul.III.73: *esitkenimde.* | JSul.I.16: *esitkenimde.*

95 JSul.III.73: *osol.* | JSul.I.16: *osol.*

96 JSul.III.73: *tigenir.* | JSul.I.16: *tigenir.*

97 JSul.III.73: *ginеḥin.* | JSul.I.16: *ginеḥin.*

98 JSul.III.73: *ʒymaty.* | JSul.I.16: *ʒymaty.*

99 JSul.III.73: *dusman.* | JSul.I.16: *dusman.*

100 JSul.III.73: *olʒalama.* | JSul.I.16: *olʒalama.*

101 JSul.III.73: *ec.* | JSul.I.16: *ec.*

102 JSul.I.16: deest.

103 A reference to a legend according to which in the time of the destruction of the Temple, 80,000 priests were burnt at the stake, see Ginzberg (1928: VI: 427).

104 JSul.III.73: *persecute with anger.* | JSul.I.16: *persecute with anger.*

105 Lit. 'have filled their stomachs'.

106 JSul.I.16: *persecute with anger.*

[32] [6] alma avaldaġylaj, alaj haliginede[107] öč[108] alyrmen öčünnü[109] da munajtuvčularyn[110]

[33] [7] da dušmanlaryn[111] ol vaḥtta taspolurlar ḥyššymyndan[112] Adonajnyn[113]. Quvġun

[34] [8] ačuvbyla[114] da ⌊tasetkin⌉[115] alarny e H tübünden[116] ol köklernin[117].

[35] [9] ⌊כן תרדפם בסערך ובסופתך ו׳⌉[118]

107 JSul.III.73: *halide.* | JSul.I.16: *halide.*

108 JSul.III.73: *ec.* | JSul.I.16: *ec.*

109 JSul.III.73: *ecinni.* | JSul.I.16: *ecinni.*

110 JSul.III.73: *munajtuvcularyn.* | JSul.I.16: *munajtuvcularyn.*

111 JSul.III.73: *dusmanlaryn.* | JSul.I.16: *dusmanlaryn.*

112 JSul.III.73: *ḥyssymyndan.* | JSul.I.16: *ḥyssymyndan.*

113 JSul.III.73: *H-nyn.* | JSul.I.16: *H-nyn.*

114 JSul.III.73: *acuv byla.* | JSul.I.16: *acuv byla.*

115 JSul.III.73: טָש אֵטְכִין. | JSul.I.16: טַש אֵטְכִין.

116 JSul.III.73: *tibinden.* | JSul.I.16: *tibinden.*

117 JSul.I.16: *keklernin.*

118 Psalm 83:15. | JSul.III.73: כן תרדפם וגו׳: תם הפשט:. (Psalm 83:15) | JSul.I.16: כֵּן תִּרְדְּפֵם בְּסַעֲרֶךָ וּבְסוּפָתְךָ תְבַהֲלֵם: מַלֵּא פְנֵיהֶם קָלוֹן וִיבַקְשׁוּ שִׁמְךָ הָ: יֵבֹשׁוּ וְיִבָּהֲלוּ עֲדֵי עַד וְיַחְפְּרוּ וְיֹאבֵדוּ: וְיֵדְעוּ כִּי אַתָּה שִׁמְךָ הָ לְבַדֶּךָ עֶלְיוֹן עַל כָּל הָאָרֶץ: בָּרוּךְ הָ לְעוֹלָם אָמֵן וְאָמֵן. (Psalm 83:15–18, Psalm 89:52).

[32] [6] as (I did) before, so will I now take your revenge'; and your oppressors
[33] [7] and enemies will perish from the anger of the Lord. Persecute
[34] [8] with anger and eradicate them, O Lord, from under the skies'.
[35] [9] ⌊So persecute them with your tempest, and with your storm ...⌉[119]

119 Psalm 83:15. | JSul.III.73: *'So persecute them ...' and so on. The end of the* peshat. (Psalm 83:15). | JSul.I.16: *'So persecute them with your tempest, and make them afraid with your storm. Fill their faces with shame; that they may seek your name, O Lord. Let them be confounded and troubled forever; yea, let them be put to shame, and perish: That men may know that you, whose name alone is the Lord, are the most high over all the earth. Blessed be the Lord forevermore. Amen, and Amen.'* (Psalm 83:15–18, Psalm 89:52).

# PART 3

# *A* peshat *of Mordechai ben Nisan*

∵

**Text number:** № 5
**Karaim incipit:** *Jasły da zabun bolǧan*
**Hebrew incipit:** אֲנוּנָה אֲנִי וַעֲגוּמָה *ʾănūnå ʾănī waʿăḡūmå*
**Dedication:** Shabbats of the month Tammuz
**Language:** Early Mod.SWKar., Mod.SWKar.
**Number of copies:** 6

| Accession no. | Place of origin of copy | Date of copy | Copyist | Folios |
|---|---|---|---|---|
| JSul.III.03 | Halych | shortly after 1805 | Unknown 7 | 99 rº–100 rº |
| JSul.I.45 | Halych | 1st half of the 19th c. | Jeshua Josef Mordkowicz | 122 vº–123 vº |
| ADub.III.61 | Halych | 1850/1851 | Jeshua Josef Mordkowicz | 111 vº–112 rº |
| JSul.III.69 | Halych | ca. 1851 (before 1866) | Jeshua Josef Mordkowicz | 218 vº–219 vº |
| JSul.III.79 | Halych | ca. 1851 (before 1866) | Jeshua Josef Mordkowicz | 268 rº–269 vº |
| JSul.I.01c | Halych | 2nd half of the 19th c. | Jeshua Josef Mordkowicz | 132 vº–133 rº |

## 1 Introductory Remarks

This *peshat* is one of four pre-18th-century Karaim *peshatim* of the *piyyut* in question, see *peshatim* № 1, 24, and 26. All six copies are vocalized.

There are no major differences between the texts. The only dissimilarities arise from the fact that the copyist, i.e. Jeshua Josef Mordkowicz, had a tendency to make improvements, including in the style, e.g. by eliminating repetitions. These minor discrepancies show that the texts in mss. JSul.III.03 and JSul.III.69 share a number of unique, common features, the same being true of the texts in JSul.I.45, ADub.III.61, JSul.III.79, and JSul.I.01c (as it is also the case with *peshat* № 1).

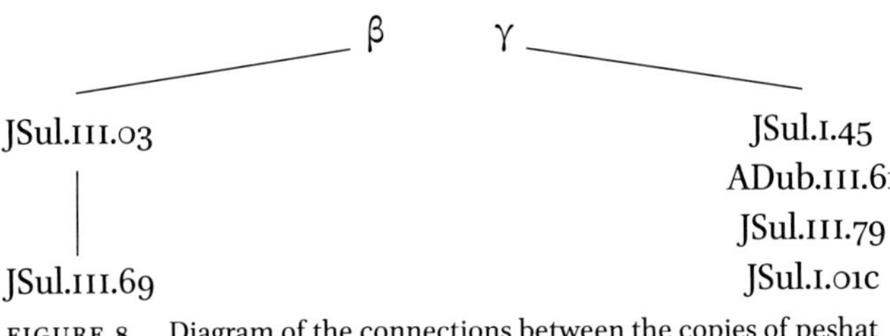


FIGURE 8 Diagram of the connections between the copies of peshat № 5

## 2 Transcription[1] and Translation

99 rº [1] [21] ⌊וזה תרגום שני לפיוט זה עשאו אמו כמוהרר מרדכי בעס מאמר מרדכי היד
נבת: באמו ההו
[2] [22] כמוהרר ניסן הזקן נבת: אנונה אני⌉[2]
[3] [23] Jasly da zabun bolġan boldum acuvlu[3] da syzlavlu, ḥor da synyq
[4] [24] kemisilgen galutta da avruvlu. Siver bolġanym
[5] [25] ücün[4] Tenrime hali boldum jerenci indelgen ki jazyġym boldu
[6] [26] ullu, qojdu meni verenlikke da[5] har kin[6] men[7] bolamen syzlavlu.
[7] [27] ⌊דוה וזבה⌉[8]. Syzlavlu da jerenci etilgen indeldim e Tenrim
[8] [28] ki tigel ⌊ḥor etme⌉[9] ḥor ettin meni. Birelttin[10] meni dinsizler
99 vº [9] [1] arasyna da kemistin[11] meni, da sirdin meni qyblalaryn alnyndan

---

1 Based on JSul.III.03.

2 JSul.I.45: פשט שני לפיוט אנונה מאמו כמוהרר מרדכי היד נבת בכמוהרר ניסן הזקן מגדול ליטא זל. | ADub.III.61: וזה פשט שני לפיוט אנונה חבורו של אמו ההו כמוהרר מרדכי היד ותמד בעס מאמר מרדכי ושאר ספריו: בכמוהרר ניסן הזקן הטרוקי נבת ועטייזש: אנונה אני. | JSul.III.69: פשט שני לפיוט אנונה תרגמו אמו הרר מרדכי בעס מאמר מרדכי ושאר ספריו היד ותמד באמו ההו כמוהרר ניסן הטרוקי הזקן יעמש. | JSul.III.79: יזה פשט שני לפיוט הנל חבורו של אמו ההו כמוהרר מרדכי היד ותמד בעס מאמר מרדכי באמו הרר ניסן הטרוקי יעמש. | JSul.I.01c: פשט שני לפיוט אנונה תרגמו אמו ההו כמוהרר מרדכי בעס דוד מרדכי היד ותמד: בן אמו כמוהרר ניסן הטרוקי יעמש.

3 JSul.I.45: *jadavlu.*

4 ADub.III.61: *icin.* | JSul.III.69: *icin.* | JSul.III.79: *icin.* | JSul.I.01c: *icin.*

5 JSul.I.45: *ki.* | ADub.III.61: *ki.* | JSul.III.79: *ki.* | JSul.I.01c: *ki.*

6 JSul.I.45: *kün.*

7 JSul.III.69: deest.

8 JSul.I.45: דוה. | JSul.III.69: דוה. | JSul.III.79: דוה. | JSul.I.01c: דוה.

9 JSul.I.45: desunt. | ADub.III.61: desunt. | JSul.III.79: desunt. | JSul.I.01c: *ḥor etmek*; the use of the *-mek*-form is possibly a result of scribal error.

10 JSul.I.45: *bireltesen.* | ADub.III.61: *bireltesen.* | JSul.III.79: *bireltesen.* | JSul.I.01c: *bireltesen.*

11 JSul.I.45: *kemisesen.* | ADub.III.61: *kemisesen.* | JSul.III.79: *kemisesen.* | JSul.I.01c: *kemisesen.*

12 JSul.I.45: *The second peshat of the* piyyut (*with the incipit*) ʾănūnå *of our master, our teacher, his honour, the Rav, Rabbi Mordechai, may the Lord avenge his blood, may his soul lodge in Eden, the son of his honour, the Rav, Rabbi Nisan the aged, from the great* (*ones*) [i.e., scholars] [מגדול ליטא in the text; possibly a textual corruption for מגדולי ליטא] *of Lithuania, may his memory be a blessing.* | ADub.III.61: *And this is the second* peshat *of the* piyyut (*with the incipit*) ʾănūnå *of our master, our teacher, the great and honourable sage, his honour, the Rav, Rabbi Mordechai, may the Lord avenge his blood, his place of rest shall be glorious, the author of the book Maʿamar Mordechai and his other books, the son of his honour, the Rav, Rabbi Nisan the aged, may his soul lodge in Eden; and may his name be remembered for good!* (*Incipit:*) ʾănūnå ʾănī. | JSul.III.69: *The second* peshat *of the* piyyut (*with the incipit*) ʾănūnå,

[1] [21] ⌊An this is the second interpretation of the *piyyut* delivered by our master, our teacher, his honour, the Rav, Rabbi Mordechai, the author of the book *Maʾamar Mordechai*, may the Lord avenge his blood, may his soul lodge in Eden, the son of our master, our teacher, the great and honourable sage, 99 rº
[2] [22] his honour, the Rav, Rabbi Nisan the aged, may his soul lodge in Eden. (Incipit:) *ʾănūnå ʾănī*⌉[12]
[3] [23] (1). I have became mournful and infirm, irate[13] and suffering; left dishonourable and broken
[4] [24] in exile, and full of pain. ⌊After being loved
[5] [25] by my God⌉[14], I have become (one) called now repulsive, for my sin was
[6] [26] great, it has ⌊devastated me⌉[15] and[16] I was suffering every day.
[7] [27] (3). I was called sufferer and repulsive, O God,
[8] [28] for You have certainly[17] rejected me completely. You made me wander
[9] [1] among the godless and ⌊You have abandoned⌉[18] me and have driven from before Your countenance 99 vº

---

*which our master translated, our teacher, the Rav, Rabbi Mordechai the author of the book Maʾamar Mordechai and his other books, may the Lord avenge his blood, his place of rest shall be glorious, the son of our master, our teacher, the great and honourable sage, his honour, Rabbi Nisan of Troki the aged, may he rest in peace.* | JSul.III.79: *And this is the second* peshat *of the* piyyut (*with the incipit*) ʾănūnå, *the composition of our master, our teacher, the great and honourable sage, his honour, the Rav, Rabbi Mordechai, may the Lord avenge his blood, his place of rest shall be glorious, the author of the book Maʾamar Mordechai, the son of our master, our teacher, the Rav, Rabbi Nisan of Troki, may he rest in peace.* | JSul.I.01c: *The second* peshat *of the* piyyut (*with the incipit*) ʾănūnå, *which our master translated, our teacher, the great and honourable sage, his honour, the Rav, Rabbi Mordechai, the author of Dod Mordechai, may the Lord avenge his blood, his place of rest shall be glorious, the son of our master, our teacher, his honour, the Rav, Rabbi Nisan of Troki, may he rest in peace.*

13 JSul.I.01c: *tired.*

14 Lit. 'to my (state of) being loved for my God'.

15 Lit. 'put me into devastation'.

16 JSul.I.45: *for.* | ADub.III.61: *for.* | JSul.III.79: *for.* | JSul.I.01c: *for.*

17 JSul.I.45: deest. | ADub.III.61: deest. | JSul.III.79: deest.

18 JSul.I.45: *You abandon.* | ADub.III.61: *You abandon.* | JSul.III.79: *You abandon.* | JSul.I.01c: *You abandon.*

[10] [2] da jat ḥanlyqlar arasyna cactyn meni. Ki[19] sensen Tenrim da[20]

[11] [3] küpligim[21] nek bulaj uzaq zaman kemisesen meni. ונחתֹּני.

[12] [4] Kemistin meni buzuqluqqa qojdun meni da sirdin meni aziz ornundan.

[13] [5] Avur tisler byla synyqtyrdyn[22] meni da titrettin meni

[14] [6] qorqunclu[23] körimlerinden[24]. E aruv enajatly[25] Tenri eger

[15] [7] gergede qazylsam qacma alnyndan, andada kicin[26] könderir[27] meni

[16] [8] necik klesen da tutar on qudratyn qolumdan. [28]ימ֗ינך.

[17] [9] Ez kicin[29] byla küplegin[30] meni da bosatqyn avur jazyqlarymny,

[18] [10] ki artyġac enkejtedi meni dušman[31] da izedi[32] saġyslarymny.

[19] [11] Dinsiz dusman qysyqlyq etedi mana da juvuz etedi[33] ullu[lu]ġumnu[34],

[20] [12] da sen e H negince cydarsen bunu. [35]⌜מתי תוציא⌟.

[21] [13] Negince e bijim Tenrim cyġarmassen ⌞rastlyqqa teremni⌝[36] menim.

[22] [14] E qorqunclu Tenrim[37] ⌞qulaq salġyn⌝[38] jalbarmaġyma da veren etkin

[23] [15] dusmanlarymny menim. Küplegin[39] meni da jarlyġasly bolajym

[24] [16] ki jystyrylmaġy[40] ücün[41] jyjynlarymnyn menim, sana telmertemen

---

19 JSul.I.45: deest. | ADub.III.61: deest. | JSul.III.79: deest. | JSul.I.01c: deest.

20 JSul.I.45: deest. | ADub.III.61: deest. | JSul.III.79: deest. | JSul.I.01c: deest.

21 JSul.III.03: a hypercorrect form of *kipligim.* | JSul.I.45: a hypercorrect form of *kipligim.* | ADub.III.61: *kipligim.* | JSul.III.69: *kipligim.* | JSul.III.79: *kipligim.* | JSul.I.01c: *kipligim.*

22 JSul.I.45: *syndyrdyn.* | ADub.III.61: *syndyrdyn.* | JSul.III.79: *syndyrdyn.* | JSul.I.01c: *syndyrdyn.*

23 JSul.I.45: *avur.* | ADub.III.61: *avur.* | JSul.III.79: *avur.* | JSul.I.01c: *avur.*

24 ADub.III.61: *kerimlerinden.* | JSul.III.69: *kerimlerinden.* | JSul.III.79: *kerimlerinden.* | JSul.I .01c: *kerimlerinden.*

25 JSul.III.03: *enaj atly.* | JSul.I.45: deest. | ADub.III.61: deest. | JSul.III.69: *enaj atly.* | JSul.III.79: *enaj atly.* | JSul.I.01c deest.

26 JSul.I.45: *kücün.*

27 JSul.I.45: *kenderir.* | ADub.III.61: *kenderir.* | JSul.III.69: *kenderir.* | JSul.III.79: *kenderir.* | JSul.I.01c: *kenderir.*

28 JSul.I.45: ימ֗ינך תסעָדני.

29 JSul.I.45: *kücün.*

30 JSul.III.03: a hypercorrect form of *kiplegin.* | JSul.I.45: a hypercorrect form of *kiplegin.* | ADub.III.61: *kiplegin.* | JSul.III.69: *kiplegin.* | JSul.III.79: *kiplegin.* | JSul.I.01c: *kiplegin.*

31 JSul.I.45: *dusman.* | ADub.III.61: *dusman.* | JSul.III.69: *dusman.* | JSul.III.79: *dusman.* | JSul.I.01c: *dusman.*

32 JSul.I.45: *izedir.* | ADub.III.61: *izedir.* | JSul.III.69: *izedir.* | JSul.III.79: *izedir.* | JSul.I.01c: *izedir.*

33 JSul.I.01c: *etedir.*

34 JSul.I.45: *ulluluġumnu.* | ADub.III.61: *ulluluġumnu.* | JSul.III.69: *ulluluġumnu.* | JSul.III.79: *ulluluġumnu.*

35 JSul.I.45: מתֹּי. | JSul.III.69: מתֹּי. | JSul.III.79: מתֹּי. | JSul.I.01c: מתֹּי.

36 JSul.I.45: *rastlyġymny.* | ADub.III.61: *rastlyġymny.* | JSul.III.69: *rastlyġymny.* | JSul.III.79: *rastlyġymny.* | JSul.I.01c: *rastlyġymny.*

[10] [2] and spread me between foreign kingdoms. ⌊Given that⌋[42] You are my God and[43]
[11] [3] strength, why do You keep abandoning me for such a long time? (4).
[12] [4] You have abandoned me, You have ⌊destructed me⌋[44] and have driven me from Your holy place.
[13] [5] You have depressed[45] me with heavy dreams and made me tremble (with fear)
[14] [6] from their terrible[46] sight. O ⌊pure-eyed God⌋[47], even if
[15] [7] I would be buried in a grave to escape from before You, even there Your power will drive me,
[16] [8] if You would wish so, and Your right hand would catch my hand. (4).
[17] [9] Strengthen me with Your own power and absolve my heavy sins
[18] [10] for the enemy is humiliating me too much and is breaking my thoughts.
[19] [11] The godless enemy oppresses me and lowers my greatness,
[20] [12] and You, O God: how long will You tolerate this? (5).
[21] [13] How long will You not ⌊turn to righteousness my rights⌋[48]?
[22] [14] Listen[49] to my cry, O my[50] awesome God, and destroy
[23] [15] my enemies. Strengthen me and let me be rescued
[24] [16] since for the sake of gathering my congregation I direct

---

37 JSul.I.45: *Tenri.* | ADub.III.61: *Tenri.* | JSul.III.79: *Tenri.*

38 JSul.I.45: *qajyrġyn esitivinni.* | ADub.III.61: *qajyrġyn esitivinni.* | JSul.III.79: *qajyrġyn esitivinni.* | JSul.I.01c: *qajyrġyn esitivinni.*

39 JSul.III.03: a hypercorrect form of *kiplegin.* | JSul.I.45: a hypercorrect form of *kiplegin.* | ADub.III.61: *kiplegin.* | JSul.III.69: *kiplegin.* | JSul.III.79: *kiplegin.* | JSul.I.01c: *kiplegin.*

40 JSul.III.69: *ystyrylmaġy.* | JSul.III.79: *ystyrylmaġy.* | JSul.I.01c: *ystyrylmaġy.*

41 ADub.III.61: *icin.* | JSul.III.69: *icin.* | JSul.III.79: *icin.* | JSul.I.01c: *icin.*

42 JSul.I.45: deest. | ADub.III.61: deest. | JSul.III.79: deest. | JSul.I.01c: deest.

43 JSul.I.45: deest. | ADub.III.61: deest. | JSul.III.79: deest. | JSul.I.01c: deest.

44 Lit. 'put me into destruction'.

45 JSul.I.45: *broke.* | ADub.III.61: *broke.* | JSul.III.79: *broke.* | JSul.I.01c: *broke.*

46 JSul.I.45: *uneasy.* | ADub.III.61: *uneasy.* | JSul.III.79: *uneasy.* | JSul.I.01c: *uneasy.*

47 JSul.I.45: *pure God.* | ADub.III.61: *pure God.* | JSul.I.01c: *pure God.* || The absence of *enejatly* in these mss. is perhaps a result of a scribal error.

48 I.e., *find me innocent when You judge me.* || JSul.I.45: *give out my righteousness (to me).* | ADub.III.61: *give out my righteousness (to me).* | JSul.III.69: *give out my righteousness (to me).* | JSul.III.79: *give out my righteousness (to me).* | JSul.I.01c: *give out my righteousness (to me).*

49 JSul.I.45: *turn Your ear.* | ADub.III.61: *turn Your ear.* | JSul.III.79: *turn Your ear.* | JSul.I.01c: *turn Your ear.*

50 JSul.I.45: deest. | JSul.III.79: deest. | JSul.I.01c: deest.

[25] [17] közlerimni[51] e bijim menim. [52]⌜עי֔ני מצפות לך⌟.
[26] [18] Közlerim[53] telmerediler sana juluvcu[54] meni galuttan küclü[55] Tenrim.
[27] [19] Qutqarġyn meni dušmanlarymdan[56] e H Tenrim küpligim[57] menim.
[28] [20] E joqtan bar etivcim baqqyn kökten[58] da ⌞qulaq salġyn⌝[59] avazymny[60]
[29] [21] menim. E H har ⌞erten byla⌝[61] esitkin avazym byla firjatymny
[30] [22] menim. [62]⌜קוֹ֔לי שׁע֖ה⌟. Avazymny qabul etkin da ⌞köz[63]
[31] [23] jummaġyn⌝[64] jalbarmaġymdan. Klegin e H qutqarma meni da
[32] [24] ʒaḥtlaġyn boluslugʼuma dusmanlarymdan. Körgin[65] ullu zavalymny[66]
[33] [25] menim da sirtkin jaslarymny közlerimden[67]. E H esitkin
[34] [26] tefilemni bijik köklerinden[68]. [69]⌜תפִּ֔לתי שמע֖ה⌟.
[35] [27] Tefilemni esitkin e H Tenri da qajtqyn acuvundan[70]
[36] [28] da qaruv bergin mana. E qajjam Tenri[71] jaman islerime kere[72]
100 rº [37] [1] tere qylmaġyn mana. Savaġatyna köre[73] ḥajifsingin meni da
[38] [2] firjatym kelsin alnyna. E H ajtamen qoltqamda ḥajifsingin
[39] [3] meni ki alaj usajdy[74] sana. [75]⌜חנ֔ני צור֔י⌟.

---

51 ADub.III.61: *kezlerimni.* | JSul.III.69: *kezlerimni.* | JSul.III.79: *kezlerimni.* | JSul.I.01c: *kezlerimni.*

52 JSul.I.45: עי֔ני. | ADub.III.61: עי֔ני. | JSul.III.69: עי֔ני. | JSul.III.79: עי֔ני. | JSul.I.01c: עי֔ני.

53 ADub.III.61: *kezlerim.* | JSul.III.69: *kezlerim.* | JSul.III.79: *kezlerim.* | JSul.I.01c: *kezlerim.*

54 ADub.III.61: *e juluvcu.*

55 ADub.III.61: *kicli.* | JSul.III.69: *kicli.* | JSul.III.79: *kicli.* | JSul.I.01c: *kicli.*

56 JSul.I.45: *dusmanlarymdan.* | ADub.III.61: *dusmanlarymdan.* | JSul.III.69: *dusmanlarymdan.* | JSul.III.79: *dusmanlarymdan.* | JSul.I.01c: *dusmanlarymdan.*

57 JSul.III.03: a hypercorrect form of *kipligim.* | JSul.I.45: a hypercorrect form of *kipligim.* | ADub.III.61: *kipligim.* | JSul.III.69: *kipligim.* | JSul.III.79: *kipligim.* | JSul.I.01c: *kipligim.*

58 ADub.III.61: *kekten.* | JSul.III.69: *kekten.* | JSul.III.79: *kekten.* | JSul.I.01c: *kekten.*

59 JSul.I.45: *qajyrġyn esitivinni.* | ADub.III.61: *qajyrġyn esitivinni.* | JSul.III.79: *qajyrġyn esitivinni.* | JSul.I.01c: *qajyrġyn esitivinni.*

60 JSul.I.45: *avazyma.* | ADub.III.61: *avazyma.* | JSul.III.69: *avazymny.* | JSul.III.79: *avazyma.* | JSul.I.01c: *avazyma.*

61 ADub.III.61: *erten bylada.* | JSul.III.79: *ertenbylada.* | JSul.I.01c: *ertenbylada.*

62 JSul.I.45: קוֹ֔לי. | JSul.III.69: קוֹ֔לי. | JSul.III.79: קוֹ֔לי. | JSul.I.01c: קוֹ֔לי.

63 JSul.III.69: *kez.*

64 JSul.I.45: *jummaġyn enaj atynny.* | ADub.III.61: *jummaġyn enaj atynny.* | JSul.III.79: *jummaġyn enaj atynny.* | JSul.I.01c: *jummaġyn enaj atynny.*

65 ADub.III.61: *kergin.* | JSul.III.69: *kergin.* | JSul.III.79: *kergin.* | JSul.I.01c: *kergin.*

66 JSul.I.45: *zelimni.* | ADub.III.61: *zelimni.* | JSul.III.79: *zelimni.* | JSul.I.01c: *zelimni.* || The word *zelim* is perhaps related to EKar. *zalim* ~ *zalym* 'cruel; tyrant', but the meaning of the latter word does not fit in with the context.

[25] [17] my eyes at You, O, Lord of mine. (6).
[26] [18] My eyes ⌊look with hope at You[176], my[77] saviour from the exile, my powerful God.
[27] [19] Save me from my enemies, O Lord God my strength.
[28] [20] O my creator from nothing, look (at me) from the heaven and listen[78] to my voice.
[29] [21] O Lord, hearken to my voice and my cry every morning.
[30] [22] (7). Accept my voice and do not close Your eyes[79]
[31] [23] to my entreaty[80]. Wish, O Lord, to save me and
[32] [24] hurry to be my providence against my enemies. See my great misery[81]
[33] [25] and wipe my tears from my eyes[82]. O Lord, hearken
[34] [26] to my prayer from Your[83] high heavens. (8).
[35] [27] Hearken to my prayer, O Lord God, and stop Your anger[84]
[36] [28] and reply to me. O, powerful God do not judge me according to my evil deeds.
[37] [1] Have mercy on me with Your benevolence 100 r°
[38] [2] and let my prayer come before You. O Lord, I say in my prayer: have mercy
[39] [3] on me for this is what is becoming to You. (9).

---

67 JSul.I.45: *jizlerimden.* | ADub.III.61: *izlerimden.* | JSul.III.69: *kezlerimnden.* | JSul.III.79: *kezlerimnden.* | JSul.I.01c: *kezlerimnden.*

68 ADub.III.61: *keklerinden.* | JSul.III.69: *keklerinden.* | JSul.III.79: *keklerinden.* | JSul.I.01c: *keklerimden*; a scribal error.

69 JSul.I.45: תְּפִלָּתִי. | JSul.III.69: תְּפִלָּתִי. | JSul.III.79: תְּפִלָּתִי. | JSul.I.01c: תְּפִלָּתִי.

70 JSul.I.01c: *qaḥyryndan.*

71 JSul.I.01c: *Tenrim.*

72 JSul.I.45: *köre.*

73 JSul.I.45: *kere.* | JSul.III.69: *kere.* | JSul.III.79: *kere.* | JSul.I.01c: *kere.*

74 ADub.III.61: *usajdyr.* | JSul.III.79: *usajdyr.* | JSul.I.01c: *usajdyr.*

75 JSul.I.45: חָנֵּנִי. | JSul.III.69: חָנֵּנִי. | JSul.III.79: חָנֵּנִי. | JSul.I.01c: חָנֵּנִי.

76 Or: *miss You.*

77 ADub.III.61: *O my.*

78 JSul.I.45: *turn Your ear.* | ADub.III.61: *turn Your ear.* | JSul.III.79: *turn Your ear.* | JSul.I.01c: *turn Your ear.*

79 JSul.I.45, ADub.III.61, JSul.III.79, JSul.I.01c: expressed with a synonym.

80 Or: *prayer.*

81 JSul.I.45: *tyrant* [?]. | ADub.III.61: *tyrant* [?]. | JSul.III.79: *tyrant* [?]. | JSul.I.01c: *tyrant* [?]. || See the respective commentary in the transcription (fn. 66).

82 JSul.I.45: *face.* | ADub.III.61: *face.*

83 JSul.I.01c *my*; a scribal error.

84 JSul.I.01c: *wrath.*

[40] [4] Ḥajifsingin meni jaratuvcum da ḥabarly[85] etkin meni ajtadoġac ki
[41] [5] bošattym[86] jazyqlarynny. Jystyrġyn[87] meni jat jerlerden da
[42] [6] menim istine ojatqyn ḥajifsinmeklerinni. Köpligine[88]
[43] [7] köre[89] savaġatynnyn[90] qabul etkin tefilesin jalbaruvcularynnyn. E
[44] [8] Tenrim köpligine[91] köre[92] savaġatynnyn qaruv bergin mana ʒomart-
[45] [9] lyġyndan[93] qajjamlyġy byla jarlyġašynnyn[94]. [95]⸢הטה הׄ אזנך⸣.

---

85 JSul.III.79: *jaḥsy ḥabarly.*

86 JSul.I.45: *bosattym.* | ADub.III.61: *bosattym.* | JSul.III.69: *bosattym.* | JSul.III.79: *bosattym.* | JSul.I.01c: *bosattym.*

87 ADub.III.61: *ystyrġyn.* | JSul.III.69: *ystyrġyn.* | JSul.III.79: *ystyrġyn.* | JSul.I.01c: *ystyrġyn.*

88 ADub.III.61: *kepligine.* | JSul.III.69: *kepligine.* | JSul.III.79: *kepligine.* | JSul.I.01c: *kepligine.*

89 ADub.III.61: *kere.* | JSul.III.69: *kere.* | JSul.III.79: *kere.* | JSul.I.01c: *kere.*

90 JSul.I.45: *jarlyġasynnyn.* | ADub.III.61: *jarlyġasynnyn.* | JSul.III.79: *jarlyġasynnyn.* | JSul.I .01c: *jarlyġasynnyn.*

91 ADub.III.61: *kepligine.* | JSul.III.69: *kepligine.* | JSul.III.79: *kepligine.* | JSul.I.01c: *kepligine.*

92 ADub.III.61: *kere.* | JSul.III.69: *kere.* | JSul.III.79: *kere.* | JSul.I.01c: *kere.*

93 JSul.I.45: deest. | ADub.III.61: deest. | JSul.III.69: deest. | JSul.III.79: deest. | JSul.I.01c: deest.

94 JSul.I.45: *jarlyġasynnyn.* | ADub.III.61: *jarlyġasynnyn.* | JSul.III.69: *jarlyġasynnyn.* | JSul.III .79: *jarlyġasynnyn.* | JSul.I.01c: *jarlyġasynnyn.*

95 Psalm 86:1. | JSul.I.45: הַטֵּה הׄ אָזְנֶךָ עֲנֵנִי וגו׳. (Psalm 86:1; אָזְנֶךָ *pro* אָזְנְךָ). | ADub.III.61: הַטֵּה הׄ אָזְנֶךָ עֲנֵנִי וגו׳. (Psalm 86:1; אָזְנֶךָ *pro* אָזְנְךָ). | JSul.III.69: הַטֵּה הׄ אָזְנְךָ וגו׳. (Psalm 86:1). | JSul.III.79: הַטֵּה הׄ אָזְנְךָ עֲנֵנִי וגו׳. (Psalm 86:1). | JSul.I.01c: הַטֵּה הׄ אָזְנְךָ עֲנֵנִי וגו׳. (Psalm 86:1).

[40] [4] My creator, have mercy on me and make me ⌊receive news[96]⌉[97] by saying:
[41] [5] 'I absolved your sins'. Gather me from the foreign lands and
[42] [6] send[98] Your mercies on me. According to the abundance
[43] [7] of Your mercy[99] accept the prayer of those who pray to You. O
[44] [8] God of mine, according to the abundance of Your mercy, reply to me, ⌊in Your generosity⌉[100],
[45] [9] with the power of Your grace. ⌊'Bow down your ear, O Lord.'⌉[101]

96 JSul.III.79: *good news.*
97 Lit. 'be of news'. | JSul.III.79: lit. 'be of good news'.
98 Lit. 'wake up'.
99 JSul.I.45: *grace.* | ADub.III.61: *grace.* | JSul.III.79: *grace.* | JSul.I.01c: *grace.*
100 JSul.I.45: desunt. | ADub.III.61: desunt. | JSul.III.69: desunt. | JSul.III.79: desunt. | JSul.I.01c: desunt.
101 Psalm 86:1. | JSul.I.45: *'Bow down your ear, O Lord, hear me …,' and so on.* (Psalm 86:1). | ADub.III.61: *'Bow down your ear, O Lord, hear me …,' and so on.* (Psalm 86:1). | JSul.III.69: *'Bow down your ear, O Lord …,' and so on.* (Psalm 86:1). | JSul.III.79: *'Bow down your ear, O Lord, hear me …,' and so on.* (Psalm 86:1). | JSul.I.01c: *'Bow down your ear, O Lord, hear me …,' and so on.* (Psalm 86:1).

# PART 4

## *A* peshat *of Moshe ben Icchak Cic-Ora*

∵

**Text number:** № 6
**Karaim incipit:** *Men synyq ummasy Jisra'elnin*
**Hebrew incipit:** אֲנִי יְשֵׁנָה וְלִבִּי עֵר *'ănī yšēnå wlibbī 'ēr*
**Dedication:** Pesach (while reading the Hallel ha-Gadol)
**Language:** MSWKar. with MNWKar. vocalization, MSWKar., Early Mod.SWKar
**Number of copies:** 7

| Accession no. | Place of origin of copy | Date of copy | Copyist | Folios |
|---|---|---|---|---|
| ADub.III.78 | Kukizów | ca. 1750 | Unknown 2 | 284 r°–285 r° |
| JSul.I.53.13 | Halych | mid-18th c. (ca. 1762) | Unknown 3 | 7 r°–7 v° |
| JSul.I.01b | Halych | 2nd half of the 18th c. | Mordechai ben Shemuel | 108 r°–108 v° |
| JSul.III.64a | Halych | between 1840 and 1851 | Unknown 10 | 10 v°–11 v° |
| JSul.III.72 | Halych | before 1851 | Jeshua Josef Mordkowicz | 7 v°–8 v° |
| JSul.I.37.02 | Lutsk | mid-19th c. | Unknown 11 | 6 v°–8 v° |
| F305-08 | Poniewież (?) | 2nd half of the 19th c. | Unknown 13 | 180 r°–181 r° |

## 1 Introductory Remarks

All seven copies are vocalized. The text in ADub.III.78 was originally written in South-Western Karaim, cf. the clearly SWKar. *jazyqlarynyzġa* [69–70] and *tüzünüz* [70], however, a Middle North-Western Karaim vocalization has been added to it by another hand using different ink and a different quill pen.

There are numerous differences between the copies. Many unique features found in JSul.I.37.02 are also present in the copy in JSul.I.01b, and, to a lesser extent, also in the copy in ms. JSul.I.53.13; see e.g. *edim qajġylarymdan* vs. *qajġylarymdan edim* (15), *baryredim* vs. *baryredim šaloš regalimde* (28), *avaz* vs. *avazy* (48), *syjyt etemen da firjat etemen* vs. *syjyt etemin* (~ *etemen*) *da firjat etemen* (63), *qyjyn* vs. *qyjynlar* (64), *jazyqlarynyzny* vs. *jazyqlarynyzġa* (70), as well as *üč* (~ *üc*) *qurlalar* vs. *üč* (~ *ic*) *qurlalar jylda* (27), *qaltradym* vs. *qaltradym da ǯaḥtladym* (~ *ʒaḥtladym*) (37), *janada* vs. *jana* (~ *jane*) (55), *ačy galutta* vs. *galutta* (61), *Tenridedi* vs. *Tenrige* (66), *ündelgenler* vs. *atalġanlar* (73), and *'olalar da šelamimler* vs. *'olalar* (75). The versions of the *peshat* copied in JSul.III.64 and JSul.III.72 are very similar to each other as well as to the text in ADub.III.78: there are a number of fragments that are shared exclusively by these three copies, see e.g. *qajġylarymda edim* vs. *edim qajġylarymda* (15), the use of *šaloš regalimde* in line 28, *avazy* vs. *avaz* (48), *syjyt etemin* vs. *syjyt etemen da firjat etemen* (62–63), *qyjynlar* vs. *qyjyn* (64), *jazyqlarynyzğa* vs. *jazyqlarynyzny* (70), *da burundaġylaj zemer da šira avazy* vs. *zemerler da širalar burundaġylaj* vs. *da burundaġylaj zemerler da širalar* (76–77). The versions in ms. ADub.III.78 and F305-08 also stand very close to each other (see, e.g., *syjyt etemen* in 62–63, or *güneḥ* in line 65), but there are some unique differences between them, too, see: *barġejsiz* vs. *barġejbiz* (35), *qondarġejsiz* vs. *qondarġejbiz* (36), *sivivine* vs. *süv́a-rińa* (39), *ne* vs *ki* (52), *qutlamaġynda* vs. *tojlamaġynda* (53), *qyryjlaryna* vs. *dört qyryjlaryna* (58), etc. Based on these differences, the relationship between the manuscripts is as follows:

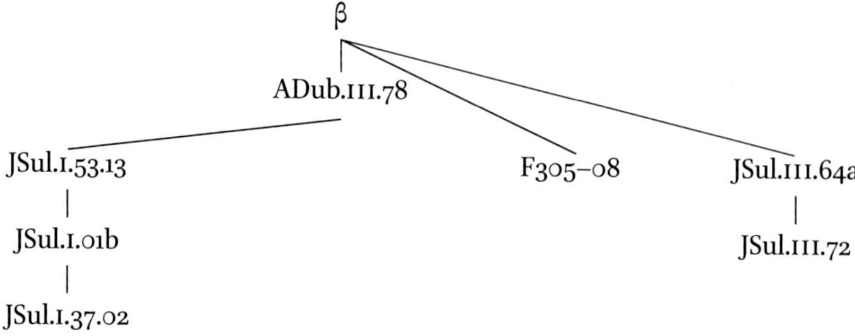


FIGURE 9 Diagram of the connections between the copies of peshat № 6

## 2 Transcription[1] and Translation

284 r° ⌊לעתה אכתוב תרגום פיוט אנ״י יש״נה שתרגמו מלשון [1] [1]
קדש ללשון קדר אדוני אסרפי[2] החכם כמה״רר [2] [2]
משה נ״ע בא״מ הנכבד כ״מ יצחק צי״ץ אורה זלה״ה [3] [3]
אני ישינה⌉[3] [4] [4]

[5] [5] Men synyq ummasy Jisra'elnin tarlyġy
[6] [6] ičińa[4] galutnun uqšatyldym[5] juq-
[7] [7] lejdoġan[6] qatynġa. Vale jüŕagim[7] ojovdu[8]
[8] [8] ešitip[9] ünün[10] Tenrinin tutunulġan navi-

---

1 Based on ADub.III.78.

2 Uncertain reading.

3 JSul.I.53.13: [...] להבין ולדעת כל עמי הארץ הוציאו כמה פיוטי׳ לתרגמם בלשון קדר וזה התרגום ר״ל פשט על פיוט ההלל שהוא אנ״י ישנ״ה ולב״י ע״ר הוציא לאורה התקשרות מאמריו במליצותיו היקרי׳ בסודות גבוהי׳ ותרגמו החכם השלם והכולל מו״ ה״ו כמוה״רר משה נ״ע בא״ד הנכבד כמ״ער יצחק המשכיל המכונה ציוצ״יורא זצ״ל והוא פשט נכון ונאה ומתוק מדבש ונ״צ דברי פי חכם חן תנצב״ה וזצוק״ל והקוראו בזמנו כדרכו כמנהגו שאברכה מ״י ומ״י׳. | JSul.I.01b: בעזרת האל אכתוב פשט יפה ומתוק שפתים ישק דברי פי חכם חן על פיוט אני ישנה ולבי ער הקריא בתוך פיוט הלל הגדול שחברו בזוך זבלו וסלת חכמתו א״ד החכם כמה״רר משה יע״מש בא״ד כמ״ר יצחק צי״ץ אור״ה נ״ע׳. | JSul.III.64a: וזה הפשט לפיוט אני ישנה תרגמו בטוב טעם החכם השלם שפתים ישק במליצתו כמוה״רר משה נב״ת בכמ״ע יצחק הנכבד ממשפחת צי״ץ אורה יע״מש׳. | JSul.III.72: וזה הפשט לפיוט אני ישנה עשוי במליצה יקרה ונכונה: מחכם מחוכם בתורה נאמנה: מו״ה ר״ר משה הנכבד יע״מש בכ״מ יצחק ממשפחת צי״ץ אורה נב״ת:. | JSul.I.37.02: ואם תרצה תא״מ גם את פשטו של זה הפיוט שתרגמו החכם כמוה״רר משה צי״ץ אורה נ״ע בכמ״ע יצחק נב״ת: וזהו הפשט היקר אשר לשבחו אין מחקר:. | F305-08: *Da daġy bu pešaty pijutnun ki Hallel Hagadolnun.*

4 JSul.I.53.13: *ičine.* | JSul.I.01b: *ičine.* | JSul.III.64a: *icine.* | JSul.III.72: *icine.* | JSul.I.37.02: *üčüne* or *ücüne.*

5 JSul.III.64a: *uqsatyldym.* | JSul.III.72: *uqsatyldym.*

6 JSul.I.53.13: *juqlajdoġan.* | JSul.I.01b: *juqlajdoġan.* | JSul.III.64a: *juqlajdoġan.* | JSul.III.72: *juqlajdoġan.* | JSul.I.37.02: *juqlajdoġan.*

7 JSul.I.53.13: *jüregim menim.* | JSul.I.01b: *jüregim menim.* | JSul.III.64a: *jiregim menim.* | JSul.III.72: *jüregim menim.* | JSul.I.37.02: *jüregim menim.*

8 F305-08: *ojavdyr.*

9 JSul.III.64a: *esitip.* | JSul.III.72: *esitip.*

10 JSul.III.64a: *inin.* | JSul.III.72: *inin.* | JSul.I.37.02: *inin.*

11 I.e., *Hebrew.*

12 I.e., *Karaim*; *Qedar* is a Biblical term for an Ishmaelite tribe (see Genesis 25:13) which in early modern Hebrew often refers to the Turks.

13 JSul.I.53.13: [...] *In order to make all the ignoramuses understand and know, you will select some* piyyutim *translated into the language of Qedar* [i.e., into Karaim]*; and this is the interpretation, i.e., a* peshat, *of a* piyyut *for Hallel, of the one* (*with the incipit*) ʾănī yšēnå wlibbī ʿēr, *which brought to light in poetic and dear words the alliance of his writings, in his dear*

[1] [1] ⌊Now, I will write the translation of the *piyyut* (with the incipit) *ʾănī* 284 r°
*yšēnå*, which (he) translated from ⌊the

[2] [2] holy language[111] into ⌊the language of Qedar[112] of my master [...?],
the hakham, his honour, the Rav, Rabbi

[3] [3] Moshe, may his soul rest in Eden, the son of our respected master,
our teacher, his honour, Icchak Cic Ora, may his memory be a
blessing for his life of the World to Come.

[4] [4] (Incipit:) *ʾănī yšēnå:*[113]

[5] [5] (1). We[14], the broken people of Israel

[6] [6] in the misery of exile, have become similar

[7] [7] to the one who sleeps by a woman, but my heart is awake

[8] [8] after having heard the voice of God: the freedom promised

---

*eloquent language, in elevated secrets and which is an interpretation of the complete and perfect hakham, our teacher, the great and honourable sage, his honour, the Rav, Rabbi Moshe, may his soul rest in Eden, the son of our respected master Icchak, whose honourable repose is Eden, ha-Maskil called Cücöra* [~ Cücöre] [sic!], *may the memory of the righteous be a blessing. And it is a proper and fine and pleasant peshat, and a banner to Zion, the words of a wise man's mouth are gracious* [cf., Ecclesiastes 10:12]—*'may his soul be bound in the bond of life'* [cf., 1 Samuel 25:29], *may the memory of the righteous and holy be a blessing—and back then read as a prayer; you will be treated according to your own deeds.* | JSul.I.01b: *With the help of the Lord I will write a beautiful and pleasant* peshat, *which will kiss lips, the words of a wise man's mouth are gracious* [cf., Ecclesiastes 10:12], (*a* peshat) *of the* piyyut (*with the incipit*) ʾănī yšēnå wlibbī ʿēr *read aloud among the* piyyutim *with the Hallel ha-Gadol, delivered by the bright light of clarity of the flour sifter of his wisdom, our master, the hakham, his honour, the Rav, Rabbi Moshe, may he rest in peace, the son of our master, the honourable teacher, Rabbi Icchak Cic Ora, may his soul rest in Eden.* | JSul.III.64a: *And this is the* peshat *of the* piyyut (*with the incipit*) ʾănī yšēnå, *lips that will kiss, an interpretation with good taste of the complete hakham, his honour, the Rav, Rabbi Moshe may his soul lodge Eden, the son of Icchak, the respected, whose honourable repose is Eden, from the Cic Ora family, may he rest in peace.* | JSul.III.72: *This is the* peshat *of the* piyyut (*with the incipit*) ʾănī yšēnå, *a poetic, dear yet proper* (*interpretation*) *of the subtle hakham faithful in the Torah, our teacher, the Rav, Rabbi Moše, the respected, may he rest in peace, the son of the honourable sir Icchak from the Cic Ora family, may his soul lodge Eden.* | JSul.I.37.02: *And, if you prefer, you will also say the* peshat *of this* piyyut [i.e., of the Hebrew original copied above in the manuscript], *which the hakham, his honour, the Rav, Rabbi Moše Cic Ora translated, may his soul rest in Eden, the son of Icchak, whose honourable repose is Eden, may his soul lodge Eden. And this is the beloved peshat which is to praise the unsearchable.* | F305-08 (the heading is in Karaim): *And also this* peshat *of the* piyyut *which is for Hallel Hagadol.*

14 Lit. 'I'.

[9] [9] leri[15] ašyra[16] azatlyq Jisra’elge[17]. ⌊Ajtqan
[10] [10] je‘ud ki dağyn körünür[18] ⌊⌊š[a]loš regalimd́a⌋[19] erkegin⌋[20]
[11] [11] Jerušalajimd́a[21]. Jana[22] širalarbyla[23] da zemerlerbyla
[12] [12] ešittirirler[24] avazlaryn[25] maḥtavlarġa, ki
[13] [13] anlyqqa jaratyldyn[26] maḥ{ta}v[27] berme küčlü[28]
[14] [14] Tenrige.⌋[29] [30]⌈אני בּ֞מלכות כּ֞שדים⌋.
[15] [15] Men galutunda Bavelnin ⌊qajġylarymdan edim⌋[31] jadağan,
[16] [16] vale ešitip[32] naviligin Dani’elnin ki hadirdi[33]
[17] [17] julunma[34] galuttan[35] tolup jetmiš[36] jyl edim
[18] [18] esimde[37] quvanġan. Tözḿajinč́a[38] učun[39]
[19] [19] zamannyn ol bij Koreš symarlady ki bolġej[40] üvü[41]
[20] [20] Tenrinin Jerušalajimd́a[42] qondarylġan, ančaq[43] bu
[21] [21] eksiklik boldu miqdašymda naviligi Ḥagajnyn
[22] [22] ki beš[44] nerśa[45] burun bolġan ⌊bet hamiqdašta⌋[46]

---

15 JSul.I.01b: *navilerin.* | F305-08: *naviĺari.*
16 JSul.I.53.13: *asyra.* | JSul.III.64a: *asyra.* | JSul.III.72: *asyra.*
17 F305-08: *Jisra’elǵa.*
18 JSul.III.64a: *kerinir.* | JSul.III.72: *kerinir.* | JSul.I.37.02: *kerinir.*
19 ADub.III.78: *šeloš regalimd́a*; a scribal error. | JSul.I.53.13: *šaloš regalimde.* | JSul.I.01b: *šaloš regalimde.* | JSul.III.64a: *šaloš regalimde.* | JSul.III.72: *šaloš regalimde.* | JSul.I.37.02: see next footnote.
20 JSul.I.37.02: *erkegin šaloš regalimge.*
21 JSul.I.53.13: *Jerušalajimde.* | JSul.I.01b: *Jerušalajimde.* | JSul.III.64a: *Jerušalajimde.* | JSul.III.72: *Jerušalajimde.* | JSul.I.37.02: deest.
22 JSul.I.37.02: *da janada.*
23 JSul.I.53.13: *širalar.* | JSul.I.01b: *širalar.* | JSul.III.64a: *širalar.* | JSul.III.72: *širalar.*
24 JSul.I.53.13: *ešitilir.* | JSul.I.01b: *ešitilir.* | JSul.III.64a: *esitilir.* | JSul.III.72: *esitilir.*
25 JSul.I.53.13: *avazlaryn*; a scribal error, instead of *avazlary.* | JSul.I.01b: *avazlaryn*; a scribal error, instead of *avazlary.* | JSul.III.64a: *avazlary.* | JSul.III.72: *avazlary.*
26 JSul.III.64a: *jaratyldym.* | JSul.III.72: *jaratyldym.* | JSul.I.37.02: *jaratyldym.*
27 The segment *-ta-* was inserted interlinearly by another hand.
28 JSul.III.64a: *kicli.* | JSul.III.72: *küclü.* | JSul.I.37.02: or: *küclü.*
29 F305-08: desunt; a scribal error.
30 JSul.I.53.13: אֲנִי. | JSul.I.01b: אני במלכות. | JSul.III.64a: אֲנִי. | JSul.III.72: אֲנִי. | F305-08: desunt.
31 JSul.I.53.13: *edim qajġylarymdan.* | JSul.I.01b: *edim qajġylarymdan.* | JSul.I.37.02: *edim qajġylarymdan.*
32 JSul.III.64a: *esitip.* | JSul.III.72: *esitip.*
33 JSul.I.53.13: *hadirdi Jisra’elge.*
34 JSul.I.53.13: *julunmaq.* | JSul.I.01b: *julunmaq.* | JSul.III.64a: *julunmaq.* | JSul.III.72: *julunmaq.* | JSul.I.37.02: *julunmaq.*
35 JSul.I.53.13: deest. | JSul.I.01b: deest. | JSul.III.72: deest. | JSul.I.37.02: deest.
36 JSul.III.64a: *jetmis.* | JSul.III.72: *jetmis.*
37 JSul.I.37.02: *esimden.* | F305-08: *esimd́a.*

[9] [9] to Israel through the[47] prophets.
[10] [10] ⌊The said promise[48] that Your man will appear again at[49] the Three Pilgrimage Festivals
[11] [11] in Jerusalem. Once[50] again, by means of songs and poems[51]
[12] [12] the voices for praise will be made be heard, since
[13] [13] (it is) for this ⌊you have been[152] created: to praise the powerful
[14] [14] God.[153] (2)
[15] [15] In the Babylonian exile I have become weary because of my troubles,
[16] [16] but after having heard the prophecy of Daniel—(namely) that
[17] [17] the liberation ⌊from the exile[154] is ready (to come) after seventy years would end—I have become
[18] [18] joyful in my mind. Without awaiting the end of this
[19] [19] time period, Cyrus the ruler has commissioned that there may be a house
[20] [20] of God built in Jerusalem, but
[21] [21] there has been a lack ⌊in my temple prophesied by Haggai[155],
[22] [22] namely there had been ⌊five things[156] in the[57] former Temple

38 JSul.I.53.13: *tözmejinče.* | JSul.I.01b: *tözmejinče.* | JSul.III.64a: *tezmejince.* | JSul.III.72: *tezmejince.* | JSul.I.37.02: *tözmejinče* or *tözmejince.*
39 JSul.III.64a: *ucun.* | JSul.III.72: *ucun.* | JSul.I.37.02: or: *ucun.*
40 JSul.I.53.13: *bolġaj.* | JSul.I.01b: *bolġaj.* | JSul.III.64a: *bolġaj.* | JSul.III.72: *bolġaj.* | JSul.I.37.02: *bolġaj.*
41 JSul.III.64a: *ivi.* | JSul.III.72: *ivi.* | JSul.I.37.02: *ivi.*
42 JSul.I.53.13: *Jerušalajimde.* | JSul.I.01b: *Jerušalajimde.* | JSul.III.64a: *Jerušalajimde.* | JSul.III.72: *Jerušalajimde.* | JSul.I.37.02: *Jerušalajimde.*
43 JSul.III.64a: *ancaq.* | JSul.III.72: *ancaq.* | JSul.I.37.02: or: *ancaq.*
44 JSul.III.64a: *bes.* | JSul.III.72: *bes.* | JSul.I.37.02: *bes.*
45 JSul.I.53.13: *nerse.* | JSul.I.01b: *nerse.* | JSul.III.64a: *nerse.* | JSul.III.72: *nerse.* | JSul.I.37.02: *nerse.*
46 JSul.I.37.02: *miqdašymda.*
47 JSul.I.01b: *Your.*
48 Lit. 'announcement'.
49 JSul.I.37.02: lit. 'to'.
50 JSul.I.37.02: *and yet.*
51 Lit. '*zemirot*'; i.e., paraliturgical poems.
52 JSul.III.64a: *was I.* | JSul.III.72: *was I.* | JSul.I.37.02: *was I.*
53 F305-08: desunt.
54 JSul.I.53.13: desunt. | JSul.I.01b: desunt. | JSul.III.72: desunt. | JSul.I.37.02: desunt.
55 Lit. 'my temple, the prophecy of Haggai'. | Cf. Haggai 1:1–2, Haggai 7–8.
56 Most likely a reference to the Babylonian Talmud, according to which the Second Temple lacked five things that had been present in the First Temple: the Ark of the Covenant, the eternal flame, the Shekinah, the Holy Spirit, and the *Urim* and *Thummim* (see Barton 1906: 97).
57 JSul.I.37.02: *my.*

284 v° [23] [1] haligińa[58] bolmady tabulġan. [59]⌜געֿיתי בעֿצלות⌟.
[24] [2] Mivrej[60] da öküre[61] čaġyrdym[62] ki bar
[25] [3] išlerim[63] boldu kedergi[64]. Süründüm[65] jerim-
[26] [4] den[66] ač[67] da jalanġač[68] kijiz da topraq töšegi[69]
[27] [5] jylajdoġač[70] saġynyp ki üč[71] qurlalar jylda[72]
[28] [6] baryredim ⌞š[a]loš regalimde⌝[73] Jerušalajimge[74] čyġarma[75]
[29] [7] ʿolalar da šelamimlernin[76] keregi[77]. Ančaq[78] tutu-
[30] [8] nulġan[79] sözü[80] Tenrinin ki kemišmesti[81] raḥmet-
[31] [9] lemekten[82] ⌞ummasyn Jisraʾelnin⌝[83] ol edi jüregim-
[32] [10] nin[84] šatyrlyġy[85]. [86]⌜הדֿוד שלֿח חגֿי⌟.
[33] [11] Raḥmetlevčü[87] Tenri tügetip[88] galutun jetmiš[89]
[34] [12] jylnyn ijdi Ḥagaj[90] navisin[91] ḥabar berme[92] ulusu-
[35] [13] na Jisraʾelnin, ki[93] uže[94] zamandyr[95] ki barġejsiz[96]

58 JSul.I.53.13: *haligine.* | JSul.I.01b: *haligine.* | JSul.III.64a: *haligine.* | JSul.III.72: *haligine.* | JSul.I.37.02: *haligine.*

59 JSul.I.53.13: געֿיתי. | JSul.III.64a: געיתי. | JSul.III.72: געֿיתי. | F305-08: desunt.

60 JSul.I.53.13: *müvrej.* | JSul.I.01b: *müvrej.* | JSul.I.37.02: *müvrej.* | F305-08: *müvrej.*

61 JSul.III.64a: *ekire.* | JSul.III.72: *ekire.* | JSul.I.37.02: *ekire.* | F305-08: *öküŕa.*

62 JSul.III.64a: *caġyrdym.* | JSul.III.72: *caġyrdym.* | JSul.I.37.02: or: *caġyrdym.*

63 JSul.I.01b: *išĺarim*; a NWKar. form. | JSul.III.64a: *islerim.* | JSul.III.72: *islerim.* | JSul.I.37.02: *üšlerim*, a hypercorrect form of *išlerim.* | F305-08: *išĺarim.*

64 F305-08: *keďargi.*

65 JSul.I.53.13: *süründim.* | JSul.III.64a: *sirindim.* | JSul.III.72: *sirindim.* | JSul.I.37.02: *süründim.*

66 JSul.I.53.13: *jörimden*; a hypercorrect form of *jerimden.* | F305-08: *jerimďan.*

67 JSul.III.64a: *ac.* | JSul.III.72: *ac.* | JSul.I.37.02: or: *ac.*

68 JSul.III.64a: *jalanġac.* | JSul.III.72: *jalanġac.* | JSul.I.37.02: *jalanġac.*

69 JSul.III.64a: *tesegi.* | JSul.III.72: *tesegi.* | JSul.I.37.02: *tešegi.* | F305-8: *tössagi.*

70 JSul.III.64a: *jylajdoġac.* | JSul.III.72: *jylajdoġac.* | JSul.I.37.02: or: *jylajdoġac.* | F305-08: *jylej-doġoč.*

71 JSul.III.64a: *ic.* | JSul.III.72: *ic.* | JSul.I.37.02: or: *üc.*

72 JSul.I.01b: deest. | JSul.I.37.02: deest.

73 ADub.III.78: *šeloš regalimde.* | JSul.I.53.13: desunt. | JSul.I.01b: desunt. | JSul.III.64a: *šaloš regalimde.* | JSul.III.72: *šaloš regalimde.* | JSul.I.37.02: desunt. | F305-08: *šaloš regalimďa.*

74 F305-08: *Jerušalajimġa.*

75 JSul.III.64a: *cyġarma.* | JSul.III.72: *cyġarma.* | JSul.I.37.02: or: *cyġarma.*

76 JSul.I.37.02: *šelamimler.* | F305-08: *šelamimĺarnin.*

77 F305-08: *keŕagi.*

78 JSul.III.64a: *ancaq.* | JSul.III.72: *ancaq.* | JSul.I.37.02: or: *ancaq.*

79 JSul.I.53.13: *tutunġan.* | JSul.I.01b: *tutunġan.* | JSul.III.64a: *tutunġan.* | JSul.III.72: *tutunġan.* | JSul.I.37.02: *tutunġan.*

[23] [1] that were not to be found (in it) now. (3). 284 vº
[24] [2] I have been crying roaringly and howlingly that all
[25] [3] my work ⌊was put to one side⌋[97], I was driven out from my land,
[26] [4] hungry and naked, felt and earth has been (my) bed,
[27] [5] (and) I have been recalling cryingly that three times a year
[28] [6] I used to go ⌊to the Three Pilgrimage Festivals⌋[98] to Jerusalem to offer
[29] [7] burnt offerings and peace offerings required. But the promised[99]
[30] [8] word of God, (saying) that He will not stop having pity
[31] [9] ⌊on the people of Israel⌋[100]—this was the
[32] [10] joy of my heart. (4).
[33] [11] The merciful God, after He had ended the exile of seventy
[34] [12] years, has sent His[101] prophet Haggai to announce to the people
[35] [13] of Israel, that[102] 'It is high time that you[103] shall go

---

80 JSul.III.64a: *sezi.* | JSul.III.72: *sözi.* | JSul.I.37.02: *sezi.*
81 JSul.III.64a: *kemismesti.* | JSul.III.72: *kemismesti.* | F305-08: *kemišḿastir.*
82 F305-08: *raḥmetĺamakḱan.*
83 JSul.I.37.02: desunt.
84 JSul.III.64a: *jiregimnin.* | F305:08: *jüŕagimnin.*
85 JSul.III.64a: *satyrlyġy.* | JSul.III.72: *satyrlyġy.*
86 JSul.I.53.13: הדֹּוד. | JSul.III.64a: הדֹּוד. | JSul.III.72: הדוד. | F305-08: desunt.
87 JSul.III.64a: *raḥmetlevci.* | JSul.III.72: *raḥmetlevcü.* | JSul.I.37.02: or: *raḥmetlevcü.* | F305-08: *raḥmetĺavčü.*
88 JSul.III.64a: *tigetip.* | JSul.III.72: *tigetip.* | F305-08: *tüǵatip.*
89 JSul.III.64a: *jetmis.* | JSul.III.72: *jetmis.*
90 F305-08: *Hagajny.*
91 JSul.I.37.02: *navini.*
92 F305-08: *berḿa.*
93 JSul.I.53.13: *ajtadoġač ki.*
94 JSul.III.64a: *ize.* | JSul.III.72: *uze.* | JSul.I.37.02: or: *uze.*
95 JSul.I.01b: *zamandy.* | JSul.III.64a: *zamandy.* | JSul.I.37.02: *zamandy.*
96 JSul.I.53.13: *barġajsiz.* | JSul.I.01b: *barġajsiz.* | JSul.III.64a: *barġajsiz.* | JSul.III.72: *barġajsiz.* | JSul.I.37.02: *barġajsiz.* | F305:08: *barġejbiz.*
97 Uncertain interpretation of *boldu kedergi.*
98 JSul.I.53.13: desunt. | JSul.I.01b: desunt. | JSul.I.37.02: desunt.
99 JSul.I.53.13, JSul.I.01b, JSul.III.64a, JSul.III.72, JSul.I.37.02: expressed with a synonym.
100 JSul.I.37.02: desunt.
101 JSul.I.37.02: deest.
102 JSul.I.53.13: *saying, that.*
103 F305-08: *we.*

[36] [14] da qondarġejsiz[104] ⌊{bet}[105] [ha]miqdašny⌉[106] da šaharyn[107]
Jerušalajimnin.
[37] [15] Ešitip[108] bu ḥabarny qaltradym ⌊da ǯaḥtladym[109]⌉[110]
[38] [16] da symarladym özüḿa[111] aġalyq[112] Zerubavelni
[39] [17] urluġun[113] Davidnin, tez qondardym da sivivine[114]
[40] [18] hadirledim[115] orun šeẖinasyna Tenrimnin[116].
[41] [19] [117]⌈זרוב֞בל ור֞עיו ב֞נו⌋.
[42] [20] Ol zamanny neni ki qondardy Zerubavel da ǯymaty[118]
[43] [21] hale[119] boldu verenlikke[120]. Qajsy orunda[121]
[44] [22] čyġaryre[di][122] ʿolalar da debeḥalar da boluredi
[45] [23] alnynda[123]
285 rº [46] [1] alnynda Tenrinin qabulluq[q]a[124], ne orunda
[47] [2] ki[125] postanovtetti[126] Ezra da Neḥamja[127] ki[128] eksil-
[48] [3] mesedi[129] qarban da šira avazy[130] ešittirmekke[131],

---

104 JSul.I.53.13: *qondarġajsiz.* | JSul.I.01b: *qondarġajsiz.* | JSul.III.64a: *qondarġajsiz.* | JSul.III.72: *qondarġajsiz.* | JSul.I.37.02: *qondarġajsiz.* | F305:08: *qondarġejbiz.*

105 Added on the right margin probably by the copyist.

106 ADub.III.78: *{bet} miqdašny.* | JSul.I.53.13: *bet hamiqdašny.* | JSul.I.01b: *bet hamiqdašny.* | JSul.III.64a: *bet hamiqdašny.* | JSul.III.72: *bet hamiqdašny.* | JSul.I.37.02: *bet hamiqdašny.*

107 JSul.III.64a: *saharyn.* | JSul.III.72: *saharyn.* | JSul.I.37.02: *saharyn.*

108 JSul.III.64a: *esitip.* | JSul.III.72: *esitip.*

109 JSul.III.64a: *ʒaḥtladym.* | JSul.III.72: *ʒaḥtladym.*

110 JSul.I.01b: desunt. | JSul.I.37.02: desunt.

111 JSul.I.53.13: *özüme.* | JSul.I.01b: *özüme.* | JSul.III.64a: *ezime.* | JSul.III.72: *ezime.* | JSul.I.37.02: deest.

112 F305-08: *ahalyq.*

113 JSul.I.37.02: *urluġundan.*

114 ADub.III.78: spelled סִיוֹבִינֵיא. | JSul.I.53.13: סיוּביוּנֵיא *süvüne* < *süvüvüne*; either a scribal error or a result of haplology. | JSul.I.01b: *süvüvüne*; spelled סֶיוּוּנֵיא. | JSul.III.64a: שִׁיוִוינֶיא *sivine* < *sivivine*; either a scribal error or a result of haplology. | JSul.III.72: שִׁיוִוינֵיא *sivine* < *sivivine*; either a scribal error or a result of haplology. | JSul.I.37.02: *süvüne bardym da*; סיוּביוּנֵיא *süvüne* < *süvüvüne* (either a scribal error or a result of haplology). | F305-08: *süvárińa.*

115 F305-08: *hadirĺadim.*

116 JSul.III.64a: *Tenrinin.* | JSul.III.72: *Tenrinin.* | JSul.I.37.02: *Tenrinin.*

117 JSul.I.53.13: זרוּבֿבל. | JSul.I.01b: זרובבל ורעיו. | JSul.III.64a: זרובבל. | JSul.III.72: זרוֹבבל. | F305-08: desunt.

118 JSul.III.64a: *ʒymaty.* | JSul.III.72: *ʒymaty.* | JSul.I.37.02: or: *ʒymaty.* | F305-08: *ǯymaty anyn.*

119 JSul.I.53.13: *haligine.* | JSul.I.01b: *haligine.* | JSul.III.64a: *haligine.* | JSul.III.72: *haligine.* | JSul.I.37.02: *haligine.*

120 F305-08: *veŕanlikḱa.*

[36] [14] and build the Temple and the city of Jerusalem'.
[37] [15] After having heard this news, I have trembled ⌊and hurried⌉[132]
[38] [16] and summoned ⌊to me⌉[133] the superior Zerubbabel
[39] [17] the[134] offspring of David, (and) I have built (it) quickly and
[40] [18] prepared[135] to His liking the place for the divine Presence of my[136] God.
[41] [19] (5).
[42] [20] That which Zerubbabel and his congregation built in that time
[43] [21] now[137] has become destroyed. The place in which
[44] [22] burnt offerings and sacrifice ⌊used to be offered⌉[138] and they used to find
[45] [23] [139]
[46] [1] acceptance before God, (the place) in which 285 r°
[47] [2] Ezra and Nehemiah decided that
[48] [3] offerings would never disappear and the voices of songs will never stop to be heard,

121 JSul.I.37.02: *orunda ki.*

122 ADub.III.78: *čyġaryre*; a scribal error. | JSul.I.53.13: *čyġaryredim.* | JSul.I.01b: *čyġaredi.* | JSul.III.64a: *cyġaredi.* | JSul.III.72: *cyġaredi.* | JSul.I.37.02: *čyġaryredi* or *cyġaryredi.*

123 Catchword.

124 ADub.III.78: *qabulluqa*; probably a scribal error. | JSul.I.53.13: *qabulluqqa.* | JSul.I.01b: *qabulluqa.* | JSul.III.64a: *qabulluqqa.*

125 JSul.I.01b: deest. | JSul.III.64a: deest.

126 JSul.I.37.02: *postanovteti*; a scribal error.

127 JSul.I.53.13: *Neḥemja.* | JSul.I.01b: *Neḥemja.* | JSul.III.64a: *Neḥemja.* | JSul.III.72: *Neḥemja.* | JSul.I.37.02: *Neḥemja.*

128 JSul.I.01b: deest. | JSul.I.37.02: deest.

129 F305-08: *eksilḿasedi.*

130 JSul.I.53.13: *avaz.* | JSul.I.01b: *avaz.* | JSul.I.37.02: *avaz.*

131 JSul.III.64a: *esittirmekke.* | JSul.III.72: *esittirmekke.* | F305-08: *ešittirḿakḱa.*

132 JSul.I.01b: desunt. | JSul.I.37.02: desunt.

133 JSul.I.37.02: desunt.

134 JSul.I.37.02: *from the.*

135 JSul.I.37.02: *went and prepared.*

136 JSul.III.64a: deest. | JSul.III.72: deest. | JSul.I.37.02: deest.

137 JSul.I.53.13, JSul.I.01b, JSul.III.64a, JSul.III.72, JSul.I.37.02: expressed with a synonym.

138 JSul.I.53.13: *I used to offer.* | JSul.I.01b: *he offered*; probably a scribal error. | JSul.III.64a: *he offered*; probably a scribal error. | JSul.III.72: *he offered*; probably a scribal error.

139 Catchword in the Karaim text: 'before Him'.

haligine[140] čaġyramyn[141] galutta da jalbaramyn[142] da joḥtur[143] ešitmek[144] tefila[145] etmekke[146]. [147]⌜טוב̈ ט̈עם זכרי̈ה בחנ̈וכה⌟. Rast ǯanbyla[148] qajtqanlarynda Tenrige[149] ne[150] ullu quvanč[151] edi qutlamaġynda[152] bet hamiqdašnyn, vale nečik[153] jazyqly boldular ol bijler[154] da kohenler[155] alarnyn jazyqlary üčün[156] jane[157] jesirlikke[158] bardy ulusu Jisra'elnin. Qolu ašyra[159] Titosnun[160] ⌞boldu veren⌝[161] bajit šeni da ulanlary Jisra'elnin tozuldular qyryjlaryna[162] tarafnyn. Vaj bizge[163] boldu[164] ki ḥorlanabiz da munajabiz bolup qullary ullu bijnin. [165]⌜בקר̈אי ל̈ו ולא⌟. Ullu tarlyqlar čydejdoġan[166] ⌞bu[167] galutta[168]⌝[169] bolalmejmyn[170] tapma onġalmaq özüḿa[171]. Syjyt

140 F305-08: *haligińa.*

141 JSul.I.53.13: *čaġyramen.* | JSul.I.01b: *čaġyramen.* | JSul.III.64a: *caġyramen.* | JSul.III.72: *caġyramen.* | JSul.I.37.02: *čaġyramen* or *caġyramen.*

142 JSul.I.53.13: *jalbaramen.* | JSul.I.01b: *jalbaramen.* | JSul.III.64a: *jalbaramen.* | JSul.III.72: *jalbaramen.* | JSul.I.37.02: *jalbaramen.*

143 JSul.III.64a: *joḥtu.* | JSul.III.72: *joḥtu.* | JSul.I.37.02: *joḥtu.*

144 JSul.III.64a: *esitmek.* | F305-08: *ešitḿak.*

145 JSul.III.64a: *tefile.* | JSul.III.72: *tefile.* | JSul.I.37.02: *tefile.*

146 F305-08: *etḿakḱa.*

147 JSul.I.53.13: טוֹ̈ב טעָ̈ם. | JSul.I.01b: טוב טעם זכריה. | JSul.III.64a: טוב טעם. | JSul.III.72: טוֹ̈ב. | F305-08: desunt.

148 JSul.III.64a: *ʒan byla.* | JSul.III.72: *ʒan byla.* | JSul.I.37.02: *ǯan byla* or *ʒan byla.*

149 F305-08: *Tenriǵa.*

150 F305-08: *ki.*

151 JSul.III.64a: *quvanc.* | JSul.III.72: *quvanc.* | JSul.I.37.02: or: *quvanc.*

152 F305-08: *tojlamaġyna.*

153 JSul.III.64a: *necik.* | JSul.III.72: *necik.* | JSul.I.37.02: or: *necik.*

154 F305-08: *bijĺar.*

155 F305-08: *kohenĺar.*

156 JSul.III.64a: *icin.* | JSul.III.72: *ücün.* | JSul.I.37.02: or: *ücün.*

157 JSul.I.53.13: *jana.* | JSul.I.01b: *janada.* | JSul.III.64a: *jana.* | JSul.III.72: *jana.* | JSul.I.37.02: *janada.*

158 F305-08: *jesirlikḱa.*

159 JSul.I.53.13: *asyra.* | JSul.III.64a: *asyra.* | JSul.III.72: *asyra.* | JSul.I.37.02: *asyra.*

160 Heb. טיטוס, i.e., Titus (full name: Titus Flavius Sabinus Vespasianus).

161 JSul.I.53.13: *veren boldu.* | JSul.I.01b: *veren boldu.* | JSul.III.64a: *veren boldu.* | JSul.III.72: *veren boldu.* | JSul.I.37.02: *veren boldu.* | F305-08: *boldu veŕan.*

162 JSul.I.53.13: *qyryjlarynda.* | JSul.III.64a: *qyryjlarynda.* | JSul.III.72: *qyryjlarynda.* | JSul.I.37.02: *qyryjlarynda.* | F305-08: *dört qyryjlaryna.*

[49] [4] (in that place), now, I cry in exile and pray,
[50] [5] and there is no listening to praying.
[51] [6] (6).
[52] [7] When they have returned with just heart to God
[53] [8] there[172] was such a great joy ⌊when the Temple was consecrated⌋[173].
[54] [9] But when the lords and the priests have become sinful,
[55] [10] because of their sins
[56] [11] the people of Israel have gone into captivity once[174] again. With the hands of Titus
[57] [12] the Second Temple has been destroyed and the children of Israel
[58] [13] have been dispersed throughout[175] the edges[176] of the land[177]. ⌊It was⌋[178] woe
[59] [14] betide us for we are condemned and troubled
[60] [15] after becoming the servants of a strong ruler. (7).
[61] [16] (While) suffering great miseries ⌊in this[179] exile[180]⌋[181]
[62] [17] I cannot find remedy[182] for myself. I grieve[183]

---

163 F305-08: *bizǵa.*

164 JSul.I.53.13: deest. | JSul.I.01b: deest. | JSul.III.64a: deest. | JSul.III.72: deest. | JSul.I.37.02: deest.

165 JSul.I.53.13: כקראי לו. | JSul.I.01b: כקראי לו ולא ענני. | JSul.III.64a: כקראי. | JSul.III.72: כקראי. | JSul.I.37.02: כקראי לו ולא ענני. | F305-08: deest.

166 JSul.I.53.13: *čydajdoġan.* | JSul.I.01b: *čydajdoġan.* | JSul.III.64a: *cydajdoġan.* | JSul.III.72: *cydajdoġan.* | JSul.I.37.02: *čydajdoġan* or *cydajdoġan.* | F305-08: *čydejdoġoč.*

167 JSul.III.72: deest.

168 JSul.I.01b: *ačy galutta.* | JSul.I.37.02: *ačy galutta* or *acy galutta.*

169 JSul.III.64a: *galutta bu.*

170 JSul.I.53.13: *bolalmajmen.* | JSul.I.01b: *bolalmajmen.* | JSul.III.64a: *bolalmajmen.* | JSul.III.72: *bolalmajmen.* | JSul.I.37.02: *bolalmajmen.*

171 JSul.I.53.13: *özüme.* | JSul.I.01b: *özüme.* | JSul.III.64a: *ezime.* | JSul.III.72: *ezime.* | JSul.I.37.02: *ezime.*

172 F305-08: *which.*

173 F305-08: *when the* [opening] *of the Temple was celebrated.*

174 JSul.I.01b: *yet once.* | JSul.I.37.02: *yet once.*

175 Lit. 'to'. | JSul.I.53.13: *in.* | JSul.III.64a: *in.* | JSul.III.72: *in.* | JSul.I.37.02: *in.*

176 F305-08: *four edges.*

177 Lit. 'place'.

178 JSul.I.53.13: desunt. | JSul.I.01b: desunt. | JSul.III.64a: desunt. | JSul.III.72: desunt. | JSul.I.37.02: desunt.

179 JSul.III.72: deest.

180 JSul.I.01b: *bitter exile.* | JSul.I.37.02: *bitter exile.*

181 JSul.III.64a: different word order.

182 Lit. 'healing'.

183 JSul.I.53.13: *grieve and cry.* | JSul.I.01b: *grieve and cry.* | JSul.I.37.02: *grieve and cry.*

[63] [18] etemin[184] šeme[185] tabarmen[186] zaman ešitmek[187] tefilama[188],
[64] [19] ki köp[189] qyjynlar[190] körem[in][191] jazyq qylġanym üčün[192]
[65] [20] eki anča[193] güneḥ[194] qylġanyma. Ančaq[195] yšančym[196]
[66] [21] Tenrige[197] ki tügeliče[198] unutmas[199] raḥmetleme[200].
[67] [22] [201]⌜מצוֹ֞ת ד֞ודי שא֞לתי⌟.
285 vº [68] [1] Ajttym Tora oḥuvčularġa[202] da anlavču-
[69] [2] larġa[203] tešuva qylyp da mode bolup jazyqla-
[70] [3] rynyzġa[204] tüzünüz[205] tanalar ornuna tügel[206]
[71] [4] tefilalar[207]. Šahat[208] saġynyp šertin[209] Avraham[210]
[72] [5] Jicḥaq[211] da[212] Ja'aqovnun julur bizni bu galuttan da
[73] [6] qalmazbiz[213] galutta Jisra'el atalġanlar[214]. Šahat[215]
[74] [7] qajtaryr bizni jerimizge[216] da bet hamiqdašta
[75] [8] čyġarybiz[217] 'olalar[218], kohenĺar[219] da[220] Leviler[221] ⌞maḥtav

---

184 JSul.I.53.13: *etemen da firjat etemen.* | JSul.I.01b: *etemen da firjat etemen.* | JSul.III.64a: *etemen*; not vocalized. | JSul.III.72: *etemen.* | JSul.I.37.02: *etemen da firjat etemen.* | F305-08: *etamin.*

185 JSul.I.37.02: *seme.*

186 F305-08: *tabarmyn.*

187 JSul.III.64a: *esitmek.* | JSul.III.72: *esitmek.* | F305-08: *ešittirma.*

188 JSul.I.53.13: *tefilame.* | JSul.I.01b: *tefilame.* | JSul.III.64a: *tefileme.* | JSul.III.72: *tefileme.* | JSul.I.37.02: *tefileme.*

189 JSul.III.64a: *kep.* | JSul.III.72: *kep.*

190 JSul.I.53.13: *qyjyn.* | JSul.I.01b: *qyjyn.* | JSul.I.37.02: *qyjyn.*

191 ADub.III.78: the vowel point of the last segment is not clearly visible. | JSul.I.53.13: *köremen.* | JSul.I.01b: *köremen.* | JSul.III.64a: *keremen.* | JSul.III.72: *keremen.* | JSul.I.37.02: *köremen.* | F305-08: *köramin.*

192 JSul.III.64a: *icin.* | JSul.III.72: *icin.* | JSul.I.37.02: or: *ücün.*

193 JSul.III.64a: *anca.* | JSul.III.72: *anca.* | JSul.I.37.02: or: *anca.*

194 JSul.I.53.13: *jazyq.* | JSul.I.01b: *jazyq.* | JSul.III.64a: *jazyq.* | JSul.III.72: *jazyq.* | JSul.I.37.02: *jazyq.* | F305-8: *güńaḥ.*

195 JSul.III.64a: *ancaq.* | JSul.III.72: *ancaq.* | JSul.I.37.02: or: *ancaq.*

196 JSul.III.64a: *ysancym.* | JSul.III.72: *ysancym.* | JSul.I.37.02: *ysancym.*

197 JSul.I.01b: *Tenridedi.* | JSul.I.37.02: *Tenridedi.* | F305-08: *Tenrida.*

198 JSul.III.64a: *tigelice.* | JSul.III.72: *tigelice.* | JSul.I.37.02: *tigeliče* or *tigelice.* | F305-08: *tüǵaliča.*

199 JSul.I.01b: *unutmasty.* | JSul.III.64a: *unutmasty.* | JSul.III.72: *unutmasty.* | JSul.I.37.02: *unutmasty.*

200 F305-08: *raḥmetĺama.*

201 JSul.I.53.13: מִצּוֹת. | JSul.III.64a: מצוֹת. | JSul.III.72: מצוֹת. | F305-08: desunt.

202 JSul.III.64a: *uḥuvcularġa.* | JSul.III.72: *uḥuvcularġa.* | JSul.I.37.02: *uḥuvčularġa* or *uḥuvcularġa.*

203 JSul.III.64a: *anlavcularġa.* | JSul.III.72: *anlavcularġa.* | JSul.I.37.02: or: *anlavcularġa.*

204 JSul.I.53.13: *jazyqlarynyzny.* | JSul.I.01b: *jazyqlarynyzny.* | JSul.I.37.02: *jazyqlarynyzny.* | F305-08: *jazyqlarny.*

205 JSul.III.64a: *tiziniz.* | JSul.III.72: *tiziniz.* | F305-08: *tüzüjüz.*

206 JSul.III.64a: *tigel.* | JSul.III.72: *tigel.* | JSul.I.37.02: *tigel.*

[63] [18] and perhaps I will ⌞live to see⌝[222] the times (when there will be) listening to my prayer,
[64] [19] for I see great suffering because of my sinning:
[65] [20] (so much as) for twice as much sinning[223]. But ⌞I hope
[66] [21] to God⌝[224] that He will not forget completely to have mercy.
[67] [22] (8).
[68] [1] I have told the readers of the Law and to (the men of) understanding 285 v°
[69] [2] (that) after doing repentance and confessing your[225] sins
[70] [3] you shall compose true prayers instead of (offering) bullocks.
[71] [4] Perhaps, remembering the covenant of Abraham,
[72] [5] Isaac[226], and[227] Jacob, He will save us from this[228] exile and
[73] [6] we will be no longer called[229] 'Israel in captivity'. Perhaps,
[74] [7] He will bring us back to our land and in the Temple
[75] [8] we will bring ⌞burnt offerings⌝[230], the priests ⌞and the⌝[231] Levites

---

207 JSul.I.53.13: *tefilaler.* | JSul.I.01b: *tefilaler.* | JSul.III.64a: *tefileler.* | JSul.III.72: *tefileler.* | JSul.I.37.02: *tefileler.*

208 JSul.III.64a: *sahat.* | JSul.III.72: *sahat.*

209 JSul.III.64a: *sertin.* | JSul.III.72: *sertin.* | JSul.I.37.02: *sertin.*

210 JSul.III.64a: *Avrahamnyn.* | JSul.III.72: *Avrahamnyn.* | F305-08: *Avrahamnyn.*

211 JSul.III.64a: *da Jicḥaqnyn.* | JSul.III.72: *Jicḥaqnyn.* | F305-08: *Jicḥaqnyn.*

212 JSul.I.37.02: deest.

213 JSul.III.64a: *qalmabiz.* | JSul.III.72: *qalmabiz.* | JSul.I.37.02: *qalmabiz.*

214 JSul.I.01b: *ündelgenler.* | JSul.I.37.02: *indelgenler.*

215 JSul.III.64a: *sahat.* | JSul.III.72: *sahat.*

216 F305-08: *jerimizǵa.*

217 JSul.I.53.13: *čyǵaryrbiz.* | JSul.I.01b: *čyǵaryrbiz.* | JSul.III.64a: *cyǵarybiz.* | JSul.III.72: *cyǵarybez*; a scribal error. | JSul.I.37.02: *čyǵaryrbiz* or *cyǵaryrbiz.* | F305-08: *čyǵaryrbiz.*

218 JSul.I.01b: *'olalar da šelamimler.* | JSul.I.37.02: *'olalar da šelamimler.*

219 JSul.I.53.13: *kohenler.* | JSul.I.01b: *kohenler.* | JSul.III.64a: *kohenler.* | JSul.I.37.02: *kohenler.*

220 JSul.I.53.13: deest. | JSul.I.01b: deest. | JSul.III.64a: deest. | JSul.III.72: deest. | JSul.I.37.02: deest.

221 F305-08: *Levililar.*

222 Lit. 'achieve; reach'.

223 JSul.I.53.13, JSul.I.01b, JSul.III.64a, JSul.III.72, JSul.I.37.02: expressed with a synonym.

224 JSul.I.01b: *my hope is in God.* | JSul.I.37.02: *my hope is in God.* | F305-08: *my hope is in God.*

225 F305-08: deest.

226 JSul.III.64a: *and Isaac.*

227 JSul.I.37.02: deest.

228 Or: *the.*

229 JSul.I.01b, JSul.I.37.02: expressed with a synonym.

230 JSul.I.01b: *burnt offerings and peace offerings.* | JSul.I.37.02: *burnt offerings and peace offerings.*

231 JSul.I.53.13: desunt. | JSul.I.01b: desunt. | JSul.III.64a: desunt. | JSul.III.72: desunt. | JSul.I.37.02: desunt.

[76] [9] ajtyrlar Tenriġa⌉[232] ⌊da burundaġylaj zemer[233]
[77] [10] da šira[234] avazy[235]⌉[236] ešittirirler[237].
[78] [11] ⌊סליק סליק סליק⌉[238]

232 JSul.i.53.13: *maḥtav ajtyrlar Tenrige.* | JSul.i.01b: *maḥtav ajtyrlar Tenrige.* | JSul.iii.64a: *maḥtav ajtyrlar Tenrige.* | JSul.iii.72: *jumus eterler Tenrige.* | JSul.i.37.02: *maḥtav ajtyrlar Tenrige.* | F305-08: *maḥtav Tenriġa ajtyrlar.*

233 JSul.i.53.13: *zemerler.* | JSul.i.01b: *zemerler.*

234 JSul.i.53.13: *zemerler.* | JSul.i.01b: *širalar.*

235 JSul.i.01b: deest. | JSul.iii.72: *avazyn.* | JSul.i.37.02: *avaz.*

236 JSul.i.53.13: *zemerler da širalar burundaġylaj.* | F305-08: *zemer da šira avazy.*

237 JSul.iii.64a: *esittirirler.* | JSul.iii.72: *esittirirler.* | F305-08: *ešittirirĺar.*

238 JSul.i.53.13: תם הפשט נכון וישר. | JSul.i.01b: תם הפשט בעזר האל. | JSul.iii.64a: תם. | JSul.iii.72: תם. | JSul.i.37.02: תם הפשט. | F305-08: תם.

[76] [9] will praise[239] God and, ⌊as it was before,⌉[240]
[77] [10] they will make the ⌊voices of⌉[241] poems[242] and songs[243] be heard
[78] [11] ⌊End, end, end.⌉[244]

239 JSul.III.72: *serve.*

240 F305-08: desunt.

241 JSul.I.01b: desunt.

242 ADub.III.78: lit. *'zemer'*, i.e. paraliturgical poem. | JSul.I.53.13: lit. *'zemer'*, i.e. paraliturgical poem. | JSul.I.01b: lit. *'zemer'*, i.e. paraliturgical poem. | JSul.III.64a: lit. *'zemirot'*, i.e. paraliturgical poems. | JSul.III.72: lit. *'zemirot'*, i.e. paraliturgical poems. | JSul.I.37.02: lit. *'zemirot'*, i.e. paraliturgical poems.

243 ADub.III.78: lit. 'song'. | JSul.I.53.13: lit. 'song'. | JSul.I.01b: lit. 'song'.

244 JSul.I.53.13: *The peshat is finished properly.* | JSul.I.01b: *The end of the peshat, with the help of God.* | JSul.III.64a: *The end.* | JSul.III.72: *The end.* | JSul.I.37.02: *The end of the peshat.* | F305-8: *The end.*

PART 5

# *The* peshatim *of Simcha ben Chananel*

∵

**Text number:** № 7
**Karaim incipit:** *Adonajdy biji Jisra'elnin*
**Hebrew incipit:** אֲדוֹנָי מֶלֶךְ יִשְׂרָאֵל *ʾăḏōnåy meleḵ yiśråʾēl*
**Dedication:** Yom Teruah
**Language:** MSWKar., Early Mod.SWKar., Mod.SWKar.
**Number of copies:** 7

| Accession no. | Place of origin of copy | Date of copy | Copyist | Folios |
|---|---|---|---|---|
| JSul.I.54.03 | Halych (?) | turn of the 19th c. | Unknown 5 | 1 v°–2 r° |
| JSul.I.54.12 | Halych | early 19th c. | Unknown 8 | 1 v°–2 r° |
| JSul.III.72$_1$ | Halych | before 1851 | Jeshua Josef Mordkowicz | 142 v°–143 v° |
| JSul.III.72$_2$ | Halych | before 1851 | Jeshua Josef Mordkowicz | 227 r°–227 v° |
| JSul.III.67 | Halych | after ca. 1840, before 1851 | Josef b. Icchak Szulimowicz (?) | 207 r°–207 v° |
| JSul.I.46 | Halych | 1st half of the 19th c. | Jeshua Josef Mordkowicz | 5 v°–6 r° |
| JSul.III.76 | Halych | 2nd half of the 19th c. | Jeshua Josef Mordkowicz | 53 r°–53 v° |

## 1 Introductory Remarks

Two different *peshatim* of this *piyyut* are available to us. The *peshat* authored by Simcha ben Chananel has been critically edited below, based on seven vocalized copies. However, neither the age of the other *peshat*, available in RAbk.IV.15 (174 r°–174 v°) and copied (possibly in Troki) on 18 Cheshvan 5568 A.M. (i.e., 19 Nov 1808 A.D.), nor the identity of its author can be determined with any degree of certainty and therefore it has not been included in this collection.[1]

1 Its incipit is *Adonajdyr biji Jisra'elnin* (№ 108) and it was copied in Mod.NWKar. Some parts of the heading that introduces the copy in ms. RAbk.IV.15 are illegible given that the handwriting on the ragged sheet has been partially obliterated or has faded due to frequent use. The existing fragment suggests that the author of the *peshat* was a person called *Abraham the aged* or someone who was the father of *Abraham the aged*: that part of the heading which would explicate this fact is missing, see: 1–2: וזה תרגום פיוט חמישי של [...] כמוהרר׳ אברהם הזקן נבֿת אשר התחלתו אדוני מלך ישר[אל] 'And this is an interpretation of the fifth *piyyut* of [...] his honour, the Rav, Rabbi Abraham the aged, may his soul lodge in Eden, which begins (with the words) *ʾăḏōnåy meleḵ yiśr*[*åʾēl*]' (see, lines 1–2 on folio 174 r°). Exactly the same information is missing from the colophon on f. 174 v° which was damaged as a result of cutting off the right margin of the page while rebinding the prayer book.

We know that the author of this *peshat* is Simcha b. Chananel. In all the headings, with the exception of JSul.III.72$_2$, he is referred to as הנ״ל 'the above-mentioned', whereas his name is explicitly written in the headings introducing *peshat* № 13.

The copies are vocalized. The differences between the copies are not significant. At the same time, one quite interesting fact to note is that the two texts taken from JSul.III.72 differ slightly from one other, although they were copied by the same copyist: JSul.III.72$_2$ stands closer to the *peshat* copied in JSul.III.67, cf. such forms shared by these two mss. as e.g. *tarlyqtan* (3), *jalbarmaqbyla* (8), *andij* (12), *bolunuvču* (17), and *atalarnyn* (19). Perhaps there were two (or possibly even more) marginally different versions of the text in circulation.

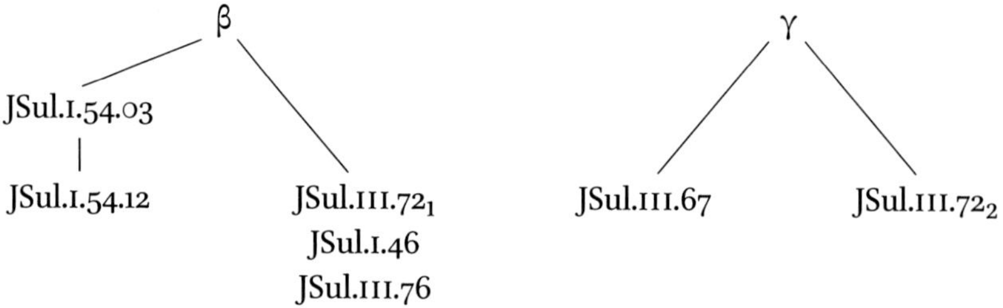


FIGURE 10 Diagram of the connections between the copies of peshat № 7

## 2 Transcription[2] and Translation

1 v°

[1] [10] ⌊וזו היא פשט פיוט השנית שהוא

[2] [11] אדוני מלך ישראל אשר תרגמו החכם הנ̈ל זצ̈ל ויעֿמש ׳ אדני מלך ישראל ׳⌉[3]

[3] [12] Adonajdy biji Jisra'elnin da bar tarlyqlardan[4] juluvčusu[5] anyn.

[4] [13] Čynyqtyrdy[6] bizni jürüme[7] tüz[8] jolbyla ⌊bermek-

[5] [14] byla⌋[9] torasyn[10] šavaġatlaryndan[11] özünün[12]. Da anyn üčün[13] borčtu[14]

[6] [15] bizge maḥtav berme anar jaḥšylyqlar[y][15] üčün[16] anyn. Zemerler-byla

[7] [16] maḥtavyn qotarajyq anyn. הודי̇ענו[17]. Bildirdi bizge Torada[18]

[8] [17] ki bu tešuva künlerinde[19] kötürgejbiz[20] avaz jalbarmaqlarbyla[21],

[9] [18] ki saġynylġajbiz alnynda anyn ošpu[22] künde[23] ol[24] ündelgen[25] Jom

[10] [19] Teru'a byla, da ki qolġajbiz ⌊alnyndan anyn⌋[26] qoltqa[27] jylamaqbyla

---

2 Based on JSul.I.54.03.

3 JSul.I.54.12: וזה הפשט לפיוט הב׳ הנקרא בקדשת ת׳ ביום הנ̈ל. | JSul.III.72$_1$: וזה פשטו של פיוט האחרון דיום תרועה שהוא אֲדוֹנָי מֶלֶךְ יִשְׂרָאֵל וגואלו להחכם הנ̈ל. | JSul.III.72$_2$: וזה פשטו של פיוט אדוני מלך ישראל: | JSul.III.67: ואם טרצה תאמר גם פשטו שתרגמו החכם הנל:. | JSul.I.46: פשט שני לפיוט אֲדֹנָי מֶלֶךְ יִשְׂרָאֵל וְגוֹאֲלוֹ הנֹאם ביום תרועה על קדושת שמע ישראל והוא ג̈כ נעשה מן המחבר הפשט הנ̈ל זצוק̈ל:.

4 JSul.III.72$_2$: *tarlyqtan.* | JSul.III.67: *tarlyqtan.*

5 JSul.I.46: *juluvcusu.* | JSul.III.76: *juluvcusu.*

6 JSul.I.46: *cynyqtyrdy.* | JSul.III.76: *cynyqtyrdy.*

7 JSul.III.67: *jirime.* | JSul.III.76: *jirime.*

8 JSul.III.72$_1$: *tiz.* | JSul.III.72$_2$: *tiz.* | JSul.III.67: *tiz.* | JSul.III.76: *tiz.*

9 JSul.I.54.12: *bermekbyla bizge.* | JSul.III.72$_1$: *bermekbyla bizge.* | JSul.III.72$_2$: *bermekbyla bizge.* | JSul.I.46: *bermek byla bizge.*

10 JSul.III.76: *aziz torasyn.*

11 JSul.I.46: *savaġatlaryndan.* | JSul.III.76: *savaġatlaryndan.*

12 JSul.III.72$_1$: *özünin.* | JSul.III.67: *ezinin.* | JSul.III.76: *ezinin.*

13 JSul.III.67: *ičin.* | JSul.I.46: *ücün.* | JSul.III.76: *icin.*

14 JSul.I.46: *borctu.* | JSul.III.76: *borctu.*

15 JSul.I.54.03: *jaḥsylyqlar*; a scribal error. | JSul.I.54.12: *jaḥsylyqlary.* | JSul.III.67: *savaġatlary.* | JSul.I.46: *jaḥsyraġy byla maḥtavlarymyznyn jaḥsylyqlary.* | JSul.III.76: *jaḥsylyqlary.*

16 JSul.III.67: *ičin.* | JSul.I.46: *ücün.* | JSul.III.76: *icin.*

17 JSul.I.54.12: deest. | JSul.III.72$_1$: הודי̇ענו להר̈ים. | JSul.III.72$_2$: deest. | JSul.III.67: הודי̇ענו להר̈ים.

18 JSul.I.46: *aziz torada.*

19 JSul.III.67: *kinlerinde.* | JSul.III.76: *kinlerinde.*

20 JSul.I.54.12: *kötirgejbiz.* | JSul.III.67: *ketirgejbiz.* | JSul.I.46: *ketirgejbiz.* | JSul.III.76: *ketirgejbiz.*

21 JSul.I.54.12: *jalbarmaqbyla.* | JSul.III.72$_2$: *jalbarmaqbyla.* | JSul.III.67: *jalbarmaqbyla.* | JSul.III.76: *jalbarmaqbyla.*

[1] [10] ⌊And this is the second *peshat* of the *piyyut* (with the incipit) 1 v°
[2] [11] *ʾăḏōnåy meleḵ yiśråʾēl,* which the above-mentioned hakham translated, may the memory of the righteous be a blessing and may he rest in peace. *ʾăḏōnåy meleḵ yiśråʾēl*(:)⌋[28]
[3] [12] The Lord is the ruler of Israel and its saviour from all the miseries[29].
[4] [13] He has accustomed us to walking the right way by giving[30]
[5] [14] His Law[31] of His own mercies. And therefore it is an obligation
[6] [15] for us to praise Him ⌊for His goodness⌋[32]. With songs
[7] [16] let us preach his praise. (2). He has announced to us in the Law[33]
[8] [17] that in these days of repentance we should lift up (our) voice in entreaties[34],
[9] [18] so that we will be remembered before Him on the day called Yom
[10] [19] Terua, and so that we (can) beg[35] before[36] Him crying

---

22 JSul.I.54.12: *ušpu.* | JSul.III.$72_1$: *ušpu.* | JSul.III.67: *ušpu.* | JSul.I.46: *uspu.* | JSul.III.76: *uspu.*

23 JSul.I.54.12: {{*kü*}} *künde.* | JSul.III.67: *kinde.* | JSul.I.46: *künnü.* | JSul.III.76: *kinde.*

24 JSul.I.54.12: deest. | JSul.III.$72_1$: deest.

25 JSul.I.54.12: *ündeledoğan.* | JSul.III.67: *indelgen.* | JSul.I.46: *indelgen.* | JSul.III.76: *indelgen.*

26 JSul.I.54.12: *any.* | JSul.III.$72_1$: *any.* | JSul.III.$72_2$: *any.* | JSul.III.67: *any.* | JSul.I.46: *any.* | JSul.III.76: *any.*

27 JSul.III.$72_1$: deest. | JSul.III.$72_2$: deest. | JSul.III.67: deest. | JSul.I.46: deest. | JSul.III.76: deest.

28 JSul.I.54.12: *And this is the second* peshat *of the* piyyut *read with the holy prayers on the above-mentioned day* [i.e., on Yom Teruah; see, № 13]. | JSul.III.$72_1$: *And this is the* peshat *of the last* piyyut *for Yom Teruah* (*with the incipit*) ʾăḏōnåy meleḵ yiśråʾēl wgōʾălō *of the above-mentioned hakham.* | JSul.III.$72_2$: *And this is the* peshat *of the* piyyut (*with the incipit*) ʾăḏōnåy meleḵ yiśråʾēl. | JSul.III.67: *And, if you prefer, say its* peshat [i.e., of the Hebrew original], *which the above-mentioned hakham translated.* | JSul.I.46: (*This is*) *the second* piyyut (*with the incipit*) ʾăḏōnåy meleḵ yiśråʾēl wgōʾălō, *the one chanted on Yom Teruah to the holy Shema Yisrael. And it is also made by the author of the above-mentioned peshat, may the memory of the righteous and holy be a blessing.*

29 JSul.III.$72_2$: *misery.* | JSul.III.67: *misery.*

30 JSul.I.54.12: *by giving us.* | JSul.III.$72_1$: *by giving us.* | JSul.III.$72_2$: *by giving us.* | JSul.I.46: *by giving us.*

31 JSul.III.76: *holy Law.*

32 JSul.III.67: *for His mercies.* | JSul.I.46: *with the best of our praises for His goodness*; lit. 'with better praises for His goodness'.

33 JSul.I.46: *holy law.*

34 Or: *prayers.* | JSul.I.54.12: *entreaty* or *prayer.* | JSul.III.$72_2$: *entreaty* or *prayer.* | JSul.III.67: *entreaty* or *prayer.*

35 Lit. 'beg a prayer'.

36 JSul.I.54.12: deest. | JSul.III.$72_1$: deest. | JSul.III.$72_2$: deest. | JSul.III.67: deest. | JSul.I.46: deest.

[11] [20] ki maḫlatetkej bar[37] jazyqlarymyzny ne ki qyldyq janġylyšlyqbyla[38]
[12] [21] hem[39] čajalyqbyla[40]. Sandyr ol[41] ulusqa[42] ki bilediler maḥtav
[13] [22] berme Tenrige bijenčbyla[43]. [44]⌜רנּו והרֿיעו⌟. ⌞{{E süver
[14] [23] qaryndašlarym da urluġu inamlylarymnyn.}}⌝[45] Anyn üčün[46] sarnanyz[47]
[15] [24] ⌞da maḥtav⌝[48]
2 r° [16] [1] da maḥtav beriniz e süver[49] qaryndašlarym[50] da urluġu atalarymnyn[51],
[17] [2] Tenrige ol aškara[52] boluvču[53] šeḫinasybyla tavy üstüne[54]
[18] [3] Sinajnyn. Qyjasa byrġylarbyla da šofarbyla kötür[ün]üz[55] avaz jalbarmaq-
[19] [4] larbyla sözübyla[56] avzunuznun[57] e ulanlary üč[58] atalarymnyn[59].
[20] [5] Tüzüjüz[60] tefilaler[61] alnynda ol bijnin Adonajnyn[62]. [63]⌜נוֿדה לשמו⌟.
[21] [6] Šükür[64] etejik[65] süver[66] ǯanbyla[67] syjly šemine anyn, ošpu[68] künde[69]
[22] [7] ki ol burunġu künüdü[70] tešuva künlerinin[71]. Ki bu on künler[72]

---

37 JSul.I.54.12: deest. | JSul.III.72$_1$: deest. | JSul.III.72$_2$: deest. | JSul.III.67: deest. | JSul.III.76: deest.

38 JSul.I.46: *janġylyslyq byla.* | JSul.III.76: *janġylyslyq byla.*

39 JSul.III.72$_2$: *da.*

40 JSul.I.46: *cajalyq byla.* | JSul.III.76: *cajalyq byla.*

41 JSul.III.72$_2$: *andij.* | JSul.III.67: *andij.* | JSul.III.76: *andij.*

42 JSul.III.72$_2$: *ulušqa*; a scribal error or a hypercorrect form of *ulusqa.*

43 JSul.I.46: *bijenc byla.* | JSul.III.76: *bijenc byla.*

44 JSul.I.54.12: deest. | JSul.III.72$_2$: רנֿו. | JSul.III.76: רנֿו.

45 Crossed out and hardly legible; a scribal error; absent from the other mss., too. Cf. line 16.

46 JSul.III.67: *ičin.* | JSul.I.46: *ücün.* | JSul.III.76: *icin.*

47 JSul.I.54.12: *sarnajyz.* | JSul.III.72$_1$: *sarnajyz.*

48 Catchwords.

49 JSul.III.67: *siver.* | JSul.I.46: *siver.* | JSul.III.76: *siver.*

50 JSul.I.46: *qaryndaslarym.* | JSul.III.76: *qaryndaslarym.*

51 JSul.I.54.12: *inamlylarymnyn.* | JSul.III.72$_1$: *inamlylarymnyn.* | JSul.III.72$_2$: *inamlylarymnyn.* | JSul.III.67: *inamlylarymnyn.* | JSul.I.46: *inamlylarymnyn.* | JSul.III.76: *inamlylarymnyn.* || Cf. *inamlylarymnyn* crossed out in JSul.I.54.03 in line 23.

52 JSul.III.72$_1$: *askara.* | JSul.I.46: *asqara.* | JSul.III.76: *asqara.*

53 JSul.III.72$_1$: *boluvču.* | JSul.III.72$_2$: *bolunuvču.* | JSul.III.67: *bolunuvču.* | JSul.I.46: *bolunuvcu.* | JSul.III.76: *bolunuvčuġa.*

54 JSul.I.46: *istine.* | JSul.III.67: *istine.* | JSul.III.76: *istine.*

55 JSul.I.54.12: *kötürüjüz.* | JSul.III.72$_1$: *kötürüniz.* | JSul.III.72$_2$: *kötürünüz.* | JSul.III.67: *ketiriniz.* | JSul.I.46: *kötiriniz.* | JSul.III.76: *ketiriniz.*

[11] [20] to forgive all[73] our sins that we committed by mistake
[12] [21] and by haughtiness. Praise to the people who know (how) to praise
[13] [22] God with joy. (3). {{O my beloved
[14] [23] brethren, the offspring of my faithful.}} Therefore laud
[15] [24] ⌊and praise⌋[74]
[16] [1] and praise, O my beloved brethren and the offspring of my forefathers[75], 2 r°
[17] [2] to God who appeared through his divine Presence on Mount
[18] [3] Sinai. As if (lifted) by a trumpet or *shofar*[76] thus lift up your voice in
[19] [4] entreaties, in words of your mouth, O, sons of my[77] three patriarchs.
[20] [5] Compose your prayers before the Lord God. (4).
[21] [6] We shall thank His honourable name with a loving heart in this very day,
[22] [7] which is the first day of the days of repentance. For in[78] these ten days[79],

---

56 JSul.III.67: *sezi byla.* | JSul.III.76: *sezi byla.*

57 JSul.III.67: *avuznun.*

58 JSul.III.67: *ič.* | JSul.I.46: *ic.* | JSul.III.76: *ic.*

59 JSul.III.$72_1$: *atalarymnyn.* | JSul.III.$72_2$: *atalarnyn.* | JSul.III.67: *atalarnyn.* | JSul.I.46: *atalarnyn.*

60 JSul.III.$72_2$: *tüzünüz.* | JSul.III.67: *tiziniz.* | JSul.I.46: *tüzünüz.* | JSul.III.76: *tiziniz.*

61 JSul.III.$72_2$: *tefileler.* | JSul.III.67: *tefileler.* | JSul.I.46: *tefileler.* | JSul.III.76: *tefileler.*

62 JSul.III.$72_1$: *H-nyn.* | JSul.III.67: *H-nyn.* | JSul.I.46: *H-nyn.* | JSul.III.76: *H-nyn.*

63 JSul.I.54.12: deest. | JSul.III.$72_2$: נודׂה. | JSul.III.76: נודׂה.

64 JSul.III.67: *šikir.* | JSul.III.76: *sikir.*

65 JSul.I.54.12: *etejiz*; probably a scribal error. | JSul.III.$72_1$: *etejiz*; probably a scribal error.

66 JSul.III.67: *siver.* | JSul.I.46: *siver.* | JSul.III.76: *siver.*

67 JSul.I.46: *ʒan byla.* | JSul.III.76: *ʒan byla.*

68 JSul.III.67: *ušpu.* | JSul.I.46: *uspu.* | JSul.III.76: *uspu.*

69 JSul.III.67: *kinde.* | JSul.III.76: *kinde.*

70 JSul.III.67: *kinidi.* | JSul.III.76: *kinidi.*

71 JSul.III.67: *kinlerinin.* | JSul.III.76: *kinlerinin.*

72 JSul.I.54.12: *kün uturu.* | JSul.III.$72_1$: *kün.* | JSul.III.$72_2$: *kün.* | JSul.III.67: *kin.* | JSul.I.46: *kün.* | JSul.III.76: *kin.*

73 JSul.I.54.12: deest. | JSul.III.$72_1$: deest. | JSul.III.$72_2$: deest. | JSul.III.67: deest.

74 Catchwords in the Karaim text.

75 JSul.III.$72_1$: *faithful.* | JSul.III.$72_2$: *faithful.* | JSul.III.67: *faithful.* | JSul.I.46: *faithful.*

76 A musical horn prominently used in Rabbanite liturgy; a symbol of Yom Teruah.

77 JSul.III.$72_2$: deest. | JSul.III.67: deest. | JSul.I.46: deest.

78 JSul.I.54.12: *facing*; lit. 'against'.

79 A reference to the Ten Days of Repentance, Heb. עֲשֶׂרֶת יְמֵי תְּשׁוּבָה.

[23] [8] on sözlerine[80] köre[81] anoẖinin ki ajtty aškarġanda[82] šeẖinasy
[24] [9] anyn alamlanġan tümenleribyla[83] aziz malaẖlarynyn, ki bolgajbiz
[25] [10] aruvlar güneḥlerimizden[84] alnynda Adonajnyn[85] kelmegi alnyna
[26] [11] ol qorqunčlu[86] ol[87] jarġu künnün[88]. [89]⸢חײנו מטוֹבו⸣. Tiri ⸤tuttu [bizni]⸥[90]
[27] [12] jaḥšylyġyndan[91] özünün[92] da šavaġatybyla[93] joqtan bar etti bizni,
[28] [13] oldu jem berüvčü[94] bar tenge da qursaqtan čyqqačoq[95] qulluġuna
[29] [14] özünün[96] ündedi[97] bizni[98]. Jalbarmaq avazymyzny ešitkej[99] da bar
[30] [15] jazyqlarymyzdan ajyrġaj bizni. Ol bij biji dunjanyn qaruv
[31] [16] bergej bizge ne vaḥtny[100] čaġyrsaq[101] anar da bergej jaḥšyġa[102] bar
[32] [17] tüslü[103] kleklerimizni. [104]⸢הָ֗ אֵין כָּמוֹךָ ׳ שְׁמַע יִשְׂרָאֵל הָ֗ אהא⸣.

---

80 JSul.III.67: *sezlerine.* | JSul.III.76: *sezlerine.*

81 JSul.I.54.12: deest. | JSul.III.$72_1$: *köredi.* | JSul.III.67: *kere.* | JSul.III.76: *kere.*

82 JSul.III.76: *asqarġanda.*

83 JSul.III.67: *timenleri byla.* | JSul.I.46: *timenleri byla.* | JSul.III.76: *timenleri byla.*

84 JSul.III.67: *gineḥlerimizden.* | JSul.I.46: *gineḥlerimizden.* | JSul.III.76: *gineḥlerimizden.*

85 JSul.III.67: *H-nyn.* | JSul.I.46: *H-nyn.* | JSul.III.76: *H-nyn.*

86 JSul.I.46: *qorqunclu.* | JSul.III.76: *qorqunclu.*

87 JSul.I.54.12: *ullu.* | JSul.III.$72_1$: *ullu.* | JSul.III.76: deest.

88 JSul.I.54.12: *kününün.* | JSul.III.67: *kinnin.* | JSul.III.76: *kinnin.*

89 JSul.III.$72_2$: חײנו. | JSul.III.76: חײנו.

90 JSul.I.54.12: *tuttu bizni.* | JSul.III.$72_1$: *tutnu bizni; tutnu* is a result of scribal error. | JSul.III.$72_2$: *tuttu bizni.* | JSul.III.67: *tutuvču bizni.* | JSul.I.46: *tuttu bizni.* | JSul.III.76: *tuttu bizni.*

91 JSul.I.46: *jaḥsylyġyndan.* | JSul.III.76: *jaḥsylyġyndan.*

92 JSul.III.$72_1$: *özinin.* | JSul.III.67: *ezinin.* | JSul.III.76: *ezinin.*

93 JSul.I.46: *savaġaty byla.* | JSul.III.76: *savaġaty byla ezinin.*

94 JSul.III.$72_1$: *berivčü.* | JSul.III.$72_2$: *berivčü.* | JSul.III.67: *berivči.* | JSul.I.46: *berivcü.* | JSul.III.76: *berivci.*

95 JSul.I.46: *cyqqacoq.* | JSul.III.76: *cyqqacoq.*

96 JSul.III.67: *ezinin.* | JSul.III.76: *ezinin.*

97 JSul.III.67: *indedi.* | JSul.I.46: *indedi.* | JSul.III.76: *indedi.*

98 JSul.I.46: *biznü*, a hypercorrect form of *bizni.*

99 JSul.I.46: *esitkej.* | JSul.III.76: *esitkej.*

100 JSul.I.54.12: *vaḥtta.* | JSul.III.$72_1$: *vaḥtta.* | JSul.III.$72_2$: *vaḥtta.* | JSul.I.46: *vaḥtta.*

101 JSul.I.54.12: *ki čaġyrsaq.* | JSul.III.$72_1$: *ki čaġyrsaq.* | JSul.III.$72_2$: *ki čaġyrsaq.* | JSul.III.67: *ki čaġyrsaq.* | JSul.I.46: *ki caġyrsaq.* | JSul.III.76: *ki caġyrsaq.*

102 JSul.I.46: *jaḥsyġa.* | JSul.III.76: *jaḥsyġa.*

103 JSul.I.54.12: deest. | JSul.III.$72_1$: deest. | JSul.III.67: deest. | JSul.I.46: deest. | JSul.III.76: deest.

104 1Chronicles 17:20; Deuteronomy 6:4. | JSul.I.54.12: ה֗ אין כמוך ואין אלהים זולתך בכל אשר שמענו באזנינו (1Chronicles 17:20). | JSul.III.$72_1$: הָ֗ אֵין כָּמוֹךָ וְאֵין אֱלֹהִים זוּלָתֶךָ בְּכָל אֲשֶׁר שָׁמַעְנוּ בְּאָזְנֵינוּ: שְׁמַע יִשְׂרָאֵל וגו׳: (1Chronicles 17:20; Deuteronomy 6:4). | JSul.III.$72_2$: ותאמר הָ֗ אֵין כָּמוֹךָ וְאֵין אֱלֹהִים ׳ שְׁמַע יִשְׂרָאֵל ׳ (1Chronicles 17:20; Deuteronomy 6:4). | JSul.III.67: הָ֗ אֵין כָּמוֹךָ וְאֵין אֱלֹהִים זוּלָתֶךָ בְּכָל אֲשֶׁר־שָׁמַעְנוּ בְּאָזְנֵינוּ: שְׁמַע יִשְׂרָאֵל הָ֗ אֱלֹהֵינוּ הָ֗ אֶחָד: אֶחָד אֱלֹהֵינוּ גָּדוֹל אֲדוֹנֵנוּ קָדוֹשׁ וְנוֹרָא שְׁמוֹ לְעוֹלָם וָעֶד: (1Chronicles 17:20; Deuteronomy 6:4; *Siddur* 1836:

[23] [8] according to the Ten Commandments of *Anoḵi*[105] that He said when his divine Presence appeared

[24] [9] marked by the vast number of holy angels, we shall be

[25] [10] clear from sins before the Lord, before the coming of

[26] [11] the frightful[106] Judgment Day. (5). He has kept us alive

[27] [12] by means of his own goodness and in his mercy He has created us from nothing,

[28] [13] He has become provider to every living being and as soon as we have left the bosom,

[29] [14] He called us to (join) His own service. May He hearken to our voices of entreaty and

[30] [15] may he separate us from our sins. May the Lord, the Lord of the world, answer

[31] [16] us when we call Him and may He turn into good

[32] [17] our wishes ⌊of all kind⌋[107]. ⌊'O Lord, there is none like you. Hear, O Israel: the Lord our God is one Lord.'⌋[108]

---

II 68 vº). | JSul.I.45: הָ אֵין כָּמוֹךָ וְאֵין אֱלֹהִים זוּלָתֶךָ בְּכָל אֲשֶׁר שָׁמַעְנוּ בְּאָזְנֵינוּ: שְׁמַע יִשְׂרָאֵל הָ אֱלֹהֵינוּ הָ אֶחָד (1 Chronicles 17:20; Deuteronomy 6:4). | JSul.III.76: יְיָ אֵין כָּמוֹךָ וְאֵין אֱלֹהִים זוּלָתֶךָ בְּכָל אֲשֶׁר שָׁמַעְנוּ בְּאָזְנֵינוּ: שְׁמַע יִשְׂרָאֵל יְהוָֹה אֱלֹהֵינוּ יְהוָֹה אֶחָד: אֶחָד אֱלֹהֵינוּ גָּדוֹל אֲדוֹנֵנוּ קָדוֹשׁ וְנוֹרָא שְׁמוֹ לְעוֹלָם וָעֶד: (1 Chronicles 17:20; Deuteronomy 6:4).

105 I.e., *of God*; lit. 'of myself', cf. the use of אָנֹכִי '(*pers. pron.*) I' in אָנֹכִי יְהוָה אֱלֹהֶיךָ 'I am the Lord your God' (Deuteronomy 5:6).

106 JSul.III.$72_1$: *frightful, great.*

107 Lit. 'various'.

108 1 Chronicles 17:20; Deuteronomy 6:4. | JSul.I.54.12: *'O Lord, there is none like you, neither is there any God beside you, according to all that we have heard with our ears.'* (1 Chronicles 17:20). | JSul.III.$72_1$: *'O Lord, there is none like you, neither is there any God beside you, according to all that we have heard with our ears. Hear, O Israel ...', and so on.* (1 Chronicles 17:20; Deuteronomy 6:4). | JSul.III.$72_2$: *And you will say, 'O Lord, there is none like you, neither is there any God. Hear, O Israel.'* (1 Chronicles 17:20; Deuteronomy 6:4). | JSul.III.67: *'O Lord, there is none like you, neither is there any God beside you, according to all that we have heard with our ears. Hear, O Israel: the Lord our God is one Lord. Our God is one, our great Lord, holy and terrifying is His name for ever and for eternity.'* (1 Chronicles 17:20; Deuteronomy 6:4; *Siddur* 1836: II 68 vº). | JSul.I.46: *'O Lord, there is none like you, neither is there any God beside you, according to all that we have heard with our ears. Hear, O Israel: the Lord our God is one Lord.'* (1 Chronicles 17:20; Deuteronomy 6:4). | JSul.III.76: *'O Lord, there is none like you, neither is there any God beside you, according to all that we have heard with our ears. Hear, O Israel: the Lord our God is one Lord.'* (1 Chronicles 17:20; Deuteronomy 6:4).

**Text number:** № 8
**Karaim incipit:** *Biji dunjanyn bijik da jalġyz Tenri*
**Hebrew incipit:** מֶלֶךְ רָם וְיָחִיד *melek̲ råm wyåḥīd̲*
**Dedication:** Shabbat Shirah
**Language:** Early Mod.SWKar., Mod.SWKar.
**Number of copies:** 6

| Accession no. | Place of origin of copy | Date of copy | Copyist | Folios |
|---|---|---|---|---|
| JSul.III.03 | Halych | shortly after 1805 | Unknown 7 | 85 r°–86 r° |
| JSul.I.45 | Halych | 1st half of the 19th c. | Jeshua Josef Mordkowicz | 101 r°–102 r° |
| ADub.III.61 | Halych | 1850/1851 | Jeshua Josef Mordkowicz | 94 v°–95 v° |
| JSul.III.69 | Halych | ca. 1851 (before 1866) | Jeshua Josef Mordkowicz | 157 v°–159 r° |
| JSul.III.79 | Halych | ca. 1851 (before 1866) | Jeshua Josef Mordkowicz | 198 v°–200 v° |
| JSul.I.54.15 | Unknown | turn of the 20th c. | Unknown 15 | 1 r°–1 v° |

## 1 Introductory Remarks

According to the headings introducing the Hebrew original, the author of the Hebrew *piyyut* was Moshe Levi b. Eliyahu (a member of the Karaim community in Kale, i.e. *Qyrq Jer*), who was also known as Moshe b. Eliyahu Levi (died 1667; see Akhiezer 2003: 740).[109] The copy in JSul.I.54.15 contains the initial fragment of the *peshat* only. All six copies are vocalized.

Textually, the copies are closely related to one other. The differences between them primarily concern the lexicon and certain morphological structures. Based on the existing discrepancies we can say that the text in ms. JSul.III.03 stands out somewhat from the other manuscripts (even from JSul.III.69), unlike, for instance, *peshatim* № 1 or 5, in which case the versions in JSul.III.03 and JSul.III.69 are somewhat more similar to to each other. In this *peshat*, only one unique feature is shared by the above-mentioned two texts, see *kücün* vs. *quvatyn* (16) (it also ought to be mentioned that JSul.III.03 and the fragmentary version in JSul.I.54.15 were not, unlike the other texts, copied by Jeshua Josef Mordkowicz). There are a number of forms and constructions, including apparent errors, that appear only in ms. JSul.III.03, see: *atyna* (10), *quvatynyn*

109 The most elaborate headings are those found in JSul.III.03 (84 v°) and JSul.I.45 (100 v°). In JSul.I.54.15 the given name of the author of the *peshat* is mentioned (1 r°) only.

(16), *Flistimnin* (25), *nerselerni* (26), *abrajlyq köpligi byla bilivnin* (29), *budu* (35), *qovuluštular* (38), *bilmediler* (39), *jesisi* (41), *merkavyn* (42), *birgesine* (42), *Mošenin alnynda* (44), *merkavlaryn* (46), *battylar* (20), and *išleme* (55). It seems, therefore, that the texts in mss. JSul.I.45, ADub.III.61, JSul.III.69, and JSul.III.79 were copied on the basis of a slightly modified and corrected version (compared to the text in JSul.III.03) or that they contain amendments that were introduced at a later date by the person who copied them. The fragment in ms. JSul.I.54.15 is too short to affiliate it, but it seems to have been copied from a different manuscript than the others, see e.g. *aškarylmaġy* (or *askarylmaġy*) (7), *mizmorlar* (9), *Adonajnyn* (13), and *širalar* (14); moreover, it might have been a manuscript used in one of several North-Western Karaim communities, see *oḥudular* (15) featuring the clearly NWKar. *o-*. Finally, it is highly probable that ms. JSul.I.54.15 was copied in Lutsk, given that it is very different from all other South-Western Karaim texts copied in Halych. The relationship between these copies is presented below:

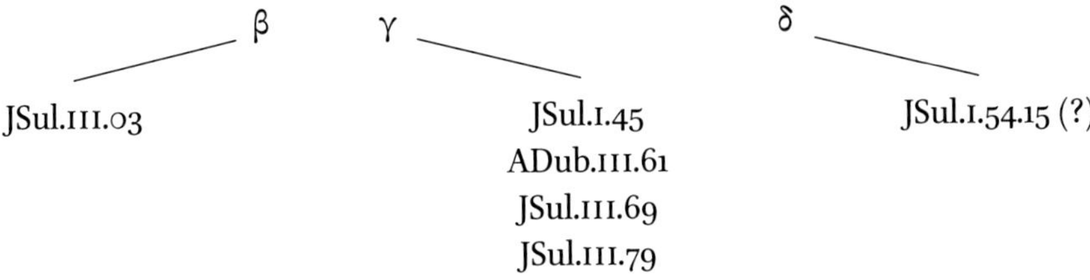


FIGURE 11 Diagram of the connections between the copies of peshat № 8

## 2 Transcription[110] and Translation

85 rº [1] [4] ⸤אם תרצה להאריך תאם גם פשטו שתרגמו החכם כמוה̃רר שמחה החזן דקה̃ק
יפה יער בכמ̃ע חננאל
[2] [5] הזקן יעמ̃ש: מלך רם ויחיד:⸣[111]

[3] [6] Biji dunjanyn bijik da jalġyz Tenri oldu Tenrisi Jisraʾelnin,
[4] [7] ijdi Mošeni inamly elčini[112] paroġa bolma juluvču[113]
[5] [8] ulusun Jisraʾelnin erki tibinden anyn. Alaj juluġaj biznide
[6] [9] bu galuttan da körgizgej[114] bizge qondarylmaġyn Jerušalajimnin ki anda
[7] [10] bolur askarmaġy[115] šeẖinasynyn. Da nečik[116] šira uḥudu Moše
[8] [11] ulanlary byla Jisraʾelnin alaj čyġyp[117] bu galuttan qotaryrlar ulluluqlaryn
[9] [12] Tenrinin[118]. [119]⸢שבחוֹד נתְנו⸣. Šira[ly][120] mizmor[121] byla
[10] [13] maḥtavlar berdiler ullu syjly atyna[122] Tenrinin, ijgende paro

110 Based on JSul.III.03.

111 JSul.I.45: ואם תרצה תאמר גם פשטו שתרגמו בזוך חכמתו אמ̃ו הה̃ו כמה̃רר שמחה החזן דקה̃ק יפה יער נב̃ת: בכמ̃עד חננאל הזקן מתושבי קה̃ק דראזניע יעמ̃ש:. | ADub.III.61: ואם תרצה תאמר גם פשטו שתרגמו אמ̃ו הה̃ו כמוה̃רר שמחה החזן דקה̃ק קוקיזוב יעמ̃ש: בכמ̃ע חננאל הזקן מן דראזניע נב̃ת:. | JSul.III.69: ואם תרצה תאמר גם פשטו שתרגמו הר̃ר שמחה החזן דקה̃ק קוקיזוב זצו̃קל בכמ̃ חננאל הזקן מן דראזניע יעמ̃ש:. | JSul.III.79: ואם תרצה תאמר גם פשטו שתרגמו החכם השלם והכולל כמוה̃רר שמחה החזן דקה̃ק קוקיזוב תנצב̃הה: בכמ̃ע חננאל הזקן אתושבי דראזניע יעמ̃ש:. | JSul.I.54.15: וזה פשט לפיוט מֶלֶךְ רָם וְיָחִיד אֵל אֱלֹהֵי יִשְׂרָאֵל תרגמו החכם השלם כמוהרר׳ שמחה החזן נע׳ דקק׳ יפה יער בכמע׳ חננאל הד׳ הדרעזני זצל׳:.

112 Or: *elcini.* | JSul.I.45: *elcisin.* | ADub.III.61: *elcini.* | JSul.III.69: *elcini.* | JSul.III.79: *elcini.* | JSul.I.54.15: *elčisin.*

113 Or: *juluvcu.* | JSul.I.45: *juluvcu.* | ADub.III.61: *juluvcu.* | JSul.III.69: *juluvcu.* | JSul.III.79: *juluvcu.*

114 ADub.III.61: *kergizgej.* | JSul.III.69: *kergizgej.* | JSul.III.79: *kergizgej.* | JSul.I.54.15: *kergizgej.*

115 ADub.III.61: *asqarmaġy.* | JSul.III.69: *asqarmaġy.* | JSul.III.79: *asqarmaġy.* | JSul.I.54.15: *aškarylmaġy* or *askarylmaġy.*

116 Or: *necik.* | JSul.I.45: *necik.* | ADub.III.61: *necik.* | JSul.III.69: *necik.* | JSul.III.79: *necik.*

117 Or: *cyġyp.* | JSul.I.45: *cyġyp.* | ADub.III.61: *cyġyp.* | JSul.III.69: *cyġyp.* | JSul.III.79: *cyġyp.*

118 JSul.III.69: *H Tenrinin.*

119 JSul.I.45: שבחֹות. | ADub.III.61: שבחות. | JSul.III.69: שבחֹות. | JSul.III.79: שבֿחות. | JSul.I.54.15: deest.

120 JSul.III.03: *širalar*; a scribal error; see also JSul.I.54.15. | JSul.I.45: *širaly.* | ADub.III.61: *širaly.* | JSul.III.79: *širaly.* | JSul.I.54.15: *širalar*; a scribal error.

121 JSul.I.54.15: *mizmorlar.*

122 JSul.I.45: *šemine.* | ADub.III.61: *šemine.* | JSul.III.69: *šemine.* | JSul.III.79: *šemine.* | JSul.I.54.15: *šemine.*

123 I.e., *the* peshat *of the Hebrew original*; see ff. 84 vº–85 rº.

124 I.e., *Kukizów.*

[1] [4] ⌊If you prefer, you may say also ⌊its *peshat*⌉[123], which the hakham, his honour, the Rav, Rabbi Simcha the hazzan of the holy community of ⌊*Yefeh Yaʿar*⌉[124] translated, the son of Chananel, whose honourable repose is Eden, 85 r°
[2] [5] the aged, may he rest in peace. (Incipit:) *meleḵ råm wyåḥīḏ.*⌉[125]
[3] [6] The lord of the world, the great and the only God—He is the God of Israel,
[4] [7] He sent Moses, ⌊the trustworthy⌉[126] envoy, to the Pharaoh to be the redeemer of
[5] [8] the people of Israel from his reign. Thus may He redeem us, too,
[6] [9] from this exile and may He show us the edifice of Jerusalem for (it is) there (where)
[7] [10] His divine Presence will appear. And as Moses had sung the song
[8] [11] with the sons of Israel, so after leaving this exile will be praised the greatness
[9] [12] of God. (2). With an extolling[127] psalm[128] sung
[10] [13] they praised the great and honourable name of God, when the Pharaoh sent

---

125 JSul.I.45: *And, if you prefer, say its* peshat [i.e., of the Hebrew original], *which the pure hakham translated, our master, our teacher, the great and honourable sage, his honour, the Rav, Rabbi Simcha the hazzan of the holy community of Yefeh Yaʿar* [i.e., Kukizów], *may his soul lodge in Eden, the son of Chananel, the aged, the hazzan of the holy community of Derażne, whose honourable repose is Eden, may he rest in peace.* | ADub.III.61: *And, if you prefer, say its* peshat [i.e., of the Hebrew original], *which our master translated, our teacher, the great and honourable sage, his honour, the Rav, Rabbi Simcha the hazzan of the holy community of Kukizów, may his soul lodge in Eden, the son of Chananel, the aged, the hazzan from Derażne, whose honourable repose is Eden, may his soul lodge in Eden.* | JSul.III.69: *And, if you prefer, say its* peshat [i.e., of the Hebrew original], *which the Rav, Rabbi Simcha translated, may the memory of the righteous and holy be a blessing, the hazzan of the holy community of Kukizów, the son of the honourable Chananel, the aged, from Derażne, may he rest in peace.* | JSul.III.79: *And, if you prefer, say its* peshat [i.e., of the Hebrew original], *which the complete hakham translated, his honour, the Rav, Rabbi Simcha the hazzan of the holy community of Kukizów, 'may his soul be bound in the bond of life'* [cf., 1Samuel 25:29], *the son of Chananel, the aged, whose honourable repose is Eden, a resident of Derażne, may he rest in peace.* | JSul.I.54.15: *And this is the* peshat *of the* piyyut (*with the incipit*) meleḵå [sic!] råm wyåḥīḏ ʾēl ʾělohē yiśråʾēl *the interpretation the complete hakham, his honour, the Rav, Rabbi Simcha the hazzan of the holy community of Yefeh Yaʿar* [i.e., Kukizów], *his soul is in Eden, the son of Chananel, whose honourable repose is Eden, the preacher of Derażne, may the memory of the righteous be a blessing.*

126 JSul.I.45: *his trustworthy.* | JSul.I.54.15: *his trustworthy.*

127 JSul.III.03: *songs*; a scribal error. | JSul.I.54.15: *songs*; a scribal error.

128 JSul.I.54.15: *psalms*; a scribal error.

[11] [14] osol[129] ol ulusnu qulluġundan[130] özünün[131], qajjam etme sözün[132]
[12] [15] navisinin ol Tenrinin ki tensi edi tivinčigine[133] ol mušqnun[134].
[13] [16] Da ajttylar ajtadoġač[135] alnynda H-nyn[136] osol[137] sözlerin[138] ol
[14] [17] širanyn ol ušpunun[139]. [140]⌜הנה שוררו⌟. Muna šira[141]
[15] [18] uḥudular[142] da anlattylar tamaša karanjalaryn ne ki qyldy, ki
[16] [19] paroġa da čerivine[143] anyn[144] kötirilgen[145] quvatynyn[146] küčün[147] körgizdi[148].
[17] [20] Hem[149] qorquv byla da qobuv byla jarlyġašyn[150] anyn qotardylar[151] ki qyrġanda
[18] [21] tunġučlaryn[152] Micrinin[153] Jisra'elni qolundan čajpavčunun[154] qutqardy.
[19] [22] Šira uḥujum H-ġa ki ullu{lu}q qylma ulluluq qyldy.
[20] [23] [155]⌜לך נאה תהלתם⌟. Sana maḥtav [berdiler][156] bar ǯanlary[157] byla,
[21] [24] sunġanda[158] osol bujruġunnu Jam Suf istine küčlü[159] jelin byla,

---

129 JSul.I.54.15: or: *ošol.*
130 JSul.III.69: *erki tibinden.*
131 ADub.III.61: *ezinin.* | JSul.III.69: *ezinin.* | JSul.III.79: *ezinin.* | JSul.I.54.15: *ezinin.*
132 ADub.III.61: *sezin.* | JSul.III.69: *sezin.* | JSul.III.79: *sezin.* | JSul.III.69: *sezin.*
133 Or: *tivincigine.* | JSul.I.45: *tivincigine.* | ADub.III.61: *kivincigine.* | JSul.III.69: *tivincigine.* | JSul.III.79: *tivincigine.*
134 JSul.I.45: *musqnun.* | ADub.III.61: *musqnun.* | JSul.III.79: *musqnun.* | JSul.I.54.15: *mušqnun* or *musqnun.* || < Heb. מוּשְׁק 'musk' (the Arabic origin of WKar. *mušq* put forward in KarRPS is less probable).
135 Or: *ajtadoġac.* | JSul.I.45: *ajtadoġac.* | ADub.III.61: *ajtadoġac.* | JSul.III.69: *ajtadoġac.* | JSul.III.79: *ajtadoġac.*
136 JSul.I.54.15: *Adonajnyn.*
137 JSul.I.54.15: *ošol.*
138 JSul.I.45: *sezlerin.* | JSul.III.69: *sezlerin.* | JSul.III.79: *sezlerin.* | JSul.I.54.15: *sezlerin.*
139 JSul.I.45: *uspunun.* | ADub.III.61: *uspunun.* | JSul.III.69: *uspunun.* | JSul.III.79: *uspunun.* | JSul.I.54.15: *ošpunun.*
140 JSul.I.45: הנה. | ADub.III.61: הנה. | JSul.III.69: הנה. | JSul.III.79: הנה. | JSul.I.54.15: deest.
141 JSul.I.54.15: *širalar.*
142 JSul.I.54.15: *oḥudular.*
143 Or: *cerivine.* | JSul.I.45: *cerivine.* | ADub.III.61: *cerivine.* | JSul.III.69: *cerivine.* | JSul.III.79: *cerivine.*
144 Ms. JSul.I.54.15 ends here.
145 JSul.I.45: *ketirilgen.* | ADub.III.61: *ketirilgen.* | JSul.III.69: *ketirilgen.* | JSul.III.79: *ketirilgen.*
146 JSul.I.45: *qudratynyn.* | ADub.III.61: *qudratynyn.* | JSul.III.69: *qudratynyn.* | JSul.III.79: *qudratynyn.*
147 Or: *kücün.* | JSul.I.45: *quvatyn.* | ADub.III.61: *quvatyn.* | JSul.III.69: *kicin.* | JSul.III.79: *quvatyn.*
148 ADub.III.61: *kergizdi.* | JSul.III.69: *kergizdi.* | JSul.III.79: *kergizdi.*
149 ADub.III.61: *ham.* | JSul.III.69: *ham.* | JSul.III.79: *ham.*

[11] [14] the people from ⌊his captivity⌋[160] to (let them) abide firmly the words
[12] [15] of the prophet of God, which was equal to ⌊a bundle of musk⌋[161].
[13] [16] And they said before the Lord the words of
[14] [17] this very song. (3). Lo, they sang the song
[15] [18] and they related the wondrous punishments He had done, that
[16] [19] He had shown the strength[162] of his lifted arm[163] to the Pharaoh and his army.
[17] [20] ⌊They have preached⌋[164] His grace both with fear and fright, for when He killed
[18] [21] the firstborns of Egypt, He saved Israel from the hand of their destroyers.
[19] [22] I sing the song to the Lord who surely did great things.
[20] [23] (4). They praise[d][165] You with their whole hearts
[21] [24] when, with Your strong wind, You gave Your order over the Red Sea

150 JSul.I.45: *jarlyġasyn.* | ADub.III.61: *jarlyġasyn.* | JSul.III.69: *jarlyġasyn.* | JSul.III.79: *jarlyġasyn.*

151 ADub.III.61: *qotarġajlar.*

152 Or: *tunġuclaryn.* | JSul.I.45: *tunġuclaryn.* | ADub.III.61: *tunġuclaryn.* | JSul.III.79: *tunġuclaryn.*

153 Or: *Micrinin.* | JSul.I.45: *Micrinin.* | ADub.III.61: *Micrinin.* | JSul.III.79: *Micrinin.*

154 Or: *cajpavcunun.* | JSul.I.45: *cajpavcunun.* | ADub.III.61: *cajpavcunun.* | JSul.III.69: *cajpavcunun.* | JSul.III.79: *cajpavcunun.*

155 JSul.I.45: לֿ֞ד נאֹ֞ה. | ADub.III.61: לֿ֞ד. | JSul.III.69: לֿ֞ד. | JSul.III.79: לֿ֞ד.

156 JSul.III.03: *berediler*; a scribal error. | JSul.I.45: *berdiler.* | ADub.III.61: *berediler*; a scribal error. | JSul.III.69: *berediler*; a scribal error. | JSul.III.79 *berediler*; a scribal error.

157 Or: *ʒanlary.* | JSul.I.45: *ʒanlary.* | ADub.III.61: *ʒanlary.* | JSul.III.69: *ʒanlary.* | JSul.III.79: *ʒanlary.*

158 ADub.III.61: *sunġanynda.* | JSul.III.69: *sunġanynda.* | JSul.III.79: *sunġanynda.*

159 Or: *küclü.* | JSul.I.45: *küclü.* | ADub.III.61: *kicli.* | JSul.III.69: *kicli.* | JSul.III.79: *kicli.*

160 Lit. 'from his own captivity'. | JSul.III.69: *under his rule.*

161 Cf. צְרוֹר הַמֹּר דּוֹדִי לִי בֵּין שָׁדַי יָלִין 'A bundle of myrrh is my beloved unto me; he shall lie all night between my breasts' (Song of Songs 1:13). In the Karaite translating tradition Heb. מֹר 'myrrh' is rendered by 'musk', i.e., WKar. *mušq* 'musk' < Heb. מוּשְׁק id. According to Frank (2004: 153), the bundle of musk is a symbol of the times of prosperity until the destruction of the First Holy Temple.

162 JSul.I.45, ADub.III.61, JSul.III.79: expressed with a synonym.

163 In all other mss. expressed with a synonym.

164 ADub.III.61: *may they preach.*

165 JSul.III:03: *praise*; a scribal error. | JSul.I.45: *praised.* | ADub.III.61: *praise*; a scribal error. | JSul.III.69: *praise*; a scribal error. | JSul.III.79 *praise*; a scribal error.

[22] [25] jarčyqlama[166] da ujutma ol tengizni asyrma Jisra'el[167] quru
[23] [26] byla. Vale paronu da čerivin[168] anyn qyjasa kötirip[169] saldy
[24] [27] tengizge atny atlanuvčusu[170] byla. [171]⌈ולא נחם אלחים⌋.
[25] [28] Da köndermedi[172] alarny Tenri jolu byla Flistimnin[173] köpligi[174] byla
85 vº [26] [1] usnun da kelesi nerselerni[175] bilmeknin, anyn üčün[176] ki
[27] [2] körmegejler[177] čerivni[178] vaḫtynda ol kečmeknin[179]. Da iliš[180]
[28] [3] bermek üčün[181] alarġa Torany tamaša etti keneš[182] ulġajtty
[29] [4] [biliv][183] köpligi[184] byla [abrajlyqnyn][185]. Küčümdü[186] da
maḫtavumdu
[30] [5] Tenri da boldu mana jarlyġasqa bolusluġu anyn.
[31] [6] [187]⌈יצא כבודו⌋. Čyqty[188] šeḫinasy Tenrinin alynlarynda
[32] [7] alarnyn küngiz[189] jolnu körgizmek[190] üčün[191] alarġa baġanasy byla
[33] [8] bulutnun, da turġuzma alar istine jaryġyn keče[192] byla
[34] [9] baġanasy byla otnun. Qajyrdy alarny tavyna Sinajnyn ullu
[35] [10] etme any micvalary byla Toranyn. Budu[193] Tenrim da orun
[36] [11] hadirlejim šeḫinasyna Tenrisidi atamnyn da bijikligin qotarajym
[37] [12] anyn. [194]⌈הנּה נהפּך⌋. Muna čivirildi[195] jüregi[196] paronun

---

166 Or: *jarcyqlama.* | JSul.I.45: *jarcyqlama.* | ADub.III.61: *jarcyqlama.* | JSul.III.79: *jarcyqlama.*
167 JSul.III.69: *Jisra'elni.* | JSul.III.79: *osol Jisra'el.*
168 Or: *cerivin.* | JSul.I.45: *cerivin.* | ADub.III.61: *cerivin.* | JSul.III.69: *cerivin.* | JSul.III.79: *cerivin.*
169 ADub.III.61: *ketirip.* | JSul.III.69: *ketirip.* | JSul.III.79: *ketirip.*
170 Or: *atlanuvcusu.* | JSul.I.45: *atlanuvcusu.* | ADub.III.61: *atlanuvcusu.* | JSul.III.69: *atlanuvcusu.* | JSul.III.79: *atlanuvcusu.*
171 JSul.I.45: ולֹא נחֹם. | ADub.III.61: וֹלֹא נחֹם. | JSul.III.69: ולֹא. | JSul.III.79: ולֹא נחֹם.
172 JSul.I.45: *kendermedi.* | JSul.III.69: *kendermedi.* | JSul.III.79: *kendermedi.*
173 JSul.I.45: *Flistimnin jerinin.* | ADub.III.61: *jerinin Flistimnin.* | JSul.III.69: *jerinin Flistimnin.* | JSul.III.79: *jerinin Flistimnin.*
174 ADub.III.61: *kepligi.* | JSul.III.69: *kepligi.* | JSul.III.79: *kepligi.*
175 JSul.I.45: *nerselernin.* | ADub.III.61: *nerselernin.* | JSul.III.69: *nerselernin.* | JSul.III.79: *nerselernin.*
176 Or: *ücün.* | JSul.I.45: *ücün.* | ADub.III.61: *icin.* | JSul.III.69: *icin.* | JSul.III.79: *icin.*
177 ADub.III.61: *kermegejler.* | JSul.III.69: *kermegejler.* | JSul.III.79: *kermegejler.*
178 Or: *cerivni.* | JSul.I.45: *cerivni.* | ADub.III.61: *cerivni.* | JSul.III.69: *cerivni.* | JSul.III.79: *cerivni.*
179 Or: *kecmeknin.* | JSul.I.45: *kecmeknin.* | JSul.III.69: *kecmeknin.* | JSul.III.79: *kecmeknin.*
180 JSul.I.45: *ilis.* | ADub.III.61: *ilis.* | JSul.III.69: *ilis.* | JSul.III.79: *ilis.*
181 Or: *ücün.* | JSul.I.45: *ücün.* | ADub.III.61: *icin.* | JSul.III.69: *icin.* | JSul.III.79: *icin.*
182 JSul.I.45: *kenes.* | ADub.III.61: *kenes.* | JSul.III.69: *kenes.* | JSul.III.79: *kenes.*
183 JSul.III.03: *abrajlyq* | JSul.I.45: *biliv.* | ADub.III.61: *biliv.* | JSul.III.69: *biliv.* | JSul.III.79: *biliv.* || See *abrajlyqnyn* in the same line.
184 ADub.III.61: *kepligi.* | JSul.III.69: *kepligi.* | JSul.III.79: *kepligi.*

[22] [25] to split and to make the sea suitable for guiding Israel overland.
[23] [26] But He lifted and cast Pharaoh and his army
[24] [27] into the sea, horses along with their riders. (5).
[25] [28] And God did not lead them along the way (through) Philistia[197], with great
[26] [1] wisdom and with the knowledge of the future events[198], so that 85 v°
[27] [2] they would not see (any) armies in the time of their march. And in order to
[28] [3] give them the Law in heritage, He showed them (His) counsel (and) increased
[29] [4] (their) knowledge with great wisdom. My strength and my fame is
[30] [5] God and His support (has become) my salvation.
[31] [6] (6). God's divine Presence went out before
[32] [7] them in a pillar of a cloud to show them the way by day
[33] [8] and—to set them light by night—
[34] [9] in a pillar of fire. He turned them towards Mount Sinai
[35] [10] to make it great by the commandments of the Law. This is my God and
[36] [11] I prepare the place for His divine Presence, He is the God of my father and I preach his greatness.
[37] [12] (7). And, lo, the heart of Pharaoh changed,

---

185 JSul.III.03: deest. | JSul.I.45: *abrajlyqnyn.* | ADub.III.61: *abrajlyqnyn.* | JSul.III.69: *abrajlyqnyn.* | JSul.III.79: *abrajlyqnyn.*

186 Or: *kücümdü.* | JSul.I.45: *kicimdi.* | ADub.III.61: *kicimdi.* | JSul.III.69: *kicimdi.* | JSul.III.79: *kicimdi.*

187 JSul.I.45: יצ֯א. | ADub.III.61: יצ֯א כבו֯דו. | JSul.III.69: יצ֯א. | JSul.III.79: יצ֯א.

188 Or: *cyqty.* | JSul.I.45: *cyqty.* | ADub.III.61: *cyqty.* | JSul.III.69: *cyqty.* | JSul.III.79: *cyqty.*

189 JSul.I.45: *kingiz.* | ADub.III.61: *kingiz.* | JSul.III.69: *kingiz.* | JSul.III.79: *kingiz.*

190 ADub.III.61: *kergizmek.* | JSul.III.69: *kergizmek.* | JSul.III.79: *kergizmek.*

191 Or: *ücün.* | JSul.I.45: *ücün.* | ADub.III.61: *icin.* | JSul.III.69: *icin.* | JSul.III.79: *icin.*

192 Or: *kece.* | JSul.I.45: *kece.* | ADub.III.61: *kece.* | JSul.III.69: *kece.* | JSul.III.79: *kece.*

193 JSul.I.45: *budur.* | ADub.III.61: *budur.* | JSul.III.69: *budur.* | JSul.III.79: *budur.*

194 JSul.III.69: הנ֯ה. | JSul.III.79: הנ֯ה.

195 Or: *civirildi.* | JSul.I.45: *civirildi.* | ADub.III.61: *civirildi.* | JSul.III.69: *civirildi.* | JSul.III.79: *civirildi.*

196 ADub.III.61: *jiregi.* | JSul.III.69: *jiregi.* | JSul.III.79: *jiregi.*

197 JSul.I.45: *the land of Philistia.* | ADub.III.61: *the land of Philistia.* | JSul.III.69: *the land of Philistia.* | JSul.III.79: *the land of Philistia.*

198 Lit. 'things'.

[38] [13] da jüregi[199] ulusunun, quvma alarny ajtadoġač[200] qobuluštular[201] alar
[39] [14] da bilme[j]diler[202] jolun ornunun. Da Tenri qattyrdy jüreklerin[203]
[40] [15] alarnyn tekmek[204] üčün[205] alar istine qaḥyryn özünün[206]. H
[41] [16] čöriv[207] jesisi[di][208] H-dy kensi šemi anyn. [209]⌜קם ואסר רכבו⌟.
[42] [17] Turdu da jerledi paro merkavyn[210] da birgesine[211] aġalyqlary anyn[212]
[43] [18] quvma Jisra'elni arttyrdylar tanmaqlaryn. Da ulanlary Jisra'elnin
[44] [19] kördiler[213] da arttyrdylar ⌞Mošenin alnynda⌝[214] jylamaqlaryn. Da
[45] [20] H bujurdu da kötirdiler[215] ezenler tolġunlaryn, da oqlajyn
[46] [21] atty tengizge paronu da čerivün[216] da bar merkavlaryn[217].
[47] [22] [218]⌜טוב ה׳ מושיע⌟. Jaḥsydy H ki ol qutqarady taspolmaqtan
[48] [23] isanuvčularny[219] bolušluġuna[220] anyn, da dušmanlaryn[221] ⌞alarnyn kesti[222]⌝[223]
[49] [24] kesilmegi kibik qamušnun[224] da qoġanyn[225]. Ullu tamašalyq[226] tamaša[227]
[50] [25] ettiler bar ol qatyš[228] el nečik[229] kördiler[230] qorqunčlu[231] quvatyn

---

199 ADub.III.61: *jiregi.* | JSul.III.69: *jiregi.* | JSul.III.79: *jiregi.*

200 Or: *ajtadoġac.* | JSul.I.45: *ajtadoġac.* | ADub.III.61: *ajtadoġac.* | JSul.III.69: *ajtadoġac.* | JSul.III.79: *ajtadoġac.*

201 JSul.I.45: *qobulusqandylar.* | ADub.III.61: *qobulusadylar.* | JSul.III.69: *qobulusadylar.* | JSul.III.79: *qobulusadylar.*

202 JSul.III.03: *bilmediler*; a scribal error. | JSul.I.45: *bilmejdiler.* | ADub.III.61: *bilmejdiler.* | JSul.III.69: *bilmejdiler.* | JSul.III.79: *bilmejdiler.*

203 ADub.III.61: *jireklerin.* | JSul.III.69: *jireklerin.* | JSul.III.79: *jireklerin.*

204 ADub.III.61: *tekme.* | JSul.III.69: *tekme.* | JSul.III.79: *tekme.*

205 Or: *ücün.* | JSul.I.45: *ücün.* | ADub.III.61: deest. | JSul.III.69: deest. | JSul.III.79: deest.

206 JSul.I.45: *ezinin.* | ADub.III.61: *ezinin.* | JSul.III.69: *ezinin.* | JSul.III.79: *ezinin.*

207 Or: *cöriv*; a hypercorrect form of *čeriv* or *ceriv*; cf. *čerivün* ~ *cerivün* in line 46. | JSul.I.45: *ceriv.* | ADub.III.61: *ceriv.* | JSul.III.69: *ceriv.* | JSul.III.79: *ceriv.*

208 JSul.III.03: *jesisi*; perhaps a scribal error. | JSul.I.45: *jesisidi.* | ADub.III.61: *jesisidi.* | JSul.III.69: *jesisidi.* | JSul.III.79: *jesisidi.*

209 JSul.I.45: קם ואסר. | ADub.III.61: קם ואסר. | JSul.III.69: קם. | JSul.III.79: קם.

210 JSul.I.45: *markavyn ezinin.* | ADub.III.61: *markavyn ezinin.* | JSul.III.69: *markavyn ezinin.* | JSul.III.79: *markavyn ezinin.*

211 JSul.I.45: *birgesine anyn.* | ADub.III.61: *birgesine anyn.* | JSul.III.69: *birgesine anyn.* | JSul.III.79: *birgesine anyn.*

212 JSul.I.45: deest. | JSul.III.69: deest.

213 ADub.III.61: *kerdiler.* | JSul.III.69: *kerdiler.* | JSul.III.79: *kerdiler.*

214 JSul.I.45: *alnynda Mošenin.* | ADub.III.61: *alnynda Mošenin.* | JSul.III.69: *alnynda Mošenin.* | JSul.III.79: *alnynda Mošenin.*

215 ADub.III.61: *ketirdiler.* | JSul.III.69: *ketirdiler.* | JSul.III.79: *ketirdiler.*

216 Or: *cerivün.* | JSul.I.45: *cerivin.* | ADub.III.61: *cerivin.* | JSul.III.69: *cerivin.* | JSul.III.79: *cerivin.*

[38] [13] as well as the heart of his people, to pursue them, saying, 'They got lost

[39] [14] and they ⌊do not know⌋[232] the way(s) of the land.' And God hardened their hearts

[40] [15] to pour His own wrath on them. The Lord

[41] [16] owns an army: its[233] name is The Lord. (8).

[42] [17] Pharaoh raised and harnessed his chariot and (so did together) with him his superiors

[43] [18] to pursue Israel; they did wrong yet again. And the sons of Israel

[44] [19] saw (this) and they continued to cry before Moses. And

[45] [20] the Lord gave an order and the rivers lifted up their waves and

[46] [21] threw Pharaoh and his army and all his chariots like an arrow into the sea.

[47] [22] (9). Good is the Lord who,

[48] [23] with His help, has saved from destruction those who hoped and cut out their enemies

[49] [24] like cutting out reed and rush.

[50] [25] All the rabble was greatly bewildered when they saw the frightful strength

---

217 JSul.I.45: *markavlaryn.* | ADub.III.61: *markavlaryn.* | JSul.III.69: *markavlaryn.* | JSul.III.79: *markavlaryn.*

218 JSul.I.45: טוֹב הׄ. | ADub.III.61: טוֹב הׄ. | JSul.III.69: טוֹב. | JSul.III.79: טוֹב הׄ.

219 Or: *isanuvcularny.* | JSul.I.45: *isanuvcularny.* | ADub.III.61: *isanuvcularny.* | JSul.III.69: *isanuvcularny.* | JSul.III.79: *isanuvcularny.*

220 JSul.I.45: *bolusluġuna.* | ADub.III.61: *bolusluġuna.* | JSul.III.69: *bolusluġuna.* | JSul.III.79: *bolusluġuna.*

221 JSul.I.45: *dusmanlaryn.* | ADub.III.61: *dusmanlaryn.* | JSul.III.69: *dusmanlaryn.* | JSul.III.79: *dusmanlaryn.*

222 JSul.I.45: *köstü*; a hypercorrect form of *kesti.*

223 JSul.III.69: *kesti alarnyn.*

224 JSul.I.45: *qamusnun.* | ADub.III.61: *qamusnun.* | JSul.III.69: *qamusnun.* | JSul.III.79: *qamusnun.*

225 ADub.III.61: *qohanyn.*

226 JSul.I.45: *tamasalyq.*

227 JSul.I.45: *tamasa.*

228 JSul.I.45: *qatys.* | ADub.III.61: *qatys.* | JSul.III.69: *qatys.* | JSul.III.79: *qatys.*

229 Or: *necik.* | JSul.I.45: *necik.* | ADub.III.61: *necik.* | JSul.III.69: *necik.* | JSul.III.79: *necik.*

230 ADub.III.61: *kerdiler.* | JSul.III.69: *kerdiler.* | JSul.III.79: *kerdiler.*

231 Or: *qorqunclu.* | JSul.I.45: *qorqunclu.* | ADub.III.61: *qorqunclu.* | JSul.III.69: *qorqunclu.* | JSul.III.79: *qorqunclu.*

232 JSul.III.03: *did not know*; a scribal error.

233 Lit. 'its own'.

| | [51] | [26] | Tenrinin, nečik[234] sajlama aġalyqlary paronun battylar[235] ortasynda |
|---|---|---|---|
| | [52] | [27] | Jam Sufnun. [236]ְרֹם נִשָּׂא[. E ullu Tenri da ketirilgen[237] |
| | [53] | [28] | belgili boldun {{aruv}}[238] ulusuna Jisra'elnin[239] ki kleden aruv da paq |
| | [54] | [29] | išleme[240] |
| 86 rº | [55] | [1] | išleme[241] alarny micvalary byla aziz Toranyn. Da terske |
| | [56] | [2] | tersligine köre[242] teledin neginče[243] ki tasny kibik qojdun |
| | [57] | [3] | jüregin[244] anyn. Ol vaḥtta aldy jalyn örkekler[in]in[245] Jisra'elnin |
| | [58] | [4] | Nilge taslamaġynyn. Da anyn üčün[246] any özünde[247] darjalar |
| | [59] | [5] | qapladylar nečik[248] tas kibik endiler ortasyna teren suvlarnyn. |
| | [60] | [6] | [וַתֹּאמֶר יְמִינְךָ הָ׳ נֶאְדָּרִי בַכֹּחַ[249 וכו' עם כל התפלה עד סופו:[250 |

---

234 Or: *necik*. | JSul.I.45: *nečik*. | ADub.III.61: *necik*. | JSul.III.69: *necik*. | JSul.III.79: *necik*.
235 JSul.I.45: *battyryldylar*. | ADub.III.61: *battyryldylar*. | JSul.III.69: *battyryldylar*. | JSul.III.79: *battyryldylar*.
236 JSul.III.69: נִשָּׂא. | JSul.III.79: נִשָּׂא.
237 JSul.I.45: *kötirilgen*.
238 Redundant word. | ADub.III.61: deest. | JSul.III.69: deest. | JSul.III.79: deest.
239 ADub.III.61: *Jisra'elge*. | JSul.III.69: *Jisra'elge*. | JSul.III.79: *Jisra'elge*.
240 Catchword.
241 JSul.I.45: *etme*. | ADub.III.61: *etme*. | JSul.III.69: *etme*. | JSul.III.79: *etme*.
242 ADub.III.61: *kere*. | JSul.III.69: *kere*. | JSul.III.79: *kere*.
243 Or: *negince*. | JSul.I.45: *negince*. | ADub.III.61: *negince*. | JSul.III.69: *negince*. | JSul.III.79: *negince*.
244 ADub.III.61: *jiregin*. | JSul.III.69: *jiregin*. | JSul.III.79: *jiregin*.
245 JSul.III.03: a hypercorrect form of *erkekler[in]in*; the *-lerinin > lerin* change took place due to scribal error or haplology. | JSul.I.45: *erkeklerinin*. | ADub.III.61: *erkeklerinin*. | JSul.III.69: *erkeklerinin*. | JSul.III.79: *erkeklerinin*.
246 Or: *üčün*. | JSul.I.45: *üčün*. | ADub.III.61: *icin*. | JSul.III.69: *icin*. | JSul.III.79: *icin*.
247 JSul.I.45: *ezinde*. | ADub.III.61: *ezinde*. | JSul.III.69: *ezinde*. | JSul.III.79: *ezinde*.
248 Or: *necik*. | JSul.I.45: *necik*. | ADub.III.61: *necik*. | JSul.III.69: *necik*. | JSul.III.79: *necik*.
249 Exodus 15:6.
250 JSul.I.45: יְמִינְךָ הָ׳ נֶאְדָּרִי בַכֹּחַ יְמִינְךָ הָ׳ וגו' (Exodus 15:6). | ADub.III.61: וַתֹּאמֶר יְמִינְךָ הָ׳ נֶאְדָּרִי בַכֹּחַ וגו' (Exodus 15:6). | JSul.III.69: יְמִינְךָ הָ׳ נֶאְדָּרִי בַכֹּחַ וגו' (Exodus 15:6). | JSul.III.79: יְמִינְךָ הָ׳ נֶאְדָּרִי בַכֹּחַ וגו' (Exodus 15:6).

[51] [26] of God, as the chosen superiors of Pharaoh sank[251] in the middle
[52] [27] of the Red Sea. (10). O, great and elevated God,
[53] [28] You have become known to the {{clean}} people of Israel for You wanted
[54] [29] ⌊to make⌋[252]
[55] [1] to make them clean and pure with your commandments of the holy Law. And 86 rº
[56] [2] You paid to the disobedient according to their obstinacy (that they had shown), until You made his[253] heart to be like a stone.
[57] [3] Then He took the due of the men of Israel
[58] [4] for casting (them) into the Nile. And for this reason did the seas
[59] [5] cover him, too: like a stone did they descend in the middle of the deep waters.
[60] [6] ⌊And you will say ⌊'Your right hand, O Lord, has become glorious in power'⌋[254] and so forth with all the prayers until the end.⌋[255]

---

251 JSul.I.45: *were sunk.* | ADub.III.61: *were sunk.* | JSul.III.69: *were sunk.* | JSul.III.79: *were sunk.*
252 Catchword in the Karaim text.
253 I.e., *Pharaoh's.*
254 Exodus 15:6.
255 JSul.I.45: *'Your right hand, O Lord, has become glorious in power. Your right hand, O Lord ...' and so forth.* (Exodus 15:6). | ADub.III.61: *And you will say 'Your right hand, O Lord, has become glorious in power. Your right hand ...' and so forth.* (Exodus 15:6). | JSul.III.69: *'Your right hand, O Lord, has become glorious in power ...' and so forth.* (Exodus 15:6). | JSul.III.79: *'Your right hand, O Lord, has become glorious in power ... and so forth.'* (Exodus 15:6).

**Text number:** № 9
**Karaim incipit:** *E H Tenrim sen basladyn körgizme mana*
*E Adonaj Tenri sen basladyn kergizme mana*
**Hebrew incipit:** אֲדוֹנָי אֱלֹהִים אַתָּה הַחִלּוֹתָ *ʾăḏonåy ʾělohīm ʾattå haḥillōṯå*
**Dedication:** Parashat Va'etchanan (Deuteronomy 3:23–7:11)
**Language:** Early Mod.SWKar., Mod.SWKar.
**Number of copies:** 5

| Accession no. | Place of origin of copy | Date of copy | Copyist | Folios |
|---|---|---|---|---|
| JSul.III.03 | Halych | shortly after 1805 | Unknown 7 | 107 v°–108 r° |
| JSul.I.45 | Halych | 1st half of the 19th c. | Jeshua Josef Mordkowicz | 144 r°–145 r° |
| ADub.III.61 | Halych | 1850/1851 | Jeshua Josef Mordkowicz | 137 r°–137 v° |
| JSul.III.69 | Halych | ca. 1851 (before 1866) | Jeshua Josef Mordkowicz | 294 v°–295 v° |
| JSul.III.79 | Halych | ca. 1851 (before 1866) | Jeshua Josef Mordkowicz | 177 v°–178 v° |

## 1 Introductory Remarks

In four manuscripts, the author of the *peshat*, i.e. Simcha b. Chananel, is referred to as "the above-mentioned", which means that the reader is redirected to the heading of *peshat* № 11 (in JSul.III.79) and № 23 (in ADub.III.61, JSul.I.45, and JSul.III.03). The Hebrew original was written by Shelomo ben Aharon of Poswol (see Tuori 2013: 425).

All five copies are vocalized. The texts are quite similar to each other. There are, again, some portions of text that appear in JSul.III.03, only, cf. *aziz torada* vs. *torada* (27), *edi da bardy* vs. *edi bardy* (28), *lešon haqodešni* vs. *lešon haqodeš byla* (30), and *söz byla* vs. *til byla* (30). All other differences are less significant as far as the relationship between the manuscripts is concerned:

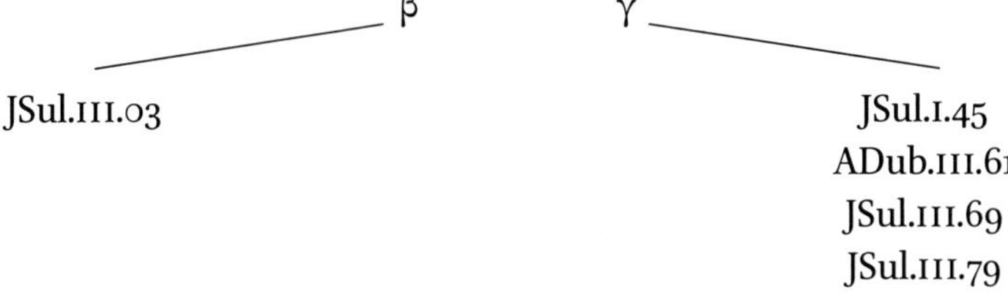


FIGURE 12 Diagram of the connections between the copies of peshat № 9

## 2 Transcription[256] and Translation

107 vº [1] [7] ⸢פשט לפיוט פרשת ואתחנן שהוא ה׳ אלהים אתה החילות להחכם הנ̃ל יע̃מש⸣[257]
[2] [8] E H[258] Tenrim[259] sen basladyn körgizme[260] mana qabaqlaryn bijik uslarnyn.
[3] [9] Turġuzdun meni küp[261] syjyncta da kördim[262] balquvlu sodlaryn
[4] [10] micvalarnyn. Qoltqa byla asajym ol Jardenni da körejim[263] jerni ki
[5] [11] ol tamašady[264] közlerinde[265] körivcilerinin[266]. Budur tefilesi Mošenin
[6] [12] navisinin ol Tenrinin. [267]⸢הקדשתיך מר̇חם⸣.
[7] [13] Qaruv beredi šeẖina ajtadoġac ki tuvmasyndan burun aziz
[8] [14] ettim seni da balquv boldu sana cyqqacoq qursaqtan.
[9] [15] Haligine saġynġyn ki raḥmetlevcü[268] Tenrinin sözü[269] qajjamdy da qalġyn
[10] [16] bu is ücün[270] alnymda jalbarmaqtan. Ki joġarġy Tenri
[11] [17] tivildi adam kibik ol[271] fašman[272] etme sözün[273] qajjam etmeqten. Da
[12] [18] daġyn küclü[274] Tenrisi Jisra'elnin aldamasty any fašman[275] etmesti
[13] [19] hašša[276] bolġaj anar sözün[277] tivsirmekten. [278]⸢ראש הפסגה⸣.

---

256 Based on JSul.III.03.

257 JSul.I.45: פשט לפיוט פרשת ואתחנן שהוא אד̇ני אלהים אתה תרגמו החכם המתרגם הנ̃ל. | ADub.III.61: וזה הפשט לפיוט פרשת ואתחנן שהוא אֲדֹנָי אֱלֹהִים אַתָּה הַחִלּוֹתָ תרגמו ג̃כ החכם האלהי המתרגם הנ̃ל הש̃ית יתן לו מהלכים בין העומדים לפניו אמן: | JSul.III.69: ואם תרצה תאמר גם פשטי שתרגמו החכם השלם כמוה̃רר שמחה החזן נב̃ת בכ̃מ חננאל הזקן יע̃מש: | JSul.III.79: פשט לפיוט פרשת ואתחנן תרגמו החכם האלהי הנ̃ל תשה̃עמ: אדני אלהים.

258 JSul.III.69: *Adonaj.*

259 JSul.III.69: *Tenri.*

260 ADub.III.61: *kergizme.* | JSul.III.69: *kergizme.* | JSul.III.79: *kergizme.*

261 JSul.III.03: a hypercorrect form of *kip.* | JSul.I.45: *kip.* | ADub.III.61: *kip.* | JSul.III.69: *kip.* | JSul.III.69: *kip.*

262 ADub.III.61: *kerdim.* | JSul.III.69: *kerdim.* | JSul.III.79: *kerdim.*

263 JSul.I.45: *kerejim.* | ADub.III.61: *kerejim.* | JSul.III.69: *kerejim.* | JSul.III.79: *kerejim.*

264 JSul.I.45: *tamasady.* | JSul.III.79: *tamasady.*

265 JSul.I.45: *kezlerinde.* | ADub.III.61: *kezlerinde.* | JSul.III.69: *kezlerinde.* | JSul.III.79: *kezlerinde.*

266 JSul.I.45: *kerivcilerinin.* | ADub.III.61: *kerivcilerinin.* | JSul.III.69: *kerivcilerinin.* | JSul.III.79: *kerivcilerinin.*

267 JSul.I.45: הקֹּדשתיך. | ADub.III.61: הקד̇שתיך. | JSul.III.69: הקד̇שתיך. | JSul.III.79: הקד̇שתיך.

268 ADub.III.61: *raḥmetlevci.* | JSul.III.69: *raḥmetlevci.* | JSul.III.79: *raḥmetlevci.*

269 JSul.I.45: *sezi*; spelled שֵׂיזִי. | ADub.III.61: *sezi.* | JSul.III.69: *sezi.* | JSul.III.79: *sezi.*

270 ADub.III.61: *icin.* | JSul.III.69: *icin.* | JSul.III.79: *icin.*

[1] [7] ⌊A *peshat* of a *piyyut* for the parashat Va'etchanan, of that (with the incipit) *H 'ĕlohīm 'attå haḥillōṯå*, of the above-mentioned hakham, may he rest in peace.[1279] 107 v°

[2] [8] O my Lord God, You have began to show me the gates of great wisdom.

[3] [9] You have settled me in a strong shelter and I have seen the shiny secrets

[4] [10] of the commandments. I beg You, may I cross the Jordan and may I see the land which

[5] [11] is a miracle in the eyes of those who see. This is the prayer of Moses

[6] [12] the prophet of God. (2).

[7] [13] The divine Presence answered, saying, 'I had sanctified you even before your birth

[8] [14] and there was light for you as soon as you left the bosom.

[9] [15] Now, remember that the word of the merciful God is durable and

[10] [16] abstain from praying for this matter before me. For the God up above

[11] [17] is not like a man that He ⌊would begrudge[1280] to abide firmly His word. And

[12] [18] even the powerful God of Israel will not delude him and will not begrudge (His word),

[13] [19] heaven protect Him from changing His word. (3).

---

271 ADub.III.61: *ol hassa bolġaj.*

272 ADub.III.61: *fasman.* | JSul.III.69: *fasman.* | JSul.III.79: *fasman.*

273 ADub.III.61: *sezin.* | JSul.III.69: *sezin.* | JSul.III.79: *sezin.*

274 ADub.III.61: *kicli.* | JSul.III.69: *kicli.* | JSul.III.79: *kicli.*

275 JSul.I.45: *fasman.* | ADub.III.61: *fasman.* | JSul.III.69: *fasman.* | JSul.III.79: *fasman.*

276 JSul.I.45: *hassa.* | ADub.III.61: *hassa.* | JSul.III.69: *hassa.* | JSul.III.79: *hassa.*

277 ADub.III.61: *sezin.* | JSul.III.69: *sezin.* | JSul.III.79: *sezin.*

278 JSul.I.45: ראֹשׁ. | JSul.III.69: ראֹשׁ. | JSul.III.79: ראֹשׁ.

279 JSul.I.45: *A* peshat *of a* piyyut *for the parashat Va'etchanan, of that* (*with the incipit*) 'ăḏonåy 'ĕlohīm 'attå, *which the above-mentioned hakham, the translator, translated.* | ADub.III.61: *And this is the* peshat *of a* piyyut *for the parashat Va'etchanan, of that* (*with the incipit*) 'ăḏonåy 'ĕlohīm 'attå haḥillōṯå, *also the translation of the above-mentioned divine hakham, the translator, God!, blessed be he, 'may places to walk will be given to him among those that stand before Him'* [see, Zechariah 3:7], *amen.* | JSul.III.69: *And, if you prefer, say its* peshat [i.e., of the Hebrew original], *which the pure hakham translated, his honour, the Rav, Rabbi Simcha the hazzan, may his soul lodge in Eden, the son of the honourable Chananel, the aged, may he rest in peace.* | JSul.III.79: *A* peshat *of a* piyyut *for the parashat Va'etchanan, which the above-mentioned divine hakham translated, 'the layer of dew came up on his lodge'* [cf., Exodus 16:13–14]. (*Incipit:*) 'ăḏonåy 'ĕlohīm.

280 ADub.III.61: *would, God forbid, begrudge.*

[14] [20] Basyna ol singirnin mingin da körgin[281] osol[282] ol jerni bijik ornun-
[15] [21] dan. Ant ettim berme any urluğuna Abrahamnyn bolusluğu
[16] [22] Tenrisinin boldu birgesine[283] avaldan. Da alġyn osol Jehošuany da
[17] [23] ⌞küplegin[284] any da kicejtkin⌟[285] any ki ağalyqqa qojarmen any ajyryp
[18] [24] anyn istine alheminden[286]. Da symarlady any H ⌞bolma ağalyq⌟[287]
[19] [25] ulusu istine ki ol edi jumuscusu Mošenin jaslyqlaryndan.
[20] [26] [288]⌜נִיבֹו לֹא חשׂך⌟. Sözün[289] ezinin[290] ajamady tizimeqten bizge
[21] [27] tatlylyġyn ajtmaqlarynyn. Da acty közün[291] aqylymyznyn tenestir-
[22] [28] geninde jaratylmaġyn jernin da bijik köklernin[292]. Cyqmaqqa
[23] [29] Micriden[293]
108 rº [24] [1] Micriden da anyn istine bunjat etti kebisi micvalaryn da resim-
[25] [2] lerin özünün[294]. Saruv saruv istine belgi belgi istine bujurdu
[26] [3] saqlama micvalaryn Torasynyn. [295]⌜הביאני במצרף⌟.
[27] [4] Kijirdi meni[296] sizgirmegine aruv dinnin da ivretti mana aziz[297] Torada
[28] [5] ki oldu Tenri körtilik[298] byla bir indeledoğan. Edi da[299] bardy
[29] [6] da bolurda da barlyġy anyn eksilmejdoğan. Qajyryr uluslarġa
[30] [7] aruv söznü[300] ⌞lešon haqodešni⌟[301] ezge ⌞söz byla⌟[302] qosulmajdo-ġan. Ol

281 ADub.III.61: *kergin.* | JSul.III.69: *kergin.* | JSul.III.79: *kergin.*
282 JSul.III.79: deest.
283 ADub.III.61: *birgesine anyn.* | JSul.III.79: *birgesine anyn.*
284 JSul.III.03: a hypercorrect form of *kiplegin.* | JSul.I.45: *kiplegin.* | JSul.III.69: *kiplegin.* | JSul.III.79: *kiplegin.*
285 ADub.III.61: *kicejtkin any da kiplegin.*
286 JSul.III.69: *senin alheminden.*
287 JSul.III.79: *ağalyq bolma.*
288 JSul.I.45: נ֗יבו. | JSul.III.69: נ֗יבו. | JSul.III.79: נ֗יבו.
289 ADub.III.61: *sezin.* | JSul.III.69: *sezin.* | JSul.III.79: *sezin.*
290 JSul.I.45: deest.
291 ADub.III.61: *kezin.* | JSul.III.69: *kezin.* | JSul.III.79: *kezin.*
292 ADub.III.61: *keklernin.* | JSul.III.69: *keklernin.* | JSul.III.79: *keklernin.*
293 Catchword.
294 JSul.I.45: *ezinin.* | ADub.III.61: *ezinin.* | JSul.III.69: *ezinin.* | JSul.III.79: *ezinin.*
295 JSul.I.45: הב֗יאני. | ADub.III.61: הב֗יאני. | JSul.III.69: הב֗יאני. | JSul.III.79: הב֗יאני.
296 JSul.III.69: *bizni.*
297 JSul.I.45: deest. | ADub.III.61: deest. | JSul.III.69: deest. | JSul.III.79: deest.
298 JSul.III.03: a hypercorrect form of *kertilik.* | ADub.III.61: *kertilik.* | JSul.III.69: *kertilik.* | JSul.III.79: *kertilik.*

[14] [20] Climb to the top of the summit and see the[303] land from a high place.
[15] [21] I swore to give it to the offspring of Abraham, the support
[16] [22] of God was with him all along. And take Joshua and
[17] [23] ⌊strengthen and reinforce⌋[304] him, for I put him into power by assigning
[18] [24] on him some of your inspiration.' And the Lord ordered him to be a superior
[19] [25] of the people, because he was the assistant[305] of Moses from their early age.
[20] [26] (4). He has not begrudged His own[306] words to formulate
[21] [27] speeches of sweetness (addressed) to us. And He has opened the eyes of our reason when He equalised
[22] [28] the creation of the earth and the high heavens with leaving
[23] [29] Egypt[307]
[24] [1] Egypt, and for this reason He laid foundations for many commandments 108 rº
[25] [2] and statutes of Him. Order over order, sign over sign—He ordered
[26] [3] to keep His commandments of the Law. (5)
[27] [4] He has introduced me into refining clear faith and He has taught me in the holy[308] Law
[28] [5] that He is the God whose name is one with the truth. He was and[309] is
[29] [6] and will be, and His existence is eternal. He turns to the nations
[30] [7] with[310] clear words in the Holy Language not mixed[311] with any other language. On that

299 JSul.I.45: deest. | ADub.III.61: deest. | JSul.III.69: deest. | JSul.III.79: deest.
300 JSul.I.45: *sözni.* | ADub.III.61: *sezni sezleme.* | JSul.III.69: *sezni sezleme.* | JSul.III.79: *sezni sezleme.*
301 JSul.III.03: *lešon haqodešni.* | JSul.I.45: *lešon haqodeš byla.* | ADub.III.61: *lešon haqodeš byla.* | JSul.III.69: *lešon haqodeš byla.* | JSul.III.79: *lešon haqodeš byla.*
302 JSul.I.45: *tilbyla.* | ADub.III.61: *til byla.* | JSul.III.69: *til byla.* | JSul.III.79: *til byla.*
303 JSul.III.79: *the.*
304 ADub.III.61: *reinforce and strengthen.*
305 Lit. 'workman, labourer; servant'.
306 JSul.I.45: deest.
307 Catchword in the Karaim text.
308 JSul.I.45: deest. | ADub.III.61: deest. | JSul.III.69: deest. | JSul.III.79: deest.
309 JSul.I.45: deest. | ADub.III.61: deest. | JSul.III.69: deest. | JSul.III.79: deest.
310 ADub.III.61: *to speak.* | JSul.III.69: *to speak.* | JSul.III.79: *to speak.*
311 Lit. 'joined'.

[31] [8] künde[312] bolur[313] H bir da birligi šeminin[314] avzunda bar elinin dunjanyn

[32] [9] bolur saǧynyladoǧan. [315]⌈ביום ההוא יהיה ה׳: שמע ישראל ה׳ אלהינו וגו׳⌋.

312 ADub.III.61: *kinde.* | JSul.III.69: *kinde.* | JSul.III.79: *kinde.*

313 ADub.III.61: *ol bolur.* | JSul.III.79: *ol bolur.*

314 JSul.I.45: *šeminin anyn.* | ADub.III.61: *šeminin anyn.*

315 Zechariah 14:9; Deuteronomy 6:4. | JSul.I.45: ביום ההוא יהיה ה׳ אחד וגו׳: שמע ישראל וגו׳: (Zechariah 14:9; Deuteronomy 6:4). | ADub.III.61: בַּיּוֹם הַהוּא יִהְיֶה הָ֫ אֶחָד וגו׳: (Zechariah 14:9). | JSul.III.69: בַּיּוֹם הַהוּא יִהְיֶה הָ֫ אֶחָד וּשְׁמוֹ אֶחָד: שְׁמַע יִשְׂרָאֵל וגו׳ (Zechariah 14:9; Deuteronomy 6:4). | JSul.III.79: וְיָהָיָה הָ֫ לְמֶלֶךְ עַל כָּל הָאָרֶץ וגו׳ (Zechariah 14:9).

[31] [8] day will be the Lord one and the oneness of His name will be
[32] [9] mentioned in the mouths of all nations of the world. ⌊In that day
shall there be Lord. Hear, O Israel: the Lord our God, and so forth.⌉[316]

316 Zechariah 14:9; Deuteronomy 6:4. | JSul.I.45: *'In that day shall there be one Lord …' and so on. 'Hear, O Israel …' and so on.* (Zechariah 14:9; Deuteronomy 6:4). | ADub.III.61: *'In that day shall there be one Lord …' and so on.* (Zechariah 14:9). | JSul.III.69: *'In that day shall there be one Lord, and his name one. Hear, O Israel …' and so on.* (Zechariah 14:9; Deuteronomy 6:4). | JSul.III.79: *'And the Lord shall be king over all the earth.'* (Zechariah 14:9).

| | |
|---|---|
| **Text number:** | № 10 |
| **Karaim incipit:** | *E Tenrisi dunjanyn ol jaratuvcu* |
| **Hebrew incipit:** | אֱלֹהֵי עוֹלָם הָעוֹשֶׂה כֹּל *ʾělohē ʿōlåm håʿōśe kol* |
| **Dedication:** | Parashat Ki Tavo (Deuteronomy 26:1–29:8) |
| **Language:** | Early Mod.SWKar., Mod.SWKar. |
| **Number of copies:** | 5 |

| Accession no. | Place of origin of copy | Date of copy | Copyist | Folios |
|---|---|---|---|---|
| JSul.III.03 | Halych | shortly after 1805 | Unknown 7 | 108 r°–108 v° |
| JSul.I.45 | Halych | 1st half of the 19th c. | Jeshua Josef Mordkowicz | 145 r°–145 v° |
| ADub.III.61 | Halych | 1850/1851 | Jeshua Josef Mordkowicz | 139 v°–140 r° |
| JSul.III.69 | Halych | ca. 1851 (before 1866) | Jeshua Josef Mordkowicz | 299 v°–300 v° |
| JSul.III.79 | Halych | ca. 1851 (before 1866) | Jeshua Josef Mordkowicz | 182 v°–183 r° |

## 1 Introductory Remarks

In the copies, the author of the *peshat* is referred to as "the above mentioned" which means that the reader is redirected to the headings of *peshatim* № 9 (in JSul.III.69), № 11 (in JSul.III.79), and № 23 (ADub.III.61, JSul.I.45, JSul.III.03).

All five copies are vocalized and are relatively similar to each other. The text in ms. JSul.III.03, being the only one not copied by Jeshua Josef Mordkowicz, shares slightly more unique portions of text with the versions in JSul.I.45 and JSul.III.69. In turn, the other two texts, i.e. the ones in mss. ADub.III.61 and JSul.III.79, constitute a separate group that share specific passages not found elsewhere, see: *ki keltirdi* vs. *anyn icin ki keltirdi* (16–17), *maqoviceler byla* vs. *maqoviceler tigel kerk byla* (17), *Jisraʾelni* vs. *Jisraʾelni bar jaḥsy byla* (23), *sarnarlar* vs. *dağynda ol kelesi zamanda sarnarlar* (26). The differences noted above show that even Jeshua Josef Mordkowicz must have used different originals in his work and that linguistically he kept improving the *peshat* over the course of time, cf. also *torany* vs. *aziz torany* (6), *aziz jerinin Jisraʾelnin* vs. *jerinin Jisraʾelnin* (7), or *da* vs. *ol vaḥtny* vs. *ol vaḥtta* (24). The above observations provide the basis for the following interconnections between the edited versions (cf. № 11) illustrated below:

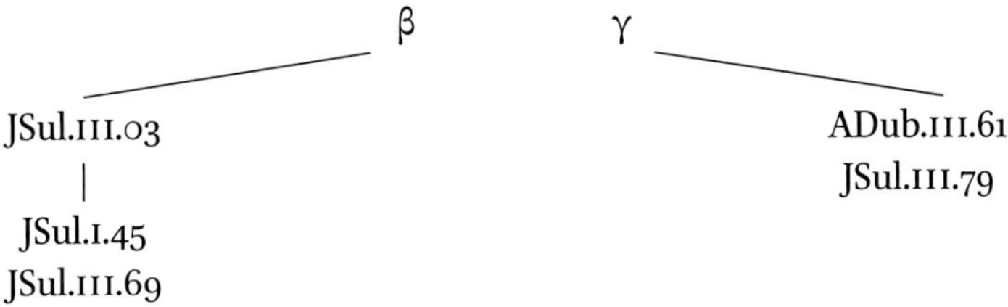


FIGURE 13 Diagram of the connections between the copies of peshat № 10

## 2 Transcription[317] and Translation

108 rº [1] [10] ⸤פשט לפיוט פרשת כי תבוא שהוא אלהי עולם העושה כל להרב הנ̃ל יע̃מש:
וזהו:⸣[318]

[2] [11] E Tenrisi dunjanyn ol jaratuvcu bar jaratylmyslarny tügel[319]
[3] [12] joqtan barġa da jaratmasyndan burun dunjany qajjamlyġynny[320]
[4] [13] körgizdün[321]. Qursaqtan cyqqacoq aziz ettin qorquvcularynny
[5] [14] da qulluġuna özinnin[322] alarny juvuttun. Ḥajifsinip berdin alarġa
[6] [15] Torany[323] cynyqtyrma alarny kecinme[324] ḥasydlyq byla da bijik
[7] [16] orunlary istine aziz[325] jerinin Jisra'elnin atlanġyzdyrdyn, osol
[8] [17] uvlunnu osol jalġyzaġynny ki sivdin. [326]⸢הבינֹותם לאחֹר⸣.
[9] [18] Aqyllattyn alarny ki bujurdun Torada ki kelip sortun jerine Jisra'elnin
[10] [19] da galut byla ilesip sortun any, keltirme ilkinden bar
[11] [20] jemisnin janġyrtma alarny. Da keltirgejler ol orunġa ki
[12] [21] anda synyqtyradylar baslarny da tizijdiler jüreklerni[327], ki
[13] [22] toḥtatma šemin özünün[328] anda sajlady H Tenrin senin any.
[14] [23] [329]⸢רחֹמי אֹל⸣. Raḥmetlerin qotarsynlar küclü[330] Tenrinin ol kep[331]
[15] [24] tamasa[332] isli indeledoġan, ki sonġulary alarnyn ullu boldu ḥotej

317 Based on JSul.III.03.
318 JSul.I.45: פשט לפיוט כי תבוא שהוא אלהי עולם העושה כל תרגמו החכם האלהי הנ̃ל. | ADub.III.61: וזה הפשט לפיוט פרשת כי תבוא שהוא אֱלֹהֵי עוֹלָם הָעוֹשֶׂה כֹּל מֵאֶפֶס תרגמו החכם השלם ואם תרצה תאמר פשטו שתרגמו אמ̃ו הר̃ר שמחה הנ̃ל תנצב̃הה. | JSul.III.69: המתרגם הנ̃ל תמ̃ן אמן. | JSul.III.79: וזה הפשט לפיוט פרשת כי תבוא תרגמו החכם הנ̃ל יע̃מש: אלהי עולם וגו׳.
319 JSul.I.45: *tigel.* | ADub.III.61: *tigel.* | JSul.III.69: *tigel.* | JSul.III.79: *tigel.*
320 JSul.III.79: *azizliginni.*
321 JSul.I.45: *körgizdin.* | ADub.III.61: *kergizdin.* | JSul.III.69: *kergizdin.* | JSul.III.79: *kergizdin.*
322 JSul.I.45: *ezinnin.* | ADub.III.61: *ezinnin.* | JSul.III.69: *ezinnin.* | JSul.III.79: *ezinnin.*
323 ADub.III.61: *aziz Torany.* | JSul.III.69: *aziz Torany.* | JSul.III.79: *aziz Toranny.*
324 JSul.I.45: *kecindirme ezlerin.*
325 JSul.I.45: deest. | ADub.III.61: deest. | JSul.III.69: deest. | JSul.III.79: deest.
326 JSul.I.45: הבינֹותם. | ADub.III.61: הבינֹותם. | JSul.III.69: הבינֹותם. | JSul.III.79: הבינֹותם.
327 ADub.III.61: *jireklerni.* | JSul.III.69: *jireklerni.* | JSul.III.79: *jireklerni.*
328 ADub.III.61: *ezinin.* | JSul.III.69: *ezinin.* | JSul.III.79: *ezinin.*
329 JSul.I.45: רחֹמי. | JSul.III.69: רחֹמי. | JSul.III.79: רחֹמי.
330 ADub.III.61: *kicli.* | JSul.III.69: *kicli.* | JSul.III.79: *kicli.*
331 JSul.I.45: *köp.*
332 JSul.I.45: *tamaša.* | ADub.III.61: *tamaša.* | JSul.III.79: *tamaša.*
333 JSul.I.45: *A peshat of a* piyyut *for the* parashat *Ki Tavo, of that* (*with the incipit*) 'ĕlohē 'ōlåm hå'ōśe kol, *which the above-mentioned divine hakham translated.* | ADub.III.61: *And this is*

[1] [10] ⌊A *peshat* of a *piyyut* for the parashat Ki Tavo, of that (with the incipit) *ʾĕlohē ʿōlåm håʿōśe kol*, of the above-mentioned sir, may he rest in peace. And this is it:⌋[333]
[2] [11] O God of the world, the creator of all creatures from complete
[3] [12] nothing into existence; and before the creation of the world You had
[4] [13] shown your permanency[334]. As soon as they left the bosom, You sanctified
[5] [14] those who fear You and You have brought them to Your own service. You have had mercy and given them
[6] [15] the Law[335] in order to accustom them ⌊to act⌋[336] with piety and
[7] [16] You have made them ride on the high places of the holy[337] land of Israel
[8] [17] Your son, the only one that You loved. (2).
[9] [18] You have admonished them that You have ordered in the Law that after arriving to the land of Israel,
[10] [19] after having shared the exile, they shall bring from the first of each
[11] [20] fruits to renew them. And may they bring (them) to that place
[12] [21] where they ⌊(bowed) their heads in humility⌋[338] and lifted up their hearts because
[13] [22] the Lord your God chose it to put His own name there.
[14] [23] (3). Preach the mercies of the powerful God,
[15] [24] called as ⌊the one wondrous in deeds⌋[339], ⌊for their end is great though

*the* peshat *of the* piyyut *for the parashat Ki Tavo, of that* (*with the incipit*) ʾĕlohē ʿōlåm håʿōśe kol mēʾepes, *which the above-mentioned complete hakham, the translator, translated; 'Bring my sould out of trouble'* [see, Psalm 143:11]. | JSul.III.69: *And, if you prefer, say its* peshat [i.e., of the Hebrew original], *which our above-mentioned master, teacher translated, the Rav, Rabbi Simcha, 'may his soul be bound in the bond of life'* [cf., 1Samuel 25:29], *amen.* | JSul.III.79: *And this is the* peshat *of the* piyyut *for the parashat Ki Tavo, which the above-mentioned hakham translated, may he rest in peace.* (*Incipit:*) ʾĕlohē ʿōlåm *and so on.*

334 JSul.III.79: *holiness.*
335 ADub.III.61: *holy Law.* | JSul.III.69: *holy Law.* | JSul.III.79: *holy Law.*
336 JSul.I.45: *to make them act*; probably a scribal error.
337 JSul.I.45: deest. | ADub.III.61: deest. | JSul.III.69: deest. | JSul.III.79: deest.
338 Lit. 'humiliated their heads'.
339 Lit. 'that of many wondrous deeds'.

[16] [25] baslyqlary alarnyn kici ⌞edi bolġan⌟[340]. Da šükür[341] etsinler ki[342]
[17] [26] keltirdi alarny jerge maqoviceler byla[343] qondarylġan. Da budu[344]
[18] [27] jemisi ol jernin ki ol sit da bal aġadoġan[345]. [346]⌜נוֹעם ה֜⌟.
[19] [28] Ceber savaġatlaryn H-nyn qotarsynlar da oncany keltirsinler
108 vᵒ [20] [1] ivine H-nyn syj byla qursalġan. Da ajtsynlar eksittim ol
[21] [2] qodešni ivimden kötirg[e]ni[347] ücün[348] bigilgenlerni[349] bolsun šeminin
[22] [3] aziz Tenrinin maḥtavy qotarylġan. Alġyslady ulusun özünün[350]
[23] [4] Jisra'elni[351] da baslaryn dušmanlarynyn[352] qojdu kesilgen. Da necik
[24] [5] körtilik[353] jerden bitse da[354] rastlyq köklerden[355] bolur baġynadoġan.
[25] [6] [356]⌜נִבָּא בֶּן בוּזִי⌟. Navilik etti Jeḥezekel uvlu Buzinin
[26] [7] ki tavlary jerinin Jisra'elnin[357] sarnarlar[358], da jemislerin kötirirler[359]
[27] [8] ulusuna {H-nyn} necik cyġyp galuttan kelme qajrylsalar. Olturġuzulurlar
[28] [9] avaldaġylaj da adam da tuvar köbisi[360] alar istine toḥtarlar.

---

340 Probably and inverted pluperfect form, instead of *bolġan edi*.

341 ADub.III.61: *šikir* or *sikir*. | JSul.III.69: *šikir* or *sikir*. | JSul.III.79: *šikir* or *sikir*.

342 ADub.III.61: *anyn icin ki*. | JSul.III.79: *anyn icin ki*.

343 ADub.III.61: {*tigel kerk byla*} {{*byla*}}. | JSul.III.79: *tigel kerk byla*.

344 ADub.III.61: *budur*. | JSul.III.69: *budur*.

345 JSul.III.79: *aqtyradoġan*.

346 JSul.I.45: נוֹעם. | ADub.III.61: נוֹעם ה׳ יספרו. | JSul.III.69: נוֹעם. | JSul.III.79: נוֹעָם.

347 JSul.III.03: *kötirgini*; a scribal error. | JSul.I.45: *kötirgeni*. | ADub.III.61: *ketirgeni*. | JSul.III.69: *ketirgeni*. | JSul.III.79: *ketirgeni*.

348 ADub.III.61: *icin*. | JSul.III.69: *icin*. | JSul.III.79: *icin*.

349 JSul.I.45: *bikregenlerni*.

350 JSul.I.45: *ezinin*. | ADub.III.61: *ezinin*. | JSul.III.69: *ezinin*. | JSul.III.79: *ezinin*.

351 ADub.III.61: *Jisra'elni bar jaḥsy byla*. | JSul.III.79: *Jisra'elni bar jaḥsy byla*.

352 JSul.I.45: *dusmanlarynyn*. | ADub.III.61: *dusmanlarnyn*. | JSul.III.69: *dusmanlarnyn*. | JSul.III.79: *dusmanlarynyn*.

353 ADub.III.61: *kertilik*. | JSul.III.69: *kertilik*. | JSul.III.79: *kertilik*.

354 JSul.I.45: *ol vaḥtyna*. | ADub.III.61: *ol vaḥtta*. | JSul.III.69: *ol vaḥtta*. | JSul.III.79: *ol vaḥtta*.

355 ADub.III.61: *keklerden*. | JSul.III.69: *keklerden*. | JSul.III.79: *keklerden*.

356 JSul.I.45: נִבָּא. | JSul.III.69: נִבָּא. | JSul.III.79: נִבָּא.

357 JSul.III.79: deest; a scribal error.

358 ADub.III.61: *daġynda ol kelesi zamanda sarnarlar*. | JSul.III.79: *daġynda ol kelesi zamanda sarnarlar*.

359 JSul.I.45: *ketirirler*. | ADub.III.61: *ketirirler*. | JSul.III.69: *ketirirler*. | JSul.III.79: *ketirirler*.

360 JSul.I.45: *kebisi*. | ADub.III.61: *kebisi*. | JSul.III.69: *kebisi*. | JSul.III.79: *kebisi*.

[16] [25] their beginning had been small⌉[361]. And they shall ⌊be thankful⌉[362] that[363]

[17] [26] He has brought them to the land ⌊built with capitals⌉[364] and these are

[18] [27] the fruits of the land flowing[365] with milk and honey. (4).

[19] [28] May they praise the pleasant mercies of the Lord and bring the tithe (of their produce)

[20] [1] to the house of Lord surrounded by fame. And they should say that 108 vº

[21] [2] ⌊'I have rid the holy(-produce) from my house'⌉[366] ⌊for lifting those who are bent[367]⌉[368], may the

[22] [3] praise of the name of the holy God be preached. He has blessed His own people,

[23] [4] Israel[369], and He has made the heads of their[370] enemies be cut off, and when

[24] [5] truth will sprout from earth, also[371] righteousness will ⌊look down⌉[372] from the heavens.

[25] [6] (5). Ezekiel the son of Buzi prophesied

[26] [7] that the mountains of the land ⌊of Israel⌉[373] will sing[374] and will bring

[27] [8] their fruits to the people of the Lord as they come to return after leaving the exile. They will inhabit them

[28] [9] as they did before, and many men and beasts will stay on them.

---

361 Cf. Deuteronomy 26:5.

362 Lit. 'thank'.

363 ADub.III.61: *because.* | JSul.III.79: *because.*

364 ADub.III.61: *built (with) capitals of true beauty.* | JSul.III.79: *built (with) capitals of true beauty.*

365 JSul.III.79: *poured.*

366 Cf. Deuteronomy 26:13.

367 JSul.I.45: *hunched.*

368 Uncertain translation.

369 ADub.III.61: *Israel with all kind of goods.* | JSul.III.79: *Israel with all kind of goods.*

370 ADub.III.61: deest. | JSul.III.69: deest.

371 JSul.I.45: *then.* | ADub.III.61: *then.* | JSul.III.69: *then.* | JSul.III.79: *then.*

372 Lit. 'will be looked down'.

373 JSul.III.79: desunt; a scribal error.

374 ADub.III.61: *sing even in the forthcoming times.* | JSul.III.79: *sing even in the forthcoming times.*

[29] [10] Da siz e tavlary jerinin[375] Jisra'elnin bitisinizni berirsiz[376] da ulusum
[30] [11] bar nametten tojarlar. [377]⌈וּפֶרְיֶכֶם תִּשְׂאוּ לְעַמִּי יִשְׂרָאֵל וגו׳:⌋

375 JSul.III.79: deest.

376 ADub.III.61: *berisiz*. | JSul.III.79: *berisiz*.

377 Ezekiel 36:8. | JSul.I.45: ופריכם תשאו לעמי ישראל וגו׳: . (Ezekiel 36:8). | ADub.III.61: וּפֶרְיְכֶם תִּשְׂאוּ לְעַמִּי יִשְׂרָאֵל וגו׳: . (Ezekiel 36:8). | JSul.III.69: וּפֶרְיְכֶם תִּשְׂאוּ לְעַמִּי יִשְׂרָאֵל כִּי קֵרְבוּ לָבוֹא: כִּי יְרַחֵם ה׳ אֶת יַעֲקֹב וּבָחַר עוֹד בְּיִשְׂרָאֵל וְהִנִּיחָם עַל אַדְמָתָם וְנִלְוָה הַגֵּר עֲלֵיהֶם וְנִסְפְּחוּ עַל בֵּית יַעֲקֹב: שְׁמַע אֵלַי יַעֲקֹב וְיִשְׂרָאֵל מְקֹרָאִי: שְׁמַע יִשְׂרָאֵל ה׳ אֱלֹהֵינוּ ה׳ אֶחָד: (Ezekiel 36:8; Isaiah 14:1, 48:12; Deuteronomy 6:4). | JSul.III.79: וּפֶרְיֶכֶם תִּשְׂאוּ לְעַמִּי יִשְׂרָאֵל וגו׳. (Ezekiel 36:8).

[29] [10] And you, O mountains of ⌊the land of[1378] Israel, give your fruits and may my people
[30] [11] be satisfied with all kinds of goods. ⌊And yield your fruit to my people of Israel, and so forth.[1379]

---

378 JSul.III.79: desunt.

379 Ezekiel 36:8. | JSul.I.45: *'And yield your fruit to my people of Israel …', and so forth.* (Ezekiel 36:8). | ADub.III.61: *'And yield your fruit to my people of Israel …', and so forth.* (Ezekiel 36:8). | JSul.III.69: *'And yield your fruit to my people of Israel for they are soon to come. For the Lord will have mercy on Jacob, and will yet choose Israel, and set them in their own land: and the strangers shall be joined with them, and they shall cling to the house of Jacob. Hearken unto me, O Jacob and Israel, my called. Hear, O Israel: The Lord our God is one Lord.'* (Ezekiel 36:8; Isaiah 14:1, 48:12; Deuteronomy 6:4). | JSul.III.79: *'And yield your fruit to my people of Israel …', and so forth.* (Ezekiel 36:8).

**Text number:** № 11
**Karaim incipit:** *E ummasy Jisra'elnin inanuvcular bir Tenrige*
**Hebrew incipit:** אַנְשֵׁי אֱמוּנָה בְּתוֹרַת אֵל *'anšē 'ĕmūnå bṯōraṯ 'ēl*
**Dedication:** Parashat Bechukotai (Leviticus 26:3–27:34)
**Language:** Early Mod.SWKar., Mod.SWKar.
**Number of copies:** 5

| Accession no. | Place of origin of copy | Date of copy | Copyist | Folios |
|---|---|---|---|---|
| JSul.III.03 | Halych | shortly after 1805 | Unknown 7 | 106 rº–106 vº |
| JSul.I.45 | Halych | 1st half of the 19th c. | Jeshua Josef Mordkowicz | 142 vº–143 vº |
| ADub.III.61 | Halych | 1850/1851 | Jeshua Josef Mordkowicz | 135 vº–136 rº |
| JSul.III.69 | Halych | ca. 1851 (before 1866) | Jeshua Josef Mordkowicz | 288 rº–289 rº |
| JSul.III.79 | Halych | ca. 1851 (before 1866) | Jeshua Josef Mordkowicz | 175 rº–176 rº |

## 1 Introductory Remarks

In mss. JSul.III.03 and JSul.I.45, the author of the *peshat* is referred to as "the above-mentioned", i.e. the reader is redirected to the heading of *peshat* № 23. All five copies are vocalized.

The few discrepancies between the copies are either amendments or preferential changes, see e.g. *kecinseniz* vs. *kecinsiniz* (3), *ketseniz* vs. *ketsiniz* (5), *indelgen* vs. *indeledoġan* (28), *qojġun* vs. *qojunġun* (34), the amended hypercorrect forms with erroneously used *ö* and *ü*, as well as *Torasyndan* ~ *aziz Torasyndan* (3), *micvalarny* ~ *aziz micvalarny* (17), *guflarymyzny* ~ *osol guflarymyzny* (21), *jerlerden* ~ *jerlerinden* (25), *kelegemde* ~ *kelegemde menim e* (26), *Abrahamnyn* ~ *Abrahamnyn da* (26), *negince ki* ~ *negince* (27), *kelgej* ~ *kelir* (27), *avaldaġy* ~ *avalġy* (31), and *turarmen* ~ *turamen* (42). The versions in ADub.III.61 and JSul.III.79 bear some similarities to one other, cf. the expressions *aziz micvalarnyn* (17), *osol guflar* (21), and *negince ki kelir* (27), used only in those two manuscripts.

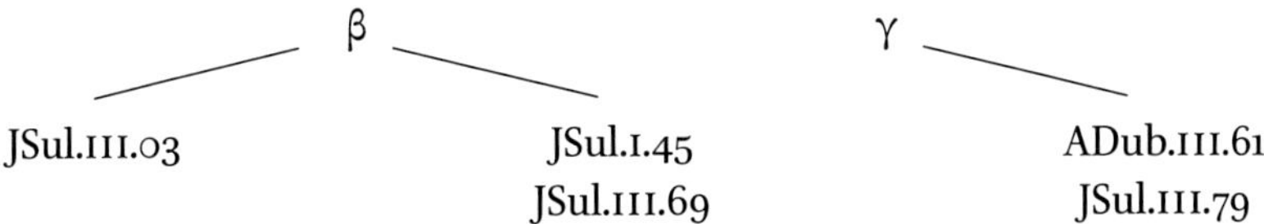


FIGURE 14 Diagram of the connections between the copies of peshat № 11

## 2 Transcription[380] and Translation

106 rº [1] [11] ⌊פשט לפיוט אם בחוקותי שהוא אנשי אמונה בתורת אל להחכם הנ̃ל נ̃ע:⌉[381]
[2] [12] E ummasy Jisra'elnin inanuvcular bir Tenrige eger jazylġan-
[3] [13] da köre[382] Torasyndan[383] Tenrinin kecins[e]niz[384], zoḫe
[4] [14] bolursiz körme[385] hašgaḥasyn Tenrinin bu dunjada da ʒanlarynyz
[5] [15] asajyslanyrlar ʿolam habada necik bu dunjadan elip kets[e]niz[386].
[6] [16] Kötiriniz[387] qollarynyzny aziz Tenrinin alnynda da syjly šemine H-nyn
[7] [17] maḥtav beriniz. Bulaj ajtady šeḫina menmen H ⌊Tenriniz süznün[388]⌉[389]
[8] [18] jaḥsy jal berivcü[390] süzge[391] eger resimlerim byla jiriseniz.
[9] [19] ⌈הִנֵּה מַה רַב⌉[392]. Muna esinizni qojunuz ne köptiler[393] nametleri
[10] [20] jaḥsylyqlarynyn, ki astrady saqlavcularġa sertin da arytuvcularġa
[11] [21] jazyqly islerden guflaryn ezlerinin. Da ḥor etivciler
[12] [22] sözlerin[394] anyn bolurlar talavġa da aclyqqa bu dunjada alajoq
[13] [23] elimlerinden sortun bolurlar ḥorluqlaryna dunjanyn, da
[14] [24] qajtaryr har birine jalyn islerinin. ⌈רׂחצו הלבׂ⌉[395].

---

380 Based on JSul.III.03.

381 JSul.I.45: וזה פשטו של פיוט פרשת בחקותי שהוא אנשי אמונה תרגמו החכם הנ̃ל. | ADub.III.61: וזה הפשט לפיוט פרשת אם בחוקותי שהוא אַנְשֵׁי אֱמוּנָה בְּתוֹרַת אֵל תִּדְרוֹכוּ תרגמו אמוה̃רר שמחה המתרגם הנ̃ל תשה̃עמ ונ̃בת. | JSul.III.69: ואם תרצה תא̃מ גם פשטו שתרגמו אמ̃ו הה̃ו כמוה̃רר שמחה החזן דקה̃ק קוקיזוב זצו̃קל בכ̃מ חננאל הזקן מן דראזניע. | JSul.III.79: פשט זה לפיוט פרשת בחקותי תרגמו אמ̃ו החכם השלם כמוה̃רר שמחה החזן דקה̃ק קוקיזוב זצו̃קל בכ̃מ חננאל הזקן מן דראזניע ישמ̃ש: אנ̇שי אמו̇נה.

382 ADub.III.61: *kere.* | JSul.III.69: *kere.* | JSul.III.79: *kere.*

383 JSul.III.79: *aziz Torasyndan.*

384 JSul.III.03: *kecinsiniz*; probably a scribal error; cf., however, *ketsiniz* in line 5. | JSul.I.45: *kecinseniz.* | ADub.III.61: *kecinseniz.* | JSul.III.69: *kecinseniz.* | JSul.III.79: *kecinseniz.*

385 ADub.III.61: *kerme.* | JSul.III.69: *kerme.* | JSul.III.79: *kerme.*

386 JSul.III.03: *ketsiniz*; probably a scribal error; cf., however, *kecinsiniz* in line 3. | JSul.I.45: *ketseniz.* | ADub.III.61: *ketseniz.* | JSul.III.69: *ketseniz.* | JSul.III.79: *ketseniz.*

387 JSul.I.45: *ketiriniz.* | ADub.III.61: *ketiriniz.* | JSul.III.69: *ketiriniz.* | JSul.III.79: *ketiriniz.*

388 JSul.III.03: a hypercorrect form of *siznin.* | ADub.III.61: *siznin.* | JSul.III.69: *siznin.* | JSul.III.79: *siznin.*

389 JSul.I.45: desunt.

390 JSul.I.45: *berivci.* | ADub.III.61: *berivci.* | JSul.III.69: *berivci.* | JSul.III.79: *berivci.*

391 JSul.III.03: a hypercorrect form of *sizge.* | JSul.I.45: *sizge.* | ADub.III.61: *sizge.* | JSul.III.69: *sizge.* | JSul.III.79: *sizge.*

392 JSul.I.45: הנ̇ה. | JSul.III.69: הנ̇ה. | JSul.III.79: הנ̇ה.

393 ADub.III.61: *keptiler.* | JSul.III.69: *keptiler.* | JSul.III.79: *keptiler.*

394 ADub.III.61: *sezlerin.* | JSul.III.69: *sezlerin.* | JSul.III.79: *sezlerin.*

395 JSul.I.45: רח̇צו. | JSul.III.69: רח̇צו. | JSul.III.79: רח̇צו.

[1] [11] ⌞A *peshat* of a *piyyut* for (the parashat) Bechukotai, of that (with the incipit) *ʾanšē ʾĕmūnå bṯōraṯ ʾēl*, of the above-mentioned hakham, may his soul rest in Eden.[1396] 106 rº

[2] [12] O, community of Israel, the believers of one God, if

[3] [13] you act according to what is written in the Law[397] of God,

[4] [14] you will have the honour of seeing the providence of God in ⌞this world[1398], and your souls

[5] [15] will relish in the ⌞World to Come[1399], when you go away from this world after dying.

[6] [16] Lift up your arms before the holy God and praise the honourable name of God.

[7] [17] So did the divine Presence say: 'I am ⌞your Lord God[1400]

[8] [18] who gives reward to you if you walk with my statutes.'

[9] [19] (2). Lo, pay attention how numerous are the goods

[10] [20] of His goodness, that He has kept[401] for those who obey His covenant and who cleanse

[11] [21] their own bodies from sinful deeds. And those who reject

[12] [22] His words will be (doomed) to destruction and hunger in this world and, in the same way,

[13] [23] after their death, they will be the shame of the world, and

[14] [24] the dues for their deeds will be returned to each one of them. (3).

---

396 JSul.I.45: *And this is a* peshat *of the* piyyut *for (the parashat) Bechukotai, of that (with the incipit)* ʾanšē ʾĕmūnå, *which the above-mentioned hakham translated.* | ADub.III.61: *And this is a* peshat *of the* piyyut *for (the parashat) Bechukotai, of that (with the incipit)* ʾanšē ʾĕmūnå bṯōraṯ ʾēl tidrōḵū, *which our master and teacher, the above-mentioned Rav, Rabbi Simcha, the translator, translated, 'the layer of dew came up on his lodge'* [cf., Exodus 16:13–14], *may his soul lodge in Eden.* | JSul.III.69: *And, if you prefer, say its* peshat [i.e., of the Hebrew original], *which our master, our teacher translated, the great and honourable sage, his honour, the Rav, Rabbi Simcha, the hazzan of the holy community of Kukizów, may the memory of the righteous and holy be a blessing, the son of the honourable Chananel, the aged, from Derażne.* | JSul.III.79: *This is a* peshat *of a* piyyut *for the parashat Bechukotai, which our master, our teacher, the complete hakham, his honour, the Rav, Rabbi Simcha translated, the hazzan of the holy community of Kukizów, may the memory of the righteous and holy be a blessing, the son of Chananel, the aged, from Derażne, may he rest in peace. (Incipit:)* ʾanšē ʾĕmūnå.

397 JSul.III.79: *holy Law.*

398 Cf. Heb. עוֹלָם הַזֶּה 'this World'.

399 Cf. Heb. עוֹלָם הַבָּא 'the World to Come'.

400 JSul.I.45: *the Lord.*

401 Lit. 'hidden'.

[15] [25] Juvunuz jüreklerinizni[402] jaman saġyslardan da arytynyz ezinizni
[16] [26] jaman islerden ki uvuclarda. Saqlanyz kecinme da qylma
[17] [27] micvalarny[403] ki jazyldy eki luḥotlarda, ki eger bulaj qylsanyz
[18] [28] jaḥsynyz bolur qatlanġan ki gufluq köreklerinìz[404] berilġen bolur
106 v° [19] [1] süzge[405] bu dunjada, alajoq ʒanlarynyz asajyslanyrlar ʿolam habada.
[20] [2] [406]⌜נתיב יושר⌝. Tiz izni sajlanyz ezinizge köcindirme[407]
[21] [3] jaḥsy qylyqlar byla guflarynyzny[408]. Bunluq byla zoḫe bolursiz
[22] [4] basqycy asyra ol inamlyqnyn jaryqqa cyġarma aqyllyq saġys-
[23] [5] larynyzny. Aziz orunda kensa ivinde jalbarma Tenrige
[24] [6] qojunuz kavvanalarynyzny, anyn ücün[409] bezmesti klegim sizden
[25] [7] da jomdarymen galut jerlerden[410] tozulġanlarynyzny. [411]⌜חסו בצלי⌝.
[26] [8] Bulaj ajtady šeḫina syjynynyz kelegemde[412] ulanlary Abrahamnyn
[27] [9] Icḥaqnyn[413] da Jaʿaqovnun küclü[414] aġalyqlarnyn, negince ki[415] kelgej[416]
[28] [10] šabat byla da jovel byla indel[gen][417] galuttan julunmaġy bu
[29] [11] jeʿudlarġa inanuvcularnyn. Qajsy jürek[418] küp[419] isanady da
[30] [12] tezedi bu navilikni any abrarmen da caġyrymen[420] azatlyq
[31] [13] ulanlaryna Jisra'elnin, da saġynymen[421] alarġa sertin avaldaġy[422]

402 ADub.III.61: *jireklerinizni.* | JSul.III.69: *jireklerinizni.* | JSul.III.79: *jireklerinizni.*
403 ADub.III.61: *aziz micvalarny.* | JSul.III.79: *aziz micvalarny.*
404 JSul.III.03: a hypercorrect form of *kerekleriniz.* | JSul.I.45: *kerekleriniz.* | ADub.III.61: *kerekleriniz.* | JSul.III.69: *kerekleriniz.* | JSul.III.79: *kerekleriniz.*
405 JSul.III.03: a hypercorrect form of *sizge.* | JSul.I.45: *sizge.* | ADub.III.61: *sizge.* | JSul.III.69: *sizge.* | JSul.III.79: *sizge.*
406 JSul.I.45: נתיב. | JSul.III.69: נתיב. | JSul.III.79: נתיב.
407 JSul.III.03: a hypercorrect form of *kecindirme.* | ADub.III.61: *kecindirme.* | JSul.III.69: *kecindirme.* | JSul.III.79: *kecindirme.*
408 ADub.III.61: *osol guflarynyzny.* | JSul.III.79: *osol guflarynyzny.*
409 ADub.III.61: *icin.* | JSul.III.69: *icin.* | JSul.III.79: *icin.*
410 JSul.III.79: *jerlerinden.*
411 JSul.I.45: חסו. | JSul.III.69: חסו. | JSul.III.79: חסו.
412 JSul.III.69: *kelegemde menim e.*
413 ADub.III.61: *da Icḥaqnyn.*
414 ADub.III.61: *kicli.* | JSul.III.69: *kicli.* | JSul.III.79: *kicli.*
415 JSul.I.45: deest.
416 JSul.I.45: *kelir.* | ADub.III.61: *kelir.*
417 JSul.III.03: *indeledoġan*; the present participle does not fit in with the context; see, mss. JSul.I.45 and JSul.III.69. | JSul.I.45: *indelgen.* | ADub.III.61: *indeledoġan*; the present participle does not fit in with the context; see, mss. JSul.I.45 and JSul.III.69. | JSul.III.69: *indelgen.* | JSul.III.79: *indeledoġan*; the present participle does not fit in with the context; see, mss. JSul.I.45 and JSul.III.69.

[15] [25] 'Purify your hearts from evil thoughts and cleanse yourselves
[16] [26] from evil deeds that are in your hands. Mind to do
[17] [27] the commandments[423] that were written on the two tables and act (according to them), for if you do so,
[18] [28] your goods will be doubled because your bodily necessities will be given
[19] [1] to you in this world and so will your souls relish in the World to Come. 106 vº
[20] [2] (4). Chose for yourselves the right way to lead
[21] [3] your bodies by good customs; by this you will have the honour of
[22] [4] revealing your thoughts of wisdom through the steps of confidence.
[23] [5] ⌊Have intention⌋[424] to pray to God at the holy place of the *kenesa*[425],
[24] [6] that is why you will not be an abomination to my intention,
[25] [7] and I will gather from the places of exile those of you who had been dispersed.' (5).
[26] [8] So did the divine Presence say: 'Shelter yourselves in my shadow, sons[426] of Abraham,
[27] [9] Isaac[427] and Jacob, the powerful superiors, until
[28] [10] the liberation from the exile ⌊may come⌋[428], called with (the name of) Sabbath and with (the name of) Jubilee[429]—
[29] [11] (the liberation) of those who believe in the promises[430]. I will protect the heart which believes strongly and
[30] [12] awaits the prophecy, and I will call for freedom
[31] [13] for the sons of Israel, and I will mention them the covenant of the ancient[431]

---

418 ADub.III.61: *jirek.* | JSul.III.69: *jirek.* | JSul.III.79: *jirek.*

419 JSul.III.03: a hypercorrect form of *kip.* | JSul.I.45: *kip.* | ADub.III.61: *kip.* | JSul.III.69: *kip.* | JSul.III.79: *kip.*

420 JSul.III.79: *caġyryrmen.*

421 JSul.III.69: *saġynyrmen.* | JSul.III.79: *saġynyrmen.*

422 ADub.III.61: *avalġy.* | JSul.III.69: *avalġy.*

423 ADub.III.61: *holy commandments.* | JSul.III.79: *holy commandments.*

424 Lit. 'place your intention'.

425 I.e., *Karaite shrine.* || Lit. 'house of *kenesa*'.

426 JSul.III.69: *O, sons.*

427 ADub.III.61: *and Isaac.*

428 JSul.I.45: *will come.* | ADub.III.61: *will come.*

429 Cf. Leviticus 25:8–55.

430 Lit. 'announcement'.

431 ADub.III.61, JSul.III.69: expressed with a synonym.

[32] [14] ic atalarnyn. [432]⌜זרֿע ידידי⌟. E urluğu süver[433]
[33] [15] qullarymnyn bajlanġyn quvat byla tizetme islerinni da tešuva
[34] [16] alnymda janġyrtma. Esinni [qojġun][434] ki qyjasy aqyllyq
[35] [17] ʒanynnyn qyjasy kibikti malaẖlarynyn bijik Tenrinin azizlikte
[36] [18] bolma, da eger klesen ol aziz malaẖlarġa tenesme,
[37] [19] köreklidi[435] bar islerinde rastlyq byla kecinme.
[38] [20] [436]⌜קראתיך בצדק⌟. Caġyrdym seni rastlyq byla qullu-
[39] [21] ġuma e qaldyġy inamly qullarymnyn. Tenestirdim seni syjda
[40] [22] jolduzlaryn kibik bijik köklerimnin[437]. Kelir vaḥt ki senin ücün[438]
[41] [23] eksitirmen[439] alnymdan bar ḥanlyqlaryn ol jernin. Haligine
[42] [24] turarmen[440] ulluluġumnu körgizme[441] ajtady šeẖinasy H-nyn.
[43] [25] ⌜עַתָּה אָקוּם יֹאמַר ה׳ עַתָּה אֵרוֹמָם עַתָּה אֶנָּשֵׂא: וכו׳:⌟[442]

---

432 JSul.I.45: זרֿע. | JSul.III.69: זרֿע. | JSul.III.79: זרֿע.

433 JSul.I.45: *siver.* | ADub.III.61: *siver.* | JSul.III.69: *siver.* | JSul.III.79: *siver.*

434 JSul.III.03: *qojunġun*; the reflexive form does not fit in with the contetxt; most probably a scribal error. | JSul.I.45: *qojġun.* | ADub.III.61: *qojġun.* | JSul.III.69: *qojġun.* | JSul.III.79: *qojġun.*

435 JSul.III.03: a hypercorrect form of *kereklidi.* | JSul.I.45: *kereklidi.* | ADub.III.61: *kereklidi.* | JSul.III.69: *kereklidi.* | JSul.III.79: *kereklidi.*

436 JSul.I.45: קראֿתיך. | JSul.III.69: קראֿתיך. | JSul.III.79: קראֿתיך.

437 ADub.III.61: *keklerimnin.* | JSul.III.69: *keklerimnin.* | JSul.III.79: *keklerimnin.*

438 ADub.III.61: *icin.* | JSul.III.69: *icin.* | JSul.III.79: *icin.*

439 JSul.I.45: *eksitimen.* | ADub.III.61: *eksitimen.* | JSul.III.79: *eksitimen.*

440 JSul.I.45: *turamen.*

441 ADub.III.61: *kergizme.* | JSul.III.79: *kergizme.*

442 Isaiah 33:10. | JSul.I.45: עתה אקום יאמר ה׳: וגו׳ (Isaiah 33:10). | ADub.III.61: עַתָּה אָקוּם יֹאמַר ה׳ וגו׳: תם הפשט (Isaiah 33:10). | JSul.III.69: עַתָּה אָקוּם יֹאמַר ה׳ עַתָּה אֵרוֹמָם עַתָּה אֶנָּשֵׂא: תם: וַיִּגְבַּה ה׳ צְבָאוֹת בַּמִּשְׁפָּט וְהָאֵל הַקָּדוֹשׁ נִקְדָּשׁ בִּצְדָקָה: קָדוֹשׁ קָדוֹשׁ קָדוֹשׁ ה׳ צְבָאוֹת מְלֹא כָל הָאָרֶץ כְּבוֹדוֹ: (Isaiah 33:10, 5:16, 6:3). | JSul.III.79: עַתָּה אָקוּם וגוא: וַיִּגְבַּה ה׳ צְבָאוֹת: קָדוֹשׁ קָדוֹשׁ קָדוֹשׁ ה׳ צְבָאוֹת: (Isaiah 33:10, 5:16, 6:3).

[32] [14] three patriarchs. (6). O offspring of my beloved
[33] [15] servants, commit (yourselves) strongly to better your deeds and to
[34] [16] renew (your) repentance before me. Pay attention that, in order to join[443] the holiness, the value of wisdom
[35] [17] of your soul[444] (must) be like the value (of that) of angels of the God up (above),
[36] [18] and if you wish to compare with the holy angels,
[37] [19] it is necessary to act with righteousness[445] in all your matters.
[38] [20] (7). I have called you with justice to (join)
[39] [21] my service, O, remnants of my faithful servants. I have made your fame compare with
[40] [22] the stars of my heavens up (above). The time will come that I will
[41] [23] wipe out from before me all the kingdoms of Earth. Now
[42] [24] I will[446] stand to show my greatness.'—said the divine Presence of God.
[43] [25] ⌞Now will I rise, says the Lord; now will I be exalted; now will I lift up myself, and so forth.⌝[447]

443 Lit. 'be in'.
444 Or: *heart.*
445 Or: *justice.*
446 JSul.I.45: deest.
447 Isaiah 33:10. | JSul.I.45: *'Now will I rise, says the Lord ...' and so on.* (Isaiah 33:10). | ADub.III.61: *'Now will I rise, says the Lord ...' and so on. The end of the peshat.* (Isaiah 33:10). | JSul.III.69: *The end. 'Now will I rise, says the Lord; now will I be exalted; now will I lift up myself. But the Lord of hosts shall be exalted in justice, and God who is holy shall be sanctified in righteousness. Holy, holy, holy, is the Lord of hosts: the whole earth is full of his glory.'* (Isaiah 33:10, 5:16, 6:3). | JSul.III.79: *'Now will I rise ...' and so on. 'But the Lord of hosts shall be exalted. Holy, holy, holy, is the Lord of hosts.'* (Isaiah 33:10, 5:16, 6:3).

| | |
|---|---|
| **Text number:** | № 12 |
| **Karaim incipit:** | *Eger ajtsam šira oḥujum* |
| **Hebrew incipit:** | אִם אָמְרִי אָשִׁירָה לְאֵלִי וְאַנְוֵהוּ *ʾim ʾåmrī ʾåšīrå lʾēlī wʾanwēhū* |
| **Dedication:** | Sukkot (on Shemini Atzeret) |
| **Language:** | MSWKar., Early Mod.SWKar., Mod.SWKar. |
| **Number of copies:** | 5 |

| Accession no. | Place of origin of copy | Date of copy | Copyist | Folios |
|---|---|---|---|---|
| JSul.I.54.03 | Halych (?) | turn of the 19th c. | Unknown 5 | 3 rº–4 rº |
| JSul.I.38.09 | Halych (?) | turn of the 19th c. | Unknown 4 | 5 rº–6 vº |
| JSul.III.72 | Halych | before 1851 | Jeshua Josef Mordkowicz | 144 rº–145 vº |
| JSul.III.67 | Halych | after ca. 1840, before 1851 | Josef b. Icchak Szulimowicz (?) | 249 rº–250 vº |
| JSul.III.76 | Halych | 2nd half of the 19th c. | Jeshua Josef Mordkowicz | 115 vº–116 vº |

## 1 Introductory Remarks

Four complete copies are available to us together with one additional, partly vocalized text that has survived in fragments in JSul.I.38.09. In JSul.III.72, the author of the *peshat*, i.e. Simcha ben Chananel, is referred to as "the above-mentioned", i.e. the reader is redirected to the heading of *peshat* № 14 in folio 141 vº. In ms. JSul.III.72, the heading of *peshat* № 16, i.e. the one that precedes the *peshat* edited here, only contains the given name *Simcha* (see 143 vº).

According to the heading introducing the Hebrew original in JSul.III.67 (248 vº–249 rº), the author of the Hebrew original was "the hakham, his honour, Rabbi Jeshua [spelled ישועה], the aged".

All five copies are vocalized and are very similar to each other. The differences between them are due for the most part to amendments or errors introduced by the copyists themselves. Mss. JSul.I.54.03 and JSul.I.38.09, i.e. the oldest versions, are somewhat similar to each other textually, see *sensen qajjam* vs. *sen qajjamsen* [12], *bir jaratylmyš* vs. *jaratylmyš* [23], *könderivčü da kečindirüvčü* vs. *könderüvčü* (~ *kenderivči* ~ *kenderivci*) [26], *bujruġun anyn* vs. *bujruġun* [28], and *da* vs. *ki* [34]. At the same time, the two manuscripts mentioned above contain the largest number of fragments not repeated elsewhere (including errors): in ms. JSul.I.54.03, see *esin* [21], *dunja* [24], *resimin* [27], *tolġunlary* [29], *joḥtu kim ki* [29], *obalarynyn* [39], *butar* [32], *tügelligine* [41], *umasyn* [50], and *ušaj-doġan* [52], whereas in JSul.I.38.09, see the absence of the word *enke* in line 6, the absence of the fragment *ese(de) ol jyllar da aštylar* in line 14, the absence of the word *üč* in line 21, as well as *miskin* [6], *aqylnyn* [10], *bar jyjynlaryn* [30], *köplügü* [36], *özleri* [38], *arslannyn* [32].

In the other three copies we find far fewer discrepancies unique to them alone. In ms. JSul.III.67 it is the fragments *jaratylmyšyn* vs. *jaratylmaġyn* [18], *baġatyrlyġynyn* vs. *baġatyrlyġynnyn* [22], *tefileler ornuna* vs. *tefileler* [54], and *yštyrma* vs. *östürme* [39] which makes this copy stand out from all the others, the latter three forms possibly being scribal errors. The copies in mss. JSul.III.72 and JSul.III.76 are the most similar to each other (they were created by the same copyist). Finally, mss. JSul.I.54.03, JSul.I.38.09, and JSul.III.72 contain a few forms exhibiting the NWKar. *ŋ > *j* change, which might suggest that those texts were copied on the basis of North-Western Karaim originals, see *birgeje* [16], *qatyjda* [16] in JSul.I.54.03 and JSul.I.38.09, *kleklerijnin* [17] in JSul.I.54.03, and *saja* [46, 55] in JSul.III.72. This is also supported by the use in those three sources of the verb *oḥu-* 'to read' with the initial *o-* characteristic of North-Western Karaim, see *oḥujum* [3], *oḥujmen* [53].

To sum up, we can assume the following pattern of interconnections:

FIGURE 15 Diagram of the connections between the copies of peshat № 12

## 2 Transcription[448] and Translation

3 r° [1] [1] ⌊⌊פשטים לפיוט של חג הסכות⌉⌉[449]
[2] [2] וזה פשט פיוט אם֞ אמ֞רי הנ֞אמ ביום מועד שמיני עצרת ושר[450] תרגמו החכם הנ֞ל נ֞ע⌉[451]
[3] [3] Eger ajtsam šira oḥujum[452] Tenrime da bijikligin[453] qotarajym
[4] [4] anyn, muna men tentekmen da nedir küčüm[454] ki bolalġajmen
[5] [5] ⌊maḥtavyn[455] ajtalma[456]⌉[457] anyn[.][458] Közlerimizde kiči[459] boldum birisi kibik
[6] [6] enke[460] usta miskinrek[461] elnin, qotarmaqtan ulluluġun[462] bijnin ol
[7] [7] bijlernin[463]. Minler byla minler da tümenler[464] byla tümenleri[465]
[8] [8] aziz malaḫlarnyn, azizligi da küčün[466] qotaradylar bijnin dunjalarnyn[.][467]
[9] [9] Jarlydy kiši[468] da jadaġandy da qotarmaqtan ulluluġun[469] Tenrinin qysqardy
[10] [10] küčü[470] aqylynyn[471], ančaq[472] kereklidi anar ki alnynda Tenrisinin dunjanyn

448 Based on JSul.I.54.03. The clause- and sentence-endings are reconstructed in comparison with the other copies.

449 A title introducing a series of *peshatim*.

450 *Pro* אשר or ואשר.

451 JSul.I.38.09: הא לך פשט לפיוט ראשון של יום שמיני עצרת שהוא אִם אָמְרִי אָשִׁירָה לְאֵלִי וְאַ שעשאו וחברו החכם כמוה֞רר שמחה החזן דקה֞ק יפה יע֞ר נב֞ת בכ֞מ חננאל הזקן נ֞ע. | JSul.III.72: וזה פשטו של פיוט הראשון של יום שמיני עצרת שהוא פיוט אִם אָמְרִי אָשִׁירָה: ג֞כ לחכם הנ֞ל. | JSul.III.67: ואם תרצה תאמר פשטו שתרגמו החכם כ֞מוהר֞ר שמחה החזן דק֞ק כוכיזוב נב֞ת בכ֞מ חננאל מתושבי קה֞ק דעראזניע יעמ֞ש. | JSul.III.76: ופה אכתוב פשטו הפיוטים הנפתבים לעיל שתרגמם אמ֞ו הר֞ר שמחה החזן בכ֞מע חננאל הזקן נב֞ת: וזה הפשט לפיוט אִם אָמְרִי המיוסד על קדושה ראשונה.

452 JSul.III.67: *uḥujum.* | JSul.III.76: *uḥujum.*

453 JSul.III.72: *bijikligim*; a scribal error.

454 JSul.III.67: *kičim.* | JSul.III.76: *kicim.*

455 JSul.III.72: *maḥtavlaryn.*

456 JSul.III.72: deest.

457 JSul.III.76: *qotarma maḥtavlaryn.*

458 Clause- or sentence-ending indicated in JSul.III.72.

459 JSul.I.38.09: *küčü*; a hypercorrect form of *kiči.* | JSul.III.76: *kici.*

460 JSul.I.38.09: deest.

461 JSul.I.38.09: *miskin.*

462 JSul.III.67: *ulluġun* < *ulluluġun* due to haplology. | JSul.III.76: *ulluġun* < *ulluluġun* due to haplology.

463 Clause- or sentence-ending indicated in JSul.III.72.

464 JSul.III.67: *timenler.* | JSul.III.76: *timenler.*

465 JSul.III.72: *timenleri.* | JSul.III.67: *timenleri.* | JSul.III.76: *timenleri.*

466 JSul.III.67: *kičin.* | JSul.III.76: *kicin.*

[1] [1] ⌊*Peshatim* of *piyyutim* for Sukkot.[1473] 3 r°

[2] [2] ⌊And this is a *peshat* of a *piyyut* (with the incipit) *ʾim ʾåmrī*, of the one chanted on the holiday of Shemini Atzeret, which the above-mentioned hakham translated, may his soul rest in Eden[1474]

[3] [3] When[475] I say, I sing the song to my God and I preach His greatness,

[4] [4] lo, I am a fool, for ⌊what kind of strength should I have[1476] to[477] be able

[5] [5] ⌊to speak out His praise[1478]? I have become small in our eyes like the

[6] [6] one of the people most[479] impoverished in wisdom, because of preaching the greatness of the Lord of the

[7] [7] lords. ⌊Many thousands[1480] and ⌊many tens of thousands[1481] of

[8] [8] holy angels preach the holiness and the power of the Lord of the worlds.

[9] [9] Miserable is the man and weary, too, from preaching the greatness of God,

[10] [10] the strength of his mind is declining, but it is needful for him to

---

467 Sentence-ending indicated in JSul.I.38.09, JSul.III.72, JSul.III.76.

468 JSul.III.76: *kisi*.

469 JSul.III.67: *ulluġun* < *ulluluġun* due to haplology.

470 JSul.III.67: *kiči*. | JSul.III.76: *kici*.

471 JSul.I.38.09: *aqylnyn*.

472 JSul.III.76: *ancaq*.

473 A title introducing a series of *peshatim*.

474 JSul.I.38.09: *May the* peshat *of the first* piyyut *for the day of Shemini Atzeret follow here, of that* (*with the incipit*) ʾim ʾåmrī ʾåširå lʾēlī wʾanwēhū, *done and written by his honour, the Rav, Rabbi, hakham Simcha the hazzan of the holy community of Yefeh Yaʿar* [i.e., Kukizów], *the son of the honourable sir Chananel, the aged, may his soul rest in Eden.* | JSul.III.72: *And this is a* peshat *of the first* piyyut *for the day of Shemini Atzeret, of that* (*with the incipit*) ʾim ʾåmrī ʾåširå, *also of the above-mentioned.* | JSul.III.67: *And, if you prefer, say its* peshat [i.e., of the Hebrew original], *which the hakham, his honour, the Rav, Rabbi Simcha translated, the hazzan of the holy community of Kukizów, may his soul lodge in Eden, the son of the honourable Chananel, a resident of the holy community of Derażne, may he rest in peace.* | JSul.III.76: *And here I will write down the* peshatim *of the above* piyyutim, *which our master and teacher, the Rav, Rabbi Simcha the hazzan translated, the son of Chananel, the aged, whose honourable repose is Eden, may his soul lodge in Eden. And this is the* peshat *of the* piyyut (*with the incipit*) ʾim ʾåmrī, *based on the first holy* (piyyut).

475 Lit. 'if'.

476 Lit. 'what kind of power is that of mine'.

477 Lit. 'that I may'.

478 JSul.III.76: *to preach His praise*.

479 JSul.I.38.09: deest.

480 Lit. 'thousands and thousands'.

481 Lit. 'tens of thousands and tens of thousands'.

[11] [11] tökkej[482] gilejin jüreg[i]nin[483][,][484] da ajtqaj muna sen e Adonaj[485] aziz Tenrim

[12] [12] avaldandy[486] barlyġyn senin[487] da ⌞sensen qajjam⌝[488] sofuna dejin bar sofnun da senin

[13] [13] qajjamlyġyn bylady qajjamlyġy bijik köklernin[489] da juvuz jernin[.][490] Da eger

[14] [14] köp[491] boldular ⌞ese[492] ol jyllar da aštylar[493]⌝[494] esede vaḥtlary ol kelesi

[15] [15] nerselernin, da sen tüvšürülmessen[495] da seni tüvšürmesler[496] vaḥtlary

[16] [16] zamanlarnyn[.][497] Jat[498] joḥtu[499] qatyjda[500] da joḥtu birgeje[501] bolušluġu[502] özge[503]

[17] [17] tenrinin[,][504] da joḥtu[505] kim ki kečiktirgej[506] bolunmaġyn bar kleklerijnin[507][.][508]

[18] [18] Usajttyn ⌞ulanlaryn adamnyn⌝[509] bilme seni körmekbyla[510] jaratylmaġyn[511]

[19] [19] qorqunčlu[512] jaratylmyšlarynnyn[513][,][514] ki bolalmajdylar körme[515] kensiliginni[516]

---

482 JSul.III.67: *tekkej.* | JSul.III.76: *tekkej.*

483 JSul.I.54.03: *jüregenin*; a scribal error. | JSul.I.38.09: *jüreginin.* | JSul.III.72: *jüreginin.* | JSul.III.67: *jireginin.* | JSul.III.76: *jüreginin.*

484 Clause- or sentence-ending indicated in JSul.III.72.

485 JSul.I.38.09: *H.* | JSul.III.67: *H.* | JSul.III.76: *H.*

486 JSul.III.67: *avaldaġylaj.*

487 JSul.III.67: *anyn.*

488 JSul.III.72: *sen qajjamsen.* | JSul.III.67: *sen qajjamsen.* | JSul.III.76: *sen qajjamsen.*

489 JSul.III.67: *keklernin.* | JSul.III.76: *keklernin.*

490 Sentence-ending indicated in JSul.I.38.09, JSul.III.72, and JSul.III.76.

491 JSul.III.67: *kep.* | JSul.III.76: *kep.*

492 JSul.III.72: *esede.* | JSul.III.76: *esede.*

493 JSul.III.67: *astylar.* | JSul.III.76: *astylar.*

494 JSul.I.38.09: desunt; a scribal error.

495 JSul.III.72: *tüvsürülmessen.* | JSul.III.67: *tivširilmessen* or *tivsirilmessen.* | JSul.III.76: *tivsirilmessen.*

496 JSul.III.72: *tüvsürmesler.* | JSul.III.67: *tivsirmesler.* | JSul.III.76: *tivsirmesler.*

497 Sentence-ending indicated in JSul.I.38.09, JSul.III.72, and JSul.III.76.

498 JSul.I.38.09: From this fragment on the text is not vocalized.

499 JSul.I.38.09: *joḥtur.* | JSul.III.72: *joḥtur.* | JSul.III.67: *joḥtur.* | JSul.III.76: *joḥtur.*

500 JSul.III.72: *qatynda.* | JSul.III.67: *qatynda.* | JSul.III.76: *qatynda.*

501 JSul.III.72: *birgene.* | JSul.III.67: *birgene.* | JSul.III.76: *birgene.*

502 JSul.III.76: *bolusluġu.*

503 JSul.III.67: *ezge.* | JSul.III.76: *ezge.*

[11] [11] reveal[517] the sorrow of his heart before the God of the world and that he may say, 'Lo, You, O Lord my holy God,

[12] [12] Your existence lasts since long ago and You are eternal until the end of all ends and with Your

[13] [13] permanence (comes) the permanence of the high heavens and low earth.' And even if

[14] [14] the years[518] would become numerous and the time of the future events ˻would pass˼[519],

[15] [15] You would not be changed and the ˻course of time˼[520] would not change You (either).

[16] [16] There is no other (god) besides You and with You there is no salvation

[17] [17] of other god, and there is no one who could stop[521] all Your wishes to come into being.

[18] [18] You made the sons of man wise in order to let them know You by seeing the creation

[19] [19] of the fearful creatures, for they are not able to see Your nature,

504 Clause- or sentence-ending indicated in JSul.I.38.09.

505 JSul.III.72: *johtur.* | JSul.III.67: *johtur.* | JSul.III.76: *johtur.*

506 JSul.III.76: *keciktirgej.*

507 JSul.I.38.09: *kleklerinnin.* | JSul.III.72: *kleklerinnin.* | JSul.III.67: *kleklerinnin.* | JSul.III.76: *kleklerinnin.*

508 Sentence-ending indicated in JSul.I.38.09, JSul.III.72, and JSul.III.76.

509 JSul.I.38.09: originally *adam{nyn} ulanlaryn*; the word order has been changed by the copyist to *ulanlaryn adamnyn* (this is indicated with barely visible marks).

510 JSul.III.67: *kermekbyla.* | JSul.III.76: *kermek byla.*

511 JSul.III.67: *jaratylmyšyn.*

512 JSul.III.76: *qorqunclu.*

513 JSul.III.76: *jaratylmyslarynnyn.*

514 Clause- or sentence-ending indicated in JSul.I.38.09.

515 JSul.III.67: *kerme.* | JSul.III.76: *kerme.*

516 JSul.I.38.09: *künšülügünnü*; a hypercorrect form of *kensiliginni*; probably copied based on a non-vocalized text, in which *-e-* in *ken* had been written with the letter *yodh*, which was then misinterpeted as *-i-* and changed to a hypercorrect *-ü-*; cf., in the same text, *körgünlerinde* in line 25.

517 Lit. 'to pour'.

518 JSul.I.38.09: deest; a scribal error.

519 JSul.I.38.09: desunt; a scribal error.

520 Lit. 'times of the times'.

521 Or: *delay.*

[20] [20] jyjyny malaẖlarnyn jovšem[522] ki aqyly adamlarnyn[523][.][524] Senin barlyġyn[525] qajjamdy

[21] [21] jaratylmaġyndan burun üč[526] dunjalarnyn[,][527] da esin[528] qojuvču[529] išlerine[530]

[22] [22] bil[i]r[531] qotarma ulluluġun baġatyrlyġynnyn[532][.][533] Da anlyqbyla bilediler

[23] [23] ki joḥtu[534] bir[535] jaratylmyš[536] ki bolmaġaj jaratuvčusu[537] anyn[,][538] da bijik da

[24] [24] juvuzda dunja[539] bolmaġajedi[540] eltingenler eger bolmasyjdy[541] eltivčüsü[542]

3 v° [25] [1] alarnyn[.][543] Körgenlerinde[544] ki sanbyla čyġadylar bar čörüvü[545] ol[546] köklernin[547][,][548]

[26] [2] tanyjdylar da biled[i]ler[549] ki bardy alarġa könderivčü[550] ⌊da kečindirüvčü[551]⌉[552]

[27] [3] da maḥtavlar čaġyradylar[553] syjly šemine anyn[.][554] Tengizge qojdu resimin[555]

---

522 JSul.III.72: *jovsem.* | JSul.III.76: *jovsem.*

523 JSul.I.38.09: *adamnyn.*

524 Sentence-ending indicated in JSul.I.38.09, JSul.III.72, and JSul.III.76.

525 JSul.I.38.09: *birligin.*

526 JSul.I.38.09: deest. | JSul.III.67: *ič.* | JSul.III.76: *ic.*

527 Clause- or sentence-ending indicated in JSul.I.38.09.

528 JSul.I.38.09: *ol esin.* | JSul.III.72: *ol esin.* | JSul.III.67: *ol esin.*

529 JSul.III.76: *qojuvcu.*

530 JSul.I.38.09: *üšlerine*; a hypercorrect form of *išlerine.* | JSul.III.76: *islerine.*

531 JSul.I.54.03: *biler*; the *biler* < *bilir* change might be morphonological in nature, see Musaev (1964: 281). | JSul.I.38.09: no vocalization; see JSul.III.72. | JSul.III.72: *bilir.* | JSul.III.67: *bilir.* | JSul.III.76: *bilir.*

532 JSul.I.38.09: *baġatyrlyqlarynnyn* | JSul.III.67: *baġatyrlyġynyn*; possibly a scribal error.

533 Sentence-ending indicated in JSul.I.38.09, and JSul.III.72.

534 JSul.I.38.09: *joḥtur.* | JSul.III.72: *joḥtur.* | JSul.III.67: *joḥtur.* | JSul.III.76: *joḥtur.*

535 JSul.III.72: deest. | JSul.III.67: deest. | JSul.III.76: deest.

536 JSul.III.76: *jaratylmys.*

537 JSul.III.76: *jaratuvcusu.*

538 Clause- or sentence-ending indicated in JSul.I.38.09.

539 JSul.I.38.09: *dunjada.* | JSul.III.72: *dunjada.* | JSul.III.67: *dunjada.* | JSul.III.76: *dunjada.*

540 JSul.III.72: *bolmaġajady*; < *bolmaġajedi* or a scribal error; cf. *bolmasajady* (24), and *syndaralyr* (29). | JSul.III.67: *bolmaġyjdy.* | JSul.III.76: *bolmaġyjdy.*

541 JSul.III.72: *bolmasajady*; < *bolmasajedi* or a scribal error; cf. *bolmaġajady* (24), and *syndaralyr* (29).

[20] [20] the circle of angels and, particularly, the wisdom of men[556]. Your existence is durable

[21] [21] since before the creation of the three worlds; and he who pays attention to Your[557] deeds

[22] [22] will know (how) to preach the greatness of Your[558] powerfulness. And for this reason they know

[23] [23] that there is ⌊not even one⌋[559] creature that would have no creator, and in the high

[24] [24] and low world there would be no one sent if there was no one to send

[25] [1] them. When they see all the armies of heavens to emerge numerously, 3 vº

[26] [2] they learn and know that they[560] have a sender ⌊and adviser⌋[561]

[27] [3] and they praise His honourable name. And He has put His[562] statute in the sea

---

542 JSul.III.72: *eltüvčüsü.* | JSul.III.67: *eltivčisi.* | JSul.III.76: *eltivcisi.*

543 Sentence-ending indicated in JSul.I.38.09, JSul.III.72, and JSul.III.76.

544 JSul.I.38.09: *körgünlerinde*; a hypercorrect form of *körgenlerinde*; probably copied on the basis of a non-vocalized text, in which *-e-* in *-gen* had been written with the letter *yodh* which was then misinterpeted as *-i-* and changed to a hypercorrect *-ü-*. | JSul.III.67: *kergenlerinde.* | JSul.III.76: *kergenlerinde.*

545 JSul.I.38.09: *čerivi.* | JSul.III.72: *čerüvü.* | JSul.III.67: *čerivi.* | JSul.III.76: *cerivi.*

546 JSul.III.76: deest.

547 JSul.III.67: *keklernin.* | JSul.III.76: *keklernin.*

548 Clause- or sentence-ending indicated in JSul.I.38.09.

549 JSul.I.54.03: *biledeler*; a scribal error. | JSul.I.38.09: no vocalization. | JSul.III.72: *bilediler.* | JSul.III.67: *bilediler.* | JSul.III.76: *bilediler.*

550 JSul.III.72: *könderüvčü.* | JSul.III.67: *kenderivči.* | JSul.III.76: *kenderivci.*

551 JSul.I.38.09: *kečindirivči.*

552 JSul.III.72: desunt. | JSul.III.67: desunt. | JSul.III.76: desunt.

553 JSul.III.67: *čağyradlar.* | JSul.III.76: *cağyradylar.*

554 Sentence-ending indicated in JSul.I.38.09, JSul.III.72, and JSul.III.76.

555 JSul.I.38.09: *resim.* | JSul.III.72: *resim.* | JSul.III.67: *resim.* | JSul.III.76: *resim.*

556 JSul.I.38.09: *man.*

557 JSul.III.67: *His.*

558 JSul.III.67: *His.*

559 JSul.III.72: *no.* | JSul.III.67: *no.* | JSul.III.76: *no.*

560 I.e., *the armies of heavens.*

561 JSul.III.72: desunt. | JSul.III.67: desunt. | JSul.III.76: desunt.

562 JSul.I.38.09: deest. | JSul.III.72: deest. | JSul.III.67: deest. | JSul.III.76: deest.

[28] [4] da tüvsürmejdi[563] bujruğun anyn[564] da asmajdy[565] qumun ček[566] qojğanynyn[,][567]

[29] [5] da čuvlasalar[568] [obalary][569] anyn da Tenriden özge[570] ⌊{joḥtu kim} ki⌋[571] syndyralyr[572] ulluluğun[573]

[30] [6] [tolğunlarynyn][574][.][575] Joqtan jaratty[576] jyjynlaryn[577] bar tiri ǯannyn[578], da jembyla

[31] [7] da beslenmekbyla jetkiliklerin beredi alarnyn[.][579] Qorqunčludu[580] ol

[32] [8] berm[e]gi[581] sartyn tavlar üstüne[582] butar[583] jemin arslanlarnyn[584] da bar

[33] [9] minleri jyllarnyn köz[585] jumčuğu[586] teklidi alnynda anyn[.][587] Jaḥšy[588] Tenridi

[34] [10] da[589] ol bošatady[590] jazyqlaryn andijlernin ki umsunadylar šava-ġatyna[591]

[35] [11] anyn[.][592] Da beredi klegin qulunun neginče[593] ki tügellegej[594] sözün[595] qoltqalarynyn[.][596]

---

563 JSul.I.38.09: *tüvšürmejdi.* | JSul.III.72: *tüvsürmejdi.* | JSul.III.67: *tivsirmejdi.* | JSul.III.76: *tivsirmejdi.*

564 JSul.III.72: deest. | JSul.III.67: deest. | JSul.III.76: deest.

565 JSul.I.38.09: *ašmajdy.* | JSul.III.72: *ašmajdy.*

566 JSul.III.76: *cek.*

567 Clause- or sentence-ending indicated in JSul.I.38.09.

568 JSul.I.38.09: *čuvlasalarda.* | JSul.III.76: *cuvlasalar.*

569 JSul.I.54.03: *tolġunlary*; cf. next line. | JSul.I.38.09: *obalary.* | JSul.III.72: *obalary.* | JSul.III.67: *obalary.* | JSul.III.76: *obalary.*

570 JSul.III.72: *ezge.* | JSul.III.67: *ezge.* | JSul.III.76: *ezge.*

571 JSul.I.38.09: *kim.* | JSul.III.72: *kim.* | JSul.III.67: *kim.* | JSul.III.76: *kim ol.*

572 JSul.III.72: *syndaralyr*; a scribal error.

573 JSul.III.67: *ulluġun* < *ulluluġun* due to haplology.

574 JSul.I.54.03: *obalarynyn*; cf. previous line. | JSul.I.38.09: *tolġunlarynyn.* | JSul.III.72: *tolġun-larynyn.* | JSul.III.67: *tolġunlarynyn.* | JSul.III.76: *tolġunlarynyn.*

575 Sentence-ending indicated in JSul.I.38.09, JSul.III.72, and JSul.III.76.

576 JSul.III.76: *jarattyn.*

577 JSul.I.38.09: *bar jyjynlaryn.*

578 JSul.III.76: *ʒannyn.*

579 Clause- or sentence-ending indicated in JSul.I.38.09, and JSul.III.72.

580 JSul.III.76: *qorquncludu.*

581 JSul.I.54.03: *bermigi*; a scribal error. | JSul.I.38.09: no vocalization. | JSul.III.72: *bermegi.* | JSul.III.67: *bermegi.* | JSul.III.76: *bermegi.*

[28] [4] and does not change His order and does not cross the sand set for frontier,

[29] [5] and if their waves[597] would roar, and apart from God ⌊there is no one⌋[598] who would be able to break the greatness

[30] [6] of the graves[599]. He created from nothing a plenty of all (kind of) living souls, and,

[31] [7] by (giving them) food and by feeding them, He gave them affluence. Awesome is He

[32] [8] because of what He gave at the mountains, prey[600] food of lions[601]; and all

[33] [9] the thousands of years are like a twinkling of an eye before Him. A good God is He,

[34] [10] ⌊and He⌋[602] absolves the sins of those[603] who wait for His mercy.

[35] [11] And He fulfils the wish of His servant as long as he fulfils the words of prayers.

---

582 JSul.III.67: *istine.* | JSul.III.76: *istine.*

583 JSul.I.38.09: *jyrtuv.* | JSul.III.72: *jyrtuv.* | JSul.III.67: *jyrtuv.* | JSul.III.76: *jyrtuv.*

584 JSul.I.38.09: *arslannyn*; clause- or sentence-ending indicated here.

585 JSul.III.67: *kez.* | JSul.III.76: *kez.*

586 JSul.III.76: *jumcuġu.*

587 Sentence-ending indicated in JSul.I.38.09, JSul.III.72, and JSul.III.76.

588 JSul.III.76: *jaḥsy.*

589 JSul.III.72: *ki.* | JSul.III.67: *ki.* | JSul.III.76: *ki.*

590 JSul.III.76: *bosatady.*

591 JSul.III.76: *savaġatyna.*

592 Clause- or sentence-ending indicated in JSul.I.38.09.

593 JSul.III.76: *negince.*

594 JSul.I.38.09: *tigellegej.* | JSul.III.67: *tigellegej.* | JSul.III.76: *tigellegej.*

595 JSul.III.67: *sezin.* | JSul.III.76: *sezin.*

596 Sentence-ending indicated in JSul.I.38.09, JSul.III.72, and JSul.III.76.

597 JSul.I.38.09: *graves.* | JSul.III.72: *graves.* | JSul.III.67: *graves.* | JSul.III.76: *graves.* || Cf. line 30.

598 JSul.I.38.09: desunt; a scribal error. | JSul.III.72: desunt; a scribal error. | JSul.III.67: desunt; a scribal error. | JSul.III.76: desunt; a scribal error.

599 JSul.I.38.09: *waves.* | JSul.III.72: *waves.* | JSul.III.67: *waves.* | JSul.III.76: *waves.* || Cf. line 29.

600 In all other mss. expressed with a synonym.

601 JSul.I.38.09: *a lion.*

602 JSul.III.72: *who*; lit. 'that'. | JSul.III.67: *who*; lit. 'that'. | JSul.III.76: *who*; lit. 'that'.

603 Lit. 'such (persons)'.

[36] [12] Jaratty bar jaratylmyšlarny[604] rastlyġybyla da köplügübyla[605] qajjamlyġynyn[.][606]
[37] [13] Arymajdy da jadamajdy joḥtu[607] tergev köplügüne[608] aqylynyn[.][609] Jajdy
[38] [14] bulutun jüzleri[610] üstüne[611] dunjanyn berme jamġurun jernin[,][612] bögöv-
[39] [15] retme[613] qurġaq pusta orunlarny[614] da östürme[615] ⌊jaš[616] ot⌋[617] alajoq
[40] [16] čyġysyn[618] barda bitislernin[619][.][620] Astylar[621] bar ol künler[622] da jetelmedi
[41] [17] kišide[623] tügelligine[624] maḥtavlarynyn. Tügendiler[625] suvlary ol tengiznin
[42] [18] da aš{k}armady[626] ulluluġu[627] syjynyn[.][628] Anlatmaqtan[629] širasyn qysqardylar
[43] [19] sözleri[630] bar ⌊tillernin[631], da qotarmaqtan maḥtavyn jadadylar erinleri
[44] [20] bar⌋[632] avuzlarnyn[633]. Köp[634] b[o]ldular[635] išlerin[636] e Adonaj[637] ki qyldyn köplü-

604 JSul.I.38.09: *jaratylmyšlaryn.* | JSul.III.67: *jaratylmyšlaryn.* | JSul.III.76: *jaratylmyslarny.*
605 JSul.I.38.09: *köplügü.* | JSul.III.72: *köplügi byla.* | JSul.III.67: *kepligibyla.* | JSul.III.76: *kepligi byla.*
606 Clause- or sentence-ending indicated in JSul.I.38.09.
607 JSul.III.72: *joḥtur.* | JSul.III.67: *joḥtur.* | JSul.III.76: *joḥtur.*
608 JSul.III.72: *köpligine.* | JSul.III.67: *kepligine.* | JSul.III.76: *kepligine.*
609 Sentence-ending indicated in JSul.I.38.09, JSul.III.72, and JSul.III.76. | JSul.I.54.03: no indication.
610 JSul.I.38.09: *özleri*; a scribal error. | JSul.III.67: *jizleri.* | JSul.III.76: *izleri.*
611 JSul.III.67: *istine.* | JSul.III.76: *istine.*
612 Clause- or sentence-ending indicated in JSul.I.38.09.
613 JSul.III.72: *begevretme.* | JSul.III.67: *begevretme.* | JSul.III.76: *begevretme.*
614 The text in JSul.I.38.09 ends here.
615 JSul.III.72: *estirme.* | JSul.III.67: *yštyrma*; probably a scribal error. | JSul.III.76: *estirme.*
616 JSul.III.72: *jas.*
617 JSul.III.76: *jasot.*
618 JSul.III.76: *cyġysyn.*
619 JSul.III.72: *bitišlerinin.* | JSul.III.67: *bitišlerinin.*
620 Sentence-ending indicated in JSul.III.72, and JSul.III.76.
621 JSul.III.67: *aštylar.*

[36] [12] He created all ⌊the creatures⌋[638] justly and by the abundance of His power,

[37] [13] He does not weaken or tire, there is no depth (comparable) to the abundance of His wisdom. He spread

[38] [14] His cloud over the surface of the world to give the earth rain to water

[39] [15] the dry deserts and to grow[639] grass as well as

[40] [16] sprouts of all (kind of) plants. All those days passed and

[41] [17] nobody was able to reach the perfection of praising Him. The waters of the sea came to their end

[42] [18] and the greatness of His glory did not reveal itself. Because of explaining[640] His song,

[43] [19] the words of all tongues[641] have been shortened, ⌊and because of preaching His glory the lips

[44] [20] of all⌋[642] mouths have weakened[643]. Your works were many, O Lord, that You have done

622 JSul.III.67: *kinler.* | JSul.III.76: *kinler.*

623 JSul.III.76: *kiside.*

624 JSul.III.72: *tügelligin.* | JSul.III.67: *tigelligin.* | JSul.III.76: *tigelligin.*

625 JSul.III.67: *tigendiler.* | JSul.III.76: *tigendiler.*

626 JSul.III.76: *asqarmady.*

627 JSul.III.72: *ulluġun* < *ulluluġun* due to haplology.

628 Sentence-ending indicated in JSul.III.72, and JSul.III.76.

629 JSul.III.72: *anlamaqtan.* | JSul.III.76: *anlamaqtan.*

630 JSul.III.67: *sezleri.* | JSul.III.76: *sezleri.*

631 JSul.III.76: *tigellernin*; a scribal error.

632 JSul.III.67: desunt; probably due to homeoarchy.

633 Sentence-ending indicated in JSul.III.72, and JSul.III.76.

634 JSul.III.67: *kep.* | JSul.III.76: *kep.*

635 JSul.I.54.03: *buldular*; a scribal error. | JSul.III.72: *boldular.* | JSul.III.67: *boldular.* | JSul.III.76: *boldular.*

636 JSul.III.76: *islerin senin.*

637 JSul.III.72: *H.* | JSul.III.67: *H.* | JSul.III.76: *H.*

638 JSul.I.38.09: *His creatures.* | JSul.III.67: *His creatures.*

639 JSul.III.67: *gather*; probably a scribal error.

640 JSul.III.72: *understanding.* | JSul.III.76: *understanding.*

641 JSul.III.67: deest; a scribal error.

642 JSul.III.67: desunt; a scribal error.

643 JSul.III.67: deest; a scribal error.

[45] [21] gübyla[644] aqylnyn. Toldu ol jer jaratylmyšlaryndan[645] da išidi[646] bujruq-

[46] [22] larynnyn[647] čerüvü[648] ol köklernin[649][.][650] Šira qotaradylar sana[651] bar jaratylmy-

[47] [23] šlary[652] juvuz dunjanyn sözübyla[653] erinlernin, neginče[654] ki ijgejsen

[48] [24] ajtmaq[655]

4 r° [49] [1] ajtmaq da yštyrgajsen[656] ǯanlaryn[657] özüne[658] da guflaryn qajtarma ornuna

[50] [2] jesodlarynyn[.][659] A osoblive[660] umasyn[yn][661] Jisra'elnin sözlejdiler[662] erinleri

[51] [3] alarnyn sarnav sözleri[663] da qoltqalaryn maḥtavlarnyn[664], ki juluġajsen ǯanlaryn[665]

[52] [4] enmekten gehinnomġa da guflaryn tarlyqlaryndan galutnun ušajdoġan[lar][666]

[53] [5] terenliklerine teren suvlarnyn[667]. Alajoq mende qulun zemer uḥujmen[668]

[54] [6] sana[669] da sarnajmen tefileler[670] sözübyla[671] erinlerimnin. E Tenri janġy

644 JSul.III.67: *kepligibyla.* | JSul.III.76: *kepligi byla.*
645 JSul.III.76: *jaratylmyslaryndan.*
646 JSul.III.76: *isidi.*
647 JSul.III.67: *bujruqlarynyn.*
648 JSul.III.72: *čörüvü.* | JSul.III.67: *čerivi.* | JSul.III.76: *cerivi.*
649 JSul.III.72: *keklernin.* | JSul.III.76: *keklernin.*
650 Sentence-ending indicated in JSul.III.72, and JSul.III.76.
651 JSul.III.72: *saja.*
652 JSul.III.76: *jaratylmyslary.*
653 JSul.III.67: *sezibyla.* | JSul.III.76: *sezi byla.*
654 JSul.III.76: *negince.*
655 Catchword.
656 JSul.III.67: *jyštyrġajsen.* | JSul.III.76: *ystyrġajsen.*
657 JSul.III.76: *ʒanlaryn.*
658 JSul.III.67: *ezine.* | JSul.III.76: *ezine.*
659 Sentence-ending indicated in JSul.III.72, and JSul.III.76.
660 JSul.III.67: *osovlive.*

[45] [21] with the abundance of wisdom, the earth has been filled with Your creatures and
[46] [22] the army of heavens is the work of Your[672] orders. All the creatures
[47] [23] of the low world preach a song to You with the words of their lips until You may send a
[48] [24] statement[673]
[49] [1] statement and You may gather all their souls to (take them to) Yourself and to return their bodies to the place 4 r°
[50] [2] of their origin. And especially the lips of the congregation of Israel say
[51] [3] the words of joy and the prayers of praise[674], that You may save their souls
[52] [4] from descending to hell and their bodies from the miseries of the exile that are like
[53] [5] the depth of the deep waters. So do I, too, Your servant, sing the poem[675]
[54] [6] to You and sing prayers[676] with the words of my lips. O, Lord, a new

---

661 JSul.I.54.03: *umasyn*; probably a scribal error. | JSul.III.72: *umasynyn.* | JSul.III.67: *umasynyn.* | JSul.III.76: *umasynyn.*

662 JSul.III.67: *sezlejdiler.* | JSul.III.76: *sezlejdiler.*

663 JSul.III.67: *sezleri.* | JSul.III.76: *sezleri.*

664 JSul.III.67: *maḥtavlarynyn.*

665 JSul.III.76: *ʒanlaryn.*

666 JSul.I.54.03: *ušajdoğan.* | JSul.III.72: *ušajdoğanlar.* | JSul.III.67: *ušajdoğanlar.* | JSul.III.76: *usajdoğanlar.*

667 Sentence-ending indicated in JSul.III.72, and JSul.III.76.

668 JSul.III.72: *oḥujmen.*

669 JSul.III.72: *saja.*

670 JSul.III.67: *tefileler ornuna.*

671 JSul.III.67: *sezi byla.* | JSul.III.76: *sezi byla.*

672 JSul.III.67: deest; probably a scribal error.

673 Catchword in the Karaim text.

674 JSul.III.67: *their praise.*

675 Lit. '*zemer*', i.e., a paraliturgical poem.

676 JSul.III.67: (*it*) *instead of prayers.*

[55] [7] šira ajtamen alnynda qyblalarynnyn. ⸤כתוב ⸤אלהים שיר חדש אשירה
[56] [8] לך⸣677 ׳ ⸤ותאם אין כאל ישורון⸣678 וכל הקדושה ׳⸣679

677 Psalm 144:9.

678 Deuteronomy 33:26.

679 JSul.III.72: אֵל נַעֲרָץ בְּסוֹד קְדוֹשִׁים רַבָּה: אֵין כָּאֵל יְשׁוּרוּן. (Psalm 89:7; Deuteronomy 33:26). | JSul.III.67: אֱלֹהִים שִׁיר חָדָשׁ אָשִׁירָה לָּךְ: אֵין כָּאֵל יְשׁוּרוּן רֹכֵב שָׁמַיִם בְּעֶזְרֶךָ וּבְגַאֲוָתוֹ שְׁחָקִים: מְעֹנָה אֱלֹהֵי קֶדֶם וּמִתַּחַת זְרוֹעוֹת עוֹלָם וַיְגָרֶשׁ מִפָּנֶיךָ אוֹיֵב וַיֹּאמֶר הַשְׁמֵד: וַיִּשְׁכֹּן יִשְׂרָאֵל בֶּטַח בָּדָד עֵין יַעֲקֹב אֶל אֶרֶץ דָּגָן וְתִירוֹשׁ אַף שָׁמָיו יַעַרְפוּ טָל: אַשְׁרֶיךָ יִשְׂרָאֵל מִי כָמוֹךָ עַם נוֹשַׁע בַּה׳ מָגֵן עֶזְרֶךָ וַאֲשֶׁר חֶרֶב גַּאֲוָתֶךָ וְיִכָּחֲשׁוּ אוֹיְבֶיךָ לָךְ וְאַתָּה עַל בָּמוֹתֵימוֹ תִדְרוֹךְ: וַיֹּאמֶר אֵלִיָּהוּ לְאַחְאָב עֲלֵה אֱכוֹל וּשְׁתֵה כִּי קוֹל הֲמוֹן הַגָּשֶׁם: וַיַּעֲלֶה אַחְאָב לֶאֱכוֹל וְלִשְׁתּוֹת וְאֵלִיָּהוּ עָלָה אֶל רֹאשׁ הַכַּרְמֶל וַיִּגְהַר אַרְצָה וַיָּשֶׂם פָּנָיו בֵּין בִּרְכָּיו: וַיֹּאמֶר אֶל נַעֲרוֹ עֲלֵה נָא הַבֵּט דֶּרֶךְ יָם וַיַּעַל וַיַּבֵּט וַיֹּאמֶר אֵין מְאוּמָה וַיֹּאמֶר שׁוּב שֶׁבַע פְּעָמִים: וַיְהִי בַּשְּׁבִיעִית וַיֹּאמֶר הִנֵּה עָב קְטַנָּה כְּכַף אִישׁ עוֹלָה מִיָּם וַיֹּאמֶר עֲלֵה אֱמוֹר אֶל אַחְאָב אֱסֹר וָרֵד וְלֹא יַעַצָרְכָה הַגָּשֶׁם: וַיְהִי עַד כֹּה וְעַד כֹּה וְהַשָּׁמַיִם הִתְקַדְּרוּ עָבִים וְרוּחַ וַיְהִי גֶּשֶׁם גָּדוֹל וַיִּרְכַּב אַחְאָב וַיֵּלֶךְ יִזְרְעֶאלָה: וּמֵעוֹלָם לֹא שָׁמְעוּ לֹא הֶאֱזִינוּ עַיִן לֹא רָאָתָה אֱלֹהִים זוּלָתְךָ יַעֲשֶׂה לִמְחַכֵּה לוֹ: לְמִי תְדַמְּיוּנִי וְתַשְׁווּ וְתַמְשִׁלוּנִי וְנִדְמֶה: וְאֶל מִי תְדַמְּיוּנִי וְאֶשְׁוֶה יֹאמַר קָדוֹשׁ: וְאַתָּה קָדוֹשׁ יוֹשֵׁב תְּהִלּוֹת יִשְׂרָאֵל:. (Psalm 144:9; Deuteronomy 33:26–29; 1Kings 18:41–45; Isaiah 64:4; Isaiah 46:5; Isaiah 40:25; Psalm 22:3; the vocalization is slightly different than in standard Biblical Hebrew). | JSul.III.76: אֵין כָּאֵל יְשׁוּרוּן וגו׳ (Deuteronomy 33:26).

[55] [7] song I sing before Your countenance; ⌊as it is written: ⌊'I will sing a new song unto You, O God'[1680].

[56] [8] And you will say ⌊'There is none like unto the God of Jeshurun'[1681] and all the holy (prayers)[1682].

---

680 Psalm 144:9.

681 Deuteronomy 33:26.

682 JSul.III.72: *'God is greatly to be feared in the assembly of the saints. There is none like unto the God of Jeshurun.'* (Psalm 89:7; Deuteronomy 33:26). | JSul.III.67: *'I will sing a new song unto you, O God. There is none like unto the God of Jeshurun, who rides upon the heaven to your help, and in his excellency on the clouds. The eternal God is your refuge, and underneath are the everlasting arms: and he shall thrust out the enemy from before you; and shall say, "Destroy them." Israel then shall dwell in safety alone: the fountain of Jacob shall be upon a land of grain and wine; also his heavens shall drop down dew. Happy are you, O Israel: who is like unto you, O people saved by the Lord, the shield of your help, and who is the sword of your excellency! And your enemies shall submit unto you; and you shall tread upon their high places. And Elijah said unto Ahab, "Get you up, eat and drink; for there is a sound of abundance of rain." So Ahab went up to eat and to drink. And Elijah went up to the top of Carmel; and he cast himself down upon the earth, and put his face between his knees, And said to his servant, "Go up now, look toward the sea." And he went up, and looked, and said, "There is nothing." And he said, "Go again seven times." And it came to pass at the seventh time, that he said, "Behold, there arises a little cloud out of the sea, like a man's hand." And he said, "Go up, say unto Ahab, Prepare your chariot, and get you down, that the rain stops you not." And it came to pass in a little while, that the heaven was black with clouds and wind, and there was a great rain. And Ahab rode, and went to Jezreel. For since the beginning of the world men have not heard, nor perceived by the ear, neither has the eye seen, O God, besides you, what he has prepared for him that waits for him. To whom will you liken me, and make me equal, and compare me, that we may be alike? To whom then will you liken me, or shall I be equal? says the Holy One. But you are holy, O you that inhabit the praises of Israel.'* (Psalm 144:9; Deuteronomy 33:26–29; 1 Kings 18:41–45; Isaiah 64:4; Isaiah 46:5; Isaiah 40:25; Psalm 22:3). | JSul.III.76: *'There is none like unto the God of Jeshurun …' and so on.* (Deuteronomy 33:26).

**Text number:** № 13
**Karaim incipit:** *Johtur senin kibik kičli da qorqunčlu Tenri*
**Hebrew incipit:** מִי כָּמוֹךָ אַדִּיר וְנוֹרָא *mī kåmōḵå ʾaḏīr wnōrå*
**Dedication:** Parashat Haazinu (Deuteronomy 32:1–32:52)
**Language:** Early Mod.SWKar., Mod.SWKar.
**Number of copies:** 3

| Accession no. | Place of origin of copy | Date of copy | Copyist | Folios |
|---|---|---|---|---|
| JSul.VII.22.02.13 | Unknown | 1st half of the 19th c. | Unknown 9 | 1 r°–1 v° |
| ADub.III.61 | Halych | 1850/1851 | Jeshua Josef Mordkowicz | 142 v°–143 r° |
| JSul.III.69 | Halych | ca. 1851 (before 1866) | Jeshua Josef Mordkowicz | 304 r°–304 v° |
| JSul.III.79 | Halych | ca. 1851 (before 1866) | Jeshua Josef Mordkowicz | 185 r°–186 r° |

## 1 Introductory Remarks

The Karaim text is an exact translation of the Hebrew original as copied in ms. JSul.III.79 (161 r°–161 v°). Ms. JSul.VII.22.02.13 contains a non-vocalized copy, whereas the other two texts are vocalized.

Textually, the three versions are very similar to each other. There are slightly more similarities between the versions in mss. ADub.III.61, on the one hand, and JSul.III.69 and JSul.III.79, on the other (they were copied by the same person), see *qajjam* vs. *inamly* (12), the conjuction *eger* (13), not used in the copies of Jeshua Josef Mordkowicz, *jazylġanġa kere torada* vs. *toraġa kere* (13–14), *belgilerinni* vs. *belgilerni* (16), or *tozduruvču* vs. *tozdurdun* (25). JSul.III.69 are almost identical except the fragment *avazlaryn ajny da kujasny keklerni da jerni* (13) which is present only in JSul.III.69, *belgilerinni* vs. *belgilerni* (16), *azatlyqqa cyġardyn* vs. *juludun* (18), and *kemisseler aziz Torany* vs. *kemiskenlerinde Torany* (23–24). Interestingly enough, we also find fragments that position the *peshatim* in mss. JSul.VII.22.02.13 and JSul.III.79 closer to each other, see *tanyqlaryn* vs. *sezlerin da tanyqlaryn* (7), *byla* vs. *istine* (11), *torany* vs. *uḥuma torany* (24) and *dunjanyn* vs. *ol dunjanyn* (25). There are no portions of text that are the same in JSul.VII.22.02.13 and ADub.III.61, only. The following diagram of interconnections between these texts (not the manuscripts) is possible:

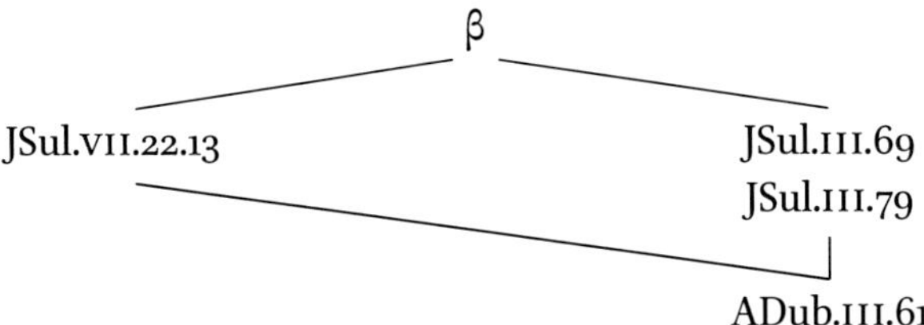


FIGURE 16 Diagram of the connections between the copies of peshat № 13

## 2 Transcription[683] and Translation

1 rº [1] [1] ⸤וזה הפשט לפיוט פרשת האזינו להר̈ר שמחה החזן נ̈ע⸣[684]

[2] [2] Joḥtur senin kibik kičli[685] da qorqunčlu[686] Tenri
[3] [3] jaratuvču[687] ič[688] dunjalarny. Joḥtur senin
[4] [4] kibik ol anlatuvču[689] baslyqtan sonġunu da askartuvcu[690] avaldan
[5] [5] bar jasyryn nerselerni. Joḥtur senin kibik bašlyġy[691] sezle{ri}nnin
[6] [6] kertidi avzunda bar ol jaratylmyšlarnyn[692]. Joḥtur senin
[7] [7] kibik inamly boldular tanyqlaryn[693] ki tanyq turġuzdun
[8] [8] ulanlaryna anyn ki kerdi tišinde[694] basqyčny[695] turġuz[u]lġan-
[9] [9] ny[696]. Joḥtur senin kibik haligi tanyqlaryna avaldan u[q]šatty[n][697]
[10] [10] alarny. Joḥtur senin kibik kičinni[698] kergizdin jaratylmy-
[11] [11] šlaryn[699] byla[700] ki jarattyn peratlarny da kelallarny. Joḥtur
[12] [12] senin kibik belgiledin qajjam[701] tanyqlar ešittirmevčiler[702]

683 Based on JSul.VII.22.02.13.

684 ADub.III.61: וזה הפשט לפיוט פרשת האזינו שהוא מִי כָֽמוֹךָ אַדִיר וְנוֹרָא תרגמו החכם השלם המתרגם הנ̈ל ה̈ה כמוה̈רר שמחה החזן בכ̈מ חננאל מן דראזניע יע̈מש. | JSul.III.69: ואם תרצה תא̈מ גם פשטו שתרגמו ה̈ר שמחה החזן דקה̈ק קוקיזוב נב̈ת: בכ̈מ חננאל הזקן מן דראזניע יע̈מש:. | JSul.III.79: פשט לפיוט פרשת האזינו תרגמו החכם כמוה̈רר שמחה החזן דקה̈ק קוקיזוב נב̈ת בכ̈מ חננאל הזקן יע̈מש.

685 ADub.III.61: *kicli.* | JSul.III.69: *kicli.* | JSul.III.79: *kicli.*

686 ADub.III.61: *qorqunclu.* | JSul.III.69: *qorqunclu.* | JSul.III.79: *qorqunclu.*

687 ADub.III.61: *jaratuvcu.* | JSul.III.69: *jaratuvcu.* | JSul.III.79: *jaratuvcu.*

688 ADub.III.61: *ic.* | JSul.III.69: *ic.* | JSul.III.79: *ic.*

689 ADub.III.61: *anlatuvcu.* | JSul.III.69: *anlatuvcu.* | JSul.III.79: *anlatuvcu.*

690 ADub.III.61: *asqartuvcu.* | JSul.III.69: *asqartuvcu.* | JSul.III.79: *asqartuvcu.*

691 ADub.III.61: *baslyġy.* | JSul.III.69: *baslyġy.* | JSul.III.79: *baslyġy.*

692 ADub.III.61: *jaratylmyslarnyn.* | JSul.III.69: *jaratylmyslarnyn.* | JSul.III.79: *jaratylmyslar-nyn.*

693 ADub.III.61: *sezlerin da tanyqlaryn.*

694 ADub.III.61: *tisinde.* | JSul.III.69: *tisinde.* | JSul.III.79: *tisinde.*

695 ADub.III.61: *basqycny.* | JSul.III.69: *basqycny.* | JSul.III.79: *basqycny.*

696 JSul.VII.22.02.13: *turġuzlġanny*; a scribal error. | ADub.III.61: *turġuzulġanny.* | JSul.III.69: *turġuzulġanny.* | JSul.III.79: *turġuzulġanny.*

697 JSul.VII.22.02.13: *ušatty*; a scribal error; cf., however, *juludu* in lines 18 and 33. | ADub.III.61: *uqsattyn.* | JSul.III.69: *uqsattyn.* | JSul.III.79: *uqsattyn.*

698 ADub.III.61: *kicinni.* | JSul.III.69: *kicinni.* | JSul.III.79: *kicinni.*

699 ADub.III.61: *jaratylmyslaryn.* | JSul.III.69: *jaratylmyslaryn.* | JSul.III.79: *jaratylmyslaryn.*

700 ADub.III.61: *istine.*

[1] [1] ⌞And this is the *peshat* of a *piyyut* for parashat Haazinu of the Rav, Rabbi, hazzan Simcha, may his soul rest in Eden(:)⌝[703] 1 r°
[2] [2] There is none like You, powerful and awesome God,
[3] [3] the creator of the three worlds. There is none like You,
[4] [4] who explain (everything) from the beginning until the end and who reveal all along
[5] [5] everything ⌞that is secret⌝[704]. There is none like You, the basic matter of Your words
[6] [6] is a truth in the mouth of all creatures. There is none like You,
[7] [7] Your witnesses[705] became trustworthy for You have put up a witness
[8] [8] for the sons of ⌞him⌝[706] who has seen in his dream the ladder put up.
[9] [9] There is none like You, You have equalised the present witnesses with those from long ago.
[10] [10] There is none like You, You have shown Your power through[707] the creatures of Yours,
[11] [11] for You have created single things and general principles. There is none
[12] [12] like You, You have marked as eternal[708] witnesses those who did not let (anyone) hear

---

701 ADub.III.61: *inamly.* | JSul.III.69: *inamly.* | JSul.III.79: *inamly.*

702 ADub.III.61: *esittirmevciler.* | JSul.III.69: *esittirmevciler.* | JSul.III.79: *esittirmevciler.*

703 ADub.III.61: *An this is the* peshat *of a* piyyut *for the parashat Haazinu, of that* (*with the incipit*) mī kåmōḵå ʾaḏīr wnōrå, *which the above-mentioned complete hakham, the translator, the great sage, his honour, the Rav, Rabbi Simcha, the hazzan translated, the son of the honourable sir Chananel from Derażne, may he rest in peace.* | JSul.III.69: *And, if you prefer, say its* peshat [i.e., of the Hebrew original], *which the hakham, his honour, the Rav, Rabbi Simcha translated, the hazzan of the holy community of Kukizów, may his soul lodge in Eden, the son of the honourable sir Chananel, the aged, may he rest in pleace.* | JSul.III.79: *A* peshat *of a* piyyut *for the parashat Haazinu, which the hakham, his honour, the Rav, Rabbi Simcha translated, the hazzan of the holy community of Kukizów, may his soul rest in Eden, the son of the honourable sir Chananel, the aged, may he rest in pleace.*

704 Lit. 'secret things'.

705 ADub.III.61: *words and witnesses.*

706 I.e., *Jacob.*

707 ADub.III.61: *in.*

708 ADub.III.61: *trustworthy.* | JSul.III.79: *trustworthy.*

[13] [13] [avazlaryn][709]. Joḥtur senin kibik eger[710] ⌊keči[nseler jazyl]ġanġa⌋[711]
[14] [14] ⌊kere Torada⌋[712] jer berir bitišin[713] da [kekler][714] [jav]durur-
[15] [15] lar[715] jamġurlarny da endirirler čyqny[716]. Joḥtur senin kibik
[16] [16] quršadyn[717] belgilerinni[718] jizleri[719] istine dunjanyn qylma
[17] [17] alarny. Joḥtur senin kibik juluvču[720] ulusunnu da qullar
[18] [18] erkinden Micriden[721] juludu[n][722] alarny. Joḥtur senin kibik
[19] [19] jerinde midbarnyn hadirledin yzlaryn Jisra'elnin da
[20] [20] baġanasy byla bulutnun da otnun [ke]nderdin[723] alarny.
[21] [21] Joḥtur senin kibik da veren pusta orunda edi ⌊qujašlary[724]
[22] [22] da kelegeleri⌋[725] da jetkirdi alarġa bar kerekni. Joḥtur senin
[23] [23] kibik bilivči[726] ne qylarlar da ne učrar[727] alarny kemiškenlerin-
[24] [24] de[728] Torany[729]. Joḥtur senin kibik dert taraflarynda
1 v° [25] [1] dunjanyn[730] tozduruvču[731] alarny. Joḥtur senin kibik kerip
[26] [2] qyjynlaryn tajmaq vaḥtta ajaqlary ḥajifsinip galuttan
[27] [3] čyġaryrsen[732] alarny. Joḥtur senin kibik kerip jarlyġašynny[733]

709 Uncertain reconstruction. || JSul.VII.22.02.13: deest; probably a scribal error. | ADub.III.61: *avazlarny.* | JSul.III.69: *avazlaryn ajny da kujasny keklerni da jerni.* | JSul.III.79: *avazlaryn*; probably a scribal error.

710 ADub.III.61: deest. | JSul.III.69: deest. | JSul.III.79: deest.

711 JSul.VII.22.02.13: an ink stain makes these two words partially illegible. | ADub.III.61: *kecinseler.* | JSul.III.69: *kecinseler.* | JSul.III.79: *kecinseler.*

712 ADub.III.61: *toraġa kere.* | JSul.III.69: *toraġa kere.* | JSul.III.79: *toraġa kere.*

713 ADub.III.61: *bitisin.* | JSul.III.69: *bitisin.* | JSul.III.79: *bitisin.*

714 JSul.VII.22.02.13: an ink stain makes this fragment illegible. | ADub.III.61: *kekler.* | JSul.III.69: *kekler.* | JSul.III.79: *kekler.*

715 ADub.III.61: *javdururlar.* | JSul.III.69: *javdururlar.* | JSul.III.79: *javdururlar.*

716 ADub.III.61: *cyqny.* | JSul.III.69: *cyqny.* | JSul.III.79: *cyqny.*

717 ADub.III.61: *qursadyn.* | JSul.III.69: *qursadyn.* | JSul.III.79: *qursadyn.*

718 ADub.III.61: *belgilerni.* | JSul.III.79: *belgilerni.*

719 ADub.III.61: *izleri.* | JSul.III.69: *izleri.* | JSul.III.79: *izleri.*

720 ADub.III.61: *juluvcu.* | JSul.III.69: *juluvcu.* | JSul.III.79: *juluvcu.*

721 JSul.VII.22.02.13: corrected by the copyist; originally: *Micrinin.* | ADub.III.61: *Micriden.* | JSul.III.69: *Micriden.* | JSul.III.79: *Micriden.*

722 JSul.VII.22.02.13: probably a scribal error; cf., however, *juludu[n]* in line 33 and *uqšatty[n]* in line 9. | ADub.III.61: *cyġardyn.* | JSul.III.79: *azatlyqqa cyġardyn.* | JSul.III.79: *juludun.*

723 JSul.VII.22.02.13: an ink stain makes the beginning of the word illegible. | ADub.III.61: *kenderdin.* | JSul.III.69: *kenderdin.* | JSul.III.79: *kenderdin.*

724 ADub.III.61: *qujaslary.* | JSul.III.69: *qujaslary.* | JSul.III.79: *qujaslary.*

725 ADub.III.61: originally: *kelegeleri da qujaslary*; the word order has been corrected by the copyist.

726 ADub.III.61: *bilivci.* | JSul.III.69: *bilivci.* | JSul.III.79: *bilivci.*

727 ADub.III.61: *ucrar.* | JSul.III.69: *ucrar.* | JSul.III.79: *ucrar.*

[13] [13] ⌊[their voices]⌋[734]. There is none like You, if they [act] according to ⌊what is [written]
[14] [14] in⌋[735] the Law, the earth will give its fruits and the [heavens] will make
[15] [15] rains [fall] and will lower dew. There is none like You,
[16] [16] You have surrounded Your[736] signs over the surface of the earth, in order to do
[17] [17] them. There is none like You, the saviour of Your people and servants,
[18] [18] You have saved[737] them from the rule of Egypt. There is none like You,
[19] [19] You have prepared the way for Israel in the desert and
[20] [20] with a pillar of a cloud and of fire You have led them.
[21] [21] There is none like You, and in the desolated desert they had sun
[22] [22] and shadow and all that was needed was delivered to them. There is none like You,
[23] [23] who know what do those do who ⌊abandon the Law⌋[738] and what will happen to them.
[24] [24] There is none like You,
[25] [1] ⌊who have scattered them⌋[739] in the four directions of the world. There is none like You, 1 vº
[26] [2] after having seen their suffering, after having mercy on their legs, in the moment of (their) faltering You will draw them out from the exile.
[27] [3] There is none like You, after having seen Your mercy,

---

728 ADub.III.61: *kemiskenlerinde.* | JSul.III.79: *kemisseler.* | JSul.III.79: *kemiskenlerinde.*

729 ADub.III.61: *uḥuma torany.* | JSul.III.69: *aziz Torany.*

730 ADub.III.61: *ol dunjanyn.*

731 ADub.III.61: *tozdurdun.* | JSul.III.69: *tozdurdun.* | JSul.III.79: *tozdurdun.*

732 ADub.III.61: *cyġaryrsen.* | JSul.III.69: *cyġaryrsen.* | JSul.III.79: *cyġaryrsen.*

733 ADub.III.61: *jarlyġasynny.* | JSul.III.69: *jarlyġasynny.* | JSul.III.79: *jarlyġasynny.*

734 Uncertain translation. | JSul.VII.22.02.13: deest; probably a scribal error. | JSul.III.69: *their voices: the moon, the sun, the heavens, and the earth.* Probably an interpretative addition inserted by the copyist of JSul.III.69. | JSul.III.79: *their voices.*

735 ADub.III.61: deest. | JSul.III.79: deest.

736 ADub.III.61: deest. | JSul.III.79: deest.

737 ADub.III.61: *took.*

738 ADub.III.61 *stop reading the Law.* | JSul.III.69: *would abandon the holy Law.*

739 ADub.III.61: *You have scattered them.* | JSul.III.69: *You have scattered them.* | JSul.III.79: *You have scattered them.*

[28] [4] sarnarlar ulusu Jisra'elnin da bašururlar[740] alarġa bar
[29] [5] qyjnavčular[741] alarny. Joḥtur senin kibik ajtuvču[742] da
[30] [6] tigellevči[743] bar išlerni[744]. Joḥtur senin kibik mohorun
[31] [7] senin belgilidi[745] da sensen juluvču[746] alarny. Joḥtur senin
[32] [8] [kibik][747] julunmušlary[748] Adonajnyn[749] ajtyrlar širasy byla maḥtav-
[33] [9] larynyn. Joḥtur senin kibik ki qolundan dušmannyn[750] juludu[n][751]
[34] [10] alarny. [752]⌈[753]⌈גואלנו ה׳ צבאות שמו ק׳⌋ ׳ תם⌋.

740 ADub.III.61: *basururlar.* | JSul.III.69: *basururlar.* | JSul.III.79: *basururlar.*

741 ADub.III.61: *qyjnavcular.* | JSul.III.69: *qyjnavcular.* | JSul.III.79: *qyjnavcular.*

742 ADub.III.61: *ajtuvcu.* | JSul.III.69: *ajtuvcu.* | JSul.III.79: *ajtuvcu.*

743 ADub.III.61: *tigellevci.* | JSul.III.69: *tigellevci.* | JSul.III.79: *tigellevci.*

744 ADub.III.61: *islerni.* | JSul.III.69: *islerni.* | JSul.III.79: *islerni.*

745 ADub.III.61: *belgidi alarda.* | JSul.III.69: *belgilidi alarda.* | JSul.III.79: *belgilidi alarda.*

746 ADub.III.61: *juluvcu.* | JSul.III.69: *juluvcu.* | JSul.III.79: *juluvcu.*

747 JSul.VII.22.02.13: deest; a scribal error. | ADub.III.61: *kibik.* | JSul.III.69: *kibik.* | JSul.III.79: *kibik.*

748 ADub.III.61: *julunmuslary.* | JSul.III.69: *julunmuslary.* | JSul.III.79: *julunmuslary.*

749 ADub.III.61: *H-nyn.* | JSul.III.69: *H-nyn.* | JSul.III.79: *H-nyn.*

750 ADub.III.61: *dusmannyn.* | JSul.III.69: *dusmannyn.* | JSul.III.79: *dusmannyn.*

751 JSul.VII.22.02.13: probably a scribal error; cf., however, *juludu*[*n*] in line 18 and *uqšatty*[*n*] in line 9. | ADub.III.61: *juludun.* | JSul.III.69: *juludun.* | JSul.III.79: *juludun.*

752 ADub.III.61: יִמְרוּ גְּאוּלֵי ה׳ אֲשֶׁר גְּאָלָם מִיַּד צָר׃ גֹּאֲלֵנוּ ה׳ צְשָׁקִי׃ (Psalm 107:2; Isaiah 47:4). | JSul.III.69: יִמְרוּ גְּאוּלֵי ה׳ אֲשֶׁר גְּאָלָם מִיַּד צָר׃ גֹּאֲלֵנוּ ה׳ צְבָאוֹת שְׁמוֹ קְדוֹשׁ יִשְׂרָאֵל׃ (Psalm 107:2; Isaiah 47:4). | JSul.III.79: יִמְרוּ גְּאוּלֵי ה׳ אֲשֶׁר גְּאָלָם מִיַּד צָר׃ גֹּאֲלֵנוּ ה׳ צְבָאוֹת שְׁמוֹ קְדוֹשׁ יִשְׂרָאֵל׃ (Psalm 107:2; Isaiah 47:4).

753 Isaiah 47:4.

[28] [4] the people of Israel will sing, and all their tormentors will bow down before them.
[29] [5] There is none like You, who say and
[30] [6] fulfil all the works. There is none like You, Your seal
[31] [7] is well-known[754] and You are their saviour. There is none [like][755] You,
[32] [8] those saved by the Lord will sing a song of praise.
[33] [9] There is none like You, for You have saved them from the hands of the enemy.
[34] [10] ⌊⌊As for our redeemer, the Lord of hosts is his name, the Holy One of Israel.⌋[756] The end.⌋[757]

754 ADub.III.61: *a sign among them.* | JSul.III.69: *well-known among them.* | JSul.III.79: *well-known among them.*

755 ADub.III.61: deest; a scribal error.

756 Isaiah 47:4.

757 ADub.III.61: *'Let the redeemed of the Lord say so, whom he has redeemed from the hand of the enemy. As for our redeemer, the Lord of hosts is his name, the Holy One of Israel.'* (Psalm 107:2; Isaiah 47:4). | JSul.III.69: *'Let the redeemed of the Lord say so, whom he has redeemed from the hand of the enemy. As for our redeemer, the Lord of hosts is his name, the Holy One of Israel.'* (Psalm 107:2; Isaiah 47:4). | JSul.III.79: *'Let the redeemed of the Lord say so, whom he has redeemed from the hand of the enemy. As for our redeemer, the Lord of hosts is his name, the Holy One of Israel.'* (Psalm 107:2; Isaiah 47:4).

**Text number:** № 14
**Karaim incipit:** *Joḥtur Tenrisi kibik Jisra'elnin*
**Hebrew incipit:** אֵין כָּאֵל יְשׁוּרוּן יָחִיד וְנֶאֱמָן *'ēn kå'el yšūrūn yåḥīd wne'ĕmån*
**Dedication:** Yom Teruah
**Language:** MSWKar., Early Mod.SWKar., Mod.SWKar.
**Number of copies:** 6

| Accession no. | Place of origin of copy | Date of copy | Copyist | Folios |
|---|---|---|---|---|
| JSul.I.54.03 | Halych (?) | turn of the 19th c. | Unknown 5 | 1 r°–1 v° |
| JSul.I.54.12 | Halych | early 19th c. | Unknown 8 | 1 r°–1 v° |
| JSul.III.72 | Halych | before 1851 | Jeshua Josef Mordkowicz | 141 v°–142 v° |
| JSul.III.67 | Halych | after ca. 1840, before 1851 | Josef b. Icchak Szulimowicz (?) | 205 v°–206 r° |
| JSul.I.46 | Halych | 1st half of the 19th c. | Jeshua Josef Mordkowicz | 5 r°–5 v° |
| JSul.III.76 | Halych | 2nd half of the 19th c. | Jeshua Josef Mordkowicz | 51 v°–52 r° |

## 1 Introductory Remarks

The authorship of the Hebrew original is attributed to Aharon ben Josef ha-Rofe (ca. 1250–1320), see e.g. JSul.III.67 (205 r°). All six copies are vocalized.

The differences between the copies are minor and are the result of the copyists' own textual improvements. Even the copies made by Jeshua Josef Mordkowicz—i.e. in mss. JSul.III.72, JSul.I.46, and JSul.III.76—contain different linguistic solutions. This makes saying anything specific about their relationship very difficult; it seems that JSul.I.54.03 contains two significant unique features (cf. *öz* vs. *ullu* in line 11, *byrġyġa* vs. *šofarġa* in line 24; cf. however, the word *byrġyġa* crossed out in JSul.I.54.12 and corrected into *šofarġa*), whereas the rest of the copies are equally distant or close to each other.

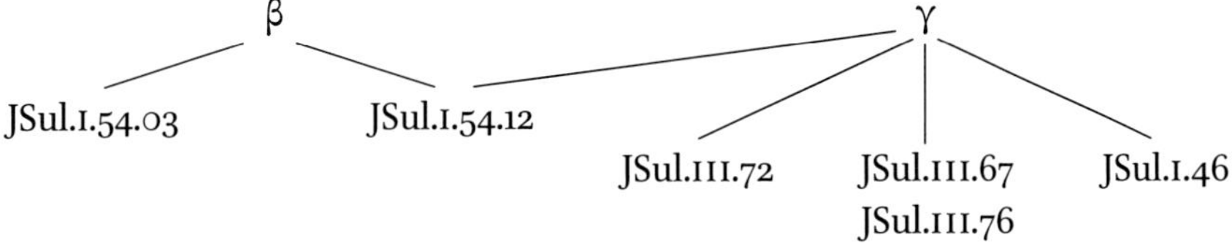


FIGURE 17 Diagram of the connections between the copies of peshat № 14

## 2 Transcription[758] and Translation

1 r° [1] [1] ⌊בשם יחיד ומיוחד המציל מהרג מטים[759] ׳ אחל לכתוב פשטי פיוטים ׳ הנאמרים ביום מ[760]

[2] [2] מועד ה יום תרועה שהוא יום ראשון לתשובה ויום דין ומשפטים ׳ אשר תרגמם החכם

[3] [3] האלהי הפשטן הגדול שבחכמים כמוֹ̃הרר שמחה החזן דק̃ק קוקיזוב יע̃א בכ̃מע חננאל

[4] [4] זצ̃לה ׳ וזהו הפשט על פיוט הראשון שהוא ׳ אי̇ן כא̇ל ישו̇רון ׳⌉[761]

[5] [5] Joḥtur Tenrisi kibik Jisra'elnin jalġyz[762] inamly Tenri oldu

[6] [6] jaratuvčusu[763] dunjanyn, ojatma abajly ulusun qajtma

[7] [7] tešuva byla belgiledi zaman janġaj Tišrinin. Ünü[764] Adonajnyn[765] hörmet-

[8] [8] byla[766] jyštyrma[767] tul tüvül[768] ündelgen[769] ulusu[n][770] Jisra'elnin. Šofarbyla

---

758 Based on JSul.I.54.03.

759 Unclear reading.

760 The letter *mem* anticipates the first word in the next line; it is, in fact, a catchword.

761 JSul.I.54.12: הא לך פשטים יורים לפיוט יום תרועה הנקרא בפי המון בני ישראל יום ראש השנה שתרגמם ללשון קדר החכם כמ̃הר שמחה החזן נב̃ת בכ̃מע חננאל ז̃ל. | JSul.III.72: ואלו הפשטים לפיוטי יום תרועה ולפיוטי יום א דחג הסכות ולפיוטי יום שמיני עצרת שתרגם החכם השלם הפשטן תנעלה כמו̃הרר שמחה החזן יע̃מש בכ̃מ חננאל זצ̃ל: וזה הראשון לפיוט ראשון של יום תרועה שהוא אין כאל ישורון. | JSul.III.67: ואם תרצה גם פשטו שתרגמו ה̃ה כמו̃הרר שמחה החזן נ̃ע: בן כ̃מ חננאל מק̃ק כוכיזוב ז̃ל: כמו שאכתוב במעבר לדף זה א. | JSul.I.46: בעזרת המשגיח בכללים ובפרטים: אכתוב פשטים לפיוטים: של יום מועד ראש השנה החרותים: תרגמם אמ̃ו כמו̃הרר שמחה החזן דק̃הק יפה יער נב̃ת בכ̃מע חננאל הזקן יע̃מש: וזה הראשון לפיוט אין כאל ישרון יחיד ונאמן א תחל ות̃אם. | JSul.III.76: ואם תרצאה תאמר גם פשטו שתרגם החכם השלם והפילוסוף התורני כמו̃הרר שמחה החזן דק̃הק קוקיזוב נב̃ת בכ̃מ חננאל הזקן מן דראזניע יע̃מש.

762 JSul.III.72: *jalġyz da.* | JSul.III.67: *jalġyz da.* | JSul.I.46: *jalġyz* {*da*}. | JSul.III.76: *jalġyz da.*

763 JSul.I.46: *jaratuvcusu.* | JSul.III.76: *jaratuvcusu.*

764 JSul.III.67: *ini.* | JSul.III.76: *ini.*

765 JSul.III.67: *H-nyn.* | JSul.I.46: *H-nyn.* | JSul.III.76: *H-nyn.*

766 JSul.III.67: *hermetbyla.* | JSul.I.46: *hermet byla.* | JSul.III.76: *hermet byla.*

767 JSul.I.46: *ystyrma.* | JSul.III.76: *ystyrma.*

768 JSul.III.67: *tivil.* | JSul.I.46: *tivil.* | JSul.III.76: *tivil.*

769 JSul.III.67: *indelgen.* | JSul.I.46: *indelgen.* | JSul.III.76: *indelgen.*

770 JSul.I.54.03: *ulusu*; a scribal error. | JSul.I.54.12: *ulusun.* | JSul.III.72: *ulusun.* | JSul.III.67: *ulusun.* | JSul.I.46: *ulusun.* | JSul.III.76: *ulusun.*

771 The meaning of מטים is unclear.

772 JSul.I.54.12: *And here are for you* (*some*) peshatim *of* piyyutim *for Yom Teruah read by many of the sons of Israel on Rosh Hashanah, the translation into the language of Qedar* [i.e., in Karaim] (*made by*) *his honour, Rabbi Simcha the hazzan, may his soul lodge in the Garden, the son of Chananel, whose honourable repose is Eden, may his memory be a blessing.*

[1] [1] ⌊In the name of the Unique, who saves the […?][771] from slaughter. I shall begin to write *peshatim* of *piyyutim* recited on the 1 r°

[2] [2] holiday of Yom Teruah, which is the first day of the Days of Repentance and the day of judgement, which the divine hakham translated,

[3] [3] the great exegete among the hakhamim, his honour, the Rav, Rabbi Simcha, the hazzan of the holy community of Kukizów, may the Lord protect it, the son of Chananel, whose honourable repose is Eden,

[4] [4] may the memory of the righteous be for the life of the World to Come. And this is the *peshat* of the *piyyut*, of that (with the incipit) *ʾēn kåʾel yšūrūn.*[1772]

[5] [5] There is none like the God of Israel, the ⌊only trustworthy[1773] God, He is

[6] [6] the creator of the world.

[7] [7] The ⌊coming of the month of Tishri[1774] has marked that (it is time for) the honourable people to be woken up to return with penance. The voice of the Lord

[8] [8] will blow the *shofar*[775] with esteem to gather the people of Israel called as the non-widowed[776]

---

| JSul.III.72: *On the other hand (here are) the* peshatim *of* piyyutim *for Yom Teruah and of* piyyutim *for the first day of the Feast of Sukkot and of* piyyutim *for Shemini Atzeret, which the complete hakham, the exalted exegete, his honour, the Rav, Rabbi Simcha the hazzan traslated, may he rest in peace, the son of the honourable sir Chananel, may the memory of the righteous be a blessing.* | JSul.III.67: *And, if you prefer, (here is) its* peshat [i.e., of the Hebrew original], *which the great sage, his honour, the Rav, Rabbi Simcha the hazzan translated, may his soul rest in Eden, the son of the honourable sir Chananel from the holy community of Kukizów, may his memory be a blessing, as I will write it down on the other side of this page.* | JSul.I.46: *With the help of the One who has providence over the general things and all the details, I will write down the* peshatim *of the* piyyutim *inscribed for the holiday of Rosh Hashanah, which our master and teacher, his honour, the Rav, Rabbi Simcha translated, the hazzan of the holy community of Yefeh Yaʿar* [i.e., Kukizów], *may his soul lodge in the Garden, the son of Chananel, the aged, whose honourable repose is Eden, may he rest in peace.* | JSul.III.76: *And, if you prefer, say its* peshat [i.e., of the Hebrew original], *which the complete hakham and the Torah-based philosopher, his honour, the Rav, Rabbi Simcha translated, the hazzan of the holy community of Kukizów, may his soul lodge in Eden, the son of the honourable sir Chananel, the aged, from Derażne, may he rest in peace.*

773 JSul.III.72: *only and trustworthy.* | JSul.III.67: *only and trustworthy.* | JSul.I.46: *only and trustworthy.* | JSul.III.76: *only and trustworthy.*

774 Lit. 'the time of the month of Tishri'.

775 A musical horn prominently used in Rabbanite liturgy; a symbol of Yom Teruah.

776 I.e., *not left by God.*

[9] [9] tartar da baryr tavullarbyla olturuvčusu[777] tarafynyn temannyn. [778]הניא.

[10] [10] Qajsy Tenri tyjdy saġyšlaryn[779] uluslarnyn[780] da kenešlerin[781] alarnyn buzdu

[11] [11] öz[782] küčübyla[783], ol čaġyrġaj[784] azatlyq uvluna[785] özünün[786] ki üze[787]

[12] [12] qaratetti any qynġyrlyġyna[788] köre[789] sanbyla. Bolġaj klek alnyndan

[13] [13] anyn ki bügün[790] jazylġaj tirlikke[791] da ačuv[792] andan keterilgej[793] jazyqlaryn

[14] [14] bošatmaqbyla[794]. Kelir šeẖinasy Adonajnyn[795] qyčqyrmaqbyla[796] Adonaj[797] šofar

[15] [15] avazybyla. [798]⌜רננת פליטה⌟. Sarnavlaryn qutulmaqnyn sarnarlar

[16] [16] ǯymaty[799] jyjynlarymnyn, ömürlük[800] ḥorluqqa[801] bolurlar jyjynlary

[17] [17] dušmanlarymnyn[802] da munajtuvčularymnyn[803], da tirliklerine ʿolam

[18] [18] habanyn bolurlar ǯymaty[804] üč[805] atalarymnyn[806]. Bunun üčün[807] qyčqyrmaqlar-

---

777 JSul.I.46: *olturuvcusu.* | JSul.III.76: *olturuvcusu.*

778 JSul.I.54.12: deest. | JSul.III.72: הניא מחשבות עמים. | JSul.III.67: הניא מחשבות.

779 JSul.I.54.12: *saġyslaryn.* | JSul.I.46: *saġyslaryn.* | JSul.III.76: *saġyslaryn.*

780 JSul.I.54.12: *uluslarnyn avaldan.* | JSul.III.67: *uluslarnyn avaldan.* | JSul.III.76: *uluslarnyn avaldan.*

781 JSul.I.54.12: *keneslerin.* | JSul.I.46: *keneslerin.* | JSul.I.46: *keneslerin.*

782 JSul.I.54.12: *ullu.* | JSul.III.72: *ullu.* | JSul.III.67: *ullu.* | JSul.I.46: *ullu.* | JSul.III.76: *ullu.*

783 JSul.III.67: *kičibyla.* | JSul.I.46: *kücübyla.* | JSul.III.76: *kici byla.*

784 JSul.I.46: *caġyrġaj.* | JSul.III.76: *caġyrġaj.*

785 JSul.I.46: *ulusuna.*

786 JSul.III.67: *ezinin.* | JSul.III.76: *ezinin.*

787 JSul.III.67: *ize.* | JSul.III.76: *ize.*

788 JSul.I.54.12: {{*sanbyla*}} *qynġyrlyġyna.*

789 JSul.III.67: *kere.* | JSul.III.76: *kere.*

790 JSul.III.67: *bigin.* | JSul.III.76: *bigin.*

791 JSul.I.54.12: *tirlikḱa.*

792 JSul.I.46: *acuv.* | JSul.III.76: *qaḥyr.*

793 JSul.III.67: *ketkej.* | JSul.I.46: *ketkej.* | JSul.III.76: *ketkej.*

794 JSul.I.46: *bosatmaqbyla.* | JSul.III.76: *bosatmaq byla.*

795 JSul.III.67: *H-nyn.* | JSul.I.46: *Tenrinin.* | JSul.III.76: *Tenrinin.*

796 JSul.I.46: *qycqyrmaq byla.* | JSul.III.76: *qycqyrmaq byla.*

797 JSul.III.67: *H.* | JSul.I.46: *H.* | JSul.III.76: *H.*

798 JSul.I.54.12: desunt. | JSul.III.72: רננת פלטה (פלטה *pro* פליטה). | JSul.I.46: רננת פלטה (פלטה *pro* פליטה). | JSul.III.76: רננת.

799 JSul.I.46: *ʒymaty.* | JSul.III.76: *ʒymaty.*

[9] [9] and in storms will come the one sitting on His southern[808] side. (2).
[10] [10] The God, who has silenced[809] the thoughts of nations and destroyed
[11] [11] their intentions with his own[810] power, He shall call for freedom for His own son[811] since
[12] [12] He has punished him[812] numerously, breaking him[813] off, according to his[814] faults. ⌞May there be a desire before him[815]⌝[816]
[13] [13] that he[817] may be destined for life, and may the anger[818] against him ⌞be removed⌝[819]
[14] [14] with the remission of his[820] sins. The divine Presence of ⌞the Lord⌝[821] will come with the calling
[15] [15] voice of the *shofar* of the Lord. (3). Songs of salvation will sing
[16] [16] the community of my congregations, to eternal misery[822] will the crowds
[17] [17] of my enemies and oppressors be (destined), and to life in the world
[18] [18] to come will the community[823] of my[824] three patriarchs be (destined). For this reason

800 JSul.I.54.12: *ömirlik.* | JSul.III.72: *ömürlik.* | JSul.III.67: *emirlik.* | JSul.I.46: *emirlik.* | JSul.III.76: *emirlik.*
801 JSul.III.72: *tirlikke.*
802 JSul.I.46: *dusmanlarymnyn.* | JSul.III.76: *dusmanlarymnyn.*
803 JSul.I.46: *munajtuvcularymnyn.* | JSul.III.76: *munajtuvcularymnyn.*
804 JSul.III.67: *ǯymaty* {{*ulanlarynyn*}}. | JSul.I.46: *ʒymaty.* | JSul.III.76: *ʒymaty ulanlarynyn.*
805 JSul.III.67: *ič.* | JSul.I.46: *ic.* | JSul.III.76: *ic.*
806 JSul.III.72: *atalarymyznyn.*
807 JSul.III.67: *ičin.* | JSul.I.46: *ücün.* | JSul.III.76: *icin.*
808 I.e., *right-hand*; cf. the linguistic connection in Hebrew between 'right' and 'left' with 'south' and 'north', respectively (see Frank 2004: 158).
809 JSul.I.54.12: *long ago silenced.* | JSul.III.67: *long ago silenced.* | JSul.III.76: *long ago silenced.*
810 JSul.I.54.12: *great.* | JSul.III.72: *great.* | JSul.III.67: *great.* | JSul.I.46: *great.* | JSul.III.76: *great.*
811 JSul.I.46: *people.*
812 JSul.I.46: *them*; i.e., *the people*, see line 11.
813 JSul.I.46: *them*; i.e., *the people*, see line 11.
814 JSul.I.46: *their*; i.e., *the people's*, see line 11.
815 JSul.I.46: *them*; i.e., *the people*, see line 11.
816 I.e., *may the will lead him.*
817 JSul.I.46: *they*; i.e., *the people*, see line 11.
818 I.e., *the anger of God.* || JSul.III.76: expressed with a synonym.
819 JSul.III.67: *leave.* | JSul.I.46: *leave.* | JSul.III.76: *leave.*
820 JSul.I.46: *their*; i.e., *the people's*, see line 11.
821 JSul.I.46: *God.* | JSul.III.76: *God.*
822 Or: *disgrace.* || JSul.III.72: *life*; a scribal error.
823 JSul.III.67: *community* {{*of the sons*}}. | JSul.III.76: *community of the sons.*
824 JSul.III.72: *our.*

[19] [19] byla[825] maḥtav[826] beriniz alnynda Adonajnyn[827]. [828]⌜נֿא יהֿיה⌟. Da ajtynyz
[20] [20] qol{t}qabyla bolġaj bizge šemi[829] anyn alamġa da kip[830] vežaġa[831], körgüzgej[832]
[21] [21] bizgede[833] tamašalyqlar[834] nečik[835] körgüzdü[836] ⌞atalarymyzġa Jam Sufbyla
[22] [22] Migdol[837] arasyna⌝[838] nečik[839] töledi[840] öčler[841] paroġa. Azasqanlaryn[842]
[23] [23] Jisra'el[843] ulusunun jomdarġaj[844] ki qalmaġaj biriside[845] alardan čajnavġa[846].
[24] [24] Ol künde[847] tartylyr[848] ullu byrġyġa[849]. [850]⌜חנון ימנן עיחו⌟
1 vº [25] [1] Ḥajifsünme[851] ḥajifsüngej[852] Tenri[853] qaldyqlarymyz[854] üstüne[855] da ulusu
[26] [2] anyn artyq tajmaġaj. Syjyt etken[i][856] üčün[857] galut vaḥtlarynda
[27] [3] bijlik vaḥtlarynda[858] meleẖ hamašijaḥnyn bizni bijendirgej. Zeẖutun Avraham-
[28] [4] nyn da Icḥaqnyn[859] bizge saġynġaj[860], da jomdarma azašqanlarymyzny[861] galut

---

825 JSul.I.54.12: *qyčqyrmaqbyla.* | JSul.III.72: *qyčqyrmaqbyla.* | JSul.III.67: *qyčqyrmaqbyla.* | JSul.I.46: *qycqyrmaqlar byla.* | JSul.III.76: *qycqyrmaq byla.*
826 JSul.I.46: *maḥtavlar.* | JSul.III.76: *maḥtavlar.*
827 JSul.III.72: *H-nyn.* | JSul.III.67: *ol bijnin H-nyn.* | JSul.I.46: *H-nyn.* | JSul.III.76: *ol bijnin H-nyn.*
828 JSul.I.54.12: desunt. | JSul.III.72: נֿא יהֿיה לנֿו שמֿו. | JSul.III.67: נאֿ יהֿיה לנֿו שמֿו.
829 JSul.I.54.12: *syjly šemi.* | JSul.III.67: *syjly šemi.* | JSul.I.46: *syjly šemi.* | JSul.III.76: *syjly šemi.*
830 JSul.I.46: *köp*; perhaps a scribal error. | JSul.III.76: *kep*; perhaps a scribal error.
831 JSul.I.46: *vezaġa.* | JSul.III.76: *vezaġa.*
832 JSul.I.54.12: *körgizgej.* | JSul.III.72: *körgizgej.* | JSul.III.67: *kergizgej.* | JSul.I.46: *körgizgej.* | JSul.III.76: *kergizgej.*
833 JSul.I.54.12: *bizge.* | JSul.III.72: *bizge.* | JSul.III.67: *bizge.*
834 JSul.III.76: *tamasalyqlar.*
835 JSul.III.67: *ki nečik.* | JSul.I.46: *necik.* | JSul.III.76: *ki necik.*
836 JSul.I.54.12: *körgizdi.* | JSul.III.72: *körgizdi.* | JSul.III.67: *kergizdi.* | JSul.I.46: *körgizdü.* | JSul.III.76: *kergizdi.*
837 Heb. מִגְדֹּל 'Migdol (a place name)', see Exodus 14:2.
838 JSul.III.67: *Jam Sufbyla Migdol arasyna atalarymyzġa*; different word order.
839 JSul.I.46: *necik.* | JSul.III.76: *necik.*
840 JSul.I.54.12: {{*körgizdi*}} {*töledi*}. | JSul.III.67: *teledi*; written erroneously with *shewa*: טֵילְידִי. | JSul.I.46: *teledi.* | JSul.III.76: *teledi.*
841 JSul.III.67: *ečler.* | JSul.I.46: *ecler.* | JSul.III.76: *ecler.*
842 JSul.I.54.12: *azašqanlaryn.* | JSul.III.67: *azašqanlaryn.*
843 JSul.I.54.12: *Jisra'elnin.*
844 JSul.I.46: *ystyrġaj.*
845 JSul.III.76: *biride.*

[19] [19] praise with shouts[862] before the Lord[863]. (4). And say
[20] [20] in a prayer that His Name[864] may be a banner and a strong tower for us, may He show
[21] [21] wonders ⌊also to⌉[865] us as he has shown (them) to our fathers between
[22] [22] the Red Sea and Migdol, when he repaid vengeance to the Pharaoh.
[23] [23] May He gather[866] the strays of the people of Israel so that not even one is left for mockery from among them.
[24] [24] On that day it will be blown into a great trumpet[867]. (5).
[25] [1] May God[868] have certainly mercy on ⌊us, remnants⌉[869], and 1 v°
[26] [2] may His people not waver any more. Because of their[870] grief in the times of exile
[27] [3] may He please us in the times of the King Messiah.
[28] [4] May He ⌊remind us⌉[871] the merit of Abraham

---

846 JSul.I.54.12: *čajnavlarġa.* | JSul.I.46: *cajnavġa.*
847 JSul.III.67: *kinde.* | JSul.III.76: *kinde.*
848 JSul.I.46: *ol tartylyr.* | JSul.III.76: *ol tartylyr.*
849 JSul.I.54.12: {{*byrġyġa*}} *šofarġa.* | JSul.III.72: *šofarġa.* | JSul.III.67: *šofarġa.* | JSul.III.76: *šofarġa.*
850 JSul.I.54.12: desunt. | JSul.III.72: חנ֫ון יח֫נן שא֫ריתנו. | JSul.III.67: חנ֫ון יחנ֫ן. | JSul.I.46: חנ֫ון יח֫נן. | JSul.III.76: חנ֫ון. || Cf. חָנוֹן יְחֻנָּן שְׁאֵרִיתֵנוּ וְעַמּוֹ (JSul.III.67, f. 205 r°).
851 JSul.III.67: *ḥajifsinme.* | JSul.I.46: *ḥajifsinme.* | JSul.III.76: *ḥajifsinme.*
852 JSul.III.72: *ḥajifsingej.* | JSul.III.67: *ḥajifsingej.* | JSul.I.46: *ḥajifsingej.* | JSul.III.76: *ḥajifsingej.*
853 JSul.III.67: deest.
854 JSul.I.54.12: *qaldyqlarymyz*{{*ny*}}. | JSul.III.67: *az qaldyġymyz.* | JSul.III.76: *az qaldyġymyz.*
855 JSul.III.67: *istine.* | JSul.I.46: *istine.* | JSul.III.76: *istine.*
856 Or: *etkenleri.* | JSul.I.54.12: *etken.* | JSul.III.72: *etken.* | JSul.III.67: *etkenleri.* | JSul.I.46: *etkeni.* | JSul.III.76: *etkeni.*
857 JSul.III.67: *ičin.* | JSul.I.46: *üčün.* | JSul.III.76: *icin.*
858 JSul.I.54.12: *vaḥtynda.* | JSul.I.46: *vaḥtynda.* | JSul.III.76: *vaḥtynda.*
859 JSul.III.67: *Icḥaqnyn* {{*da Jaʿaqovnun*}}.
860 JSul.I.54.12: *bügün saġynġaj.*
861 JSul.I.46: *azasqanlarymyzny.* | JSul.III.76: *azasqanlarymyzny.*
862 JSul.I.54.12: *shout.* | JSul.III.72: *shout.* | JSul.III.67: *shout.* | JSul.III.76: *shout.*
863 JSul.III.67: *Lord God.* | JSul.III.76: *Lord God.*
864 JSul.I.54.12: *honourable Name.* | JSul.III.67: *honourable Name.* | JSul.I.46: *honourable Name.* | JSul.III.76: *honourable Name.*
865 JSul.I.54.12: desunt. | JSul.III.72: desunt. | JSul.III.67: desunt.
866 JSul.I.46: expressed with a synonym.
867 JSul.I.54.12: {{*trumpet*}} *shofar.* | JSul.III.72: *shofar.* | JSul.III.67: *shofar.* | JSul.III.76: *shofar.*
868 JSul.III.67: *He.*
869 JSul.III.67: *us, few remnants.* | JSul.III.76: *us, few remnants.*
870 JSul.III.67: *all their.*
871 JSul.I.54.12: *remind us today.*

[29] [5] jerlerinden tutunġanyna köre[872] šofarġa ullu avazbyla tarttyrġaj[873].
[30] [6] [874]⌈קרב יקרב⌋. Juvutma juvutqaj jarlyġašymyzny[875] süverlikbyla[876]. Da
[31] [7] ešittirgej[877] bizge quvanč[878] avazy[n][879] köp[880] ḥajifsünmekbyla[881]. Ullu
[32] [8] quvatly[882] ⌊anyn erkindedi⌉[883] ol tengiz da ol jerde[884] tolularybyla[885].
[33] [9] Küčlü[886] Tenri syrynda aziz malaḫlarnyn ullulugu qotaryl[a]dy[887] syjbyla.
[34] [10] ⌊כַּכָּתוּב⌋ ⌈אֵל נַעֲרָץ בְּסוֹד קְדוֹשִׁים רַבָּה וגו׳⌉[888]⌉[889]

872 JSul.III.67: *kere.* | JSul.III.76: *kere.*
873 JSul.I.54.12: *tartyrġaj.* | JSul.III.67: *tartyrġaj.*
874 JSul.I.54.12: desunt. | JSul.III.76: קרֿב.
875 JSul.I.46: *jarlyġasymyzny.* | JSul.III.76: *jarlyġasymyzny.*
876 JSul.III.67: *siverlikbyla.* | JSul.I.46: *siverlik byla.* | JSul.III.76: *siverlik byla.*
877 JSul.I.54.12: *ešitirgej.* | JSul.I.46: *esittirgej.* | JSul.III.76: *esittirgej.*
878 JSul.I.46: *bijenc.*
879 JSul.I.54.03: *avazy.* | JSul.I.54.12: *avazy.* | JSul.III.72: *avazy.* | JSul.III.67: *avazy.* | JSul.I.46: *avazyn.* | JSul.III.76: *avazyn.*
880 JSul.III.67: *kep.* | JSul.III.76: *kep.*
881 JSul.I.54.12: *ḥajifsinmekbyla.* | JSul.III.72: *ḥajifsinmekbyla.* | JSul.III.67: *ḥajifsinmekbyla.* | JSul.I.46: *ḥajifsinmek byla.* | JSul.III.76: *ḥajifsinmek byla.*
882 JSul.I.46: *quvatly Tenri.* | JSul.III.76: *quvatly Tenri.*
883 JSul.I.46: *anyndy.*
884 JSul.I.54.12: *jer.* | JSul.III.72: *jer.* | JSul.I.46: *jer.*
885 JSul.III.67: *bar tolularybyla.* | JSul.III.76: *bar tolulary byla.*
886 JSul.III.67: *kičli.* | JSul.I.46: *küclü.* | JSul.III.76: *kicli.*
887 JSul.I.54.03: *qotaryldy.* | JSul.I.54.12: *qotarylady.* | JSul.III.72: *qotarylady.* | JSul.III.67: *qotarylady.* | JSul.I.46: *qotarylady.* | JSul.III.76: *qotarylady.*
888 Psalm 89:7.
889 JSul.I.54.12: אל נערץ בסוד קדושים רבה ונורא עכ״ס (Psalm 89:7). | JSul.III.72: אֵל נַעֲרָץ בְּסוֹד קְדוֹשִׁים וגו׳. (Psalm 89:7). | JSul.III.67: אֵל נַעֲרָץ בְּסוֹד קְדוֹשִׁים רַבָּה וְנוֹרָא עַל כָּל סְבִיבָיו: הָ אֱלֹהֵי צְבָאוֹת מִי כָמוֹךָ חֲסִין יָהּ וֶאֱמוּנָתְךָ סְבִיבוֹתֶיךָ: אֵין קָדוֹשׁ כַּהָ כִּי אֵין בִּלְתֶּךָ וְאֵין צוּר כֵּאלֹהֵינוּ. (Psalm 89:7; 1Samuel 2:2). | JSul.I.46: אֵל נַעֲרָץ בְּסוֹד קְדוֹשִׁים וגו׳. (Psalm 89:7). | JSul.III.76: תם.

[29] [5] and Isaac and, in order to gather all our strays from the lands of exile according to His promise, may He make us blow into the trumpet with great voice.

[30] [6] (6). May He certainly bring closer our salvation and love and

[31] [7] may ⌊He make us hear the voice of joy[890]⌉[891] with great mercy.

[32] [8] Almighty[892], ⌊He rules⌉[893] the sea and the also[894] land along with that[895] they are filled with.

[33] [9] Powerful God, His greatness is preached with reverence in the secret of the holy angels.

[34] [10] ⌊As it is written: ⌊'God is greatly to be feared in the assembly of the saints.'⌉[896]⌉[897]

---

890 JSul.I.46: expressed with a synonym.

891 Another, less probable interpretation of this part of the sentence, assuming *avazy* in place of *avazyn*: JSul.I.54.03: or: *the voice of joy be heard for us.* | JSul.I.54.12: or: *the voice of joy be heard for us.* | JSul.III.72: or: *the voice of joy be heard for us.* | JSul.III.67: or: *the voice of joy be heard for us.*

892 JSul.I.46: *God Almighty.* | JSul.III.76: *God Almighty.*

893 JSul.I.46: *His is.*

894 JSul.I.54.12: deest. | JSul.III.72: deest. | JSul.I.46: deest.

895 JSul.III.67: *everything that.* | JSul.III.76: *everything that.*

896 Psalm 89:7.

897 JSul.I.54.12: *'God is greatly to be feared in the assembly of the saints, and to be had in reverence of all them who are about him.'* (Psalm 89:7). | JSul.III.72: *'God is greatly to be feared in the assembly of the saints …' and so on.* (Psalm 89:7). | JSul.III.67: *'God is greatly to be feared in the assembly of the saints, and to be had in reverence of all them who are about him. O Lord God of hosts, who is a strong Lord like unto you? or to your faithfulness round about you? There is none holy as the Lord: for there is none beside you: neither is there any rock like our God.'* (Psalm 89:7–8; 1 Samuel 2:2). | JSul.I.46: *'God is greatly to be feared in the assembly of the saints …' and so on.* (Psalm 89:7). | JSul.III.76: *The end.*

**Text number:** № 15
**Karaim incipit:** *Kelip sortun Jisra'el*
**Hebrew incipit:** אַחֲרֵי בא יְשוּרוּן *'aḥărē bo yšūrūn*
**Dedication:** Parashat Shlach (Numbers 13:1–15:41)
**Language:** Early Mod.SWKar., Mod.SWKar.
**Number of copies:** 5

| Accession no. | Place of origin of copy | Date of copy | Copyist | Folios |
|---|---|---|---|---|
| JSul.III.03 | Halych | shortly after 1805 | Unknown 7 | 106 v°–107 v° |
| JSul.I.45 | Halych | 1st half of the 19th c. | Jeshua Josef Mordkowicz | 143 v°–144 r° |
| ADub.III.61 | Halych | 1850/1851 | Jeshua Josef Mordkowicz | 136 v°–137 r° |
| JSul.III.69 | Halych | ca. 1851 (before 1866) | Jeshua Josef Mordkowicz | 291 r°–291 v° |
| JSul.III.79 | Halych | ca. 1851 (before 1866) | Jeshua Josef Mordkowicz | 176 v°–177 v° |

## 1 Introductory Remarks

In JSul.III.03, JSul.I.45, ADub.III.61, and JSul.III.79, Simcha ben Chananel is referred to as 'the above-mentioned': in JSul.III.03 and JSul.I.45, his name is included in the headings of *peshat* № 23, whereas in ADub.III.61 and JSul.III.79, this is written in the headings of *peshat* № 11. All copies are vocalized.

Since the oldest text is the only one not copied by Jeshua Josef Mordkowicz, the differences we find in the rest of the copies are apparently the result of textual improvements introduced by Mordkowicz. Some of these are significant, see, for instance, the different versions of the fragment *jalbarmaqlar ol acuv vaḥtynda* (24–25), as well as the word *muna* (7) replaced by the passage *qaruv beredi šeḫina ajtadoğac muna* in mss. ADub.III.61 and JSul.III.69. At the same time, however, we can also observe discrepancies between the latter two texts, e.g. *jiridiler* vs. *jiridiler saruvu artyna Tenrinin* (15). Finally, there are also fragments which indicate a close affinity between ADub.III.61 and JSul.III.79, cf. *jalbarmaqlar byla ol buzuqluq vaḥtta* vs. *jalbarmaqlar byla ol buzulmaq vaḥtynda* (24–25).

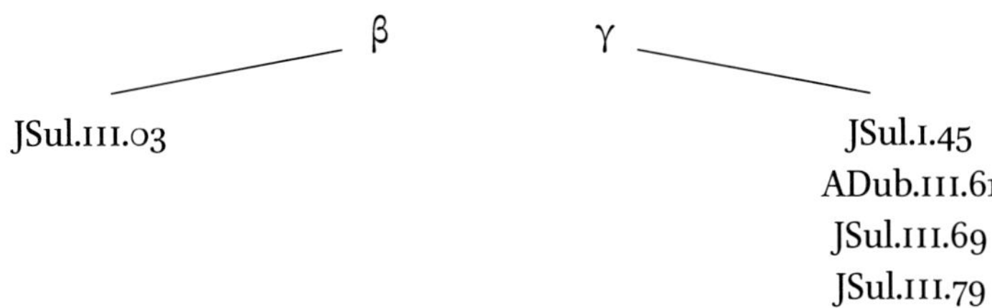


FIGURE 18 Diagram of the connections between the copies of peshat № 15

## 2 Transcription[898] and Translation

106 v° [1] [26] ⌟פשט לפיוט פרשת שלח לך שהוא אחרי בוא ישורון תרגמו החכם הנ̈ל נב̈ת:⌜[899]
[2] [27] Kelip sortun Jisra’el cegine ⌞Qadeš Barne‘anyn⌝[900], ajtyldy
[3] [28] anar bujruġundan Tenrinin barġyn meresl[e]gin[901] ol
[4] [29] jerni[902]
107 r° [5] [1] jerni da barca qajda ki qajrylsan qaltratysen jyjynyn dusmanlarynnyn[903],
[6] [2] da cajsylama osol ol jerni kledi ajtmaġy byla ullu quvatly
[7] [3] qutqaruvcu Tenrinin. Muna[904] jadamady qudraty H-nyn qutqarmaqtan
[8] [4] isanuvcularny bolusluġuna anyn. [905]⌜הוט̇ב הדב̇ר⌟.
[9] [5] Jaḥsy köründi[906] ol söz[907] közlerinde[908] Mošenin da sajlady tuvuslu
[10] [6] elni ortasyndan ol ʒymatnyn, birer kisi birer kisi bar
[11] [7] ševetlerinden Tenrinin, da maḥtamaqlaryndan sortun ki ol jer
[12] [8] aġadoġan sit da bal ol da körgizip[909] sortun jemisin anyn.
[13] [9] Civirildiler civirilmegi kibik jaltaj jajnyn. [910]⌜רו̇ח חן⌟.
[14] [10] Sirin söz[911] edi avzunda Jehošu‘anyn uvlunun Nunnun da Kalevnin
[15] [11] ki alar körtilik[912] byla jiridiler[913] da tyjdylar ulusnu ajtadoġač ne[k][914]

---

898 Based on JSul.III.03.

899 JSul.I.45: פשט לפיוט פרשת שלח לך שהוא אחרי בוא ישורון תרגמו החכם הנ̈ל. | ADub.III.61: וזה הפשט לפיוט פרשת שלח לך א̇חרי בוא ישורון תרגמו החכם המתרגם הנ̈ל נפשו תהא צרורה בצרור החיים ואם תרצה תאמר גם פשטו תרגמו אמ̈ו כמה̈רר שמחה החזן בעיר קוקיזוב נב̈ת בכמו̈הע̈מ חננאל הזקן יע̈מש. | JSul.III.79: וזה הפשט לפיוט פרשת שלח לך תרגמו החכם המתרגם הנזכר לעיל תנצ̈בהה: אַחֲרֵי בוֹא יְשׁוּרוּן.

900 Heb. קָדֵשׁ בַּרְנֵעַ ‘Kadesh-barnea (place name)’; see Numbers 34:4.

901 JSul.III.03: *meresligin*; a scribal error; cf., however, JSul.III.79. | JSul.I.45: *mereslegin.* | ADub.III.61: *mereslegin.* | JSul.III.69: *mereslegin.* | JSul.III.79: *meresligin*; a scribal error; cf., however, JSul.III.03.

902 Catchword.

903 JSul.III.79: *dusmanlarnyn.*

904 ADub.III.61: *qaruv beredi šeḫina ajtadoġac muna.* | JSul.III.69: *qaruv beredi šeḫina ajtadoġac muna.*

905 JSul.I.45: הוט̇ב. | JSul.III.69: הוט̇ב. | JSul.III.79: הוט̇ב.

906 JSul.I.45: *körindi.* | ADub.III.61: *kerindi.* | JSul.III.69: *kerindi.* | JSul.III.79: *kerindi.*

907 ADub.III.61: *sez.* | JSul.III.69: *sez.* | JSul.III.79: *sez.*

908 ADub.III.61: *kezlerinde.* | JSul.III.69: *kezlerinde.* | JSul.III.79: *kezlerinde.*

909 ADub.III.61: *kergizip.* | JSul.III.69: *kergizip.* | JSul.III.79: *kergizip.*

910 JSul.I.45: רו̇ח.

911 ADub.III.61: *sez.* | JSul.III.69: *sez.* | JSul.III.79: *sez.*

912 JSul.III.03: a hypercorrect form of *kertilik.* | JSul.I.45: a hypercorrect form of *kertilik.* | ADub.III.61: *kertilik.* | JSul.III.69: *kertilik.* | JSul.III.79: *kertilik.*

[1] [26] ⌞A *peshat* of a *piyyut* for the parashat Shlach, of that (with the incipit) *ʾaḥărē ḇo yšūrūn*, which the above-mentioned hakham translated, may his soul lodge in Eden.[1915] 1 r°

[2] [27] After Israel had arrived to the border of Kadesh Barnea, they were told

[3] [28] by an order of God: 'Go and inherit the

[4] [29] land[916]

[5] [1] land and anywhere you would turn you will make the crowds of ⌞your enemies[1917] tremble', 107 r°

[6] [2] and they wished to spie out the land (accompanied) by the words of the greatly powerful

[7] [3] God the redeemer. Lo[918], the hand of the Lord has not weakened by saving

[8] [4] those who believed in His providence. (2).

[9] [5] These words seemed good in the eyes of Moses, and he chose brave

[10] [6] men from among the congregation, one man from each

[11] [7] of all tribes of God, and after ⌞they had praised[1919] that the land is

[12] [8] flowing with milk and honey and after they had seen its fruits,

[13] [9] ⌞they turned away like a cunning bow[1920]. (3).

[14] [10] Sweet words were in the mouth of Jehoshua the son of Nun and Kalev

[15] [11] who were walking[921] with truth and they admonished the people, saying, 'Why

---

913 JSul.I.45: *jüridiler.* | ADub.III.61: *jiridiler saruvu artyna Tenrinin.*

914 JSul.III.03: *ne*; most probably a scribal error. | JSul.I.45: *nek.* | ADub.III.61: *nek.* | JSul.III.69: *nek.* | JSul.III.79: *nek.*

915 JSul.I.45: *A* peshat *of a* piyyut *for the parashat Shlach, of that* (*with the incipit*) ʾaḥărē ḇo yšūrūn, *which the above-mentioned hakham translated.* | ADub.III.61: *And this is the* peshat *of a* piyyut *for the parashat Shlach* (*with the incipit*) ʾaḥărē ḇo yšūrūn, *which the above-mentioned hakham the translator translated, 'may his soul be bound in the bond of life'* [cf., 1Samuel 25:29]. | JSul.III.69: *And, if you prefer, say its* peshat [i.e., of the Hebrew original], *which our master, our teacher, his honour, the Rav, Rabbi Simcha translated, the hazzan in the town of Kukizów, may his soul lodge in Eden, the son of the honourable sir Chananel, 'dew on his lodge'* [cf., Exodus 16:13–14], *the aged, may he rest in peace.* | JSul.III.79: *And this is the* peshat *of the* piyyut *for the parashat Shlach, which the above-mentioned hakham the translator translated, 'may his soul be bound in the bond of life'* [cf., 1Samuel 25:29]. (*Incipit:*) ʾaḥărē ḇo yšūrūn.

916 Catchword in the Karaim text.

917 JSul.III.79: *enemies.*

918 JSul.III.79: *and the divine Presence replied, saying, 'Lo.*

919 Lit. 'their praise'.

920 Lit. 'they turned away like the turning of a cunning bow'.

921 ADub.III.61: *walking after the commandments of God.*

[16] [12] tersejesiz, da inanmajsiz sözüne[922] Tenrinin da hörmetli[923]
[17] [13] bujruġuna anyn tanasiz. Da dusmandan ketti kelegesi anyn
[18] [14] istinden ne seskenesiz[924]. Tek H-ġa tanmanyz ki anyn bolusluġu
[19] [15] byla biz alarny jenerbiz. [925]⌜נמֹר ריֹחם⌟.
[20] [16] Tivsirildi aqyllary alarnyn {{necik esittiler}} necik esittiler
[21] [17] terelerin Tenrinin, ki ajtty qajjamdyr[926] H da toludu[927] syjyndan[928]
[22] [18] dunja da jasyryn orunlary anyn. Alaj eksilir saġynclary
[23] [19] alarnyn alnyndan enajatlarynyn[929], da barlary taspolġajediler
[24] [20] bir köz[930] jumcuġuna eger Moše sajlanmusu turmasyjdy ⌞jalbar-maqlar [byla]
[25] [21] ol acuv vaḫtynda⌟[931] alnynda Tenrinin. [932]⌜חיֹ וקיֹים אמֹר⌟.
[26] [22] Tiri da qajjam Tenri ajtty ummasyna[933] Jisra'elnin daġyn bu[934]
[27] [23] belgi byla bolur qajjamlyġy jaryġynnyn[935], hadirlegin ezine cicit
[28] [24] dert mivisi istine jabunurunnun da jaryrlar közleri[936] aqylynnyn.
[29] [25] Közlerin[937] anyn istine baqsynlar da saġynġyn osol bar micvalaryn
[30] [26] H Tenrinnin[938], da bolurlar közlerin[939] baġuvcular qolajly islerni da
[31] [27] qajrylmassen jaman saġyslary artyna ⌞jaman jecerinnin⌟[940].
[32] [28] [941]⌜קוי עדתי⌟. Tezgin e ʒymatym ki hanuzda[942]

---

922 JSul.I.45: *sözine.* | ADub.III.61: *sezine.* | JSul.III.69: *sezine.* | JSul.III.79: *sezine.*

923 JSul.I.45: *hermetli.* | ADub.III.61: *hermetli.* | JSul.III.69: *hermetli.* | JSul.III.79: *hermetli.*

924 JSul.III.03: שֵׁישְׁכֵינֵישִׁיז. | JSul.I.45: סֶישְׁכֵינֵישִׁיז. | ADub.III.61: שֶׁישְׁכֶינֶישִׁיז. | JSul.III.69: שֶׁישְׁכֵינֶישִׁיז. | JSul.III.79: שֶׁישְׁכֵינֵישִׁיז.

925 JSul.I.45: נמֹר. | JSul.III.69: נמֹר.

926 ADub.III.61: *qajjamdy.*

927 JSul.III.79: *toludur.*

928 JSul.III.79: *syjyndan anyn.*

929 In all copies written separately, i.e., *enaj atlarynyn.*

930 ADub.III.61: *kyz*, most likely < *kez* due to the Mod.SWKar. [ḱy] ~ [kė] alternation. | JSul.III.69: *kez.* | JSul.III.79: *kez.*

931 JSul.I.45: *ol buzuqluq vaḥtynda jalbarmaqlar byla.* | ADub.III.61: *jalbarmaqlar byla ol buzulmaq vaḥtta.* | JSul.III.69: *jalbarmaqlar byla ol qaḥyr vaḥtynda.* | JSul.III.79: *jalbarmaqlar byla ol buzulmaq vaḥtynda.*

932 JSul.I.45: חֹי. | ADub.III.61: חֹי וקֹיים. | JSul.III.69: חֹי. | JSul.III.79: חֹי וקֹיים.

933 JSul.III.79: *ulusuna.*

934 ADub.III.61: *buda.*

935 A mistranslation as a result of confusing אוֹרְךָ 'I will instruct you' with its homonym, i.e., with אוֹרְךָ 'your light'.

936 ADub.III.61: *kezleri.* | JSul.III.69: *kezleri.* | JSul.III.79: *kezleri.*

937 ADub.III.61: *kezlerin.* | JSul.III.69: *kezlerin.* | JSul.III.79: *kezlerin.*

938 JSul.III.79: *Tenrinin.*

939 ADub.III.61: *kezlerin senin.* | JSul.III.69: *kezlerin senin.* | JSul.III.79: *kezlerin senin.*

940 JSul.I.45: *jecer hara'nyn.* | ADub.III.61: *jecer hara'nyn.* | JSul.III.69: *jecer hara'nyn.* | JSul.III.79: *jecer hara'nyn.* || A calque of Heb. יֵצֶר הָרַע 'evil inclination', see Genesis 6:5, 8:21.

[16] [12] do you turn away and (why) do you not believe the words of God, and

[17] [13] betray His honourable order? His shadow[943] went from above the enemies

[18] [14] (so) what are you trembling (for)? But do not betray the Lord for with His providence

[19] [15] we will defeat them.' (4).

[20] [16] Their mind changed when they heard

[21] [17] the laws of God who said 'Powerful is the Lord, and

[22] [18] the world and His secret[944] places are filled with His fame'. So does their memory vanish

[23] [19] before God's eyes, and all of them would have perished

[24] [20] ⌊in a blink of an eye⌋[945] if Moses, His chosen one, would not ⌊stand (and say) entreaties⌋[946]

[25] [21] before God ⌊in the times of anger[947]⌋[948]. (5).

[26] [22] The living and powerful God said to the community[949] of Israel, 'And with this

[27] [23] sign will ⌊he power of your light come into being⌋[950], prepare for yourselves fringes

[28] [24] for the four corners of your quilt and the eyes of wisdom will shine!

[29] [25] May your eyes look at Him and remember all the commandments

[30] [26] of your[951] Lord God, and ⌊may your eyes care about⌋[952] the right issues and

[31] [27] do not turn after the evil thoughts of the evil inclination.

[32] [28] (6). Expect, O my congregation, that, still,

---

941 JSul.I.45: חבֿי. | JSul.III.69: קוֹי. || See Heb. קַוִּי עֲדָתִי (JSul.III.69: 290 v°) and קַוִּי עֲדָתִי (JSul.III.79: 153 r°).

942 JSul.I.45: *hanuz.* | ADub.III.61: *hanuz.* | JSul.III.69: *hanuz.* | JSul.III.79: *hanuz.*

943 I.e., *protection.*

944 Or: *hidden.*

945 I.e., *in an instant.*

946 Lit. 'stand with entreaties'.

947 JSul.III.69: expressed with a synonym.

948 JSul.I.45: *in the times of depravity* (~ *destruction*). | ADub.III.61: *in the times of depravity* (~ *destruction*). | JSul.III.79: *in the times of depravity* (~ *destruction*).

949 JSul.III.79: *people.*

950 A mistranslation of the Hebrew original as a result of confusing אוֹרְךָ 'I will instruct you' with its homonym, i.e., אוֹרְךָ 'your light'.

951 JSul.III.79: *the.*

952 Lit. 'may your eyes be carers about'.

107 v° [33] [1] qajtarymen seni ornuna. Tezgin ki dağyn küplermen[953] seni da
[34] [2] kicejtirmen seni jarytmaqbyla qyblalarymny sana. Tezgin ki dağyn
[35] [3] süvermen[954] seni da bijenc byla juvu[tur]men[955] seni jerine. Kici köz[956]
[36] [4] jumcuġuna[957] kemistim seni galutta da ullu raḥmetler byla jystyrymen[958]
[37] [5] seni da emirlik jarlyġas toḥtatyrmen istine. ⌊בשצף קצף
[38] [6] הסתרתי פני רגע ממך וכו׳: גואלנו ה׳ צבאות:⌉[959]

---

953 JSul.III.03: a hypercorrect form of *kiplermen*. | JSul.I.45: *kiplermen*. | ADub.III.61: *kiplermen*. | JSul.III.69: *kiplermen*. | JSul.III.79: *kiplermen*.

954 JSul.I.45: *sivermen*. | ADub.III.61: *sivermen*. | JSul.III.69: *sivermen*. | JSul.III.79: *sivermen*.

955 JSul.III.03: *juvurtumen*; a scribal error: *juvurt-* '1. to fertilize animals; 2. to make run, to drive' does not fit in with the context (morphologically a form like *juvurtumen* might be explained as an abbreviated future tense form with the future tense marker *-r-* syncopated); see also mss. JSul.III.69 and JSul.III.79. | JSul.I.45: *juvuturmen*. | ADub.III.61: *juvuturmen*. | JSul.III.69: *juvurtumen*. | JSul.III.79: *juvurtumen*.

956 ADub.III.61: *kez*. | JSul.III.69: *kez*. | JSul.III.79: *kez*.

957 JSul.III.69: *jumcuqqa*.

958 JSul.I.45: *ystyryrmen*. | ADub.III.61: *ystyryrmen*. | JSul.III.69: *ystyryrmen*. | JSul.III.79: *ystyryrmen*.

959 Isaiah 54:8; Isaiah 47:4. | JSul.I.45: בשצף קצף הסתרי פני וגו׳: גואלנו ה׳ וגו׳ (Isaiah 54:8; Isaiah 47:4). | ADub.III.61: תם: בְּשֶׁצֶף קֶצֶף הִסְתַּרְתִּי פָּנַי רֶגַע מִמֵּךְ וגו׳. (Isaiah 54:8). | JSul.III.69: בְּשֶׁצֶף קֶצֶף הִסְתַּרְתִּי פָּנַי רֶגַע מִמֵּךְ וּבְחֶסֶד עוֹלָם רִחַמְתִּיךְ אָמַר גֹּואֲלֵךְ ה׳: גּוֹאֲלֵנוּ ה׳ צְבָאוֹת שְׁמוֹ קְדוֹשׁ יִשְׂרָאֵל. (Isaiah 54:8; Isaiah 47:4). | JSul.III.79: בְּשֶׁצֶף קֶצֶף הִסְתַּרְתִּי וגו׳: גּוֹאֲלֵנוּ ה׳ צְבָאוֹת שְׁמוֹ קְדוֹשׁ יִשְׂרָאֵל. (Isaiah 54:8; Isaiah 47:4).

[33] [1] I will bring you back to your place. Expect that I will even strengthen you and 107 v°
[34] [2] reinforce you by lightening up my countenance for you. Expect that
[35] [3] I will even love you and bring you in joy closer to your land. ⌊For a moment⌉[960]
[36] [4] I have left you in exile but with great mercy I will gather you
[37] [5] and eternal salvation will I place on you’. ⌊‘In a little wrath
[38] [6] I hid my face from you for a moment …’, et cetera. ‘As for our redeemer, the Lord of hosts …’.⌉[961]

---

960 Lit. ‘for a tiny blink of an eye’.

961 Isaiah 54:8; Isaiah 47:4. | JSul.I.45: *‘In a little wrath I hid my face.’* (Isaiah 54:8; Isaiah 47:4). | ADub.III.61: *‘I hid my face from you for a moment …’ and so on.* (Isaiah 54:8). | JSul.III.69: *‘In a little wrath I hid my face from you for a moment; but with everlasting kindness will I have mercy on you, says the Lord your Redeemer. As for our redeemer, the Lord of hosts is his name, the Holy One of Israel.’* (Isaiah 54:8; Isaiah 47:4). | JSul.III.79: *‘In a little wrath I hid …’ and so on. ‘As for our redeemer, the Lord of hosts is his name, the Holy One of Israel.’* (Isaiah 54:8; Isaiah 47:4).

**Text number:** № 16
**Karaim incipit:** *Kicli Tenri syrynda aziz malaḫlarnyn*
**Hebrew incipit:** אֵל נַעֲרָץ בְּסוֹד מַלְאֲכֵי שְׁבִיבוֹ *ʾēl naʿărå̄ṣ bsōḏ malʾăḵē šḇīḇō*
**Dedication:** Parashat Eikev (Deuteronomy 7:12–11:25)
**Language:** Mod.SWKar.
**Number of copies:** 3

| Accession no. | Place of origin of copy | Date of copy | Copyist | Folios |
|---|---|---|---|---|
| ADub.III.61 | Halych | 1850/1851 | Jeshua Josef Mordkowicz | 137 vº–138 vº |
| JSul.III.69 | Halych | ca. 1851 (before 1866) | Jeshua Josef Mordkowicz | 295 vº–296 vº |
| JSul.III.79 | Halych | ca. 1851 (before 1866) | Jeshua Josef Mordkowicz | 178 vº–179 vº |

## 1 Introductory Remarks

In the headings, the name of Simcha ben Chananel, i.e. the author of the *peshat*, is referred to as 'Simcha the above-mentioned' or 'the above-mentioned', which means that the reader is redirected to the heading of *peshat* № 23 in ms. ADub.III.61, to the introduction to *peshat* № 9 in ms. JSul.III.69, and to the heading introducing *peshat* № 11 in ms. JSul.III.79.

The three copies are vocalized and there are almost no significant differences between them. The dissimilarities we find are mostly due to minor improvements made by the copyist. The only significant discrepancy, namely the portion of the text *kici byla jajynyn da qylycynyn ki* (24–25) that is worded differently in JSul.III.69 (as *qylycy byla ani jaj byla*), suggests that the copies in ADub.III.61 and JSul.III.79 have a stronger affinity with each other. Cf. also *bijnin* vs. *anyn* (5).

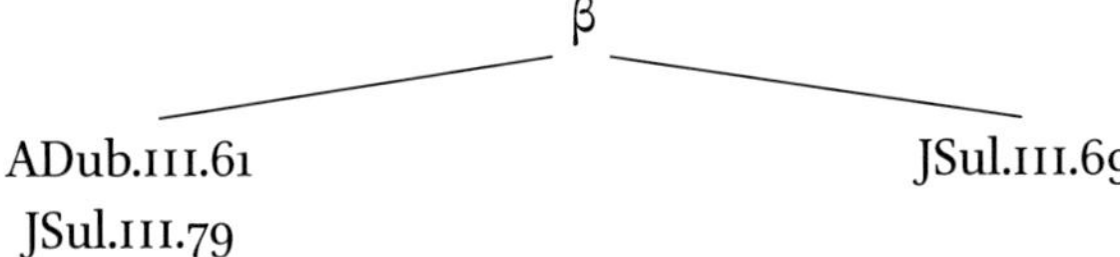


FIGURE 19 Diagram of the connections between the copies of peshat № 16

## 2 Transcription[962] and Translation

137 vº [1] [22] ⸤זה הפשט לפיוט פרשת עקב שהוא אֵל נַעֲרָץ בְּסוֹד מַלְאֲכֵי שְׁבִיבוֹ: תרגמו
[2] [23] מורנו הר״ר שמחה המתרגם הנ״ל זצוק״ל:⸣[963]
[3] [24] Kicli Tenri syrynda aziz malaẖlarnyn, oldur qojuvcu
[4] [25] aziz alhamin[964] icinde Mošenin siverinin,
[5] [26] oldu inamly kitivci da hammese avzunda maḥtavy[965] bijinin[966].
[6] [27] nobat[967]
138 rº [7] [1] Nobat kibik tatyjdylar erinleri anyn da solaqtaġy cyjbal kibik
[8] [2] tatlydylar sezleri avzunun, oldu ivretivci ulusuna
[9] [3] Tenrinin tiz jolnu jaḥsy etmek icin[968] anar sonġusunda kinlerinin.
[10] [4] Saruv saruv istine bujurdu ⸤saqlama anar⸣[969] micvalarny atlanġyzdyr-
[11] [5] maq icin any bijik orunlary istine aqylnyn, saqlaġany icin[970]
[12] [6] juvuq ulusu Tenrinin Jisra'el qylma terelerin Toranyn[971]. Saqlar anar
[13] [7] H sertin da savaġatny da tojdurur any[972] nametinden asajyslyq-
[14] [8] larynyn. Sarnavlary byla qutulmaqnyn bar jamandan qursar any keterir
[15] [9] bar qyjynyn anyn. Kicli alġyslarny ne ki jazdy Torada
[16] [10] toḥtatyr basy istine anyn. Alġyslar jemisin qursaġynyn da[973]
[17] [11] atlanyr teveleri istine dusmanlarynyn. Keterir andan bar

962 Based on ADub.III.61.
963 JSul.III.69: ואם תרצה תאמר גם פשטו שתרגמו החכם המתרגם כמוהרר שמחה הנ״ל יעמ״ש. | JSul.III.79: פשט לפיוט פרשת עקב תרגמו החכם הקדוש הנ״ל זצ״ל: לא נערצ.
964 JSul.III.69: *alhemin.* | JSul.III.79: *alhemin.*
965 JSul.III.69: *maḥtavu.* | JSul.III.79: *maḥtavu.*
966 JSul.III.69: *anyn.*
967 Catchword.
968 JSul.III.79: deest.
969 JSul.III.69: *anar saqlama.* | JSul.III.79: *anar saqlama.*
970 JSul.III.79: *ücin.*
971 JSul.III.79: *torasynyn.*
972 JSul.III.69: *any H.*
973 JSul.III.69: deest. | JSul.III.79: deest.
974 JSul.III.69: *And, if you prefer, say its* peshat [i.e., of the Hebrew original], *which the above-mentioned hakham the translator, his honour, the Rav, Rabbi Simcha translated, may he rest in peace.* | JSul.III.79: *A* peshat *of a* piyyut *for the parashat Eikev, which the above-mentioned holy hakham translated, may the memory of the righteous be a blessing.* (*Incipit:*) ʾēl naʿărâṣ.
975 Lit. 'put His inspiration into His beloved Moses'.
976 I.e., *Moses.*
977 JSul.III.69: *Him.*

[1] [22] ⌊And this is the *peshat* of a *piyyut* for the parashat Eikev, of that (with the incipit) *ʾēl naʿărås̱ bsōd̠ malʾăḵē šḇīḇō*, which 137 vº

[2] [23] our teacher, the above-mentioned Rav, Rabbi Simcha the translator translated, may the memory of the righteous and holy be a blessing.⌋[974]

[3] [24] The powerful God, (hidden) in the secret of holy angels, is who ⌊has filled

[4] [25] His beloved Moses with His holy inspiration⌋[975]:

[5] [26] he[976] is the trustworthy shepherd, and the praise of Lord[977] is always in his mouth.

[6] [27] [978]

[7] [1] His[979] lips are tasty like the flowing honey and 138 rº

[8] [2] his words are sweet like honey in the honeycomb; he is the one who teaches the people

[9] [3] of God the right way in order to do good to Him until the last of their days.

[10] [4] Instruction by instruction—he ordered to keep his commandments in order to seat

[11] [5] them[980] on the high places of wisdom (and) in order to guard

[12] [6] Israel, the dear people of God, to act (according to) ⌊the Law⌋[981]. The Lord will keep

[13] [7] His covenant and His mercy for them and will[982] satisfy them with the goods of pleasures.

[14] [8] With songs of salvation will He protect[983] them from any evil and

[15] [9] will take away all their suffering. He will place strong blessings, which He wrote in the Law,

[16] [10] on their heads. He will bless the fruits of their bosom and[984]

[17] [11] He will mount ⌊the camels of⌋[985] their enemies. He will take away from them all

---

978 Catchword in the Karaim text: ‘flowing honey’.

979 I.e., *Moses's*.

980 I.e., *the people of God*.

981 JSul.III.79: *His law*.

982 JSul.III.69: *the Lord will*.

983 Lit. ‘surround, enclose’.

984 JSul.III.69: deest. | JSul.III.79: deest.

985 Possibly a mistranslation in the Karaim text, cf. Deuteronomy 33:29.

[18] [12] ḥastalyqny da berir alarny anduvculary istine anyn.
[19] [13] Erklenir uluslar istine tivil ⌊kici byla jajynyn da qylycynyn
[20] [14] ki⌋[986] ancaq boluslugu byla Tenrisinin. Bolalyr ⌊tas etme⌋[987] alarny[988]
[21] [15] tigeller kleklerin jireginin, ki jarlyġasy H-nyn bolur qalqany da
[22] [16] kipligi anyn. Jonma abaqlaryn alarnyn kivdirir suqlanmastyr[989]
[23] [17] kerkine kimisinin da altynynyn. Maḥtavu Tenrinin bolur avzunda
[24] [18] anyn turġanyndan sortun da baslyġynda jatmaġynyn, anyn icin ki
[25] [19] burun qyjnady any da andan sortun asatty any da man byla
[26] [20] tojdurdu aclyġyn anyn. Quvat byla bajlandyrdy any hermet
[27] [21] byla qursady any ki tizetti any micvalary byla Toranyn
[28] [22] tensi etme any malaḫlary byla keklernin. Anyn icin kerek-
[29] [23] lidi ki kicin da azizligin qotarġaj astrylyġy byla bar kavvanasynyn.
[30] [24] Ceber šira[990] byla maḥtav bergej kicli Tenrige da qorqunclu bar
[31] [25] malaḫlar istine ol toḥtavcular civrelerinde aziz taḥtynyn.
[32] [26] Da ajtqaj e H Tenri jaratuvcu ceba'otnu joḥtur senin kibik kicli
138 vº [33] [1] Tenri jyjynynda aziz malaḫlarnyn[991]. ⌊הָ׳ אֱלֹהֵי צְבָאוֹת מִי
[34] [2] כָּמוֹךָ חֲסִין יָהּ וגו׳:⌉[992]

986 JSul.III.69: *qylycy byla ani jaj byla*.
987 ADub.III.61: טַש אֶיטְמֶיא. | JSul.III.69: טַס אֶיטְמֶיא. | JSul.III.79: טַש אֶיטְמֶיא.
988 JSul.III.69: *any*. | JSul.III.79: *any*.
989 JSul.III.69: *suqlanmasty*. | JSul.III.79: *suqlanmasty*.
990 JSul.III.79: *širalar*.
991 JSul.III.79: *malaḫlarynyn*.
992 Psalm 89:8. | JSul.III.69: ותֹּאמ הָ׳ אֱלֹהֵי צְבָאוֹת מִי כָמוֹךָ חֲסִין יָהּ וגו׳ (Psalm 89:8). | JSul.III.79: הָ׳ אֱלֹהֵי צְבָאוֹת מִי כָמוֹךָ וגו׳ (Psalm 89:8).

[18] [12] the diseases and will put[993] those to ⌊the ones that guard[994] them⌋[995].
[19] [13] He[996] will rule over nations not with ⌊the power of⌋[997] his bow and sword,
[20] [14] but by the providence of his God. He will be able to destroy them[998]
[21] [15] (and) will make the wishes of his heart come true, for the Lord's grace will be the shield and
[22] [16] the strength of him. He will burn down their carved idols (and) will not desire
[23] [17] the beauty of their silver and gold. The praise of God will be in his mouth,
[24] [18] after he wakes up and before[999] lying down, for
[25] [19] earlier, He had tormented him and after that fed him manna and
[26] [20] filled his hunger. He has girded him with strength and
[27] [21] has surrounded him with esteem and bettered him with the commandments of the Law
[28] [22] to make him equal to the angels of heavens. Therefore, it is necessary
[29] [23] to preach the power and holiness of all His intentions assiduously.
[30] [24] With a pleasant song[1000] may the powerful God be praised who is awesome
[31] [25] over all angels that dwell around His holy throne.
[32] [26] And may it be said ⌊'O Lord God the creator of hosts, there is no god strong like You
[33] [1] in the circles of angels[1001]'⌋[1002]. ⌊'O Lord God of hosts, who 138 v°
[34] [2] is a strong Lord like unto you?' and so on.⌋[1003]

993 Lit. 'give'.
994 I.e., *keep captive.*
995 I.e., *all future enemies.*
996 I.e., *Moses.*
997 JSul.III.69: desunt.
998 I.e., *the nations.* || JSul.III.69: *it.* | JSul.III.79: *it.*
999 Lit. 'at the beginning of'.
1000 JSul.III.79: *songs.*
1001 JSul.III.79: *His angels.*
1002 Cf. Psalm 89:8.
1003 Psalm 89:8. | JSul.III.69: *'O Lord God of hosts, who is a strong Lord like unto you? …' and so on.* (Psalm 89:8). | JSul.III.79: *'O Lord God of hosts, who is …' and so on.* (Psalm 89:8).

**Text number:** № 17
**Karaim incipit:** *Maḥtavludu ol Tenri Adonaj*
*Maḥtavludu ol Tenri H*
*Maḥtavludur ol Tenri H*
**Hebrew incipit:** בָּרוּךְ הָאֵל הָ׳ *bårūḵ hå'ēl H*
**Dedication:** Sukkot (on Shemini Atzeret)
**Language:** MSWKar., Early Mod.SWKar., Mod.SWKar.
**Number of copies:** 3

| Accession no. | Place of origin of copy | Date of copy | Copyist | Folios |
|---|---|---|---|---|
| JSul.I.54.03 | Halych (?) | turn of the 19th c. | Unknown 5 | 4 rº–4 vº |
| JSul.III.72 | Halych | before 1851 | Jeshua Josef Mordkowicz | 145 vº–146 rº |
| JSul.III.76 | Halych | 2nd half of the 19th c. | Jeshua Josef Mordkowicz | 116 vº–117 rº |

## 1 Introductory Remarks

In all three analysed manuscripts, Simcha ben Chananel, the author of the *peshat*, is refered to as "the above-mentioned": his name is explicitly mentioned in the headings introducing *peshatim* № 14 (mss. JSul.I.54.03 and JSul.III.72) and № 12 (JSul.III.76). All three copies are vocalized.

The versions in JSul.III.72 and JSul.III.76 are very similar to each other (having been copied by the same person), see *čerivü* vs. *bar čerivü* (3), *toranyn* vs. *aziz toranyn* (7), *künlernin* vs. *künlerinin* (8), *ḥyǯlavčularyna vs. bujurdu ḥyǯlavčularyna* (9), *ündelgen* vs. *ündeledoġan* (10), *künlerni* vs. *künlerde* (12), *kim* vs. *da kim* (14), and *jarčyqlavčusu tengizlernin* vs. *jarčyqlavču suvlaryn tengizlernin* (20). At the same time, in ms. JSul.III.72 we find erroneous forms that have either been corrected or not repeated by the same scribe in JSul.III.76, cf. *javdurtuvčusu* vs. *javduruvčusu* (15), *erenlerimiznin* vs. *erinlerimiznin* (22), *ornuna hammeše 'ola qarbanlarynyn* vs. *ornuna hammeselik qarbanlarynyn* (23), which is an argument supporting the view that JSul.III.76 is a more recent manuscript than JSul.III.72 (see also № 19). Based on the above we arrive at the following diagram of the relationships between the three copies:

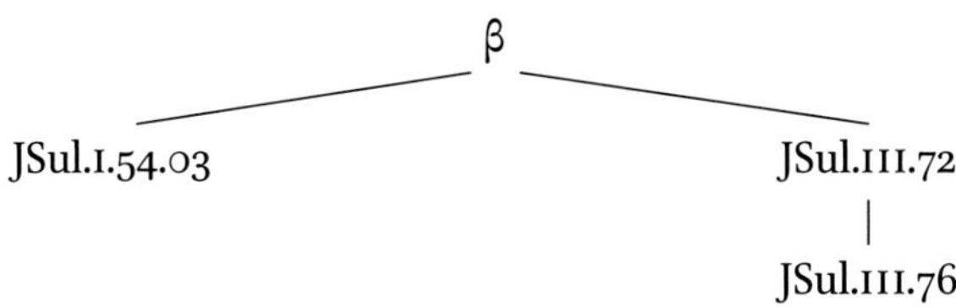


FIGURE 20 Diagram of the connections between the copies of peshat № 17

## 2 Transcription[1004] and Translation

4 rº

[1] [8] ⸤גם זה פשט פיוט ברוך האל ה́ הנ̃אמ

[2] [9] ביום מועד שמיני עצרת ׳ תרגמו החכם הנ̃ל נ̃ע⸣[1005]

[3] [10] Maḫtavludu[1006] ol Tenri Adonaj[1007] ki ol bijikrekti čerivü[1008]

[4] [11] üstüne[1009] bijiktegi köklernin[1010], ki sajlady {{bizn}}

[5] [12] bizni jaḫšyraq[1011] bar uruvlaryndan ol uluslarnyn, da berdi bizge

[6] [13] tügel[1012] töreler[1013] tüzülgenler[1014] učsuz[1015] usundan anyn, da körkejtti[1016]

[7] [14] bizni jaḫšyraq[1017] bar ol ummalardan micvalarybyla Toranyn[1018]. Da bujurdu

[8] [15] bizge qylma aziz moʿedlerin bijenčli[1019] künlernin[1020], da baryndan sortun

[9] [16] ḥyǯlavčularyna[1021] yštyrylyp[1022] tefile etme bet hamiqdašta {{künü}}

[10] [17] kününde[1023] Šemini ʿAceret ündelgen[1024] moʿednin. Bu kün[1025] aziz ündel-

[11] [18] miš[1026] künüdü[1027] tügenmeginin[1028] šaloš regalim moʿedlerinin. Zeḫut bolur

[12] [19] bizge bar ol künlerni[1029] alnynda Tenrinin, ki saqlasaq qylma bar

---

1004 Based on JSul.I.54.03.

1005 JSul.III.72: וזה פשטו של פיוט השני של יום שמיני עזרת שהוא ברוך האל ה́ על קדושת גואלנו ה́ להחכם הנ̃ל נ̃ע. | JSul.III.76: וזהו פשטו של פיוט בָרוּךְ הָאֵל הָ́ הנאמר ביום שמיני עצרת תרגמו המתקן פשט הנ̃ל זצו̃קל.

1006 JSul.III.76: *maḥtavludur.*

1007 JSul.III.72: *H.* | JSul.III.76: *H.*

1008 JSul.III.72: *bar čerüvü* or *bar cerüvü.* | JSul.III.76: *bar cerivi.*

1009 JSul.III.76: *istine.*

1010 JSul.III.76: *keklernin.*

1011 JSul.III.76: *jaḥsyraq.*

1012 JSul.III.76: *tigel.*

1013 JSul.III.76: *tereler.*

1014 JSul.III.76: *tizilgenler.*

1015 JSul.III.72: or: *ucsuz.* | JSul.III.76: *ucsuz.*

1016 JSul.III.72: *körkejti*; probably a scribal error. | JSul.III.76: *kerkejtti.*

1017 JSul.III.76: *jaḥsyraq.*

1018 JSul.III.72: *aziz toranyn.* | JSul.III.76: *aziz toranyn.*

1019 JSul.III.72: or: *bijencli.* | JSul.III.76: *bijencli.*

1020 JSul.III.72: *künlerinin.* | JSul.III.76: *kinlerinin.*

1021 JSul.III.72: *bujurdu ḥyǯlavčularyna or bujurdu ḥyʒlavcularyna.* | JSul.III.76: *bujurdu ḥyʒlavcularyna.*

[1] [8] ⌊In addition, this is a peshat of the *piyyut* (with the incipit) *bårūḵ hå'ēl H*, the one chanted 4 rº

[2] [9] on the holiday of Shemini Atzeret, which the above-mentioned hakham translated, may his soul rest in Eden.⌋[1030]

[3] [10] Praised is the Lord God who is above ⌊the army⌋[1031]

[4] [11] of the heavens above, who has chosen

[5] [12] us to be better than all the tribes of nations and has given us

[6] [13] complete laws prepared by His endless wisdom and beautified

[7] [14] us more than all the nations with the commandments of the Law[1032]. And He has ordered

[8] [15] us to celebrate[1033] the ⌊holy holidays of the joyful days⌋[1034] and (has ordered)

[9] [16] them[1035] who celebrated those (days) to pray in the temple after all (those days)

[10] [17] on the day of the holiday called Shemini Atzeret. That day

[11] [18] is the day of completion of the Three Pilgrimage Festivals, called holy. It will be a merit

[12] [19] of ours before God if, in those days, we would take care to do all

---

1022 JSul.III.72: *jystyrylyp.* | JSul.III.76: *ystyrylyp.*

1023 JSul.III.76: *kininde.*

1024 JSul.III.72: *ündeledoğan.* | JSul.III.76: *indeledoğan.*

1025 JSul.III.76: *kin.*

1026 JSul.III.72: *ündelmis.* | JSul.III.76: *indelmis.*

1027 JSul.III.76: *kinidi.*

1028 JSul.III.72: *tügenmegi.* | JSul.III.76: *tigenmegi.*

1029 JSul.III.72: *künlerde.* | JSul.III.76: *kinlerde.*

1030 JSul.III.72: *And this is a* peshat *of the second* piyyut *for the day of Shemini Atzeret, of that* (*with the incipit*) bårūḵ hå'ēl H, (*said*) *to the holy* gō'ălēnū H [see, Isaiah 47:4], (*the interpretation*) *of the above-mentioned hakham, may his soul rest in Eden.* | JSul.III.76: *And this is a* peshat *of the* piyyut (*with the incipit*) bårūḵ hå'ēl H, *the one chanted on the day of Shemini Atzeret, which the above-mentioned reformer of peshatim translated, may the memory of the righteous and holy be a blessing.*

1031 JSul.III.72: *all armies.* | JSul.III.76: *all armies.*

1032 JSul.III.72: *holy Law.* | JSul.III.76: *holy Law.*

1033 Lit. 'do'.

1034 I.e., *the intermediate days of Sukkot* (cf. the dedication of this *piyyut*); cf. also PBHeb. מוֹעֵד 'half-holy-day, intermediate days of Pesach and Sukkot'.

1035 JSul.III.72: *He ordered them.* | JSul.III.76: *He ordered them.*

[13] [20] ol bijik resimlerin aziz Toranyn, qorqma Adonaj[1036] Tenrimizden ki

[14] [21] oldu jaratuvčusu[1037] üč[1038] dunjalarnyn. Ol jamġur berse kim[1039] tyjalyr

[15] [22] da beklese bulutlarny ki{m} barmodu javdurtuvčusu[1040] alarnyn. Oldu

[16] [23] qondaruvču[1041] bijik köklerde[1042] jergelerin galgallarynyn. Alajoq bavyn

4 vº [17] [1] özünün[1043] qojdu juvuz dunjada bolma erklenmekleri tübüne[1044] alarnyn.

[18] [2] Oldu čaġyruvču[1045] suvlaryna ol tengiznin da tögedi[1046] alarny jüzleri[1047] üstüne[1048]

[19] [3] jernin avazybyla kök[1049] kökremeklerinin[1050]. Anyn kleginden bašqa[1051] beremodular[1052]

[20] [4] ol kökler[1053] tamčylaryn[1054] jamġurlarnyn. Muna oldu Tenrimiz jarčyqlavčusu[1055]

[21] [5] tengizlernin[1056]. Anyn üčün[1057] umsunajyq anar tügelligibyla[1058] jüreknin[1059],

[22] [6] da anyn syjly šemine šükür[1060] etejik tefileleribyla[1061] erinlerimiznin[1062]

[23] [7] erteli kečeli[1063] qozulary ornuna[1064] ʿola qarbanlarynyn. Nečik[1065] jazylġandy

---

1036 JSul.III.72: *H.* | JSul.III.76: *H.*

1037 JSul.III.72: or: *jaratuvcusu.* | JSul.III.76: *jaratuvcusu.*

1038 JSul.III.72: or: *üc.* | JSul.III.76: *ic.*

1039 JSul.III.72: *da kim.* | JSul.III.76: *da kim.*

1040 The verbal base is *javdurt-*, a double causative form, i.e. *jav.dur.t-.* || JSul.III.72: *javduruvčusu* or *javduruvcusu.* | JSul.III.76: *javduruvcusu.*

1041 JSul.III.72: *qundaruvču* or *qundaruvcu*; a scribal error. | JSul.III.76: *qondaruvcu.*

1042 JSul.III.76: *keklerde.*

1043 JSul.III.76: *ezinin.*

1044 JSul.III.76: *tibine.*

1045 JSul.III.72: or: *caġyruvcu.* | JSul.III.76: *caġyruvcu.*

1046 JSul.III.76: *tegedi.*

1047 JSul.III.76: *izleri.*

1048 JSul.III.76: *istine.*

1049 JSul.III.76: *kek.*

1050 JSul.III.76: *kekremeklerinin.*

1051 JSul.III.76: *basqa.*

1052 JSul.III.72: *beremodlar.*

1053 JSul.III.76: *kekler.*

1054 JSul.III.72: or: *tamcylaryn.* | JSul.III.76: *tamcylaryn.*

[13] [20] the great statutes of the holy Law and to fear our Lord God, for

[14] [21] He is the creator of the three worlds. ⌊When He makes the rain fall⌋[1066], who is able to stop it?

[15] [22] And when[1067] He locks the clouds, is there anyone (able) to ⌊make them rain⌋[1068]? He is

[16] [23] the creator[1069] of the line of (celestial) spheres in high heavens and so

[17] [1] did He place His bonds on the low world to be under their[1070] command. 4 v°

[18] [2] He is who calls the waters of the sea and He pours them on the surface of the earth

[19] [3] with the sound of thunders of the sky. Would the heavens give

[20] [4] drops of rains without His will? Lo, He is our God who splits

[21] [5] the seas[1071]. For this reason we shall ⌊rest our hopes in⌋[1072] Him with whole hearts

[22] [6] and we shall thank His honourable name with prayers of our lips[1073]

[23] [7] ⌊in lieu of⌋[1074] ⌊burnt offerings⌋[1075] of lamb (offered) in the mornings and night. As it is written:

---

1055 JSul.III.72: *jarčyqlavču* or *jarcyqlavcu*. | JSul.III.76: *jarcyqlavcu*.

1056 JSul.III.72: *suvlaryn tengizlernin*. | JSul.III.76: *suvlaryn tengizlernin*.

1057 JSul.III.72: or: *ücün*. | JSul.III.76: *icin*.

1058 JSul.III.76: *tigelligi byla*.

1059 JSul.III.76: *jireknin*.

1060 JSul.III.76: *sikir*.

1061 JSul.III.72: *tefilaleri byla*.

1062 JSul.III.72: *erenlerimiznin*; most probably a scribal error.

1063 JSul.III.72: *kečeli* or *keceli*. | JSul.III.76: *keceli*.

1064 JSul.III.72: *ornuna hammeše*; the use of *hammeše* instead of *hammešelik* is perhaps a result of a scribal error (cf. JSul.III.76). | JSul.III.76: *ornuna hammeselik*.

1065 JSul.III.72: *nečik* or *necik*. | JSul.III.76: *necik*.

1066 Lit. 'if He gives rain'.

1067 Lit. 'if'.

1068 JSul.III.72, JSul.III.76: expressed with a synonym.

1069 Lit. 'builder'.

1070 I.e., *of the celestial spheres*.

1071 JSul.III.72: *the waters of seas*. | JSul.III.76: *the waters of seas*.

1072 Or: *wait for*.

1073 JSul.III.72: *men*; rather a scribal error: cf. *erin* 'lip' vs. *eren* 'man, person of trust'.

1074 JSul.III.72: *always in lieu of*; however, the use of *hammeše* 'always' instead of *hammešelik* 'endless' might be an error; see the next footnote and the respective commentary in the transcription.

1075 JSul.III.76: *endless burnt offerings*.

[24] [8] šükür[1076] etsinler cadiqler ullu da qorqunčlu[1077] syjly šemine Tenrinin.

[25] [9] ⌞ככתוב יודו שמך גדול ונורא קדוש הוא: יודו לה׳ חסדו ׳⌝[1078]

1076 JSul.III.76: *sikir*.

1077 JSul.III.72: or: *qorqunclu*. | JSul.III.76: *qorqunclu*.

1078 Psalm 99:3; Psalm 107:8. | JSul.III.72: כַּכָּתוּב יוֹדוּ שִׁמְךָ גָּדוֹל וְנוֹרָא קָדוֹשׁ הוּא: וכו׳. | JSul.III.76: כַּכָּתוּב יוֹדוּ שִׁמְךָ גָּדוֹל וְנוֹרָא קָדוֹשׁ הוּא.

[24] [8] 'May the just thank the great and awesome honourable name of God.'

[25] [9] As it is written: ⌊'Let them praise Your great and awesome name; for it is holy. O that men would praise the Lord for his goodness.'⌋[1079]

1079 Psalm 99:3; Psalm 107:8. | JSul.III.72: *'O that men would praise the Lord for his goodness …' et cetera.* (Psalm 107:8). | JSul.III.76: *'O that men would praise the Lord for his goodness.'* (Psalm 107:8).

**Text number:** № 18
**Karaim incipit:** *Necik joḥtu tensi qajjam Tenrige*
**Hebrew incipit:** אֵין עֲרוֹךְ לְאֵל יָהּ *ʾēn ʿărōḵ lʾēl yåh*
**Dedication:** Parashat Vayikra (Leviticus 1:1–5:26)
**Language:** Early Mod.SWKar.
**Number of copies:** 1

| Accession no. | Place of origin of copy | Date of copy | Copyist | Folios |
|---|---|---|---|---|
| JSul.I.45 | Halych | 1st half of the 19th c. | Jeshua Josef Mordkowicz | 140 rº–141 rº |

## 1 Introductory Remarks

The only known copy is vocalized. *Peshat* № 29 is an interpretation of the same *piyyut*, but it was written by another person (by Mordechai ben Shemuel).

## 2 Transcription and Translation

140 rº [1] [6] וזה הפשט הראשון לפיוט פרשת ויקרא שהוא אין ערוך לאל יה תרגמו
[2] [7] אמ̃ו הה̃ו כמוה̃רר שמחה החזן נב̃ת בכמ̃עד חננאל הזקן יעמ̃ש:
[3] [8] Necik joḥtu tensi qajjam Tenrige alaj joḥtu tensi
[4] [9] tamaša islerine anyn. Ulluluġun anyn
[5] [10] syjyndyralmajdylar kökler da ol juvuz dunjada toludu
[6] [11] šeḫinasy anyn. Fikiri har kisinin jetelmesti kelme
[7] [12] tergeme syrlaryn anyn. Ancaq tamaša micvalaryn
[8] [13] Torasynyn ivrendik avzundan Moše rabenunun inamly
[9] [14] navisinin. Turġuzulup sortun miškan eki keruvim
[10] [15] arasyndan esitiredi inin Tenrinin, ki bolalmady
[11] [16] kelme ohel moʿedge ki bulutbyla boldu toḥtamaġy
[12] [17] qorqunclu šeḫinasynyn Tenrinin. Ki joḥtu andij
[13] [18] adam dunjada ki bolġaj rast da ki jazyqly bolmaġaj
[14] [19] jamanlyġy sartyn ⌊jaman jecerinin[1080], anlyq byla ki eki ʒan-
[15] [20] lary byla tensidi bar tilsiz tirilerge da alar
140 vº [16] [1] hammeše cyġysynda da kirisinde anyn. Ancaq
[17] [2] aqyllyq ʒan byla bergen adamġa Tenriden ajyryc
[18] [3] boldu alardan da anyn byla ol tilsiz tiriler isti-
[19] [4] ne boldu syjy anyn. Muna jazyqly bolġanda qarban
[20] [5] keltirsin tuvarny özü kibik tirini da jengillenir
[21] [6] igi anyn, tirini da esedoġanny ki ol remezdi qarban-
[22] [7] ġa tirkisi byla aruv etme any jemese murdar
[23] [8] etme any. Da köreklidi[1081] ki saġys etkej ki tegil-
[24] [9] megi kibik qanynyn da kivmegi kibik javynyn ol ʿola-

1080 A calque of Heb. יֵצֶר הָרַע 'the evil inclination', see Genesis 6:5 and 8:21.
1081 A hypercorrect form of *kereklidi*.
1082 Expressed with *rabenu*, i.e., Heb. רַבֵּינוּ 'our rabbi'.
1083 Lit. 'with this'.
1084 I.e., *the good soul and the evil soul*.
1085 I.e., *the animals and plants*.
1086 I.e., *the two souls*.
1087 I.e., *from the animals and plants*.
1088 I.e., *a (sacrifice of) livestock and plants*.
1089 Or: *sacrificial table*.
1090 Lit. 'thinks'.

[1] [6] And this is the first *peshat* of the *piyyut* for the parashat Vayikra, of that (with the incipit) *ʾēn ʿărōḵ lʾēl yåh*, which 140 r°
[2] [7] our master, our teacher, the great and honourable sage, his honour, the Rav, Rabbi Simcha the hazzan translated, may his soul lodge in Eden, the son of Chananel, the aged, whose honourable repose is Eden, may he rest in peace.
[3] [8] As there is nothing equal to God, so there is nothing equal
[4] [9] to His wondrous deeds.
[5] [10] The heavens are not able to hold His greatness and the low world is full of
[6] [11] His divine Presence. The intellect of all men will not be enough to come
[7] [12] and fathom His secret. But we have learned the wondrous commandments
[8] [13] of His Law through the mouth of ⌞our master⌝[1082], Moses, His trustworthy
[9] [14] prophet. After the Tabernacle had been put up,
[10] [15] he heard the voice of God (coming) from between the two cherubim, since he could not
[11] [16] come into the tent of meeting, since it became the place of dwelling
[12] [17] by the cloud of the awesome divine Presence of God. For there is no such
[13] [18] man in the world that would be just and who would not be sinful,
[14] [19] because of the evil of the evil inclination, ⌞and also⌝[1083] since
[15] [20] with one's ⌞two souls⌝[1084] one is equal to all ⌞the mute living beings⌝[1085] and they[1086]
[16] [1] are (with one) always: at the time of his departure and arrival. But 140 v°
[17] [2] the wisdom and the heart given to the man from God
[18] [3] have been separated ⌞from them⌝[1087], and with that His fame
[19] [4] has been over the mute. Lo, in his sinfulness, one shall
[20] [5] bring sacrifice, cattle, living like him himself, and
[21] [6] his burden will become lighter: ⌞a living or growing (sacrifice)⌝[1088] for it is an allegory of sacrifice—
[22] [7] of making him(self) clean with his sacrifice[1089] or desecrating
[23] [8] him(self). And it is necessary that he ⌞is convinced⌝[1090] that like pouring
[24] [9] the blood and like burning the fat of the burnt offering,

[25] [10] nyn alaj tegilgej qany da kivgej javy ol jazyqly boluvcu
[26] [11] adamnyn, ki bir tirlü dert bunjattan boldu jaratylmaq-
[27] [12] lary alarnyn, bir ivretiv kohenge da ʒymatqa da
[28] [13] nasige da ulusuna ol jernin. Da kereklidi ki ol
[29] [14] jazyqly boluvcu tekkej gilejin jalbarmaqlar byla alnynda
[30] [15] bir jaratuvcusunun, da qabul etkej ʒany isti-
[31] [16] ne ki qajtmaġaj artyq jaman islerine qajtqanlaj
[32] [17] it qusqununa ezinin. Ki synyq ʒanly kisiden
[33] [18] begenedi Tenri jaḥsyraq bujvolundan šelamim debeḥa-
[34] [19] synyn, da jazyqly bolmajyn keltirse tirkisin
[35] [20] ezeknin da tavada islengen[1091] da quvurġan da panv́ada
[36] [21] islengen qabul etedi Tenri ʒomartlyqlar keltirge-
[37] [22] ninin. Bundij kecinmekler byla kecinivcü zoẖe
[38] [23] bolady kerme jarlyġasyn H-nyn, sandyr andij kisige
[39] [24] ki körtü ʒan byla jalbarsa alnynda Tenrisinin,
[40] [25] andijnin ʒanyn qabul eter Tenri tivincigine ol
[41] [26] tirliknin[1092]
141 r° [42] [1] tirliknin da toḥtatyr any tibinde aziz taḥtynyn.
[43] [2] ⌊Ki juvuqtur hašgahasy H-nyn tigelleme klegin qorquv-
[44] [3] cularynyn.⌉[1093] [1094]⌈אַךְ קָרוֹב לִירֵאָיו יִשְׁעוֹ וגו׳:⌋

---

1091 Spelled אִישְׁלֵינְגֵן; the letter *shin* is used also for noting [s] in this text, see יֶמֶישֶׁי *jemese* in line 22 and כֵילְטִירְשֶׁיא *keltirse* in line 34.

1092 Catchword.

1093 Psalm 85:9.

1094 Psalm 85:9.

1095 Lit. 'to pour'.

1096 Lit. 'takes on his soul'; a calque of Russ. *на душу взять* 'to take responsibility for; to pledge'.

1097 Expressed with Kar. *bujvol* < Russ. *буйвол* 'bufallo'. Given that all animal sacrifices in the Torah are of domestic animals, here it is perhaps used in the meaning of 'bull'. Cf. also 29:32.

[25] [10] so should be poured the blood and should be burned the fat of a sinful
[26] [11] man, for their creation had the same four fundaments.
[27] [12] There is one teaching for the priest and for the congregation and
[28] [13] for the princes and for the people of the earth. And it is necessary that the
[29] [14] sinful reveals[1095] the sorrow of his heart in prayers before the
[30] [15] only creator, and that he pledges[1096]
[31] [16] not to come back any more to his evil deeds like a dog who comes back
[32] [17] to its own vomit. For a contrite hearted man pleases
[33] [18] God more than a sacrifice of a buffalo[1097] (offered) for peace offerings;
[34] [19] and if someone not being sinful brings his sacrifice of ⌊wheat (flour)⌉[1098]
[35] [20] prepared in a pan and fried or prepared in a (shallow) cauldron,
[36] [21] God will accept the generosity of the one who brought (it).
[37] [22] ⌊The one who behaves so⌉[1099] has the honour
[38] [23] of seeing the grace[1100] of the Lord; He thinks of such men
[39] [24] who pray before God with true heart,
[40] [25] God will accept the soul of such (men) ⌊(to be bound) in the bundle
[41] [26] ⌊of life⌉[1101]
[42] [1] of life⌉[1102] and He will place him near His holy throne. 141 r°
[43] [2] For the providence of the Lord is near to perform the wish of those that fear
[44] [3] him. ⌊'Surely His salvation is near those that fear him …' and so on.⌉[1103]

---

1098 Cf. *özek un* 'wheat flour' in 29:33.

1099 Lit. 'the one who behaves with such a behaviour'.

1100 Or: *salvation*.

1101 Catchword in the Karaim text.

1102 Lit. 'for the bundle of life' (see, 1Samuel 25:29).

1103 Psalm 85:9.

**Text number:** № 19
**Karaim incipit:** *Qajjam avalġy Tenri*
**Hebrew incipit:** יֹושֵׁב קֶדֶם *yōšēḇ qeḏem*
**Dedication:** Sukkot (on Shemini Atzeret)
**Language:** MSWKar., Early Mod.SWKar., Mod.SWKar.
**Number of copies:** 3

| Accession no. | Place of origin of copy | Date of copy | Copyist | Folios |
|---|---|---|---|---|
| JSul.I.54.03 | Halych (?) | turn of the 19th c. | Unknown 5 | 4 vº–5 rº |
| JSul.III.72 | Halych | before 1851 | Jeshua Josef Mordkowicz | 146 vº–147 rº |
| JSul.III.76 | Halych | 2nd half of the 19th c. | Jeshua Josef Mordkowicz | 117 rº–117 vº |

## 1 Introductory Remarks

The author of the *peshat* is refered to as "the above-mentioned" in the copies found: Simcha ben Chananel's name is included in the respective headings of *peshatim* № 14 (in mss. JSul.I.54.03 and JSul.III.72) and № 12 (in ms. JSul.III.76). All three copies are vocalized.

The differences between the texts are minor. Copied by the same person, the texts in JSul.III.72 and JSul.III.76 are more similar to each other, see *ḥyǯynyn ol Sukotnun* vs. *ḥyǯynyn ol macalarnyn da jedi künü* (~ *kini*) *ol Sukotnun* (6–7), *har* vs. *har bir* (5, 25), *bizni* vs. *bizge* (9), *ǯanymyzny* vs. *ǯanlarymyzny* (~ *zanlarymyzny*) (10), *tüzüjüz* vs. *töginiz* (~ *teginiz*) (12), *tefilelerbyla* vs. *tefilabyla* (~ *tefile byla*) (12), *jalbarmaqlarbyla* ~ *jalbarmaqbyla* (13), *ol* vs. *ošol* (~ *osol*) *ol* (23), *sahardan* vs. *sahardan da saladan* (25), *avzuda* ~ *avzundan* (27), and *bolġaj qotarylġan* ~ *qotarylġaj* (28). There are two erroneous forms in JSul.III.72 that are not repeated in JSul.III.76, namely *'Aceret* vs. *'Aceretnin* (7), *ündemekbyla* vs. *indelmekbyla* (7), which suggests that JSul.III.76 is a more recent manuscript (cf. № 17). The relationship between the copies can be presented thus:

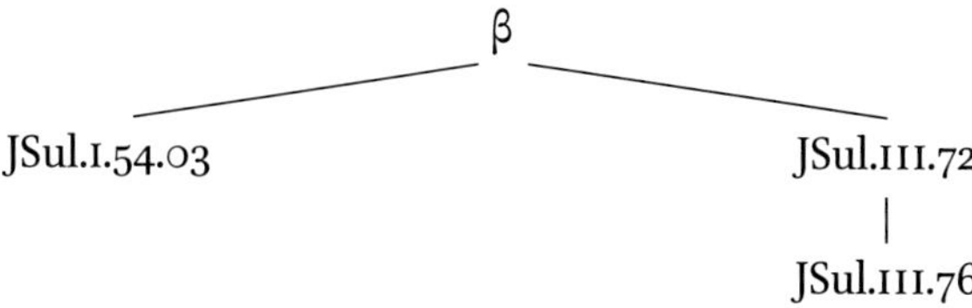


FIGURE 21 Diagram of the connections between the copies of peshat № 19

## 2 Transcription[1104] and Translation

4 v° [1] [10] ⌊גם זה פשט של פיוט יוֹשֵׁב קדֻם ליום מועד הנ̃ל להחכם הנ̃ל נ̃ע׳⌉[1105]

[2] [11] {יוֹשֵׁב}[1106]. Qajjam avalġy Tenri čyġarġanda[1107] atalarymyzny jerinden Micrinin

[3] [12] ullu tamašalyqlarbyla, jürüttü[1108] alarny[1109] pusta jerde

[4] [13] midbarda qyrq jyl da qaplady alarny bulut byla. Da anyn üčün[1110]

[5] [14] bujurdu bizge qylma moʿedler üč[1111] keretler har[1112] jylda saġynma

[6] [15] savaġatlaryn anyn maḥtavlarbyla, ki oldu jedi künü[1113] ḥyǯynyn[1114] ol Sukot-

[7] [16] nun[1115] da Šemini ʿAceretnin[1116] [ö]zü[1117] [ö]züne[1118] moʿed ündelmekbyla[1119].

[8] [17] {דֶּרֶךְ}[1120]. Jolubyla tirliknin jürüttü[1121] bizni bermegibyla bizge[1122] aziz

[9] [18] Torany da kijindirdi biz[ge][1123] ḥörmet[1124] küčlü[1125] micvalarybyla.

[10] [19] Ömürlük[1126] tirlik byla asajyšlatty[1127] ǯanymyzny[1128] qojġanynda[1129] bizge

---

1104 Based on JSul.I.54.03.

1105 JSul.III.72: גם זה פשט לפיוט חמישי של יום שמיני עצרת על קדושת שמע ישראל שהוא יוֹשֵׁב קֶדֶם. | JSul.III.76: פשט שליש לפיוט יושב קדם הנאמר ביום והוא כמו כן להחכם הנ̃ל שמיני אצרת תרגמו הר̃ר שמחה הנ̃ל תנצ̃בה.

1106 JSul.III.72: deest. | JSul.III.76: deest.

1107 JSul.III.76: *čyġarġanda.*

1108 JSul.III.76: *jiritti.*

1109 JSul.III.76: *bizni*; a scribal error; cf. the sentence-ending fragment: *qaplady alarny bulut byla.*

1110 JSul.III.76: *icin.*

1111 JSul.III.76: *ic.*

1112 JSul.III.72: *har bir.* | JSul.III.76: *har bir.*

1113 JSul.III.76: *kini.*

1114 JSul.III.76: *ḥyʒynyn.*

1115 JSul.III.72: *macalarnyn da jedi künü ol Sukotnun.* | JSul.III.76: *macalarnyn da jedi kini ol Sukotnun.*

1116 JSul.III.72: *ʿAceret.*

1117 JSul.I.54.03: *üzü*; a scribal error or a result of assimilation. | JSul.III.72: *özü.* | JSul.III.76: *ezi.*

1118 JSul.I.54.03: *üzüne*; a scribal error or a result of assimilation. | JSul.III.72: *özüne.* | JSul.III.76: *ezine.*

1119 JSul.III.72: *ündemekbyla.* | JSul.III.76: *indelmekbyla.*

1120 JSul.III.72: דֶּרֶךְ חַיִּים. | JSul.III.72: דֶּרֶךְ חַיִּים.

1121 JSul.III.76: *jiritti.*

[1] [10] ⌊In addition, this is a *peshat* of a *piyyut* (with the incipit) *yōšēḇ qeḏem* for the above-mentioned holiday of the above-mentioned hakham, may his soul rest in Eden.⌉[1130] 4 vº
[2] [11] When the ancient powerful God took our fathers[1131] from the land of Egypt
[3] [12] with great wonders He led them[1132] in the desert,
[4] [13] in the steppes, for forty years and covered them with a cloud. And for this reason
[5] [14] He has ordered us to celebrate[1133] holidays three times every[1134] year to remember
[6] [15] His mercies with praise, since these are the seven days of the feasts named[1135] the Feast of Sukkot
[7] [16] and of Shemini Atzeret.
[8] [17] (2). He led us along the way of life by giving us[1136] the holy
[9] [18] Law, and clothed us in glory by His powerful commandments.
[10] [19] He made our soul[1137] relish eternal life when He put on us

---

1122 JSul.III.72: deest. | JSul.III.76: deest.

1123 JSul.I.54.03: *bizni*; probably a scribal error. | JSul.III.72: *bizge*. | JSul.III.76: *bizge*.

1124 JSul.III.76: *hermet*.

1125 JSul.III.76: *kicli*.

1126 JSul.III.76: *emirlik*.

1127 JSul.III.76: *asajyslatty*.

1128 JSul.III.72: *ǯanlarymyzny*. | JSul.III.76: *ʒanlarymyzny*.

1129 JSul.I.54.03: *qojaġanynda*; a scribal error. | JSul.III.72: *qojġanynda*. | JSul.III.76: *qojġany byla*.

1130 JSul.III.72: *In addition, this is the fifth* peshat *of a* piyyut *for Shemini Atzeret to the holy Shema Yisrael, of that* (*with the incipit*) yōšēḇ qeḏem, *and it is also* (*an interpretation*) *of the above-mentioned hakham*. | JSul.III.76: *The third* peshat *of the* piyyut (*with the incipit*) yōšēḇ qeḏem, *the one chanted on the day of Shemini Atzeret, which the above-mentioned Rav, Rabbi Simcha translated, 'may his soul be bound in the bond of life'* [cf., 1Samuel 25:29].

1131 Or: *ancestors*.

1132 JSul.III.76: *us*.

1133 Lit. 'do'.

1134 JSul.III.72: *every single*. | JSul.III.76: *every single*.

1135 Lit. 'with itself's name'.

1136 JSul.III.72: deest. | JSul.III.76: deest.

1137 JSul.III.72: *souls*. | JSul.III.76: *souls*.

[11] [20] saqlav jürüme[1138] resimleri byla. Bunun üčün[1139] e ulusu Jisraʾelnin

[12] [21] sajlanmušlary[1140] anyn tüzüjüz[1141] alnynda anyn gilejinizni tefileler-byla[1142]

[13] [22] da jalbarmaqlarbyla[1143], ošpu[1144] künde ündeledoġan[1145] Šemini ʿAceret byla.

[14] [23] {נוֹרא}[1146]. Qorqunčlu[1147] da küčlü[1148] Tenri zynharlady bizge Torada

5 rº [15] [1] avalġy zamandan, saqlama micvalaryn özünün[1149] da ḥyǯlama[1150] har jylda üč[1151]

[16] [2] keretler saġynčyna[1152] čyqmaqnyn[1153] Micriden. Da bu künnü[1154] ündedi[1155] ʿAceret

[17] [3] jyštyrynyp[1156] tefile etme bet hamiqdašta arynyp bar jazyqlardan. Da

[18] [4] barysyn b[u]n[u][1157] qyldy tüvül[1158] öz[1159] fajdasy üčün[1160] ančaq[1161] ki jaḥšy[1162] bolġaj

[19] [5] bizge bar ol künlerni[1163] qorq[q]anymyz[1164] üčün[1165] Adonaj Tenrimizden.

[20] [6] {רחוּם}[1166]. Raḥmetlevčü[1167] da ḥajüfsünüvčü[1168] Tenri janġyrtma künlerimizni[1169]

[21] [7] avaldaġylaj küvüllengej[1170]. Nečik[1171] qondarġanda ˪Šlomo hameleḫ˩[1172] burunġu

[22] [8] bet hamiqdašny Šemini ʿAceret kününde[1173] ijdi ošol[1174] ol ulusnu

---

1138 JSul.III.76: *jirime.*
1139 JSul.III.76: *icin.*
1140 JSul.III.76: *sajlanmuslary.*
1141 JSul.III.72: *töginiz.* | JSul.III.76: *teginiz.*
1142 JSul.III.72: *tefilabyla.* | JSul.III.76: *tefile byla.*
1143 JSul.III.72: *jalbarmaqbyla.* | JSul.III.76: *jalbarmaq byla.*
1144 JSul.III.72: *ušpu.* | JSul.III.76: *uspu.*
1145 JSul.III.76: *indelgen.*
1146 JSul.III.72: נוֹרא ואיוֹם. | JSul.III.72: נוֹרא ואיום.
1147 JSul.III.76: *qorqunclu.*
1148 JSul.III.76: *kicli.*
1149 JSul.III.76: *ezinin.*
1150 JSul.III.76: *ḥyʒlama.*
1151 JSul.III.76: *ic.*
1152 JSul.III.76: *saġyncyna.*
1153 JSul.III.76: *cyqmaqnyn.*
1154 JSul.III.76: *kinni.*
1155 JSul.III.76: *indedi.*
1156 JSul.III.72: *jyštyrylyp.* | JSul.III.76: *ystyrynyp.*
1157 JSul.I.54.03: *bünü*; a scribal error. | JSul.III.72: *bunu.* | JSul.III.76: *bunu.*

[11] [20] an obligation[1175] to walk with His statutes. For this reason, O, people of Israel,
[12] [21] His chosen ones, compose[1176] before Him your confession in prayers
[13] [22] and entreaties—in this day called Shemini Atzeret.
[14] [23] (3). The awesome and powerful God has instructed us in the Law
[15] [1] since long ago to keep His own commandments and to celebrate three times each year 5 r°
[16] [2] in the memory of leaving Egypt. And He has named this day Atzeret
[17] [3] in order to assemble and pray in the temple and to get purified from sins. And
[18] [4] He has not done all these (things) for His own benefit, but in order that
[19] [5] all these days may be good for us, ⌊(in order) that we fear the Lord our God⌋[1177].
[20] [6] (4). Merciful and gracious God, may it be decided
[21] [7] to restore ⌊our days of old⌋[1178]. And in the way (the people) blessed the Lord when King Solomon built the First
[22] [8] Temple (and) sent the people on the day of Shemini Atzeret

1158 JSul.III.76: *tivil.*
1159 JSul.III.76: *ez.*
1160 JSul.III.76: *icin.*
1161 JSul.III.76: *ancaq.*
1162 JSul.III.76: *jaḥsy.*
1163 JSul.III.76: *kinlerni.*
1164 JSul.I.54.03: *qorqanymyz*; probably a scribal error. | JSul.III.72: *qorqqanymyz.* | JSul.III.76: *qorqqanymyz.*
1165 JSul.III.76: *icin.*
1166 JSul.III.72: רחֿום וחנֿון.
1167 JSul.III.76: *raḥmetlevci.*
1168 JSul.III.72: *ḥajifsünüvčü.* | JSul.III.76: *ḥajifsinivci.*
1169 JSul.III.76: *kinlerimizni.*
1170 JSul.III.76: *kivillengej.*
1171 JSul.III.76: *necik.*
1172 Heb. שְׁלֹמֹה הַמֶּלֶךְ, i.e., King Solomon the son of David called Jedidiah.
1173 JSul.III.76: *kininde.*
1174 JSul.III.76: *osol.*
1175 Lit. 'guard'.
1176 JSul.III.72: lit. 'pour'. | JSul.III.76: lit. 'pour'.
1177 I.e., *in order that we should remain alive to have the opportunity to fear Him.*
1178 Lit. 'our days as they were in the past'.

[23] [9] čatyrlaryna[1179] da alġyšladylar[1180] {{alar}} ol[1181] bijni alaj qondarylġanda
[24] [10] kelesi bet hamiqdaš meleẖ hamašijaḥ avzundan bar kol Jisra'el[nin][1182] alġyšlanġaj[1183].
[25] [11] Kertiden kötürgej[1184] alam da har[1185] sahardan[1186] da har[1187] valajattan t[o]zulġanlaryn[1188]
[26] [12] Jisra'elnin jomdarġaj. Da bolġaj Adonaj[1189] jalġyz [ö]zü[1190] bij bar ol jer
[27] [13] üstüne[1191] da barlyġyda birligi[1192] anyn avzunda[1193] bar tennin
[28] [14] ⌊bolġaj qotarylġan[1194]. [1195]⌈והיה ה׳ למלך על כל הארץ׳⌋

1179 JSul.III.76: *catyrlaryna.*
1180 JSul.III.76: *alġysladylar.*
1181 JSul.III.72: *ošol ol.* | JSul.III.76: *osol ol.*
1182 JSul.I.54.03: *Jisra'el*; a scribal error. | JSul.III.72: *Jisra'elnin.* | JSul.III.76: *Jisra'elnin.*
1183 JSul.III.76: *alġyslanġaj.*
1184 JSul.III.72: *kötirgej.* | JSul.III.76: *ketirgej.*
1185 JSul.III.72: *har bir.* | JSul.III.76: *har bir.*
1186 JSul.III.72: *sahardan da saladan.* | JSul.III.76: *sahardan da saladan.*
1187 JSul.III.76: *har bir.*
1188 JSul.I.54.03: *tuzulġanlaryn*; probably a scribal error a result of assimilation. | JSul.III.72: *tozulġanlaryn.*
1189 JSul.III.72: *H.* | JSul.III.76: *H.*
1190 JSul.III.72: *özü.* | JSul.III.76: *ezi.*
1191 JSul.III.76: *istine.*
1192 JSul.I.54.03: *birliginin*; a scribal error. | JSul.III.72: *birligi.* | JSul.III.76: *birligi.*
1193 JSul.III.72: *avzundan.* | JSul.III.76: *avzundan.*

[23] [9] to (dwell in) their tents, so may, (in the times) when

[24] [10] the next Temple will be built, ⌊all the Israel⌉[1196] be blessed through the mouth of the King Messiah.

[25] [11] May the banners be truly lifted and may they gather from every[1197] city[1198] and every[1199] province of the dispersion of

[26] [12] of Israel. ⌊And the only Lord, Himself, shall be king over all the earth⌉[1200];

[27] [13] and His existence and His oneness shall be preached in the mouth of all people.

[28] [14] ⌊And the Lord shall be king over all the earth.⌉[1201]

---

1194 JSul.III.72: *qotarlylġaj.* | JSul.III.76: *qotarlylġaj.*

1195 Zechariah 14:9. | JSul.III.72: וְהָיָה הָ׳ לְמֶלֶךְ עַל כָל הָאָרֶץ בַּיּוֹם הַהוּא יִהְיֶה הָ׳ אֶחָד וּשְׁמוֹ אֶחָד: שְׁמַע יִשְׂרָאֵל. (Zechariah 14:9; Deuteronomy 6:4). | JSul.III.76: וְהָיָה הָ׳ לְמֶלֶךְ עַל כָּל הָאָרֶץ בַּיּוֹם הַהוּא יִהְיֶה הָ׳ אֶחָד וּשְׁמוֹ אֶחָד. (Zechariah 14:9).

1196 JSul.III.72: *the whole of Israel.* | JSul.III.76: *the whole of Israel.*

1197 JSul.III.72: *every single.* | JSul.III.76: *every single.*

1198 JSul.III.72: *city and village.* | JSul.III.76: *city and village.*

1199 JSul.III.76: *every single.*

1200 Zechariah 14:9.

1201 Zechariah 14:9. | JSul.III.72: *'And the Lord shall be king over all the earth: in that day shall there be one Lord, and his name one. Hear, O Israel.'* (Zechariah 14:9; Deuteronomy 6:4). | JSul.III.76: *'And the Lord shall be king over all the earth: in that day shall there be one Lord, and his name one.'* (Zechariah 14:9).

**Text number:** № 20
**Karaim incipit:** *Qajjam Tenri juluvčumuz biznin*
**Hebrew incipit:** אָמֵן גוֹאֲלֵנוּ *ʾåmēn gōʾălēnū*
**Dedication:** The first day of Sukkot
**Language:** MSWKar., Early Mod.SWKar., Mod.SWKar.
**Number of copies:** 5

| Accession no. | Place of origin of copy | Date of copy | Copyist | Folios |
|---|---|---|---|---|
| JSul.I.54.03 | Halych (?) | turn of the 19th c. | Unknown 5 | 2 r°–2 v° |
| JSul.I.38.09 | Halych (?) | turn of the 19th c. | Unknown 4 | 4 r°–5 r° |
| JSul.III.72 | Halych | before 1851 | Jeshua Josef Mordkowicz | 143 v°–144 r° |
| JSul.III.67 | Halych | after ca. 1840, before 1851 | Josef b. Icchak Szulimowicz (?) | 223 v°–224 r° |
| JSul.III.76 | Halych | 2nd half of the 19th c. | Jeshua Josef Mordkowicz | 94 v°–95 r° |

## 1 Introductory Remarks

In JSul.I.54.03, Simcha ben Chananel, the composer of the *peshat*, is referred to as “the above-mentioned”, i.e., the reader is redirected to *peshat* № 14. JSul.I.38.09 contains a non-vocalized copy; the other four texts are vocalized.

There are almost no significant differences between the analysed copies. In each of them we find a few unique minor and seemingly *ad hoc* amendments. Perhaps it is the text in ms. JSul.III.76 that stands out the most, cf. *jaḫsylyqlarynyn* vs. *ašajyšlyqlarynyn* (4), *bulutnu* vs. *bulut* (8), *ribbimiznin* vs. *rabenunun* (10), *H jaratuvcusu* vs. *jaratuvčusu* (21), *qyjnavcularymyznyn* vs. *qyjnavčularymnyn* ~ *qyjnavčularnyn* (24), and *aziz malaḫlarnyn* vs. *malaḫlarnyn* (26). Based on the few differences we can propose the following diagram:

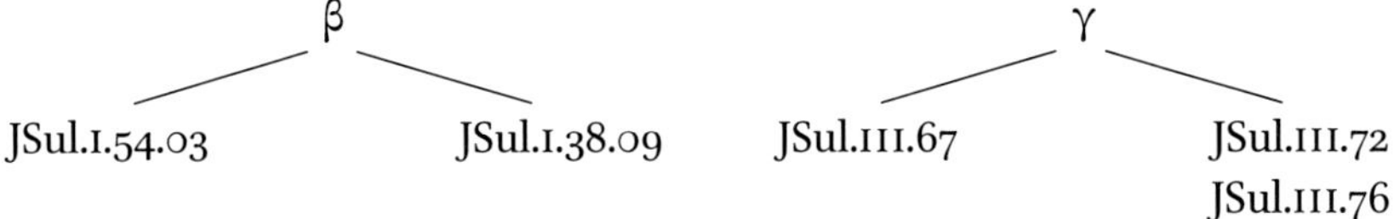


FIGURE 22 Diagram of the connections between the copies of peshat № 20

## 2 Transcription[1202] and Translation

2 rº [1] [8] ⸤וזה פשט של פיוט אמן גואלנו הנאם ביום א׳ דחג הסכות שתרגמו גב החכם הנל זל⸣[1203]

[2] [9] Qajjam Tenri juluvčumuz[1204] biznin oldu biji ol bijlernin[,][1205] anyn

[3] [10] küčü[1206] qotarylady avzunda bar sarnavčularnyn[1207]. Tamčylaryndan[1208]

[4] [11] čyqlarynyn[1209] tojdurdu bizni nametlerinden ašajyšlyqlarynyn[1210].

[5] [12] Oldu berüvčü[1211] aryġanġa küč[1212] da arttyrdy[1213] quvatyn ḥalsyzlarnyn.

[6] [13] Saġyndy šertin[1214] üč[1215] atalarnyn, da čyġardy[1216] bizni {{qol}} qolundan

2 vº [7] [1] ḥaneslilernin[1217] da coʿanlylarnyn[1218], da jürüttü[1219] bizni midbarda baġanasy-

[8] [2] byla otnun da bulutlarnyn[1220]. Jajdy bulut[1221] üstümüzge[1222] qaplavġa

---

1202 Based on JSul.I.54.03.

1203 JSul.I.38.09. הא לך פשט לפיוט רביעי דיום א׳ סכות שהוא אָמֵן גוֹאֲלֵנוּ שעשאו וחברו החכם כמוהרר שמחה נע חזן דקהק קוכיזוב יצו בכמע חננאל הזקן נבת. | JSul.III.72: וזה פשטו של פיוט דיום א׳ דסוכות שהוא אָמֵן גוֹאֲלֵנוּ להחכם הרר שמחה הנל. | JSul.III.67: ואם תרצה תאמר גם פשטו שתרגמו כמוהרר שמחה החזן נע בכמ חננאל יעמש. | JSul.III.76: וזה פשטו שתרגמו החכם השלם אמוהרר שמחה החזן דקהק קוקיזוב בכמ חננאל חזקן יעמש.

1204 JSul.III.67: *juluvčumuz* or *juluvcumuz*. | JSul.III.76: *juluvcumuz*.

1205 In JSul.I.38.09, JSul.III.72, JSul.III.67, and JSul.III.76, clause-ending marks (a *sof pasuq* or a *gershayim*) are used here.

1206 JSul.III.67: *kiči* or *kici*. | JSul.III.76: *kici*.

1207 JSul.III.67: or: *sarnavcularnyn*. | JSul.III.76: *sarnavcularnyn*.

1208 JSul.III.67: *tamčylaryn* or *tamcylaryn*; the lack of the ablative case is probably due to a scribal error. | JSul.III.76: *tamcylaryndan*.

1209 JSul.III.67: *čyqlarnyn* or *cyqlarnyn*. | JSul.III.76: *cyqlarynyn*.

1210 JSul.III.76: *jaḥsylyqlarynyn*.

1211 JSul.I.38.09: *berivčü*. | JSul.III.72: *berivčü*. | JSul.III.67: *berivči* or *berivci*. | JSul.III.76: *berivci*.

1212 JSul.III.67: *kič* or *kic*. | JSul.III.76: *kic*.

1213 JSul.I.38.09: *artyrdy* or *artyrady*; not vocalized. | JSul.III.67: *arttyrady*. | JSul.III.76: *arttyrady*.

1214 JSul.III.67: *sertin*. | JSul.III.76: *sertin*.

1215 JSul.III.67: *ič* or *ic*. | JSul.III.76: *ic*.

1216 JSul.III.67: or: *cyġardy*.

1217 A Kar. *-li* derivative of Heb. חָנֵס 'Hanes; a place in Egypt', see Isaiah 30:4.

1218 A Kar. *-ly* derivative of Heb. צֹעַן 'Zoan; a place in Egypt', see Isaiah 30:4.

[1] [8] ⌊And this is a *peshat* of the *piyyut* (with the incipit) *ʾåmēn gōʾălēnū*, the one chanted on the first day of the feast of Sukkot, which the above-mentioned hakham translated, too, may his memory be a blessing.⌉[1223] 2 rº
[2] [9] The powerful God, our saviour, He is the Lord of the lords[1224]; His
[3] [10] power is preached in the mouth of all who praise. With the drops
[4] [11] of His[1225] dew, He has satisfied us with the goods of pleasures[1226].
[5] [12] He is the one who gives strength to the weary and has increased[1227] the power of the exhausted.
[6] [13] He has remembered the covenant of the three patriarchs and has taken us from the hands
[7] [1] of the people ⌊of Hanes and Zoan⌉[1228] and has led us in the desert 2 vº
[8] [2] in a pillar of fire and (in a pillar) of clouds[1229]. He has spread a cloud over[1230] us to be it a cover

---

1219 JSul.III.67: *jiritti.* | JSul.III.76: *jiritti.*

1220 JSul.III.72: *bulutnun.*

1221 JSul.III.76: *bulutnu.*

1222 JSul.III.67: *istimizde.* | JSul.III.76: *istimizge.*

1223 JSul.I.38.09: *May the* peshat *of the forth* piyyut *concerning the first day of Sukkot follow here, of that (with the incipit)* ʾåmēn gōʾălēnū, *done and written by his honour, the Rav, Rabbi, hakham Simcha, may his soul rest in Eden, the hazzan of the holy community of Kukizów, may his Rock and our Redeemer preserve it* [i.e., the community; יעֿ̃א would rather be expected here], *the son of the honourable sir Chananel, the aged, may his soul lodge in Eden.* | JSul.III.72: *And this is a* peshat *of the* piyyut *concerning the first day of Sukkot, of that (with the incipit)* ʾåmēn gōʾălēnū, *of the above-mentioned Rav, Rabbi, hakham Simcha.* | JSul.III.67: *And, if you prefer, say its* peshat [i.e., of the Hebrew original], *which his honour, the Rav, Rabbi Simcha the hazzan translated, may his soul rest in Eden, the son of the honourable sir Chananel, may he rest in peace.* | JSul.III.76: *And this is its* [i.e., of the Hebrew original] peshat, *which the complete hakham, our master, our teacher, the Rav, Rabbi Simcha translated, the hazzan of the holy comunity of Kukizów, the son of the honourable sir Chananel, the aged, may he rest in peace.*

1224 In all mss. but JSul.I.54.03, there is a sentence- or clause-ending mark used here (a *sof pasuq* or *gershayim*).

1225 JSul.III.67: deest.

1226 JSul.III.76: *good.*

1227 JSul.I.38.09: *increased* or *increases.* | JSul.III.67: *increases.* | JSul.III.76: *increases.*

1228 I.e., *of Egypt*; see Isaiah 30:4.

1229 JSul.III.72: *cloud.*

1230 JSul.III.67: *above.*

[9] [3] da könderdi[1231] bizni sarnavlarybyla tynčlyqlarnyn[1232]. Sodlaryn Tora-
[10] [4] synyn ülüš[1233] berdi bizge qolu ašyra[1234] Moše rabenunun[1235] inamly[1236] elčisinin[1237].
[11] [5] Bijenčli[1238] da quvančly[1239] moʿedlerni qylma b[u]jurdu[1240] bizge zamanlaryn-
[12] [6] da belgili vaġdalarynyn[1241], qylma Sukot jašaradoġan[1242] da begevre-jdoġan[1243]
[13] [7] tallarybyla özennin[1244], da jemiši[1245] byla[1246] syjly aġačnyn[1247] da
[14] [8] özgede[1248] ǯynslarnyn[1249], anyn üčün[1250] ki bilgejler sondraġy dorlar
[15] [9] jaḥšylyqlaryn[1251] Tenrinin ki qyldy eline burunġu dorlarnyn[1252], ki
[16] [10] Sukotta olturġuzdu bizni quvanma köplügübyla[1253] bijenč-
[17] [11] lernin[1254], ašatty[1255] bizge man da perepelice[1256] da berdi
[18] [12] bizge hörmet[1257] da köplügün[1258] mallarnyn, sözledi[1259] skalaġa[1260] da
[19] [13] berdi suv[1261] ⌊ičme[1262] bizg[e][1263]⌉[1264] qurġaq orunlarynda midbarnyn,
[20] [14] javdurdu bizge da tojdurdu bizni nametinden[1265] ol astralġan

---

1231 JSul.III.67: *kenderdi.* | JSul.III.76: *kenderdi.*
1232 JSul.III.67: or: *tynclyqlarnyn.* | JSul.III.76: *tynclyqlarnyn.*
1233 JSul.III.67: *iliš.* | JSul.III.76: *ilis.*
1234 JSul.III.72: *asyra.* | JSul.III.67: *asyra.* | JSul.III.76: *asyra.*
1235 JSul.III.76: *ribbimiznin.*
1236 JSul.III.76: *oldu inamly*; *oldu* '*lit.* it is' calques Lat. *id est* 'i.e.' or its Slavonic equivalents.
1237 JSul.III.67: *elčisin* or *elcisin*; a scribal error. | JSul.III.76: *elcisinin.*
1238 JSul.III.67: or: *bijencli.* | JSul.III.76: *bijencli.*
1239 JSul.III.67: or: *quvancly.* | JSul.III.76: *quvancly.*
1240 JSul.I.54.03: *bojurdu*; a scribal error. | JSul.I.38.09: not vocalized. | JSul.III.72: *bujurdu.* | JSul.III.67: *bujurdu.*
1241 The possessive suffix expresses most likely definiteness here. | JSul.I.38.09: *vaġdalarnyn.* | JSul.III.67: *vaġdalarnyn.* | JSul.III.76: *vaġdalarnyn.*
1242 JSul.III.72: *jasaradoġan.* | JSul.III.67: *jasaradoġan.* | JSul.III.76: *jasaradoġan.*
1243 JSul.III.72: *bögövrejdoġan.*
1244 JSul.III.67: *ezennin.* | JSul.III.76: *ezennin.*
1245 JSul.III.76: *jemisi.*
1246 JSul.I.38.09: probably *byla*; spelled ביל.
1247 JSul.III.67: or: *aġacnyn.* | JSul.III.76: *aġacnyn.*
1248 JSul.III.67: *ezgede.* | JSul.III.76: *ezgede.*
1249 JSul.III.67: or: *ʒynslarnyn.* | JSul.III.76: *ʒynslarnyn.*
1250 JSul.III.67: *ičin* or *icin.* | JSul.III.76: *icin.*
1251 JSul.III.76: *jaḥsylyqlaryn.*

[9] [3] and has sent us with songs of peace. He has given us the secrets of His Law
[10] [4] in a heritage through the hands ⌊our master⌋[1266], Moses, His[1267] trustworthy envoy.
[11] [5] He has ordered us to celebrate the joyful and cheerful holidays during
[12] [6] the well-known dates, to celebrate Sukkot, thriving and delighting in
[13] [7] the dew of rivers and the fruits of illustrious trees and
[14] [8] also other species, so that the posterity know
[15] [9] all the goodness of God that He has done to the people of the first generations[1268], that
[16] [10] on Sukkot He settled us to rejoice with an abundance of joy,
[17] [11] (that) He has fed us with manna and quail and has given
[18] [12] us honour and an abundance of goods[1269], (that) He has talked to the rock and
[19] [13] has given us water[1270] to drink at the dry places of the desert,
[20] [14] He has made rain for us and satisfied us with the wealth of His[1271] hidden

1252 JSul.I.38.09: *dornun.*
1253 JSul.I.38.09: *köpligi byla.* | JSul.III.72: *köpligibyla.* | JSul.III.67: *kepligi byla.* | JSul.III.76: *kepligi byla.*
1254 JSul.III.67: or: *bijenclernin.* | JSul.III.76: *bijenclernin.*
1255 JSul.III.67: *asatty.* | JSul.III.76: *asatty.*
1256 JSul.I.38.09: probably *perepelice*; spelled פריפליציא.
1257 JSul.III.67: *hermet.* | JSul.III.76: *hermet.*
1258 JSul.III.67: *kepligin.* | JSul.III.76: *kepligin.*
1259 JSul.III.67: *sezledi.* | JSul.III.76: *sezledi.*
1260 JSul.I.38.09: this word is vocalized.
1261 JSul.III.67: *suvlaryn.*
1262 JSul.III.67: or: *icme.* | JSul.III.76: *icme.*
1263 JSul.I.54.03: *bizgi*; a scribal error. | JSul.I.38.09: *bizge.* | JSul.III.72: *bizge.* | JSul.III.67: *bizge.* | JSul.III.76: *bizge.*
1264 JSul.I.38.09: *bizge ičme.*
1265 JSul.I.38.09: *nametinde*; a scribal error.
1266 Expressed with *rabenu*, i.e., Heb. רַבֵּינוּ 'our rabbi'.
1267 JSul.III.76: *in other words, His.*
1268 JSul.I.38.09: *generation.*
1269 Or: *cattle.*
1270 JSul.III.67: *waters.*
1271 JSul.III.67: deest.

[21] [15] jaḥšylyqlarynyn[1272]. Alaj haliginede turġaj jaratuvčusu[1273] bijiktegi
[22] [16] köklernin[1274], haliginede[1275] ⌊bijikligin körgüzgej⌋[1276] qylma tamašalyq-
[23] [17] laryn[1277] urluġu üčün[1278] inamly üč[1279] atalarymnyn[1280] juluma bizni
[24] [18] galuttan da qutqarma bizni qolundan qyjnavčularymnyn[1281].
[25] [19] Qajjam Tenri syjly taḥty üstüne[1282] d[a][1283] ullulugun körgüzüv-
[26] [20] čü[1284] syrynda šinanim[1285] ündeledoġan[1286] malaẖlarnyn[1287].
[27] [21] ⌊כַּכָּתוּב⌋ ⌊יוֹשֵׁב עַל כִּסֵּא רָם וְנִשָּׂא׳⌉[1288]⌉[1289]

1272 JSul.III.76: *jaḥsylyqlarynyn.*
1273 JSul.I.54.03: spelled יַירַטוּבְ,צוּסוּ. | JSul.I.38.09: *jaratuvčusu.* | JSul.III.72: *jaratuvčusu.* | JSul.III.67: or: *jaratuvcusu.* | JSul.III.76: *H jaratuvcusu.*
1274 JSul.III.67: *keklernin.* | JSul.III.76: *keklernin.*
1275 JSul.I.38.09: *haligine.* | JSul.III.67: *haligine.* | JSul.III.76: *haligine.*
1276 JSul.I.38.09: *bijikligin körgüzgej haliginede ullu*[lu]*ġun körgizgej; ulluġun* < *ulluluġun* as a result of haplology. | JSul.III.72: *bijikligin körgizgej haliginede ulluluġun körgüzgej.* | JSul.III.67: *bijikligin kergizgej haligine ulluluġun kergizgej.* | JSul.III.76: *bijikligin kergizgej haligine ulluluġun kergizgej.*
1277 JSul.III.72: *tamašalyqlar.* | JSul.III.67: *tamašalyqlar.* | JSul.III.76: *tamasalyqlar.*
1278 JSul.III.67: *ičin* or *icin.* | JSul.III.76: *icin.*
1279 JSul.III.67: *ič* or *ic.* | JSul.III.76: *ic.*
1280 JSul.III.72: *atalarnyn.* | JSul.III.76: *atalarnyn.*
1281 JSul.III.72: *qyjnavčularnyn.* | JSul.III.67: *qyjnavčularnyn or qyjnavcularnyn.* | JSul.III.76: *qyjnavcularymyznyn.*
1282 JSul.III.67: *istine.* | JSul.III.76: *istine.*
1283 JSul.I.54.03: *di;* a scribal error. | JSul.I.38.09: not vocalized. | JSul.III.72: *da.* | JSul.III.67: *da.* | JSul.III.76: *da.*
1284 JSul.III.72: *körgizüvčü.* | JSul.III.67: *kergizivči* or *kergizivci.* | JSul.III.76: *kergizivci.*
1285 Heb. שְׁנְאַנִּים 'the Shinannim', i.e., a medieval epithet for angels, an order of angels according to 14th-century kabbalistic works, more precisely according to *Massekhet Azilut* and *Berit Menuchah*; see e.g. Blau & Kohler (1901: 591). We find *Shinannim* mentioned also in the zemmer *ś'ī zimrå napšī* of Mordechai ben Icchak Łokszyński (see *Siddur* 1890–1892: IV: 205–206; Tuori 2013: 370) or in RAbk.IV.03 (346 v°) in a list of the ten orders of angels (see Muchowski 2013a: 312–313).
1286 JSul.I.38.09: *indeledoġan.* | JSul.III.67: *indeledoġan.* | JSul.III.76: *indeledoġan.*
1287 JSul.III.76: *aziz malaẖlarnyn.*
1288 Isaiah 6:1.

[21] [15] goods. Thus may now ⌊be elevated⌋[1290] the creator[1291] of the heavens above,
[22] [16] may He, also[1292] now, ⌊show His highness⌋[1293] in order to do His[1294] wonders
[23] [17] to the offspring of my[1295] three patriarchs, in order to redeem us
[24] [18] from exile and save us from the hand of my[1296] tormentors.
[25] [19] O, powerful God, on His honourable throne and the one who shows His greatness
[26] [20] in the secret of angels[1297] called the Shinannim!
[27] [21] ⌊As it is written: ⌊'Sitting upon a throne, high and lifted up'⌋[1298]⌋[1299]

---

1289 JSul.I.38.09: יושב על כסא רם ונשא ושוליו מלאים אה״ שרפים עומדים ׳ וקרא זה אל זה ואמר ״ קדוש קדוש קדוש הֹ צבאות ״. (Isaiah 6:1, 6:2, 6:3). | JSul.III.72: יֹשֵׁב עַל כִּסֵּא רָם וְנִשָּׂא: קָקָֽק הָ צְבָאוֹת. (Isaiah 6:1, 6:3). | JSul.III.67: יֹשֵׁב עַל כִּסֵּא רָם וְנִשָּׂא: שְׂרָפִים עוֹמְדִים מִמַּעַל לוֹ: וְקָרָא זֶה אֶל זֶה וְאָמַר: קָדוֹשׁ קָדוֹשׁ קָדוֹשׁ הָ צְבָאוֹת מְלֹא כָל הָאָרֶץ כְּבוֹדוֹ. (Isaiah 6:1, 6:2, 6:3). | JSul.III.76: יֹשֵׁב עַל כִּסֵּא רָם וְנִשָּׂא וְשׁוּלָיו מְלֵאִים אֶת הַהֵיכָל: שְׂרָפִים עוֹמְדִים מִמַּעַל לוֹ שֵׁשׁ כְּנָפַיִם לְאֶחָד בִּשְׁתַּיִם יְכַסֶּה פָנָיו וּבִשְׁתַּיִם יְכַסֶּה רַגְלָיו וּבִשְׁתַּיִם יְעוֹפֵף: וְקָרָא זֶה אֶל זֶה וְאָמַר קָדוֹשׁ קָדוֹשׁ קָדוֹשׁ הָ צְבָאוֹת מְלוֹא כָל הָאָרֶץ כְּבוֹדוֹ. (Isaiah 6:1–3).

1290 Lit. 'rise'.

1291 JSul.III.76: *Lord creator*.

1292 JSul.I.38.09: deest. | JSul.III.67: deest. | JSul.III.76: deest.

1293 JSul.I.38.09: *show His highness, may He, also now, show His greatness.* | JSul.III.72: *show His highness, may He, also now, show His greatness.* | JSul.III.67: *show His highness, may He show now His greatness.* | JSul.III.76: *show His highness, may He show now His greatness.*

1294 JSul.III.72: deest. | JSul.III.67: deest. | JSul.III.76: deest.

1295 JSul.III.72: deest. | JSul.III.76: deest.

1296 JSul.III.72: deest. | JSul.III.67: deest. | JSul.III.76: *our*.

1297 JSul.III.76: *holy angels*.

1298 Isaiah 6:1.

1299 JSul.I.38.09: *'Sitting upon a throne, high and lifted up, and his train filled the temple. Above it stood the seraphim. And one cried unto another, and said, "Holy, holy, holy, is the Lord of hosts."'* (Isaiah 6:1, 6:2, 6:3). | JSul.III.72: *'Sitting upon a throne, high and lifted up. Holy, holy, holy, is the Lord of host.'* (Isaiah 6:1, 6:3). | JSul.III.67: *'Sitting upon a throne, high and lifted. Above it stood the seraphim. And one cried unto another, and said, "Holy, holy, holy, is the Lord of hosts: the whole earth is full of his glory."'* (Isaiah 6:1, 6:2, 6:3). | JSul.III.76: *'Sitting upon a throne, high and lifted up, and his train filled the temple. Above it stood the seraphim: each one had six wings; with two he covered his face, and with two he covered his feet, and with two he did fly. And one cried unto another, and said, "Holy, holy, holy, is the Lord of hosts: the whole earth is full of his glory."'* (Isaiah 6:1–3).

**Text number:** № 21
**Karaim incipit:** *Sensen aziz Tenri da qajjam*
**Hebrew incipit:** אַתָּה קָדוֹשׁ יוֹשֵׁב תְּהִלּוֹת בְּנֵי אֵיתָן *ʾattå qåḏōš yōšēḇ thillōṯ bnē ʾēṯån*
**Dedication:** Parashat Re'eh (Deuteronomy 11:26–16:17)
**Language:** Mod.SWKar.
**Number of copies:** 3

| Accession no. | Place of origin of copy | Date of copy | Copyist | Folios |
|---|---|---|---|---|
| ADub.III.61 | Halych | 1850/1851 | Jeshua Josef Mordkowicz | 138 vº–139 rº |
| JSul.III.69 | Halych | ca. 1851 (before 1866) | Jeshua Josef Mordkowicz | 296 vº–297 vº |
| JSul.III.79 | Halych | ca. 1851 (before 1866) | Jeshua Josef Mordkowicz | 179 vº–180 vº |

## 1 Introductory Remarks

In the headings that introduce the copies of this *peshat*, Simcha ben Chananel is referred to as "the above-mentioned". His name is included in the headings of *peshatim* № 23 (in ADub.III.61), № 9 (in JSul.III.69), and № 11 (in JSul.III.79). All three copies are vocalized

There are hardly any differences between the texts. The few discrepancies that do exist (not counting apparent scribal errors), are minor amendments, see *micvalarny* vs. *ol micvalarny* vs. *ol aziz micvalarny* (10), and *qaranjalarnyn* vs. *qarġyslarnyn da qaranjalarnyn* (16).

## 2 Transcription[1300] and Translation

138 v° [1] [3] ⌊וזה הפשט לפיוט פרשת ראה שהוא אַתָּה קָדוֹשׁ יוֹשֵׁב תְּהִלּוֹת בְּנֵי אֵיתָן: תרגמו
[2] [4] גֹּ֗ב החכם האלהי יעֹ֗מש:⌋[1301]

[3] [5] Sensen aziz Tenri da qajjam qabul etivci maḥtavlaryn ulan-
[4] [6] larynyn Jisra’elnin, ol sajlavcu ʒanlaryn qurquvcularyn-
[5] [7] nyn da tiz etivci izin jollarynyn. Kerdiler seni suvlary Jam Sufnun
[6] [8] qaltradylar necik jarcyqladyn any battyrma elin Micrinin da
[7] [9] qavsattyn basyn paronun livjatanġa usaġannyn[1302]. Berdin[1303] qollary asyra
[8] [10] Moše rabenunun ivretivler Jisra’elge ki jirigejler kecindirmek-
[9] [11] leri byla alarnyn, alġysny da qarġysny berdin alnynda sajlanmus-
[10] [12] larynnyn. Eger tynlasalar da qylsalar ⌊[ol] micvalarny⌋[1304] bolurlar Josef hacadiq
[11] [13] kibik ki tapty osol qaryndaslaryn tizinde Dotannyn[1305]. Da eger
[12] [14] kemisseler qulluġun Tenrinin bolurlar taspolmaqqa taspolmaġy kibik
[13] [15] Datannyn[1306] da Aviramnyn[1307]. Tavy istine Gerizimnin[1308] ajtyldy
[14] [16] alġyslary qajjam etivcilerge micvalarny da tanyqlyqlaryn alarnyn.
[15] [17] Da tavy istine ‘Evalnyn[1309] belgirtildi qarġyslar qajjam etmevci-
[16] [18] lerge kepligi byla tisli qaranjalarnyn[1310]. Sandyr andij ʒanlarġa
[17] [19] ki sajladylar tizlikni da qojdular jaḥsy jolġa saġyslaryn ezlerinin.

---

1300 Based on ADub.III.61.

1301 JSul.III.69. ואם תרצה תאֹ֗מ גם פשטו שתרגמו המתרגם הנֹ֗ל תנצֹ֗בהה. | JSul.III.79: וזה הפשט לפיוט פרשת ראה אנכי תרגמו המתרגם האלהי והתורני הנֹ֗ל יעֹ֗מש.

1302 JSul.III.79: *uqsaġannyn.*

1303 JSul.III.69: *berdi*; a scribal error.

1304 ADub.III.61: *micvalarny.* | JSul.III.69: *ol micvalarny.* | JSul.III.79: *ol aziz micvalarny.*

1305 Heb. דֹּתָן ‘Dothan (place name)’, see Genesis 37:17.

1306 Heb. דָּתָן, i.e., Dathan the son of Eliab, see Numbers 16:1–33.

1307 Heb. אֲבִירָם, i.e., Abiram the son of Eliab, see Numbers 16:1–33.

1308 Heb. הַר גְּרִיזִּים ‘Mount Gerizim’, see Deuteronomy 11:29.

1309 Heb. הַר עֵיבָל ‘Mount Ebal’, see Deuteronomy 11:29.

1310 JSul.III.79: *qarġyslarnyn da qaranjalarnyn.*

1311 JSul.III.69: *And, if you prefer, say its* peshat [i.e., of the Hebrew original], *which the above-mentioned translator translated, ‘may his soul be bound in the bond of life’* [cf., 1 Samuel 25:29]. | JSul.III.79: *And this is the* peshat *of a* piyyut *for the parashat Re’eh, which the above-mentioned divine translator and ha-Torani translated, may he rest in peace.*

1312 JSul.III.69: *He has given*; a scribal error.

1313 Expressed with *rabenu*, i.e., Heb. רַבֵּינוּ ‘our rabbi’.

[1] [3] ⌊And this is the *peshat* of the *piyyut* for the parashat Re'eh, of that (with the incipit) *'attå qåḏōš yōšēḇ thillōṯ bnē 'ēṯån*, also the interpretation 138 v°
[2] [4] of the divine hakham, may he rest in peace.⌉[1311]
[3] [5] You are the holy and powerful God, the one who accepts the praises
[4] [6] of the children of Israel, the one who chooses the souls of those who fear
[5] [7] You and the one who straightens the path of their ways. The waters of the Red Sea have seen You,
[6] [8] they have trembled as You have split it in order to sink the people of Egypt and
[7] [9] you have destroyed the head of Pharaoh resembling the Leviathan. ⌊You have given⌉[1312] through the hands
[8] [10] of ⌊our master⌉[1313], Moses, the teachings for Israel that they should walk ⌊with their guidance⌉[1314],
[9] [11] You have given Your blessing and curse before Your chosen
[10] [12] ones: if they would obey and do the commandments[1315], they will be like Joseph the just,
[11] [13] who found his brothers in the plain of Dothan. But if
[12] [14] they would abandon the service of God, they will be just as the destruction
[13] [15] of Dathan and Abiram. On Mount Gerizim
[14] [16] His blessings have been voiced to those who have strengthened the commandments and ⌊their witnesses⌉[1316].
[15] [17] And on Mount Ebal curses have been appointed for those who have not
[16] [18] strengthened (them)[1317]; (they have been appointed) with an abundance of ⌊all kind of⌉[1318] punishments[1319]. Praise to those[1320] souls,
[17] [19] who have chosen rightfulness and have placed their own thoughts on the right way.

---

1314 I.e., *with the guidance of the teachings.*
1315 JSul.III.79: *the holy commandments.*
1316 I.e., *those who saw Moses bringing the commandments.*
1317 I.e., *the commandments and their witnesses.*
1318 Lit. 'various'.
1319 JSul.III.79: *curses and punishments.*
1320 Lit. 'such'.

[18] [20] Anlyq byla kemistiler ʒurumun gernin aruvluğu byla yzlarynyn
[19] [21] da qyjasa jazdylar anar get bitigin ki kemistiler jamanlyġyn
[20] [22] ⌊[jaman] islerinin⌉[1321]. Da tersligi byla qylġanlary icin jazyqlar tizijdiler
[21] [23] alnynda Tenrinin bar ʒan byla tigel tešuvalaryn ezlerinin.
[22] [24] Anyn icin jaḥsy ijis bergej ijisi jaḥsy islerinin ijisi kibik
[23] [25] otjamlarynyn sarajdaġy baġnyn. Haligine qahallaryn senin širalary
[24] [26] byla maḥtavlarynyn, qoladylar qyblalaryn Tenrinin ki ʒaḥtlaġaj
[25] [27] julunmaq[1322]
139 r° [26] [1] julunmaq alarġa avurluqlaryndan galutlarynyn, aziz toḥtar orunlarynda kenesa ivlerinde joġarġy Tenrinin, hammese qoladylar
[27] [2] larynda kenesa ivlerinde joġarġy Tenrinin, hammese qoladylar
[28] [3] gufluq da ʒanlyq juluvlaryn ki juluġaj ulusun Jisra'elnin galuttan
[29] [4] saġynyp alarġa sertin ic atalarnyn.
[30] [5] ⌊פְּדוּת שָׁלַח לְעַמּוֹ צִוָּה לְעוֹלָם בְּרִיתוֹ וגו׳:⌉[1323]

1321 ADub.III.61: *islerinin*; a scribal error. | JSul.III.69: *jaman islerinin.* | JSul.III.79: *jaman islerinin.*

1322 Catchword.

1323 Psalm 111:9. | JSul.III.69: פְּדוּת שָׁלַח לְעַמּוֹ: צַהֲלִי וָרֹנִּי: גּוֹאֲלֵנוּ הָ׳ צְבָקְ׳:. (Psalm 111:9, Isaiah 12:6, Isaiah 47:4). | JSul.III.79: פְּדוּת שָׁלַח לְעַמּוֹ צִוָּה לְעוֹלָם בְּרִיתוֹ וגו׳. (Psalm 111:9).

1324 ADub.III.61: deest; a scribal error.

[18] [20] By this, due to the cleanness of their ways they have abandoned the punishment of the grave
[19] [21] as if they wrote a letter of divorce that they have abandoned the evil
[20] [22] of [evil][1324] deeds. And as for those who do disobediently sins,
[21] [23] they wholeheartedly arrange their own proper repentance before God.
[22] [24] For this reason, a good sacrifice he shall give, a sacrifice of good deeds, like the sacrifice
[23] [25] of incense in a palace garden. Now, Your communities ask
[24] [26] the countenance of God, with songs of praise, that He may advance their
[25] [27] salvation[1325]
[26] [1] salvation from the burden of their exile; in the holy dwelling places 139 r°
[27] [2] of the God up above, in His temples they[1326] always ask
[28] [3] for their physical and spiritual redemption, that may He save the people of Israel from exile,
[29] [4] reminding them the covenant of the three patriarchs.
[30] [5] ⌊'He sent redemption unto his people: he has commanded his covenant forever …' and so on.⌉[1327]

---

1325 Catchword in the Karaim text.

1326 I.e., *the communities of God.*

1327 Psalm 111:9. | JSul.111.69: *'He sent redemption unto his people. Cry out and shout. As for our redeemer, the Lord of hosts is his name, the Holy One of Israel.'* (Psalm 111:9, Isaiah 12:6, Isaiah 47:4). | JSul.111.79: *'He sent redemption unto his people: he has commanded his covenant forever …' and so on.* (Psalm 111:9).

**Text number:** № 22
**Karaim incipit:** *Siviniz qulluġun H-nyn*
**Hebrew incipit:** אֶהֱבוּ אֶת הָ׳ דּוֹר יְשָׁרִים *ʾehĕḇū ʾeṯ H dōr yšårīm*
**Dedication:** Parashat Shoftim (Deuteronomy 16:18–21:9)
**Language:** Mod.SWKar.
**Number of copies:** 3

| Accession no. | Place of origin of copy | Date of copy | Copyist | Folios |
|---|---|---|---|---|
| ADub.III.61 | Halych | 1850/1851 | Jeshua Josef Mordkowicz | 139 rº–139 vº |
| JSul.III.69 | Halych | ca. 1851 (before 1866) | Jeshua Josef Mordkowicz | 298 rº–298 vº |
| JSul.III.79 | Halych | ca. 1851 (before 1866) | Jeshua Josef Mordkowicz | 180 vº–181 vº |

## 1 Introductory Remarks

Simcha ben Chananel is referred to as the "above-mentioned" in the headings of its Karaim *peshatim*. His name is provided in the headings introducing *peshatim* № 23 (in ADub.III.61), № 9 (in JSul.III.69), and № 11 (in JSul.III.79). All three copies are vocalized.

There are only a few differences between the versions, all of them being textual improvements introduced by the same copyist. An interesting feature in JSul.III.69 and JSul.III.79 is the use of Karaim words instead of their Slavonic-origin equivalents used in ADub.III.61, see *hodnyj tanyqlar* vs. *inamly tanyqlar* (14) and *povynnyj ceriv* vs. *borc cerivi* (24). The textual differences are evenly distributed between the copies.

## 2 Transcription[1328] and Translation

139 rº ⌊וזה הפשט לפיוט פרשת שופטים שהוא אֱהֶבוּ אֶת הָ' דוֹר יְשָׁרִים: גֿב תרגמו
החכם המתרגם הנ̃ל יעֿמש:⌉[1329]

Siviniz qulluġun H-nyn doru tizlernin aruv Jisraʾeller. Tyntylynyz jazyqly islerden eziniz da tyntynyz ekincilernide da tutunuz rastlyqny da tereni da qylynyz tiz isler. Klegin Tenrinin qylynyz da beriniz tere ivlerde[1330] inamly jirekli tereciler da tajaqcylar, ki bolġajlar tizlikni quvuvcular da ki izlerge iz etmegejler. Almaqny šoḥad ḥor etsinler maġat soqurlar kibik jaryqta qarmanyrlar, da sezlerin rastlarnyn da paqlarnyn qynġyrajtyrlar. Da eksitsinler macevany da qujas sufatlarny da Ašeralarny[1331] ʿavoda zaraġa islengenler. Da qulluq etivcini da basuruvcunu[1332] cerivine ol keklernin alajoq qyluvcu ezine qujma abaqlar, tas byla taslansyn anar kere necik tanyqlyq berseler hodnyj[1333] tanyqlar, da bar avur da jasyryn tereler. Arasyna kini qannyn borclu qan byla nendijde bolsa talas sezler, keltirilsinler tere[1334] tergevci uslularġa ki alardylar jetmis zaqen ⌊bet din hagadol⌉[1335] indeledoġanlar.
Da biji[1336] Jisraʾelnin bolmasyn tanyġyzsyz elden ki alardylar ol jat ummalar. Da tabulmasynlar Jisraʾelde ulanlaryn ezlerinin ʿavoda

1328 Based on ADub.III.61.

1329 JSul.III.69. ואם תרצה תאמ גם פשטו שתרגמו הר̃ר שמחה הנ̃ל נב̃ת. | JSul.III.79: וזה הפשט לפיוט פרשת שוׂפֿטים ושׂוׂטרים תרגמו המתרגם האלהי הנ̃ל נב̃ת: אהבו את ה̓.

1330 JSul.III.69: *ivlerde aġaraqlar.* | JSul.III.79: *ivlerde aġaraqlar.*

1331 Heb. אֲשֵׁרָה 'Asherah; a Canaaite and Phoenician godess of fortune and prosperity'.

1332 JSul.III.79: *basuruvcu*; a scribal error.

1333 JSul.III.69: *inamly.* | JSul.III.79: *inamly.*

1334 ADub.III.61: *teren*; a scribal error. | JSul.III.69: *tere.* | JSul.III.79: *tere.*

1335 Heb. בֵּית דִּין הַגָּדֹל 'Supreme Court of Justice'; a reference to the court mentioned in Deuteronomy 17:8–13.

1336 JSul.III.79: *meleḫ ki.*

1337 JSul.III.69: *And, if you prefer, say its* peshat [i.e., of the Hebrew original], *which the above-mentioned Rav, Rabbi Simcha translated, may his soul lodge in Eden.* | JSul.III.79: *And this is the* peshat *of a* piyyut *for the parashat Shoftim, which the above-mentioned divine translator translated, may his soul lodge in Eden.*

1338 Lit. 'give the courthouses'.

1339 JSul.III.69: *chiefs: judges and supervisors.* | JSul.III.79: *chiefs: judges and supervisors.*

1340 I.e., *do not show partiality*; cf. Deuteronomy 16:19.

1341 *Asherah* is a Canaanite and Phoenician goddess of fortune and prosperity.

[1] [6] ⌊And this is the *peshat* of a *piyyut* for the parashat Shoftim, of that (with the incipit) *ʾehĕḇū ʾeṯ H dōr yšårīm*, also the interpretation 139 rº
[2] [7] of the above-mentioned hakham, the translator, may he rest in peace.⌉[1337]
[3] [8] The generation of the righteous, the clean (people) of Israel: love the service of the Lord!
[4] [9] Examine yourselves (in search) of sinful deeds and examine
[5] [10] the others, too, and keep justice and the law and do right
[6] [11] deeds. Do the wish of God and ⌊provide the courthouses (with)⌉[1338]
[7] [12] ⌊judges and supervisors⌉[1339] of trustworthy hearts, that they may
[8] [13] observe the righteousness and ⌊pay no attention to faces⌉[1340].
[9] [14] They should disdain accepting bribe lest they grope in brightness like the blind and
[10] [15] distort the words of the clean and pure. And they should remove
[11] [16] the idol-images, the images of sun and the Asherahs[1341] of those who do idolatry.
[12] [17] And those who serve and bow down before the army of
[13] [18] the heavens, likewise those who make for themselves molten idols, should be stoned with stones
[14] [19] based on that what worthy[1342] witnesses and all
[15] [20] the weighty and secret laws would testify. If there be any words of quarrel ⌊between the innocent and the guilty[1343]⌉[1344],
[16] [21] they should be taken to the wise investigators of the law
[17] [22] that are called the ⌊seventy elders⌉[1345] of the ⌊Supreme Court of Justice⌉[1346].
[18] [23] And may the lord[1347] of Israel be not from unknown men, since those are foreign
[19] [24] nations. And may there be no one among (the sons of) Israel who would lead his own child[1348]

---

1342 JSul.III.69: *trustworthy*. | JSul.III.79: *trustworthy*.

1343 Or: *debtor*.

1344 Lit. 'between the envious blood and guilty (~ owing) blood'.

1345 Cf. Numbers 11:16, 24–25.

1346 I.e., *Bet Din ha-Gadol*; a reference either to the supreme court mentioned in Deuteronomy 17:8–13.

1347 JSul.III.79: *king*.

1348 Or: *son*.

[20] [25] zaraġa ot asyra asyruvcular, da soruvcu qamdan da bildeciden
[21] [26] da ystyruvcu ystyrmaqlar. Navi ⌊qaryndaslary arasyndan⌋[1349]
139 v° [22] [1] turġuzur H ⌊ol [navi]⌋[1350] anlatyr alarġa jasyryn nerselerni ne ki bolunurlar.
[23] [2] Da ⌊rešut cerivinde⌋[1351] cyqmasynlar bes sanalġanlar, ki ancaq
[24] [3] ⌊povynnyj cerivde⌋[1352] cyqsyn ḥatanda ḥuʒurasyndan bolmasyn kiniler.
[25] [4] Da kelip orusma sahar byla kereklidi burundan sezleme bazlyq
[26] [5] sezler. Da eger bazlasmasalar[1353] kereklidi ki vatylġajlar ol erkek-
[27] [6] ler, da qyran tabulsa tizde da[1354] kim eltirdi any bilmeseler,
[28] [7] qartlary juvuqraq saharnyn ol qyranġa buzovun[1355] syġyrnyn alsynlar,
[29] [8] ki tartmady bojunsada da afilu bosta ketirip qojmasynlar.
[30] [9] Da ol Tenri eksitir borcun ol kini qannyn eger qylsaq aruv
[31] [10] da jaḥsy isler. Joḥtur Tenrisi kibik Jisra'elnin da[1356] kim anyn kibik
[32] [11] ivretivci ki anyn alnynda asqarady bar jasyryn isler. Anyn
[33] [12] icin ševaḥ ajtajyq anar da uḥujuq alnynda anyn zemerler da
[34] [13] širalar. Ki bijikligin kergizdi rastlyq qylmaqbyla[1357] da juvuz etedi

---

1349 JSul.III.69: *qaryndaslaryndan.*

1350 JSul.III.69: *ol navi.*

1351 A calque of Heb. מִלְחֶמֶת רְשׁוּת 'a war that that the Torah does not obligate, nor forbid; a permitted war (according to the Jewish law)'.

1352 JSul.III.69: *borc cerivinde.* | JSul.III.79: *borc cerivinde.* || Both terms, i.e., *povynnyj ceriv* and *borc cerivi*, calque Heb. מִלְחֶמֶת מִצְוָה 'war by commandment; a war that does not require permisson and the Torah makes compulsory, obligatory war'.

1353 JSul.III.79: *bazlašmasalar.*

1354 ADub.III.61: *dam*; a scribal error. | JSul.III.69: *da.* | JSul.III.79: *da.*

1355 JSul.III.79: *tisi buzovun.*

1356 JSul.III.79: *dam*; a scribal error.

1357 JSul.III.69: *byla.*

1358 Lit. 'asking'.

1359 JSul.III.69: deest.

1360 I.e., *from the Jewish people.*

1361 ADub.III.61: deest. | JSul.III.79: deest.

1362 Cf. Heb. מִלְחֶמֶת רְשׁוּת 'a war that the Torah does not obligate, nor forbid; lit. *permitted war'.*

1363 See Deuteronomy 20:5–8, where four such categories are listed. The fifth category is, according to *Ṭuv Ṭa'am*, the one to be found in Deuteronomy 24:5 (Wasserman 2017, personal communication).

1364 ADub.III.61: lit. 'war of duty', 'compulsory war'. | JSul.III.69: lit. 'war of a debt', 'debt war'.

[20] [25] through fire to idolatry and no one ⌞seeking answers from⌟[1358] sorcerers and soothsayers

[21] [26] and gathering assemblies. From among[1359] ⌞the brethren of the prophet⌟[1360]

[22] [1] will the Lord lift ⌞the prophet⌟[1361], He will relate them the secret events that will take place. 139 vº

[23] [2] And to a ⌞permitted war⌟[1362] ⌞five numbered (categories of people) must not go⌟[1363], since (it is) only

[24] [3] the ⌞obligatory war⌟[1364] to which even the groom[1365] should go from his (marital) chamber, and there should be no innocent ones.

[25] [4] And after one arrives to siege[1366] a city, it is necessary first to say words of peace,

[26] [5] and if they would not conclude peace, it is binding that only men may be killed.

[27] [6] And if there is a dead on the field that it would be not known who killed him,

[28] [7] the elders of the closest city should take a calf[1367] of cattle for the dead,

[29] [8] which has not pulled a yoke, ⌞and they may not lift (a yoke with the calf) even if unharnessed⌟[1368].

[30] [9] And God will reduce the guilt of the innocent blood if we will do clean

[31] [10] and good deeds. There is none like the God of Israel: Who is a teacher like Him?,

[32] [11] for all the secret things are evident before Him. For this reason

[33] [12] we shall praise Him and sing before Him poems[1369] and

[34] [13] songs. For He has shown His greatness by doing[1370] justice and He has lowered

---

|| Cf. Heb. מִלְחֶמֶת מִצוָה 'a war that does not require permisson and the Torah makes compulsory, obligatory war; lit. *war by commandment*'.

1365 Or: *fiancé* (~ *the youth*).

1366 Lit. 'fight'.

1367 JSul.III.79: *female calf*.

1368 The use of the negative verb form *not lift* is probably an error. The original fragment, namely Heb. לֹא מָשְׁכָה בְעוֹל וְאִם הֵרִים (see JSul.III.79: 158 rº), should rather be interpreted as 'even if it has lifted (a yoke)'—i.e., *lifted*, but not *pulled*. I.e., the commented passage should rather read *even if it lifted (a yoke) unharnessed*.

1369 Lit. '*zemirot*', i.e., paraliturgical poems.

1370 JSul.III.69: deest.

[35] [14] bijliklerni da bijik etedi andijlerni qajsylary juvuz ʒan byla
[36] [15] alnynda Tenrinin[1371] jirijdiler.
[37] [16] ⌞וַיִּגְבַּה הָ֑ צְבָאוֹת בַּמִּשְׁפָּט וְהָאֵל הַקָּדוֹשׁ וגו׳:⌝[1372]

1371 JSul.III.69: *anyn*. | JSul.III.79: *anyn*.

1372 Isaiah 5:16. | JSul.III.69. תם: וַיִּגְבַּה הָ֑ צְבָאוֹת בַּמִּשְׁפָּט וְהָאֵל הַקָּדוֹשׁ וגו׳. (Isaiah 5:16). | JSul.III.79: וַיִּגְבַּה הָ֑ צְבָאוֹת בַּמִּשְׁפָּט וגו׳. (Isaiah 5:16).

[35] [14] the high ones and has elevated those who walk with humble heart

[36] [15] before God.

[37] [16] ⌞'But the Lord of hosts shall be exalted in justice, and God who is holy ...' and so on.⌝[1373]

1373 Isaiah 5:16. | JSul.III.69: *The end. 'But the Lord of hosts shall be exalted in justice, and God who is holy ...' and so on.* (Isaiah 5:16). | JSul.III.79: *'But the Lord of hosts shall be exalted in justice ...' and so on.* (Isaiah 5:16).

**Text number:** № 23
**Karaim incipit:** *Sizge caġyramen igit sözlerin e syjly erenler*
**Hebrew incipit:** אֲלֵיכֶם אֶקְרָא אִישִׁים *ʾălēḵem ʾeqrå ʾīšīm*
**Dedication:** Parashat Kedoshim (Leviticus 19:1–20:27)
**Language:** Early Mod.SWKar., Mod.SWKar.
**Number of copies:** 3

| Accession no. | Place of origin of copy | Date of copy | Copyist | Folios |
|---|---|---|---|---|
| JSul.III.03 | Halych | shortly after 1805 | Unknown 7 | 105 v°–106 r° |
| JSul.I.45 | Halych | 1st half of the 19th c. | Jeshua Josef Mordkowicz | 141 v°–142 v° |
| ADub.III.61 | Halych | 1850/1851 | Jeshua Josef Mordkowicz | 135 r°–135 v° |

## 1 Introductory Remarks

The Hebrew original was also interpreted by Shemuel ben Josef ha-Mashbir, see *peshat* № 27. All three copies are vocalized.

The differences between the edited texts concern amendments introduced by the copyist in ADub.III.61, cf. *erenler* vs. *Jisraʾeller* (3), *ezgelernide* vs. *ekincilernide* (5), *icimizden* vs. *jiregimizden* (10), *abajlyq byla* vs. *syj byla da abajlyq byla* (12), and *jalġyz H bir* vs. *H jalġyz ezi biji* (28). Based on the few difference we can propose the following diagram:

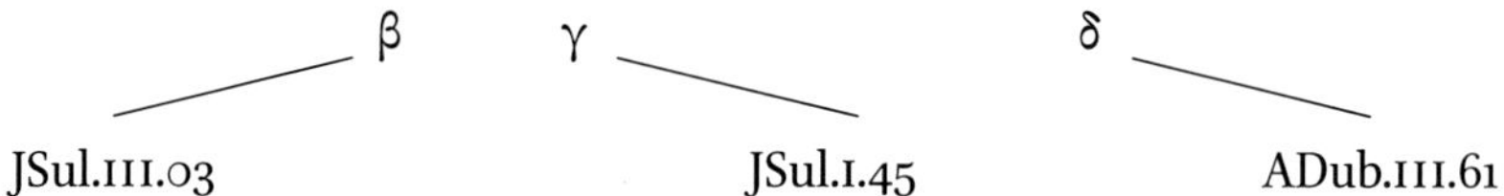


FIGURE 23 Diagram of the connections between the copies of peshat № 23

## 2 Transcription[1374] and Translation

105 vº [1] [11] ⌊פשט שני לפיוט פרשת קדושים שהוא אליכם אקרא אישים לה֞הו כמו֞הרר
[2] [12] שמחה החזן בכ֞מ חננאל הזקן מתושבי קה֞ק דרעזניא:⌉[1375]
[3] [13] Sizge caġyramen igit sözlerin[1376] e syjly erenler[1377].
[4] [14] Tyntylynyz eziniz jazyqly islerden da tynty-
[5] [15] nyz ezgelernide[1378] necik erenler alaj qatynlar. Quvunuz qylma
[6] [16] micvalaryn Tenrinin anyn ücün[1379] eliminizden sortun bolursiz
[7] [17] azizler. Hammeše saruvlaryn Tenrinin saqlama bolunuz ʒaḥtlavcu-lar,
[8] [18] ki alar bar klevcilerine izlengendiler. Qajrylmanyz ol heclik-
[9] [19] lerge ki alar tuzaq kibik tuzaqlajdylar. Köteriniz[1380] ⌊jaman jecerni⌉[1381]
[10] [20] icinizden[1382] da otlu qarbanlar ornuna qylynyz tigel tešuvalar.
[11] [21] Kisi dostuna bolmanyz tanuvcular. Syjly šeminden Tenrinin
[12] [22] qorqunuz anyn ücün[1383] bolursiz hermetbyla da abajlyq[1384] byla
[13] [23] cergelgenler. Siverlikte kecininiz kisi qaryndasy byla
[14] [24] anyn ücün[1385] bolmassiz savaġatlaryndan Tenrinin taslanġanlar. Da
[15] [25] eki tislü[1386] saġysny ki oldu ol[1387] avuz byla jaḥsyny sözlemek[1388]
[16] [26] da icte jamanny saġys etmek bundij isni ḥor etiniz ancaq
[17] [27] ol körtilikni[1389] bolunuz izlevciler. Nek byrclanyrsiz[1390] gufluq

---

1374 Based on JSul.III.03.

1375 JSul.I.45. פשט לפיוט פרשת קדושים שהוא אליכם אקרא אישים תרגמו אמ֞ו הה֞ו כמו֞הרר שמחה החזן דקה֞ק יפה יער ז֞ל בכמ֞ע חננאל הזקן יע֞מש. | ADub.III.61: פשט שני לפיוט פרשת קדושים תהיו תרגמו אמ֞ו הר֞ר שמחה החזן דקה֞ק קוקיזוב יע֞מש: בן כמ֞ע חננאל הזקן מתושבי קה֞ק דרעזניא נב֞ת.

1376 JSul.I.45: *sözleri*; a scribal error. | ADub.III.61: *sezlerin*.

1377 ADub.III.61: *Jisra'eller*.

1378 ADub.III.61: *ekincilernide*.

1379 ADub.III.61: *icin*.

1380 A hypercorrect form of *keteriniz*. | JSul.I.45: *keteriniz*. | ADub.III.61: *keteriniz*.

1381 A calque of Heb. יֵצֶר הָרַע 'evil inclination', see Genesis 6:5, 8:21.

1382 ADub.III.61: *jireginizden*.

1383 ADub.III.61: *icin*.

1384 ADub.III.61: *syjbyla da abajlyq byla*.

1385 ADub.III.61: *icin*.

1386 JSul.I.45: *tirli*. | ADub.III.61: *tirli*.

1387 ADub.III.61: deest.

1388 ADub.III.61: *sezlemek*.

1389 A hypercorrect form of *kertilikni*. | JSul.I.45: *körtini*; a hypercorrect form of *kertini*. | ADub.III.61: *kertilikni*.

[1] [11] ⌊The second *peshat* of a *piyyut* for the parashat Kedoshim, of that (with the incipit) *ʾălēḵem ʾeqrå ʾīšīm*, of the great and honourable sage, his honour, the Rav, Rabbi 139 r°
[2] [12] Simcha the hazzan, the son of his honour, the Rav, Rabbi Chananel a resident of the holy community of Derażne.⌋[1391] .
[3] [13] I call to you with the words of advice, O, honourable men!
[4] [14] Examine yourselves (in search) of sinful deeds and examine
[5] [15] the others, too, (both) men and women. Hurry to do
[6] [16] the commandments of God, because then, after your death, you will be
[7] [17] holy. Hasten always to keep the orders of God,
[8] [18] for they are sought by all those who wish them. Do not turn
[9] [19] towards vanities for they snare like a trap. Remove the evil inclination
[10] [20] from ⌊inside you⌋[1392] and in place of burnt offerings do true penance.
[11] [21] Do not be godless to each other. Fear the honourable name of God
[12] [22] because then you will be enfolded by esteem and with regard[1393].
[13] [23] Treat your brethren with love
[14] [24] because then you will be not abandoned by the mercies of God. And
[15] [25] (reject having) two different thoughts, i.e. to say (something) good with mouth
[16] [26] but to think (something) evil inside: reject such deeds, but
[17] [27] be a searcher of the truth. Why would you disgrace yourselves by bodily

---

1390 JSul.I.45: *byrclanysiz.* | ADub.III.61: *byrclanysiz.*

1391 JSul.I.45: *A* peshat *of a* piyyut *for the parashat Kedoshim, of that (with the incipit)* ʾălēḵem ʾeqrå ʾīšīm, *which our master, our teacher, the great and honourable sage, his honour, the Rav, Rabbi Simcha translated, the hazzan of the holy community of Yefeh Yaʿar* [i.e., Kukizów], *may his memory be a blessing, the son of the Chananel, the aged, whose honourable repose is Eden, may he rest in peace.* | ADub.III.61: *The second* peshat *of a* piyyut *for the parashat Kedoshim, which our teacher, our master, the Rav, Rabbi Simcha translated, the hazzan of the holy community of Kukizów, may he rest in peace, the son of the Chananel, the aged, whose honourable repose is Eden, the resident of the holy community of Derażne, may his soul lodge in Eden.*

1392 ADub.III.61: *your heart.*

1393 ADub.III.61: *fame and with regard.*

[18] [28] ginehler byla da anyn ücün[1394] ʒanlarynyz ʒurum ketirirler.
[19] [29] Köteriniz[1395]
106 rº [20] [1] Köteriniz[1396] aqlafyn jüreknin[1397] ki ol aqlafy kibikti jemisinin ağacnyn
[21] [2] javuqlar da qatylar. Beriniz es [kelme][1398] aziz hermetli orun-
[22] [3] ğa kenesa ivine tizime alnynda Tenrinin syjly tefileler.
[23] [4] Birligin qotarynyz syjly šeminin Terninin hammeše da maḥtav
[24] [5] berme anar bolunuz juvuvcular. Ki ol uluslarğa qajyryr
[25] [6] aruv sözni[1399] ki oldu ol[1400] lešon haqodeš da ol vaḥtta eksilirler
[26] [7] dusmanlar qulluğun Tenrinin unutturuvcular. Da qulluq etme
[27] [8] anar bir sağysbyla bolurlar izlevciler. Da ol künde[1401] bolur
[28] [9] ⌊jalġyz H bir⌉[1402] bar dunjada da anyn birligine inanyrlar bar
[29] [10] umalar. ⌊בַּיּוֹם הַהוּא יִהְיֶה ה׳ אֶחָד וגו׳: שמע ישראל:⌉[1403]

---

1394 ADub.III.61: *icin*.

1395 Catchword.

1396 A hypercorrect from of *keteriniz*. | JSul.I.45: *keteriniz*. | ADub.III.61: *keteriniz*.

1397 ADub.III.61: *jireknin*.

1398 JSul.III.03: *qylma*; a scribal error. | JSul.I.45: *kölme*; a hypercorrect form of *kelme*. | ADub.III.61: *kelme*.

1399 ADub.III.61: *sezni*.

1400 JSul.I.45: deest. | ADub.III.61: deest.

1401 ADub.III.61: *kinde*.

1402 ADub.III.61: *H jalġyz ezi biji*.

1403 Zechariah 14:9, Deuteronomy 6:4. | JSul.I.45: וְהָיָה ה׳ לְמֶלֶךְ וגו׳: שמע ישראל. (Zechariah 14:9, Deuteronomy 6:4). | ADub.III.61: וְהָיָה ה׳ לְמֶלֶךְ עַל כָּל הָאָרֶץ וגו׳. (Zechariah 14:9).

1404 Catchword in the Karaim text.

[18] [28] sins because of which your souls would bear punishment?

[19] [29] Remove[1404]

[20] [1] Remove the unbelief[1405] of your heart, for that unbelief[1406] is like the hidden and hard fruit of a tree. 106 rº

[21] [2] Think sensible (and) come to the holy, esteemed place,

[22] [3] ⌊to the *kenesa*⌉[1407], to compose your honourable prayers before God.

[23] [4] Preach the oneness of the honourable name of God, always, and

[24] [5] be the one who approaches Him to praise (Him). For He directs[1408] to the nations

[25] [6] clear words, i.e. the Holy Language, and then

[26] [7] the enemies that made the service of God forgotten will vanish. And

[27] [8] the seekers of His service with unanimous[1409] thought will remain[1410]. And on that day,

[28] [9] the Lord[1411] will be the only one[1412] in the whole world and all the nations will believe in His oneness.

[29] [10] ⌊'In that day shall there be one Lord …' and so on. 'Hear, o Israel.'⌉[1413]

---

1405 Lit. 'foreskin'; Kar. *aqlaf* 'foreskin' is used in collocations to mean 'unbeliever; unbelieving'; in this case, it is probably understood as 'unbelief', 'uncleanness'; cf. SWKar. *aqlaf jirekliler* 'those with hearts of unbelievers; those with unbelieving hearts' (KarRPS 57, s.v. *аклаф*). See, next footnote. Cf. Deuteronomy 30:6.

1406 Lit. 'foreskin'; see, previous footnote.

1407 I.e., *to a Karaite shrine*; lit. 'to the house of *kenesa*'.

1408 Lit. 'turns'.

1409 Lit. 'one'.

1410 Lit. 'be'.

1411 ADub.III.61: *Lord himself.*

1412 ADub.III.61: *lord.*

1413 Zechariah 14:9, Deuteronomy 6:4. | JSul.I.45: *'And the Lord shall be king …' and so on. 'Hear, o Israel …'.* (Zechariah 14:9, Deuteronomy 6:4). | ADub.III.61: *'And the Lord shall be king over all the earth …' and so on.* (Zechariah 14:9).

**Text number:** № 24
**Karaim incipit:** *Ummasy Jisra'elnin zallenedi alnynda Tenrinin*
*Ummasy Jisra'elnin zellenedi alnynda Tenrinin*
**Hebrew incipit:** אֲנוּנָה אֲנִי וַעֲגוּמָה *'ănūnå 'ănī wa'ăgūmå*
**Dedication:** Shabbats of the month Tammuz
**Language:** Early Mod.SWKar., Mod.SWKar.[1414]
**Number of copies:** 7

| Accession no. | Place of origin of copy | Date of copy | Copyist | Folios |
|---|---|---|---|---|
| JSul.III.03 | Halych | shortly after 1805 | Unknown 7 | 101 v°–102 r° |
| JSul.I.45 | Halych | 1st half of the 19th c. | Jeshua Josef Mordkowicz | 125 v°–127 r° |
| ADub.III.61 | Halych | 1850/1851 | Jeshua Josef Mordkowicz | 113 v°–114 v° |
| JSul.III.69 | Halych | ca. 1851 (before 1866) | Jeshua Josef Mordkowicz | 221 v°–222 v° |
| JSul.III.79 | Halych | ca. 1851 (before 1866) | Jeshua Josef Mordkowicz | 272 r°–274 r° |
| JSul.I.01c | Halych | 2nd half of the 19th c. | Jeshua Josef Mordkowicz | 133 r°–134 r° |
| JSul.I.11 | Lutsk | 1878 | Zecharia ben Chanania Rojecki | 96 v°–99 r° |

## 1 Introductory Remarks

This *peshat* is one of four pre-18th-century Karaim *peshatim* of the *piyyut* starting with the words *'ănūnå 'ănī wa'ăgūmå*. The other three are *peshatim* № 1, 5, and 26. The copy in ms. JSul.I.11, i.e. a manuscript copied in Lutsk in 1878 by a native-speaker of North-Western Karaim, contains a number of north-western forms or hybrid forms that exhibit both South- and North-Western Karaim features. All copies are vocalized.

The texts can be arranged into two groups which share unique features. The versions of the *peshat* copied in JSul.III.03, JSul.III.69, and JSul.I.11 are very close to one other (and originate, most likely, from one copy or from copies closely related to one other). The other copies, i.e. the ones we found in JSul.I.45, ADub.III.61, JSul.III.79, and JSul.I.01c, constitute another group that share a number of affinities; cf. *jerlerimnin* vs. *jerimnin* (6), *murdarlyqlary* vs. *murdarlyġy* (7), *astry sivilgen* vs. *sivilgen* (8), *indeldim* vs. *murdar indeldim* (10), *ḥor etme ḥor ettin* vs. *ḥor ettin* (11), *hec abaqlarġa* vs. *abaqlarġa* (12), *ḥanlyqlary* vs.

1414 With a number of North-Western Karaim forms in JSul.I.11.

*gojlary* (13), *ol jerlernin* vs. *jerlernin* (14), *küp Tenrim menim* vs. *Tenrisi quvatymnyn* (14–15), *galutta kemisesen* vs. *kemisesen* (15), *miqdašynnyn* vs. *ivinnin* (17), *qorquvundan* vs. *qorquvlaryndan* (18), *könderir* vs. *jeter* (20), *qorqunclu* vs. *e qorqunclu* (29), *Tenrim* vs. *Tenri* (34), *joqtan bar etivcim* vs. *jaratuvcum* (35), *baqqyn istime* vs. *baqqyn* (35), *esitkin* vs. *tynlaġyn* (36), *jaslarymny* vs. *jasymny* (40), *jaratuvcum* vs. *e H jaratuvcum* (48), and *da qunusqun bolusluġuma menim* (38–39) not present in JSul.I.45, ADub.III.61, JSul.III.79, and JSul.I.01c. Moreover, the similarities (including errors), shared by JSul.III.03 and JSul.I.11 only, show that these two copies are even more closely related to one other (which corresponds to the fact that these are the only two manuscripts not copied by Jeshua Josef Mordkowicz), see *Tenrim* vs. *e Tenrim* (11), *tislerin* vs. *tisler* (18), and *qazynsam* vs. *qazylsam* (19). Besides these, there are also a few isolated discrepancies in mss. JSul.I.45, ADub.III.61, JSul.III.69, and JSul.I.01c that are a result of Jeshua Josef Mordkowicz's amendments. The relationship between these texts (not the manuscripts!) can be presented as follows:

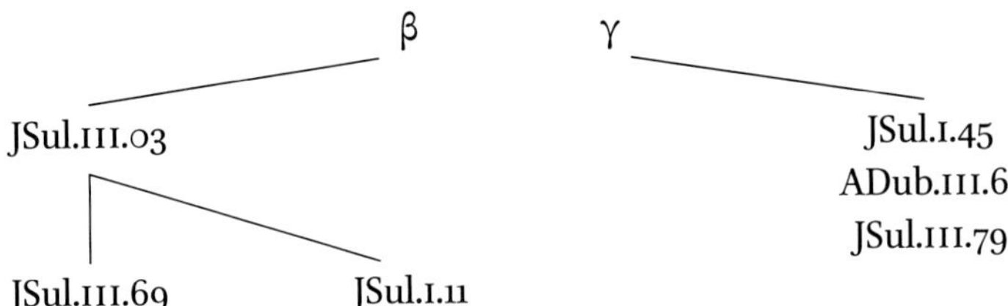


FIGURE 24 Diagram of the connections between the copies of peshat № 24

## 2 Transcription[1415] and Translation

101 v° [1] [2] ⌞וזה פשט רביעי לפיוט אנונה אני ועגומה אמ̃ו כמוה̃רר שמחה בכ̃מ חננאל נב̃ת:

[2] [3] אנונה אני ועגומה:⌝[1416]

[3] [4] Ummasy Jisra'elnin zallenedi[1417] alnynda Tenrinin da

[4] [5] ajtady jasly menmen[1418] da taryqqan qryvda

[5] [6] ketirgen[1419] dusmanlarymdan[1420] da acyrġandyrylġan[1421]. Ḥorlanġan da juvuz

[6] [7] ortasynda galut jerlerimnin[1422] kemisilgen, byrclanġan[1423] boldum

[7] [8] murdarlyqlary[1424] byla[1425] gojlarnyn[1426] bolġanym ornuna ez jerimde[1427]

[8] [9] azizlikte Tenrime astry[1428] sivilgen. Jazyqlarym ücün[1429]

---

1415 Based on JSul.III.03.

1416 JSul.I.45: פשט רביעי לפיוט אנונה עשאו כמוה̃רר שמחה החזן בכ̃מע חננאל הזקן יע̃מש. | ADub.III.61: פשט רביעי לפיוט אנונה תרגמו החכם האלהי אמוה̃רר שמחה החזן דקה̃ק קוקיזוב זצ̃וקל בכ̃מע חננאל מן דראזניע יש̃מש: אנ̃ונה אנ̃י ועג̃ומה. | JSul.III.69: פשט רביעי לפיוט אנונה תרגמו אמ̃ו הה̃ו כמוה̃רר שמחה החזן דקה̃ק קוקיזוב יע̃מש בכ̃מ חננאל הזקן מתושבי דראזניע יש̃י עמה̃ן. | JSul.III.79: פשט רביעי לפיוט אנונה תרגמו החכם הנעלה כמוה̃רר שמחה החזן דקה̃ק קוקיזוב נב̃ת בכ̃מע חננאל הזקן מן דראזניע יע̃מש: אנ̃ונה אנ̃י ועג̃ומה. | JSul.I.01: פשט שלישי לפיוט אנונה תרגמו אמ̃ו הר̃ר שמחה החזן דקה̃ק קוקיזוב תמ̃ד בכ̃מ חננאל הזקן יע̃מש. | JSul.I.11: תרגם זה אנ̃ונה אנ̃י ועגומ̃ה תרגם כהרר׳ שמחה החזן בכ̃מ חננאל מן דראז̃נה יעמש״ זצ̃וקל.

1417 ADub.III.61: *zellenedi.* | JSul.III.79: *zellenedi.* | JSul.I.01: *zellenedi.* | JSul.I.11: or: *żellenedi.*

1418 JSul.I.11: *menmin.*

1419 JSul.I.45: *kötirgen.*

1420 JSul.I.11: *dušmanlarymdan.*

1421 JSul.I.11: or: *ačyrġandyrylġan.*

1422 JSul.I.45: *jerimnin.* | ADub.III.61: *jerimnin.* | JSul.III.79: *jerimnin.* | JSul.I.01: *jerimnin.*

1423 JSul.I.11: or: *byrčlanġan.*

1424 JSul.I.45: *murdarlyġy.* | ADub.III.61: *murdarlyġy.* | JSul.III.79: *murdarlyġy.* | JSul.I.01: *murdarlyġy.*

1425 JSul.I.45: *ücüne.* | ADub.III.61: *icine.* | JSul.III.69: *icine.* | JSul.III.79: *icine.* | JSul.I.01: *icine.* | JSul.I.11: *icine* or *ičine.*

1426 ADub.III.61: *ceja gojlarnyn.*

1427 JSul.I.11: *jerimda.*

1428 JSul.I.45: deest. | ADub.III.61: deest. | JSul.III.79: deest. | JSul.I.01: deest.

1429 ADub.III.61: *icin.* | JSul.III.69: *icin.* | JSul.III.79: *icin.* | JSul.I.01: *icin.* | JSul.I.11: or: *üčün.*

1430 JSul.I.45: *The fourth* peshat *of the* piyyut (*with the incipit*) 'ănūnå *delivered by his honour, the Rav, Rabbi Simcha, the hazzan, the son of the Chananel, the aged, whose honourable repose is Eden, may he rest in peace.* | ADub.III.61: *The fourth* peshat *of the* piyyut (*with*

[1] [2] ⌊And this is the fourth *peshat* of the *piyyut* (with the incipit) *ʾănūnå ʾănī*, delivered by of our master, our teacher, his honour, the Rav, Rabbi Simcha the son of the honourable sir Chananel, may his soul lodge in Eden. 101 v°

[2] [3] (Incipit:) *ʾănūnå ʾănī wa'ăḡūmå*[1430]

[3] [4] The nation of Israel repents before God and

[4] [5] says: 'I am mournful and worried, suffering wrong

[5] [6] from my enemies and wearied. Condemned

[6] [7] and abandoned ⌊in the midst of the degrading[1431] lands[1432] of my exile. I have become disgraced

[7] [8] by[1433] the uncleanness of the Gentile[1434], instead of being in my own land

[8] [9] in sanctity, ⌊very much[1435] loved by my God. Because of my sins,

---

*the incipit*) ʾănūnå, *which the divine hakham translated, our master, our teacher, the Rav, Rabbi Simcha, the hazzan of the holy community of Kukizów, may the memory of the righteous and holy be a blessing, the son of the Chananel, whose honourable repose is Eden, from Derażne, may he rest in peace.* (*Incipit:*) ʾănūnå ʾănī wa'ăḡūmå. | JSul.III.69: *The fourth* peshat *of the* piyyut (*with the incipit*) ʾănūnå, *which our master, our teacher, his honour, Rabbi Simcha translated, the hazzan of the holy community of Kukizów, may he rest in peace, the son of the honourable Chananel, the aged, a resident of Derażne may the Lord protect it* [i.e., the community of Derażne] *in a pillar of cloud.* | JSul.III.79: *The fourth* peshat *of the* piyyut (*with the incipit*) ʾănūnå, *which the exalted hakham, his honour, the Rav, Rabbi Simcha translated, the hazzan of the holy community of Kukizów, may his soul lodge in Eden, the son of Chananel, the aged, from Derażne, the honourable repose of wich is Eden, may he rest in peace.* (*Incipit:*) ʾănūnå ʾănī wa'ăḡūmå. | JSul.I.01: *The third* peshat *of the* piyyut (*beginning with the word*) ʾănūnå, *which our master, our teacher, the Rav, Rabbi Simcha translated, the hazzan of the holy community of Kukizów, his place of rest shall be glorious, the son of the honourable sir Chananel, the aged, may he rest in peace.* | JSul.I.11: *This is an interpretation* (*of the* piyyut *beginning with the words*) ʾănūnå ʾănī wa'ăḡūmå, *the interpretation* (*of*) *his honour, the Rav, Rabbi Simcha, the hazzan, the son of Chananel from Derażne, may he rest in peace, may the memory of the righteous and holy be a blessing.*

1431 Lit. 'in the degrading midst of the'.

1432 Or: *places.* | JSul.I.45: *land* (~ *place*). | ADub.III.61: *land* (~ *place*). | JSul.III.79: *land* (~ *place*). | JSul.I.01: *land* (~ *place*).

1433 JSul.I.45: *in.* | ADub.III.61: *in.* | JSul.III.69: *in.* | JSul.III.79: *in.* | JSul.I.01: *in.* | JSul.I.11: *in.*

1434 ADub.III.61: *the shameless* (~ *cruel*) *Gentile.*

1435 JSul.I.45: desunt. | ADub.III.61: desunt. | JSul.III.79: desunt. | JSul.I.01: desunt.

[9] [10] berdi[1436] meni Tenrim[1437] qajġyly har kün[1438] ḥastalanġan.
[1439]⌈דוֹה וזבֿה⌋.
[10] [11] Ḥastalanġan da zavly[1440] kibik ⌊[murdar] indeldim⌋[1441] gojlardan anyn üсün[1442]
[11] [12] ki sen Tenrim[1443] ⌊ḥor etme[1444]⌋[1445] ḥor ettin meni. Tinkelttin
[12] [13] meni qulluq etivciler[1446] arasyna hec[1447] abaqlarġa da jerimden[1448]
[13] [14] tasladyn[1449] meni, da sirdin meni qyblalaryn alnyndan da ḥanlyqlary[1450]
[14] [15] arasyna ol[1451] jerlernin[1452] tozdurdun meni. Ki sensen ⌊küp[1453] Tenrim
[15] [16] menim⌋[1454] nek bulaj uzaq zaman galutta[1455] kemisesen[1456] meni.
[16] [17] [1457]זנחתֿני. Kemistin meni buzuqluq qyldyn mana da
[17] [18] sirdin meni ornundan miqdašynnyn[1458]. Synyqtyrdyn meni qorqunclu[1459]
[18] [19] tislerin[1460] byla da alġasattyn meni qorquvundan[1461] kerimlerinnin[1462].

---

1436 JSul.I.01: *qojdu.* || The interchangeable use of *qoj-* 'to put' and *ber-* 'to give' is a semantic calque of Heb. נָתַן '1. to give; 2. to permit; 3. to deliver; 4. to put, to set; 5. to make'—known also from Biblical texts.

1437 JSul.I.45: *Tenri.* | ADub.III.61: *Tenri.* | JSul.III.79: *Tenri.* | JSul.I.11: *Tenri.*

1438 ADub.III.61: *kin.* | JSul.III.69: *kin.* | JSul.III.79: *kin.* | JSul.I.01: *kin.* | JSul.I.11: כִּיוּן *kün*, the vocalization suggests Mod.NWKar. [*ḱuń*].

1439 JSul.I.45: דוֹה. | JSul.III.69: דוֹה. | JSul.III.79: דוֹה. | JSul.I.01: דוֹה. | JSul.I.11: דוה.

1440 ADub.III.61: *zavly qatyn.*

1441 JSul.III.03: *indeldim.* | JSul.I.45: *murdar indeldim.* | ADub.III.61: *murdar indeldim.* | JSul.III.69: *indeldim.* | JSul.III.79: *murdar indeldim.* | JSul.I.01: *murdar indeldim.* | JSul.I.11: *indeldim.*

1442 ADub.III.61: *icin.* | JSul.III.69: *icin.* | JSul.III.79: *icin.* | JSul.I.01: *icin.* | JSul.I.11: or: *üčün.*

1443 JSul.I.45: *e Tenrim.* | ADub.III.61: *e Tenrim.* | JSul.III.69: *e Tenrim.* | JSul.III.79: *e Tenrim.* | JSul.I.01: *e Tenrim.*

1444 JSul.I.11: *etḿa.*

1445 JSul.I.45: desunt. | ADub.III.61: desunt. | JSul.III.79: desunt. | JSul.I.01: desunt.

1446 JSul.I.11: אֵיטִיבְצִיוּלֵיר *etivcüĺar* or *etivčüĺar* (a hybrid form).

1447 JSul.I.45: deest. | ADub.III.61: deest. | JSul.III.79: deest. | JSul.I.01: deest. | JSul.I.11: or: *heč.*

1448 JSul.I.11: *jerimd́an.*

1449 JSul.I.11: *tašladyn.*

1450 JSul.I.45: *gojlary.* | ADub.III.61: *gojlary.* | JSul.III.79: *gojlary.* | JSul.I.01: *gojlary.*

1451 JSul.I.45: deest. | ADub.III.61: deest. | JSul.III.79: deest. | JSul.I.01: deest.

1452 JSul.I.11: *jerĺarnin.*

1453 A hypercorrect form of *kip.* | JSul.III.69: *kip.* | JSul.I.11: *küp*; a hypercorrect form of *kip.*

1454 JSul.I.45: *Tenrisi quvatymnyn.* | ADub.III.61: *Tenrisi quvatymnyn.* | JSul.III.79: *Tenrisi quvatymnyn.* | JSul.I.01: *Tenrisi quvatymnyn.*

[9] [10] my[1463] God has made me concerned and ill every day. (2).
[10] [11] I have been called by the Gentile unclean[1464], like a sufferer or ⌊one with a discharge⌋[1465], for
[11] [12] You, my[1466] God, have certainly[1467] rejected me. You have made me wander
[12] [13] among those who serve paltry[1468] idols and
[13] [14] You have cast me out from my land and have driven me from before Your countenance and
[14] [15] have scattered me among the kingdoms[1469] of those[1470] lands. Given that You are my powerful God,
[15] [16] why do You keep me for so long time in exile?
[16] [17] (3). You have abandoned me, ⌊destructed me⌋[1471] and
[17] [18] have driven me from the place of Your shrine[1472]. You have depressed me with Your[1473] frightful
[18] [19] dreams and terrified me with the fear of Your visions.

---

1455 JSul.I.45: deest. | ADub.III.61: deest. | JSul.III.79: deest. | JSul.I.01: deest.
1456 JSul.I.11: כֵּימִיסֵיסִין *kemisesin* (a hybrid form).
1457 ADub.III.61: זנחתני פרצתני.
1458 JSul.I.45: *ivinnin.* | ADub.III.61: *ivinnin.* | JSul.III.79: *ivinnin.* | JSul.I.01: *ivinnin.*
1459 JSul.I.11: or: *qorqunčlu.*
1460 JSul.I.45: *tisler.* | ADub.III.61: *tisler.* | JSul.III.69: *tisler.* | JSul.III.79: *tisler.* | JSul.I.01: *tisler.* | JSul.I.11: טִיסְלַירִין *tisĺarin* (a hybrid form).
1461 JSul.I.45: *qorquvlaryndan.* | ADub.III.61: *qorquvlaryndan.* | JSul.III.79: *qorquvlaryndan.* | JSul.I.01: *qorquvlaryndan.*
1462 JSul.I.11: כֵּירִימְלַירִינְנִין *kerimĺarinnin* (a hybrid form).
1463 JSul.I.45: deest. | ADub.III.61: deest. | JSul.III.79: deest. | JSul.I.11: deest.
1464 JSul.III.03: deest. | JSul.III.69: deest. | JSul.I.11: deest.
1465 ADub.III.61: *a women having a discharge.*
1466 JSul.I.45: *O my.* | ADub.III.61: *O my.* | JSul.III.69: *O my.* | JSul.III.79: *O my.* | JSul.I.01: *O my.*
1467 JSul.I.45: deest. | ADub.III.61: deest. | JSul.III.79: deest. | JSul.I.01: deest.
1468 JSul.I.45: deest. | ADub.III.61: deest. | JSul.III.79: deest. | JSul.I.01: deest.
1469 JSul.I.45: *Gentile* or *nations.* | ADub.III.61: *Gentile* or *nations.* | JSul.III.79: *Gentile* or *nations.* | JSul.I.01: *Gentile* or *nations.*
1470 Or: *the.* | JSul.I.45: deest. | ADub.III.61: deest. | JSul.III.79: deest. | JSul.I.01: deest.
1471 Lit. 'You did destruction to me'.
1472 JSul.I.45: *house.* | ADub.III.61: *house.* | JSul.III.79: *house.* | JSul.I.01: *house.*
1473 JSul.I.45: deest. | ADub.III.61: deest. | JSul.III.69: deest. | JSul.III.79: deest. | JSul.I.01: deest.

[19] [20] E aruv enajatly[1474] Tenri[1475] eger gergede[1476] qazynsam[1477] qacma[1478]

[20] [21] alnyndan qyblalarynnyn, dağyn andada qudratyn könderir[1479] meni

[21] [22] da tutar meni kücü[1480] on qudratynnyn. יְמִינְךָ.

[22] [23] On qudratyn küplesin[1481] meni asyrmaq byla avurluğun gineḥlerimnin[1482],

[23] [24] ki astry juvuz boldum da izildiler fikirleri[1483] sağyslarymnyn,

[24] [25] dusman[1484] qysyqlyq etedi[1485] mana da juvuz etti ektemligin[1486]

[25] [26] bijikliklerimnin[1487], da sen e H bilesen[1488] qacanġadejin bolur avurluğu

[26] [27] galutumnun. [1489]⸢מָתַי תוֹצִיא⸣. Galutta avurluqlar[1490]

[27] [28] cydağanymny keredoğac[1491] e bij[i][1492] dunjanyn qacan cyġaryrsen[1493]

[28] [29] rastlyqqa[1494]

102 rº [29] [1] rastlyqqa jarğularymny. Qorqunclu[1495] Tenri ⸤qabul etkin jalbarmaqlarymny[1496]⸥[1497]

[30] [2] da veren etkin galutta qyjnavcularymny[1498], küplegin[1499] meni da

---

1474 In all copies written separately, i.e., *enaj atly*; see our remark on page 108.

1475 JSul.I.45: deest. | ADub.III.61: deest.

1476 JSul.I.11: גֵּירְגֵּידְיא *gerged́a* (a hybrid form).

1477 JSul.I.45: *qazylsam.* | ADub.III.61: *qazylsam.* | JSul.III.69: *qazylsam.* | JSul.III.79: *qazylsam.* | JSul.I.01: *qazylsam.*

1478 JSul.I.11: or: *qačma.*

1479 JSul.I.45: *jeter.* | ADub.III.61: *jeter.* | JSul.III.69: *kenderir.* | JSul.III.79: *jeter.* | JSul.I.01: *jeter.* | JSul.I.11: *kenderir.*

1480 ADub.III.61: *kici.* | JSul.III.69: *kici.* | JSul.III.79: *kici.* | JSul.I.01: *kici.* | JSul.I.11: or: *küču.*

1481 A hypercorrect form of *kiplesin.* | JSul.I.45: *kiplesin.* | ADub.III.61: *kiplesin.* | JSul.III.69: *kiplesin.* | JSul.III.79: *kiplesin.* | JSul.I.01: *kiplesin.* | JSul.I.11: כיוּפְּלַיסִין *küpĺasin* (a hypercorrect form of NWKar. *kipĺasin*).

1482 JSul.I.11: גִינֵיחְלַירִימְנִין *gineḥĺarimnin* (a hybrid form).

1483 JSul.I.11: *fikirĺari.*

1484 JSul.I.11: *dušman.*

1485 JSul.I.11: *eťadi.*

1486 JSul.I.11: אֵיקְטַימְלִיגִין *ekťamligin* (a hybrid form).

1487 JSul.I.11: *bijikliḱĺarimnin.*

1488 JSul.I.11: בִילֵיסִין *bilesin* (a hybrid form).

1489 JSul.I.45: מָתַי. | ADub.III.61: מָתַי. | JSul.III.69: מָתַי. | JSul.I.01: מָתַי. | JSul.I.11: מָתַי.

1490 JSul.I.11: *avurluḥlar.*

1491 JSul.I.11: כֵּירֵידוֹגוֹן *keredoġon* (a hybrid form).

[19] [20] O pure-eyed God, even if I would ⌞bury myself⌝[1500] in a grave to escape
[20] [21] from before Your countenance, even there Your hand would drive[1501] me,
[21] [22] and the power of Your right hand would catch me. (4).
[22] [23] May Your right hand strengthen me by forgiving the burden of my sins
[23] [24] for I have become very unworthy and the concepts of my thoughts have been broken;
[24] [25] the enemy has oppressed me and lowered the highness of my pride,
[25] [26] but You, O Lord, know until when will last the burden
[26] [27] of my exile. (5). Seeing that I have borne the burdens in exile,
[27] [28] O Lord of the world, ⌞when will You turn[1502]
[28] [29] ⌞to righteousness⌝[1503]
[29] [1] to righteousness my verdicts⌝[1504]? Awesome God, ⌞accept my entreaties[1505]⌝[1506] 102 r°
[30] [2] and destroy my tormentors in the exile, strengthen me and

1492 JSul.III.03: *bij*; a scribal error. | JSul.I.45: *biji.* | ADub.III.61: *biji.* | JSul.III.69: *biji.* | JSul.III.79: *biji.* | JSul.I.01: *biji.* | JSul.I.11: *biji.*

1493 JSul.I.45: *cyġarysen.* | JSul.III.79: *cyġarysen.* | JSul.I.11: or: *čyġaryrsen.*

1494 Catchword.

1495 JSul.I.45: *e qorqunclu.* | ADub.III.61: *e qorqunclu.* | JSul.III.79: *e qorqunclu.* | JSul.I.01: *e qorqunclu.* | JSul.I.11: or: *qorqunčlu.*

1496 JSul.III.69: *jalbarmaġymny.* | JSul.I.11: *jalbarmaġymny.*

1497 JSul.I.45: *qajyrġyn esitivinni jalbarmaġyma.* | ADub.III.61: *qajyrġyn esitivinni jalbarmaġyma.* | JSul.III.79: *qajyrġyn esitivinni jalbarmaġyma.* | JSul.I.01: *qajyrġyn esitivinni jalbarmaġyma.*

1498 JSul.I.11: or: *qyjnavčularymny.*

1499 A hypercorrect form of *kiplegin.* | JSul.I.45: *kiplegin.* | ADub.III.61: *kiplegin.* | JSul.III.69: *kiplegin.* | JSul.III.79: *kiplegin.* | JSul.I.01: *kiplegin.* | JSul.I.11: כיופְלֵיגִין *küplegin* (a hybrid and hypercorrect form).

1500 JSul.I.45: *be buried.* | ADub.III.61: *be buried.* | JSul.III.69: *be buried.* | JSul.III.79: *be buried.* | JSul.I.01: *be buried.*

1501 JSul.I.45: *reach.* | ADub.III.61: *reach.* | JSul.III.79: *reach.* | JSul.I.01: *reach.*

1502 Lit. 'take out', 'draw out'.

1503 Catchword in the Karaim text.

1504 I.e., *when will You find me innocent when You judge me.*

1505 JSul.III.69: *entreaty.* | JSul.I.11: *entreaty.*

1506 JSul.I.45: *turn Your ear to my entreaty.* | ADub.III.61: *turn Your ear to my entreaty.* | JSul.III.79: *turn Your ear to my entreaty.* | JSul.I.01: *turn Your ear to my entreaty.*

[31] [3] jarlyġaslanajym ki jistirmek[1507] ücün[1508] ⌊jyjynyn qahallarymnyn⌋[1509], jalbarmaqlar
[32] [4] byla sana kötiremen[1510] osol[1511] közlerimni[1512]. [1513]⌈עי֗ני מצפ֗ות⌋.
[33] [5] Közlerim[1514] telmerediler[1515] sana e Tenrim bar tarlyqtan juluvcu[1516] meni.
[34] [6] Juluġun meni uturu[1517] turuvcularymdan[1518] e H Tenrim[1519] arttyruvcu[1520]
[35] [7] ḥalimni. E ⌊joqtan bar etivcim[1521]⌋[1522] baqqyn istime[1523] da qabul
[36] [8] etkin tefilemni[1524]. E H har erten bylalarda esitkin[1525] avazymny.
[37] [9] [1526]⌈קו֗לי שע֗ה⌋. Avazymny qabul etkin da jummaġyn enajatynny[1527]
[38] [10] jalbarmaġymdan. Klegin[1528] e H qutqarma meni ⌊da qunusqun
[39] [11] bolusluġuma menim⌋[1529] da jyraq ketmegin[1530] menden[1531]. Körgin[1532] qryvda
[40] [12] cydaġanymny[1533] gojlardan da sirtkin jaslarymny[1534] közlerimden[1535].

---

1507 JSul.I.45: *ystyrmaq.* | ADub.III.61: *ystyrmaq.* | JSul.III.69: *ystyrmaq.* | JSul.III.79: *ystyrmaq.* | JSul.I.01: *ystyrmaq.* | JSul.I.11: *jyštyrmaq.*

1508 ADub.III.61: *icin.* | JSul.III.69: *icin.* | JSul.III.79: *icin.* | JSul.I.01: *icin.* | JSul.I.11: or: *üčün.*

1509 JSul.I.45: *galut jerlerden tozulġanlarymny.* | ADub.III.61: *galut jerlerden tozulġanlarymny.* | JSul.III.79: *galut jerlerimden tozulġanlarymny.* | JSul.I.01: *galut jerlerden tozulġanlarymny.*

1510 ADub.III.61: *ketiremen.* | JSul.III.69: *ketiremen.* | JSul.III.79: *ketiremen.* | JSul.I.01: *ketiremen.* | JSul.I.11: *ketiremen.*

1511 JSul.I.11: *ošol.*

1512 ADub.III.61: *kezlerimni.* | JSul.III.69: *kezlerimni.* | JSul.III.79: *kezlerimni.* | JSul.I.01: *kezlerimni.* | JSul.I.11: כיוזְלֵירִימְנִי *közlerimni* (possibly a hybrid form).

1513 JSul.I.45: עי֗ני. | ADub.III.61: עי֗ני. | JSul.III.79: עי֗ני. | JSul.I.01: עי֗ני.

1514 ADub.III.61: *kezlerim.* | JSul.III.69: *kezlerim.* | JSul.III.79: *kezlerim.* | JSul.I.01: *kezlerim.* | JSul.I.11: *kezlerim.*

1515 JSul.I.11: טֵילְמֵירֵידִילַיר *telmerediĺar* (a hybrid form).

1516 JSul.I.11: or: *juluvču.*

1517 JSul.I.11: *utru.*

1518 JSul.I.11: or: *turuvčularymdan.*

1519 JSul.I.45: *Tenri.* | ADub.III.61: *Tenri.* | JSul.III.79: *Tenri.* | JSul.I.01: *Tenri.*

1520 JSul.I.11: or: *arttyruvču.*

1521 JSul.I.11: *etivčüm.*

1522 JSul.I.45: *jaratuvcum.* | ADub.III.61: *jaratuvcum.* | JSul.III.79: *jaratuvcum.* | JSul.I.01: *jaratuvcum.*

1523 JSul.I.45: deest. | ADub.III.61: deest. | JSul.III.79: deest. | JSul.I.01: deest. | JSul.I.11: *üstüḿa.*

[31] [3] let me be rescued since for the sake of gathering ⌊the congregation of my communities⌋[1536]
[32] [4] I lift my eyes to You with entreaties. (6).
[33] [5] My eyes ⌊miss You⌋[1537], O God of mine, my saviour from all the misery.
[34] [6] Save me from my foes, O Lord God ⌊of mine⌋[1538], who increases
[35] [7] my abilities. O my creator ⌊from nothing⌋[1539], look ⌊at me⌋[1540] and accept
[36] [8] my prayer. O Lord, hearken to my voice every morning.
[37] [9] (7). Accept my voice and do not close Your eyes[1541]
[38] [10] to my entreaty. Wish, O Lord, to save me and ⌊raise
[39] [11] for the sake of my providence⌋[1542] and do not go far from me. See that I have suffered
[40] [12] wrong from the Gentile and wipe my tears from my eyes.

1524 JSul.I.11: *tefilamny.*
1525 JSul.I.45: *tynlağyn.* | ADub.III.61: *tynlağyn.* | JSul.III.79: *tynlağyn.* | JSul.I.01: *tynlağyn.* | JSul.I.11: *ešitkin.*
1526 JSul.I.45: קוֹלִי. | ADub.III.61: קוֹלִי. | JSul.III.69: קוֹלִי. | JSul.III.79: קוֹלִי. | JSul.I.01: קוֹלִי.
1527 JSul.I.45: *esitivinni.*
1528 JSul.I.11: *kĺagin.*
1529 JSul.I.45: desunt. | ADub.III.61: desunt. | JSul.III.79: desunt. | JSul.I.01: desunt.
1530 JSul.I.11: *ketḿagin.*
1531 JSul.I.11: *mendán.*
1532 ADub.III.61: *kergin.* | JSul.III.69: *kergin.* | JSul.III.79: *kergin.* | JSul.I.01: *kergin.* | JSul.I.11: *kirgin kergin*; a scribal error.
1533 JSul.I.11: or: *čydağanymny.*
1534 JSul.I.45: *jasymny.* | ADub.III.61: *jasymny.* | JSul.III.79: *jasymny.* | JSul.I.01: *jasymny.*
1535 ADub.III.61: *kezlerimden.* | JSul.III.69: *kezlerimden.* | JSul.III.79: *kezlerimden.* | JSul.I.01: *kezleri{m}den.* | JSul.I.11: כיוֹזְלֶירִימדַין *közlerimdán* (a hybrid form).
1536 JSul.I.45: *from the places of exile those of you who had dispersed.* | ADub.III.61: *from the places of exile those of you who had dispersed.* | JSul.III.79: *from the places of exile those of you who had dispersed.* | JSul.I.01: *from the places of exile those of you who had dispersed.*
1537 Or: *look at You with hope.*
1538 JSul.I.45: desunt. | ADub.III.61: desunt. | JSul.III.79: desunt. | JSul.I.01: desunt.
1539 JSul.I.45: desunt. | ADub.III.61: desunt. | JSul.III.79: desunt. | JSul.I.01: desunt.
1540 JSul.I.45: desunt. | ADub.III.61: desunt. | JSul.III.79: desunt. | JSul.I.01: desunt.
1541 JSul.I.45: *ears*; a scribal error: the verb *jum-* 'close; squint' can be used with reference to eyes, only.
1542 JSul.I.45: desunt. | ADub.III.61: desunt. | JSul.III.79: desunt. | JSul.I.01: desunt.

[41] [13] E H tynlaġyn jalbarmaġymny da japmaġyn esitivinni[1543] tefilemden[1544].

[42] [14] [1545]⌜תפלתי שמעה⌟. Tefilemni[1546] qabul etkin da qajtqyn

[43] [15] da qaruv bergin mana. E raḥmetli Tenri[1547] jamanlyġyna köre[1548] jaman

[44] [16] islerimnin jarġu jarmaġyn meni da islerime köre[1549] telemegin

[45] [17] mana. Firjatymny qabul etkin da savaġatyn byla ḥajifsingin[1550]

[46] [18] meni da kelsin tefilem[1551] alnyna. Men ajtamen e H sirinlik[1552]

[47] [19] sunġun mana. [1553]⌜חנני צורי⌟. Sirinlik[1554] tapsyn

[48] [20] tefilem[1555] alnynda jaratuvcum[1556] da ḥabar bergin mana ajtadoġac[1557]

[49] [21] bosattym[1558] avurluġun gineḥlerinnin[1559]. Jystyrġyn[1560] meni jat jerlerden[1561]

[50] [22] da istime qyzyssynlar cuvlamaqlary[1562] ḥajifsinmeklerinnin.

[51] [23] Köpligi[1563] byla jarlyġasynnyn[1564] qabul etkin tefilesin[1565] jalbaruvcularynnyn[1566].

[52] [24] E Tenrim köpligi[1567] byla savaġatynnyn tynlaġyn sarnamaqlarymny[1568] da

---

1543 JSul.I.11: *ešitivinni.*

1544 JSul.I.11: *tefilamdan.*

1545 JSul.I.45: תפלתי. | ADub.III.61: תפלתי. | JSul.III.69: תפלתי. | JSul.III.79: תפלתי. | JSul.I.01: תפלתי. | JSul.I.11: תפלתי.

1546 JSul.I.11: *tefilamny.*

1547 JSul.III.69: *bij da kicli Tenri.*

1548 ADub.III.61: *kere.* | JSul.III.69: *kere.* | JSul.III.79: *kere.* | JSul.I.01: *kere.* | JSul.I.11: *kere.*

1549 JSul.I.45: *kere.* | ADub.III.61: *kere.* | JSul.III.69: *kere.* | JSul.III.79: *kere.* | JSul.I.01: *kere.* | JSul.I.11: *kere.*

1550 JSul.I.11: *ḥajyfsunġun.*

1551 JSul.I.11: *tefilam.*

1552 JSul.I.11: *širinlik.*

1553 JSul.I.45: חנני. | ADub.III.61: חנני. | JSul.III.69: חנני. | JSul.III.79: חנני. | JSul.I.01: חנני.

1554 JSul.I.11: *širinlik.*

1555 JSul.I.11: *tefile.*

1556 JSul.I.45: *e H jaratuvcum.* | ADub.III.61: *senin e H jaratuvcum.* | JSul.III.79: *senin e H jaratuvcum.* | JSul.I.01: *senin e H jaratuvcum.* | JSul.I.11: or: *jaratuvčum.*

1557 JSul.I.11: *ajtadoġoc* or *ajtadoġoč.*

1558 JSul.I.11: *bošattym.*

1559 JSul.III.79: *gineḥlerimnin*; a scribal error.

[41] [13] O Lord, listen to my entreaty and do not close Your ears to my prayer.
[42] [14] (8). Accept my prayer and turn back
[43] [15] and reply to me. O merciful God[1569], do not judge me according to the evil
[44] [16] of my evil deeds and do not pay to me according to my deeds.
[45] [17] Accept my cry and have mercy on me with Your benevolence,
[46] [18] and let my prayer come before You. I say, O Lord, reach out Your approval
[47] [19] to me. (9). May my prayer find
[48] [20] approval before You, ⌞my creator⌝[1570], and ⌞announce to me⌝[1571],
[49] [21] "I have absolved the burden of your sins". Gather me[1572] from the foreign lands
[50] [22] and may the thunders of Your mercies be worried about me.
[51] [23] With[1573] the abundance of Your grace accept the prayer of those[1574] who pray to You.
[52] [24] O God of mine, with the abundance of Your mercy listen to me singing and

---

1560 JSul.I.45: *ystyrġyn.* | ADub.III.61: *ystyrġyn.* | JSul.III.69: *ystyrġyn.* | JSul.III.79: *ystyrġyn.* | JSul.I.01: *ystyrġyn.*

1561 JSul.I.11: ייֵרְלַירְדֵין *jerĺarden* (a hybrid form).

1562 JSul.I.11: or: *čuvlamaqlary.*

1563 JSul.I.45: *ki köpligi.* | ADub.III.61: *kepligi.* | JSul.III.69: *kepligi.* | JSul.III.79: *kepligi.* | JSul.I.01: *kepligi.* | JSul.I.11: *köpligi.*

1564 JSul.III.03: or: *jarlyġašynnyn.* | JSul.I.11: *jarlyġašynnyn.*

1565 JSul.I.11: *tefilasyn.*

1566 JSul.III.69: *barda jalbaruvcularynnyn.* | JSul.I.11: or: *jalbaruvčularynnyn.*

1567 ADub.III.61: *kepligi.* | JSul.III.69: *kepligi.* | JSul.III.79: *kepligi.* | JSul.I.01: *kepligi.* | JSul.I.11: *köpligi.*

1568 JSul.I.11: *sarnamaḥlarymny.*

1569 JSul.III.69: *Lord and powerful God.*

1570 JSul.I.45: *O Lord, my creator.* | ADub.III.61: *O Lord, my creator.* | JSul.III.79: *O Lord, my creator.* | JSul.I.01: *O Lord, my creator.*

1571 Lit. 'announce to me, saying'.

1572 I.e., *Israel.*

1573 JSul.I.45: *for with.*

1574 JSul.III.69: *all of those.*

[53] [25] qaruv bergin mana körtiligi[1575] byla jarlyġasynnyn[1576].

[54] [26] ⸤אלהים ברב חסדך וכו׳: הטה ה׳ אזנך ענני:⸣[1577]

1575 A hypercorrect form of *kertiligi*. | ADub.III.61: *kertiligi*. | JSul.III.69: *kertiligi*. | JSul.III.79: *kertiligi*. | JSul.I.01: *kertiligi*. | JSul.I.11: *kertiligi*.

1576 JSul.I.11: *jarlyġašynnyn*.

1577 Psalm 69:13; Psalm 86:1. | JSul.I.45: הטה ה׳ אזנך ענני וגו׳. (Psalm 86:1). | ADub.III.61: תם: ותאמר הַטֵּה הָ׳ אָזְנְךָ עֲנֵנִי כִּי עָנִי וְאֶבְיוֹן אָנִי. (Psalm 86:1). | JSul.III.69: אֱלֹהִים בְּרָב חַסְדֶּךָ וגו׳ וכל המזמור ר״ל הַטֵּה הָ׳ אָזְנְךָ עֲנֵנִי כִּי עָנִי וְאֶבְיוֹן אָנִי וגו׳. (Psalms 69:13, 86:1). | JSul.III.79: הַטֵּה הָ׳ אָזְנְךָ עֲנֵנִי וגו׳. (Psalm 86:1). | JSul.I.01: הטה ה׳ אזנך וגו׳. (Psalm 86:1). | JSul.I.11: אלהים ברב חסדך ענני ב״א. (Psalms 69:13).

[53] [25] answer me with the truth of Your grace.'

[54] [26] ⌊'O God, in the multitude of your mercy …' and so forth. 'Bow down your ear, O Lord, hear me.'⌋[1578]

1578 Psalm 69:13; Psalm 86:1. | JSul.I.45: *'Bow down your ear, O Lord, hear me …' and so on.* (Psalm 86:1). | ADub.III.61: *'Bow down your ear, O Lord, hear me: for I am poor and needy.'* (Psalm 86:1). | JSul.III.69: *And you will say 'O God, in the multitude of your mercy …' and so on, and whole psalm, i.e., 'Bow down your ear, O Lord, hear me: for I am poor and needy …' and so on.* (Psalms 69:13, 86:1). | JSul.III.79: *'Bow down your ear, O Lord, hear me …' and so on.* (Psalm 86:1). | JSul.I.01: *'Bow down your ear, O Lord …' and so on.* (Psalm 86:1). | JSul.I.11: *'O God, in the multitude of your mercy hear me, in the truth of your salvation.'* (Psalm 69:13).

# PART 6

# *A* peshat *of Josef ben Shemuel ben Josef ha-Mashbir*

∴

| | |
|---|---|
| **Text number:** | № 25 |
| **Karaim incipit:** | *Maḥtavludu joġarġy Tenri jaratuvcu köklerni*<br>*Maḥtavludur joġarġy Tenri jaratuvcu köklerni* |
| **Hebrew incipit:** | יִשְׁתַּבַּח אֵל עֶלְיוֹן *yištabbaḥ ʾēl ʿelyōn* |
| **Dedication:** | Parashat Vayelech (Deuteronomy 31:1–31:30) |
| **Language:** | Early Mod.SWKar., Mod.SWKar. |
| **Number of copies:** | 7 |

| Accession no. | Place of origin of copy | Date of copy | Copyist | Folios |
|---|---|---|---|---|
| JSul.III.03 | Halych | shortly after 1805 | Unknown 7 | 109 r°–109 v° |
| JSul.I.45 | Halych | 1st half of the 19th c. | Jeshua Josef Mordkowicz | 146 r°–147 r° |
| JSul.I.46 | Halych | 1st half of the 19th c. | Jeshua Josef Mordkowicz | 99 v°–100 v° |
| ADub.III.61 | Halych | 1850/1851 | Jeshua Josef Mordkowicz | 141 r°–142 r° |
| JSul.III.07 | Halych | 2nd half of the 19th c. | Jeshua Josef Mordkowicz | 114 v°–115 r° |
| JSul.III.69 | Halych | ca. 1851 (before 1866) | Jeshua Josef Mordkowicz | 302 v°–303 v° |
| JSul.III.79 | Halych | ca. 1851 (before 1866) | Jeshua Josef Mordkowicz | 184 r°–185 r° |

## 1 Introductory Remarks

All seven copies are vocalized. The versions copied in ADub.III.61 and JSul.III.79 are slightly more similar to each other than to the other copies, but their shared affinities cannot be considered significant, see *aziz Toranyn* vs. *Toranyn* (16), *tajġan vaḥtta* vs. *ne vaḥtny tajsa* (31), *azizligin da qajjamlyġyn* vs. *azizligin* (35). The copies in JSul.I.46 and JSul.III.07 also share some features, see, e.g., *barġȧ jaratty* vs. *bar etti* (9) or the lack of *jerinin* (20). The copy in JSu.I.45 stands somewhat closer to the *peshatim* in ADub.III.61 and JSul.III.79, see, e.g., *ivinde* vs. (*orunda*) *kensa ivinde* (37). Finally, there are some unique similarities between JSul.III.03 and JSul.III.69, too, see, e.g., *har birisinin* vs. *har bir tirinin* (11). The relationship between these texts can be presented as follows:

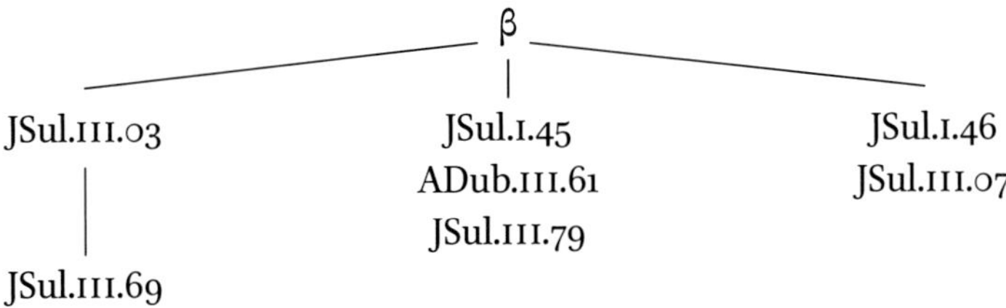


FIGURE 25 Diagram of the connections between the copies of peshat № 25

## 2 Transcription[1] and Translation

109 r° [1] [15] ⸤וזה הפשט לפיוט פרשת וילך שהוא ישתבח אל עליון עשאו אד̃ היניק וחכים
ה̃ה

[2] [16] אמ̃ו כמוה̃רר יוסף המשכיל החריף נב̃ת בא̃ז כמוה̃רר שמואל החזן ואב̃ד דקה̃ק
הליץ יעמ̃ש⸣[2]

[3] [17] Maḥtavludu[3] joġarġy Tenri jaratuvcu köklerni[4] da bar

[4] [18] jyjynlaryn alarnyn, da cyġaruvcu san

[5] [19] byla cerivlerin da barlaryn at byla caġyrady qylma qulluġun

[6] [20] anyn. Könderedi[5] kücübyla[6] bijiktegi cerivni da toḥtavcularyn

[7] [21] juvuz dunjanyn da qajjamlyqta tutady peratlaryn da kelallaryn alarnyn.

[8] [22] Acady osol jaḥsylyġyn qudratynyn[7] da tolturady kleklerin bar

[9] [23] tiri tennin. Savaġaty byla joqtan ⸤barġa jaratty⸣[8] alarny da

[10] [24] raḥmetleri byla malaẖlyq ustan tüzüdü[9] aqyllaryn alarnyn.

---

1 Based on JSul.III.03.

2 JSul.I.45: וזה הפשט לפיוט פרשת וילך שהוא ישתבח אל אליון אד̃ ההו̃ כמוה̃רר יוסף המשכיל
והוא נעשה :JSul.I.46 | .נב̃ת: בן אז̃ כמוה̃רר שמואל החזן דקה̃ק האליץ יעמ̃ש: אם ושרצונך תא̃מ
מזוך שכלו הצלול של אד̃ היניק וחכים ה̃ה כמוה̃רר יוסף המשכיל נב̃ת בא̃ז ההו̃ כמוה̃רר שמואל
החזן ואב̃ד דקה̃ק האליץ יעמ̃ש: אם תרצה תא̃מ אותו כדי להבין את טוב טעם מליצתו עמו הארץ
ואם תרצה תאמר גם פשטו שתרגמו אד̃ו דודי חיניק :ADub.III.61 | .הבלתי מבינים לשונ הקדש:
וחכים החכם כמוה̃רר יוסף נב̃ת: בן אד̃ו זקני הגאון המרומם כמוה̃רר שמואל החזן ואב̃ד דקה̃ק
וזהו פשטו שתרגמו אד̃ היניק וחכים כמוה̃רר יוסף נב̃ת כמוה̃רר :JSul.III.07 | .האליץ תנצב̃הה
וזהו פשטו שתרגמו אד̃ היניק והכים אד̃ו מוה̃רר יוסף זצ̃ל בא̃ז :JSul.III.69 | .שמואל החזן יעמ̃ש
וזהו פשטו של :JSul.III.79 | .כמוה̃רר שמואל החזן בא̃ז מוה̃רר יוסף המשביר בר לע̃נ תשה̃עמ:
.פיוט פרשת וילך משה תרגמו אד̃ מוה̃רר יוסף היניק וחכים נב̃ת בא̃ז כמוה̃רר שמואל החזן זצו̃קל:

3 JSul.I.45: *maḥtavludur.* | JSul.I.46: *maḥtavludur.* | ADub.III.61: *maḥtavludur.* | JSul.III.07: *maḥtavludur.* | JSul.III.69: *maḥtavludur.* | JSul.III.79: *maḥtavludur.*

4 ADub.III.61: *keklerni.* | JSul.III.07: *keklerni.* | JSul.III.69: *keklerni.* | JSul.III.79: *keklerni.*

5 ADub.III.61: *kenderedi.* | JSul.III.07: *kenderedi.* | JSul.III.69: *kenderedi.* | JSul.III.79: *kenderivci.*

6 ADub.III.61: *kici byla.* | JSul.III.07: *kici byla.* | JSul.III.69: *kici byla.* | JSul.III.79: *kici byla.*

7 JSul.I.45: *q[udrat]ynyn.*

8 JSul.I.46: *bar etti.* | JSul.III.07: *bar etti.*

9 JSul.I.45: *tizidi.* | JSul.I.46: *tizidi.* | ADub.III.61: *tizidi.* | JSul.III.07: *tizidi.* | JSul.III.69: *tizidi.* | JSul.III.79: *tizidi.*

10 JSul.I.45: *And this is the* peshat *of the* piyyut *for the parashat Vayelech (with the incipit)* yištabbaḥ ʾēl ʿelyōn, *done by my master, the wise learned sage, his honour, the Rav, Rabbi Josef ha-Maskil, may his soul lodge in Eden, the son of our aged master, his honour, the Rav, Rabbi Shemuel, the hazzan of the holy community of Halych, may he rest in peace. If you want you will say:* | JSul.I.46: *And this* [i.e., the Hebrew original] *became clarified and completely transparent by (the work) of my master, the young and wise scholar, the great sage, his honour, the Rav, Rabbi Josef ha-Maskil, may his soul lodge in Eden, the son of our aged master, the great and honourable sage, his honour, the Rav, Rabbi Shemuel the hazzan and the chief*

[1] [15] ⌊And this is the *peshat* of a *piyyut* for the parashat Vayelech (with the incipit) *yištabbaḥ ʾēl ʿelyōn*, done by my master, the young scholar and the wise, the great sage, 109 r°

[2] [16] our master and teacher, his honour, the Rav, Rabbi Josef ha-Maskil, the sharp(-minded), may his soul lodge in Eden, the son of his honour, the Rav, Rabbi Shemuel the hazzan and the chief justice of the holy community of Halych, may he rest in peace.[110]

[3] [17] Praised is the God above, the creator of the heavens and all

[4] [18] their armies[11] and the one who reveals

[5] [19] in (great) numbers His armies and calls them all by name to serve

[6] [20] Him. With His power He leads His army in the heavens and (leads) those who dwell

[7] [21] on the low world, and He holds in permanency their single things and principles.

[8] [22] He opens His goodness of His power and satisfies the wishes of all

[9] [23] living beings. With His grace, He ⌊has created them[112] from nothing and

[10] [24] with His mercies He constructed their reason based on angelic wisdom.

---

*justice of the holy community of Halych, may he rest in peace. And if you prefer, you will say this so that the ignoramuses who do not understand the holy language understand the good taste of this poetic interpretation.* | ADub.III.61: *And, if you prefer, say its* peshat [i.e., of the Hebrew original], *which my aged master translated, my uncle, the young and wise scholar, the hakham, his honour, the Rav, Rabbi Josef, may his soul lodge in Eden, the son of my aged master, the gifted (~ Gaon* [?]) *and exalted, his honour, the Rav, Rabbi Shemuel, the hazzan and the chief justice of the holy community of Halych, 'may his soul be bound in the bond of life'* [cf., 1Samuel 25:29]. | JSul.III.07: *And this is its* [i.e., of the Hebrew original] peshat, *which my master, the young and wise scholar, his honour, the Rav, Rabbi Josef translated, may his soul lodge in Eden, the son of our aged master, his honour, the Rav, Rabbi Shemuel, the hazzan, may he rest in peace.* | JSul.III.69: *And this is its* [i.e., of the Hebrew original] peshat, *which my master translated, the young and wise scholar, my master and teacher, the Rav, Rabbi Josef, may the memory of the righteous be a blessing, the son of our aged master, his honour, the Rav, Rabbi Shemuel, the hazzan, the son of our teacher, the Rav, Rabbi Josef who provides pure grain* [i.e., Josef ha-Mashbir; cf. Genesis 42:3] *for the elevation of the soul, 'the layer of dew came up on his lodge'* [cf., Exodus 16:13–14]. | JSul.III.79: *And this is the* peshat *of a* piyyut *for the parashat Vayelech Moshe, which our master, our teacher, the Rav, Rabbi Josef translated, the young and wise scholar, may his soul lodge in Eden, the son of our aged master, his honour, the Rav, Rabbi Shemuel, the hazzan, may the memory of the righteous and holy be a blessing.*

11 Lit. 'crowds'.

12 JSul.I.46: expressed with a synonym. | JSul.III.07: expressed with a synonym.

[11] [25] Beredi jemlerin har birinin[13] vaḫtynda baslap aġaraqlaryndan
[12] [26] enke kicireklerinedejin alarnyn. Qullar erkinden cyġardy[14]
[13] [27] ulusun da juludu[15] alarny galutundan Micrinin. Jarcyqlady Jam Sufnu
[14] [28] alynlaryndan da könderdi[16] alarny tynclyq byla quruda jüzleri[17]
109 vº [15] [1] istine küclü[18] suvlarnyn. Keltirdi alarny ⌊tavyna Sinajnyn⌋[19]
[16] [2] da esittirdi alarġa on sözlerin[20] Toranyn[21] da iliš[22]
[17] [3] berdi alarġa terelerin aziz micvalarynyn. Tigelledi körklerin[23]
[18] [4] syjy byla kohenliknin da ajryqsy etti alarny arasyndan bar
[19] [5] uluslarnyn. Bildi jürimeklerin[24] alarnyn midbarda qyrq jyl
[20] [6] negince ki keltirdi alarny ceklerine[25] jerinin[26] šiva ʿamamimnin.
[21] [7] Da juvuq bolġanlarynda ol jerge Moše rabenu inamlysy
[22] [8] ivinin tizetti da qolajlady yzlaryn alarnyn. Zynharlady
[23] [9] alarny ajtadoġac ki tojġanlaryndan sortun nametlerinden
[24] [10] Tenrinin azmaġajlar jonma abaqlary artyna olturuvcularynyn
[25] [11] ol jernin. Ki bu jalġan emunany ilis aldylar atalary avaldan
[26] [12] hanuz zamanyndan Teraḥnyn atasynyn Avrahamnyn. Ancaq jalġyz
[27] [13] birligine H-nyn isanġajlar urluġu Jisraʾelnin da anar qojġajlar
[28] [14] har vaḫt umsunclaryn ezlerinin. Ki oldu quvatlary da
[29] [15] küplikleri[27] oldu kücü[28] ḥallarynyn. Oldu gorallary da tijiš[29]

---

13 JSul.I.45: *bir tirinin.* | JSul.I.46: *bir tirinin.* | ADub.III.61: *bir tirinin.* | JSul.III.07: *bir tirinin.* | JSul.III.79: *bir tirinin.*

14 JSul.I.45: *juludu.* | ADub.III.61: *juludu.* | JSul.III.07: *juludu.*

15 JSul.I.45: *cyġardy.* | JSul.III.07: *cyġardy.*

16 ADub.III.61: *kenderdi.* | JSul.III.07: *kenderdi.* | JSul.III.69: *kenderdi.* | JSul.III.79: *kenderdi.*

17 JSul.I.45: *izleri.* | ADub.III.61: *izleri.* | JSul.III.07: *izleri.* | JSul.III.69: *izleri.* | JSul.III.79: *izleri.*

18 ADub.III.61: *kicli.* | JSul.III.07: *kicli.* | JSul.III.69: *kicli.* | JSul.III.79: *kicli.*

19 JSul.I.45: *Sinaj tavyna.* | JSul.I.46: *Sinaj tavyna.* | JSul.III.07: *Sinaj tavyna.*

20 ADub.III.61: *sezlerin.* | JSul.III.07: *sezlerin.* | JSul.III.69: *sezlerin.* | JSul.III.79: *sezlerin.*

21 ADub.III.61: *aziz Toranyn.* | JSul.III.79: *aziz Toranyn.*

22 JSul.I.45: *ilis.* | JSul.I.46: *ilis.* | ADub.III.61: *ilis.* | JSul.III.07: *ilis.* | JSul.III.69: *ilis.* | JSul.III.79: *ilis.*

23 ADub.III.61: *kerklerin.* | JSul.III.07: *kerklerin.* | JSul.III.69: *kerklerin.* | JSul.III.79: *kerklerin.*

24 ADub.III.61: *jirimeklerin.* | JSul.III.07: *jirimeklerin.* | JSul.III.69: *jirimeklerin.* | JSul.III.79: *jirimeklerin.*

25 JSul.III.07: *cegine.*

26 JSul.I.46: deest. | JSul.III.07: deest.

27 A hypercorrect form of *kiplikleri.* | JSul.I.45: *kiplikleri.* | ADub.III.61: *kiplikleri.* | JSul.III.07: *kiplikleri.* | JSul.III.69: *kiplikleri.* | JSul.III.79: *kiplikleri.*

28 JSul.I.45: *kici.* | ADub.III.61: *kici.* | JSul.III.07: *kici.* | JSul.III.69: *kici.* | JSul.III.79: *kici.*

29 ADub.III.61: *tijis.* | JSul.III.07: *tijis.* | JSul.III.69: *tijis.* | JSul.III.79: *tijis.*

[11] [25] In due course, He has provided food for ⌊every single (being)⌉[30], starting from the old
[12] [26] and ending with the smallest of them. He has taken[31] His people from slavery[32]
[13] [27] and saved[33] them from the exile of Egypt. He has split the Red Sea
[14] [28] before them and lead them with peace overland over the surface
[15] [1] of the mighty waters. He has led them to Mount Sinai 109 v°
[16] [2] and made them hear the ten words of the Law[34] and has given them in heritage
[17] [3] the laws of the holy commandments. He has crowned[35] their beauty
[18] [4] with fame of priesthood and sanctified them from among all the
[19] [5] nations. He has known their wandering[36] for forty years in the desert
[20] [6] until He brought them to the borders of the land of the ⌊seven nations⌉[37].
[21] [7] And when they were close to that land, ⌊our master⌉[38], Moses, steadfast
[22] [8] in His house, straightened and made easier their ways. He has instructed
[23] [9] them by saying that after being satisfied with the goods
[24] [10] of God, may they not go astray after carved idols of those who inhabit
[25] [11] the land. For their fathers have come into possession of this false religion from ancient times
[26] [12] as far as in the times of Terah the father of Abraham. But only
[27] [13] in the oneness of Lord may the offspring of Israel believe, and may they
[28] [14] always place their hopes in it, for that is their power and
[29] [15] strength, that is the power of their potential. That is their fate and their due

---

30 JSul.I.45: *living being.* | JSul.I.46: *living being.* | ADub.III.61: *living being.* | JSul.III.07: *living being.* | JSul.III.79: *living being.*

31 JSul.I.45: *saved.* | ADub.III.61: *saved.* | JSul.III.07: *saved.*

32 Lit. 'rule of slaves', i.e., 'rule where they were being kept as slaves'.

33 JSul.I.45: *took.* | JSul.III.07: *took.*

34 ADub.III.61: *holy Law.* | JSul.III.79: *holy Law.*

35 Lit. 'accomplished', 'finished'.

36 Lit. 'walking'.

37 A reference to the seven nations that inhabited the land of Canaan in the time of Exodus, i.e., the Hittites, the Girgashites, the Amorites, the Canaanites, the Perizzites, the Hivites, and the Jebusites (see Deuteronomy 7:1).

38 Expressed with *rabenu*, i.e., Heb. רַבֵּינוּ 'our rabbi'.

[30] [16] ilisleri toḥtaġanlarynda tarlyqlarynda galutlarynyn. Anyndy
[31] [17] ec almaq jaman telev qajtarma[39] umalarġa ⌊ne vaḥtny tajsa⌉[40]
[32] [18] kücü[41] mazallarynyn. Ol cyġaryr ulusun qaranġylyqlaryndan avur
[33] [19] galutnun[42] da jarytyr tumanlaryn alarnyn. Anyn ücün[43] povinnost[t]u[44]
[34] [20] ki alar[45] da ulanlary[46] da ulanlary ulanlarynynda jystyrynmaġy[47]
[35] [21] byla qahallarynyn, šükür[48] etkejler[49] aziz šemine da azizligin[50]
[36] [22] ajtqajlar maḥtavlary byla erinlerinin[51], da ki esittirgejler
[37] [23] sarnav avazlaryn aziz hermetli ivinde[52] da birligin da qajjam-
[38] [24] lyġyn qotarġajlar[53] pasuġu byla Šemaʿ Jisraʾelnin.
⌊שמע ישראל הׄ אלהינו הׄ אחד:⌉[54] [25] [39]

39 JSul.III.07: *teleme.*

40 ADub.III.61: *tajġan vaḥtta.*

41 ADub.III.61: *kici.* | JSul.III.07: *kici.* | JSul.III.69: *kici.* | JSul.III.79: *kici.*

42 JSul.III.69: *galutlarynyn.*

43 JSul.III.07: *icin.* | ADub.III.61: *icin.* | JSul.III.69: *icin.* | JSul.III.79: *icin.*

44 JSul.III.03: *povinostu*; possibly a scribal error. | JSul.I.45: *povinnosttu.* | JSul.I.46: *povinnosttu.* | ADub.III.61: *borctu.* | JSul.III.07: *borctu.* | JSul.III.69: *borctu.* | JSul.III.79: *borctu.*

45 ADub.III.61: *alar ezleri.*

46 ADub.III.61: *ulanlary alarnyn.* | JSul.III.79: *ulanlary alarnyn.*

47 JSul.I.45: *ystyrynmaġy.* | JSul.I.46: *ystyrynmaġy.* | ADub.III.61: *ystyrynmaġy.* | JSul.III.07: *ystyrylmaġy.* | JSul.III.69: *ystyrylmaġy.* | JSul.III.79: *ystyrynmaġy.*

48 ADub.III.61: *sikir.* | JSul.III.07: *sikir.* | JSul.III.69: *sikir.* | JSul.III.79: *sikir.*

49 JSul.I.45: *bergejler.* | JSul.I.46: *bergejler.* | JSul.III.07: *bergejler.* | JSul.III.69: *bergejler.*

50 JSul.III.79: *azizligin da qajjamlyġyn.* | ADub.III.61: *azizligin da qajjamlyġyn.*

51 JSul.I.46: *ezlerinin*; possibly a scribal error.

52 JSul.I.46: *kensa ivinde.* | JSul.III.07: *orunda kensa ivinde.*

53 JSul.III.69: *qotarġajlar barlary.* | JSul.III.07: *ajtqajlar.* | JSul.III.79: *qotarġajlar barlary.*

54 Deuteronomy 6:4. | JSul.I.45: שמע ישראל הׄ אלהינו הׄ אחד:. (Deuteronomy 6:4). | JSul.I.46: שְׁמַע יִשְׂרָאֵל הָ אֱלֹהֵינוּ הָ אֶחָד. (Deuteronomy 6:4). | ADub.III.61: שְׁמַע יִשְׂרָאֵל הָ אֱלֹהֵינוּ הָ אֶחָד. (Deuteronomy 6:4). | JSul.III.07: שְׁמַע יִשְׂרָאֵל הָ אֱלֹהֵינוּ הָ אֶחָד. (Deuteronomy 6:4). | JSul.III.69: שמע ישראל הׄ אלהינו הׄ אחד. (Deuteronomy 6:4). | JSul.III.79: שְׁמַע יִשְׂרָאֵל הָ אֱלֹהֵינוּ הָ אֶחָד. (Deuteronomy 6:4).

[30] [16] share in the time they dwelled in their misery of their exile. To Him belongs (the right)
[31] [17] to take revenge, ⌊to return[55] the evil⌋[56] to the nations when the
[32] [18] strength of their constellations[57] would stagger. He will draw His people out from the darkness of the hard
[33] [19] exile and will light up their cloud. For this reason it is an obligation
[34] [20] that they[58] and their children and even the children of their children along with the gathering
[35] [21] of their communities thank[59] His holy name and
[36] [22] mention[60] His holiness[61] by the praise of their lips[62] and that they make
[37] [23] the voices of joy be heard in ⌊His holy, honourable house⌋[63] and
[38] [24] they praise[64] His oneness and His eternity with the ⌊Biblical verse of *Shema Yisrael*⌋[65]. ⌊Hear, O Israel: The Lord our God is one Lord.⌋[66]

---

55 JSul.III.07: *repay*.

56 Lit. 'to return the evil payment', 'to repay the evil payment'.

57 Cf. 28:26–28.

58 ADub.III.61: *they themselves*.

59 JSul.I.45: *give thanks*. | JSul.I.46: *give thanks*. | JSul.III.07: *give thanks*. | JSul.III.69: *give thanks*.

60 Lit. 'say'.

61 ADub.III.61: *holiness and power* (~ *eternity*). | JSul.III.79: *holiness and power* (~ *eternity*).

62 JSul.I.46: *own*; possibly a scribal error.

63 JSul.I.46: *His* (~ *the*) *holy, honourable temple* (~ *kenesa*). | JSul.III.07: *His* (~ *the*) *holy, honourable place, in the temple* (~ *kenesa*).

64 JSul.III.07: *mention*; lit. 'say'. | JSul.III.69: *all praise*. | JSul.III.79: *all praise*.

65 I.e., Deuteronomy 6:4.

66 Deuteronomy 6:4. | JSul.I.45: *'Hear, O Israel: The Lord our God is one Lord.'* (Deuteronomy 6:4). | JSul.I.46: *'Hear, O Israel: The Lord our God is one Lord.'* (Deuteronomy 6:4). | ADub.III.61: *'Hear, O Israel: The Lord our God is one Lord.'* (Deuteronomy 6:4). | JSul.III.07: *'Hear, O Israel: The Lord our God is one Lord.'* (Deuteronomy 6:4). | JSul.III.69: *'Hear, O Israel: The Lord our God is one Lord.'* (Deuteronomy 6:4). | JSul.III.79: *'Hear, O Israel: The Lord our God is one Lord.'* (Deuteronomy 6:4).

# PART 7

## *The* peshatim *of Shemuel ben Josef ha-Mashbir*

∵

**Text number:** № 26
**Karaim incipit:** *Men zavally Jisra'el*
**Hebrew incipit:** אֲנוּנָה אֲנִי וַעֲגוּמָה *'ănūnå 'ănī wa'ăgūmå*
**Dedication:** Shabbats of the months Tammuz and Av
**Language:** MSWKar., Early Mod.SWKar., Mod.SWKar.
**Number of copies:** 7

| Accession no. | Place of origin of copy | Date of copy | Copyist | Folios |
|---|---|---|---|---|
| JSul.I.01b | Halych | 2nd half of the 18th c. | Mordechai ben Shemuel | 126 rº–126 vº |
| JSul.III.63 | Halych | ca. 1778 (before 1797) | Jeshua Mordkowicz | 35 vº–36 vº |
| JSul.III.03 | Halych | shortly after 1805 | Unknown 7 | 100 rº–101 vº |
| JSul.I.45 | Halych | 1st half of the 19th c. | Jeshua Josef Mordkowicz | 123 vº–125 rº |
| ADub.III.61 | Halych | 1850/1851 | Jeshua Josef Mordkowicz | 112 rº–113 vº |
| JSul.III.69 | Halych | ca. 1851 (before 1866) | Jeshua Josef Mordkowicz | 219 vº–221 vº |
| JSul.III.79 | Halych | ca. 1851 (before 1866) | Jeshua Josef Mordkowicz | 269 vº–272 rº |

## 1 Introductory Remarks

This text is one of four pre-18th-century Western Karaim *peshatim* of the *piyyut* with the incipit *'ănūnå 'ănī wa'ăgūmå*, cf. *peshatim* № 1, 5, and 24. All the copies are vocalized, yet the vowel points in JSul.I.01b have been added to the text very likely by another hand.

Many differences can be observed between the seven copies. To begin with, there are a number of unique features to be found in the text copied in ms. JSul.I.01b, cf. e.g. *köplügünde* vs. *köplügünden* (~ *köpliginden* ~ *kepliginden*) (5), *jerlerinde tüslü* vs. *tüslü* (~ *tisli*) *jerlerinde* (11), *arasynda* vs. *arasyndan* (14), *qajtma tešuvabyla jazyġymdan sana* vs. *jazyġymdan tešuvabyla qajtma sana* (19–20), *görde* vs. *görge* (~ *gerge* ~ *gergede*) (21), *raḥemtlevčü da qutqaruvču* vs. *raḥemtlevčü* (~ *raḥemtlevcü* ~ *raḥemtlevci*) (24), *dušman qysyqlyq etedi mana astry* vs. *astry dušman qysyqlyq etedi mana* (27), *da* vs. *ki* (30), *tüslü* vs. *türlü* (~ *tirli*) (32), *qaḥirlerinbyla* vs. *qaḥyrynbyla* (37), *inam* vs. the (apparently) erroneously copied *inaq* (38), &c. The latter discrepancy shows the texts in JSul.III.63, JSul.III.03, JSul.I.45, ADub.III.61, JSul.III.69, and JSul.III.79 form a separate group in which the word *inam* has been copied as *inaq*. There are also some portions of text that are characteristic of the version copied in JSul.III.63 only, see, for instance, *Adonajnyn* vs. *H-nyn* (5), *ḥorluqqa* vs. *ḥorluqlarġa* (12), *munajtuvčularymnyn* vs. *qyjnavčularymnyn* (32), *saġynmaġyn* vs. *saġynmaġyn mana* or *ojatqyn* vs. *ojatqajsen* (56). Also worth mentioning are a few similarities shared exclusively by mss. JSul.I.01b and JSul.III.63, namely *klegin* vs. *klegen* (16), *balqytma* vs. *cyġarma* (31), *qulaq salġyn* vs. *qajyrġyn esitivinni* (31), *utru* vs. *uturu* (37). Finally, there are a number of textual features that, on the one hand, the texts in JSul.III.03 and JSul.III.69, and, on the other, the text in ms. JSul.I.45 share with those copied in mss. JSul.I.01b, JSul.III.63, ADub.III.61, and JSul.III.79.

It should be pointed out that the word *süvümlü* (7) in ms. JSul.I.01b is spelled סִיווּמְלִיו. The presence of the vowel sign *chiriq* under *samekh* suggests that the vowel points must have been added to the text later by another person who, in this case only, vocalized the first syllable according to Modern South-Western Karaim phonology. Additionally, the clearly NWKar. word form *özüjnün* (43) used in mss. JSul.III.63 suggests that its copyist worked with a copy that ultimately originated from a manuscript written in the north-western dialect. It is important to note that Josef ha-Mashbir, the father of the author of the *peshat*, was a speaker of North-Western Karaim (see 2.1.1).

The connections between the texts are encapsulated in the diagram below:

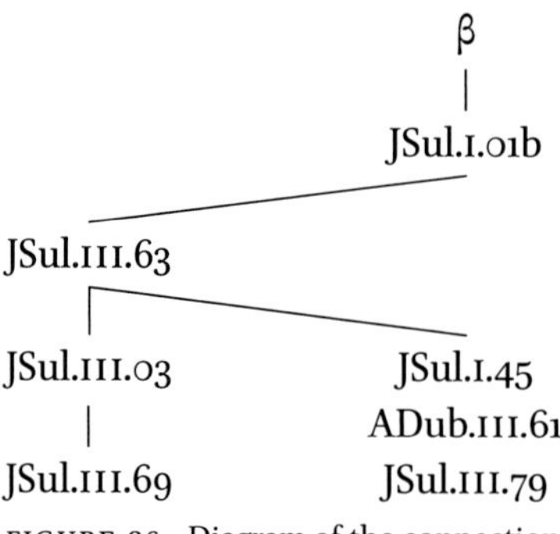


FIGURE 26 Diagram of the connections between the copies of peshat № 26

## 2 Transcription[1] and Translation

126 r° [1] [13] ⸂ופה אכתוב פשט על פיוט אנונה אני הנאמר בשבתות האבלות ובשבת תשובה שנהגו לקראו החזנים

[2] [14] בימות בדרכו ואם שהם שלשה מינים אבחר מכלם של אדמוה כמהרר שמואל החזן זצל באד מו הח כמוהרר יוסף על[...]⸃[2]

[3] [15] Men zavally Jisra'el bilinemen jazyġyma[3] oltura galutta küčlü[4] jasta da

[4] [16] ačuvlu[5], ki bar bu tarlyqlar učradylar[6] meni ki olturġanymda jerimde

[5] [17] köplügünde[7] bar nametnin ḥor ettim qulluġun H-nyn[8] ol aziz da ol qorqun-

---

1 Based on JSul.I.01b.

2 JSul.III.63: ובזה בשם אלהי קדם מעונה ׳ ובעזרתו אחל לכתוב פשט חבור אנונה ׳ הנסמנת לפניך בתפלת אלו השבתות של חדש תמוז ואב שבשבתות השנה: והוא אשר תרגמו אז מוהרר שמואל החזן נע באז מו ההוה כמוהרר יוסף המשביר בר נע ׳ תחל ותאמ בקול עציב ומר ונמהר ובלב נכאב ׳ אנונה אני ׳. | JSul.III.03: תרגום שלישי לפיוט הנל עשאו אז ההו כמוהרר שמואל החזן יעמש באז ההו כמוהר יוסף המשביר בר לען נבת. | JSul.I.45: פשט שלישי לפיוט אנונה עשאו אז ההו כמוהרר שמואל החזן זל באז כמוהרר יוסף המשביר זל. | ADub.III.61: פשט שלישי לפיוט אנונה יקר ונעים מאד במליצתו עשאו ותרגמו בזוך הכמתו אז מוהרר שמואל החזן ואבד דקחק נבת באז מוהרר יוסף המשביר בר לען יעמש. | JSul.III.69: וזה הפשט השלישי לפיוט אנונה תרגמו אז מוהרר שמואל החזן נבת בן אז מו הרר יוסף המשביר בר לען יעמש: אנונה אני ועגומה. | JSul.III.79: פשט שלישי לפיוט אנונה תרגמו אז החכם האלהי והתורני כמהרר שמואל החזן ואבד דקהק האליץ נבת באז מוהרר יוסף המשביר בר לען זצוקל.

3 JSul.III.63: *jazyqlaryma.* | JSul.III.03: *jazyqlaryma.* | JSul.III.69: *jazyqlaryma.*

4 JSul.III.03: *küclü.* | JSul.I.45: *küclü.* | ADub.III.61: *kicli.* | JSul.III.69: *kicli.* | JSul.III.79: *kicli.*

5 JSul.III.03: *acuvlu.* | JSul.I.45: *acuvlu.* | ADub.III.61: *acuvlu.* | JSul.III.69: *acuvlu.* | JSul.III.79: *acuvlu.*

6 JSul.III.03: *ucradylar.* | JSul.I.45: *ucradylar.* | ADub.III.61: *ucradylar.* | JSul.III.69: *ucradylar.* | JSul.III.79: *ucradylar.*

7 JSul.III.63: *köplügünden.* | JSul.III.03: *köpliginden.* | JSul.I.45: *köpliginden.* | ADub.III.61: *kepliginden.* | JSul.III.69: *kepliginden.* | JSul.III.79: *kepliginden.*

8 JSul.III.63: *Adonajnyn.*

9 JSul.III.63: *And this is in the name of ancient God! And with His help I will start to write a* peshat *of the composition* (*with the incipit*) ʾănūnå, *which is indicated before you* (*in the prayerbook*) *in the prayer of these Shabbats, of the months Tammuz and Av, out of the Shabbats of the year. An it is that which our aged master, our teacher, the wise and important Rav, Rabbi Shemuel the hazzan translated, may his soul rest in Eden, the son of our aged Master, our teacher, the great and honourable sage, his honour, the Rav, Rabbi Josef who provides pure grain* [i.e., Josef ha-Mashbir; cf. Genesis 42:3], *may his soul rest in Eden. You should start and say, with a sad and bitter and grieving* [lit. bitter and hasty; the author of this heading used rhyming words, cf. Habakkuk 1:6] *voice and an anguished heart:* ʾănūnå ʾănī. | JSul.III.03: *The third translation of the above mentioned* piyyut *delivered by our aged master, the great and honourable sage, his*

[1] [13] ⌊And here, I will write down a *peshat* of the *piyyut* (with the incipit) *ʾănūnå ʾănī*, the one recited on Shabbats (in the time of) mourning and on Shabbat Teshuva, that *hazzanim* used to read in their own way 126 rº

[2] [14] on weekdays; and although there be three kinds (of *peshatim* of this *piyyut*), I will choose of all of them that of our master, our teacher Rabbi, his honour, the Rav, Rabbi Shemuel, the aged, may the memory of the righteous be a blessing, the son of our master, our teacher, the wise, his honour, the Rav, Rabbi Josef […].⌉[9]

[3] [15] (1). I, miserable Israel, I am conscious of my sin[10] dwelling in exile, in great grief and

[4] [16] bitter, for all these worries happen to me because, when I dwelt in my land

[5] [17] in[11] abundance of any goods, I disdained the service of the holy and feared Lord.

---

*honour, the Rav, Rabbi Shemuel the hazzan, may he rest in peace, the son of our aged master, the great and honourable sage his honour, the Rav, Rabbi Josef who provides pure grain* [i.e., Josef ha-Mashbir; cf. Genesis 42:3] *for the elevation of the soul, may his soul lodge in Eden.* | JSul.I.45: *The third peshat of the* piyyut (*beginning with the word*) ʾănūnå *delivered by our aged master, the great and honourable sage, his honour, the Rav, Rabbi Shemuel, the hazzan, may his memory be a blessing, the son of our aged master, his honour, the Rav, Rabbi Josef ha-Mashbir, may his memory be a blessing.* | ADub.III.61: *The third* peshat *of the the beloved and very pleasant* piyyut (*beginning with the word*) ʾănūnå, *in a poetic interpretation delivered by the pure hakham, our aged master, our teacher, the Rav, Rabbi Shemuel, the hazzan and the chief justice of the holy community of Halych, may his soul lodge in Eden, the son of our aged master, our teacher, Rabbi Josef who provides pure grain* [i.e., Josef ha-Mashbir; cf. Genesis 42:3] *for the elevation of the soul, may he rest in peace.* (*Incipit:*) ʾănūnå ʾănī waʿăgūmå. | JSul.III.69: *And this is the third* peshat *of the* piyyut (*beginning with the word*) ʾănūnå, *which our aged Master, our teacher, the Rav, Rabbi Shemuel the hazzan translated, may his soul lodge in Eden, the son of our aged master, our teacher, the Rav, Rabbi Josef who provides pure grain* [i.e., Josef ha-Mashbir; cf. Genesis 42:3] *for the elevation of the soul, may he rest in peace.* | JSul.III.79: *The third* peshat *of the* piyyut (*beginning with the word*) ʾănūnå, *which our aged master, the divine hakham and ha-Torani, his honour, the Rav, Rabbi Shemuel translated, the hazzan and the chief justice of the holy community of Halych, may his soul lodge in Eden, the son of our aged master, our teacher, the Rav, Rabbi Josef who provides pure grain* [i.e., Josef ha-Mashbir; cf. Genesis 42:3] *for the elevation of the soul, may the memory of the righteous be a blessing.*

10 JSul.III.63: *sins.* | JSul.III.03: *sins.* | JSul.III.69: *sins.*

11 JSul.III.63: *because of.* | JSul.III.03: *because of.* | JSul.I.45: *because of.* | ADub.III.61: *because of.* | JSul.III.69: *because of.* | JSul.III.79: *because of.*

[6] [18] člu[12]. Da bunarköre[13] dağyn[14] olda ḥorlady meni da bezdi klegi anyn menden neki[15] burundan

[7] [19] edim anar astry süvümlü[16]. Vale haligine qaḥyrybyla qojdu meni qajǧyly da harkün[17]

[8] [20] men[18] bolamen syzlavlu. [19]⌜דוה וזבה⌟. Qajyrdym ense aziz[20] zynharlamaqlaryna

[9] [21] tügel[21] Torannyn[22] jabušqanym[23] byla murdar qulluğuna jat tenrilernin da murdar

[10] [22] bolundum alar byla neginče[24] ki ḥor ettim da byrčlattym[25] syjly ǯanymny[26].

[11] [23] Bu jazyq üčün[27] tünkelttin[28] meni ⌞jerlerinde tüslü⌟[29] umalarnyn qulluq etiv-

[12] [24] čülernin[30] ʿavoda zarağa da ullu ḥorluqlarğa[31] qollarynda alarnyn kemištin[32] meni.

[13] [25] Da dağyn[33] čeber[34] jerimden[35] ki ülüš[36] beribedin any mana sürdün[37] meni andan da ḥanlyqlar

[14] [26] arasynda[38] tozdurdun ulanlarymny. Ki muna sensen kipligim[39] tar

---

12 JSul.III.03: *qorqunclu.* | JSul.I.45: *qorqunclu.* | ADub.III.61: *qorqunclu.* | JSul.III.69: *qorqunclu.* | JSul.III.79: *qorqunclu.*

13 ADub.III.61: *bunar kere.* | JSul.III.69: *bunar kere.* | JSul.III.79: *bunar kere.*

14 JSul.III.79: *dağy.*

15 JSul.III.03: *ne ornuna ki.* | JSul.III.79: *ne [ornuna] ki.*

16 JSul.I.01b: spelled סִיווּמְלִיו. | JSul.III.03: *sivimli.* | JSul.I.45: *sivimli.* | ADub.III.61: *sivimli.* | JSul.III.69: *sivimli.* | JSul.III.79: *sivimli.*

17 JSul.III.63: *har kin.* | ADub.III.61: *har kin.* | JSul.III.69: *har kin.* | JSul.III.79: *har kin.*

18 JSul.III.63: deest. | JSul.I.45: deest. | ADub.III.61: deest.

19 JSul.III.03: ד̋בה וזב̋ה. | JSul.I.45: דוֹה. | JSul.III.69: דוֹה. | JSul.III.79: דוֹה.

20 JSul.III.03: deest. | ADub.III.61: deest. | JSul.III.69: deest.

21 JSul.III.03: *aziz.* | JSul.I.45: *tigel.* | ADub.III.61: *tigel.* | JSul.III.69: *tigel.* | JSul.III.79: *tigel.*

22 JSul.III.03: *toranyn.* | JSul.I.45: *toranyn.* | ADub.III.61: *toranyn.*

23 JSul.III.03: *jabusqanym.* | JSul.I.45: *jabusqanym.* | ADub.III.61: *jabusqanym.* | JSul.III.69: *jabusqanym.* | JSul.III.79: *jabusqanym.*

24 JSul.III.03: *negince.* | JSul.I.45: *negince.* | ADub.III.61: *negince.* | JSul.III.69: *negince.* | JSul.III.79: *negince.*

25 JSul.III.03: *byrclattym.* | JSul.I.45: *byrclattym.* | ADub.III.61: *byrclattym.* | JSul.III.69: *byrclattym.* | JSul.III.79: *byrclattym.*

26 JSul.III.03: *ʒanymny.* | JSul.I.45: *ʒanymny.* | ADub.III.61: *ʒanymny.* | JSul.III.69: *ʒanymny.* | JSul.III.79: *ʒanymny.*

27 JSul.III.03: *ücün.* | JSul.I.45: *ücün.* | ADub.III.61: *icin.* | JSul.III.69: *icin.* | JSul.III.79: *icin.*

28 JSul.III.03: *tinkelttin.* | JSul.I.45: *tinkelttin.* | ADub.III.61: *tinkelttin.* | JSul.III.69: *tinkelttin.* | JSul.III.79: *tinkelttin.*

[6] [18] And therefore He has condemned me, too, and His will has found me repulsive; me, who originally

[7] [19] had been very much dear to Him. But now, in His wrath, he made me concerned and every day

[8] [20] I am full of pain. (2). And I have turned my back on the holy[40] instructions

[9] [21] of Your[41] immaculate[42] Law by joining the unclean service to strange gods, and I have become impure

[10] [22] by this, until I have disdained and besmirched my noble heart[43].

[11] [23] For this sin You have made me wander in the various lands of those nations that serve

[12] [24] paganism, and in the hands of them in great disgrace

[13] [25] have You have left me. And also from[44] my pleasant land which You have given me as a legacy You have cast me out and

[14] [26] You have scattered my children among kingdoms. So, lo, You are my strength[45] in my times of want,

---

29 JSul.III.63: *tüslü jerlerinde.* | JSul.III.03: *tisli jerlerinde.* | JSul.I.45: *tisli jerlerinde.* | ADub.III.61: *tisli jerlerinde.* | JSul.III.69: *tisli jerlerinde.* | JSul.III.79: *tisli jerlerinde.*

30 JSul.III.03: *etivcilernin.* | JSul.I.45: *etivcilernin.* | ADub.III.61: *etivcilernin.* | JSul.III.69: *etivcilernin.* | JSul.III.79: *etivcilernin.*

31 JSul.III.63: *ḥorluqqa.*

32 JSul.III.03: *kemistin.* | JSul.I.45: *kemistin.* | ADub.III.61: *kemistin.* | JSul.III.69: *kemistin.* | JSul.III.79: *kemistin.*

33 JSul.III.03: *daġy.* | JSul.III.69: *daġy.* | JSul.III.79: *daġyn.*

34 JSul.III.03: *ceber.* | JSul.I.45: *ceber.* | ADub.III.61: *ceber.* | JSul.III.69: *ceber.* | JSul.III.79: *ceber.*

35 JSul.III.63. *jerimden de.* | JSul.I.45: *jerimden de.* | ADub.III.61: *jerimdende.* | JSul.III.79: *jerimdende.*

36 JSul.III.03: *ilis.* | JSul.I.45: *ilis.* | ADub.III.61: *ilis.* | JSul.III.69: *ilis.* | JSul.III.79: *ilis.*

37 JSul.III.03: *sirdin.* | JSul.I.45: *sirdin.* | ADub.III.61: *sirdin.* | JSul.III.69: *sirdin.* | JSul.III.79: *sirdin.*

38 JSul.III.63: *arasyna.* | JSul.III.03: *arasyna.* | JSul.I.45: *arasyna.* | ADub.III.61: *arasyna.* | JSul.III.69: *arasyna.* | JSul.III.79: *arasyna.*

39 JSul.III.03: *küpligim da bolusluġum*; *küpligim* is a hypercorrect form of *kipligim.* | JSul.I.45: *küpligim da bolusluġum*; *küpligim* is a hypercorrect form of *kipligim.* | ADub.III.61: *kipligim da bolusluġum.* | JSul.III.69: *kipligim da bolusluġum.* | JSul.III.79: *kipligim da bolusluġum.*

40 JSul.III.03: deest. | ADub.III.61: deest. | JSul.III.69: deest.

41 JSul.III.03: deest. | JSul.I.45: deest. | ADub.III.61: deest.

42 JSul.III.03: *holy.*

43 Or: *soul.*

44 JSul.III.63: *even from.* | JSul.I.45: *even from.* | ADub.III.61: *even from.* | JSul.III.79: *even from.*

45 JSul.III.03: *strength and providence.* | JSul.I.45: *strength and providence.* | ADub.III.61: *strength and providence.* | JSul.III.69: *strength and providence.* | JSul.III.79: *strength and providence.*

[15] [27] vaḥtymda nekbu haligine uzaq zaman galutta ynǯytasen[46] meni.
[16] [28] [47]⌈זנחתּני פרצתּני⌋. Da sen Tenrim[48] rastsen bar ol qaranjabyla kelgen[49] üstüme[50] ḥotej
[17] [29] ki kemištind[e][51] ese[52] da sürdün[53] alnyndan da ham ki buzdun[54] ese aziz da körklü[55]
[18] [30] üvümüznü[56] bet hamiqdašynny. Qačan[57] ki tynlamadym ügütlerine[58] hörmetli[59]
[19] [31] navilerinnin ki qorquturediler[60] da a[d]epl[ere]diler[61] meni ⌊qajtma tešuvabyla
126 vº [20] [1] jazyġymdan sana⌋[62] jaḥšy[63] etmek üčün[64] aqibatymny. E aruv enajatly[65] ne bolunajym
[21] [2] köplügünden[66] jazyqlarymnyn ki muna eger ajtsam tačanajym[67] {görde}[68] šahat[69] anda qaḥyryn
[22] [3] jetmegejedi meni. Kertiden[70] muna joḥtu birde orun ki jašyryn[71] bolġaj senden da daġyn

---

46 JSul.III.03: *ynǯytasen.* | JSul.I.45: *ynǯytasen.* | ADub.III.61: *ynǯytasen.* | JSul.III.69: *ynǯytasen.* | JSul.III.79: *ynǯytasen.*

47 JSul.I.45: זנחתּני. | ADub.III.61: זנחתּני. | JSul.III.69: זנחתּני. | JSul.III.79: זנחתּני.

48 JSul.III.03: *e Tenrim.*

49 JSul.III.63: *kelgin*; a scribal error.

50 JSul.III.03: *istime.* | JSul.I.45: *istimizge.* | ADub.III.61: *istimizge.* | JSul.III.69: *istime.* | JSul.III.79: *istimizge.*

51 JSul.I.01b: *kemištindin*; a scribal error. | JSul.III.63: *kemištin de.* | JSul.III.03: *kemistinde.* | JSul.I.45: *kemistinde.* | ADub.III.61: *kemistin de.* | JSul.III.69: *kemistinde.* | JSul.III.79: *kemistinde.*

52 JSul.III.03: *ese meni.*

53 JSul.III.63: *sürdün meni.* | JSul.III.03: *sirdinde ese.* | JSul.I.45: *sirdin.* | ADub.III.61: *sirdinde ese.* | JSul.III.69: *sirdinde ese.* | JSul.III.79: *sirdinde ese.*

54 JSul.III.03: *buzdunda.* | JSul.I.45: *buzdunda.* | JSul.III.69: *buzdunda.* | JSul.III.79: *buzdunda.*

55 ADub.III.61: *kerkli.* | JSul.III.69: *kerkli.* | JSul.III.79: *kerkli.*

56 JSul.III.03: *ivimizni.* | JSul.I.45: *ivimiznü.* | ADub.III.61: *ivimizni.* | JSul.III.69: *ivimizni.* | JSul.III.79: *ivimizni.*

57 JSul.III.03: *qacan.* | JSul.I.45: *qacan.* | ADub.III.61: *qacan.* | JSul.III.69: *qacan.* | JSul.III.79: *qacan.*

58 JSul.III.03: *igitlerine.* | JSul.I.45: *igitlerine.* | ADub.III.61: *igitlerine.* | JSul.III.69: *igitlerine.* | JSul.III.79: *igitlerine.*

59 JSul.III.03: *hermetli.* | JSul.I.45: *hermetli.* | ADub.III.61: *hermetli.* | JSul.III.69: *hermetli.* | JSul.III.79: *hermetli.*

60 JSul.III.63: *qorquturediler meni.*

61 JSul.I.01b: two ink stains make the reading diffcult. | JSul.III.63: *edeplerediler*; possibly misspelled, the second vowel point is amended, cf., however, EKar. *eǯäplä-*. | JSul.III.03: *adeplerediler.* | JSul.I.45: *adeplerediler.* | ADub.III.61: *adeplerediler.* | JSul.III.69: *adeplerediler.* | JSul.III.79: *adeplerediler.*

62 JSul.III.63: *jazyġymdan tešuvabyla qajtma sana.* | JSul.III.03: *jazyġymdan tešuvabyla*

[15] [27] why do You harm me now in exile for so long?

[16] [28] (3). And You, ⌊my God[172], You are righteous with all those punishments that came upon me[73]—even if

[17] [29] You would abandon me and ⌊drive (me)[174] from before You and[75] even if You would destroy our holy and beautiful

[18] [30] house, Your temple. When I have not listened to the advices of the honourable

[19] [31] prophets who ⌊frightened (me)[176] and imposed atonement on me in order to (make me) return to You with penance

[20] [1] to improve my confidence. O pure-eyed (God), what shall happen to me 126 vº

[21] [2] because of the abundance of my sins, for, lo, if I say 'I shall hide away in[77] a grave because, perhaps, Your wrath

[22] [3] would not reach me (there)', then, indeed, (I should know) that, lo, there is not even a place that remains as a secret (hidden) from You and even

---

*qajtma sana.* | JSul.I.45: *jazyġymdan tešuvabyla qajtma sana.* | ADub.III.61: *jazyġymdan tešuvabyla qajtma sana.* | JSul.III.69: *jazyġymdan tešuvabyla qajtma sana.* | JSul.III.79: *jazyġymdan tešuvabyla qajtma sana.*

63 JSul.III.03: *jaḥsy.* | JSul.I.45: *jaḥsy.* | ADub.III.61: *jaḥsy.* | JSul.III.69: *jaḥsy.* | JSul.III.79: *jaḥsy.*

64 JSul.III.03: *ücün.* | JSul.I.45: *ücün.* | ADub.III.61: *icin.* | JSul.III.69: *icin.* | JSul.III.79: *icin.*

65 JSul.III.03: *enaj atly.* | JSul.I.45: *enaj atly.* | ADub.III.61: *enaj atly.* | JSul.III.69: *enaj atly.* | JSul.III.79: *enaj atly.*

66 JSul.III.03: *köpliginden.* | JSul.I.45: *köpliginden.* | ADub.III.61: *kepliginden.* | JSul.III.69: *kepliginden.* | JSul.III.79: *kepliginden.*

67 JSul.III.03: *tacanajym.* | JSul.I.45: *tacanajym.* | ADub.III.61: *tacanajym.* | JSul.III.69: *tacanajym.* | JSul.III.79: *tacanajym.*

68 JSul.III.63: *görge.* | JSul.III.03: *gerge.* | JSul.I.45: *gergede.* | ADub.III.61: *gerge.* | JSul.III.69: *gerge.* | JSul.III.79: *gerge.*

69 JSul.III.03: *sahat.* | JSul.I.45: *sahat.* | ADub.III.61: *sahat.* | JSul.III.69: *sahat.* | JSul.III.79: *sahat.*

70 JSul.III.03: *körtiden*; a hypercorrect form of *kertiden.* | JSul.I.45: *körtiden*; a hypercorrect form of *kertiden.*

71 JSul.III.63: *jasyryn.* | JSul.III.03: *jasyryn.* | JSul.I.45: *jasyryn.* | ADub.III.61: *jasyryn.* | JSul.III.69: *jasyryn.* | JSul.III.79: *jasyryn.*

72 JSul.III.03: *O God of mine.*

73 JSul.I.45: *us.* | JSul.III.79: *us.*

74 JSul.III.63: *drive me.* | JSul.III.03: *even if You would drive me.* | ADub.III.61: *even if You would drive me.* | JSul.III.69: *even if You would drive me.* | JSul.III.79: *even if You would drive me.*

75 JSul.III.03: *and even.* | JSul.I.45: *and even.* | JSul.III.69: *and even.* | JSul.III.79: *and even.*

76 JSul.III.63: *frightened me.*

77 JSul.III.63: *into.* | JSul.III.03: *into.* | JSul.I.45: *even into.* | ADub.III.61: *into.* | JSul.III.69: *into.* | JSul.III.79: *into.*

[23] [4] andada[78] on qudratyn[79] jeter meni. [80]⌜ימינך תסעדני⌟. Ančaq[81] bilgenimbyla ki

[24] [5] sensen jalġyz[82] raḥmetlevčü[83] da sürtüvčü[84] güneḥlerin[85] qajtuvčularnyn[86] rast ǯanbyla[87]

[25] [6] sana daġyn[88] menimde qoltqamdy senden[89] ki küčlü[90] jayzqlarymny alnyndan tabergin. Da

[26] [7] tutunġanyna köre[91] navilerin ašyra[92] kötürme[93] meni topraqtan da juvuzluġumdan

[27] [8] tezče[94] klegin. Baqqyn endi aziz ornundan ki ⌞dušman qysyqlyq etedi mana astry⌟[95]

[28] [9] neginče[96] ki[97] endirdi jerge[98] körkümnü[99] anyn üčün[100] bolušluġunnu[101] ijgin. Ki

[29] [10] qačanġadejin[102] e H čydarsen[103] dušmannyn[104] ḥaraplamaġyn. [105]⌜מתי תוציא אדון⌟.

---

78 JSul.III.03: deest; a scribal error.

79 JSul.III.63: *qundaratyn*; a scribal error.

80 JSul.III.03: ימֿינך. | JSul.I.45: ימֿינך. | JSul.III.69: ימֿינך. | JSul.III.79: ימֿינך.

81 JSul.III.03: *ancaq.* | JSul.I.45: *ancaq.* | ADub.III.61: *ancaq.* | JSul.III.69: *ancaq.* | JSul.III.79: *ancaq.*

82 JSul.III.63: deest.

83 JSul.III.63: *raḥmetlevčü da qutqaruvču.* | JSul.III.03: *raḥmetlevcü.* | JSul.I.45: *raḥmetlevcü.* | ADub.III.61: *raḥmetlevci.* | JSul.III.69: *raḥmetlevci.* | JSul.III.79: *raḥmetlevci.*

84 JSul.III.03: *sirtivcü.* | JSul.I.45: *sirtivcü.* | ADub.III.61: *sirtivci.* | JSul.III.69: *sirtivci.* | JSul.III.69: *sirtivci.*

85 JSul.III.03: *gineḥlerin.* | JSul.I.45: *gineḥlerin.* | ADub.III.61: *gineḥlerin.* | JSul.III.69: *gineḥlerin.* | JSul.III.79: *gineḥlerin.*

86 JSul.III.03: *qajtuvcularnyn.* | ADub.III.61: *qajtuvcularnyn.* | JSul.III.69: *qajtuvcularnyn.* | JSul.III.79: *qajtuvcularnyn.*

87 JSul.III.03: *ʒan byla.* | JSul.I.45: *ʒan byla.* | ADub.III.61: *ʒan byla.* | JSul.III.69: *ʒan byla.* | JSul.III.79: *ʒan byla.*

88 JSul.III.03: *daġy.* | JSul.I.45: *daġy.* | ADub.III.61: *daġy.* | JSul.III.69: *daġy.* | JSul.III.79: *daġy.*

89 JSul.III.63: *sendin*; a scribal error, cf. *senden* in line 22.

90 JSul.III.03: *küclü.* | JSul.I.45: *küclü.* | ADub.III.61: *kicli.* | JSul.III.69: *kicli.* | JSul.III.79: *kicli.*

91 ADub.III.61: *kere.* | JSul.III.69: *kere.* | JSul.III.79: *kere.*

92 JSul.III.03: *asyra.* | JSul.I.45: *asyra.* | ADub.III.61: *asyra.* | JSul.III.69: *asyra.* | JSul.III.79: *asyra.*

93 JSul.III.03: *kötirme.* | JSul.I.45: *kötirme.* | ADub.III.61: *ketirme.* | JSul.III.69: *ketirme.* | JSul.III.79: *ketirme.*

94 JSul.III.03: *tezce.* | JSul.I.45: *tezce.* | ADub.III.61: *tezce.* | JSul.III.69: *tezce.* | JSul.III.79: *tezce.*

[23] [4] there[106] Your right hand will reach me. (4). But since I know that
[24] [5] You are the only[107] one who ⌊has pity on⌋[108] those who return to You with an upstanding heart and who blots out their sins,
[25] [6] I also do have a request to You that You may throw out from before You my sins and
[26] [7] (that), according to Your promise, You may wish to lift me up swiftly from the ground and from my lowness.
[27] [8] See now from Your holy place that the enemy has oppressed me very much
[28] [9] until he lowered my beauty to earth[109], and therefore send Your providence[110]. For
[29] [10] how long will You tolerate the insults of the enemy? (5).

95 JSul.III.63: *astry dušman qysyqlyq etedi mana.* | JSul.III.03: *astry dusman qysyqlyq etedi mana.* | JSul.I.45: *astry dusman qysyqlyq etedi mana.* | ADub.III.61: *astry dusman qysyqlyq etedi mana.* | JSul.III.69: *astry dusman qysyqlyq etedi mana.* | JSul.III.79: *astry dusman qysyqlyq etedi mana.*

96 JSul.III.03: *negince.* | JSul.I.45: *negince.* | ADub.III.61: *negince.* | JSul.III.69: *negince.* | JSul.III.79: *negince.*

97 JSul.I.45: deest. | ADub.III.61: deest. | JSul.III.79: deest.

98 JSul.III.79: *gerge*; perhaps a scribal error.

99 JSul.III.03: *körkimni.* | JSul.I.45: *körkimni.* | ADub.III.61: *kerkimni.* | JSul.III.69: *kerkimni.* | JSul.III.79: *kerkimni.*

100 JSul.III.03: *ücün.* | JSul.I.45: *ücün.* | ADub.III.61: *icin.* | JSul.III.69: *icin.* | JSul.III.79: *icin.*

101 JSul.III.03: *bolusluġumnu.* | JSul.I.45: *bolusluġunnu.* | ADub.III.61: *bolusluġumnu.* | JSul.III.69: *bolusluġumnu.* | JSul.III.79: *bolusluġumnu.*

102 JSul.III.03: *qacanġa dejin.* | JSul.I.45: *qacanġadejin.* | ADub.III.61: *qacanġadejin.* | JSul.III.69: *qacanġadejin.* | JSul.III.79: *qacanġadejin.*

103 JSul.III.03: *cydarsen.* | JSul.I.45: *cydarsen.* | ADub.III.61: *cydarsen.* | JSul.III.69: *cydarsen.* | JSul.III.79: *cydarsen.*

104 JSul.III.03: *dušmannyn.* | JSul.I.45: *dusmannyn.* | ADub.III.61: *dusmannyn.* | JSul.III.69: *dusmannyn.* | JSul.III.79: *dusmannyn.*

105 JSul.III.03: מתּי. | JSul.I.45: מתּי. | ADub.III.61: מתּי. | JSul.III.69: מתּי. | JSul.III.79: מתּי.

106 JSul.III.03: deest; a scribal error.

107 JSul.III.63: deest.

108 JSul.III.63: *has pity on and saves.*

109 JSul.III.79: *the grave*; perhaps a scribal error, cf. *jer* 'earth' and *ger* 'grave'.

110 JSul.III.03: *my providence.* | ADub.III.61: *my providence.* | JSul.III.69: *my providence.* | JSul.III.79: *my providence.*

[30] [11] Ki nek bu jašyrdyn[111] enajatynny[112] menden [ki][113] čyqmajsen[114] čörivleme[115] čörivlerimni[116] burundaġy-

[31] [12] laj da jaryqqa balqytma[117] törelerimni[118]. E qorqunčlu[119] Tenri qulaqsalġyn[120] bu syjytly

[32] [13] tefilamny[121] da veren etkin tüslü[122] qyjynlarbyla qyjnavčula-rymny[123]. Da alajoq tefilasyn[124]

[33] [14] jyjynlarynyn barda qahallarymnyn qabul etkin da jarlyġašynbyla[125] kiplegin[126] meni, ki muna

[34] [15] ⌊erteden da kečeden⌋[127] sana jalġyzġa telmertemen közlerimni[128]. [129]⌈עיני מצפות⌋.

[35] [16] E Tenrim qutqaruvčum[130] da juluvčum[131] bu eki galuttan[132] daġy[133] buda avur galutumdan

[36] [17] jyštyrma[134] azašqanlarymny[135] senden tüvül[136] özgege[137] qojamen yšančymny[138], ki ojatqaj-

---

111 JSul.III.63: *jasyrdyn.* | JSul.III.03: *jasyrdyn.* | JSul.I.45: *jasyrdyn.* | ADub.III.61: *jasyrdyn.* | JSul.III.69: *jasyrdyn.* | JSul.III.79: *jasyrdyn.*

112 JSul.III.03: *enaj atynny.* | JSul.I.45: *enaj atynny.* | ADub.III.61: *enaj atynny.* | JSul.III.69: *enaj atynny.* | JSul.III.79: *enaj atynny.*

113 JSul.I.01b: *da*; probably a scribal error. | JSul.III.63: *ki.* | JSul.III.03: *ki.* | JSul.I.45: *ki.* | ADub.III.61: *ki.* | JSul.III.69: *ki.* | JSul.III.79: *ki.*

114 JSul.III.63: spelled with the letter *kaph.* | JSul.III.03: *cyqmajsen.* | JSul.I.45: *cyqmajsen.* | ADub.III.61: *cyqmajsen.* | JSul.III.69: *cyqmajsen.* | JSul.III.79: *cyqmajsen.*

115 JSul.III.63: *čörüvleme.* | JSul.III.03: *cerivleme.* | JSul.I.45: *cerivleme.* | ADub.III.61: *cerivleme.* | JSul.III.69: *cerivleme.* | JSul.III.79: *cerivleme.*

116 JSul.III.63: *čörüvlerimni.* | JSul.III.03: *cerivlerimni.* | JSul.I.45: *cerivlerimni.* | ADub.III.61: *cerivlerimni.* | JSul.III.69: *cerivlerimni.* | JSul.III.79: *cerivlerimni.*

117 JSul.III.03: *cyġarma.* | JSul.I.45: *cyġarma.* | ADub.III.61: *cyġarma.* | JSul.III.69: *cyġarma.* | JSul.III.79: *cyġarma.*

118 JSul.III.03: *terelerimni.* | JSul.I.45: *terelerimni.* | ADub.III.61: *terelerimni.* | JSul.III.69: *terelerimni.* | JSul.III.79: *terelerimni.*

119 JSul.III.03: *qorqunclu.* | JSul.I.45: *qorqunclu.* | ADub.III.61: *qorqunclu.* | JSul.III.69: *qorqunclu.* | JSul.III.79: *qorqunclu.*

120 JSul.III.03: *qajyrġyn esitivinni.* | JSul.I.45: *qajyrġyn esitivinni.* | ADub.III.61: *qajyrġyn esitivinni.* | JSul.III.69: *qajyrġyn esitivinni.* | JSul.III.79: *qajyrġyn esitivinni.*

121 JSul.III.63: *tefilemni.* | JSul.III.03: *tefileme.* | JSul.I.45: *tefilemni.* | ADub.III.61: *tefileme.* | JSul.III.69: *tefileme.* | JSul.III.79: *tefileme.*

122 JSul.III.63: *türlü.* | JSul.III.03: *tirli.* | JSul.I.45: *tirli.* | JSul.III.69: *tirli.* | JSul.III.79: *tirli.*

123 JSul.III.63: *munajtuvčularymny.* | JSul.III.03: *qyjnavcularymny.* | JSul.I.45: *qyjnavcularymny.* | ADub.III.61: *qyjnavcularymny.* | JSul.III.69: *qyjnavcularymny.* | JSul.III.79: *qyjnavcularymny.*

124 JSul.III.63: *tefilesin.* | JSul.III.03: *tefilesin.* | JSul.I.45: *tefilesin.* | ADub.III.61: *tefilesin.* | JSul.III.69: *tefilesin.* | JSul.III.79: *tefilesin.*

125 JSul.III.03: *jarlyġasyn byla.* | JSul.I.45: *jarlyġasyn byla.* | ADub.III.61: *jarlyġasyn byla.* | JSul.III.69: *jarlyġasyn byla.* | JSul.III.69: *jarlyġasyn byla.*

[30] [11] So why did You hide Your eyes from me so that You shall not rise to be in command of my army as it was before

[31] [12] and to illumine[139] my laws. O awesome God, listen[140] to my prayer full of grief

[32] [13] and destroy my oppressors with all kind of suffering. And, likewise,

[33] [14] accept the prayer of the congregations of all my communities, and strengthen me with Your mercy, for, lo,

[34] [15] in the mornings and at night I direct my eyes to only You. (6).

[35] [16] O God of mine, my redeemer and my saviour from the two exiles, also even from this hard exile of mine

[36] [17] I trust You and no one else apart from You, that You will gather my strays, so that You may arouse

---

126 JSul.III.03: *küplegin*; a hypercorrect form of *kiplegin.* | JSul.I.45: *küplegin*; a hypercorrect form of *kiplegin.*

127 JSul.III.03: *erteden da keceden.* | JSul.I.45: *ertede da kecede.* | ADub.III.61: *ertede da kecede.* | JSul.III.69: *erteden da keceden.* | JSul.III.79: *ertede da kecede.*

128 JSul.III.63: *ošol közlerimni.* | JSul.III.03: *osol közlerimni.* | ADub.III.61: *kezlerimni.* | JSul.III.69: *osol kezlerimni.* | JSul.III.79: *kezlerimni.*

129 JSul.III.63: עיני מצפות לך. | JSul.I.45: עיני. | ADub.III.61: עיני. | JSul.III.69: עיני. | JSul.III.79: עיני.

130 JSul.III.03: *qutqaruvcum.* | JSul.I.45: *qutqaruvcum.* | ADub.III.61: *qutqaruvcum.* | JSul.III.69: *qutqaruvcum.* | JSul.III.79: *qutqaruvcum.*

131 JSul.III.03: *juluvcum.* | JSul.I.45: *juluvcum.* | ADub.III.61: *juluvcum.* | JSul.III.69: *juluvcum.* | JSul.III.79: *juluvcum.*

132 JSul.III.63: *galutlarymdan.* | JSul.III.03: *galutumdan.* | JSul.III.69: *galutumdan.* | JSul.III.79: *galutumdan.*

133 JSul.III.63: *dağyn.* | ADub.III.61: *dağyn.*

134 JSul.III.03: *jystyrma.* | JSul.I.45: *jystyrma.* | ADub.III.61: *ystyrma.* | JSul.III.69: *ystyrma.* | JSul.III.79: *ystyrma.*

135 JSul.III.63: spelled with the letter *kaph.* | JSul.III.03: *azasqanlarymny.* | JSul.I.45: *azasqanlarymny.* | ADub.III.61: *azasqanlarymny.* | JSul.III.69: *azasqanlarymny.* | JSul.III.79: *azasqanlarymny.*

136 JSul.III.03: *tivil.* | JSul.I.45: *tivil.* | ADub.III.61: *tivil.* | JSul.III.69: *tivil.* | JSul.III.79: *tivil.*

137 JSul.III.03: *ezgege.* | JSul.I.45: *ezgege.* | ADub.III.61: *ezgege.* | JSul.III.69: *ezgege.* | JSul.III.79: *ezgege.*

138 JSul.I.01b: or: *išančymny.* | JSul.III.63: or: *išančymny.* | JSul.III.03: *ysancymny* or *isancymny.* | JSul.I.45: *ysancymny* or *isancymny.* | ADub.III.61: *ysancymny* or *isancymny.* | JSul.III.69: *ysancymny* or *isancymny.* | JSul.III.79: *ysancymny* or *isancymny.*

139 Lit. 'illumine to light'. | JSul.III.03: *reveal.* | JSul.I.45: *reveal.* | ADub.III.61: *reveal.* | JSul.III.69: *reveal.* | JSul.III.79: *reveal.*

140 JSul.III.03: *turn Your ear.* | JSul.I.45: *turn Your ear.* | ADub.III.61: *turn Your ear.* | JSul.III.69: *turn Your ear.* | JSul.III.79: *turn Your ear.*

[37] [18] sen künülügünnü[141] da jasanġajsen[142] qaḥirlerinbyla[143] öč[144] alma utru[145] turuvčularymdan[146]

[38] [19] ki har vaḥt tavullajyn saġyšlajdylar[147] tozdurma meni. Da sözüne[148] köre[149] inam[150] qulla-

[39] [20] rynnyn ijgin rast elčimni[151] da anyn qolu ašyra[152] tezče[153] ǯaḥtlaġyn[154] jarlyġašymny[155],

[40] [21] ki sana e H ešittiremen[156] har vaḥt jalbarmaq avazymny. [157]⌜קוֹלִי שְׁעֵה⌟.

[41] [22] Qoltqabyla[158] e tynlavču[159] tefilasyn[160] miskinlernin menimde bu syjytly jalbarmaġymdan

[42] [23] enajatynny[161] jummaġyn, ki süvgen[in]de[162] jerinni toḥtatma šeẖinanny anda süvgün[163]

[43] [24] menide qulluġuna özünnün[164] da bulušluġuma[165] ǯaḥtlaġyn[166]. Körgün[167] endi qynġyrlyq[168]

---

141 < MSWKar. **könülügünnü* 'Your justice' (assimilation), cf. our remarks in the glossary (s.v. *künülük*). || JSul.III.63: *künülemeginni*; a scribal error. | JSul.III.03: *kinilemeginni*; a scribal error. | JSul.I.45: *kinilegenni*; a scribal error. | ADub.III.61: *kiniliginni*. | JSul.III.69: *kinilimegenni*; a scribal error. | JSul.III.79: *kiniliginni*.

142 JSul.III.03: *jašanġajsen*; a hypercorrect form of *jasanġajsen*.

143 JSul.III.63: *qaḥyrynbyla*. | JSul.III.03: *qaḥyryn byla*. | JSul.I.45: *qaḥyryn byla*. | ADub.III.61: *qaḥyryn byla*. | JSul.III.69: *qaḥyryn byla*. | JSul.III.79: *qaḥyryn byla*.

144 JSul.III.03: *ec*. | JSul.I.45: *ec*. | ADub.III.61: *ec*. | JSul.III.69: *ec*. | JSul.III.79: *ec*.

145 JSul.III.03: *uturu*. | JSul.I.45: *uturu*. | ADub.III.61: *uturu*. | JSul.III.69: *uturu*. | JSul.III.79: *uturu*.

146 JSul.III.03: *turuvcularymdan*. | JSul.I.45: *turuvcularymdan*. | ADub.III.61: *turuvcularymdan*. | JSul.III.69: *turuvcularymdan*. | JSul.III.79: *turuvcularymdan*.

147 JSul.III.03: *saġyslajdylar*. | JSul.I.45: *saġyslajdylar*. | ADub.III.61: *saġyslajdylar*. | JSul.III.69: *saġyslajdylar*. | JSul.III.79: *saġyslajdylar*.

148 JSul.III.03: *sözine*. | JSul.I.45: *sözine*. | ADub.III.61: *sezine*. | JSul.III.69: *sezine*. | JSul.III.79: *sezine*.

149 JSul.III.03: *köre*. | ADub.III.61: *kere*. | JSul.III.69: *kere*. | JSul.III.79: *kere*.

150 JSul.III.63: *inaq*; most probably a scribal error repeated in all the other manuscripts. | JSul.III.03: *inaq*; most probably a scribal error. | JSul.I.45: *inaq*; most probably a scribal error. | ADub.III.61: *inaq*; most probably a scribal error. | JSul.III.69: *inaq*; most probably a scribal error. | JSul.III.79: *inaq*; most probably a scribal error.

151 JSul.III.03: *elcinni*. | JSul.I.45: *elcimizni*. | ADub.III.61: *elcimizni*. | JSul.III.69: *elcinni*. | JSul.III.79: *elcimizni*.

152 JSul.III.03: *asyra*. | JSul.I.45: *asyra*. | ADub.III.61: *asyra*. | JSul.III.69: *asyra*. | JSul.III.79: *asyra*.

153 JSul.III.03: *tezce*. | JSul.I.45: *tezce*. | ADub.III.61: *tezce*. | JSul.III.69: *tezce*. | JSul.III.79: *tezce*.

[37] [18] Your justice and arm Yourself with Your wrath to take revenge on my foes

[38] [19] who devise all the time (how to) to scatter me like a storm. And according to the word of Your servants of faith

[39] [20] send my[169] just envoy and through his hand swiftly advance my salvation,

[40] [21] for I make You hear my voice of entreaty all the time. (7).

[41] [22] I beg You, He who listens to the prayer of the poor, do not

[42] [23] close Your eyes even to my entreaty full of grief: that in Your love to the land (strong enough) to put Your divine Presence there, do want[170]

[43] [24] me, too, for the service of You Yourself and hurry to help me. See now that I have borne (all the) faults[171]

---

154 JSul.III.03: *zaḥtlaġyn.* | JSul.I.45: *zaḥtlaġyn.* | ADub.III.61: *zaḥtlaġyn.* | JSul.III.69: *zaḥtlaġyn.* | JSul.III.79: *zaḥtlaġyn.*

155 JSul.III.03: *jarlyġasymny.* | JSul.I.45: *jarlyġasymny.* | ADub.III.61: *jarlyġasymny.* | JSul.III.69: *jarlyġasymny.* | JSul.III.79: *jarlyġasynny.*

156 JSul.III.03: *esittiremen.* | JSul.I.45: *esittiremen.* | ADub.III.61: *esittiremen.* | JSul.III.69: *esittiremen.* | JSul.III.79: *esittiremen.*

157 JSul.III.03: קוֹלִי. | JSul.I.45: קוֹלִי. | JSul.III.69: קּוֹלִי. | JSul.III.79: קוֹלִי.

158 JSul.III.03: *qoltqa* [*byla*].

159 JSul.III.03: *tynlavcu.* | JSul.I.45: *tynlavcu.* | ADub.III.61: *tynlavcu.* | JSul.III.69: *tynlavcu.* | JSul.III.79: *tynlavcu.*

160 JSul.III.63: *tefilesin.* | JSul.III.03: *tefilesin.* | JSul.I.45: *tefilesin.* | ADub.III.61: *tefilesin.* | JSul.III.69: *tefilesin.* | JSul.III.79: *tefilesin.*

161 JSul.III.03: *enaj atynny.* | JSul.I.45: *enaj atynny.* | ADub.III.61: *enaj atynny.* | JSul.III.69: *enaj atynny.* | JSul.III.79: *enaj atynny.*

162 JSul.I.01b: *süvgende.* | JSul.III.03: *sivgende.* | JSul.I.45: *sivgende.* | ADub.III.61: *sivgende.* | JSul.III.69: *sivgende.* | JSul.III.79: *sivgeninde.*

163 JSul.III.03: *sivgin.* | JSul.I.45: *sivgin.* | ADub.III.61: *sivgin.* | JSul.III.69: *sivgin.* | JSul.III.79: *sivgin.*

164 JSul.III.63: *özüjnün*; a NWKar. form. | JSul.III.03: *ezinnin.* | JSul.I.45: *ezinnin.* | ADub.III.61: *ezinnin.* | JSul.III.69: *ezinnin.* | JSul.III.79: *ezinnin.*

165 JSul.III.03: *bolusluġuma.* | JSul.I.45: *bolusluġuma.* | ADub.III.61: *bolusluġuma.* | JSul.III.69: *bolusluġuma.* | JSul.III.79: *bolusluġuma.*

166 JSul.III.03: *zaḥtlaġyn.* | JSul.I.45: *zaḥtlaġyn.* | ADub.III.61: *zaḥtlaġyn.* | JSul.III.69: *zaḥtlaġyn.* | JSul.III.79: *zaḥtlaġyn.*

167 JSul.III.03: *körgin.* | JSul.I.45: *körgin.* | ADub.III.61: *kergin.* | JSul.III.69: *kergin.* | JSul.III.79: *kergin.*

168 JSul.III.03: *qyjyn.* | JSul.III.69: *qyjyn.*

169 JSul.III.03: *Your.* | JSul.I.45: *our.* | ADub.III.61: *our.* | JSul.III.69: *Your.* | JSul.III.79: *our.*

170 Lit. 'love'.

171 JSul.III.03: *suffering.* | JSul.III.69: *suffering.*

[44] [25] čydaġanymny[172] da sürtkün[173] jüzlerimden[174] jylamaq[175] jašlarymny[176] köplügünden[177] rusvajlyġyn[yn][178]

[45] [26] dušmanlarymnyn[179] da qollaryndan[180] syjly da abajly ǯanymny[181] qutqarġyn. Azizligi üčün[182] bu

[46] [27] qorqunčlu[183] šeminnin tynlama firjatymny ešitivünnü[184] salġyn.

[47] [28] [185]⌈תפלתי שמעה⌋. Qajtqyn endi qaḥyr ačuvundan[186] fašman[187] etme ol[188] jaman üčün[189]

[48] [29] da qaruv bergin mana ajtadoġač[190] qorqmaġyn zavally[191] Jisra'el ki ešittim[192] {bu} telfilanny[193],

128 r°[194] [49] [1] da qalyn bulutnu kibik sürtkün[195] jamanlyġyn jerenči[196] išlerimnin[197] ki alarġa köre[198]

[50] [2] töre[199] etmegejsen meni. Da bu rast firjatym jetsin alnyna senin da ǯomartly-

[51] [3] ġyndan[200] qudratyjnyn[201] ajamaġyn menden šavaġatynny[202], ki muna qotaramen maḥtavunnu

---

172 JSul.III.03: *cydaġa{ny}mny.* | JSul.I.45: *cydaġanymny.* | ADub.III.61: *cydaġanymny.* | JSul.III.69: *cydaġanymny.* | JSul.III.79: *cydaġanymny.*

173 JSul.III.03: *sirtkin.* | JSul.I.45: *sirtkin.* | ADub.III.61: *sirtkin.* | JSul.III.69: *sirtkin.* | JSul.III.69: *sirtkin.*

174 JSul.III.03: *közlerimden.* | JSul.I.45: *izlerimden.* | ADub.III.61: *izlerimden.* | JSul.III.69: *kezlerimden.* | JSul.III.79: *izlerimden.*

175 JSul.III.63: *jalamaq*; a scribal error.

176 JSul.III.03: *jaslarymny.* | JSul.I.45: *jaslarymny.* | ADub.III.61: *jaslarymny.* | JSul.III.69: *jaslarymny.* | JSul.III.79: *jaslarymny.*

177 JSul.III.03: *köpligin{den}.* | JSul.I.45: *köpliginden.* | ADub.III.61: *kepliginden.* | JSul.III.69: *kepliginden.* | JSul.III.79: *kepliginden.*

178 JSul.III.63: *rusvajlyġynyn.* | JSul.III.03: *rusvajlyġynyn.* | JSul.I.45: *rusvajlyġynyn.* | ADub.III.61: *rusvajlyġynyn.* | JSul.III.69: *rusvajlyġynyn.* | JSul.III.79: *rusvajlyġynyn.*

179 JSul.III.03: *dusmanlarymnyn.* | JSul.I.45: *dusmanlarymnyn.* | ADub.III.61: *dusmanlarymnyn.* | JSul.III.69: *dusmanlarymnyn.* | JSul.III.79: *dusmanlarymnyn.*

180 JSul.III.63: *qollaryndan alarnyn.* | JSul.III.03: *qollaryndan alarnyn.* | ADub.III.61: *qollaryndan alarnyn.* | JSul.III.69: *qollaryndan alarnyn.* | JSul.III.79: *qollaryndan alarnyn.*

181 JSul.III.03: *ʒanymny.* | JSul.I.45: *ʒanymny.* | ADub.III.61: *ʒanymny.* | JSul.III.69: *ʒanymny.* | JSul.III.79: *ʒanymny.*

182 JSul.III.03: *ücün.* | JSul.I.45: *ücün.* | ADub.III.61: *icin.* | JSul.III.69: *icin.* | JSul.III.79: *icin.*

183 JSul.III.03: *qorqunclu.* | JSul.I.45: *qorqunclu.* | ADub.III.61: *qorqunclu.* | JSul.III.69: *qorqunclu.* | JSul.III.79: *qorqunclu.*

184 JSul.III.63: *ešitüvünnü.* | JSul.III.03: *esitivinni.* | JSul.I.45: *esitivinni.* | ADub.III.61: *esitivinni.* | JSul.III.69: *esitivinni.* | JSul.III.79: *esitivinni.*

185 JSul.I.45: תפִּלתי. | ADub.III.61: תפִּלתי. | JSul.III.69: תפִּלתי. | JSul.III.79: תפִּלתי.

186 JSul.III.03: *acuvundan.* | JSul.I.45: *acuvundan.* | ADub.III.61: *acuvundan.* | JSul.III.69: *acuvundan.* | JSul.III.79: *acuvundan.*

187 ADub.III.61: *fasman.* | JSul.III.69: *fasman.* | JSul.III.79: *fasman.*

[44] [25] and wipe out my tears from my faces[203] that I have cried because of the abundance of disgrace

[45] [26] (I have received from) my enemies, and save my honourable and respected soul from their hands. Because of the holiness

[46] [27] of Your awesome name, open up Your ears to hear my cry.

[47] [28] (8). Return now, do not begrudge evil Your angry wrath

[48] [29] and reply to me, saying, 'Do not fear, miserable[204] Israel, for I have heard Your prayer',

[49] [1] and, like a thick cloud, blot out the evil of my repulsive deeds, so that You may not 128 r°

[50] [2] judge me according to them. And may this upstanding cry of mine come[205] before You and, because of the generosity

[51] [3] of Your power, do not begrudge me Your mercy, for, lo, I preach Your praise

---

188 JSul.I.45: deest. | ADub.III.61: deest. | JSul.III.79: deest.

189 JSul.III.03: *ücün.* | JSul.I.45: *ücün.* | ADub.III.61: *icin.* | JSul.III.69: *icin.* | JSul.III.79: *icin.*

190 JSul.III.03: *ajtadoġac.* | JSul.I.45: *ajtadoġac.* | ADub.III.61: *ajtadoġac.* | JSul.III.69: *ajtadoġac.* | JSul.III.79: *ajtadoġac.*

191 JSul.I.45: *e zavally.* | ADub.III.61: *e zavally.* | JSul.III.79: *e zavally.*

192 JSul.III.03: *esittim.* | JSul.I.45: *esittim.* | ADub.III.61: *esittim.* | JSul.III.69: *esittim.* | JSul.III.79: *esittim.*

193 JSul.III.63: *telfilenni.* | ADub.III.61: *telfilenni.* | JSul.III.03: *telfilenni.* | JSul.I.45: *telfilenni.* | JSul.III.69: *telfilenni.* | JSul.III.79: *telfilenni.*

194 Folio 127 r° contains a list of personal names (written by another person), which does not constitute a part of the *peshat*. It was drawn up on a much smaller sheet of paper and inserted into the manuscript between folios 126 and 128. Folio 127 v° is left empty.

195 JSul.III.03: *sirtkin.* | JSul.I.45: *sirtkin.* | ADub.III.61: *sirtkin.* | JSul.III.69: *sirtkin.* JSul.III.79: *sirtermen.*

196 JSul.III.03: *jerenci.* | JSul.I.45: *jerenci.* | ADub.III.61: *jerenci.* | JSul.III.69: *jerenci.* | JSul.III.79: *jerenci.*

197 JSul.III.03: *islerimnin.* | JSul.I.45: *islerimnin.* | ADub.III.61: *islerimnin.* | JSul.III.69: *islerimnin.* | JSul.III.79: *islerimnin.*

198 ADub.III.61: *kere.* | JSul.III.69: *kere.* | JSul.III.79: *kere.*

199 JSul.I.45: *tere.* | ADub.III.61: *tere.* | JSul.III.69: *tere.* | JSul.III.79: *tere.*

200 JSul.III.03: *ʒomartlyġyndan.* | JSul.I.45: *ʒomartlyġyndan.* | ADub.III.61: *ʒomartlyġyndan.* | JSul.III.69: *ʒomartlyġyndan.* | JSul.III.79: *ʒomartlyġyndan.*

201 JSul.I.01b: a NWKar. form. | JSul.III.63: *qudratynnyn.* | JSul.III.03: *qudratynnyn.* | JSul.I.45: *qudratynnyn.* | ADub.III.61: *qudratynnyn.* | JSul.III.69: *qudratynnyn.* | JSul.III.79: *qudratynnyn.*

202 JSul.III.03: *savaġatynny.* | JSul.I.45: *savaġatynny.* | ADub.III.61: *savaġatynny.* | JSul.III.69: *savaġatynny.* | JSul.III.79: *savaġatynny.*

203 JSul.III.03: *eyes.* | JSul.III.69: *eyes.* | JSul.III.79: *eyes.*

204 JSul.I.45: *O miserable.* | ADub.III.61: *O miserable.* | JSul.III.79: *O miserable.*

205 Lit. 'reach'.

[52] [4] da ajtamen ⌊qoltqabyla e H⌉[206] ḥajifsingün[207] meni. [208]⌈חנני צורי⌋.
[53] [5] E ḥajifsünüvcü[209] Tenri bošatuvču[210] güneḥni[211] da tanmaqny
sağynmağyn mana[212] burunğu
[54] [6] jazyqlarymny da jubančly[213] ḥabar ešittirgin[214] ki tügendi[215] artyq
uču[216] güneḥl[e]-
[55] [7] rimnin[217]. Bar türlü[218] otračlardan[219] jondarma azašqanlarymyzny[220] aziz šaharyna[221]
[56] [8] Jerušalajimge ojatqyn[222] raḥmetlerinni je‘udlaryna köre[223]
navilerinnin. Da
[57] [9] qabulluqqa bolsun bu[224] jalbarmaq tefilam[225] alnynda qyblalarynnyn qarbanlary
[58] [10] ornuna tanalarnyn. Kertiligibyla[226] jarlyğašynnyn[227] e Tenrim[228]
qaruv bergin
[59] [11] mana köplügünden[229] šavağatynnyn[230]. [231]⌈ותאמר התה הׄ אזנך עני׳
וכו׳:⌋.

206 ADub.III.61: *e H qoltqabyla.*

207 JSul.III.63: *ḥajifsüngün.* | JSul.III.03: *ḥajifsingin.* | JSul.I.45: *ḥajifsingin.* | ADub.III.61: *ḥajifsingin.* | JSul.III.69: *ḥajifsingin.* | JSul.III.79: *ḥajifsingin.*

208 JSul.I.45: חׇנֵּנִי. | JSul.III.69: חׇנֵּנִי. | JSul.III.79: חׇנֵּנִי.

209 JSul.III.03: *ḥajifsinivcü.* | JSul.I.45: *ḥajifsinivcü.* | ADub.III.61: *ḥajifsinivci.* | JSul.III.69: *ḥajifsinivci.* | JSul.III.79: *ḥajifsinivci.*

210 JSul.III.03: *bosatuvcu.* | JSul.I.45: *bosatuvcu.* | ADub.III.61: *bosatuvcu.* | JSul.III.69: *bosatuvcu.* | JSul.III.79: *bosatuvcu.*

211 JSul.III.03: *jazyqny.* | JSul.I.45: *gineḥni.* | ADub.III.61: *gineḥni.* | JSul.III.69: *jazyqny.* | JSul.III.79: *gineḥni.*

212 JSul.III.63: deest.

213 JSul.III.03: *jubancly.* | JSul.I.45: *jubancly.* | ADub.III.61: *jubancly.* | JSul.III.69: *jubancly.* | JSul.III.79: *jubancly.*

214 JSul.III.63: *ešittirgin mana.* | JSul.III.03: *esittirgin mana.* | JSul.I.45: *esittirgin.* | ADub.III.61: *esittirgin mana.* | JSul.III.69: *esittirgin mana.* | JSul.III.79: *esittirgin mana.*

215 JSul.III.03: *tigendi.* | JSul.I.45: *tigendi.* | ADub.III.61: *tigendi.* | JSul.III.69: *tigendi.* | JSul.III.79: *tigendi.*

216 JSul.III.03: *ucu.* | JSul.I.45: *ucu.* | ADub.III.61: *ucu.* | JSul.III.69: *ucu.* | JSul.III.79: *ucu.*

217 JSul.I.01b: *güneḥlirimnin*; a scribal error; spelled גִיוּנֵיחְלִירְימְנִין. | JSul.III.63: *güneḥlerinnin.* | JSul.III.03: *gineḥlerinnin.* | JSul.I.45: *güneḥlerimnin.* | ADub.III.61: *gineḥlerinnin.* | JSul.III.69: *gineḥlerinnin.* | JSul.III.79: *gineḥlerimnin.*

218 JSul.III.03: *tirli.* | JSul.I.45: *tirli.* | ADub.III.61: *tirli.* | JSul.III.69: *tirli.* | JSul.III.79: *tirli.*

219 JSul.III.03: *otraclardan.* | JSul.I.45: *otraclardan.* | ADub.III.61: *otraclardan.* | JSul.III.69: *otraclardan.* | JSul.III.79: *otraclardan.*

220 JSul.III.63: *azašqanlarymny.* | JSul.III.03: *azasqanlarymny.* | JSul.I.45: *azasqanlarymny.* | ADub.III.61: *azasqanlarymny.* | JSul.III.69: *azasqanlarymny.* | JSul.III.79: *azasqanlarymny.*

[52] [4] and I say, 'I beg You, O Lord, have mercy on me.' (9).

[53] [5] O gracious God who absolves of sins and transgression, do not ⌊remind me[1232] my past

[54] [6] sins; and make me hear the joyful news: that ⌊my sinning has already come to its end[1233].

[55] [7] Arouse[234] Your mercies to gather my strays from ⌊all the[1235] isles into the holy city of

[56] [8] Jerusalem, according to the promises[236] of Your prophets. And

[57] [9] may my lamentation find acceptance before Your countenance

[58] [10] (brought) instead of a sacrifice lamb. Reply to me, O God of mine, with the truth of Your grace,

[59] [11] with the abundance of Your mercy. ⌊And you will say: 'Bow down your ear, O Lord, hear me ...', and so forth.[1237]

---

221 JSul.III.03: *šaharyna.* | JSul.I.45: *saharyna.* | ADub.III.61: *saharyna.* | JSul.III.69: *saharyna.* | JSul.III.79: *saharyna.*

222 JSul.III.63: *ojatqajsen.*

223 ADub.III.61: *kere.* | JSul.III.69: *kere.* | JSul.III.79: *kere.*

224 JSul.I.45: deest. | ADub.III.61: deest. | JSul.III.79: deest.

225 JSul.III.63: *tefilem.* | JSul.III.03: *tefilem.* | JSul.I.45: *tefilem.* | ADub.III.61: *tefilem.* | JSul.III.69: *tefilem.* | JSul.III.79: *tefilem.*

226 JSul.III.03: *körtiligi byla*; *körtiligi* is a hypercorrect form of *kertiligi.* | JSul.I.45: *körtiligi byla*; *körtiligi* is a hypercorrect form of *kertiligi.*

227 JSul.III.03: *jarlyġasynnyn.* | JSul.I.45: *jarlyġasynnyn.* | ADub.III.61: *jarlyġasynnyn.* | JSul.III.69: *jarlyġasynnyn.* | JSul.III.79: *jarlyġasynnyn.*

228 JSul.I.45: *Tenri.* | ADub.III.61: *Tenri.* | JSul.III.79: *Tenri.*

229 JSul.III.03: *köpliginden.* | JSul.I.45: *köpliginden.* | ADub.III.61: *kepliginden.* | JSul.III.69: *kepliginden.* | JSul.III.79: *kepliginden.*

230 JSul.III.03: *savaġatynnyn.* | JSul.I.45: *savaġatynnyn.* | ADub.III.61: *savaġatynnyn.* | JSul.III.69: *savaġatynnyn.* | JSul.III.79: *savaġatynnyn.*

231 JSul.III.63: הטה ה̇ אזנך ענני כי עני וכל המזמור. | JSul.III.03: הטה ה̇ אזנך ענני. | JSul.I.45: הטה ה̇. | ADub.III.61: תם הטה ה̇ אזנך וגו׳. | JSul.III.69: הטה ה̇ וגו׳. | JSul.III.79: הַטֵה הָ̇ אָזְנְךָ וגו׳.

232 JSul.III.63: *remember.*

233 Lit. 'the end of my sins already came its end'.

234 JSul.III.63: *may You arouse.*

235 Lit. 'various'.

236 Lit. 'announcements'.

237 Psalm 86:1. | JSul.III.63: *'Bow down your ear, O Lord, hear me for I am poor ...', and the whole psalm.* (Psalm 86:1). | JSul.III.03: *'Bow down your ear, O Lord, hear me.'* (Psalm 86:1). | JSul.I.45: *'Bow down, O Lord.'* (Psalm 86:1). | ADub.III.61: *The end. 'Bow down your ear, O Lord ...', and so on.* (Psalm 86:1). | JSul.III.69: *'Bow down, O Lord ...', and so on.* (Psalm 86:1). | JSul.III.79: *'Bow down your ear, O Lord ...', and so on.* (Psalm 86:1).

**Text number:** № 27
**Karaim incipit:** *Sizge caǧyramen igit sezlerim e syjly Jisraʾeller*
*Sizge caǧyramen igit sezlerim e syjly erenler*
**Hebrew incipit:** אֲלֵיכֶם אֶקְרָא אִישִׁים *ʾălēḵem ʾeqrå ʾīšīm*
**Dedication:** Parashat Kedoshim (Leviticus 19:1–20:27)
**Language:** Mod.SWKar.
**Number of copies:** 4

| Accession no. | Place of origin of copy | Date of copy | Copyist | Folios |
|---|---|---|---|---|
| ADub.III.61 | Halych | 1850/1851 | Jeshua Josef Mordkowicz | 134 vº–135 rº |
| JSul.III.69 | Halych | ca. 1851 (before 1866) | Jeshua Josef Mordkowicz | 286 vº–287 rº |
| JSul.III.79 | Halych | ca. 1851 (before 1866) | Jeshua Josef Mordkowicz | 174 rº–175 rº |
| JSul.I.37.03 | Halych (?) | between 1851 and 1866 | Unknown 12 | 16 vº |

## 1 Introductory Remarks

Another interpretation of the same *piyyut* is provided by *peshat* № 23. All four copies are vocalized and there are almost no differences between them. The existing discrepenacies are minor, cf. *Jisraʾeller* vs. *erenler* (3), *islerinizde eziniz* vs. *islerinizde eziniz* vs. *islerinizde* (4), *kleklerice* vs. *klegice* (8), *islerde* vs. *islerinde* (18).

## 2 Transcription[238] and Translation

134 v° [1] [3] ⌊וזה הפשט היקר לפיוט פרשת קדושים שהוא אֲלֵיכֶם אֶקְרָא אִשִׁים תרגמו אדו׳
זקני מוהֿרר

[2] [4] שמואל החזן ואבֿד דקֿהק האליץ יעמֿש באֿז מוהֿרר יוסף המשביר בר לעֿנ
תנצבֿהה:⌉[239]

[3] [5] Sizge caġyramen igit sezlerim e syjly Jisra'eller[240].

[4] [6] Tyntylynyz ⌊islerinizde eziniz⌉[241] da tyntynyz

[5] [7] ekincilernide necik erenler alaj qatynlar. Quvunuz bar

[6] [8] kiciniz byla qylma jaḥsy islerni ki elgeninizden sortun bolġajsiz

[7] [9] azizler. Da negince tirisiz bu dunjada qajjam etme micvalaryn

[8] [10] Tenrinin bolunuz ʒaḥtlavcular, ki aziz micvalary Toranyn kleklerice[242]

[9] [11] qyluvcularynyn izlengendiler. Anyn icin qajrylmanyz jazyqly

[10] [12] saġyslarġa maġat bolursiz alar icine tuzaqlanġanlar. Cyġarynyz[243]

[11] [13] icinizden jamanlyġyn jecerinin jireginiznin da ornunda debeḥasynyn

[12] [14] qarbanlarnyn qylynyz jaḥsy isler[244]. Da kecininiz kertilik byla kisi

[13] [15] dostu byla da savut aluv isinde bolmanyz biri birinizni alda-

[14] [16] tuvcular. Atyndan Tenrinin qorqunuz bar islerinizde da syjbyla

---

238 Based on ADub.III.61.

239 JSul.III.69: וזה פשטו שתרגמו אזֿ החכם השלם כמוהֿרר שמואל החזן זצוֿקל באֿז כמוהֿרר יוסף המשביר בר לעֿנ נבֿת וזיֿיא. | JSul.III.79: וזה הפשט לפיוט פרשת קדושים תרגמו אזֿ החכם האלהי כמוהֿרר שמואל החזן זצוֿקל באֿז כמוהֿרר יוסף המשביר נבֿת. | JSul.I.37.03: פשט לפ׳ קדושים שהוא אֲלֵיכֶם אֶקְרָא א׳: תרגמו אזֿ אמו כמהֿרר שמואל החזן ואבד׳ דקהל הק׳ יעמֿש: באז׳ מוהרר יוסף בר לעֿם נבר תשהֿעמ׳.

240 JSul.I.37.03: *erenler.*

241 JSul.III.69: *eziniz islerinizde.* | JSul.III.79: *islerinizde.*

242 JSul.I.37.03: *klegice.*

243 JSul.III.69: *cyharynyz.*

244 Ms. JSul.I.37.03 ends here.

245 I.e., *Josef ha-Mashbir*; cf. Genesis 42:3.

246 Cf., 1 Samuel 25:29.

247 JSul.I.69: *And this is* its [i.e., of the Hebrew original] peshat *which our aged master, the complete hakham, his honour, the Rav, Rabbi Shemuel the hazzan translated, may the memory of the righteous and holy be a blessing, the son ouf our aged master, his honour, the Rav, Rabbi Josef who provides pure grain* [i.e., Josef ha-Mashbir; cf. Genesis 42:3] *for the elevation of the soul, may his soul lodge in Eden, may his merit protect us, Amen!* | JSul.III.79: *And this is the* peshat *of the* piyyut *for the parashat Kedoshim, which our aged master the divine hakham, his honour, the Rav, Rabbi Shemuel the hazzan translated, may the memory of the righteous and holy be a blessing, the son of our aged master, his honour, the Rav, Rabbi Josef ha-Mashbir, may his soul lodge in Eden.* | JSul.I.37.03: *A* peshat *of the* (piyyut *with the*

[1] [3] ⌞And this is the dear *peshat* of the *piyyut* for the parashat Kedoshim, of (the one with the incipit) *ʾălēḵem ʾeqrå ʾīšīm*, which my aged master, our teacher, sir and Rabbi 134 v°

[2] [4] Shemuel the hazzan translated, the president of court of the holy community of Halych, may he rest in peace, the son of our aged master ⌞Josef who provides pure grain⌟[245] for the elevation of his soul, ⌞'may his soul be bound in the bond of life'⌟[246].⌟[247]

[3] [5] I call to you with the words of advice, O, honourable Israelites[248].

[4] [6] Examine your own[249] deeds and examine

[5] [7] the others, too, (both) men and women. Hurry with all

[6] [8] your power to do good deeds in order to be holy after your death.

[7] [9] And as long as you live in this world, be one of those who hurry to strengthen the words of

[8] [10] God's commandments, for the holy commandments of the Law

[9] [11] are sought according to the wishes[250] of those who do them. Because of this do not turn towards sinful

[10] [12] thoughts lest you will be snared in them. Remove[251]

[11] [13] from inside you the evil inclination of your heart, and instead of the sacrifice

[12] [14] of offerings do good deeds. Treat your neighbour with truth,

[13] [15] and do not be a deceiver to each other in the matters (connected to) ⌞taking any item⌟[252].

[14] [16] Fear the honourable name of God in all your deeds and

---

*incipit*) ʾălēḵem ʾeqrå ʾī[šīm] *for the parashat Kedoshim, which our aged master, our teacher, our master, his honour, the Rav, Rabbi Shemuel translated, the hazzan and president of court of the holy community* (*of Halych*), *may he rest in peace, the son of our aged master, our teacher, the Rav, Rabbi Josef ha-Mashbir, pure with the pure* [cf., 2 Samuel 22:27], *'the layer of dew came up on his lodge'* [cf., Exodus 16:13–14].

248 JSul.I.37.03: *men.*

249 JSul.I.37.03: deest.

250 JSul.I.37.03: *wish.*

251 Lit. 'pull out'.

252 Uncertain interpretation of Kar. *savut aluv*; cf. *savut* '1. vessel, dish; 2. weapon' and *aluv* '1. taking; 2. robbery'. See the use of NWKar. *savut* in ADub.III.73 (179 v°): *da ol upraq ki bolsa anda ḥastalyġy cara'atnyn junlu upraqta jemeśa üskülülü upraqta, jemeśa osnovada jemeśa utokta üskülünün jemeśa junnun jemeśa terida jemeśa nendijda terili savutta* [...] 'And the garment: if there is the disease of leprosy in it—in garment of wool or in garment of linen; either in the warp or in the woof of the linen or of the wool, or in leather or in any item made of leather [...]' (Leviticus 13:47–48).

[15] [17] da abajlyq byla bolunuz qaplanġanlar. Siverliknin quvusun iciriniz
[16] [18] kisi qaryndasyna da muft dusmanlyqny bolmanyz saqlavcular.
[17] [19] Da jaman saġyslarny ḥor etiniz da ol kertilikni bolunuz
[18] [20] izlevciler, ki nek bu jazyqly islerde[253] guflarynyznyn bolsunlar
[19] [21] ʒanlarynyz byrclanġanlar. Da qatylyġyna[254] aqlafynyn jemis bitti-
[20] [22] redoġan aġacnyn aqlaflary jireginiznin bolmasyn uqsaġanlar. Ancaq
[21] [23] es qojunuz ki aziz ʒanlarynyz ol kelgen gufunuzġa jyjynyndan[255]
[22] [24] aziz malaḫlarnyn qorqunclu taḥty tibine Tenrinin bolġajlar
[23] [25] syjynuvcular. Qotarynyz birligin atynyn pasuġu byla Šemaʿ Jisraʾelnin
[24] [26] da[256]
135 rº [25] [1] da maḥtav berme eki keret kinde bolunuz pilnovat etivciler,
[26] [2] ki bu jal icin cyġaryr sizni galuttan aziz jerinizge da ol
[27] [3] vaḥtta civirir aruv sez bar gojlarġa ki birligine anyn jalġyznyn
[28] [4] caġyrġajlar, da ki bir kivil byla qulluġuna anyn kelgejler da
[29] [5] basurġajlar. Ki ol zamanda bilinir ulluluġu bijliginin bar dunjada
[30] [6] da anar jalġyzġa basururlar bar ullu bijler.
[31] [7] ⸢וְיִהְיָה הָ לְמֶלֶךְ עַל כָל הָאָרֶץ וגו׳:⸣[257]

253 JSul.III.69: *islerinde*.
254 JSul.III.69: *qatylyġyn*; a scribal error.
255 JSul.III.69: *jyjyndan*; a scribal error.
256 Catchword.
257 Zechariah 14:9. | JSul.III.69: וְהָיָה הָ לְמֶלֶךְ עַל כָל הָאָרֶץ בַיּוֹם הַהוּא וגו׳: שְׁמַע יִשְׂרָאֵל הָ אֱלֹהֵינוּ וגו׳. (Zechariah 14:9; Deuteronomy 6:4). | JSul.III.79: וְהָיָה הָ לְמֶלֶךְ עַל כָל הָאָרֶץ: שְׁמַע יִשְׂרָאֵל הָ אֱלֹהֵינוּ הָ אֶחָד. (Zechariah 14:9; Deuteronomy 6:4).
258 Lit. 'a guardian of hostility'.
259 Lit. 'foreskin'; Kar. *aqlaf* 'foreskin' is used in collocations to mean 'unbeliever; unbelieving'; in this case, it is probably understood as 'unbelief', 'uncleanness'; cf. SWKar. *aqlaf jirekliler* 'those with hearts of unbelievers; those with unbelieving hearts' (KarRPS 57, s.v. *аклаф*). Cf. Deuteronomy 30:6.
260 Lit. 'be not equalised'.
261 Lit. 'foreskin'. See our explanation in fn. 259.
262 Uncertain translation.

[15] [17] be covered with fame and regard. Give your neighbour drink from the goblet of love

[16] [18] and do not be hostile[258] without a reason.

[17] [19] And reject the evil thoughts and be a searcher of the truth,

[18] [20] for why should your souls be disgraced with the sinful deeds of your body?

[19] [21] ⌊And may the uncircumcision[259] of your heart ⌊not be like⌉[260] the hardness of the uncircumcision[261]

[20] [22] of trees giving fruits⌉[262]. But

[21] [23] pay attention that may your holy souls that ⌊have entered⌉[263] your bodies from the circles

[22] [24] of holy angles find shelter near the awesome throne of God.

[23] [25] Preach the oneness of His name with with the ⌊Biblical verse of *Shema Yisrael*⌉[264]

[24] [26] and[265]

[25] [1] and be one of those who mind to praise twice a day. 135 r°

[26] [2] Because for this payment He will bring you out from the exile to your holy places and then

[27] [3] He will turn with clean words to those gentiles who would call His single oneness,

[28] [4] and to those who would join[266] ⌊in great numbers⌉[267] His service and

[29] [5] would bow down. Because then will be the greatness of His kingdom known in all the world,

[30] [6] and all the great lords will bow only to Him.

[31] [7] ⌊And the Lord shall be king over all the earth.⌉[268]

---

263 Lit. 'come'.

264 I.e., Deuteronomy 6:4.

265 Catchword in the Karaim text.

266 Lit. 'have come into'.

267 Lit. 'not with one'; i.e., 'not one strong'.

268 Zechariah 14:9. | JSul.III.69: *'And the Lord shall be king over all the earth: in that day ...' and so on. 'Hear, O Israel: The Lord our God ...' and so on.* (Zechariah 14:9; Deuteronomy 6:4). | JSul.III.79: *'And the Lord shall be king over all the earth. Hear, O Israel: The Lord our God is one Lord.'* (Zechariah 14:9; Deuteronomy 6:4).

# PART 8

## *The* peshatim *of Mordechai ben Shemuel*

∵

**Text number:** № 28
**Karaim incipit:** *E qajjam Tenrisi Ja'aqovnun*
**Hebrew incipit:** אֱלֹהֵי יִשְׂרָאֵל נְשַׁבְּחָךְ וּנְפָאֲרָךְ *ʾĕlohē yiśråʾēl nšabbḥåḵ ūnpåʾăråḵ*
**Dedication:** The first day of Pesach
**Language:** Early Mod.SWKar., Mod.SWKar.
**Number of copies:** 6

| Accession no. | Place of origin of copy | Date of copy | Copyist | Folios |
|---|---|---|---|---|
| JSul.III.03 | Halych | shortly after 1805 | Unknown 7 | 110 r°–110 v° |
| JSul.III.72 | Halych | before 1851 | Jeshua Josef Mordkowicz | 141 r°–141 v° |
| JSul.III.67 | Halych | after ca. 1840, before 1851 | Josef b. Icchak Szulimowicz (?) | 55 v°–56 r° |
| JSul.III.73 | Halych | mid-19th c. | Jeshua Josef Mordkowicz | 68 r°–68 v° |
| JSul.I.54.09 | Halych | mid-19th c. | Jeshua Josef Mordkowicz | 1 r°–1 v° |
| JSul.III.64b | Halych | 1st half of the 20th c. | Abraham b. Icchak Josef Leonowicz | 20 v°–21 r° |

## 1 Introductory Remarks

All six copies are vocalized. As far as similarities between the texts are concerned, the versions in JSul.III.03, JSul.III.67, and JSul.III.73 are closer to each other, see *neslar* (a scribal error) vs. *nisanlar* (11), *belgi* vs. *belgiler* (12), *kelgeninde* vs. *klegeninde* (12), *symarlady* vs. *symarladyn* (16). The same is true of the copies in JSul.III.72 and JSul.I.54.09, see *nisanlar* vs. *neslar* (11), *erkitibine ese* vs. *ese(k) erkitübine* (26), *sana jalġyzġa* vs. *muna sana jalġyzġa* (27), *tezče mašijaḥymyzny goʾel* vs. *goʾel* (28). Finally, the text we find in JSul.III.64 stands closer to the fomer group, see the presence of *indeledoġan* (6), *neslar* (11), *kelgeninde* (12), *erkitibine ese* (26), *muna* (27), *goʾel* (28), as well as *javrunumuzdan* vs. *javrumdan* (21), and *haligine biz* vs. *biz haligine* (26). The relationship between the copies can be presented as follows:

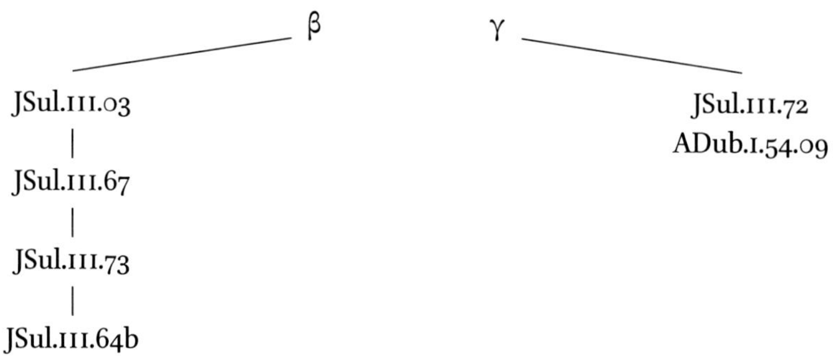


FIGURE 27 Diagram of the connections between the copies of peshat № 28

## 2 Transcription[1] and Translation

110 r° [1] [1] ⌊והא לך פשט יקר לפיוט אלהי ישראל נשבחך ונפארך הנאמר במועד יום חג
[2] [2] המצות על קדושת ואתה קדוש שהיא קדושה ראשונה: תרגמו בטוב טעמו החכם
[3] [3] האלהי אשר בין קהלות בני מקרא {יצא} שמו: הה אז גאוני ורוזני חכם התורני ופלוסוף
[4] [4] האלהי השלם והכולל פליאות חכמתו אין מי יוכל למלל כש כמוהרר מרדכי החוזה צאנ
[5] [5] נבת באז כמער שמואל החסיד והסגן הזקן ונשוא פנים יעמש: וזהו הפשט⌉[2]

[6] [6] E qajjam Tenrisi Ja‘aqovnun indeledoğan[3] šemi byla Jisra’elnin
[7] [7] šükürlük[4] da maḥtav berejik sana jaḥsyraġy[5] byla maḥtav-
[8] [8] larymyznyn. Qotarma qotarajyq jarlyġasynny[6] da hammeše[7] saġyn-
[9] [9] dyrajyq tamašalyqlaryn[8] joqtan bar etivcimiznin[9]. Raḥemtlerin
[10] [10] ajalmadylar bizden tizetkenin byla yzlarymyzny micvalary byla

---

1 Based on JSul.III.03.

2 JSul.III.72: [...] וזה הראשון לפיוט הראשון שלמועד יום הראשון של חג המצות שהוא אלהי ישראל נשבחק: תרגמו והוציאו לאורה אז מוה הוה כמהר מרדכי החוזה נע באז הנכבד והנעלה כמר שמואל החסיד והנשיא נבת. | JSul.III.67: ואם תרצה תאמר גם פשטו שתרגמו אמו כמוהרר מרדכי נבת בן אמו כמוהרר שמואל החסיד יעמש. | JSul.III.73: ואם תרצה תאמר גם פשטו שתרגמו אז ההו כמוהרר מרדכי החזן נבת באז כמער שמואל החסיד והסגן יעמש. | JSul.I.54.09: וזה הפשט לפיוט אֱלֹהֵי יִשְׂרָאֵל נְשַׁבְּחָךְ הנאמר ביום [...] של חג המצות על קדושה ראשונה: תרגמו אז החכם המרומם מוהרר מרדכי החזן ואבד תשהעם באז כמער שמואל החסיד תנצבהה. (A short fragment is damaged.) | JSul.III.64b: וזה פשטו של פיוט אלהי ישראל נשבחך הנאמר על קדושה הראשנה ביום א׳ של פסח תרגמו אמו כמהרר מרדכי החזן דקק האליץ נבת: בכמער שמואל החסיד זצוקל.

3 JSul.III.72: *indelgen.* | JSul.III.67: *indelgen.*

4 JSul.III.67: *šikirlik* or *sikirlik.* | JSul.I.54.09: *sikirlik.* | JSul.III.64b: *sikirlik.*

5 JSul.III.72: *jaḥšyraġy.*

6 JSul.III.72: *jarlyġašynny.*

7 JSul.III.64b: *hammese.*

8 JSul.III.67: *tamasalyqlaryn.* | JSul.III.64b: *tamasalyqlaryn.*

9 JSul.III.72: *etivčümüznin.*

10 I.e., *Pesach.*

11 I.e., *Karaims.*

12 Cf., Isaiah 9:15: זָקֵן וּנְשׂוּא־פָנִים 'the elder and honourable'.

13 JSul.III.72: *And this is the very first* piyyut *for the first day of the feast of unleavened bread the one* (*with the incipit*) ’ĕlohē yiśrå’ēl nšabbḥåḵ, *an interpretation published by our aged master, our teacher Rabbi, his honour, the magnificent and important Rabbi Mordechai, the seer, may his soul rest in Eden, the son of our aged master, the respected and the exalted, our honourable teacher, Rabbi Shemuel, the pious and the leader, may his soul lodge in Eden.* | JSul.III.67: *And if you prefer, its* peshat [i.e., of the Hebrew original] *will you also say, which our master, our teacher, his honour, the Rav, Rabbi Mordechai translated, may his soul lodge in Eden, the son of our master, our teacher, his honour, the Rav, Rabbi Shemuel,*

[1] [1] ⌊And this, for you, is the beloved *peshat* of the *piyyut* (with the incipit) *ʾĕlohē yiśråʾēl nšabbḥåḵ ūnp̄åʾăråḵ* follows, the one recited on the ⌊Feast 110 r°

[2] [2] of Unleavened Bread[110] in addition to the Kedushah *wʾattå qådōš*; he translated it with his good sense, the

[3] [3] divine hakham, his name is known among the communities of ⌊the sons of the Scripture[111]: the great sage, our aged master, the genius and noble, the Torah-based hakham,

[4] [4] and the divine philosopher, complete and comprehesive, the wonder of his wisdom cannot be expressed (in words), his glorious name, his honour, the Rav, Rabbi Mordechai, the seer,

[5] [5] may his soul lodge in Eden, the son of our aged master Shemuel, whose honourable repose is Eden, the pious hazzan, the officiant, the ⌊elder and honourable[112], may he rest in peace. And this is the *peshat*:[113]

[6] [6] O, powerful God of Jacob called by the name of Israel,

[7] [7] we shall give thanks to You and praise You with the best[14] of

[8] [8] praises. We do preach Your grace and always recall

[9] [9] the wonders of our creator from nothing.

[10] [10] We were not begrudged Your mercies as[15] our ways have been straightened with the commandments

---

*the pious, may he rest in peace.* | JSul.III.73: *And if you prefer, its* peshat [i.e., of the Hebrew original] *will you also say, which our aged master, the great and honourable sage, his honour, the Rav, Rabbi Mordechai the hazzan translated, may his soul lodge in Eden, the son of Shemuel, whose honourable repose is Eden, the pious and dignitary, may he rest in peace.* | JSul.I.54.09: *And this is a* piyyut (*with the incipit*) ʾĕlohē yiśråʾēl nšabbḥåḵ *said on the* (*first*) *day of the feast of unleavened bread as the first Kedushah* [i.e., prayer], *which our aged master, the elevated hakham, our teacher, the Rav, Rabbi Mordechai translated, the hazzan and the chief justice, 'the layer of dew came up on his lodge'* [cf., Exodus 16:13–14], *the son of our aged master Shemuel, whose honourable repose is Eden, the pious, 'may his soul be bound in the bond of life'* [cf., 1Samuel 25:29]. | JSul.III.64b: *And this is the* peshat *of the* piyyut (*with the incipit*) ʾĕlohē yiśråʾēl nšabbḥåḵ, *the one recited about primary sanctity on the first day of Pesach, which our master, our teacher, his honour, the Rav, Rabbi Mordechai translated, the hazzan of the holy community of Halych, may his soul lodge in Eden, the son of Shemuel, whose honourable repose is Eden, the pious, may the memory of the righteous and holy be a blessing.*

14 Lit. 'better'.

15 Lit. 'with', 'by'.

[11] [11] da resimleri byla aziz Toranyn. Qorquncluluqlar[16] n[i]s[an]lar[17] byla
[12] [12] da ⌊belgi byla⌋[18] arttyrdyn kelgeninde[19] juluma bizni galutundan
[13] [13] Micrinin. Sağynġanyn byla bizge sertin Abrahamnyn antetken
[14] [14] anar nevu'asynda Betarimnin[20]. Da inamly navini Moše rabenunu
[15] [15] sajladyn rast elcige[21] da jalyny byla {otnun} ortasyndan ol senenin
[16] [16] bilindin anar šemi byla ehjenin. Torany[22] symarlady[n][23] bizge qolu
[17] [17] asyra anyn ajyrmaq ücün[24] bizni ḥanlyqlaryndan ol jernin, da
[18] [18] burunġu diburnu[25] on sözlerden[26] ki oldu ⌊*anoḫi H elohejḫa*⌋[27] sağyncy byla
[19] [19] ⌊cyqmaqnyn[28] Micriden⌋[29] qojdu[n][30] fundament tasyn anyn. Da tislerin[31] raša'a
[20] [20] paronun ki turdu elip sortun Josef syndyrdyn tisli[32] qulluqlar
[21] [21] byla sirindirivcü[33] kücün[34] ḥalimnin. Jigin[35] dusmannyn[36] javrunumuzdan[37]
[22] [22] keterdin da jaryttyn tumanyn qaranġylyġymyznyn[38]. Juluv ijdin[39] ulusuna

---

16 JSul.III.72: *qorqunčluluqlar.* | JSul.III.67: *qorqunculuqlar*; a scribal error.

17 JSul.III.03: *neslar*; a scribal error. | JSul.III.72: *nisanlar.* | JSul.III.67: *neslar*; a scribal error. | JSul.III.73: *neslar*; a scribal error. | JSul.I.54.09: *nisanlar.* | JSul.III.64b: *neslar*; a scribal error.

18 JSul.III.72: *belgilerbyla.* | JSul.I.54.09: *belgiler byla.* | JSul.III.64b: *belgiler byla.*

19 JSul.III.72: *klegeninde.* | JSul.III.67: *klegeninde.* | JSul.I.54.09: *klegeninde.*

20 Cf. Heb. בְּתָרִים 'parts', a reference to Mount Betarim, the site of the covenant of the pieces between Abraham and God.

21 JSul.III.72: *elčige.*

22 JSul.III.72: *Tora.*

23 JSul.III.03: *symarlady*; possibly a scribal error. | JSul.III.72: *symarladyn.* | JSul.III.67: *symarlady*; possibly a scribal error. | JSul.III.73: *symarlady*; possibly a scribal error. | JSul.I.54.09: *symarladyn.* | JSul.III.64b: *symarladyn.*

24 JSul.III.72: *üčün.* | JSul.III.67: *icin.* | JSul.I.54.09: *icin.* | JSul.III.64b: *icin.*

25 JSul.III.64b: erroneously spelled דְבוּרְנוּ; cf. also תְּלִי in line [27].

26 JSul.III.67: *sezlerden.* | JSul.I.54.09: *sezlerden.* | JSul.III.64b: *sezlerden.*

27 A quotation of Heb. אָנֹכִי יְהוָה אֱלֹהֶיךָ 'I am the Lord your God' (Exodus 20:2; Deuteronomy 5:6).

28 JSul.III.72: *čyqmaqnyn.*

29 JSul.III.67: {{*cyqmaqnyn Micriden*}} *cyqmaqnyn Micriden.*

30 JSul.III.03: *qojdu*; possibly a scribal error. | JSul.III.72: *qojdun.* | JSul.III.67: *qojdu*; possibly a scribal error. | JSul.III.73: *qojdu*; possibly a scribal error. | JSul.I.54.09: *qojdu*; possibly a scribal error. | JSul.III.64b: *qojdun.*

31 JSul.III.72: *tišlerin.* | JSul.III.64b: *kislerin.*

32 JSul.III.72: *tüslü.*

33 JSul.III.72: *süründirivčü.* | JSul.III.67: *sirindirivci.* | JSul.I.54.09: *sirindirivci.* | JSul.III.64b: *sirindirivci.*

[11] [11] and the statutes of the holy Law. You have increased the fear by (showing) omens

[12] [12] and signs when You came to redeem us from the exile

[13] [13] of Egypt by mentioning us the covenant of Abraham promised

[14] [14] him in the ⌊prophecy of Betarim[140]. And You have chosen the trustworthy prophet, ⌊our master[141], Moses,

[15] [15] to be a just envoy and with the flame of fire (coming) from inside the bush

[16] [16] ⌊You have[142] revealed Yourself to him under[43] the name *ehyēh*[44]. You have handed over to us the Law through his hands

[17] [17] in order to separate us from the kingdoms of earth, and ⌊You have[145] laid

[18] [18] the first speech of the ten commandments, which is 'I am the Lord your Lord', along with the remembrance

[19] [19] of leaving Egypt, (to be) its foundation stone. And

[20] [20] You have broken ⌊the teeth[146] of the wicked Pharaoh who arose after Joseph had died,

[21] [21] who[47] has brought the power of my abilities to a fall by all kind of captivities. You have removed from our[48] shoulder the burden of the enemies

[22] [22] and You have lighted up the cloud of our darkness. You have sent[49] redemption to the people

---

34 JSul.III.72: *küčün.* | JSul.III.67: *kicin.* | JSul.I.54.09: *kicin.* | JSul.III.64b: *kicin.*

35 JSul.III.73: *igin.* | JSul.I.54.09: *igin.* | JSul.III.64b: *igin.*

36 JSul.III.72: *dušmannyn.*

37 JSul.III.67: *javrunumdan.*

38 JSul.III.67: *qarangylymyznyn*; a scribal error.

39 JSul.III.64b: *berdin.*

40 I.e., *Covenant of the Pieces.*

41 Expressed with *rabenu*, i.e., Heb. רַבֵּינוּ 'our rabbi'.

42 JSul.III.03: *He has*; possibly a scribal error. | JSul.III.67: *He has*; possibly a scribal error. | JSul.III.73: *He has*; possibly a scribal error.

43 Lit. 'with'.

44 Heb. אֶהְיֶה 'name of God' < אֶהְיֶה אֲשֶׁר אֶהְיֶה 'I am that I am' (Exodus 3:14); an epithet of God, see also Tuori (2013: 411).

45 JSul.III.03: *He has*; possibly a scribal error. | JSul.III.67: *He has*; possibly a scribal error. | JSul.III.73: *He has*; possibly a scribal error. | JSul.I.54.09: *He has*; possibly a scribal error.

46 I.e., *the power.*

47 I.e., *the Pharaoh.*

48 JSul.III.67: *my.*

49 JSul.III.64b: *given.*

[23] [23] Jisra'elge televinden[50] tigenmejdoġan[51] jaḥsylyqlarynnyn[52]. Da dusmanlaryn[53]
[24] [24] on ⌊qaranjalar byla⌋[54] vattyn da bermedin tajma ajaqlarymyzġa biznin.
[25] [25] Alaj barda dusmanlarymyzġa[55] da tar berivcilerimizge[56] telegin[57] jaman
[26] [26] televlerin[58] alarnyn. Da ḥotej ⌊haligine biz⌋[59] ⌊erkitibine ese⌋[60]
[27] [27] mazalnyn indelgen[61] Teli muna[62] sana jalġyzġa da tivil[63] mazalġa isanabiz
[28] [28] da köp[64] jaḥsylyqlaryna[65] senin. Da qolabiz ki ijgejsen bizge go'el[66]
[29] [29] Jisra'elni ki sensen körtü[67] juluvcumuz[68] biznin. E inamly Tenri
[30] [30] sözlerinde[69] özünnin[70] tezce[71] qajjam etkin bizge naviligin
110 vº [31] [1] Ješajanyn. Ki bulaj ajtty H küclü[72] Tenri küplügimiz[73] biznin:
[32] [2] Tez zamanda julurmen galuttan ivin[74] Ja'aqovnun urluġun Abrahamnyn.
[33] [3] ⌊כי כה אמר הׄ אלהים מצרים וגו׳:⌋[75]

50 JSul.III.72: *tölevinden.*
51 JSul.III.72: *tügenmejdoġan.*
52 JSul.III.72: *jaḥšylyqlarynnyn.* | JSul.I.54.09: *jaḥsylyqlarynyn*; a scribal error.
53 JSul.III.72: *dušmanlaryn.*
54 JSul.III.72: *qaranjabyla.*
55 JSul.III.72: *dušmanlarymyzġa.*
56 JSul.III.72: *berivčülerimizge.*
57 JSul.III.72: *tölegin.*
58 JSul.III.72: *tölevlerin.*
59 JSul.I.54.09: *biz haligine.*
60 JSul.III.72: *esek erki tübine.* | JSul.I.54.09: *ese erki tibine.*
61 JSul.III.03: spelled אִינְדֵּילְיגִין; a scribal error. | JSul.III.72: *ündelgen.*
62 JSul.III.72: deest. | JSul.I.54.09: deest.
63 JSul.III.72: *tüvül.*
64 JSul.III.67: *kep.* | JSul.I.54.09: *kep.* | JSul.III.64b: *kep.*
65 JSul.III.72: *jaḥšylyqlaryna.*
66 JSul.III.72: *tezče mašijaḥymyzny go'el.* | JSul.I.54.09: *tezce mašijaḥymyzny go'el.*
67 JSul.III.03: a hypercorrect form of *kerti.* | JSul.III.72: *kerti.* | JSul.III.67: *kerti.* | JSul.I.54.09: *kerti.* | JSul.III.64b: *kerti.*
68 JSul.III.72: *juluvčumuz.*
69 JSul.III.67: *sezlerinde.* | JSul.I.54.09: *sezlerinde.* | JSul.III.64b: *sezlerinde.*
70 JSul.III.67: *ezinnin.* | JSul.III.73: *özinnin.* | JSul.I.54.09: *ezinnin.* | JSul.III.64b: *ezinin*; a scribal error.
71 JSul.III.72: *tezče.*
72 JSul.III.72: *küčlü.* | JSul.III.67: *kicli.* | JSul.I.54.09: *kicli.* | JSul.III.64b: *kicli.*

[23] [23] of Israel from the reserves[76] of Your never-ending goodness. And You

[24] [24] have beaten Your enemies with ten punishments and You have not let our legs stagger.

[25] [25] Thus have You returned to all of our enemies and to our oppressors the evil[77]

[26] [26] (received from) them. And even if we would be now mentioned under the rule

[27] [27] of constellation called Teli[78], lo[79], we believe only in You, not in constellation(s),

[28] [28] and in the multitude of Your goodness. And we beg You that You may send us the redeemer[80]

[29] [29] of Israel for You are our true saviour. O trustworthy God,

[30] [30] in Your own words confirm to us the prophecy of

[31] [1] Isaiah. For thus said the Lord the powerful God our strength: 110 vº

[32] [2] Soon I will save from the exile the house of Jacob the offspring

[33] [3] of Abraham. ⌊'For thus says the Lord God, "Into Egypt ..."', and so on.⌉[81]

---

73 JSul.III.03: a hypercorrect form of *kipligimiz*. | JSul.III.72: *kipligimiz*. | JSul.III.67: *kipligimiz*. | JSul.III.73: *küpligimiz*; a hypercorrect form of *kipligimiz*. | JSul.I.54.09: *kipligimiz*. | JSul.III.64b: *kipligimiz*.

74 JSul.III.72: *üvün*.

75 Isaiah 52:4. | JSul.III.72: כִּי כֹה אָמַר הָ׳ אֱלֹהִים מִצְרַיִם יָרַד עַמִּי בָּרִאשׁוֹנָה וכו׳. (Isaiah 52:4; בָּרִאשֹׁנָה *pro* בָּרִאשׁוֹנָה). | JSul.III.67: כִּי כֹה אָמַר הָ׳ אֱלֹהִים מִצְרַיִם יָרַד עַמִּי בָּרִאשׁוֹנָה לָגוּר שָׁם וְאַשּׁוּר בְּאֶפֶס עֲשָׁקוֹ [...]. (Isaiah 52:4; בָּרִאשׁוֹנָה *pro* בָּרִאשֹׁנָה). Followed by a number of other quotations in Hebrew from the Book of Isaiah (Isaiah 52:5–6, 29:22–23, 8:13, etc.). | JSul.III.73: The Karaim text is followed by a separate text in Hebrew containing quotations, among others from Isaiah 52:5–6, 29:22–23, 8:13, etc. The order of the quotations is the same as in JSul.III.67. | JSul.I.54.09: כִּי כֹה אָמַר הָ׳ אֱלֹהִים מִצְרַיִם יָרַד עַמִּי וגו׳. (Isaiah 52:4). | JSul.III.64b: כִּי כֹה אַמָר הָ׳ אֱלֹהִים וכ׳ו. (Isaiah 52:4; אַמָר *pro* אָמַר). || Under the text in JSul.I.54.09, we find the following annonation written in *Kurrentschrift* in dark brown ink: *Josef Mardkowicz ist geschrieben disen*.

76 Lit. 'payments'.

77 Lit. 'evil payments'.

78 One of the constellations in heaven.

79 JSul.III.72: deest. | JSul.I.54.09: deest.

80 JSul.III.72: *soon our Messiah redeemer*. | JSul.I.54.09: *soon our Messiah redeemer*.

81 Isaiah 52:4. | JSul.III.72: *'For thus says the Lord God, "My people went down at first into Egypt ..."', and so forth*. (Isaiah 52:4). | JSul.III.67: *'For thus says the Lord God, "My people went down at first into Egypt to sojourn there; and the Assyrian oppressed them without cause."'* (Isaiah 52:4). Followed by other quotations in Hebrew from the Book of Isaiah. | JSul.I.54.09: *'For thus says the Lord God, "My people went down into Egypt ...,"' and so on*. [cf., Isaiah 52:4] *Josef Mardkowicz wrote this*. | JSul.III.64b: *'For thus says the Lord God.'* (Isaiah 52:4).

**Text number:** № 29
**Karaim incipit:** *Necik joḥtu tensi küclü Tenrige*
*Necik joḥtur tensi küclü Tenrige*
**Hebrew incipit:** אֵין עֲרוֹךְ לְאֵל יָהּ *ʾēn ʿărōḵ lʾēl yåh*
**Dedication:** Parashat Vayikra (Leviticus 1:1–5:26)
**Language:** Early Mod.SWKar., Mod.SWKar.
**Number of copies:** 6

| Accession no. | Place of origin of copy | Date of copy | Copyist | Folios |
|---|---|---|---|---|
| JSul.III.03 | Halych | shortly after 1805 | Unknown 7 | 105 r°–105 v° |
| JSul.I.45 | Halych | 1st half of the 19th c. | Jeshua Josef Mordkowicz | 141 r°–141 v° |
| ADub.III.61 | Halych | 1850/1851 | Jeshua Josef Mordkowicz | 133 v°–134 v° |
| JSul.III.69 | Halych | ca. 1851 (before 1866) | Jeshua Josef Mordkowicz | 283 v°–284 v° |
| JSul.III.79 | Halych | ca. 1851 (before 1866) | Jeshua Josef Mordkowicz | 172 v°–174 r° |
| JSul.I.37.03 | probably Halych | between 1851 and 1866 | Unknown 12 | 12 v°–13 v° |

## 1 Introductory Remarks

*Peshat* № 18 is another interpretation of the *piyyut* starting with the words *ʾēn ʿărōḵ lʾēl yåh*. All six copies are vocalized. The text copied in ms. JSul.III.03 bears a number of unique features, such as e.g. *qadaġanlar* vs. *qadaġalar* (10), *kisi* vs. *adam* (15), *sibasynyn sartyn* vs. *sibasyndan* (16), *ʒandan* vs *ʒanavardan* (23), *qarbanyn* vs. *qarbanlaryn* (25), *avanlyqny* vs. *ol jazyqny* (31), and shares a few common textual elements with the text copied in JSul.I.45, see *körme* vs. *kirme* (12) and *istine* vs. *icine* (33). Additionally, the texts in ADub.III.61 and JSul.III.79 also have a number of unique features in common, see *jazyqly bolmaġaj* vs. *bolġaj jazyqsyz* (15), *ʒanyndan anyn* vs. *ʒanyndan* (18), *jalbaruvcularnyn* vs. *jalbaruvcularynyn* (36), and *andij* vs. *har bir* (36). Based on the above, the relationship between the copies can be presented as follows (cf. № 30):

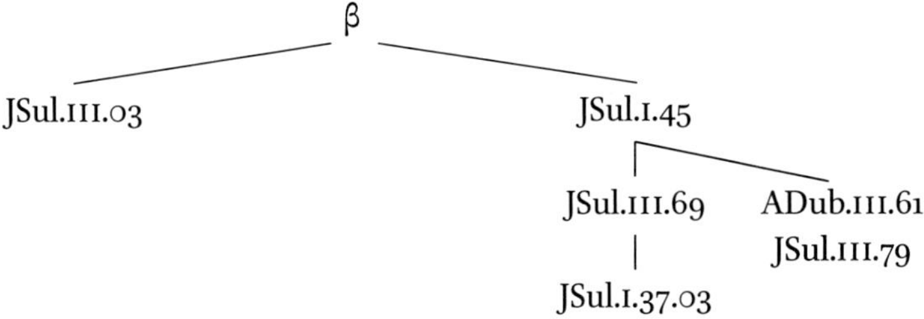


FIGURE 28 Diagram of the connections between the copies of peshat № 29

## 2 Transcription[82] and Translation

105 r° [1] [1] ⌈ובעזרת סומך ידי מטים: אכתוב פשטי הפיוטים: מחכמים מחוכמים לפיוטם:
[2] [2] מזוך שכלם חרותים: כדי להבין הגיון לשוננו הקדושה לאזני עמי הארץ הפשוטים[83]:
[3] [3] וזו יצאה ראשונה: מחכם האלהי בעל תבונה: הוא אז ההו כמוהרר מרדכי החוזה צאנ
[4] [4] נבת באז כמער שמואל החסיד יעמש בגן עדנה: לפיוט אין ערוך לאל יה ה כונן
[5] [5] שמים בתבונה: תחל ותאמ בקול נגינה:⌉[84]
[6] [6] Necik joḥtu[85] tensi küclü[86] Tenrige alaj joḥtu[87] qyjas tamasa[88]
[7] [7] islerine anyn. Ol tabulġandy bar orunda bir tirli
[8] [8] ceksiz da qyjassyz da ol dunja toldu syjyndan anyn. Fikiri har bir
[9] [9] kisinin tisikkendi kelgeninde tergeme syryn anyn. Aʒajyp
[10] [10] dinler da tamaša[89] tereler qadaġanlar[90] ivrendik avzundan inamly
[11] [11] navisinin. Turġuzup sortun Moše rabenu ol miškanny caġyrdy

82 Based on JSul.III.03.

83 The reading and hence the interpretation of this word remains obscure.

84 JSul.I.45: פשט שני לפיוט אין ערוך עשאו אז ההו כמוהרר מרדכי החזן באז כמער שמואל החסיד זל. | ADub.III.61: וזה הפשט היקר לפיוט פרשת ויקרא שהוא אֵין עֲרוֹךְ לְאֵל יָה תרגמו אדו׳ זקני החכם המרומם והכולל כקשת כמוהרר מרדכי החזן ואבד דקהלתנו נבת כמער שמואל החסיד נבת. | JSul.III.69: וזהו פשטו שתרגמו אז ההו מוהרר מרדכי החזן זצוקל באז כמער שמואל החסיד והגביר הנעלה יעמש. | JSul.III.79: וזה הפשט לפיוט פרשת ויקרא שהוא אין ערוך לאל יה תרגמו אז החכם האלהי הקדוש כקשת כמוהרר מרדכי החזן נבת באז כמער שמואל החסיד יעמש. | JSul.I.37.03: פשט לפ׳ ויקרא שתרמו אדוני דודי פארי והודי אמו׳ כמוהרר מרדכי החזן זצוקל: באז כמר שמואל החסיד הגביר הנעלה ונפ׳ זל: אֵין עֲרוֹךְ לְאֵל יָה.

85 JSul.I.45: *joḥtur.* | ADub.III.61: *joḥtur.* | JSul.III.69: *joḥtur.* | JSul.I.37.03: *joḥtur.*

86 ADub.III.61: *kicli.* | JSul.III.69: *kicli.* | JSul.III.79: *kicli.* | JSul.I.37.03: *kicli.*

87 ADub.III.61: *joḥtur.*

88 JSul.I.45: *tamaša.* | ADub.III.61: *tamaša.* | JSul.III.69: *tamaša.* | JSul.III.79: *tamaša.*

89 JSul.I.37.03: *tamasa.*

90 JSul.I.45: *qadaġalar.* | ADub.III.61: *qadaġalar.* | JSul.III.69: *qadaġalar.* | JSul.III.79: *qadaġalar.* | JSul.I.37.03: *qadaġalar.*

91 Proverbs 3:19.

92 JSul.I.45: *The second* peshat *of the* piyyut (*with the incipit*) ʾēn ʿărōḵ, *delivered by our aged master, the great and honourable sage, his honour, the Rav, Rabbi Mordechai, the hazzan, the son of our aged master, his honour, Rabbi Shemuel the pious, may his memory be a blessing.* | ADub.III.61: *And this is the* peshat *of the beloved* piyyut *for the parashat Vayikra, of the one* (*with the incipit*) ʾēn ʿărōḵ l'ēl yåh, *which my aged master translated, the elevated hakham, his holy and glorious name being his honour, the Rav, Rabbi Mordechai, the hazzan and the chief justice of our community, may his soul lodge in Eden, the son of his honour, Rabbi Shemuel, the pious, may his soul lodge in Eden.* | JSul.III.69: *And this is its* [i.e., of the Hebrew original] peshat, *which our aged master, the great and honourable sage, our teacher, Rabbi*

[1] [1] ⌊And with the help of (God, who) supports the hands of those that falter, I will write *peshatim* of *piyyutim*, from wise men, wisened to *piyyutim* 105 r°

[2] [2] inscribed from the purity of their intelligence, so that to make the sense of the holy language understandable for the ears of the simple ignoramuses.

[3] [3] And here goes out the first one, (the work) of the divine hakham, possessor of understanding, our aged master, the great and honourable sage, his honour, the Rav, Rabbi Mordechai, the seer,

[4] [4] may his soul lodge in Eden, the son of our aged master, his honour, Rabbi Shemuel, the pious, may he rest in his resting place in the Garden of Pleasure, (the *peshat*) of the *piyyut* (with the incipit) *ʾēn ʿărōḵ lʾēl yåh*. ⌊The Lord

[5] [5] has established the heavens by understanding.[191] You should start and sing it aloud:[192]

[6] [6] As there is nothing equal to the powerful God, so is there no number (that could compare) to the (number) of His wondrous

[7] [7] deeds. He is (to be found) in all the places

[8] [8] with no limits and countlessly and the world is filled with His fame. The intellect of all

[9] [9] men is fallen when they come to fathom His secret.

[10] [10] We have learned the amazing faith and wondrous ⌊laws ordered (to us)[193] through the mouth of the trustworthy

[11] [11] prophet. After ⌊our master[194], Moses, had put up the Tabernacle

---

*Mordechai the hazzan translated, may the memory of the righteous and holy be a blessing, the son of our aged master, his honour, Rabbi Shemuel, the pious and the elevated master, may he rest in peace.* | JSul.III.79: *And this is the* peshat *of a* piyyut *for the parashat Vayikra, of the one (with the incipit)* ʾēn ʿărōḵ lʾēl yåh, *which our aged master, the divine and holy hakham translated, his holy and glorious name being his honour, the Rav, Rabbi Mordechai, the hazzan, may his soul lodge in Eden, the son of our aged master, his honour, Rabbi Shemuel, the pious, may he rest in peace.* | JSul.I.37.03: Peshat *for the parashat Vayikra, which my master translated, my magnificent and glorious uncle, my master, my teacher, his honour, the Rav, Rabbi Mordechai, the hazzan, may the memory of the righteous and holy be a blessing, the son of our aged master, our honourable teacher, Rabbi Shemuel, the pious master, the lofty and the deceased, may his memory be a blessing.*

93 JSul.I.45: *laws, orders.* | ADub.III.61: *laws, orders.* | JSul.III.69: *laws, orders.* | JSul.III.79: *laws, orders.* | JSul.I.37.03: *laws, orders.*

94 Expressed with *rabenu*, i.e., Heb. רַבֵּינוּ 'our rabbi'.

[12] [12] any H arasyndan eki ol keruvimlernin. Da bolalmady k[i]rme[95]
[13] [13] ohel moʿedge alnyndan ol bulutnun da qorquvundan šeḫinasynyn
[14] [14] H-nyn. Da anda askartty[96] anar Tenri ʿenjanlaryn[97] kisinin da
[15] [15] ucurun anyn. Ki joḥtu[98] rast kisi[99] dunjada ki ⌊bolġaj jazyqsyz⌋[100]
[16] [16] ⌊sibasynyn {sartyn}⌋[101] tuvarlyq ʒanynyn. Ki eki jecerler esediler anar
[17] [17] birge esmegi byla gufunun da alar qursajdylar cyġysyn da
[18] [18] kelisin anyn, basqa aqyllyq ʒanyndan[102] qajsy byla syjlandy ki
[19] [19] oldu ol indelgen cyraġy Tenrinin. Da bolġany sartyn jaratylġan
[20] [20] dert jesodlardan protyvnyjlar[103] biri birine[104] ketermek ücün[105]
[21] [21] jazyġyn da ⌊jengil etmek⌋[106] ücün[107] jigin[108] murdarlyġynyn, bujurdu
[22] [22] juvutma qarban usajdoġandan ezine klegim ajtma tiri
[23] [23] ʒandan[109] da esedoġandan arytmaq ücün[110] murdarlyġyn ʒanynyn.
[24] [24] Ki saġyslanġaj qany qarbanynyn qany kibik juvutuvcusunun da javy
[25] [25] javy kibik[111] juvutqanda otlu qarbanyn[112] ezinin[113], ki necik adam
[26] [26] alaj tuvar bir ucur tibinedi tivsirilmegi sartyn dört[114]

---

95 JSul.III.03: *körme*; a scribal error. | ADub.III.61: *kirme.* | JSul.III.69: *kirme.* | JSul.III.79: *kirme.* | JSul.I.37.03: *kirme.*

96 JSul.I.45: *asqartty.* | ADub.III.61: *asqartty.* | JSul.III.69: *asqartty.* | JSul.III.79: *asqartty.* | JSul.I.37.03: *asqartty.*

97 JSul.I.45: ʿ[*i*]*njanlaryn*; spelled: עְנִיַןלַרִין. | ADub.III.61: *ʿinjanlaryn.* | JSul.III.69: *ʿinjanlaryn.* | JSul.III.79: *ʿinjanlaryn.* | JSul.I.37.03: *ʿinjanlaryn.*

98 ADub.III.61: *joḥtur.* | JSul.III.69: *joḥtur.*

99 JSul.I.45: *adam.* | ADub.III.61: *adam.* | JSul.III.69: *adam.* | JSul.III.79: *adam.* | JSul.I.37.03: *adam.*

100 ADub.III.61: *jazyqly bolmaġaj.* | JSul.III.79: *jazyqly bolmaġaj.*

101 JSul.I.45: *sibasyndan.* | ADub.III.61: *sibasyndan.* | JSul.III.69: *sibasyndan.* | JSul.III.79: *sibasyndan.* | JSul.I.37.03: *sibasyndan.*

102 ADub.III.61: *ʒanyndan anyn.* | JSul.III.79: *ʒanyndan anyn.*

103 Or: *protivnyjlar.*

104 JSul.I.37.03: *birisine.*

105 ADub.III.61: *icin.* | JSul.III.69: *icin.* | JSul.III.79: *icin.* | JSul.I.37.03: *icin.*

106 JSul.I.45: *jengilletmek.*

107 ADub.III.61: *icin.* | JSul.III.69: *icin.* | JSul.III.79: *icin.* | JSul.I.37.03: *icin.*

108 JSul.III.69: *igin.* | JSul.I.37.03: *igin.*

109 JSul.I.45: *ʒanavardan.* | ADub.III.61: *ʒanavardan.* | JSul.III.69: *ʒanavardan.* | JSul.III.79: *ʒanavardan.* | JSul.I.37.03: *ʒanavardan.*

110 ADub.III.61: *icin.* | JSul.III.69: *icin.* | JSul.III.79: *icin.* | JSul.I.37.03: *icin.*

111 ADub.III.61: *kibik anyn.*

[12] [12] the Lord called Him from between the two cherubim. And he could not [enter][115]

[13] [13] the tent of meeting ⌊because of the cloud in front of it⌋[116] and because of the fear of the divine Presence

[14] [14] of the Lord. And there God revealed him the task of the man and

[15] [15] his fate. For there is no just man[117] in the world that ⌊would be without sins⌋[118]

[16] [16] because of his animal soul, for the ⌊two inclinations⌋[119] grow in[120] one

[17] [17] along with the growth of one's body, and they surround one's departure and

[18] [18] arrival: (everything) except the wise heart for which he was respected for:

[19] [19] it is called the torch of God. And because of his (state of) being created

[20] [20] from four origins contrary to each other, in order to remove

[21] [21] his sins and to make lighter the burden of his uncleanness, He has ordered

[22] [22] to offer sacrifice from what is appropriate to Him, ⌊i.e.⌋[121] ⌊from what lives

[23] [23] and grows⌋[122], to purify the uncleanness of his soul.

[24] [24] And may the blood of the sacrifice be considered to be the blood of the one who offers it and its fat

[25] [25] to be like his fat when he brings his own burnt offering[123]; for man

[26] [26] and beast ⌊share the same fate⌋[124] because of their four contradictory

---

112 JSul.I.45: *qarbanlaryn.* | ADub.III.61: *qarbanlaryn.* | JSul.III.69: *qarbanlaryn.* | JSul.III.79: *qarbanlaryn.* | JSul.I.37.03: *qarbanlaryn.*

113 JSul.I.45: *özünün.*

114 JSul.I.45: *dert.* | ADub.III.61: *dert.* | JSul.III.69: *dert.* | JSul.III.79: *dert.* | JSul.I.37.03: *dert.*

115 JSul.III.03: *look into*; probably a scribal error. | JSul.I.45: *look into*; probably a scribal error.

116 Uncertain translation, cf. Exodus 40:35.

117 JSul.I.45, ADub.III.61, JSul.III.69, JSul.III.79, JSul.I.37.03: expressed with a synonym.

118 ADub.III.61: *would not be sinful.* | JSul.III.79: *would not be sinful.*

119 I.e., *the vegetative soul and feeling soul.*

120 Lit. 'to', 'for'.

121 Lit. 'I want to say'.

122 Lit. 'from living beings and from that grows'; i.e., *from livestock and plants.*

123 JSul.I.45: *offerings.* | ADub.III.61: *offerings.* | JSul.III.69: *offerings.* | JSul.III.79: *offerings.* | JSul.I.37.03: *offerings.*

124 Lit. 'are under one fate'.

[27] [27] eḫijotlarynyn. Bir ivretiv berdi Tenri kohenge da ʒymatqa
[28] [28] ulusuna[125] ol jernin da nasisine anyn, da alajoq bujurdu ki
[29] [29] tekkej gilejin ol keltirivcü[126] qarban alnynda bir Tenrinin jara-
[30] [30] tuvcusunun, da ki qabul etkej ʒanyna qajtmasqa qylma
105 v° [31] [1] artyq avanlyqny[127] qajtqanlaj it qusqununa ezinin. Da tivil
[32] [2] semiz bujvollary šelamimlernin ancaq synyq jürek[128] da aruv ʒan
[33] [3] klegidi Tenrinin, alajoq tirkisi özek[129] unnun panv́a istine[130]
[34] [4] da tava istine qabuldu Tenrige eger bolsa ʒomartlyġyndan
[35] [5] aruv jüreknin[131]. Bundijdi jolu H-nyn tabulma qoltqasyna jalbaruv-
[36] [6] cularynyn[132]. Anar köre[133] sandy[134] ⌊har bir⌋[135] kisige ki caġyrsa kertilik[136]
[37] [7] byla šemine anyn. Ʒany anyn bolur tivinciginde ol tirliknin
[38] [8] juvuq taḥtyna Tenrinin. Ki juvuqtu[137] H bar caġyruvcuġa anar
[39] [9] rast ʒan byla da tigel kavvana byla bar astrylyġyndan jüreginin[138].
[40] [10] ⌊כַּכָּתוּב אַךְ קָרוֹב לִירֵאָיו יִשְׁעוֹ לִשְׁכּוֹן כָּבוֹד בְּאַרְצֵנוּ: בָּרוּךְ כְּבוֹד ה׳ וגו׳:⌉[139]

125 JSul.III.69: *da ulusuna.* | JSul.I.37.03: *da ulusuna.*

126 ADub.III.61: *keltirivci.* | JSul.III.69: *keltiravci*; a scribal error. | JSul.III.79: *keltirivci.* | JSul.I.37.03: *keltirivci.*

127 JSul.I.45: *ol jazyqny.* | ADub.III.61: *ol jazyqny.* | JSul.III.69: *ol jazyqny.* | JSul.III.79: *ol jazyqny.* | JSul.I.37.03: *ol jazyqny.*

128 ADub.III.61: *jirek.* | JSul.III.69: *jirek.* | JSul.III.79: *jirek.* | JSul.I.37.03: *jirek.*

129 JSul.I.45: *ezek.* | ADub.III.61: *ezek.* | JSul.III.69: *ezek.* | JSul.III.79: *ezek.* | JSul.I.37.03: *ezek.*

130 ADub.III.61: *icine.* | JSul.III.69: *icine.* | JSul.III.79: *icine.* | JSul.I.37.03: *icine.*

131 ADub.III.61: *jireknin.* | JSul.III.69: *jireknin.* | JSul.III.79: *jireknin.* | JSul.I.37.03: *jireknin.*

132 ADub.III.61: *jalbaruvcularnyn.*

133 ADub.III.61: *kere.* | JSul.III.69: *kere.* | JSul.III.79: *kere.* | JSul.I.37.03: *kere.*

134 ADub.III.61: *sandyr.* | JSul.III.69: *sandyr.* | JSul.III.79: *sandyr.* | JSul.I.37.03: *sandyr.*

135 ADub.III.61: *andij.* | JSul.III.79: *andij.*

136 JSul.I.45: *körtilik*; a hypercorrect form of *kertilik*.

137 ADub.III.61: *juvuqtur.* | JSul.III.69: *juvuqtur.* | JSul.III.79: *juvuqtur.* | JSul.I.37.03: *juvuqtur.*

138 ADub.III.61: *jireginin.* | JSul.III.69: *jireginin.* | JSul.III.79: *jireginin.* | JSul.I.37.03: *jireginin.*

139 Psalm 85:9; Ezekiel 3:12. | JSul.I.45: אך קרוב ליראיו וגו׳. (Psalm 85:9). | ADub.III.61: אַךְ קָרוֹב לִירֵאָיו יִשְׁעוֹ וגו׳. (Psalm 85:9). | JSul.III.69: אַךְ קָרוֹב לִירֵאָיו יִשְׁעוֹ לִשְׁכּוֹן כָּבוֹד בְּאַרְצֵנוּ: בָּרוּךְ כְּבוֹד ה׳ מִמְּקוֹמוֹ:. (Psalm 85:9; Ezekiel 3:12). | JSul.III.79: אַךְ קָרוֹב וגו׳: בָּרוּךְ כְּבוֹד ה׳ מִמְּקוֹמוֹ:. (Psalm 85:9; Ezekiel 3:12). | JSul.I.37.03: אַךְ טוֹב וָחֶסֶד [:] בָּרוּךְ כְּבוֹד ה׳: תם. (Psalm 23:6; Ezekiel 3:12).

140 JSul.III.69: *and to.* | JSul.I.37.03: *and to.*

141 Lit. ‘pour’.

142 Lit. ‘take on his soul’; a calque of Russ. *на душу взять* ‘to pledge; to take responsibility for’.

143 JSul.I.45: *sin.* | ADub.III.61: *sin.* | JSul.III.69: *sin.* | JSul.III.79: *sin.* | JSul.I.37.03: *sin.*

[27] [27] qualities. God has given one teaching to the priest and to the congregation,
[28] [28] to[140] the people of the earth and to its princes; and so has He ordered that
[29] [29] one who brings sacrifice shall reveal[141] the sorrow of his heart before the only God the creator,
[30] [30] and that he shall pledge[142] not to come back to doing
[31] [1] evil[143] any more, like a dog who comes back to its own vomit. And it is not 105 v°
[32] [2] the peace offerings of fat buffalos[144] but the contrite heart and pure soul
[33] [3] what God wishes, likewise, the sacrifice of wheat flour on[145] a (shallow) cauldron
[34] [4] or on a pan is acceptable to God if it would (come) from the generosity
[35] [5] of a clean heart. ⌊Such is the Lord's way to be found in the prayers of those who pray to Him[146].
[36] [6] He thinks of every[147] men that would call with truth
[37] [7] His name. The soul of those will be ⌊(bound) in the bundle of life⌋[148]
[38] [8] near the throne of God. For the Lord is close to all those who call Him
[39] [9] with just soul and with intention without blemish with all the zeal of his heart.
[40] [10] ⌊Surely his salvation is near those that fear him; that glory may dwell in our land. Blessed be the glory of the Lord.⌋[149]

144 Expressed with Kar. *bujvol* < Russ. *буйвол* 'bufallo'. Given that all animal sacrifices in the Torah are of domestic animals, here it is perhaps used in the meaning of 'bull'. Cf. 17:33.

145 ADub.III.61: *in.* | JSul.III.69: *in.* | JSul.III.79: *in.* | JSul.I.37.03: *in.*

146 The respective Karaim fragment is somewhat obscure; cf. Isaiah 55:6.

147 ADub.III.61: *such a.* | JSul.III.79: *such a.*

148 Psalm 85:9.

149 Psalm 85:9; Ezekiel 3:12. | JSul.I.45: *'Surely [his salvation] is near those that fear him …' and so on.* (Psalm 85:9). | ADub.III.61: *'Surely his salvation is near those that fear him …', and so on.* (Psalm 85:9). | JSul.III.69: *'Surely his salvation is near those that fear him; that glory may dwell in our land. Blessed be the glory of the Lord from his place.'* (Psalm 85:9; Ezekiel 3:12). | JSul.III.79: *'Surely [his salvation] is near …', and so on. 'Blessed be the glory of the Lord from his place.'* (Psalm 85:9; Ezekiel 3:12). | JSul.I.37.03: *'Surely goodness and mercy … Blessed be the glory of the Lord.'* (Psalm 23:6; Ezekiel 3:12).

**Text number:** № 30
**Karaim incipit:** *Sensen Tenri astry kötirilgen*
**Hebrew incipit:** אַתָּה אֵל מִתְנַשֵּׂא *ʾattå ʾēl mit̠naśśē*
**Dedication:** Parashat Nitzavim (Deuteronomy 29:9–30:20)
**Language:** Early Mod.SWKar., Mod.SWKar.
**Number of copies:** 5

| Accession no. | Place of origin of copy | Date of copy | Copyist | Folios |
|---|---|---|---|---|
| JSul.III.03 | Halych | shortly after 1805 | Unknown 7 | 108 v°–109 r° |
| JSul.I.45 | Halych | 1st half of the 19th c. | Jeshua Josef Mordkowicz | 145 v°–146 r° |
| ADub.III.61 | Halych | 1850/1851 | Jeshua Josef Mordkowicz | 140 r°–141 r° |
| JSul.III.69 | Halych | ca. 1851 (before 1866) | Jeshua Josef Mordkowicz | 301 r°–301 v° |
| JSul.III.79 | Halych | ca. 1851 (before 1866) | Jeshua Josef Mordkowicz | 183 r°–184 r° |

## 1 Introductory Remarks

All five copies are vocalized. There are only a few differences between them. Textually, the versions of this *peshat* as copied in JSul.III.03 and JSul.I.45 are almost identical (the only discrepancy is *uruvunda* vs. *uruvundada* in line 16). Likewise, there are hardly any dissimilarities between the copies in ADub.III.61 and JSul.III.79, the only one being *uqsalyrmo* vs. *uqsalyr* (26). The relationship between these versions is set out in the diagram below (cf. № 29):

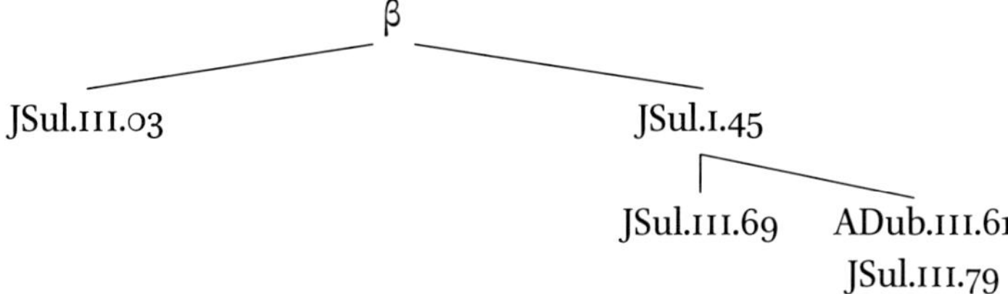


FIGURE 29 Diagram of the connections between the copies of peshat № 30

## 2 Transcription[150] and Translation

108 vº [1] [12] ⌊פשט לפיוט פרשת נצבים שהוא אתה אל מתנשא תרגמו אז̃ הה̃ו כמוה̃רר מרדכי

[2] [13] החוזה זא̃נ ואב̃ד דקה̃ק האליץ נב̃ת: בא̃ז כמא̃ר שמואל החסיד והסגן הזקן ונ̃פ יע̃מש:⌉[151]

[3] [14] Sensen Tenri astry kötirilgen[152] da qajjam olturuvcu[153] taḥty

[4] [15] istine bijliknin, ol turġuzuvcu tizivin ic

[5] [16] avullarynyn Jisra'elnin utru[154] tizivine ic ḥeleklerinin ol meci'utnun.

[6] [17] Aġaraqlarynyz aġaraqlary ševetleriniznin qartlarynyz da bar ol

[7] [18] ʒymatynyz tartylġan künlerinden[155] berešitnin[156], turdular bar ol janġy

[8] [19] dor tuvġanlar midbarda ulludan kicigedejin alnynda Mošenin,

[9] [20] kirme sertke H byla ki qojdu da tüzüdü[157] alynlarynda alarnyn,

[10] [21] turġuzmaq ücün[158] alarny özüne[159] ulusuna alġysly ilisnin,

[11] [22] kümler[160] bardy anda da alardanda sortun kelisi dorlarnyn. Vale

---

150 Based on JSul.III.03.

151 JSul.I.45: פשט לפיוט פרשת נצבים שהוא אתה אל מתנשא עשאו אז̃ הה̃ו כמוה̃רר מרדכי החזן נב̃ת: בא̃ז כמ̃ער שמואל החסיד יהסגן יע̃מש:. | ADub.III.61: וזה הפשט לגיוט נצבים שהוא אַתָּה לֵא מִתְנַשֵּׂא תרגמו אז̃ איש אלהים קדוש כק̃שת כמוה̃רר מרדכי החזן ואב̃ד דקהלתנו הק̃ נב̃ת בא̃ז כמ̃ער שמואל החסיד והצדיק התמים גביר מרומם וזקן ונשוא פנים תצב̃הה:. | JSul.III.69: ואם תרצה תא̃מ גם פשטו שתרגמו אז̃ החכם המרומם מוה̃רר מרדכי החזן ואב̃ד דקה̃ק זצו̃קל בא̃ז כמ̃ער שמואל החסיד והגביר הנעלה נב̃ת:. | JSul.III.79: פשט זה לפיוט פרשת אתם נצבים תרגמו אז̃ הה̃ו כמוה̃רר מרדכי החזן ואב̃ד דקה̃ק תשה̃עמ בא̃ז כמ̃ער שמואל החסיד והגביר הנעלה והמרומם יע̃מש:.

152 JSul.I.45: *ketirilgen.* | ADub.III.61: *ketirilgen.* | JSul.III.69: *ketirilgen.* | JSul.III.79: *ketirilgen.*

153 ADub.III.61: deest. | JSul.III.69: deest. | JSul.III.79: deest.

154 JSul.I.45: *uturu.* | ADub.III.61: *uturu.* | JSul.III.69: *uturu.* | JSul.III.79: *uturu.*

155 ADub.III.61: *kinlerinden.* | JSul.III.69: *kinlerinden.* | JSul.III.79: *kinlerinden.*

156 A quotation of the first word of the the book of Genesis, i.e., of Heb. בְּרֵאשִׁית 'in the beginning'.

157 JSul.I.45: *tizidi.* | ADub.III.61: *tizidi.* | JSul.III.69: *tizidi.* | JSul.III.79: *tizidi.*

158 ADub.III.61: *icin.* | JSul.III.69: *icin.* | JSul.III.79: *icin.*

159 ADub.III.61: *ezine.* | JSul.III.69: *ezine.* | JSul.III.79: *ezine.*

160 JSul.I.45: *kimler.* | ADub.III.61: *kimler.* | JSul.III.69: *kimler.* | JSul.III.79: *kimler.*

161 Cf. Isaiah 9:15: זָקֵן וּנְשׂוּא־פָנִים 'the elder and honourable'.

162 JSul.I.45: *A* peshat *of a* piyyut *for the parashat Nitzavim* (*with the incipit*) 'attå 'ēl mitnaśśē, *delivered by our aged master, the great and honourable sage, his honour, the Rav, Rabbi Mordechai, the hazzan, may his soul lodge in Eden, the son of our aged master, his honour, Rabbi, Shemuel, the pious officiant, may he rest in peace.* | ADub.III.61: *And this is the* peshat *of the* piyyut (*with the incipit*) 'attå 'ēl mitnaśśē, *which our aged master, the holy man of God translated his holy and glorious name being his honour, the Rav, Rabbi Mordechai, the hazzan and the chief justice of our holy community, may his soul lodge in Eden, the son of our aged master, his honour, Rabbi Shemuel, the pious and just, the innocent elevated master,*

[1] [12] ⌊A *peshat* of the *piyyut* for the parashat Nitzavim (with the incipit) *ʾattå ʾēl miṯnaśśē*, which our aged master, the great and honourable sage, his honour, the Rav, Rabbi Mordechai translated, 108 vº

[2] [13] the seer and the chief justice of the holy community of Halych, may his soul lodge in Eden, the son of our aged master, his honour, Rabbi Shemuel, the pious and the officiant ⌊elder and the honourable⌉[161], may he rest in peace:⌉[162]

[3] [14] You are the most[163] elevated and powerful God ⌊who sits⌉[164]

[4] [15] on the throne of the kingdom, the one who has set the arrangement of ⌊the three

[5] [16] camps of Israel⌉[165] against the arrangement of the three parts of the realities.

[6] [17] Your chiefs, the leaders of Your tribes, Your elders and all Your

[7] [18] congregation which exists ⌊from the days of the beginning on⌉[166] stood—all the new

[8] [19] generation that was born in the desert, both great and small—before Moses

[9] [20] to enter a covenant with the Lord that He has put and arranged before them,

[10] [21] to appoint[167] them be for Him His own people of the blessed share:

[11] [22] them who were there and also the forthcoming generations (who would come) after them. But he

---

*the elder and honourable, 'may his soul be bound in the bond of life'* [cf., 1Samuel 25:29]. | JSul.III.69: *And if you prefer you will also say its* [i.e., of the Hebrew original] peshat, *which our aged master, the elevated hakham, our teacher, Rabbi Mordechai translated, the hazzan and the chief justice of the holy community, may the memory of the holy and righteous be a blessing, the son of our aged master, his honour, Rabbi Shemuel, the pious and the elevated master, may his sould lodge in Eden.* | JSul.III.79: *This is a* peshat *of a* piyyut *for the parashat Nitzavim, which our aged master, the great and honourable sage, his honour, the Rav, Rabbi Mordechai translated, the hazzan and the chief justice of the holy community, 'the layer of dew came up on his lodge'* [cf., Exodus 16:13–14], *the son of his honour, Rabbi Shemuel, the pious, the elevated and exalted master, may he rest in peace.*

163 Lit. 'very'.

164 ADub.III.61: deest. | JSul.III.69: deest. | JSul.III.79: deest.

165 A reference to the three camps in the wilderness during the Exodus: the camp of the Indwelling presence of God, the camp of the Levites, and the camp of the Israelites.

166 I.e., *from the creation of the universe*; lit. 'from the days of the Book of Genesis on', 'from the days of Bereshit on'.

167 Lit. 'set', 'put up'.

[12] [23] kimnin ⌊bolsa ʒany⌋[168] bolġanysqan qorquvunda H-nyn, da alġyslanmus
[13] [24] bolsa ezi özüne[169] kelninden[170] fikirinin, ajtma savluq bolur
[14] [25] mana ḥotej barsamda tersligi byla jüregimnin[171], ⌊tas etmek⌋[172] ücün[173]
[15] [26] aqyllyq ʒanyn[174] tolturġany byla kleklerin tuvarlyq ʒanynyn, oloq
[16] [27] saʿatny[175] titinlenir qaḥyry da acuvu H-nyn anda da uruvunda[176]
[17] [28] anyn. Da ajyryr any H jamanġa bolmajyn onġalmaq syzlavuna
[18] [29] jarasynyn[177]
109 rº [19] [1] jarasynyn, ki qajryldy yzyndan jaryq Toranyn tunġan klegi
[20] [2] artyna ⌊jaman jecerinin⌋[178]. Körtiden[179] sandyr andij kisige
[21] [3] qajsynyn qurulġandy hammeše[180] jajy Torasynyn da emunasynyn,
[22] [4] da klegi anyn tutušqandy[181] süverligine[182] joġarġy Tenrinin. Anar
[23] [5] köre[183] küclü[184] Tenri küp[185] quvaty byla tutar on qolundan anyn.
[24] [6] Da daġy egirek[186] baryndan sivilir tigel ʿavodasy byla ezinin,
[25] [7] eger tekse suvnu kibik gilejin da qylsa any kavvansy byla jüreginin[187].
[26] [8] Ki kim uqsalyrmo[188] H-ġa da ol bijlik bitin dunjada anyndy

---

168 ADub.III.61: *ʒany bolsa.* | JSul.III.79: *ʒany bolsa.*

169 JSul.I.45: *özine.* | ADub.III.61: *ezine.* | JSul.III.69: *ezine.* | JSul.III.79: *ezine.*

170 ADub.III.61: *kelninde.* | JSul.III.69: *kelninde.* | JSul.III.79: *kelninde.*

171 ADub.III.61: *jiregimnin.* | JSul.III.69: *jiregimnin.* | JSul.III.79: *jiregimnin.*

172 JSul.III.03: טָשׁ אֵיטְמֵיק. | JSul.I.45: טַס אֵיטְמֶיק. | ADub.III.61: טַשׁ אֶיטְמֶיק. | JSul.III.69: טַשׁ אֶיטְמֶיק. | JSul.III.79: טַס אֵיטְמֶיק.

173 ADub.III.61: *icin.* | JSul.III.69: *icin.* | JSul.III.79: *icin.*

174 ADub.III.61: *ʒanyn ezinin.* | JSul.III.79: *ʒanyn ezinin.*

175 ADub.III.61: *sahatny.*

176 JSul.I.45: *uruvundada.* | ADub.III.61: *uruvundada.* | JSul.III.69: *uruvundada.* | JSul.III.79: *uruvundada.*

177 Catchword.

178 A calque of Heb. יֵצֶר הָרַע 'evil inclination', see Genesis 6:5, 8:21.

179 JSul.III.03: a hypercorrect form of *kertiden.* | JSul.I.45: a hypercorrect form of *kertiden.* | ADub.III.61: *kertiden.* | JSul.III.69: *kertiden.* | JSul.III.79: *kertiden.*

180 ADub.III.61: deest. | JSul.III.79: deest.

181 JSul.I.45: *tutusqandy.* | ADub.III.61: *tutusqandy.* | JSul.III.69: *tutusqandy.* | JSul.III.79: *tutusqandy.*

182 JSul.I.45: *siverligine.* | ADub.III.61: *siverligine.* | JSul.III.69: *hammeše siverligine.* | JSul.III.79: *siverligine.*

183 ADub.III.61: *kere.* | JSul.III.69: *kere.* | JSul.III.79: *kere.*

184 ADub.III.61: *kicli.* | JSul.III.69: *kicli.* | JSul.III.79: *kicli.*

185 JSul.III.03: a hypercorrect form of *kip.* | JSul.I.45: *kip.* | ADub.III.61: *kip.* | JSul.III.69: *kip.* | JSul.III.79: *kip.*

186 JSul.I.45: *edirek.*

[12] [23] who would have a soul[189] confused regarding the fear of Lord and
[13] [24] would ⌊consider himself⌉[190] blessed[191] by[192] the heart of his thinking to say: '⌊I will be (kept in good) health⌉[193]
[14] [25] even if I would walk with the disobedience of my heart in order to destroy
[15] [26] the[194] soul of wisdom by satisfying the wishes of the animal soul', in that very
[16] [27] hour the wrath and anger of God will fume at him and at his tribe[195],
[17] [28] and the Lord will destine him for evil, there being no remedy[196] for the
[18] [29] wound[197]
[19] [1] wound of his disease, for he has diverged from the path of the bright Law (going) after the darkened wishes[198] 109 rº
[20] [2] of the evil inclination. Indeed, (the Lord) thinks of such men
[21] [3] whose bow of the Law and faith is always[199] drawn,
[22] [4] and his ⌊wishes are⌉[200] fastened[201] together with the love of the God above.
[23] [5] According to that will the powerful God hold his right hand with His great strength.
[24] [6] And his service will even be loved more than everything (else),
[25] [7] if he would pour[202] the sorrow of his heart like water and would do that with the assiduousness of his heart.
[26] [8] For ⌊is there anybody who will be like⌉[203] God? And the kingdom of the entire world belongs only to Him.

---

187 ADub.III.61: *jireginin.* | JSul.III.69: *jireginin.* | JSul.III.79: *jireginin.*
188 JSul.III.79: *uqsalyr.*
189 Or: *heart.*
190 Lit. 'be for himself'.
191 Lit. 'a blessed one'.
192 ADub.III.61: *in.* | JSul.III.69: *in.* | JSul.III.79: *in.*
193 Lit. 'health will be for me'.
194 ADub.III.61: *his own.* | JSul.III.79: *his own.*
195 JSul.I.45: *tribe, too.* | ADub.III.61: *tribe, too.* | JSul.III.69: *tribe, too.* | JSul.III.67: *tribe, too.*
196 Lit. 'healing'.
197 Catchword in the Karaim text.
198 Lit. 'wish'.
199 ADub.III.61: deest. | JSul.III.79: deest.
200 Lit. 'wish is'.
201 JSul.III.69: *always fastened.*
202 I.e., *reveal.*
203 JSul.III.79: *who will be like.*

[27] [9] jalġyznyn. Da bar isleri anyn tizdü[204] da körtidü[205] da joḥtu[206]
[28] [10] avanlyq midalarynda anyn. Oldu bijik kötirivcü[207] da juvuz
[29] [11] etivcü[208] da anyn erkindedi bar bijlikleri jernin. Da kim
[30] [12] barmodu anyn kibik bar tabulġanlarynda üc[209] dunjalarnyn, ki ol
[31] [13] astry kötirilgendi[210] basyna bar maḥtavlarnyn da alġysnyn.
[32] [14] ⌞כי מי אל מבלעדי הֿ: ואתה קדוש:⌟[211]

204 JSul.I.45: *tizdi.* | ADub.III.61: *tizdi.* | JSul.III.69: *tizdi.* | JSul.III.79: *tizdi.*

205 JSul.III.03: a hypercorrect form of *kertidi.* | JSul.I.45: *körtidi*; a hypercorrect form of *kertidi.* | ADub.III.61: *kertidi.* | JSul.III.69: *kertidi.*

206 ADub.III.61: *joḥtur.* | JSul.III.79: *joḥtur.*

207 ADub.III.61: *ketirivci.* | JSul.III.69: *ketirivci.* | JSul.III.79: *ketirivci.*

208 ADub.III.61: *etivci.* | JSul.III.69: *etivci.* | JSul.III.79: *etivci.*

209 JSul.I.45: *ic.* | ADub.III.61: *ic.* | JSul.III.69: *ic.* | JSul.III.79: *ic.*

210 JSul.I.45: *ketiriligendi.* | ADub.III.61: *ketiriligendi.* | JSul.III.69: *ketiriligendi.* | JSul.III.79: *ketiriligendi.*

211 2 Samuel 22:32; Psalm 22:3. | JSul.I.45: כִּי מִי אֵל מִבַּלְעֲדֵי הָ֗ וגו׳: (2 Samuel 22:32). | ADub.III.61: כִּי מִי אֵל מִבַּלְעֲדֵי הָ֗: (2 Samuel 22:32). | JSul.III.69: כִּי מִי אֱלוֹהַּ מִבַּלְעֲדֵי הָ֗ וּמִי צוּר מִאֱ֗ :

[27] [9] And all His deeds are right and just, and there is no
[28] [10] evil in His measures[212]. He is who lifts up high and lowers,
[29] [11] and He rules all the kingdoms of the Earth. And is there anybody
[30] [12] like Him among those who are to be found in the three worlds, for He
[31] [13] is greatly exalted above any praise and blessing.
[32] [14] ⌊For who is God, except the Lord? But you are holy.⌉[213]

---

.מִבַּלְעֲדֵי יְיָ: אֵין קָדוֹשׁ כַּיְיָ כִּי אֵין בִּלְתֶּךָ: וְאַתָּה קָדוֹשׁ יוֹשֵׁב תְּהִלּוֹת יִשְׂרָאֵל: (2 Samuel 22:32; Psalm 18:31; 1 Samuel 2:2; Psalm 22:3). | JSul.III.79: .כִּי מִי אֵל מִבַּלְעֲדֵי יְיָ: כִּי מִי אֱלוֹהַּ מִבַּלְעֲדֵי יְיָ וגו׳: (2 Samuel 22:32; Psalm 18:31).

212 Or: *character.*

213 2 Samuel 22:32. | JSul.I.45: *'For who is God, except the Lord? …', and so on.* (2 Samuel 22:32). | ADub.III.61: *'For who is God, except the Lord? and who is a rock, except our God?'* (2 Samuel 22:32). | JSul.III.69: *'For who is God, except the Lord? For who is God except the Lord? There is none holy as the Lord: for there is none beside you. But you are holy, O you that inhabit the praises of Israel.'* (2 Samuel 22:32; Psalm 18:31; 1 Samuel 2:2; Psalm 22:3). | JSul.III.79: *'For who is God, except the Lord? For who is God except the Lord? …', and so on.* (2 Samuel 22:32; Psalm 18:31).

# Lexicographical Addenda

Lemmatised below are those words that are absent from the Karaim–Russian–Polish dictionary (KarRPS). Published in 1974 the latter work features ca. 17,400 entries and it still remains the most elaborate compilation of the Karaim lexicon. Nevertheless, it is far from being an exhaustive presentation of the Karaim lexicon, given that it contains lemmas from all three dialects of Karaim and each dialectal form received a separate enty. From a methodological point of view, it was, obviously, the right decision to make, but, at the same time, this number gives us an average of 5,800 words per dialect. By way of comparison, the Kirghiz–Russian dictionary of Judachin (1985) comprises 40,000 entries, its Russian–Kirghiz equivalent (Judachin 1957) boasts 51,000, whereas the Crimean Karaim–English dictionary of Aqtay & Jankowski (2015) contains more than 10,000.

Since its publication a few lexicographical additions have been made to the Western Karaim content of KarRPS. We should mention here W. Zajączkowski's brief article (1977), or Németh's glossaries (2011b: 96–98, 2015c: 88–91). There is, however, still much to do in this respect, the lexicographical addenda presented here being another response to this need.

In the glossary, the lemmas are presented in the context in which they are attested. Our glossary is based on the content of the oldest versions of each religious poem: if the context remained unchanged in the other copies of the respective *peshat*, we only quote the oldest manuscript. Archaic variants of words lemmatized in KarRPS that are explicable in terms of regular phonological or phonetic sound changes are not included in the glossary. Proper nouns are not included in the glossary, either, the only exception being names of holidays and feasts.

**A, ʿA**

**ʿAceret** SW 'Shemini Atzeret'

*jedi künü ḥyǯynyn ol macalarnyn da jedi künü ol Sukotnun da ʿA. özü özüne moʿed ündelmekbyla* (19:7); *bu künnü ündedi ʿA. jyštyrynyp* (19:16)

⩩ Heb. שְׁמִינִי עֲצֶרֶת 'Shemini Atzeret (a holiday)', NWKar. *aceret* 'the seventh day of Pesach' ⇒ **Šemini ʿAceret**

**afilu** SW 'even if'

*ki tartmady bojunsada da a. bosta ketirip qojmasynlar* (22:29)

⩩ Heb. אֲפִילוּ ~ אֲפִלּוּ 'even, even if, even though'

**ahah** SW 'woe!'

*a. H qyjasa unuttun ki sensen jaratuvcum* (1:18); *sen e H rast jarġucu a. kemistin bosatma jazyqlarymny* (1:21); *a. aruv enajatly Tenri* (1:25); *a. tergevčü fikirlerin aruv*

 | DOI:10.1163/9789004419377_014

*jüreknin* (3:42); *a. aziz atam kör ki bijenčli jürekbyla tözemen alġyšynny da bošatlyġynny* (3:93)

ℛ Heb. אֲהָהּ 'woe!, alas!, ah!'

**'amamim** see **šiva 'amamim**

**anlat-** SW 'to relate, to tell'

**-tylar:** *muna šira uḥudular da a. tamaša karanjalaryn ne ki qyldy, ki paroġa da čerivine anyn* (8:15)

**-yr:** *navi qaryndaslary arasyndan turġuzur H ol* [*navi*] *a. alarġa jasyryn nerselerni ne ki bolunurlar* (22:22)

ℛ WKar. *anlat-* '1. to explain; 2. to inform; 3. to call'

**anoẖi** SW 'I (*an epithet of God*)'

**-nin:** *sözlerine köre a.* (7:23)

ℛ Heb. אָנֹכִי '(*pers. pron.*) I'; used as an epithet of God

**artyq** SW '1. already; 2. (*with neg. verb*) any more'

*arttyrmasty a. dusman olʒalama jerinden seni* (4:30); *da ulusu anyn a. tajmaġaj* (14:26); *ki qajtmaġaj a. jaman islerine qajtqanlaj it qusqununa ezini* (18:31); *jubančly ḥabar ešittirgin ki tügendi a. uču güneḥl*[*e*]*rimnin* (26:54); *qajtmasqa qylma a. avanlyqny qajtqanlaj it qusqununa ezinin* (29:31)

ℛ WKar. *artyq* 'more'; EKar. *artyq* '1. more; 2. already'

**'avoda zara** SW 'idolatry'

**-ġa:** *eksitsinler macevany da qujas sufatlarny da ašeralarny 'a. z. islengenler* (22:11); *tabulmasynlar Jisra'elde ulanlaryn ezlerinin 'a. z. ot asyra asyruvcular* (22:19–20); *bu jazyq üčün tünkelttin meni jerlerinde tüslü umalarnyn qulluq etivčülernin 'a. z.* (26:12)

ℛ Heb. עֲבוֹדָה זָרָה 'idolatry, paganism'

## B

**bajit šeni** SW 'the Second Temple'

*qolu ašyra Titosnun boldu veren b. š.* (6:57)

ℛ Heb. בַּיִת שֵׁנִי, in fact בֵּית־הַמִּקְדָּשׁ הַשֵּׁנִי 'the Second Temple'

**barly|q** SW 'existence'

**-ġy:** *edi da bardy da bolurda da b. anyn eksilmejdoġan* (9:29); *da bolġaj Adonaj jalġyz* [*ö*]*zü bij bar ol jer üstüne da b. da birligi anyn avzunda bar tennin bolġaj qotarylġan* (19:27)

**-ġyn:** *sen e Adonaj aziz Tenrim avaldandy b. senin da sensen qajjam sofuna dejin bar sofnun* (12:12); *senin b. qajjamdy jaratylmaġyndan burun üč dunjalarnyn* (12:20)

ℛ Kar. *bar* 'extistence, being'

**beḥira** SW 'choice'

**-ma:** *ol tirlikni da ol ölümnü bergeninde Torany menim b. berdin* (3:53)

ℛ Heb. בְּחִירָה 'choice; option'

**ber-: kle|k ber-** SW 'to fulfil a wish'
**-edi:** *da b. klegin qulunun neginče ki tügellegej sözün qoltqalarynyn* (12:35)
⚘ Kar. *ber-* 'to give', SWKar. *klek* 'wish'
**berešit** SW '*fig.* beginning; the moment of creation of the universe'
**-nin:** *bar ol ʒymatynyz tartylġan künlerinden b.* (30:7)
⚘ Heb. בְּרֵאשִׁית '1. in the beginning (*the first word of the the Book of Genesis*); 2. Book of Genesis'
**bet** see **bet din hagadol**
**bet din hagadol** SW 'Supreme Court of Justice'
*alardylar jetmis zaqen b. d. h. indeledoġanlar* (22:17)
⚘ Heb. בֵּית דִּין הַגָּדוֹל 'Supreme Court of Justice' (see Deuteronomy 17:8–13)
**bet hamiqdaš** SW '1. temple; 2. the Temple in Jerusalem, the Holy Temple'
*qondarylġanda kelesi b. h.* (19:24)
**-ny:** *nečik qondarġanda Šlomo hameleḥ burunġu b. h. Šemini 'Aceret kününde* (19:22)
**-nyn:** *rast ǯanbyla qajtqanlarynda Tenrige ne ullu quvanč edi qutlamaġynda b. h.* (6:53)
**-ta:** *beš nerśa burun bolġan b. h. haligińa bolmady tabulġan* (6:22); *šahat qajtaryr bizni jerimizge da b. h. čyġarybiz 'olalar* (6:74); *tefile etme b. h.* (17:9); *jyštyrynyp tefile etme b. h.* (19:17)
**-ymda:** *bes nerse burun bolġan b. m. haligine bolmady tabulġan* (6:22)
**-ynny:** *aziz da körklü üvümüznü b. h.* (26:18)
⚘ Heb. בֵּית הַמִּקְדָּשׁ 'temple; the Temple in Jerusalem, the Holy Temple'
**bikre-** SW 'to bend, to stoop'
**-genlerni:** *e raḥmetlevcü Tenri qacan qajrylysen mana da ullu qajǵylarymdan juvutyrsen meni, e küplevcü b. juvuz etivcü ektemlerni* (3:67)
⚘ SWKar. *bikrej-* 'to stoop', NWKar. *büḱŕaj-* 'to bend'
**bitik: get bitigi** SW 'letter of divorce'
**-in:** *jazdylar anar g. b.* (21:19)
⚘ Heb. גֵּט 'letter of divorce (a short form of גֵּט אִשָּׁה)'
**bu**$^{\mathrm{I}}$ W def. art. 'the'
*jeter bolġajdy mana b. acuvun* (1:33); *vaj bizǵa ki b. jazyǵymyz üčün bolduq Tenrimizǵa ujatlylar da iḿančliĺar* (2:10); *körgüz mana b. šavaġatyjny* (3:80); *qutqarǵyn any bu ačy galuttan* (3:117)
⚘ Kar. *bu* 'this' ⇒ **ol, osol, osol ol, ošol, ošol ol**
**bu**$^{\mathrm{II}}$ SW expressive particle
*qacanġadejin b. talasmassen talaslarymny* (1:37)
⚘ Kar. *bu* (dem. pron.) 'this' | Cf. Pol. *to*$^{\mathrm{I}}$ (dem. pron.) 'this', to$^{\mathrm{II}}$ expressive particle
**bujvol** SW '1. buffalo; ? 2. bull'
**-lary:** *tivil semiz b. šelamimlernin* (29:32)
**-undan:** *b. šelamim debeḥasynyn* (18:33)

⸙ Russ. *буйвол* 'buffalo'; NWKar. *bujvol* 'buffalo'. Given that all animal sacrifices in the Torah are of domestic animals, in lines 18:33 and 29:32 it is perhaps used in the meaning of 'bull'.

## C

**ceba'ot** SW 'armies, hosts'

-**nu:** *da ajtqaj e H Tenri jaratuvcu c.* (16:32)

⸙ Heb. צְבָאוֹת 'armies, hosts'; pl. of צָבָא

**cercek** SW 'ridicule'

-**ke:** *bolduq c. bar uluslarġa* (2:15)

⸙ SWKar. *cercik* 'ridicule' ⇒ **čerček, čerćak**

**ceriv: borc cerivi** SW 'obligatory war'

-**nde:** *p. c. cyqsyn ḥatanda ḥuzurasyndan* (22:24)

⸙ Cf. Heb. מִלְחֶמֶת מִצְוָה 'a war that does not require permisson and the Torah makes compulsory, obligatory war; lit. *war by commandment*'

**ceriv: povynnyj ceriv** SW 'obligatory war'

-**de:** *p. c. cyqsyn ḥatanda ḥuzurasyndan* (22:24)

⸙ Cf. Heb. מִלְחֶמֶת מִצְוָה 'a war that does not require permisson and the Torah makes compulsory, obligatory war; lit. *war by commandment*'

**ceriv: rešut cerivi** SW 'a permitted war'

-**nde:** *r. c. cyqmasynlar bes sanalġanlar* (22:23)

⸙ Cf. Heb. מִלְחֶמֶת רְשׁוּת 'a war that that the Torah does not obligate, nor forbid; a permitted war (according to the Jewish law)'

**cicit** SW 'fringe'

*hadirlegin ezine c. dert mivisi istine jabunurunnun* (15:27)

⸙ Heb. צִיצִית 'fringe, tassel'

## Č

**čajnav** NW 'mockery'

-**lar:** *bolduq čerćakḱa bar uluslarġa kültkü da č.* (2:16)

⸙ SWKar. *cajnav* 'ridicule, mockery'

**čerček** SW 'ridicule'

-**ke:** *bolduq č. bar uluslarġa* (2:15)

⸙ SWKar. *cercik* 'ridicule' ⇒ **cercek, čerćak**

**čerćak** NW 'ridicule'

-**ḱa:** *bolduq č. bar uluslarġa kültkü da čajnavlar*

⸙ SWKar. *cercik* 'ridicule' ⇒ **cercek, čerček**

## D

**dibur** SW 'speech'
  **-nu:** *burunġu d. on sözlerden ki oldu* anoḫi H elohejḫa (28:18)
  ⸙ Heb. דִּבּוּר 'speech'

## ʒ

**ʒanavar: tiri ʒanavar** SW 'living creature, animal'
  **-dan:** *bujurdu juvutma qarban usajdoġandan ezine klegim ajtma t. ʒ. da esedoġandan arytmaq ücün murdarlyġyn ʒanynyn* (29:22–23)
  ⸙ Pers. جانوار *ǧānwār* 'animal; beast' (Steingass 1892: 353); EKar. *ǯanavar* 'animal; beast'

## E, 'E

**eḫijot** SW 'qualities'
  **-larynyn:** *necik adam alaj tuvar bir ucur tibinedi tivsirilmegi sartyn dört e.* (29:27)
  ⸙ Heb. אֵיכֻיּוֹת 'qualities', pl. of אֵיכוּת
**ehje** SW '*ehyēh* (an epithet of God)'
  **-nin:** *jalyny byla otnun ortasyndan ol senenin bilindin anar šemi byla e.* (28:16)
  ⸙ Heb. אֶהְיֶה 'name of God' < אֶהְיֶה אֲשֶׁר אֶהְיֶה 'I am that I am' (Exodus 3:14); an epithet of God
**eksilmejdoġan** SW 'eternal'
  *edi da bardy da bolurda da barlyġy anyn e.* (9:29)
  ⸙ SWKar. *eksil-* 'to disappear, to diminish'
**emirlik** SW 'eternal'
  *e. ḫorluqqa bolurlar jyjynlary dušmanlarymnyn* (14:16); *e. jarlyġas toḫtatyrmen istine* (15:37); *e. tirlik byla asajyšlatty ʒanlarymyzny* (19:10)
  ⸙ SWKar. *emirlik* 'eternity' ⇒ **ömürlük, ömirlik, ömürlik**
**emuna** 'faith, religion'
  **-ny:** *bu jalġan e. ilis aldylar atalary avaldan* (25:25)
  **-synyn:** *körtiden sandyr andij kisige qajsynyn qurulġandy hammeše jajy Torasynyn da e.* (30:21)
  ⸙ Heb. אֱמוּנָה '1 faith; 2. belief'
**'enjan** SW 'task'
  **-laryn:** *da anda askartty anar Tenri 'e. kisinin da ucurun anyn* (29:14)
  ⸙ Heb. עִנְיָן 'occupation, task' ⇒ **'injan**
**enke** SW superlat. suff. 'most'
  *közlerimizde kiči boldum birisi kibik e. usta miskinrek elnin* (12:6)
  ⸙ EKar. *enke* '(superlat. suff.) most'

**eslet-** SW 'to remind'

**-edirler**: *ančaq raḥmetlerin e. meni jalbarma sana anlavču saġyšlaryn fikirlerimnin* (3:10)

**-ediler**: *ančaq raḥmetlerin e. meni jalbarma sana e anlavču saġyšlaryn fikirlerimnin* (3:10)

⚘ EKar. *esle-* 'to remember'

**ezge** SW *abl.* 'apart from'

*Tenriden e. kim synd[y]ralyr ulluluġun tolġunlarynyn* (12:29)

⚘ SWKar. *ezge* 'other' ⇒ **özge**

G

**galgal** SW 'globe, celestial sphere'

**-larynyn**: *oldu qondaruvču bijik köklerde jergelerin g.* (17:16)

⚘ MHeb. גַּלְגַּל 'globe, celestial sphere' (Jastrow 1903: II 245); WKar. *galgal* 'circle'. The Ar. origin of the world put forward in KarRPS (158) seems hardly probable. BHeb. גַּלְגַּל '1. wheel; 2. whirl; 3. whirlwind' (cf. Psalm 77:18) cannot be treated as the word's etymon in 17:16.

**get** see **bitik: get bitigi**

**go'el** SW 'redeemer'

*qolabiz ki ijgejsen bizge g. Jisra'elni* (28:28)

⚘ Heb. גּוֹאֵל 'redeemer, deliverer'

**goj** SW '1. gentile; 2. Gentile; 3. nation'

*tas etkin bar g. qyjnavcularymny* (1:40)

**-lar**: *byrclandym murdarlyqta ol g. kibik ki alar arasyna tozdurdun jyjynlarymny* (1:17)

**-lardan**: *ajyrmaq ücün meni murdar g.* (1:37); *ḥastalanġan da zavly kibik murdar indeldim g.* (24:10); *körgin qryvda cydaġanymny g.* (24:40)

**-larġa**: *ol vaḥtta civirir aruv sez bar g. ki birligine anyn jalġyznyn caġyrġajlar* (27:27)

**-larnyn**: *baqqyn muft cydaġanymny acytmaqlaryna ceja g.* (1:58); *byrclanġan boldum murdarlyqlary byla g.* (24:7)

**-lary**: *sirdin meni qyblalaryn alnyndan da g. arasyna* (24:13)

⚘ Heb. גּוֹי '1. nation, pleople; 2. Gentile'

H, Ḥ, Ḫ

**ha: ha mana** SW 'woe is me'

*h. m. ki jazyġybyla atamnyn tolġatyldym da anam güneḥibyla issitti meni ḥamilalyġynda* (3:39)

**hacadiq** SW 'the just (an epithet)'

*bolurlar Josef h. kibik ki tapty osol qaryndaslaryn tizinde Dotannyn* (21:10)

♣ Heb. צַדִּיק 'just'; used with the Heb. definite article

**hagadol** see **bet din hagadol**

**ḥajot** SW 'living'

*qondarġyn veren bolġan miqdašynny ki edi qondarylġan qyjasyba kise kavodnun da ol ḥ. qodešnin ki ediler navilerge körüngenler* (3:122)

♣ Heb. הַיּוֹת 'living, life'

**hamašijaḥ** see **meleḥ: meleḥ hamašijaḥ**

**hameleḥ: Šlomo hameleḥ** SW 'King Solomon'

*nečik qondarġanda Š. h. burunġu bet hamiqdašny* (19:21)

♣ Heb. שְׁלֹמֹה הַמֶּלֶךְ, i.e., King Solomon the son of David called Jedidiah; used with the Heb. definite article; SWKar. *meleḥ* 'king' ⇒ **meleḥ**

**hamiqdaš** see **bet hamiqdaš**

**haqodeš** SW 'sanctity'

**-nin**: *qondarġyn veren bolġan miqdašynny ki edi qondarylġan qyjasy byla kise kavodnun da ol ḥajot h. ki ediler navilerge körüngenler* (3:166)

♣ Heb. קֹדֶשׁ 'holiness, sanctity'; used with the Heb. definite article ⇒ **lešon haqodeš, qodeš**

**ḥasydlyq** SW 'piety'

*ḥajifsinip berdin alarġa Torany cynyqtyrma alarny kecinme ḥ byla* (10:6)

♣ Heb. חָסִיד 'pious'

**ḥešbon** SW 'account'

**-unda**: *rast bolusen sözleme birgeme töre sözleri jarġu kününnün ḥ.* (3:31)

♣ Heb. חֶשְׁבּוֹן 'account, reckoning, calculation'

**hodnyj** SW 'worthy'

*tas byla taslansyn anar kere necik tanyqlyq berseler h. tanyqlar* (22:14)

♣ Ukr. arch. годний 'worthy' (in today's Ukrainian: *colloq.*) (ISUJa 1: 543; SUM 2: 104)

**ḥokimlik** SW 'ruthlessness'

*ḥ. sirdiler istimizge* (2:25)

♣ SWKar. *ḥoḫimlik* 'ruthlessness' ⇒ **ḥökümlük**

**ḥökümlük** NW, SW 'ruthlessness'

*ḥ. süŕadiĺar üstümüzǵa* (2:25)

♣ SWKar. *ḥoḫimlik* 'ruthlessness' ⇒ **ḥokimlik**

## I, ˈI

**iḥcuvun** SW '?'

*jasly hem taryqqan ʒanly tisli qajġydan boldum men ol i. bolġan Tenrige* (1:5)

♣ Perhaps, a compound consisting of *iḥ* (see KarRPS 195, s.v. *uux*) meaning most probably 'holy' (related to Tkc. *yjyq* ~ *ijiq* etc., see Räsänen 1969: 164; ÈSTJa I 649–650) and, perhaps, MPol. *czuban* 'shepherd' (SPolXVI IV: 1) (with an *u—a* > *u—u* assimilation in Karaim).

**'injan** SW 'task'

**-laryn:** *da anda asqartty anar Tenri 'i. kisinin da ucurun anyn* (29:14)

⚘ Heb. עִנְיָן 'occupation, task' ⇒ **'enjan**

## J

**jaḥšyraq** ~ **jaḥsyraq** SW 'more'

*j. 'oladan da debeḥadan süvesen synyq ǯanny* (3:103)

⚘ SWKar. *jaḥsyraq* 'better'

**javdurt-** SW 'to make rain fall'

**-uvčusu:** *beklese bulutlarny kim barmodu j. alarnyn* (17:15)

⚘ SWKar. *javdur-* 'to make rain fall'; used with the causative *-t-*

**jazyl-** SW 'to be destined'

**-ġaj:** *bolġaj klek alnyndan anyn ki bügün j. tirlikke* (14:13)

⚘ Kar. *jazyl-* 'to be written'

**jecer** SW 'inclination'

**-im:** *qunušturady meni jaman j.* (3:21)

**-inin:** *jazyqly bolmaġaj jamanlyġy sartyn jaman j.* (18:14); *cyġarynyz icinizden jamanlyġyn j. jireginiznin* (27:11); *klegi jaman j.* (30:20)

**-innin:** *qajrylmassen jaman saġyslary artyna jaman j.* (15:31)

**-ler:** *eki j. esediler anar* (29:16)

**-ni:** *köteriniz jaman j. icinizden* (23:9)

⚘ Heb. יֵצֶר 'inclination', Heb. יֵצֶר הָרַע 'evil inclination' (Genesis 6:5, 8:21); SWKar. *jecer* 'character, texture' ⇒ **jecer hara'**

**jecer hara'** SW 'evil inclination'

**-nyn:** *qajrylmassen jaman saġyslary artyna j. h.* (15:31)

⚘ Heb. יֵצֶר הָרַע 'evil inclination' (Genesis 6:5, 8:21); SWKar. *jecer* 'character, texture' ⇒ **jecer**

**jengil et-** SW 'to make lighter'

**-mek:** *j. e. ücün jigin murdarlyġynyn* (21:21)

⚘ SWKar. *jengil et-* 'to disrespect'

**jesod** SW 'origin'

**-lardan:** *da bolġany sartyn jaratylġan dert j. protyvnyjlar biri birine* (29:20)

**-larynyn:** *qajtarma ornuna j.* (12:50)

⚘ Heb. יְסוֹד 'origin, source'

**Jom Teru'a** SW 'Yom Teruah'

*saġynylġajbiz alnynda anyn ošpu künde ol ündelgen J. T.* (7:9–10)

⚘ Heb. יוֹם תְּרוּעָה 'Yom Teruah'

**jovsem** SW 'particularly'

*ki bolalmajdylar körme kensiliginni jyjyny malaẖlarnyn j. ki aqyly adamlarnyn* (12:20)

☙ Pol. *i owszem* '1. (*arch.*) furthermore, in adition, what is more, and even; 2. (*arch.*) especially, particularly' (SStp 5: 709–710) ⇒ **jovšem**

**jovšem** SW 'particularly'

*ki bolalmajdylar körme kensiliginni jyjyny malaẖlarnyn j. ki aqyly adamlarnyn* (12:20)

☙ Pol. *i owszem* '1. (*arch.*) furthermore, in adition, what is more, and even; 2. (*arch.*) especially, particularly' (SStp 5: 709–710) ⇒ **jovsem**

## K

**kelal** SW 'principle'

**-larny:** *jarattyn peratlarny da k.* (13:11)

**-laryn:** *qajjamlyqta tutady peratlaryn da k. alarnyn* (25:7)

☙ Heb. כְּלָל '1. general rule, rule, principle; 2. sum, total; 3. community'

**keruvim** SW 'cherubim'

*turġuzulup sortun miškan eki k. arasyndan esitiredi inin Tenrinin* (18:9)

**-lerni:** *turġan künlerinde heẖalynda joġarġy Tenrinin körgenlerinde ol k.* (4:11)

**-lernin:** *turġuzup sortun Moše rabenu ol miškanny caġyrdy any H arasyndan eki ol k.* (29:12)

☙ Heb. כְּרֻבִים 'cherubim'

**kini** SW 'innocent'

*arasyna k. qannyn borclu qan byla nendijde bolsa talas sezler* (22:15); *da ol Tenri eksitir borcun ol k. qannyn* (22:30)

**-ler:** *povynnyj cerivde cyqsyn ḥatanda ḥuzurasyndan bolmasyn k.* (22:24)

☙ < SWKar. *keni* 'innocent' < MSWKar. **könü* id. (it is not the SWKar. *kini* 'envious' used here); cf. Heb. דָם הַנָּקִי 'innocent blood' in the Hebrew original of *peshat* № 22. Cf. also *kini* and *könü* used in two translations of Deuteronomy 24:5: *Ki alsa kiši janġy qatyn čyqmasyn čerüvge da ašmasyn anyn ašyra heč nemede könü bolsun üvünde bir jyl da bijendirsin ošol qatynyn ki aldy* (ADub.III.73: 319 v°) and *Ki alsa kisi janġy qatyn cyqmasyn cerivge ani asmasyn anyn istine hec qystavlu nerse kini bolsun ivine bir jyl da bijendirsin osol qatynyn ki aldy* (JSul.III.01: 213 v°), cf. 'When a man has taken a new wife, he shall not go out to war, neither shall he be charged with any matter; he shall be free at home one year and make happy his wife whom he has taken' (Deuteronomy 24:5). ⇒ **kinilik, künülük**

**kinili|k** SW 'justice'

**-ginni:** *ki ojatqajsen k. da jasanġajsen qaḥyryn byla ec alma uturu turuvcularymdan* (26:37)

☙ < MSWKar. **könülük* 'justice' > SWKar. *kenilik* id. > SWKar. *kinilik* id. It is not SWKar. *kinilik* < MSWKar. *künülük* 'envy; passion' used in the referenced text. For further information see **kini.** ⇒ **kini, künülük**

**kise** SW 'throne'

*qondarġyn veren bolġan miqdašynny ki edi qondarylġan qyjasyba k. kavodnun da ol ḥajot qodešnin ki ediler navilerge körüngenler* (3:122)

☙ Heb. כִּסֵּא 'throne'

**kle ki** SW *'even if'

*ahah aruv enajatly Tenri k. k. eger gergede qazylsam* (1:25); *ḥorladym da qajjam etmedim alarny k. k. jalyn alarnyn bildimde ese* (3:20)

☙ The meaning is reconstructed on the basis of *ḥotej* 'even though' used in place of *kle ki* in the other copies of *peshat* № 3.

**kol** SW 'whole'

*avzundan bar k. Jisra'el[nin] alġyšlanġaj* (19:24)

☙ Heb. כֹּל 'all, whole, the whole of'

**künülü|k** SW 'justice'

**-günnü:** *ki ojatqajsen k. da jasanġajsen qaḥirlerinbyla öč alma utru turuvčularymdan* (26:37)

☙ < MSWKar. **könülük* 'justice' > SWKar. *kenilik* id. > SWKar. *kinilik* id. It is not SWKar. *kinilik* < MSWKar. *künülük* 'envy; passion' used in the referenced text. For further information see **kini.** ⇒ **kini, kinilik**

L

**lešon haqodeš** SW 'the Holy Language; Hebrew'

*qajyryr uluslarġa aruv sezni sezleme l. h. byla ezge til byla qosulmajdoġan* (9:30); *ol uluslarġa qajyryr aruv sözni ki oldu ol l. h.* (23:25)

**-ni:** *qajyryr uluslarġa aruv söznü l. h. ezge söz byla qosulmajdoġan* (9:30)

☙ Heb. לְשׁוֹן הַקֹּדֶשׁ 'the Holy Tongue'; appellation attributed to the Hebrew language

M

**maceva** SW 'idol image'

**-ny:** *da eksitsinler m. da qujas sufatlarny da ašeralarny* (22:11)

☙ BHeb. מַצֵּבָה 'idol image'; SWKar. *maceva* 'tombstone'

**maḥtav ber-** SW 'to praise'

**-diler:** *maḥtavlar b. ullu syjly atyna Tenrinin* (8:10); *sana m. b. bar ʒanlary byla* (8:20)

**-ejik:** *šükürlük da m. b. sana* (28:7)

**-gej:** *ceber šira byla m. b. kicli Tenrige* (16:30)

**-iniz:** *m. b. e süver qaryndašlarym da urluġu atalarymnyn Tenrige* (7:16); *syjly šemine H-nyn m. b.* (11:7); *qyčqyrmaqlarbyla m. b. alnynda Adonajnyn* (14:19)

**-me:** *borčtu bizge m. b. anar jaḥšylyqlary üčün anyn* (7:6); *sandyr ol ulusqa ki bilediler* *m. b. Tenrige bijenčbyla* (7:12–13); *da m. b. anar bolunuz juvuvcular* (23:23–24); *m. b. eki keret kinde bolunuz pilnovat etivciler* (27:25)

⚘ SWKar. *maḥtav* 'praise' ⇒ **maḥtavlar ber-**

**maḥtavlar ber-** SW 'to praise'

**-diler:** *m. b. ullu syjly atyna Tenrinin* (8:10); *sana m. b. bar ʒanlary byla* (8:20)

⚘ SWKar. *maḥtav* 'praise' ⇒ **maḥtav ber-**

**maqovice** SW 'capital'

**-ler:** *da šükür etsinler ki keltirdi alarny jerge m. byla qondarylġan* (10:17)

⚘ Russ. *маковица* 'capital'; NWKar. *makovća* 'capital'

**mašijaḥ** W 'Messiah'

**-yndan:** *da ešittirgin bizġa m. ḥabarlar* (2:47)

**-ymyzdan:** *da ešittirgin bizge m. jubančly ḥabarlar* (2:47)

⚘ Heb. מָשִׁיחַ '1. the anointed; 2. Messiah'; SWKar. *masijaḥ* 'Messiah'

**mazal** SW 'constellation'

**-ġa:** *da ḥotej haligine biz erkitibine ese mazalnyn indelgen Teli muna sana jalġyzġa da tivil m. isanabiz* (28:27)

**-larynyn:** *anyndy ec almaq jaman telev qajtarma umalarġa ne vaḥtny tajsa kücü m.* (25:32)

**-nyn:** *da ḥotej haligine biz erkitibine ese m. indelgen Teli muna sana jalġyzġa da tivil mazalġa isanabiz* (28:27)

⚘ Heb. מַזָּל 'constellation, zodiac'; EKar. *mazal* 'constellation', NWKar. *mazal* 'luck'

**meci'ut** SW 'reality'

**-nun:** *turġuzuvcu tizivin ic avullarynyn Jisra'elnin utru tizivine ic ḥeleklerinin ol m.* (30:5)

⚘ Heb. מְצִיאוּת '1. existence, essence; 2. reality, actuality'

**meleḫ: meleḫ hamašijaḥ** SW 'King Messiah'

*m. h. avzundan bar kol Jisra'el alġyšlanġaj* (19:24)

**-nyn:** *bijlik vaḥtlarynda m. h.* (14:27)

⚘ Heb. מֶלֶךְ הַמָּשִׁיחַ 'King Messiah' ⇒ **hameleḫ**

**merkav** SW 'chariot'

**-laryn:** *atty tengizge paronu da čerivün da bar m.* (8:46)

**-yn:** *turdu da jerledi paro m. da birgesine aġalyqlary anyn* (8:42)

⚘ Heb. מֶרְכָּב '1. chariot, carriage'; WKar. *markav* 'two-wheeled chariot'

**mida** SW 'measure; ? character'

**-larynda:** *joḥtu avanlyq m. anyn* (30:28)

**-larynny:** *ivretejim gineḥlilerge jaḥsy m.* (3:80)

⚘ Heb. מִדָּה '1. measure; 2. character'

**mizbeaḥ** W 'altar'

*joḥtu bügün bizġa ni m. ani mizbeaḥ ani kohen tüťatüvčü otjamlar* (2:17)

**-yn:** *da tügel qarbanlarny anda čyġaryrlar m. üstüne tanalar* (3:127)

⚘ Heb. מִזְבֵּחַ 'altar'; WKar. *mizbaḥ* 'altar'

**miškan** SW 'Tabernacle'
*turġuzulup sortun m. eki keruvim arasyndan esitiredi inin Tenrinin* (18:9)
**-ny**: *turġuzup sortun Moše rabenu ol m.* (29:11)
⚘ Heb. מִשְׁכָּן '1. dwelling-place, habitation; 2. tabernacle'

**muḥtac** SW 'worried'
**-lar**: *firjat etebiz sana e H biz jarlylar m.* (2:42–43)
**-larny**: *unutmaġyn firjatlarybyla miskin m.* (3:118)
⚘ SWKar. *muḥtaclyq* 'worry' ⇒ **muḥtač**

**muḥtač** W 'worried'
**-lar**: *firjat etabiz sana H biz jarlylar m.* (2:42–43)
**-larny**: *unutmaġyn firjatlarybyla miskin m.* (3:118)
⚘ SWKar. *muḥtaclyq* 'worry' ⇒ **muḥtac**

## N

**negince** SW interr. pron. 'until when, how long'
*sen e H n. cydarsen bunu* (5:20); *n. e bijim Tenrim cyġarmassen rastlyqqa teremni menim* (5:21)
⚘ SWKar. *negince* 'as long as, until'

**nevu'a** SW 'prophecy'
**-synda**: *saġynġanyn byla bizge sertin Abrahamnyn antetken anar n. Betarimnin* (28:14)
⚘ Heb. נְבוּאָה 'prophecy'; *nevu'asy Betarimnin* 'prophecy of Betarim', a reference to the Covenant of the Pieces

**ni** W 'neither'
*ullu azizligimizd́an joḥtu bügün bizǵa n. miqdaš ani mizbeaḥ ani kohen tüt́atüvčü otjamlar* (2:17)
⚘ Pol. *ni* 'neither', Russ. *ни* id.

**nobat** SW 'flowing honey'
*n. kibik tatyjdylar erinleri anyn da solaqtaġy cyjbal kibik tatlydylar sezleri avzunun* (16:7)
⚘ Possibly related to Heb. נֹפֶת 'flowing honey, honey from the comb'

## O, ʿO

**ohel moʿed** SW 'tent of meeting'
**-ge**: *bolalmady kelme o. m. ki bulutbyla boldu toḥtamaġy qorqunclu šeḫinasynyn Tenrinin* (18:11); *bolalmady kirme o. m. alnyndan ol bulutnun* (29:13)
⚘ Heb. אֹהֶל מוֹעֵד 'tent of meeting; tabernacle of meeting'

**ol** W def. art. 'the'
*jasly hem taryqqan ʒanly tisli qajǵydan boldum men o. iḥcubun* (1:5); *birisi kibik o.*

*nekeslernin* (1:8); *byrclandym murdarlyqta o. gojlar kibik* (1:17); *ačyrġandyrdyq any saqlamajyn šertin o. kesilġan birġamizġa eki keŕatĺar* (2:34); *ajttylar ajtadoġač alnynda H-nyn osol sözlerin o. širanyn ol ušpunun* (8:13); *passim*

⸙ SWKar. *ol* dem. pron. 'that' ⇒ **bu$^{I}$, osol, osol ol, ošol, ošol ol**

**'olam haba** SW 'the World to Come'

**-da:** *ʒanlarynyz asajyslanyrlar 'o. h.* (11:5, 11:19)

**-nyn:** *da tirliklerine 'o. h. bolurlar ǯymaty üč atalarymnyn* (14:17–18)

⸙ Heb. עוֹלָם הַבָּא 'the World to Come'

**oldu** SW 'that is, in other words'

*berdi bizge qolu asyra Moše ribbimiznin o. inamly elcisinin* (20:10)

⸙ A calque of Lat. *id est* 'i.e.' or its Slavonic equivalents, cf., e.g. Pol. *to jest* id.

**oloq** SW 'that very, exactly that'

*o. sa'atny titinlenir qaḥyry da acuvu H-nyn* (30:15)

⸙ SWKar. *ol* 'that' + *oq* (intensifying (specifying) particle)

**oq** SW intensifying or specifying particle

*alajo. köpligine köre jarlyġasynnyn qabul etkin tefilesin barda jalbaruvcularnyn* (1:73); *olo. sa'atny titinlenir qaḥyry da acuvu H-nyn* (30:15); *alajo. közler körme nedi jaḥšy da nedi jaman* (3:53); *alajo. öz aruvluġun üčün* (3:58); *alajo. meni ačy ǯanly qulunnu* (3:96); *alajo. šavaġatyndan öz kleginbyla tüzetkin Cijjonnu* (3:115); *alajo. raḥmetlerinbyla qondar* (3:118); *bu dunjada alajo. elimlerinden sortun* (11:12); *alajo. ʒanlarynyz asajyslanyrlar 'olam habada* (11:19); *östürme jaš ot alajo. čyġysyn barda bitislernin* (12:39); *qulluq etivcini da basuruvcunu cerivine ol keklernin alajo. qyluvcu ezine qujma abaqlar* (22:13); *alajo. tefilasyn jyjynlarynyn barda qahallarymnyn qabul etkin* (26:32); *alajo. bujurdu ki tekkej* (29:28); *da aruv ʒan klegidi Tenrinin, alajo. tirkisi özek unnun panva istine* (29:33)

⸙ SWKar. *ol* 'that' + *oq*, *alaj* 'thus' + *oq*

**osoblive** SW 'especially'

*o. umasynyn Jisra'elnin sözlejdiler erinleri alarnyn sarnav sözleri* (12:50)

⸙ Pol. *osobliwie* '(*arch.*) especially, particularly' (SStp 5: 655) ⇒ **osovlive**

**osol** SW def. art. 'the'

*sana telmertemen o. közlerimni* (1:43); *e Tenri savaġatyn byla körtilikke cyġarġyn o. bar jaḥsy ḥabarlarny* (1:75); *ajttylar ajtadoġač alnynda H-nyn o. sözlerin ol širanyn ol ušpunun* (8:13); *bajlanġyn qaḥyr byla qarat etme o. barda qonsularymny* (4:6); *esitkenimde o. firjatynny* (4:30); *da alġyn o. Jehošuany* (9:16); *bijik orunlary istine aziz jerinin Jisra'elnin atlanġyzdyrdyn, o. uvlunnu o. jalġyzaġynny ki sivdin* (10:7–8); *passim*

⸙ SWKar. *osol* '(*dem. pron.*) that' ⇒ **bu$^{I}$, ol, osol ol, ošol, ošol ol**

**osol: osol ol** SW def. art. 'the'

*ijgende paro o. o. ulusnu qulluġundan özünün* (8:11); *basyna ol singirnin mingin da körgin o. o. jerni bijik ornundan* (9:14); *ijdi osol ol ulusnu* (19:22); *da cajsylama o. o. jerni kledi ajtmaġy byla ullu quvatly qutqaruvcu Tenrinin* (15:6)

⚘ SWKar. *osol* '(*dem. pron.*) that' + *ol* '(*dem. pron.*) that' ⇒ **bu[I], ol, osol ol, ošol, ošol ol**

**osovlive** SW 'especially'

*o. umasynyn Jisra'elnin sezlejdiler erinleri alarnyn sarnav sözleri* (12:50)

⚘ Pol. *osobliwie* '(*arch.*) especially, particularly' (SStp 5: 655) ⇒ **osoblive**

**ošol** W def. art. 'the'

*qajtarġyn H o. qajtuvumuznu* (2:48); *ešitkenimde o. firjatynny* (4:30); *ajttylar ajtadoġač alnynda Adonajnyn o. sezlerin ol širanyn ol ošpunun* (8:13)

⚘ NWKar. *ošol* '(*dem. pron.*) that' ⇒ **bu[I], ol, osol, osol ol, ošol ol**

**ošol**: **ošol ol** SW def. art. 'the'

*ijdi o. o. ulusnu* (19:22)

⚘ NWKar. *ošol* '(*dem. pron.*) that' + *ol* '(*dem. pron.*) that' ⇒ **bu[I], ol, osol, osol ol, ošol**

**ošpu** SW 'this'

*saġynylġajbiz alnynda anyn o. künde ol ündelgen Jom Teru'a byla* (7:9); *o. künde ki ol burunġu künüdü tešuva künlerinin* (7:21); *o. künde ündeledoġan Šemini 'Aceret byla* (19:13)

**-nun**: *ajttylar ajtadoġač alnynda Adonajnyn ošol sezlerin ol širanyn ol o.* (8:13)

⚘ SWKar. *uspu* 'this'

## Ö

**ökün-** NW 'to yearn'

-'**abiz**: *ö. sana tarlyġymyzdan galutta ökünǵanĺaj ačy ʒanly tullar* (2:44)

-**ǵanĺaj**: *ökünábiz sana tarlyġymyzdan galutta ö. ačy ʒanly tullar* (2:44)

⚘ SWKar. *ekin-* 'to yearn, to miss'

**ömirlik** SW 'eternal'

*ö. ḥorluqqa bolurlar jyjynlary dušmanlarymnyn* (14:16)

⚘ SWKar. *emirlik* 'eternity' ⇒ **emirlik, ömürlik, ömürlük**

**ömürlik** SW 'eternal'

*ö. tirlikke bolurlar jyjynlary dušmanlarymnyn* (14:16)

⚘ SWKar. *emirlik* 'eternity' ⇒ **emirlik, ömirlik, ömürlük**

**ömürlük** SW 'eternal'

*ö. ḥorluqqa bolurlar jyjynlary dušmanlarymnyn* (14:16); *ö. tirlik byla asajyšlatty ʒanymyzny* (19:10)

⚘ SWKar. *emirlik* 'eternity' ⇒ **emirlik, ömirlik, ömürlik**

**özge** SW *abl.* 'apart from'

*Tenriden ö. joḥtu kim ki syndyralyr ulluluġun* [*tolġunlarynyn*] (12:29)

⚘ SWKar. *ezge* 'other' ⇒ **ezge**

## P

**panv́a** SW 'a shallow cauldron; pan'

*tirkisi özek unnun p. istine da tava istine qabuldu Tenrige* (29:33)

-**da**: *keltirse tirkisin ezeknin da tavada islengen da quvurġan da p. islengen qabul etedi Tenri ʒomartlyqlar keltirgeninin* (18:35)

✤ MPol. *panwia* 'a pan, a shallow cauldron' (Linde 1811: 623, s.v. *panew*; SStp. 4: 22, s.v. *panew*).

**pasu|q** SW 'Biblical verse'

-**ġu**: *birligin da qajjamlyġyn qotarġajlar p. byla Šema' Jisra'elnin* (25:38); *qotarynyz birligin atynyn p. byla Šema' Jisra'elnin* (27:23)

✤ Heb. פָּסוּק '1. Biblical verse; 2. sentence'; SWKar. *pasuq* '1. sentence; 2. verse'

**perat** SW 'single thing'

-**larny**: *jarattyn p. da kelallarny* (13:11)

-**laryn**: *qajjamlyqta tutady p. da kelallaryn alarnyn* (25:7)

✤ Heb. פְּרָט 'single thing, detail, unit'

**pilnovat et-** SW 'to mind'

-**ivciler**: *maḥtav berme eki keret kinde bolunuz p. e.* (27:25)

✤ Pol. *pilnować* 'to mind, to take care' →← Ukr. *пильнувати* id.

**postanovtet-** SW 'to decide'

-**ti**: *ne orunda ki p. Ezra da Neḥamja ki eksilmesedi qarban da šira avazy* (6:47)

✤ Russ. *постановить* ~ (arch.) *постановити* 'to decide', Ukr. *постановити* id.

**povinnost** SW 'obligation'

-**tu**: *p. ki alar da ulanlary da ulanlary ulanlarynynda jystyrynmaġy byla qahallarynyn, šükür etkejler aziz šemine* (25:33)

✤ Russ. *повинность* 'obligation, duty'

**povynnyj** see **ceriv: povynnyj ceriv**

**protyvnyj** SW 'contrary'

-**lar**: *jaratylġan dert jesodlardan p. biri birine* (29:20)

✤ Russ. *противный* 'contrary, opposite', Ukr. *противний* id.

**pusta: pusta orun** SW 'desert'

-**larny**: *bögövretme qurġaq p. o. da östürme jaš ot* (12:39)

-**da**: *joḥtur senin kibik da veren p. o. edi qujašlary da kelegeleri da jetkirdi alarġa bar kerekni* (13:21)

✤ SWKar. *pusta jer* 'desert'

## Q

**qabul kör-** SW 'to accept'

-**gin**: *har caġyrġanymda sana e H avazymny q. k.* (1:54)

✤ SWKar. *qabul* 'acceptance', SWKar. *ker-* 'to see'

**qahal** SW 'community'

**-larymnyn:** *jistirmek ücün jyjynyn q.* (24:31); *tefilasyn jyjynlarynyn barda q. qabul etkin* (26:33)

**-laryn:** *haligine q. senin širalary byla maḥtavlarynyn, qoladylar qyblalaryn Tenrinin* (21:23)

**-larynyn:** *alar da ulanlary da ulanlary ulanlarynynda jystyrynmaġy byla q.* (25:35)

**-ym:** *vale küplegin meni da jarlyġaslanajym ki daġy q. ücün necik özüm ücün tizijmen sana jalbarmaqlarymny* (1:41)

⚘ Heb. קָהָל 'assembly, gathering; congregation, community'

**qajjam et-** SW *'to confirm'

**-kin:** *inamly Tenri sözlerinde özünnin tezce q. e. bizge naviligin Ješajanyn* (28:30)

⚘ WKar. *qajjam et-* 'to strengthten'

**qarban** W 'offering, sacrifice'

*da ki zoẖe tüvülbiz juvutma sana q. har kün* (2:53); *ne orunda ki postanovtetti Ezra da Neḥamja ki eksilmesedi q. da šira avazy* (6:48); *muna jazyqly bolġanda q. keltirsin tuvarny özü kibik tirini* (18:19); *bujurdu juvutma q. usajdoġandan ezine* (29:22); *tekkej gilejin ol keltirivcü q. alnynda bir Tenrinin jaratuvcusunun* (29:29)

**-ġa:** *muna jazyqly bolġanda qarban keltirsin* [...] *tirini da esedoġanny ki ol remezdi q. tirkisi byla aruv etme any jemese murdar etme any* (18:21–22)

**-lar:** *köteriniz jaman jecerni icinizden da otlu q. ornuna qylynyz tigel tešuvalar* (23:10)

**-larny:** *tügel q. anda čyġaryrlar mizbeaḥyn üstüne* (3:126)

**-larnyn:** *cyġarynyz icinizden jamanlyġyn jecerinin jireginiznin da ornunda debeḥasynyn q. qylynyz jaḥsy isler* (27:12)

**-lary:** *qabulluqqa bolsun bu jalbarmaq tefilam alnynda qyblalarynnyn q. ornuna tanalarnyn* (26:57)

**-larynyn:** *šükür etejik tefileleribyla erinlerimiznin erteli kečeli qozulary ornuna ʿola q.* (17:23)

**-yn:** *juvutqanda otlu q. ezinin* (29:25)

**-ynyn:** *saġyslanġaj qany q. qany kibik juvutuvcusunun* (29:24)

⚘ Heb. קָרְבָּן 'offering, sacrifice, oblation'

**qatys: qatys el** SW 'rabble, gathered mass'

*ullu tamasalyq tamasa ettiler bar ol q. e. necik kördiler qorqunclu quvatyn Tenrinin* (8:50)

⚘ Cf., *Da ol qatyš el ki ortasynda anyn küśandiĺar küśanč da qajttylar daġyn ulanlary Jisraʾelnin da ajttylar kim ašatsajdy bizġa et?* (ADub.III.73: 229 v°) and *Da ol qatys el ki ortasynda anyn kisendiler kisenc da qajttylar da jyladylar daġyn uvullary Jisraʾelnin da ajttylar kim asattyrsyjdy bizge et?* (JSul.III.01: 157 v°) 'And the gathered mass who were among them had a longing, and the children of Israel, as well, went back and cried, and they said, "Who will feed us meat?"' (Numbers 11:4); EKar. *qatyš* 'rally, crowd' (Aqtay & Jankowski 2015: 296). ⇒ **qatyš el**

**qatyš: qatyš el** SW 'rabble, gathered mass'

*ullu tamašalyq tamaša ettiler bar ol q. e. nečik kördiler qorqunčlu quvatyn Tenrinin* (8:50)

☘ EKar. *qatyš* 'rally, crowd' (Aqtay & Jankowski 2015: 296); for more information, see, **qatys el**

**qobulus-** SW 'to get lost'

**-adylar:** *q. alar da bilmejdiler jolun ornunun* (8:38)

**-qandylar:** *q. alar da bilmejdiler jolun ornunun* (8:38)

☘ SWKar. *kobulus-* 'to confuse' ⇒ **qobuluš-**

**qobuluš-** SW 'to get lost'

**-tular:** *q. alar da bilme[j]diler jolun ornunun* (8:38)

☘ SWKar. *kobulus-* 'to confuse' ⇒ **qobulus-**

**qodeš** W '1. holy; 2. sanctity'

*syjyt eťadiĺar kohenĺar kijüvčü q. upraqlar* (2:21)

**-ni:** *ajtsynlar eksittim ol q. ivimden* (10:21)

**-nin:** *qondarġyn veren bolġan miqdašynny ki edi qondarylġan qyjasyba kise kavodnun da ol ḥajot q. ki ediler navilerge körüngenler* (3:122)

☘ Heb. קֹדֶשׁ 'a holy object; holiness, sanctity' ⇒ **haqodeš, lešon haqodeš**

**qoj-** SW 'to change into; to make something be something or some kind of'

**-du:** *q. meni rast terecim qajġyly ullu satyrlyġym ornuna* (1:10); *alġyslady ulusun özünün Jisra'elni da baslaryn dušmanlarynyn q. kesilgen* (10:23); *jazyqlarym icin q. meni Tenrim qajġyly* (24:9); *vale haligine qaḥyrybyla q. meni qajġyly* (26:7)

**-dun:** *terske tersligine köre teledin neginče ki tasny kibik q. jüregin anyn* (8:56)

☘ WKar. *qoj-* '1. to lay down, to place; 2. to consider, to think'; influenced by Heb. נָתַן '1. to give; 2. to permit; 3. to deliver; 4. to put, to set; 5. to make'

**qryvda: qryvda ketir-** SW 'to suffer wrong'

**-gen:** *jasly menmen da taryqqan q. k. dusmanlarymdan* (24:4–5)

☘ Ukr. *кривда* 'harm, wrong'; SWKar. *ketir-* 'to lift, to raise'

**qynġyrlyq** SW 'fault'

*körgün endi q. čydaġanymny da sürtkün jüzlerimden jylamaq jašlarymny* (26:43)

☘ EKar. *qyŋġyrlyq* '1. fault; 2. lie; lawlessness'; SWKar. *qynġyrlyq* 'incorrectness'

## R

**rabenu** SW 'our master'

*Moše r. inamlysy ivinin* (25:21); *turġuzup sortun Moše r. ol miškanny* (29:11)

**-nu:** *inamly navini Moše r. sajladyn rast elcige* (28:14)

**-nun:** *tamaša micvalaryn Torasynyn ivrendik avzundan Moše r. inamly navisinin* (18:8); *sodlaryn Torasynyn ülüš berdi bizge qolu ašyra Moše r. inamly elčisinin* (20:10); *berdin qollary asyra Moše r. ivretivler Jisra'elge* (21:8)

☘ Heb. רַבֵּינוּ 'our rabbi'

**regalim** see **šaloš regalim**
**rešut** see **ceriv: rešut cerivi**

S

**san: sanbyla** SW 'numerously'
*s. čyġadylar bar čörüvü ol köklernin* (12:25); *čaġyrġaj azatlyq uvluna özünün ki üze qaratetti any qynġyrlyġyna köre s.* (14:12)
⁂ Kar. *san* 'number', WKar. *byla* '(*postp.*) with'
**sene** SW 'bush'
-**nin**: *jalyny byla otnun ortasyndan ol s. bilindin anar šemi byla ehjenin* (28:15)
⁂ Heb. סְנֶה 'bush'
**siviv** SW 'liking'
-**ine**: *tez qondardym da s. hadirledim orun šeḫinasyna Tenrimnin* (6:39)
⁂ SWKar. *siv-* 'to like, to love' ⇒ **süvüv**
**sizgir-** SW 'to refine'
-**megine**: *kijirdi meni s. aruv dinnin* (9:27)
⁂ SWKar. *sizgir-* 'to strain (to filter)'
**sod** SW 'secret'
-**laryn**: *turġuzdun meni küp syjyncta da kördim balquvlu s. micvalarnyn* (9:3); *s. Torasynyn ülüš berdi bizge qolu ašyra Moše rabenunun inamly elčisinin* (20:9)
⁂ Heb. סוֹד 'secret'; NWKar. *sod* 'secret'
**Sukot** SW 'Sukkot'
*qylma S.* (20:12)
-**nun**: *jedi künü ḥyǯynyn ol S. da Šemini 'Aceretnin* [*ö*]*zü* [*ö*]*züne mo'ed ündelmekbyla* (19:7); *jedi künü ḥyǯynyn ol macalarnyn da jedi künü ol S. da 'Aceret özü özüne mo'ed ündelmekbyla* (19:7)
-**ta**: *S. olturġuzdu bizni* (20:16)
⁂ Heb. סֻכּוֹת 'Sukkot'
**sun-: bujruknu sun-** SW 'to give order'
-**ġanda**: *sana maḥtav* [*berdiler*] *bar ǯanlary byla, s. osol bujruġunnu Jam Suf istine küčlü jelin byla* (8:21)
-**ġanynda**: *sana maḥtav* [*berdiler*] *bar ʒanlary byla, s. osol bujruġunnu Jam Suf istine kicli jelin byla*
⁂ Kar. sun- '1. to spread; 2. to stretch, to reach out', Kar. *bujruq* 'order'.
**süvüv** SW 'liking'
-**üne**: *tez qondardym da s. hadirledim orun šeḫinasyna Tenrimnin* (6:39)
⁂ SWKar. *siv-* 'to like, to love' ⇒ **siviv**

## Š

**šaloš regalim** W 'Three Pilgrimage Festivals'
-**de**: *ajtqan je'ud ki dağyn körünür š. r. erkegin Jerušalajimde* (6:10)
-**d́a**: *ajtqan je'ud ki dağyn körünür š[a]loš r. erkegin Jerušalajimd́a* (6:10)
-**ge**: *ajtqan je'ud ki dağyn kerinir erkegin š. r.* (6:10)
⚘ Heb. שָׁלֹשׁ רְגָלִים 'Three Pilgrimage Festivals'

**šeḫina** SW 'the divine Presence (of God)'
*alaj ajtady š. muna men turarmen ec alma avaldağylaj* (4:31); *qaruv beredi š. ajtadoġac* (9:7); *bulaj ajtady š. menmen H Tenriniz süznün* (11:7); *bulaj ajtady š. syjynynyz kelegemde* (11:26)
-**nny**: *toḥtatqyn endi e bijim qorqunčlu š.* (3:115); *ki süvgen[in]de jerinni toḥtatma š. anda süvgü* (26:42)
-**sy**: *maḥtav beriniz [...] Tenrige ol aškara boluvču š. byla tavy üstüne Sinajnyn* (7:17); *ki bu on künler on sözlerine köre anoḫinin ki ajtty aškarġanda š. anyn* (7:23); *čyqty š. Tenrinin alynlarynda alarnyn küngiz jolnu körgizmek üčün alarġa bağanasy byla bulutnun* (8:31); *haligine turarmen ulluluğumnu körgizme ajtady š. H-nyn* (11:42); *kelir š. Adonajnyn qyčqyrmaqbyla Adonaj šofar avazybyla* (14:14); *da ol juvuz dunjada toludu š. anyn* (18:6)
-**syna**: *hadirledim orun š. Tenrimnin* (6:40); *budu Tenrim da orun hadirlejim š.* (8:36)
-**synyn**: *körgizgej bizge qondarylmağyn Jerušalajimnin ki anda bolur askarmağy š.* (8:7); *bolalmady kelme ohel mo'edge ki bulutbyla boldu toḥtamağy qorqunclu š. Tenrinin* (18:12); *bolalmady k[i]rme ohel mo'edge alnyndan ol bulutnun da qorquvundan š. H-nyn* (29:13)
⚘ Heb. שְׁכִינָה 'God, the divine Presence'

**šelamim** W *pl. t.* 'peace offering'
*ki synyq ʒanly kisiden begenedi Tenri jaḥsyraq bujvolundan š. debeḥasynyn* (18:33)
-**ler**: *joḥtu galutumuzda cyġarmaq 'olalar da š.* (2:20); *baryredim Jerušalajimge cyġarma 'olalar da š. keregi* (6:29) ⇒ -**ĺar**
-**lernin**: *baryredim š[a]loš regalimde Jerušalajimge čyġarma 'olalar da š. keregi* (6:29); *da tivil semiz bujvollary š.* (29:32)
-**ĺar**: *joḥtu galutumuzda čyġarmaq 'olalar da š.* (2:20) ⇒ -**ler**
⚘ Heb. שְׁלָמִים, the pl. of Heb. שֶׁלֶם 'peace offering'

**Šemini 'Aceret** SW 'Shemini Atzeret'
*kününde Š. 'A. ündelgen mo'ednin* (17:10); *ošpu künde ündeledoġan Š. 'A. byla* (19:13); *Š. 'A. kününde ijdi ošol ol ulusnu čatyrlaryna* (19:22)
-**nin**: *jedi künü ḥyǯynyn ol Sukotnun da Š. 'A. [ö]zü [ö]züne mo'ed ündelmekbyla* (19:7)
⚘ Heb. שְׁמִינִי עֲצֶרֶת 'Shemini Atzeret (a holiday)' ⇒ **'Aceret**

**šeni** see **bajit šeni**

**ševaḥ** SW 'praise'

*š. ajtajyq anar* (22:33)

⁂ Heb. שֶׁבַח 'praise'

**šinanim** SW 'Shinannim'

*syrynda š. ündeledoğan malaḫlarnyn* (20:26)

⁂ Heb. שִׁנְאַנִּים 'the Shinannim' (a pl. of שִׁנְאָן 'angel'), i.e., a medieval epithet for angels; an order of angels according to 14th-century kabbalistic works, more precisely according to *Massekhet Azilut* and *Berit Menuchah*; see, e.g., Blau & Kohler (1901: 591)

**šira** SW 'song'

*nečik š. uḥudu Moše* (8:7); *eksilmesedi qarban da š. avazy ešittirmekke* (6:48); *š. avazy ešittirirler* (6:77); *muna š. uḥudular da anlattylar tamaša karanjalaryn ne ki qyldy* (8:14); *š. uḥujum H-ğa ki ulluluq qylma ulluluq qyldy* (8:19); *eger ajtsam š. oḥujum* (12:3); *š. qotaradylar sana bar jaratylmyšlary juvuz dunjanyn sözübyla erinlernin* (12:46); *e Tenri janġy š. ajtamen alnynda qyblalarynnyn* (12:55); *ceber š. byla maḥtav bergej kicli Tenrige* (16:30)

**-lar:** *š. byla da zemerlerbyla ešittirirler avazlaryn maḥtavlarġa* (6:11); *zemerler da š. burundaġylaj ešittirirler* (6:77); *muna š. oḥudular da anlattylar tamaša karanjalaryn ne ki qyldy* (8:14); *ceber š. byla maḥtav bergej kicli Tenrige* (16:30); *uḥujuq alnynda anyn zemerler da š.* (22:34)

**-lary:** *š. byla maḥtavlarynyn* (21:23)

**-nyn:** *ajtadoġač alnynda H-nyn osol sözlerin ol š. ol ušpunun* (8:14)

**-sy:** *julunmušlary Adonajnyn ajtyrlar š. byla maḥtavlarynyn* (13:32)

**-syn:** *anlatmaqtan š. qysqardylar sözleri bar tillernin* (12:42)

⁂ Heb. שִׁירָה 'song, hymn'

**šiva ʿamamim** SW 'seven nations'

**-nin:** *keltirdi alarny ceklerine jerinin š. ʿa.* (25:20)

⁂ Heb. שִׁבְעָה עֲמָמִים 'seven nations'

**šofar** SW '*shofar* (a musical horn)'

*byrġylarbyla da š. byla* (7:18); *š. byla tartar da baryr tavullarbyla olturuvčusu tarafynyn temannyn* (14:8); *kelir šeḫinasy Adonajnyn qyčqyrmaqbyla Adonaj š. avazybyla* (14:14)

**-ġa:** *ol künde tartylyr ullu š.* (14:24); *š. ullu avazbyla tarttyrġaj* (14:29)

⁂ Heb. שׁוֹפָר 'trumpet'

**T**

**tal** SW 'dew'

**-lary:** *begevrejdoġan t. byla özennin* (20:13)

⁂ Heb. טַל 'dew'

**tenufa** SW '(wave) offering'
-**nyn**: *töšü kibik ol t.* (3:106)
♣ Heb. תְּנוּפָה '(wave) offering'
**tere**: **tere qyl**- SW 'to judge'
-**maġyn**: *jaman islerime kere t. q. mana* (5:37)
♣ SWKar. *tere et*- 'to judge', Kar. *qyl*- 'to do'
**teruma** SW '*terumah*, priestly dues form produce'
-**nyn**: *inčigi kibik ol t.* (3:107)
♣ Heb. תְּרוּמָה '*terumah*, priestly dues form produce; contribution to be set apart for priests'
**tešuva qyl**- SW 'to do repentance'
-**yp**: *t. q. da mode bolup jazyqlarynyzġa tüzünüz tanalar ornuna tügel tefilalar* (6:69)
♣ SWKar. *tešuva* 'repentance', Kar. *qyl*- 'to do'
**tiri ʒan** SW 'living creature, animal'
-**nyn**: *joqtan jaratty jyjynlaryn bar t. ʒ.* (12:30)
-**dan**: *bujurdu juvutma qarban usajdoġandan ezine klegim ajtma t. ʒ. da esedoġandan arytmaq ücün murdarlyġyn ʒanynyn* (29:22–23)
♣ SWKar. *tiri ʒan* 'living soul' ⇒ **tiri ǯan**
**tiri ǯan** SW 'living creature, animal'
-**nyn**: *joqtan jaratty jyjynlaryn bar t. ǯ.* (12:30)
♣ SWKar. *tiri ʒan* 'living soul' ⇒ **tiri ʒan**
**tirli**: **bir tirli** SW '(*with a neg. verb or with a priv. form*) not a, none'
*inckelikleri[ne] micvalarynnyn teneselmes alarġa b. t. bahaly nerse* (3:19); *ol tabulġandy bar orunda b. t. ceksiz da qyjassyz da ol dunja toldu syjyndan anyn* (29:7)
♣ Kar. *bir* 'one', SWKar. *tirli* 'various, diverse' ⇒ **bir türlü, bir tüslü**
**türlü**: **bir türlü** SW '(*with a neg. verb*) not a, none'
*inčkelikleri[ne] micvalarynnyn tenešelmes alarġa b. t. bahaly nerse* (3:19)
♣ Kar. *bir* 'one', SWKar. *tirli* 'various, diverse' ⇒ **bir tirli, bir tüslü**
**tüslü**: **bir tüslü** SW '(*with a neg. verb*) not a, none'
*inčkeliklerine micvalarynnyn tenešelmes alarġa b. t. bahaly nerse* (3:19)
♣ Kar. *bir* 'one', SWKar. *tisli* 'various' ⇒ **bir tirli, bir türlü**

## Y

**ynʒyt**- SW 'to harm'
-**asen**: *nekbu haligine uzaq zaman galutta y. meni* (26:15)
♣ SWKar. *ynʒyrt*- 'to torment', EKar. *ynǯyt*- 'to harm, to insult' ⇒ **ynǯyt**-
**ynǯyt**- SW 'to harm'
-**asen**: *nekbu haligine uzaq zaman galutta y. meni* (26:15)
♣ SWKar. *ynʒyrt*- 'to torment', EKar. *ynǯyt*- 'to harm, to insult' ⇒ **ynʒyt**-

## Z

**zabun bol-** SW 'to be helpless, to be infirm'

**-ġan:** *jasly da z. b. boldum acuvlu da syzlavlu* (5:3)

♣ Pers. زبون *zabūn* 'infirm, helpless' (Johnson 1852: 649; Steingass 1892: 610)

**zahürmen** P 'wormwood'

*qojdular uv ašyma da z.* (4:19)

♣ Pers. زهرمار *zahr mār* '(*compound*) snake venom' (Steingass 1892: 630, 1139); SWKar. *zahirme* ~ *zahirmen* id., NWKar. *zah́urḿar* id.

**zallen-** SW 'to repent'

**-edi:** *ummasy Jisra'elnin z. alnynda Tenrinin* (24:3)

♣ Pol. *żałować* 'to regret; to sympathise'; NWKar. *želle-* ~ *žeŋĺa-* id. ⇒ **zellen-**

**zellen-** SW 'to repent'

**-edi:** *ummasy Jisra'elnin z. alnynda Tenrinin* (24:3)

♣ Pol. *żałować* 'to regret; to sympathise'; NWKar. *želle-* ~ *žeŋĺa-* id. ⇒ **zallen-**

**zaqen** SW 'elder'

*alardylar jetmis z. bet din hagadol indeledoġanlar* (22:17)

♣ Heb. זָקֵן '1. old, old man; 2. elder; 3. scholar'

**zavly** SW 'one with a discharge'

*vaj mana ki ucrandym jazyqlaryma da jyġys hem z. qatyn kibik ajrycly boldum bar azizlikten* (1:12); *ḥastalanġan da z. kibik murdar indeldim gojlardan* (24:10); *ḥastalanġan da z. qatyn kibik murdar indeldim gojlardan* (24:10)

♣ Heb. זָב '*adj.* one that has a flux (or gonorrhoea)' + *-ly* derivative suffix; SWKar. *zavlyq* 'secretion, discharge'

**zelim** SW '?'

**-ni:** *körgin ullu z.* (5:32)

♣ Perhaps related to EKar. *zalim* ~ *zalym* 'cruel; tyrant', but the meaning of the latter word does not fit in with the context.

**zellen-** SW 'to repent'

**-edi:** *ummasy Jisra'elnin z. alnynda Tenrinin* (24:3)

♣ Pol. *żałować* 'to regret; to sympathise'; NWKar. *želle-* ~ *žeŋĺa-* id. ⇒ **zallen-**

**zoḫe: zoḫe et-** SW 'to honour'

**-kejsen:** *resimlerinni üvretkin mana ki jaryqlanma jaryġybyla qyblalarynnyn z. e. meni* (3:16)

♣ Heb. זוֹכֶה 'won, deserved' (the Heb. origin of *zoḫe* is not indicated in KarRPS); SWKar. *zoḫe bol-* 'to have the honour; to deserve'

# Hebrew Abbreviations

The index below contains a list of abbreviations included in the edited manuscripts. In most cases, they were used for meanings that are also well known from non-Karaite Hebrew sources. Hence, our main source of information was the dictionaries of Buxtorf (1708 [1985]), Jastrow (1903), Stern (1926), Händler & Kahan (1938 [1967]), Ashkenazi & Yarden (1965), and Baader (1999). However, the way some abbreviations are deciphered deviates from their usual meaning indicated in the works above. For instance, the abbreviation אז̃ is usually employed to express Heb. אָבִי זְקֵנִי 'my grandfather' (see e.g. Ashkenazi & Yarden 1965: 25; Stern 1926: 11, s.v. א"ז or Baader 1999: 24, s.v. אא"ז). In the edited materials, however, we can observe that some copyists used it with reference to different persons. It is very probable therefore that this particular abbreviation tended to be used to express Heb. אֲדוֹנֵנוּ זְקֵנֵינוּ 'our older master' or אֲדֹנִי זְקֵנִי 'my aged master' (*mutatis mutandis*, the same refers to באז̃.), cf. the expression אדו' זקני and אדוני זקני used in the headings of peshat № 1 in mss. JSul.III.69 (216 v°) and JSul.III.79 (265 v°). To keep it simple, only the cantillation sign *zarqa* (˜) and (if *zarqa* was rarely used in the respective abbreviation) the *geresh* (′) is included in the list below.

א

| | |
|---|---|
| אב̃ד | אַב־בֵּית־דִּין 'president of court; chief justice' |
| אד̃ | 1. אֲדֹנִי 'my master'; 2. אֲדוֹנֵנוּ 'our master'; 3. אֲדֹנִי דוֹדִי 'my master, my uncle' |
| אדו' | 1. אֲדֹנִי 'my master'; 2. אֲדוֹנֵנוּ 'our master' |
| אד̃מוה | אֲדוֹנֵנוּ מוֹרֵנוּ הָרַב 'our master, our teacher Rabbi' |
| אה̃ | אֶת־הַהֵיכָל 'the temple' (cf. Isaiah 6:1) |
| אה̃א | אֱלֹהֵינוּ ה̃ אֶחָד 'our God, the Lord is one'; see also ה̃ |
| אח̃כ | אַחַר־כָּךְ 'afterwards, thereafter' |
| אז̃ | 1. אֲדוֹנֵנוּ זְקֵנֵינוּ 'our aged master'; 2. אֲדֹנִי זְקֵנִי 'my aged master' |
| אמ̃ו | אֲדוֹנֵנוּ מוֹרֵנוּ 'our master, our teacher' |
| אמוה̃רר | אֲדוֹנֵנוּ מוֹרֵנוּ הָרַב רַבִּי 'our master, our teacher, the Rav, Rabbi' |

ב

| | |
|---|---|
| בא̃ | בֶּאֱמֶת יִשְׁעֶךָ 'in the truth of your salvation' (cf. Psalm 69:14) |
| בא̃ד | 1. בֶּן אֲדוֹנֵנוּ 'the son of our master'; 2. בֶּן אֲדֹנִי 'the son of my master' |
| באז̃ | 1. בֶּן אֲדוֹנֵנוּ זְקֵנֵינוּ 'the son of our aged master'; 2. בֶּן אֲדֹנִי זְקֵנִי 'the son of my aged master'; see also אז̃ |
| באמ̃ | 1. בֶּן אֲדוֹנֵנוּ מוֹרֵנוּ 'the son of our master, our teacher'; 2. בֶּן אֲדֹנִי מוֹרִי 'the son of my master, my teacher' |

| | |
|---|---|
| בכ״מ | בֶּן כְּבוֹד מַעֲלַת 'the son of the honourable (*the person's name*)' |
| בכ״מע | בֶּן כְּבוֹד מְנוּחָתוֹ עֵדֶן 'the son of (*the person's name*), whose honourable repose is Eden' |
| בכמ״עד | בֶּן כְּבוֹד מְנוּחָתוֹ עֵדֶן 'the son of (*the person's name*), whose honourable repose is Eden' |
| בכמ״ער | בֶּן כְּבוֹד מְנוּחָתוֹ עֵדֶן 'the son of the Rav (*the person's name*), whose honourable repose is Eden' |
| בע״ס | בַּעַל סֵפֶר 'the author of the book (*the book's title*)' |

ג

| | |
|---|---|
| ג״כ | גַּם כֵּן 'also, too' |

ד

| | |
|---|---|
| דקה״ק | דִּקְהִלָּה קְדוֹשָׁה 'of the holy community' |
| דקק׳ | דִּקְהִלָּה קְדוֹשָׁה 'of the holy community' |

ה

| | |
|---|---|
| ה׳ | a designation of the tetragrammaton |
| ה׳ָ | a designation of the tetragrammaton |
| הד׳ | הַדַּרְשָׁן 'the preacher' |
| ה״ה | הֶחָכָם הַגָּדוֹל 'the great sage' |
| הה״ו | הֶחָכָם הַגָּדוֹל וְהַנִּכְבָּד 'the great and honourable sage' |
| ההו״ה | הֶחָכָם הַגָּדוֹל וְהַנִּכְבָּד 'the great and honourable sage' |
| הו״ה | הַמְפוֹאָר וְהֶחָשׁוּב 'the magnificent and important' |
| ה״ח | הֶחָכָם 'the wise' |
| הי״ד | הַשֵּׁם יִקֹּם דָּמוֹ 'may the Lord avenge his blood' |
| הנא״מ | הַנֶּאֱמַר 'the one chanted (*lit.* the one said)' |
| ה״ל | הַלָּשׁוֹן 'the passage' |
| הנ״ל | 1. הַנִּזְכָּר לְעֵיל 'the above-mentioned'; 2. הַנִּמְצָא לְעֵל 'found above' |
| הנק׳ | הַנִּקְרָא 'which is read' |
| הע״מ | הַטַּל עַל מְלוֹנוֹ 'dew on his lodge' (?); see also תשה״עמ |
| הק״ק | הַקְּהִלָּה הַקְּדוֹשָׁה 'the holy community' |
| הר״ר | הָרַב רַבִּי 'the Rav, Rabbi' |
| השי״ת | הַשֵּׁם יִתְבָּרֵךְ 'God, blessed be he' |

ו

| | |
|---|---|
| ואבֿד | see אבֿד (with Heb. וְ 'and'). |
| ואחֿכ | see אחֿכ (with Heb. וְ 'and'). |
| וגו' | וְגוֹמֵר 'and so forth' |
| וזײַא | see זײַא (with Heb. וְ 'and'). |
| ועטײַזש | see עטײַזש (with Heb. וְ 'and'). |
| ויעמֿש | see יעמֿש (with Heb. וְ 'and'). |
| וכו' | וְכֻלֵּה ~ וְכֻלֵּיהּ ~ וְכֻלְהוּ 'and so forth' |
| וכול' | וְכֻלֵּה ~ וְכֻלֵּיהּ ~ וְכֻלְהוּ 'and so forth' |
| ולמֿעט | see למֿעט (with Heb. וְ 'and'). |
| ונב' | see נב' (with Heb. וְ 'and'). |
| ונבֿת | see נבֿת (with Heb. וְ 'and'). |
| ונֿפ | 1. see נֿפ (with Heb. וְ 'and'); 2. וּנְשׂוּא־פָנִים 'and honourable' (cf. Isaiah 9:15) |
| ונֿצ | see נֿצ (with Heb. וְ 'and'). |
| ותֿאמ | see תֿאמ (with Heb. וְ 'and'). |
| ותֿמן | see תֿמן (with Heb. וְ 'and'). |

ז

| | |
|---|---|
| זֿיא | זְכוּתוֹ יָגֵן עָלֵינוּ אָמֵן 'may his merit protect us, Amen!' |
| זײַא | for זֿיא. |
| זֿל | זִכְרוֹנוֹ לִבְרָכָה 'may his memory be a blessing' |
| זצוֿקל | זֵכֶר צַדִּיק וְקָדוֹשׁ לִבְרָכָה 'may the memory of the righteous and holy be a blessing' |
| זצֿל | זֵכֶר צַדִּיק לִבְרָכָה 'may the memory of the righteous be a blessing' |
| זצלֿהה | זֵכֶר צַדִּיק לְחַיֵּי הָעוֹלָם הַבָּא 'may the memory of the righteous be for the life of the World to Come' |

י

| | |
|---|---|
| יעֿא | 1. יָגֵן עָלֶיהָ אֱלֹהִים 'may the Lord protect it' (precation on mentioning an inhabited place); 2. יְכוֹנְנֶהָ עֶלְיוֹן אָמֵן 'may the Lord establish it. Amen' (precation on mentioning an inhabited place) |
| יעֿי | יָגֵן עָלֶיהָ יְהוָה 'may the Lord protect it' |
| יעמֿש | יָנוּחַ עַל מִשְׁכָּבוֹ שָׁלוֹם 'may he rest in peace; may peace rest on his place of repose' |
| יצֿו | יִשְׁמְרֵהוּ צוּרוֹ וְגוֹאֲלֵנוּ 'may his Rock [i.e. the Lord, the Rock of Israel; see 2 Samuel 23:3] and our Redeemer preserve him/it' |

כ

| | |
|---|---|
| כ״ג | כֹּהֵן גָּדוֹל 'High Priest' |
| כגק״שת | a combination of כ״ג and קש״ת |
| כהר׳ | כְּבוֹד הָרַבִּי 'his honour, Rabbi' |
| כהרר׳ | כְּבוֹד הָרַב רַבִּי 'his honour, the Rav, Rabbi' |
| כמה״רר | כְּבוֹד מַעֲלַת הָרַב רַבִּי 'his honour, the Rav, Rabbi' |
| כמ״הר | כְּבוֹד מַעֲלַת הָרַבִּי 'his honour, Rabbi' |
| כמוה״רר | כְּבוֹד מַעֲלַת וְהָרַב רַבִּי 'his honour, the Rav, Rabbi' |
| כמ״ר | כְּבוֹד מוֹרֵנוּ רַבִּי 'our honourable teacher, Rabbi' |
| כמ״עד | כְּבוֹד מְנוּחָתוֹ עֵדֶן '(*the person's name*), whose honourable repose is Eden' (used after *the son of*) |
| כק״ש | כְּבוֹד קְדֻשַּׁת שֵׁם תִּפְאַרְתּוֹ 'his holy and glorious name' |
| כק״שת | כְּבוֹד קְדֻשַּׁת שֵׁם תִּפְאַרְתּוֹ 'his holy and glorious name' |
| כ״ש | כְּבוֹד שֵׁם 'his glorious name' |

ל

| | |
|---|---|
| לה״הו | see הה״ו (with Heb. לְ 'belonging to'). |
| להר״ר | see הר״ר (with Heb. לְ 'belonging to'). |
| למ״עט | לְמַעֲשִׂים טוֹבִים 'for good deeds' |
| למ״ת | see מ״ת (with Heb. לְ 'at, by'). |
| לע״נ | לְעִלּוּי נִשְׁמַת 'for the elevation of the soul [i.e., to Heaven]' |
| לפ׳ | ... לְפָרָשַׁת 'of the parashat (*the parashah's name*)' |

מ

| | |
|---|---|
| מ״אֱ | מִבַּלְעֲדֵי אֱלֹהֵינוּ 'except our God' (cf. 2 Samuel 22:32) |
| מו״ה | מוֹרֵנוּ הָרַב 'our teacher Rabbi' |
| מוה״רר | 1. מוֹרֵנוּ הָרַב רַבִּי 'our teacher, the Rav, Rabbi'; 2. מוֹרֵנוּ וְרַבֵּנוּ הָרַב רַבִּי 'our teacher and our master, the Rav, Rabbi' |
| מ״ו | מוֹרֵנוּ 'our teacher' |
| מ״י ומ״י | מַעֲשֶׂיךָ יְקָרְבוּךָ וּמַעֲשֶׂיךָ יְרַחֲקוּךָ 'you will be treated according to your own deeds' (cf. Mishnah: Eduyot 5:7) |
| מ״ת | מַתַּן תּוֹרָה 'the giving of the Law (on Mount Sinai)' |

נ

| | |
|---|---|
| נב׳ | נַפְשׁוֹ בְּגַן ~ נַפְשׁוֹ בְּעֵדֶן 'his soul is in Eden' |
| נב״ת | נַפְשׁוֹ בְּגַן תָּלִין ~ נַפְשׁוֹ בְּעֵדֶן תָּלִין 'may his soul lodge in Eden' |

| | |
|---|---|
| נ״י | נֵרוֹ יָאִיר 'may his light shine' (words of respect after mentioning a living person) |
| נע' | נִשְׁמָתוֹ עֵדֶן 'may his soul rest in Eden' |
| נ״ע | נִשְׁמָתוֹ עֵדֶן 'may his soul rest in Eden' |
| נ״פ | נִפְטָר 'deceased' |
| נ״צ | נֵס־צִיּוֹנָה 'a banner to Zion' |
| נרו' | נַטְרֵיהּ רַחֲמָנָא וּפַרְקֵיהּ 'may God protect him and save him' |

ע

| | |
|---|---|
| עט״יזש | עַל טוֹב יִזָּכֵר שְׁמוֹ 'and may his name be remembered for good' (cf. Mishnah Megillah 4:9) |
| עכ״ס | עַל־כָּל־סְבִיבָיו 'of all them who are about him' (Psalm 89:8) |
| עמ״הן | עַמּוּד הֶעָנָן 'pillar od cloud' (?) |
| עמ״ת | עַל מִצְוֹת תְּפִלִּין 'on the commandment to don phylacteries' (?) |

פ

| | |
|---|---|
| פיוטי׳ | פִּיּוּטִים *'piyyutim'* |

צ

| | |
|---|---|
| צא״נ | צוּרָה אֱנוֹשִׁית 'human form' |
| צְשָׁקְי: | צְבָאוֹת שְׁמוֹ קְדוֹשׁ יִשְׂרָאֵל '[…] of hosts is his name, the Holy One of Israel' (Isaiah 47:4) |

ק

| | |
|---|---|
| קה״ק | קְהִלָּה קְדוֹשָׁה 'holy community' |
| קי' | קְדוֹשׁ יִשְׂרָאֵל 'the Holy One of Israel' (an epithet of God) |
| קָקָק | קָדוֹשׁ קָדוֹשׁ קָדוֹשׁ 'holy, holy, holy' (cf. Isaiah 6:3) |
| קש״ת | קְדֻשַּׁת שֵׁם תִּפְאֶרֶת 'the holy and glorious name (of)' (used with כמוה״רר) |

ר

| | |
|---|---|
| ר״ל | רוֹצֶה לוֹמַר 'id est' |

## ת

| | |
|---|---|
| ת׳ | 1. תְּפִלָּה ‘prayer’; 2. תְּפִלּוֹת ‘prayers’ |
| תא̃מ | תֹּאמַר ‘you will say’ |
| תו̃בב | תִּבָּנֶה וְתִכּוֹנֵן בִּמְהֵרָה בְּיָמֵינוּ אָמֵן ‘may it be rebuilt and re-established speedily in our days’ (said on mentioning Jerusalem) |
| תמ̃ך | תְּהִי מְנוּחָתוֹ כָּבוֹד ‘his place of rest shall be glorious’ (cf. Isaiah 11:10) |
| תמ̃ן | תּוֹצִיא מִצָּרָה נַפְשִׁי ‘bring my soul out of trouble’ (cf. Psalm 143:11) |
| תנצ̃בהה | for תנצ̃בהח |
| תנצ̃בה | תְּהִי נִשְׁמָתוֹ צְרוּרָה בִּצְרוֹר הַחַיִּים ‘may his soul be bound in the bond of life’ (cf. 1 Samuel 25:29) |
| תנצ̃בהח | תְּהִי נִשְׁמָתוֹ צְרוּרָה בִּצְרוֹר הַחַיִּים ‘may his soul be bound in the bond of life’ (cf. 1 Samuel 25:29) |
| תשה̃עמ | תַּעַל שִׁכְבַת הַטַּל עַל מְלוּנוּ ‘the layer of dew came up on his lodge’ (cf. Exodus 16:13–14), cf. also הע̃מ |

# Bibliography

## Referenced Handwritten Primary Sources

**Introductory remarks:** All the manuscripts referenced in the present monograph are listed below. The *peshatim* that constitute the textual base of this book are kept among others, in three Polish private collections: in the private archives of Aleksander Dubiński (1924–2002), Józef Sulimowicz (1913–1973), and Rafał Abkowicz (1896–1992). The first component of the accession numbers assigned to the materials kept in these archives is, by the same token, a reference to the respective holding (cf. ADub., JSul., and RAbk.). The names of persons mentioned in the references below are included in the General Index. If known, the number of folios of each item is indicated; if it consists of both printed and handwritten manuscripts, the number of the printed folios is given first, followed by the number of handwritten folios, see e.g. ADub.III.61.


ADub.III.61 = A prayer book in Hebrew and South-Western Karaim. A copy of volume 1 of *Siddur* (1737) bound together with handwritten additions copied in 1850/1851 in Halych by ⇒ **Jeshua Josef Mordkowicz.** 141 + 145 folios.

ADub.III.68 = A collection of religious texts translated into North-Western Karaim (Haggadah, some fragments of the Haftarah, *zemirot*, prayers, blessings). Copied in the years 1881–1882 by ⇒ **Semjon Osipovič Chorčenko** (*Семенъ Осиповичъ Хорченко*, born 1868, died 1923) in Troki. 64 folios.

ADub.III.69 = A translation of the Book of Psalms into North-Western Karaim. Copied between 28 Oct 1928 and 29 Jun 1929 in Troki by ⇒ **Ananiasz Zajączkowski.** 194 folios.

ADub.III.73 = A translation of the Torah, the Book of Ruth, the Book of Jeremiah, Ecclesiastes, and the Book of Esther into North-Western Karaim. The Torah was copied between 25 Mar 1720 and 31 May 1720 whereas the other books were copied ca. 1720 (more precisely after 31 May 1720, before 27 Mar 1723). Copied in Kukizów by ⇒ **Simcha ben Chananel.** 385 folios.

ADub.III.78 = A prayer book in Hebrew, South-Western and North-Western Karaim. The work of several copyists created in the 18th and 19th centuries (ca. 1750 at the earliest, see folios 118 v° and 251 v°). Several manuscripts bound together. Copied in Halych and (probably) Lutsk. 625 folios.

ADub.III.82 = A translation of the Torah and fragments (Haftarah) of the books of Joshua, Judges, 1–2 Kings, Isaiah, Jeremiah, Ezekiel, Hosea, Joel, Obadiah, Micah, Habakkuk, and Zechariah into South-Western Karaim. Copied by ⇒ **Jeshua Josef Mordkowicz** most probably in Halych in the 2nd half of the 19th century. 289 folios.

ADub.III.102.08 = A fragmented collection of prayers in Hebrew and South-Western

Karaim. Copied in Halych in the second half of the 19th century and at the turn of the 20th by several copyists of unknown identity. 57 folios.

AGKŁ = *Archiwum Gminy Karaimskiej w Łucku*. The archive of the Karaim community in Lutsk containing birth, marriage, and death certificates (1869–1947). Stored in the private collection of Anna Sulimowicz-Keruth (Warsaw).

B 263 = A manuscript in Hebrew (*Bet Avraham*) written in 1662 in Troki by Abraham ben Yoshiyahu (1636–1667) with brief North-Western additions from 1671 (a *qinah* authored by ⇒ **Zarach ben Natan** in 1649). Stored in the Institute of Oriental Manuscripts of the Russian Academy of Sciences in Saint Petersburg.

B 282 = An Eastern Karaim translation of the books of Psalms, Proverbs, Job, Daniel, Ezra, and Nehemiah. Copied around the turn of the 19th century. Kept in the Institute of Oriental Manuscripts of the Russian Academy of Sciences (Saint Petersburg). 117 folios.

Evr I Bibl 143 = A translation of the books of Exodus (from Exo 21:11 on), Leviticus, and Numbers (until Num 28:15), copied in a Turkic tongue in the 15th century. Stored in the National Library of Russia in Saint Petersburg. 104 folios. Full text available online at: http://web.nli.org.il/sites/NLI/English/digitallibrary/pages/viewer.aspx?presentorid=MANUSCRIPTS&docid=PNX_MANUSCRIPTS000151708-1#|FL38639157 (accessed 8 Oct 2017).

Evr I 699 = A commentary on the precepts of the faith written by Icchak ben Abraham of Troki (commentary on Eliyahu Bashyachi's *Adderet Eliyyahu*) in Hebrew and North-Western Karaim. Stored in the National Library of Russia in Saint Petersburg. Copied by ⇒ **Mordechai ben Icchak** (perhaps ⇒ **Mordechai ben Icchak Łokszyński**) in the 17th century. 18 folios. Full text available online at: http://web.nli.org.il/sites/NLI/English/digitallibrary/pages/viewer.aspx?&presentorid=MANUSCRIPTS&docid=PNX_MANUSCRIPTS000151518-1#|FL38617465 (accessed on 1 Nov 2017).

Evr II A 1185 = A collection of *piyyutim* and other religious texts written in Hebrew (18th century). Stored in the National Library of Russia in Saint Petersburg. 13 folios. Full text: http://web.nli.org.il/sites/NLI/Hebrew/digitallibrary/pages/viewer.aspx?presentorid=MANUSCRIPTS&docid=PNX_MANUSCRIPTS000144651-1#|FL49541471 (accessed on 28 Oct 2018).

F305-08 = A collection of religious texts, primarily *piyyutim*, and the translations of some of the books of the Tanakh into Hebrew and North-Western Karaim. The work of an unknown copyist in the second half of the 19th century. Copied most likely in Poniewież or in Troki. Stored in the Wroblewski Library of the Lithuanian Academy of Sciences. 322 folios.

F305-09 = A collection of religious texts, primarily *piyyutim*, *zemirot*, and prayers in Hebrew and North-Western Karaim. It also contains a translation of the Book of Esther into North-Western Karaim. Copied by an unknown person in the second half of the 19th century. Stored in the Wroblewski Library of the Lithuanian Academy of Sciences. 57 folios.

F305-11 = A collection of religious texts for Yom Kippur in Hebrew and North-Western Karaim. It also contains a translation of the Book of Jonah and of the Haftarot into North-Western Karaim. Copied by an unknown person in 1878. Stored in the Wroblewski Library of the Lithuanian Academy of Sciences. 308 folios.

F305-41 = A collection of religious texts, primarily elegies for the Shabbats of the month Tammuz as well as songs and prayers for Yom Kippur in Hebrew and North-Western Karaim. It also contains Bible translations: the Book of Lamentations, the Book of Hosea (4:1–11:9), Ecclesiastes (1–9), the Book of Deuteronomy (31:16–32:43), and the Book of Jeremiah (5:1–5:9). It is the work of three unknown copyists: folios 1 r°–65 v° were copied most probably in the 18th century; folios 66 r°–143 v° stem from the 19th century, folio 143 vo was copied by a third person in the 19th century. Stored in the Wroblewski Library of the Lithuanian Academy of Sciences. 143 folios.

F305-49 = A 19th-century North-Western Karaim translation of the Haggadah. Copied by an unknown person. Critically edited by Jankowski (2019). 18 folios.

F305-67 = A collection of religious texts in Hebrew and North-Western Karaim, primarily *zemirot* and *piyyutim*. It also contains a translation of the Song of Songs, and the Book of Jeremiah. The work of several copyists created in the 18th and 19th centuries. Stored in the Wroblewski Library of the Lithuanian Academy of Sciences. 240 folios.

F305-220 = A collection of religious texts in South-Western Karaim. Copied in Halych in the 19th century by ⇒ **Jeshua Josef Mordkowicz.** Owned by a person called ⇒ **Rafael ben Jehoshua Grigulevič** (from Panevėžys, see 1 r°). 20 folios.

Gaster Hebrew MS 170 = An Eastern Karaim translation of some portions of the Torah (Genesis 1:1–Deuteronomy 32:51) and the Book of Lamentations (4:11–5:22). Copied in the beginning of the 19th century. 245 folios. Full text available online at: https://luna.manchester.ac.uk/luna/servlet/s/a0jk2m.

JER NLI 4101-8 = A collection of religious texts in Hebrew and North-Western Karaim. Copied in Lutsk by an unkown person. Stored in The National Library of Israel. 455 folios. Full text available online at: https://web.nli.org.il/sites/NLI/Hebrew/digitallibrary/pages/viewer.aspx?presentorid=MANUSCRIPTS&docid=PNX_MANUSCRIPTS002582472-1.

JSul.I.01a–c = A prayer book in Hebrew, South-Western and North Western Karaim. The work of a number of copyists created in the 17th–19th centuries and then bound together, among them: JSul.I.01a copied in Halych between 1685 and 1700 by ⇒ **Josef ha-Mashbir ben Shemuel ha-Rodi**, JSul.I.01b copied in Halych in the 2nd half of the 18th century by ⇒ **Mordechai ben Shemuel**, and JSul.I.01c copied in the 2nd half of the 19th century by ⇒ **Jeshua Josef Mordkowicz.** The manuscript as a whole was most likely copied in Kukizów, Halych, and Lutsk. 318 folios.

JSul.I.02 = A collection of religious songs (*zemirot*) in Hebrew, Karaim, and Polish. Copied in Lutsk in the 19th century (sometime between 1807 and 1832 with a few later additions) by ⇒ **Mordechai ben Josef of Lutsk.** 289 folios.

JSul.I.04 = A translation of the Book of Job into South-Western Karaim. Copied in Lutsk in 1814 by ⇒ **Jaakov ben Icchak Gugel.** 126 folios.

JSul.I.11 = A prayer book in Hebrew, South- and North Western Karaim. Copied in Lutsk in 1878 mostly by ⇒ **Zecharia ben Chanania Rojecki.** Ordered by ⇒ **Icchak ben Nisan ben Moshe Firkowicz** in Lutsk. Folio 52 vº includes an additional fragment copied by ⇒ **Abraham ben Nisan Icchak Firkowicz.** Folios 53 rº–55 rº copied by an unknown person. 132 folios.

JSul.I.16 = A prayer book in Hebrew, and South-Western Karaim. Copied in Halych at the turn of the 20th century by an unknown person. 456 folios.

JSul.I.17 = A collection of religious songs and prayers. The work of several copyists in Halych and (probably) Lutsk dating from the 2nd half of the 19th century. Two copyists are identified: folios 11 rº (bottom)–96 rº and 178 rº–194 vº were copied by ⇒ **Jeshua Josef Mordkowicz**; folios 171 rº–177 rº were copied by ⇒ **Shemuel ben Josef.** 285 folios.

JSul.I.19 = A prayer book in Hebrew, South-Western and North Western Karaim. Copied most likely in Lutsk at the turn of the 19th century, by several unknown persons. 225 folios.

JSul.I.37.02 = A collection of *piyyutim* in Hebrew with one additional *peshat* in South-Western Karaim. Copied in the 19th century by an unknown person, most probably in Lutsk (the paper and its shape is characteristic of Lutsk). 8 folios.

JSul.I.37.03 = A fragment of a collection of *piyyutim* in Hebrew and South-Western Karaim. Copied sometime between 1851 and 1866 in Halych by a nephew of ⇒ **Abraham ben Levi Leonowicz.** 16 folios.

JSul.I.37.05 = Fragments of a collection of *zemirot* in Hebrew and South-Western Karaim. Copied around the turn of the 19th century, very likely in Lutsk, by an unknown person. 10 folios.

JSul.I.37.06 = A fragmented collection of *zemirot* in Hebrew and South-Western Karaim. Copied around the turn of the 19th century, very probably in Lutsk, by an unknown person. 10 folios.

JSul.I.37.09 = A fragmented collection of religious songs in Hebrew and South-Western Karaim. Copied most likely in the mid-18th century by an unknown person. 10 folios.

JSul.I.37.17 = A collection of *piyyutim* in Hebrew and South-Western Karaim. Copied before 1840 in Halych by an unknown person. 6 folios.

JSul.I.38.04 = A *qinah* written in South-Western Karaim, with North-Western Karaim elements. Copied around the turn of the 19th century, very probably in Lutsk, by an unknown person. 2 folios.

JSul.I.38.06 = Fragments of a collection of *zemirot* in Hebrew and South-Western Karaim. Probably copied in the early 19th century by an unknown person. 1 folio.

JSul.I.38.09 = Fragments of a collection of prayers and *piyyutim* in Hebrew and South-Western Karaim. Copied in Halych at the turn of the 19th century most probably by an unknown person. 6 folios.

JSul.I.38.11 = A fragmented collection of religious songs in Hebrew and South-Western Karaim. Copied between 1738 and 1744 by an unknown person. 2 folios.

JSul.I.38.21 = A *qinah* written in Hebrew and South-Western Karaim. Copied in 1807, most likely in Lutsk, by an unknown person. 2 folios.

JSul.I.45 = A payer book in Hebrew and South-Western Karaim. A copy of volume 1 of *Siddur* (1528/1529) bound together with handwritten additions copied in Halych in the 1st half of the 19th century (after ca. 1825) by ⇒ **Jeshua Josef Mordkowicz.** 103 + 153 folios.

JSul.I.46 = A prayer book in Hebrew and South-Western Karaim. A copy of volume 4 of *Siddur* (1528/1529) bound together with handwritten additions copied in Halych in the 1st half of the 19th century (after ca. 1825) by ⇒ **Jeshua Josef Mordkowicz.** 147 + 111 folios.

JSul.I.49.48 = A translation of one *piyyut* into North-Western Karaim. Copied in Vilnius after 1928 by ⇒ **Eliezer Josef ben Josef Łobanos** (born 1878, died 1947). 1 folio.

JSul.I.50.06 = A translation of the Book of Esther into South-Western Karaim along with a collection of *piyyutim* into both Hebrew and South-Western Karaim. Copied ca. 1815 in Lutsk by an unknown copyist. 36 folios.

JSul.I.53.12 = An elegy of ⇒ **Zarach ben Natan of Troki** in Hebrew and its Karaim translation. Copied in Halych in the 19th century by an unknown copyist. 2 folios.

JSul.I.53.13 = A fragment of a prayer book in Hebrew and South-Western Karaim. A copy of volume 1 of *Siddur* (1737) bound together with handwritten additions. What remained from this item is page נט of the printed *siddur* and 10 folios of handwritten text copied in the mid-18th century (probably ca. 1762) by an unknown person, most probably in Halych (from where this item was brought to Poland in 1964). 1 + 10 folios.

JSul.I.54.03 = A collection of *piyyutim* in Hebrew and South-Western Karaim. Copied at the turn of the 19th century by an unknown person, most probably in Halych. 5 folios.

JSul.I.54.09 = A South-Western Karaim *peshat* of a Hebrew *piyyut*. Copied in the mid-19th century in Halych by ⇒ **Jeshua Josef Mordkowicz.** 1 folio.

JSul.I.54.12 = Two South-Western Karaim *peshatim* of Hebrew *piyyutim*. Copied in the early 19th century in Halych by an unknown person. 3 folios.

JSul.I.54.15 = A South-Western Karaim *peshat* of a Hebrew *piyyut*. Copied at the turn of the 20th century by an unknown person, most probably in Lutsk. 2 folios.

JSul.II.02 = A prayer book in Hebrew from the turn of the 18th century. Copied by an unknown person. 53 folios.

JSul.III.01 = A South-Western Karaim translation of the Torah and Haftarot. Copied in Halych in the mid-19th century by ⇒ **Jeshua Josef Mordkowicz.** 298 folios.

JSul.III.02 = An Eastern Karaim translation of the Former Prophets, the books of Ruth, Esther, Proverbs (the latter has survived in fragments). Copied before 1687 (but after 1648). 244 folios.

JSul.III.03 = A prayer book in Hebrew and South-Western Karaim. A copy of volume 1 of *Siddur* (1737) bound together with handwritten additions copied in Halych shortly after 1805 by an unknown person. 122 + 120 folios.

JSul.III.05 = A prayer book in Hebrew and North-Western Karaim. Copied by unknown persons in Kukizów in the 2nd half of the 18th century. 655 folios.

JSul.III.07 = A prayer book in Hebrew and South-Western Karaim. A copy of volume 1 of *Siddur* (1737) bound together with handwritten additions copied in Halych in the 2nd half of the 19th century by ⇒ **Jeshua Josef Mordkowicz** (except 1 folio which was copied by an unknown person). 209 + 125 folios.

JSul.III.30 = A prayer book in Hebrew and South-Western Karaim. A copy of volume 2 of *Siddur* (1836) bound together with handwritten additions copied in Halych in the mid-19th century by ⇒ **Jeshua Josef Mordkowicz.** 178 + 6 folios.

JSul.III.63 = A prayer book in Hebrew and South-Western Karaim. A copy of volume 1 of *Siddur* (1737) bound together with handwritten additions copied ca. 1788 (1797 the latest) in Halych by ⇒ **Jeshua ben Mordechai Mordkowicz.** 169 + 39 folios.

JSul.III.64 = A prayer book in Hebrew and South-Western Karaim. Copies of volumes 2 and 3 of *Siddur* (1737) bound together with handwritten additions written between the 1st half of the 19th century and 1938 in Halych by one of the brothers of ⇒ **Jeshua Josef Mordkowicz** (folios 1 r°–17 v°, 26 r°–31 v°) and by ⇒ **Abraham ben Icchak Josef Leonowicz.** 168 pages + 56 folios + 31 folios.

JSul.III.65 = 18th-century handwritten additions in Hebrew and South-Western Karaim bound together with volume 4 of *Siddur* (1737). The folio קכ verso contains an annotation with the date 10 Tevet 5553 A.M., i.e. 25 December 1792. Copied in Halych. It contains various religious works and a South-Western translation of the Book of Esther. 214 + 22 folios.

JSul.III.66 = A prayer book in Hebrew and South-Western Karaim. A copy of volume 3 of *Siddur* (1737) bound together with handwritten additions copied at the turn of the 19th century in Halych by two unknown copyists. 106 + 188 folios.

JSul.III.67 = A prayer book in Hebrew and South-Western Karaim. Copied after ca. 1840 and before 1851 in Halych by an unknown copyist (perhaps ⇒ **Josef ben Icchak Szulimowicz**). 271 folios.

JSul.III.69 = A prayer book in Hebrew and South-Western Karaim. Copied ca. 1851 (1866 at the latest) in Halych by ⇒ **Jeshua Josef Mordkowicz** (except some Hebrew fragments which were copied by an unknown person). 779 folios.

JSul.III.72 = A prayer book in Hebrew and South-Western Karaim. Copied in the 1st half of the 19th century (before 1851) in Halych by ⇒ **Jeshua Josef Mordkowicz.** 261 folios.

JSul.III.73 = A prayer book in Hebrew and South-Western Karaim. A copy of volume 2 of *Siddur* (1737) bound together with handwritten additions copied in the mid-19th century in Halych by ⇒ **Jeshua Josef Mordkowicz.** 114 + 140 folios.

JSul.III.74 = A fragment of a prayer book in Hebrew and South-Western Karaim. A copy of volume 2 of *Siddur* (1804) bound together with handwritten additions copied in the 19th century by ⇒ **Jeshua Josef Mordkowicz.** 22 + 99 folios.

JSul.III.76 = A prayer book in Hebrew and South-Western Karaim. Copied in the 2nd half of the 19th century in Halych by ⇒ **Jeshua Josef Mordkowicz.** 244 folios.

JSul.III.77 = A prayer book in Hebrew and South-Western Karaim. Copied between 1856 and 1866 in Halych by ⇒ **Jeshua Josef Mordkowicz.** 336 folios.

JSul.III.79 = A prayer book in Hebrew and South-Western Karaim. Copied ca. 1851 (1866 at the latest) in Halych by ⇒ **Jeshua Josef Mordkowicz.** 391 folios.

JSul.VI.12.01 = A collection of *zemirot* in North-Western Karaim. Copied in the 20th century by an unknown person. 6 folios.

JSul.VII.22.02.13 = One South-Western Karaim *peshat* of a *piyyut*. Copied in the 1st half of the 19th century by an unknown person. The place where this manuscript was created is unknown. 1 folio.

MNém.I.01 = A private letter in Polish sent by Aleksander Mardkowicz (1875–1944) to prof. Tadeusz Kowalski (1889–1948). Sent 5 June 1930 from Lutsk. Stored in Kraków in the private archive of Michał Németh. 2 folios.

JSul.VII.22.22.03 = A private letter written in South-Western Karaim and sent by ⇒ **Mordechai ben Icchak Bezikowicz** to ⇒ **Shemuel ben Icchak.** Sent 16 Sept 1904 from Odessa. Edited in Németh (2011b) under accession number $3^{(78)}$. 1 folio.

RAbk.IV.03 = A prayer book and a collection of folk literautre in Hebrew and North-Western Karaim. Copied at the beginning of the 19th century in Troki by three copyists, among them ⇒ **Chanania ben Josef Kobecki** (born ca. 1783) (folios 1 r°–144 v° (except of folio 11), 166 r°–194 v°), ⇒ **Mordechai ben Josef** (folios 145 r°–165 v°, folios 195 r°–379 r°). 379 folios.

RAbk.IV.04 = An interpretation of a *piyyut* in North-Western Karaim. Kopied in 1914 by ⇒ **Icchak Boaz Firkowicz.** 2 folios.

RAbk.IV.15 = A prayer book in Hebrew and North-Western Karaim. The work of many copyists (one of them is identified: ⇒ **Chanania Abraham ben David Abkowicz,** born 1814 or 1817, died 1876, hazzan in Troki in 1844–1876) bound together. Copied in the 18th century and in the 1st half of the 19th century. The place where it was created is unknown. 183 folios.

TKow.01 = A translation of the Torah into North-Western Karaim. A partially-vocalised manuscript copied by Simcha ben Chananel, the copyist of ADub.III.73. It was finished on 7 December 1722 A.D. Kept in Kraków in the private archive of the inheritors of the late ⇒ **Tadeusz Kowalski**'s (1889–1948) private archive. Mistakenly described by Kowalski (1929: 289) and ⇒ **Ananiasz Zajączkowski** (1939b: 94) as a manuscript created in 1723 in Derazhne. The place of its creation was misinterpreted by Kowalski on the basis of the fact that Simcha referred to himself in an annotation on folio 2 v° as "Simcha the son of Chananel of Derażne" (it is the copyist's father who was “of Derazhne”, not the copyist). The whereabouts of this manuscript were unknown until 15 November 2019 when it was re-discovered by the present author and Anna Sulimowicz-Keruth. 350 folios.

### Referenced Printed Primary Sources


Abkowicz, Aleksander. 1926. Kyna. Aziź sahyncyna abajły katynymnyn.—*Myśl Karaimska* 1(3): 22.

Abrahamowicz, Zecharja. 1931. Tachanun ułłu king′e.—*Karaj Awazy* 2: 28.

Bizikowicz, Jehuda [= יהודה ביזיקוויץ] & Firkowicz, Icchak Boaz [= יצחק־בעז פירקוויץ] (ed.). 1909. תהלות ישראל. תוספות לתפילות הקראים. *Tihilot Israel. Литургическія пѣснопѣнія караимовъ*. Berdičev" [ברדיטשוב].

Dubiński, Simcha (ed.). 1895. צקון לחש: איזה סליחות ווידוים וגם קינות לשבתות תמוז מתרגמים בשפת קדר. *Чакун лахаш, т.е. Излияние мольбы*. Vilnius [*non vidi*].

Firkovičius, Mykolas (ed.). 1993. *Karaj koltchalary. Karaimų maldos*. Vilnius.

Firkovičius, Mykolas (ed.). 1998. *Karaj dińliliarniń jalbarmach jergialiari. 1 bitik. Ochumach üčiuń kieniesada*. Vilnius.

Firkovičius, Mykolas (ed.). 1999. *Karaj dińliliarniń jalbarmach jergialiari. 2 bitik. Ochumach üčiuń adieť vahdalarynda*. Vilnius.

Firkowicz, Szymon [= pen name *Szafir*]. 1931. Psalm XXIII.—*Karaj Awazy* 1: 17.

Firkowicz, Szymon (ed.). 1935. *Kołtchałar. Krótkie modlitwy karaimskie*. Wilno.

Leonowicz, Abraham [= Abraham b. Levi Leonowicz]. 1930–1931. Ačy kyna avur syjyt arttyrajym.—*Myśl Karaimska* 2(3–4): 14–16 [published in: Kowalski, Tadeusz (1930–1931)].

Leonowicz, Josef. 1936a. Kynasy Ribbi Szałomnun Zacharjasiewicznin.—*Karaj Awazy* 10: 4 [published in: Zarachowicz (1930)].

Leonowicz, Josef. 1936b. Kynasy Ribbi Awrahamnyn Leonowicznin oł Szofetnin.—*Karaj Awazy* 10: 4–5 [published in: Zarachowicz (1930)].

Leonowicz, Simha. 1936. Kynasy Ribbi Jeszua Josef Mordkowicznin.—*Karaj Awazy* 10: 5–6 [published in: Zarachowicz (1930)].

Łobanos, Josief. 1927. Kyna.—*Sahyszymyz* 1: 4.

Łobanos, Josief. 1930–1931. Kyna jarych da ałhyszły sahynczyna Achiezer Zajączkowskiniń oł manhygnyn.—*Myśl Karaimska* 2(3–4): 57–58.

Malecki, Pinchas ben Aharon [= פנחס בן אהרן מאליצכי] (ed.). 1890. רָנֵּי פַלֵּט. *Рунне Паллеть т.е. Пѣсни о спасеніи души*. Vilnius.

Malecki, Pinchas ben Aharon [= פנחס בן אהרן מאליצכי] (transl.). 1900. סדר הלל הקטן כמנהג בני מקרא קדש. *Седеръ галлель Гаккатанъ. Славословіе на пасху по обряду караимовъ*. Vilnius.

Mardkowicz, Aleksander (ed.). 1930. *Zemerłer* (*Karaj sezinde*). Łuck.

Mardkowicz, Aleksander. 1932a. Kart sifcekłer. Eki zemeri ribbi Josefnin uwłunun Jeszuanyn.—*Karaj Awazy* 2(4): 18–21.

Mardkowicz, Aleksander. 1932b. Mosze Derje. Sahyncyna ułłu jircynyn.—*Karaj Awazy* 3(5): 18–22.

Mardkowicz, Aleksander (ed.). 1933a. Kyna.—*Karaj Awazy* 6: 11–12.

Mardkowicz, Aleksander. 1936. Kart sifcekłer. Miśkin dzan. Tizidi ribbi Josef uwłu Jeszuanyn Deraźnadan.—*Karaj Awazy* 10: 6–7.

Mickiewicz, Zacharjasz [= זכריה מיצכיוויץ] & Rojecki, Elijahu [= אליהו רואצכי] (transl.). 1888. ספר חמשה חומשי תורה מתורגם ללשון קדרי לבני מקרא קודש המורגלת בפי קהלות הקראים הדרים בגלילות רוסיא. *Хамиша хумше тора, т. е., пятикнижіе ветхаго завѣта, переведенное на караимское нарѣчіе посредствомъ Захарія Михайлова Мицкевича и Илья Исаева Роецкаго*. Vilnius.

*Siddur* (1528/1529) = Cornelius Adelkind (publisher). 1528/1529. סדר התפלות למנהג קהל הקראים. Vol. 1–4. Venice. [See Walfish (2011: 452; poz. 5324)].

*Siddur* (1734) = Afedah Jeraqa, Shabetaj Jeraqa, Menaḥem Tzadik Jerušalmi [= שבתי ירקא, אפדה ירקא, מנחם צדיק ירושלמי] (publishers). 1737. סדר ההפטרות ושאר הדברים המקבצים. Vol. 1–2. Kale. [See Walfish (2011: 460; poz. 5380)].

*Siddur* (1737) = Afedah Jeraqa, Shabetaj Jeraqa [= אפדה ירקא, שבתי ירקא] (publishers). 1737–1742. סדר התפלות למנהג קהלות הקראים. Vol. 1–4. Kale. [See Walfish (2011: 452; poz. 5325)].

*Siddur* (1804) = סדורי התפלות לכל השנה כפי מנהג קהלות הקראים הדרים בגלילות קירים וקוסטנטינא ופולין וליטא. Vol. 1–3. Kale. [See Walfish (2011: 453; poz. 5326)].

*Siddur* (1836) = Mordechai Tiriškan [= מרדכי טירישקן, Мордхай Тиришкан] (publisher). 1836. סדור התפלות כמנהג הקראים. *Молитвенний книги по обряду караимов*. Vol. 1–4. Evpatorija. [See Walfish (2011: 453; poz. 5327)].

*Siddur* (1890–1892) = Jaakov Šišman [= יעקב (בן יוסף) שישמן, Яков (Иосифович) Шишман] (publisher). 1890–1892. סדור התפלות כמנהג הקראים. *Сидуръ гатефилотъ кемингагъ гакараимъ, т. е. Молитвенная Книга по обряду караимовъ*. Vol. 1–4. Vilna. [See Walfish (2011: 454; poz. 5331)].

Szulimowicz, Nowach & Zarachowicz, Zarach (ed.). 1927. ירמיה. [Halych].

## Referenced Scholarly Literature

Abrahamowicz, Zygmunt. 2001. Dzieje Karaimów w Haliczu.—*Przegląd Orientalistyczny* 198–199: 3–16 [Prepared for print by Stefan Gąsiorowski].

Akhiezer, Golda. 2003. The history of the Crimean Karaites during the sixteenth to eighteenth centuries.—Polliack, Meira (ed.). *Karaite Judaism. A guide to its history and literary sources*. Leiden, Boston, 729–757.

Akhiezer Golda & Markon Isaak Dov Ber. 2007. Joseph ben Samuel ben Isaac ha-

Mashbir.—Skolnik, Fred & Berenbaum, Michael (eds.). *Encyclopaedia Judaica. Second Edition*. Vol. 11. Detroit, New York, San Francisco, New Haven (Connecticut), Waterville (Maine), London: 425.

Altbauer, Moshé. 1979–1980. O tendencjach dehebraizacji leksyki karaimskiej i ich wynikach w Słowniku karaimsko-rosyjsko-polskim.—Ševčenko, Ihor & Sysyn, Frank E. (eds.). *Eucharosterion: Essays presented to Omeljan Pritsak on his sixtieth birthday by his colleagues and students* (= *Harvard Ukrainian Studies* 3/4, part 1). Cambridge [Massachusetts, USA]: 51–60.

Aqtay, Gülayhan. 2009. *Eliyahu ben Yosef Qılcı's anthology of Crimean Karaim and Turkish literature. Critical edition with introduction, indexes and facsimile*. (= *Yıldız Dil ve Edebiyat Dizisi* 8). Vol. 1–2. İstanbul.

Aqtay, Gulayhan & Jankowski, Henryk. 2015. *A Crimean Karaim–English dictionary*. (= *Prace Językoznawcze* 2). Poznań.

Ashkenazi Shmuel, Yarden Dov [= שמואל אשכנזי, דוב ירדן]. 1965. אוצר ראשי תיבות בלשון ובספרות מימי קדם ועד ימינו. *Ozar Rashe Tevot. Thesaurus of Hebrew abbreviations*. Jerusalem.

Baader, Fritz Henning. 1999. *Kurzwort- und Abkürzungslexikon. Hebräisch-Deutsch und Hebräisch-Englisch*. Schömberg.

Bałaban, Majer. 1909. *Spis Żydów i Karaitów ziemi Halickiej i powiatów Trembowelskiego i Kołomyjskiego w r. 1765*. Kraków.

Bałaban, Majer. 1927. *Studja historyczne*. Warszawa.

Barton, George A. 1906. Temple, the Second.—Singer, Isidore et al. (eds.). *The Jewish Encyclopedia*. Vol. 12. New York, London: 97–98.

Baskakov, Nikolaj Aleksandrovič & Zajączkowski, Ananiasz & Šapšal, Seraja Markovič (eds.). 1974. *Karaimsko-russko-pol'skij slovar'. Słownik karaimsko-rosyjsko-polski*. Moskva.

van Bekkum, Wouter Jacques. 1998. *Hebrew Poetry from Late Antiquity. Liturgical Poems of Yehudah. Critical Edition with Introduction and Commentary*. (= *Ancient Judaism and Early Christianity* 43). Leiden.

Berta, Árpád. 1996. *Deverbale Wortbildung im Mittelkiptschakisch-Türkischen*. (= *Turcologica* 24). Wiesbaden.

Berta, Árpád. 1998. Middle Kipchak.—Johanson, Lars & Csató, Éva Ágnes (eds.). *The Turkic languages*. New York.

Bilodid, Ivan Kostjantynovyč et al. (eds.). (1970–1980). *Slovnyk ukrajins'koji movy*. Vol. 1–11. Kyjiv.

Birnbaum, Salomo Asher. 1954–1957. *The Hebrew scripts. Part one: The text. Part two: The plates*. London.

Birnbaum, Salomo Asher & Diringer, David & Federbush, Zvi Hermann & Maimon, Jacob & Naveh, Joseph & Shunary, Jonathan. 2007. Alphabet, Hebrew.—Berenbaum, Michael & Skolnik, Fred (eds.). *Encyclopaedia Judaica*. Vol. 1 (2nd ed.). Detroit: 689–728.

Blau, Ludwig & Kohler, Kaufmann. 1901. Angelology.—Singer, Isidore et al. (eds.). *The Jewish Encyclopedia*. Vol. 1. New York, London: 583–597.

Briquet, Charles-Moïse. 1907. *Les filigranes. Dictionnaire historique des marques de papier dès leur apparition vers 1282 jusqu'en 1600 avec 39 figures dans le texte et 16,112 fac-similés de filigranes*. Vol. 1–4. Genève.

Buxtorf, Johannes. 1708 [1985]. *De abbreviaturis Hebraicis liber novus et copiosus. Cui accesserunt operis talmudici brevis recensio, eiusdemque librorum & capitum index: item Bibliotheca Rabbinica ordine alphabetico disposita, cum adpendice eidem inserta*. Herborn [reprinted by Georg Olms Verlag: Hildesheim, Zürich, New York. 1985].

Cegiołka [= Smętek], Dorota. 2019. A South-Western Karaim Bible Translation of the Book of Genesis in Manuscript no. JSul.III.01.—*Almanach Karaimski* 8: 9–33.

Csató, Éva Ágnes. 1995. Zur Silbenharmonie des Nordwest-Karaimischen.—*Acta Orientalia Academiae Scientiarum Hungaricae* 48.3: 329–337.

Csató, Éva Ágnes. 1999. Syllabic harmony in Turkic: The evidence of code-copying.—Brendemoen, Bernt & Lanza Elizabeth & Ryen, Else (eds.). *Language encounters across time and space. Studies in language contact*. Oslo: 341–352.

Csató, Éva Ágens. 2011. A typological coincidence: Word order properties in Trakai Karaim biblical translations.—Erguvanlı-Taylan, Eser & Rona, Bengisu (eds.). *Puzzles of language. Essays in honour of Karl Zimmer* (= *Turcologica* 86). Wiesbaden: 169–186.

Csató, Éva Ágens. 2012. Lithuanian Karaim.—*Journal of Engangered Languages* 1 (winter): 33–45.

Csató, Éva Ágens & Johanson, Lars. 2016. Some phonological and morphological features of spoken Halich Karaim.—Zimonyi, István & Karatay, Osman (eds.): *Central Eurasia in the Middle Ages. Studies in honour of Peter B. Golden*. Wiesbaden: 57–68.

Černych, Pavel Jakovlevič. 1999 [1993]. *Istoriko-ètimologičeskij slovaŕ sovremennogo russkogo jazyka*. Vol. 1–4. 3rd edition. Moskva.

Danon, M. Abraham. 1921. Fragments Turcs de la Bible et des Deutérocanoniques.—*Journal Asiatique* 12: 97–122.

Deutsch, Gotthard. 1905. Piyyuṭ.—Singer, Isidore et al. (eds.). *The Jewish Encyclopedia*. Vol. 10. New York, London: 65–68.

Drimba, Vladimir. 2000. *Codex Comanicus. Édition diplomatique avec fac-similés*. București.

Drüll, Dagmar. 1980, *Der Codex Cumanicus. Entstehung und Bedeutung* (= *Geschichte und Gesellschaft. Bochumer Historische Studien* 23). 2nd edition. Weinsberg.

Dubiński, Aleksander. 1959. Początki zainteresowań językiem i literaturą karaimską w nauce europejskiej do końca XIX wieku.—*Przegląd Orientalistyczny* 2(30): 135–144 [Reprinted in: Dubiński, Aleksander. 1994. *Caraimica. Prace karaimoznawcze*. (Edited by Tadeusz Majda). Warszawa: 63–72].

Dubiński, Aleksander. 1965a. Die magisch-weissagerische Terminologie im Karaimischen.—*Ural-altaische Jahrbücher* 36: 311–325.

Dubiński, Aleksander. 1965b. Terminy wróżbiarskie w karaimskich przekładach Biblii.—*Euhemer* 6.49: 12–23.

Dubiński, Aleksander. 1978. Phonetische Merkmale des Łuck-Halicz Dialektes der karaimischen Sprache.—*Rocznik Orientalistyczny* 39.2: 33–44.

Dubiński, Aleksander. 1993. Lokalizacja języka karaimskiego w świetle jego rozwoju historycznego.—*Przegląd Orientalistyczny* 165–166: 37–42 [Reprinted in: Dubiński, Aleksander. 1994. *Caraimica. Prace karaimoznawcze.* (Edited by Tadeusz Majda). Warszawa: 113–120].

Džanmavov, Jusip Džangišievič. 1967. *Deepričastija v kumykskom literaturnom jazyke (sravnitelno s drugimi tjurkskimi jazykami)*. Moskva.

Eljaševič, Vjačeslav Alekseevič. 2016. "Pinkas Medinat Kefe": Novyj istočnik po istorii karaimov Krymskogo chanstva rannego novogo vremeni.—*Vostok* 5: 42–52.

Engel, Edna. 2013. Script, history of development.—Khan, Geoffrey et al. (eds.). *Encyclopedia of Hebrew language and linguistics*. Vol. 3. Leiden, Boston: 485–502.

ÈSTJa see Sevortjan, Èrvand Vladimirovič (ed.) (1974).

Fahn, Reuven. 1929. ספר הקראים. כתבי ראובן פאהן. Lwów [*non vidi*].

Firkovičius, Mykolas. 1994. *David Bijnin machtav čozmachlary. Psalmės*. Vilnius.

Firkovičius, Mykolas. 2000. *Šelomonun mašallary. Süleyman'ın Meselleri. Patarlių knyga (Proverbia)*. (= *Türk Dil Kurumu Yayınları* 771). Ankara.

Fleischer, Ezra. 2007. Piyyut.—Skolnik, Fred & Berenbaum, Michael (eds.). *Encyclopaedia Judaica. Second Edition*. Vol. 16. Detroit, New York, San Francisco, New Haven (Connecticut), Waterville (Maine), London: 192–195.

Frank, Daniel. 2004. *Search scripture well: Karaite Exegetes and the Origins of the Jewish Bible Commentary in the Islamic East*. (= *Études sur le Judaïsme Médiéval* 29). Leiden, Boston.

Friedman, Richard Elliott. 2003. *The Bible with sources revealed. A new view into the Five Books of Moses*. New York.

Fürst, Julius. 1896. *Geschichte des Karäerthums von 1575 bis 1865 der gewöhnlichen Zeitrechnung. Die letzten vier Abschnitte. Eine kurze Darstellung seiner Entwicklung, Lehre und Literatur*. Leipzig.

von Gabain, Annemarie. 1959. Die Sprache des Codex Cumanicus.—Deny, Jean & Grønbech, Kaare & Scheel, Helmuth & Togan, Zeki Velidi (eds.). *Philologiae Turcicae Fundamenta*. Vol. 1. Wiesbaden: 46–73.

Garkavec, Aleksandr. 2002. *Kypčakskoe piśmennoe nasledie. Tom 1. Katalog i teksty pamjatnikov armjanskim piśmom*. Almaty.

Gąsiorowski, Stefan. 2008. *Karaimi w Koronie i na Litwie w XV–XVIII wieku*. Kraków, Budapest.

Gintsburg, Iona I. 2003. *Catalog of Jewish manuscripts in the Institute of Oriental Studies of the Russian Academy of Sciences. Memorial edition*. New York.

Ginzberg, Louis. 1928. *The legends of the Jews*. Vol. 6. Philadelphia.

Grishchenko, Aleksander. 2017. Personal communiaction: an e-mail sent on 29 Apr 2017.

Grishchenko, Aleksander. 2018. *The edited Slavonic-Russian Pentateuch from the fifteenth century: The preliminary results of the linguistic and textological study*. Moscow.

Grønbech, Kaare. 1942. *Komanisches Wörterbuch. Türkischer Wortindex zu Codex Cumanicus*. København.

Grzegorzewski, Jan. 1903. Ein türk-tatarischer Dialekt in Galizien. Vokalharmonie in den entlehnten Wörtern der karaitischen Sprache in Halicz. (Mit Einleitung, Texten und Erklärungen zu den Texten).—*Sitzungsberichte der kais*[*erlichen*] *Akademie der Wissenschaften in Wien. Philosophisch-historische Klasse* 146: 1–80.

Grzegorzewski, Jan. 1916–1918. Caraimica. Język Łach-Karaitów.—*Rocznik Oryentalistyczny* 1/2: 252–296.

Hamp, Eric P. 1976. Palatalization and harmony in Gagauz and Karaite.—Heissig, Walther & Krueger, John Richard & Oinas Felix J. & Schütz, Edmond. (eds.). *Tractata altaica Denis Sinor sexagenario optime de rebus altaicis merito dedicata*. Wiesbaden: 211–213.

Harkavy, Albert & Strack, Hermann Leberecht. 1875. *Catalog der hebräischen Bibelhandschriften der Kaiserlichen Öffentlichen Bibliothek in St. Petersburg. Erster und zweiter Theil*. St. Petersburg, Leipzig.

Harviainen, Tapani. 1991. *De Karaitis Lithuaniae*: Transcriptions of recited biblical texts, description of the pronunciation tradition, and the peculiarities of shewa.—Kronholm, Tryggve (ed.). *Festskrift till Gösta Vitestam*. (= *Orientalia Suecana* 38–39). Stockholm, Odense: 36–44.

Harviainen, Tapani. 1992. The Karaites of Lithuania at the present time and the pronunciation of Hebrew among them: A preliminary survey.—Dotan, Aron (ed.). *Proceedings of the Ninth International Congress of the International Organization for Masoretic Studies 1989*. (= *Masoretic Studies* 7). Atlanta: 53–69.

Harviainen, Tapani. 1997. Three Hebrew primers, the pronunciation of Hebrew among the Karaims in the Crimea, and shewa.—Wardini, Elie (ed.). *Built on solid rock. Studies in Honour of Professor Ebbe Egede Knudsen on the occasion of his 65th birthday April 11th 1997*. Oslo: 102–114.

Harviainen, Tapani. 2013. Karaite Pronunciation Traditions: Modern.—Khan, Geoffrey et al. (eds.). *Encyclopedia of Hebrew Language and Linguistics*. Vol. 2. Leiden, Boston: 453–457.

Harviainen, Tapani & Hopeavuori, Keijo & Nieminen, Kai. 1998. *Rannalla päärynäpuu. Liettuan karaiimien runoutta*. Helsinki.

Händler, George H. & Kahan, Israel Issar. 1938 [1967]. *Lexikon der Abbreviaturen. Bearbeitet und mit einem Verzeichnis der Mischna-Abschnitte von J. Kahan*. 2nd edition (reprographic copy). Hildesheim [Göttingen]. [A supplement to: Dalman, Gustaf H. 1967 [1938]. *Aramäisch-neuhebräisches Handwörterbuch zu Targum, Talmud und Midrasch*. Hildesheim [Göttingen]].

Henderson, Ebenezer. 1826. *Biblical researches and travels in Russia; including a tour in the Crimea and the Passage of the Caucasus: With observations on the state of the Rabbinical and Karaite Jews, and the Mohammedan and pagan tribes, inhabiting the southern provinces of the Russian Empire*. London.

Hollender, Elisabeth. 2008. Piyyut commentary in medieval Ashkenaz. (= *Studia Judaica* 42). Berlin, New York.

Ianbay, Iala. 2016. *Krimchak dictionary*. Wiesbaden.

ISUJa see Tymčenko, Jevgen Kostjantynovyč (ed.) (1930–1932).

Jacobs, Joseph. 1901. Manuscripts.—Singer, Isidore et al. (eds.). *The Jewish Encyclopedia*. Vol. 8. New York, London: 303–315.

Janhunen, Juha. & Rybatzki, Volker (eds.). 1999. *Writing in the Altaic world*. (= *Studia Orientalia* 87). Helsinki.

Jankowski, Henryk. 1994. Jak krymscy Karaimowie czytali *pataḥ* i co z tego wynika?—Górska, Elżbieta & Ostafin, Barbara (eds.). *Studia orientalia Thaddaeo Lewicki oblata. Materiały sesji naukowej poświęconej pamięci Profesora Tadeusza Lewickiego. Kraków, 17–18 listopada 1993*. Kraków: 107–114.

Jankowski, Henryk. 1997. A Bible translation into the northern Crimean dialect of Karaim.—*Studia Orientalia* 82: 1–82.

Jankowski, Henryk. 2003. Position of Karaim among the Turkic languages.—*Studia Orientalia* 95: 131–150.

Jankowski, Henryk 2008. The question of the existence of the Crimean Karaim and its relation to Western Karaim.—Bairašauskaitė, Tamara & Kobeckaitė, Halina & Miškinienė, Galina (eds.). *Orientas Lietuvos Didžiosios Kunigaikštijos visuomenės tradicijoje: totoriai ir karaimai*. (= *Straipsnių rinkinys, parengtas pranešimų, skaitytų tarptautinėje mokslo konferencijoje „610-osios totorių ir karaimų įsikūrimo Lietuvos Didžiojoje Kunigaikštijoje metinės" 2007 m. rugsėjo 13–15 d. Vilniaus universitete, pagrindu*). Vilnius: 162–168.

Jankowski, Henryk. 2009. Translations of the Bible into Karaim.—*Religion Compass* 3/4: 502–523.

Jankowski, Henryk. 2011. Two prayers for the Day of Atonement in translation into the Luck-Halicz dialect of Karaim.—Shapira, Dan & Lasker, Daniel J. (with the assistance of Akhiezer, Golda & Kizilov, Mikhail) (eds.). *Eastern European Karaites in the last generations*. Jerusalem: 156–170.

Jankowski, Henryk 2012. Literatura krymskokaraimska.—*Przegląd Orientalistyczny* 241/1: 50–67.

Jankowski, Henryk. 2014. Two Karaim religious poems by Isaac ben Abraham Troki.—*Karaite Archives* 2: 35–57.

Jankowski, Henryk. 2015a. Karaim and Krymchak.—Kahn, Lily & Rubin, Aaron D. (eds.). *Handbook of Jewish languages*. Leiden, Boston: 451–488.

Jankowski, Henryk. 2015b. Reconstruction of Old Kipchak.—[editors not indicated]. *Proceedings of the 12th Seoul International Altaistic Conference. Multidimensional understandings of languages and cultures of Altaic people*. Seoul: 271–292.

Jankowski, Henryk. 2015c. Response to Mikhail Kizilov's critical notes on my article.—*Karaite Archives* 3: 187–194. [cf. Kizilov (2015a)].

Jankowski, Henryk. 2018. Translation of the Tanakh into Crimean Karaim: History, Manuscripts, and Language.—Kahn, Lily (ed.). *Jewish languages in historical perspective*. (= *Studies in Judaica* 17). Leiden, Boston.

Jankowski, Henryk. 2019. Hagada trockokaraimska.—*Almanach Karaimski* 8: 35–140.

Jankowski, Henryk & Aqtay, Gulayhan & Cegiołka, Dorota & Çulha, Tülay & Németh, Michał. 2019. *The Crimean Karaim Bible. Volume 1: Critical edition of the Pentateuch, Five Scrolls, Psalms, Proverbs, Job, Daniel, Ezra and Nehemiah. Volume 2: Translation*. (= *Turcologica* 119). Wiesbaden.

Jastrow, Marcus. 1903. *A dictionary of the Targumim, the Talmud Babli and Yerushalmi, and the Midrashic literature*. Vol. 1–2. London, New York.

Johnson, Francis. 1852. *A dictionary, Persian, Arabic, and English*. London.

Judachin, Konstantin Kuźmič (ed.). 1957. *Orusča-kyrgyzča sözdük. Russko-kyrgyzskij slovaŕ*. Moskva.

Judachin, Konstantin Kuźmič. 1985. *Kirgizsko-russkij slovaŕ*. Vol. 1–2. Moskva.

KarRPS see Baskakov, Nikolaj Aleksandrovič & Zajączkowski, Ananiasz & Šapšal, Seraja Markovič (eds.) (1974).

Khan, Geoffrey. 2020. *The Tiberian pronunciation tradition of Biblical Hebrew*. Vol. 1–2. Cambridge.

KirgRussS see Judachin, Konstantin Kuźmič (1985).

Kizilov, Mikhail. 2007. Two piyyutim and a rhetorical essay in the northern (Troki) dialect of the Karaim language by Isaac ben Abraham of Troki.—*Judaica* 63.1/2: 64–75.

Kizilov, Mikhail. 2009. The Karaites of Galicia. An ethnoreligious minority among the Ashkenazim, the Turks, and the Slavs 1772–1945. (= *Studia Judaeoslavica* 1). Leiden, Boston.

Kizilov, Mikhail. 2015a. Reuven Fahn and Isaac Troki: A research note on two articles published in *Karaite Archives* 2 (2014).—*Karaite Archives* 3: 175–186.

Kizilov, Mikhail. 2015b. *The sons of scripture. The Karaites in Poland and Lithuania in the Twentieth Century*. Warszawa, Berlin.

Klemensiewicz, Zenon. 1974 [2002]. *Historia języka polskiego*, Warszawa [7th edition].

Kobeckaitė, Halina. 2019. *Ijov. Jobo Knyga. Kniga Ioba*. Trakai.

Kowalski, Tadeusz. 1929. *Karaimische Texte im Dialekt von Troki*. (= *Prace Komisji Orjentalistycznej Polskiej Akademji Umiejętności* 11). Kraków.

Kowalski, Tadeusz. 1930–1931. Z pożółkłych kart.—*Myśl Karaimska* 2(3–4): 12–25.

König, Eduard. 1910. *Hebräisches und aramäisches Wörterbuch zum Alten Testament mit Einschaltung und Analyse aller schwer erkennbaren Formen, Deutung der Eigennamen sowie der massoretischen Randbemerkungen und einem deutsch-hebräischen Wortregister*. Leipzig.

Lidzbarsky, Mark. 1901. Alphabet, the Hebrew.—Singer, Isidore et al. (eds.). *The Jewish Encyclopedia*. Vol. 1. New York, London: 439–454.

Linde, Samuel Bogumił. 1807–1814. *Słownik języka polskiego*. Vol. 1–4. Warszawa.

Machcińska, Małgorzata. 2015. *Lieszon hak-kodiesz. Zagadnienia pisowni i wymowy hebrajszczyzny Karaimów polsko-litewskich.* (= *Prace Karaimoznawcze* 3). Poznań.

Mann, Jacob. 1931 [1972]. *Texts and Studies in Jewish History and Literature. Volume II: Karaitica*. New York [second edition: 1972].

[Mardkowicz, Aleksander]. 1932c. Ribbiłer, kajsyłar hazzanłyk ettiłer Łuckada basłap burunhu jarymyndan XIX jizjilnyn.—*Karaj Awazy* 5: 16.

Mardkowicz, Aleksander. 1933b. Sahyncyna "babinecnin".—*Karaj Awazy* 6: 1–6.

Mardkowicz, Aleksander. 1935. *Karaj sez-bitigi. Słownik karaimski. Karaimisches Wörterbuch*, Łuck.

Mayenowa, Maria Renata et al. (eds.). 1969. *Słownik polszczyzny XVI wieku*. Vol. 4. Wrocław, Warszawa, Kraków.

Medvedeva, L. Ja. 1988. O kollekcii karaimskich i krymčakskich rukopisej v LO Instituta vostokovedenija AN SSSR.—*Sovetskaja Tjurkologija* 6: 89–102.

Muchowski, Piotr. 2013a. *Folk literature of the Polish-Lithuanian Karaites. Abkowicz 3 manuscript, part 2*. Paris.

Muchowski, Piotr. 2013b. *Pas Yeda'* and *Mass' ha-'Am*: The lost works of Avraham ben Yoshiyahu (Abraham Ezyaszewicz).—*Karaite Archives* 85–112.

Muchowski, Piotr. 2017. Hebrajszczyzna karaimska. 'Święty język' Karaimów polsko-litewskich.—Muchowski, Piotr & Tomal, Maciej & Witkowski, Rafał. 2017. *Karae Edom. Studia nad historią i kulturą Karaimów I Rzeczypospolitej.* (= *Prace Karaimoznawcze* 8). Poznań: 274–299.

Muchowski, Piotr & Tomal, Maciej & Sulimowicz, Anna & Witkowski, Maciej & Yariv, Arie. 2017. *Dokumenty historii Karaimów polsko-litewskich. Edycja krytyczna wybranych rękopisów w językach hebrajskim, łacińskim i polskim.* (= *Prace Karaimoznawcze* 7). Poznań.

Munkácsi, Bernát. 1909. Karäisch-tatarische Hymnen aus Polen.—*Keleti Szemle* 10: 185–210.

Musaev, Kenesbaj Musaevič. 1964. *Grammatika karaimskogo jazyka. Fonetika i morfologija*. Moskva.

Musaev, Kenesbaj Musaevič. 1977. *Kratkij grammatičeskij očerk karaimskogo jazyka*. Moskva.

Münz-Manor, Ophir. 2011. Figurative Language in Early Piyyut.—Van Bekkum, Wout & Katsumata, Naoya (eds.). *Giving a diamond. Essays in honor of Joseph Yahalom on the occasion of his seventieth birthday*. Leiden: 51–67.

Németh, Michał. 2009. Errors with and without purpose: A. Mardkowicz's transcription of Łuck-Karaim letters in Hebrew script.—*Studia Linguistica Universitatis Iagellonicae Cracoviensis* 126: 97–106.

Németh, Michał. 2010. North-Western and Eastern Karaim features in a manuscript found in Łuck.—Mańczak-Wohlfeld, Elżbieta & Podolak, Barbara (eds.). *Studies on the Turkic world. A Festschrift for Professor St. Stachowski on the occasion of his 80th birthday*. Kraków: 75–94.

Németh, Michał. 2011a. A different look at the Lutsk Karaim sound system.—*Studia Linguistica Universitatis Iagellonicae Cracoviensis* 128: 69–101.

Németh, Michał. 2011b. *Unknown Lutsk Karaim letters in Hebrew script. A critical edition*. (= *Studia Turcologica Cracoviensia* 12). Kraków.

Németh, Michał. 2011c. *Zwięzła gramatyka języka zachodniokaraimskiego (z ćwiczeniami)*. (= *Prace Karaimoznawcze* 1). Poznań.

Németh, Michał. 2013a. Ananiasz Zajączkowski's doctoral thesis: The original manuscript of *Sufiksy imienne i czasownikowe w języku zachodniokaraimskim*.—*Folia Orientalia* 50: 115–156.

Németh, Michał. 2013b. Karaim letters of Jehoszafat Kapłanowski. I. Critical edition.—*Studia Linguistica Universitatis Iagellonicae Cracoviensis* 130: 237–257.

Németh, Michał. 2013c. Karaim letters of Jehoszafat Kapłanowski. II. Linguistic analysis.—*Studia Linguistica Universitatis Iagellonicae Cracoviensis* 130: 259–276.

Németh, Michał. 2014a. A historical phonology of Western Karaim. Alveolars and front labials in the south-western dialect.—*Studia Linguistica Universitatis Iagellonicae Cracoviensis* 131/3: 247–267.

Németh, Michał. 2014b. A historical phonology of Western Karaim. The evolution of consonant harmony in the north-western dialect.—*Studia Linguistica Universitatis Iagellonicae Cracoviensis* 131/4: 353–369.

Németh, Michał. 2014c. An early North-Western Karaim Bible translation from 1720. Part 1. The Torah.—*Karaite Archives* 2: 109–141.

Németh, Michał. 2015a. A historical morphology of Western Karaim. The *-p edi* past tense in the south-western dialect.—*Acta Orientalia Academiae Scientiarum Hungaricae* 68.2: 215–228.

Németh, Michał. 2015b. A historical phonology of Western Karaim. The process of its diversification into dialects.—*Studia Linguistica Universitatis Iagiellonicae Cracoviensis* 132: 167–185.

Németh, Michał. 2015c. An early North-Western Karaim Bible translation from 1720. Part 2. The Book of Ruth.—*Karaite Archives* 3: 49–102.

Németh, Michał. 2016a. A Crimean Karaim handwritten translation of the Book of Ruth dating from before 1687. Another contribution to the history of Crimean Karaim and to the question of the *stemma codicum* of the Eupatorian printed edition of the Tanakh from 1841.—*Türk Dilleri Araştırmaları* 26: 161–217.

Németh, Michał. 2016b. Batı Karaycasının Lehçelere Ayrılma Süreci ve Dönemselleştirilmesi.—Eker, Süer & Ülkü, Çelik Şavk (eds.). *Tehlikedeki Türk Dilleri. III. Cilt 4. Disiplinlerarası Yaklaşımlar. Endangered Turkic Languages. III. Vol. 4. Interdisciplinary Approaches*. Ankara, Astana: 264–276.

Németh, Michał. 2016c. Rękopisy i druki karaimskie w polskich zbiorach prywatnych. Nowe perspektywy badań karaimoznawczych.—*Almanach Karaimski* 5: 61–101.

Németh, Michał. 2018a. An early North-Western Karaim text dating from before 1700. A linguist's contribution to the biography of Josef ha-Mashbir.—*Almanach Karaimski* 7: 83–98.

Németh, Michał. 2018b. A historical phonology of Western Karaim. The process of its diversification into dialects. Part 2. Supplementary data on the absolute and relative chronology of sound changes.—*Rocznik Orientalistyczny* 71/2: 146–161.

Németh, Michał. 2020. Gustaf Peringer's Karaim Biblical Material Revisited. A Linguistic Commentary on a Text Sample from 1691.—[forthcoming in a Festschrift, Kraków].

Németh, Michał. 2021. *The Western Karaim Torah. A critical edition of a manuscript from 1720*. Leiden, Boston [forthcoming in *Languages of Asia*, Brill].

Németh, Michał. [forthcoming]. *A historical morphology of Western Karaim. The two pluperfect tenses in diachronic and areal perspective.*—[submitted to *Journal of Language Contact* in 2020].

Nemoy, Leon. 1952. Karaite anthology. Excerpts from the early literature. (= *Yale Judaica Series* 7). New Haven, London.

Nevins, Andrew & Vaux, Bert. 2004. Consonant harmony in Karaim.—Csirmaz, Aniko & Lee, Youngjoo & Walter, Mary Ann (eds.). *The Proceedings of the 1st Workshop on Altaic in Formal Linguistics*. (= MIT *Working Papers in Linguistics* 46). Cambridge: 175–194.

Nosonovskij, Michail & Šabarovskij, Vladimir [= Šabarovśkyj, Volodymyr]. 2004. Karaimskaja obščina 16–18 vv. v Deražnom na Volyni.—*Vestnik Evrejskogo universiteta* 9: 29–50.

Nosonovsky, Michael. 2007. Judeo-Turkic encounters in Hebrew epitaphs from Ukraine: Naming patterns.—Alpargu, Mehmet & Öztürk, Yücel (eds.). *Omeljan Pritsak armağanı. A tribute to Omeljan Pritsak*. (= *Sakarya Üniversitesi Yayınları* 51) Sakarya: 283–301.

Olach, Zsuzsanna. 2013. *A Halich Karaim translation of Hebrew biblical texts*. (= *Turcologica* 98). Wiesbaden.

Olach, Zsuzsanna. 2014. A comparative study of two evening prayers written in Karaim.—Demir, Nurettin. & Karakoç, Birsel & Menz, Astrid (eds.). *Turcology and linguistics*. Ankara: 313–326.

Olach, Zsuzsanna. 2016a. A "Lovely morning prayer": a new edition of a Karaim version.—*Karaite Archives* 4: 77–116.

Olach, Zsuzsanna. 2016b. A South-Western Karaim morning prayer.—Eker, Süer & Ülkü, Çelik Şavk (eds.). *Endangered Turkic languages 4. Interdisciplinary approaches*. Ankara, Astana: 293–306.

Olach, Zsuzsanna. 2016c. Emergence of a new written culture: The use of Hebrew script among the Krimchaks and the Karaim.—*Acta Orientalia Vilnensia* 13: 61–78.

Olach, Zsuzsanna. 2017. Karaim translations of the Song of Moses as sources of Karaite Religious Concepts.—Csáki, Éva & Ivanics, Mária & Olach, Zsuzsanna (eds.). *Role of religions in the Turkic culture. Proceedings of the 1st International Conference on the Role of Religions in the Turkic Culture held in September 9–11, 2015 in Budapest.* Budapest.

Petuchowski, Jakob J. 2004. *Theology and poetry. Studies in the medieval piyyut.* Oxford.

Poppe, Nicholas. 1965. *Introduction to Altaic Linguistics.* (= *Ural-Altaische Bibliothek* 14). Wiesbaden.

Poznański, Samuel. 1916. Karäische Kopisten und Besitzer von Handschriften.—*Hebrœische Bibliographie* 19.4/6: 79–122.

Poznański, Samuel. 1912–1919. Karäisch-tatarische Literatur.—*Keleti Szemle* 13 (1912–1913): 37–47, 360; *Keleti Szemle* 14 (1913–1914): 223–224; *Keleti Szemle* 18 (1918–1919): 150–151.

Poznański, Samuel (ed.). 1920. ספר זכר צדיקים או קצור אגדה להקראי מרדכי בן יוסף סולטאנסקי. *Zecher Caddikim. Kronika historyczna Karaity Mordechaja Sułtańskiego.* Warszawa.

Piccard = *Piccard watermark collection.* URL: https://www.piccard-online.de/start.php (accessed 9 Oct 2017).

Pritsak, Omeljan. 1959a. Das Karaimische.—Deny, Jean & Grønbech, Kaare & Scheel, Helmuth & Togan, Zeki Velidi (eds.). *Philologiae Turcicae Fundamenta.* Vol. 1. Wiesbaden: 318–340.

Pritsak, Omeljan. 1959b. Das Kiptschakische.—Deny, Jean & Grønbech, Kaare & Scheel, Helmuth & Togan, Zeki Velidi (eds.). *Philologiae Turcicae Fundamenta.* Vol. 1. Wiesbaden: 75–87.

Polinsky, Maria S. 1991. The Krymchaks: history and texts.—*Ural-Altaische Jahrbücher. Ural-Altaic Yearbook* 63: 123–154.

von Rohden, Frauke. 2004. Karäisches Gedenken der Khmelnytsky-Verfolgungen: ein Piyut von 1650.—*Judaica* 60.2: 159–169.

Radloff, Wilhelm. 1888. Bericht über eine Reise zu den Karaimen der westlichen Gouvernements.—*Bulletin de l'Académie Impériale des Sciences de St-Pétersbourg* 32: 173–182.

Räsänen, Martti. 1949. *Zur Lautgeschichte der türkischen Sprachen.* (= *Studia Orientalia* 15). Helsinki.

Räsänen, Martti. 1957. *Materialien zur Morphologie der türkischen Sprachen* (= *Studia Orientalia* 21). Helsinki.

Räsänen, Martti. 1969. *Versuch eines etymologischen Wörterbuchs der Türksprachen.* (= *Lexica Societatis Fenno-Ugricae* 17.1). Helsinki.

Rudkowski, Sergjusz. 1932. *Krwawe echo Humania na Wołyniu* (*rzeź kotowska 1768 r.*). *Podanie.* Łuck.

Sevortjan, Èrvand Vladimirovič (ed.). 1974. *Ètimologičeskij slovaŕ tjurkskich jazykov* (*obščetjurkskie i mežtjurkskie osnovy na glasnye*). Moskva.

Shapira Dan. 2002. Some new data on the Karaites in Wolhynia [sic!] and Galicia in the 18th century.—Novochaťko, Leonid & Fedoruk, Oleksandr & Berehovśkyj, Oleksandr (eds.). *Karajimy Halyča: Istorija ta kuĺtura. Materialy mižnarodnoji konferenciji, Halyč, 6–9 veresnja 2002*. Ĺviv, Halyč.

Shapira, Dan. 2003. The Turkic languages and literatures of the East European Karaites.—Polliack, Meira (ed.). *Karaite Judaism. A guide to its history and literary sources*. Leiden, Boston: 657–728.

Shapira, Dan. 2006. סיגול לשוני בתרגומי התנ"ך ללשונות תורכיות של הקראים.—מסורות [= *Massoroth*] 13–14: 253–278.

Shapira, Dan. 2013. The Karaim translation of the Book of Nehemia copied in the 17th century's Crimea and printed in 1840/1841 at Gözleve, on the copyist of the manuscript, and some related issues.—*Karaite Archives* 1: 133–198.

Shapira, Dan. 2014. A new Karaite-Turkish manuscript from Germany: New light on genre and language in Karaite and Rabbanite Turkic Bible translations in the Crimea, Constantinople and elsewhere.—*Karaite Archives* 2: 143–176.

Shapira, Dan. 2018. Review of: Taube, Moshe (introd., ed. and trans.). 2016. *The logika of the Judaizers. A fifteenth-century Ruthenian translation from Hebrew. Critical edition of the Slavic texts presented alongside their Hebrew sources with introduction, English translation, and commentary*. Jerusalem.—*Aleph* 18.2: 295–312.

Shapira, Dan. 2019. An Unknown Jewish Community of the Golden Horde.—Hao, Chen (ed.). *Competing Narratives between Nomadic People and their Sedentary Neighbours. Papers of the 7th International Conference on the Medieval History of the Eurasian Steppe Nov. 9–12, 2018 Shanghai University, China*. (= *Studia Uralo-Altaica* 53). Szeged: 281–294.

SPolXVI see Mayenowa, Maria Renata et al. (eds.) (1969).

SStp. see Urbańczyk, Stanisław et al. (ed.) (1953–2002).

Stachowski, Kamil. 2009. The discussion on consonant harmony in northwestern Karaim.—*Türkbilig* 18: 158–193.

Stachowski, Kamil. 2015. Remarks on the phonology of the transitional period of Northwestern Karaim.—*Dil Araştırmaları* 10: 29–42.

Steingass, Francis Joseph. 1892. *A Comprehensive Persian-English dictionary, including the Arabic words and phrases to be met with in Persian literature*. London.

Steinschneider, Moritz. 1871. Karaitische Handschriften. Anhang.—*Hebræische Bibliographie* 11: 37–46.

Stern, Adolf [= יונה שטערן]. 1926. ספר ראשי תיבות. *Handbuch der Hebräischen Abbreviaturen*. Sighetul-Marmaţiei.

Sulimowicz, Anna. 2013a. Listy do Łucka. Aleksander Mardkowicz jako adresat korespondencji Ananiasza Zajączkowskiego.—*Almanach Karaimski* 2: 37–60.

Sulimowicz, Anna. 2013b. Mieczek i Siunek.—*Awazymyz* 1(38): 4–13.

Sulimowicz, Anna. 2014. A document on the economic status of the Lutsk Karaites in the mid-19th century.—*Karaite Archives* 2: 177–200.

Sulimowicz, Anna. 2015. Nieznany przekład Roty na język karaimski.—*Almanach Karaimski* 4: 101–116.

Sulimowicz, Anna. 2016. Inner hierarchy in the Halicz Karaite community based on a document from the 1830s.—*Karaite Archives* 4: 129–152.

Sulimowicz, Józef. 1972. Materiał leksykalny krymskokaraimskiego zabytku językowego (druk z 1734 r.).—*Rocznik Orientalistyczny* 35/1: 37–76.

Sulimowicz, Józef. 1973. Materiał leksykalny krymskokaraimskiego zabytku językowego (druk z 1734 r.). II.—*Rocznik Orientalistyczny* 36/1: 47–107.

SUM see Bilodid, Ivan Kostjantynovyč et al. (eds.) (1970–1980).

Šabarovśkyj, Volodymyr. 2013. *Karajimy na Volyni (štrychy do portreta zahadkovogo narodu)*. Lućk.

Šapšal, Seraja Markovič [= Г. С.]. 1918. *Kratkij očerk" tjurksko-karaimskoj literatury.—Izvěstija karaimskago Duchovnago Pravlenija* 2/1: 6–10; 2/2: 13–17.

Tentzel, Wilhelm Ernst (ed.). 1691. *Monatliche Unterredungen einiger guten Freunde von allerhand Büchern und andern annemlichen Geschichten; allen Liebhabern der Curiositäten zur Ergetzligkeit und Nachsinnen heraus gegeben*. Lepizig.

Tryjarski, Edward. 2017. *Armeno-Kipchak studies. Collected papers*. (= *Prace Orientalistyczne* 43). Warszawa.

Tuori, Riikka. 2013. *Karaite zěmīrōt in Poland-Lithuania. A study of paraliturgical Karaite Hebrew poems from the seventeenth and eighteenth centuries*. Helsinki.

Tymčenko, Jevgen Kostjantynovyč (ed.). (1930–1932). *Istoryčnyj slovnyk ukrajinśkogo jazyka*. Vol. 1. Charkiv.

Urbańczyk, Stanisław et al. (ed.). 1953–2002. *Słownik staropolski*. Vol. 1–11. Warszawa (vol. 1–10/3), Kraków (vol. 2/4–11), Wrocław (vol. 2/5–10/3), Gdańsk (vol. 6/3–10/3), Łódź (vol. 8/6–10/3).

VEWT see Räsänen, Martti (1969).

Walfish, Barry Dov (with Kizilov, Mikhail). 2011. *Bibliographia Karaitica. An annotated bibliography of Karaites and Karaism*. (= *Études sur le Judaïsme Médiéval* 43). Leiden, Boston.

Wasserman, Gabriel. 2016. *Royal attire. לְבוּשׁ מַלְכוּת. On Karaite and Rabbanite beliefs Ḥakham Mordecai ben Nisan*. [*Sine loco*].

Wasserman, Gabriel. [forthcoming]. *You are Holy / Atta Qadosh: Liturgical poems for each Torah portion by the thirteenth-century Byzantine Karaite sage Aaron ben Joseph*, Daly City (California; The Karaite Press). [*Non vidi*].

Weinreich, Uriel. 1963. Four riddles in bilingual dialectology.—*American contributions to the Fifth International Congress of Slavicists. Vol. I. Linguistic contributions*. The Hague: 335–359.

Yardeni, Ada. 1997. *The book of Hebrew script. History, palaeography, script styles, calligraphy & design*. Jerusalem.

Zaborski, Andrzej. 2000. Tadeusz Kowalski (1889–1948).—Michalik, Jan & Walecki,

Wacław (eds.). *Uniwersytet Jagielloński. Złota księga wydziału filologicznego*. Kraków 2000: 409–417.

Zajączkowska-Łopatto, Emilia. 2013. Listy Ananiasza Zajączkowskiego do Jego Ekscelencji Hadży Seraji Chana Szapszała.—*Almanach Karaimski* 2: 5–17.

Zajączkowska-Łopatto, Emilia. 2014. Ananiasz Zajączkowski—orientalistyka przede wszystkim.—*Almanach Karaimski* 3: 133–148.

Zajączkowski, Ananiasz. 1926. Literatura karaimska.—*Myśl Karaimska* 3: 7–17.

Zajączkowski, Ananiasz. 1929. Unikanie wyrażeń antropomorficznych w przekładach karaimskich.—*Myśl Karaimska* 2.2: 9–24.

Zajączkowski, Ananiasz. 1931. *Krótki wykład gramatyki języka zachodnio-karaimskiego (narzecze łucko-halickie)*. Łuck.

Zajączkowski, Ananiasz. 1931–1932 [1934]. Przekłady trenów Jeremjasza w narzeczu trocko-karaimskim.—*Rocznik Orjentalistyczny* 8: 181–192.

Zajączkowski, Ananiasz. 1932. *Sufiksy imienne i czasownikowe w języku zachodnio-karaimskim (przyczynek do morfologii języków tureckich)*. (= *Polska Akademja Umiejętności. Prace Komisji Orjentalistycznej* 15). Kraków.

Zajączkowski, Ananiasz. 1934a. Karaimi na Wołyniu.—*Rocznik Wołyński* 3: 149–191.

Zajączkowski, Ananiasz. 1934b. Przekłady trenów Jeremjasza w narzeczu trocko-karaimskim (tekst i słowniczek).—*Rocznik Orjentalistyczny* 10: 158–177.

Zajączkowski, Ananiasz. 1939a. Karaj tili.—*Onarmach* 3: 2–3.

Zajączkowski, Ananiasz. 1939b. Najstarsza wiadomość o języku tureckim Karaimów w Polsce (z XVII w.).—*Myśl Karaimska* 12 (1937–1938): 90–99.

Zajączkowski, Ananiasz. 1947. Terminologia muzułmańska a tradycje nomadów w słownictwie karaimskim.—*Myśl Karaimska. Seria Nowa* 2: 24–39.

Zajączkowski, Ananiasz. 1953. *Studia orientalistyczne z dziejów słownictwa polskiego*. (= *Prace Wrocławskiego Towarzystwa Naukowego* 49, seria A). Wrocław.

Zajączkowski, Ananiasz. 1954. *Słownik arabsko-kipczacki z okresu Państwa Mameluckiego Bulġat al-muštāq fī luġat at-turk wa-l-qifǯāq. Część II. Verba*. (= *Prace Orientalistyczne* 1). Warszawa.

Zajączkowski, Ananiasz. 1961. *Karaims in Poland. History. Language. Folklore. Science*. Warszawa, Paris.

Zajączkowski, Ananiasz. 1964. Die karaimische Literatur.—Bazin, Louis & Bombacı, Alessio & Deny, Jean & Gökbilgin, Tayyib & İz, Fahir & Scheel, Helmuth (eds.). *Philologiae Turcicae Fundamenta*. Vol. 2. Wiesbaden: 793–801.

Zajączkowski, Włodzimierz. 1965. Ein Bruchstück des hebräisch-karaimischen Wörterbuches.—*Ural-Altaische Jahrbücher* 36: 429–433.

Zajączkowski, Włodzimierz. 1966. Karaimisch–tschuwaschische Parallelen.—[editors not indicated]. *Reşid Rahmeti Arat için*. (= *Türk Kültürünü Araştırma Enstitüsü Yayınları* 19 (seri I, sayı A2)). Ankara: 429–432.

Zajączkowski, Włodzimierz. 1973a. Łucki Józef Salomon.—Rostworowski, Emanuel et al. (eds.). *Polski Słownik Biograficzny*. Vol. 18. Wrocław: 512–513.

Zajączkowski, Włodzimierz. 1973b. Łucki Sima Izaak.—Rostworowski, Emanuel et al. (eds.). *Polski Słownik Biograficzny*. Vol. 18. Wrocław: 513.

Zajączkowski, Włodzimierz. 1976. Mordechaj ben Nisan.—Rostworowski, Emanuel (ed.). *Polski Słownik Biograficzny*. Vol. 21. Wrocław: 764.

Zajączkowski, Włodzimierz. 1977. Beitrag zur Erforschung des karaimischen Wortschatzes.—*Folia Orientalia* 18: 199–204.

Zajączkowski, Włodzimierz. 1980. Karaimische Übersetzungen des Alten Testament.—*Folia Orientalia* 21: 160–161.

Zarachowicz, Zarach. 1925. Josef Mordkowicz (1802–1884). (W 40-tą rocznicę zgonu).—*Myśl Karaimska* 1(2): 20–23.

Zarachowicz, Zarach. 1930. Ic kyna.—*Karaj Awazy* 10: 3–6.

Zarachowicz, Zarach. 1935. Łuwachy hazzanłarnyn Halicta.—*Karaj Awazy* 8: 23.

Zilynśkyj, Ivan. 1979. *A phonetic description of the Ukrainian language*. Cambridge [USA].

Żylko, Fedot Trochymovyč. 1958. *Hovory ukrajinśkoji movy*. Kyjiv.

# Facsimiles

The facsimile of JER NLI 4101-8 is available online, see ***Referenced handwritten primary sources***. All other facsimila are presented below.

FACS. 1 ADub.III.61: 94 verso–95 recto

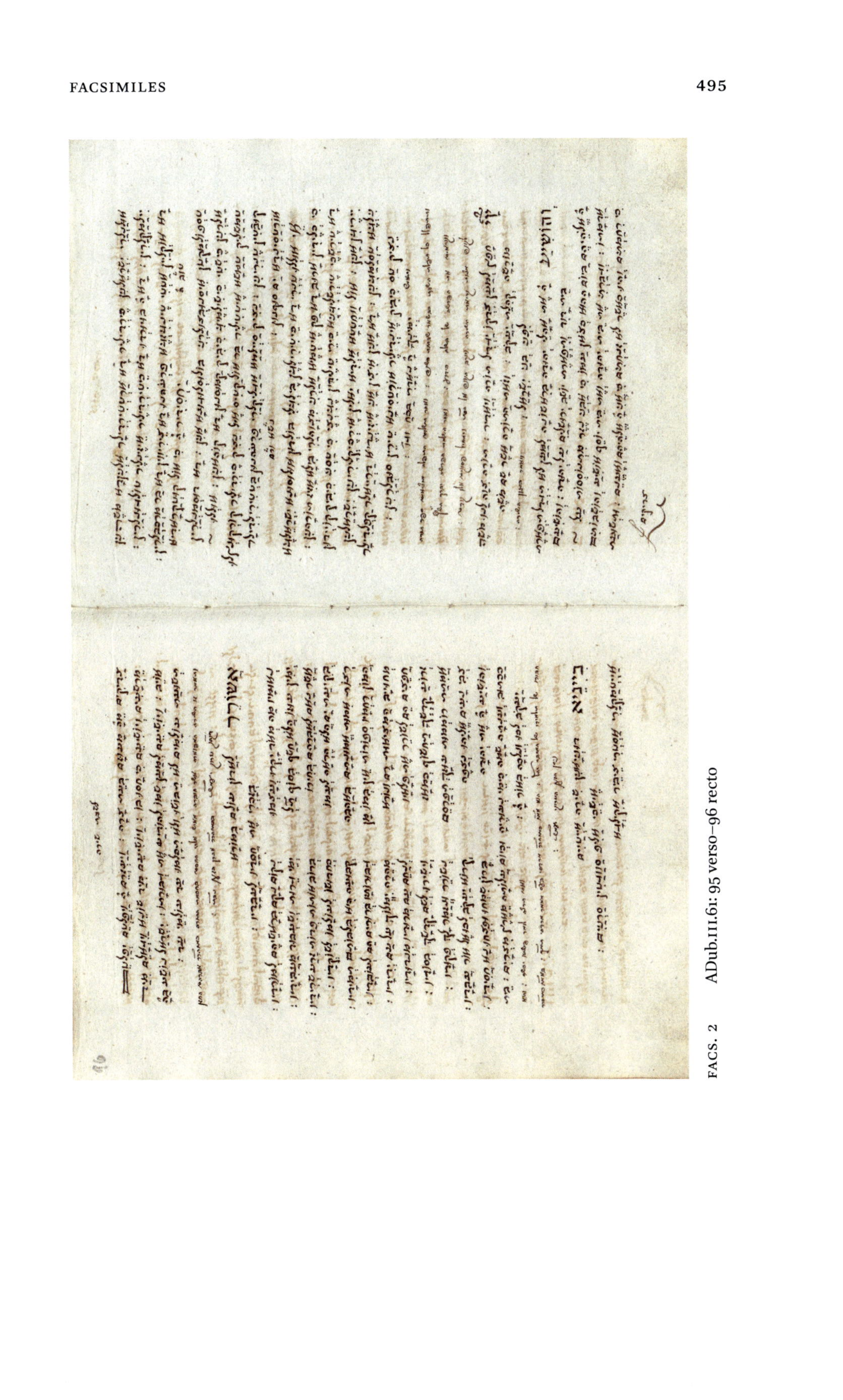

FACS. 2 ADub.III.61: 95 verso–96 recto

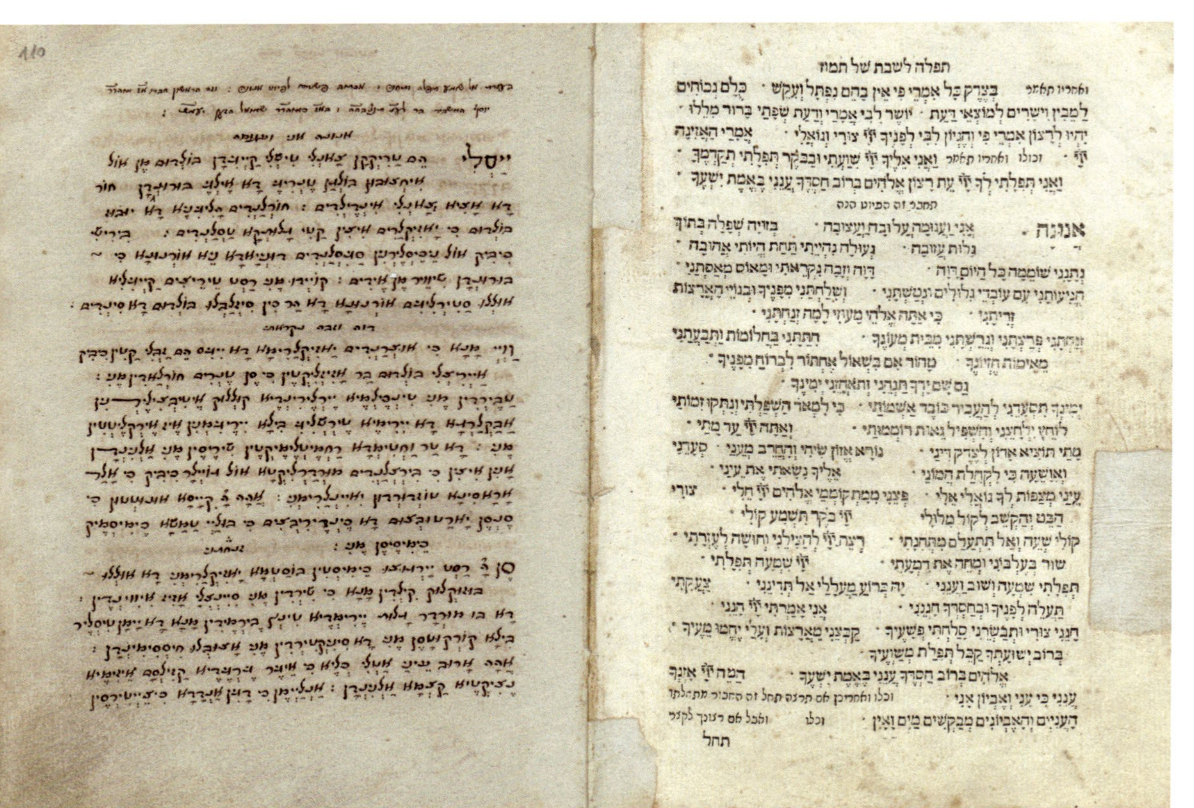

FACS. 3 ADub.III.61: 110 recto and *Siddur* (1736–1737: 86 verso)

FACS. 4 ADub.III.61: 110 verso–111 recto

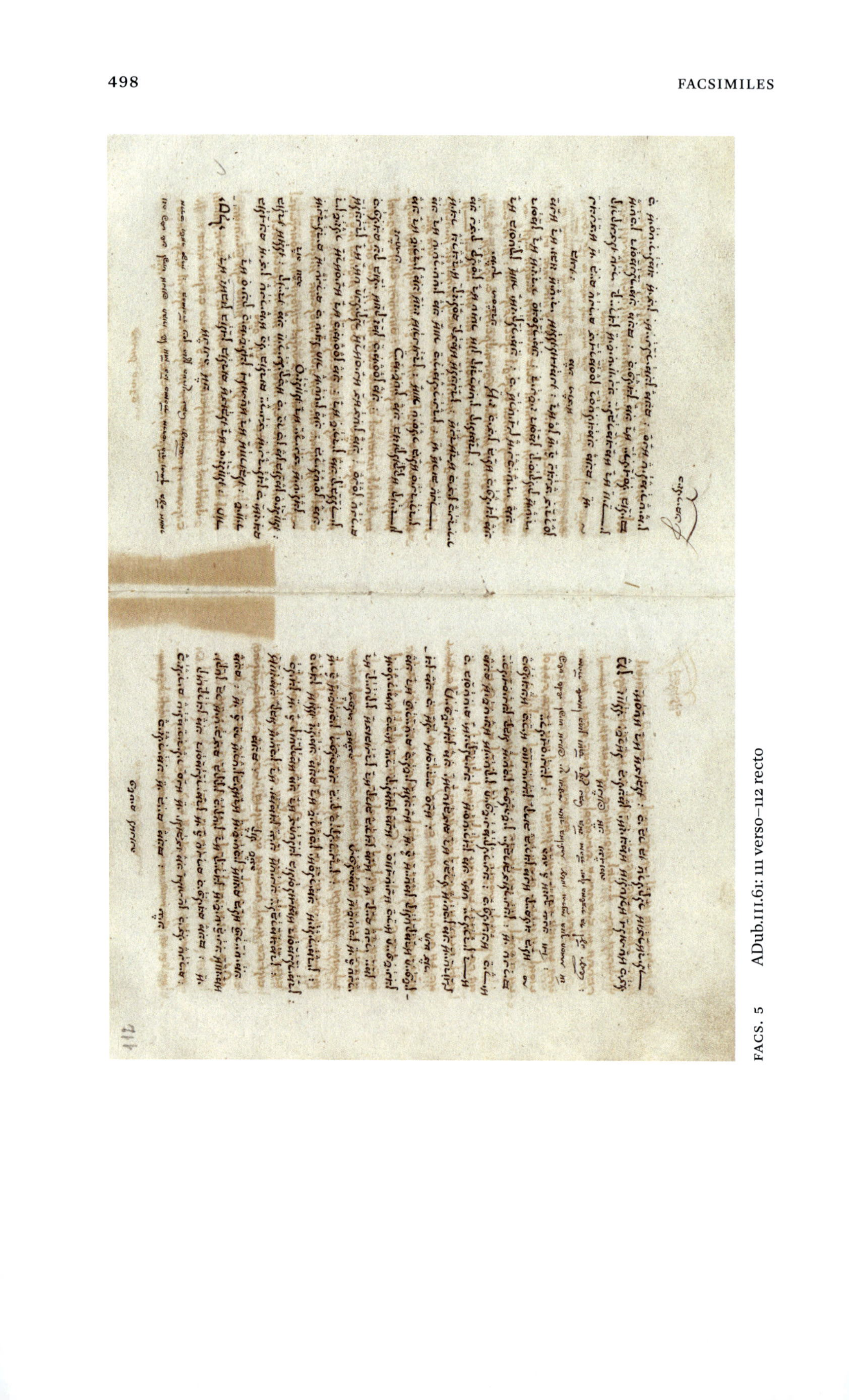

FACS. 5 ADub.III.61: 111 verso–112 recto

FACS. 6 ADub.III.61: 112 verso–113 recto

FACS. 7 ADub.III.61: 113 verso–114 recto

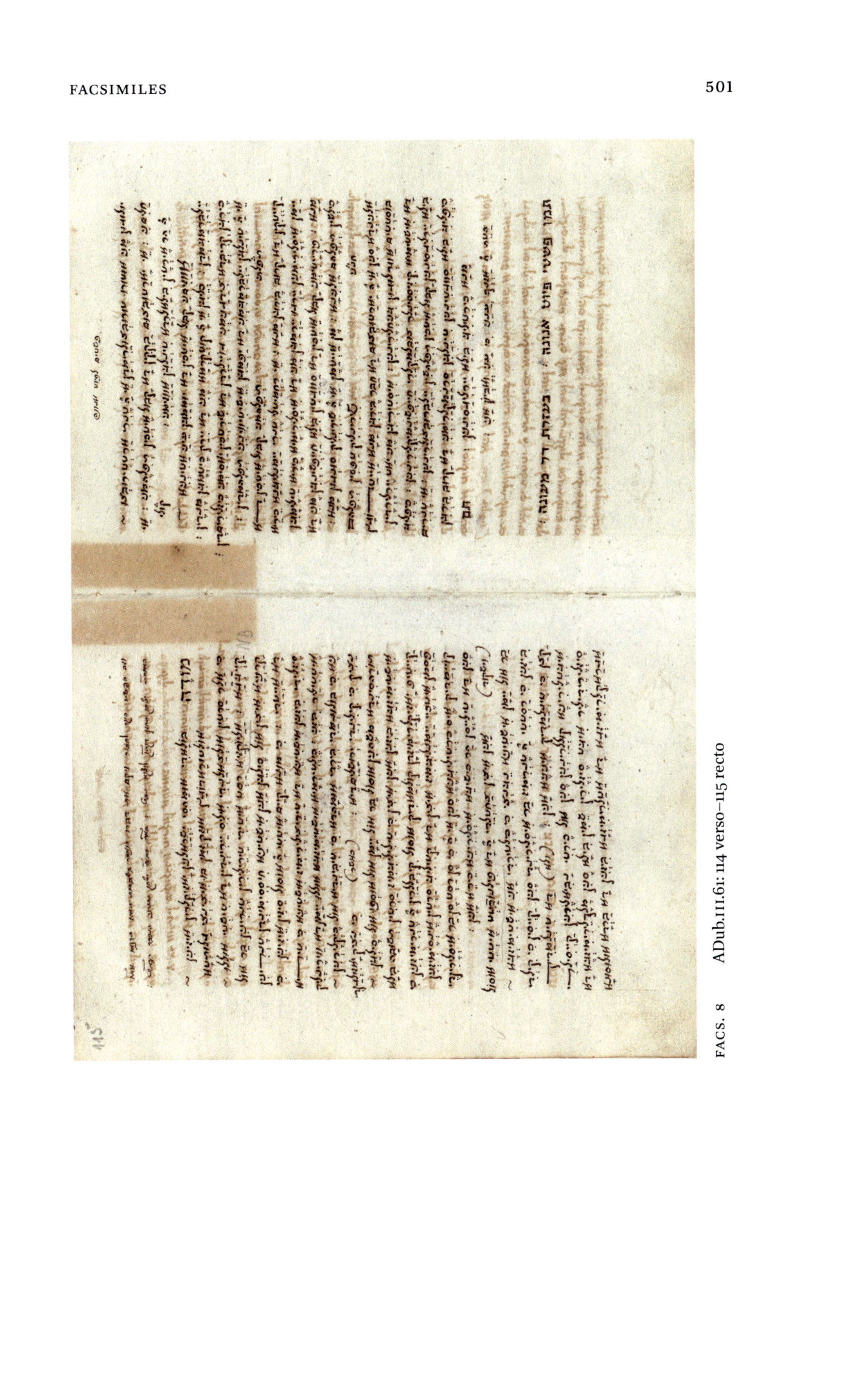

FACS. 8 ADub.III.61: 114 verso–115 recto

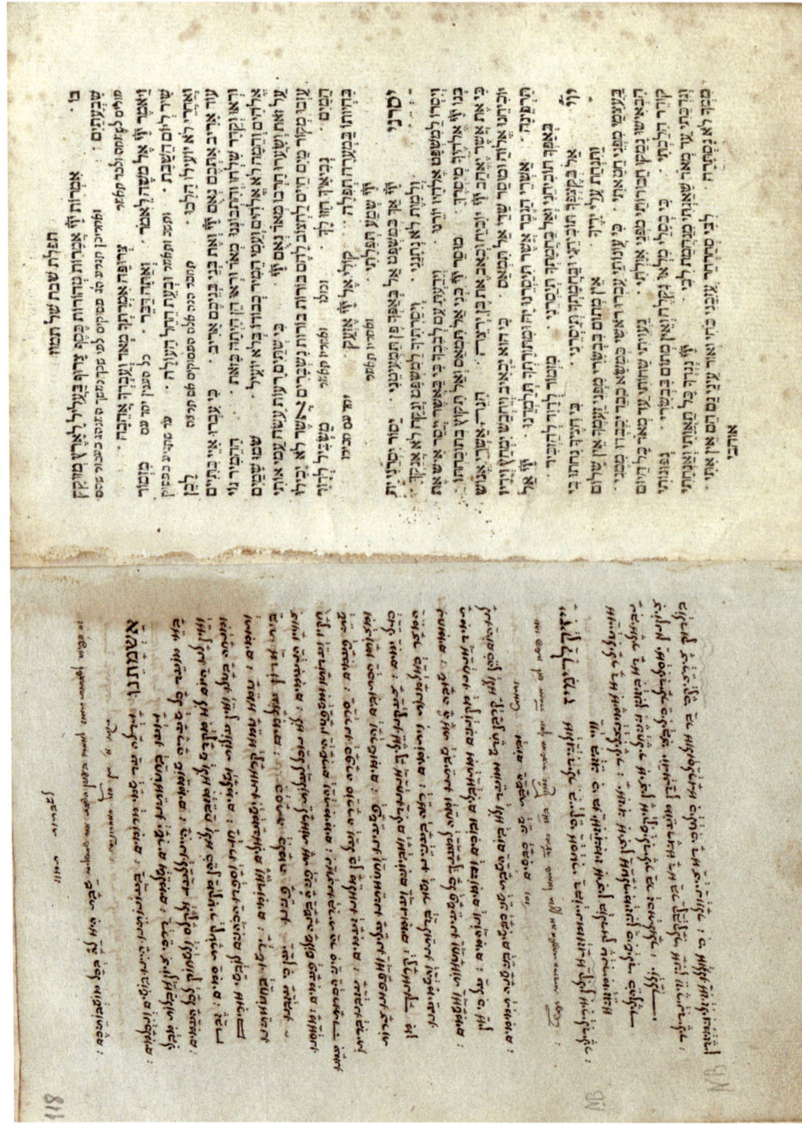

FACS. 9 ADub.III.61: 118 recto and *Siddur* (1736–1737: 89 verso)

FACS. 10 ADub.III.61: 118 verso and *Siddur* (1736–1737: 90 recto)

FACS. 11 ADub.III.61: 133 verso–134 recto

FACS. 12 ADub.III.61: 134 verso–135 recto

FACS. 13 ADub.III.61: 135 verso–136 recto

FACS. 14 ADub.III.61: 136 verso–137 recto

FACS. 15 ADub.III.61: 137 verso–138 recto

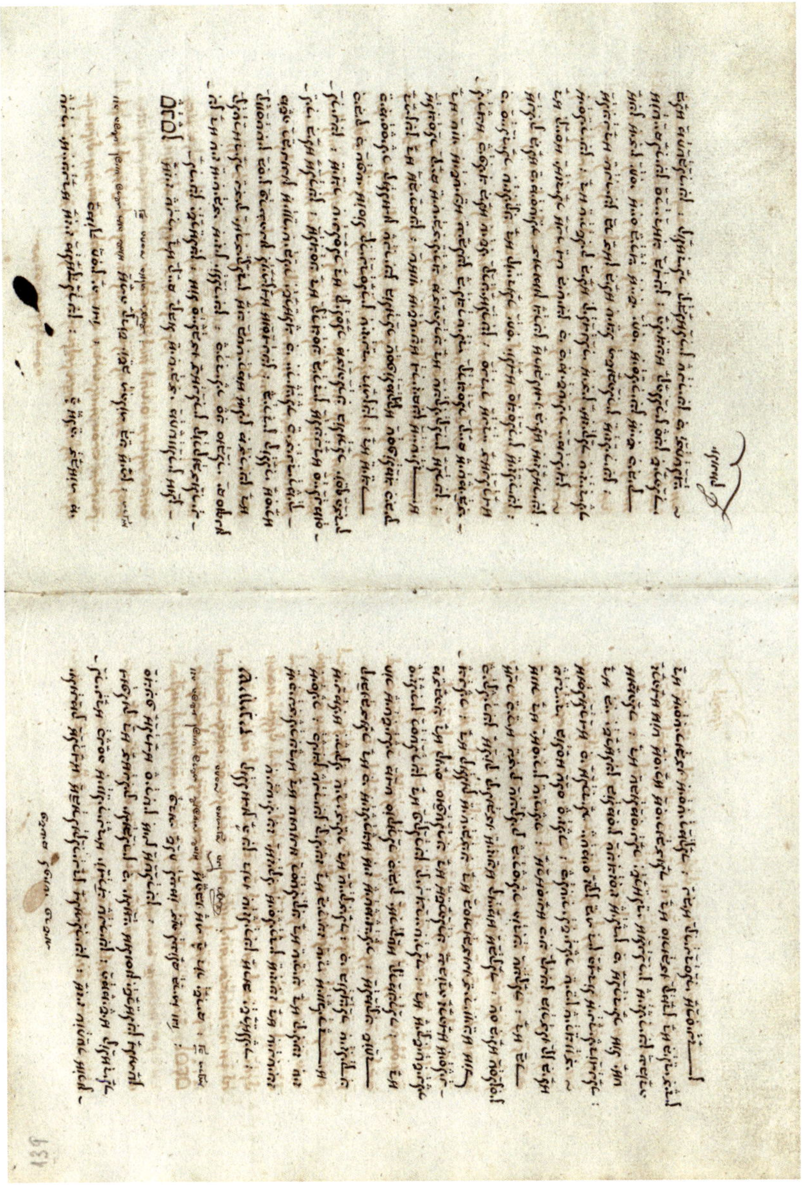

FACS. 16 ADub.III.61: 138 verso–139 recto

FACS. 17 ADub.III.61: 139 verso–140 recto

FACS. 18 ADub.III.61: 140 verso–145 recto

FACS. 19 ADub.III.61: 141 verso–142 recto

FACS. 20 ADub.III.61: 142 verso–143 recto

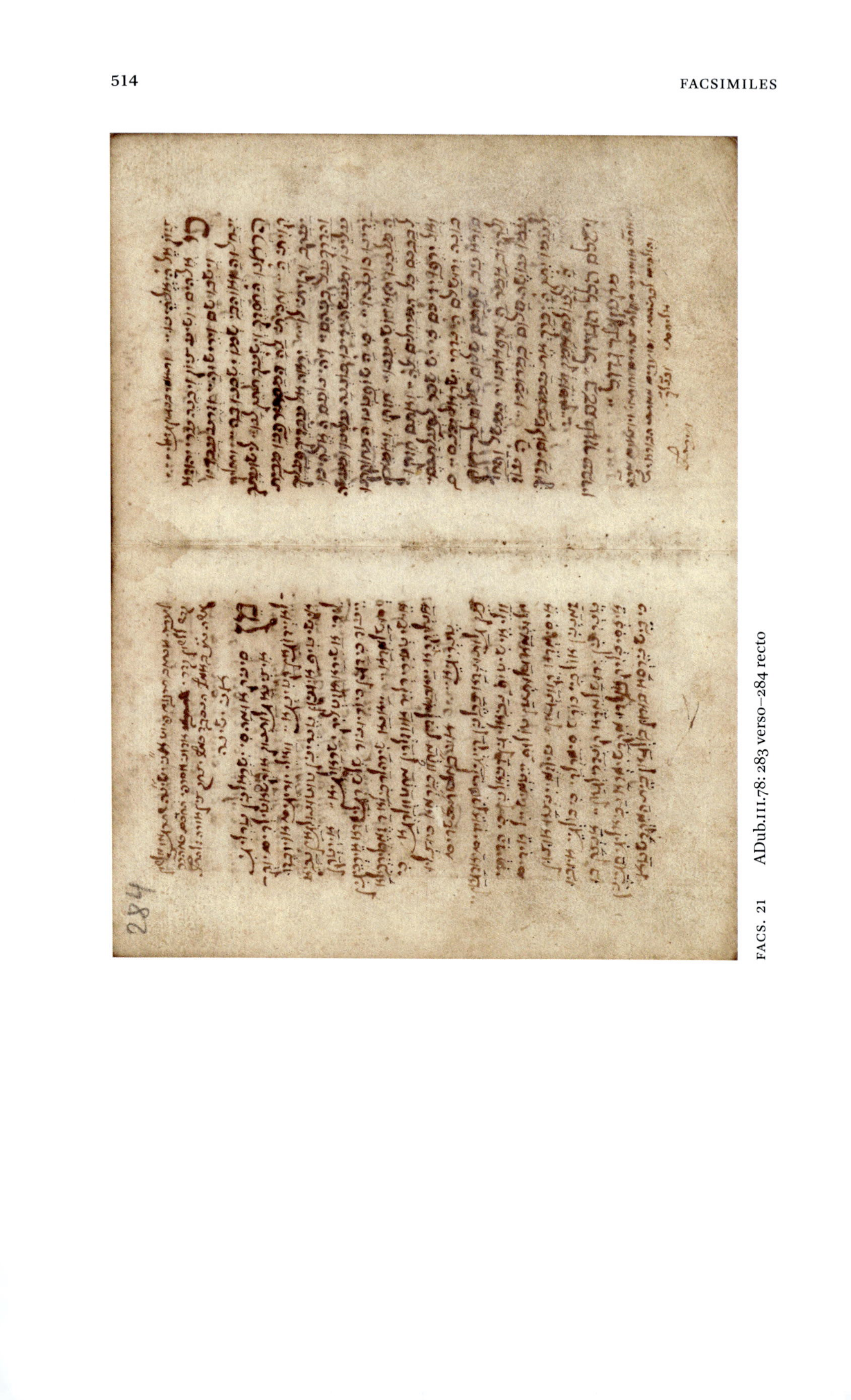

FACS. 21 ADub.III.78: 283 verso–284 recto

FACS. 22 ADub.III.78: 284 verso–285 recto

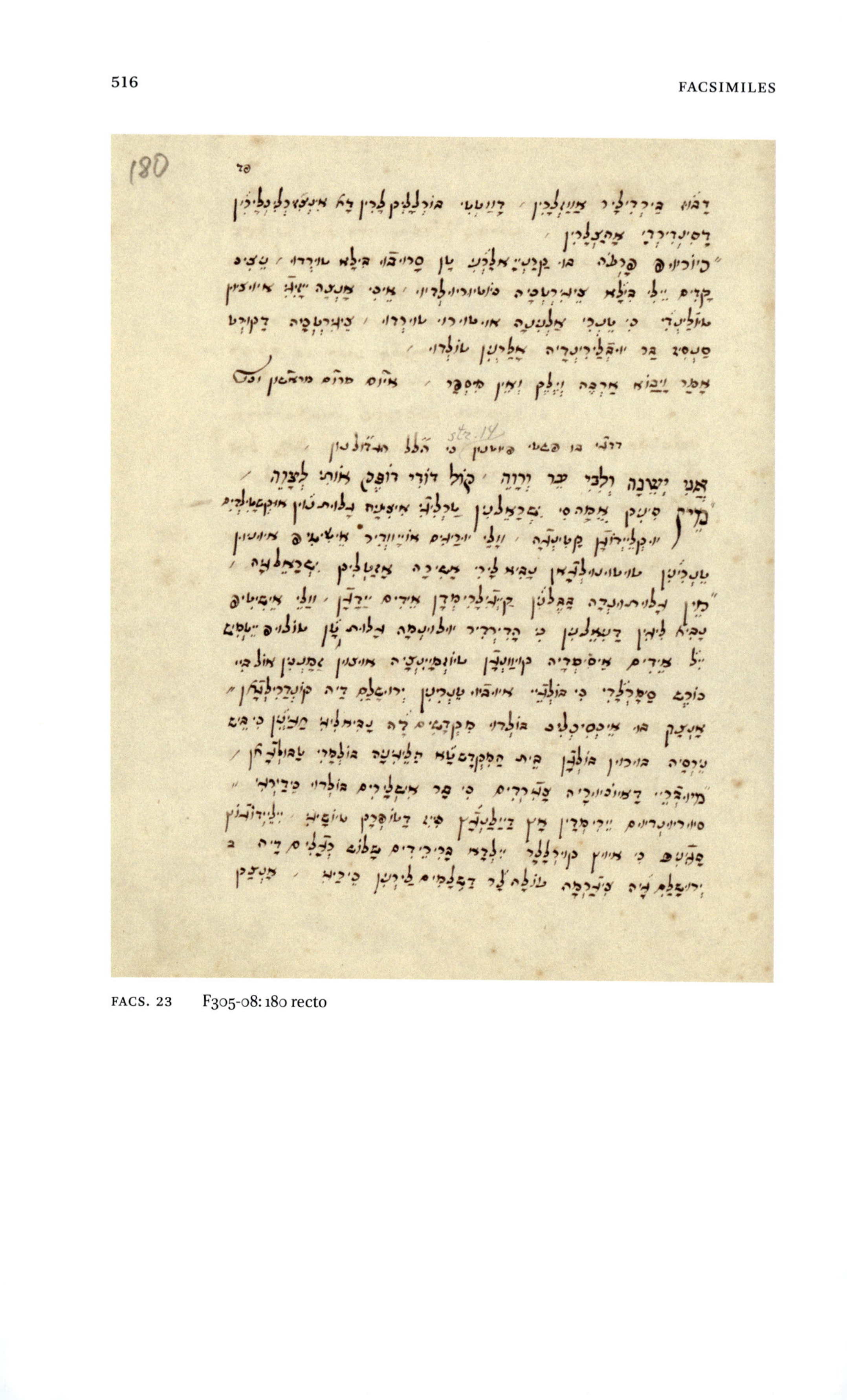

FACS. 23 F305-08: 180 recto

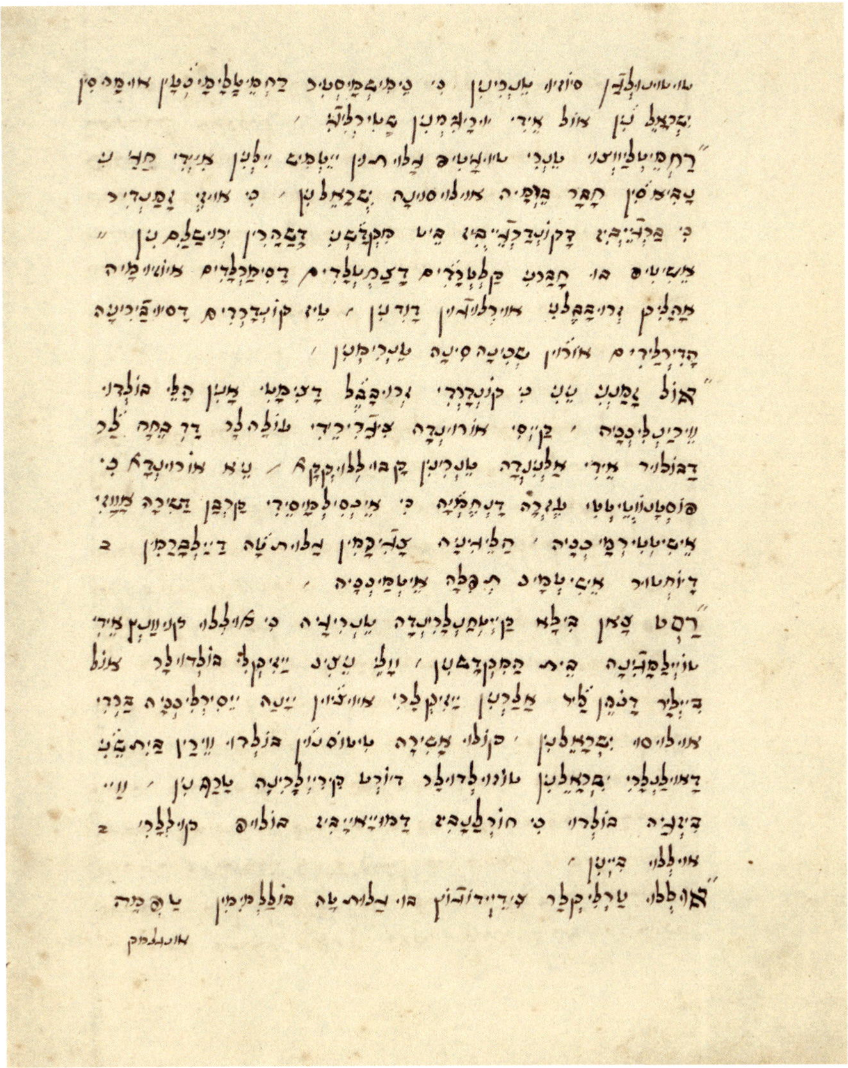

FACS. 24 F305-08: 180 verso

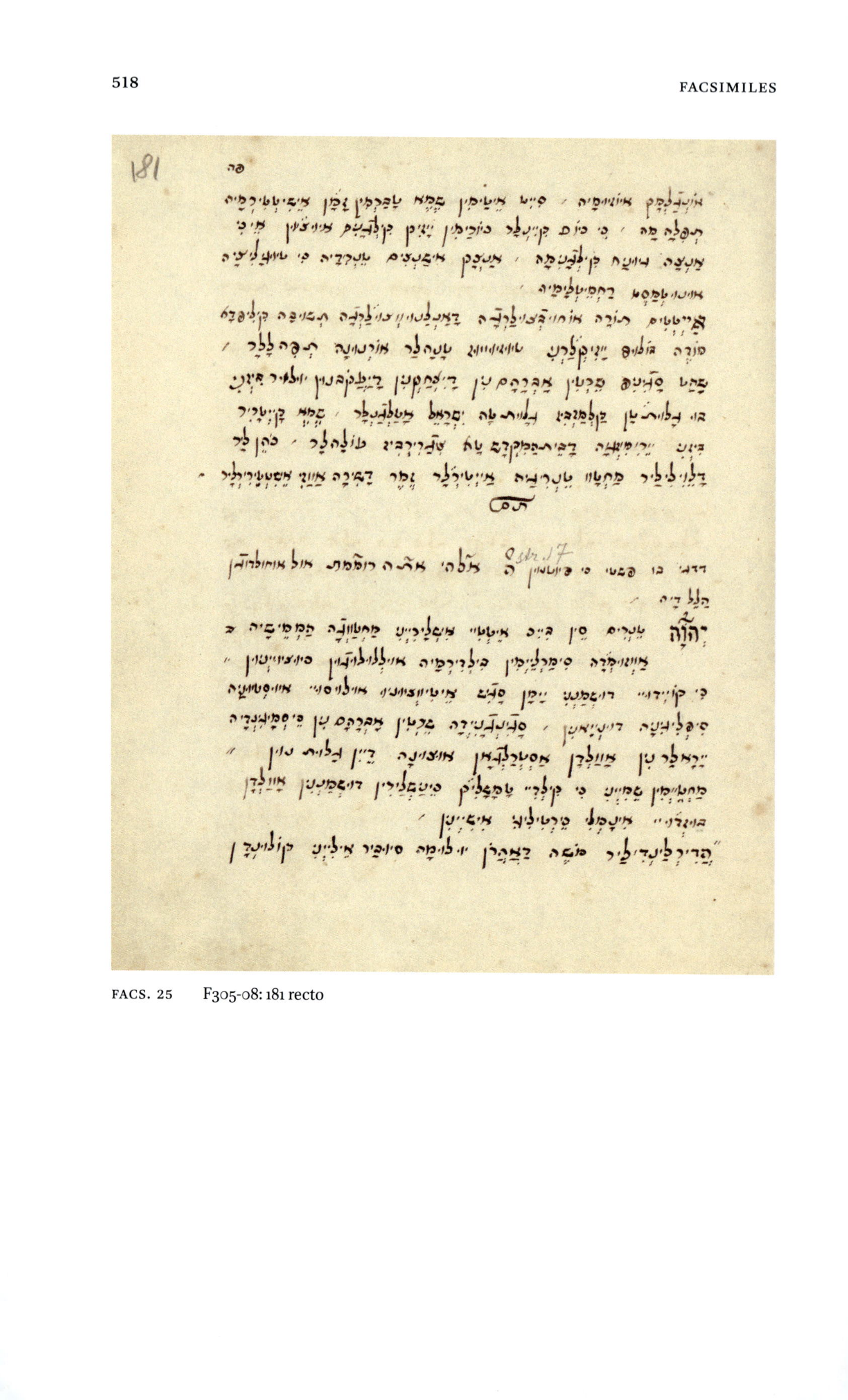

FACS. 25 F305-08: 181 recto

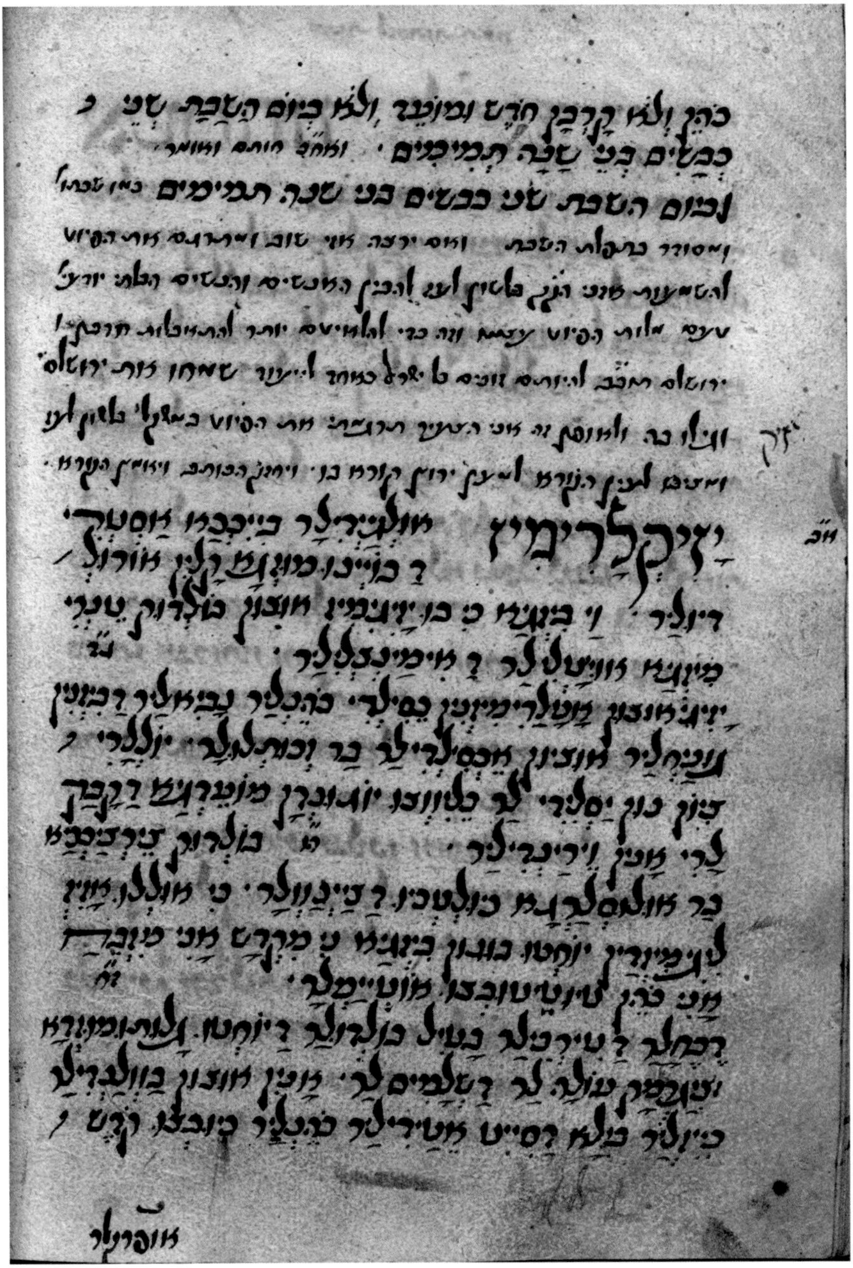

FACS. 26 JSul.I.01a: 118 verso

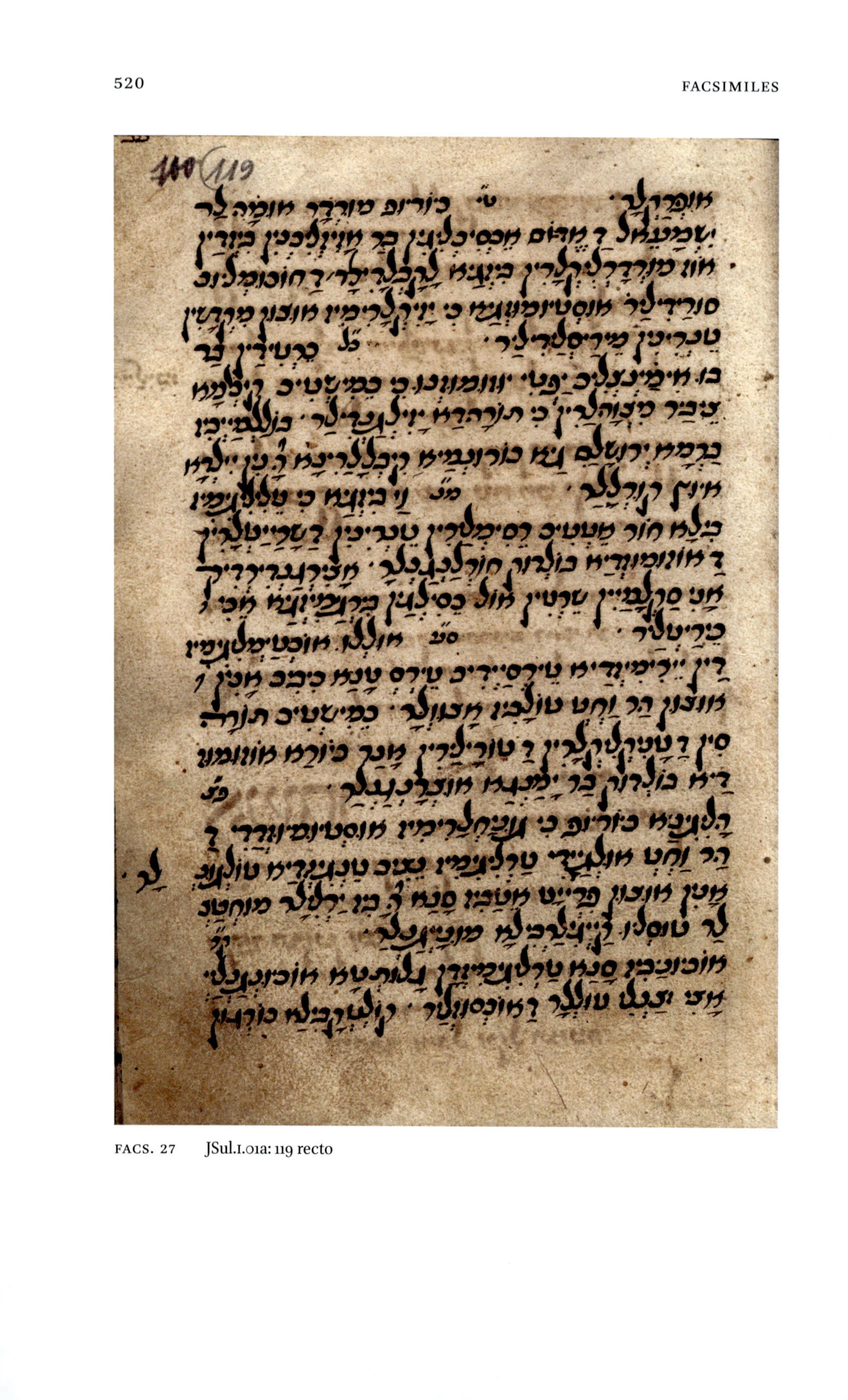

FACS. 27 JSul.I.01a: 119 recto

FACS. 28 JSul.I.01a: 119 verso

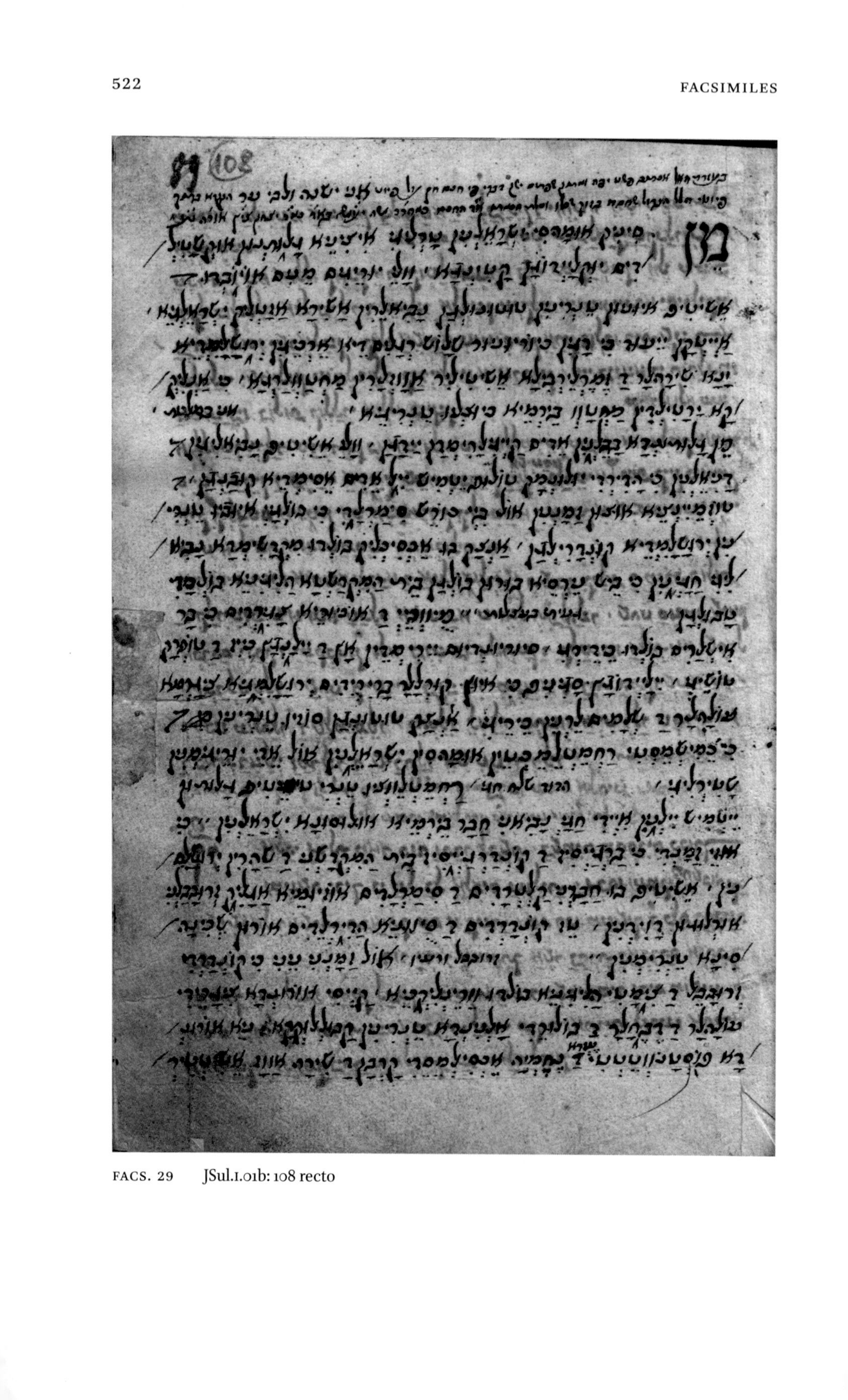

FACS. 29 JSul.1.01b: 108 recto

FACS. 30 JSul.I.01b: 108 verso

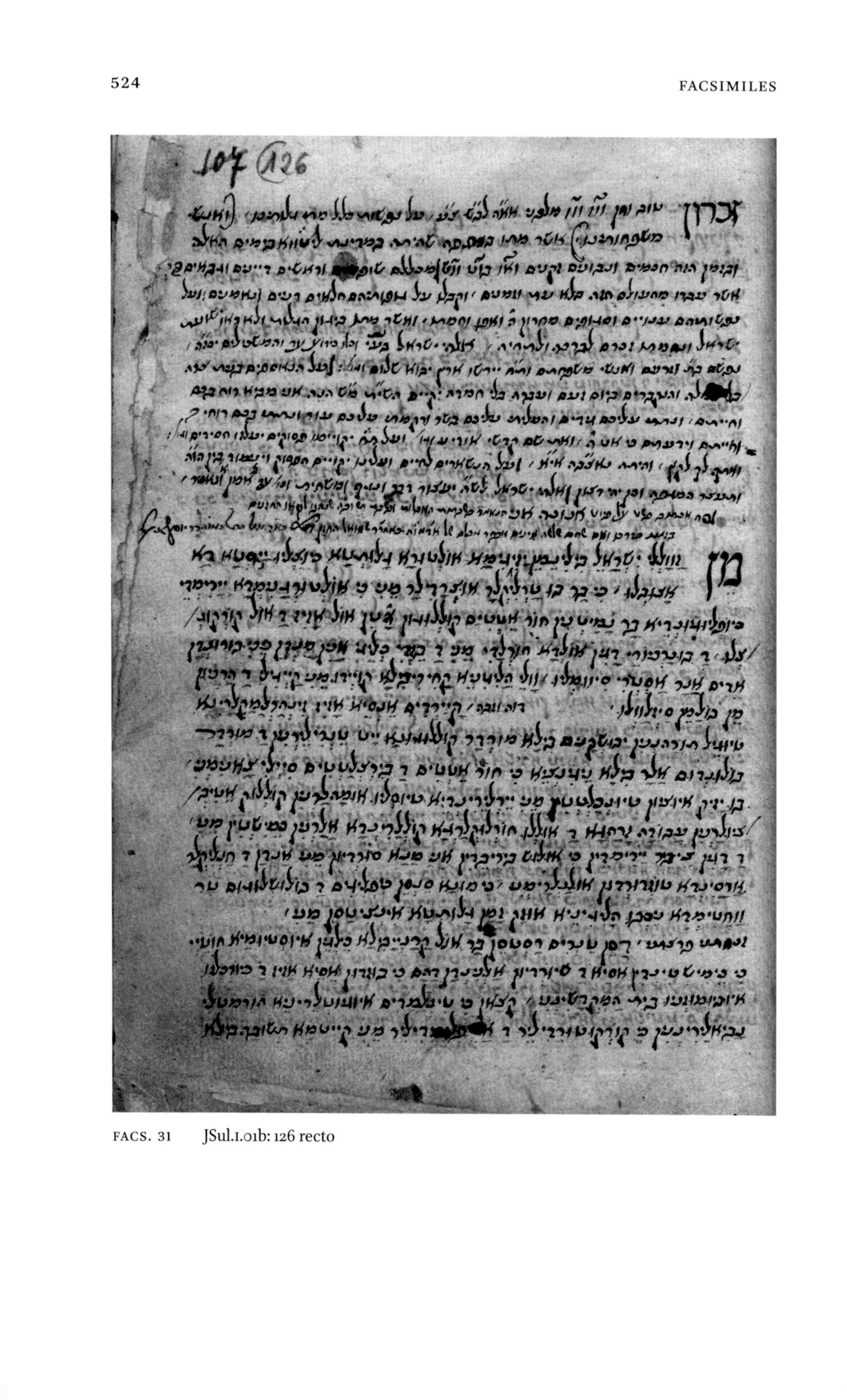

107 (126)

FACS. 31 JSul.1.01b: 126 recto

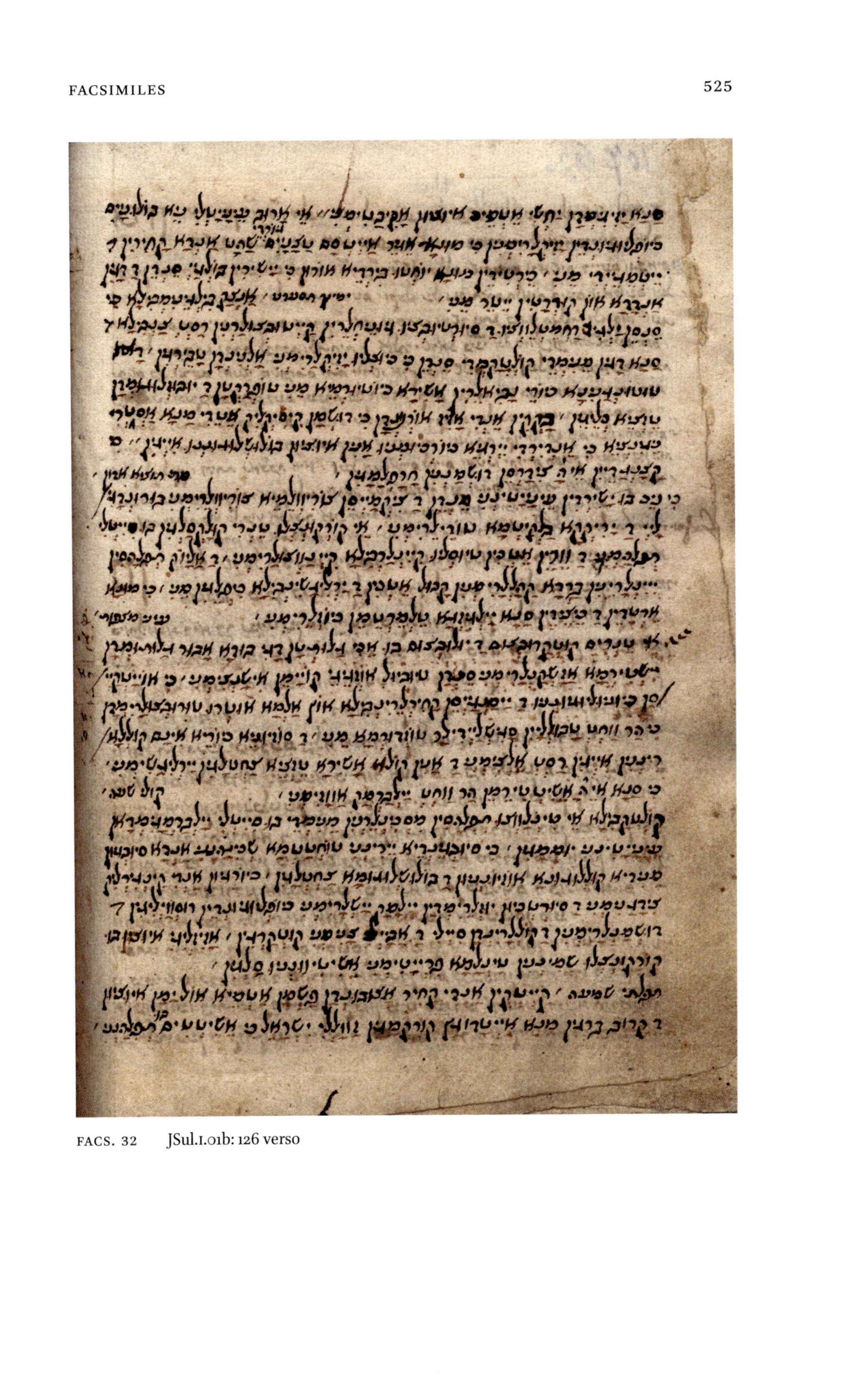

FACS. 32 JSul.I.01b: 126 verso

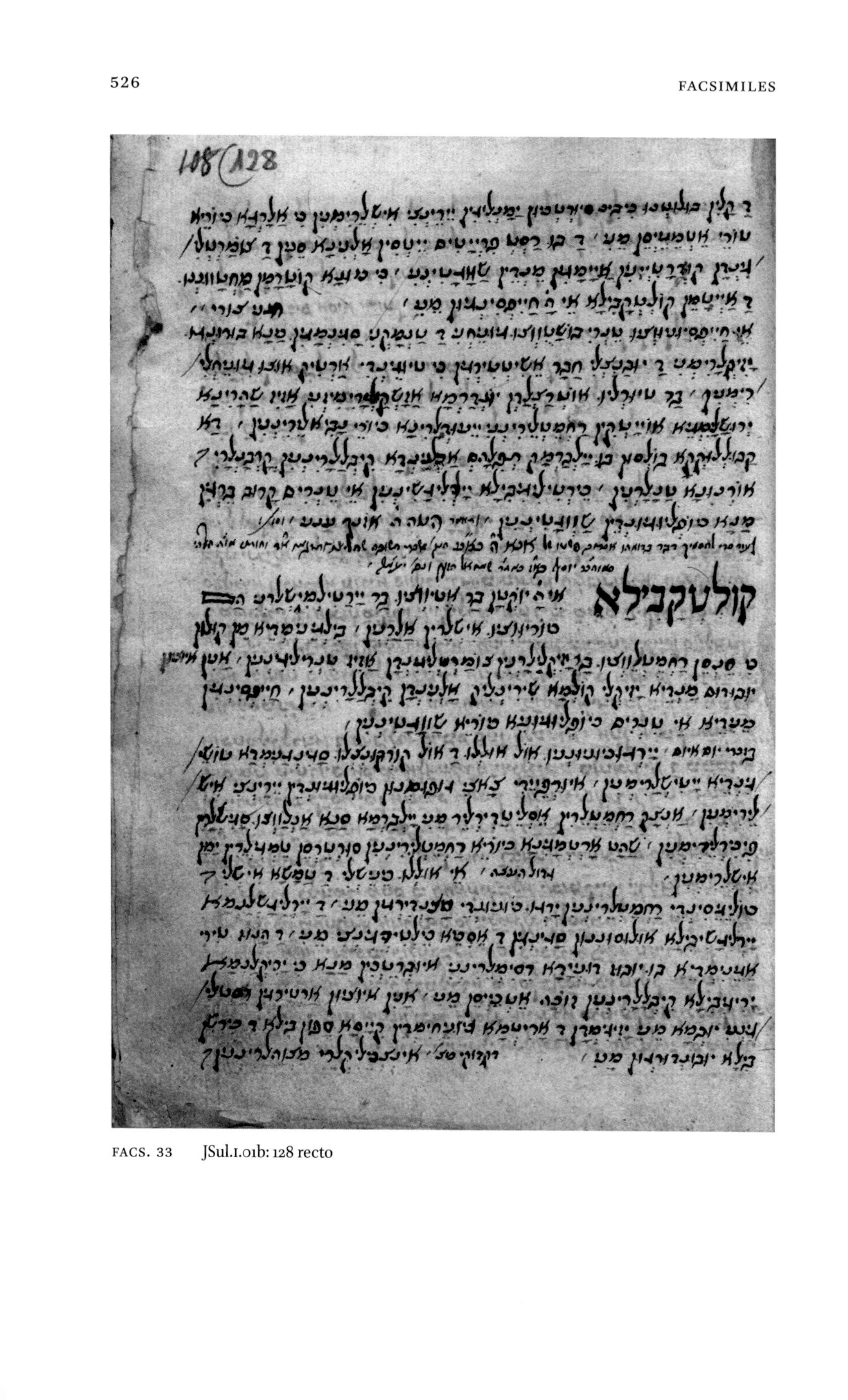

FACS. 33 JSul.I.01b: 128 recto

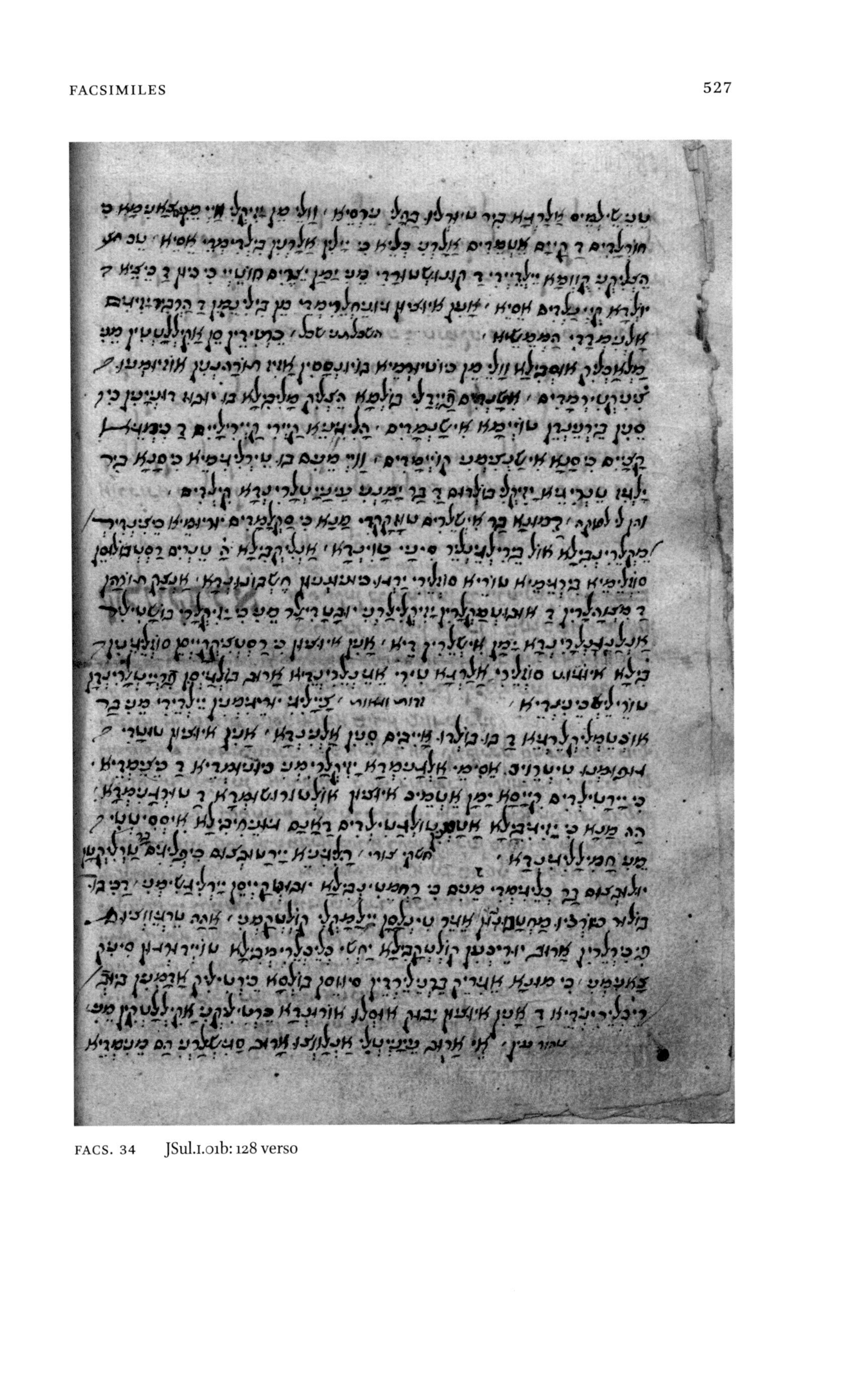

FACS. 34 JSul.I.01b: 128 verso

FACS. 35 JSul.I.01b: 129 recto

FACS. 36 JSul.I.01b: 129 verso

FACS. 37 JSul.I.01b: 130 recto

FACS. 38 JSul.I.01c: 131 recto

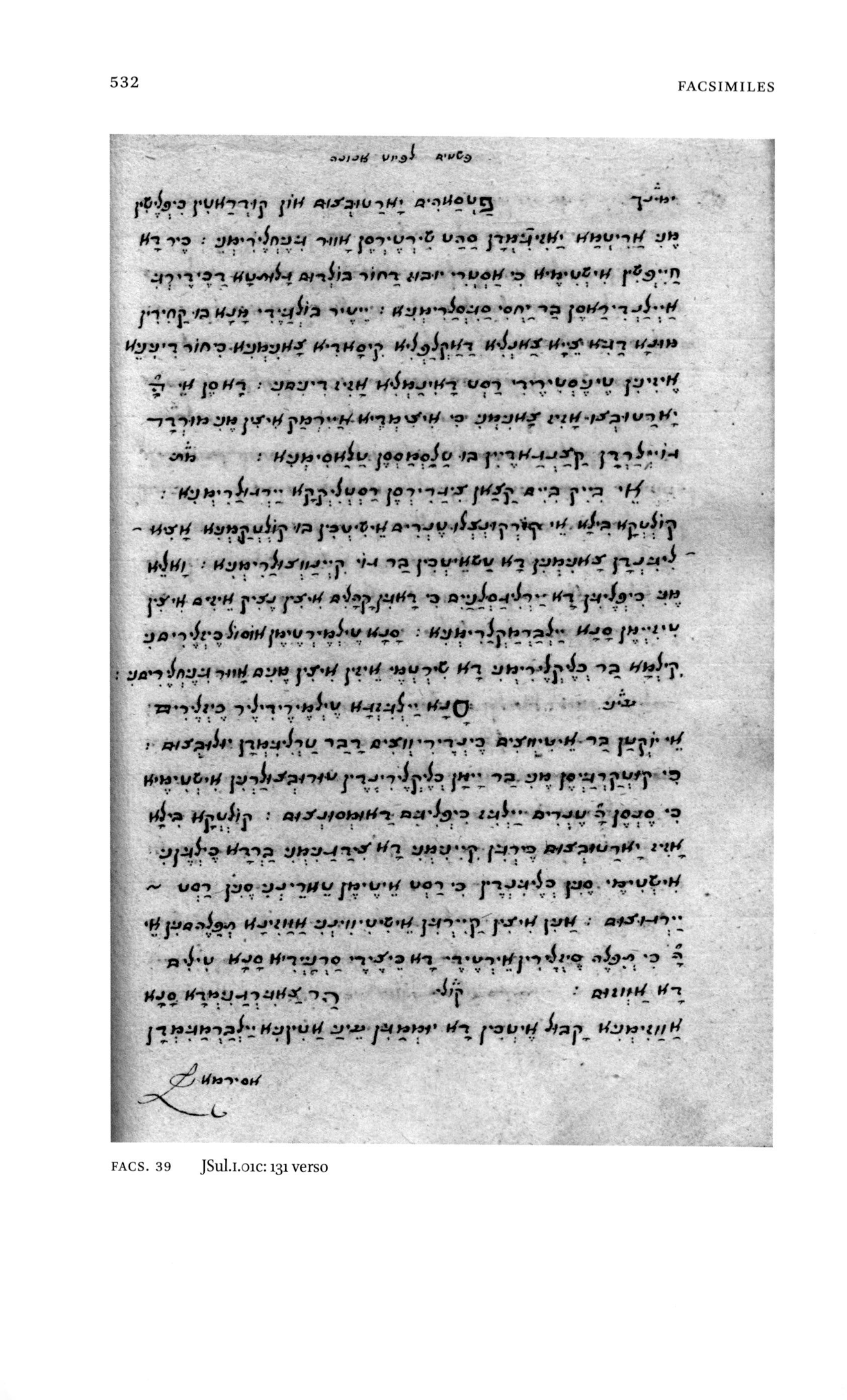

FACS. 39 JSul.1.01c: 131 verso

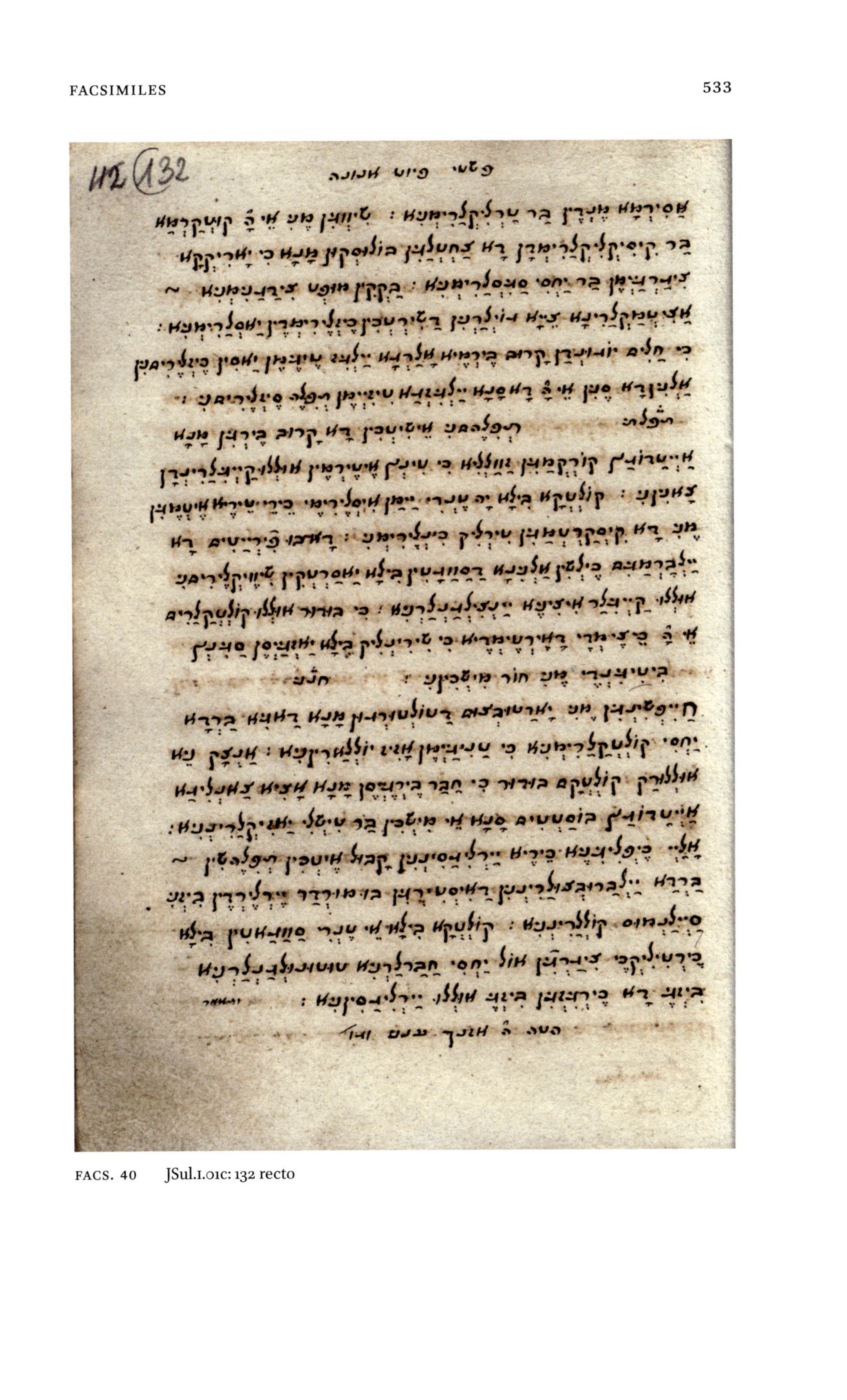

FACS. 40 JSul.I.01c: 132 recto

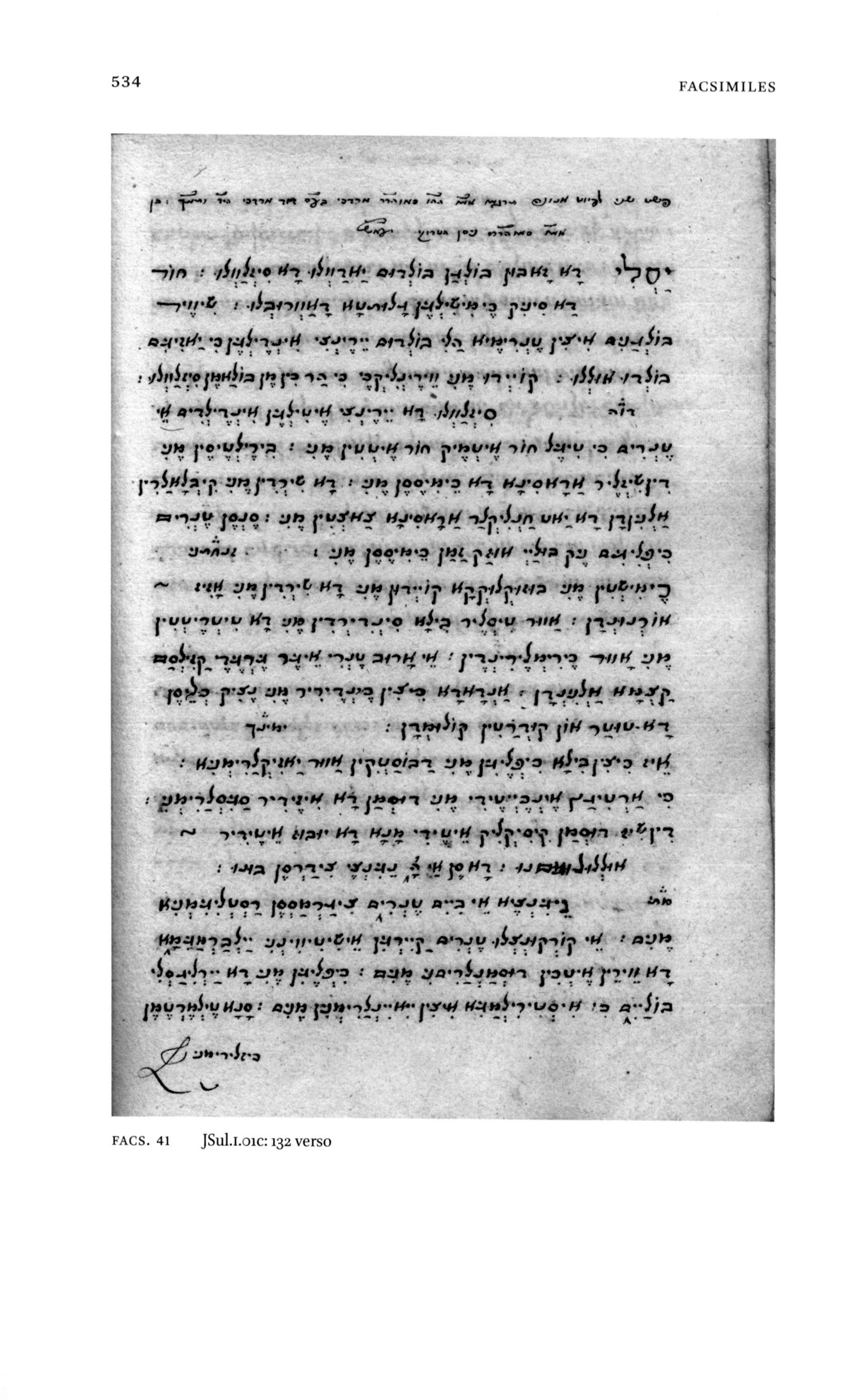

FACS. 41 JSul.I.01c: 132 verso

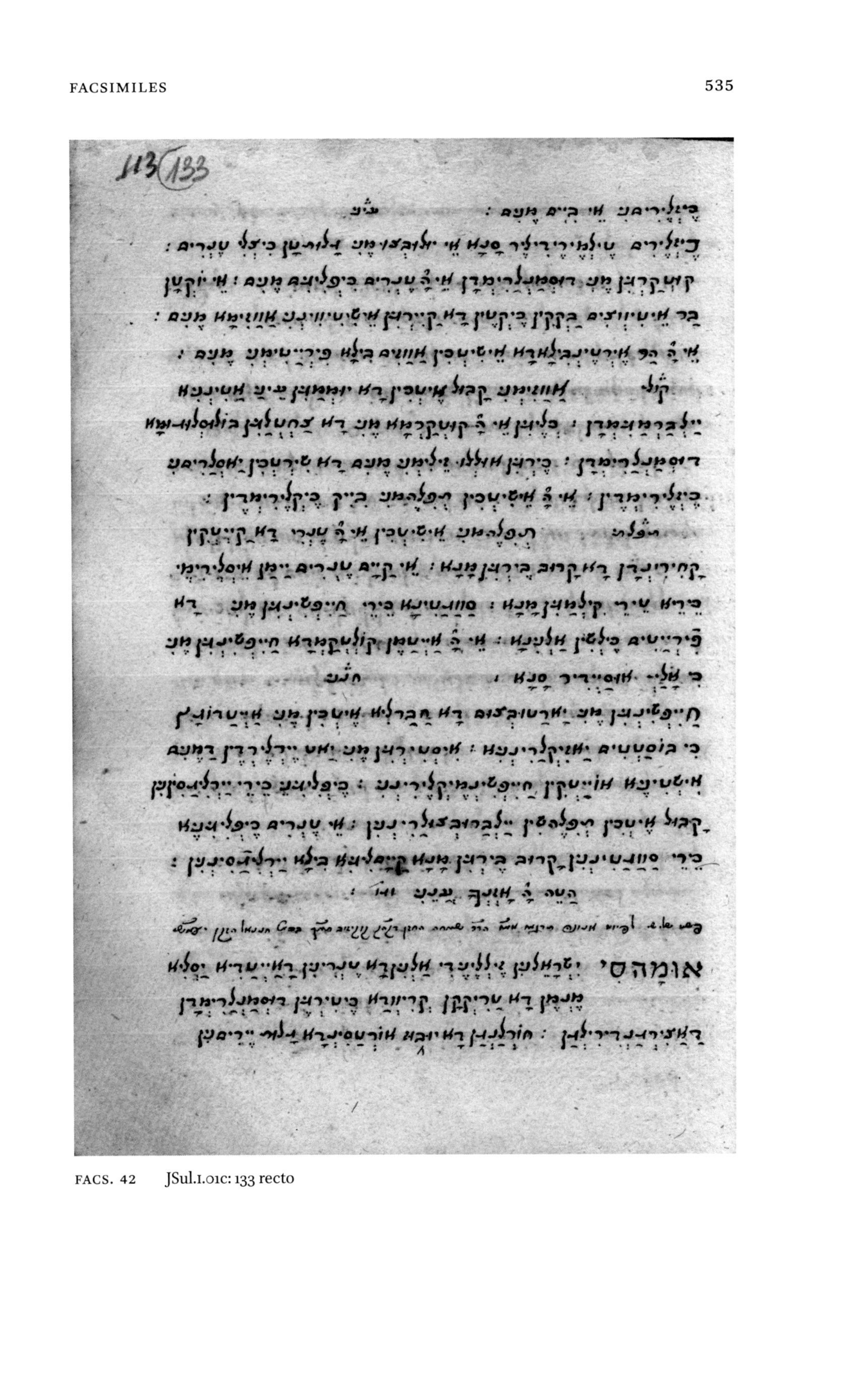

113 (133)

FACS. 42 JSul.I.01c: 133 recto

FACS. 43 JSul.I.01c: 133 verso

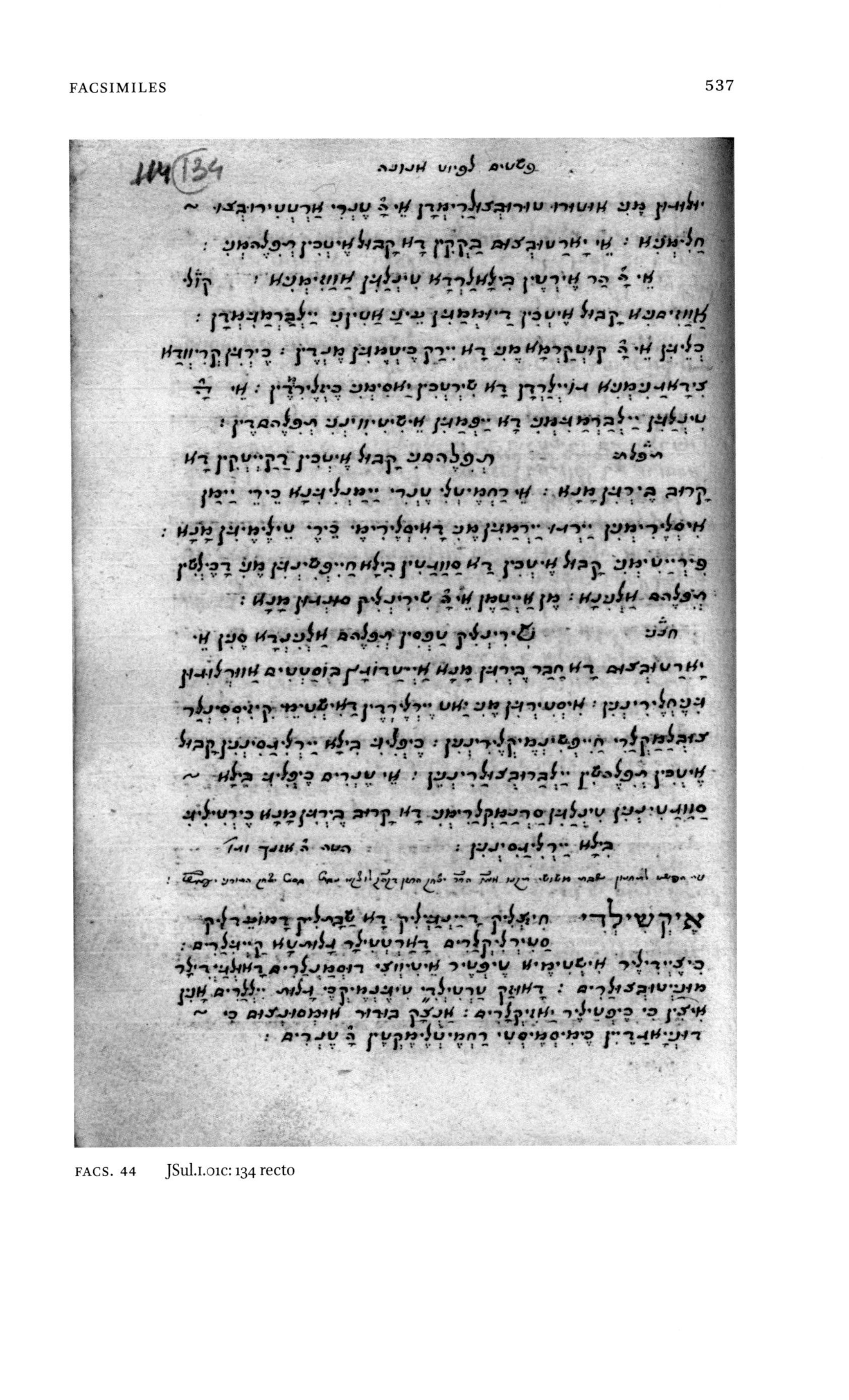

FACS. 44 JSul.I.01c: 134 recto

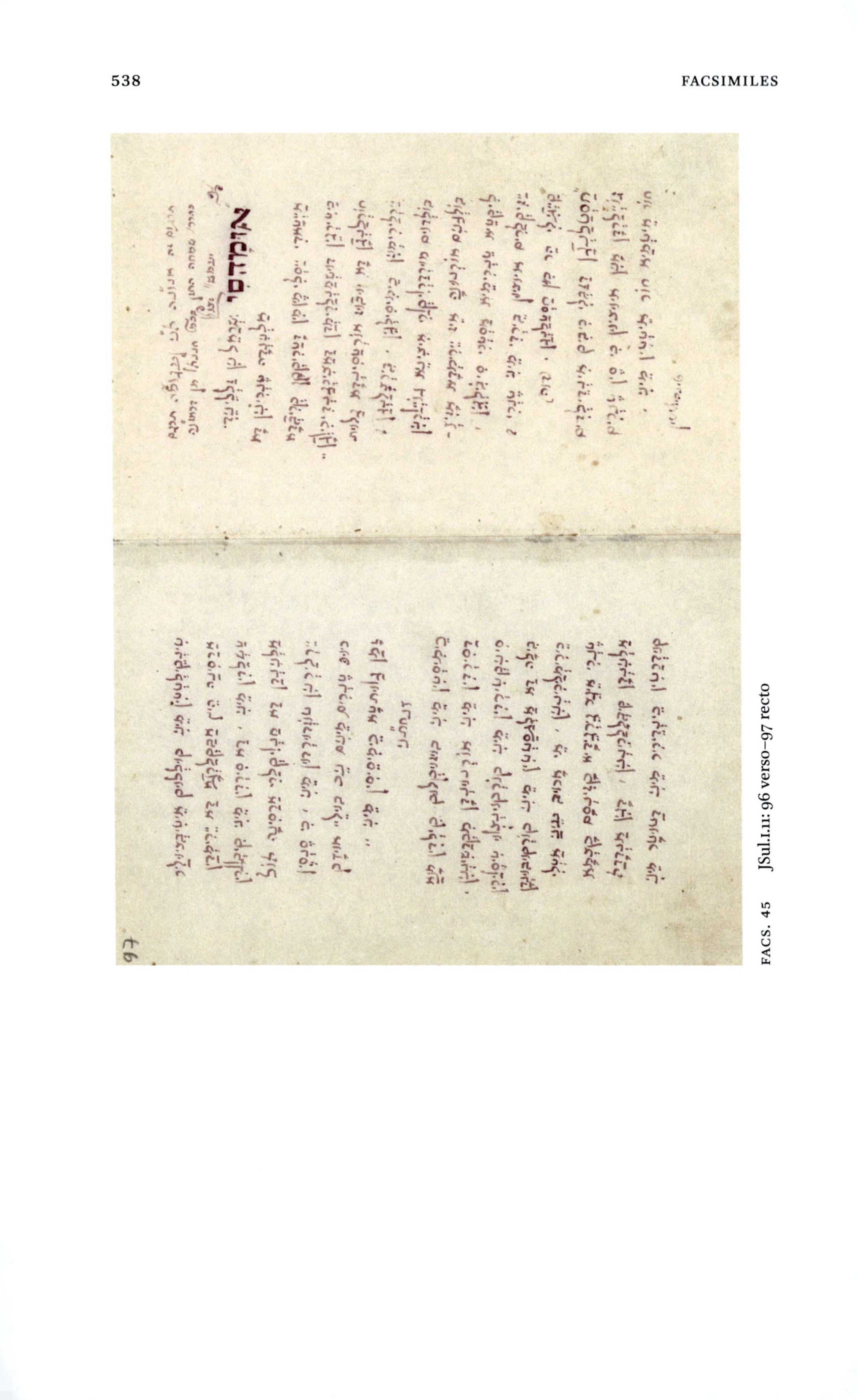

FACS. 45 JSul.1.11: 96 verso–97 recto

FACS. 46 JSul.I.11: 97 verso–98 recto

FACS. 47 JSul.1.11: 98 verso–99 recto

FACS. 48 JSul.1.11: 102 verso–103 recto

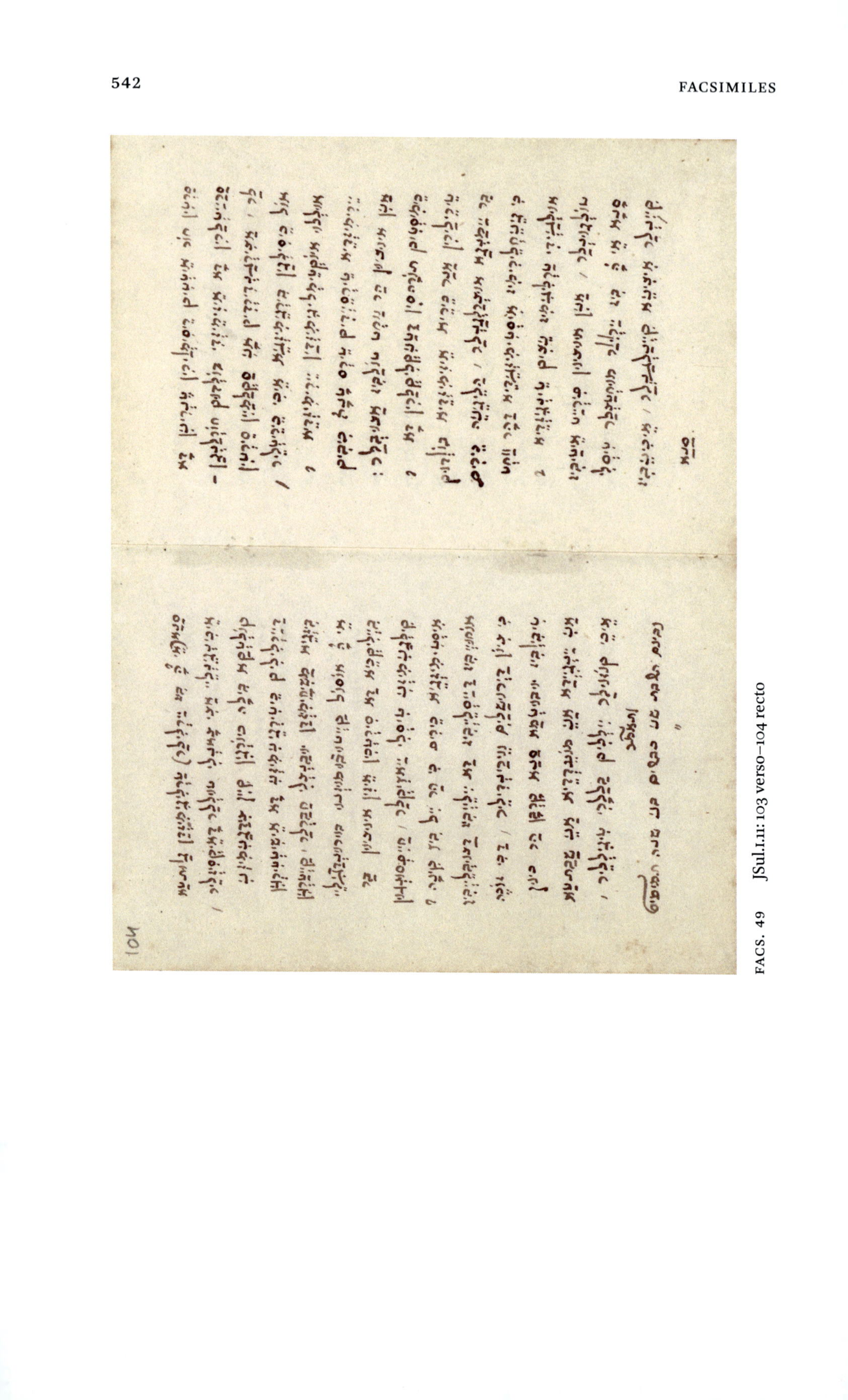

FACS. 49 JSul.1.11: 103 verso–104 recto

FACS. 50 JSul.I.16: 288 recto

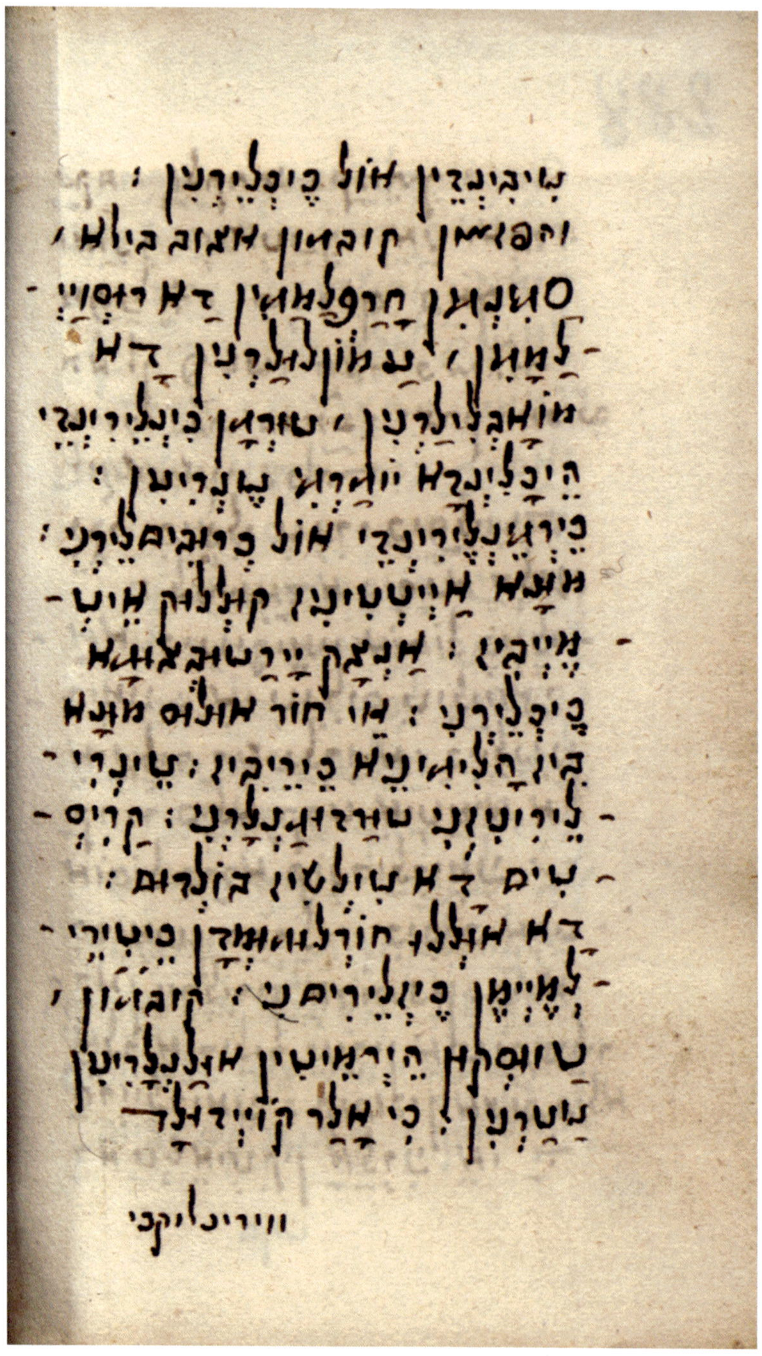

FACS. 51 JSul.I.16: 288 verso

289

FACS. 52 JSul.I.16: 289 recto

FACS. 53 JSul.I.16: 289 verso

FACS. 54 JSul.I.16: 290 recto

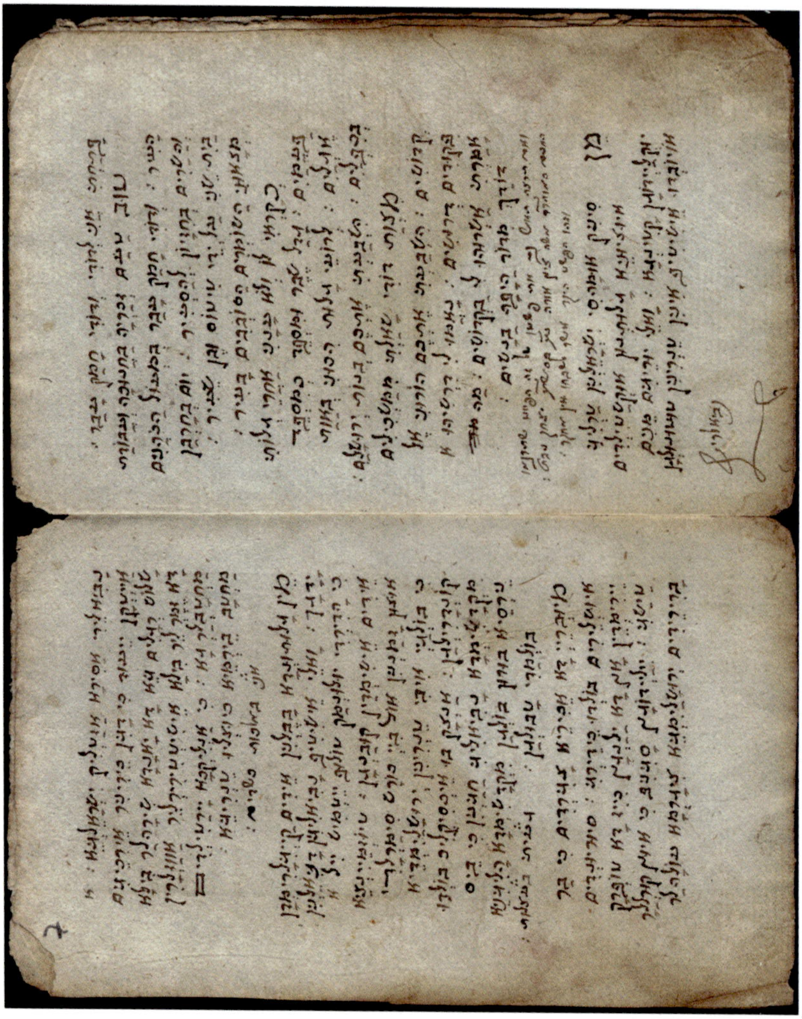

FACS. 55 JSul.I.37.02: 6 verso–7 recto

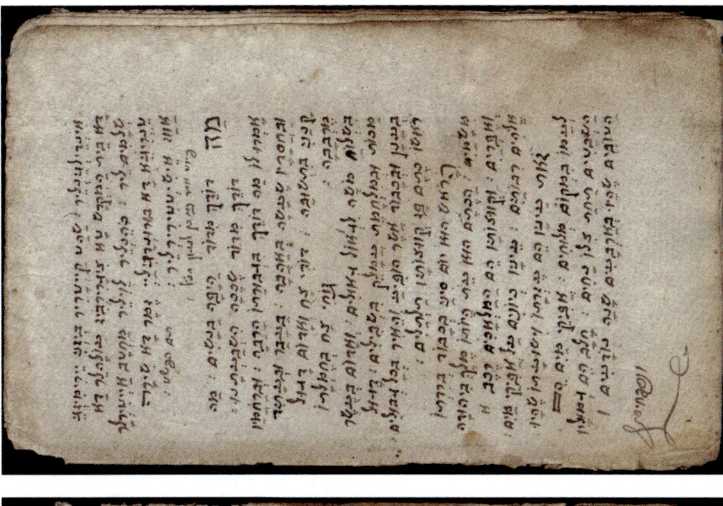

FACS. 57 JSul.I.37.02: 8 verso

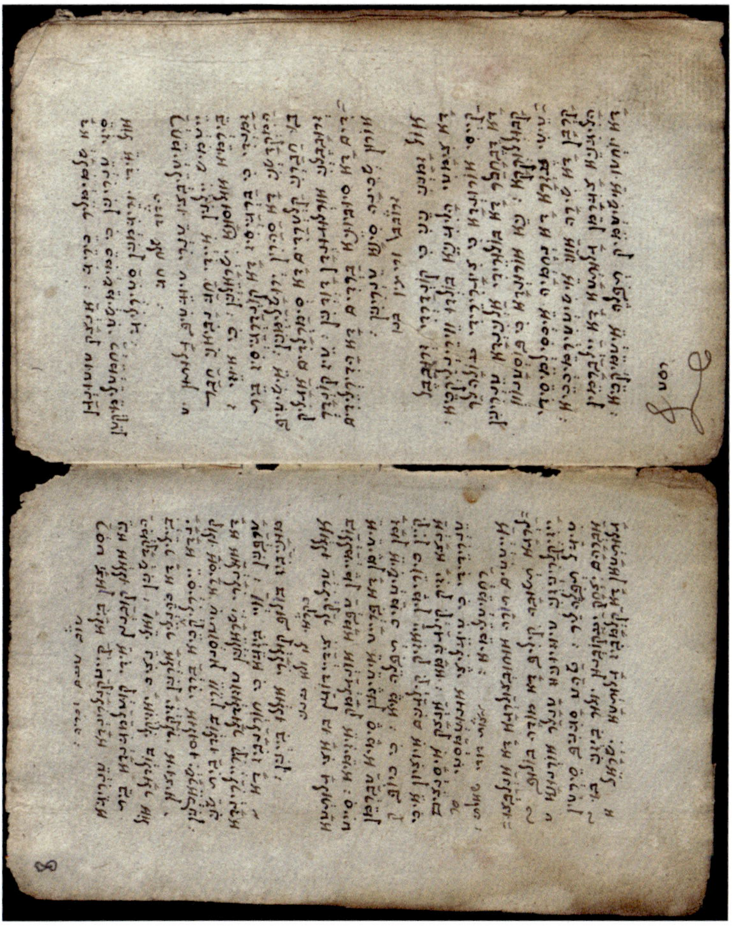

FACS. 56 JSul.I.37.02: 7 verso–8 recto

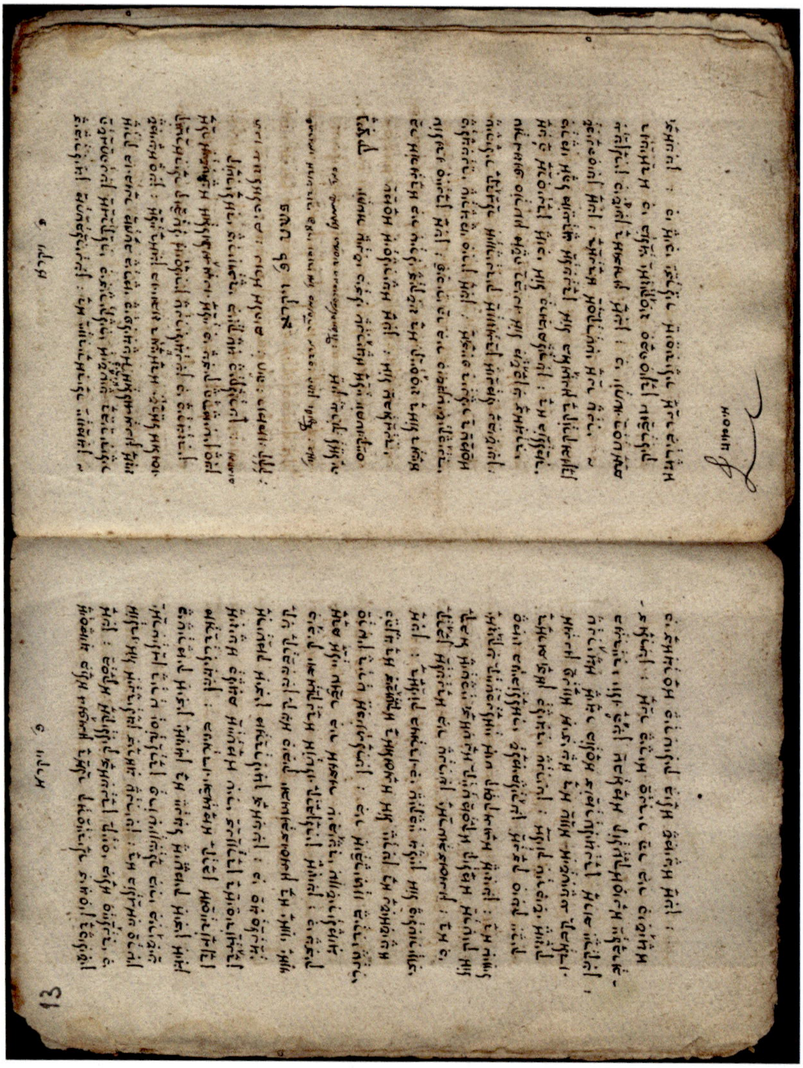

FACS. 58 JSul.I.37.03: 12 verso–13 recto

FACS. 59 JSul.I.37.03: 13 verso–14 recto

FACS. 60 JSul.I.37.03: 16 verso

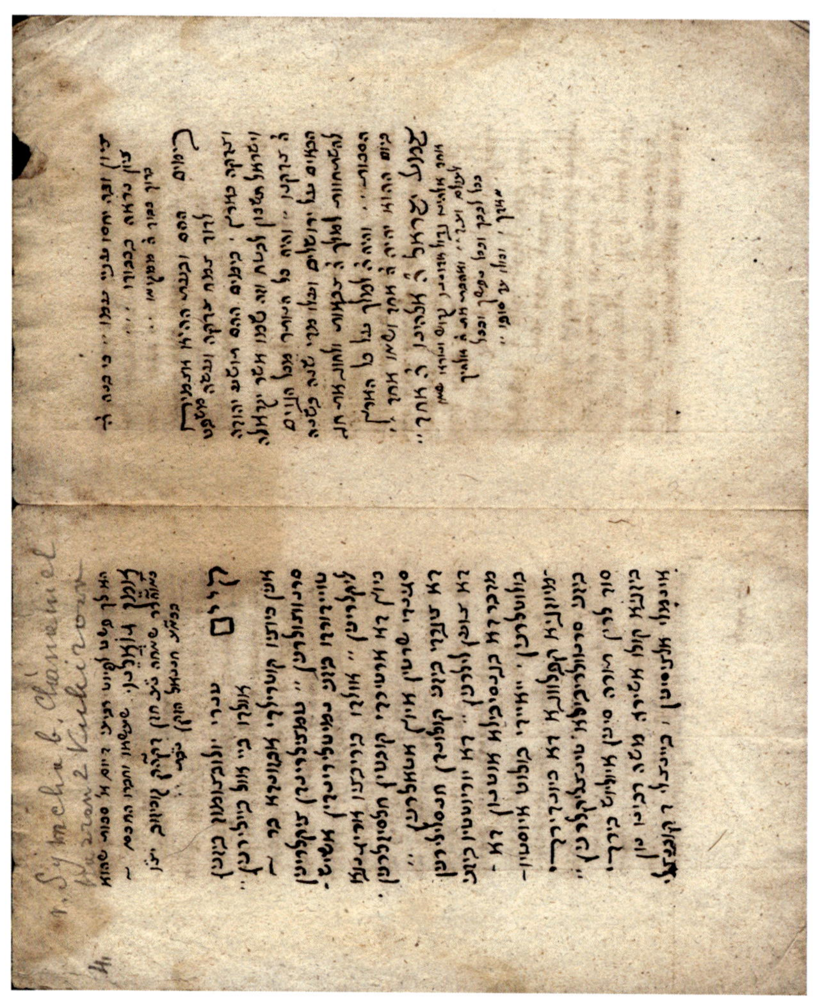

FACS. 61 JSul.1.38.09: 3 verso–4 recto

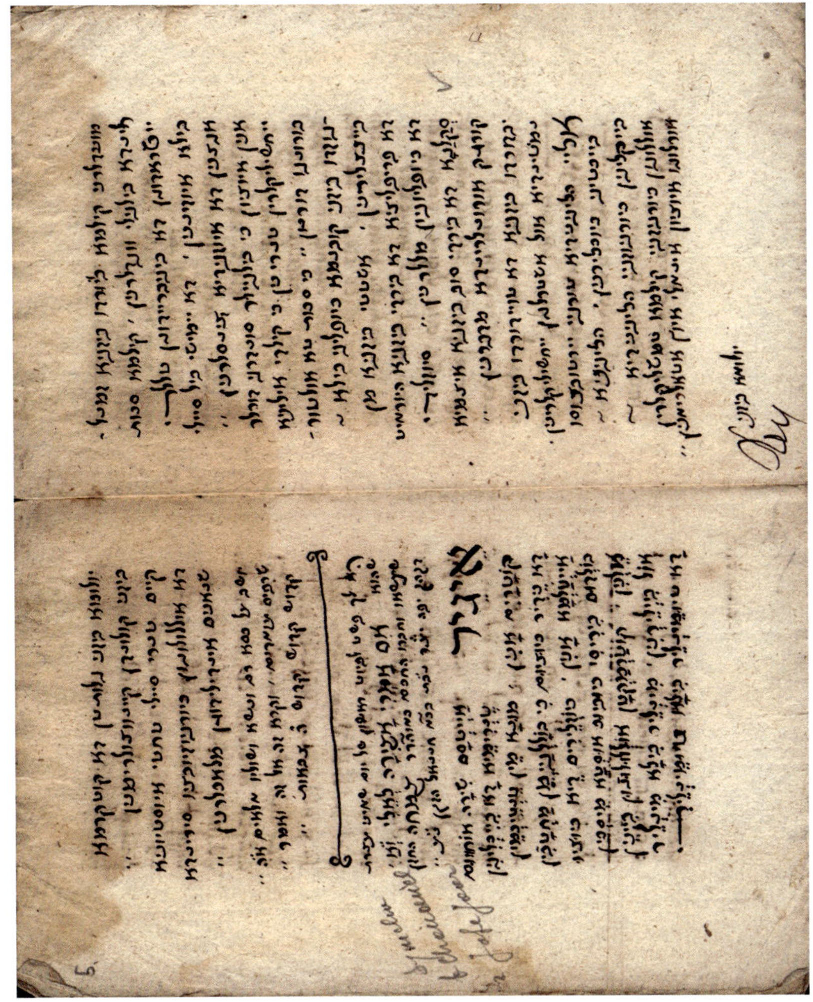

FACS. 62 JSul.1.38.09: 4 verso–5 recto

FACS. 64 JSul.I.38.09: 6 verso

FACS. 63 JSul.I.38.09: 5 verso–6 recto

FACS. 65 JSul.I.45: 100 verso–101 recto

FACS. 66 JSul.1.45: 101 verso–102 recto

FACS. 67 JSul.I.45: 102 verso–103 recto

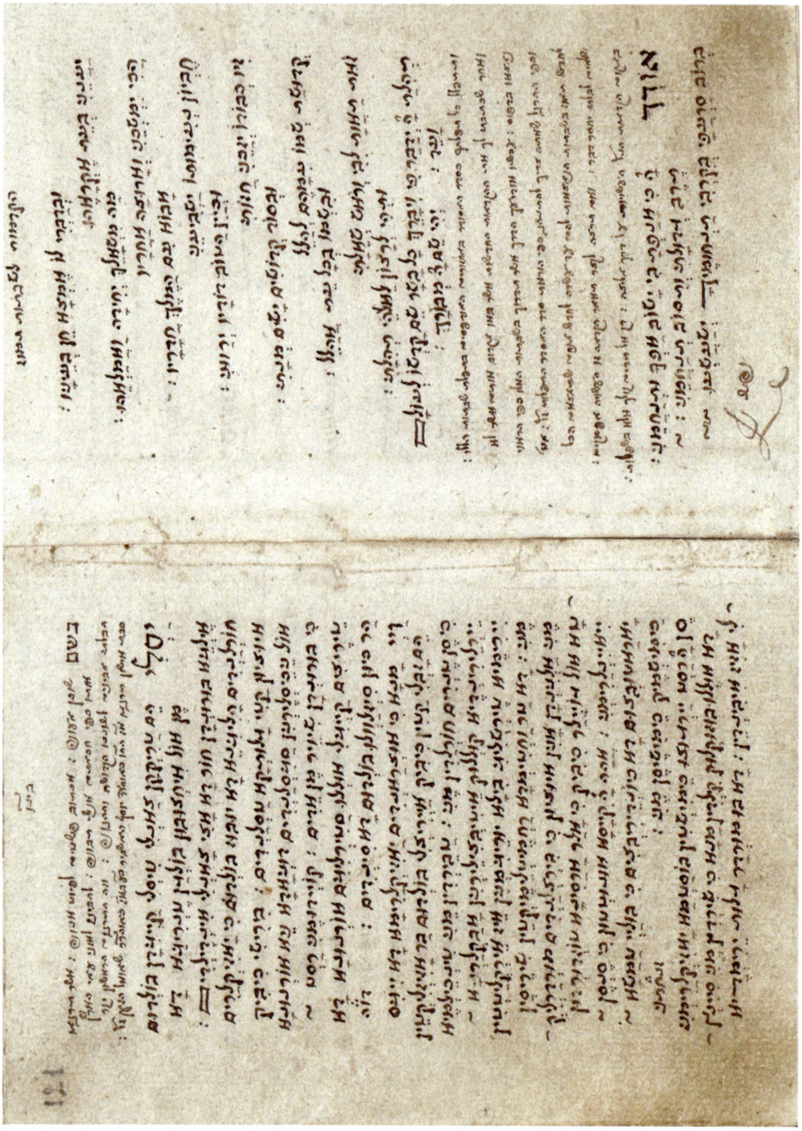

FACS. 68 JSul.I.45: 120 verso–121 recto

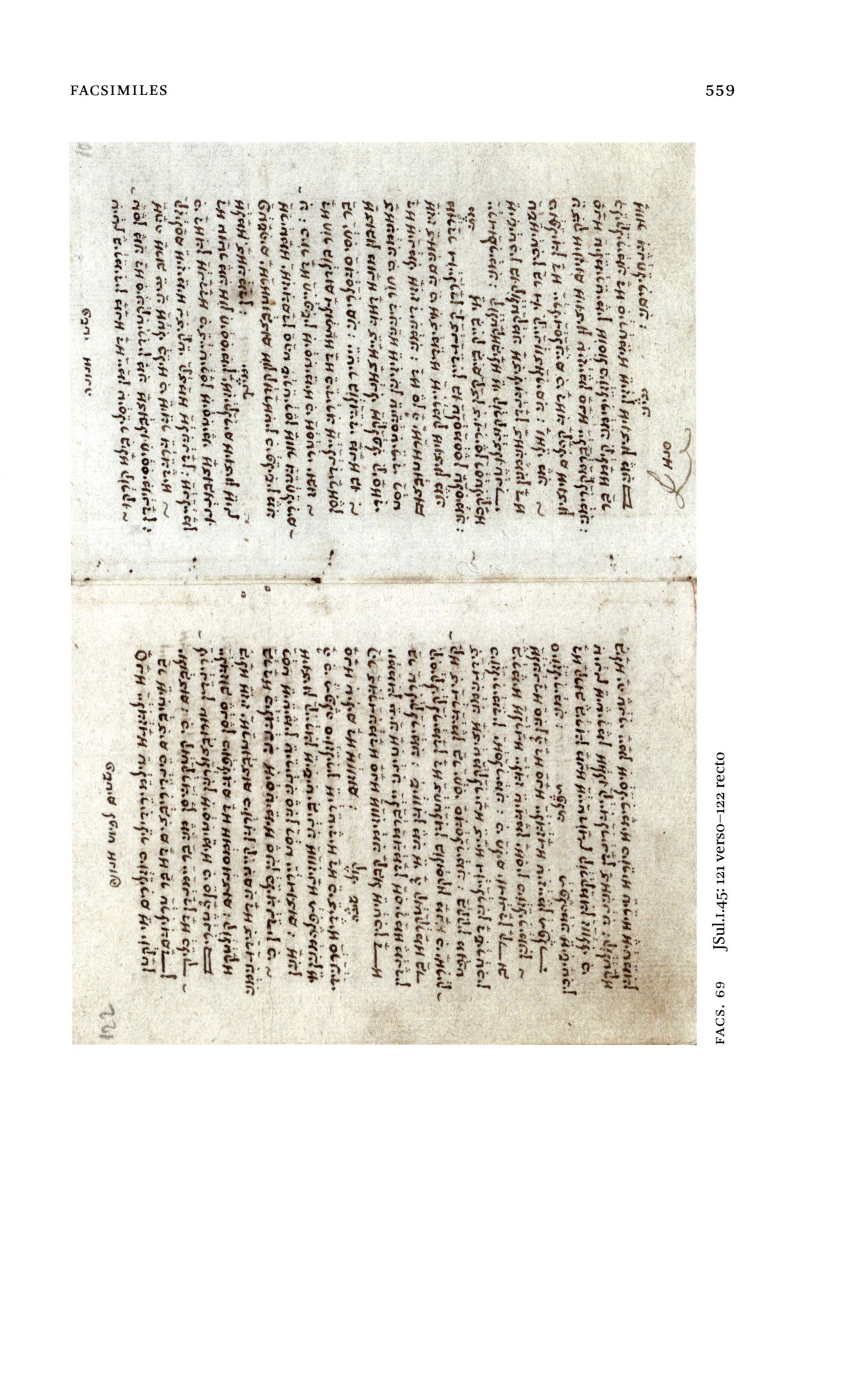

FACS. 69 JSul.I.45: 121 verso–122 recto

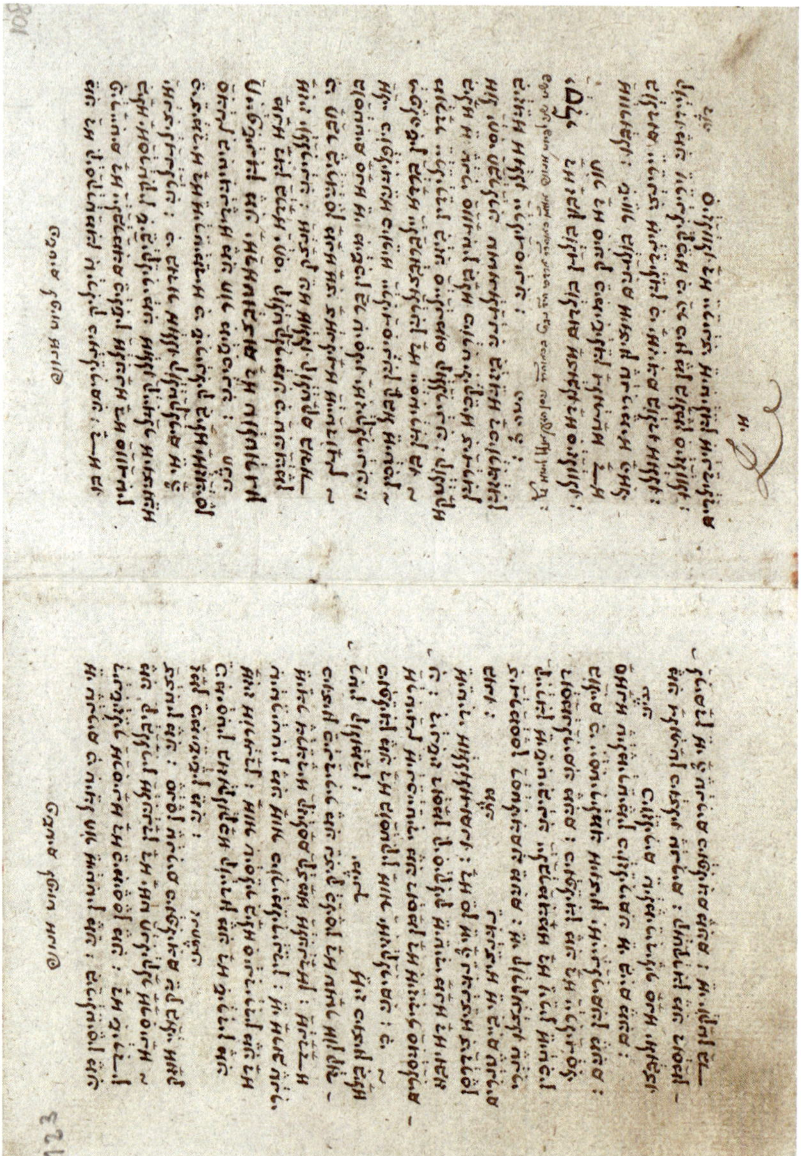

FACS. 70 JSul.1.45: 122 verso–123 recto

FACS. 71 JSul.I.45: 123 verso–124 recto

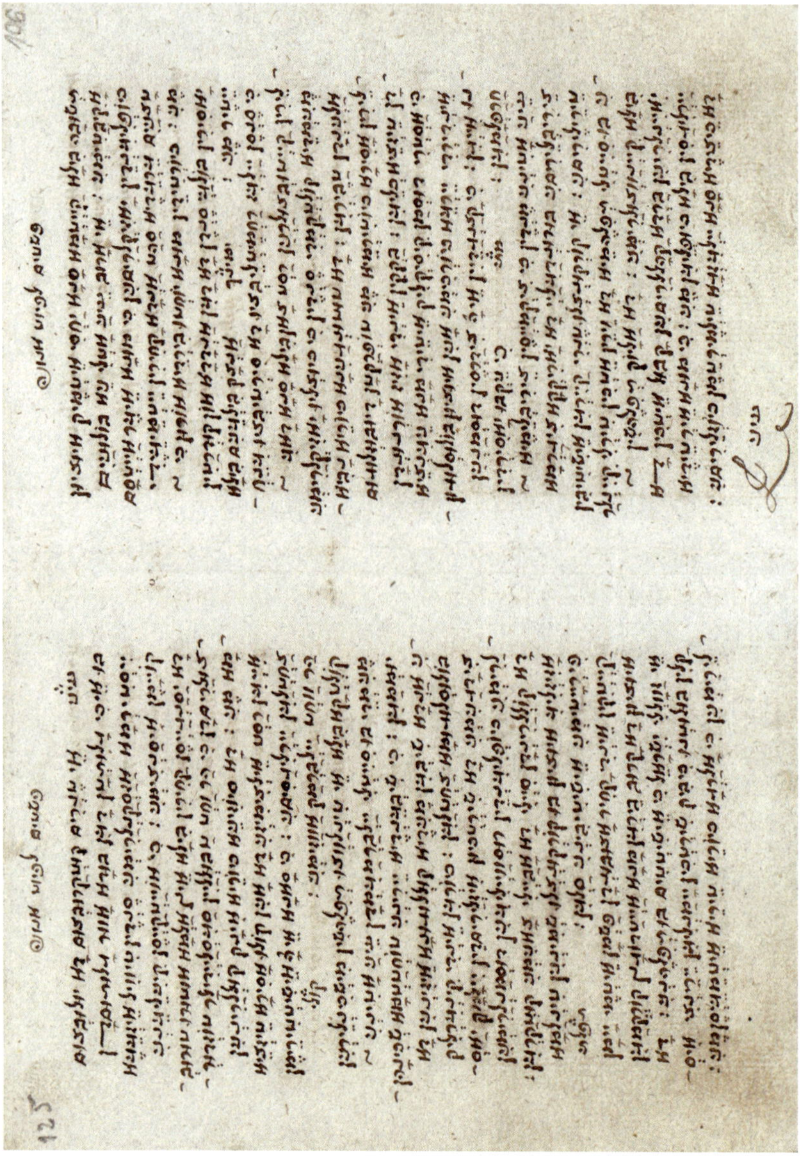

FACS. 72 JSul.I.45: 124 verso–125 recto

FACS. 73 JSul.1.45: 125 verso–126 recto

FACS. 74 JSul.1.45: 126 verso–127 recto

FACS. 75 JSul.I.45: 138 verso–139 recto

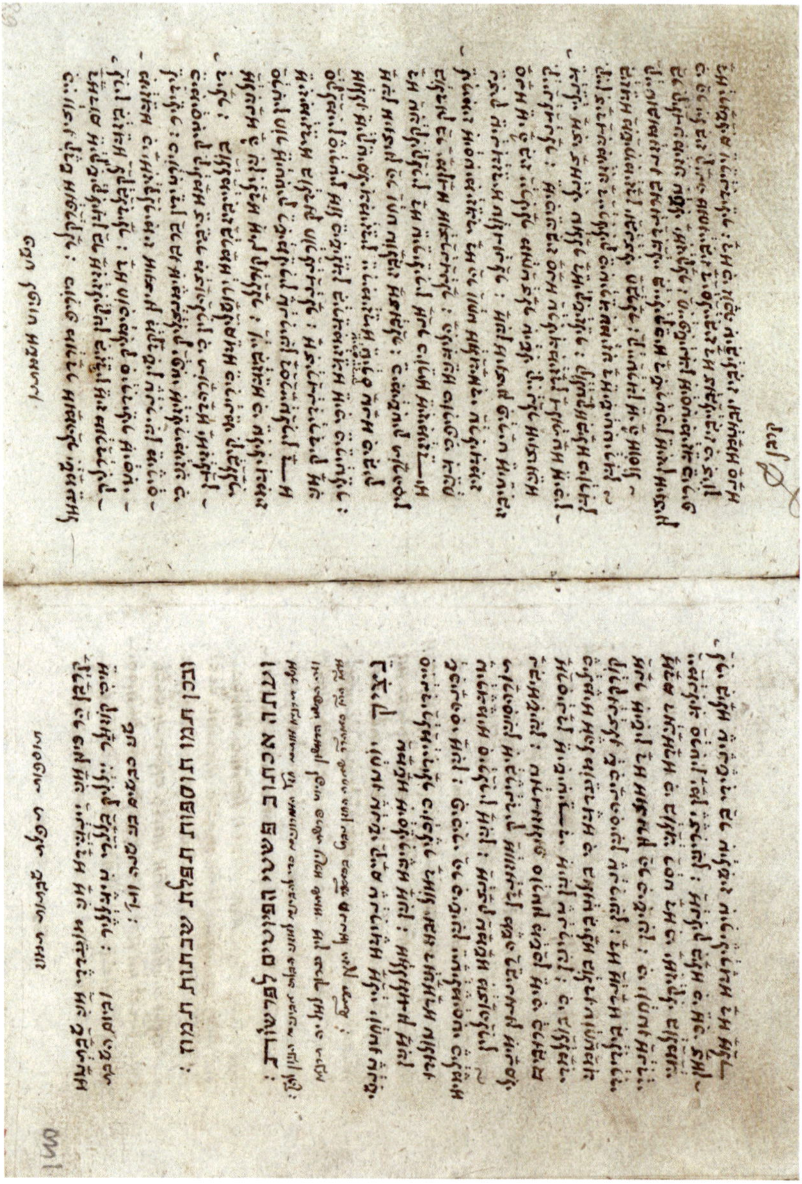

FACS. 76 JSul.I.45: 139 verso–140 recto

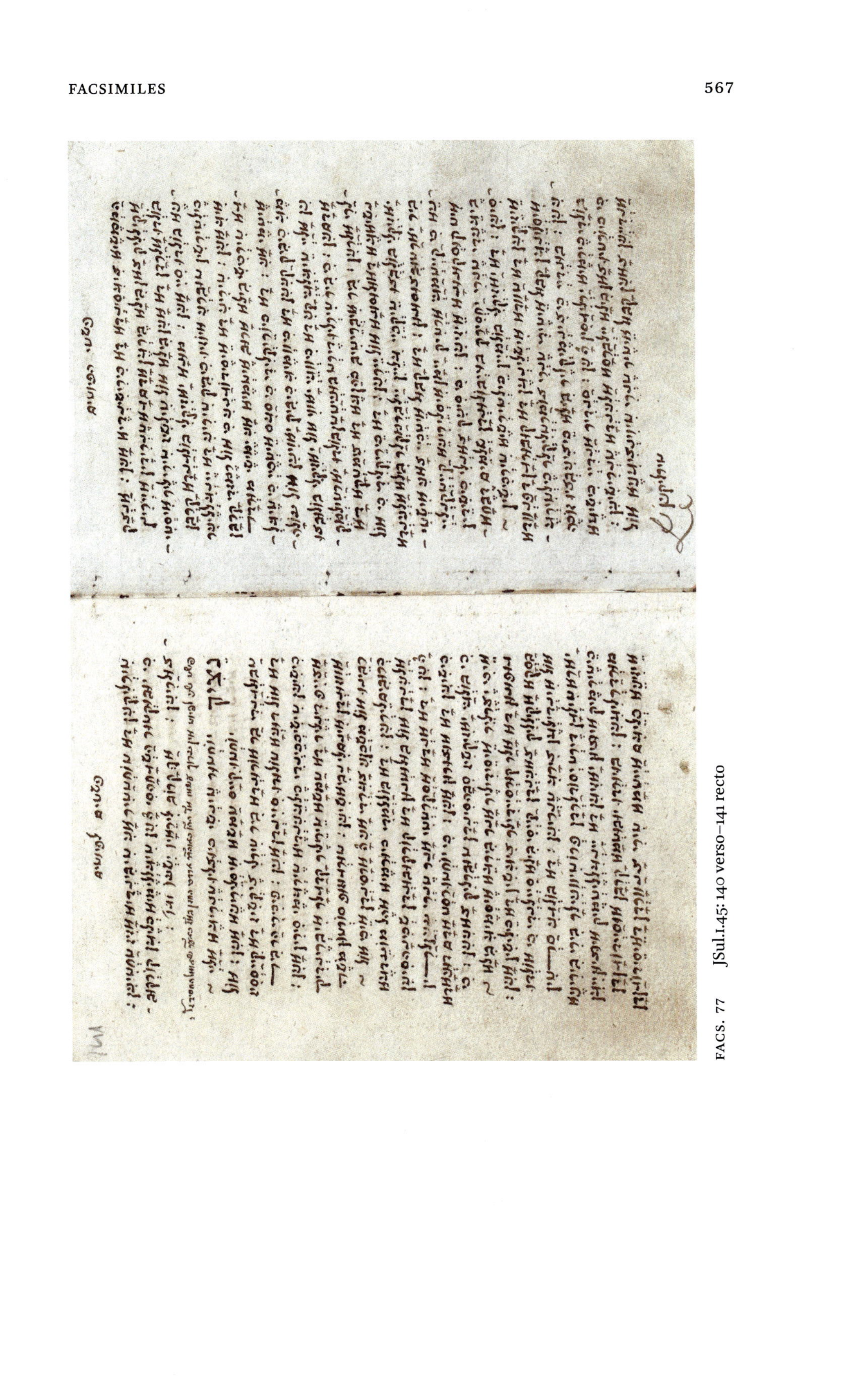

FACS. 77 JSul.I.45: 140 verso–141 recto

FACS. 78 JSul.1.45: 141 verso–142 recto

FACS. 79 JSul.I.45: 142 verso–143 recto

FACS. 80 JSul.I.45: 143 verso–144 recto

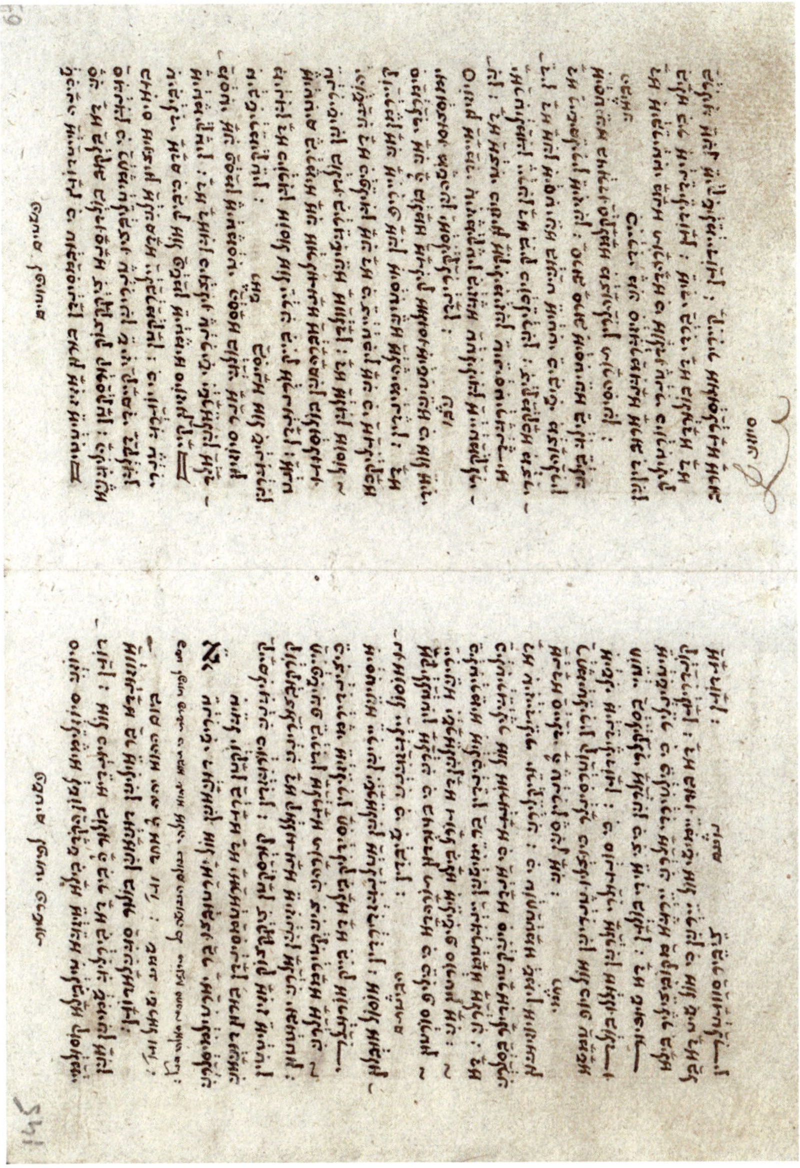

FACS. 81 JSul.I.45: 144 verso–145 recto

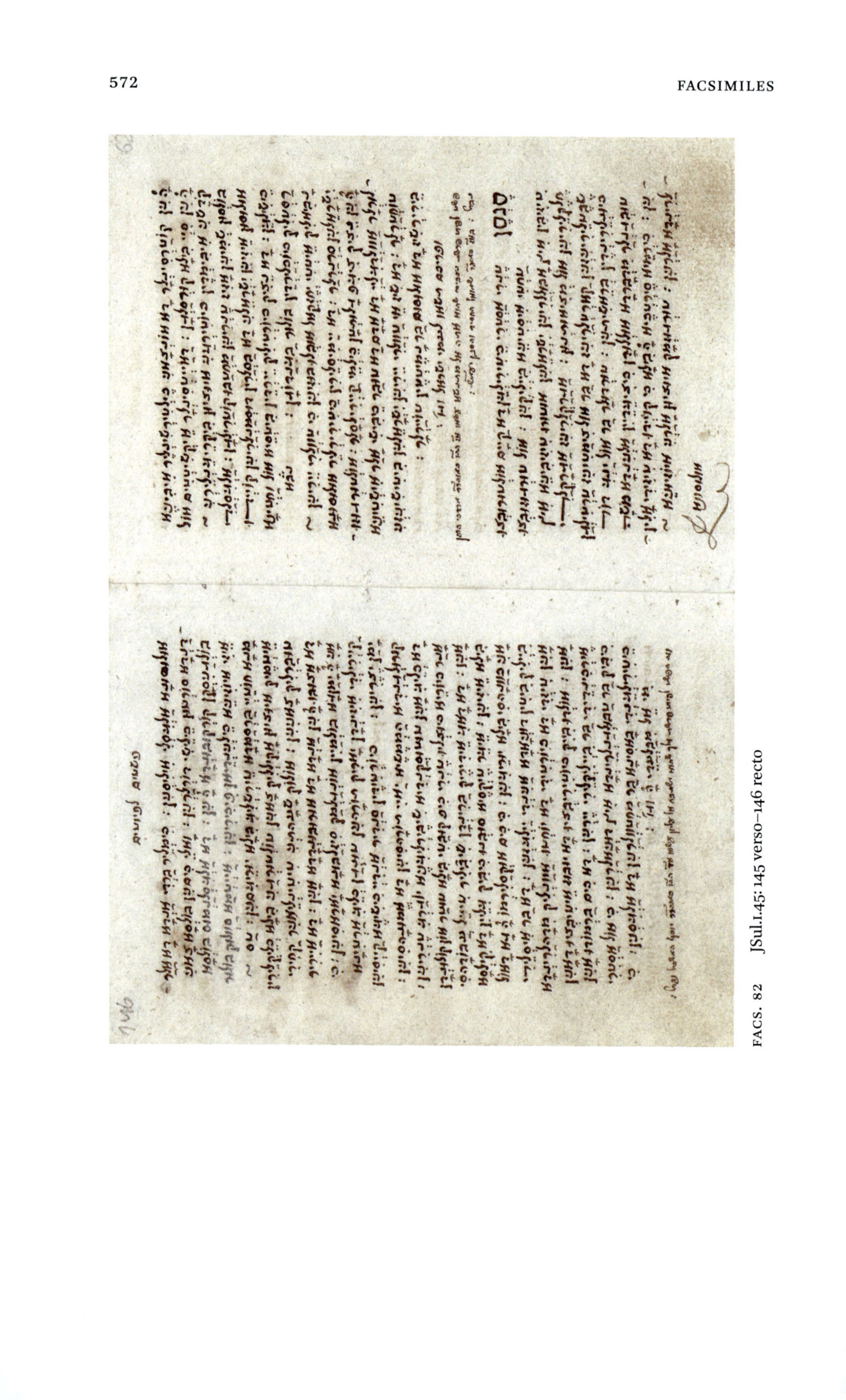

FACS. 82 JSul.I.45: 145 verso–146 recto

FACS. 83 JSul.I.45: 146 verso–147 recto

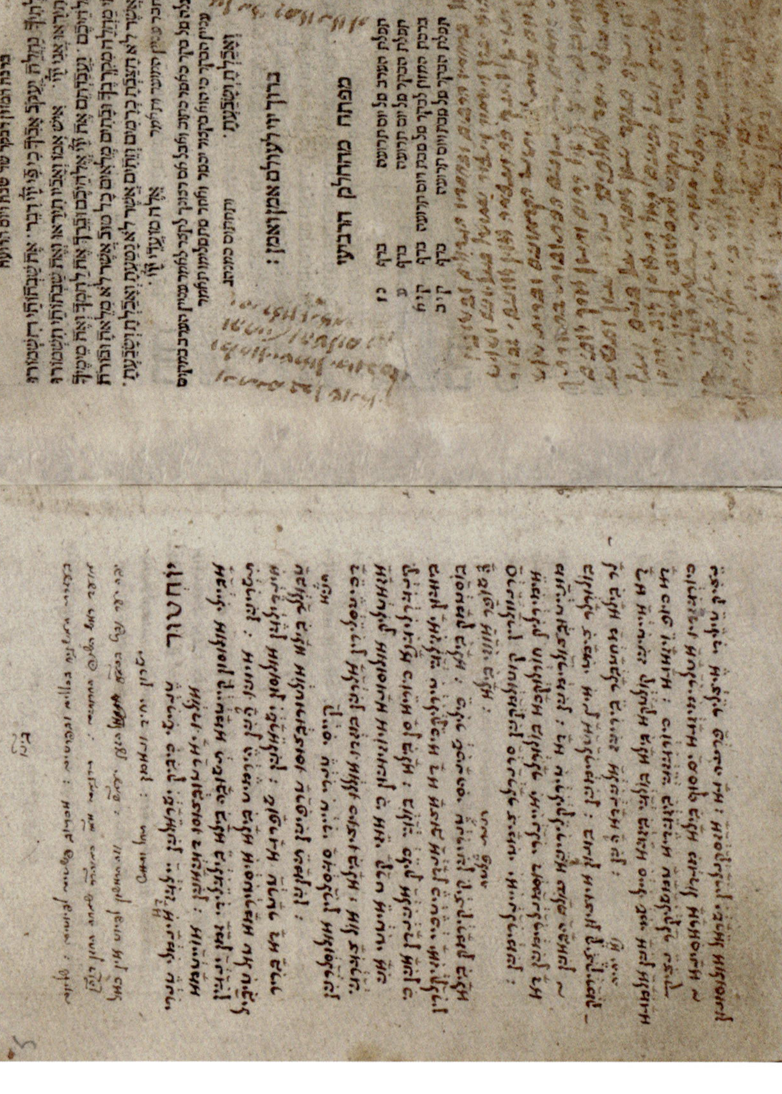

FACS. 84 JSul.1.46: 5 recto and *Siddur* (1528: 120 verso)

FACS. 85 JSul.1.46: 5 verso–6 recto

FACS. 86 JSul.1.46: 94 verso–95 recto

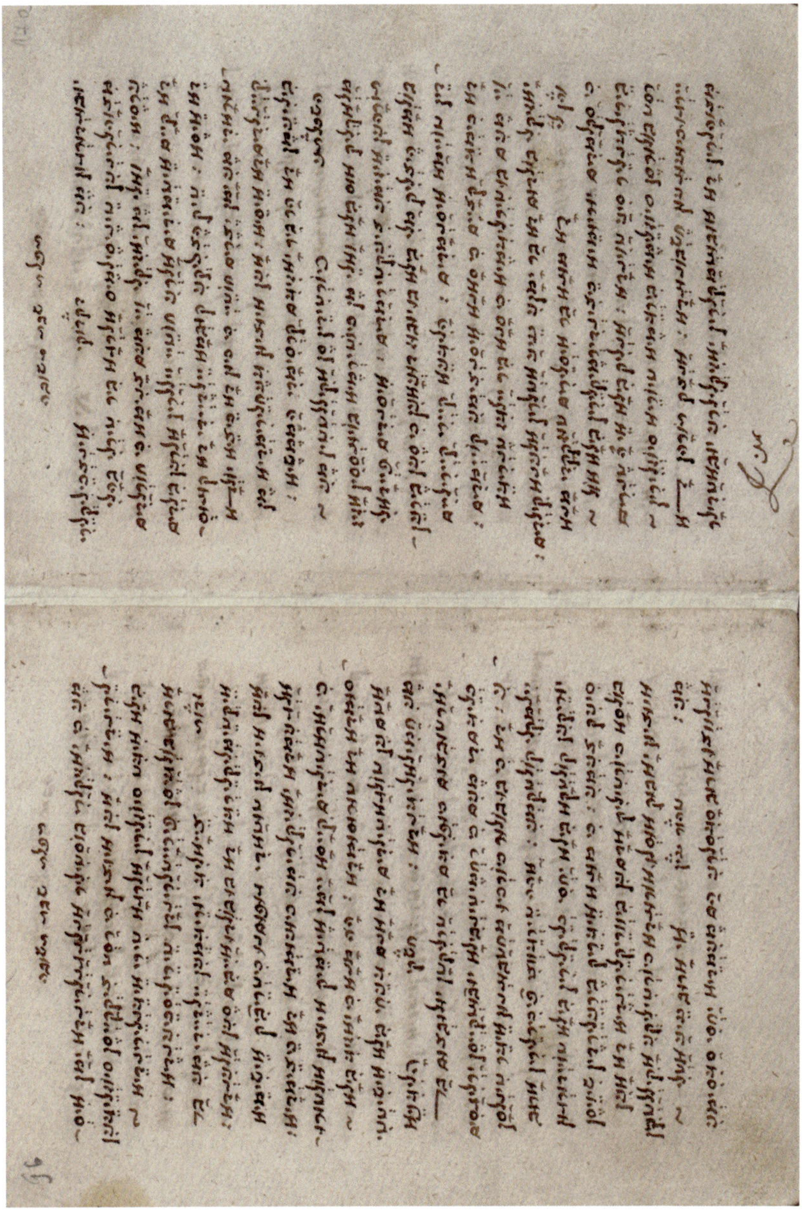

FACS. 87 JSul.I.46: 95 verso–96 recto

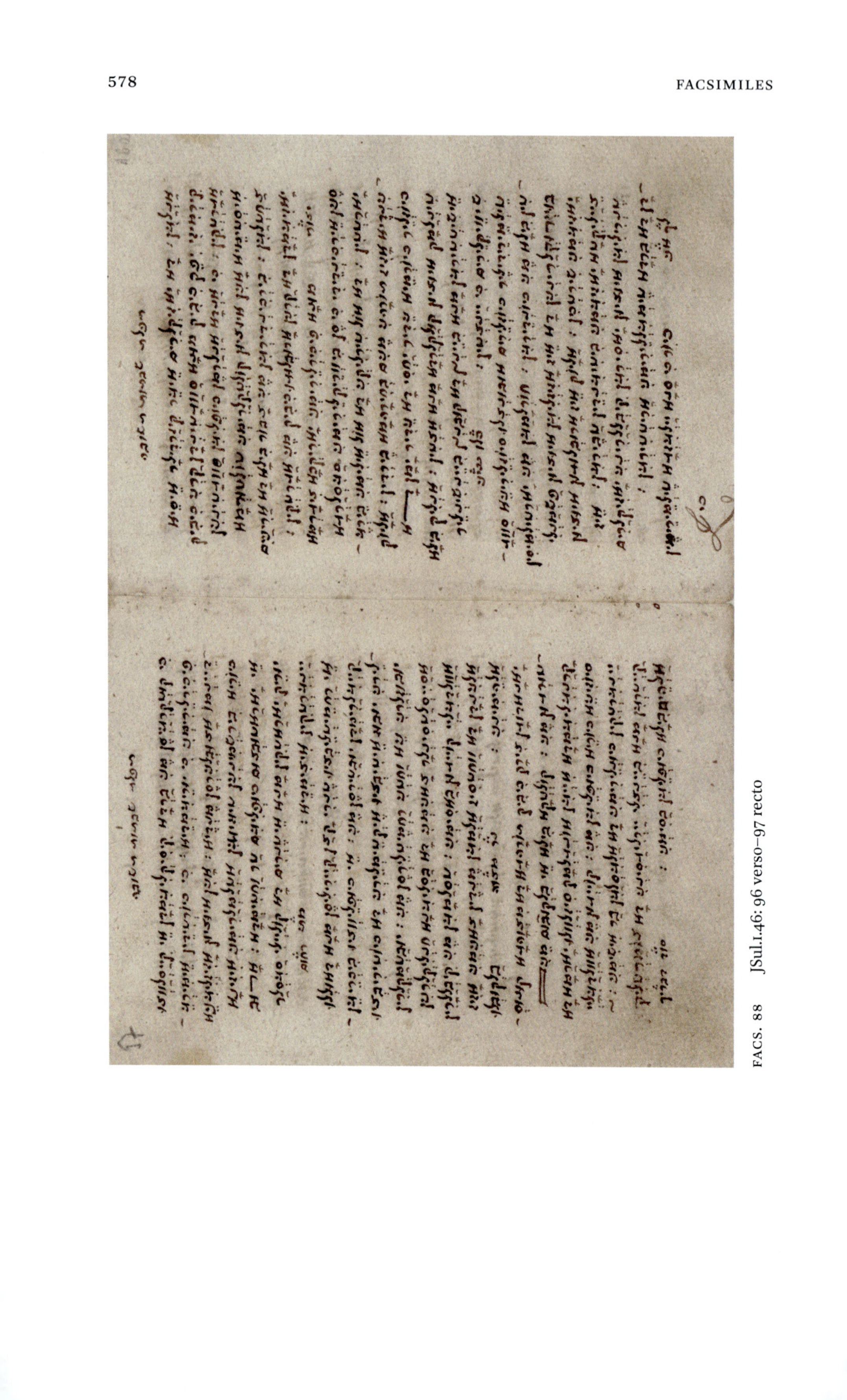

FACS. 88 JSul.1.46: 96 verso–97 recto

FACS. 89 JSul.I.46: 97 verso–98 recto

FACS. 90 JSul.I.46: 98 verso–99 recto

FACS. 91 JSul.1.46: 99 verso–100 recto

FACS. 92 JSul.1.46: 100 verso–101 recto

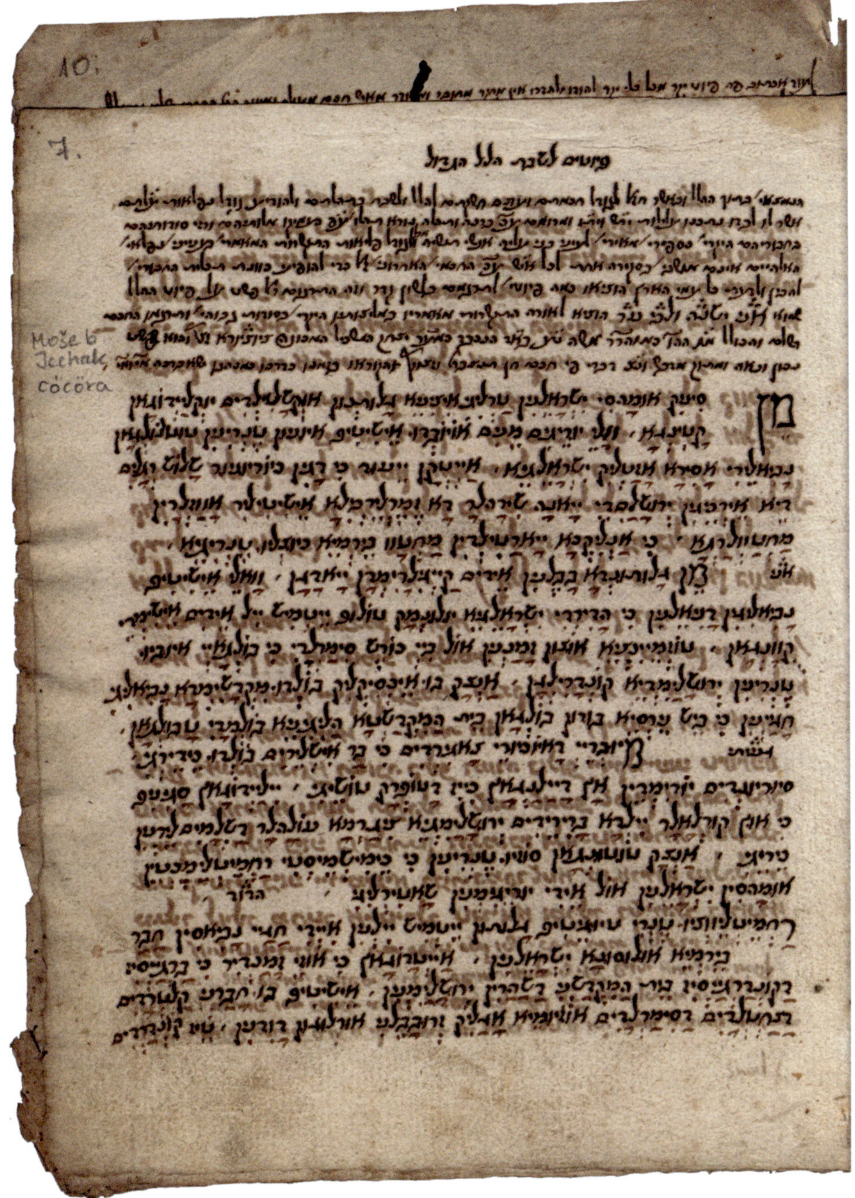

FACS. 93 JSul.I.53.13: 7 recto

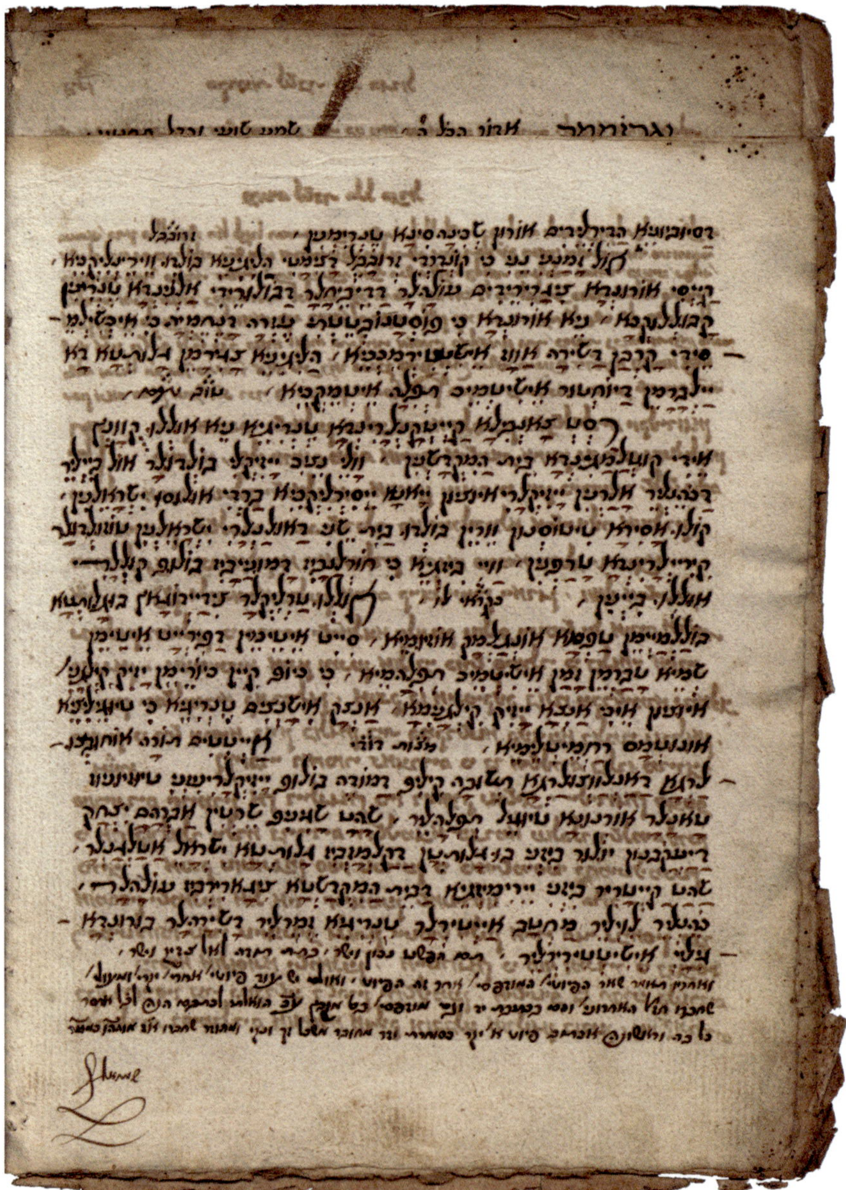

FACS. 94 JSul.1.53.13: 7 verso

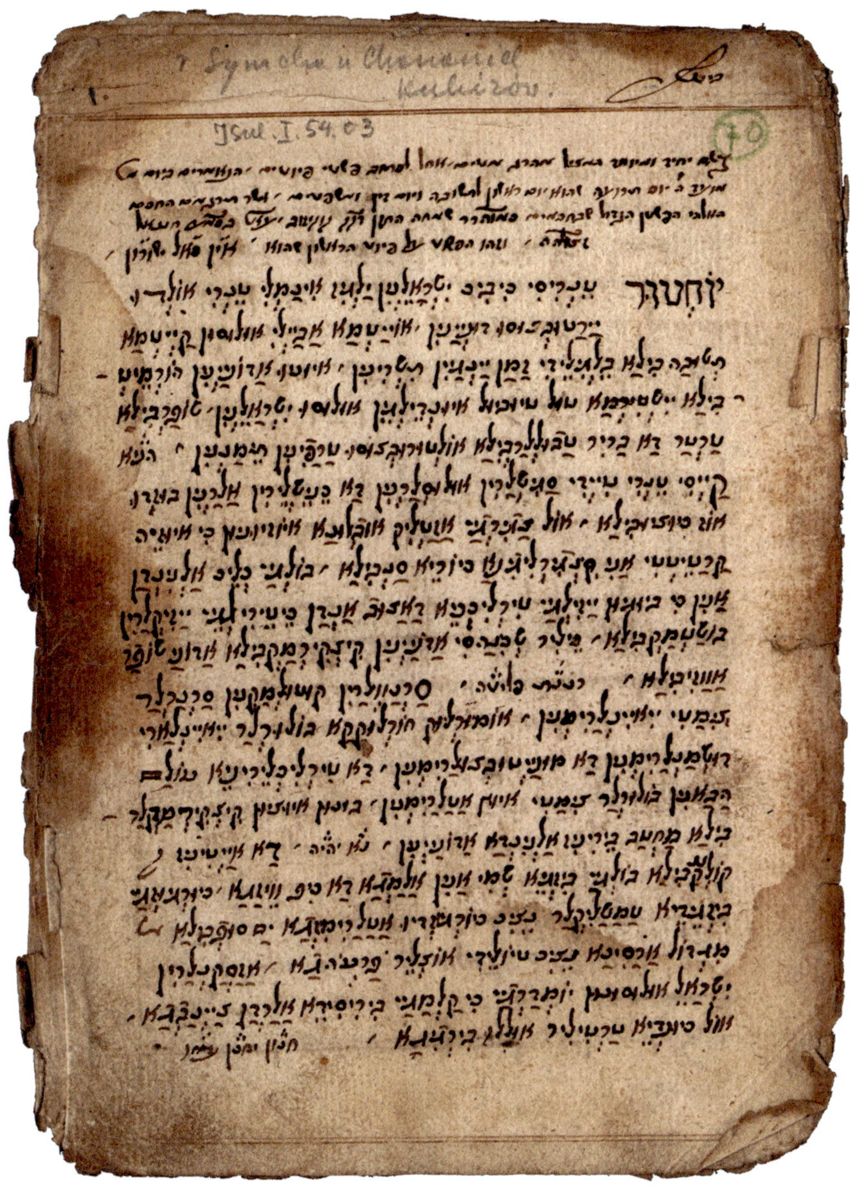

FACS. 95 JSul.I.54.03: 1 recto

FACS. 96 JSul.1.54.03: 1 verso–2 recto

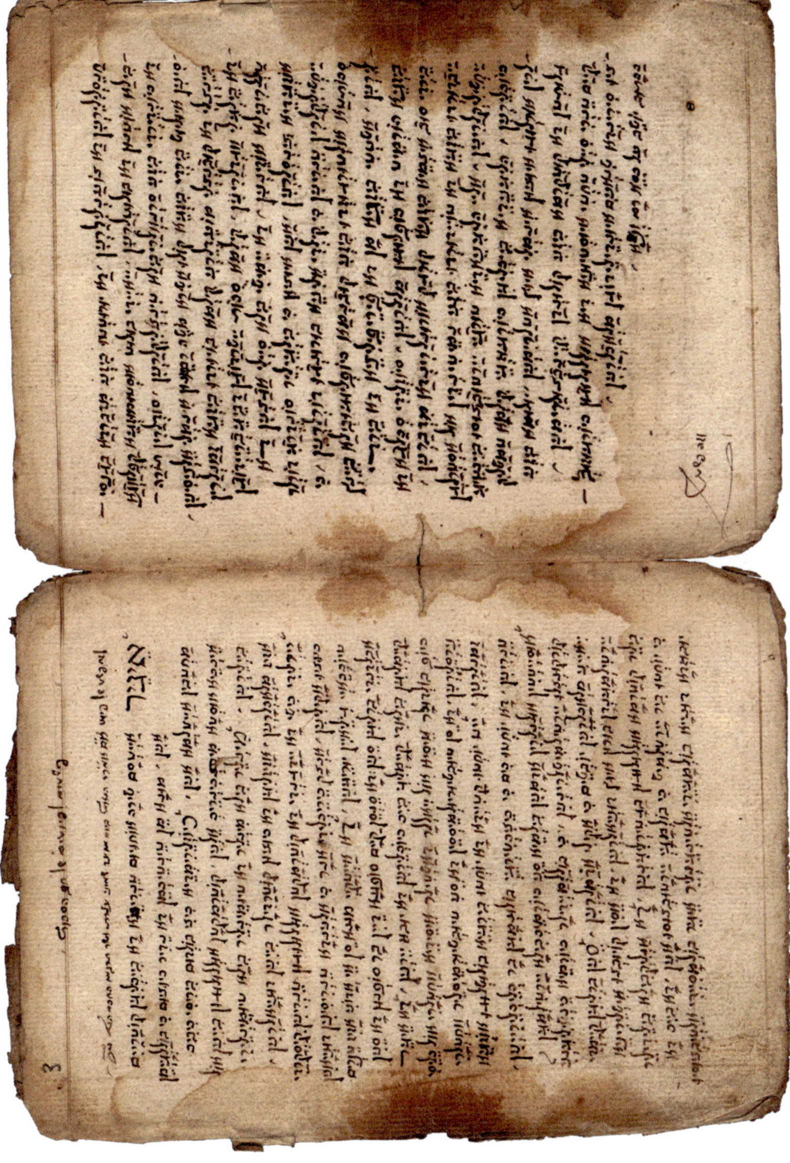

FACS. 97 JSul.I.54.03: 2 verso–3 recto

FACS. 98 JSul.1.54.03: 3 verso–4 recto

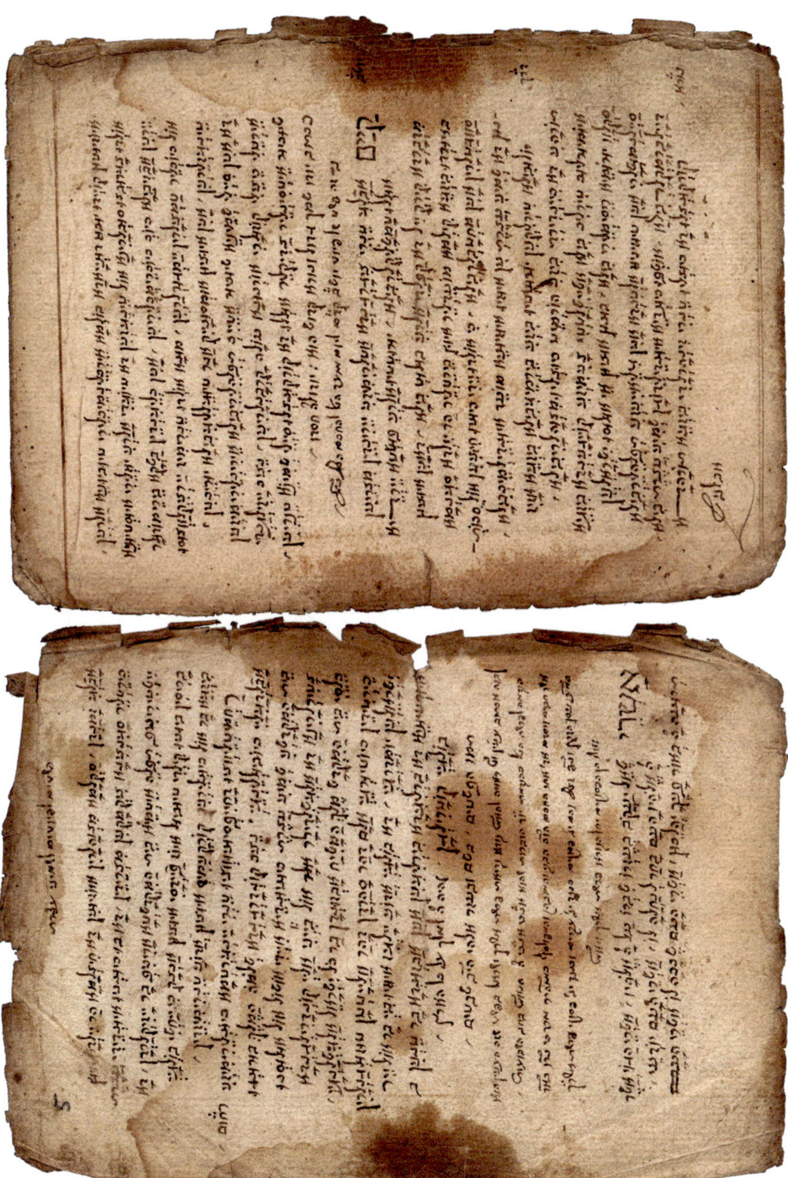

FACS. 99 JSul.I.54.03: 4 verso–5 recto

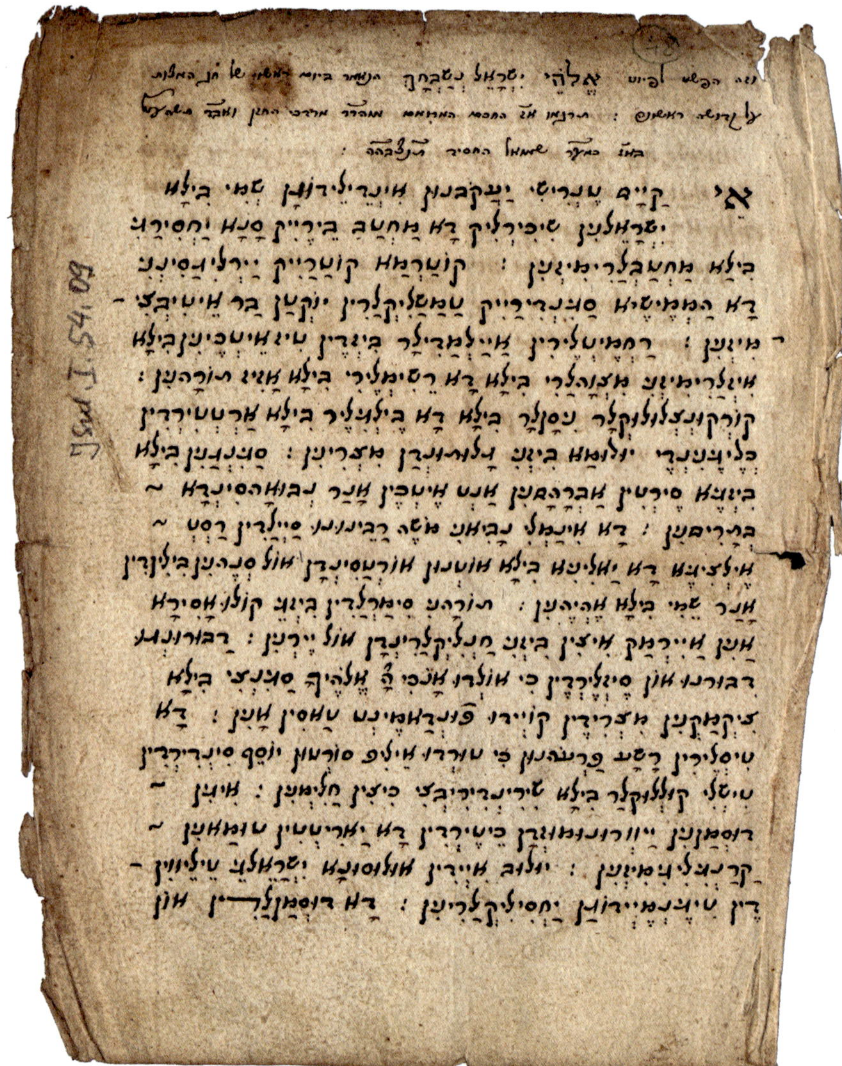

FACS. 100 JSul.I.54.09: 1 recto

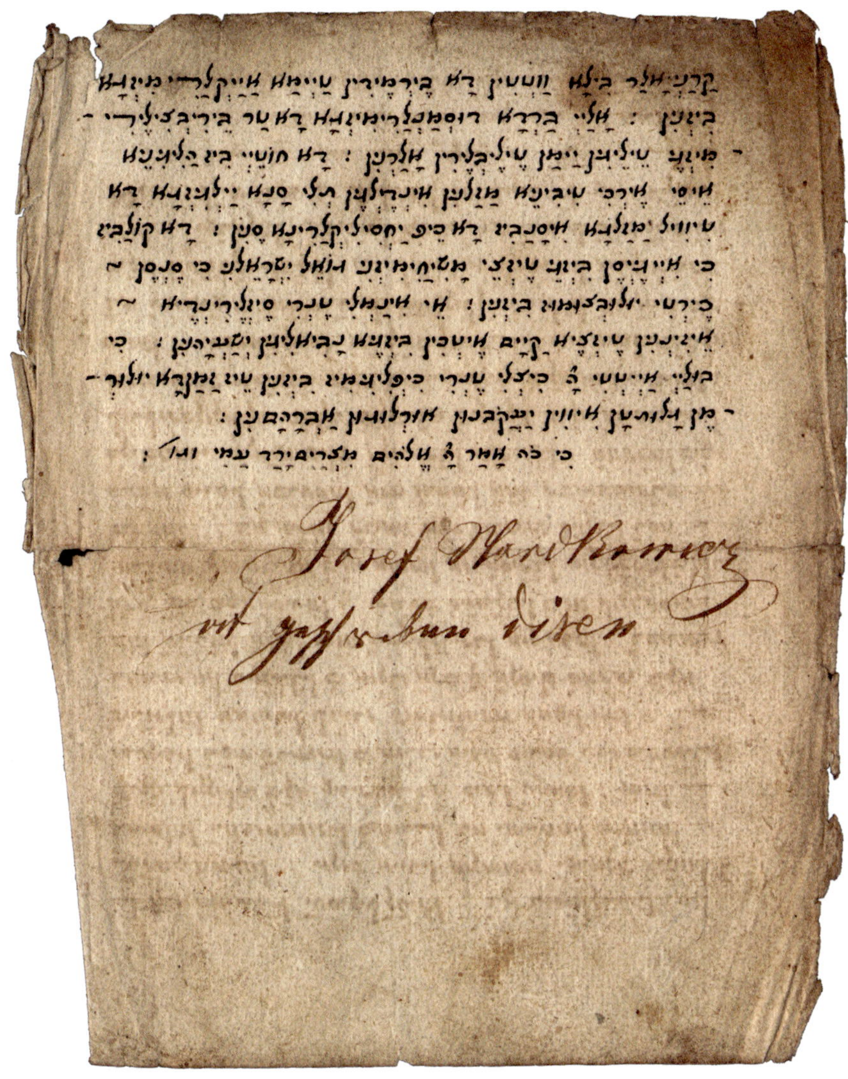

FACS. 101 JSul.I.54.09: 1 verso

FACS. 102 JSul.I.54.12: 1 recto

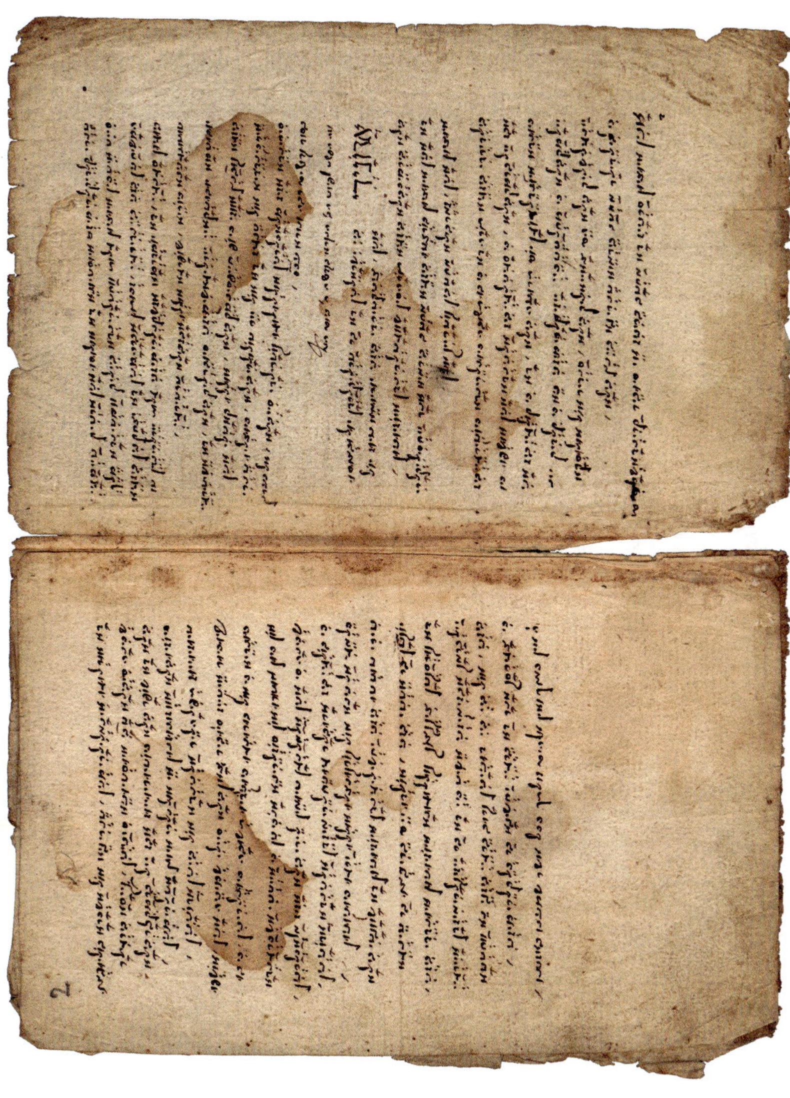

FACS. 103 JSul.I.54.12: 1 verso–2 recto

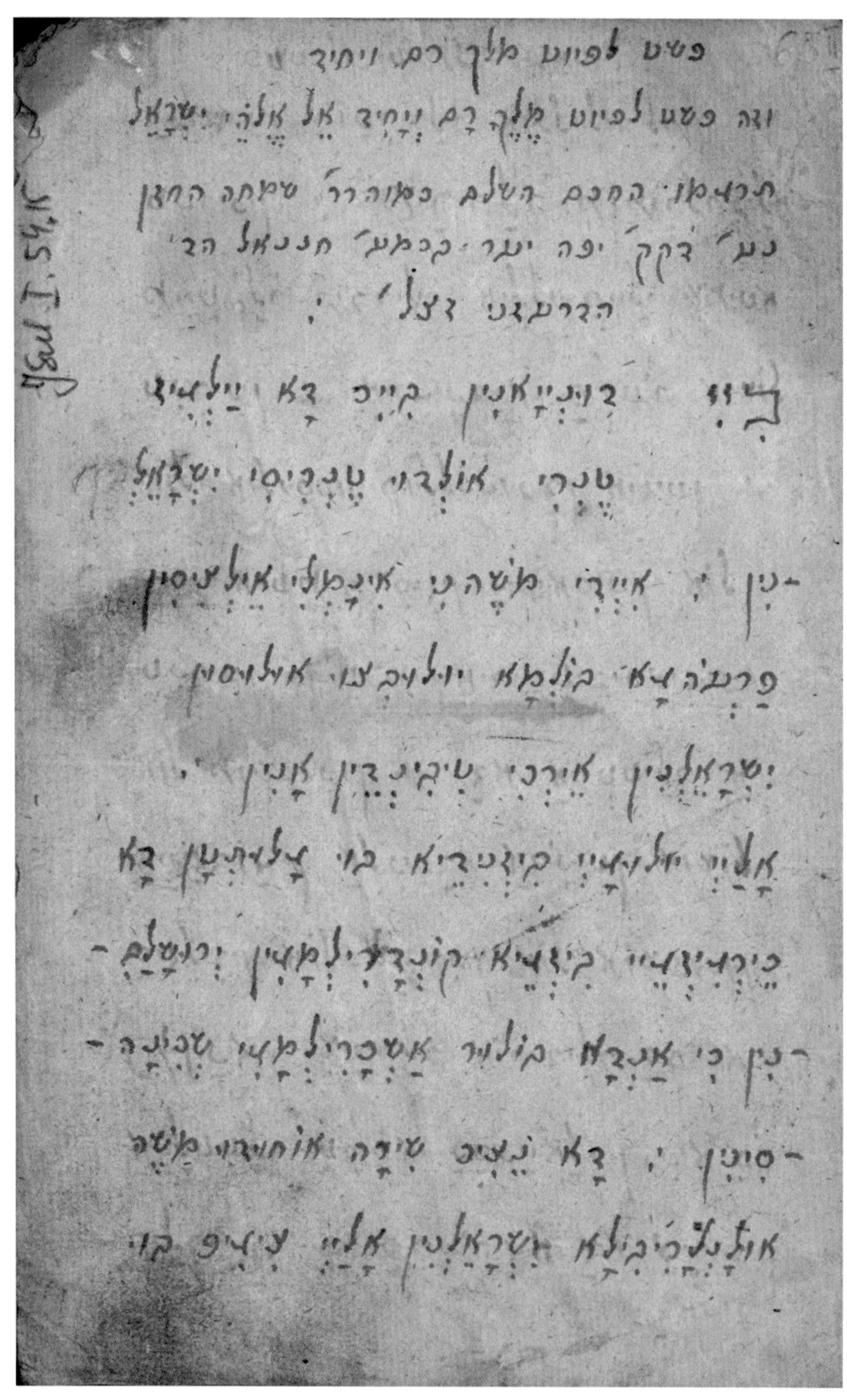

פשט לפיוט מלך רם ויחיד

וזה פשט לפיוט מֶלֶךְ רָם וְיָחִיד אֵל אֱלֹהֵי יִשְׂרָאֵל

FACS. 104 JSul.1.54.15: 1 recto

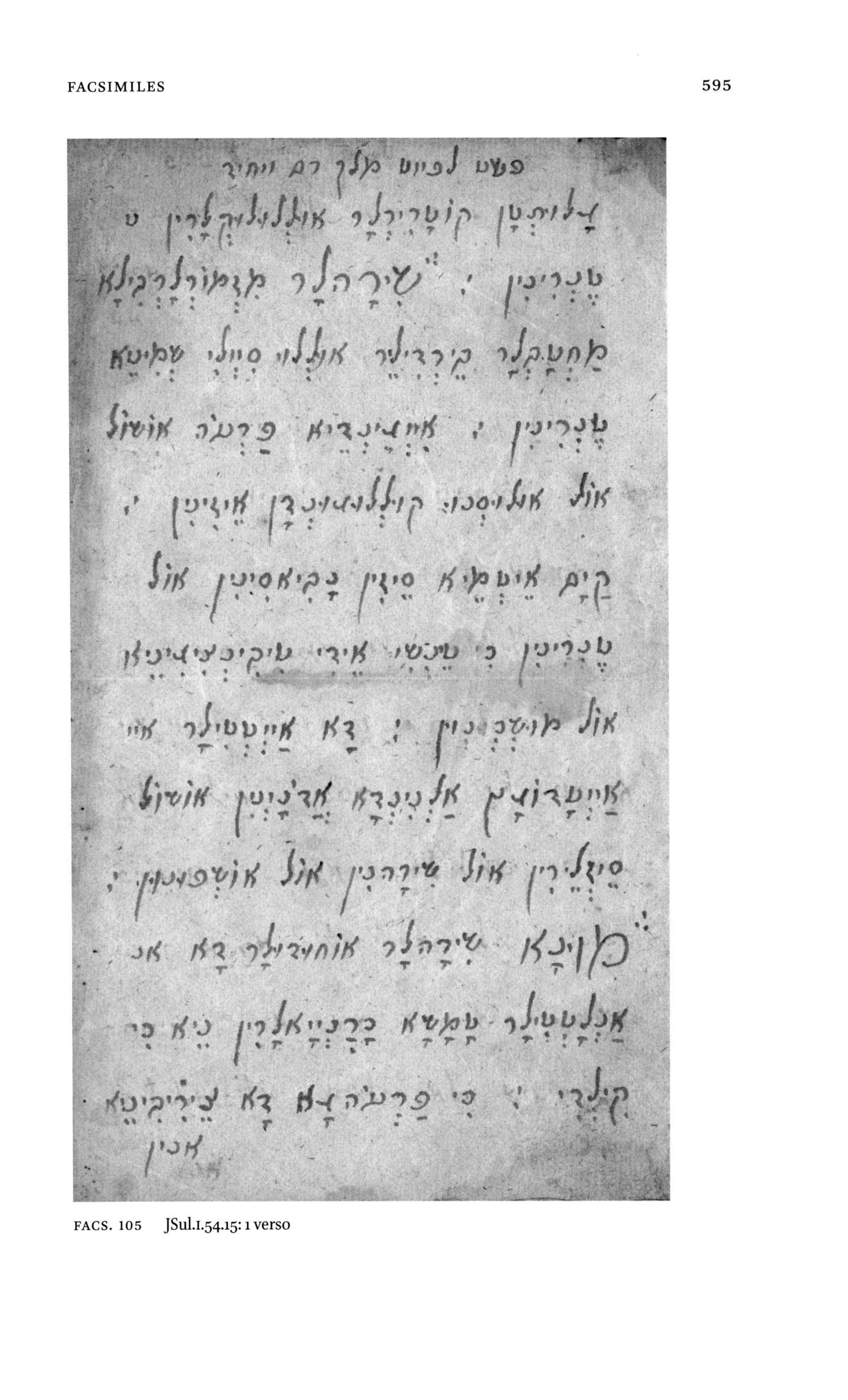

פשט לפיוט מלך רם ווחיד

FACS. 105 JSul.I.54.15: 1 verso

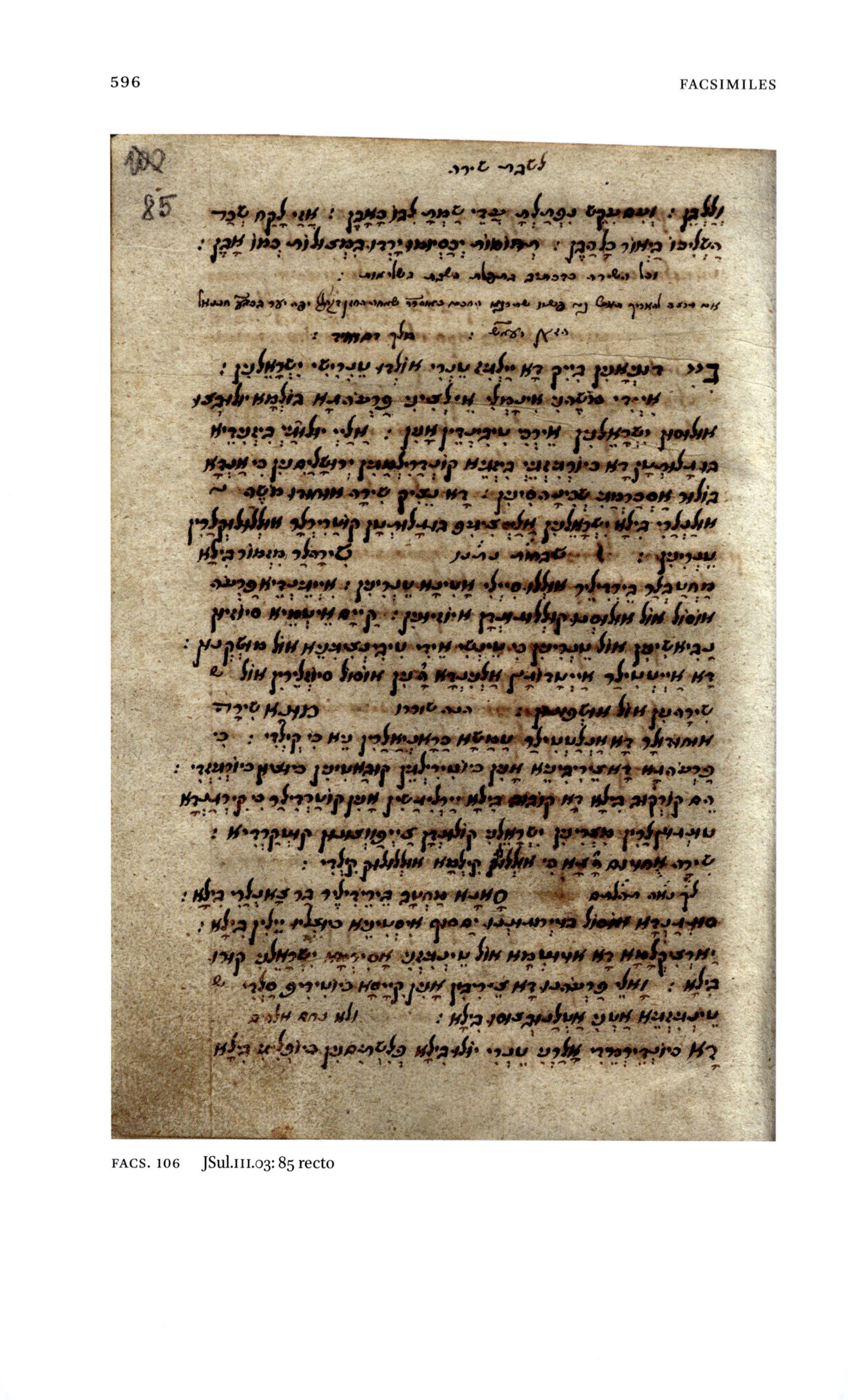

FACS. 106 JSul.III.03: 85 recto

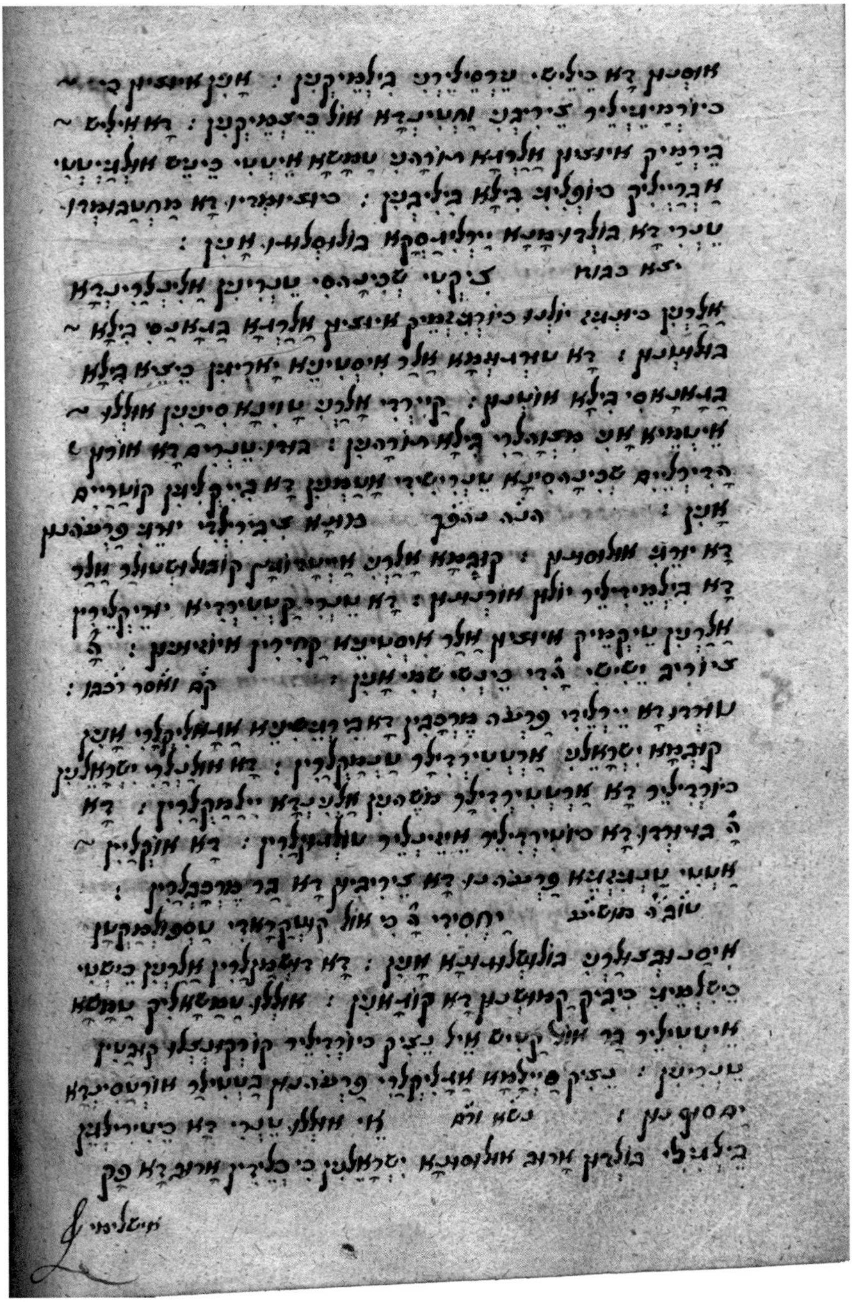

FACS. 107 JSul.III.03: 85 verso

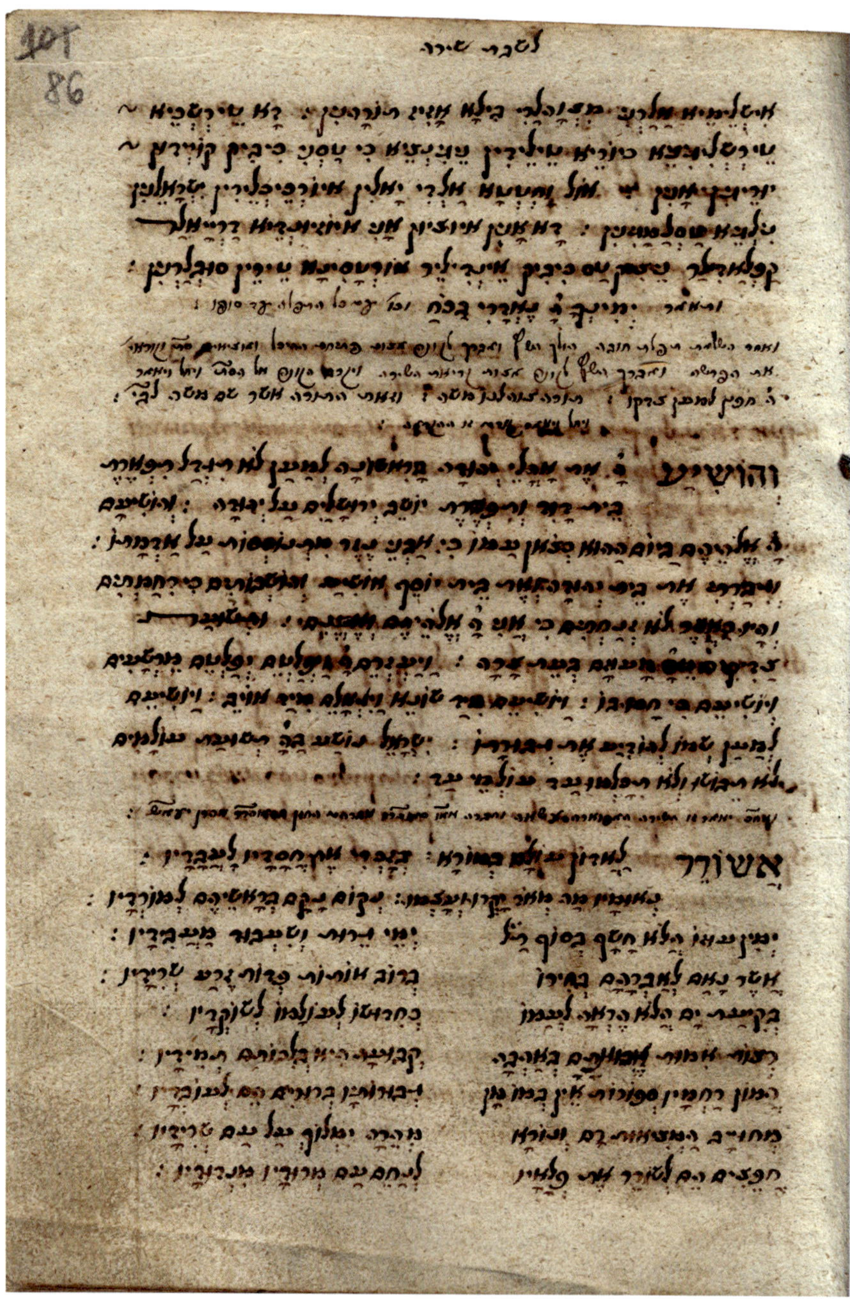

FACS. 108 JSul.III.03: 86 recto

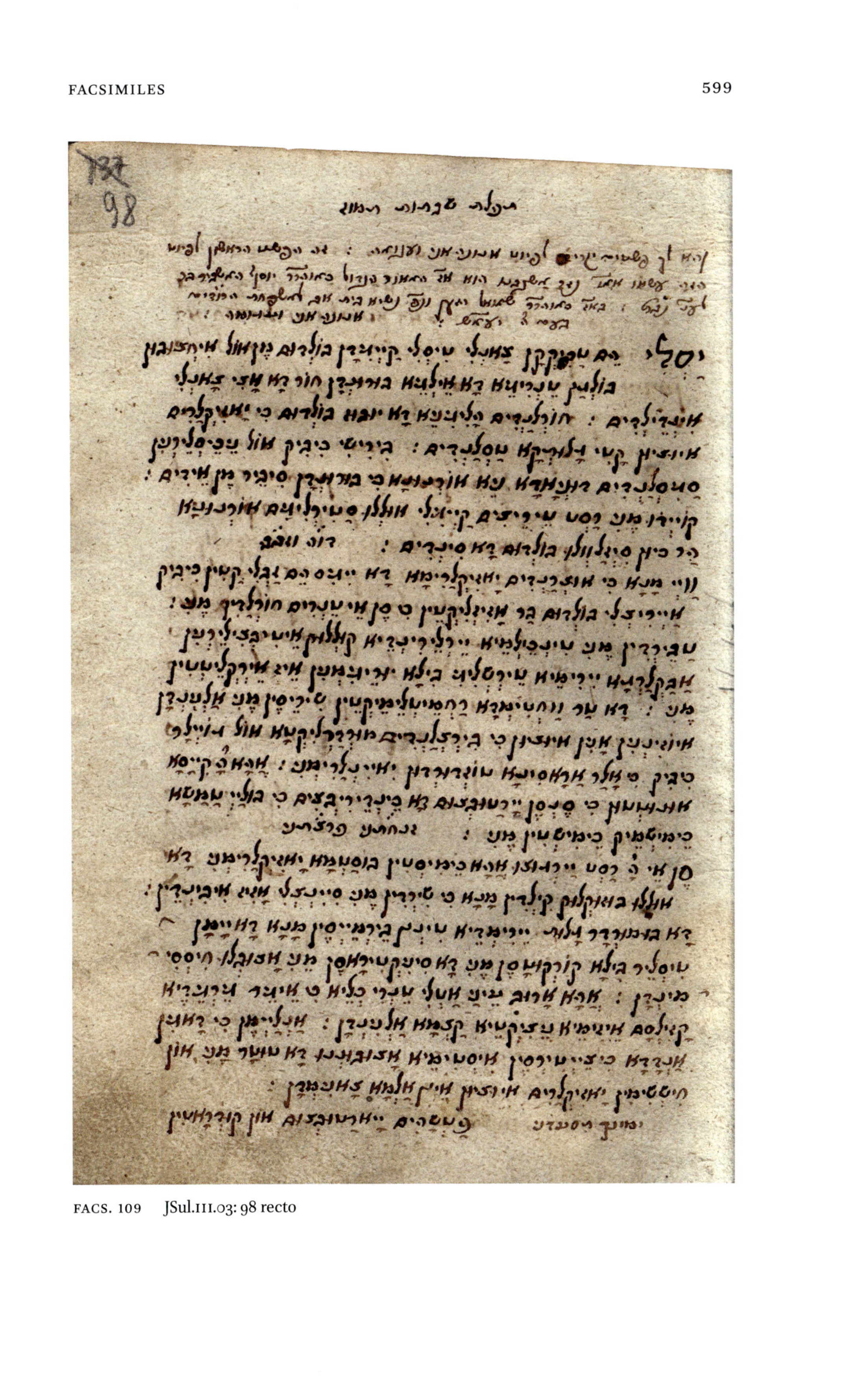

FACS. 109 JSul.III.03: 98 recto

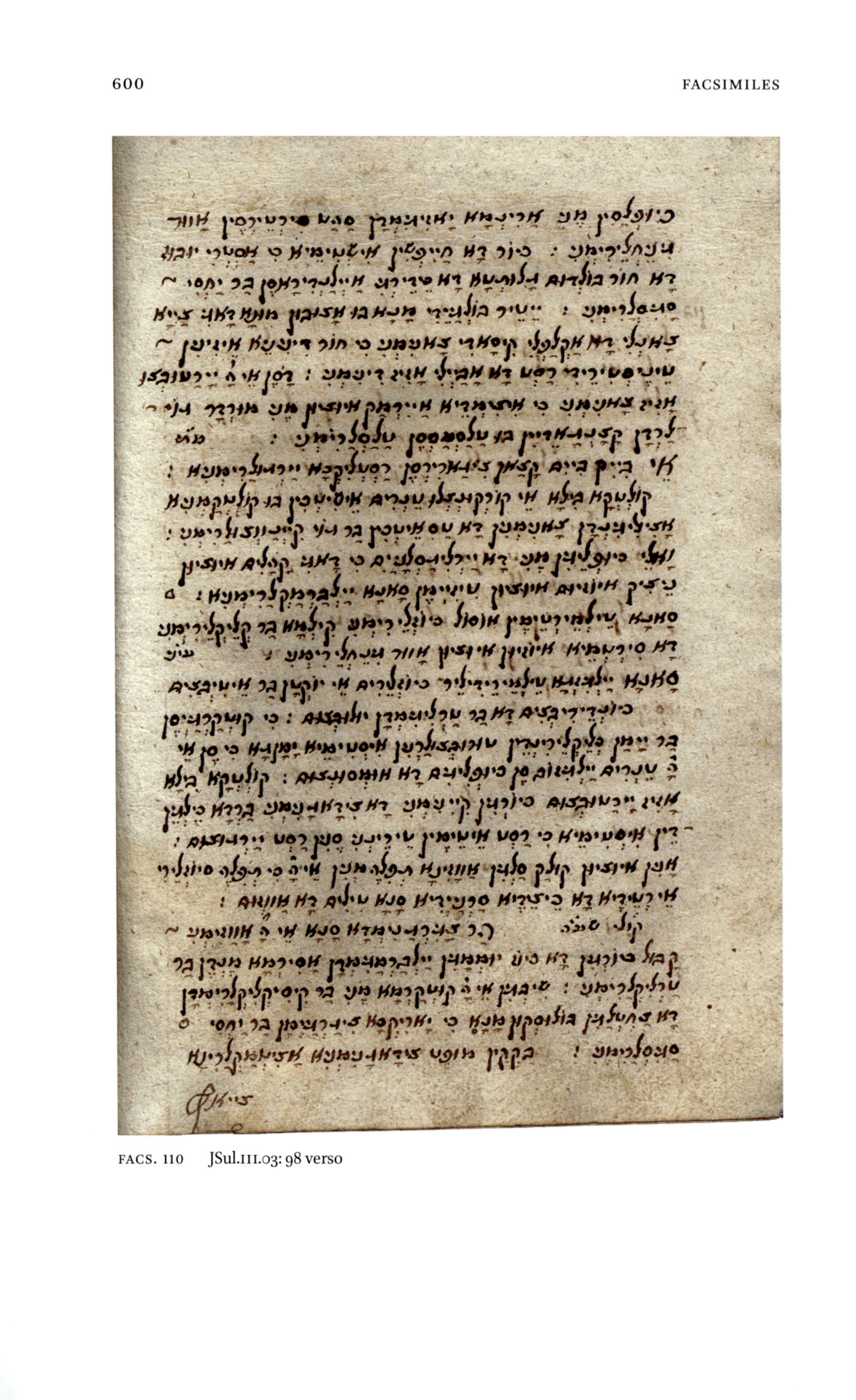

FACS. 110 JSul.III.03: 98 verso

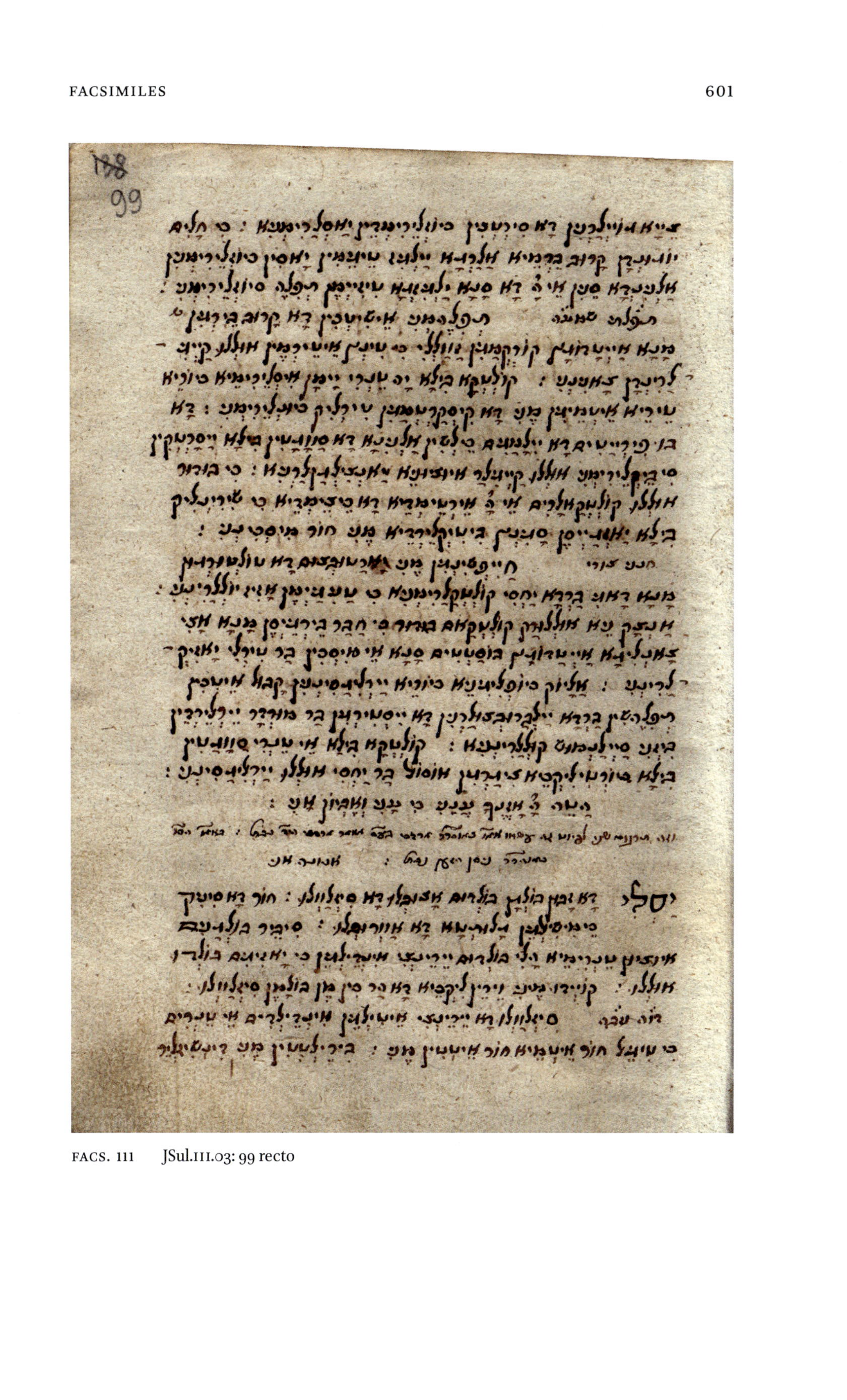

FACS. 111 JSul.III.03: 99 recto

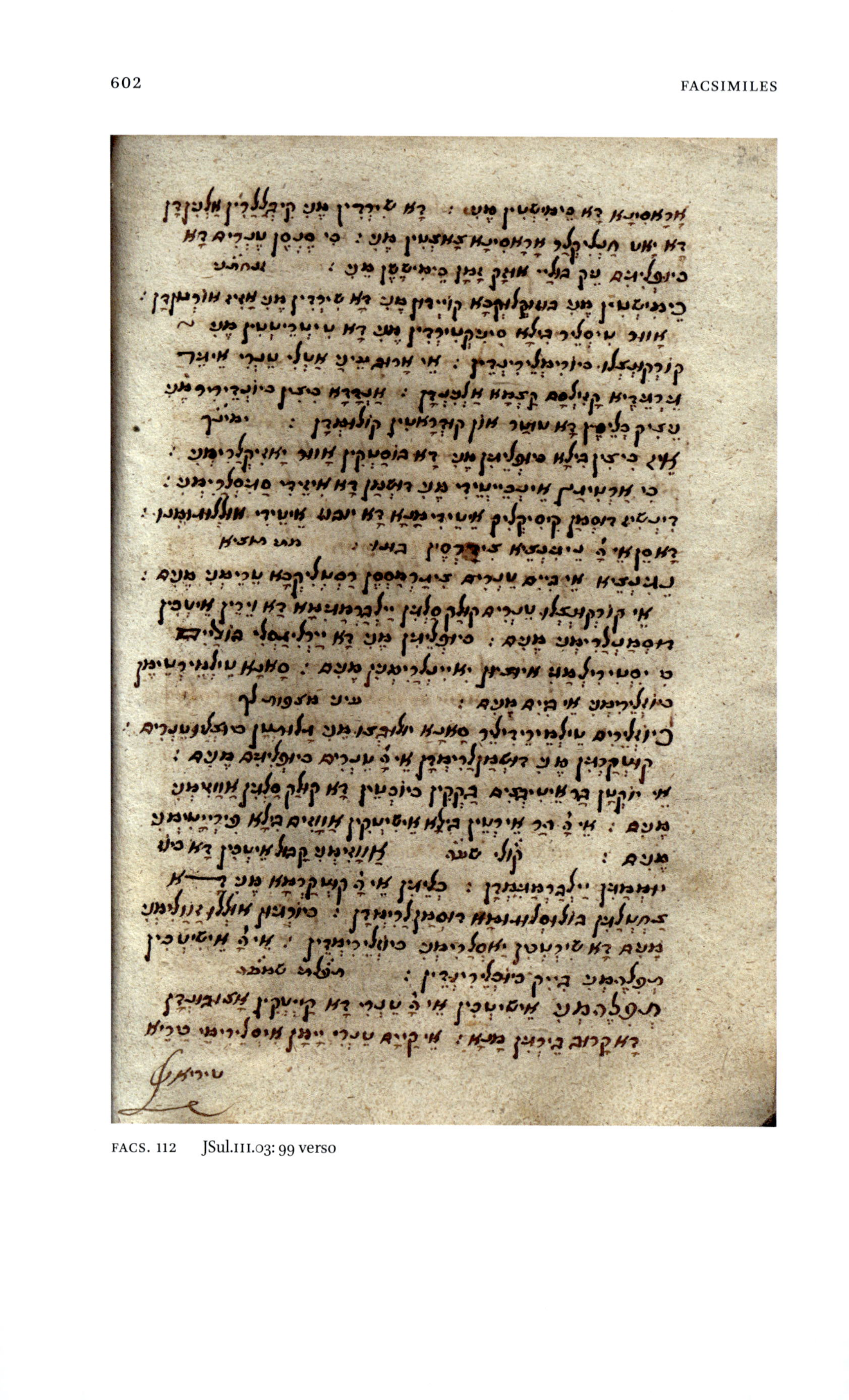

FACS. 112 JSul.III.03: 99 verso

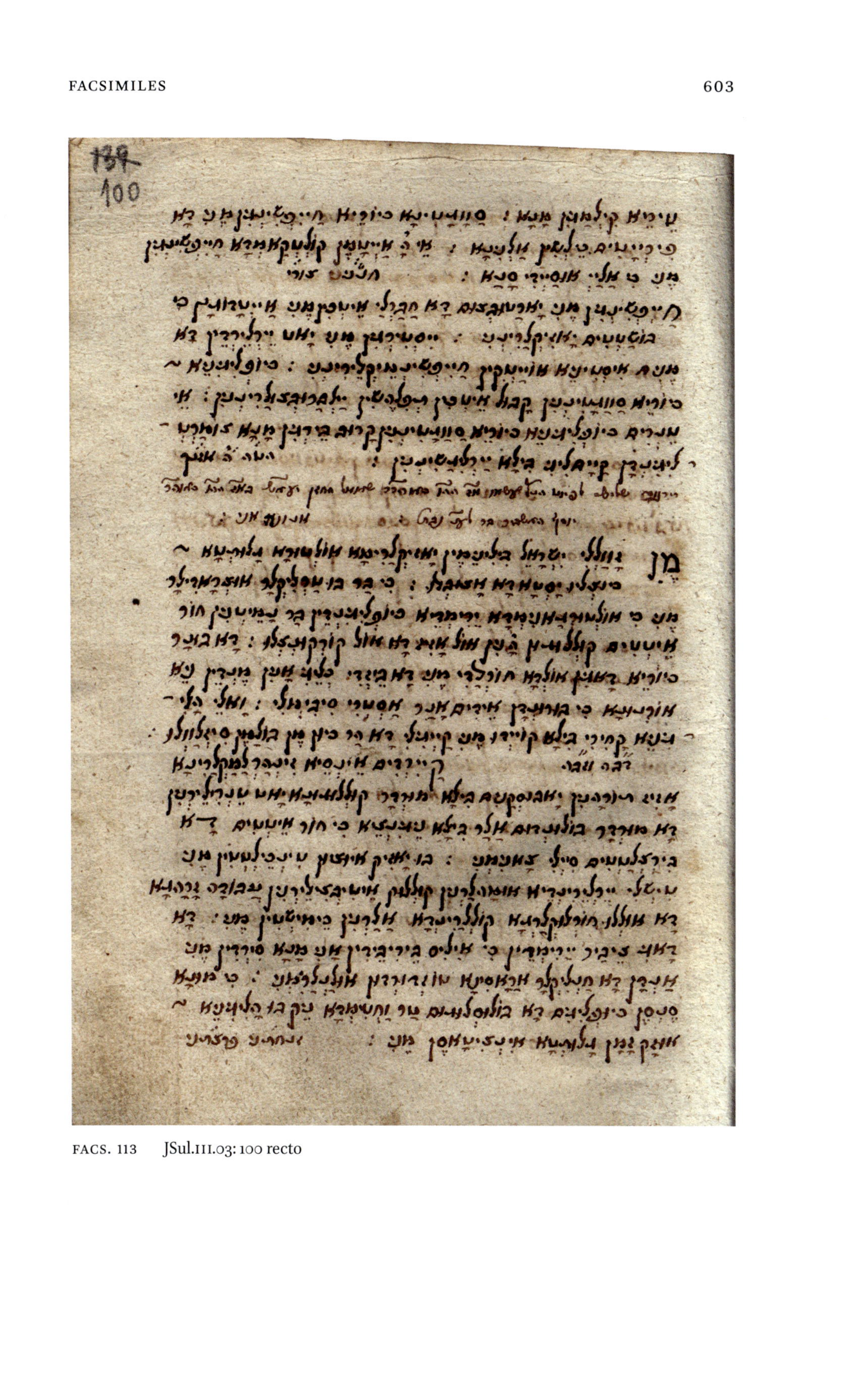

FACS. 113 JSul.III.03: 100 recto

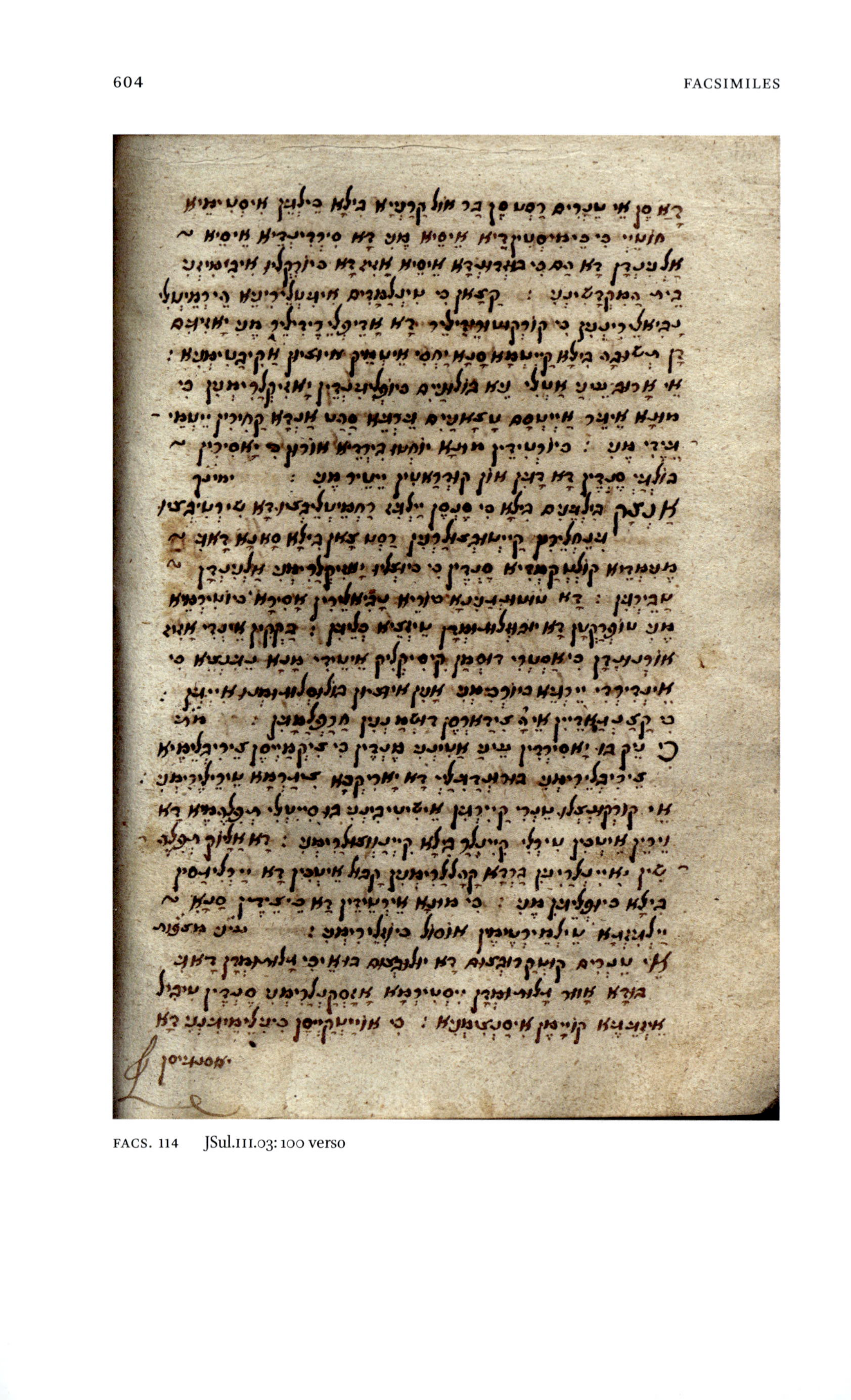

FACS. 114 JSul.III.03: 100 verso

FACS. 115 JSul.III.03: 101 recto

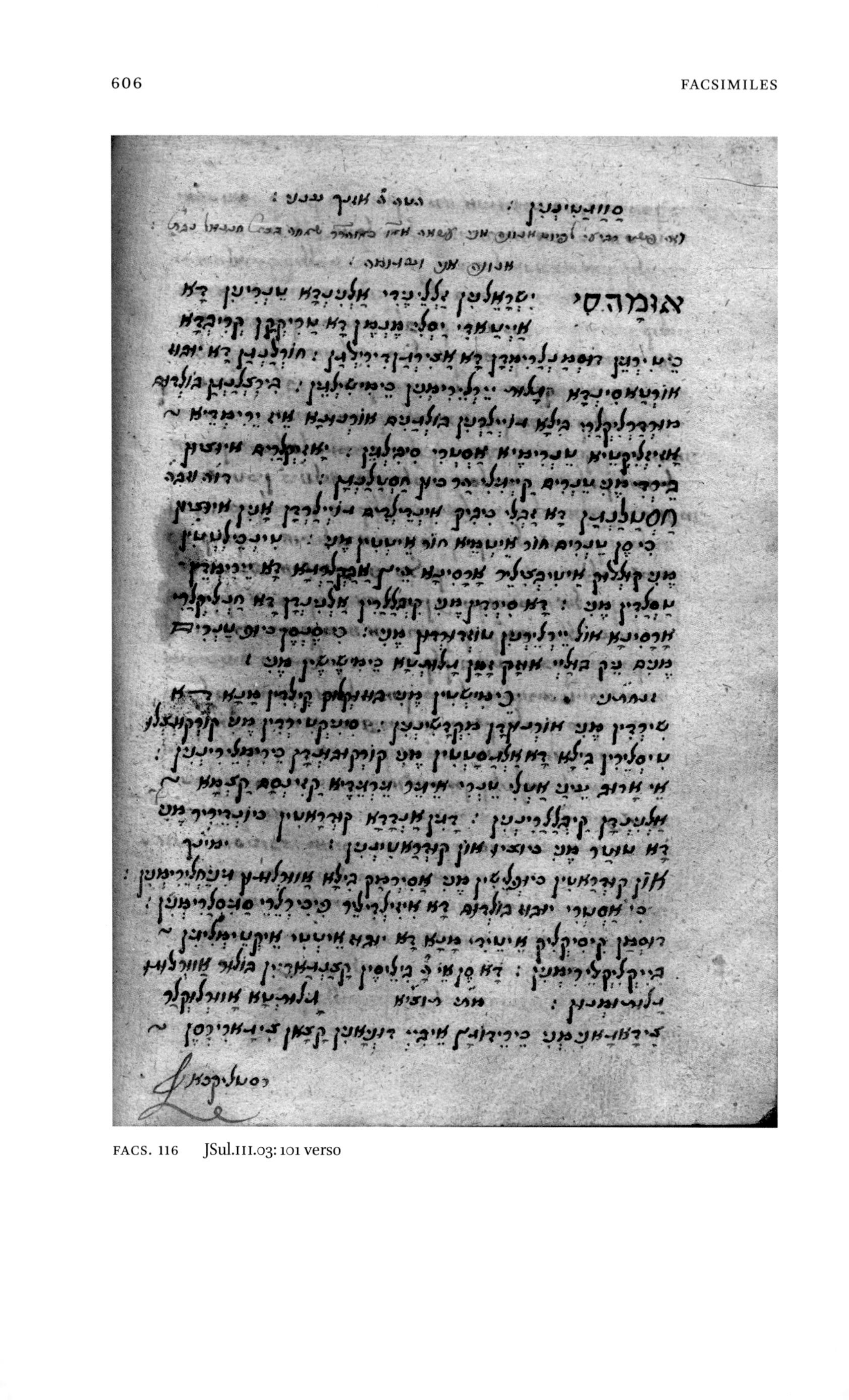

FACS. 116 JSul.III.03: 101 verso

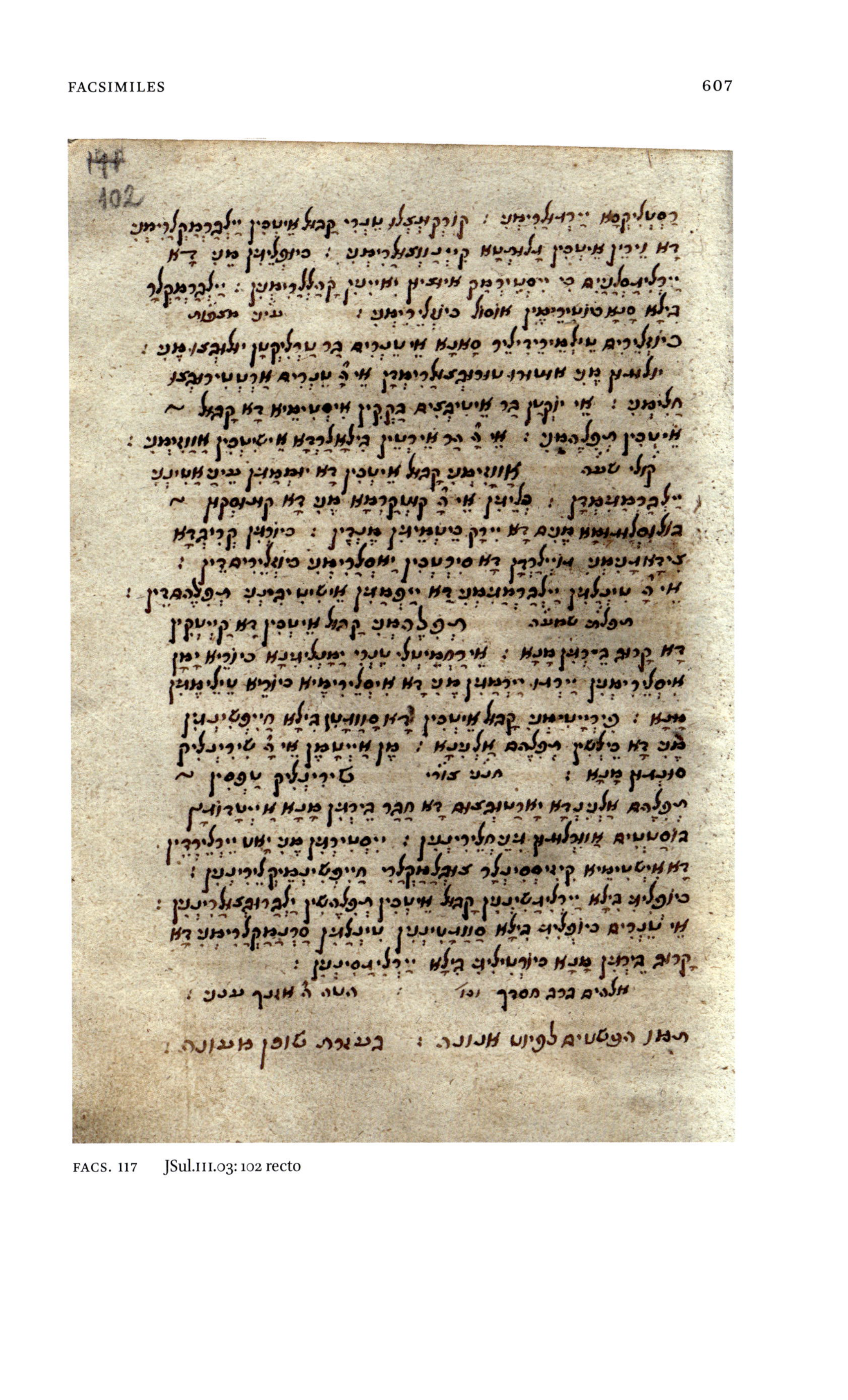

FACS. 117 JSul.III.03: 102 recto

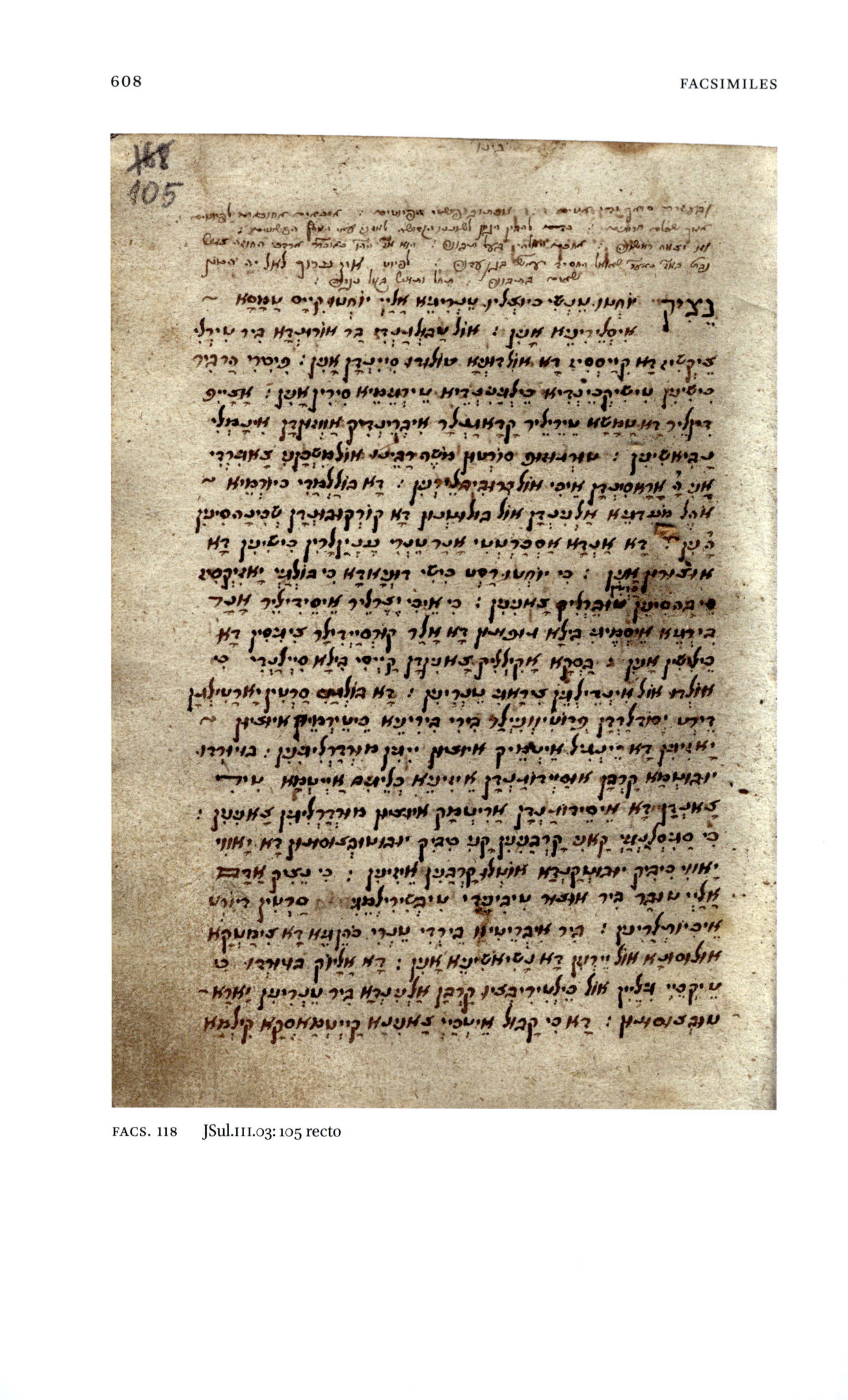

FACS. 118 JSul.III.03: 105 recto

FACS. 119 JSul.III.03: 105 verso

FACS. 120 JSul.III.03: 106 recto

FACS. 121 JSul.III.03: 106 verso

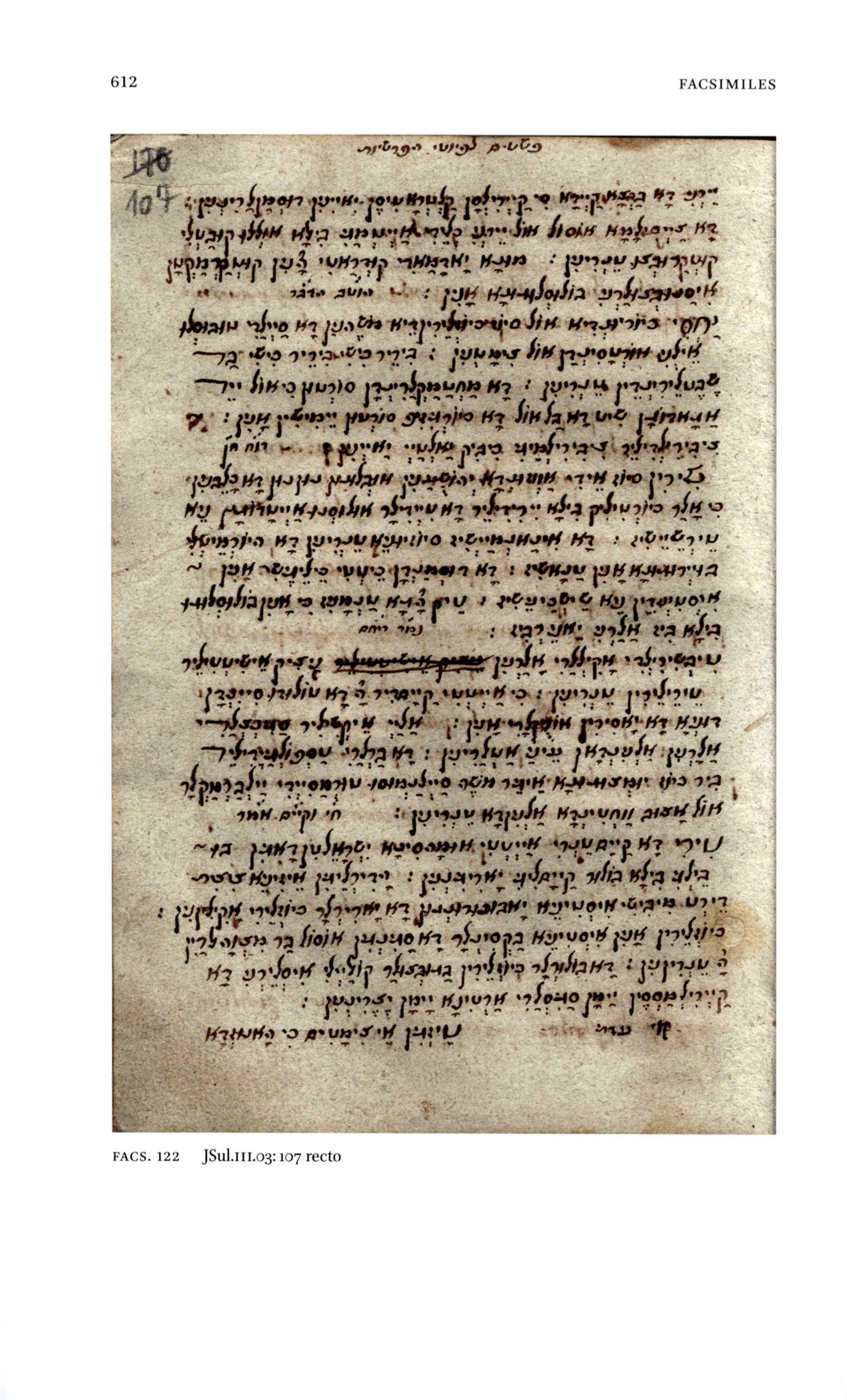

FACS. 122 JSul.III.03: 107 recto

FACS. 123 JSul.III.03: 107 verso

FACS. 124 JSul.III.03: 108 recto

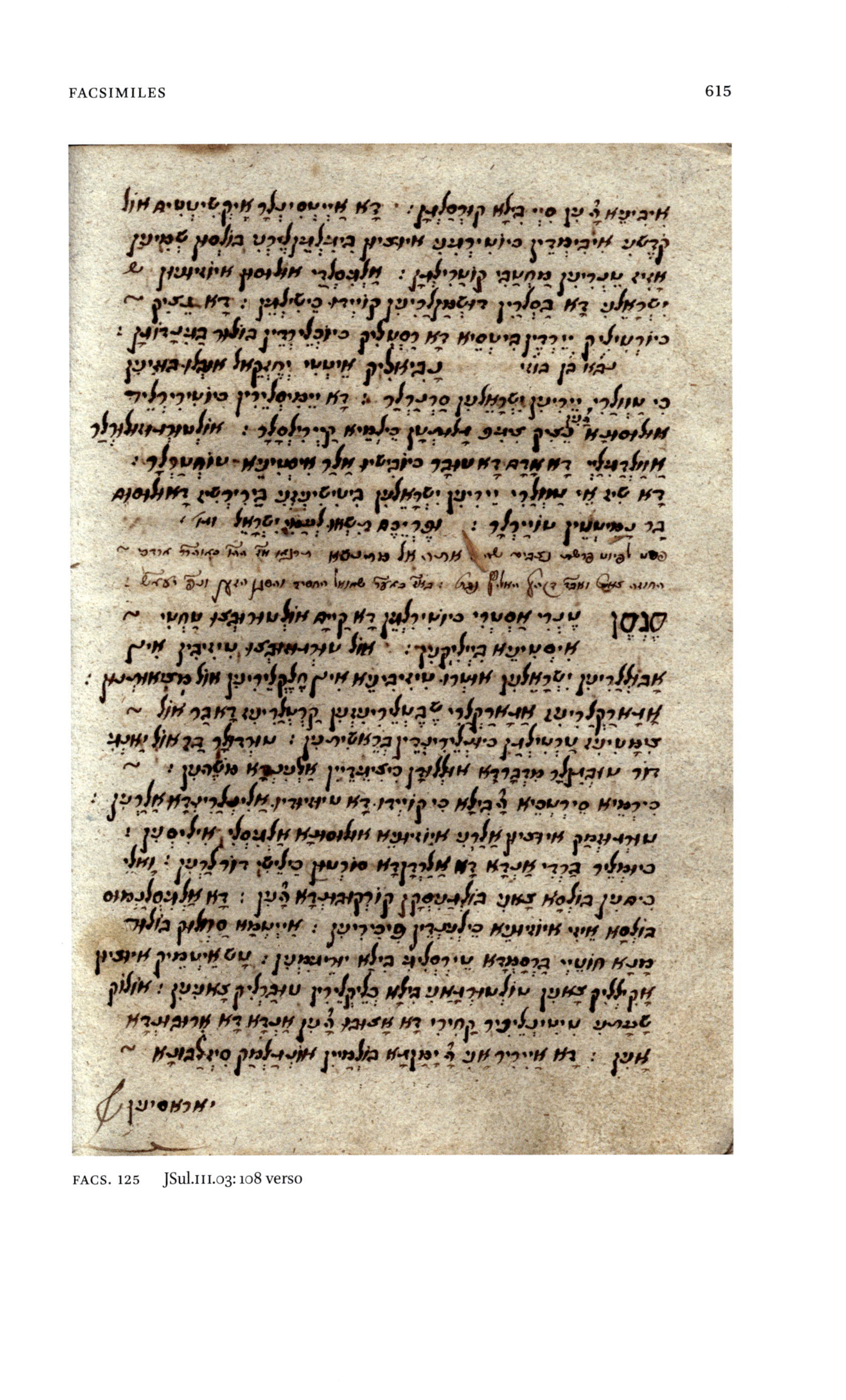

FACS. 125 JSul.III.03: 108 verso

FACS. 126 JSul.III.03: 109 recto

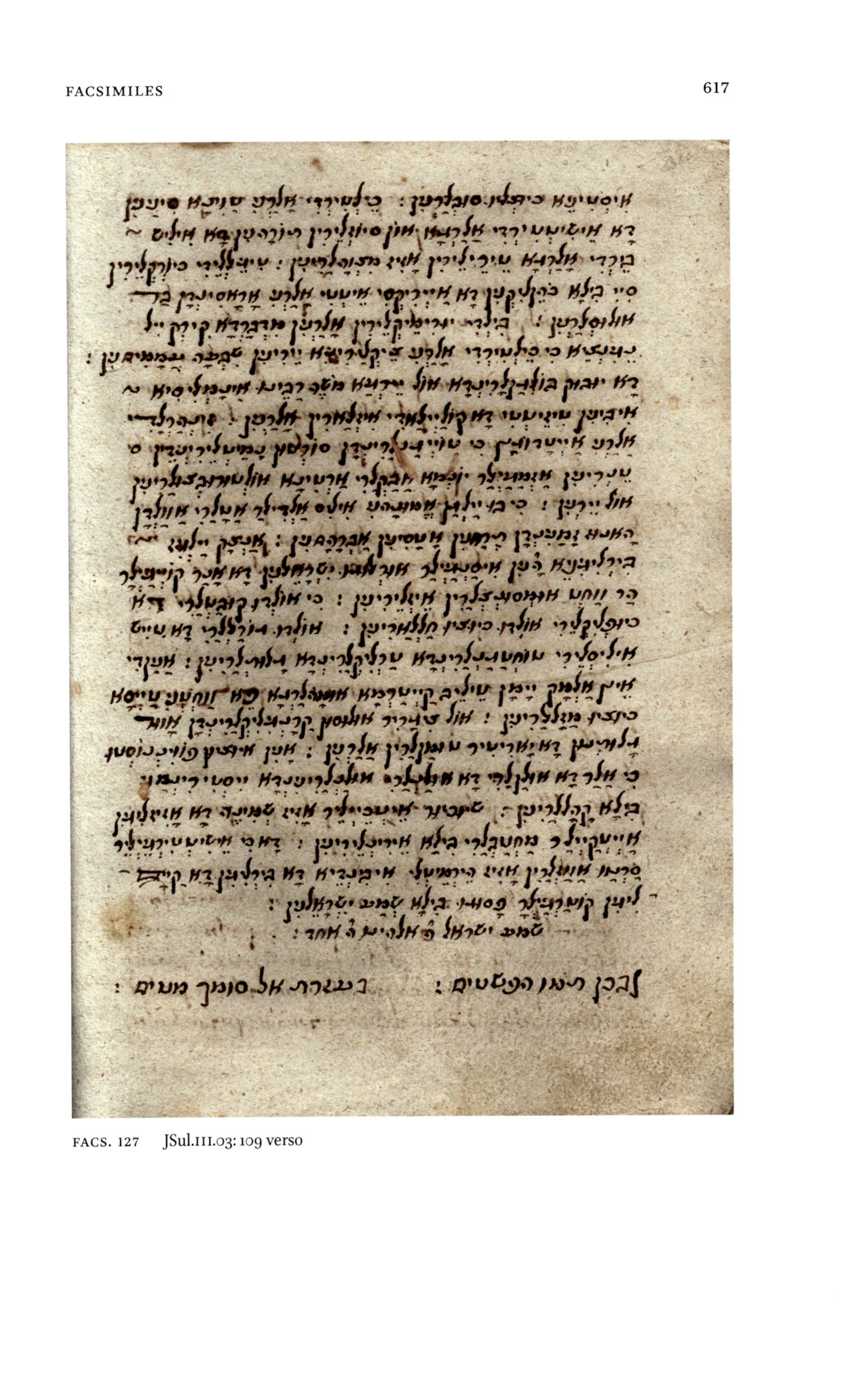

שמע ישראל ה' אלהינו ה' אחד :

נבכן תמו הפסוקים : בעזרת אל סומך [illegible] :

FACS. 127 JSul.III.03: 109 verso

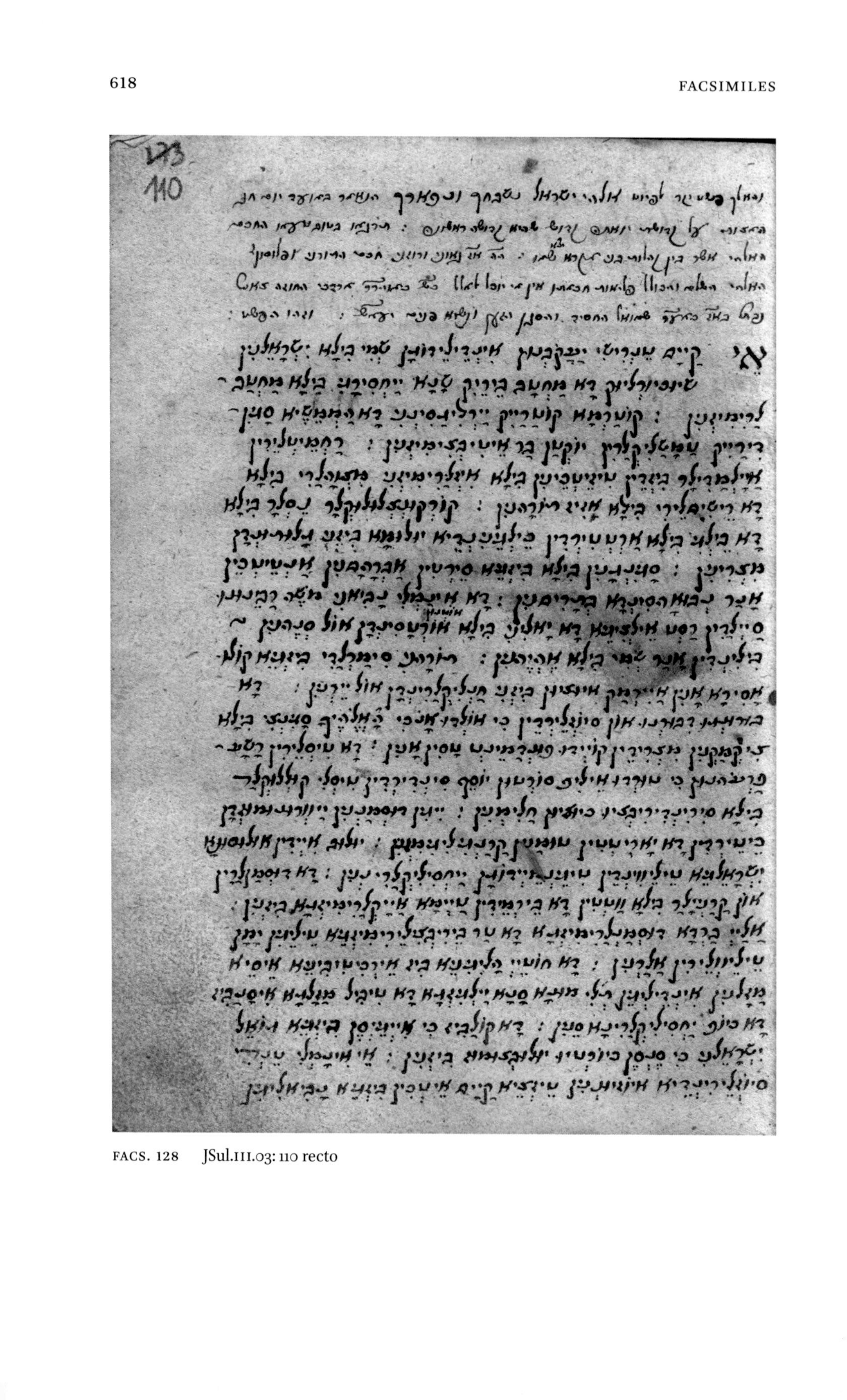

FACS. 128 JSul.III.03: 110 recto

[illegible]

[illegible]

כי כה אמר ה' אלהים מצרים וגו' :

[illegible]

ישתבח אל עליון קונה שמים וחילם : המוציא במספר
צבאם ובשם יקרא לכלם : סובל עליונים
ותחתונים ברעם ובכלם : פותח את ידו ומשביע לכל חי משאלם
בחסדו בראם וברחמיו פעלם : נותן אכלם בעתו למענם
ועד עולם : מעביר עבדים העלה ממצרים ואולם :
רוקע הים בכחו ושבר מי מנוחות נהלם : דברי תורתו השמיעם
ומשפטיו הנחילם : כלל יפים בהודו ומכל עם הבדילם : ירעם
לכרם במדבר עד הביאם אל גבולם : ושם נאמן ביתו אשרם
ויישר מסלולם : כזם לכל יזנו אחרי אלהי העמים ופסלם : אשר
שקר נחלום אבותם מעולם : אך כי בה' יבטחו ולו ישימו כסלם :
כי הוא עזם ומעוזם הוא כחם וחילם : הוא חלקם וגורלם הוא
נחלתם וחבלם : לו נקם ושלם לעת תמוט רגלם : הוא יוציאם
מחשכם ויאיר אפלם : לכן הם ובניהם ובני בניהם במקהלם :
יברכו שמו ויקדישוהו במהללם : ייחדו אומר וישמיעו ברון
קולם : שמע ישראל ה' אלהינו ה' אחד :

[illegible]

FACS. 129 JSul.III.03: 110 verso

FACS. 130 JSul.III.07: 110 verso

FACS. 131 JSul.III.07: 111 recto

FACS. 132 JSul.III.07: 111 verso

FACS. 133 JSul.III.07: 112 recto

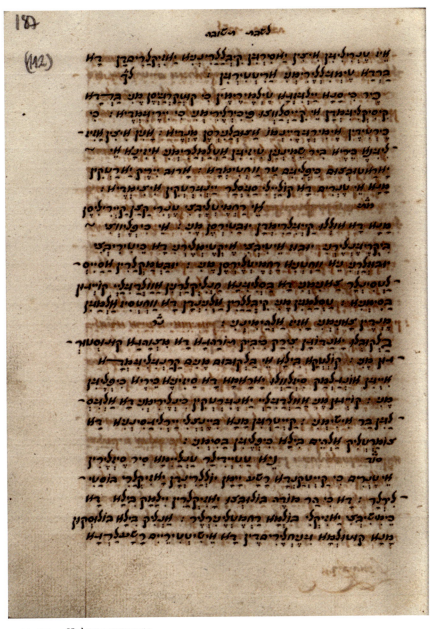

FACS. 134 JSul.III.07: 112 verso

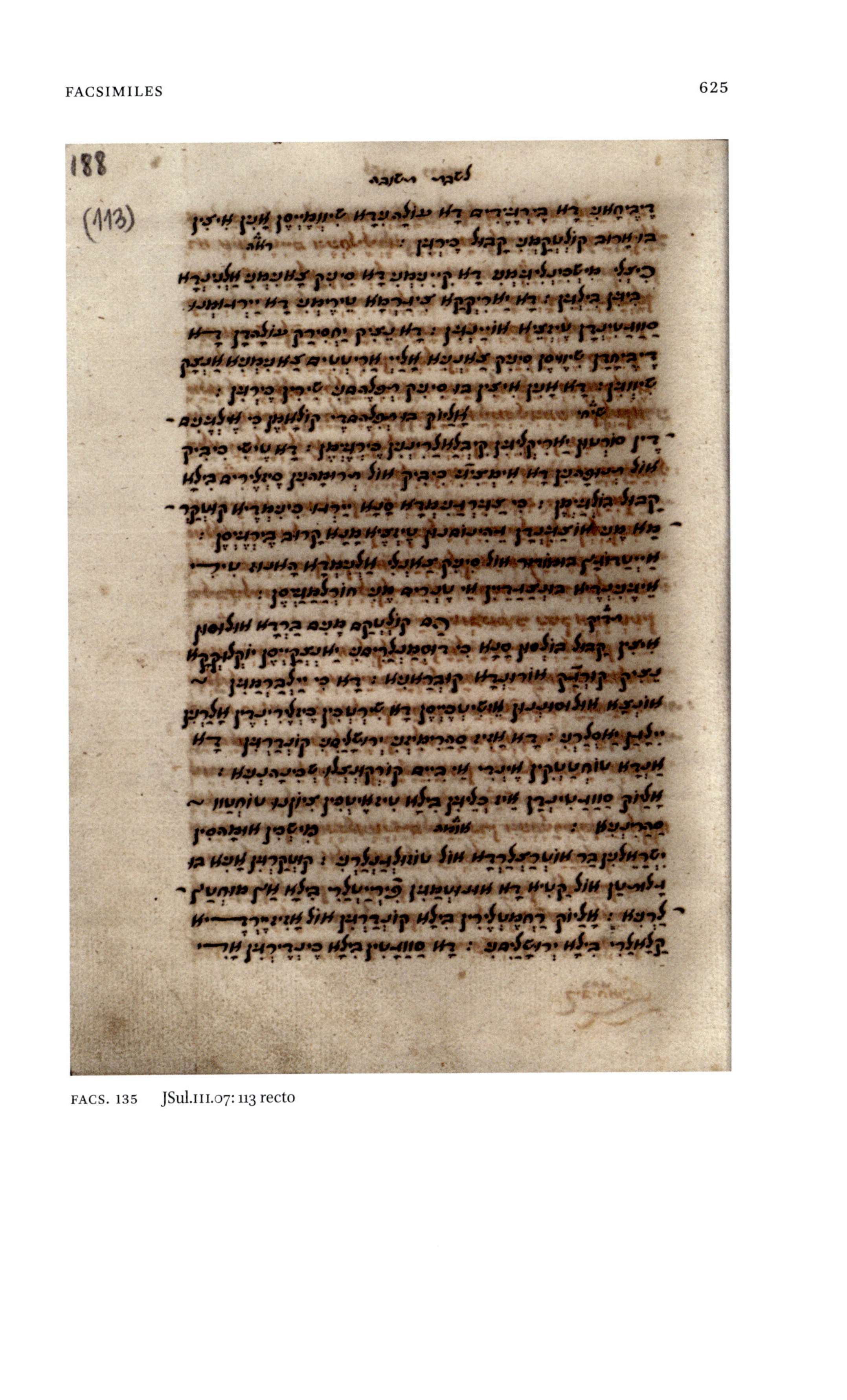

FACS. 135 JSul.III.07: 113 recto

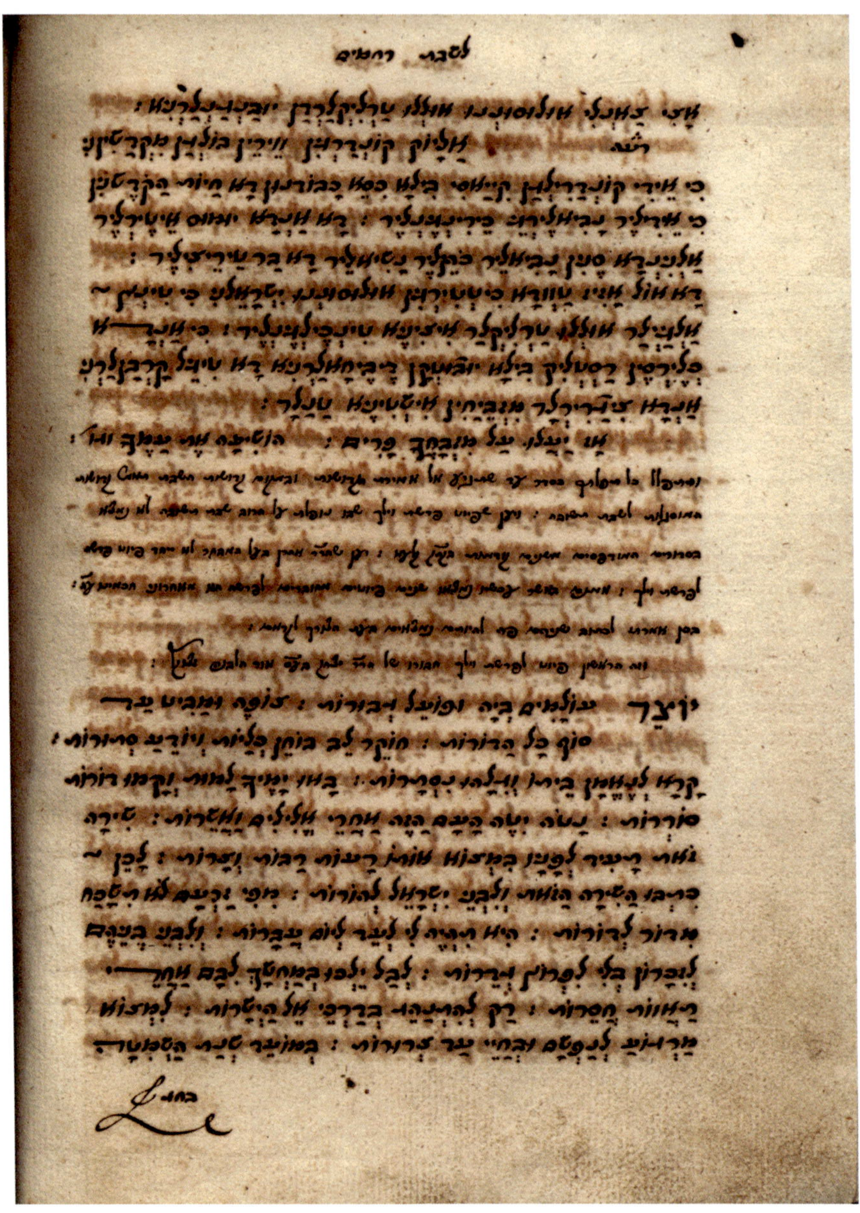

FACS. 136 JSul.III.07: 113 verso

189

(114)

בחר הסוכות את כל התורה לקרות : באמונה כל קהל ישראל להבר
מחשבותם הרעות ולזרות : הנה יהושע ריחתו ללמדם חקים
ותורות : והוא ינחיל אותם את הארץ המיועדת בגזרות :
מי כאלהינו נותן הישרות : מגיד מראשית אחרית ומדבר
אזהרות : ברוממות אמרותיו אמרות טהורות : יחיד ויקיים
הבטחותיו הנגזרות : יגזור אומר לקבץ גליות פזורות : יגאלם
גאולה נצחית מוציא אסירים בכושרות : ברחי ישראל וכנס ~
ליפה נוף משוש כל עיירות : ואהבתו תכסה על כל פשעינו ~
בימי כפרות : אין קדוש כה׳ כי אין בלתו עושה עתרות : כי הוא
קדוש ישראל יושב תהלות ואמירות : אין קדוש כה׳ כי אין בלתך :
ואתה קדוש יושב תהלות ישראל :

פיוט שני לפרשת וילך חברו [illegible] יוסף הקדוש בעל המעונות [illegible]
[illegible] הקדוש [illegible] יסדו על קדושה שאנו [illegible] [illegible] :

ישתבח אל עליון קונה שמים וחילם : ומוציא במספר
צבאם ובשם יקרא לכלם : סובל עליונים ותחתונים
פרטם וכללם : פותח את ידו ומשביע לכל חי משאלם : בחסדו
ברא וברחמיו פעלם : נותן אכלם בעתו למקטנם ועד
גדולם : מגיד עבדים העלה עמו וממצרים גאלם : רגע
הים בכחו ועל מי מנוחות נהלם : דברי תורתו השמיעם
ומשפטיו הנחילם : כלל יפים בהודו ומבדל עם הבדילם : ירעם
לבטח במדבר עד הביאם אל גבולם : ושם נאמן ביתו אשרם
וייסר מסלולם : ביום לבל יזנו אחרי אלהי העמים ופסלם :
אשר שקר נחלום אבותם מעולם : אך כי בה׳ יבטחו ולו ישימו
כסלם : כי הוא עזם ומעוזם הוא כחם וחילם : הוא חלקם
וגורלם הוא נחלתם וחבלם : לו נקם ושלם לעת תמוט רגלם :
הוא יוציאם מחשכם ויאיר אפלם : לכן הם ובניהם ובני בניהם

FACS. 137 JSul.III.07: 114 recto

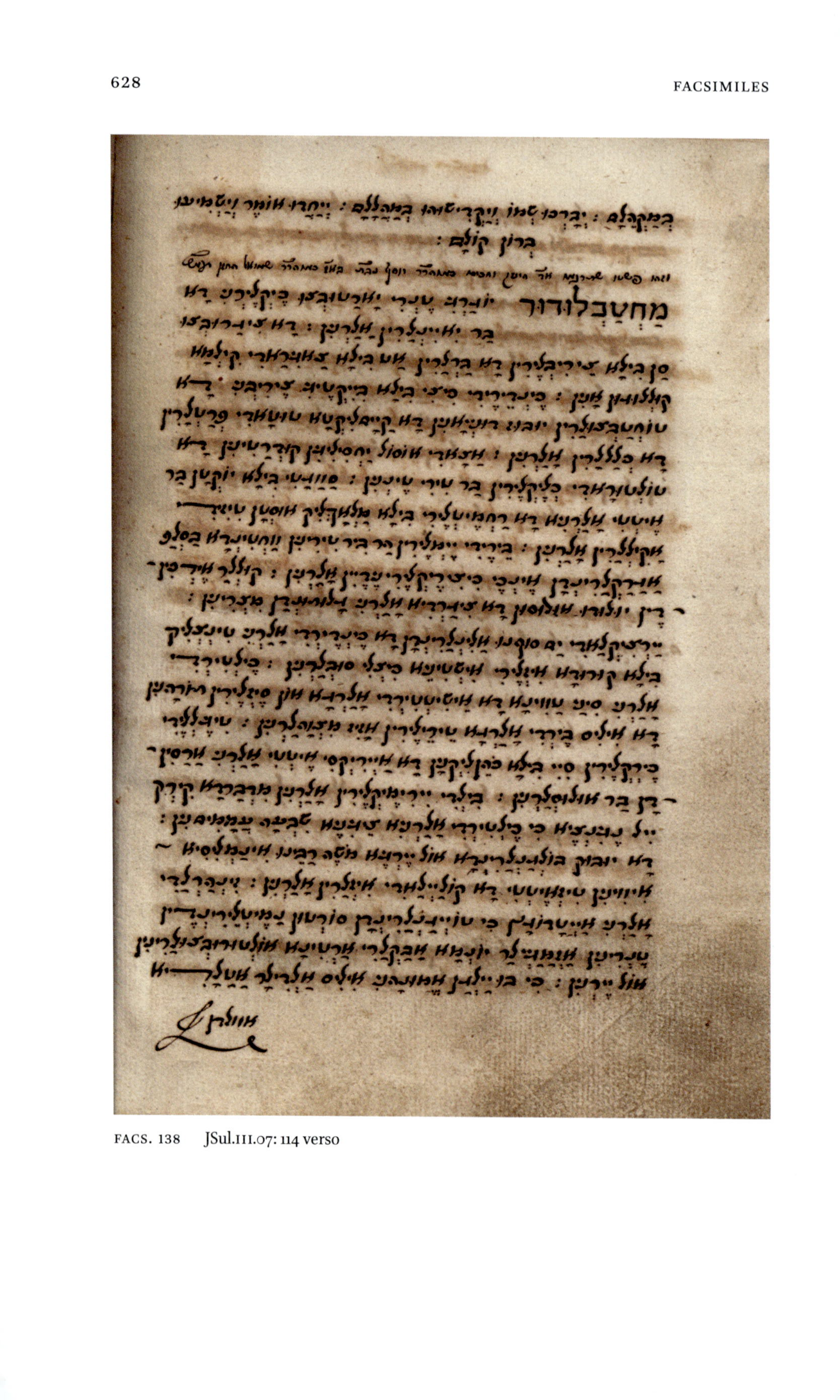

במקהלם : יברכו שמו ויברכוהו במהללם : ויחדו אומר וישמיעו

ברון קולם :

מחטבלודור

FACS. 138 JSul.III.07: 114 verso

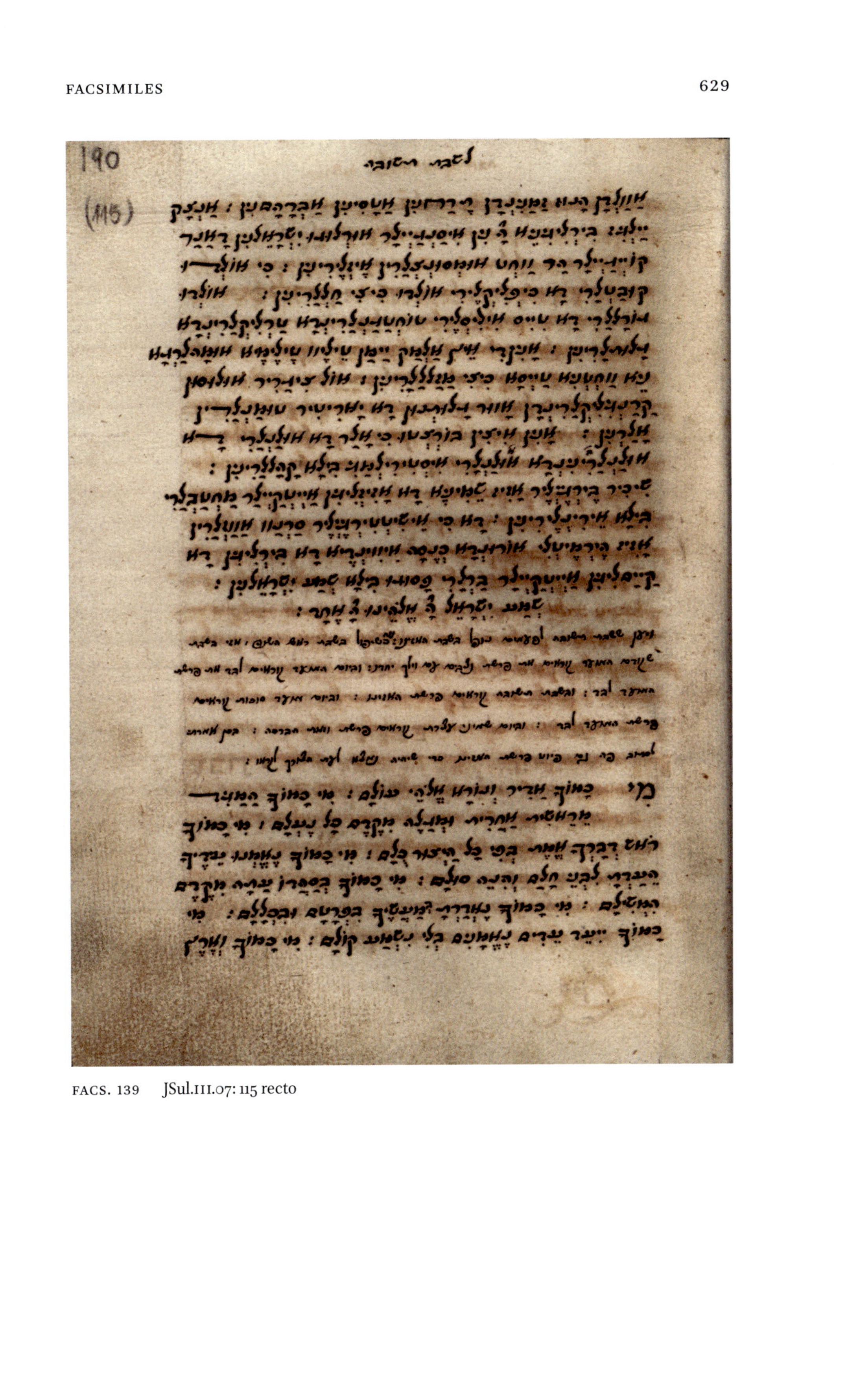

FACS. 139 JSul.III.07: 115 recto

FACS. 140 JSul.III.63: 35 verso

FACS. 141 JSul.III.63: 36 recto

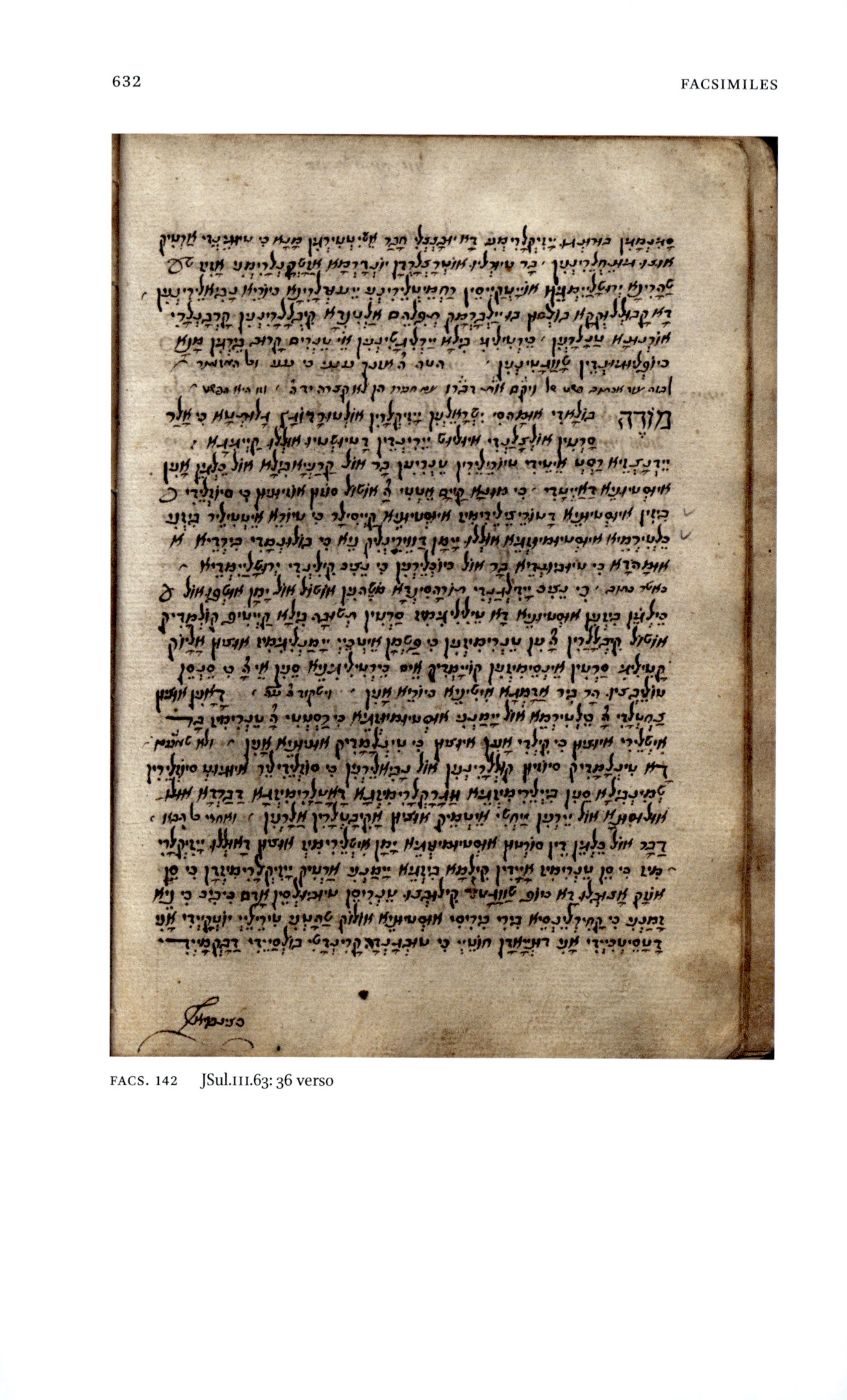

FACS. 142 JSul.III.63: 36 verso

FACS. 143 JSul.III.63: 37 recto

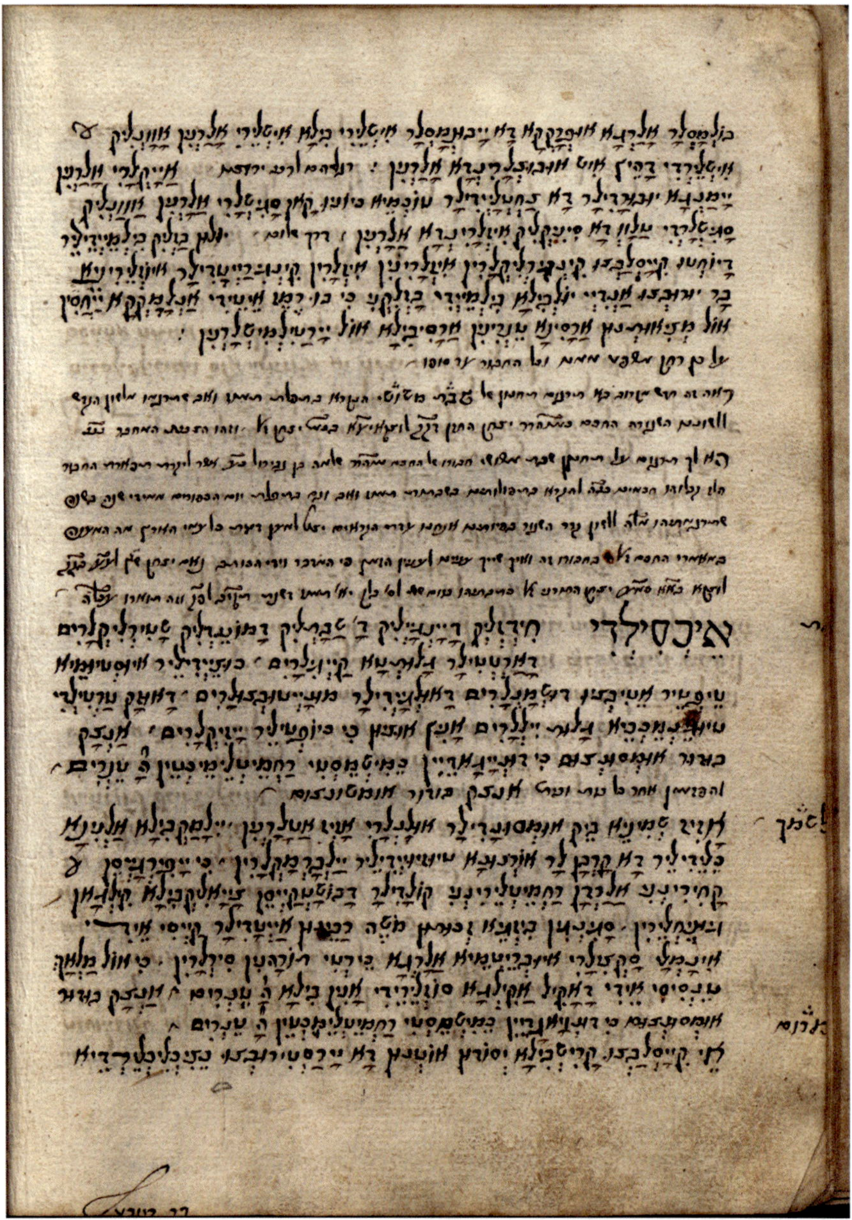

FACS. 144 JSul.III.63: 37 verso

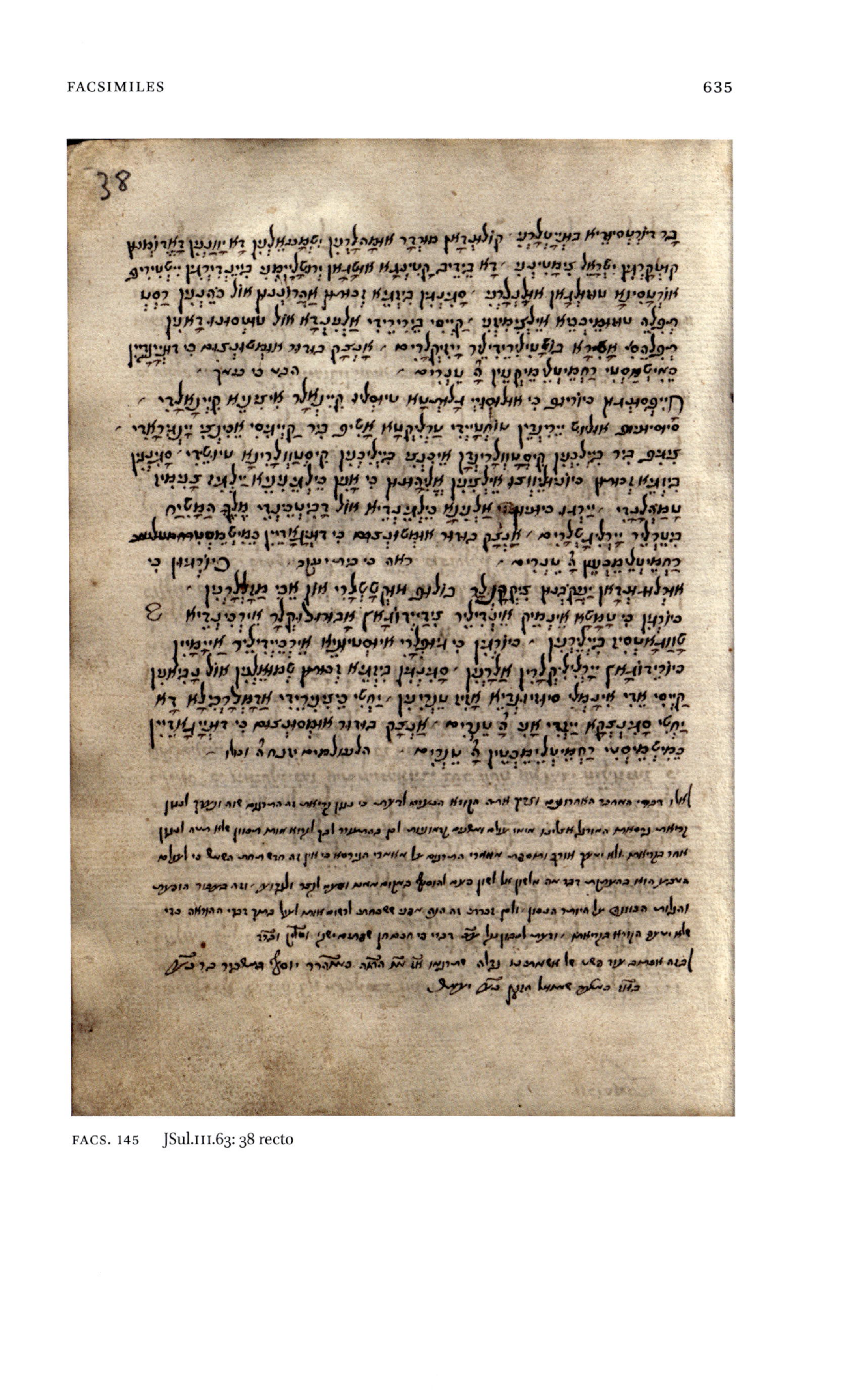

38

FACS. 145 JSul.III.63: 38 recto

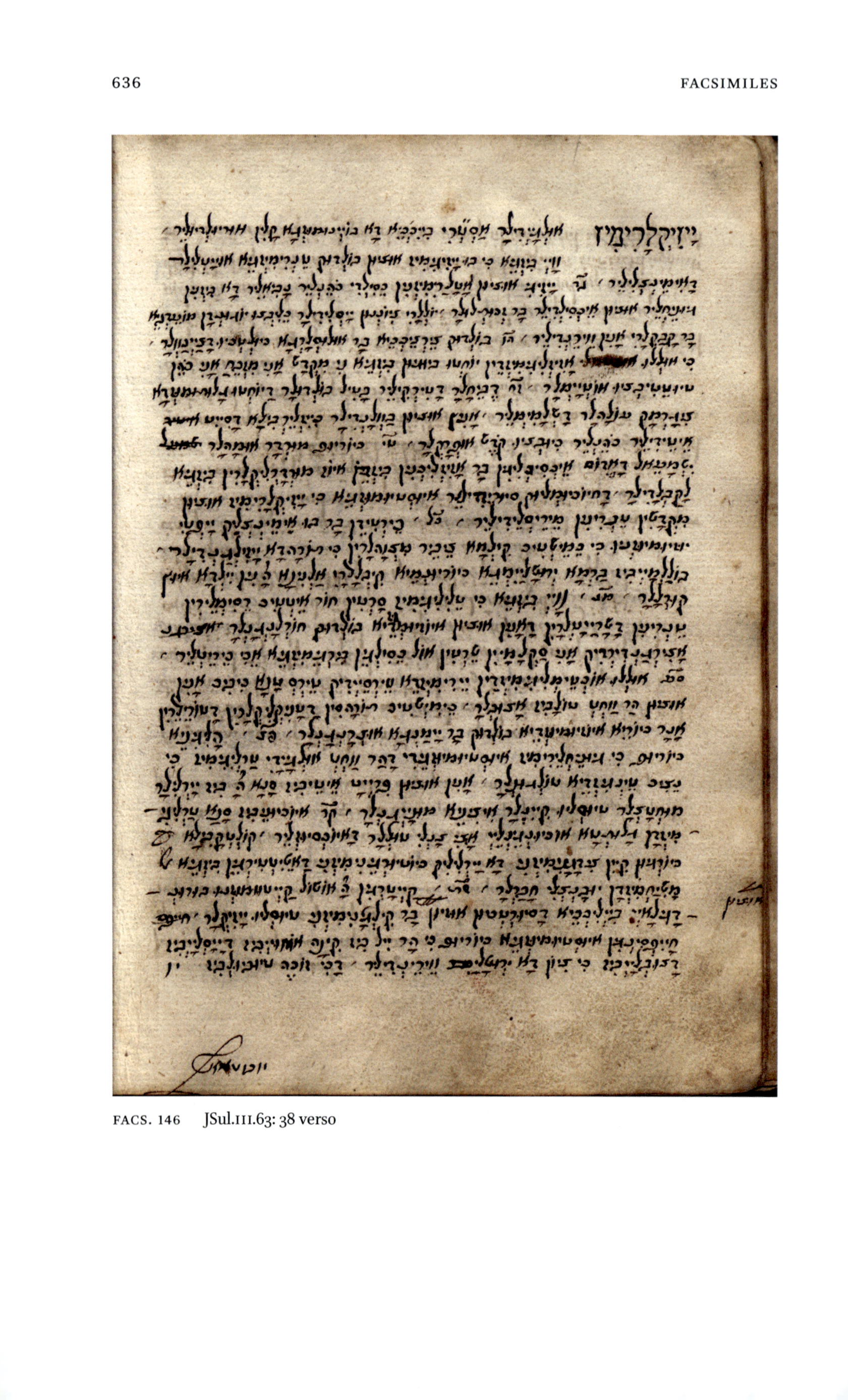

FACS. 146 JSul.III.63: 38 verso

39

FACS. 147 JSul.III.63: 39 recto

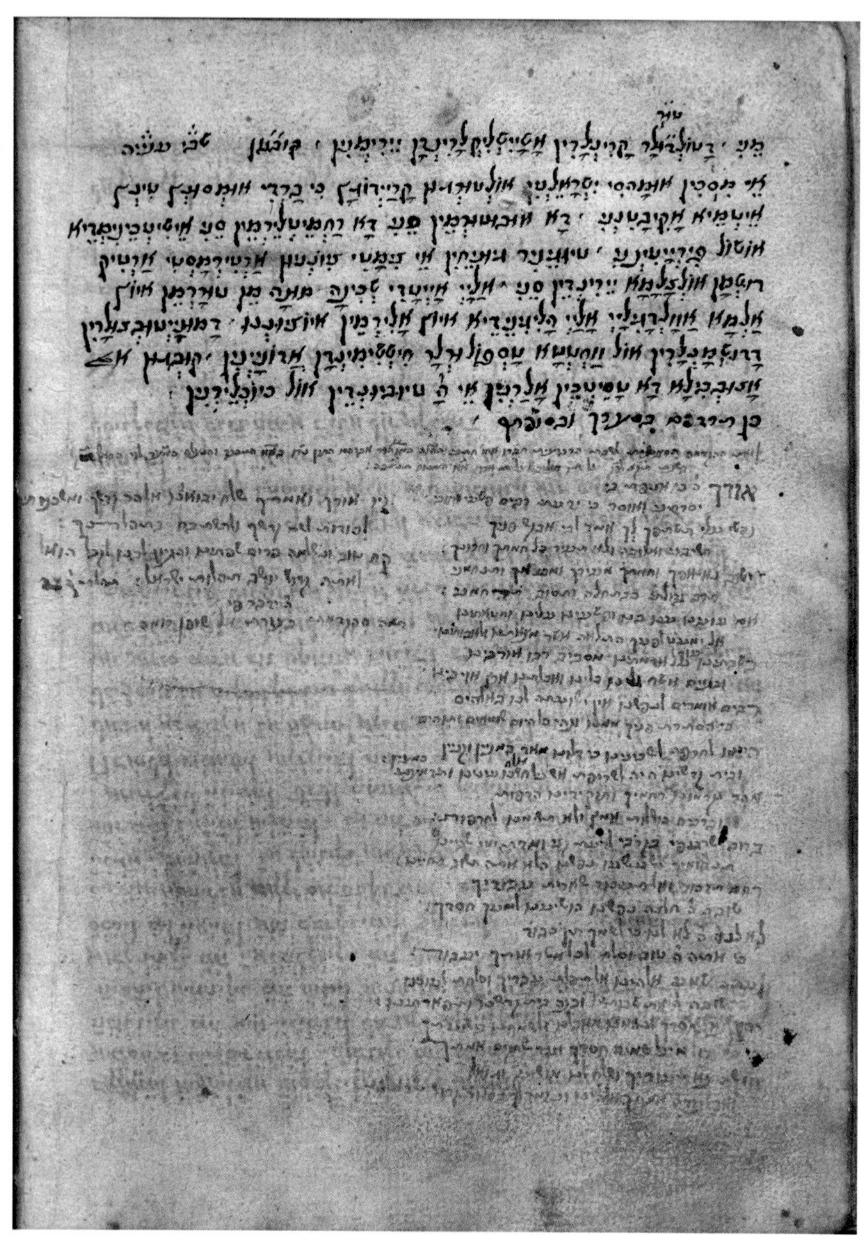

FACS. 148 JSul.III.63: 39 verso

FACS. 149 JSul.III.64a: 10 verso

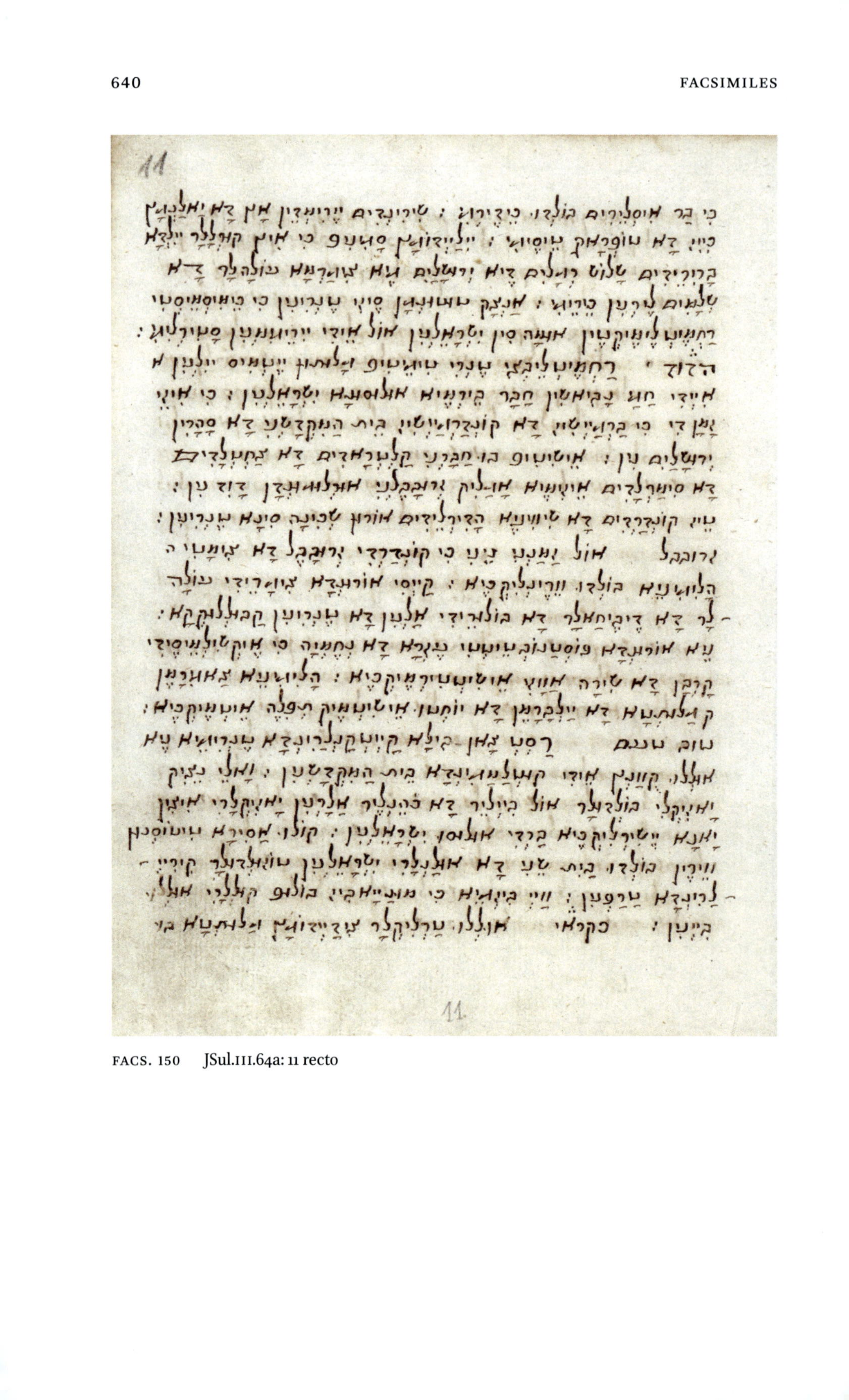

FACS. 150 JSul.III.64a: 11 recto

FACS. 151 JSul.III.64a: 11 verso

FACS. 152 JSul.III.64b: 20 verso–21 recto

FACS. 153 JSul.III.66: 133 verso–134 recto

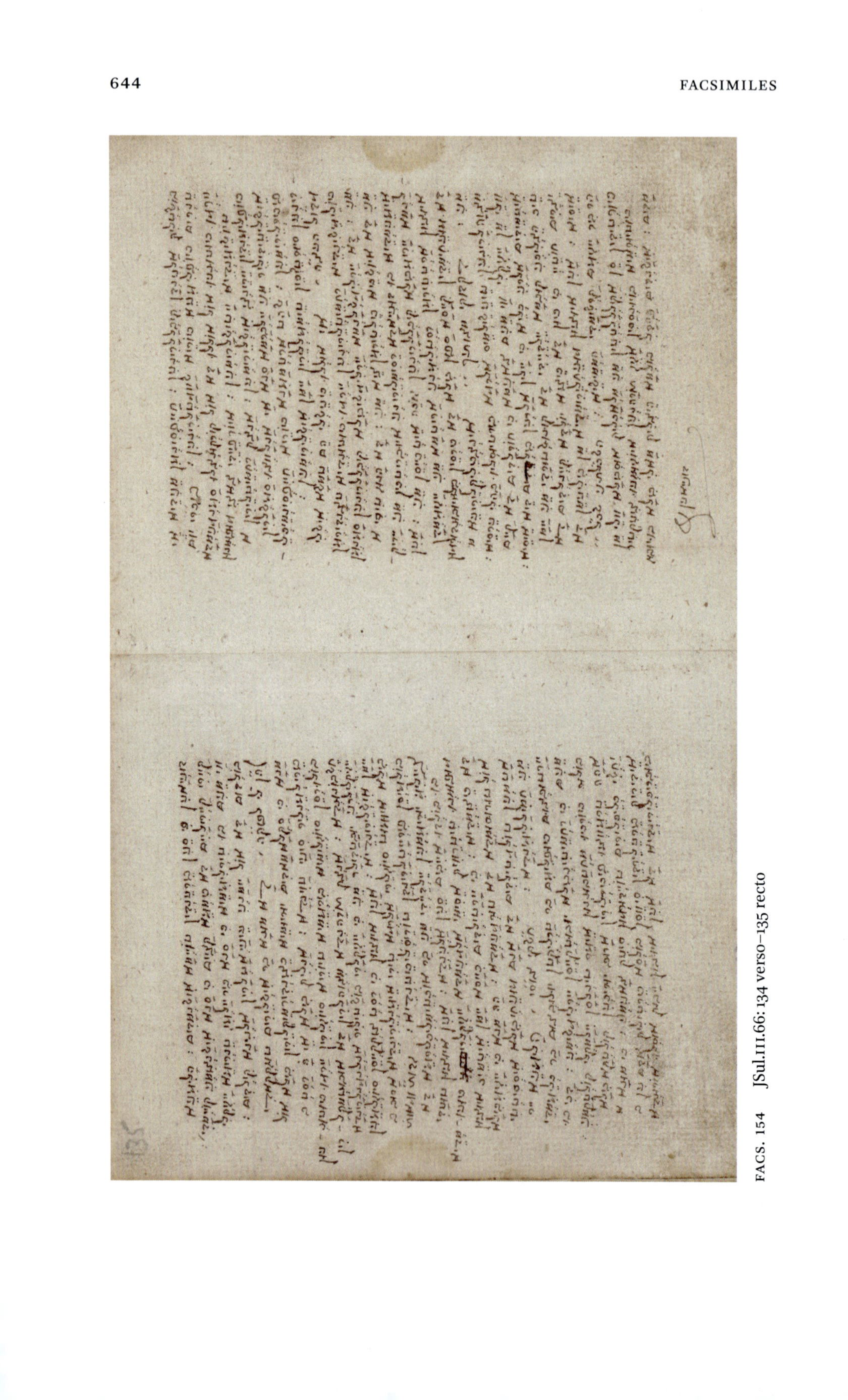

FACS. 154 JSul.III.66: 134 verso–135 recto

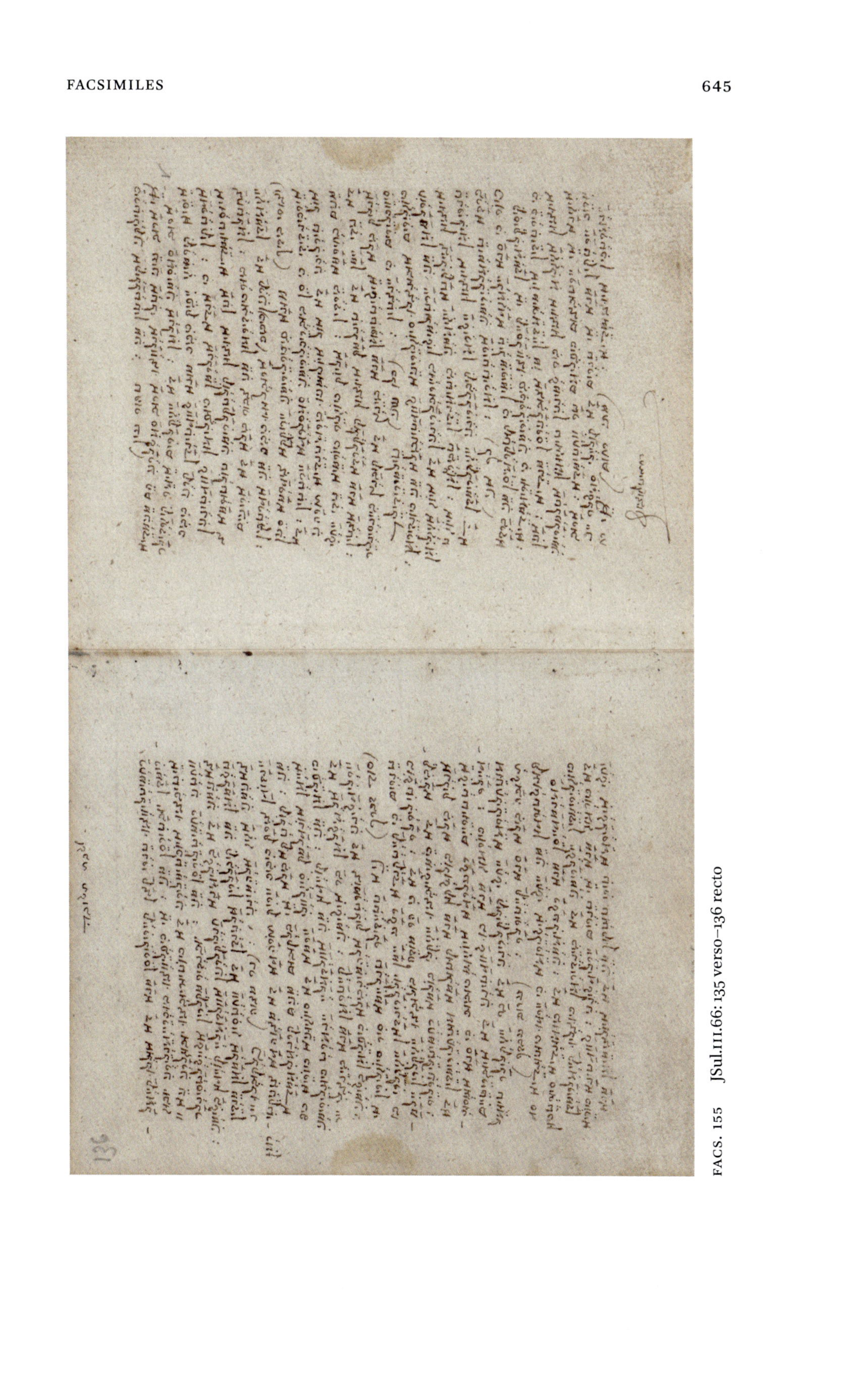

FACS. 155 JSul.III.66: 135 verso–136 recto

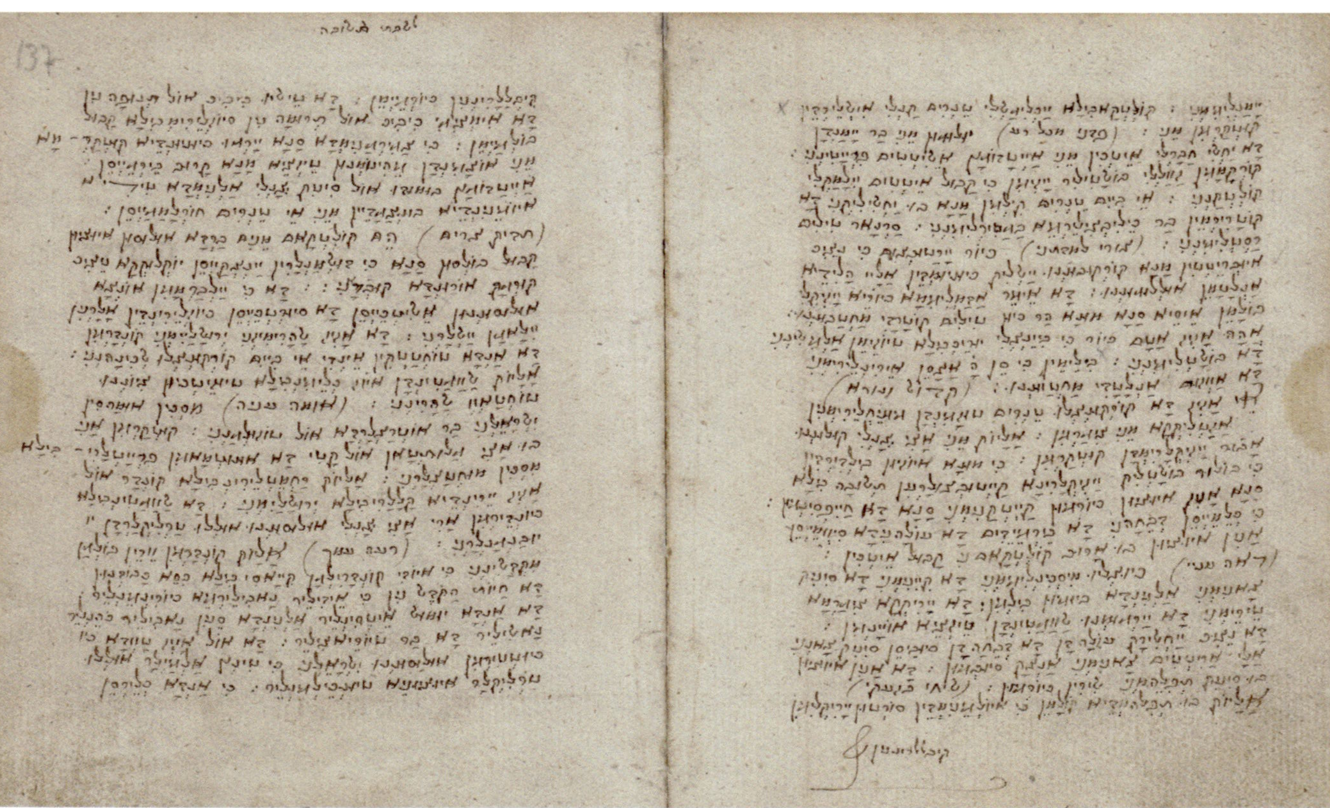

FACS. 156 JSul.III.66: 136 verso–137 recto

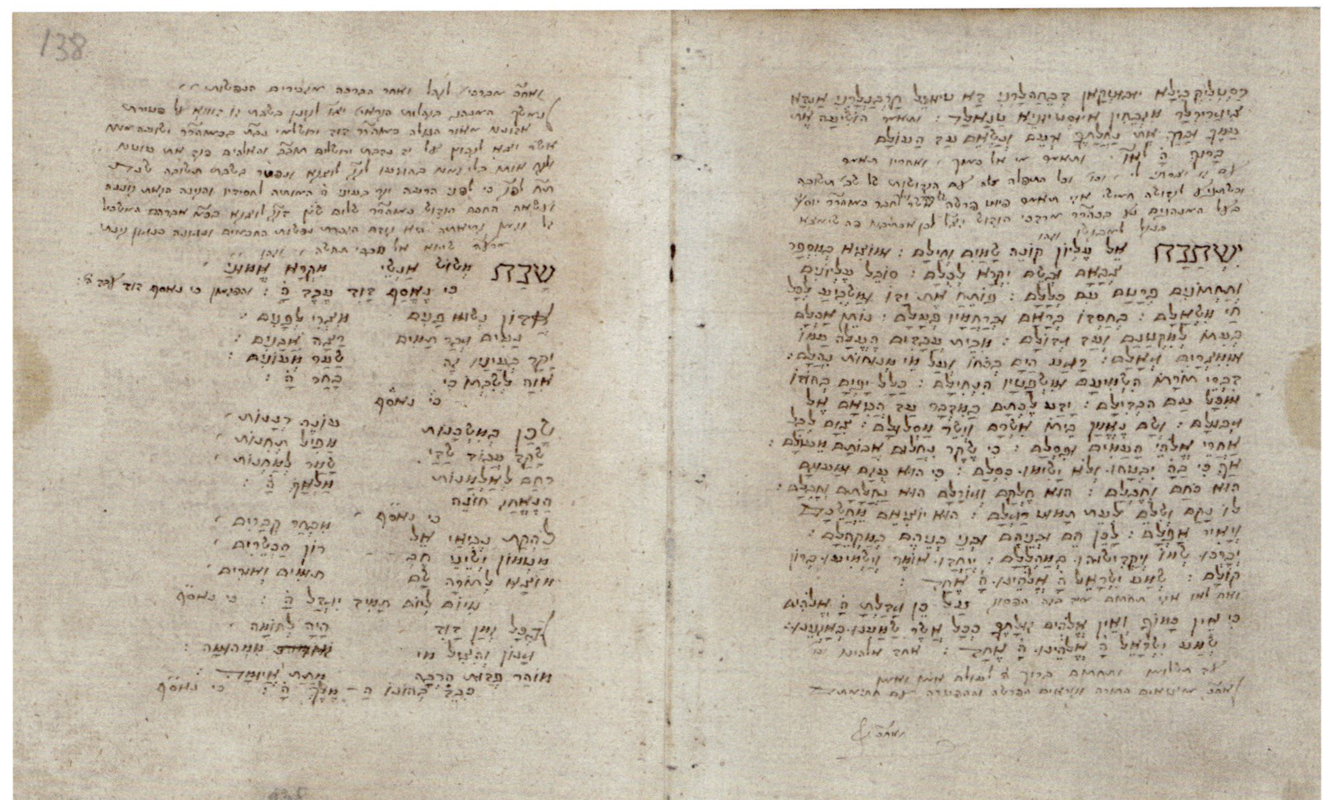

FACS. 157 JSul.III.66: 137 verso–138 recto

FACS. 158 JSul.III.67: 55 verso–56 recto

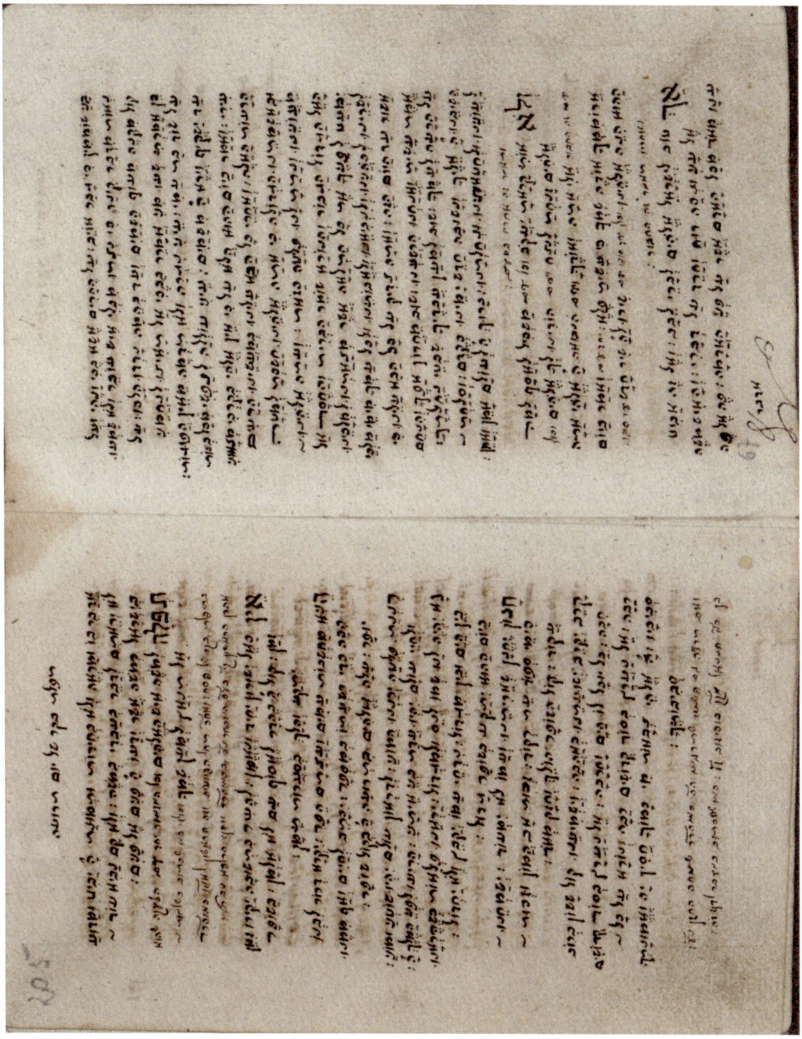

FACS. 159 JSul.III.67: 204 verso–205 recto

FACS. 160 JSul.III.67: 205 verso–206 recto

FACS. 161 JSul.III.67: 206 verso–207 recto

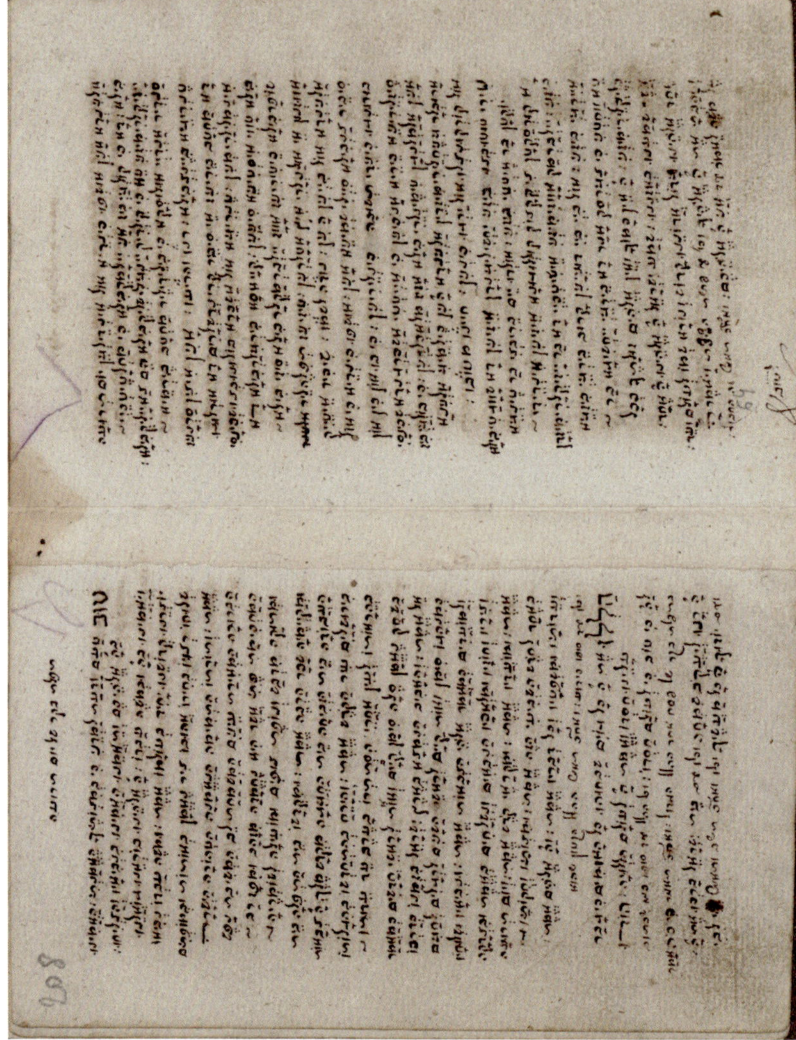

FACS. 162 JSul.III.67: 207 verso–208 recto

FACS. 163 JSul.III.67: 223 verso–224 recto

FACS. 164 JSul.III.67: 248 verso–249 recto

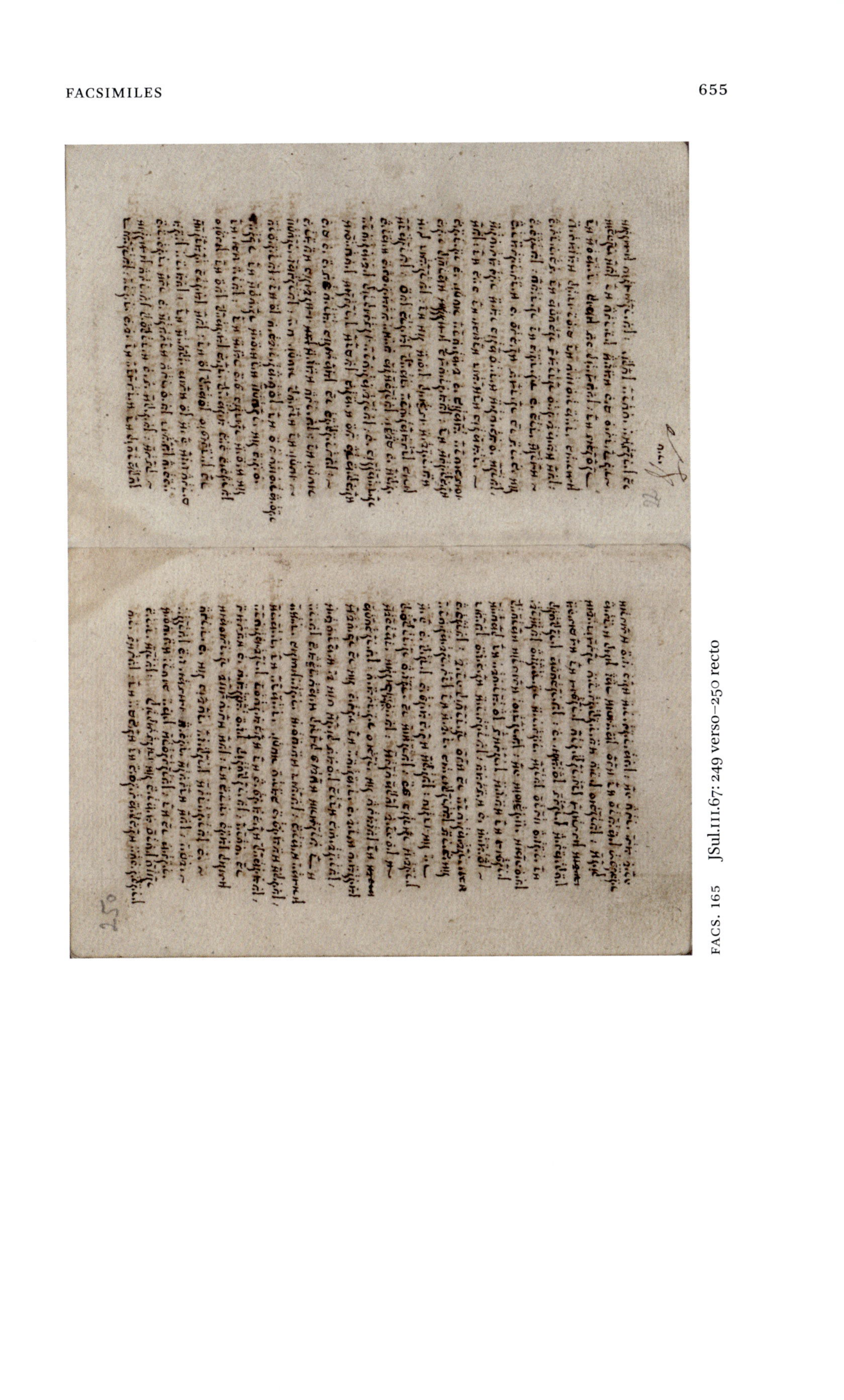

FACS. 165 JSul.III.67: 249 verso–250 recto

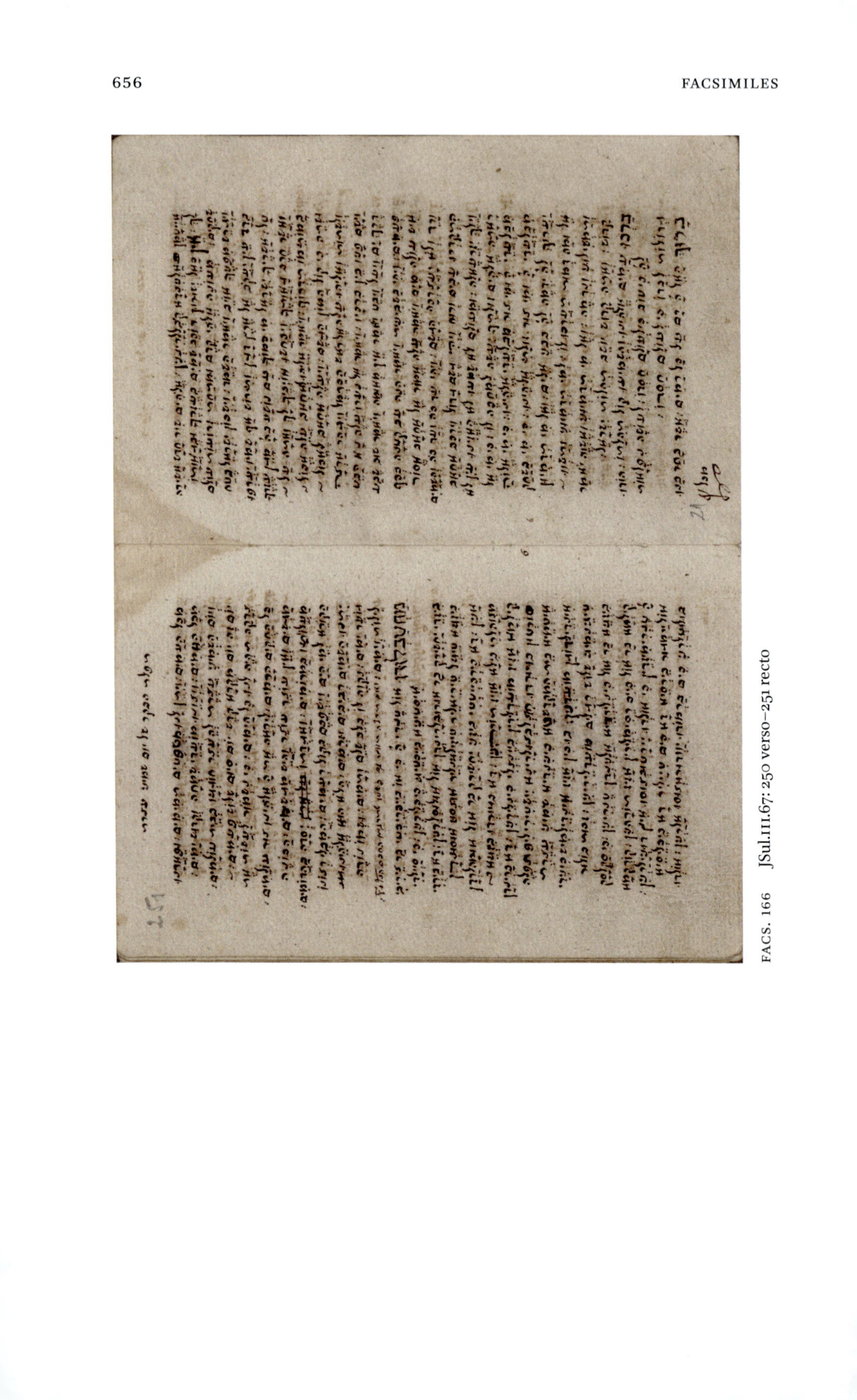

FACS. 166 JSul.III.67: 250 verso–251 recto

FACS. 167 JSul.III.69: 157 verso

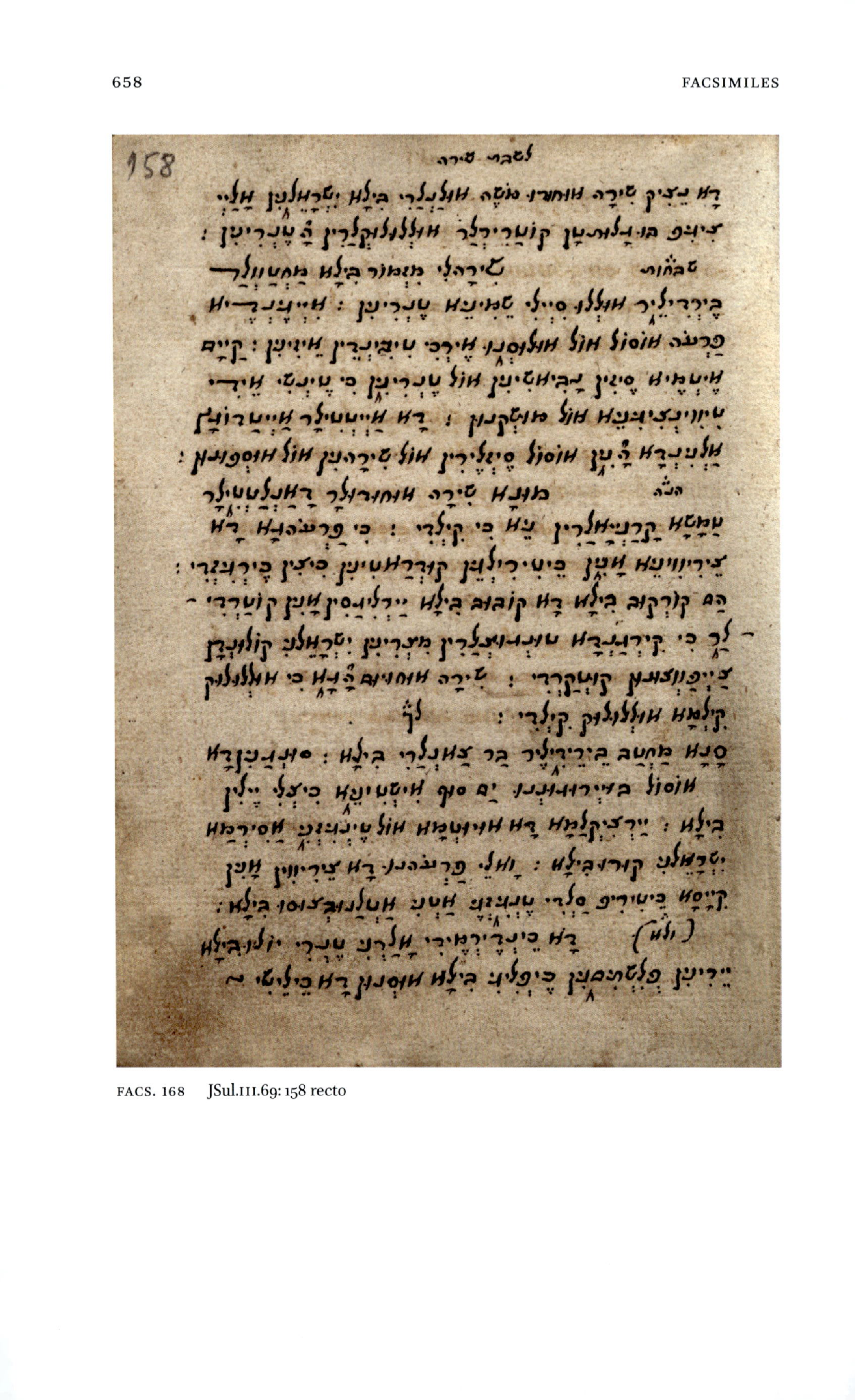

FACS. 168 JSul.III.69: 158 recto

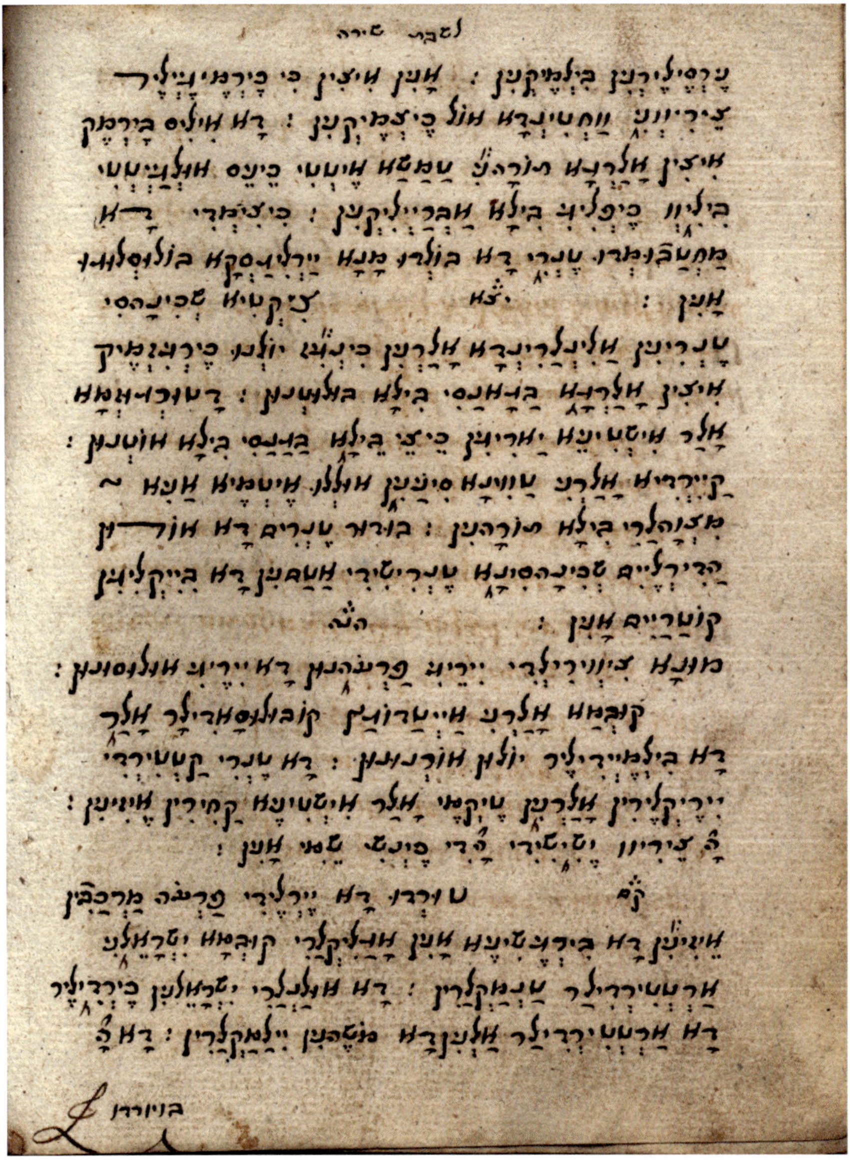

FACS. 169 JSul.III.69: 158 verso

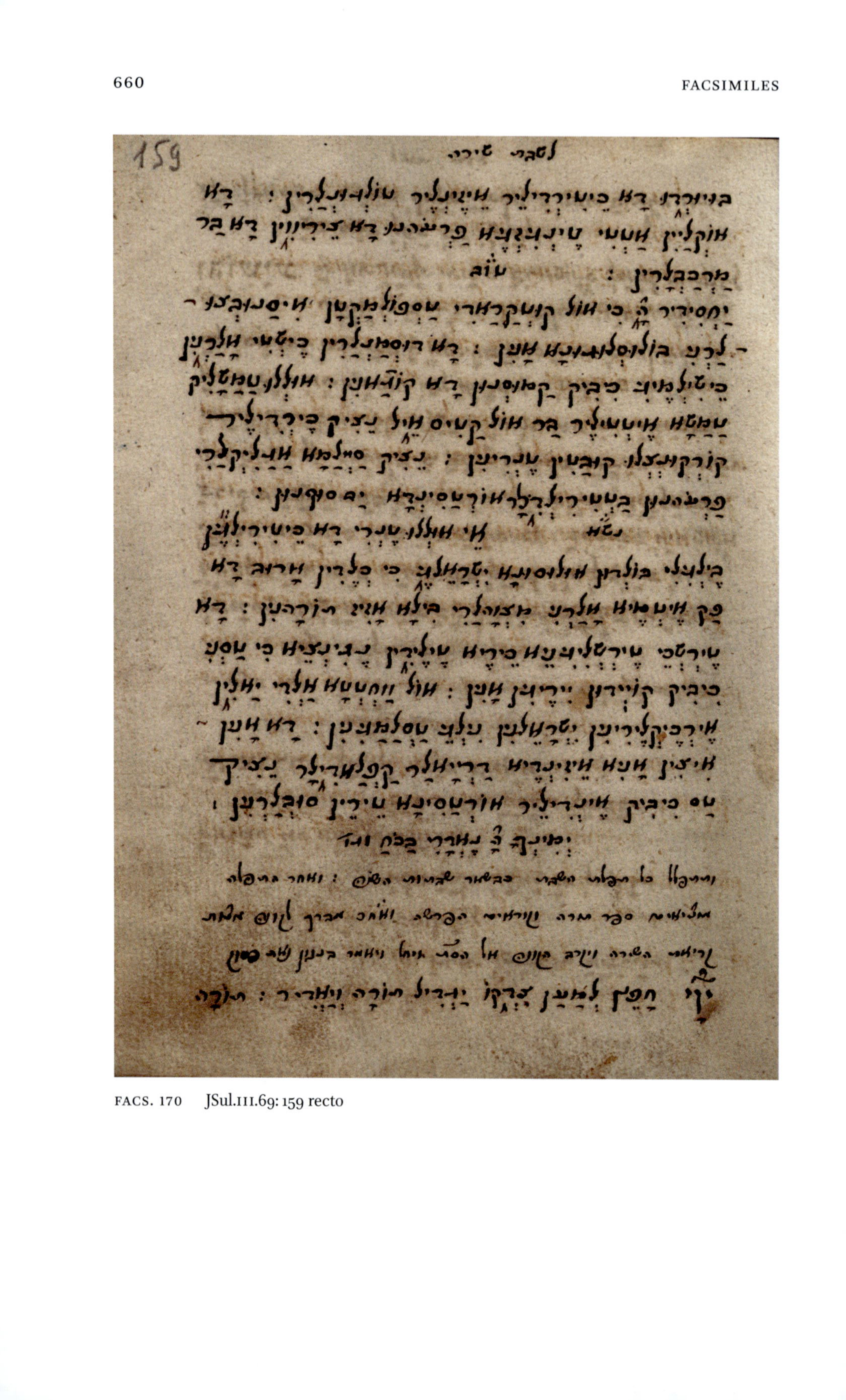

FACS. 170 JSul.III.69: 159 recto

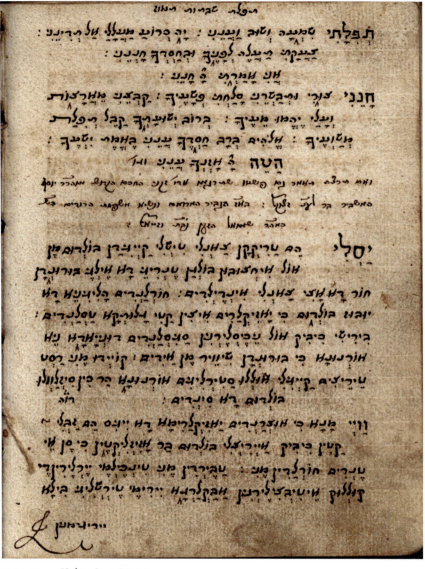

FACS. 171 JSul.III.69: 216 verso

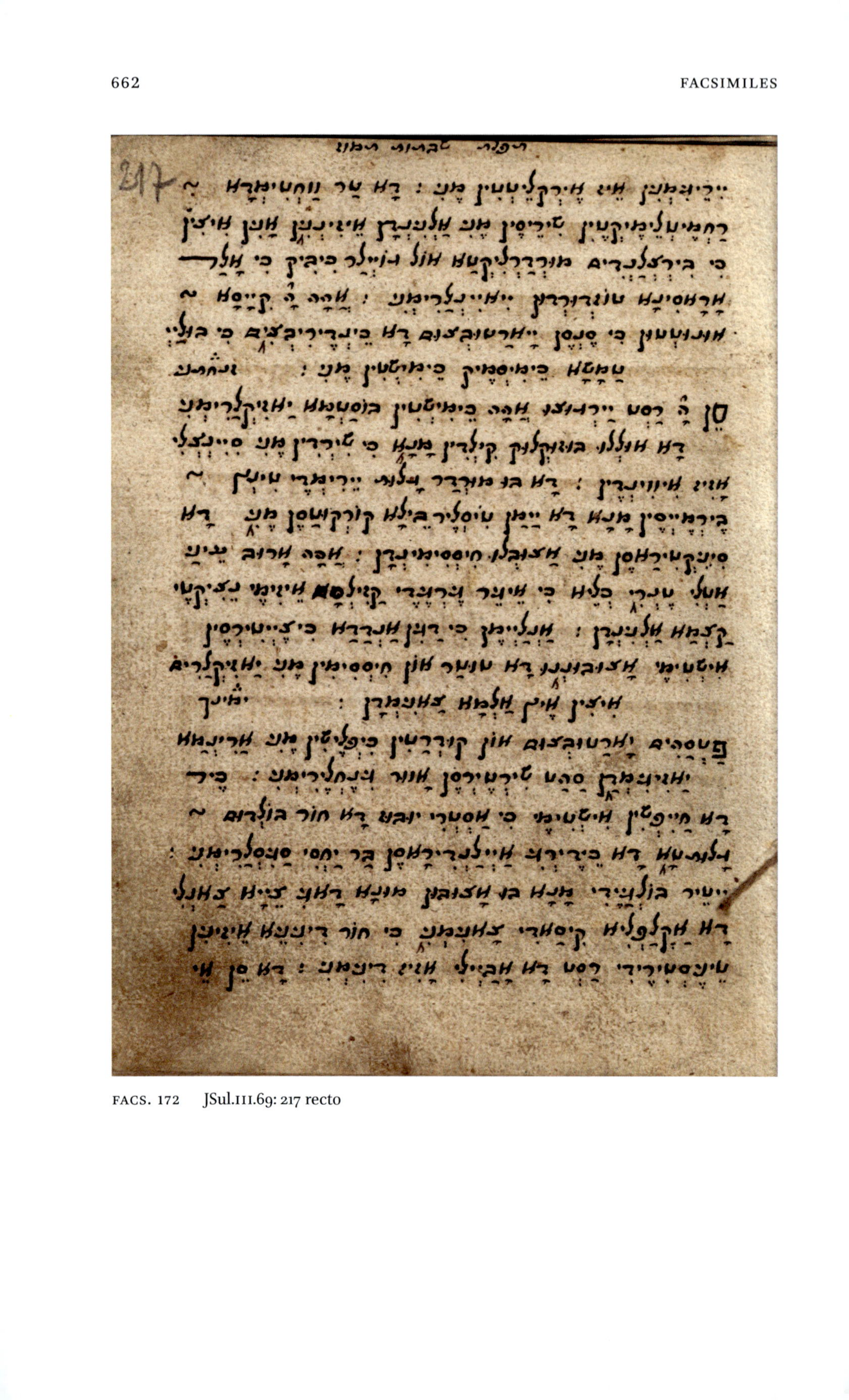

FACS. 172 JSul.III.69: 217 recto

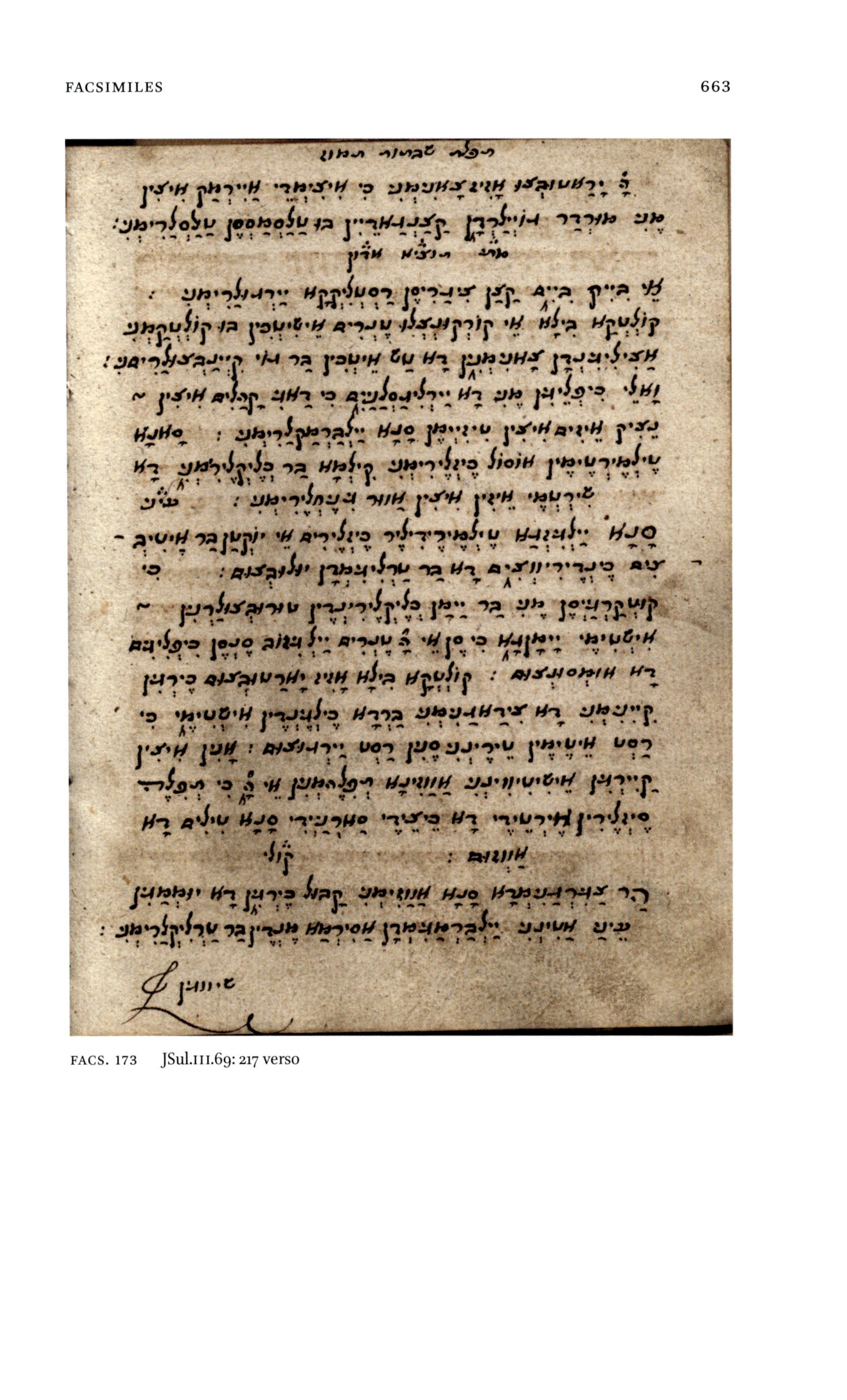

FACS. 173 JSul.III.69: 217 verso

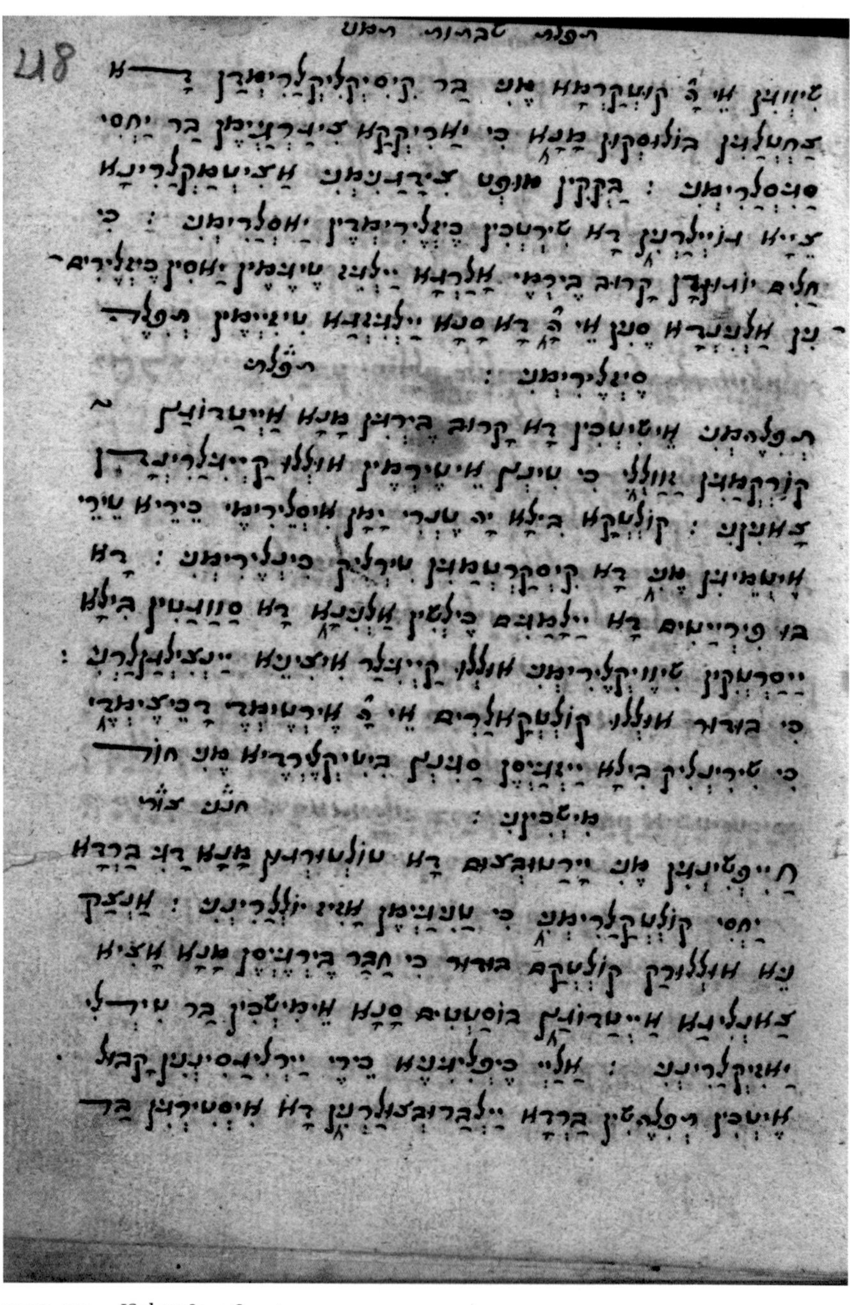

FACS. 174 JSul.III.69: 218 recto

FACS. 175 JSul.III.69: 218 verso

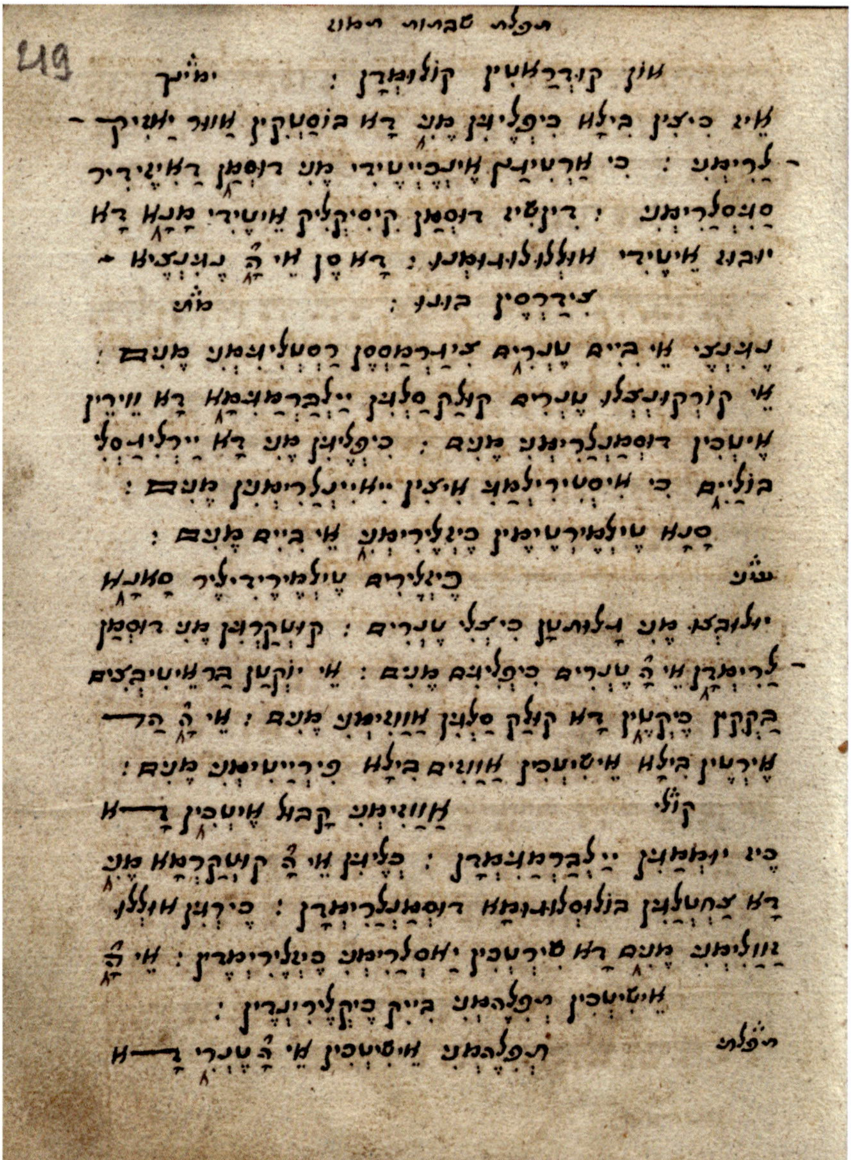

FACS. 176 JSul.III.69: 219 recto

FACS. 177 JSul.III.69: 219 verso

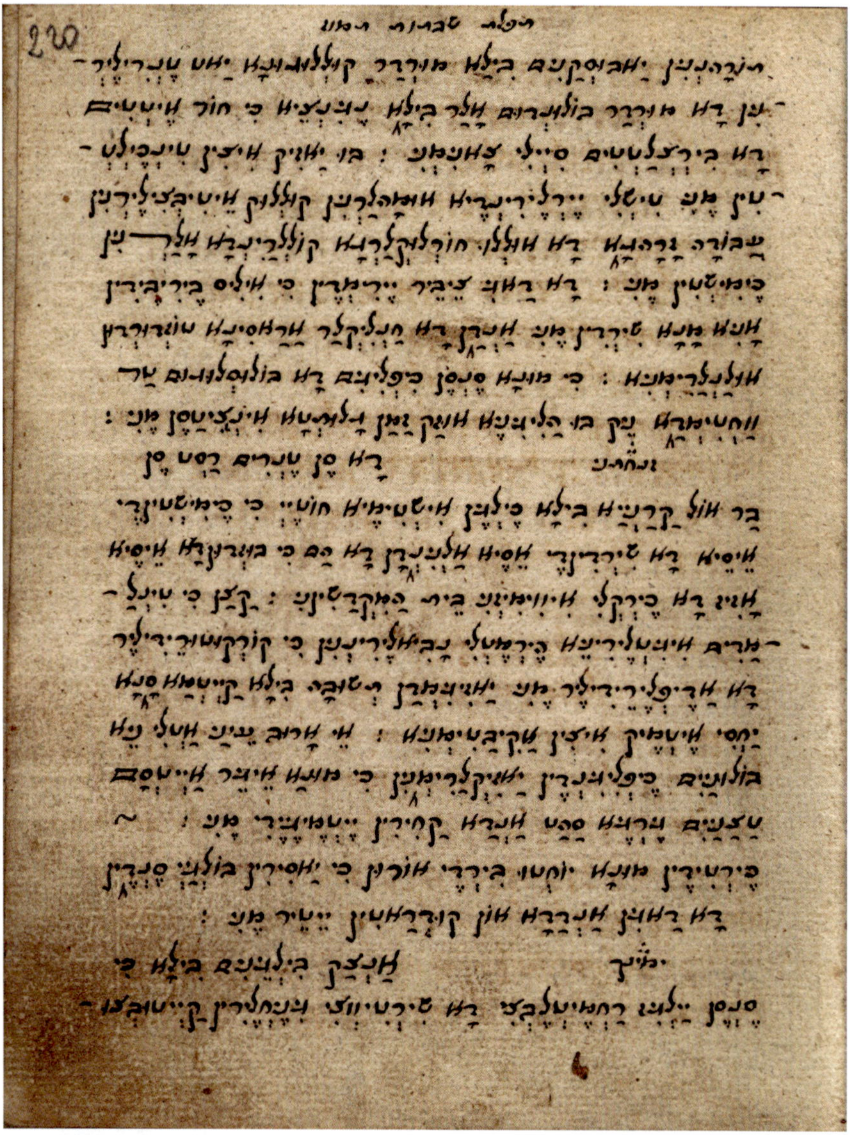

FACS. 178 JSul.III.69: 220 recto

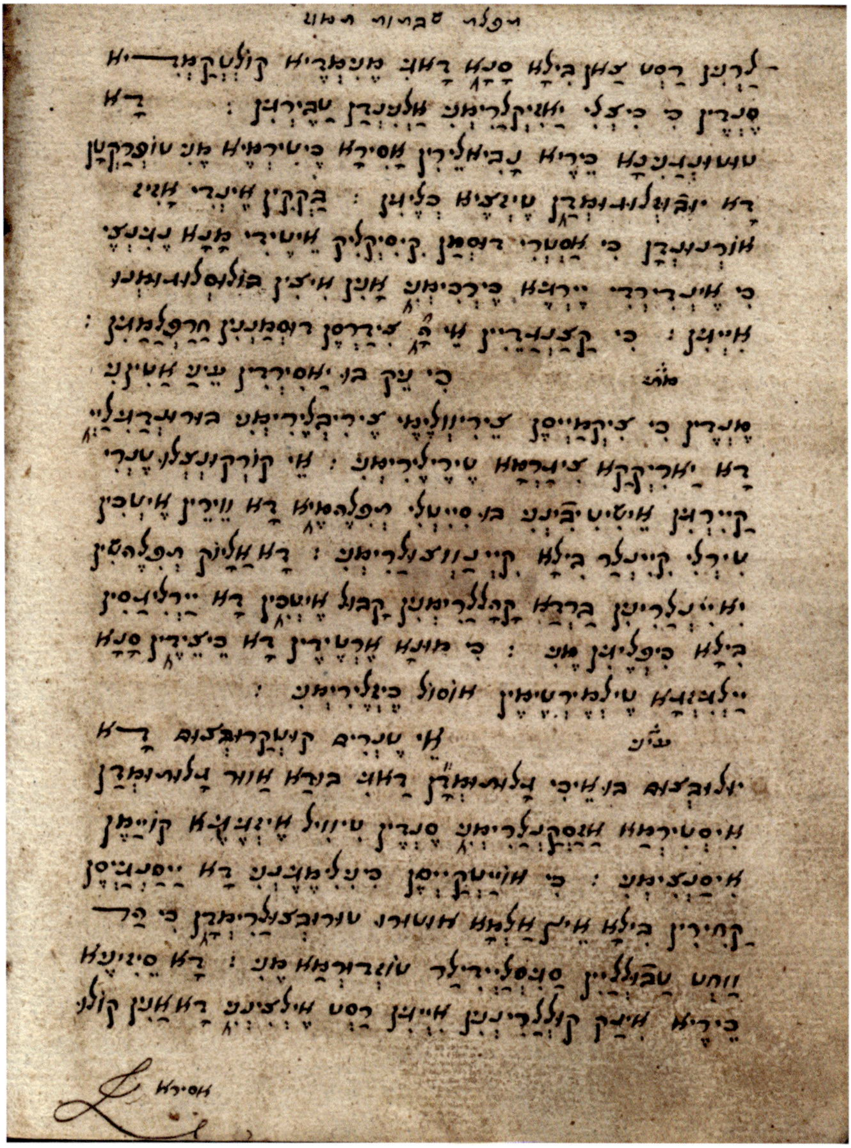

FACS. 179 JSul.III.69: 220 verso

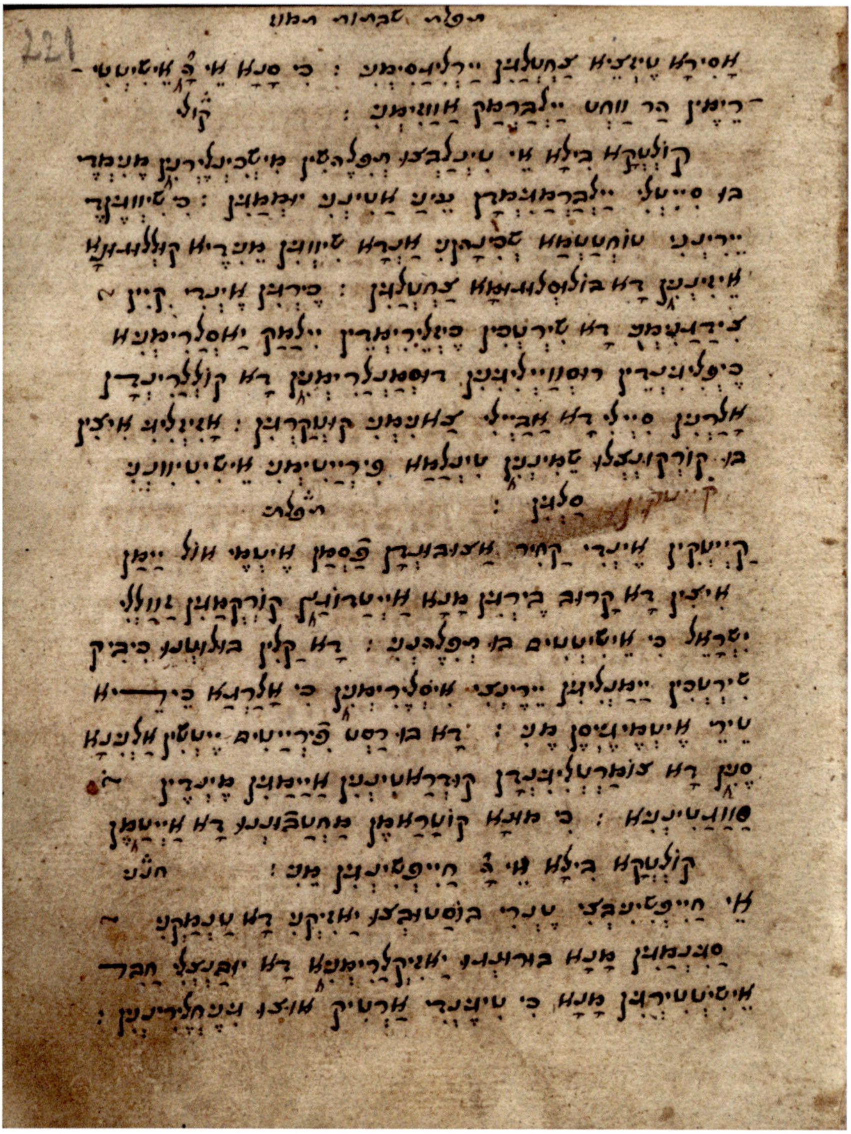

FACS. 180 JSul.III.69: 221 recto

FACS. 181 JSul.III.69: 221 verso

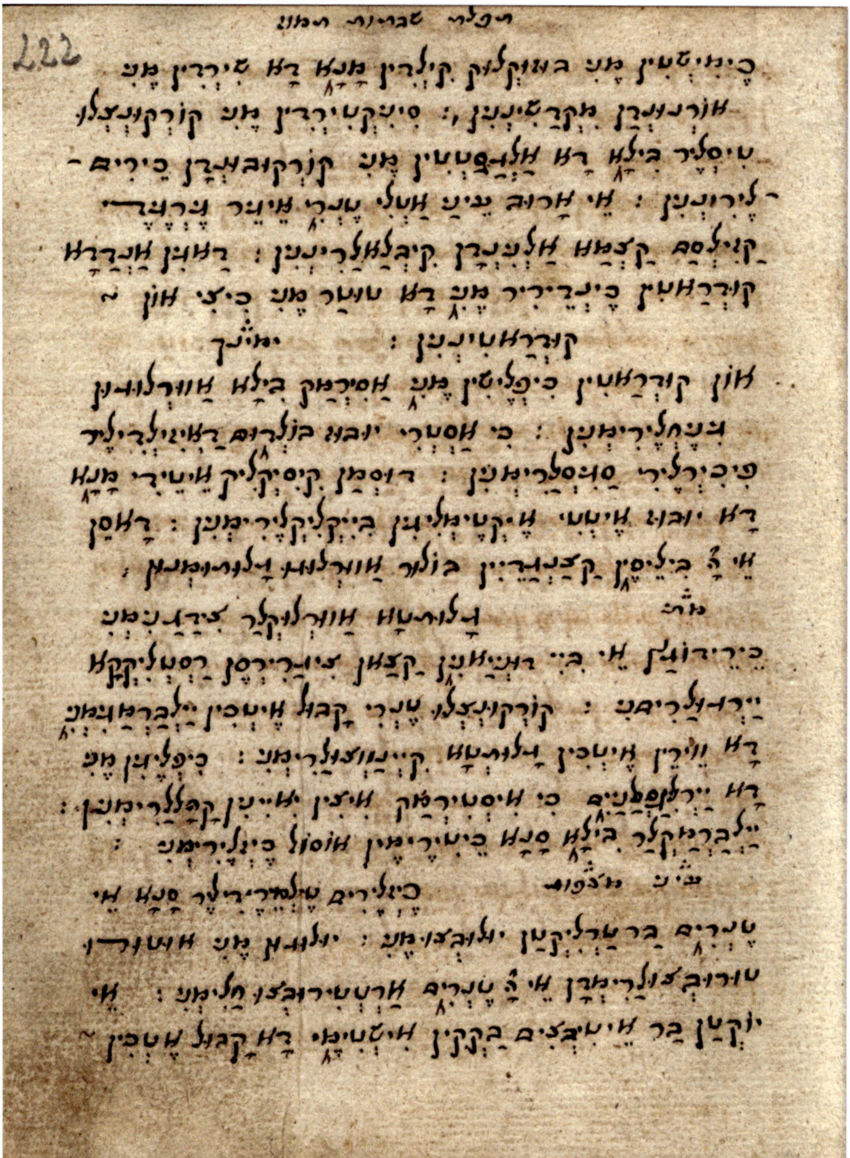

FACS. 182 JSul.III.69: 222 recto

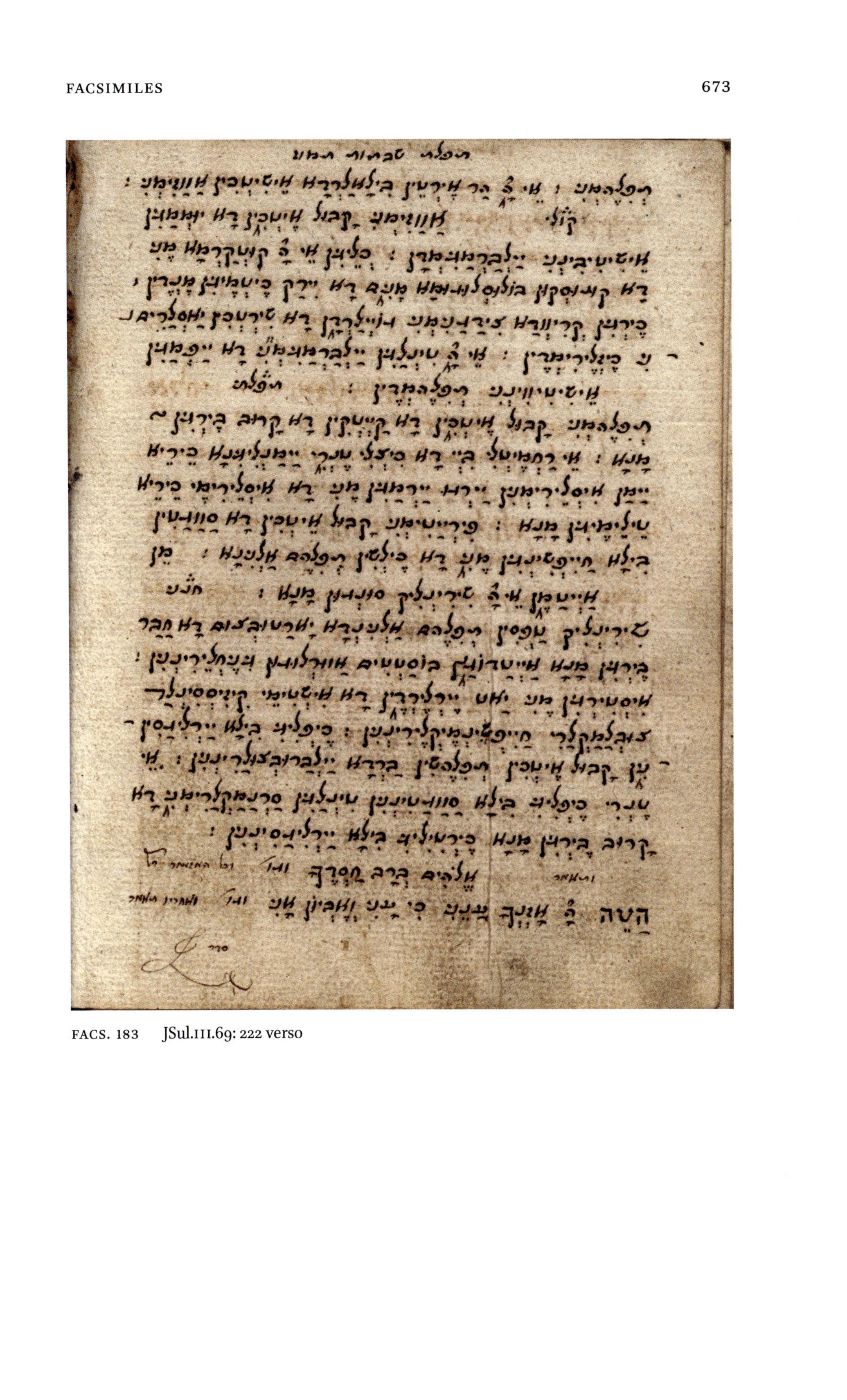

FACS. 183 JSul.III.69: 222 verso

FACS. 184 JSul.III.69: 230 recto

FACS. 185 JSul.III.69: 230 verso

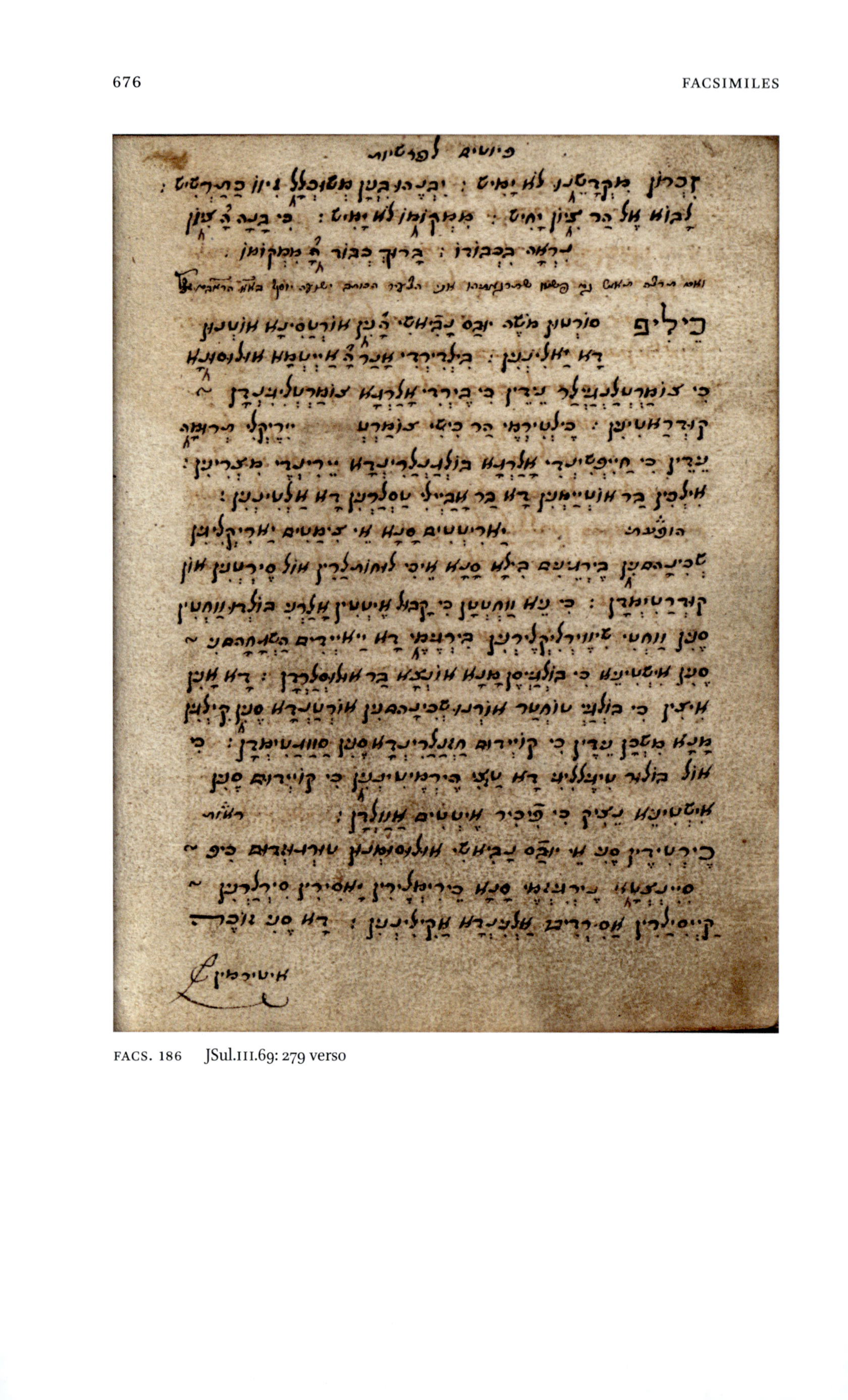

FACS. 186 JSul.III.69: 279 verso

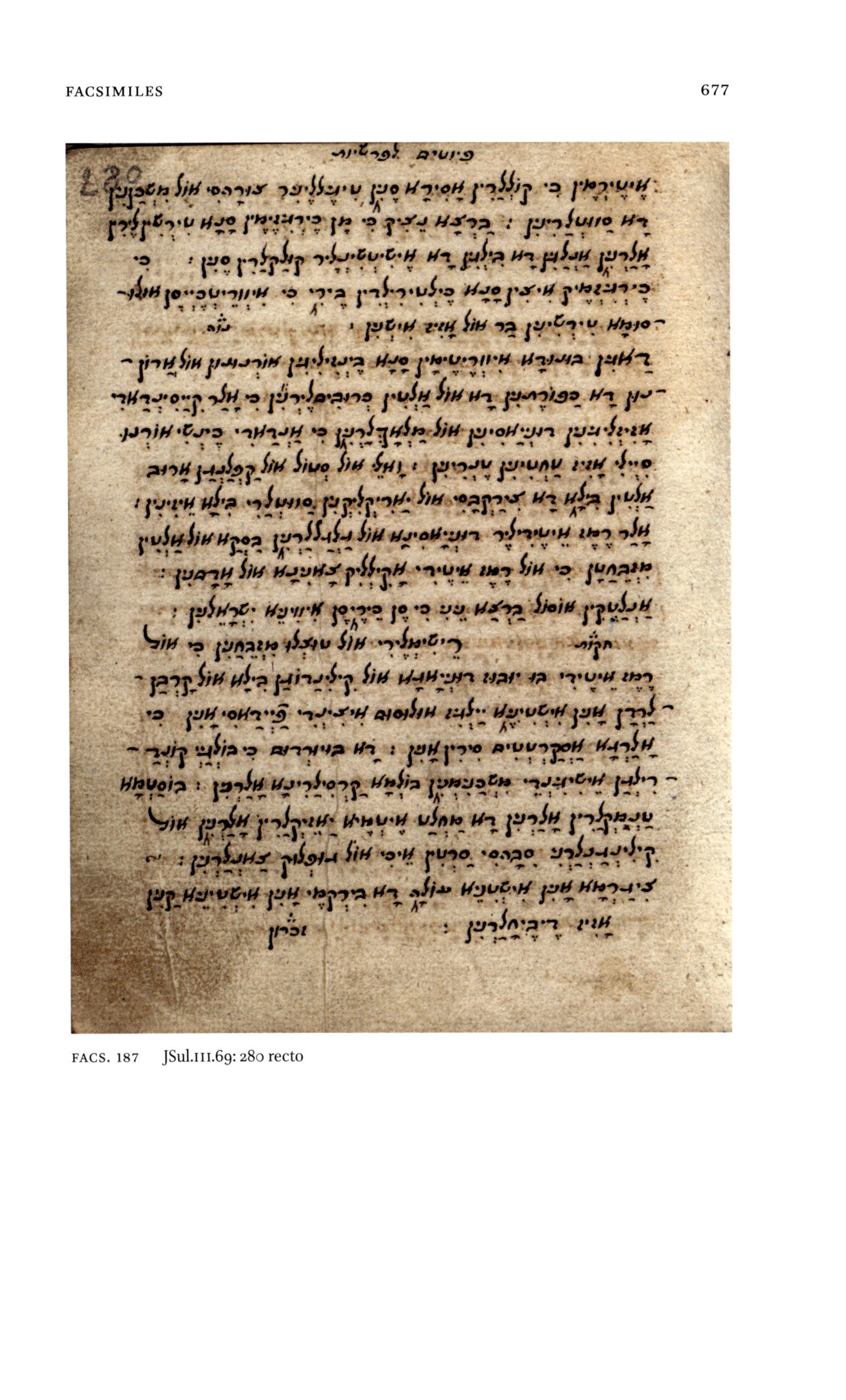

FACS. 187 JSul.III.69: 280 recto

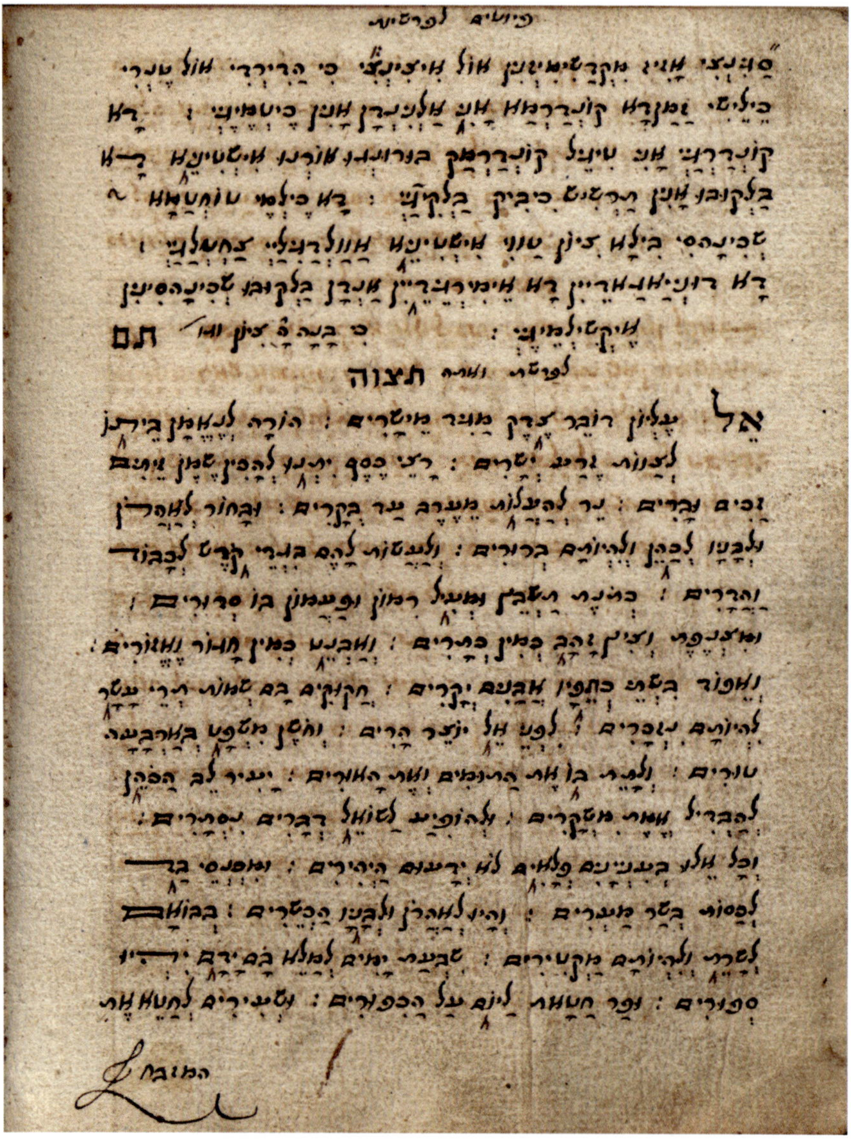

FACS. 188 JSul.III.69: 280 verso

FACS. 189 JSul.III.69: 283 verso

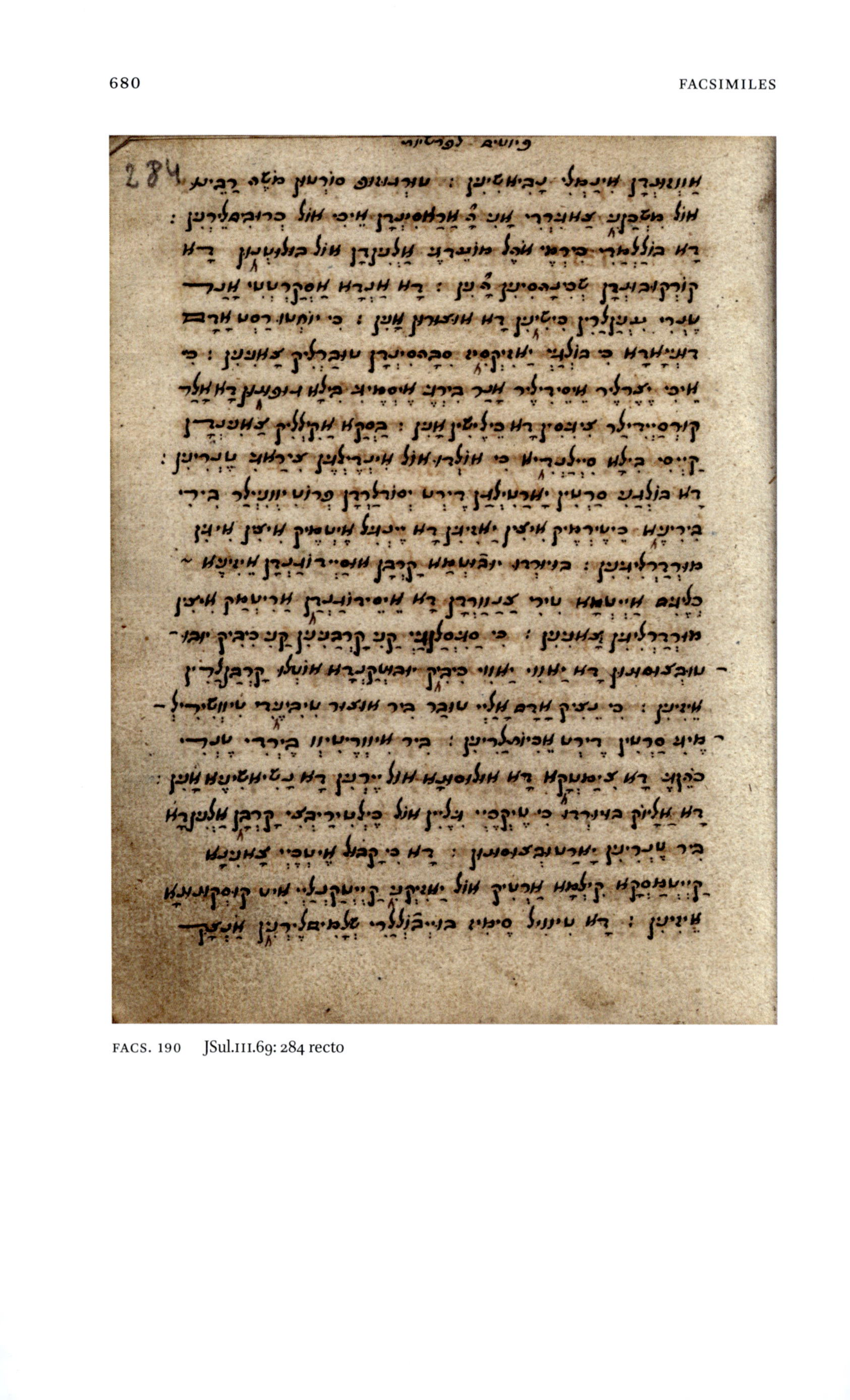

FACS. 190 JSul.III.69: 284 recto

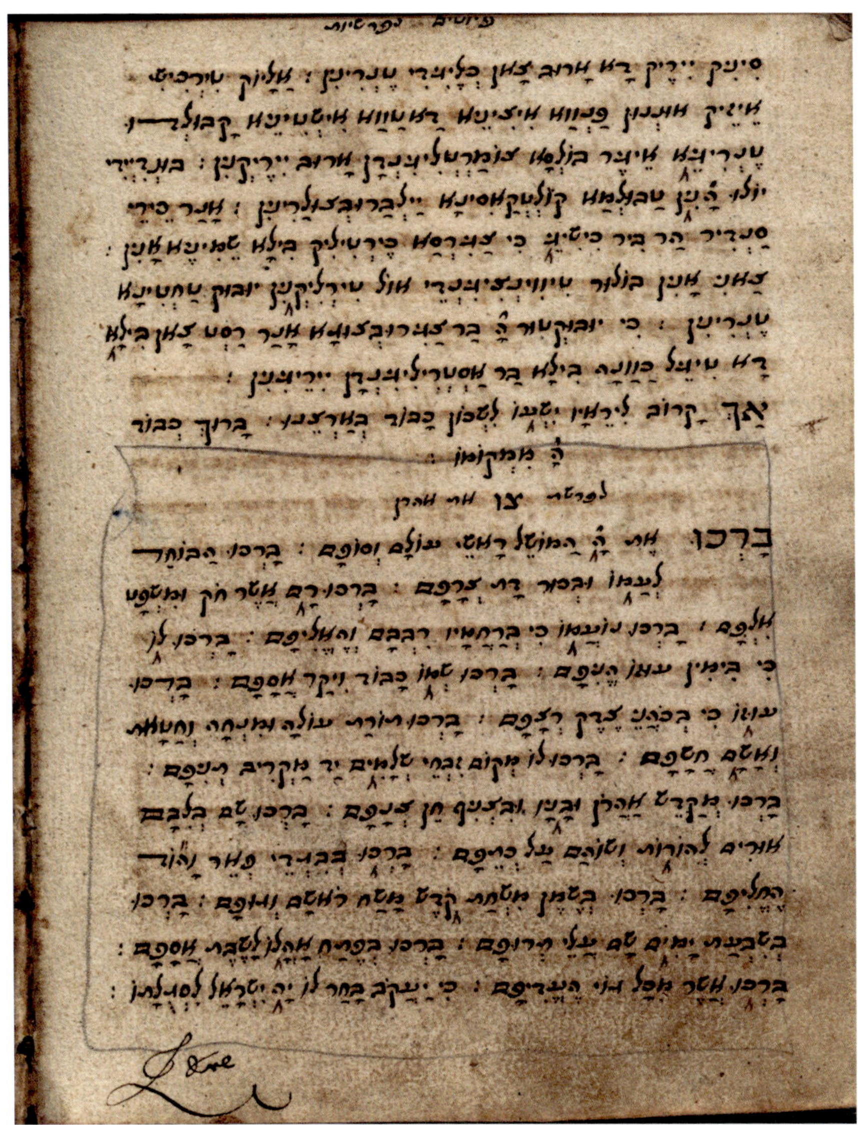

FACS. 191 JSul.III.69: 284 verso

FACS. 192 JSul.III.69: 286 verso

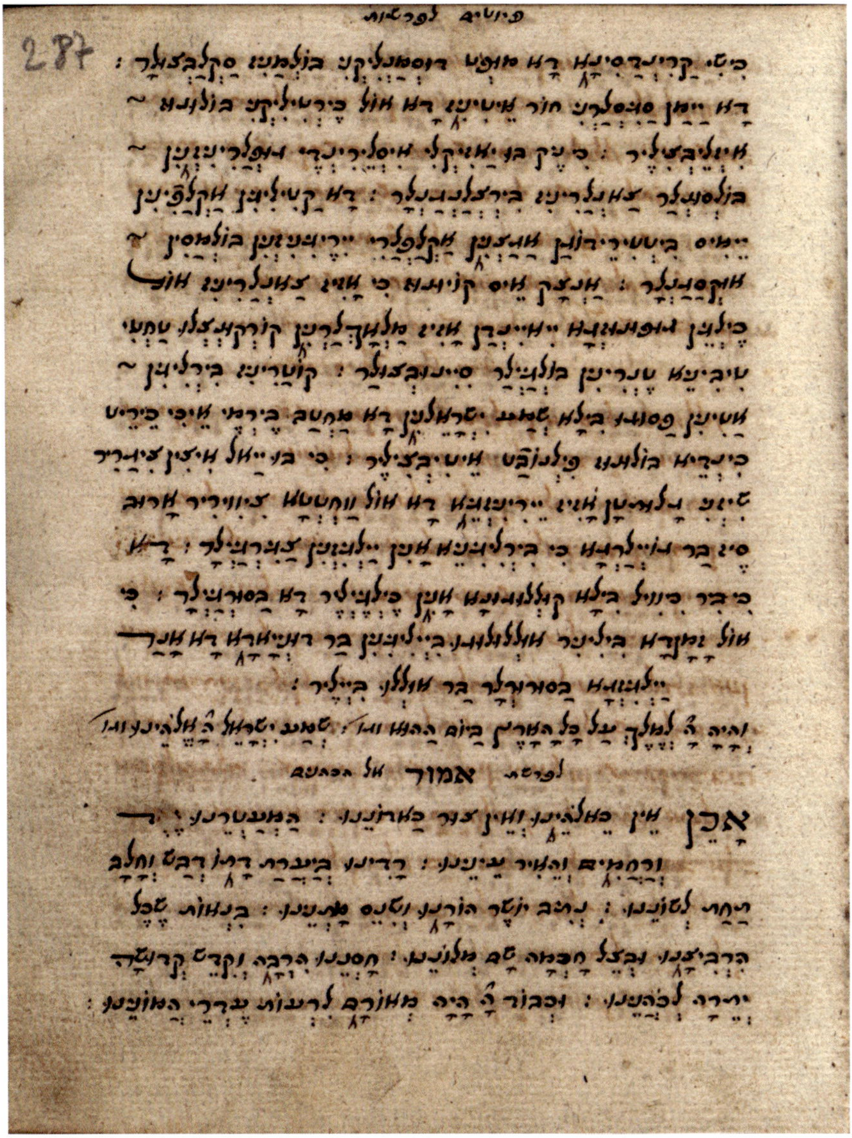
פיוטים לפרשות

והיה ה׳ למלך על כל הארץ ביום ההוא וגו׳ : שמע ישראל ה׳ אלהינו וגו׳

לפרשת אמור אל הכהנים

FACS. 193 JSul.III.69: 287 recto

FACS. 194 JSul.III.69: 288 recto

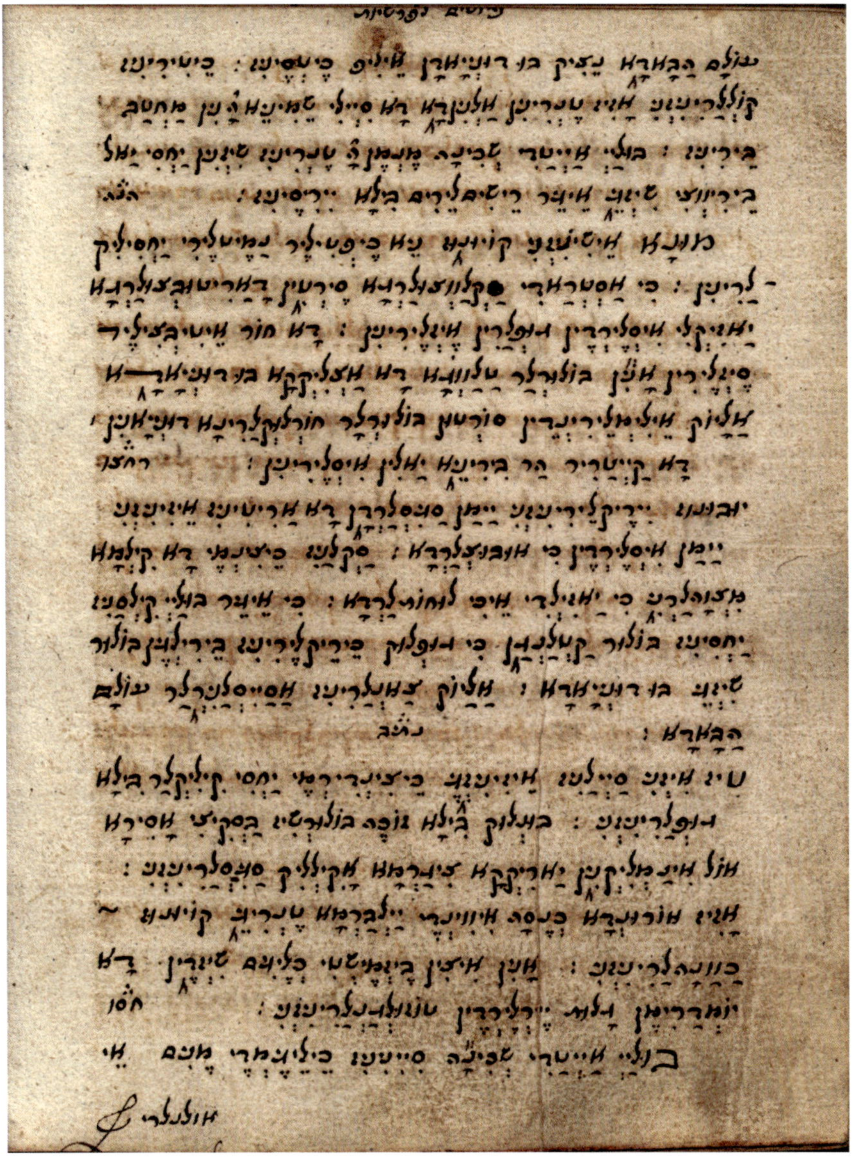

FACS. 195 JSul.III.69: 288 verso

פיוטים לפרשיות

289

תם

עתה אקום יאמר ה' עתה ארומם עתה אנשא : ויגבה ה' צבאות במשפט והאל הקדוש נקדש בצדקה : קדוש קדוש קדוש ה' צבאות מלוא כל הארץ כבודו :

לפרשת במדבר סיני

FACS. 196 JSul.III.69: 289 recto

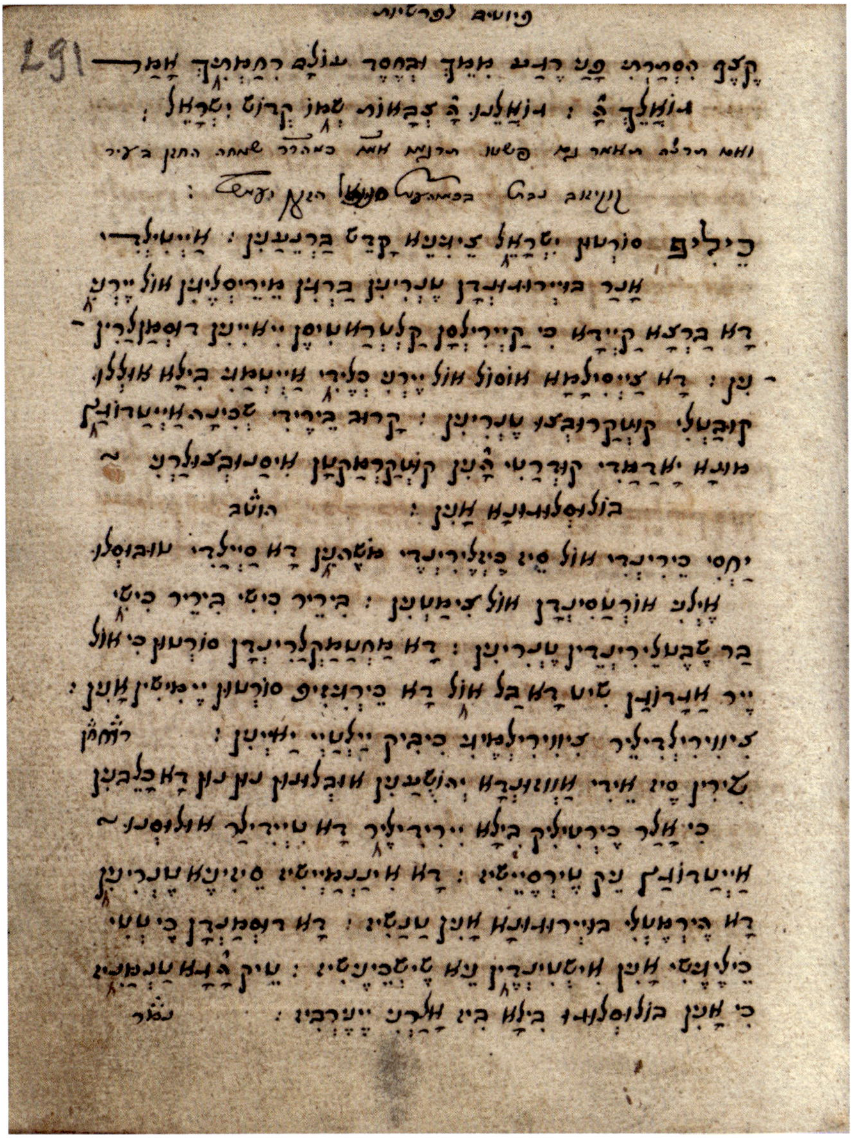

FACS. 197 JSul.III.69: 291 recto

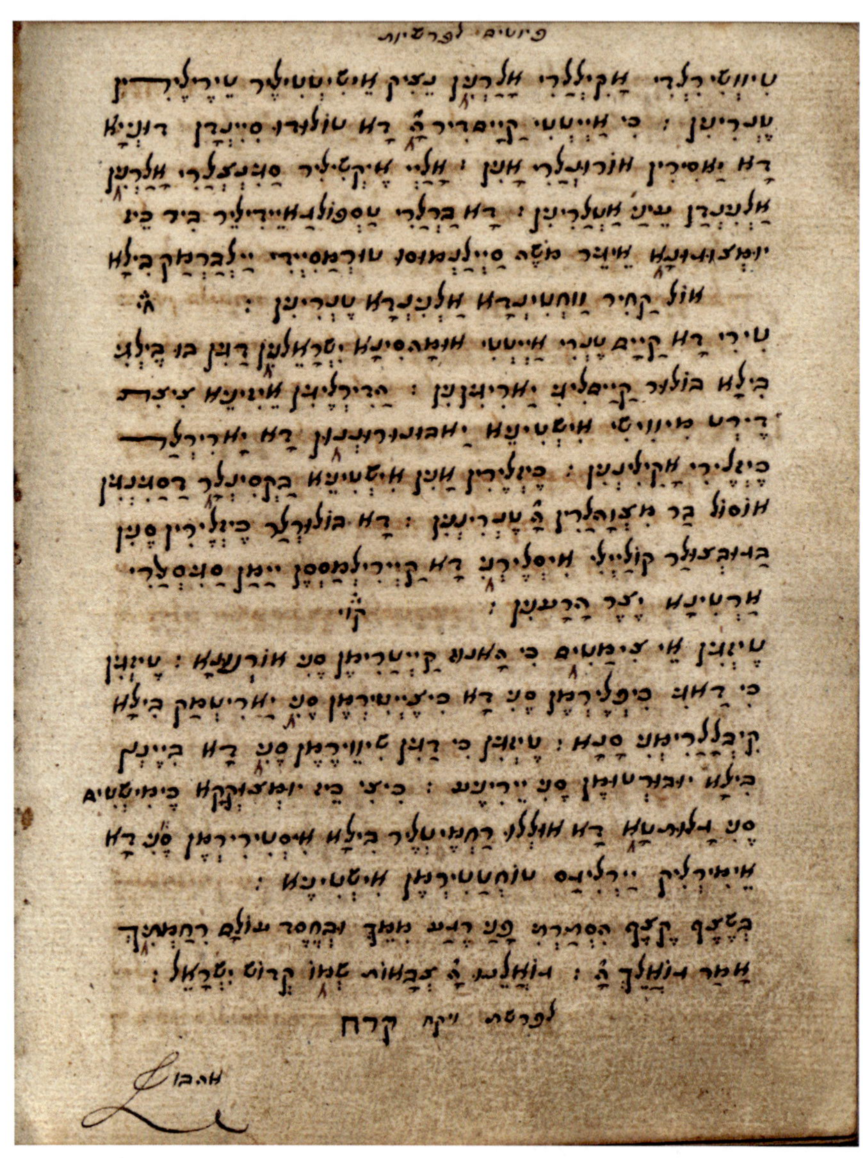

FACS. 198 JSul.III.69: 291 verso

פיוטים לפרשיות

292

אהבו את ה׳ כל חסידיו : המשלם גמול על יתר למורדיו :
רחבו מני ים חסדיו לעבדיו : נוקם עלילותיו
בעונו ירדיו : הנה בקום קרח בחמת מוקדיו : עם דתן ואבירם
ונפל בודר במועדיו : ויקנאו למשה לפרוץ גדרו ומוסדיו :
ולאהרן קדוש ה׳ ראש כהנים ופקידיו : עדי כי קרבו לפני ה׳
כי אין בלעדיו : במחתות קטרת בבית מועדיו : וירא כבוד
ה׳ לתלונות סורדיו : אל כל העדה ובאזניהם קול פחדיו : העלו
מסביב למשכני רשעי אל נודיו : פן תספו בפיר אל ואידיו :
תפתח ארץ ותבלע דתן ואבירם וילדיו : ואהבה להעטיר
רשעים מקריבי קטרת להבחין עמו ומעבדיו : ולהוקיר
כהונת אהרן ופרח המטה ויגמל שקדיו : לשבח תלמות
עם מרעיתו וצאן ידיו : יתעלה המתנשא בכסא יקרו
והודיו : יושב על כסא רם ונשא : שרפים עומדים ממעל
לו : בשתים יכסה פניו : וקרא זה אל זה ואמר : קדוש קדוש
קדוש ה׳ צבאות מלא כל הארץ כבודו :

לפרשת חקת התורה

אמון היתה תורה אצל נורא ואיום : משחקת לפניו בכל
יום : ואמרת שעשועי לבני אדם פדיום : ואהיה
שעשועים יום יום : הנה חקת פרה אדומה
באה דברה : לטהר טמאי נפש בשרפת עם עורה : נתונה
לסגן כהנים עד גמרה : אזרחה ויספרה הכינה ואם חקרה :
רם סודה כי מטמאה ומטהרת : מעין כל שכל ידיעתה

FACS. 199 JSul.III.69: 292 recto

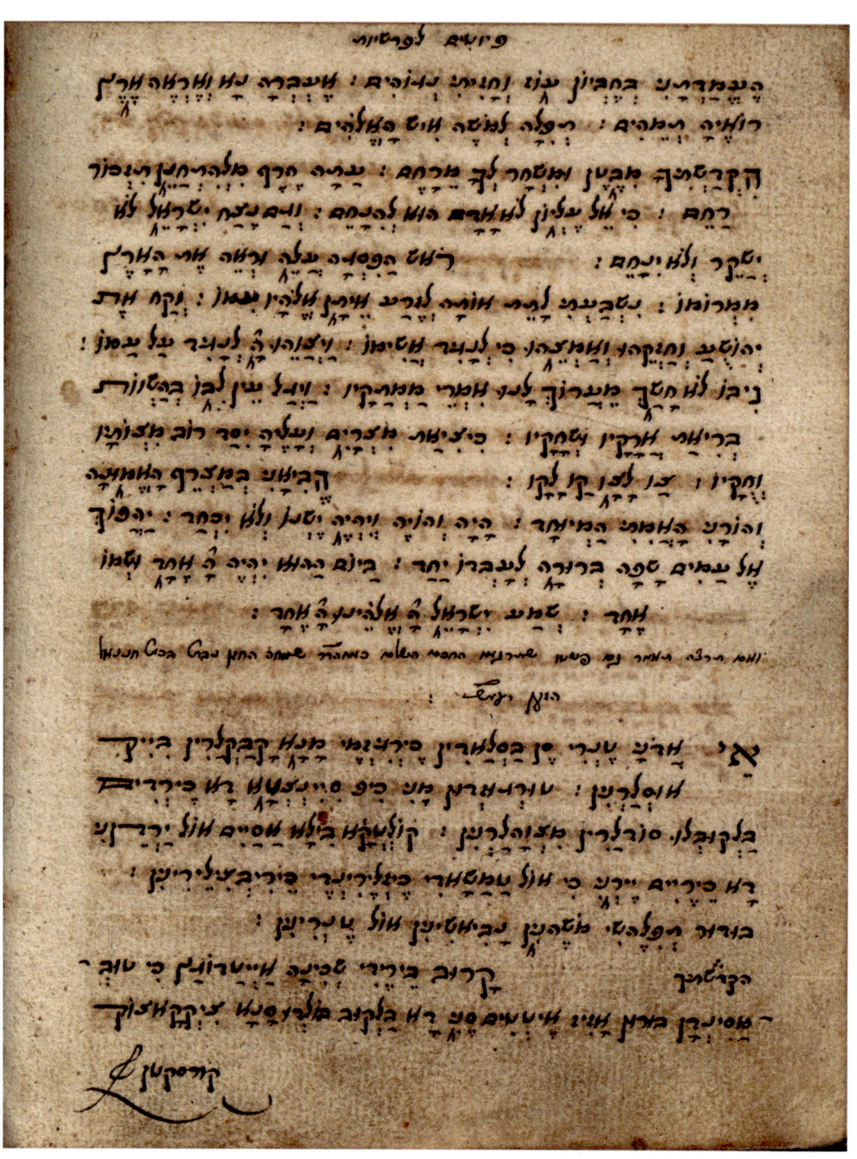

FACS. 200 JSul.III.69: 294 verso

FACS. 201 JSul.III.69: 295 recto

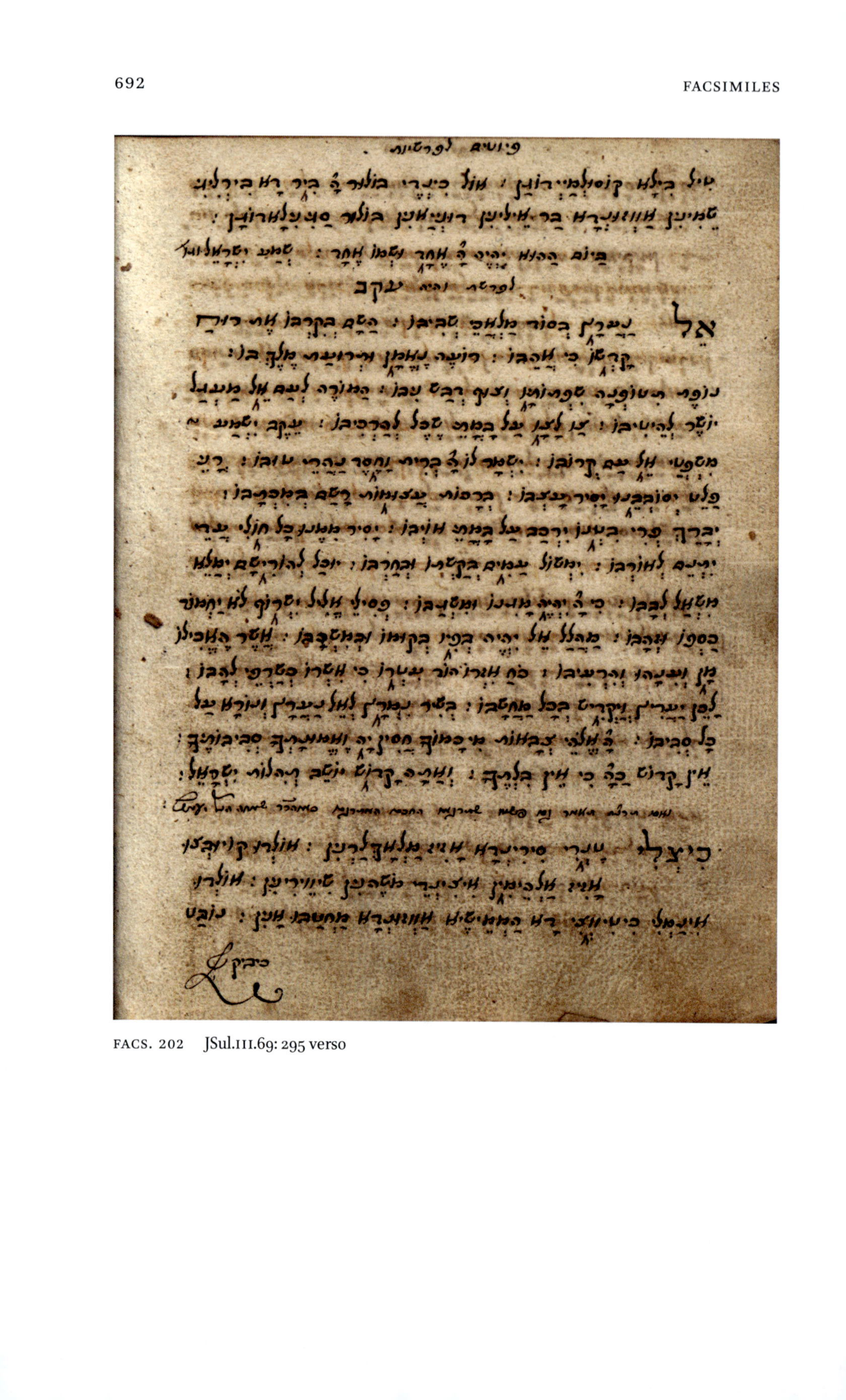

FACS. 202 JSul.III.69: 295 verso

FACS. 203 JSul.III.69: 296 recto

FACS. 204 JSul.III.69: 296 verso

FACS. 205 JSul.III.69: 297 recto

FACS. 206 JSul.III.69: 297 verso

FACS. 207 JSul.III.69: 298 recto

FACS. 208 JSul.III.69: 298 verso

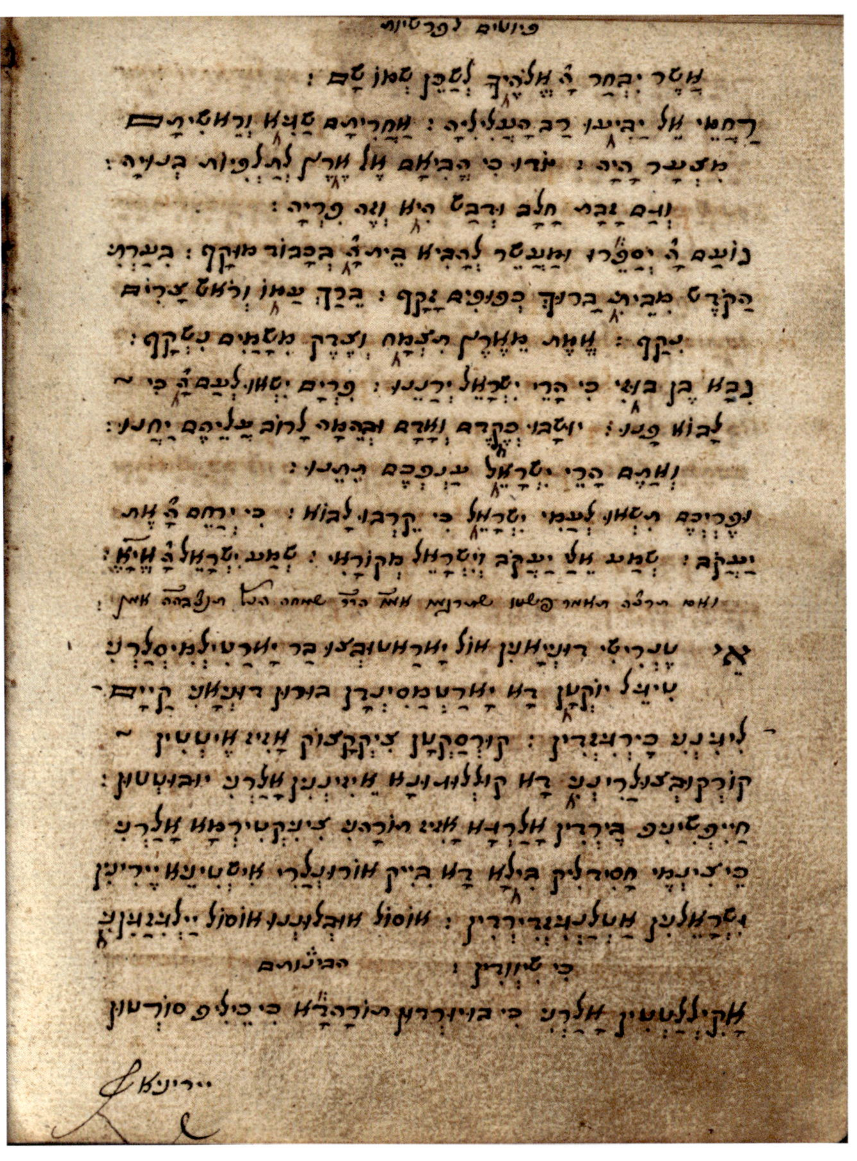

FACS. 209 JSul.III.69: 299 verso

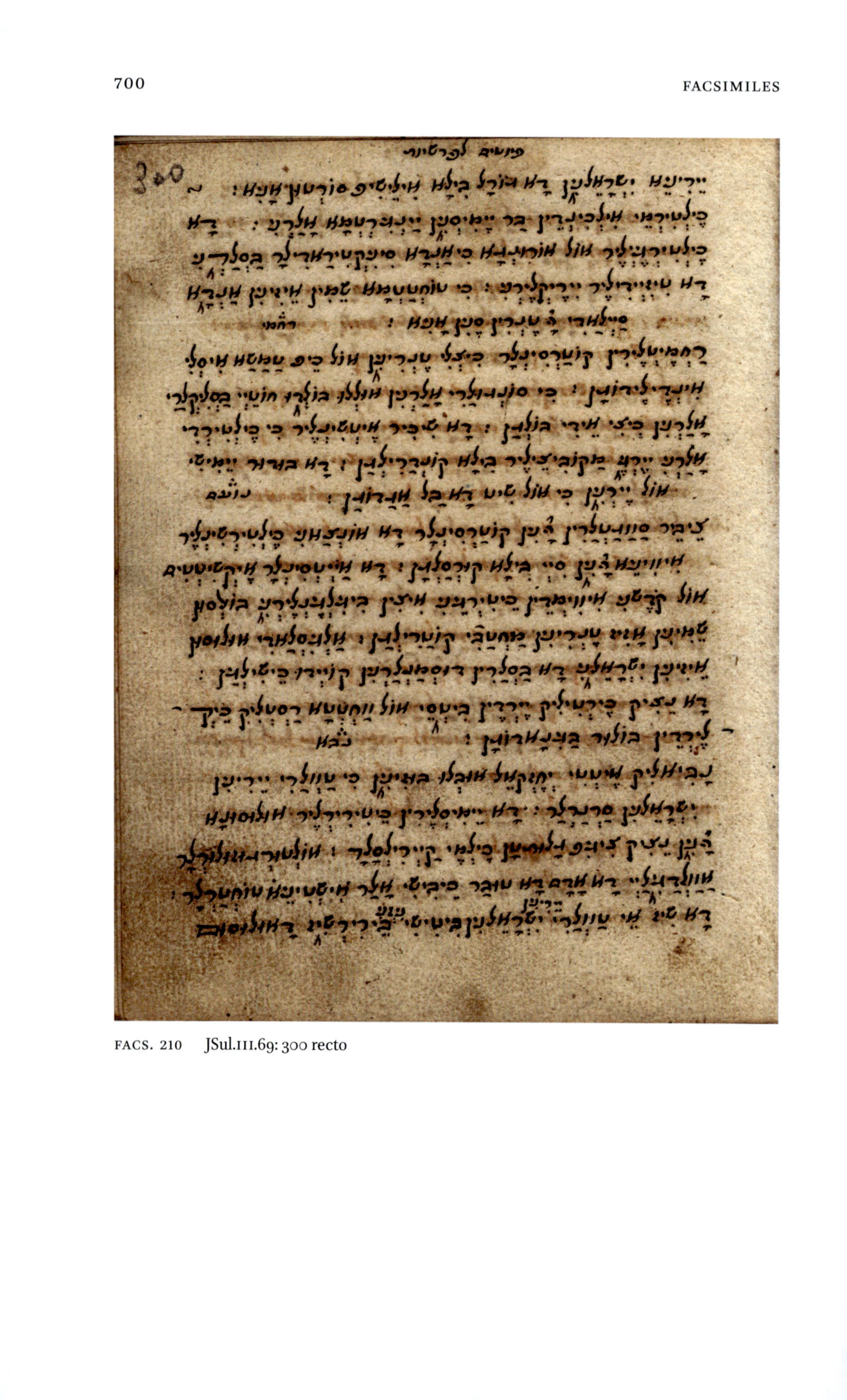

FACS. 210 JSul.III.69: 300 recto

פיוטים לפרשיות

בר נמיטען טוירלר :

ופריכם תשאו. לעמי ישראל כי קרבו לבוא : כי ירחם ה' את
יעקב ובחר עוד בישראל והניחם על אדמתם ונלוה הגר
עליהם ונספחו על בית יעקב : שמעו אלי יעקב וישראל
מקוראי : שמע ישראל ה' אלהינו ה' אחד :

לפרשת אתם נצבים

אתה אל מתנשא ויושב בכסא ממלכה : המציב לעמך
מערכה לקראת מערכה : ראשיכם זקניכם
שבטיכם ערה מימי בראשית נמשכה : נצבו כלם טף ונשיהם
חוטב עצים ושואב מימי ברכה : לעבור בברית שם להם
ערוכה : למען הקים אותם לו לעם נחלה ברוכה : לאיתנו ולדורות
הבאות אמריהם בריתו נמשכה : ואשר ישנו פה נבוכה :
והתברך בלבבו לאמר שלום יהיה לי בלי פרכה : כי בשרירות
לבי אתהלכה : למען ספות הרוה עם הצמאה : יעשן אף ה'
וחמתו בו נתכה : והבדילו ה' לרעה מאין ארוכה : כי פנה
מנורת אורה אל חשכה : אחלי אנוש קשה תעורת דרכו דרוכה :
וחשקתו לאל על תמוכה : וימינו ביתן אל סמוכה : ותמיד
לבו בעבודתו כמים ישפכה : כי מי דומה לו ולו המלוכה :
ומלאכתו באמת היא המלאכה : מעלה ומוריד ובידו המסכה
הנסוכה : ומי כמוהו מרומם על כל תהלה וברכה : כי מי אל
מבלעדי ה' : כי מי אלוה מבלעדיך : אין קדוש כה' כי אין
בלתך ואין צור כאלהינו : ואתה קדוש יושב תהלות ישראל :

סימן

FACS. 211 JSul.III.69: 300 verso

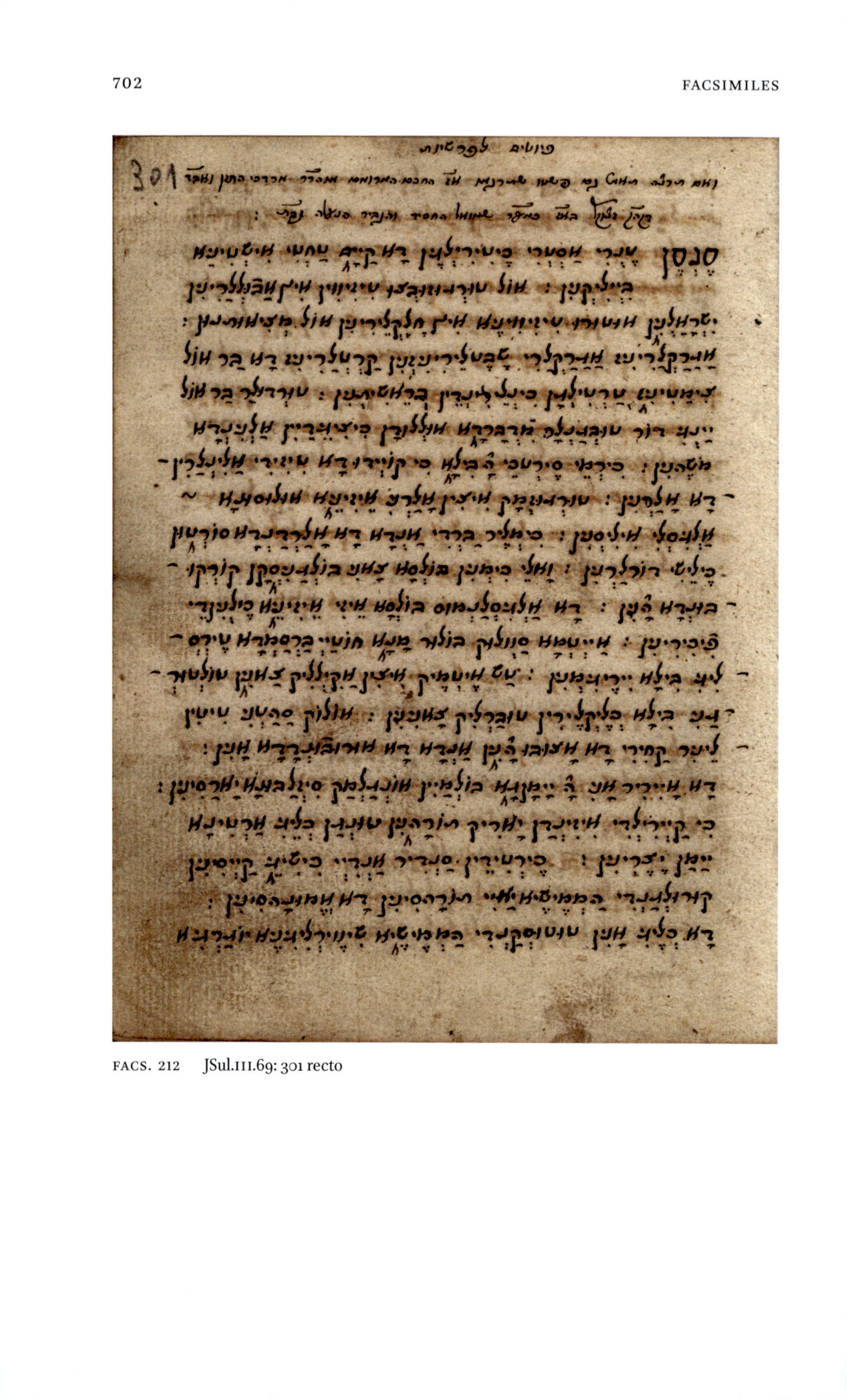

FACS. 212 JSul.III.69: 301 recto

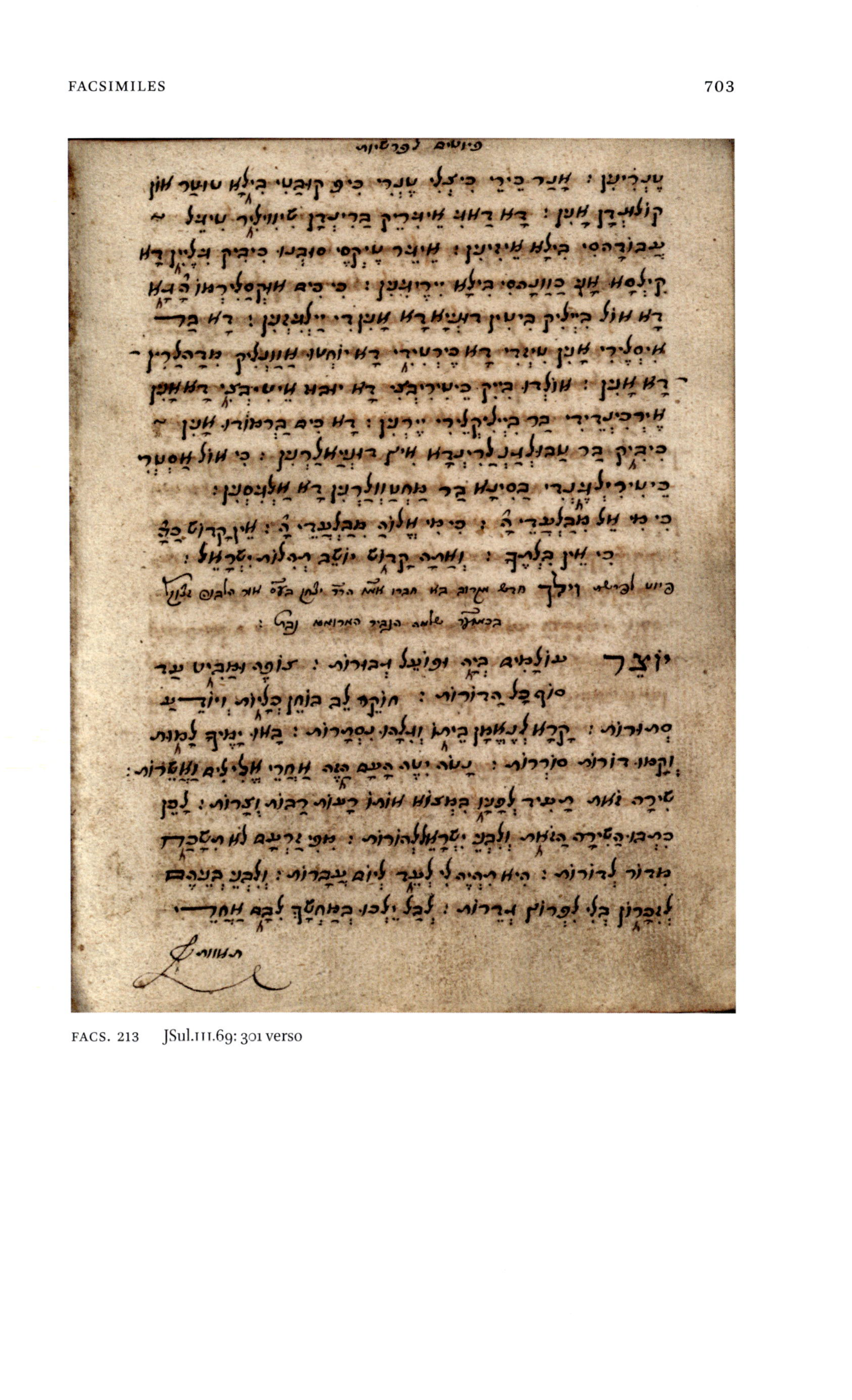

FACS. 213 JSul.III.69: 301 verso

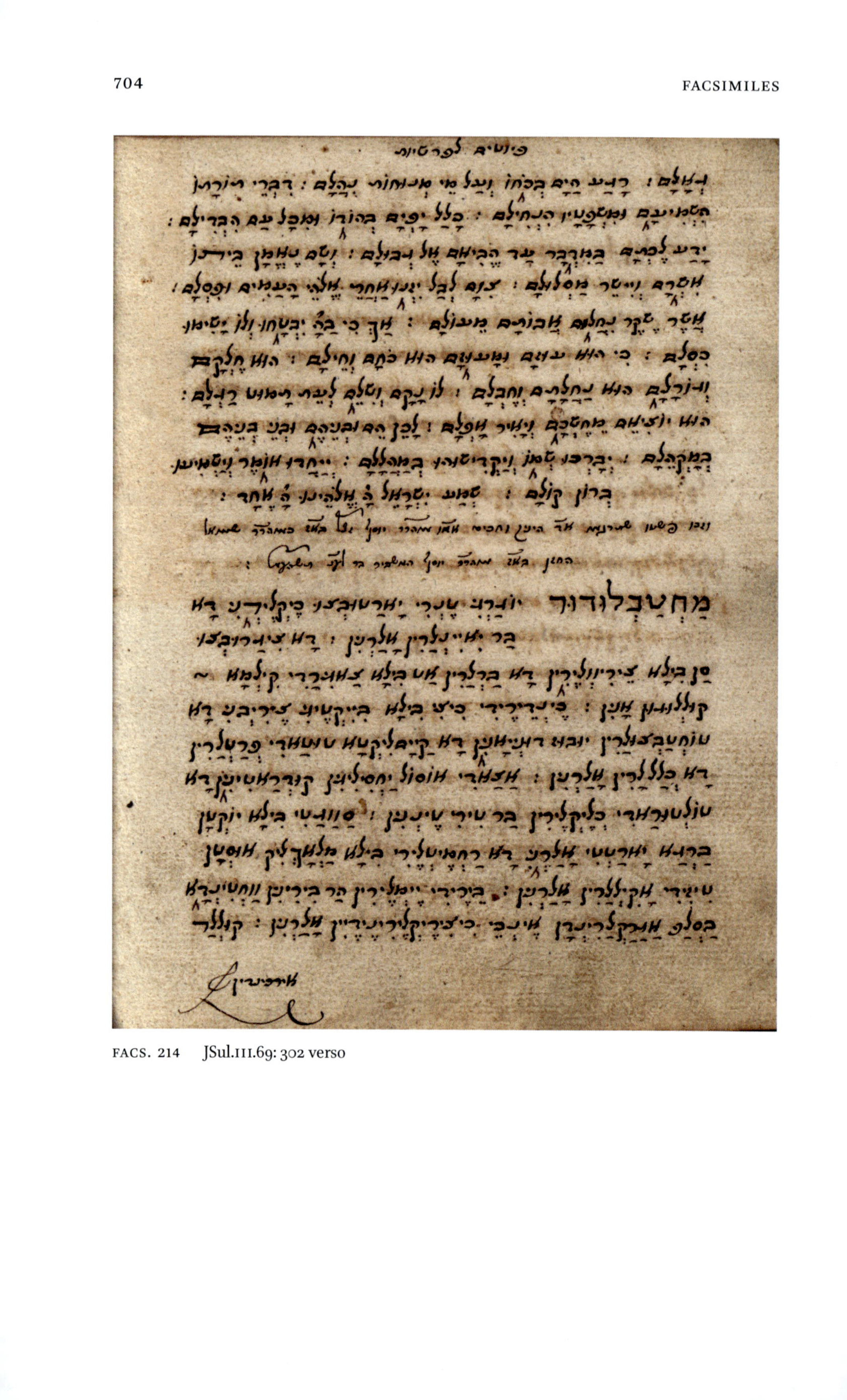

FACS. 214 JSul.III.69: 302 verso

FACS. 215 JSul.III.69: 303 recto

פיוטים לפרשיות

קהללרינין : שכיר בירנילר אגיז שמינע דאוזנלינין איטקיילר
מחטבלרי בילא אירינלרינין : דא כי איטוטירנילר סרנוו
אוזלרין אגיז הירמיטלי איוונידי דא בירלינין דא קימלינין
קושרניילר בררי פסוגו בילא שמע ישראלנין :

שמע ישראל ה׳ אלהינו ה׳ אחד :

לפרשת האזינו

מי כמוך אדיר ונורא אלהי עולם : מי כמוך המגיד
מראשית אחרית ומגלה מקדם כל נעלם : מי כמוך
ראש דברך אמת בפי כל היצור כלם : מי כמוך נאמנו שדיך
העדת לבני חלם והנה סלם : מי כמוך הסדרו עדת מקדם
המשילם : מי כמוך ערכת המעטיך בפרטם ובכללם : מי
כמוך יער עדים נאמנם בלי נשמע קולם : מי כמוך וארץ
תרנה יבלה והשמים יחנו עלם : מי כמוך סבבו אורותיך
על פני תבל לפעלם : מי כמוך פורה עמך ומביא עברים
באלם : מי כמוך בארץ מדבר פנה מסלולם : מי כמוך
ובתוהו ילל ישימון היה שמשם וצלם : מי כמוך ירבו מדי
יעבון במעברם ובמעגלם : מי כמוך מפצ בארבע פאות
חילם : מי כמוך יראה עניים לעת המשו רגלם : מי כמוך
ירננו גוים עמו וישמחו לעולם : מי כמוך אומר ואומר
בכללם : מי כמוך חותמיך נכר ואמרו העולם : מי כמוך
ואמרו השיר הלולם : מי כמוך אשר מיד צר גאלם : ואמרו
גואלנו ה׳ אשר גאלם מיד צר : גואלנו ה׳ צבאות שמו קק׳ :

FACS. 216 JSul.III.69: 303 verso

FACS. 217 JSul.III.69: 304 recto

פיוטים לפרשיות

לפרשת וזאת הברכה

FACS. 218 JSul.III.69: 304 verso

FACS. 219 JSul.III.72: 7 verso–8 recto

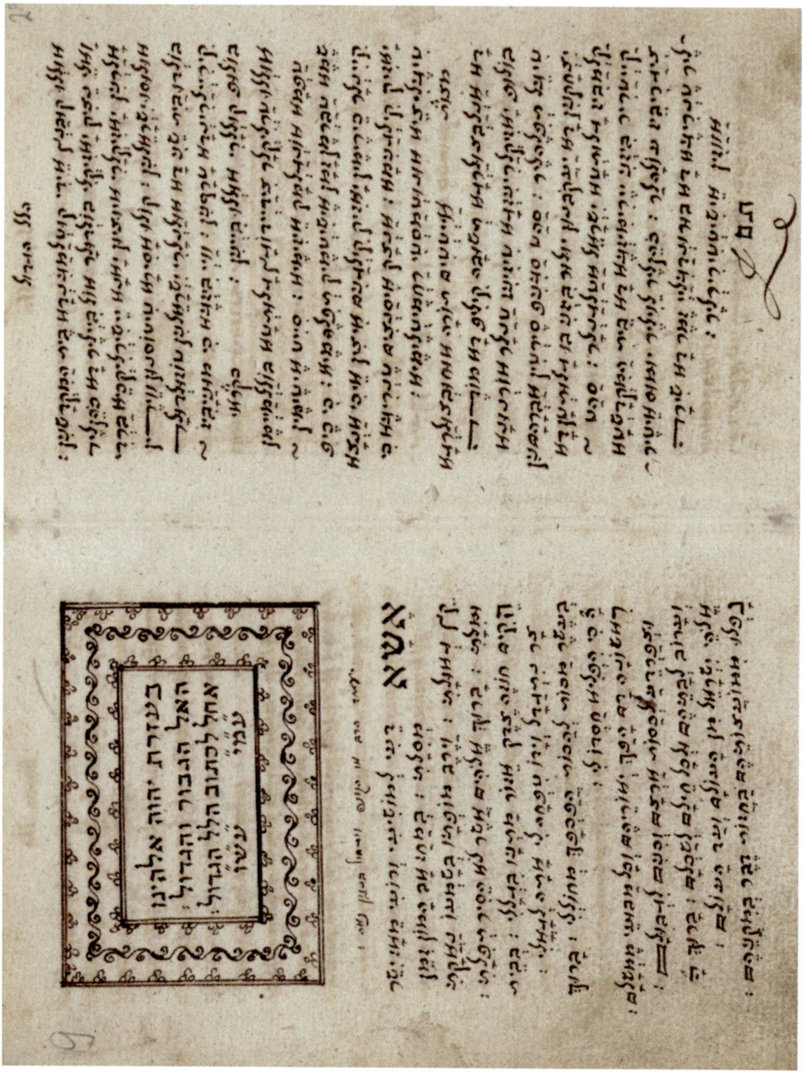

FACS. 220 JSul.III.72: 8 verso–9 recto

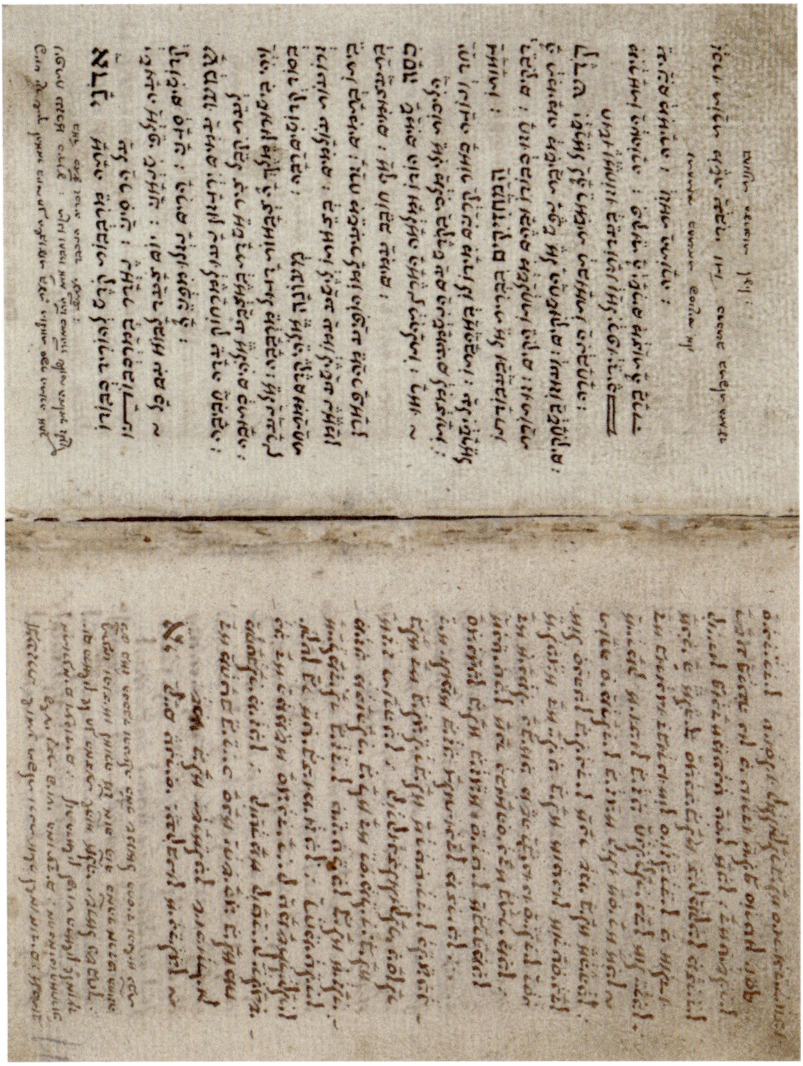

FACS. 221 JSul.III.72: 140 verso–141 recto

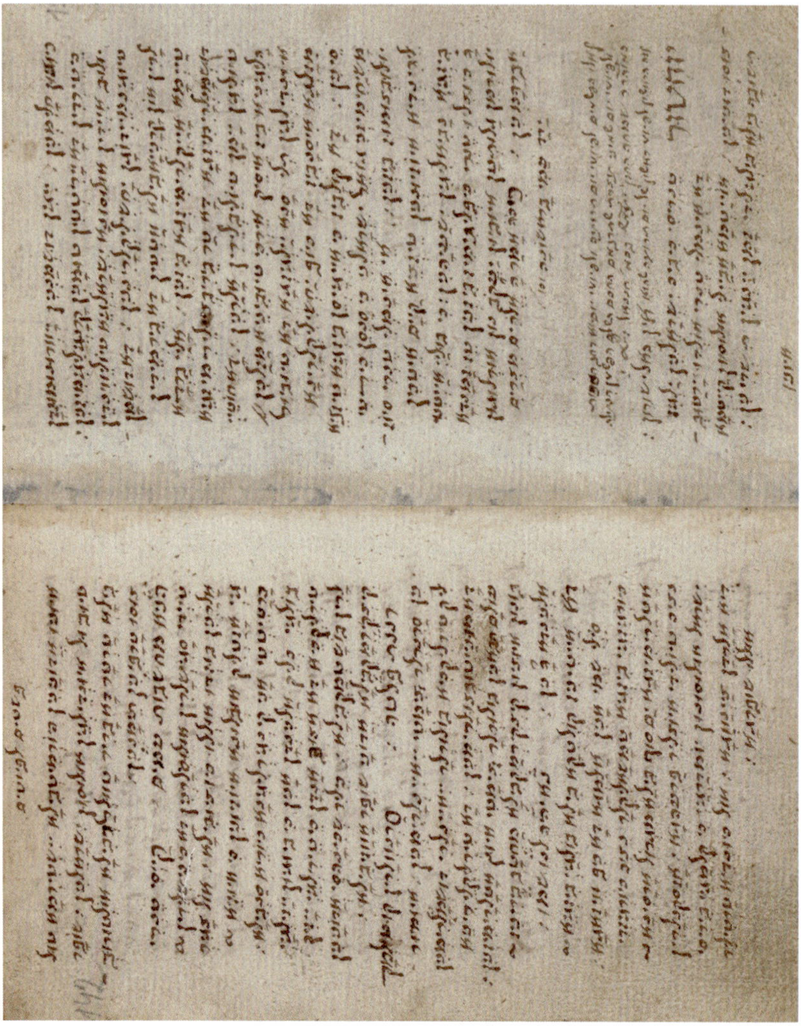

FACS. 222 JSul.III.72: 141 verso–142 recto

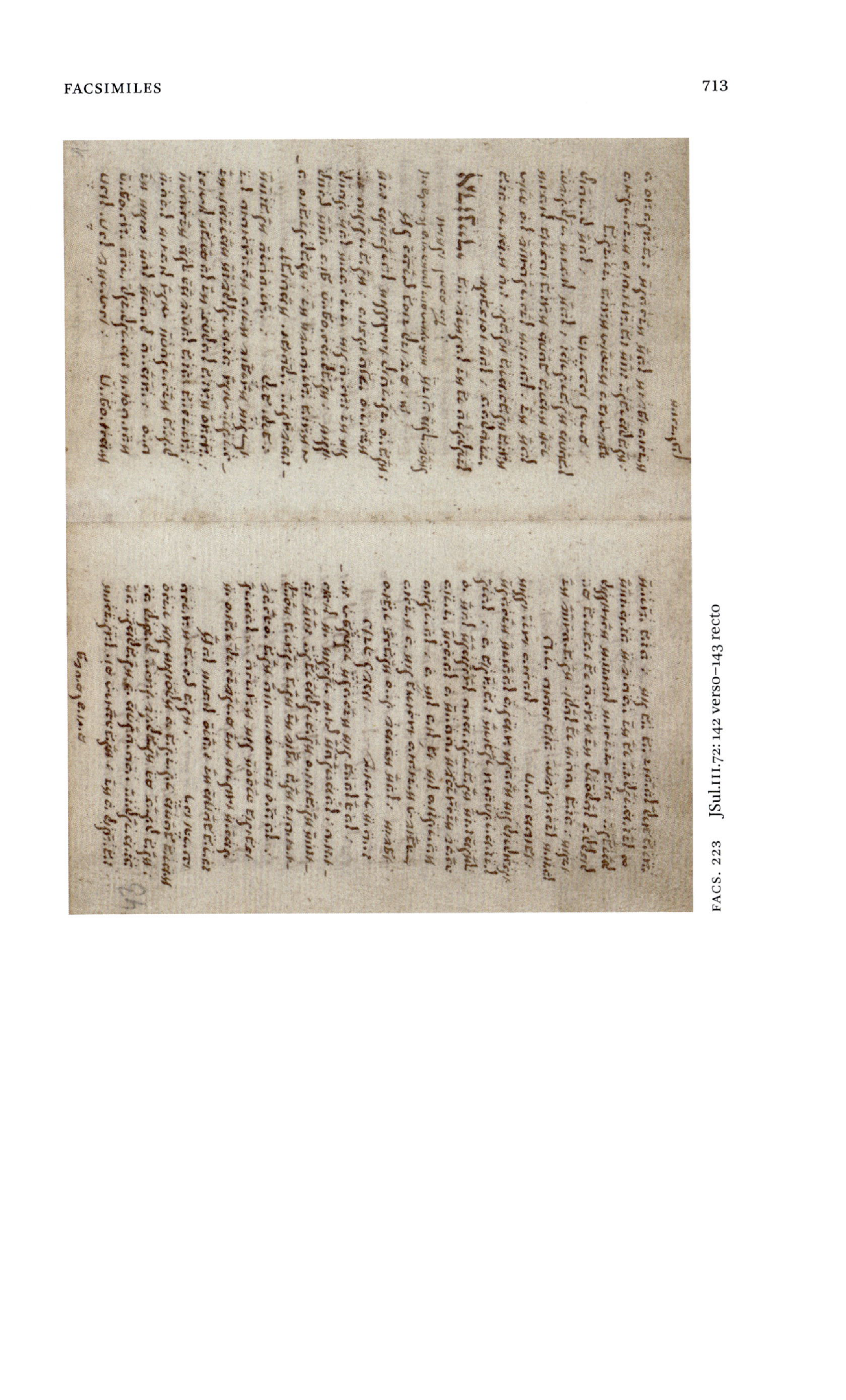

FACS. 223 JSul.III.72: 142 verso–143 recto

FACS. 224 JSul.III.72: 143 verso–144 recto

FACS. 225 JSul.III.72: 144 verso–145 recto

FACS. 226 JSul.III.72: 145 verso–146 recto

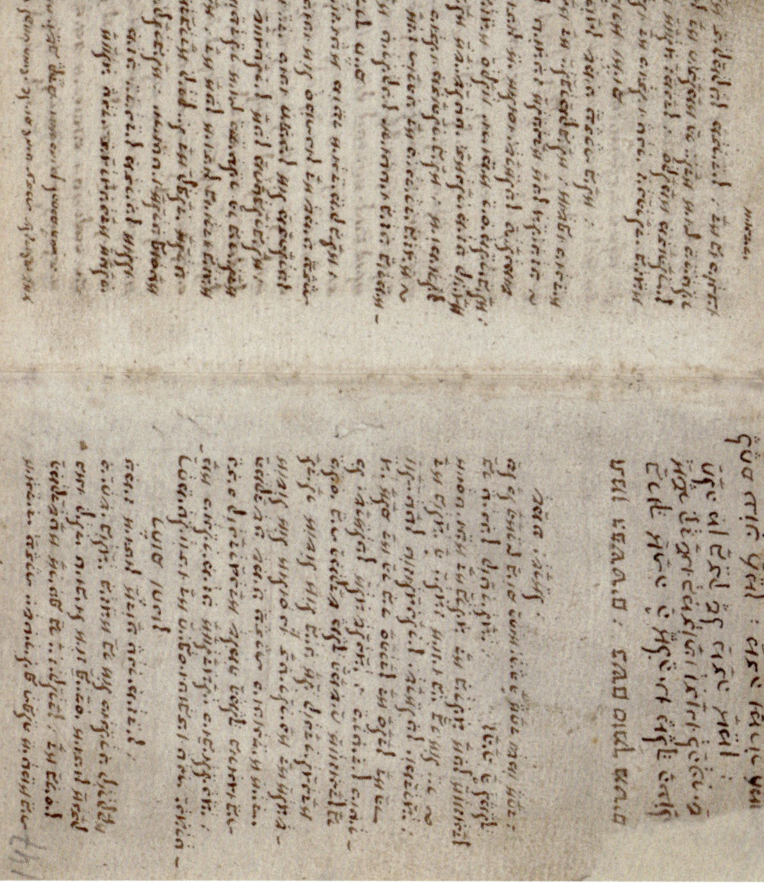

FACS. 227 JSul.III.72: 146 verso–147 recto

FACS. 228 JSul.III.72: 226 verso–227 recto

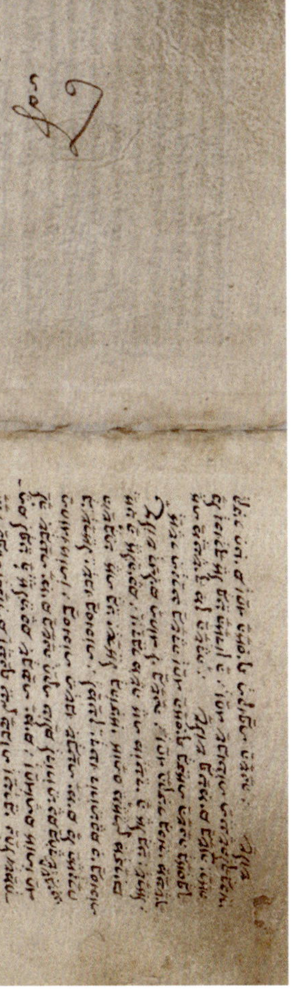

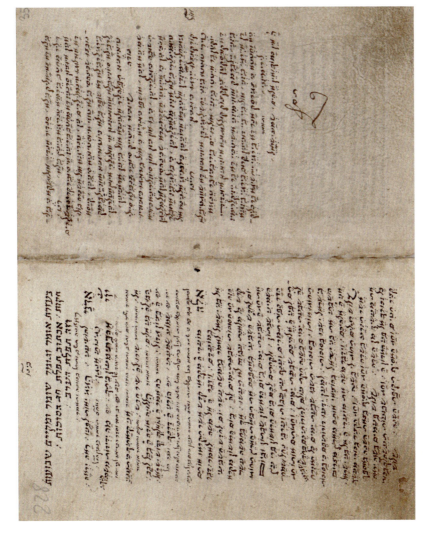

FACS. 229 JSul.III.72: 227 verso–228 recto

FACS. 230 JSul.III.73: 68 recto

תפלת בקר של פסח

[illegible]

[illegible]

כי כה אמר ה' אלהים מצרים ירד עמי בראשונה לגור שם ואשור באפס עשקו : ועתה מה לי פה נאם ה' כי לוקח עמי חנם מושלו יהילילו נאם ה' ותמיד כל היום שמי מנואץ : לכן ידע עמי שמי לכן ביום ההוא כי אני הוא המדבר הנני : לכן כה אמר ה' אל בית יעקב אשר פדה את אברהם לא עתה יבוש יעקב ולא עתה פניו יחורו : כי בראותו ילדיו מעשה ידי בקרבו יקדישו שמי והקדישו את קדוש יעקב ואת אלהי ישראל יעריצו : את ה' צבאות אותו תקדישו והוא מוראכם והוא מעריצכם : אל נערץ בסוד קדושים רבה ונורא על כל סביביו : ה' אלהי צבאות מי כמוך חסין יה ואמונתך סביבותיך : אין קדוש כה' כי אין בלתך ואין צור כאלהינו :

אין כאל ישורון רוכב שמים בעזרך ובגאותו שחקים : מעונה אלהי קדם ומתחת זרועות עולם ויגרש מפניך אויב ויאמר השמד : וישכון ישראל בטח בדד עין יעקב אל ארץ דגן ותירוש אף שמיו יערפו טל : אשריך ישראל מי כמוך עם נושע בה' מגן עזרך ואשר חרב גאותך ויכחשו אויביך לך ואתה על במותימו תדרוך : כי מי אל מבלעדי ה' ומי צור מבלעדי אלהינו : כי מי אלוה מבלעדי ה' ומי צור זולתי אלהינו : כי מי בשחק יערוך לה' ידמה לה' בבני אלים : ואל מי תדמיון אל ומה דמות תערכו לו : למי תדמיוני ותשוו ותמשלוני ונדמה : ואל מי תדמיוני ואשוה יאמר קדוש : ואתה קדוש יושב תהלות ישראל :

האל תמים דרכו אמרת ה' צרופה מגן הוא לכל החוסים בו :

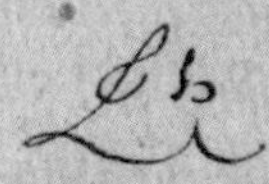

FACS. 231 JSul.III.73: 68 verso

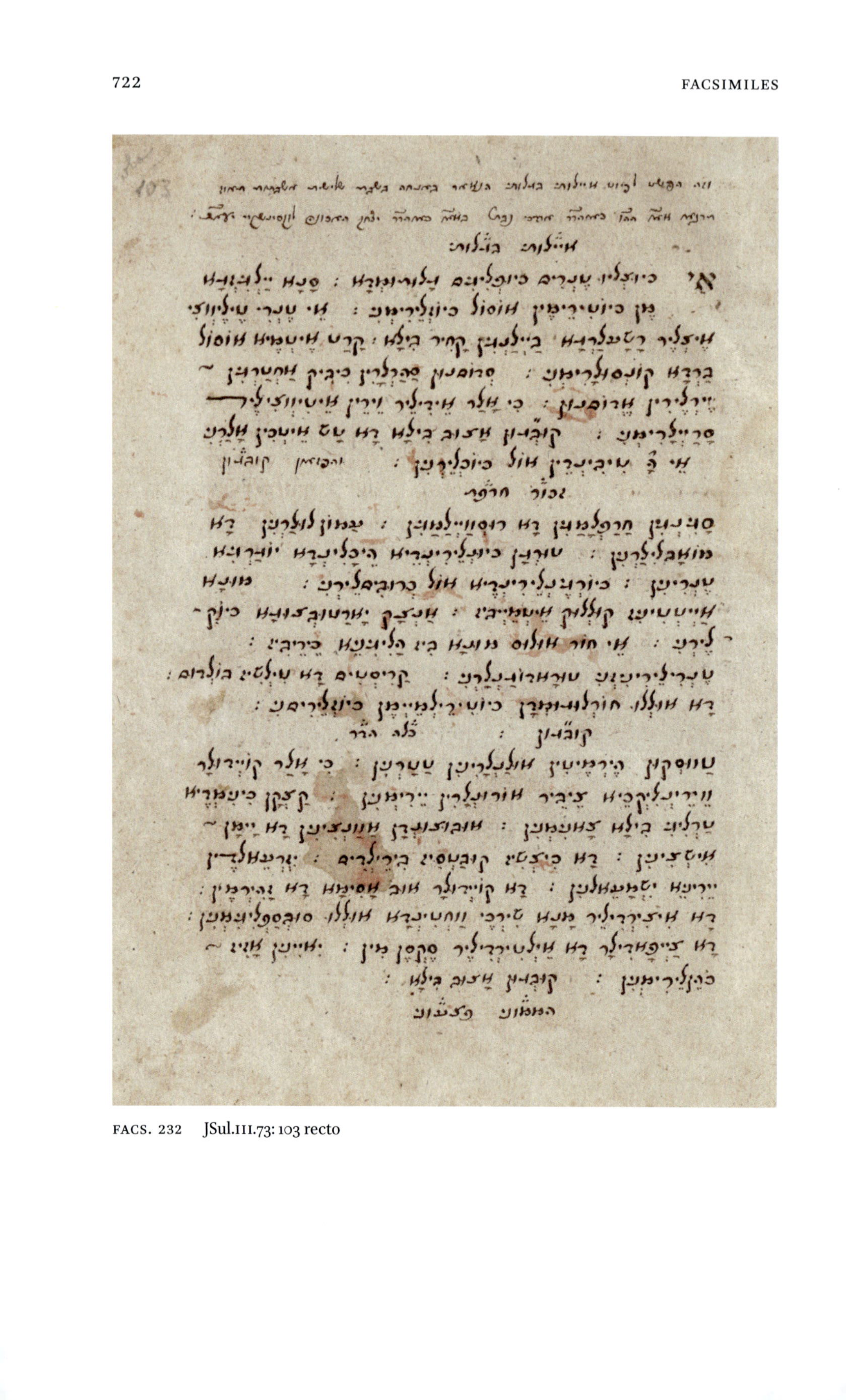

FACS. 232 JSul.III.73: 103 recto

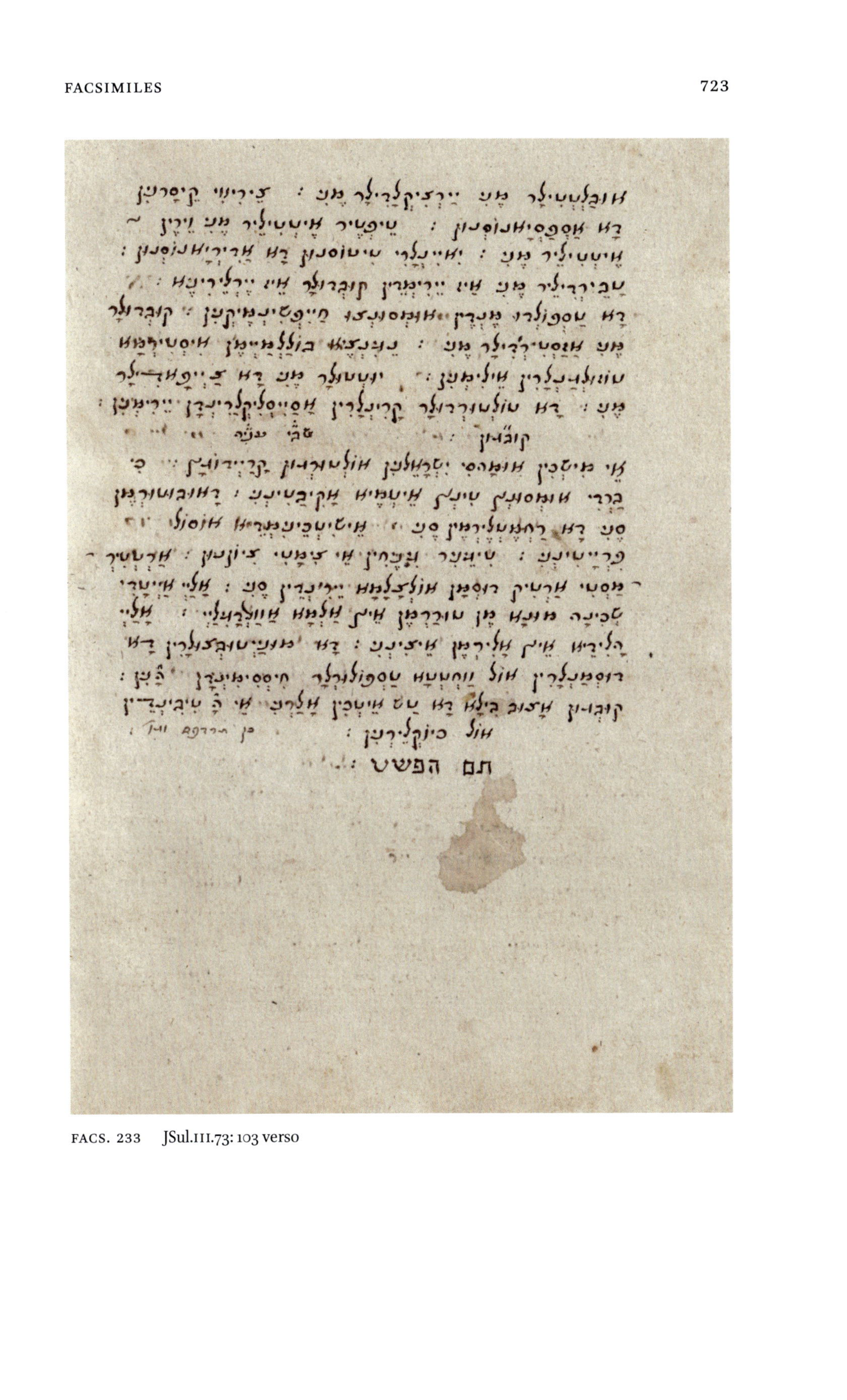

תם הפשט :

FACS. 233 JSul.III.73: 103 verso

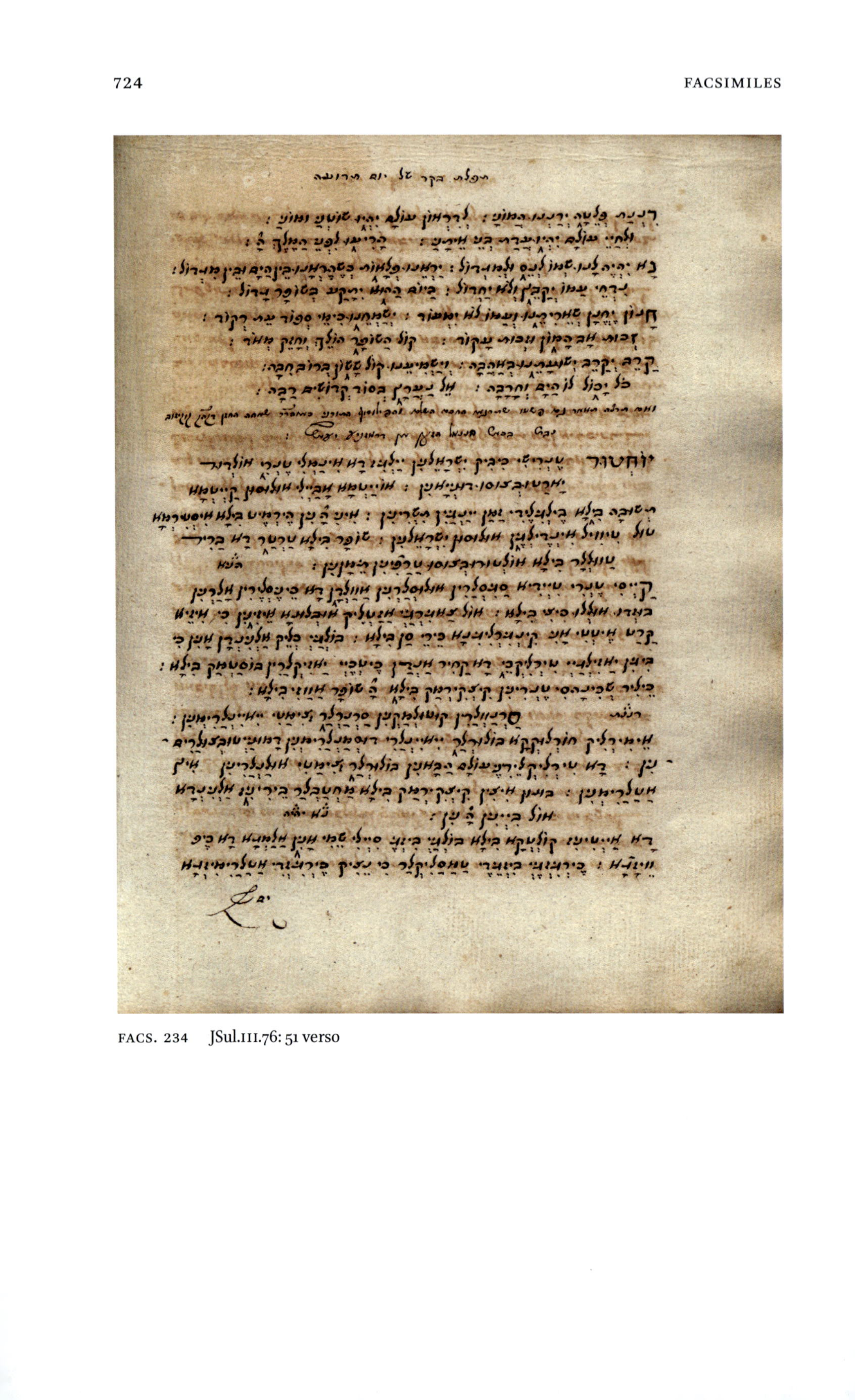

FACS. 234 JSul.III.76: 51 verso

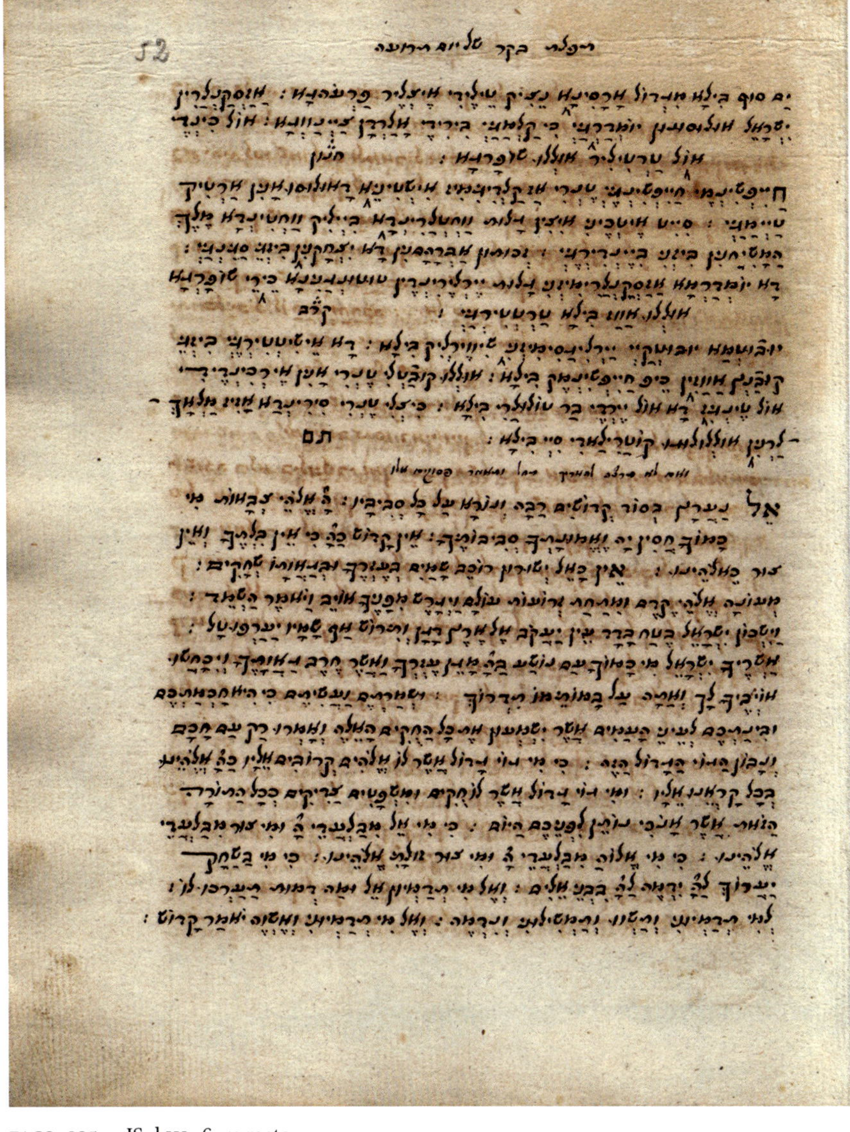

FACS. 235 JSul.III.76: 52 recto

תפלת בקר של יום תרועה

ואתה קדוש יושב תהלות ישראל :

האל התמים דרכו אמרת ה' צרופה מגן הוא לכל החוסים בו : כל אמרת
אלוה צרופה מגן הוא לחוסים בו : ואתה ה' מגן בעדי כבודי
ומרים ראשי : כי שמש ומגן ה' אלהים חן וכבוד יתן ה' לא ימנע טוב להולכים
בתמים : תמים תהיה עם ה' אלהיך : לא ימצא בך מעביר בנו ובתו באש
קוסם קסמים מעונן ומנחש ומכשף : וחובר חבר ושואל אוב וידעוני ודורש
אל המתים : וכי יאמרו אליכם דרשו אל האובות ואל הידעונים המצפצפים
והמהגים הלא עם אל אלהיו ידרוש בעד החיים אל המתים : כדנה תאמרון
להום אלהיא די שמיא וארקא לא עבדו יאבדו מארעא ומן תחות שמיא
אלה : לא כאלה חלק יעקב כי יוצר הכל הוא וישראל שבט נחלתו ה' צבאות
שמו : יודו שמך גדול ונורא קדוש הוא : יודו לה' חסדו ונפלאותיו לבני אדם :
ויודו שמים פלאך ה' אף אמונתך בקהל קדושים : פדות שלח לעמו צוה
לעולם בריתו קדוש ונורא שמו : צהלי ורני יושבת ציון כי גדול בקרבך
קדוש ישראל : גואלנו ה' צבאות שמו קדוש ישראל :

זמרו כבוד שמו שימו כבוד תהלתו : אמרו לאלהים מה נורא מעשיך
ברב עזך יכחשו לך אויביך : כל הארץ ישתחוו לך ויזמרו לך יזמרו
שמך סלה : כשמך אלהים כן תהלתך על קצוי ארץ צדק מלאה ימינך :
אשרי העם יודעי תרועה ה' באור פניך יהלכון : בשמך יגילון כל היום
ובצדקתך ירומו : כי תפארת עזמו אתה וברצונך תרום קרננו : כי
לה' מגיננו ולקדוש ישראל מלכנו : עלה אלהים בתרועה ה' בקול שופר :
זמרו אלהים זמרו זמרו למלכנו זמרו : כי מלך כל הארץ אלהים זמרו
משכיל : רוממו ה' אלהינו והשתחוו להדום רגליו קדוש הוא : קדוש קדוש
קדוש ה' צבאות מלוא כל הארץ כבודו :

אלהינו ואלהי אבותינו קיים לנו כל בשורותיך הטובות הנאמרות
מפי יחזקאל עבדך : כה אמר ה' שער החצר הפנימית
הפונה קדים יהיה סגור ששת ימי המעשה וביום השבת יפתח וביום החדש
יפתח : והשתחוו עם הארץ פתח השער ההוא בשבתות ובחדשים לפני ה' :

ואל

FACS. 236 JSul.III.76: 52 verso

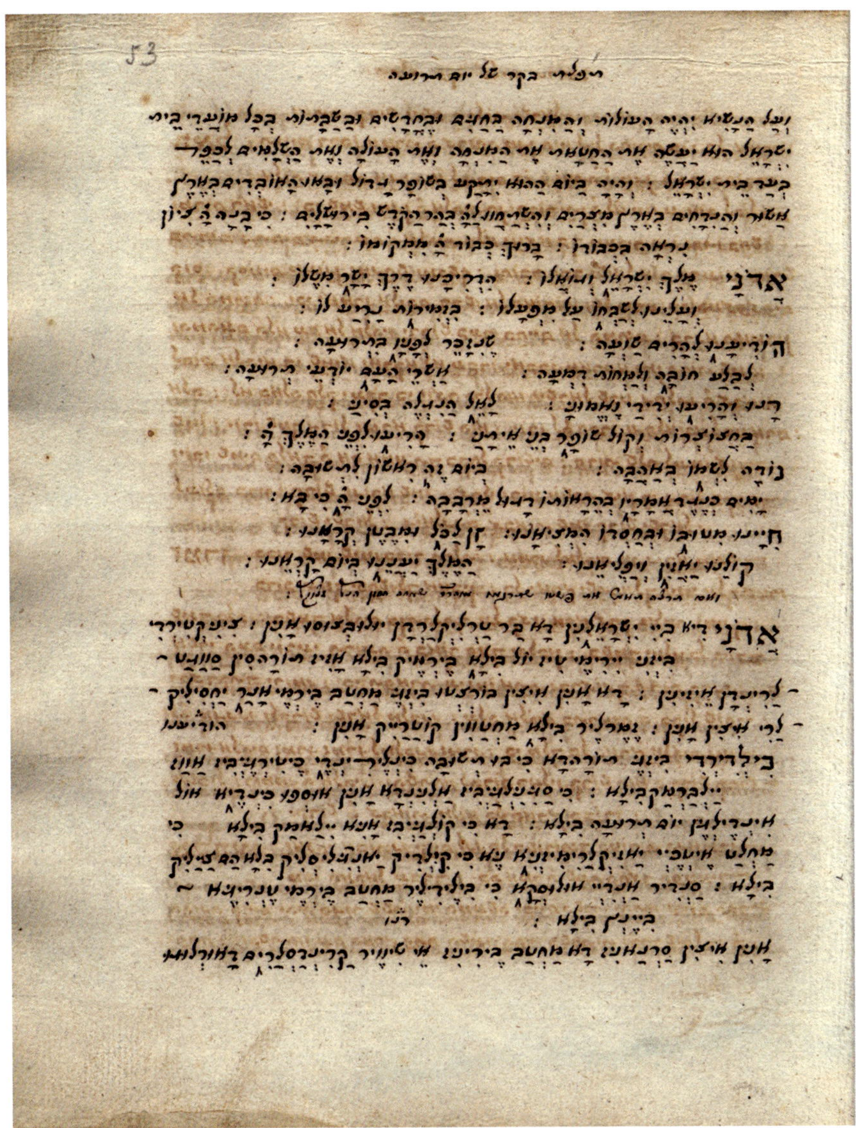

FACS. 237 JSul.III.76: 53 recto

FACS. 238 JSul.III.76: 53 verso

תפלת בקר של סוכות

ומעיננו מלוות לך להושיענו ולהצילנו : מכף מעול וחומץ נפשנו : שוסינו
ובוזזינו : מחרפינו ומגדפינו : מלחיצינו ומרחיקינו : מבקשי רעתנו להמיתנו :
צור ישראל ריבה ריבנו : לחם את לוחמינו : והרק חנית וסגור לקראת רודפינו :
והכריתם בימינו : שועלים שועלים קטנים מחבלים כרמים : ואז נודה לך ונאמר
ונשבח ונרומם ונהלל ונגדל ונהדר ונפאר זכרך בתוכנו : יה המרכבה
והנקרא דיין האלמנות בורא נמצאים אפסים לתהלה יחד המהללות ~
הנקרים דרכם סלה יהיו עומדות : הבעל גאות ובגאות ראוי לנו תמיד שמך
להודות : ככתוב יודו שמך גדול ונורא קדוש הוא : יודו לה׳ חסדו ונפלאותיו
לבני אדם : אך צדיקים יודו לשמך ישבו ישרים את פניך : ויודו שמים פלאך ה׳
אף אמונתך בקהל קדושים : ברוך שלח לעמו צוה לעולם בריתו קדוש ונורא
שמו : צהלי ורוני יושבת ציון כי גדול בקרבך קדוש ישראל : גואלנו ה׳ צבאות
שמו קדוש ישראל :

אמן גואלנו אדון האדונים : המטיב בפי כל אדונים : רסיסי טללין
השביענו במעגנים : נותן ליעף כח ועצמה לאין אונים : זכר ברית
אבותם : והוציאנו מיד חנסים וצועדים : ויוליכנו במדבר בעמוד אש ועננים :
פרש ענן למסך והנחנו ברננים : רני רוני הנחילנו על ידי ציר אמונים :
זמני גל וששון זונו לעתים מזומנים : לעשות סכה בערבי נחל רטבים ורעננים :
ובפרי עץ הדר ושאר מינים : למען ידעו דורות ראשונים ואחרונים : כי
בסוכות הושיבנו לעולה ברוב שלונים : האכילנו מן שלו ונתן לנו הוד וקניינים :
דבר לסלע ונתן מימיו נאמנים : השקיענו והשביענו מטובו הצפונים :
עתה יקום דר מעונים : עתה יתרומם עתה יתנשא בעד גרע אמונים :
לגאלנו מיד מעננים : יושב על כסא ומתנשא בסוד שאננים :

[illegible]

קיים טרי יולנה צמוא בינן אולדו בי אול ביילירנן : אמן כיצי
קוטרילאדיא אווגמרא בר סרנווצולרנן : שמציאלרינדן
ציקלרינן אויירדורדו בינה נמיטלירידן יחסיליקלרינן : אולדו בירייוצי
מרינמא כיג דא ארטשירדיא קובעין חלסיגלרנן : סמנדיא סירטין
איין אמלרנן : דא ציורדי בינה קולמדן חנסליירנן דא צונלרנן :

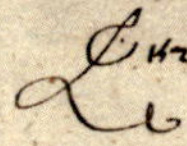

FACS. 239 JSul.III.76: 94 verso

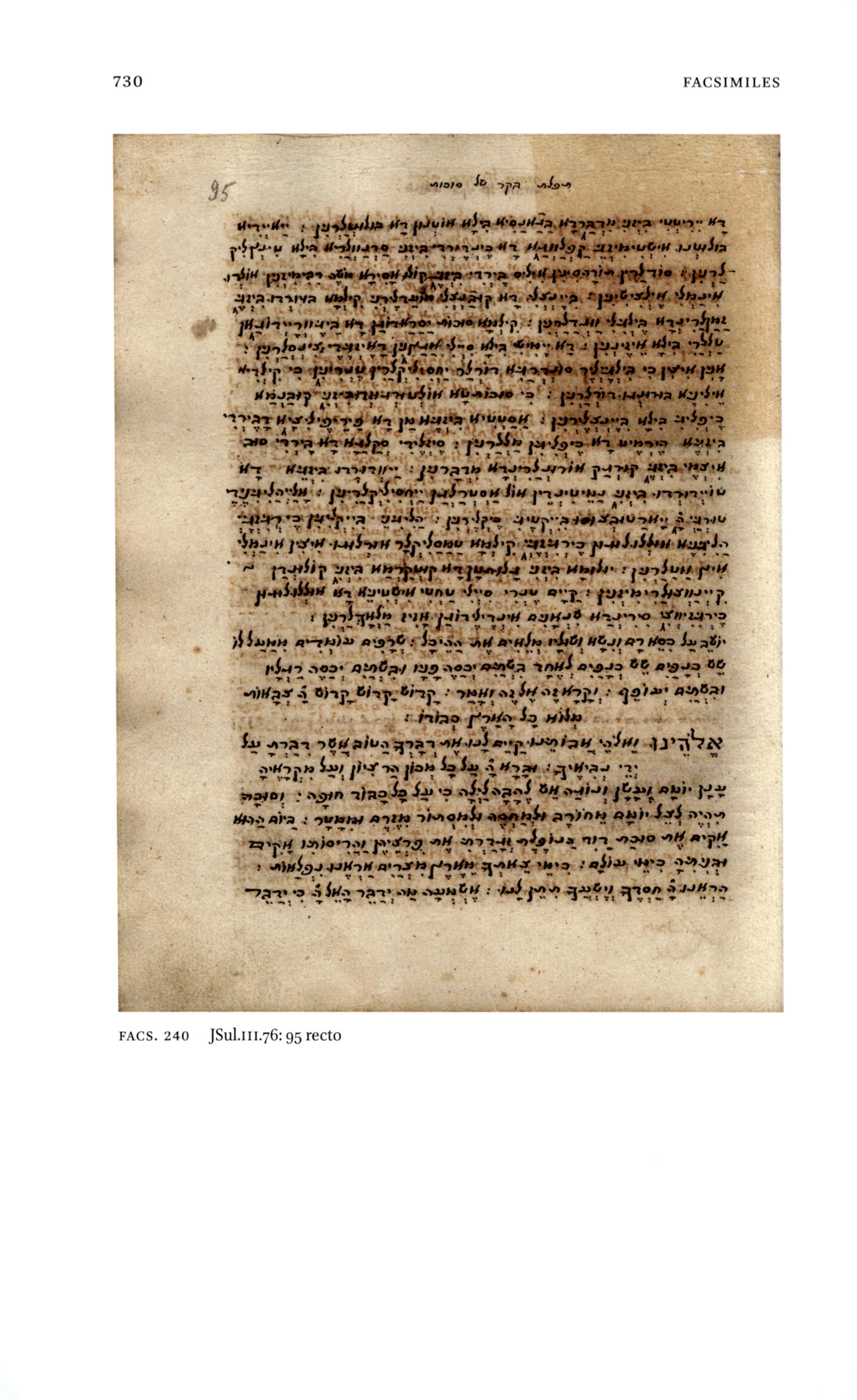

FACS. 240 JSul.III.76: 95 recto

תפלת בקר יום שמיני עצרת

יושב קדם בהושיעו אותנו מאומללה : הוליכנו בארץ ציה והסך לנו
בעננה : ולזכור חסדיו צומו בכל שנה ושנה :
רק חלק לשבעה וגם לשמונה :

דרך חיים הדריכנו והלבישנו עטרת : החיינו בחוקיו בשומו לנו משמרת :
בזאת בחיריו שפכו לפניו תפלה ועתירה : ביום השמיני עצרת :

נורא ואיום הזהירנו מימים קדמונים : שמור מצותיו ולחוג בכל שנה שלש פעמים :
ויום זה קרא עצרת בבית עולמים : ליראה את ה' אלהינו לטוב לנו כל הימים :

רחום וחנון לחדש ימינו כקדם ימלך : כמו ביום שמיני שלח את העם ויברכו את
המלך : הכי ישאו נס ויבוא נפוצותינו מכל עיר ופלך : והיה ה' למלך :
והיה ה' למלך על כל הארץ ביום ההוא יהיה ה' אחד ושמו אחד : שמע ישראל
ה' אלהינו ה' אחד :

ופה תכתוב פשטי הפיוטים המסודרים לעיל שתרגמם אמ"ו הר"ר שמחה יצחק בהמ"ע הנגאל הגאון ...
וזה הפשט לפיוט אם אמרי המיוסד על קריאה ראשונה

איגיד איטעסם סירה אוחשיוש טערימיא דא ביקליגין קוטריים אנין :
אושא אין טינטיקמן דא טריר כיכים כי בוללגיאן קוטרמא
מחשבלרין אנין : כיגלירימריא כיצי בולדום בירישי כיביק איוכי
אוסטא מישכינריק איליגין : קוטרמקטן אוללושאן בייגן אול בילירגין :
מינגליר בילא מינגליר דשימינגליר בילא שימינגלירי אזיז מלאכלרגין :
אזיגליגין דכיצין קוטראדילר בייגן דושמאלרגין : יאורלידיא כישי
דא יארואגדיא דא קוטרמקטן אוללולושאן טערינין קיסקארי כיצי אקילגין :
אנצק כירקלירי אנר כי אלנגדא טערישינין דושמאנין טיקכיי אלין יירינגין :
דא איימקיי אושאסן שי ה' אזיז טערים אולדרדיא בדליגין סנין : דסן קיימסן
סופונאדיין בר סופגון דא סנין קיימליגין בילאדיא קיימליגי בייק כיקליגין
דא יובוג יירגין : דא איינר כיפ בולדולר איסירליא אול יילר דא
אסטילר איסירליא ווחטלרי אול כיליגי ערסילירגין : דא סן טיוושירילמיססן
דא סן טיוושירמיסלר ווחטלרי זמנלרגין : יאט יוחטור קטינרא
דא יוחטו בירינצא בולוסלוגו אזיז טערינין : דא יוחטור כים כי כיציך
טירגי בולומגין בר כליקלירגין : אוסייטעין אולגלרין ארמגין

בילגוי

FACS. 241 JSul.III.76: 115 verso

FACS. 242 JSul.III.76: 116 recto

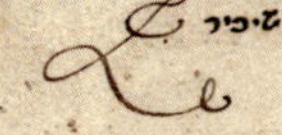

FACS. 243 JSul.III.76: 116 verso

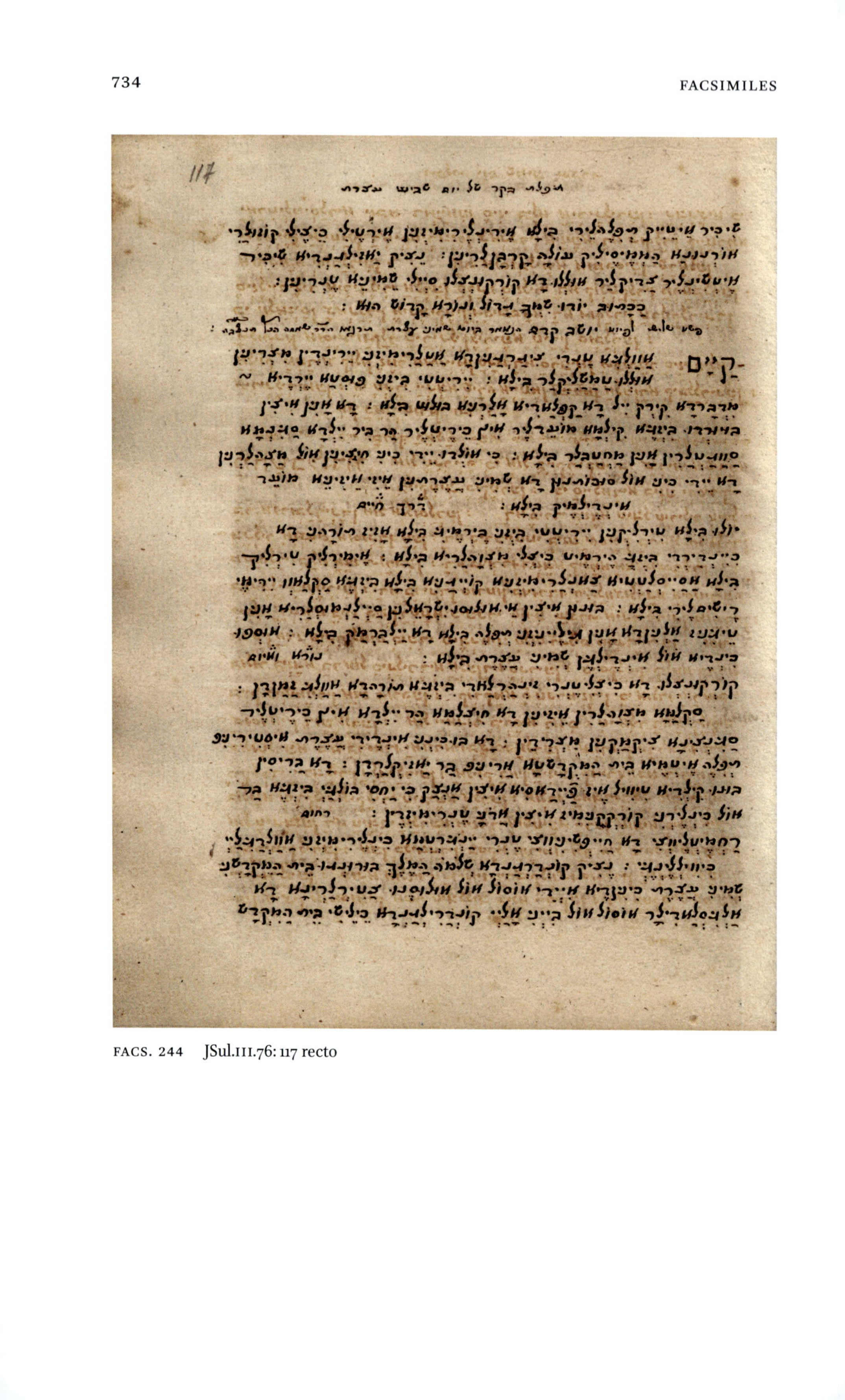

FACS. 244 JSul.III.76: 117 recto

תפלת בקר של יום שמיני עצרת

מלך המשיח אוזווערדן בר כל ישראלען אלגעסלגשי : פירשירין ~
כיטירנגי אלם דא הר ביר סהרדן דא סלאודן דא הר ביר וולייטען ~
טוזולגנלרין ישראלען יומדרגי : דא בולגי ה׳ יילנגי איטי ביי בר אול
ייר איסטינגא דא ברליגי דא בירליגי אינן אוזווערדן בר עינען קוטרילגי :
והיה ה׳ למלך על כל הארץ ביום ההוא יהיה ה׳ אחד ושמו אחד :

ואח״כ אומר אלה הקדושה בניגון הזה :

כה אמר האל ה׳ בורא השמים ונוטיהם רוקע הארץ וצאצאיה נותן
נשמה לעם עליה ורוח להולכים בה : אני ה׳ הוא שמי וכבודי לאחר
לא אתן ותהלתי לפסילים : אף ידי יסדה ארץ וימיני טפחה שמים קורא אני
אליהם יעמדו יחדו : למען ידעו ממזרח שמש וממערבה כי אפס בלעדי
אני ה׳ ואין עוד : למען יראו וידעו וישימו וישכילו כי יד ה׳ עשתה זאת וקדוש
ישראל בראה : זכרו ראשונות מעולם כי אנכי אל ואין עוד אלהים ואפס
כמוני : כי מי אל מבלעדי ה׳ ומי צור מבלעדי אלהינו : כי מי אלוה מבלעדי
ה׳ ומי צור זולתי אלהינו : כי מי בשחק יערוך לה׳ ידמה לה׳ בבני אלים :
ואומר אין קדוש כה׳ : אין כאל ישרון : מעונה אלהי קדם : וישכון ישראל :
אשריך ישראל : ויאמר אליהו לאחאב וכל הפסוקים הכתובים בקדושה ראשונה עד
אלהים זולתך יעשה למחכה לו : וכולו ואומר ואל מי תדמיון אל : ואל מי תדמיוני
ואשוה : ואל מי תדמיוני : ואתה קדוש יושב תהלות ישראל :

ואומר הקדושה השנית הכתובה לעיל :

ברכו עמים אלהינו והשמיעו קול תהלתו : הודו לה׳ : לעושה נפלאות :
ברוך האל ה׳ רם על כל רמים : וכל הפיוט ככתוב לעיל ותחתום
גואלנו ה׳ צבאות שמו קדוש ישראל : ואומר גם זה

מי כה׳ אלהינו המגביהי לשבת : המשפילי לראות בשמים ובארץ :
עושה כימה וכסיל והופך לבקר צלמות ויום לילה החשיך הקורא למי
הים וישפכם על פני הארץ ה׳ שמו : מעלה נשיאים מקצה הארץ ברקים
למטר עשה מוצא רוח מאוצרותיו : הנותן מטר על פני ארץ ושולח מים
על פני חוצות : מי לא ידע בכל אלה כי יד ה׳ עשתה זאת : רומה ה׳ בעזך
נשירה ונזמרה גבורתך : רוממו ה׳ אלהינו והשתחוו להדום רגליו קדוש

הוא

FACS. 245 JSul.III.76: 117 verso

118

תפלת בקר של יום שמיני עצרת

הוא : קדוש קדוש קדוש יי צבאות מלוא כל הארץ כבודו :
ברוך יי צורי המלמד ידי לקרב אצבעותי למלחמה : ברוך יי כי
הפליא חסדו לי בעיר מצור : וייראו ממערב את שם יי וממזרח
שמש את כבודו כי יבוא כנהר צר רוח יי נוססה בו : ייראו מיי כל הארץ
ממנו יגורו כל יושבי תבל : וייראו גוים את שם יי וכל מלכי הארץ את
כבודך : כי בנה יי ציון נראה בכבודו : ברוך כבוד יי ממקומו :
הלא תדעו הלא תשמעו הלא הוגד מראש לכם הלא הבינותם מוסדות
הארץ : היושב על חוג הארץ ויושביה כחגבים הנוטה כדוק
שמים וימתחם כאהל לשבת : הלא ידעת אם לא שמעת אלהי עולם יי בורא
קצות הארץ לא ייעף ולא ייגע אין חקר לתבונתו : דעו כי יי הוא האלהים
הוא עשנו ולו אנחנו עמו וצאן מרעיתו : דע את אלהי אביך ועבדהו
בלב שלם ובנפש חפצה כי כל לבבות דורש יי וכל יצר מחשבות מבין אם
תדרשנו ימצא לך ואם תעזבנו יזניחך לעד : יי עמכם בהיותכם עמו
אם תדרשהו ימצא לכם ואם תעזבוהו יעזוב אתכם : שמע אלי יעקב
וישראל מקוראי אני הוא אני ראשון אף אני אחרון : שמע ישראל יי
אלהינו יי אחד :
אחד אלהינו גדול אדונינו קדוש ונורא שמו לעולם ועד : ותאמר
ואהבת את יי אלהיך וכל קריאת שמע עם פרשת ציצית ואחריו תאמר חבור טוב
טעם ודעת למדני ותחבר ההעראות ומצותיו אמת : ומקראי קדש
אמת : ויום שמיני עצרת הזה אמת : ומצותיו וחקותיו ותורותיו
ומשפטיו וכול ואחריו תאמר הלל הגיון הללו את יי כל גוים ואחריו תאמר ברכת כהנים
ותאמר אחריו כי כה אמר יי רנו ליעקב שמחה וכול עם אלפות שמות :
ותשב ותאמר סמכני כאמרתך ואחיה ואחריו יהי לבי תמים בחקיך
ואחריו תאמר ויעתרה יי אלהינו אשר הוצאת ואחריו תעשה תפלה בלחש : ותאמר
הראנו יי חסדך ועוד תעשה תפלה בלחש ותקום ותתן שלום לעם ותחתום
ברוך יי לעולם אמן ואמן :
ואחר השלמת התפלה עושים תנועות ומוציאים ספר תורה וקורא פרשת האזנו : וכשיגיע ניעם
אלות פותחת ההיכל ועושה הפתיחה יפה ויאמר אשר זה התורה בגון נאה :

FACS. 246 JSul.III.76: 118 recto

FACS. 247 JSul.III.77: 191 verso

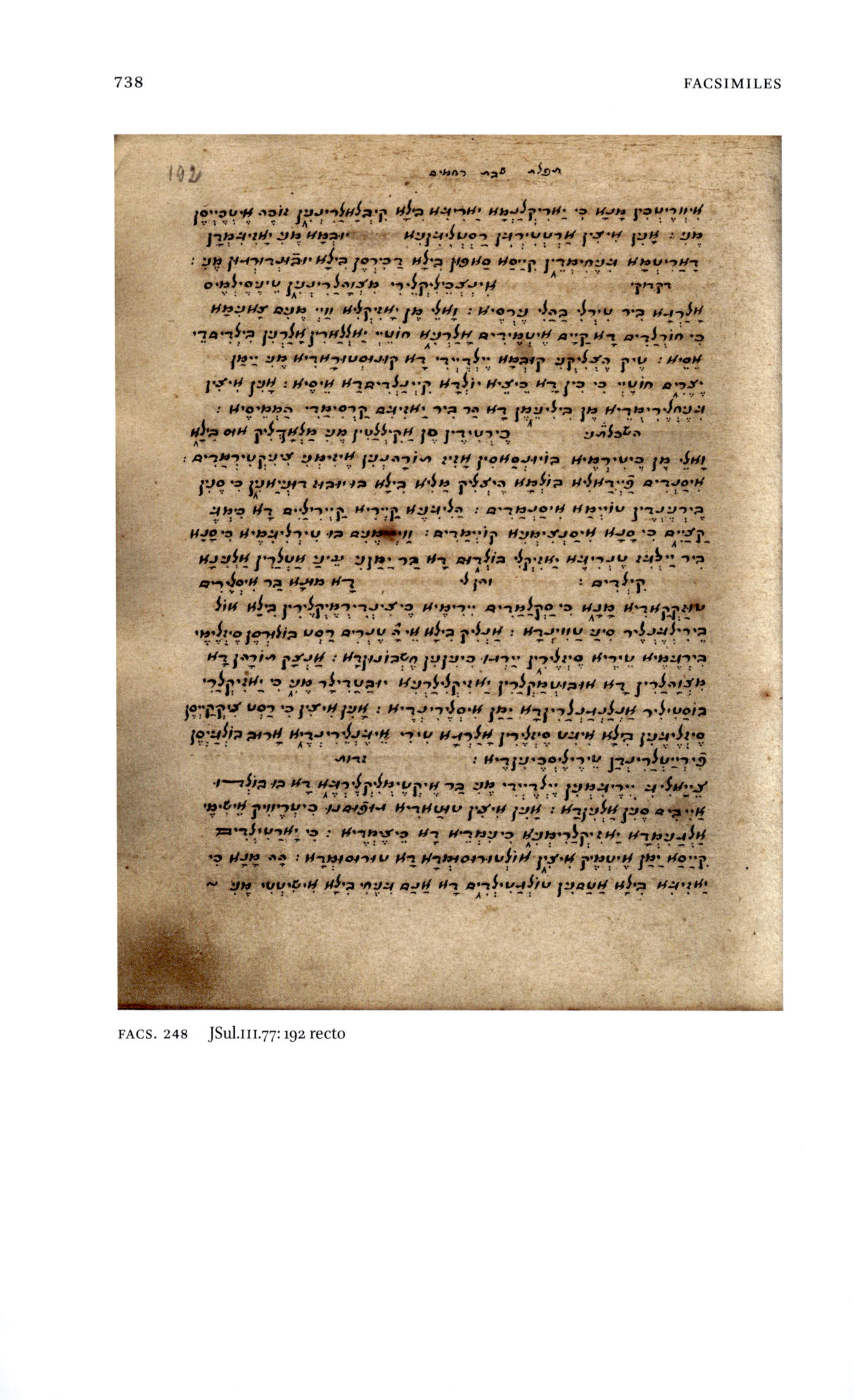

192

תפלה סבת רחמים

FACS. 248 JSul.III.77: 192 recto

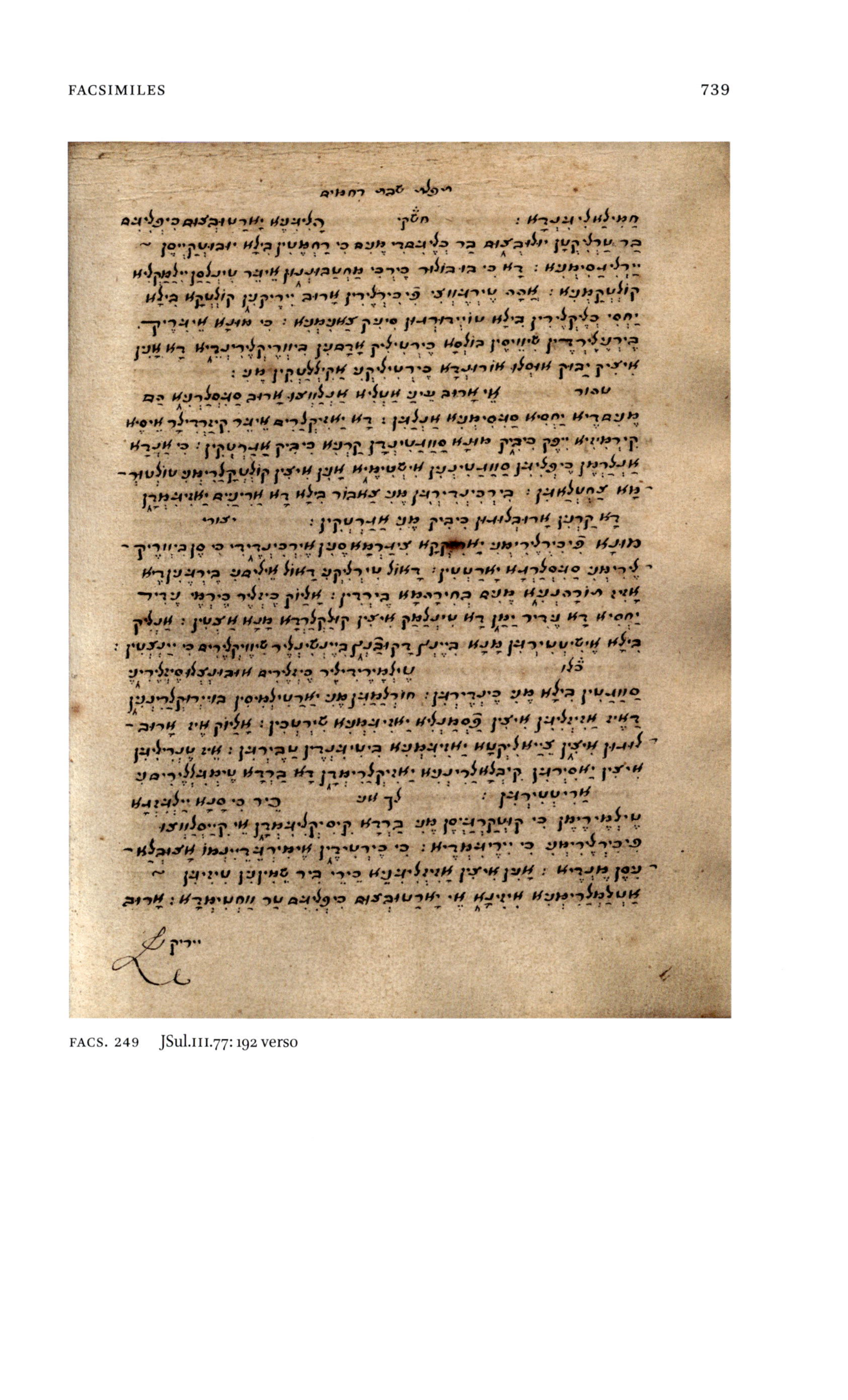

FACS. 249 JSul.III.77: 192 verso

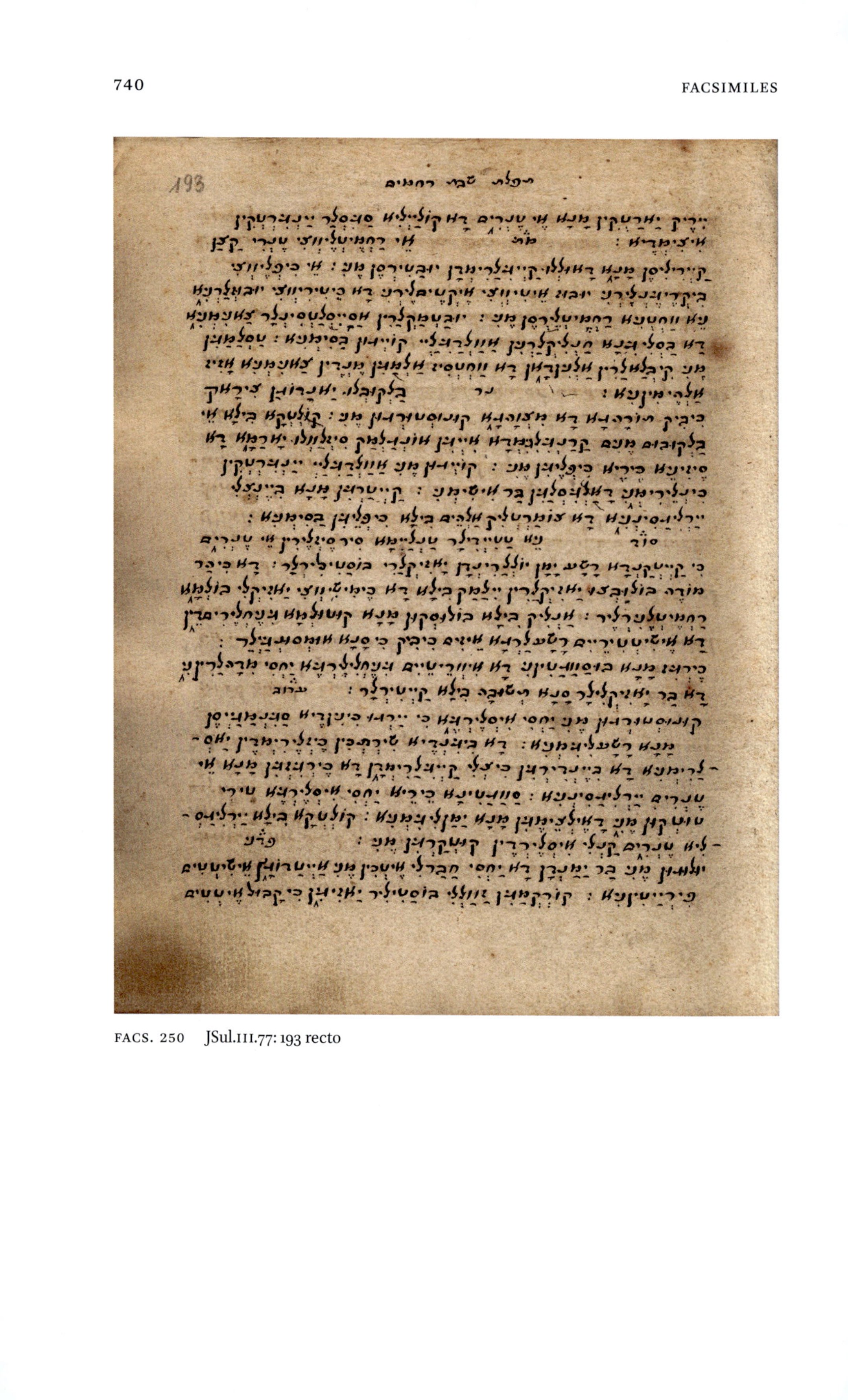

FACS. 250 JSul.III.77: 193 recto

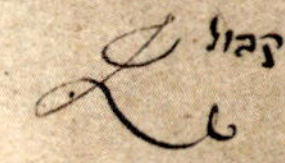

FACS. 251 JSul.III.77: 193 verso

FACS. 252 JSul.III.77: 194 recto

FACS. 253 JSul.III.79: 170 verso–171 recto

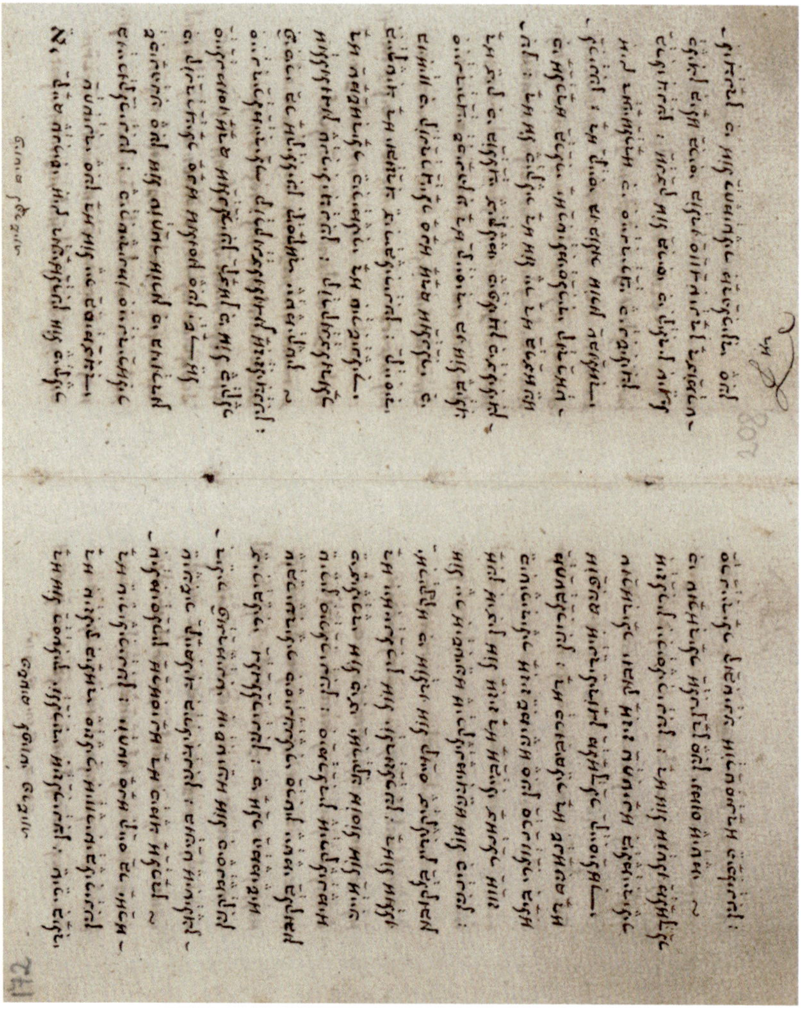

FACS. 254 JSul.III.79: 171 verso–172 recto

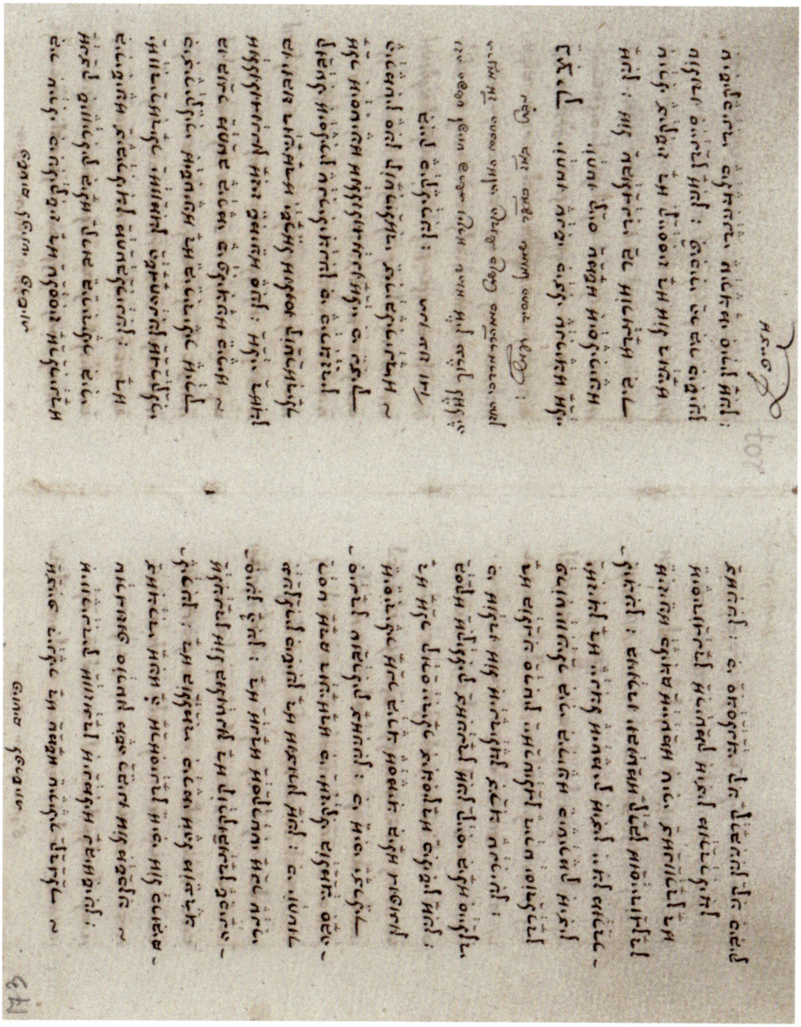

FACS. 255 JSul.III.79: 172 verso–173 recto

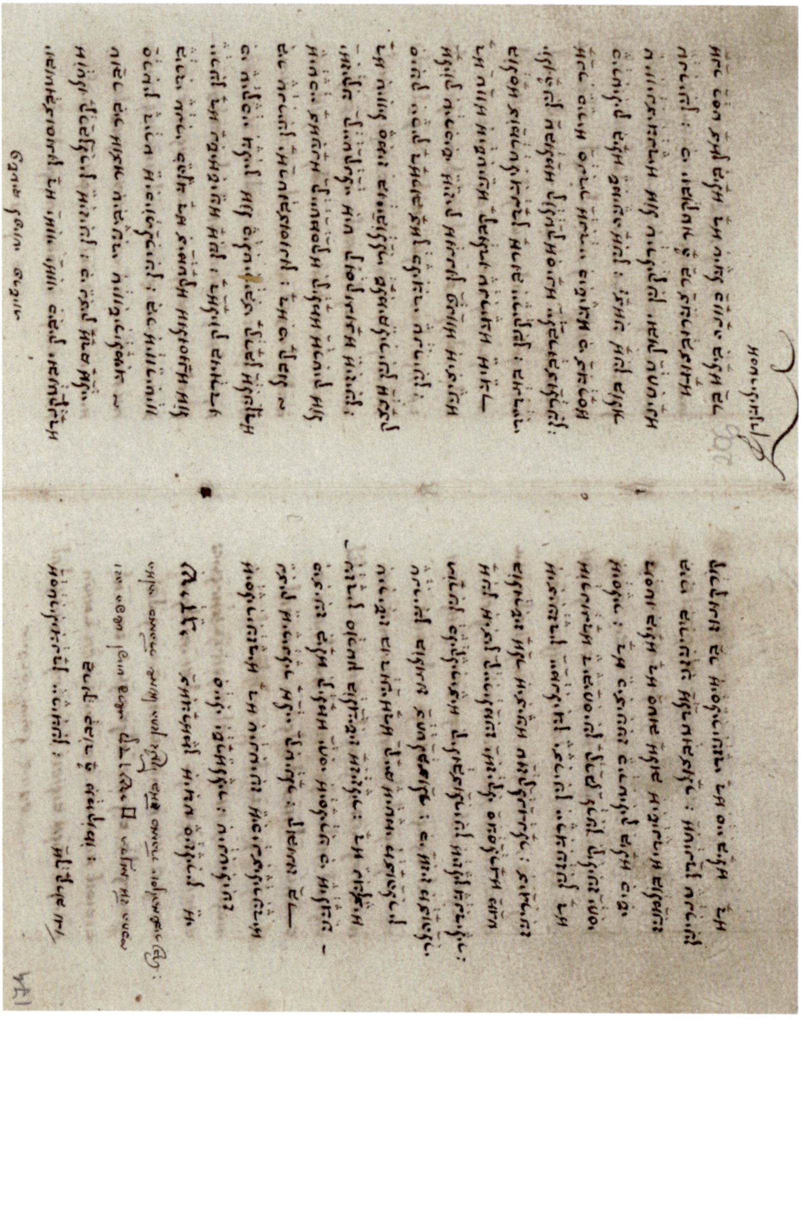

FACS. 256 JSul.III.79: 173 verso–174 recto

FACS. 257 JSul.III.79: 174 verso–175 recto

FACS. 258 JSul.III.79: 175 verso–176 recto

FACS. 259 JSul.III.79: 176 verso–177 recto

FACS. 260 JSul.III.79:177 verso–178 recto

FACS. 261 JSul.III.79: 178 verso–179 recto

FACS. 262 JSul.III.79: 179 verso–180 recto

FACS. 263 JSul.III.79: 180 verso–181 recto

FACS. 264 JSul.III.79: 181 verso–182 recto

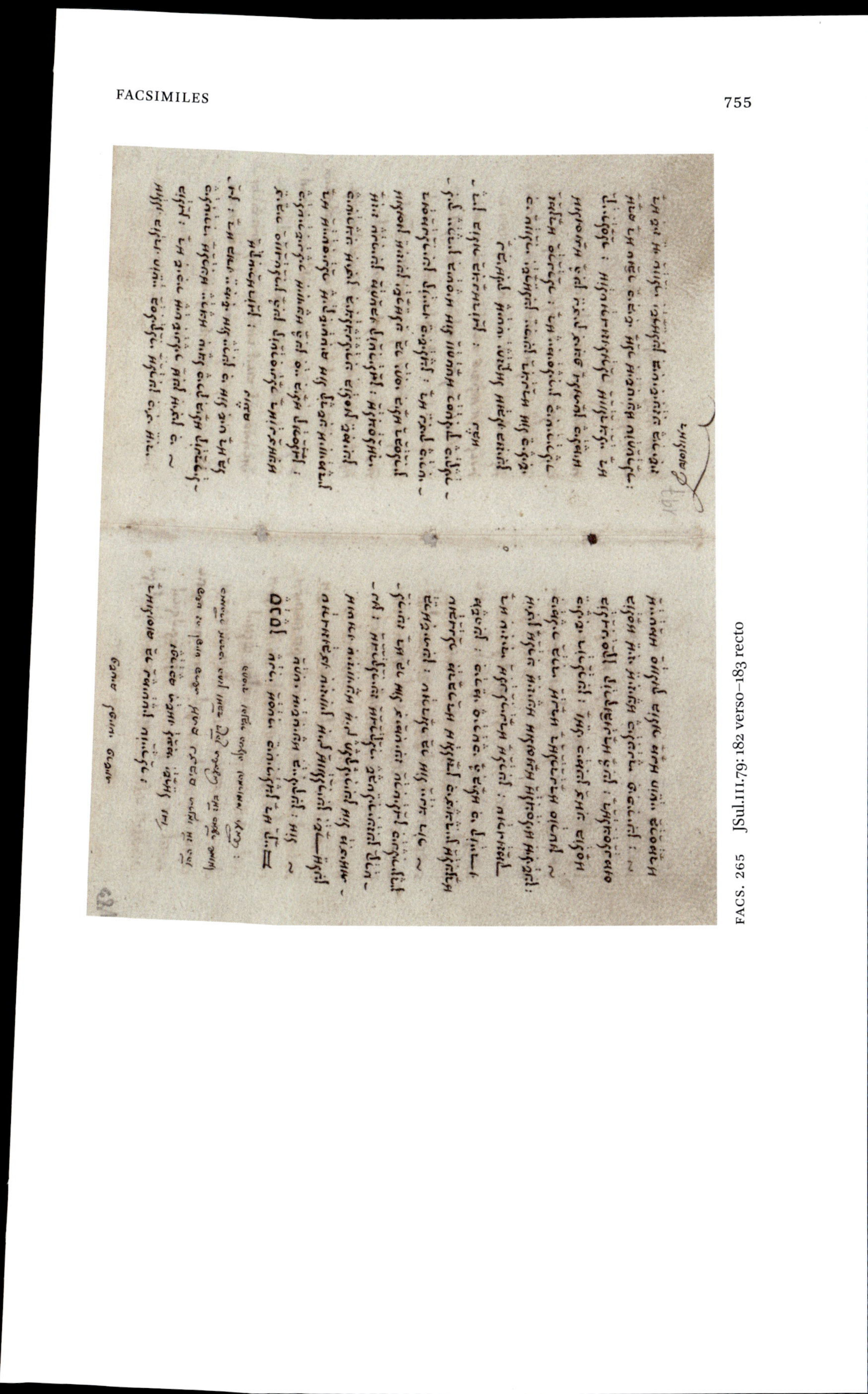

FACS. 265 JSul.III.79: 182 verso–183 recto

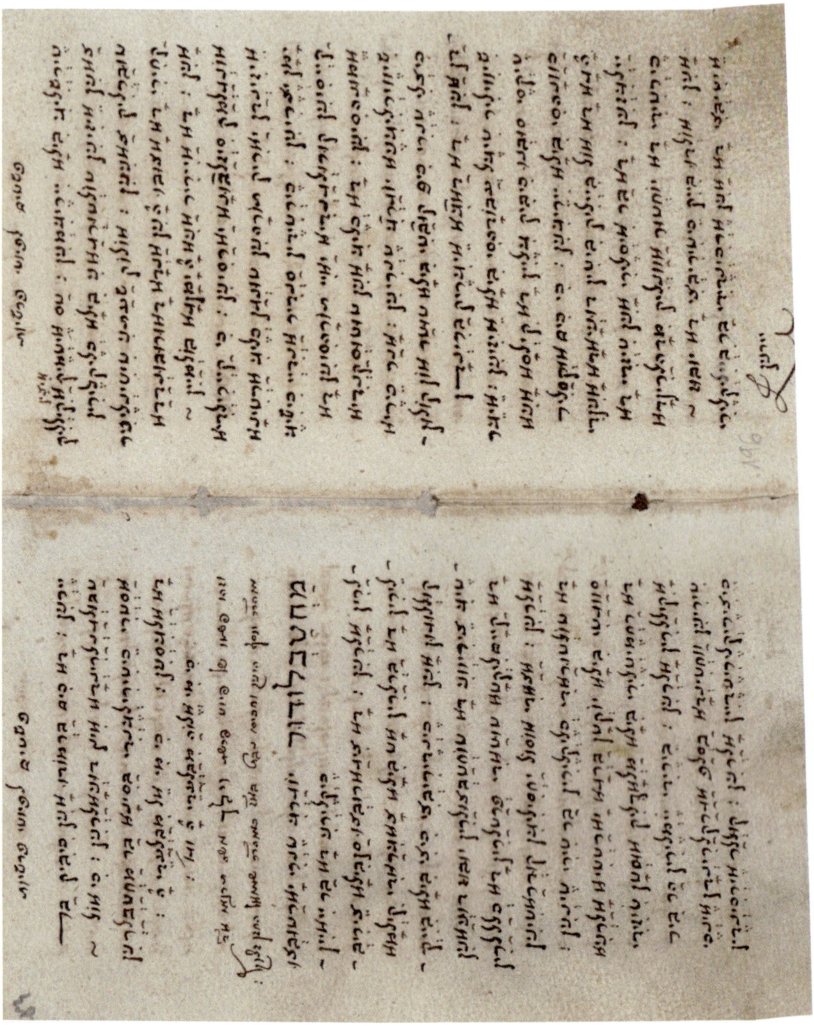

FACS. 266 JSul.III.79: 183 verso–184 recto

FACS. 267 JSul.III.79: 184 verso–185 recto

FACS. 268 JSul.III.79:185 verso–186 recto

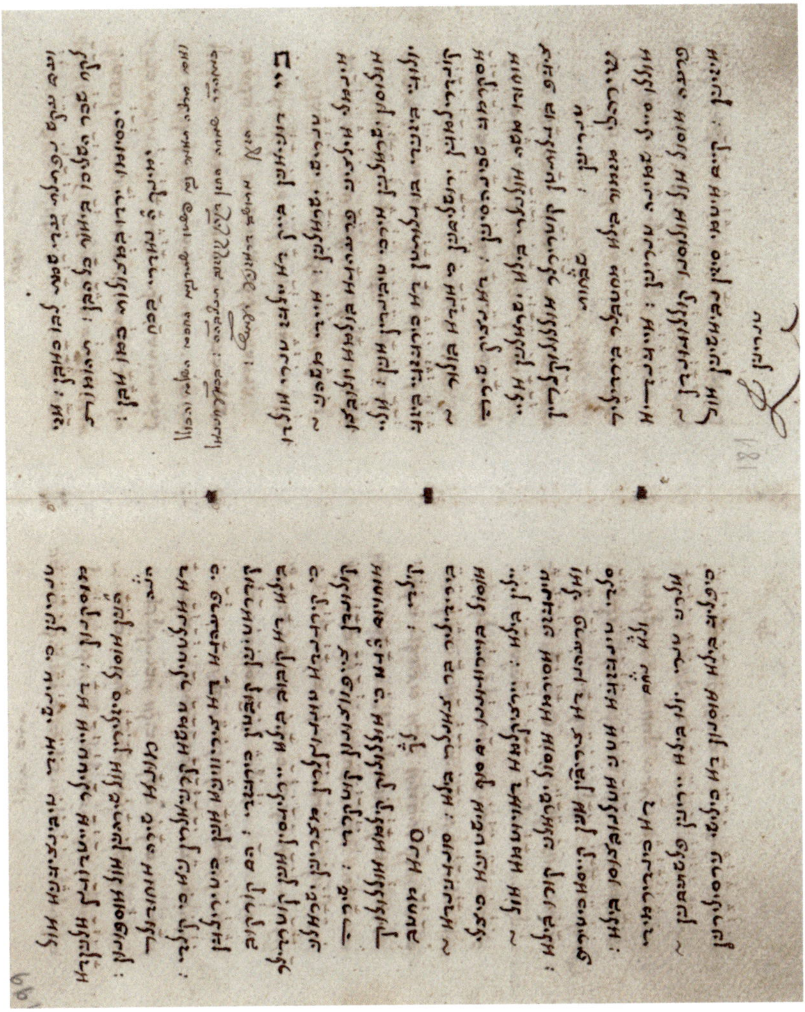

FACS. 269 JSul.III.79: 198 verso–199 recto

FACS. 270 JSul.III.79: 199 verso–200 recto

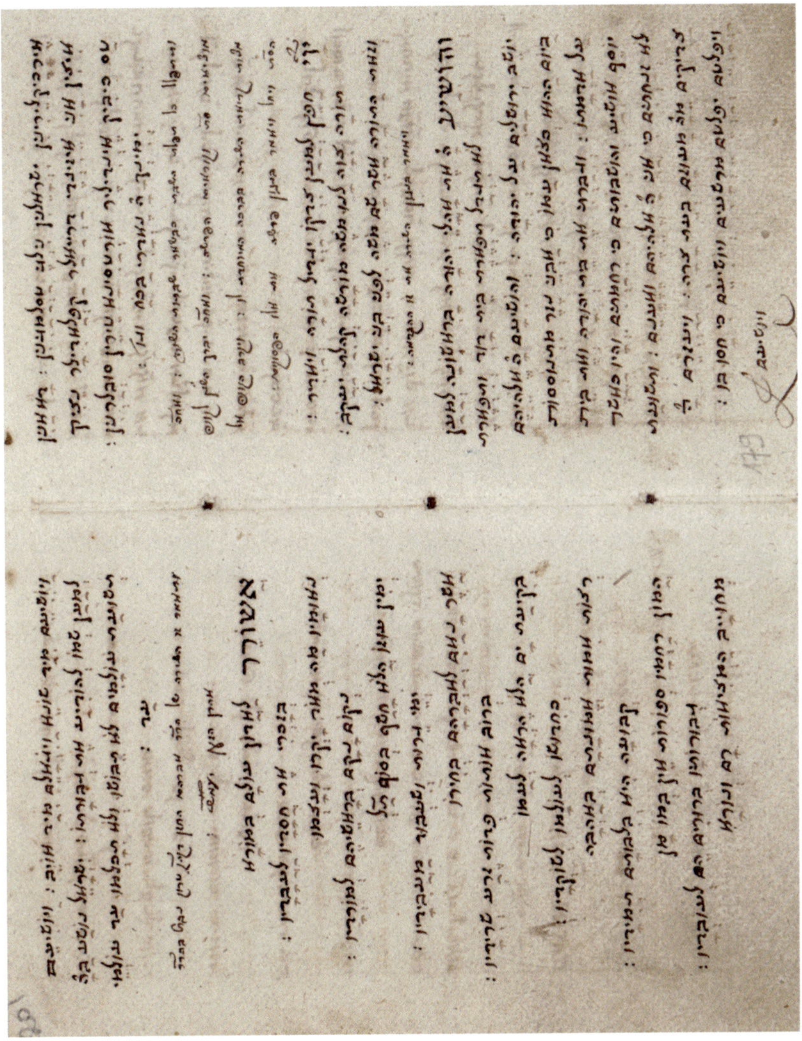

FACS. 271 JSul.III.79: 200 verso–201 recto

FACS. 272 JSul.III.79: 265 verso–266 recto

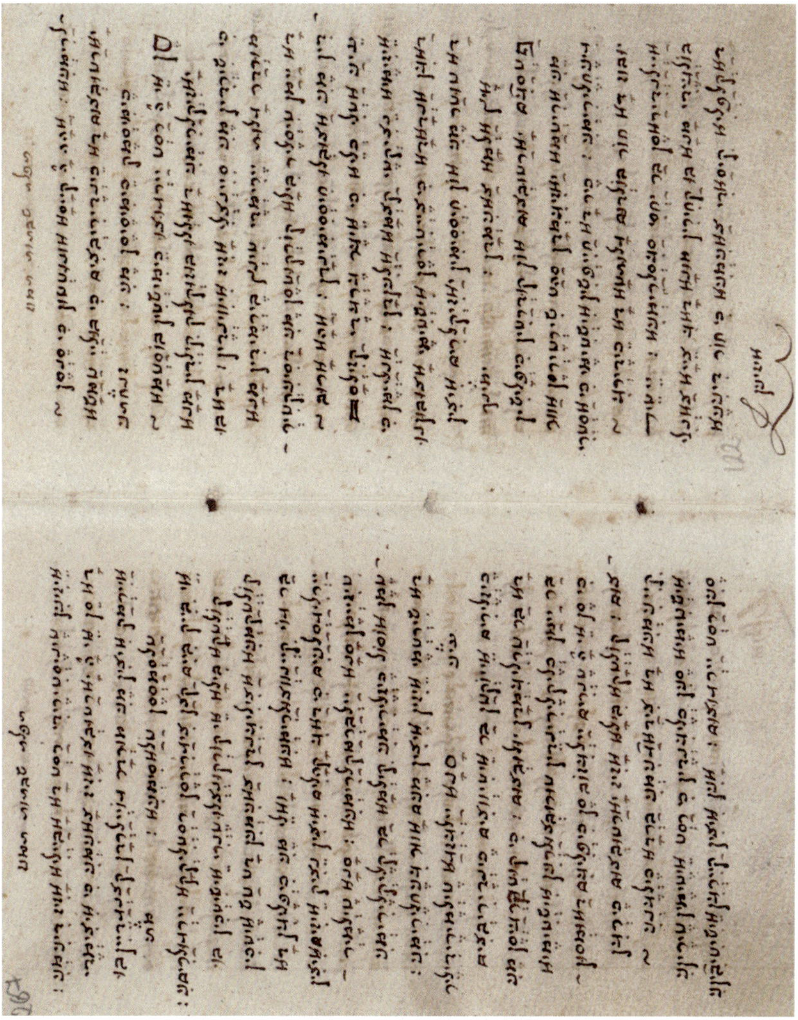

FACS. 273 JSul.III.79: 266 verso–267 recto

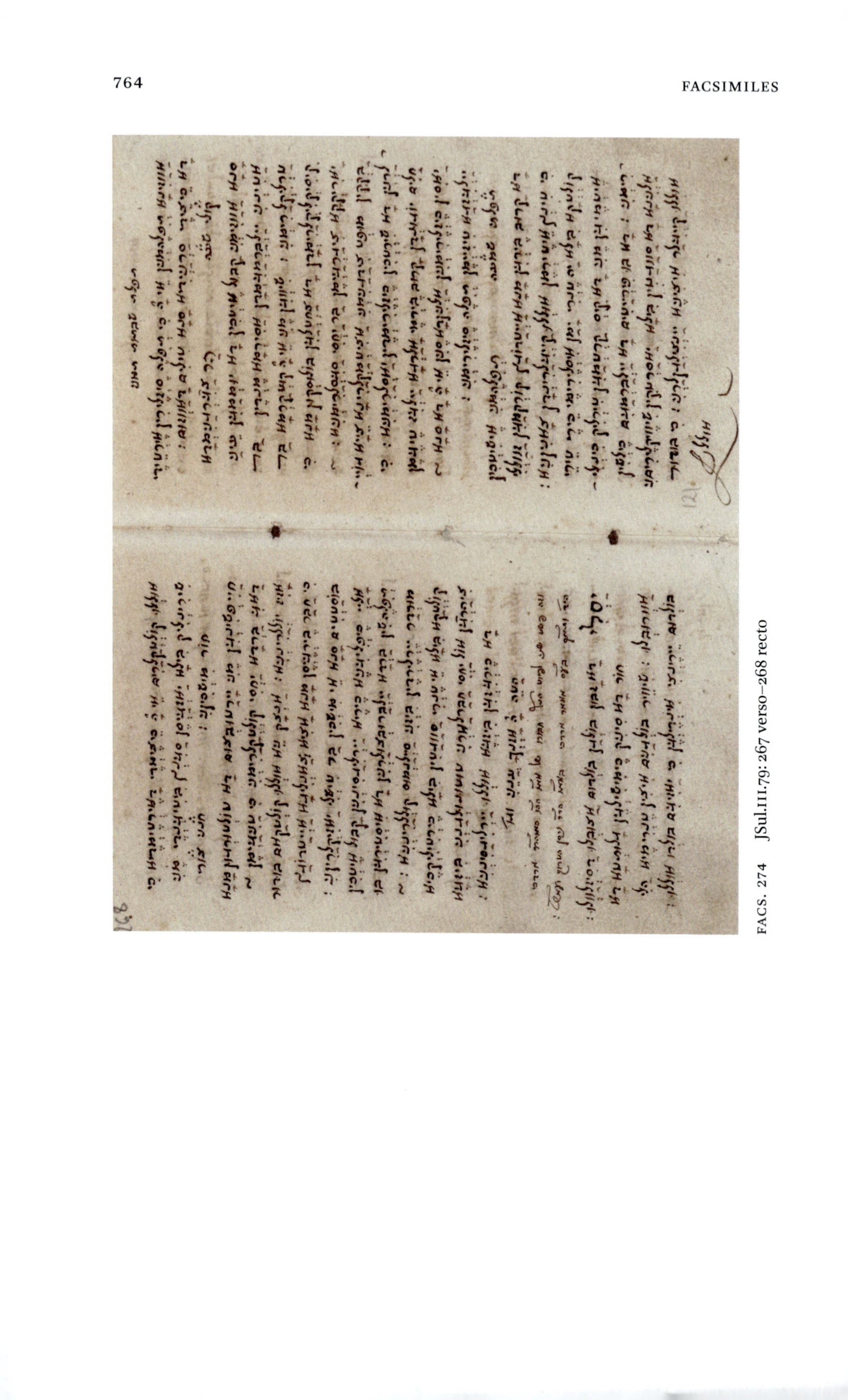

FACS. 274 JSul.III.79: 267 verso–268 recto

FACS. 275 JSul.III.79: 268 verso–269 recto

FACS. 276 JSul.III.79: 269 verso–270 recto

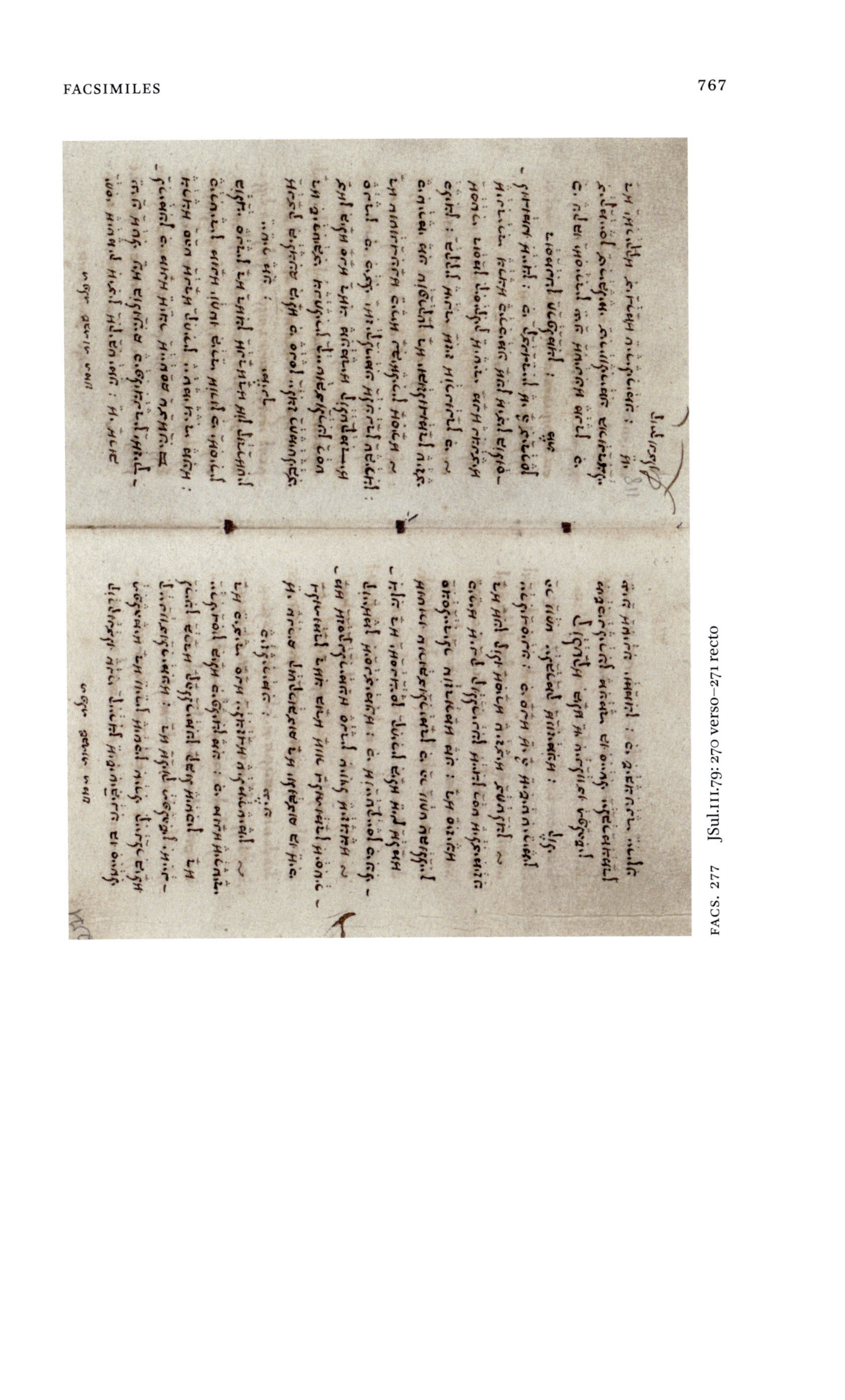

FACS. 277 JSul.III.79: 270 verso–271 recto

FACS. 278 JSul.III.79: 271 verso–272 recto

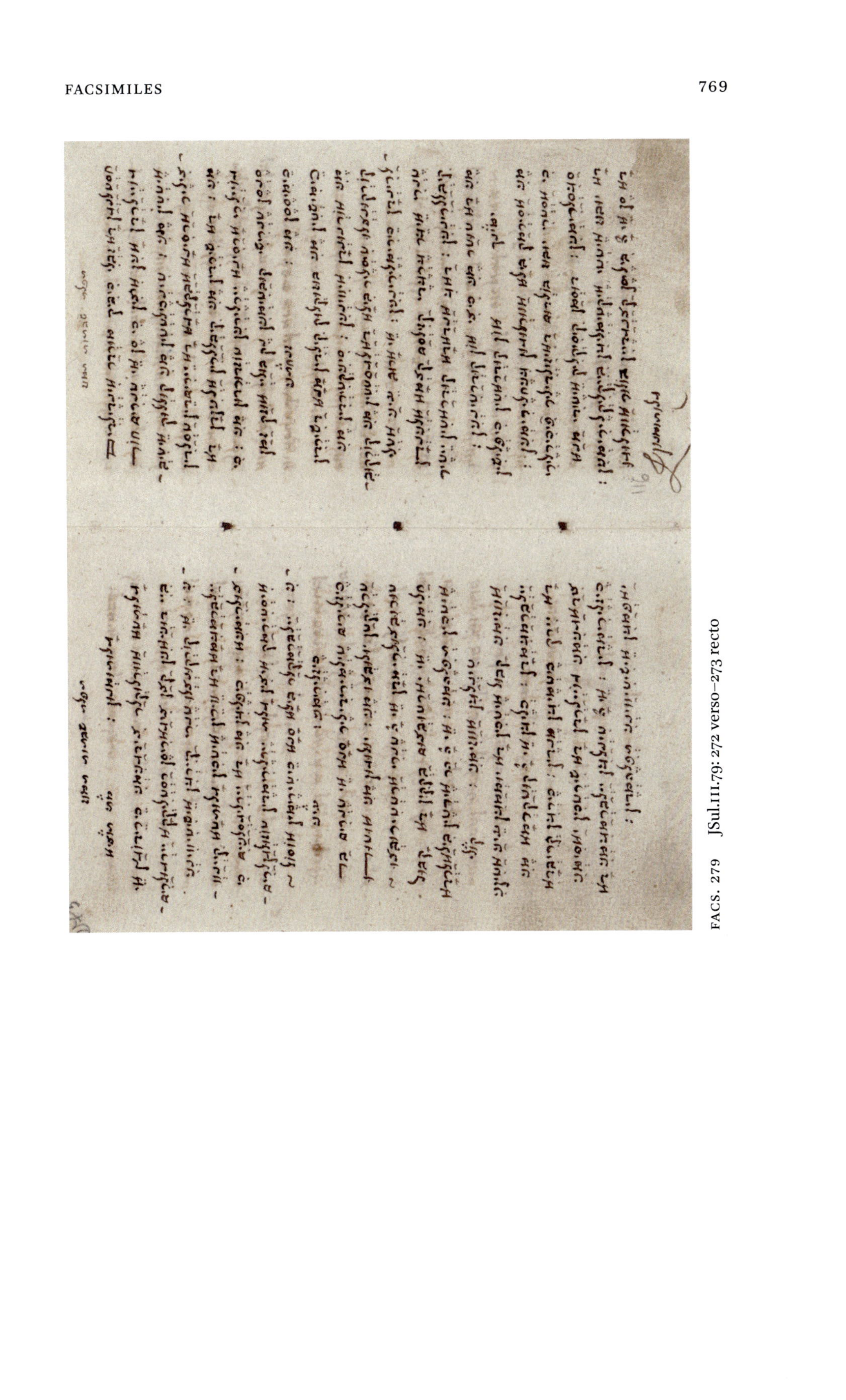

FACS. 279 JSul.III.79: 272 verso–273 recto

FACS. 280 JSul.III.79: 273 verso–274 recto

FACS. 281 JSul.III.79: 285 verso–286 recto

FACS. 282 JSul.III.79: 286 verso–287 recto

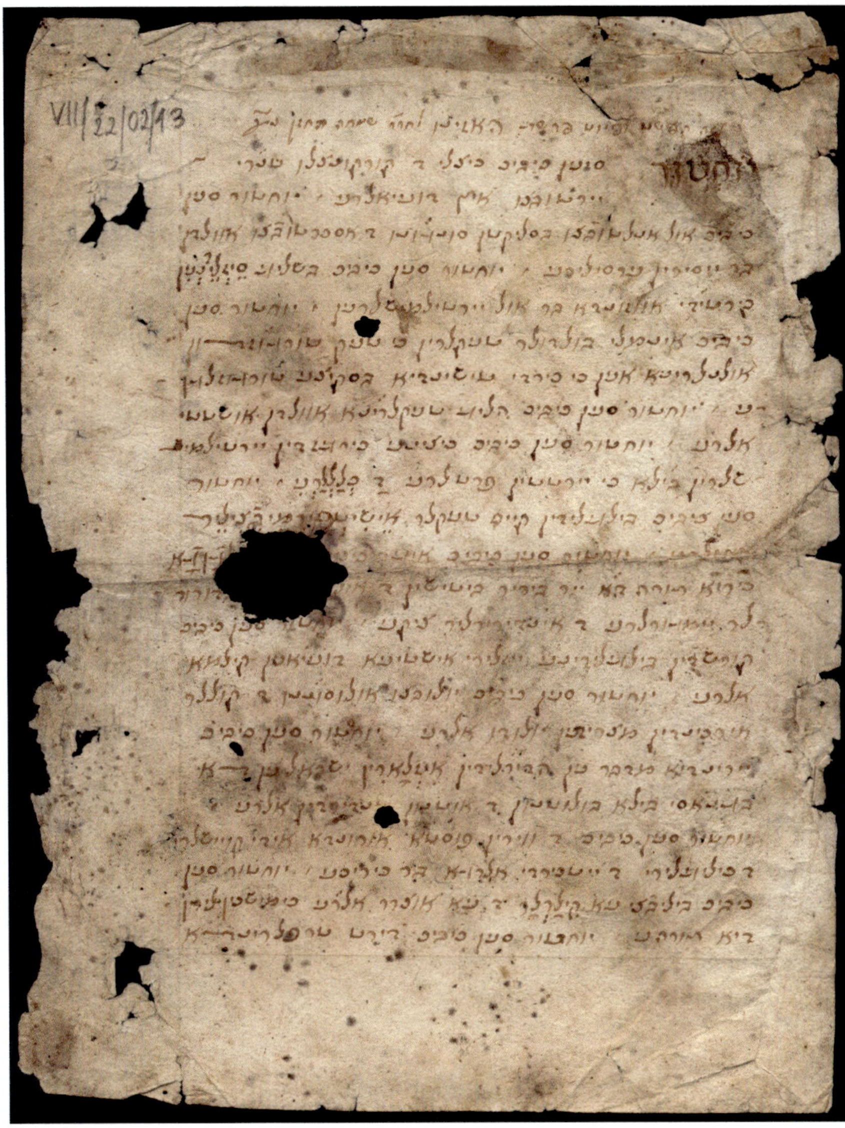

FACS. 283 JSul.VII.22.02.13: 1 recto

FACS. 284 JSul.VII.22.02.13: 1 verso

# Index of Hebrew Incipits

אַתָּה אֵל מִתְנַשֵּׂא *ʾattå ʾēl mitnaśśē* 13, 19, 433
אַתָּה אֱלֹהַי יוֹצֵר עוֹלָם *ʾattå ʾĕlohay yōṣēr ʿōlåm* 22
אַתָּה הִצַּבְתָּ גְבֻלוֹת *ʾattå hiṣṣabtå gbulōt* 15
אַתָּה כּוֹנַנְתָּ לְזֶרַע *ʾattå kōnantå lzeraʿ* 16
אַתָּה נֶאֱמַן בֵּיתִי *ʾattå neʾĕman bēṯī* 15, 21
אַתָּה קָדוֹשׁ וְנוֹרָא *ʾattå qådoš wnōrå* 16, 20
אַתָּה קָדוֹשׁ יוֹשֵׁב תְּהִלּוֹת בְּנֵי אֵיתָן *ʾattå qådōš yōšēb thillōt bnē ʾēṯån* 12, 18, 341
אַתָּה קָדוֹשׁ יוֹשֵׁב תְּהִלּוֹת יִשְׂרָאֵל *ʾattå qådōš yōšēb thillōt yiśråʾēl* 22
אַתָּה קָדוֹשׁ פּוֹעֵל גְּבוּרוֹת *ʾattå qådōš pōʿēl gbūrōt* 14, 24

בָּרוּךְ אֵל אֲשֶׁר אֵין *bårūk ʾēl ʾăšer ʾēn* 17
בָּרוּךְ הָאֵל הָ׳ *bårūk håʾēl H* 12, 24, 310
בָּרְכוּ אֶת הָ׳ *bårkū ʾeṯ H* 16

גּוֹאֲלֵנוּ גּוֹאֵל יִשְׂרָאֵל *gōʾălēnū gōʾēl yiśråʾēl* 15

וַיָּקֶם אֶת דְּבָרוֹ *wayyåqem ʾeṯ dbårō* 52n45

יָהּ שׁוֹכֵן *yåh šōkēn* 21
יוֹדוּ לַהָ׳ חַסְדּוֹ *yōdū la-H ḥasdō* 21
יָוָי אֱלֹהִים אַתָּה הַחִלּוֹתָ *YWY ʾĕlohīm ʾattå haḥillōtå* 18
יָוָי נָתַן אוֹמֶר *YWY nåṯan ʾōmer* 17

יוֹשֵׁב קֶדֶם *yōšēb qedem* 12, 24, 325
יִשְׁתַּבַּח אֵל עֶלְיוֹן *yištabbaḥ ʾēl ʿelyōn* 13, 377
יִתְגַּדֵּל אֵל עֶלְיוֹן *yitgaddal ʾēl ʿelyōn* 18

כְּרוּבִים כָּל בְּנֵי עֶלְיוֹן *krūbīm kål bnē ʿelyōn* 40n27

מִי כַהָ׳ אִבֵּי עֶדְנֵי *mī ka-H ʾibē ʿednē* 19
מִי כָהָ׳ אֱלֹהֵינוּ הַמַּגְבִּיהִי לָשֶׁבֶת *mī kå-H ʾĕlohenū hammağbīhī låšebet* 20
מִי כָהָ׳ אֲשֶׁר *mī ka-H ʾăšer* 15
מִי כָהָ׳ אֲשֶׁר לֹא יָכִילוּ *mī ka-H ʾăšer lo yåkilū* 18
מִי כָּמוֹךָ אַדִּיר וְנוֹרָא *mī kåmōkå ʾadīr wnōrå* 11, 19, 278
מֶלֶךְ עוֹלָם מִקֶּדֶם נִפְלָאוֹת עָשָׂה *melek ʿōlåm miqqedem niplåʾōt ʿåśå* 23
מֶלֶךְ רָם וְיָחִיד *melek råm wyåḥīd* 11, 226
מִמְּקוֹמוֹ הוֹפִיעַ *mimmqōmō hōpiaʿ* 15
מָרוֹם מֵרִאשׁוֹן *mårōm mērišōn* 22

נוֹדֶה לה עַל חַסְדּוֹ *nōde l-H ʿal ḥasdō* 37n19

שְׂאִי זִמְרָה נַפְשִׁי *śʾī zimrå napšī* 36, 45, 338n1285
שָׁבַת מְשׂוֹשִׂי *šåbat mśōśī* 9n21

# Index of Karaim Incipits

# Index of Biblical Verses Referenced

# Index of Linguistic and Philological Phenomena

# General Index

Printed in the United States
By Bookmasters